THE COLONIAL RECORDS OF NORTH CAROLINA
[Second Series]

Volume I *North Carolina Charters and Constitutions, 1578-1698*, edited by Mattie Erma Edwards Parker

Volume II *North Carolina Higher-Court Records, 1670-1696*, edited by Mattie Erma Edwards Parker

Volume III *North Carolina Higher-Court Records, 1697-1701*, edited by Mattie Erma Edwards Parker

Volume IV *North Carolina Higher-Court Records, 1702-1708*, edited by William S. Price, Jr.

Volume V *North Carolina Higher-Court Records, 1709-1723*, edited by William S. Price, Jr.

Volume VI *North Carolina Higher-Court Records, 1724-1730*, edited by Robert J. Cain

Volume VII *Records of the Executive Council, 1664-1734*, edited by Robert J. Cain

Volume VIII *Records of the Executive Council, 1735-1754*, edited by Robert J. Cain

Volume IX *Records of the Executive Council, 1755-1775*, edited by Robert J. Cain

Volume X *The Church of England in North Carolina: Documents, 1699-1741*, edited by Robert J. Cain

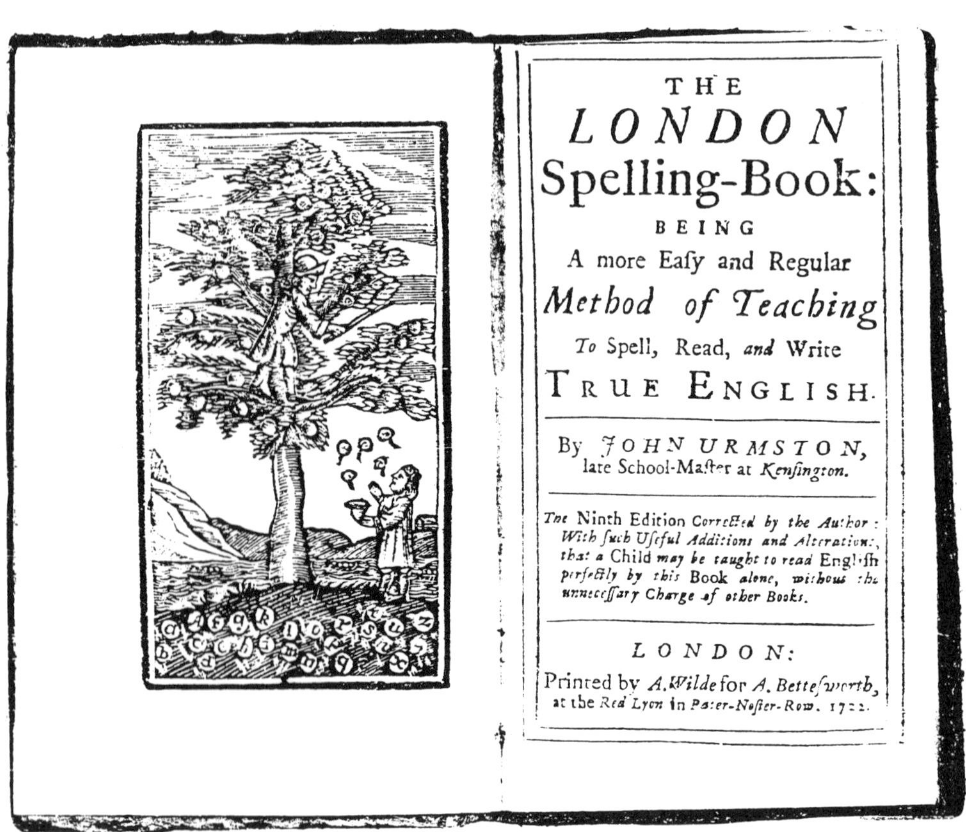

THE

LONDON

Spelling-Book:

BEING

A more Eaſy and Regular

Method of Teaching

To Spell, Read, *and* Write

TRUE ENGLISH.

By *JOHN URMSTON,*
late School-Maſter at *Kenſington.*

The Ninth Edition *Corrected by the Author: With ſuch Uſeful Additions and Alterations, that a* Child *may be taught to read* Engliſh *perfectly by this* Book *alone, without the unneceſſary Charge of other Books.*

LONDON:

Printed by *A. Wilde* for *A. Betteſworth*, at the *Red Lyon* in *Pater-Noſter-Row.* 1722.

Prior to his service as an SPG missionary in North Carolina (1710-1721), Rev. John Urmston operated a school in Kensington, London, and was author of an 82-page primer that went through a number of editions. Shown here is the frontispiece from a copy in the Biblioteca Naçional, Madrid.

THE COLONIAL RECORDS OF NORTH CAROLINA
[Second Series]

VOLUME X

THE CHURCH OF ENGLAND IN NORTH CAROLINA: DOCUMENTS, 1699-1741

ROBERT J. CAIN, *Editor*

Assisted by DENNIS ISENBARGER, LEIGH ANNA LAWING, WILLIAM A. OWENS, JR., TRUDY RAYFIELD, and SUSAN M. TRIMBLE

DIVISION OF ARCHIVES AND HISTORY
NORTH CAROLINA DEPARTMENT OF CULTURAL RESOURCES
RALEIGH
1999

Library of Congress Catalog Card Number 99-070515
ISBN 0-86526-283-7

Table of Contents

Acknowledgments ix

Introduction to the Volume xi

The Documents in this Volume xi

The Church of England in North Carolina to 1741 xiii

Editorial Method l

Abbreviations

Source References for Documents lii

Document Type lii

Citations to Printed Sources liii

List of Documents lvii

Papers of the Church of England 3

Vestry Minutes 431

Appendix. 497

Index 505

Illustrations

Frontispiece and title page of book by Rev. John Urmston . . . . . . *frontispiece*

Catalog of books in Bath Library . . . . *following lxix*

Thomas Tenison, archbishop of Canterbury 1694-1715 . . . . *do.*

Letter from Rev. Giles Ransford . . . . *do.*

Thomas Bray, founder of SPCK and SPG . . . . *do.*

William Wake, archbishop of Canterbury 1716-1737 . . . . *do.*

Interior of St. Thomas's Church, Bath . . . . *do.*

Edmund Gibson, bishop of London 1723-1748 . . . . *following 428*

Title page of "Osterwald's Catechism" . . . . *do.*

Entry from Journal of the SPG . . . . *do.*

Henry Compton, bishop of London 1675-1686, 1688-1713 . . . . . *do.*

Recommendation for Rev. Thomas Newnam . . . . *do.*

Title page of published sermon . . . . *do.*

Page from vestry minutes, St. Paul's, Edenton . . . . *facing 431*

Acknowledgments

Since the first documents were transcribed for this volume in October, 1981, a number of people have played a part in its publication. My thanks are therefore due to Terrell A. Crow, Patricia Johnson, Leigh Anna Lawing, E.T. Malone, Jr., William A. Owens, Jr., Trudy Rayfield, the late Josephine Walker, Caroline Banks Whitley, Frank Whitley, Stephena K. Williams, and Kay B. Wyche. The newest staff member, Dennis Isenbarger, has been helpful in various ways in the latter stages. I owe a special debt of gratitude to Susan M. Trimble, editorial assistant, who has performed key tasks in the creation of the present work—indexing, bibliographic research on the many arcane titles mentioned in the text, and preparing camera-ready copy—to name a few.

Although not involved directly in the process of production, others have played essential roles in bringing this work to completion: Dr. Jeffrey J. Crow, director of the Division of Archives and History, and Dr. William S. Price, Jr., former director, have been fully supportive, as have the current administrator of the Publications Section, Joe A. Mobley, and former administrators Jeffrey J. Crow and Mrs. Memory Mitchell. No editor could ask for better cooperation and encouragement than I have had over the years from these scholars.

The editor also acknowledges with thanks the following individuals who read the introduction and made valuable suggestions: Barbara T. Cain, Jeffrey J. Crow, E.T. Malone, Jr., William S. Powell, William S. Price, Jr., and Alan Watson. Any remaining errors are entirely my own. A special word of thanks also must go to The Carolina Charter Corporation, which for almost forty years has been an indispensible part of the work of the North Carolina Colonial Records Project, of which *The Colonial Records of North Carolina* [*Second Series*] is a part. The current president, Armistead Maupin, and his predecessors, George E. London, Mrs. L.Y. Ballentine, David Stick, and Francis E. Winslow, have been unstinting in their efforts on behalf of the project, as have numerous other members of the corporation.

Permission to publish selected records in its custody and ownership has been graciously granted by the United Society for the Propagation of the Gospel. Similar permission has been given by His Grace the archbishop of Canterbury and the trustees of Lambeth Palace Library; the comptrollers of Her Majesty's Stationery Office; the North Carolina Collection, University of North Carolina Library at Chapel Hill; and St. Paul's Episcopal Church, Edenton.

Since the publication of Volume IX, the Colonial Records Project has lost through death one of its stauchest supporters. Mattie Erma Edwards Parker died on July 4, 1995, at the age of eighty-nine. Mrs. Parker brought the project into being, presided over a search for North Carolina-related documents in dozens of American repositories, devised the editorial procedures still in use in the project, and edited the first three volumes in the present series. Additionally, Mrs. Parker was for many years secretary of the Carolina Charter Corporation. Her successor editors will always be grateful to her for these accomplishments, and also for her willingness, when she thought it necessary, to stand firm in defense of the project. I dedicate this volume to her memory.

Robert J. Cain
Raleigh, North Carolina
May 23, 1999

Introduction to the Volume

THE DOCUMENTS IN THIS VOLUME

The documents printed in this first of three volumes devoted to records of the Church of England in colonial North Carolina consist of letters, reports, petitions, journal entries, statutes, and similar items, as well as minutes of the vestry of the parish of St. Paul, Edenton. The majority are from the archives of the Society for the Propagation of the Gospel in Foreign Parts (SPG), an abundantly rich collection now housed in Rhodes House Library, Oxford University. Other documents are from various repositories, most notably from the Fulham Papers in the Lambeth Palace Library, and from the Public Record Office, Kew, Surrey, England. The letters are in the main originals and copybook copies sent by clergymen in the colony to the Society and to the bishop of London and archbishop of Canterbury. Transcriptions of these and of the other items printed in this volume were prepared from paper printouts from microfilm. In a number of instances it was necessary for the editor to examine the original at Rhodes House Library in order to clarify words and passages not legible on the microfilm. Paper printouts were also used for transcriptions of the vestry minutes from St. Paul's.

The correspondence and other material from the SPG are organized at Rhodes House into several series: Series B and Series C consist of originals, and Series A (which ends in 1736) consists of copybook copies. Except in the very few instances in which they were too fragmented to be printable, originals, when extant, have been used in preference to copies.

The printed annual "Abstract of the Proceedings" of the SPG, a series beginning in 1711, affords a useful brief review, colony by colony, of activities of the Society's missionaries. In a few cases these reports, which were appended to the annual anniversary sermon preached before the Society, are able to supply a summary of a letter or other document not extant in any other form.

Journals of the monthly meetings of the Society record actions taken by that body, and also contain full summaries of letters received from its missionaries and others. Relevant extracts have generally been included here in editorial notes, although they sometimes are printed as documents in their own right. In a sizeable number of instances the journals' abstracts of letters, petitions, and other documents presented to the meetings constitute the only surviving version of the document. Especially is this true of the period from October, 1735, to June, 1738, when there is an almost total absence of both originals and verbatim copies of SPG records relating to North Carolina.

Except for two brief extracts from Pasquotank Parish,[1] the only surviving vestry minutes from this period are those kept by the vestry in Chowan. Even these are not complete, as is readily apparent in several instances,[2] and it may well be that there were a number of sittings for which no record exists. That said, the fact remains that these minutes provide a unique insight into the workings of an Anglican parish in North Carolina during the first four decades of the eighteenth century. Other types of vestry records are even more rare. A few letters and petitions from vestries survive,[3] but no parish registers recording christenings, marriages, and burials have been unearthed.

One innovation in the present volume is that, unlike the first nine in this series, it includes extracts as well as entire documents. Previous volumes have with almost no exceptions printed documents in full; such a procedure for Volume X would have led to the inclusion of much material that is of marginal or no value to the story of the Church of England in colonial North Carolina.

[1]Pp. 251-252, below.

[2]Pp. 447, 448*n*. Accounts and rough minutes misplaced before they could be entered in the vestry minute book are the subject of an order of the vestry in 1734, p. 476, below. See also p. 469, below.

[3]Pp. 171-173, 309-310, 324, 353-354, 450, below.

THE CHURCH OF ENGLAND IN NORTH CAROLINA TO 1741

Virginia Dare, the first child born in America of English parents, was baptized in August, 1587, on Roanoke Island, within the bounds of what later would become the colony of North Carolina. In that same month the Indian Manteo was also baptized in Roanoke.[1] In both instances the rite was administered according to the form prescribed by the Church of England, an institution created by an English monarch half a century before and, by the time of the Roanoke settlement, securely entrenched in England by acts of Parliament. Despite this promising beginning for Anglicanism in North Carolina, more than a century elapsed before it became the official faith of the province—indeed, before the Church of England had a presence in North Carolina that can be detected definitively at this remove in time.

Permanent white settlement in North Carolina began in the 1650s, and for the next forty years it would be confined to the region above Albemarle Sound, mainly along the extensive system of rivers and creeks. Settlement gradually spread south, with the Pamlico River area receiving its first white settlers around 1691. By 1703 the Neuse was settled as well, and in the mid-1720s the Cape Fear region followed suit. The colony enjoyed no semblance of an urban center until the establishment of Bath Town near the mouth of the Pamlico River in the opening years of the eighteenth century.[2] Such decentralization proved to be inconducive to the construction of church buildings, or to the establishment of an efficient parish structure or other accouterments of a flourishing church life on the Anglican model.

So far as is known, there was no organized Anglican congregation in North Carolina during the seventeenth century. Henderson Walker, president of the Council, summed up the situation when he wrote in 1703 that "we have been Settled neer...50 years in this place, and I may justly say most part of 21 years on my owne knowledge without Priest or Altar and

[1]William S. Powell, *Dictionary of North Carolina Biography*, 6 vols. (Chapel Hill: University of North Carolina Press, 1979-1996).

[2]Hugh T. Lefler and William S. Powell, *Colonial North Carolina: A History* (New York: Charles Scribner's Sons, 1973), 29-112, hereinafter cited as Lefler and Powell, *Colonial North Carolina*.

before that time according to all that appears to me much worse."[3] The province consequently became a byword for virtual heathenism among British dominions. In the first decade of the eighteenth century a secretary of the Society for the Propagation of the Gospel, or SPG, characterized North Carolina as "this sad Country," where there was "hardly any face of Religion, no Ministers, no Churches, no Towns, nor anything but a vast scatter'd flock without Shepherds and running wild in the desert."[4] At about the same time a bishop of London argued for a substantial supplement to the salary offered prospective missionaries to North Carolina, "for," he wrote, "they must live among Barbarians." The Rev. John Blair's brief time in the colony in 1704 convinced him that he had been "sent to the most Barbarous place in the Continent,"[5] while the experiences of the SPG missionary William Gordon led him in 1708 to view North Carolina as "a Countrey but wild and Imperfect in its' Circumstances."[6] Two and a half years (1708-1710) in Pasquotank and Currituck precincts proved more than sufficient to persuade the Rev. James Adams that he had "struggled...with a Lawless and Barbarous People," while the Rev. John Urmston at about the same time denounced North Carolinians as "an InGratefull people" who were "the dreggs and Gleanings of all other Ingish Colonies." Some among the second generation of clergy in the colony saw little improvement. A disillusioned John LaPierre in 1733 saw "a lawless place, a Scattered people," affording a minister neither parsonage nor glebe.[7] Lay opinion corroborated the clerical. The aristocratic Virginian, William Byrd of Westover, whose mordant wit was directed more than once against North Carolinians, called them "Arrant Pagans" in the 1720s, and condemned Virginia's southern neighbor as being a place where "every One does what seems best in his own Eyes." He went on to ridicule Edenton, one of only two tiny villages in the province, for being, he claimed exaggeratedly, "the only Metropolis in the Christian or Mahometan World, where there is neither Church,

[3]P. 22, below.
[4]Pp. 57-58, below.
[5]Pp. 31, 48, below.
[6]P. 86, below.
[7]Pp. 104, 276, 348, below.

Chappel, Mosque, Synagogue, or any other Place of Publick Worship of any Sect or Religion whatsoever."[8]

Although opportunities for worship according to the rubrics of the Book of Common Prayer were almost nonexistent in North Carolina during the seventeenth century, they were not entirely so. The statement of Henderson Walker quoted above suggests that during the preceding twenty-one years religious services were not completely wanting. According to testimony presented in a lawsuit many years later, one "Parson John Wood," presumably an Anglican minister, is supposed to have settled at Nobbs Crook Creek in Pasquotank Precinct around 1679, where he remained some years as "parson of the Place." If the statement is accurate, and Wood was indeed in Anglican orders, he would be the first priest of the Church of England in North Carolina for which a record survives. The assertion, made in the province's Court of Chancery in 1714, claimed that Wood "came and settled upon" the land in question "about the year 1679," then "after Some considerable time" he returned to "Europe." Wood appointed an attorney to look after his affairs, including receipt of "his Tobacco due to him, he having been parson of the Place"—a phrase perhaps indicating payment of salary due from a Virginia parish, but one also at least hinting at the admittedly remote but interesting possibility of a seventeenth-century North Carolina statute, now lost, providing for the payment of clergy in tobacco.[9] In addition, visiting clergy from Virginia would at least occasionally conduct services in Albemarle, a practice persisting well into the following century. A letter of 1729 from Governor Richard Everard to the bishop of London stated that "our New Country

[8]William K. Boyd (ed.), *William Byrd's Histories of the Dividing Line Betwixt Virginia and North Carolina* (Raleigh: North Carolina Historical Commission, 1929), 96.

[9]William S. Price, Jr. (ed.), *Higher-Court Minutes, 1709-1723*, Volume V of *The Colonial Records of North Carolina* [*Second Series*] (Raleigh: Department of Cultural Resources, Division of Archives and History [projected multivolume series, 1963-], 1977), 490-491, hereinafter cited as Price, *Higher-Court Minutes, 1709-1723*. A John Wood (or "Mr. Wood") married North Carolina couples as early as 1671, with at least one of the ceremonies being performed in Accomack County in Virginia. Perquimans Precinct, Births, Marriages, Deaths, and Flesh Marks, 1659-1820, 1, 3, 5. State Archives, Division of Archives and History, Raleigh, hereinafter referred to as Perquimans Register. Nobbs Crook Creek, a tributary of the Pasquotank River, was in Pasquotank Precinct. Margaret Hofmann, *Provinces of North Carolina, 1663-1729: Abstracts of Land Patents*, (Weldon, N.C.: Roanoke News Co., 1979), 18 and passim. A standard (and frequently inaccurate) compilation of the names and careers of colonial American clergy states that a John Wood, son of a clergyman, matriculated Magdalen Hall, Oxford University, in 1658, and was in Nansemond Parish, Virginia, from 1684. Weis, *The Colonial Clergy of Virginia, North Carolina, South Carolina* (Boston: Society of the Descendants of the Colonial Clergy, 1955), 55. The name of the person who baptized Virginia Dare and Manteo is unknown. He perhaps

next Virginia is well supplyd by the indefatiguable Pains and Industry" of Rev. Nicholas Jones of Nansemond County.[10] Two years later, Governor George Burrington spoke of northern parishes of North Carolina "Paying some Neighbouring Minister for Comeing out of Virginia."[11] Clergy from Virginia also married numerous couples registered in the Perquimans Precinct register of births, marriages, and deaths.[12] Lay readers—unordained persons authorized to undertake a limited number of ecclesiastical functions—may have read prayers and sermons from time to time during the earlier period, although there is no surviving evidence that they did so.

The lords proprietors, who theoretically governed North Carolina from the time they received royal charters in 1663 and 1665 to their sale of seven-eighths of the province to the Crown in 1729, did little to encourage the growth of Anglicanism in the colony—and this despite the fact that the charter of 1663 stated as a principal motive of the proprietors their being "excited with a laudable and pious Zeal for the propagation of the Christian Faith."[13] As an inducement to settlement, the province of Carolina, comprising what in time became the two Carolinas, from the beginning enjoyed religious toleration. The charters granted by King Charles II invested the proprietors with authority to build Anglican churches and chapels and to appoint Anglican clergy. More importantly, the charters empowered the proprietors to grant "Indulgencies and Dispensations" to any in the province who did not wish to be included within the Anglican fold, and so long as they did not create disturbances they could worship, or not, as they pleased. Presumably this freedom could be extended to Catholics, and even to Jews and other non-Christians, since the power granted to the proprietors was unqualified. Similar provisions were included in several other colonial charters granted around this time, although such liberties were far from being permitted in England, or in Carolina's northern

was a ship's chaplain, since there is no evidence that the Roanoke settlers included a clergyman among their number. David Beers Quinn, *The Roanoke Voyages, 1584-1590* (London: Hakluyt Society, 1955), II, 531*n*.

[10]P. 321, below.

[11]P. 327, below.

[12]Perquimans Register, passim. Although entries do not state in which colony the ceremonies took place, the fact of their being recorded in Perquimans County makes it likely that they took place there.

[13]Mattie Erma Edwards Parker (ed.), *North Carolina Charters and Constitutions, 1578-1698*, Volume I of *The Colonial Records of North Carolina* [*Second Series*] (Raleigh: Department of Cultural Resources, Division of Archives and History [projected multivolume series, 1963-], 1963), 76, hereinafter cited as Parker, *Charters and Constitutions*.

neighbor Virginia, which in 1643 had by statute established the Church of England and thereby provoked an exodus of Catholics and Puritans from that colony. The proprietors of Carolina almost immediately made the charters' toleration clauses part of a formal compact, the Concessions and Agreement (1665), negotiated between the proprietors and a group of Barbadians intending to settle in Carolina.[14]

The philosopher John Locke, secretary to the proprietary board and associate of Anthony Ashley Cooper, later first earl of Shaftesbury, the most active and visionary of the early proprietors, is with Cooper credited with devising the "Grand Model" that was intended to provide a system of government for the infant colony. The Fundamental Constitutions of Carolina, as the instrument was named, went through a number of substantial revisions between the time of the first version of 1669 and the final one of 1698. During this period, the clauses relating to religion and the church underwent notable changes that usually reflected either the shifting composition of the proprietary board, or the prevailing political climate in England.[15] Few, however, of the elaborate provisions of the Fundamental Constitutions were ever implemented entirely, or even partially, in either the northern or southern parts of Carolina. The structure of government envisioned by the Constitutions presupposed an elite of sufficient number and quality to fill the plethora of offices to be established, and lower orders of the necessary numbers and docility to enable the essentially feudal scheme of landholding to come into being. Neither of these conditions was ever realized in proprietary Carolina.[16]

A number of the clauses relating to religion remained unchanged in each of the successive versions of the Constitutions. Being a freeman and property owner, or even a resident, was conditional on acknowledgment

---

[14]Parker, *Charters and Constitutions*, 77, 88-89, 92, 103-104, 114; Charles M. Andrews, *The Colonial Period of American History*, 4 vols. (New Haven and London: Yale University Press, 1934-1938), II, 4, and I-IV, passim, hereinafter cited as Andrews, *Colonial Period*.

[15]Parker, *Charters and Constitutions*, 128-131; Andrews, *Colonial Period*, III, 212-221; Herbert R. Paschal, "Proprietary North Carolina: A Study in Colonial Government" (unpublished doctoral dissertation, University of North Carolina, Chapel Hill, 1961), 117-118.

[16]Robert J. Cain (ed.), *Records of the Executive Council, 1664-1734*, Volume VII of *The Colonial Records of North Carolina* [*Second Series*] (Raleigh: Department of Cultural Resources, Division of Archives and History [projected multivolume series, 1963-], 1984), xv-liv, passim, hereinafter cited as Cain, *Records of the Executive Council, 1664-1734*. The Grand Model was in reality devised more for the southern colony at Ashley River, settlement of which began in 1670, than for the one at Albemarle, which had been in being for a dozen or more years when the first draft of the Constitutions was penned.

of a God and of the necessity of according Him public and solemn worship. Any seven or more persons could bring into being their own religion, with its distinctive beliefs and name—the only stipulations regarding belief and practice being that the existence of God and the necessity for public worship had to be acknowledged, and that there be some procedure whereby an adherent could "bear witness to truth" by a solemn oath or its equivalent. One could become a member of a sect by formally enrolling in the subscription book of whichever one he chose, and membership in some "Church or Profession" was a precondition to officeholding and even to enjoying "any benefit or protection of the Law." Other clauses, no doubt inspired by the intense religious turmoil in England during its civil war a generation before, prohibited the ridiculing of any faith or the disturbance of its services, or speaking "Irreverently or seditiously" of the government or governor during such services. The Constitutions were at pains to address the question of whether or not a slave enjoyed any enhanced standing in law by virtue of becoming a church member. He did not.[17]

In addition to those clauses remaining essentially the same in all versions of the Fundamental Constitutions, there were others that changed significantly over the period from 1669 to 1698. The first reference to the Church of England appeared in the third version of the Constitutions (1670):

> As the Country comes to be sufficiently Planted and Distributed into fit Divisions, it shall belong to the Parliament to take care for the building of Churches and the public Maintenance of Divines, to be employed in the Exercise of Religion according to the Church of England, which, being the only true and Orthodox, and the National Religion of all the King's Dominions, is so also of Carolina, and therefore, it alone shall be allowed to receive public Maintenance by Grant of Parliament.[18]

In the two versions of 1682 (January and August), drawn up in the midst of the crisis in England over the impending accession of the Catholic duke

[17]Parker, *Charters and Constitutions*, 148-150, 163-164, 181-183, 202-204, 227-229, 238-240.
[18]Parker, *Charters and Constitutions*, 181.

of York to the crowns of England and Scotland, which saw the proprietor and eminent protestant champion, Lord Shaftesbury, forced to flee the country in November, the characterization of the Church of England as "the only true and Orthodox, and the National Religion of all the King's Dominions" changed to the much less grandiloquent "religion of the Government of England." Omitted also was the declaration that Anglicanism was the faith "also of Carolina," although the statement of its exclusive right to "public Maintenance by Grant of Parliament" was retained. The second version of 1682 then proceeded to permit each "church or Congregation of Christians, not of the communion of the Church of Rome" to tax its own members annually up to a penny per acre of land and twelve pence per poll, and it enjoined the taxation of anyone for the support of any church except the one to which he belonged. It also for the first time prohibited clergy of any denomination from being a member of the legislature or from holding any civil office.[19] Both versions of 1682 also made acknowledgment of belief in an afterlife a condition of being a property–owning free inhabitant of Carolina.[20]

The version of the Fundamental Constitutions most unabashedly promoting Anglicanism was that of 1698, the last in the series. It probably was more than simple coincidence that this one appeared only a year after the accession of John Grenville, first earl of Bath, to the leadership of the proprietary board as palatine. Bath's son, John Grenville, first baron Granville of Potheridge, inherited his father's proprietary share in 1701 and also became palatine in that year. Lord Granville was a zealous churchman, and it is probable that even before becoming palatine he influenced the drafting of the last Constitutions. Whereas the various Constitutions from 1669 to 1682 contained from 111 to 125 clauses, the one of 1698 had only forty-one, and of these fully sixteen dealt with religion. Restored to a place of prominence in 1698 was the statement that the Church of England was "the only true and orthodox, and the National Religion of the King's Dominions," even as it was "also of Carolina." The provision allowing seven or more to constitute a "church or profession" was retained, although, as if to make the point that religious toleration

[19]Parker, *Charters and Constitutions*, 202, 227-228

[20]Parker, *Charters and Constitutions*, 202, 227. The first required affirmation of "a future being after this Life," while the second added to the end of this formulation the codicil "of happiness or misery."

was at best a distasteful expedient, the lengthy preamble to the clause, stressing the positive benefits of toleration, for the first time did not appear in the Constitutions. Also dropped was the clause prohibiting clergymen from holding secular office or serving in the assembly. More significantly, the power of a group constituting a "church or profession" to tax its adherents was entirely omitted, as was the ban on taxing for the support of a church other than the one to which the taxpayer belonged. By 1698, then, the constitutional mechanisms were in place at least to allow, if not to require, the formal establishment of the Church of England as the officially sanctioned faith in Carolina, and on a basis similar to that by which it was established in the mother country. Such an eventuality awaited only the enactment of enabling legislation in the assemblies of Carolina, north and south.[21]

The Fundamental Constitutions in their various manifestations remained almost entirely in the realm of theory. This fact was in effect recognized by the lords proprietors, as evidenced in such things as the promulgation of several sets of "Temporary Laws" in the 1670s and the issuance of formal instructions to successive governors at the beginning of their administrations. The stated purpose of the Temporary Laws was to provide an interim form of government until Carolina acquired sufficient population to enable the Constitutions to be implemented. The laws came, however, to be considered by the proprietors an integral part of the colony's governmental system until the opening years of the next century.

[21]M. Eugene Sirmans, *Colonial South Carolina: A Political History, 1663-1786* (Williamsburg: Institute of Early American History and Culture, 1966), 76-77, characterizes Lord Granville, as "an aggressive Anglican" and quotes a contemporaneous source describing him as "an inflexible bigot for the High-church." Parker, *Charters and Constitutions*, 149-150, 181, 203, 228, 238. The preamble stated well the case for religious toleration, especially in a colonial context: "But Since the natives of that place, who will be concerned in our plantation, are utterly strangers to Christianity, whose Idolatry, Ignorance, or mistake gives us no right to Expel or use them ill; and those who remove from other parts to plant there will unavoidably be of differenct opinions concerning matters of Religion, the liberty whereof they will expect to have allowed them, and it will not be Reasonable for us, on this account, to keep them out; that civil peace may be maintained amidst the diversity of opinions, and our agreement and compact with all men may be duly and faithfully observed, the volution [violation] whereof, upon what pretense soever, cannot be without great offence to Almighty God, and great scandal to the true Religion, which we profess; and also, that Jews, heathens, and other disenters from the purity of Christian Religion may not be scared and kept at a distance from it, but, by having an opportunity of acquainting themselves with the truth and Reasonableness of its doctrine, and the peaceableness and Inoffensiveness of its professors, may, by good usage and persuasion, and all those Convincing methods of Gentleness and meeknes suitable to the Rules and design of the gospel, be won over to embrace and unfeignedly Receive the truth: therefore, any Seven or more persons agreeing in any Religion shall constitute a church or profession, to which they shall give some name to distinguish it from others."

Instructions to governors throughout the proprietary period were viewed in a similar light by the proprietors. In neither the Temporary Laws nor the instructions were there any references to church matters, but only to the mundane concerns of land policy and the organization of civil government.[22] The primacy of the proprietors' laws and instructions as attempts to communicate and implement their wishes, and the patent inability of the Fundamental Constitutions to accomplish these ends, was implicitly recognized by the proprietors when they suspended the Constitutions in 1693. The version of 1698 was a last attempt to devise a workable scheme of government based on at least some remaining shreds of the Grand Model. It was, however, never accepted in South Carolina, and apparently there was no attempt to have it promulgated in North Carolina. From 1709, instructions to new governors of both Carolinas omitted all references to the Fundamental Constitutions, although in strict theory its status as organic law was undiminished for as long as proprietary government existed—to 1719 in South Carolina, and 1729 in North Carolina.[23]

As noted previously, the lords proprietors as a body gave but meager practical assistance to the planting of Anglicanism in North Carolina throughout the period of their authority there. In 1670, the proprietary board informed the governor and Council of Albemarle that as an inducement to the establishment of a town, the first revenues they received from the colony would be devoted to building a church, a "state house" and a prison.[24] The colony's first town, Bath, did not come into being for another thirty-five years, and there is no evidence that the proprietors ever contributed to the construction of a church or other public building there. In 1712

[22]The Temporary Laws and the instructions to proprietary governors are to be found only in widely scattered sources, not all of them published. For the laws, the Temporary Laws of 1671 and 1672 are printed in Langdon Cheves (ed.), "The Shaftesbury Papers and other Records relating to Carolina...," *Collections of the South Carolina Historical Society*, V (1897), 324-325, 367, 403-405; the Temporary Agrarian Laws of 1672 are printed in William James Rivers, *A Sketch of the History of South Carolina to the Close of the Proprietary Government by the Revolution of 1719* (Charleston: McCarter & Co., 1856), 355-359. The set sent to the government of Albemarle, virtually identical to the one sent to South Carolina dated June 21, 1672, is printed in J. R. B. Hathaway (ed.), *North Carolina Historical and Genealogical Register*, III (January, 1903), 27-29. The instructions are found in Cain, *Records of the Executive Council, 1664-1734*, 335-336, 350-353, (to the governor and Council, 1670 and 1679) 442-454, 464-475, 507-524, 544-549 (to governors Edward Hyde, Charles Eden, George Burrington, and Richard Everard). Other instructions are printed in Saunders, *Colonial Records*, I, 333-338 (Captain Henry Wilkinson), 373-384 (Philip Ludwell), 391-392, 554-557, 694-696 (John Archdale, Edward Tynte, and Sir Nathaniel Johnson as governor of "Carolina").

[23]Cain, *Records of the Executive Council, 1664-1734*, xvi-xvii.

[24]Cain, *Records of the Executive Council, 1664-1734*, 339.

they wrote the General Assembly offering to contribute £200 sterling toward the building of a church "in such place as shal be thought most Suitable and convenient to all or at least the Greatest part of the Inhabitants" of the province. A statute of 1723 declared the recently established town of Edenton the beneficiary of this proprietary largesse and ordered that the funds be collected from the receiver general. The legislation then went on to specify the dimensions and other details of the building, and to provide a further £200 as the province's contribution, "that the Said Church may be handsomely and completely finished." Surviving records do not disclose whether or not the sums were ever actually paid, although in 1724 the vestry of St. Paul's ordered that a request for £200 be made both to the proprietors' receiver general and to the province's treasurer.[25] In 1725 the proprietors agreed to build a house for the minister in Edenton and to set aside 300 acres for a glebe, but this was never done.[26]

On occasion, the lords proprietors would commend a cleric to the attention of the provincial authorities, as they did the Rev. Dr. Thomas Bray in 1699, and the Rev. John Urmston in 1710. Similarly, when two clergymen in 1725 requested a recommendation to the bishop of London in order to be sent to North Carolina, the proprietors were happy to oblige and reminded the SPG that by their charter they were vested with the right to nominate ministers to livings.[27] With becoming piety, the previously mentioned letter of 1712 from the proprietors to the assembly had also undertaken to "earnestly recommend" to that body that it "Seriously consider of the state of the Church" in the province, and also that it "take care that the same may be Establish'd and that all due and necessary appointments may be made to the Ministers thereof." In fact, by that year the Church of England had already been established in North Carolina for some years, thanks to a statute enacted by the General Assembly in 1701. A pithy commentary on the lackluster role of the proprietors in ecclesiastical affairs in North Carolina is provided by the large landowner and devout churchman, Sir Nathaniel Duckenfield, when he wrote near the

[25]CO 5/290, 51, in the Public Record Office, Kew, Surrey, England, photocopies in British Records, State Archives, Raleigh; Walter Clark (ed.), *The State Records of North Carolina* (Raleigh: State of North Carolina, 1895-1906), XXV, 193, hereinafter cited as Clark, *State Records*; p. 461, below.

[26]P. 298, below. Rev. William Gordon in 1709 ridiculed the church of St. Paul's Parish as "Small, very Sorrily put together, and as ill lookd after," but not until the late 1730s did construction of an adequate building get under way. Pp. 84, 285, 461, 485, and passim, below.

[27]Pp. 3, 103, 297-298, 298*n*, below.

end of the proprietary era that the proprietors had "little of Church Affairs at Heart."[28]

At the beginning of the eighteenth century, Virginia and possibly New York were the only mainland colonies in which the Church of England had been established.[29] Following the English model, establishment acts in British America usually included the levying of a general tax in order to maintain Anglican clergy and to pay for the construction of Anglican churches. Ministers of the Church of England also enjoyed such perquisites as receiving a fee for all marriages performed in their parish, and exemption from militia duty. In addition to these privileges granted by statute, there were as well the statutory obligations to provide for the poor and to assume several administrative responsibilities, both of which functions in North Carolina will be discussed later in this essay.[30]

As has been mentioned previously, North Carolina in 1700 had enjoyed permanent white settlement for almost half a century. Over the course of that period, the region settled by Europeans expanded to encompass the entire area north of Albemarle Sound and included as well much of the Pamlico Sound region to the south. The population had grown from at most a few hundred to an estimated 10,000 whites, plus several hundred black slaves.[31] During this period of territorial expansion and increase in numbers, the only organized, sustained religious activity, apart from rites performed by indigenous peoples, had been that of the Society of Friends, or Quakers. Perquimans and Pasquotank precincts became strong centers of Quakerism following visits in 1672 by George Fox and William Edmundson, and by 1700 there were at least three weekly meetings in the area.[32]

The establishment of Anglicanism as the officially sanctioned faith in North Carolina came in November, 1701, with the enactment of the first

---

[28]P. 311, below.

[29]A Virginia act of 1643 required all ministers "to conform to the orders and constitutions of the Church of England." Andrews, *Colonial Period*, I, 234n. The establishment act passed by New York's assembly in 1693 was "an ambiguously worded statement which seemed to favor the interests of the Church of England without actually saying so." John Frederick Woolverton, *Colonial Anglicanism in North America* (Detroit: Wayne State University Press, 1984), 125, hereinafter cited as Woolverton, *Colonial Anglicanism.*

[30]Woolverton, *Colonial Anglicanism*, 16-23, and passim.

[31]William S. Price, Jr. (ed.), *North Carolina Higher-Court Records, 1702-1708*, Volume IV of *The Colonial Records of North Carolina* [*Second Series*] (Raleigh: Department of Cultural Resources, Division of Archives and History [projected multivolume series, 1963-]), 1974, xiii, hereinafter cited as Price, *Higher-Court Records, 1702-1708.*

[32]Price, *Higher-Court Records, 1702-1708*, xvi. For Quakerism generally in North Carolina see Seth B. Hinshaw, *The Carolina Quaker Experience, 1665-1985: An Interpretation* (Greensboro: North Carolina Yearly Meeting and the North Carolina Friends Historical Society, 1984).

of a succession of so-called "vestry acts." Virtually the only evidence we have concerning circumstances surrounding the event is the statement of Henderson Walker, president of the Council and staunch churchman, two years later that "with a great deale of Care and management" his administration had been able to "get an Assembly" favorable to the enterprise. The vestry of St. Paul's, Edenton, some years later recalled that the outcome "was not obtained without hard struggling," and one may well believe it.[33] Although direct evidence is lacking, it is possible that Lord Granville, who became proprietor palatine in August, 1701, was able in some manner to influence the outcome.

The North Carolina act of 1701 does not survive, nor do assembly journals or other legislative records that might throw light on details of its passage. The main provisions of the statute can, however, be inferred from various other sources. Henderson Walker characterized it as one "for building Churches and establishing of a maintenance for Ministers amongst us," while a cleric serving in the colony several years later complained that the £30 annual salary permitted ministers by the act was payable in produce of the country, equivalent to only £10 or £15 sterling.[34] The legislation also named members of the newly erected vestries. The first sitting (November 29, 1701) of the vestry of the parish of Chowan Precinct took care to note that it had been appointed by the 1701 act. The same vestry at its inaugural meeting levied a tax of 12 pence on every tithable in the precinct, an action that would necessarily have been specifically sanctioned by the statute. At the same sitting the vestry directed that a search be made for a reader and that work commence on the building of a church, and as well ordered that relief be provided to an indigent—all of which activities must have been either required or permitted by the act.[35]

Aside from those for Chowan Precinct, the dearth of vestry records makes it impossible to know precisely when and to what degree other vestries became organized and functioning. The Rev. John Blair claimed to have convened a vestry in each precinct during his few months in the colony in 1704, and in that year all four precincts in existence (Chowan, Pasquotank, Perquimans, and Currituck) were in the Albemarle region.

---

[33]Pp. 22, 172, below.
[34]Pp. 22, 65, below.
[35]Pp. 431-432, below.

Blair stated that three small churches had been built and three glebes established, and that in each of "the three Chiefe Presincts" (undoubtedly Pasquotank, Perquimans, and Chowan) a salaried reader had been employed.[36] The vestry of Pasquotank was functioning by 1706 at least, since in that year it sent a petition to the bishop of London.[37] Aside from these and a few similar scraps, nothing is known about the earliest years of vestries in North Carolina.

It is, however, certain that the act of 1701 dismayed and alarmed dissenters in the province, especially Quakers, who undertook a spirited campaign to have it repealed by the assembly or disallowed by the lords proprietors.[38] Whether or not the effort was successful is a matter of debate—due again to the scarcity of surviving sources. The historian Stephen B. Weeks contended that the proprietors had disallowed the act, basing his conclusion solely on a statement by John Blair late in 1704 that the act of 1701 had not been confirmed by the lords proprietors because they considered the £30 annual allowance to ministers insufficient. Virtually all historians of the early church in North Carolina have followed Weeks's lead.[39] A fragment of an undated letter addressed to "your Excellency" stated that Dr. Thomas Bray had written (presumably from London) that the act had been disallowed, not because of "the Littlenesse of the Provision made for the Support of A Minister," but rather because the act gave "too much power to A"—at which point the document is torn, but most likely the missing word is "vestry" or "commission." If, however, the act of 1701 was not in force after the first few years following its passage, it is difficult to explain how the vestry of Chowan could continue to levy a church tax within the parish in each of the years 1704, 1705, and 1706. One plausible explanation is that the North Carolina act of 1701 was never

[36]P. 28, below.

[37]Pp. 44-45, below.

[38]P. 22, below.

[39]Stephen B. Weeks, *Religious Development in the Province of North Carolina* (Baltimore: John Hopkins Press [Tenth Series, Volume V of the John Hopkins University Studies in Historical and Political Science], 1892), 275-276; Lawrence Fouchee London and Sarah McCulloh Lemmon, *The Episcopal Church in North Carolina, 1701-1959* (Raleigh: The Episcopal Diocese of North Carolina, 1987), 5; Sarah McCulloh Lemmon, "The Genesis of the Protestant Episcopal Diocese of North Carolina," *North Carolina Historical Review*, XXVIII (October, 1951), 427; *See also* Lefler and Powell, *Colonial North Carolina*, 195. Hugh Talmage Lefler and Albert Ray Newsome, *The History of a Southern State: North Carolina*, 3d ed. (Chapel Hill: University of North Carolina Press, 1973), 59.

repealed, and that the disallowed act referred to by Dr. Bray was in fact a South Carolina vestry act of 1704 that included a clause setting up a commission that could dismiss ministers from their incumbencies. It is highly unlikely that the North Carolina act contained a similar provision, since the only known reference that can be construed as admitting such a possibility is the fragmentary statement attributed to Dr. Bray.[40]

Paucity of records results in similar confusion over the dates of several enactments subsequent to the one of 1701. Weeks appears to have thought mistakenly that the South Carolina church act of 1704 (that colony's first) was a North Carolina creation of that year.[41] On the other hand, available evidence indicates strongly that a North Carolina act allowing vestries to remove ministers was passed in 1708, and Weeks makes no mention of it. The most noteworthy feature of the 1708 act was that vestries, rather than the governor or other authority, were empowered both to employ and to remove ministers. Clerics within the colony and in London took exception to the provision, and this act may in fact be the one referred to by Dr. Bray as having been disallowed.[42] In 1711 the Anglican-dominated assembly passed two new acts relating to the church. One of them, "An Act for the better and more effectual preserving the Queen's peace, and the establishing a good and lasting foundation of Government in North Carolina," (reenacted in 1715) came in the midst of the civil disturbance known as the Cary Rebellion and included provisions aimed at eradicating "Sedition" and promoting "religion and virtue." The measure punished "seditious words or speeches" and "scurrilous Libels against the present Government" and sought to exclude Quakers from public office in the colony by requiring officials to qualify themselves "according to the strictness of the Laws of Great Brittain now in Force"—laws that required

[40]CCR 188, State Archives, Raleigh; pp. 438-440, 445, below. The complaint of Lord Weymouth in 1706 that missionaries could be "displaced by Laymen" in "Carolina" could apply to either colony, as far as the phraseology is concerned; p. 46, below; Thomas Cooper (ed.), *The Statutes at Large of South Carolina* (Columbia: A. S. Johnston, 2 vols., 1836-37), II, 236-248.

[41]Robert J. Cain, (ed.), *North Carolina Higher-Court Minutes, 1724-1730*, Volume VI of *The Colonial Records of North Carolina* [*Second Series*] (Raleigh: Department of Cultural Resources, Division of Archives and History [projected multivolume series, 1963-], 1981), xxx, hereinafter cited as Cain, *Higher-Court Minutes, 1724-1730*.

[42]Cain, *Higher-Court Minutes, 1724-1730*, xxx; pp. 74, 91, 94, 177. The vestry of Chowan in March, 1703/4, "received" John Blair as minister, he "having the approbation of the D[eputy] Governor." By contrast, the same vestry in May, 1708, "In Observance to a late Act of Assembly...made Choice of" the Rev. William Gordon, "the Honorable presidents Approbation being Signified." Pp. 437, 442, below. Gordon, on his return to England, gave to the secretary of the SPG a copy of a North Carolina act with the partial title "An Act for electing of Vestrys." P. 91, below.

various oaths to be taken, an action in contravention of an important tenet of Quaker belief. The statute then went on to incorporate into North Carolina law "all" enactments of the British Parliament "for the Establishment of the Church," in addition to the corpus of parliamentary statutes "made for granting Indulgences to protestant dissenters."[43] Probably there were few practical effects of the sweeping language. The phraseology was vague, perhaps deliberately, and no specific English laws were cited. Nonetheless, the clause made unmistakably plain that the era of Quaker political influence was at an end.

The other act of 1711 dealt exclusively with the church. Again, the act itself has not survived, but its salient features are known or can be inferred from various sources. The missionary, John Urmston, characterized it as "a very good, and proper Act."[44] He wrote a few months after its passage that a vestry of twelve men had been appointed in each precinct, with all assemblymen being included among the number. Vestries were to choose churchwardens, who could purchase land and a house for the minister's use, as well as build churches and pay the minister a salary. Vestries also were enjoined to make every effort to provide for their parish a clergyman "approved of and allowed by the Lord Bishop of London."[45] Ministers were to be paid at least £70 in commodities,[46] and all taxable (or "tithable") persons[47] in a precinct could be assessed at least 20 pence in "Staple Commodities of the Country," payable at "places convenient upon the Water" rather than at the residence of the minister.[48] It may have been

---

[43]William L. Saunders (ed.), *The Colonial Records of North Carolina* (Raleigh: State of North Carolina, 10 volumes, 1886-1890), I, 789-790, hereinafter cited as Saunders, *Colonial Records*. On the Cary Rebellion see Price, *Higher-Court Minutes, 1709-1723*, xxi-xxv.

[44]P. 119, below. The same minister also called it "A very favourable Act ... made in order to Establish our Church." P. 165, below.

[45]P. 119, below. The inclusion of members of the assembly as ex officio vestrymen is worth noting, since numbers of them undoubtedly would have been opposed to Anglican establishment and might well have proved a disruptive influence in the vestry. The office of churchwarden was an English creation dating from at least the fifteenth century. Usually two in number for each parish, churchwardens in North Carolina were vestrymen appointed by the vestry for a term of one year in order to carry out various administrative functions, such as collecting fines, entering into contracts, and the like.

[46]Pp. 120, 446, below. It may have been the case that ministers could be paid more than the £70 voted by the vestry of Chowan in this instance. In the absence of the act, it is impossible to say.

[47]Although legislation must have addressed the question prior to 1715, the first surviving act defining a tithable is one of 1715, which was enacted because "many Doubts have & do arise at what Age persons in this Country shall be reputed Tythables." Both male and female slaves were to be taxed at age twelve, and free males at age sixteen. An act of 1723 made taxable free blacks, mulattoes, "and other Persons of mixt Blood," and also whites of either sex who married one of them. Clark, *State Records*, XXIII, 72, 106.

[48]P. 447, below.

possible that the legislation allowed, but did not require, taxation at a rate higher than the 20d (or 1s 8d) levied at the February, 1712/13, meeting of the vestry of Chowan. The minister was denied a seat in the vestry, which the missionary John Urmston considered a possibly fatal defect, "for now they are at their Liberty to allow anything or nothing."[49] Some two years after the statute was enacted, Urmston claimed that "little or nothing [has been] done persuant to the said Act" due to "the Opposition of Sectarists" and the "poverty Misery and calamitous Circumstances the Country is reduced to" — the latter being a reference to the effects of the Tuscarora War.[50]

The first North Carolina church act to survive in its entirety is the one of 1715. Included in the so-called Revisal of 1715, it appears to have been in large measure a reenactment of that of 1711. Its preamble asserted that the province was "a Member of the Kingdom of Great Britain" and that by the charter from the crown to the proprietors the Church of England was "the only Established church to have Publick encouragement in it." The preamble went on to state that passage of the act was intended to be an expression of gratitude to the SPG ("the Rtt. Honble, the Society for promoting the Christian Religion in Foreign parts") for its "Zeal for promoting our Holy Religion."

The statute erected nine parishes. In Albemarle County, there were two in each of the precincts of Chowan and Pasquotank, and one each in Currituck and Perquimans. In Bath County, the precincts of Hyde, Craven, and Beaufort each received one. Much of the act concerns attempts to ensure that vestrymen and other parish officials performed their duties—a fact suggesting that this had been a problem under previous legislation. After naming a vestry of twelve men for each parish, it imposed a fine of £3.0.0 on any of them who neglected or refused to qualify by taking the required oaths[51] and by declaring his belief that it was unlawful "upon any pretence whatever" to take up arms against the king. The vestryman, who

[49] Pp. 121, 177, 447, below. It is impossible to say whether Urmston used "allow" in the general sense of "permit," or more specifically to indicate payments to the minister.

[50] P. 165, below.

[51] Although the wording of the oaths is not given, they would undoubtedly have been the ones required of all officeholders: a denial of the legitimacy of the claims of the Stuart pretender to the throne of Great Britain, and a declaration against transubstantiation.

had to be a freeholder, was also required to make a further declaration that he would not oppose "the Liturgy of the Church of England as it is by Law established." Anyone appointed to the vestry who happened to be "a known & publick dissenter from the Church of England" was able to escape the fine. Marshals and churchwardens who did not carry out their statutory tasks could also be fined, as could vestrymen who missed meetings. In contrast to the act of 1711, that of 1715 gave ministers a seat on the vestry. Furthermore, if a vestry failed to fill a vacancy in its ranks due to the refusal of an appointee to qualify, the incumbent minister (or if the parish had none, the governor) could do so.[52]

Importantly, by the 1715 legislation churchwardens and vestries were given the responsibility of procuring a minister. The act made no reference to involvement in the selection process by the governor or any other political or ecclesiastical authority. It then went on to specify that a clergyman employed by a vestry was to be "Qualified according to the Ecclesiasticall Laws of England," as well as "able and Godly" and "of sober Life and Conversation." The vestry could compel the minister's full time residence in the parish, and the act also required him to officiate at the church or chapel in the parish at least ten Sundays annually. A minister was to be paid for his services a minimum of £50 annually by the parish, and the vestry was empowered to purchase land for a glebe and to build a church and chapels.[53]

In order to meet the expenses connected with maintaining a minister and paying "all other parish Charges," the statute empowered the vestry to levy a yearly tax of up to five shillings on all tithables in the parish. Other funds also came by way of legislation. In addition to fines and forfeitures for a plethora of infractions being in part earmarked for "the use of the parish," a portion of the proceeds from the sale of town lots in Bath, Edenton, and Beaufort was turned over to the vestries of the respective parishes. The 1715 "Act Concerning Servants and Slaves" gave churchwardens the responsibility of selling the service of female servants who bore a

[52]Pp. 188-191, below. Although not provided for in the act of 1715, vestrymen could be excused from service for "Age and Infirmity." Pp. 459-460, below.

[53]P. 192, below.

child by their master, or of any white woman who did so by a Negro, Mulatto, or Indian, with the proceeds going to the vestry. Likewise, churchwardens were directed to bind out to the age of 31 years the children born of such relationships, and the vestry was entitled to receive any "Profitts" that might be realized by the transaction.[54] Failure of the vestries in the counties of Craven and Chowan to levy a tax sufficient to build churches in New Bern and Edenton led the General Assembly itself in 1740 to impose a two-year tax for the purpose, and to appoint commissioners to oversee their construction.[55] Almost two decades later, in 1759, the assembly approved a lottery to raise funds for completing churches in the parishes of St. James and St. Philip in New Hanover County, that method being considered "a more easy Way than by an additional Tax for that Purpose." The scant number of lottery tickets sold, however, impelled the passage of a similar act in 1760, and the legislation also earmarked proceeds from the sale of slaves and other booty recovered from a Spanish privateer in the Cape Fear in 1748 for construction of the two churches.[56]

Gifts constituted another source of parochial funds. An act of 1720 mentioned "Some particular persons" who paid the salaries of the minister and reader in the Southwest Parish of Chowan, and the Rev. John LaPierre in the newly established New Hanover Precinct received his stipend by subscription among his parishioners. Governor Henderson Walker's will in 1701 bequeathed £5 toward construction of a church in Chowan, while that of the Wilmington merchant Alexander Duncan in 1767 left the substantial sum of £400 proclamation toward completing or adorning the church there. The Rev. Thomas Newnam in 1722 noted that "we are now Making a Collection thro' the Whole Parish" in order to build a church in Society Parish (Bertie Precinct), and parishioners in the vicinity of "Maherin" were employing the same means in order to supply themselves with a chapel. The councillor Richard Sanderson bequeathed a plantation, slaves, and livestock for support of a minister, and Francis Nicholson,

[54]P. 192, below. Examples of fines benefitting parishes are in Clark, *State Records*, XXV, 169, 182, 203, and of sales of town lots doing the same are in Clark, *State Records*, XXIII, 73, XXV, 177, 207. For examples of statutory fines collected by the vestry of St. Paul's, see the index to this volume, "Fines, forfeitures." The provision concerning servants and slaves is in Clark, *State Records*, XXIII, 64-65.

[55]Pp. 402-405, 413-414, below; Clark, *State Records*, XXIII, 144, with supplementary acts at pp. 231, 365-366, 466-467. In the case of New Bern, the assembly also redirected to church construction a tax laid by the vestry for hiring a minister.

[56]Clark, *State Records*, XXIII, 535-537; XXV, 391-392.

while governor of Virginia, made gifts toward church construction in North Carolina. The Rev. Ebenezer Taylor, however, drew the scorn of his fellow missionary, John Urmston, for relying exclusively on voluntary contributions for his subsistence.[57]

The church act of 1715 also addressed marriage. For decades, North Carolina's dearth of clergy had necessitated allowing magistrates to officiate at weddings—a practice drawing the hostility of clerics, since it removed a traditional and significant source of incidental income. The act of 1715 forbade marriages to be performed by laymen in parishes having resident Anglican clergymen, and also prohibited such rites when they violated ecclesiastical laws on consanguinity.[58]

The structure of church establishment in North Carolina remained essentially the same for a generation, although several significant modifications and amplifications were undertaken by legislation over the years until the next comprehensive revisal of the vestry act in 1741. An "Additional Act" of 1720 addressed the question of vacancy on a vestry by granting power to the remaining members to appoint a freeholder resident in the parish to fill the position. The 1715 act had under certain circumstances allowed the incumbent minister or the governor to make the appointment, a provision omitted from the act of 1720. Also asserting that the act of 1715 had not sufficiently empowered churchwardens to levy fines and forfeitures, the additional act remedied the defect by allowing them to distrain the goods of anyone not paying a fine or forfeiture imposed for infractions mentioned in the 1715 act, such as refusing to qualify as a vestryman or to serve as a churchwarden, or illegally uniting a couple in marriage.[59]

An enactment of 1727 reflected suspicions that funds in some parishes were being misappropriated by churchwardens and vestrymen. Parishioners were permitted (but not required) to elect two men to inspect the vestry's accounts and publish the results. The inspectors were also empowered to bring an action in the courts to recover missing funds.[60]

---

[57]Clark, *State Records*, XXV, 168. An act of assembly provided for reimbursement by the parish of the sums advanced for payment of the salaries in Chowan. Pp. 12, 22, 107, 172, 254, 282-283, 347, 449, below; J. Bryan Grimes, *North Carolina Wills and Inventories*, (Raleigh: Trustees of the Public Libraries, 1912), 164, 436, hereinafter cited as Grimes, *Wills and Inventories*.

[58]Pp. 192-193, below.

[59]Pp. 265-267, below. The act also provided for payment to the Rev. John Urmston of £110 owed him by Chowan Parish, and removed the 5s limit on the parish poll tax in order to pay for it.

[60]P. 312, below.

Parish officers were not the only ones suspected of misappropriating parish funds. The churchwardens and vestry of Pasquotank Parish complained to the SPG about the withholding of £10 contributed by Governor Nicholson, and also petitioned the president and Council to compel Edward Moseley, one of the most powerful men in the colony, to yield up the sum.[61]

A highly revealing statute was the one enacted by the General Assembly in 1729 "for Regulating Vestrys in this Government and for the better Inspecting the Vestrymen and Church Wardens Accounts of Each and Every Parish within this Government." The legislation demonstrated at least a perception that the method of choosing vestrymen according to the acts of 1715 and 1720 was seriously flawed, and that the act of 1727 did not yet provide the required degree of accountability in the management of parish funds. The statute of 1729 stated that there had been "many Complaints" by the inhabitants of "Several" unnamed parishes that parish taxes had been misapplied, and that there had been collusion by vestrymen in settling churchwardens' accounts. The cause of this unhappy turn of events was, the act's preamble asserted, the fact of "evil Disposed and averitious persons getting into Vestrys." The attempted remedy was to transform the vestry in North Carolina from an essentially self-perpetuating body with unlimited tenure into an elective one with a fixed term of two years. While vestrymen still had to be freeholders, the new act extended the franchise in vestry elections to all freemen, Anglican and non-Anglican alike, who were to be polled at designated places in each parish on alternate Easter Mondays. The new vestries could compel former churchwardens and vestrymen to account for their collections and expenditures, and if any funds were found to have been "applyed to private uses" they could be recovered by suit. Similarly, justices of the peace and others could be called to account for their collections of the various fines and forfeitures supposed to be applied to parochial purposes. Throughout the act, infractions of its provisions subjected the transgressor to stiff fines.[62]

---

[61]Cain, *Records of the Executive Council, 1664-1734*, 425; p. 250, below.

[62]Pp. 314-316, below. This important act was not included in the collection of acts edited by Walter Clark and published in *The State Records of North Carolina*, XXIII, XXV, and as a consequence has not been made use of by historians. The only known copy is among records microfilmed at the Public Record Office in London for the British Records Program of the North Carolina Colonial Records Project, a copy of which is in the North Carolina State Archives.

Beginning with the assembly's creation of the precincts of New Hanover and Tyrrell in 1729, and of their coterminous parishes of St. James's and St. Andrew's, respectively, acts erecting new precincts (or counties, after 1739) included clauses creating and naming new parishes. The statute erecting Bertie Precinct from Chowan in 1722 made no mention of a new parish, although an act of 1727 stated that Bertie Precinct had but a single parish, and then proceeded to establish a second one and to appoint a vestry for it. A few parishes were born as the result of the division of an existing one, as was the South Parish of Chowan in 1722 and St. Patrick's Parish in Johnston County in 1756, among others. The reverse of this process took place with the consolidation of the two sparsely populated parishes of St. John and St. Peter in Pasquotank County in 1756.[63] Interestingly, it appears that a vestry began functioning in the Lower Cape Fear in or around 1728, shortly before the erection of New Hanover Precinct and St. James's Parish by the General Assembly in 1729. The vestry's extralegal status meant that when it attempted to "lay an assessement upon the parrish" the action had no standing in law.[64]

In addition to legislation addressing the structure of church establishment in North Carolina, other acts dealt with an area of traditional concern to the church—individual moral behavior. The first half-century of the colony's existence after the granting of the charter of 1665 is almost devoid of surviving statute law on the subject, although court records from this time reveal that there were prosecutions for statutory offences such as adultery, "scandalous cohabiting," fornication, sabbath breaking, and bearing a child out of wedlock. The dates of various of the prosecutions show that a statute against adultery, for example, was in place by 1695, against "scandalous cohabiting" as early as 1701, and against sabbath breaking by the time of the governorship of Henderson Walker (1699-1703).[65] The revisal of 1715 and subsequent legislation included acts such as one for "the better observing the Lord's Day...And also for the

[63]P. 316, below; Clark, *State Records*, XXIII, 100, 469-471; XXV, 182-183, 210, 213.

[64]Pp. 316, 347, below.

[65]Mattie Erma Edwards Parker (ed.), *North Carolina Higher-Court Records, 1670-1696*, Volume II of *The Colonial Records of North Carolina* [*Second Series*] (Raleigh: Department of Cultural Resources, Division of Archives and History [projected multivolume series, 1963-], 1968), 328, hereinafter cited as Parker, *Higher-Court Records, 1670-1696*; Mattie Erma Edwards Parker (ed.), *Higher-Court Records, 1697-1701*, Volume III of *The Colonial Records of North Carolina* [*Second Series*] (Raleigh: Department of Cultural Resources, Division

suppressing Prophaneness, Immorality, & divers other vicious & Enormous Crimes" (1715, substantially reenacted in 1741), which provided penalties for laboring on Sunday, using profanity, drunkenness, fornication, bearing a bastard child, and cohabitation by unmarried couples "from Foreign Parts."[66] In addition to acts attempting to regulate morals and encourage decorous behavior in general, sections of others addressed similar concerns. An act of 1756 "for the Regulation of the Town of Wilmington," for example, provided for the patrolling of streets by constables during the time of divine service in order to eliminate "great Disturbances in the Streets, or near the Place where the [service] is performed." An earlier regulation for the proposed (but never established) town of Carteret on Roanoke Island forbade tavern keepers to entertain anyone on the sabbath during the time of church services, or to allow anyone in their taverns to "gett drunk on the Sabbath Day."[67] Prosecutions under such statutes continued apace in both higher and lower courts after 1715.[68]

Although most of the statutory powers and responsibilities of a vestry dealt with ecclesiastical matters exclusively, several of them related solely to civil concerns. One of these was the maintenance of standard weights and measures for the parish, a duty imposed by an act of March, 1702. The act is missing, but probably would have included periodic verification of the accuracy of weights and measures used in trade. Vestries did not, however, prove adequate to that task. An act of assembly of 1741,

---

of Archives and History [projected multivolume series, 1963-], 1971), 89, 90, 108, 109, 128, 425, 428-429, 448, 451, 466; Price, *Higher-Court Records, 1702-1708*, 334, 415; Price, *Higher-Court Records, 1709-1723*, 44. For accounts of two prosecutions in 1705, for breach of an act "against Fornication & Adultery" see Weynette P. Haun, *Old Albemarle County, North Carolina, Perquimans Precinct Court Minutes, 1688-1738* (Durham, N.C.: The Author, 1980), 72, 75. These examples are all from pre-1715 higher court records; surviving precinct court records in the North Carolina State Archives contain similar items. Only two sets of surviving proprietary instructions to governors allude to any concern with moral behavior. A private instruction to Philip Ludwell in 1691 directs him to "use your uttmost endeavour to reduce the people to a sober vertuous manner of life by punishing all debauchery and profaneness." Saunders, *Colonial Records*, I, 383. Three years later, the proprietary board suggested to John Archdale, fellow proprietor and governor of Carolina, that granting a charter to Charleston might help to "check vice and Incourage Sobriety and vertue as well as trade." CO5/289, f. 10b, photocopy from Public Record Office, London, in British Records Collection, State Archives, Raleigh.

[66]Clark, *State Records*, XXIII, 3-6, 173-175. Both acts included a provision that they were to be read publicly twice a year in each parish.

[67]Clark, *State Records*, XIII, 460, XXV, 203.

[68]Price, *Higher-Court Minutes, 1709-1723*, 44, 114, 127, 202-251 passim, 256, 288, 290, 346, 397; Cain, *Higher-Court Minutes, 1724-1730*, 324, 420, 425, 554-555; Paul M. McCain, *The County Court in North Carolina before 1750* (Durham: Duke University Press, 1954), 44-45.

complaining that "many Notorious Frauds and Deceits" were being "daily committed by false Weights and Measures," followed practice in England and assigned the duty to the county court.[69] Another civil obligation created by statute was that of overseeing the triennial "processioning" (walking the boundaries) of lands, a duty of the vestry from 1723 to 1773, when it too was assigned to the county court.[70] Similarly, vestries were in 1723 directed by legislation to pay bounties for the killing of squirrels, and could levy a special tax to that end. Subsequent legislation added other "vermin" such as wolves, panthers, and wildcats, but in 1764 the responsibility was transferred to the county court, with the bounties to be paid from county taxes.[71] Yet another non-ecclesiastical task assigned churchwardens was the payment of rewards to those who apprehended runaway slaves and servants.[72]

Maintenance of the poor was an important responsibility assigned to the vestry. Before the establishment of parishes in 1701, higher courts occasionally placed indigent children in care at public expense,[73] but it appears from scanty evidence that this may have been the only aspect of poor relief dealt with by courts at either the provincial or precinct levels during this period.[74] If this was in fact the case, they would have been but following English practice, by which the vestry, not the bench, was the body traditionally dispensing relief to the poor. The earliest surviving church act, the one of 1715, does not specify poor relief as one of the duties of parishes, although it is apparently referred to obliquely when the act mentions expenditures "Which shall properly be a parish Charge altho not mentioned in this Act."[75] The preamble to the 1720 church act included

---

[69]P. 433, below; Clark, *State Records*, XXIII, 178-180

[70]Clark, *State Records*, XXIII, 103-106, 114-115, 924.

[71]Clark, *State Records*, XXV, 198-200; the 1727 "Act to Encourage Destroying of Vermin" is cited by title only in Clark, XXV, 533, but given in full in New-York Historical Society, BV North Carolina Laws, 301-302, microfilm copy in North Carolina Colonial Records Project. Clark, *State Records*, XXIII, 288, 617-618, 784-785, 914-915, XXV, 312, 476.

[72]Clark, *State Records*, XXIII, 197-198. The act is one of 1741.

[73]Parker, *Higher-Court Records, 1697-1701*, 97-98, 109, 113, 243, 526.

[74]The minutes of Perquimans Precinct Court, 1693-1706, are printed in Saunders, *Colonial Records*, I, 386-656, passim, and reveal no assistance to indigents or others in need. An exhaustive study of public poor relief in the colony does not mention any mechanism for dispensing such aid at this time. Alan D. Watson, "Public Poor Relief in Colonial North Carolina," *North Carolina Historical Review*, LIV, no. 4 (October 1977), 347-366, hereinafter cited as Watson, "Public Poor Relief."

[75]John M. Garland, "The Nonecclesiastical Activities of an English and a North Carolina Parish: A Comparative Study," *North Carolina Historical Review*, L, no. 1 (January 1973), 35. P. 192, below.

"relief of the poor" as proper parish business, and the one of 1741 granted the vestry full authority to impose poll taxes for its various responsibilities, including "Care and Support of the Poor."[76] Another source of income for this work included various fines designated specifically for "the use of the poor" rather than for the more usual "use of the parish."[77] Private charity constituted another source of assistance to the poor. Although most such acts of benevolence would have gone unrecorded, the will (1729) bequeathing £100 currency from Thomas Harvey for "the youse & benefett of the pore & pore Children beloing to the precinck of Prequimons" survives. Governor Henderson Walker bequeathed ten barrels of corn to "tenn poore people," and the merchant John Paine left £13 proclamation money to the churchwardens "of every county in the Province" to be distributed to the poor (1767). In the extant minutes of St. Paul's Parish, Chowan County, 134 individuals are mentioned as receiving assistance from parish funds between 1712 and 1775. The minutes for St. John's Parish, Carteret County, 1742-1775, note forty-one.[78]

Even as the supplementary church acts of 1720 and 1729 had addressed what the assembly perceived as shortcomings in the ecclesiastical structure erected in 1715, so the comprehensive vestry act of 1741 sought to strengthen that edifice still further. Drawing on four decades of experience in church establishment in North Carolina, the drafters of the 1741 statute retained many distinctive features of previous legislation, but they also included a number of significant modifications. Vestries were still to be elected rather than appointed, but the electoral base was narrowed by requiring voters to be freeholders rather than the "freemen" decreed by the act of 1729. The vestry continued to be composed only of freeholders, but in place of the 1729 act's permissive "may" in the clause directing all qualified electors to meet biennially in order to choose a vestry, the act of

[76] Pp. 266, 417, below.

[77] Examples can be found in Clark, *State Records*, XXIII, 5, 10, 675-676, and XXV, 198, 210, 251. More specific still was the fine to be used for providing the poor with arms at militia musters. Clark, *State Records*, XXV, 337.

[78] Grimes, *Wills and Inventories*, 231, 325, 436. Watson, "Public Poor Relief," 348. This article exhaustively examines the various categories of "poor" and the types of relief afforded them. For individual cases dealt with by the vestry of St. Paul's, see pp. 431-494, passim, below.

1741 substituted the obligatory "shall"; it did not, however, provide sanctions for failure to do so.[79] Most of the fines and forfeitures, as well as the £50 stipend for ministers, remained the same in their stated amounts, but were denominated in the considerably more valuable proclamation money rather than in the local currency allowed by previous acts.[80] The vestry was still empowered to levy a poll tax of up to five shillings proclamation, but whereas acts prior to 1741 had not specified the means by which it was to be collected, the one of that year assigned the responsibility to the sheriff. Continuing problems in accounting for parish funds are apparent in the clause in the 1741 act requiring churchwardens to render an account annually to their vestry for all funds in their hands, and providing stiff penalties for failure to do so.[81]

The legislation of 1741, like that of 1715, laid upon the vestry and churchwardens the duty "to procure an able and Godly Minister, qualified according to the Ecclesiastical Laws of England, and a Person, of a sober Life and Conversation." The minister's stipend was to be at least £50 a year (proclamation by the 1741 act), for which sum the minister was to be "constantly" resident in the parish and was not to officiate in vacant neighboring parishes except by permission of the churchwardens and vestry.[82] The 1715 act allowed resident ministers to omit officiating in their parishes up to one-sixth of the Sundays in a year, but the act of 1741 made no similar concession.[83] The Rev. John Urmston had his salary reduced for failing to officiate "in the parts near the Indian Town" in Chowan Precinct, as ordered by the vestry of Chowan.[84] The agreement between the same vestry and the Rev. Thomas Newnam specified that the minister would officiate twenty Sundays a year in Edenton and ten at the chapel near the

---

[79]P. 414, below.

[80]"Proclamation money," or "lawful money," received its name from an attempt by the British government to prevent the inflation of colonial currency. A royal proclamation of 1704 forbade colonists to inflate the value of their money by any more than one-third of its sterling equivalent, or £133:6:8 to £100 sterling. The scheme proved unsuccessful as a device to control rates of exchange, but the proclamation rate at least became a means of specifying a value greater than that of most local currencies, including that of North Carolina. At the time of the 1741 act, £100 sterling was worth some £1,000 North Carolina money, making payments specified in proclamation money considerably more valuable than those that were not. McCusker, *Money & Exchange in Europe & America, 1600-1775* (Williamsburg: Institute of Early American History and Culture, 1978), 116-131, 215-219.

[81]P. 416, below.

[82]P. 417, below.

[83]P. 192, below.

[84]Pp. 455, 459, below.

Indian Town, with the remaining Sundays allowed Newnam "for his Attendances on other parts of the Government."[85] By the act of 1741, vestries were permitted for the first time to impose a measure of discipline on clergy who might be "notoriously guilty of any scandalous Immorality": a minimum of nine of the full complement of twelve members of the vestry could stop the salary of an offending minister, and it could be restored only by a decision in his favor in a trial in the General Court.[86] The 1741 act also enjoined the minister to preserve and keep in good repair the woodlands, house, and outbuildings on the land (or "glebe") provided by the parish for his use. None of the statutes, however, conferred on the vestry the right to remove a cleric—an action that would have been viewed by authorities at home as a serious infringement of episcopal prerogative.

Another significant difference between the establishment act of 1741 and that of 1715 is that the latter divided the colony into nine parishes, and the former into sixteen. The growth in number was not the result of creating smaller parishes, but rather of the steady expansion in the number of white settlers and in the area settled by them. The estimated 10,000 whites in 1700 had by 1740 swelled to some 40,000—a fourfold increase in less than two generations. The zone of settlement in 1740 included approximately 26,000 square miles, or half the land area of the present state, easily several times the area settled in 1700. Population density continued to be low throughout the period, offering a constant challenge to the established church to find a means of ministering to a widely dispersed flock.[87]

A major threat to Anglicanism in North Carolina in the 1740s was the unremitting growth of the dissenter population. Although their influence in provincial politics evaporated after the Cary Rebellion, the Quakers of the precincts of Perquimans and Pasquotank continued to be numerically

---

[85] P. 459, below.

[86] Pp. 417-418, below.

[87] Harry Roy Merrens, *Colonial North Carolina in the Eighteenth Century: A Study in Historical Geography* (Chapel Hill: University of North Carolina Press, 1964), 4; United States Bureau of the Census, *Historical Statistics of the United States, Colonial Times to 1970* (Washington: Government Printing Office, 2 volumes, 1975), II, 1168.

significant. Baptists were perceived as a growing threat by Governor Everard in the late 1720s,[88] and Presbyterian numbers began to climb with the increase in Scottish and Scotch-Irish immigration.[89] As early as 1714, John Urmston complained about the presence on his vestry of two Anabaptists and three "Vehement Scotchmen Presbyterians."[90]

The possibilities of North Carolina as a mission field for Anglicanism were first addressed by the Society for the Promotion of Christian Knowledge, or SPCK. The SPCK was founded in London in 1699, with Dr. Thomas Bray as the guiding force. Within a few years the organization had concentrated its efforts on the establishment of schools, distribution of literature, and similar educational enterprises, but in 1700, shortly after its founding, it sent Daniel Brett to North Carolina as a missionary, along with three libraries for the colony.[91] The length of time Brett spent in the colony is not known precisely, but it may have been as much as two years. Reports in May and October, 1703, indicate that Brett's behavior was unexceptionable during his first half year in the province. After that, according to a former president of the Council, Brett "in a most horrid manner broke out in such an extravigant Course that I must owne I am ashamed to express his Carriage it being in such an high Nature." The Rev. John Talbot, who was in the province briefly in 1703, was less inhibited in his comments. Brett was, according to Talbot, "a scandalous fellow, that has done more harm than good every where; he was the worst I think that ever came over." Although there was a marked shortage of clergy in America, "we had better have none att all than such Scandalous Beasts."[92]

The missionary organization undertaking the formidable task of meeting the twin challenges of an insufficient number of clergy and growing

---

[88]Pp. 304, 320-321, below.

[89]Cain, *Higher-Court Minutes, 1724-1730*, xxxv.

[90]P. 181, below.

[91]Pp. 4-9, below; W. O. B. Allen and Edmund McClure, *Two Hundred Years: The History of the Society for Promoting Christian Knowledge, 1698-1898* (London: SPCK, 1898), passim; Edmund McClure, *A Chapter in English Church History: Being the Minutes of the Society for Promoting Christian Knowledge for the Years 1698-1704* (London: SPCK, 1888), passim.

[92]Pp. 15, 22, below.

dissenter strength was the Society for the Propagation of the Gospel in Foreign Parts, or SPG—also founded through the efforts of Dr. Thomas Bray. Launched in London in 1701, the year in which church establishment came to North Carolina, the society counted among its members a number of the spiritual and temporal elite—higher clergy, nobility, and substantial merchants. Meeting monthly, usually in the archbishop of Canterbury's library in the church of St. Martin-in-the-Fields in London, the members of the society read letters from their missionaries and others throughout British America, and ordered the secretary to draft replies to numbers of them. The monthly meeting also received recommendations from the Standing Committee, a small body convening biweekly in the chapter house of St. Paul's Cathedral in order to prepare business for the monthly meeting. The society often referred correspondence and other matters to the committee for report and recommendation. An annual general meeting in February featured a sermon, afterwards printed along with a report on the activities of the SPG and its missionaries during the preceding year. The society also drew up regulations for the orderly conduct of its business, as well as standing orders for its missionaries.[93]

Included among the early membership of the SPG were two of the lords proprietors and a proprietary governor of North Carolina, which helped to ensure that the organization was from the first aware both of the existence of the province and of the problematic state of the church establishment there.[94] Reports to the SPG in its first year that the sole missionary at Albemarle, the notorious Daniel Brett, was "extreamly fatigud" in having to serve the settlement at Pamlico as well, prompted a resolution from the organization to send its own missionary. Beginning with the brief visit of George Keith and John Talbot in 1703, the society provided partial or total financial support to eleven of the twenty-five Anglican ministers known to have regularly served in North Carolina, however briefly, between 1701 and 1754.[95]

---

[93]C. F. Pascoe, *Two Hundred Years of the S.P.G.: An Historical Account of the Society for the Propagation of the Gospel in Foreign Parts, 1701-1900*, (London: the Society, 2 volumes, 1901), 1-99, hereinafter cited as Pascoe, *Two Hundred Years*; the sermon and report were printed annually from 1703 and 1712, respectively. Pp. 39-43, 97-102, below.

[94]Pp. 13, 243 (the proprietors Thomas Amy and Lord Carteret), and 80 (Governor Edward Hyde), below.

[95]Robert J. Cain (ed.), *Records of the Executive Council, 1735-1754*, Volume VIII of *The Colonial Records of North Carolina* [*Second Series*] (Raleigh: Department of Cultural Resources, Division of Archives and History [projected multivolume series, 1963-]), 1988, xlviii, hereinafter cited as Cain, *Records of the Executive Council, 1735-1754*.

The SPG enjoyed at best a mediocre success in recruiting clergy to take a post in North Carolina, despite the lure of an annual stipend of £80 sterling instead of the usual £50.[96] As mentioned previously, North Carolina early acquired a reputation as a post of uncommon hardship, with difficult travel, an unhealthy climate, vestries that often were ungenerous and unhelpful, very large parishes and missions, and an almost total absence of urban amenities. One minister rejected an offer from the society to go to North Carolina with the observation that reading about the province had convinced him that it was "the properest Place in the World, for a Clergy Man to go to that is either weary of his Life; or fit to appear no where else."[97] The statement, while harsh, did undoubtedly reflect the view of North Carolina prevailing among most of the Anglican clergy in both Britain and America.[98] As a consequence, the colony got its share and more of questionable clergymen throughout the colonial era—as can be amply attested by a number of the documents printed in this volume and the two to follow.

The distribution of literature constituted another means employed by the SPG to plant the faith in the American colonies. As mentioned previously, in 1700, the year prior to the founding of the SPG, the SPCK had sent to North Carolina three libraries—the gift, apparently, of Thomas Thynne, first Viscount Weymouth.[99] Daniel Brett delivered the libraries to St. Thomas parish in 1701, where for a number of years they were the object of much civic pride for the village of Bath.[100] The 1,050 books and tracts, comprising 189 titles, were intended by Dr. Bray to constitute three separate libraries—provincial, parochial, and a "laymen's library." The first was to serve the entire province, the second the incumbent minister, and the third was to be a lending library for the laity of the parish.[101] Although most of the works concerned various aspects of religion, a number of them

---

[96]Cain, *Higher-Court Minutes, 1724-1730*, xxxi; pp. 187-188, below. The Rev. Brian Hunt, however, asked to be transferred from his post in South Carolina to one in North Carolina, since the £80 paid there would enable him to "lay up somewhat for my poor little ones." P. 300, below.

[97]P. 335, below.

[98]Pp. 31, 48, 50, 57-58, 71-72, 86, 95-96, 104, 107, 114-121, 140-141, and passim, below.

[99]P. 4, below.

[100]Herbert R. Paschal, Jr., *A History of Colonial Bath*, (Raleigh: Committee on the Two Hundred and Fiftieth Anniversary, 1955), 12-17, hereinafter cited as Paschal, *Colonial Bath*; John Kenneth Gibson, "The Thomas Bray Libraries, St. Thomas Parish, Pamlico [Bath, North Carolina], 1700: A Bibliographical and Historical Analysis." (master's thesis, University of North Carolina at Chapel Hill, 1986), I/1-I/9, hereinafter cited as Gibson, "Thomas Bray Libraries."

[101]Gibson, "Thomas Bray Libraries," I/1-I/2.

also dealt with essentially secular matters such as history, biography, geography, natural sciences, and the like.[102] By the 1760s, however, all of the books had been dispersed and nothing remained of the libraries.[103]

Like the SPCK, the SPG recognized the importance of making the printed word available both to its missionaries and to the public at large. One of its earliest actions as an organization was to send Bibles and prayerbooks to several colonies, including two of each to North Carolina.[104] It subsequently made gifts of books at various times to several parishes.[105] The society also early on adopted a policy of allowing £10 to newly appointed missionaries for the purchase of books for themselves, to be selected from a list of approved works.[106] Additionally, new missionaries were given £5 worth of "practical and devotional" books and tracts, plus catechisms, for distribution to selected parishioners.[107] Even so, missionaries would ask for further gifts of books from the society, noting the general poverty in the colony. On occasion they would request spelling books for poor children, as well as works directed specifically to combatting such evils as swearing, drunkenness, and sabbath breaking. Also solicited from time to time were polemical writings refuting Quakerism, and those upholding the validity of infant baptism and other orthodox doctrine and practice.[108] Several times the SPG was treated to the spectacle of squabbles over the custody of missionary libraries, and even to accusations by clerics that both Governor Edward Hyde's widow and John Urmston sold books intended by the society to be distributed free.[109]

As viceroy of a monarch who also happened to be supreme head on earth of the Church of England, a royal governor was charged with the duty of advancing the interest of the church whenever he could. It has been noted previously that the formal instructions given by the proprietors to their new governors notably made no reference to the church. It was, however,

[102]Pp. 5-10, below.
[103]Paschal, *Colonial Bath*, 15; Gibson, I/6-I/7.
[104]P. 13, below.
[105]Pp. 70, 176, 365, 386, 412, 448, below.
[106]P. 101, below. The list is printed at pp. 33-39, below, with an addendum on pp. 409-410.
[107]Pp. 101, 172, 298, 387, below.
[108]Pp. 15-16, 198, 362, 369, 421, below.
[109]Pp. 143, 151, 160, 168, 175, 178, 180, 198, below.

otherwise when royal government was instituted in North Carolina with the arrival of Governor George Burrington in 1731. On the surface, at least, official interest in the position of the church in the province increased markedly, as indicated by instructions issued to Burrington and his successors. Indeed, concern for the advancement of Anglicanism in royal colonies had been a feature of instructions from the king to his governors for many years, and by 1731 such instructions had in large measure become standardized.[110]

Taking pride of place as the first religion clause in the governor's instructions was one granting "a Liberty of Conscience" to all not giving "Offence or Scandal" to the government. Roman Catholics, of whom there were virtually none in North Carolina, were the only group excepted from the provision.[111] The governor was then instructed to "take care" that a number of desirable things be done: that God be "Devoutly and Duly Served" throughout his government; that the Book of Common Prayer be read and the Anglican form of the Eucharist be celebrated each Sunday and holy day; that church buildings be well maintained and increased in number; that Anglican ministers be provided an adequate salary, house, and glebe; and that parishes be "So limitted and Settled as You shall find most convenient for Accomplishing this Good Work." No particular means were suggested for realizing these goals. The instructions were, however, specific in prescribing certain actions, and in proscribing others. Governors were to benefice only those ministers holding a certificate from the bishop of London attesting that they conformed to the doctrine and discipline of the Church of England and were "of good Life and Conversation." Furthermore, governors were to report to the bishop of London on anyone officiating in an Anglican church or chapel without being in orders. The instructions decreed that ministers were always to have a seat on the vestry, and any of them giving scandal in doctrine or behavior were to be

[110]Pp. 325-327, 327*n*, below. Leonard Woods Labaree (ed.), *Royal Instructions to British Governors, 1670-1776* (New York: Appleton-Century Company, 2 Volumes, 1935), II, 482-506.

[111]Cain, *Higher-Court Minutes, 1724-1730*, xxxv-xxxvi.

removed by the "proper and usual Means." Schoolmasters could not operate a school without first being licensed by the bishop of London.[112]

The instructions also ordered governors to uphold the bishop of London's jurisdiction in the colonies "So far as conveniently may be." Specifically excluded from this jurisdiction was the authority to "collate to benefices" (install ministers in parishes), as was the granting of marriage licenses and letters of probate—both of which were reserved to governors "as far as by Law We may." What powers the bishop of London did in fact possess in the colonies were not detailed—undoubtedly by design, since avoiding specificity would do much to help avoid confrontations with colonial vestries. The governor's instructions did state, however, that the bishop held a commission from the king to exercise ecclesiastical jurisdiction either in person or through a surrogate known as a "commissary."[113]

The office of episcopal commissary had been in existence in England from pre-Reformation times, having been instituted in order to assist a bishop to administer the farthest reaches of his diocese. Since no bishop of London ever visited an American colony, it was through a succession of commissaries that what modest authority he enjoyed was exercised. The first such official appointed in America was James Blair, commissary for Virginia for over fifty years (1689-1743). Thomas Bray, founder of the SPCK and SPG, was commissary for Maryland from 1695 to 1700. The first commissary appointed for the Carolinas and Bahama Islands, Gideon Johnston, was also rector of St. Philip's, Charleston, and served from 1707 until his death in 1716. The second appointee for the region was William Tredwell Bull, rector of St. Paul's, Colleton, South Carolina, from 1712 to 1723, and commissary ca. 1719 to 1723. The last was a Scot, Alexander Garden, commissary 1729-1749, and rector of St. Philip's, Charleston, 1719-1753.[114] So far as is known, none of the three ever visited North Carolina in their capacity as commissary, although reporting to the bishop of London on the state of their commissarial districts, and especially on the condition of the clergy in them, was the most important part of their duty. Even an

[112]Pp. 325-327, below.

[113]Pp. 325-326, below.

[114]George W. Williams, "Letters to the Bishop of London from the Commissaries in South Carolina," *South Carolina Historical Magazine*, 78 (January-October, 1977), 2-10; hereinafter cited as Williams, "Letters"; Woolverton, *Colonial Anglicanism*, 84-87.

instruction from the bishop of London in 1717 that "the Commissary shall strictly and punctually hold a general Visitation of the Clergy each year" was not observed in the case of North Carolina. Gideon Johnston's sole concern with the province was as a place to send a particularly troublesome priest, the Rev. Ebenezer Taylor, who despite Taylor's bitter protests was removed as rector of St. Andrew's parish near Charleston and sent as a missionary to Bath County.[115] Commissary Bull asked John Baptista Ashe, a prominent landowner and assemblyman, to prepare for him an account of the church in North Carolina. Before it could be completed, however, Bull had departed permanently for England, and there is no evidence that he ever took any notice of North Carolina beyond his request to Ashe.[116] Alexander Garden evinced somewhat more interest in the colony during his two decades as commissary. The rascally cleric Richard Marsden drew his scornful attention, as did the unsavory minister John Boyd. Garden also corresponded with the Rev. John Garzia about some books, and he recommended appointment of the Rev. James Moir as missionary in North Carolina.[117] Even so, concern with his North Carolina charge constituted only an infinitesimal portion of his correspondence with the bishop of London, virtually all of which related to the colony's southern neighbor.[118]

Royal governors' instructions included an exhortation to enforce vigorously all laws passed by the North Carolina assembly against the vices of "Blasphemy, Prophaness, Adultery, Fornication, Bigamy, Incest, Prophanation of the Lords Day, Swearing and Drunkenness," along with an order to "earnestly recommend" to the assembly that it enact such legislation if it had not already done so. In order to help ensure enforcement, governors were further directed to provide a way for churchwardens to bring court actions against those committing such crimes.[119] An extensive examination of minutes of both higher and lower courts in the colony, however, reveals prosecutions for offenses against morality brought only by secular authorities.

[115] Pp. 187*n*, 206-207, 217-221, 228-229, 232-233, below. Commissary Bray had planned a visit to North Carolina, but was in America too briefly to make the journey from Maryland. P. 1, below.

[116] Pp. 289-290, below.

[117] Pp. 322, 329, 351-353, 375-376, 378, 390-391, 394-396, below.

[118] Williams, "Letters," 132-147, 213-242, 286-317.

[119] Cain, *Records of the Executive Council, 1664-1734*, 607; Cain, *Records of the Executive Council, 1735-1754*, 515; Robert J. Cain (ed.), *Records of the Executive Council, 1755-1775*, Volume, IX of *The Colonial Records of North Carolina* [*Second Series*] (Raleigh: Department of Cultural Resources, Division of Archives and History [projected multivolume series, 1963-]), 523, 665.

Governors also were to take care not to appoint to public office anyone "whose ill Fame and conversation may occasion Scandal"—the better to entice "Infidels" to embrace Christianity. The king's instructions then went on to direct that two important groups of infidels receive particular attention: the governor was to consult with the assembly and Council about the "best Means to facilitate and Encourage the Conversion of Negroes and Indians to the Christian Religion." Although conversion of Indians and enslaved Africans had been a stated objective of the SPG from its beginning,[120] it was an activity that proprietary as well as royal governors, and most of the missionaries, appear to have done nothing to encourage during the period covered by the documents in this volume. There were a few noteworthy exceptions, however. In 1704, the missionary James Blair stated that he had often conversed with Indians in the province, and that the English speakers among them appeared "very willing and fond of being Christians." Blair urged that vigorous measures be taken to "bring over a greate many of them," especially in light of their large numbers and the necessity for keeping French influence from making inroads among them.[121] The Rev. Giles Ransford reported that he had baptized a small number of both Negroes and Indians. He also asserted that he had become proficient in the Indians' language, and offered, without result, to undertake a mission to them.[122] In the 1720s, Thomas Newnam baptized a few Negroes, who to his delight could recite "the Creed," Lord's Prayer, and Ten Commandments. He estimated the number of Indians in the settled portion of the colony at no more than 300 warriors, which would imply a total population of only around 1500. Newnam wrote that they lived in two towns by themselves, "very quiet and peaceable." He was, however, pessimistic about the prospects of successfully proselytizing among them.[123] The Rev. John Blacknall at about the same time was preaching at the Indian town in northern Chowan Precinct, and the Rev. Thomas Baylye claimed to have baptized several Indians and

---

[120]Pascoe, *Two Hundred Years*, 7-8.

[121]P. 29, below.

[122]Pp. 143, 197, below. John Urmston, the other missionary in North Carolina at this time and no friend of Ransford's, expressed deep skepticism about the latter's claims of baptizing Indians and Negroes. P. 256, below.

[123]P. 283, below.

"many" Negroes. The Rev. John Garzia also baptized a few Indians and Negroes in the 1730s.[124]

Regardless of their clear instructions on the point, neither of the royal governors during this period, George Burrington and Gabriel Johnston, ever broached to the assembly or to their councils the subject of the conversion of Indians and Negroes. Both men knew that such an exercise would have been worse than useless, since it stood no chance of sympathetic consideration in either body and would have provoked pointless controversy. Especially was this true of the idea of proselytizing black slaves. There was a mistaken but widespread and persistent belief throughout the colonies that Christians could not legally be enslaved, and that baptism therefore conferred freedom.[125] Masters also feared that Christianization would result in dangerous notions of equality, making the slaves less tractable, and even rebellious.[126]

The king's instructions to his governors also commanded them to "recommend" to the assembly that it "Enter upon proper Methods for the Erecting and maintaining of Schools" in order to teach both reading and "the principles of Religion." Governor Gabriel Johnston, a former professor of Hebrew at the University of St. Andrews, commended the idea to the General Assembly in the strongest terms, and reminded its members that the assembly had "never yet taken the least care to Erect one School, which deserves the name"—a failure that in his opinion was in large measure responsible for "the many disorders which have always Prevailed among us." The upper house readily agreed with Johnston, but the lower house made no response.[127] In 1745 the General Assembly finally created a fund for the establishment of "free schools," but before any of it could be used for its intended purpose it was diverted in order to help pay for an expedition against the Cherokee. The same fate befell £6,000 authorized "for the funding and endowing a Public School."[128] No similar effort to

---

[124]Pp. 305-306, 381, 422, below.

[125]P. 96, below. An excellent discussion of this notion is found in John C. Van Horne (ed.), *Religious Philanthropy and Colonial Slavery: The American Correspondence of the Associates of Dr. Bray, 1717-1777* (Urbana and Chicago: University of Illinois Press, 1985), 25-30, hereinafter cited as Van Horne, *Religious Philanthropy*.

[126]Van Horne, *Religious Philanthropy*, 30-31.

[127]P. 371 and 371*n*, below.

[128]Clark, *State Records*, XXIII, 394, XXV, 235, 394-5. The act of 1745 "for Laying a Tax for Sinking the Now Current Bills of Credit" provided funds only from any excess raised by the tax over the eight-year period it was to be levied. It is not known what, if anything, this sum amounted to.

provide schools at public expense was attempted during the colonial era. The assembly confined its educational activities to exempting schoolmasters from militia musters (from 1766), empowering commissioners and trustees in Edenton and New Bern to establish schools in those towns (1745, 1764), and passing an act establishing and endowing Queen's College in Charlotte (1770).[129]

Royal governors also chided successive assemblies for other sins of omission that contributed, as the governors saw it, to the chronically precarious state of Anglicanism in North Carolina. Governor Burrington argued that failure to provide glebe lands and houses for ministers was not only a "Reproach to the Country," but also constituted a deterrent to immigration into the colony.[130] In 1736, only a few years after his arrival, Governor Johnston castigated the same body for the "Deplorable and almost Total want of Devine Worship throughout the province." Johnston went on to profess his belief that

> it is Impossible to Instance . . . in any Colony belonging to a Christian Nation; where some Effectuall provision has not been made; for paying in Publick and at Stated times, That Adoration and Homage to Almighty God, so highly Becoming all Rational Creatures; and for Instructing the People in their Duty to the Supream Author of their Being, to one Another and to themselves.[131]

No legislation immediately resulted from Johnston's lambasting, nor did it several years later when he condemned as "realy Scandalous" and "a Reproach peculiar to this part of his Majesty's Dominions" the fact that there were in the entire "wide Extended province" only two places where religious services were held regularly.[132] However, as discussed previously, the vestry act of 1741 did include various features favorable to the clergy of the colony.

---

[129]Clark, *State Records*, XXIII, 232-233, 394, 605, 631, 678-680, 761, 780, 787, 823, 915, XXV, 484-485, 516, 520.

[130]Saunders, *Colonial Records*, III, 541.

[131]P. 370, below.

[132]P. 389, below.

Both royal and proprietary governors occasionally corresponded directly with ecclesiastical authorities in England. In addition to reporting on the general state of the church in the colony, governors also discussed the performance of individual clergymen—an exercise that during the waning days of proprietary rule was colored by the bitter factional strife of the period. Governor Richard Everard, in a letter to the bishop of London in 1725/6, excoriated the questionable Thomas Baylye as a troublemaker and a creature of former Governor Burrington. Everard's own protégé, John Blacknall, condemned Baylye as well.[133] George Burrington, as first royal governor, was not loath to use the occasion of writing a report to the bishop of London—a privy councillor as well as a cleric—to make representations concerning the governor's bitter political struggle with the chief justice of the colony. Burrington also sent accounts of the province's religious affairs to both the secretary of state and the Board of Trade, which proprietary governors had had no occasion to do; if governors of North Carolina before 1731 corresponded with the lords proprietors about such matters, there is no known evidence of it.[134]

At the dawn of the eighteenth century, then, the first faltering steps in Anglican establishment were being taken in North Carolina. By the end of 1741, a body of legislation had been enacted, vestries existed throughout the province, the Society for the Propagation of the Gospel in Foreign Parts was committed to providing a modest number of missionaries, and several churches and chapels had been built. A paucity of relevant records severely limits detailed knowledge of these matters, however. No single source so well illuminates the actual workings of the establishment in the province as vestry minutes. Unfortunately, to the end of 1741 this uniquely valuable record survives for only one parish. Other sources do, however, permit us to sketch at least the outline of the story of the Church of England in North Carolina during this period, and on occasion to add shading and color as well. The incomplete but extensive body of reports from missionaries to the SPG and the bishop of London, while too often self-serving, intolerant, and petty, nevertheless does provide most of what is known today about the church in colonial North Carolina.

---

[133]Pp. 303-306, below.

[134]Pp. 327-328, 330-331, 335-336, 339-340, 384-385, below.

EDITORIAL METHOD

The method employed in transcribing documents for this volume is based on rules for the "expanded method" in Frank Freidel (ed.), *Harvard Guide to American History* (Cambridge: Belknap Press of Harvard University Press, Revised Edition, 2 volumes, 1975), I, 30-31. Most abbreviations and contractions have been expanded. Those retained include all proper names, dates, titles, and abbreviations in use at the present time. If more than one expanded form fitted the context, abbreviations were retained as written. In those few instances in which it was impossible to distinguish among abbreviations, contractions, or misspellings on the part of the contemporary scribe, no expansion has been made where the literal meaning is clear. Superior letters have been brought down to the line of text.

Spelling in the manuscript has been followed, with the exception of expansions, substitution of *th* for the symbol (resembling a y) indicating the archaic letter thorn, and substitution of modern usage with respect to *i* and *j*, and *u* and *v*, which sometimes were used interchangeably in the documents. Interpolation of *sic* has been used in only a few instances. A few obvious slips of the pen, such as the repetition of words, have been silently corrected.

Capitalization in the manuscript has been followed, with some exceptions. Each heading paragraph, or notation is begun with a capital letter regardless of its form in the manuscript. A capital letter likewise follows a period ending a sentence or other passage. If a proper name is not capitalized in the manuscript, it is not capitalized in this volume unless it meets one of the above conditions.

Very limited modification has been made in *punctuation*. Periods follow entries that require them, and also all retained abbreviations. Commas separate names in lists changed from vertical to horizontal form. In a few cases the editor has deleted extremely erratic punctuation, such as colons and dashes after every few words.

Square brackets enclose material supplied editorially. Inferred readings of missing and partially missing passages are printed in roman type. Other supplied material is in italics, including the source reference for each document and such interpolations as *torn*, *illegible*, and *blank*. Words and phrases underlined in the original are also italicized.

Boldface type is used for the title and date preceding the text of each paper.

Angle brackets enclose material that occurs in the manuscript but has been transferred to a different position on the printed page. Such items chiefly include marginal notations; they are in italic type, except that roman type is used for manuscript page numbers.

The documents are divided into two sections, the first consisting of papers and the second of vestry minutes. Each section is arranged chronologically. Where no date is given in the manuscript, an approximate date, based on internal evidence, has in most instances been supplied and enclosed within square brackets.

ABBREVIATIONS USED IN SOURCE REFERENCES FOR DOCUMENTS

C	Chancery Records, Public Record Office, Kew, England
CO	Colonial Office Records, Public Record Office, Kew, England
LAM/SPG	Records of the Society for the Propagation of the Gospel in Foreign Parts in the Lambeth Palace Library, London
LAM/FUL	Records of the Bishop of London in the Lambeth Palace Library, London
NYHS	New-York Historical Society, Bound Volumes of Laws
SPG/A	Society for the Propagation of the Gospel in Foreign Parts, Entrybooks of Letters
SPG/B	Society for the Propagation of the Gospel in Foreign Parts, Letterbooks, Series B
SPG/C	Society for the Propagation of the Gospel in Foreign Parts, Letterbooks, Series C
SPG/Jou	Society for the Propagation of the Gospel in Foreign Parts, Journal
SPG/Jou/Cte	Society for the Propagation of the Gospel in Foreign Parts, Journal of the Standing Committee
SPG/Jou/App	Society for the Propagation of the Gospel in Foreign Parts, Appendix to the Journal
SPG/SAP	Society for the Propagation of the Gospel in Foreign Parts, Sermons and Abstracts of Proceedings
SS	Secretary of State Records, State Archives of North Carolina, Raleigh
T	Treasury Records, Public Record Office, Kew, England

ABBREVIATIONS USED FOR DOCUMENT TYPE

ALS	Autograph Letter, Signed
D	Document
DS	Document Signed
Dup	Duplicate
LS	Letter, Signed

ABBREVIATED CITATIONS TO PRINTED SOURCES

Acts of the Privy Council. Public Record Office, *Acts of the Privy Council of England*, 6 vols. (Hereford, England: His Majesty's Stationery Office, 1908-1912).

Andrews, *Colonial Period.* Charles M. Andrews, *The Colonial Period in American History*, 4 vols. (New Haven: Yale University Press, 1934-1938).

Boyd, *William Byrd's Histories of the Dividing Line.* William Kenneth Boyd (ed.), *William Byrd's Histories of the Dividing Line Betwixt Virginia and North Carolina* (Raleigh: Historical Commission, 1929).

Burke's Peerage. John Burke, *Genealogical and Heraldic Dictionary of the Peerage and Baronetage of the British Empire*, 8th ed. (London: Henry Colburn, 1841).

Cain, *Records of the Executive Council, 1664-1734.* Robert J. Cain (ed.), *Records of the Executive Council, 1664-1734*, vol. VII of *The Colonial Records of North Carolina* [*Second Series*] (Raleigh: Department of Cultural Resources [projected multivolume series, 1963—], 1984).

Cain, *Records of the Executive Council, 1735-1754.* Robert J. Cain (ed.), *Records of the Executive Council, 1735-1754*, vol. VIII of *The Colonial Records of North Carolina* [*Second Series*] (Raleigh: Department of Cultural Resources [projected multivolume series, 1963—], 1988).

Clark, *State Records.* Walter Clark (ed.), *The State Records of North Carolina*, 16 vols. (Raleigh and Goldsboro: State Printer, 1895-1906).

Cumming, "Turbulent Life of Captain James Wimble." William P. Cumming, "The Turbulent Life of Captain James Wimble," *North Carolina Historical Review* 46 (January 1969), 1-18.

DAB.Dictionary of American Biography, 22 vols. (New York: C. Scribner's Sons, 1928-1958).

*DNB.*Leslie Stephens (ed.), *Dictionary of National Biography*, 66 vols. (London: Smith, Elder & Co., 1885-1901).

*DNCB.*William S. Powell (ed.), *Dictionary of North Carolina Biography*, 6 vols. (Chapel Hill: University of North Carolina Press, 1979-1996).

Hofmann, *Province of North Carolina.* Margaret M. Hofmann (comp.), *Province of North Carolina, 1663-1729: Abstracts of Land Patents* (Weldon, N.C.: the compiler, 1979).

James, "Richard Marsden, Wayward Clergyman." Fleming H. James, "Richard Marsden, Wayward Clergyman," *William and Mary Quarterly*, 3d. ser., vol. XI (Oct. 1954), 578-591.

Klett, *Minutes of the Presbyterian Church*. Guy S. Klett (ed.), *Minutes of the Presbyterian Church in America, 1706-1788* (Philadelphia: Presbyterian Historical Society, 1976).

London and Lemmon, *Episcopal Church in North Carolina*. Lawrence F. London and Sarah M. Lemmon (eds.), *The Episcopal Church in North Carolina, 1701-1959* (Raleigh: The Episcopal Diocese of North Carolina, 1987).

Manross, *Fulham Papers in the Lambeth Palace Library*. William Wilson Manross (comp.), *The Fulham Papers in the Lambeth Palace Library: American Colonial Section, Calendar and Indexes* (Oxford: Clarendon Press, 1965).

Manross, *SPG Papers in the Lambeth Palace Library*. William Wilson Manross (comp.), *S.P.G. Papers in the Lambeth Palace Library: Calendar and Indexes* (Oxford: Clarendon Press, 1974).

OED. James A. H. Murray, et al. (eds.), *The Oxford English Dictionary*, corrected ed., 13 vols. (Oxford: Clarendon Press, 1933).

Parker, *Charters and Constitutions*. Mattie Erma Edwards Parker (ed.), *North Carolina Charters and Constitutions, 1578-1698*, vol. [I] of *The Colonial Records of North Carolina* [*Second Series*] (Raleigh: Department of Cultural Resources [projected multivolume series, 1963—], 1963).

Parker, *Higher-Court Records, 1697-1701*. Mattie Erma Edwards Parker (ed.), *North Carolina Higher-Court Records, 1697-1701*, vol. [III] of *The Colonial Records of North Carolina* [*Second Series*] (Raleigh: Department of Cultural Resources [projected multivolume series, 1963—], 1971).

Paschal, "Proprietary North Carolina." Herbert Richard Paschal, Jr., "Proprietary North Carolina: A Study in Colonial Government," (Ph.D. diss., University of North Carolina at Chapel Hill, 1955).

Pascoe, *Two Hundred Years of the SPG*. C. F. Pascoe, *Two Hundred Years of the S.P.G.: An Historical Account of the Society for the Propagation of the Gospel in Foreign Parts, 1701-1900*, 2 vols. (London: The Society, 1901).

Pickering, *Statutes at Large*. Danby Pickering (ed.), *The Statutes at Large from Magna Charta to the End of the Eleventh Parliament of Great Britain, Anno 1761, Continued*...46 vols. (Cambridge: John Archdeacon for Charles Bathurst, 1767).

Powell, *Gazetteer*. William S. Powell (ed.), *The North Carolina Gazetteer* (Chapel Hill: University of North Carolina Press, 1968).

Powell, *Proprietors of Carolina*. William S. Powell, *The Proprietors of Carolina* (Raleigh: Carolina Charter Tercentenary Commission, 1963).

Price, *Higher-Court Minutes, 1709-1723*. William S. Price, Jr., *North Carolina Higher-Court Minutes, 1709-1723*, vol. V of *The Colonial Records of North Carolina* [*Second Series*] (Raleigh: Department of Cultural Resources [projected multivolume series, 1963—], 1977).

Saunders, *Colonial Records*. William L. Saunders, *The Colonial Records of North Carolina*, 10 vols. (Raleigh: State of North Carolina, 1886-1890).

Sirmans, *Colonial South Carolina*. M. Eugene Sirmans, *Colonial South Carolina, A Political History, 1663-1763* (Chapel Hill: University of North Carolina Press for the Institute of Early American History and Culture, 1966).

Swann's Revisal. Samuel Swann (comp.), *Collection of All the Public Acts of Assembly in the Province of North Carolina*...(Newbern: James Davis, 1751).

Weiss, *Colonial Clergy of Virginia, North Carolina and South Carolina*. Frederick Lewis Weiss, *The Colonial Clergy of Virginia, North Carolina, and South Carolina* (Boston: n.p., 1955).

List of Documents

PAPERS

Date	Document	Page
1699 December 20	Letter from Lords Proprietors to Thomas Harvey and Council	3
[1700]	Account	4
1700	Accounts	4
1700 June 7	Warrant	5
1700 December 2	Library Catalog	5
1700 December 2	Library Catalog	9
[1702]	Report	10
1701/2 February 27	Extracts from Letters and a Report	11
1702 April 28	Journal of the Committee of the SPG	13
1702 August 21	Journal of the SPG	13
1702 December 18	Journal of the SPG	14
[1703]	Account	14
1703	Accounts	14
1703 May 3	Letter from Rev. John Talbot to [Rev. Richard] Gillingham	15
1703 September 1	Letter from Rev. John Talbot to Secretary, SPG	17
1703 September 4	Letter from Rev. George Keith to Secretary, SPG	19
1703 October 8	Letter from Charles Smith to Secretary, SPG	21
1703 October 21	Letter from Henderson Walker to Bishop of London	22
1703/4 February 18	Journal of the SPG	23
1703/4 March 13	Letter from Rev. Charles Smith to [Secretary, SPG]	24
1704 April 21	Journal of the SPG	25
1704 May 31	Testimonial	25
1704 June 6	List	26
1704 October 13	Memorandum	27
[1704 November]	Account of Mission	27
1704 November 6	Journal of the Committee of the SPG	30
1704 November 17	Journal of the SPG	30
1704 November 20	Letter from Rev. John Blair to Committee, SPG	31
ca. 1705	Petition	32
1705/6	List of Books for Missionaries	33
1706	Instructions	39
[1706]	Petition	44

1706 March 28	Journal of the SPG	45
1706 April 12	Letter from Lord Weymouth to Secretary, SPG	46
1706 April 19	Journal of the SPG	47
[1706] July 4	Letter from Bishop of London to [Secretary, SPG]	47
1706 November 15	Letter from Bishop of London to Secretary, SPG	47
1706 December 20	Letter from Bishop of London to Secretary, SPG	48
1706/7 January 17	Journal of the SPG	49
1706/7 March 22	Letter from Bishop of London to [Secretary, SPG]	49
1707 April 16	Letter from Rev. John Talbot to Secretary, SPG	50
1707 May 26	Journal of the Committee of the SPG	50
1707 July 18	Journal of the SPG	51
1707 July 22	Letter from Bishop of London to Secretary, SPG	51
1707 August 16	Letter from Bishop of London to Committee, SPG	52
1707 August 18	Testimonial	53
1707 August 20	Letter from Henry Sandford to Bishop of Elphin	53
1707 August 22, 26	Testimonials	54
1707 September 4	Letter from Bishop of London to Secretary, SPG	55
1707 September 12	Letter from Bishop of London to SPG	56
1707 September 19	Journal of the SPG	56
1707 September 22	Letter from Bishop of London to Secretary, SPG	57
1707 September 25	Letter from Secretary of the SPG to Archbishop of Tuam	57
1707 September 27	Testimonial	58
1707 September 29	Letter from Humfrey Wanley to Secretary, SPG	59
1707 September 29	Journal of the Committee of the SPG	59
1707 October 17	Journal of the SPG	60
1707 November 10	Letter from Rev. James Adams to Secretary, SPG	60
1707 November 19	Letter from Rev. William Gordon to Secretary, SPG	61
1707 November 22	Letter from Rev. James Adams to Secretary, SPG	61
1707 December 9	Letter from Rev. James Adams to Secretary, SPG	62
1707/8 January 16	Journal of the SPG	63
1708 April 1	Letter from Rev. William Gordon to Secretary, SPG	63
1708 June 10	Letter from Rev. James Adams to Secretary, SPG	64
1708 August 23	Letter from Rev. Richard Marsden to Secretary, SPG	66
1708 August 24	Letter from Vestry of Chowan to Bishop of London	68
1708 September 13	Letter from Churchwardens of Chowan to Secretary, SPG	69
1708 August 6	Letter from Churchwardens of Chowan to SPG	70
1708 September 18	Letter from Rev. James Adams to Secretary, SPG	71

1708 September 25	Letter from William Glover to Bishop of London	73
ca. 1708 September	Letter from William Glover to SPG	74
1708 December 13	Letter from Rev. William Gordon to Secretary, SPG	75
ca. 1709	Letter from Thomas Pollock to Rev. William Gordon	75
[1709 January]	Report	76
1708/9 January 21	Journal of the SPG	79
1709 March 29	Letter from Bishop of London to Secretary, SPG	79
1709 April 15	Journal of the SPG	80
1709 May 4	Testimonial	80
1709 May 13	Letter from Rev. William Gordon to SPG	81
1709 May 16	Proposal	88
1709 July 15	Journal of the SPG	89
1709 August 13	Letter from Bishop of London to Secretary, SPG	89
1709 August 15	Letter from Bishop of London to Secretary, SPG	90
1709 August 19	Journal of the SPG	90
1709 September 16	Journal of the SPG	91
1709 September 24	Letter from Secretary of the SPG to Governors	92
1709 September 26	Letter from Secretary of the SPG to Missionaries	92
1709 September 28	Letter from Rev. John Urmston to [Secretary, SPG]	93
1709 October 3	Letter from Rev. John Urmston to Secretary, SPG	94
1709 October 4	Letter from Rev. James Adams to Secretary, SPG	95
1709 October 21	Journal of the SPG	97
ca. 1710	Standing Orders	97
ca. 1710	Extract from List	102
1709/10 February 9	Letter from Lords Proprietors to Edward Tynte	103
1709/10 February 10	Letter from Rev. John Urmston to Secretary, SPG	103
1710 March 27	Letter from Rev. James Adams to _______ Hoar	104
1710 March 27	Letter from Rev. James Adams to Secretary, SPG	105
1710 September 4	Letter from Rev. James Adams to Secretary, SPG	106
1710 August 25	Testimonial	108
1710 August 26	Testimonial	109
1710 August 30	Testimonial	110
1710 October 15	Letter from Rev. John Urmston to Secretary, SPG	111
1710/11 February 8	Journal of the SPG	111
1710/11 March 21	Letter from Rev. Jacob Henderson to Secretary, SPG	111
1711 April 20	Letter from Christopher DeGraffenried to Bishop of London	112
1711 June 30	Letter from A. W. Boehm to Secretary, SPG	113
1711 July 5	Letter from Rev. Giles Ransford to Secretary, SPG	114

1711 July 7	Letter from Rev. John Urmston to Secretary, SPG	115
1711 July 17	Letter from Rev. John Urmston to Secretary, SPG	122
1711 July 26	Letter from Benjamin Bradly to Secretary, SPG	124
1711 July 30	Testimonial	125
1711 August 7	Testimonial	126
1711 August 17	Journal of the SPG	127
1711 August 27	Letter from Bishop of London to Secretary, SPG	127
1711 September 3	Letter from Rev. Benjamin Dennis to Secretary, SPG	128
1711 September 20	Letter from Rev. Robert Lasinby to Rev. Dr. Butler	130
1711 September 19	Letter from Rev. R. Mayo to Rev. Robert Lasinby	131
1711 October 19	Journal of the SPG	131
1711 December 10	Journal of the Committee of the SPG	132
1711 December 13	Letter from Rev. Giles Ransford to Secretary, SPG	132
1711 December 31	Letter from Bishop of London to [Secretary, SPG]	133
1711/2 January 9	Letter from Rev. Giles Ransford to Secretary, SPG	134
1711/2 January 12	Letter from Bishop of London to Secretary, SPG	135
1711/2 January 21	Letter from Rev. John Urmston to Bishop of London	135
1711/2 February 20	Letter from Rev. Giles Ransford to Secretary, SPG	136
1711/2 Febuary 23	Letter from Rev. Giles Ransford to Secretary, SPG	137
1712 April 29	Letter from Secretary of the SPG to Rev. John Urmston	138
1712 May 30	Letter from Edward Hyde to Rev. Giles Ransford	138
1712 May 30	Letter from Rev. John Urmston to Secretary, SPG	140
After 1712 July 23	Bond	141
1712 July 25	Letter from Rev. Giles Ransford to Secretary, SPG	142
1712 July 25	Letter from Rev. Giles Ransford to [Bishop of London]	145
1712 August 26	Letter from Rev. Miles Gale to Archbishop of York	146
1712 September 19	Journal of the SPG	147
1712 September 29	Letter from Rev. John Urmston to Bishop of London	147
1712 October 3	Letter from Bishop of London to Secretary, SPG	149
1712 October 17	Journal of the SPG	150
1712 October 22	Letter from Rev. John Urmston to John Hodges	150
1712 November 6	Letter from Secretary of the SPG to Rev. Giles Ransford	152
1712 November 6	Letter from Secretary of the SPG to Rev. John Urmston	153
1712 November 14	Letter from Alexander Spotswood to Rev. Giles Ransford	153
1712 November 24	Letter from W. Hall to [Secretary, SPG]	154
1712 December 17	Will	155

ca. 1713	Representation	156
1712/3 January 17	Letter from Bishop of London to Secretary, SPG	157
1712/3 February 17	Letter from Rev. Giles Ransford to Secretary, SPG	157
1713 June 19	Journal of the SPG	159
1713 July 13	Letter from Rev. Giles Ransford to Secretary, SPG	160
1713 May 25	Letter from Henry Duke to Rev. Giles Ransford	161
1713 November 6	Letter from Rev. John Urmston to Secretary, SPG	162
1713 November 17	Bond	163
1713 December 1	Letter from Rev. John Urmston to Francis Nicholson	164
1713 December 1	Letter from Francis Nicholson to Secretary, SPG	166
1713 October 30	Extract from Francis Nicholson to Thomas Pollock	167
1713 December 1	Letter from Rev. Giles Ransford to Francis Nicholson	168
1713 December 18	Letter from Secretary of the SPG to Rev. John Urmston	169
1713 December 18	Letter from Secretary of the SPG to Rev. Giles Ransford	170
1713/4 January 1	Letter from Rev. John Urmston to Francis Nicholson	170
1713/4 February 19	Report	171
1713/4 March 2	Letter from Vestry of Queen Anne's Creek to Secretary SPG, and Francis Nicholson	171
1714 March 30	Letter from Rev. Giles Ransford to Secretary, SPG	174
1714 March 30	Journal of the SPG	175
1714 April 12	Letter from Rev. John Urmston to Francis Nicholson	176
[1714 April]	Letter from Thomas Pollock to Francis Nicholson	179
1714 May 11	Letter from Francis Nicholson to Secretary, SPG	179
1714 May 11	List	180
1714 June 12	Letter from Rev. John Urmston to Secretary, SPG	180
1714 July 15	Letter from Edward Moseley to Francis Nicholson	182
1714 August 3	Letter from Thomas Pollock to Francis Nicholson	183
1714 August 7	Letter from Rev. John Urmston to Secretary, SPG	184
1714 September 22	Letter from Rev. John Urmston to Secretary, SPG	185
1714 October 8	Letter from Charles Eden to SPG	186
1714 December 17	Letter from Secretary of the SPG to Rev. John Urmston	187
1714 December 17	Letter from Secretary of the SPG to Rev. Giles Ransford	188
1715	Act of Assembly	188
1715	Abstract	193
1714/5 January 10	Letter from Rev. Giles Ransford to George Jefferies	196
171[5] January 19	Letter from Rev. Giles Ransford to Secretary, SPG	197

1715 April 13	Letter from Rev. John Urmston to Secretary, SPG	198
1715 April 22	Letter from Rev. Miles Gale to Secretary, SPG	199
1715 June 12	Letter from Rev. John Urmston to Secretary, SPG	200
1715 June 21	Letter from Rev. John Urmston to Secretary, SPG	202
[1715] July 17	[Letter from Rev. John Talbot to Rev. John Urmston]	203
1715 ca. August	Letter from Rev. Thomas Gale to Secretary, SPG	203
1715 September 16	Letter from Secretary of the SPG to Rev. Gideon Johnston	204
[1715] November 18	Letter from Secretary of the SPG to Charles Eden	205
1715 November 18	Letter from Secretary of the SPG to Rev. John Urmston	205
1715/6 January 27	Letter from Rev. Gideon Johnston to Secretary, SPG	206
1716 February 14	Letter from Rev. John Urmston to Secretary, SPG	208
1715/6 February 14	Letter from Rev. John Urmston to Secretary, SPG	212
1715/6 February 28	Letter from Rev. John Urmston to Secretary, SPG	214
1715/6 March 19	Letter from Rev. Francis LeJau to Secretary, SPG	215
1716 April 4	Letter from Rev. Gideon Johnston to Secretary, SPG	216
1716 April 18	Letter from Rev. Ebenezer Taylor to Secretary, SPG	217
1716 April 20	Journal of the SPG	221
1716 April 23	Letter from Secretary of the SPG to Rev. John Urmston et al.	221
1716 April 25	Letter from Edward Mashborne to Secretary, SPG	222
1716 May 10	Letter from Charles Eden to Secretary, SPG	223
1716 May 14	Letter from Secretary of the SPG to Charles Craven and Charles Eden	224
1716 May 14	Letter from Secretary of the SPG to Rev. John Urmston et al.	225
1716 May 25	Letter from Secretary of the SPG to Charles Craven and Charles Eden	225
1716 June 11	Letter from Secretary of the SPG to Rev. John Urmston et al.	226
1716 June 11	Letter from Secretary of the SPG to Vestries of Chowan, Pasquotank, and Elsewhere	227
1716 July 16	Letter from Secretary of the SPG to Missionaries in Carolina	227
1716 August 17	Letter from Rev. Giles Ransford to Secretary, SPG	228
1716 October 19	Letter from Parishioners of St. Andrews to Rev. Gideon Johnston	228
1716 November 13	Letter from Rev. John Urmston to Secretary, SPG	230
1716 November 16	Journal of the SPG	232

1716 November 22	Letter from Secretary of the SPG to Rev. Ebenezer Taylor	233
1716 December 15	Letter from Rev. John Urmston to Secretary, SPG	233
1716 December 17	Letter from Secretary of the SPG to Rev. John Urmston	235
1716/7 January 17	Letter from Charles Eden to Secretary, SPG	235
1716/7 January 29	Letter from Rev. John Urmston to Secretary, SPG	236
1716/7 February 9	Letter from Rev. John Urmston to Secretary, SPG	239
1716/7 February 23	Letter from John Jekyll to Secretary, SPG	240
1716/7 March 10	Letter from Churchwardens and Vestry of St. Thomas's to SPG	240
1717 April 20	Letter from Thomas Howard to Rev. Ebenezer Taylor	242
1717 April 22	Instructions	242
1717 April 26	Journal of the SPG	243
1717 May 1	Letter from Rev. John Urmston to Secretary, SPG	243
1717 June 22	Letter from Rev. John Urmston to Secretary, SPG	245
1717 June 22	Letter from Rev. John Urmston to Secretary, SPG	247
1717 July 19	Journal of the SPG	249
1717 August 10	Letter from Churchwardens and Vestry of Pasquotank to SPG	250
1708 October 18; 1716 May 22	Vestry Minutes	251
1717 October 23	Letter from Rev. John Urmston to Secretary, SPG	252
1717/8 January 19	Letter from Alexander Spotswood to Rev. Giles Ransford	253
1718 May 2	Letter from Rev. John Urmston to Secretary, SPG	254
1718 September 29	Letter from Rev. John Urmston to Secretary, SPG	254
1718 October 18	Letter from Rev. John Urmston to Secretary, SPG	255
1718/9 February 20	Report	258
1719 April 23	Letter from Rev. Ebenezer Taylor to Secretary, SPG	258
1719 November 20	Letter from Rev. Ebenezer Taylor to Treasurer, SPG	263
1719 December 31	Letter from Rev. John Urmston to Secretary, SPG	263
1720	Act of Assembly	265
1719/20 February 15	Letter from Rev. John Urmston to Secretary, SPG	267
1719/20 February 19	Report	268
1720 April 25	Letter from Rev. John Urmston to Secretary, SPG	268
1720/1 February 5	Letter from Rev. John Urmston to Secretary, SPG	270
1721 April 12	Letter from Charles Eden to Secretary, SPG	271
1721 May 10	Letter from Rev. John Urmston to Secretary, SPG	272
1721 May 26	Letter from Anonymous to Secretary, SPG	273

1721 June 23	Letter from Bishop of London to Treasury Board	274
1721 July 21	Letter from Rev. John Urmston to Secretary, SPG	275
1721 July 21	Journal of the SPG	276
1721 September 12	Testimonial	276
1721 September 28	Journal of the SPG	277
1721 October 23	Order	278
1721 November 7	Letter from Secretary of the SPG to Charles Eden	278
1721 November 7	Letter from Secretary of the SPG to "Vestry of Chowan"	279
1721 November 11	Order in Council	279
ca. 1722	Letter from Rev. Benjamin Pownall to the SPG	280
1721/2 January 19	Journal of the SPG	280
1721/2 February 16	Report	281
1721/2 February 16	Journal of the SPG	281
1722 June 15	Letter from Rev. John Urmston to Secretary, SPG	281
1722 June 29	Letter from Rev. Thomas Newnam to Secretary, SPG	282
1722/3 February 15	Report	284
1723 May 9	Letter from Rev. Thomas Newnam to Secretary, SPG	284
1723 September 21	Will	286
1723 November 18	Letter from Vestry of Edenton to Secretary, SPG	287
1723 November 20	Proceedings of the General Assembly	288
1723 November 28	Letter from John Lovick to Secretary, SPG	289
ca. 1724	Memorandum	289
1723 April 6	Extract of John Baptista Ashe to Rev. William Tredwell Bull	289
[1724]	Letter from Richard Hewitt to SPG	291
1724 March 26	Power of Attorney	291
1724 August 21	Journal of the SPG	292
1724 August 22	Letter from Th. Bradley to Bishop of London	295
1724 October 16	Journal of the SPG	296
1724 December 18	Journal of the SPG	297
1724/5 February 19	Report	297
1724/5 February 19	Journal of the SPG	297
1725 April 16	Journal of the SPG	298
1725 May 12	Letter from Rev. Brian Hunt to [Francis Nicholson]	299
1725 May 12	Letter from Rev. Brian Hunt to Secretary, SPG	299
1725 October 2	Letter from Secretary of the SPG to Rev. Brian Hunt	300
1725 December 3	Affidavit	301
ca. 1726	Statement	302

1725/6 January 25	Letter from Richard Everard to Bishop of London	303
1725/6 January 27	Affidavit	305
1725/6 February 18	Report	305
1726 April 15	Journal of the SPG	306
1726 May 12, 25	Letter from Rev. Thomas Baylye to Bishop of London	306
1726 May 25	Petition	309
1726 October 3	Letter from Nathaniel Duckenfield to "Reverend Sir"	310
1727	Act of Assembly	312
1728 October 25	Letter from Rev. John LaPierre to Secretary, SPG	312
1729	Act of Assembly	314
1728/9 January 24	Letter from Clergy of South Carolina to Bishop of London	316
1729 April 14	Letter from Richard Everard to [Bishop of London]	317
1729 June 28, 30	Letter from Rev. James Blair to [Bishop of London]	318
1729 July 5	Letter from Rev. James Blair to [Bishop of London]	319
1729 September 8	Letter from Rev. James Blair to [Bishop of London]	319
1729 September 19	Journal of the SPG	320
1729 October 12	Letter from Richard Everard to [Bishop of London]	320
1729 October 17	Journal of the SPG	322
[1729 November 24]	Letter from Rev. Alexander Garden to Bishop of London	322
ca. 1730	Letter from Daniel Kidlye to "Sir"	323
1729/30 January 31	Letter from Bishop of Meath to [Bishop of London]	323
1730 Easter Monday	Petition	324
1730 December 14	Instructions	325
1731 July 2	Letter from George Burrington to Duke of Newcastle	327
1731 August 20	Journal of the SPG	328
[1732]	Petition	328
1731/2 February 25	Letter from Rev. Alexander Garden to [Bishop of London]	329
1731/2 March 15	Letter from George Burrington to [Bishop of London]	330
1732 April 4	Testimonial	331
1732 April 6	Letter from Christopher Gale to Bishop of London	332
1732 April 15	Letter from Rev. Francis Peart to "Sir"	333
1732 May 6	Letter from Rev. Bevill Granville to [Bishop of London]	334
1732 May 9	Letter from Rev. Brian Berks to Secretary, SPG	334
1732 May 10	Letter from George Burrington to [Bishop of London]	335
1732 September 25	Letter from William Hay to [Bishop of London]	336

1732 October 20	Journal of the SPG	337
1732 November 29	Letter from Rev. John LaPierre to Bishop of London	337
ca. 1733	Letter from Bishop of London to Governments in Colonies	339
1732/3 January 1	Letter from George Burrington to Board of Trade	339
1732/3 February 16	Report	340
1732/3 March 17	Certificate	340
1733 April 5	Letter from Rev. John Boyd to Bishop of London	341
1733 May 5	Letter from Rev. James Blair to [Bishop of London]	342
1733 June 20	Letter from Rev. Richard Marsden to [Bishop of London]	343
1733 July 4	Proceedings of the General Assembly	345
1733 August 4	Warrant	346
1733 October 9	Letter from Rev. John LaPierre to Bishop of London	347
1734	Letter from Rev. John Boyd to Secretary, SPG	348
1734 April 23	Letter from Rev. John LaPierre to Bishop of London	349
1734 June 8	Letter from Rev. Alexander Garden to [Bishop of London]	351
1734 June 13	Answers	352
1734 October 10	Petition	353
1734/5 February 21	Report	354
1734/5 March 21	Journal of the SPG	355
1735 April 12	Letter from Rev. John Boyd to [Bishop of London]	355
1735 May 8	Petition	357
1735 May 8	Petition	357
1735 May 8	Letter from Rev. John Garzia to Bishop of London	358
1735 July 7	Letter from Rev. Richard Marsden to Bishop of London	359
1735 October 17	Journal of the SPG	362
1735/6 February 20	Report	363
1735/6 March	Memorandum	364
1735/6 March 19	Letter from Rev. John Garzia to [Bishop of London]	364
1735/6 March 19	Letter from Rev. John Garzia to Secretary, SPG	365
1736 August 16	Letter from Rev. Richard Marsden to Bishop of London	366
1736 September 22	Proceedings of the General Assembly	370
1736 November 8	Letter from Rev. Richard Marsden to [Bishop of London]	371
1736 December 17	Journal of the SPG	373
1736/7 February 18	Journal of the SPG	374
1737 April 15	Journal of the SPG	374

1737 September 6	Letter from Rev. Alexander Garden to Bishop of London	375
1737 October 9	Will	377
ca. 1738	Letter from Rev. Alexander Garden to Rev. John Garzia	378
[1738]	Account	378
1737/8 March 13	Letter from Rev. Richard Marsden to Bishop of London	381
1737/8 March 17	Journal of the SPG	382
1738 April 21	Journal of the SPG	382
1738 May 19	Journal of the SPG	382
1738 June 16	Journal of the SPG	383
1738 June 30	Letter from Gabriel Johnston to SPG	384
1738 July 20	Letter from Rev. John Garzia to Secretary, SPG	385
1738 July 20	Letter from Rev. John Garzia to SPG	386
1738 July 21	Journal of the SPG	386
1738 August 18	Journal of the SPG	387
1738 September 15	Journal of the SPG	387
1738 November 17	Journal of the SPG	388
1738/9 February 1	Letter from Rev. John Fordyce to Secretary, SPG	388
1738/9 February 8	Proceedings of the General Assembly	389
1738/9 February 16	Report	390
1739 May 4	Letter from Rev. Alexander Garden to Bishop of London	390
1739 May 18, 21	Minute; Letter from Secretary of the SPG to Bishop of London	392
1739 June 6	Letter from Rev. Richard Marsden to Secretary, SPG	393
1739 June 12	Letter from Rev. Alexander Garden to Bishop of London	394
1739 June 20	Letter from Bishop of Chester to Secretary, SPG	395
1739 July 13	Letter from Bishop of London to Secretary, SPG	395
1739 August 17	Journal of the SPG	396
1739 August 28	Letter from Secretary of the SPG to Rev. John Garzia	396
1739 August 28	Letter from Secretary of the SPG to Gabriel Johnston	397
1739 September 21	Journal of the SPG	398
1739 October 3	Letter from Vestry and Churchwardens of St. James's Parish to Archbishop of Canterbury	398
1739 October 19	Journal of the SPG	399
1739 November 16	Journal of the SPG	400

1739 November 19	Letter from Secretary of the SPG to "The Inhabitants of St. Paul's Parish, Chowan" and Elsewhere	400
ca 1740?	Letter from Rev. Gabriel Talck to Bishop of London	401
1740	Act of Assembly	402
ca. 1740 January	Statement; Bill of Exchange; Protest	405
1739/40 February 15	Report	407
1740 October 29	Letter from Rev. James Moir to Secretary, SPG	408
1740 October 30	Journal of the Committee of the SPG	409
1740 December 10	Letter from Richard Marsden to [Archbishop of Canterbury]	410
1741	Act of Assembly	413
1741	Act of Assembly	414
1740/1 February 20	Report	419
1741 March 30	Letter from Churchwardens of St. James's Parish to Secretary, SPG	419
1741 April 16	Letter from Rev. John Garzia to Secretary, SPG	420
[1741 April 16]	Notitia Parochialis	421
1741 May 25	Letter from Rev. James Moir to Secretary, SPG	422
1741 July 28	Letter from Rev. George Whitefield to Bishop of Oxford	423
1741 September 17	Letter from Bishop of Oxford to Rev. George Whitefield	426
1741 September 18	Journal of the SPG	427
1741 October 16	Journal of the SPG	428

VESTRY MINUTES

St. Paul's Parish, 1701-1741

Year	*Document*	*Page*
1701	Vestry Minutes	431
1702	Vestry Minutes	433
1703	Vestry Minutes	435
1704	Vestry Minutes	436
1705	Vestry Minutes	438
1706	Vestry Minutes	439
1707	Vestry Minutes	440
1708	Vestry Minutes	441
1709	Vestry Minutes	444
1712	Vestry Minutes	446

1713	Vestry Minutes	447
1714	Vestry Minutes	448
1715	Vestry Minutes	451
1717	Vestry Minutes	452
1719	Vestry Minutes	453
1720	Vestry Minutes	455
1722	Vestry Minutes	456
1723	Vestry Minutes	457
1724	Vestry Minutes	461
1725	Vestry Minutes	462
1726	Vestry Minutes	462
1727	Vestry Minutes	463
1728	Vestry Minutes	464
1729	Vestry Minutes	468
1731	Vestry Minutes	470
1732	Vestry Minutes	473
1733	Vestry Minutes	474
1734	Vestry Minutes	476
1735	Vestry Minutes	479
1736	Vestry Minutes	481
1737	Vestry Minutes	485
1738	Vestry Minutes	486
1739	Vestry Minutes	489
1740	Vestry Minutes	490
1741	Vestry Minutes	492

Decr. 2d. 1700. 295

A Catalogue

Of Books sent by Mr. Brett to Albemarle Settlement North Carolina Towards Raising of a Layman's Library for the Use of the Inhabitants. The Several Books to be Lent or Given by the Minister thereof according to Discretion.

100 Pastoral Letters; Being a Serious Exhortation to all persons to take Care of their Soules. +

5 Bibles.

5 Catecheticall Discourses.

5 Bp Kenn's Exposition on the Ch. Catm. +

5 Guides to a Christian.

5 Keith's Chrian Catechism.

5 The Surpassing Excellency of Chrian Knowledge.

5 The Faith and Practice of a Ch. of England man. +

5 Whole Dutys of man. +

5 Chrian Monitors B. +

100 Earnest Exhortations to the Religious Observation of ye Lord's Day. +

First page of a catalog of books sent to the "Albemarle Settlement North Carolina" by the Society for the Propagation of Christian Knowledge in 1700 and reproduced here by kind permission of the North Carolina Collection, University of North Carolina Library, at Chapel Hill. This "Layman's Library" was one of three sent together to the colony, the other two being intended to constitute a provincial library and a library for the use of the incumbent of St. Thomas's, Bath. All of them were in Bath Town, and within a few generations the 1,050 books and tracts had become entirely dispersed.

Thomas Tenison, archbishop of Canterbury from 1694 to 1715. Tenison was elected first president of the SPG, and thereafter presidents of the society were invariably archbishops of Canterbury. Presidents rarely, however, involved themselves closely in society matters. Illustration from C. F. Pascoe, *Two Hundred Years of the S.P.G.: an Historical Account of the Society for the Propagation of the Gospel in Foreign Parts, 1701-1900*, 2 vols. (London: The Society, 1901).

23

Worthy Sr Chowan N. Carolina Jany ye 10th 1714/15

I lately receiv'd a letter from Mr Taylor ye Societies Secretary, wherein he has been pleas'd to lay before me ye state of Accompts between ye Society & myself. — I have return'd my answer to both his letters by this opportunity of a Passage, with an account of ye present state of ye coun-trey, wch I hope may prove satisfactory. — I find there is considerably due to me, & upon yt Presumption have drawn on you for twelve Pounds & five shillings Sterl: Pray make punctual payment at thirty days after ye Bill is exhibited to you, for I have receiv'd ye full value from Capt William Wright of Virginia, & believe me to be Sr Your most obedient humble servant

Giles Rainsford Missionary

First page of a letter from Rev. Giles Ransford to the treasurer of the SPG, January 10, 1714/5. See page 196, below.

Dr. Thomas Bray (1656-1730), founder of both the Society for the Promotion of Christian Knowledge (1699) and the Society for the Propagation of the Gospel in Foreign Parts (1701). Illustration is of an unattributed painting held by the SPG and reproduced in C. F. Pascoe, *Two Hundred Years of the S.P.G.: an Historical Account of the Society for the Propagation of the Gospel in Foreign Parts, 1701-1900*, 2 vols. (London: The Society, 1901).

William Wake, archbishop of Canterbury from 1716 to 1737. The monthly meetings of the Society for the Propagation of the Gospel in Foreign Parts took place in his archepiscopal library in the church of St. Martin-in-the-Fields, London. Illustration from Norman Sykes, *William Wake, Archbishop of Canterbury, 1657-1737* (Cambridge, Eng.: Cambridge University Press, 1957).

Constructed in 1734, St. Thomas's Church, Bath, is the oldest church building in North Carolina. Photograph from the files of the Division of Archives and History.

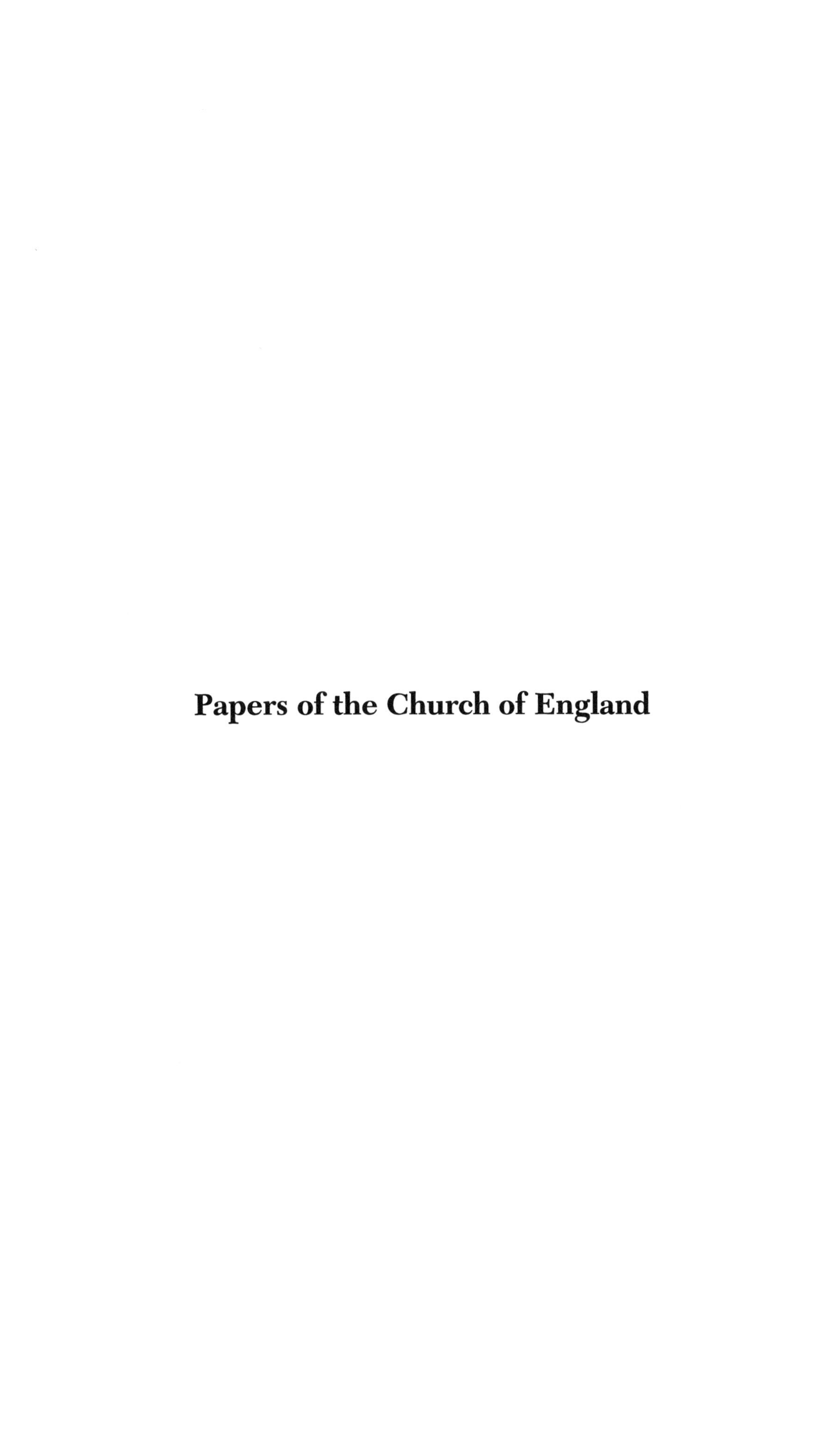

Papers of the Church of England

Papers of the Church of England

[*CO 5/289*]

Lords Proprietors to Thomas Harvey and Council
1699 December 20

<81> London Decber. the 20 1699
Gentlemen

The Reverend Doctor Bray[1] a learned pious and Charitable Man coming into America Suffragan and Comissary to the Bishop of London your Diocesan and designing to give you a Visit wee thought fit to let you know it and desire you to treat him with all kindness and respect and place the charge to the publique Account. Among other good Offices he will doe you he will be able to Mediate in any difference that may be between Virginia and Us[2] concerning which and your other Affayrs you are like Suddenly to heare from Us at large Wee are Gentlemen Your very Affectionate friends.

Bathe Palatine, Craven, Bathe for Lord Carteret, M. Ashley, Wm. Thornburg for Sir John Colleton, Tho. Amy, Wm. Thornburgh[3]

To Tho. Harvey[4] Esqr. Deputy Governour
and to our Deputys and Councill
of North Carolina

Copy.

[1]Rev. Dr. Thomas Bray (1656-1729/30) founded the Society for the Promotion of Christian Knowledge (SPCK) in 1699 and was instrumental in the establishment of the Society for the Propagation of the Gospel in Foreign Parts (SPG) in 1701. In 1700 he served briefly in Maryland as commissary to the bishop of London. As far as is known, he never visited North Carolina. *DAB*.

[2]At this time there were sharp disagreements between Virginia and North Carolina over their boundary, and also over the jurisdiction of Virginia's court of admiralty. *See* Parker, *Higher-Court Records, 1697-1701*, xxxii-xxxvii, lvi-lix.

[3]With the exception of William Thornburgh, these signatories were Lords Proprietors of Carolina: John Grenville, 1st earl of Bath (1628-1701); William Craven, 2nd earl of Craven (1668-1711); John Carteret,

2nd baron Carteret (1690-1763); Maurice Ashley (1675-1726); and Thomas Amy (d. 1704), who held two of the eight proprietary shares. Willliam Thornburgh, while not a proprietor himself, frequently acted on behalf of Sir John Colleton (1668-1754), both before and after Colleton's minority. Not represented in this list is the proprietor Joseph Blake. Powell, *Proprietors of Carolina*, passim.

[4]Thomas Harvey (d. July, 1699) held a succession of offices in North Carolina from at least 1683: justice of the county court of Albemarle, justice of the General Court, member of the council, and (1694-1699) deputy governor. *DNCB*.

[*T 38/179*]

Account
[1700]

An Account of the Expence of the Civill List for Entire year from the 25th Xber. 1699 to 25th Xber. [1700] viz.

Paid at the Rect. of his Majestys Exchequer. [...]

Paid Severall as of his Majestys Royall bounty for the charge of their passages going Chaplains Schoolmasters or in Such like quality to the West Indies Videlicet. [...]

To Danll. Brett[1] going Chaplain to Carolina. 20._._ [...]

D. As early as the reign of Charles II, royal payments had been made to clergy to help defray expenses of passage in taking up appointments in the colonies.

[1]Rev. Daniel Brett, first Anglican missionary to North Carolina. See appendix.

[*SPG/BRAY ASSOC./f12*]

Accounts
1700

London. Dr. Brays account of Benefactions and Missions and Charges relating thereunto Since his Return from MaryLand as given in by him then to a Committee of the Corporation for the Propagation of the Gospel in Foreign Parts.

Dr. Bray Dr.

To Benefactions Received Since his Return from MaryLand July 15th 1700 towards the Missionaries their Libraries and other Books to be Given and Sent in their Respective Parishes and towards other appendant Charges [...]

To Ld. Viscount Weymouth[1] for the first yeares mission 70. 0. 0

To Ld. Viscount Weymouth towards Books to be Dispersd amongst the people 300. 0. 0

To Ld. Guilford[2] for Mr. Bretts mission 3. 4. 6 [...]

London.

Per Contr. Dr. Bray Cr.

By Charges relating to the Missionaries and their Parochial Libraries and other Books Sent into the plantations [...]

<*1700 No. 2*> To Mr. Marsden[3] towards his Mission	30. 0. 0 [...]
<*Dec. 7*> By One parochial and two Layman Libraries Sent to Mr. Brett to N. Carolina and for his own Subsistense	83. 4. 0 [...]
By the Sallary for the Second yeares mission returnd to the Missionary[4] at N. Carol.	50. 0. 0 [...]

D.

[1]Sir Thomas Thynne, 1st viscount Weymouth (1640-1714), a noted high tory and patron of "nonjuring" bishops—Anglican bishops refusing to take an oath of allegiance to William and Mary in 1689. *DNB*.

[2]Francis North, 2nd baron Guildford, 1673-1729. *Burke's Peerage* (1914 ed.), 912.

[3]Rev. Richard Marsden. See appendix.

[4]Daniel Brett.

[*T 53/15*]

Warrant
1700 June 7

<*Mr. Brett Chaplaine £20*> After etc. By Vertue of the Generall Letters Patents Dormant bearing Date the 8th of Aprill 1689. These are to pray and require You to draw an Order for paying unto [*blank*] Brett Clerk or his Assignes the Sume of £20 for his passage to Carolina where he is going Chaplaine And lett the Same be satisfyed out of any his Majestys Treasure being and remaining in the Receipt of the Exchequer Applicable to the Uses of the Civill Government For which This shall be your Warrant Cockpitt Treasury Chambers 7th of June 1700. S.F., J.S., H.B., R.H. [...]

D. Similar warrants were issued on the dates indicated for payments of £20 to the following clergymen for passage to North Carolina:

Samuel Thomas, August 11, 1702 (T 53/16, 68). Although the warrant specified North Carolina, Thomas had actually been appointed missionary to South Carolina by the SPG and took up his duties there. John Blair, April 17, 1703 (T 53/16, 284); James Adams, September 26, 1707 (T 53/19, 86); John Urmston, September 1, 1709 (T 53/20, 126); Thomas Newnam (as Thomas *Newman*), October 19, 1721 (T 53/29, 203); Walter Jones and Richard Hewitt, December 17, 1724 (T 53/31, 341). These two served in Virginia rather than North Carolina. John Blacknall, June 7, 1725 (T 53/32); John Boyd, October 3, 1732 (T 53/36, 119); James Moir, November 13, 1739 (T 53/40, 201); Thomas Burgess, October 2, 1741 (T 53/40, 201).

[*NC Collection*]

Library Catalog
1700 December 2

A Catalogue Of Books sent Decr. 2d 1700 with Mr. Brett Towards Founding a Parochial Library at St. Thomas Parish in Pamplico North Carolina.

Fol.
Pool's Synopsis Criticorum 5 fol.
Medes Works fol.
Dr. Hammond's Works 4 Vol.
Maldonatus in 4 Evangelia.
Scapula Lexicon Graco Latinum Elzi viri et Hackij Ludg. Bat. 1652.
Philippia A Limborch Theologia Christiana.
The Works of the Author of the Whole Duty of man.
Ductor Dubitantium fol.
Causin's Holy Court.
Downham of Justification.
Petri Martyris Loci Communes.
Sir Richard Baker's Chronicle of the Kings of England Lond. 1679.
Howel's Lexicon Tetraglocton being an English, French, Italian Spanish Dictionary 1660.
Wilkin's Real Character.
Bp. Peirson's Exposition on the Creed.
The Merchants Map of Commerce.
Chilling'sworth's Religion of Protestants a Safe way to Salvation.
Guillim's Display of Heraldry Lond. 1660.
Laud against Fisher.
Towerson on the Creed 10 Com. Lord's Prayer and the Sacraments 4 vol. f.
Davis de Jure Uniformitatis Ecclesiasticae In which the Chief things of the Laws of nature and nations, and of the divine Law concerning the Consistency of the Ecclesiastical with the Civil State is Unfolded fol.
Cases against the Dissenters by the London Divines.
Churchhill's Divi Britannici fol.
Monasticum Anglicanum Epitomiz'd
Guillims Display of Heraldry.
The Cambridge Concordance.
Barrow's Sermons 3 vol.
Biblia 70 Interpretum Wiccelij 1697 New B.
A Church Bible.

4°
Bibliotheca Parochialis et Catechetica.
Athias's Hebrew Bible.
Littleton's Dictionary.
Turretini Compendium.
Claud's Historical Defence of the Reformation.
Sparrow's Collection of Canons with Bp. Overal's Convocation book
Parker's Demonstration of the Divine Authority of the Christian Religion and the Law of Nature
Pagit's Christianography.
Kettlewel's Measures of Christian Obedience.
A Way to gett Wealth Containing six principal Vocations.
Hoornbeck de Conversione Indorum et Gentilium.
Thorndick's Weights and Measures.
Le Grand's Historia Naturae varijs Experimentis A Ratiocinijs Elmidata Sedum Principia Stabilita in Institutione Philosophiae Edit oeden Authore 4°.
Pet. Molinaei Anatome Arminianismi.
Goodman's Penitent Pardon'd.
Stillingfleet's Irenicum.
Mr. Keith's 4 Narratives with those other Tracts against the Quakers videlicet 1. The Arguments of the Quakers more particularly of G. Keith against Bap. and the Supper Answer'd.
2. Satan Disrob'd. 3 The History of Sin and Heresy. 4 A Paralell betwixt the Faith and Doctrine of the present Quakers, and the chief Hereticks in all Ages.
5 The Quakers set in the true Light.
A Religious Conference between a minister and Parishioners concerning the Practice of Baptizing Infants by powring water on their Faces with a Vindication of Godfathers and Godmothers.
Discourses on the Notes of the Church.

8°
A Large English Bible with Apocrypha and Service.
Corpus Juris Civilis Gothofridi 8°.
H. Simon's History of the Original and Progress of Ecclesiastical Revenues with his Critical History of the Religions and Customs of the Eastern Nations.
Dr. Bull's Judicium Ecclesiae Catholicae de Necessitate Credendi J. Christum esse verum Deum.
Justimus cum Notis Variorum 8°.
Whiston's new Theory of the Earth.
Virgilius cum Notis Variorum.
Falkner's Libertas Ecclesiastica 8°.
Bp. Burnet's Abridgment of the History of the Reformation.
Horatius cum Notis Variorum.
Epictetus's Morals with Simplicius's Comment.
Wotton's Reflections upon Antient and Modern Learning.
Jurieu's History of the Council of Trent.
The Gentleman's Recreation in 4 parts videlicet Hunting, Hawking, Fowling, Fishing.
Seller's History of Palmyra.
South's Sermons 3 vol.
Osborns Advice to his son.
Five Discourses of the Author of the Snake in the Grass.
The Snake in the Grass.
The Defence of the Snake
Huetij Demonstratio Evangelica 2 Vol.
Grotius's Truth of the Christian Religion
Rawlet's Divine Poems
Bp. Sanderson of Episcopacy not prejudicial to Regal Power.
Hickman's Animadversions on Dr. Heilin's Quinquarticular History
The Oxford Grammar.
Mr. Clarks Three practical Essays on Baptism Confirmation, Repentance
Life of Bp. Bedle
The Life of Sir Thomas Smith.
Varenij Descriptio Regni Japonia et Siam. Item de Japoniorum Religione et Siamensium Et de Diversis omnium Gentium Religionibus
Galai Opuscula Muthologica Ethica et Physica Grae Lat.
Goodman's Winter Evening Conference 2 vol.
Varenij Geographia Universalis In qua Affectiones Generales Telluris Explicantur Cum Schematibus.
Kettlewel's Discourses.
Whaley's Sermons of Adultery and of the Christian Warfare.
Richardsons Canon of the N. Test. Vindicated against Toland's Amyntor
Mr. Hill's municipium Ecclesiasticum.
Drellingcourt's Christians Defence against the Fears of Death.
Hudibrass 1t and 2d parts
Bp. Wilkin's Sermons.
Bp. Spratt's History of the Conspiracy against King Ch. 2.
Peirc's pacificatorium.
Love's l'Comle's Journey through the Empire of China 8°.
Whartoni Historia de Episcopis et Decanis Londiniensibus
Sherlock's practical Discourse on Religious Assemblies.
Dr. Payn's Sermons.
Dr. Wake's Principles of the Christian Religion.
Wingate's Abridgment of all the Statutes in force til 41.
Dr. Stillingfleet's Vindication of the Trinity 8°.
L [*blank*] On the Sufferings and Satisfaction of Christ 2 pts.
Bate's Harmony of the Divine Attributes
A.Bp. Usher's power of the Prince Communicated by God the Obedience Required of the Subject.
The Second part of the whole Duty of man.

Whaley's Sermons.

Mr. Boyls Enquiry into the vulgarly Received Notion of Nature.

Verstegans Antiquities.

England's Worthies, or the Lives of the most Eminent persons from Constantine to the present Time

Mr. Math. Pool of the Nullity of the Romish Faith.

The Christian's Pattern.

Dr. Burnet's Vindication of the Authority Constitution and Laws of the Ch. and State of Scotld.

Dr. R. Sherlock's practical Christian; And Practice of Examination

Buxtorifij Lexicon Hebraicum, et Chaldaicum Basileae 1663

Juvenalis Satyre cum Notis Variorum.

Wingate's Arithmetick.

Mauric's Defence of Diocesan Episcopacy.

Guilielmi Grotij Enchiridion de Juris naturalis Principijs

A new and Easy method to Understand the Roman History with an Exact Chronology of the Reign of the Emperors for the Use of the D. of Burgundy

Turner's middle Way betwixt Necessity and Freedom.

Jenkyns of the Reasonableness of the Christian Religion 1 Vol. of the Reasonableness of the Christian Religion pt. 2.

Wingate's Abridgment of all Statutes in force and Use from the beginning of Magna Charta til 1641

Observations on a Journey to Naples wherein the frauds of Romish Monks and Priests are Discovered

Historical Collections out of several Grave Protestant Historians concerning the Changes of Religion in the Reigns of Hen. 8 Ed. 6. Queen Mary and Q. Elizab.

Dr. Scott's Works 5 Vol.

Bp. Patrick upon Repentance and the Lent Fast.

Passor's Lexicon Graeco Latinum in Nov. Test.

Dr. Holder's Discourses concerning Time for the better Understanding of the Ch. Calendar

Ars Cogitandi sive Logica In qua praeter Vulgares Regulae plura nova habentur ad Rationem dirigendam utilia

Mr. Allen's Catholicism, or several Enquiries touching Visible Ch. Membership, Ch. Communion, The Nature of Schism; And the Usefulness of National Constitutions in Religion

Busbaei Gracae Grammaticos Rudimenta 8°.

Mandey's Marrow of Measuring wherein a ready way is shewn how to Measure in Glazing, Painting, Plastering Masonry Joyners, Carpenters and Bricklayers Work; As also Land

Dugard's Vindication of the Marriage of Cozin Germans from the Censures of Unlawfulness and Inexpediency

Bovel's Pandaemonium, or Blow to Modern Sadducism.

Boyl's Medicinal Experiments, Being a Collection of Choice and Safe Remedies

The Christian Education of Children, according to the Maxims of the Sacred Scripture, and the Instructions of the Fathers of the Church

Bp. Burnet's Letters with his Reflections on Varillay's History of the Revolutions that have happen'd in Europe in matters of Religion 8°.

The Art of Heraldry in two parts Comprehending all Necessary Rules; And Giving a full Account of the Priviledges of the Gentry of England.

The Penitent or Entertainments for Lent.

An Easy method with the Deists and Jews.

Bodini Respub. Amistol. 1645.
Buxtorifij Epitome Grammatica Hebreae.
The Art of Speaking by Messieurs du port Royal.
Manger's French Grammar. The Sixteenth Ed.
The French New Testament.
Chassanaei Enchiridion Juris Civilis.
A Short Discourse on the Baptismal Covenent.
Dr. Willi's Advice to the Roman Catholicks of England.
Angliae Notitia sive praesens status Angliae Succincte Enucleatus
Ellisij Grotij de Principijs Juris Naturalis Enchiridion.
King's Inventions of Men in the Worship of God.

D. Reproduced by kind permission of the North Carolina Collection, University of North Carolina Library at Chapel Hill. The libraries comprising these titles and the ones in the following document were sent with Rev. Daniel Brett to St. Thomas Parish, Bath County, presumably arriving there in 1701. A full bibliographical analysis of the 153 titles in the present document, and the thirty-six in the one following, is given in John Kenneth Gibson, "The Thomas Bray Libraries, St. Thomas Parish, Pamlico [Bath, North Carolina], 1700: A Bibliographical and Historical Analysis" (unpublished master's thesis, University of North Carolina at Chapel Hill, 1986).

[*NC Collection*]

Library Catalog
1700 December 2

Decr. 2d 1700. A Catalogue Of Books sent by Mr. Brett to Albemarle Settlement North Carolina Towards Raising of a Layman's Library for the Use of the Inhabitants. The Several Books to be Lent or Given by the Minister thereof according to Discretion.

100 Pastoral Letters; Being a Serious Exhortation to all persons to take Care of their Soules.
5 Bibles.
5 Catecheticall Discourses.
5 Bp. Kenn's Exposition on the Ch. Catechism.
5 Guides to a Christian.
5 Keith's Christian Catechism.
5 The Surpassing Excellency of Christian Knowledge.
5 The Faith and Practice of a Ch. of England man.
5 Whole Dutys of man.
5 Christian Monitors B.
100 Earnest Exhortations to the Religious Observation of the Lord's Day.
5 Serious Exhortations to the performance of Religious Duties both publick and private.
100 Cautions against Prophane Swearing.
5 Dr. Ashton on Deathbed Repentance.
100 Christians daily Devotion.
5 Dr. Comber of Fervent and Frequent Prayer.
5 Dr. Beveridge's Sermon on the Common Prayer B.
5 Discourses on the Nature, Necessity and Benefitt of Sacraments as Seals of the Covenent of Grace.
5 Dorrington's Familiar Guide to the Holy Sacrament
5 Answers to all the Excuses, and Pretences which men ordinarily

	make for their not coming to the Communion. B.
1	Snake in the Grass.
1	Defence of the Snake.
1	Primitive Heresy Reviv'd.
1	Paralell of the Doctrine of the Quakers with the Primitive Hereticks
2	Discourses shewing who they are who are now Qualify'd to Administer Baptism and the Ld's. Supper.
100	Serious Invitations of the Quakers to return to Christianity
1	Dr. Willi's Address to the Roman Catholicks.
1	London Cases Epitomiz'd
1	Bp. King's Inventions of men in the worshop of God.
100	Ch. Catechisms with Prayers and Graces.
5	Christian Schollars In Rules and Directions for children and youth.
100	Expositions of the Ch. Catechisms with Scripture proofs.
20	Pastoral Letters shewing the necessity and Advantage of an Early Religion.
20	Introductions of the New Version of Psalms.
20	Short Discourses of the Doctrine of our Baptismal Covenent
20	Common Prayers.

D. Reproduced by kind permission of the North Carolina Collection, University of North Carolina Library at Chapel Hill. See the note for the document above. The volumes in the present catalog constituted a lending, or "layman's," library. Another catalog identical in content to this one and not printed here is also in the North Carolina Collection, and would appear to indicate that two such libraries were sent to the parish.

[*SPG/Jou/App B*]

Report
[1702]

<II.> An Account of the State of Religion in the English Plantations in North America by Colonel Dudley[1] Governor of New England. Vide Journal 19 Sept. 1701.

The Plantations on the Shore of America as they lye from South to North may be thus accounted.

South Carolina contains Seaven Thousand Souls will admit and support Three Ministers.

North Carolina. Five thousand Souls, alike Three Ministers, and both stand in need of Schools.

Virginia. Forty Thousand Souls, was by the Lord Culpepper divided into about Forty Parishs with an Establish'd Maintenance by Act of Assembly but are not fully supply'd, and the Maintenance hurt by disuse, but will be always encouraged by Colonel Nicholson the present Governor.

Maryland. Twenty Five Thousand Souls, in Twenty Six parishes. I suppos'd well supply'd by the care of Dr. Bray.

Pensilvania and the Lower Counties annext. Fifteen Thousand Souls will well support Four Ministers, one at Philadelphia, and one in each County, with dependant Schools upon each.

West Jersey. Five Thousand Souls most Quakers, may yet have one Minister, at present supported from England.

East Jersey. Six Thousand Souls in about Seaven Towns and Parishes, may at present Support Two Ministers the rest being Dissenters.

New York. Twenty Five Thousand Souls in Twenty Five Towns about Ten of them Dutch, the rest English, may have about Five Ministers, the rest Dutch Presbiterians and English Dissenters.

Connecticut. Thirty Thousand Souls, about Thirty Three Towns all Dissenters supply'd with Ministers and Schools of their own Perswasion.

Naraganset or Kings Province. Three Thousand Souls without any Ministry or Publick Form of Religion, may have two Ministers, and might well support them.

Road Island and Providence Plantations. Five Thousand Souls in Seaven Towns, at present under a Quaker Government, but might have Two Ministers and Schoolmasters, at first subsisted from hence, at least one of them.

Massachusets or New England. Seventy Thousand Souls, in Seaventy Towns, all Dissenters, that have Ministers and Schools of their own Perswasions, except one Congregation of the Church of England at Boston where there are two Ministers.

New Hampshire. Three Thousand Souls in Six Towns all Dissenters that have Ministers and Schools of their own Perswasion.

Province of Mayn. Two Thousand Souls in Six Towns (the rest of that great Province being in Ten years past wasted and driven of by the Indians) are all Dissenters, and have Ministers and Schools of their own.

In the Three last Colonies and Connecticut by an early Law providing for Ministers and Schoolmasters, I am of Opinion there are no Children to be found of Ten year old that do not read well, nor men of Twenty that do not write tolerably.

<*Qualifications of Ministers.*> The Ministers to be sent from England to any of the abovesaid Colonies must be Men of good Learning, sound Morals and should not be very young and where there is not the view of a good Support from their Hearers, must be supply'd from hence then they be not in contempt, but may be well provided for, in those Parts where the Governments are imediately dependant upon the Crown and Government of England.

D.

[1]Joseph Dudley (1647-1720), governor of Massachusetts 1702-1715. *DAB*.

[*LAM/SPG/X*]

Extracts from Letters and a Report
1701/2 February 27

An Extract out of Letters[1] lately Received from Raonoak in N. Carolina, and from the Report of a Worthy Gentleman[2] lately come thence.

1. That the Minister[3] lately Sent in does much good amongst them.

2. That he is forcd to Supply two Settlements the one calld Pamphlico and the other Raonoak 50 Miles distance for which Reason neither Settlement have the Benefit of his Ministry and he himself is extreamly fatigud in Serving both.

3. That it will therefore be a very great Charity to Supply them with another Minister And to Support him with an Allowance from hence for Some time at least, till the Inhabitants Shall make a provison for him.

4. That in Order to that, President Walker[4] the Governor of the Country Desires that a Grant may be Obtaind of his Majesty of the 1*d.* per pound Custome on the Side Trade towards the Support of a Minister, as is now done out of the Same Customes in Pensylvania.

5. They Inform us from thence that Governor Nicholson[5] has given them a Large Benefaction towards the Building of their Church. And it may not be improper in this place to take Notice that this has been his Way upon all the Continent to Lay the Foundation of Churches by a Benefaction of his own, and the People in the Several Colonies upon the Encouragment have Soon Run up their Churches, As was done at Boston Rhode Island, New York Philadelphia in Pensylvania, most eminently through Mary Land, and now in Carolina.

And indeed to do him Justice he is, as the founder so the Buttress and Support of all our Churches on the Continent for which Reason the Enemy has lately and I am Afraid Still does all that is possible to Supplant him by forming the most Wiked and falsest Calumnies against him. And it is a happy Providence that by the coming over of a most worthy Gentleman lately from those parts they are found to be false.

[*Endorsed:*]
Numbers 9, 10, 11, 12
An Extract of Letters
from Road Iland Boston etc.
27 Febr. 1701/2

D. Read at a meeting of the SPG on February 27, 1701/2. Included among "Extracts of several Letters...deliverd in by Dr. Bray" was this "Extract of Letters from Roonoak North Carolina relating to the sending one Missionary into those Parts.... The fourth Extract relating to North Carolina was again read," and it was then "Resolved that it is the Opinion of this Society that a Missionary be forthwith sent to Roonoak in North Carolina." Journal of the SPG, I, 30.

[1]Not located.

[2]Not identified.

[3]Daniel Brett.

[4]Henderson Walker (ca. 1658-1704), president of the council of North Carolina, July, 1699, to June, 1703; zealous supporter of the Anglican establishment in the colony. *DNCB.*

[5]Francis Nicholson (1655-1728), governor or lieutenant-governor of five American colonies, including Virginia (1690-1692, 1698-1705), and South Carolina (1720-1725). He was in command of the British military expedition that took Port Royal, Acadia, in 1710. A devout churchman, Nicholson left most of his estate to the SPG. *DAB.*

[*SPG/Jou/Cte*]

Journal of the Committee of the SPG
1702 April 28

<[19]> 28 April 1702 [...]

1. Agreed That it is the Opinion of this Committee, that tenn Church Bibles and as many Common Prayer Books should be sent after Mr. Keith[1] and Mr. Gordon[2] videlicet Two for New England and the Naragansetts, Two for New York, Two for East and West Jerseys, Two for Pensylvania, and Two for North Carolina. [...]

Minutes.

[1]George Keith (ca. 1638-1716) was one of the most prominent members of the Society of Friends from 1664 until his conversion to Anglicanism in 1700, in which year he was ordained by the bishop of London. In 1702 he sailed to America as the first missionary of the SPG and undertook an extensive tour of the American colonies, attacking the tenets of Quakerism. *DAB*.

[2]Patrick Gordon was the second missionary employed by the SPG, receiving his appointment in March, 1701/2. The next month he and Rev. George Keith, the Society's first missionary, sailed for America. Gordon was dead by April of the following year. Pascoe, *Two Hundred Years of the SPG*, I, 10; Manross, ed., *SPG Papers in the Lambeth Palace Library*, 44.

[*SPG/Jou/1*]

Journal of the SPG
1702 August 21

<81> 21 August 1702. [...]

<82.> 12. Dr. Humfrey Prideaux, Dean of Norwich, Dr. George Thorpe Prebendary of Canterbury, and Mr. Thomas Amy[1] one of the Proprietors of Carolina being recommended by the said Committee were proposed the first time for Members of this Society. [...]

14. Two Letters read from Mr. Keith and Mr. Gordon dated 12th of June 1702 at Boston in New England desiring the Society to appoint Mr. Talbott[2] assistant to the said Mr. Keith, in his Travells in America. [...]

Minutes.

[1]Thomas Amy (d. 1704) held a proprietary share in trust for four other proprietors, and also was by the proprietary board assigned the share of Seth Sothel upon Sothel's death in 1694. Powell, *Proprietors of Carolina*, 50. Amy was proposed for membership a second time at a meeting of September 18, and elected at a meeting of October 16. Journal of the SPG, I, 85-86.

[2]John Talbot (1645-1727), appointed an SPG missionary in September, 1702, accompanied George Keith in his travels throughout the colonies, including North Carolina. *DAB*.

[*SPG/Jou/1*]

Journal of the SPG
1702 December 18

<93> 18 December 1702. [...]

<94> 18. Part of two Letters[1] from Mr. Walker President of the Council of N. Carolina to Mr. Amy one of the Proprietors of this Province relating to the Settlement of the Church in those being read.

19. Ordered that the said Letters be referred to the said Committee and Report to be made at next Meeting.

20. Ordered that Mr. Amy be desired to attend the said Committee [...]

Minutes. The Committee's journal of December 22, 1702, records its deliberations on the order from the monthly meeting of the SPG: "Mr. Walker's Letter relating to the sending 2 Ministers to N. Carolina (where the Inhabitants will allow £60 to each) being read, Agreed that it be recommended to all the Members present at this Committee to Consider of Fit Persons to be sent into those Parts and to make a Report thereof at the next Meeting." Journal of the Committee of the SPG. No such report was noted in subsequent meetings.

[1]Not located.

[*T 38/179*]

Account
[1703]

Civill List for one Entire year, to wit, from Christmas 1701 to Christmas 1702 [...]
Her present Majestys Expence Continued [...]
To Patrick Gordon going Chaplain to North Carolina[1] 20._._
To Samll. Thomas do.[2] 20._._ [...]

D.

[1]There is no evidence that Gordon ever visited North Carolina. He was dead by April, 1703. Journal of the SPG, I, 105.

[2]Rev. Samuel Thomas served South Carolina rather than North Carolina.

[*SPG/BRAY ASSOC./f12*]

Accounts
1703

London June 1t 1703. Dr. Brays Account of Benefactions and Missions and Charges thereunto belonging since his delivery of the Last Account March 6, 1701/2 to the Corporation for the propagation of the Gospel in Foreign parts.

Dr. Bray	Dr. [...]
To The Ld. Viscount Weymouth for the Third Years Mission	50. 0. 0 [...]
Dr. Bray per Contr.	Cr. [...]
By £50 pay'd to Collonel Quarry for the Missionary in N. Carolina which according to Instructions he has in his hands to be payd to the next to be Sent.	50. 0. 0 [...]
By paper and print[ing] relating to the two Laws made in Mary Land and North Carolina[1] for preservation of the Library in the Same Collonies	3. 7. 6 [...]
By £30 to the N. Carolina Missionary[2] which with the Queens Bounty makes up the Third Years allowance for himsel £20 being deducted towards paying for the Library already Sent worth £50	30. 0. 0 [...]

D.

[1]This act has not been located. One of 1715 was wholly or in large part a reenactment of the one referred to here, and provided for a "Library Keeper" and commissioners, borrowing privileges by residents of Beaufort Precinct, and the compilation of catalogs of the library. Clark, *State Records*, XXIII, 76-79.

[2]Rev. Daniel Brett.

[*SPG/A/1*]

Rev. John Talbot to [Rev. Richard] Gillingham
1703 May 3

<*CXX.*> Mr. Talbot to Mr. Gillingham.

Virginia 3d May 1703

Dear Friend,

<*An account of his Arrival in Virginia.*> Now att last (God be praised) we are arrived att the Haven where we would be. Mr. Keith is got to his Daughter's House and I am got amongst my old Friends and Acquaintance in these Parts who are very glad to See me, especially those of the Ministry, who came over along with me. [...] <*Gov. Nicholson is building two Churches in N. Carolina and one at Newcastle.*> The Governour of Virginia is building Several more Churches; Two at N. Carolina where we are going next week, and one att New-Castle; [...] <*He is going by land to Pamplico in N. Carolina where one Bret a Scandelous Fellow had been the Minister.*> We are going now by Land to Pamplico in N. Carolina a Place where there never was any Minister, but only one Dan. Brett a Scandalous fellow, that has done more harm than good every where; he was the worst I think that ever came over. We want a great many good Ministers here in America Especially in those parts mentioned in the Scheme, but we had better have none att all than such Scandalous Beasts as Some make them Selves not only the worst of Ministers but of Men. <*The want of Books in those Parts etc.*> If you know none so good as to come, I hope you will find them that are willing to Send Some good Books would do very well

in the mean while. I am Sure there is no want of them in England they have enough and to Spare. <*He objects against Dr. Brays method of commenting on the Ch. Catechism.*> Indeed we have had many of Dr. Bray's Books, and I could wish we had more But his Way and Method is not the best for this People that we have to do withal, Quakers, and Quaker Friends; to most of them, nothing but Controversy will Serve their turn, 'tis a hard Matter to persuade to the Baptismal Covenant, on which the Dr. has writ 3 or 4 Books, one in folio, that they may be ever learning and yet never be able to come to the Knowledge of the Creed, the Lord's Prayer nor the ten Comandments.

<*The People of those parts sharp and inquisitive.*> Those that we have to deal with, are a sharp and Inquisitive People; they are not Satisfied with one Dr.'s Opinion, but must have Something that is Authentick if we hope to prevail with them.

<*Common Prayer Books etc. wanted.*> We should have Some Common Prayers Books new or old, of all Sorts and Sizes, with the 39 Articles and Some books of Homilys to Set up the Worship and Service of God till we have Ministers. Some of Dr. Comber's[1] Books would be of right good Use here to give those that ask a Reason of all things contained in our English Liturgy which has Still Stood the best Test of all Adversaries that were not blind and deaf. Above all Mr. Lesly[2] the Author of the Snake in the Grass has given Quakerism a deadly wound I hope never to be healed, and his 5 Discourses about Baptism and Episcopacy have brought many to the Church. We want 1000 of them to dispose of in the way that we goe. <*His manner of distributing Books as he Travels.*> I use to take a Walletfull of Books and carry them 100 miles about and disperse them abroad and give them to all that desired 'em, which in due time will be of good Service to the Church, 'tis a Comfort to the People in the Wilderness to see that some body takes care of them. There is a time to Sow and a time to reap which I don't desire in this World. <*He refuses to take money of the People.*> I might have money enough of the People in many Places but I would never take any of those that we goe to Proselyte, especially amongst the Quakers, I Resolved to work with my hands rather than they should say, I was a hireling and come for Money which they are very Apt to do. [...] I desire your Prayers and rest your Real Friend and Servant.

J. T.

P.S. <*The People of the Country very kind to him.*> Pray give my Service to all Friends for Indeed that [is] all I have to give 'em having my Portmanteau plunder'd by a Negro. I lost all the money I had in the World, but God be praised I have lackd not Since I came ashoar. I found Such Welcome at Some friend's or others, that I have been as it were att home, and could command much more than if I had been there, So that thô I am one that has nothing, yet I possess all things that the Country affords.

I want Bands shirts and shoes very much they are 9*s*. a pair here and not half so good as in England; a Girdle or 2 would do very well such as Mr. Barnaby Sells. I wish they would send me a Chest of Cloaths yearly to New York or Philadelphia and you could pay them for me. [...]

Copy.

[1]Thomas Comber (1645-99). Comber's most famous work, *Companion to the Temple*, was written mainly as a defense of the tenets of the Church of England against attacks from dissenters. *DNB*.

[2]Charles Leslie (1650-1722).

[*SPG/A/1*]

Rev. John Talbot to Secretary, SPG
1703 September 1

<*CXXV.*> Mr. Talbot to the Secretary.

Philadelphia 1st Sept. 1703

Sir

<*He gives account of his Journy.*> We have been the grand Circuit from N. England to N. Carolina, and are now return'd to the Center of our Business. [...]

<*Mr. K. and he have Baptiz'd many Quakers.*> Mr. Keith and I have preacht the Gospell to all Sorts and Conditions of Men, we have baptized Severall Scores of Men Women and Children, Chiefly those of his old Friends (the Rest are harden'd just like the Jews, who please not God and are contrary to all men) we have gathered Several Hundreds together for the Church of England and what is more to build houses for her Service. <*4 or 5 Churches building in Jersey etc.*> Here are 4 or 5 going forward now in this Province and the next. That att Burlington is almost finisht, Mr. Keith preacht the first Sermon in it before my Ld. Cornbury whom the Queen has made Governor of Jersey to the Satisfaction of all Christian People. <*And several in N. Carolina etc.*> Churches are going up amain where there were never any before. They are going to build 3 at N. Carolina to keep the People together lest they should fall into Heathenism, Quakerism etc. and 3 more in these lower Counties about New Castle besides those att Chester Burlington and Amboy. [...]

I was willing to travel with Mr. Keith, Indeed I was loath he should goe alone now he was for us, who I'me Sure would have had followers enough had he come against us. Besides I had another End in it, that by his free Conversation and Learn'd Disputes both with his friends and Enemies I have learn't better in a year to deal with the Quakers, then I could by Several Years study in the schools. We want more of his Narratives which would be of Good Use here where we often meet with the Quakers and their Books. <*An account of Books written against the Quakers, and much wanted in those Parts.*> More of his Answers to Robt. Barklay[1] would come well to the Clergy of Maryland and Virginia etc. Barklay's Book has done most Mischief, therefore Mr. Keith's Answer is more Requisite and Necessary. Mr. Keith has don great Service to the Church where e're he has been, by Preaching and Disputing publickly and from house to house, he has confuted many (Especially the Anabaptists) by Labor and Travel Night and Day, <*Mr. K. has printed several Books against the Anabaptists and given them away at his own charges.*> by Writing and Printing of Books mostly att his own Charge and Cost, and giving them out freely, which has been very expensive to him. By these Means People are much awaken'd, and their Eyes open'd to see the good Old Ways and they are very well pleased to find the Church att last take Such Care of her Children. For it is a Sad thing to Consider the years that are past, how Some that were born of the English, never heard of the Name of Christ, how many others were Baptized in his Name and fallen away to Heathenism, Quakerism, Atheism for want of Confirmation.

<*He laments the Want of a Bishop in those Parts.*> It Seems the Strangest thing in the World and 'tis thought History can't parallell it, or That any Place has received the word of God so many years, So many hundred Churches built, So many thousand Proselytes made, and Still remain altogether in the Wilderness as sheep without a shepherd. The Poor Church of America is worse on't in this Respect, than any of her Adversaries. <*The Advantage of the Presbyterians Independants and other Sectaries in that Respect.*> The Presbiterians here come a great way to lay hands one on Another, but after all I think they had as good stay att home for the good they do. The Independants are called by their sovereign Lord the People. The Anabaptists and Quakers pretend to the Spirit. But the Poor Church has no body upon the Spot to comfort or Confirm her Children. No body to Ordain Several that are willing to Serve, were they authorized, for the Work of the Ministry. Therfore they fall back again into the Herd of the Dissenters, rather than they will be att the Hazard and Charge to goe as far as England for Orders: So that we have Seen Several Countries, Islands, and Provinces which have hardly an Orthodox Minister amongst 'em, which might have been Supply'd had we been So happy as to See a Bishop or Suffragan Apud Americanos.

<*The Indians wonder the Squa Sachem.*> When we brought over the News that King William was dead, and Queen Anne reigned in his Stead the Indians wonder'd what was come to the English that they should have a Squaw Sachem as they Said a Woman King, however they Sent her a Present, and hop'd that she would prove a Good Mother to this Church, and Send us a God-Father or rather a Father in God with Apostolical Gravity and Authority to bless us, that we allso may be a Church for I count, No Bishop no Church, as true as No Bishop No King.

We count our Selves happy and indeed So we are under the Protection and Fatherly Care of the Right Reverend Father in God Henry Ld. Bp. of London[2] and we are all Satisfied that we can't have a greater Friend and Patron then himself. But alas! There is Such a great Gulph fixt between, that we can't pass to him nor he to us; but may he not Send a Suffragan I believe and am sure there are a great many learn'd, and good men in England, and I believe also did our gracious Queen Ann, but know the Necessities of her many good Subjects in these Parts of the World, she would allow £1000 per annum rather than so many souls should suffer and then 'twould be a hard case if there should not be found one amongst So many Pastors, and Doctors (de tot millibus unus Qui transiens adjuvet nos),[3] mean-while I don't doubt but Some learn'd and good man would goe further and do the Church more Service with £100 per annum than with a Coach and Six, 100 year hence.

<*The Works of the Author of the Snake in the Grass are much Wanted.*> The Reverend Author of the Snake in the Grass has don great Service here by his Excellent Book, no body that I know Since the Apostles dayes has managed Controversie better against all Jews, Heathens and Hereticks. Many here have desired to see the Author, however I hope we shan't want his works, especially against the Quakers, and the 5 discourses which have convinced many and are much desiderated. <*He has disperst the Books sent over by Mr. K. with good success.*> Those Boxes of Books that were Sent over last year Mr. Keith has disposed of in their Several Places as directed. I have carried Several of the Smaller Sort in a Wallet Some hundred miles and distributed them to the People as I Saw need. They have been long upon the Search of Truth in these Parts, they see thrô the Vanity and

Pretences of all Dissenters and generally Send directly to the Church. Now is the time of Harvest, we want a hundred hands for the work, mean while 2 or 3 that are well chosen will do more good there than all the rest. For we find by Sad Experience that People are better where they have none, than when they have an ill Minister. <*The Credit of the Societies abroad.*> Next unto God, our Eyes are upon the Corporation for help in this heavy Case. I dare say nothing has obtained more Reputation to the Church and Nation of England abroad than the Honorable Society for Reformation of Manners, and the Reverend and Honorable Corporation for propagating the Gospel in forreign Parts.

<*The Quakers zeal to make Proselytes.*> The Quakers Compass Sea and Land to make Proselytes, they Send out yearly a parcel of Vagabond fellows that ought to be taken up, and put in Bedlam,[4] rather than Suffered to goe about railing and raving against the Laws and Orders of Christ and his Church. For why? Their Preaching is of Cursing and Lyes, poysoning the Souls of the People with Damnable Errors, and Heresies, and not content with this, in their own Territories of Pensyvania, but they travel with Mischief over all parts as far as they can goe; over Virginia and Maryland, and agen thrô Jersey and N. York as far as N. England, but there they Stop, for they have prevented them by Good Laws and due Execution [...].

Pray be so kind as to present my humble Duty and Service to my Benefactors the Rt. Reverend my Lords the Bishops and the other Honorable Members of the Noble Corporation particularly my very good Lord the Bishop of London, whose Prayers and blessing are humbly and heartily desired by Sir your most humble and Obedient Servant.

John Talbot.

The Directions are
To John Chamberlayne[5] Esqr.
in Petty-France Westmr.

Copy.

[1]Robert Barclay (1648-90), Scottish Quaker polemicist. His most famous work was *An Apology for the True Christian Divinity, as the Same is Preached and Held Forth by the People in Scorn Called Quakers* (1676).

[2]Henry Compton, bishop of London 1675-1713.

[3]This Latin phrase may be translated "out of the many thousands may one pass over and help us."

[4]The Hospital of St. Mary of Bethlehem in London had been a lunatic asylum since the fifteenth century.

[5]John Chamberlain was secretary to the SPG from its beginning until his death in February, 1711/2.

[*LAM/SPG/XV*]

Rev. George Keith to Secretary, SPG
1703 September 4

<59> Philadelphia 4h Septemb. 1703

Worthy Sir

My humble duty presented to his Grace, my lord of Canterbury, my lord of London, and all the other right reverend Bishops, and other reverend Ministers, and other worthy members of the honourable Corporation for the propagation of the Gospel in forrain parts, together with my kind respects to your Selfe. These are to Acquaint you that by Gods help and favour, I and my worthy associat Mr. Talbot have finished our travells in Mary land, Virginia, and North Carolina, and are safely returned to this place. In all which Countries and places we mett with very kind reception, from persons of all conditions high and low, having preached in all the several parts where we travelled, both on Sundayes, and oft on week dayes, in their respective Churches the Quakers only excepted, who not only in those parts of Mary land and Virginia, but in all other parts, where we went to visit their meetings, and have friendly discourse with them, either at their meetings or at their houses were generally very uncivil and rude to us, as in new England, at Piscataway, Rhod iland, and long iland, east and west Jersey; declining generally all discourse with us and returning nothing to our kindly offers to informe them, but reproaches and railings, and grosse reflections (not only upon us but on the Church of England, and her Clergy) used by some of them, whereof we have sufficient proof. In Virginia there are but a few Quakers and very much asunder, and the tyme of their yearly meeting happend, when we were on our travel returning from North Carolina, so that we had not tymely notice to be there. The Quakers yearly meeting in Mary Land was over befor we came into that Country. The Governours of the Several Countries and provinces, where we have travelled, and other inferior magistrats and justices of peace were very kind to us, and so were all the ministers where we travelled, and kindly invited us to preach in their Churches, whenever we Came, as accordingly we did. Virginia and Mary land are generally well provided with ministers, and they are generally of good repute but in some places, ministers are wholly wanting as in Princes Anns County in virginia, and at Anapolis in Mary land. And in all North Carolina, there is not one minister, since Mr. Brett is gone, of whom I need not to say any thing, for I suppose you have heard fully of his bad Character. [...][1]

I remain, your obliedged and affect[ionate] friend.

George Keith

[*Addressed*:]
For John Chamberlain Esquire
Secretary to the Honorable
Corporation for the propagation
of the Gospel in forrain parts at
his lodging in petty france
by Mr. John Thomas at London.

[*Endorsed*:]
121
Mr. Keith. Philadelphia
4 Septemb. 1703

ALS.

[1]The remainder of this document concerns the travels of Keith and Talbot among Quakers in Maryland, the Jerseys, Pennsylvania, and New York.

[*SPG/A/1*]

Rev. Charles Smith to Secretary, SPG
1703 October 8

<*CII.*> Mr. Smith to the Secretary.

Ashelworth near
Glocester Octr. 8, 1703

Sir,

<*He doubts of his sufficiency to undertake the Mission to the 5 Nations of the Indians.*> You were pleased to permit that I should write to you about my going over to the five Nations. I have consider'd that business more throughly Since I came from London. And I find it is attended with innumerable and great difficulties and dangers. But none of these things prevail with me. This one consideration of winning Souls to God outweigheth all. And if that Blessed End by any means may be obtained, it will abundantly compensate for all difficulties whatsoever, but that which I mostly stick at, is my insufficiency and unworthiness. I want that which should fit and qualify me for so great and Apostolical an Employment. There is somewhat in me, I know not what to call it, whether Ambition for so honourable, or Zeal for so good a Work, that prompts me to it, but fear restrains me: for I dread the thoughts of running without being sent. <*But refers himself wholly to the Society etc.*> Now in this Doubt I humble refer myself to the Congregation. If his Grace the Arch-Bishop and Bishop of London together with the rest of the Reverend Society by whom I was designned for Carolina, but as I take it not absolutely appointed, shall be pleased to transfer me to the other Service, I shall humbly and chearfully accept of it. And therefore I desire to be determined by them, because I believe that God will direct and prosper their Councils. I have here Sent the Bishop of Glocester's Certificat, as was required. So with my Respectfull Salutations to you, I rest Good Sir your must humble and hearty Servant.

Charles Smith.

P.S. <*And wishes that he may be allow'd to take his Wife with him.*> My Dear Wife whom I was to consult with, about this Affair is willing to comply with, and accompany her husband. And therefore I hope that if I shall be sent unto the 5 Nations, some meet allowance will be made for her. But considering with whome I have to do, viz. Wise and Good, as well as Great Men, I rather suppose it than insist upon it.

The Directions are
To The Worshipfull John Chamberlayne
Esqr. in Petty France Westmr.
att London These present.

Copy.

[*LAM/SPG/XV*]

Henderson Walker to Bishop of London
1703 October 21

No. Carolina Octor. 21 1703

May it please your Lordshipp

The great and pious designes of your Lordship towards these American parts for the propagating of the Christian Church of which you are so pious and good pillar imboldens me to Lay before your Lordship the present Estate of North Carolina as to their Christian well being and I was the more encouraged to do it by reason that our Lords Proprietors were pleased to write to us concerning Mr. Bray your Lords Commissary comeing to Visitt us.[1]

My Lord we have been Settled neer this 50 years in this place, and I may Justly say most part of 21 years on my owne knowledge without Priest or Altar and before that time according to all that appears to me much worse. George Fox some years agoe came into these parts and by Strange Infatuations did infuse the Quakers principles into some small number of the people which did and hath continued to growe ever since very numerous by reason of their yearly sending in men to encourage and exhort 'em to their wicked principles and here was none to dispute nor to oppose them in carrying on their pernitious principles for many years till God of his infinite goodness was pleased to inspire the Reverend Dr. Bray, sometime about 4 years agoe to send in some books of his owne particular pious guift of the explanation of the Church Catichismn with some other small books to be disposed of and lent as we thought fitt did in some measure put a Stop to their Growth and about a year after did send to us a Library of books for the benefitt of this place given by the honorable the Corporation for the establishing of the Christian Religion by one Mr. Daniel Brett a Minister appointed for this place, he for about ½ a year behaved himself in a modest manner, but after that in a most horrid manner broke out in such an extravigant Course that I must owne I am ashamed to express his Carriage it being in so high Nature. It hath been a great trouble and grief to us who have a great veneration for the Church that the first Minister who was sent to us should prove soe ill as to give the Dissenters so much occasion to Charge us with him. My Lord I humbly beg you to beleive that we doe not think that the most Reverend Dr. Bray knew any thing of the Life or Conversation of the Man. We did about this time 2 year with a great deale of Care and management get an Assembly and we passed an Act[2] for building of Churches and establishing of a maintenance for Ministers amongst us, and in pursuance thereto we have built one Church and there is two more agoeing forward, and his Excellency Francis Nicholson Esqr. Governor of Virginia was pleased of his pious goodness to give us £10 to each Church. And we sent immediately Copys of that Act of Assembly to our Lords Proprietors to get the same Ratifyed, and likewise a Copy to Dr. Bray to intreat his favour with them to obtaine a Ratification which we were in hopes to obtaine this Shipping, but they not being come, we are in a great Loss. My Lord I humbly beg leave to informe you that we have an Assembly to Sitt the 3d. of November next, and there is above one half of the Burgesses that are Chosen are Quakers and have declared their designes of making voyd the Act for establishing the Church. If your Lordship out of the good and pious Care of us doth not put a Stopp to their Growth we shall the most part, especially the Children borne here become heathens. I humbly intreat your Lordship to send some worthy good man among us to regaine the Flock and to perfect us in our Duty to God and establish us by his Doctrine life and Conversation in the fundamentalls of our Christian Profession that we in our time and those as comes hereafter may bless God that he has raised up So Noble a pillar as your Lordship to regaine those who are going a Stray and put a Stop to the pernitious growing principles of these Quakers. Your Lordship may see the Copy of our Act by Dr. Bray, and I humbly begg your Lordships pardon for giveing you this trouble and take leave to Subscribe myself My Lord Your most humble and Obedient Servant.

Henderson Walker

[*Addressed:*]
To The right honorable and Rt.
Reverend Father in God Henry Lord
Bishop of London most humbly Present

[*Endorsed:*]
129
Governor Walker
N. Carolina 21 Octob. 1703.

LS.

[1]Dr. Thomas Bray was briefly in Maryland in 1700 as commissary to the bishop of London. As far as is known, he never visited North Carolina.

[2]No copy of this act is known to have survived.

[*SPG/Jou/1*]

Journal of the SPG
1703/4 February 18

<137> At the Vestry of St. Mary le Bow. 18 Februry. 1703/4 [...]

<139> 13. Mr. Bradford offer'd a Memorial from Mr. Charles Smith, to the Society, which, was read.

14. Ordered that the Treasurer do pay the said Mr. Smith the Sum of Ten Pounds towards his Charges of coming to Town etc. he having declind going among the Indians.

15. It having been proposed to the Said Mr. Smith to go to Roanoak in N. Carolina, he desired a Months time to consider of the Same, which, was agreed to by the Society. [...]

Minutes.

[*LAM/SPG/VII*]

Rev. Charles Smith to [Secretary, SPG]
1703/4 March 13

<100> Honoured Sir

The honourable Society at the general meeting concluded that a mission to the five nations about which I had bin waiting upon them was not proper for me as I was a married man. And therefore they proposed some other Place to me and particularly Roanoak in north Carolina. I was to consider of it and returne my answer by the next monthly meeting. Now I having considered of this matter, am not willing to take my wife to that unhealthfull Country. If my Service may be accepted for South Carolina for which (as I take it) I was at first enrolled I would willingly goe thither, and my wife likewise. Several creditable persons of that Country, particularly Mr. Mosely[1] the Deputy Secretary and Mr. Franklin[2] of London the Proprietor thereof, who came but very lately from those Parts, assure me that a minister is much wanting there; especially such a one as will apply himself to the instruction of youth: Which I would gladly do if ther should be occasion. My designes I hope are real to do good to Souls, if by any means I may. Indeed that which put me upon that designe at first were some unhappy debts for which I am engaged. And this I acknowledge to the honourable Society, that I may not make a shew of a more pure and perfect zeal than indeed I have. However as far as I know my owne heart my predominant motive is to do good. For I am perswaded that by the grace of God I shal be much more useful in those Parts, than I am here like to be under my unhappy and prejudicial circumstances. As for my debts, in case of my removal, I have already taken care for the discharge of them. Soe with my respects to the honourable Society and my humble thanks to them for their late bounty to me desiring that they would be pleased to accept of my poor Service, I rest Worthy Sir yr. much oblidged and humble Servant

Charles Smith

<*I would desire the favour of you to send me the answer as soon as you can.*>

Ashellworth Gl. Sh.
March 13, 1703/4

[*Addressed*:]
To The Worshipfull John Chamberlayne Esqr.
In Petty France In Westminster London
These Present

[*Endorsed*:]
139.
Mr. Smith Ashelworth
13 March 1703/4

ALS. Read at a meeting of the SPG on March 17, 1703/4, when it was ordered "that the Secretary do return him an Answer, and that the subject of his Letter be referr'd to the Committee att St. Paul's." Journal of the SPG, I, 142.

[1]Edward Moseley (ca. 1682-1749) migrated to North Carolina around 1704 and quickly became one of the most important political figures in the colony, serving at various times as councillor, assemblyman and speaker of the assembly, provincial treasurer, surveyor general, and chief justice of the General Court, among other offices. *DNCB*.

[2]It is uncertain who is meant. No one of this or a similar name was ever a proprietor.

[*SPG/Jou/1*]

Journal of the SPG 1704 April 21

<145> 21 April 1704 [...]

2. The Secretary Reported from the Committee that he had writ to Mr. Ch. Smith about going to S. Carolina, but had not yet recd. any Answer. [...]

Minutes.

[*SPG/Jou/App B*]

Testimonial 1704 May 31

<41.> The Governor of Virginia's Testimonial of Mr. George Keith. Journal. 18 Aug. 1704.

Virginia ss. Whereas I have seen a Testimonial from the Vestry of Christ Church in Philadelphia directed to the Rt. Reverend Father in God Henry Lord Bishop of London, bearing date the 7 Apr. 1704 and an Address of the Minister and Vestry of Philadelphia, directed to the Rt. Honorable and Right Reverend the Members of the Corporation for the Propagation of the Gospel in Foreign Parts, bearing date 7 Apr. 1704 and a Certificate by the Rector, Wardens and Vestry of Trinity Church in N. York, bearing date the 20th day of March 1703 in behalf of the Reverend Mr. George Keith, and knowing the said Persons, and having heard from the mouths of some of them, and by Letters from others of them the main Substance of the abovemention'd Testimonial, Address and Certificate, it makes me not in the least doubt of any, or any part of them.

<*Mr. Keith very zealous for the Church.*> And the said Mr. Keith having been twice in this her Majestys Colony and Dominion of Virginia I found him very zealous both by his preaching and discoursing, to do the same things here; as likewise when he went once to N. Carolina. And were it not that I'm in hopes his now being design'd God willing for England will be for the Interest and Service of my Holy Mother the Church of England as by Law establish'd in these parts I should be very sorry for his leaving them at present,

but he being able to give a just and full Account of all the Church affairs in this North America, both in respect of it's present Circumstance, and of the ways and means (by the Divine assistance) for it's further Increasing and flourishing in all Respects I humbly conclude will recompence his Absence.

<*Hopes Mr. Keith will return to be Mathematical and philosophy Professor in the Colledge at Virginia.*> I'm in great hopes that he will return, if not upon the same Account that he came, yet for his being Mathematical and Philosophy Professor in her Majesties Royal Colledge of Wm. and Mary. I'm heartily sorry for his Inability of Body (travelling, especially by Land, being very troublesome and inconvenient to him) as likewise that he is not 20 or 30 years younger. I most cordially wish him an happy and prosperous Voyage to England and the like Return hither. In testimony of what is herein written, I have set to my hand and caused the Seal of this her Majestys most Ancient and great Colony of Virginia to be fixed this 31st day of May In the Third year of the reign of our Soveraign Lady Queen Anne etc. Annoq Domini 1704.

Fr. Nicholson

Copy.

[*LAM/SPG/X*]

List
1704 June 6

<32> Sometime since I had Orders from a Gentleman to Deliver to Dr. Bray Forty of Mr. Dodwells[1] Praelectioners Academicae in Schola Mission or Canidemias. To be Dispos'd of where they may be realy Usefull and where not likely to be bought Of which 40 The Dr. has dispos'd of 25 as below and return'd to me the 15 remaining. [...]
1 To the Library at Pamplico in N. Carolina. [....][2]
June 6th 1704. B. Toole.

[*Endorsed:*]
List of Mr. Dodwells Books
sent the Society from an
unknown Hand by Mr. Toole

D.

[1]Presumably Henry Dodwell the elder (1641-1711), scholar and theologian, author of numerous works on historical, classical, and theological subjects. *DNB*.

[2]The remaining copies were sent to Pennsylvania, Maryland, and South Carolina, as well as to various places in Great Britain.

[LAM/SPG/XV]

Memorandum
1704 October 13

<3> I having travelled in diverse parts of North Carolina about an hundred Myles do Certifie from my own experience, that travelling in that Country is both difficult and chargeable especially to strangers it is difficult, becaus generally the roads are deep and intricate, and Cannot be travelld Safely without a guide, and convenience of lodging and provision no wyse so good as in all the other parts of America, for in North Carolina rarely is there any drink but water, and milk, and that little or none at all in winter, and by reason of many rivers that are great, the passages over them are both troublesome and very chargeable, as I found by experience.

George Keith

London 13h Octob. 1704

D.

[LAM/SPG/XV]

Account of Mission
[1704 November]

<36> A true and Just Account of my mission to North Carolina.

I was ordained In order to goe to the Plantations Aprill the 12th, 1703, and then receved the Queens Bounty of 20 pounds and Soon after My Lord Weimouths Bounty of 50 pounds, upon which I Lived In England, untill the first of 8ber., following, which together with my fitting out for such a voage and Country Consumed the most part of my money, I had Likewise five pounds sent me by my Lord of London to Portsmouth, and when I Landed in Virginia I had noe more than twinty five pounds. I Landed In Virginia Janry. 14, 1703 and as Soon as I cou'd Conveniently travell, I waited upon the Governour, and Immediately after, made the best of my way in to the Country, where I was bound. I arived amongst the Inhabitants, after a tedious and troublesome Jorney Janry. 24th 1703. I was then oblidged to buy a Couple of horses which cost me 14 pounds, one of which was for a guide because there is noe possibility, for a stranger to find his road in that Country for if he once goes astray, (it being such a desart Country) It's a great hazard if Ever he finds his road again, Besides there is mighty Inconvenciencies in traveling there, for the roads are not only deep and difficult to be found, but there are Likewise seven greate Rivers in the Country over which there is noe passing with horses Except two of them, one of which, the Quakers have setled a ferey over for there own Conveniencie, and noe body but themselves have the priveledge of it soe that at the passing over the rivers, I was obliged either to borrow or hyre horses, which was both troublesome and Chargable, In soe much that in Litle more then two months, I was oblidged to dispose of the necessaries I Caried over for my own use to satisfie my Creditors. I found In the Country a greate many

Children to be Baptised, where of I Baptised about a hundred, and there are a greate many still to be Baptised, whose parents wou'd not condescend to have them Baptised with Godfathers and Godmothers.

I married none in the Country, for that was a perquisite belonged to the magistrate, which I was not desirous to deprive them of it.

I preached twice every Sunday, and often on the week dayes, when there vestries mett, <38> or Coud apoint them to bring there Children to be Baptised.

I called a vestrie In Each Presinct, in my first progress through the Country, to whom I gave an account of my Lord Weymouthes, Charitable bounty In supporting my mission among them, and Likewise the Good desings [*sic*] of the Honorable Society had for them as I was Informed by Mr. Aime, that they had setled 80 pounds a year for the maintainance of two Clergymen amongst them. And Likewise a proposall that Doctor Bray desired me to make to them, upon there procuring of Good Gleebs he doubted not but that there might be a Setlement made, for the advantage of the Church, such as there is in the Island of Bromudas, (viz.) two slaves and a small stock in Each presinct and that to be Continued Good by the Incumbent to his Successor, which will be a lasting Estate to the Church.

They have built In the Country three small Churches and have three Gleebs, and In the three Chiefe Presincts there is a Reader Established in Each of them, to whom they allow a small sallary, who, reads morning and Evening prayer Every Lordsday, and two sermons and I took Care, to furnish them with books, from the Library, for that use before I came away.

I remained very well satisfied in the Country, till there assembly sat, which was in the first of May, where I Expected they wou'd propose a setlement, for my maintainance, and they taking noe Care of it, together with my then Circumstances, which were but very Indifferent; <39> discouraged me very much, and occasioned my first thought, of returning to England. For I was Informed before I went there, that there was 30 pounds a year; setled by Law to be payed In Each Presinct, for the maintainance of a minister. Which Law was sent over here to be confirmed by/to there Lords Proprietors, and it being supposed not be a Competencie, for a minister to live on, was sent back again without Confirmation, whereof the Quakers took the advantage, and will Endeavour to prevent any such Law passing for the future for they are the Greatest number in the assembly, and are unanimous and stand truely to one another, in whatsomever may be for there Intrest; for the Country may be divided into four sorts of People, first the Quakers who are the most powerfull Enemies to Church Goverment, but a people very poorly ignorant of what they profess; A second sort, are a great many that have noe religion but woud be Quakers, if by that they were not oblidged to lead a more moral life then they are willing to Comply to; A third sort are a sort of Presbiterians, which sort is upheld by some idle fellows, that have left there lawfull Imployments, and Preach and Baptize through the Country without any manner of orders, from any sect, or pretended Church.

A fourth sort, who are realy zealous for the intrest of the Church, are the fewest in number but the better sort of people and wou'd doe very much for the setlement of Goverment there, if not violently oposed by these three presedent sects and although they be all three of different pretensions <40> yet they all Concur together in one Common Cause to prevent any thing that will be chargable to them, as they alledge Church Goverment will be if once Established by Law. And an other greate discoragment these poor people have is a Governour who doe not in the Least Countinance, them in this bussiness, but rather discourage them.

In finding it impossible to travel through the Country at that rate I begun, I was resolved to setle in one Presinct but the people all alledging my Lord weymouths Charity was universely designed for the whole Country wou'd not Consent, to it, which bred some disturbancie amongst them, upon which I was advised by some of the best frends to the Church to Come over, and represent there Condition to the Honorable Society, not only of there want of ministers, but like wise there inabilities to maintain them. And there desires then Complying with my necessities was a powerfull and privailing argument, Considering I was then reduced, to my last stake, and knew not where or upon what account to be further suplyed.

Besides such a solitary, toylsom, and hard living as I met with there, were very sufficient discouragements; I was distant from any minister, a hundred and twenty miles, soe that if any Case of difficulty or doubt shoud hapen with whom shou'd I consult?

And for my traveling throw the Country I rid one day with an other Sunday only excepted above 30 miles a day In the worst roads that ever I saw, and have some times lyen whole nights in the woods.

I will now Endeavour to shew you how ineffectual a single mans Labours wou'd be amongst soe scatred a people. <41> In the first place Suppose him minister of one presinct (whereas there are five in the Country) and this Presinct as they are all Bounded with two Rivers, and those Rivers at least 20 Miles distant, without any Inhabitant on the Road, for they plant only on the Rivers, and they are planted In Lenth upon these rivers at least 60 miles And to give all these Inhabitants an opurtunity of hearing a sermon; and bringing there Children to be Baptised which must be on the Sabath, for they won't spare time of an other day and must be in every ten miles distances for five miles is the farthest that they will bring there Children or willingly Come themselves; soe that he must to doe his duty Effectually, be ten or twelve weeks in making his progress through one Presinct.

You may also Consider the distance that the new Colony of Pamplico is from the rest of the Inhabitants of the Country, for any man that has tryed it wou'd sooner undertake a voage from this City to Holland, then thats, for besides a sound of five miles broad, and Nothing to Cary one over but small Conoes. There are above fifty miles of desart to pass through without any human Creature Inhabiting it, I think it Likwise reasonable to Give you an account of a Greate nation of Indians, that live In that Goverment Computed to be noe less then a Hundred thousand, many of which Live amongst the English, and all as I can understand a very Civilised People.

<42> I have often Conversed with them and have been frequently In there Towns.

Those that Can Speak English amongst them seem to be very willing and fond of being Christians, and In my opinion there might be methods taken, to bring over a greate many of them.

If there was noe hopes of making them Christians, the advantage of having missioners among them wou'd redoun'd to the advantage of the Goverment; for if they shou'd once be brought over to a french Intrest, (as we have too much reason to belive there are some promoters amongst them for that End) by there late actions, It wou'd be (if not to the utter ruin) to the Great prejuducie of all the English Plantations on the Continent of America.

I have here In Briefe set down what I have to say and shall be ready to answer any questions the Honnorable Society shall think Convenient to Ask me Concerning the Country; and shall be both ready and willing to serve them any where, upon such Encoragement as I can take according to my Education, After My Lord Weymouth ceases to lay his Commands on me.

I have made a Considerable loosing voage of it this time, Both by my troublesome traveling In America, and Likwise by being taken into France; where I was prisoner of war 9 weeks, and was forced to make use of my Credite, for my sustinance; and have Lived In the same Circumstances, since I came to England, without any maner of relife which has been very troublesome to me.

<43> All which has brought me Considerably In debt, over 35 pounds, and know noe way to pay it, without my Charitable benefactor, or the Honnorable Society, Judge my Labors worthy a reward.

[*Endorsed:*]
49.
Mr. Blairs[1] Mission into N. Carolina

D.

[1]Rev. John Blair. See appendix.

[*SPG/Jou/Cte*]

Journal of the Committee of the SPG
1704 November 6

<97> 6 November 1704 [...]

1. Mr. Blaire a missionary of the Rt. Honorable The Lord Weymouth To No. Carolina, and lately return'd by the Way of France (where he had been A Prisoner 9 Weeks) attended the Committee and gave a written Acct. of his Travels in the Plantations and offer'd his Service to Return into Those or any other Parts the Society shall Appoint him, Upon Sufficient Encouragement; Agreed that this Committee will represent his Case to the Society at the next Generall Meeting. [...]

Minutes.

[*SPG/Jou/1*]

Journal of the SPG
1704 November 17

<171> 17 Novr. 1704 [...]

<173> 14. The Report of the Committee of the 6 Inst. relating To Mr. Blaire a Minister sent over by the Rt. Honorable the Ld. Weymouth at the Recommendation of Dr. Bray was read; Agreed that this matter be postpon'd till the Ld. Weymouth and Dr. Bray's Answer relating To the said Mr. Blaire be Come to hand. [...]

Minutes.

[*SPG/A/2*]

Rev. John Blair to Committee, SPG
1704 November 20

<*XIV.*> Mr. Blair to the Committee.

London 20 Novr. 1704

Honorable Gentlemen

I have for some time attended you in relation to the Business of North Carolina and would willingly and patiently attend the finishing of it; but that my present Circumstances will not allow me. <*Taken by the French by which he has contracted debts.*> I have liv'd since 1 Augt. that I was taken by the French without any manner of Supply, which has brought me Considerably in Debt to Strangers, who now Impatiently Expect their Money, and I believe some of them think by my long Delays, <*Afraid of Arrests.*> that I design to Impose upon them for which reason I dread their Arrest each Moment; My Debts Contracted in France are £8 which I am obliged to Pay in this City, £5 I Borrow'd in Portsmouth to bring me to London, £18 for Gown Cassock Shirts, Bands, Hat, Shoes and Stockins and other little Necessaries, £5 for Diet and Lodging since I Came to this City neither of which Debts I am now able to Pay, and if your Honorable Board does not think fitt to relieve me, I shall be Obliged to retire to some Private Place for my Security. <*Ld. Weymouth owes him a year's Salary desires the Society to advance it.*> My Ld. Weymouth owes me a Year's Salary and his absence I believe from This Place is the Occasion of my not being Supplied, and If this Honorable Board shall think it Convenient to advance me the Money to relieve my necessities, My Salary from My Ld. Weymouth, will repay them, when he is pleas'd to give it and if He does not pay it, I shall serve in any other Place, where the Honorable Society shall think Convenient to Send me, for the Money besides my Usage in the Plantations has been a little hard, above any other Missionary that has gone to America, for they <*Difficulties in his Mission.*> Generally have besides their £50 from the Honorable Society, at least £50 or 60 a Year from the Country they are sent to. And although I was sent to the most Barbarous place in the Continent, yet I had no more than my £50 per annum from My Ld. Weymouth, for I never Could have Expected to have got a Farthing from the Country had I staid there 7 Years longer. I humbly desire therefore that Ye would take these things to Your Consideration and let me have an Answer of what I am to Expect, and your Complyance to my Requests will not only releave me, but lay a Lasting Obligation on me to be Gentleman Your humble Servant.

John Blair

The Directions are
To the Committee etc.
at St. Pauls Chapter House.

Copy.

[*LAM/SPG/XV*]

Petition
ca. 1705

<44> To the right Honorable the Lords Spiritual and Temporall in Parliament Assembled the Humble Petition of the Queens Majesties most distressed Subjects Inhabitting near Pampticoe River in the County of Bath within her Majesties Dominions Of North Carolina.

Sheweth

That your petitioners depending upon the Royall Assureance which was given for their Encourageing the Exercise of the Protestant Religion and the benefitt of the Laws of England and the Encouragements which were published for planting in the said parts[1] setled themselves and their Familyes upon the said River, And goeing through Incredible Difficultyes from the Indians a Vast Labour and Expence recovered and Improved divers great Quantityes of Land thereabouts, They made all Due Applications to the Governours and Councell of the Lords Proprietors of those Lands For being Admitted into the previledges published as Aforesaid But instead thereof they have been treated by the said Governours and Councell with very great hardshipps neither could your petitioners' Obtain the Favour of having A Minister appointed them Though they Offerred with Cheerfullnesse to be at the Charges of Maintaining him and by reason thereof your Petitioners have been deprived of the means of Grace which their Souls Earnestly longed after And near 200 of their Children have not been Admitted to the Sacrament of Baptisme.

That your petitioners with Gods blessing on their hard Labours have made such Improvements in their said respective plantations that they are able yearly to Supply her Majesties Shipps with great Quantityes of Victualling Stores And of pitch and Tarr and with great Quantityes of Extraordinary good Masts and Planks of Oake And had your Petitioners Iron and Sailes and Rigging they could Build good Vessells there And by her Majesties Countenance and Assistance they could Carry on A very Considerable trade there and much Increase her Majesties Customs And had your petitioners the happynesse of being under her Majesties Imediate Government and protection they could be enabled to pay their duty to her Majestye in divers other perticulars of Publick Importance.

Your petitioners For the Sake and Tender Mercyes of our blessed Jesus in All humble Earnestnesse Implore your Lordshipps consideration of the Premisses And that out of your great piety and Zeal For the propagation of the Protestant Religion you would Intercede with her most Gratious Majestye on their Behalfs and that such Speedy Course may be taken For their Releife and Countenance as to your Lordshipps Renowned piety and Wisdomes shall Seem meete. And your petitioners shall ever pray etc.

[Sarah] dupis

[*Addressed:*]
To the Lords spiritual
and Temporall in Parliament Assembled
The humble petition of her Majesties
Distressed Subjects Inhabitting
in pamptico River in
North Carolina

DS. This document was read at a meeting of the SPG on March 15, 1705/6: "The Lord Bishop of Chichester gave in at the Bord a Copy of a Petition of the Inhabitants near pamplico etc. in N. Carolina, to the house of Lords desiring a minister may be sent over to them etc. Ordered that the said petition be refer'd to the Committee, who are to Report what is fit to be done therein, and the Person that brought the said petition is desir'd to attend the Committee concerning it." Journal of the SPG, I, 226.

[1]This wording suggests that the petitioners were Huguenots, who had begun to settle in the area at about this time. *See* Alonzo Thomas Dill, Jr., "Eighteenth Century New Bern, a History of the Town and Craven County, 1700-1800, Part I, Colonization of the Neuse," *North Carolina Historical Review*, XXII (January, 1945), 18-20.

[*SPG/Jou/App B*]

List of Books for Missionaries
1705/6

<27.> Bibliotheca Missionariorum.

Pools Synopsis or Bishop of Ely on the O. Testament with Hammond or Whitby on the New.
Cousins Scholastical History of the Canon of Ss.
Caves Lives
Historia Literaria
Earhard's Ecclesiastical History
Le Clerks Cotelerius
Caranza's Sum of Councils
Beoregii Code and Canonum Vindicatus
Aquina's Summs [*sic*]
Helvici Chronologia
Usserii Annales

Bp. Wilkins Natural Religion
Arian and Simplicius on Epictetus
Antonius de Seipso
Grotius de Veritate Religionis Christiana
Combers Works, or Abridgment with the Ordination Office.
Ellis and Rogers on the 39 Articles.
Bp. Nicholson on the Church Catechism
Dr. Barrow on the Lord's Prayer
Bishop Pearson on the Creed.
Bishop Andrews on the Commandments
Bishop Patricks Mensa Mystica, Aqua Genitalis, on the Sacraments.
or Kettlewell on the Sacraments
Dr. Brays Lectures or Abridgmt.
Cave's Primitive Christianity
Whole Duty of Man's Works
Faith and Practice of a Church of England Man
Lucas's Practical Divinity
Duty of Servants
Ostervald's Cause of the Corruption of Christianity his Catechism translated into English.
ABp. Tillotson's Sermons Fol.
Sandersons Sermons
Sermons at Boyles Lectures
Bp. Sanderson de Juramento Obligatione Conscientiae in 9. Casibus
Bishop Hall's Cases of Conscience
Hales Contemplations Divine and Moral 2 Vol.
Herbert's Country Parson
Visitation Charges of the Bps. of Dublin, Worcester, Bath and Wells, Lincoln, Rochester, Chester
Hornbects Summa Controvers.
Bennets London Cases
Hookers Ecclesiastical Policy
King's Inventions of Men in the Worship of God
Presbiterian and Independ. Churches in N. England brought to the Test by Keith.
Lessley's Snake in the Grass
Bennett of Schism
Barrough or Hoadly compleat
Bennett's Confutation of Popery
Vorstii Anti-Bellarminus Contractus
Rawlet's Dialogue
Dr. Edwards agt. the Socinians.
Mr. Nelson's Companion for the Fasts and Festivals etc.
Bp. of Chichesters Defence of the Liturgy agt. Mather
Bp. of St. Asaph's Exposition on the Ch. Catechism.
Bp. Stillingfleets origines Sacrae
Dean Youngs Sermons

Missionaries Library. Reviewed, Corrected and Enlarged, according to Order; 28th Feb. and 15th March 1705.

A.
Arrian on Epictetus
Antoniu. de Seipso
A. Bp. Andrews on Devotion etc.
A. Dr. Asheton of Visiting the Sick
Allen's Discourses.

B.
Bp. Beveridge Cod. Can.
—Exposition of the Catechism
—Sermons.<16 *July* 1708>
Dr. Brays Lectures on the Catech.
—Baptismal Covenant
—Bibliotheca paroch.
Bennet's London Cases
—of Schism
—Confutation of Popery
Boursrough of Schism
Birket on the N. Testament
Barrows Works
Bishop Burnet on the 39 Articles
—Pastoral Care.
—Abridgmt. of the Hist. Reform.
Bragg on the Parables
—on the Miracles
Dr. Bentley's Boyles Lectures
Dr. Bradford on Do.
Dr. Blackhall on Do.

C.
Cousins. Schol. Hist.
Caves Lives
—Histor. Liter.
—Primit. Christianity
Caranza Sum of Council
Combers Works Fol.
—on Ordination Offices
Chilingworths Works
Bp. Cumberland's Law of Nature Engl.
Clarkes Boyles Lectures
Bp. Compton London Episcopalia.

D.
Duty of Man's Works
Drelincourt on Death.

E.
Eachard's Eccles. Hist.
Dr. Jonathan Edward's agt. Socinians.
Ellis Expos. 39 Artic.

F.
Faith and Pract. of Ch. of Engl. man.

G.
Grot. de veritat Xiana. Relig.
Bp. Gardners visit. Charge
Grabes Spiritegium.
—Instin. Martyr.
Dr. Gastril's Boyles Lectures

H.
Hammonds N. Testam.
Helvici Chronolog.
Bp. Halls Cases of Conscience
Hales Contemplations
Herberts Parson
Hooker's Eccles. Policy.
Headig of Schism.
Hornecks Sermons
—Happy Ascetick.

I.

K.
ABp. King's Invention of Men
Keith's presbyt. and Indep. Churches brought to the Test etc.
King (Peter) on the Creed
Bp. Kidder's Visit. Charge
Kettlewels Discourses.

L.
Lucas Practic Divinity
—Duty of Servants
Lewis Compan. for Afflicted
Life of God in the Soul of Man.

M.
ABp. Marsh Visit Charge.

N.
Nelson's Fasts and Festivals.

O.
Ostervalds Causes of Corruption etc.
—Catechism.

P.
Pools Synopsis
Bp. Pearson on the Creed
Bp. Patrick: Xtian. Sacrifice
—Comments on the O. Testam.

Q.

R.
Rogers on the 39 Articles.
Rawlets Dialogue.

S.
Sanderson's Sermons
—Life and Cases.
Bp. Stillingfleets Orig. Sacrae
—Eccles. Cases
Bp. Sprats Visit. Charge
ABp. Sharp's (York) Sermons
Dean Stanhope's Tho. a Kempis
—Boyles Lectures.
Dean Sherlock of Death etc.
—Scripture Sufficiency.
Bp. Stratfords Visit Charge

T.
ABp. Tillotson's Sermons fol.
A-Bp. Tennisons Collect of Canons Articles etc.

U.
Usserii Annales

V.
Vorstii Anti-Bellarminus etc.

W.
Bp. Wilkins Nat. Religion.
—of Prayer and Preaching
Whitby on the N. Testamt.
Bp. Wake on the C. Catechism
Bp. Williams agt. Mather etc.
—Boyles Lectures.
Word of God best Guide
Dean Willis Address to the Rom. Cath.

Y.
Books allowed for Churches
English Bible in Folio, of the last Edition, with Worcester and Peterb. Chronology
Common Prayer Book with 39 Articles and Ordinations
Book of Homilies.
Sparrows Collection of Canons
Arch Bps. Book of Orders Injunctions etc. to be read in Churches.
Cambridge Concordance, best Edition.
Catalogue of Small Tracts etc.
Pastoral Letter, 1 and 2 part
Christian Monitor
Familiar Guide
Preparation for Death and Judgmt.
Sick Christian's Companion.
All Dr. Woodwards Small Tracts viz.
on the Lord's day
Uncleaness
Drunkeness
Swearing
Gaming
All. Dr. Asheton's Small Tracts viz.
[*blank*]
Christian Scholar
Bp. Beveridges Catechism
Faith and Practice of a Ch. of Engd. man
Gods Dominion over the Seas
Seamans Monitor
Souldiers Monitor
Duty of a Husbandman
Church Catechism explain'd
Whole Art of Catechizing
Guide of a Christian
Whole Duty of a Christian
Gibson's Family Prayer
—on the Sacrament

Common Prayer book best Companion

together with a certain Number of the following Books viz. Common Prayer books. Bp. William's Catechisms of Ch. Engd. and agt. Popish Doctrines. Bp. Beveridges Usefulness Com. Prayer. Ostervalds Catechism.

Dr. Comber's Arguments of a Roman answered by a Protestant.

D. At a meeting of the SPG on March 15, 1705/6, the Committee reported that it had reviewed "the old List of Missionaries Libraries, together with the Catalogue of small Tracts, and other Books for the use of the respective Churches to which the Missionaries were appointed," and that "having made several Amendments and Additions thereto, It was their Opinion that the said Lists so corrected were proper to be made the Standing Catalogue of the Missionaries Libraries." The Society concurred in the recommendation, contingent on the list's being presented to the archbishop of Canterbury, president of the Society, for his comments. Journal of the SPG, I, 223, 229.

[*SPG/Sermons*]

Instructions
1706

A Collection of Papers, Printed by Order of the Society for the *Propagation of the Gospel in Foreign Parts. Viz. The Charter, The Request, etc., The Qualifications of Missionaries. Instructions for the Clergy. Instructions for Schoolmasters. Prayers for the Charity-Schools.* London, Printed by *Joseph Downing,* in *Bartholomew-Close* near [*West*]-*Smithfield,* 1706. [...]

<[22]> Instructions for the Clergy employ'd by the Society for the Propagation of the Gospel in Foreign Parts.

Upon their Admission by the Society.

I. That from the Time of their Admission they lodge not in any Publick-House; but at some Bookseller's, or in other private and Reputable Families, till they shall be otherwise accommodated by the Society.

II. That till they can have a convenient Passage, they employ their Time usefully; in reading Prayers, and Preaching, as they have Opportunity; in hearing others Read and Preach; or in such Studies as may tend to fit them for their Employment.

III. That they constantly attend the standing Committee of this Society, at St. *Paul's* Chapter-House, and observe their Directions.

<[23]> IV. That before their Departure, they wait upon his Grace the Lord Arch-Bishop of *Canterbury*, their Metropolitan; and upon the Lord Bishop of *London*, their Diocesan; to receive their paternal Benediction and Instructions.

Upon their going on Board the Ship designed for their Passage.

I. That they demean themselves not only inoffensively and prudently; but so as to become remarkable Examples of Piety and Virtue to the Ships Company.

II. That whether they be Chaplains in the ships, or only Passengers, they endeavour to prevail with the Captain or Commander, to have Morning and Evening Prayer said daily, as also Preaching and Catechizing every Lords-Day.

III. That throughout their Passage, they Instruct, Exhort, Admonish, and Reprove, as they have Occasion and Opportunity, with such Seriousness and Prudence as may gain them Reputation and Authority.

<[24]> *Upon their Arrival in the Country whither they shall be sent.*

First, *With Respect to themselves.*

I. That they always keep in their View the great Design of their Undertaking, *viz.* to promote the Glory of Almighty God, and the Salvation of Men, by propagating the Gospel of our Lord and Saviour.

II. That they often consider the Qualifications requisite for those who would effectually promote this Design, *viz.* A sound Knowledge and hearty Belief of the Christian Religion, an Apostolical Zeal temper'd with Prudence, Humility, Meekness, and Patience; a fervent Charity towards Souls of Men; and finally the Temperance, Fortitude, and Constancy, which become good Soldiers of Jesus Christ.

III. That in order to the obtaining and preserving the said Qualifications, they do very frequently in their Retirements offer up fervent Prayers to Almighty God for his Direction and Assistance; converse much with the Holy Scriptures; seriously reflect upon their Ordination Vows; and consider the Account which they <[25]> are to render to the great Shepherd and Bishop of Souls, at the last Day.

IV. That they acquaint themselves thorowly with the Doctrine of the Church of *England*, as contain'd in the Articles and Homilies; its Worship and Discipline, and Rules for Behaviour of the Clergy, as contain'd in the Liturgy and Canons; and that they approve themselves accordingly, as genuine Missionaries from this Church.

V. That they endeavour to make themselves Masters in those Controversies, which are necessary to be understood in order to the preserving their Flock from the Attempts of such Gainsayers as are mixt among them.

VI. That in their outward Behaviour they are circumspect and unblameable, giving no Offence either in Word or Deed; that their Ordinary Discourse be grave and edifying; their Apparel decent, and proper for Clergy-Men; and that in their whole Conversation they be Instances and Patterns of the Christian Life.

VII. That they do not board in, or frequent Publick-houses, or lodge in Families of Evil Fame; that they wholly abstain from Gaming, and all vain Pastimes; and converse not familiarly with lewd or profane Persons, otherwise than in order to reprove, admonish, and reclaim them.

<[26]> VIII. That in whatsoever Family they shall lodge, they perswade them to join with them in daily Prayer Morning and Evening.

IX. That they be not nice about Meats and Drinks, nor immoderately careful about their Entertainment in the Places where they shall sojourn; be contented with what Health requires and the Place easily affords.

X. That as they be Frugal in Opposition to Luxury; so they avoid all Appearance of Covetousness, and recommend themselves according to their Abilities by the prudent Exercise of Liberality and Charity.

XI. That they take special Care to give [no] Offence to the Civil Government, by intermingling in the Affairs not relating to their own Calling and Function.

XII. That avoiding all Names of Distinction, they endeavour to preserve a Christian Agreement and Union one with another, as a Body of Brethren of one and the same

Church united under the Superior Episcopal Order, and all engaged in the same great Design of Propagating the Gospel; and to this End keeping up a Brotherly Correspondence, by meeting together at certain Times, as shall be most convenient for mutual Advice and Assistance.

<[27]> Secondly, *With Respect to their Parochial Cure.*

I. That they conscientiously observe the Rules of our Liturgy in the Performance of all the Offices of their Ministry.

II. That besides the stated Service appointed for Sundays and Holy-days, they do, as far as they shall find it practicable, publickly read the daily Morning and Evening Service, and decline no fair Opportunity of Preaching to such as may be Occasionally met together from Remote and Distant Parts.

III. That they perform every part of Divine Service with that Seriousness and Decency, that may recommend their Ministrations to their Flock, and excite a Spirit of Devotion in them.

IV. That the chief Subjects of their Sermons be the great Fundamental Principles of Christianity, and the Duties of a sober, righteous, and godly Life, as resulting from those Principles.

V. That they particularly preach against those Vices, which they shall observe to be most Predominant in the Places of their Residence.

VI. That they carefully instruct the People concerning the Nature and Use of the Sacraments <[28]> of Baptism and the Lord's-Supper, as the peculiar Institutions of Christ, Pledges of Communion with him, and Means of deriving Grace from him.

VII. That they duly consider the Qualifications of those adult Persons, to whom they administer Baptism; and of those likewise whom they admit to the Lord's-Supper, according to the Directions of the Rubricks in our Liturgy.

VIII. That they take a special Care, to lay a good Foundation for all of their other Ministrations, by Catechizing those under their Care, whether Children or other ignorant Persons, explaining the Catechism to them in the most easie and familiar Manner.

IX. That in their Instructing *Heathens* and *Infidels*, they begin with the Principles of natural Religion, appealing to their Reason and Conscience; and thence proceed to shew them the Necessity of Revelation, and the Certainty of that contained in the Holy Scriptures, by the plain and most obvious Arguments.

X. That they frequently visit their respective Parishioners; those of our own Communion, to keep them steady in the Profession and Practice of Religion, as taught in the Church of *England*; those that oppose us, or dissent from us, to convince and reclaim them, with a Spirit of Meekness and Gentleness.

<[29]> XI. That those whose Parishes shall be of large extent, shall, as they have Opportunity and convenience, officiate in the several Parts thereof, so that all the Inhabitants may by turns partake of their Ministrations; and that such as shall be appointed to officiate in several places, shall reside sometimes at one, sometimes at another of those Places, as the Necessities of the People shall require.

XII. That they shall, to the best of their Judgments, distribute those small Tracts given by the Society for the Purpose, amongst such of the Parishioners as shall want them most, and appear likely to make the best Use of them; and that such useful Books, of which they have not sufficient Number to give, they be ready to lend to those who will be most careful in reading and restoring them.

XIII. That they encourage the setting up of schools for the teaching of Children; and particularly by the Widows of such Clergy-Men as shall die in those Countries, if they be found capable of that Employment.

XIV. That each of them keep a Register of his Parishioners Names, Profession of Religion, Baptism, etc. according to the Scheme annex'd, No. I, for his own Satisfaction, and the Benefit of the People.

<[30]> Thirdly, *With Respect to the Society.*

I. That each of them keep a constant and regular Correspondence with the Society, by their Secretary.

II. That they send every six Months an Account of the State of their respective Parish according to the Scheme annex'd, No. II.

III. That they communicate what shall be done at the Meetings of the Clergy, when settled, and whatsoever else may concern the Society.

<[31]> *Notitia Parochialis*; To be made by each Minister soon after his Acquaintance with his People, and kept by him for his own Ease and Comfort, as well as the Benefit of his Parishioners.

I. *Names of Parishioners.*	II. *Profession of Religion.*	III. *Which of them Baptized.*	IV. *When Baptized.*	V. *Which of them Communicants.*	VI. *When they first Communicated.*	VII. *What Obstructions they meet with in their Ministrations.*

<[32]> No. II. *Notitia Parochialis*; Or, An Account to be sent Home every Six Months to the *Society* by each Minister, concerning the Spiritual State of their respective Parishes.

I. *Number of Inhabitants.*
II. *No. of the Baptized.*
III. *No. of Adult Persons Baptized this Half Year.*
IV. *No. of Actual Communicants of the Church of* England.
V. *No. of those who profess themselves of the Church of* England.
VI. *No. of Dissenters of all Sorts, particularly Papists.*

<[33]> *Instructions for Schoolmasters Employ'd by the Society*, etc.

I. That they well consider the End for which they are employ'd by the Society, *viz.* the Instructing and disposing Children to believe and live as Christians.

II. In order to this end, that they teach them to read truly and distinctly, that they may be capable of reading the Holy Scriptures, and other pious and useful Books; for the informing their Understandings, and regulating their Manners.

III. That they instruct them thorowly in the Church Catechism, teach them first to read it distinctly and exactly, then to learn it perfectly by heart, endeavouring to make them understand the sense and meaning of it, by the help of such Expositions as the Society shall send over.

IV. That they teach them to Write a plain and legible Hand, in order to the fitting them for useful Employments; with as much Arithmetick as shall be necessary to the same Purpose.

V. That they be industrious, and give constant attendance at proper School-hours.

<[34]> VI. That they daily use, Morning and Evening, short and proper Prayers with their Scholars in the School, and teach them Prayers and Graces to be used by themselves at home.

VII. That they oblige their Scholars to be constant at Church on the Lord's-Day, Morning and Afternoon, and at all other times of publick Worship; that they cause them to carry their Bibles and Prayer-Books with them instructing them how to use them there, and how to demean themselves in the several parts of Worship; that they be there present with them taking Care of their reverent and decent Behaviour, and examine them afterwards as to what they have heard and learn'd.

VIII. That when any of their Scholars are [ready] for it, they recommend them to the Minister of the Parish, to be publickly Catechiz'd in the Church.

IX. That they take especial Care of their Manners, both in their Schools and out of them warning them seriously of those Vices to which Children are most liable; teaching them to abhor Lying and Falshood, and to avoid all forms of Evil-speaking; to love Truth and Honesty; to be Modest, Gentle, Well-behav'd, Just, and Affable, and Courteous to all their Companions respectful of their Superiours, particularly to w[*illegible*] <[35]> all that Minister in holy things, and especially to the Minister of their Parish; and all this from a sense and fear of Almighty God, endeavouring to bring them in their tender Years to that sense of Religion which may render it the constant Principle of their Lives and Actions.

X. That they use all kind and gentle Methods in the Government of their Scholars, that they may be lov'd as well as fear'd by them; and that when Correction is necessary, they make the Children to understand that it is given them out of kindness, for their good, bringing them to a sense of their Fault, as well as of their Punishment.

XI. That they frequently consult with the Minister of the Parish in which they dwell, about the Methods of Managing their Schools, and be ready to be advised by him.

XII. That they do in their whole Conversation shew themselves Examples of Piety and Virtue to their Scholars, and to all whom they shall converse.

XIII. That they be ready as they have opportunity, to teach and instruct the *Indians* and *Negroes*, and their Children.

XIV. That they send to the Secretary of the Society, once in every six Months, an Account of the State of their respective Schools, the Number of their Scholars, with the Methods and Success of their Teaching.

Printed.

[*LAM/SPG/XV*]

Petition
[1706]

To the Reverend Father in God Henry Lord Bishop of London. The humble Address of the Churchwardens and Vestry of the Parish of Pascotank in North Carolina and a part of your Lordship's Diocess in behalf of themselves and the rest of the Inhabitants of the Said Parish. In all humility shew unto your Lordship.

That by reason of the distance and want of opportunity (no shipping going from this place for England) we could not according to our desires represent our deplorable condition to your Lordship, as we should long Since have done, had an opportunity presented, which at the last it hath pleased Almighty God to afford us by Sending amongst us the Reverend Mr. Richard Marsden, who in his Visitation of this Government in his passage to South-Carolina has in Charity and Commiseration to our poor Souls not Spared any Labour or pains in discharge of his Ministerial Function during the short time of his stay here, preaching not only Sundays but on the Week-days, Baptizing not only great number of Infants but Some of riper years, who have been bred up under Quaker Parents, and administring the Holy Sacrament of the Lord's Supper never before administred in this Parish, and has promised to present this our humble Address to your Lordship. The heavy burthen that we groan under is the want of a grave Sober and able Divine to be settled amongst us (which we most humbly and heartily implore And beseech your Lordship to furnish us with) qualifyed to perform those afore-mentioned Duties, which at present we are without and lament the want of, being as sheep without a shepherd, the which blessing if we could be so happy to enjoy, the Elder Sort would be more firm and stable in their holy profession, the youth (of whom there are many) well grounded in the Principles of our holy Religion, virtue and godliness of living promoted and encouraged, wickedness, Vice, immorality and prophaneness banished, the growing faction of Quakerism (of which there are many Professors in this and our neighbouring Parish) discouraged, and a number of poor Seduced ignorant Souls recovered out of the Lethargy of that detestable opinion. And God Almighty would the more plentifully shour down his blessings upon us. And altho' under our present Circumstances we are not capable of raising a full and Suitable maintenance, that a worthy Minister may deserve, yet we hope in few years, as our youth grow up, the Seduced brought over and Religion shall flourish, we shall be in a capacity to make more ample Contribution, than our present incapacity will afford; in the mean time we shall doe our utmost to encourage so good and necessary a Work. And whereas thro' your Lordship's and Several of the pious and well-disposed Nobility and Gentry's Bounty of our Native Country the Kingdom of England there has been Several presses of Books sent into this Government, the greatest part whereof are marked for St. Thomas Parish in Pamplicoe in the County of Bath and there lodged, and is so far distant from us, that wee have not any Benefit by them, Wee most humbly begg of your Lordship to bestow <47> Some Books on this Parish, Such as to your Lordship shall seem most meet and convenient for us, if not for a standing Library, Such as may be lent out to the Inhabitants thereof to be returned again to the Person to whose care and Custody the whole shall be committed.

All which we humbly lay before your Lordship's pious and serious consideration, having no other remedy and presuming upon your Lordships wonted Commiseration Charity and Pity towards the Souls of all men, and, not in the least doubting of relief, which when we shall be so happy to enjoy we shall be the more capable to offer up our hearty and unfeigned Thanks to God Almighty for so great a Blessing, and our hearty prayers, to God Almighty for your Lordship as the Instrument in procuring the Same, as also for your Health prosperity and long continuance over us, and in the mean time shall according to our bounden Duty always endeavour to approve ourselvs Your Lordship's Dutifull Sons and most humble Servants.

Thomas Relfe, Richd. Mardron Church wardens, John Jennings, Robert Wallis, William Collings, Fra. de Lemar, Samuel Davis, John Davis, William Relph, Tho. Boyd, John Wade, Phil. Tockesey.

[*Endorsed*:]
Adress of the Churchwardens
etc. of Pascotank
in N. Carolina to the
Ld. Bp. of London.

Copy.

[*SPG/Jou/1*]

Journal of the SPG
1706 March 28

<230> 28th March 1706. [...]

<232> 16. Also that having considered of the Lord Bishop of London's Letter[1] of the 4th instant, of that of Mr. Talbots of the 14th[2] and of the Petition of some of the Inhabitants of N. Carolina, relating to the great want of Ministers in those parts, they[3] had Agreed to Report as their Opinion that the Sum of £60 should be made up to Mr. Talbot for his 4th years Service ending in June next (on Condition he return in the Service of the Society) £20 of the said £60 having been already Ordered on the same Account. Agreed to. [...]

[18.] Also that they had farther Agreed to Report as their Opinion, that Mr. Talbot should be forthwith sent back to Burlington,[4] and in Case Mr. Moor[5] fail in his Attempt of setling among the Indians at Albany, that then Mr. Moor shall come back to Burlington and Mr. Talbot shall go to N. Carolina, to Preach baptize and Prepare the People there for the receiving a Residing Missionary, that Mr. Talbot continue there for 6 months, and at the Expiration thereof Return to Burlington, and Mr. Moor to Carolina and so each of 'em Alternately to serve N. Carolina and Burlington and while

they shall be employed by the Society in such Services that they receive each of them from the Society sixty Pounds per Annum. Agreed to.
<233> Also to move the Society (in case the aforesaid Proposal be Agreed to), that a proper Application may be made to the Lord Weymouth to continue his former Bounty of Supporting a Missionary in N. Carolina and that his Lordships Pleasure be known thereupon. [...]

Minutes.

[1]Not located.
[2]Not located.
[3]The Committee of the SPG.
[4]New Jersey.
[5]Rev. Thorogood Moore (d. 1708?) served churches in New York and New Jersey, and was a catechist to Indians in the area. Apparently he and a colleague were lost at sea. Manross, *SPG Papers in the Lambeth Palace Library*, 99, 108, and passim.

[*SPG/A/2*]

Lord Weymouth to Secretary, SPG
1706 April 12

<*CXLIII.*> Lord Weymouth to Mr. Chamberlayne.

L. Leat Apr. 12th 1706.

Sir.
<*The disordered State of Carolina, and the little Mr. Blair did makes his Lordship think Charity may be better employed.*> The present disordered State of Carolina gives no Encourag[ement] to Missionaries to go thither, for who shall have the Government of them, it is not fit they should be displaced by Laymen there is no Ecclesiastical Jurisdiction, nor any Care taken to have any setled there, Mr. Blair indeed did so little for what he had, that I think Charity may be better employed other wayes. I know nothing of Mr. Talbot nor his Character whether he is a converted Quaker, as Mr. keith is, or whether originally of the Church of England, I have not heard from any of the persons you hint at but do not name, though your Recomendation needs no Assistants. I thank you for the kind Visits I received from you in Town, and am very truly Sir Your most affectionate Servant

Weymouth.

Directions are
For John Chamberlayne Esqr.

Copy.

[*SPG/Jou/1*]

Journal of the SPG
1706 April 19

<234> 19th April 1706. [...]

<235> The Lord Bishop of London laid before the Bord a paper Entitled The Planters Letter[1] to the Lord Bishop of London touching the present State of N. Carolina, Ordered that the said Letter be refer'd to the Committee who are to Report their Opinion thereof at the next Meeting. [...]

Minutes. At a meeting on May 17, 1706, the SPG accepted a report from the Committee that it "appear[s] by the said Paper, that there is great want of Ministers in North Carolina, and ... that the first proper Persons that offer themselves Missionarys of the Society be sent to N. Carolina." Journal of the SPG, I, 238-239.

[1]Not located.

[*LAM/SPG/VII*]

Bishop of London to [Secretary, SPG]
[1706] July 4

Jul. 4.

Sir,

I send you a letter for Mr. Rector twenty pounds: but you must first let somebody be bound with him to me, that in case he be not upon his voyage within six months after the date of the bond it shall stand good against them.

Mr. Roberts shall attend the Committee when he please: and if Mr. Black[1] is found worthy the sooner he was dispatched the better. If he should inform my Lord Bishop of Carlile's character, I should think him fit to send to N. Carolina, and the sooner the better: for I fear he is not well able to subsist long in town. I am Sir your most humble Servant.

H. London

ALS.

[1]Rev. William Black was not appointed to serve in North Carolina, but instead was sent by the SPG to Sussex County, Delaware. Manross, *SPG Papers in the Lambeth Palace Library*, 7.

[*LAM/SPG/VII*]

Bishop of London to Secretary, SPG
1706 November 15

Sir

The shortness of the dayes, and the bad Road, hinders me from waiting upon the Committee this day, and therefore I begg you would put them in mind of some things, in which I presume they are not yet come to a resolution. [...]

3. Whether they have yet met with 2 persons fit to send to North Carolina. [...]

Your humble Servant.

H. London

Fulham
Nov. 15, 1706

[*Addressed*:]
For John Chamberlain Esqr.
in Petty France
Westminster

[*Endorsed*:]
14.
Ld. Bp. of London
15. Novemb. 1706
<*Entered*>

ALS.

[*SPG/A/3*]

Bishop of London to Secretary, SPG
1706 December 20

<XXII> Ld. Bp. of London to the Secretary
Sir,

I wou'd humbly move the Society to send Mr. Cordiner to Albany with an allowance of £50 per annum as I will take care of the rest. I do not know where he can do more good and if he might have a Schoolmaster over with him at £30 per annum it wou'd yet do more good. I shou'd think Mr. Bl[ack] and Mr. Robinson[1] fitest for N. Carolina but they cannot have less than £100 per annum each for you know they must live among Barbarians. Mr. Jenkins is surely then most proper for Apoquiminy and the other whose name I have forgot, to assist Mr. [*blank*] at Elizabeth town or Salem, In great pain I rest Sir Yours.

H. London

Decr. 20th 1706.

Copy.

[1]Not identified.

[SPG/Jou/1]

Journal of the SPG
1706/7 January 17

<262> 17th January 1706-7. [...]

4. Mr. Stubs[1] reported that he had according to order waited on the Lord Bishop of Gloucester about Mr. Talbot, the Secretary also acquainting the Bord that he had writ to his said Lordship upon that affair, and received his answer dated 23 Decr. 1706 which was read, Mr. Talbot attending at the Door was call'd in and heard what he had farther to offer in his affair, and read Several papers to the Society sign'd by the Societies Missionaries relating to a Suffragan Bishop etc., and a Paper intituled the Planters Letter, and Order of Court dispensing with the Residence of Ministers sent to Sea <263> and to the Plantations etc., then Mr. Talbot withdrew, and the Society having considered of the whole Matter, the said Gentleman was called in and askt whether he was willing to return by the first Opportunity in the Service of the Society, which he desired to consider of against the next Meeting. [...]

Minutes.

[1]Philip Stubbs (1665-1738), archdeacon of St. Albans and an ardent supporter of the work of both the SPG and the SPCK. *DNB.*

[LAM/SPG/VII]

Bishop of London to [Secretary, SPG]
1706/7 March 22

Sir

I desire you would recommend this Gentleman[1] to the Committee, who will bring a Testimonial from his Diocesan my Lord Bp. of Norwich; and if they are Satisfyed with him, I hope he may be thought a proper Person to Send to Carolina. I am Sir Your most assured Friend and Brother.

H. London

Fulham
Mar. 22d, 1706

[*Endorsed:*]
31.
Lord Bishop of London
22 March 1706/7
<*Entered*>

ALS.

[1] Not identified.

[*LAM/SPG/VII*]

Rev. John Talbot to Secretary, SPG
1707 April 16

<253> Honored Sir

I have received several Letters from my Friends in America who think Long for my Return which I was forward to do once and agen, but Satan hinder'd me by raising Lyes and Slanders in my way, But I have cleard my selfe to all that have heard me, and I hope you will Satisfye the Honorable Society that I am not the man to whom that dark Character due belong. Mr. Keith has known my doctrine and manner of Life some years, and what I have ventur'd suffer'd and acted for the Gospel of Christ abroad and at home. I desire his Letter may be read to the Honorable Board, and that they will be pleased to dispatch me the sooner the better, for the season is far spent and ships are going out and if I go at all I would go quickly. I know the wants of the poor people in America. They have need of me, or else I shoud not venture my life to do that abroad which I could do more to my own advantage at home. I shoud be glad to see some body sent to North Carolina. I hope the planters letter is not quite Forgot. Tis a sad thing to live in the Wilderness like the wild Indians [*illegible*] without God in the world.

Pray give my humble duty and Service to all the members of the Honorable Society. May God prosper their generous undertakings for the advancement of his glory and the progress of the Gospel where in I do not rest but labor and travel as a good Soldier of Je. Christ and Honored Sir, your humble Servant.

John Talbot

London Ap. 16 1707

[*Addressed:*]
<254> To John Chamberlane Esqr.
at his house in Petty France
Westminster

[*Endorsed:*]
8.D Entered
Mr. Talbot, London
16 April 1707

ALS.

[*SPG/Jou/Cte*]

Journal of the Committee of the SPG
1707 May 26

26 May 1707. [...]

1. A Letter from the Lord Bishop of London to the Committee dated Fulham 24 instant was read, recommending the Bearer Mr. Alexander Wood[1] to the Service of the Society particularly to Charles Town Carolina. Ordered that the Secretary do deliver to the said Mr. Wood one of the Printed Forms of Testimonials, and that he do procure them to be sign'd according to the Standing Orders of the Society.

2. Agreed to move the Society that in case the said Mr. Wood shall appear to be qualified for the Service, and be content to go upon the foot of the Society's Allowance, he may be sent to N. Carolina, where there is a great want of Missionaries, and whither the Society have Agreed to send the first proper Persons that offer themselves to the Service of the Society, as appears by the Minutes of 17 May 1706. n. 12.[2] [...]

Minutes.

[1]Wood arrived in South Carolina later in 1707 and served until his death in 1711. LAM/SPG/XVI, 197-199; LAM/SPG/XVII, 66-67.

[2]Journal of the SPG, I, 238-239.

[*SPG/Jou/1*]

Journal of the SPG
1707 July 18

<290> 18th July 1707. [...]

<291> Also that they[1] had Agreed to move the Society and put them in mind of the very great want of Ministers in N. Carolina, and of the promise of the Society in their Minutes to supply that Place, and for that unless some Minister can be sent to go with the next Virginia Fleet which will sail about September next, there is no likelyhood of an Opportunity to send to North Carolina in Twelve months. Agreed that it be refer'd to the Committee to consider of sending thether the first Person that shall offer his Service to the Society. [...]

Minutes.

[1]The Committee of the SPG.

[*SPG/A/3*]

Bishop of London to Secretary, SPG
1707 July 22

<LXXVII> Ld. Bp. of London to the Secretary

July 22d 1707.

Sir

If I have been more earnest in desiring your Assistance in promoting the Interest of those persons I recommended to you and in such terms your Modesty cou'd not bear: I question not, but that you will easily excuse me, when I assure you that my necessary absence constrains me to have my whole reliance upon your kindness. As to Mr. Johnston[1] I look upon him to be every way so well qualifyed and Zealously disposed, that whatever place he goes to it will be happy in him: but whether North Carolina will suit so well with his Circumstances, it will be worth while to Consult a little with him at your best leasure, and not rather to recommend him to Charles Town. You will oblige me to let me know whether Mr. Wesendunck has waited upon you: for you may safely trust him with money is Assigned for Mr. Bridge. No Man wishes better for Dr. Bray than my self, but as his merit is from the publick, judge you what an insupportable burden I shou'd draw upon my self, if I shou'd so excuse the Crown. I am Sir Your most humble Servant.

H. London

Directed
To Jno. Chamberlayne Esqr. etc.

Copy.

[1]Rev. Gideon Johnston (ca. 1671-1716) was sent to South Carolina in 1707 as commissary of the bishop of London, and served in that colony until his death.

[*LAM/SPG/VIII*]

Bishop of London to Committee, SPG
1707 August 16

Aug. 16.

Gentlemen

The bearer Mr. Mill[1] is very well recommended and desirous to take Orders and to take your directions for N. Carolina or where you please. If you find him answer your expectations, your commands shall be complyed with by Your most humble Servant.

H. London

[*Addressed*:]
To the Gentlemen of the
Committee for propagating the Gospel etc.

[*Endorsed*:]
Ld. Bp. of London
16 Aug. 1707

ALS. Read at a meeting of the Committee of the SPG on September 1, 1707, when "Mr. Francis Milne ... was acquainted that he must procure Letters Testimonial agreeable to the printed Forms." Journal of the Committee of the SPG.

[1]Rev. Francis Milne. Within a few months Milne was appointed to a vacant parish in Virginia. LAM/SPG/VIII, 72.

[*LAM/SPG/X*]

Testimonial
1707 August 18

We the Minister and Churchwardens and other parishioners whose names are here underwritten do hereby certify the Rt. Reverend the Ld. Bp. of London and the Society incorporated by charter for the propogation of the Gospel in foreign parts that the bearer hereof James Adams[1] Clerk has during the time that he has been an Assistant to Mr. Johnston the present Incumbent of the parishes of Castlemore killmovee and Killcolmon from the Latter end of the year 1702. to the day of the date hereof behav'd himself piously soberly and discreetly to the general satisfaction of both the Minister and parishioners and that he has not in that time or any other time before or after, that we cou'd hear, said or done any thing that might be a blemish to his Character. Given under our hands and seals this 18th day of August 1707.

Gideon Johnston Minister (Seal), Samll. Ball Churchwarden (Seal), Connor Hickey Ch. warden (Seal), Richd. Stuck (Seal), Stephen Lawrence (Seal), James Pratt (Seal), William Coton (Seal)

[*Endorsed:*]
10.
Mr. Adams Testimonials

DS.

[1]As is evident from this document, Adams was an "assistant," presumably curate, to Gideon Johnston in Ireland before serving in the Albemarle region of North Carolina from 1708 until his death in1710. See appendix.

[*LAM/SPG/X*]

Henry Sandford to Bishop of Elphin
1707 August 20

Castlereagh Augt. the 20th 1707

My Lord

Mr. Adams haveing recd. encouragement from the Bishop of London to preach the Gospell in America is so desirous to be employed in the good works, that he quits his

Curacie in the Diocess of Killala and the appointment he had from me to goe foorthwith to be Chaplain to yr. Society in North Carolina, which I wish with all my heart may be for his benefit which is the only consideration that cou'd make me concent to his leaving my Family, where he has behaved himself ever since he came amoungst us so well in all respects that he has justly merited the generalla love and esteeme that the best part of which I owe him, is to Testefie that his behaviour for these 5 years and ½ past (that he has taught my Children) has bin sobor civill and pious and as such a Person I begg leave to recommend him to your Lordship who am Your Lordships most faithfull and obedient humble Servant.

Hen. Sandford

The Enclosed letter I recd. from Collonel Henry Sandford this 28 day of August 1707. Wittnesse my hand.

S. Elphin

[*Addressed:*]
To the Lord Bishop of Elphin
This

ALS.

[*LAM/SPG/X*]

Testimonials
1707 August 22, 26

<66> We the Bishop of Elphin and others of the Clergy of the adjacent Dioceses of Tuam and Elphin do hereby Certifie the Right Reverend the Lord Bishop of London and the Society Incorporated by Charter for the Propagation of the Gospel in Foreign parts that the bearer hereof James Adams Clerk has during the time that he liv'd in this Diocess from the latter end of the year 1701 when he was Ordained to the day of the date hereof behav'd himself piously soberly and discreetly to the General Satisfaction of us and those with whom he hath been concern'd and that he hath not in that time or before that we cou'd hear, done or said any thing that might be the least blemish to his Character. Given under our hands and Seales this 22d day of August 1707.

August 26th 1707

Before this Gentleman was ordain'd priest, he being sent to me by the Bp. to be examind I enquird into his character, and was informed by persons of very good credit that he was of a fit, very sober and studious character. I did accordingly recommend him, I did not since hear that he did by any act or acts demerit that character.

Ed Goldsmith Dean of Elphin

I have known the Gentleman above named about Seaven years and I do beleive that he well deserves the character that has bin given him by the Dean of Elphin as wittnessing hand and Seales this 26 of Augst. 1707.

Samll. Hodson Prebend of Ballinletter; William Pullin (Seal), Thos. Reahemaine, Rector de Ballakean, in Dioces Freamene (Seal), gideon Johnston (Seal), Jon. Bullingbrooke (Seal)

DS.

[*LAM/SPG/VIII*]

Bishop of London to Secretary, SPG
1707 September 4

Sept. 4.

Sir

This war[1] is a grievious thing to our poor missioners, who are forced to be tossed and tumbled about; that it costs them and me more for a free passage, than if they had taken it in a merchant man for a price. For God's sake incline as many as you can to take compassion on them next meeting: for if we do not support them under those Discouragements, we must expect no more good men to offer their Service. I hope I have met with one very good man for N. Carolina, whom you shall see, after I have examined him a little farther. The two inclosed will inform you of three objects of our compassion. But I would be glad we might transfer Mr. Cordiner because of his family, [in one] of yr. men of war that go streight with yr. Virginia Fleet. I am Sir, your most humble servant.

H. London

[*Addressed*:]
For John Chamberlain
Esqr. at his house
in Petty France Westminster

[*Endorsed*:]
Lord Bp. of London 4th Sept.
1707. About Mr. Black Cordiner
and Jenkins and Walker.
<*Entered*>

ALS.

[1]The War of the Spanish Succession, 1702-1713.

[*LAM/SPG/VIII*]

Bishop of London to SPG
1707 September 12

Gentlemen

The Bearer Mr. Gordon[1] is one of the Persons designed for North Carolina. He is willing to undertake it, and I hope will discharge himself very well in his Mission into those parts. I therefore recommend him to you, and am Gentlemen Your very humble Servant.

H. London

Fulham
Sept. 12, 1707.

[*Addressed*:]
To the Gentlemen of the Committee
for propagating the Gospel in
foreign Parts

[*Endorsed*:]
Lord Bishop of London, Fulham
12 Sept. 1707.
<*Entered*>

ALS. Read at a meeting of the Committee of the SPG on September 15, 1707, "and the said Gentleman [William Gordon] being called in, was examined, and told that he must procure Testimonials against the next Meeting of the Committee." Journal of the Committee of the SPG.

[1]William Gordon served in North Carolina 1707-1708. See appendix.

[*SPG/Jou/1*]

Journal of the SPG
1707 September 19

<295> 19th September 1707. [...]

<296> 7. The Lord Bishop of London acquainted the Bord that two Gentlemen Mr. Gordon and Mr. Adams had attended him and offer'd their Service for North Carolina, and that the Ships for those Parts being ready to Sail, his Lordship was apprehensive that they would lose their passage unless they were presently dispatcht, Agreed that this matter be refer'd to the Committee who are to examine the Qualifications of the abovementioned Gentlemen, and to make their Report to the Lord ABp. and in case his Grace shall approve of them that they shall have an Allowance of Sixty pounds per annum each to commence from Michaelmas next, and the usual Allowances of Ten pounds and Five pounds, each for Books. [...]

Minutes.

[SPG/A/3]

Bishop of London to Secretary, SPG
1707 September 22

<CXVI> Ditto to Ditto.[1]

Sir

I desire you would acquaint the Committee for propagating the Gospel etc. that I have seen and approved the Testimonials of the Bearer Mr. Wm. Gordon, and have ordained him upon the Credit of them, believing him a Person fitly qualifyed for the Office of a Missionary. I send you here inclosed the Memorial I spoke of, which you will please to present to his Grace of Canterbury; and if you wou'd see the Causes in the Act of Assembly, you have them in the Memorial, which Mr. Evan Evans gave in on Fryday last. I am also to request you to lay before his Grace the two inclosed Certificates relating to Mr. Honyman.

Sir Your humble Servant.

H. London

Mr. Adams also comes
along with Mr. Gordon being designed
likewise for North Carolina.

Fulham
Septr. 22d 1707.
Directed. To Jno. Chamberlayne Esqr.

Copy. Read at a meeting of the Committee on September 22, 1707. William Gordon "being call'd in, inform'd the Bord that his Testimonials could not be ready til next Monday, and the Committee considering that the time of Mr. Gordon's Departure (in case he should be approved) would be very sudden, gave him a Text and appointed him to read prayers and preach on Monday morning next at St. Dunstans in the West.... The said Letter recommending Mr. James Adams, he was called in and produced the Bp. of Elphins Letters Dimissory, and a Certificate from the Dean of Elphin and other Divines, and from the Minister and Parishioners of Castlemore etc. in Ireland, where he had officiated as Curate, together with a Letter from Mr. Sandford of Castlereagh in the County of Roscommon, all giving him a very good Character, which were read then a Text was given to the said Gentleman and he was appointed to read Prayers and Preach at St. Dunstans in the West on Friday morning next." Journal of the Committee of the SPG.

[1]I.e., a letter from the bishop of London to the secretary.

[LAM/SPG/VIII]

Secretary of the SPG to Archbishop of Tuam
1707 September 25

Petty France, Westminster
25th Septr. 1707.

My Honored Lord

Your Graces Letter and another From Mr. Visey (a Son or Kinsman of your Lordships as I suppose) found me in my waiting at Windsor which was the reason why they were not Communicated to the Society before last Fryday the General Monthly Meeting. As soon as they were read I was Commanded by His Grace the Lord A. Bishop of Caterbury our president and the rest of the Members to return your Grace their Hearty thanks for your intended Benefaction of twenty pounds yearly; and as for what Lordship writes about Mr. Johnson,[1] they don't at all doubt but he will make good the Caracter your Grace has given of him, and they have all the Deference immaginable for your recommendation but having been for some time under an Obligation of sending a Couple of Missionaries to N. Carolina, where there is hardly any face of Religion, no Ministers, no Churches, no Towns, nor anything but a vast scatter'd flock without Shepherds and running wild in the desert; they cou'd not dispense with their promise of providing first for those poor Wretches, as they have don with a Salary of £60 per Annum to each Missionary notwithstanding the narrowness of their Revenue as well as Precariousness of it, seeing that it consists almost wholly of voluntary Contributions, and that our Disbursements do at present exceed our Income by near 3 or £400. My Lord, the society gave Mr. Johnson the refusal of going to this sad Country, tho' no body thought it proper for him considering his large family and other Circumstances, which we all pity the more because he is a Man (so far as appears to us who have throughly sifted him) without exceptions. I can't despair however of my Lord of Londons doing someting for him either on the Continent of America or in West Indies, I am sure no body wishes it more than My Lord Your Grace's Most faithfull humble Servant.

Jno. Chamberlayne

If your Grace wants any more Books or Papers be pleased to Command 'em at any time.

[*Endorsed:*]
25 Septemb. 1707
Copy of a Letter
to the ABp. of Tuam.

Copy.

[1]Gideon Johnston.

[*LAM/SPG/XV*]

Testimonial
1707 September 27

These are to certifie that William Gordon Clerk A. M. hath been particularly known to me these three years last bypast here at London, and I can freely recommend him (if my recommendation can have any value with the Right Reverend, Reverend, and Honourable members of the society for propagating the Gospel in forreign parts) as a person of a Sober life, good learning, and Orthodox principles, and who is zealous for her majesties government and the Church of England as by law established. And during his abode in North Britain he was regular in his life, and one with whom I have been acquainted since the year 1683. In testimony whereof I have subscribed these present at London the 27th of September 1707.

A. Middleton
Curate of St. Benedicts pauls wharf.

[*Endorsed*:]
Mr. Gordon's Testimonials.

DS.

[*SPG/Jou/App B*]

Humfrey Wanley to Secretary, SPG
1707 September 29

<104.> Mr. Gordon's Testimonials. [...]

Mr. Wanley to the Secretary. Dukestreet York buildings, 29th Sept. 1707.

Honor'd Sir

I am desired by Mr. Gordon, and some of his Friends to apprise you of his Behavior, while he was a Lodger with me in Mr. Berenclow's house, which is now about three years ago. He abode with us about 5, or 6 Months, and during that time did Demean himself (so far at least as I could gather from any thing that I heard or saw, relating to him) as might become an honest, and a Sober Man, And this Opinion was had of him by the whole Family, and has remain'd with us ever since, tho' we have not seen him above four times since he left us. I am Honor'd Sir, Your most Humble Servant.

Humfrey Wanley

Copy.

[*SPG/Jou/Cte*]

Journal of the Committee of the SPG
1707 September 29

29th Sept. 1707. [...]

3. Mr. Gordon attending produced Testimonials to the Satisfaction of the Committee.

4. Mr. Shute reported that he had heard Mr. Adams and Mr. Gordon read Prayers and Preach respectively, and that they both performed very well.

5. Agreed that it is the Opinion of the Committee that the said Mr. Adams and Mr. Gordon are proper Persons, and well qualified for the Mission.

6. Agreed that the Secretary do wait upon his Grace the Lord ABp. for his Approbation of the said Gentlemen, pursuant to the Order of the Society. [...]

Minutes.

[*SPG/Jou/1*]

Journal of the SPG
1707 October 17

<221> 17th October 1707. [...]

7. The Secretary reported from the Committee that they having Examined the Qualifications of Mr. Gordon and Mr. Adams, It was their Opinion that they are proper Persons, and well qualified for the Mission, Agreed to, and Ordered that the said Gentlemen do wait on his Grace the President, and lay before him their Testimonials. [...]

Minutes.

[*SPG/A/3*]

Rev. James Adams to Secretary, SPG
1707 November 10

<LXXXVIII> Mr. Adams to the Secretary

Bristol Novr. 10th 1707.

Sir

According to your Directions when I last waited upon you I give you this trouble. Mr. Gordon and I have got all our Goods safe a board and the Ships wait only for the first fair wind to carry them off; The Captain (Charles Stuart my Lord Mountjoys Brother) is an extream civil Gentleman, he received us very courteously and built us Cabbins as soon as he received the Order for our Passage we have received many Civilities from Mr. Bedford Minister (of Temple Church) and Mr. Shutes Brother.

I shall by the Grace of God puctually observe all the Orders and Instructions given me by the Society and as much as in me lyes endeavour to answer the pious design of that venerable and worthy body of men this is all from Sir Your very humble Servant.

James Adams

If you have any further Commands to lay upon us before the Wind serves you may direct your Letter to be left at Mr. Jno. Campbells next door to the Naggs head in Wine Street.

Copy.

[*SPG/A/3*]

Rev. William Gordon to Secretary, SPG
1707 November 19

<CXXX> Mr. Gordon to the Secretary

Sir

Mr. Adams it seems has writ to you already but since he thought fit not to Communicate to me the Contents nor tell me before he writ, I think myself Obliged to trouble you with this; we are just going a board in order to Sail this afternoon or in the Morning the wind at North, I shall as soon as I arrive make the best of my way to North Carolina, endeavour to the utmost of my power to answer the good and great end of my Mission, and Shun every thing with my best Care, may in the least tend to obstruct the same. I am Sir Your very humble Servant.

Wm. Gordon

Bristoll
Novr. 19th 1707

Superscribed
To Jno. Chamberlayne Esqr. etc.

Copy.

[*LAM/SPG/XV*]

Rev. James Adams to Secretary, SPG
1707 November 22

Sir

I hope this trouble will be no trespass upon your good humour tho' I have nothing to write but that Mr. Gordon and I are blessed be God [well] and went a board wednesday Last with the Capt. having some prospect of a favourable gale to carry us off but finding the wind settle in a contrary point we are all returned a shore till it shall please him who bringeth the winds out of his treasure to give us an opportunity of pursuing our intended voage. The Capt. continues still extremely civil to us even beyond what we cou'd in reasone expect or hope for, and may this good Luck in our first advances prove a happy omen of

Success in our Mission to be instrumental in bringing to light those that Sit in darkness and in the Shadow of Death in converting the obstinate and in every respect as well by the examplariness of our lives at the Soundness of our doctrine answering in Some measure the pious designe of so many truly charitable and good men which shall be the sincere and faithfull endeavour of Sir Your most oblig'd and humble Servant.

James Adams

Bristoll Saturday 9ber. 22d 1707

<*The first fair wind you may conclude we are gone off.*>

[*Addressed:*]
To John Chamberlayne Esqr. at his
house in petty france Westminster
London this

[*Endorsed:*]
21
Mr. Adams. Bristol
22 Novemb. 1707
Entered

ALS. Read at a meeting of the Committee on December 8, 1707. Journal of the Committee of the SPG.

[*LAM/SPG/VIII*]

Rev. James Adams to Secretary, SPG
1707 December 9

Sir

We Left Bristoll Tuesday the 25th of the Last month not Intending to touch at any port before we got within the Capes of Virginia but contrary winds drove us upon the Coast of Ireland where we were for some time before we cou'd either get from or safly make this harbour we got in here the 2d instant and we stay only for a fair wind as things happen to us you Shall according to your directions have an account of them punctually from Sir Your Most obliged and humble Servant.

James Adams

Kingsale Xber. 9th 1707.

[*Endorsed:*]
Mr. Adams. Kinsale
9 Decemb. 1707
Mr. Adams, Kingsale 9 Decr. 1707
<*Entered*>

[*Addressed*:]
John Chamberlayne Esqr. at his
house in petty france Westminster London.
these

ALS.

[*SPG/Jou/1*]

Journal of the SPG
1707/8 January 16

<308> 16th January 1707-8. [...]

<309> [8.] An Address from the Churchwardens and other Inhabitants of Pascotank in North Carolina, to the Lord Bishop of London was read. Ordered that the Secretary do write to the said Churchwardens etc. and acquaint them, that the Society has prevented[1] their Request by sending over two Clergymen to supply the Wants of the said Country, with Salaries of £60 each, but that they do expect that the Gentlemen of the Country should do what they can for them and particularly desire to know, how much the said Clergymen may probably expect from the Inhabitants of the said Pascotank etc. [...]

Minutes.

[1]*Prevent*: "To act before, in anticipation of, or in preparation for." *OED*.

[*LAM/SPG/XV*]

Rev. William Gordon to Secretary, SPG
1708 April 1

<6> Sir

We are just come to an Anchor in Linnhaven Bay after allmost three months passage and much Bad weather. I find we Shall get easier to No. Carolina from hence than we Expected whither We designe to Set forward God willing too morrow morning we are just weighing again for York River from whence it Seemes Sloops frequently goe to Carolina though the accts. I have had about the distance differ very much Some Calling it Seaven Some fifeteen others thirty Leagues and all the Mapps I have Seen are Equally imperfect; we have no very favourable Caracter of the Country and it will be hard if after So much rough weather we have mett with at Sea we Should have to doe with rugged tempers asshore but whatever inconveniences we find as we Shall allways make the best of them, So we Shall take all care to answere in every thing the good Expectations (I hope) the Honorable Society has of our Endeavours. I have no time to writ So fully as I would the opportunity by this Ship being as Sudden as accidentall therfor I hope you'll please to Excuse this abruptness. Your Very Humble Servant.

Wm. Gordon

Garland
Linhaven Bay Aprll. 1st 1708
4 in the morning

I Beg Sir Seeing I have not tim to writ home you'll be so kind as acquaint Mr. Wanley that he may Let our people know I'm very well And Safe arrived to whom my humble Service and to Mr. Hen. Hoare.

[*Addressed*:]
John Chamberlain Esqr.
at his house in Petty France Westmr.
London

[*Endorsed*:]
Mr. Gordon Linhaven
Bay in [*blank*]
1 April 1708
received 5th August
<*Entered*>

ALS. Read at a meeting of the SPG on September 17, 1708, when it was ordered "that the Secretary do write to the Capt. of the Man of War, who carried over the said Gentlemen, and return him the Thanks of the Society for his kindness to the said Gentlemen." Journal of the SPG, I, 353.

[*SPG/A/4*]

Rev. James Adams to Secretary, SPG
1708 June 10

<XLIII> Mr. Adams to the Secretary

Virginia
10th June 1708.

Sir.

Mr. Gordon and I by the good Providence of God got safe to Virginia the last day of March from whence we went into North Carolina and Address't our Selves to the President of the Council[1] who received us with all respect and Civility. The Countrey is divided into 4 large Precincts besides a large Tract of Land calld Pamptico divided into 3 Precincts more[2] I am by the President and Council appointed to settle in the Precinct call'd Pascotank and to take what care I can of the adjacent Precinct of Caratuck beside; there is no Church in Pascotank but the People upon my being Ordered among them have resolved forthwith to build a Church and two Chappels of ease the Precinct being of two great an extent to meet all at one or two places; I have been twice among the people of Carratuck precinct but cou'd not call a Vestry some of their leading Men being out of the Country and the rest unwilling to go about any Church affaires till their return. I cannot propose to make them so frequent Visits as the faithfull discharge of my duty requires till the extremity of the heat abates a little which now keeps me from undertaking long and tedious journeys. Each Precinct by Act of Assembly allows a Minister that resides among them to the value of £30 in the produce of the Countrey; which is equivalent to £10 or £15 Sterling. I found by the pious care of our now President the Posture of Affaires as to matter of Religion in a much better Condition than might have bin expected in a Place so destitute of means. I have preached some Preparatory Sermons to the Lords Supper and find many of the People well inclined to receive the Sacrament, I hope to be able to give a better account of the Countrey and People by the London Fleet. (This is by Capt. Stewart to whom Mr. Gordon and I lye under all the Obligations immaginable we eat at his own Table the whole passage and when I was sick had such care taken of me that I shou'd be the ingratefullest of men if I shou'd not upon all occasions acknowledge the kindness and Civility of that Worthy Gentleman.) I cou'd not get my goods to Carolina when I first arrived but am now come up again to Virginia to carry them down and to set out from hence again (God willing) next Morning for Carolina (blessed be God) in very good health and hope the Almighty will enable me in some measure to answer the pious design of so many good men which shall be the sincere and faithfull endeavour of Sir Your most Obliged and Humble Servant.

James Adams

P.S. Mr. Black and Mr. Jenkyns[3] are Arrived in the Burlington Man of War they left all their Cloaths and Books on Bord the Oxford which they lost at the Maderas being a Shore when she was blown from her Anchor we are in pain here for the Oxford and other Ships which are not yet Arrived, tho' the other three Men of Warr and the main Body of the Fleet came in above three weeks ago. What Orders you have at any time for me be pleas'd to direct them to be left with the Reverend Mr. Wallace[4] of Riquotan[5] who has promis'd to take care to send them down to me. There is a Pretty Library of Books in Pamptico a part of North Carolina sent thither by Dr. Bray when he was in this Country.

Copy. Read at a meeting of the SPG on September 17, 1708, when it was ordered "that the Secretary do write to the Capt. of the Man of War, who carried over the said Gentlemen, and return him the Thanks of the Society for his kindness to the said Gentlemen." Journal of the SPG, I, 353.

[1]William Glover (d. before October, 1712) held various offices in the colony after his removal to North Carolina from Virginia prior to 1690. From 1700 to 1712 he was a member of the council. As that body's president he was acting governor from October, 1707, to October, 1708, by virtue of which position he was a protagonist in the so-called Cary Rebellion. *DNCB*.

[2]At this time the area north of Albemarle Sound was divided into the precincts of Currituck, Pasquotank, Perquimans, and Chowan. Bath County was erected in 1696 and comprised the precincts of Wickham, Pamtecough, and Archdale, which within a few years were renamed Hyde, Beaufort, and Craven, respectively.

[3]Revs. William Black and Thomas Jenkins.

[4]Rev. James Wallace, or Wallis.

[5]I.e., Kiquotan, Virginia.

[*SPG/A/4*]

Rev. Richard Marsden to Secretary, SPG
1708 August 23

<LV.> Mr. Marsden to the Secretary.

Honor'd Sir,

I request you to Communicate the following Letter to the Society for propagating the Gospel in Forreign parts; I make bold to give you this trouble being Secretary to the Society.

Sir. Since my Ordination by my Lord of London is eight years, which time I have spent in America, for I was sent directly by my Lord to Maryland and did officiate in St. Michael's parish on the Eastern Shoar for six Years and three quarters or thereabouts to the satisfaction and content of all my parishioners.

Then desirous to return to England did resolve to see North and South Carolina, I staid in N. Carolina five weeks before had an Opportunity for a Passage to the other; in which time I preached ten Sermons, and administred the Communion to the President and ten more that were desirous to receive, and baptised One hundred forty and four Children and nine Adult persons that had been educated Quakers. I received a Letter from the President and Council to my Lord of London requesting Ministers to be sent and also a petition from the Vestry of Pascotank desiring one for a Precinct, and a Letter from the president directed to me giving an Account of the State of Religion there, which Letters and petition I sent inclosed to my diocesan per the first opportunity which doubt not has received and laid them before the Honorable Society.

I arrived at Charles Town in S. Carolina the 17th day of July 1707 after had preached was earnestly desired to undertake to supply St. Philips Parish by Governor and Chief of the parishioners, until received an Answer to a Letter they had sent to the Bp. of London requesting Dr. Bray for their Minister, I had officiated three Months when the Reverend Mr. Maule arrived here, and the Reverend Mr. Wood who was recommended by my Lord to the abovesaid parish; then the Parishioners being desirous to have liberty to elect their Minister, the Governour and the rest of the Commissioners of the Church Act, issued out an Order accordingly and the 1st of December (the Governor being present and presenting me) was unanimously elected Rector of St. Philips Charles Town; but after had been at the Charges of hiring a Sloop to send to Maryland for my wife and Children, and thirty pounds in paling in Gardens, and fencing (for the Ground that belong'd to the Minister's house did lie Common) Church, Mansehouse, Glebeland, all was neglected after the removal of Mr. Edward Marston. It was my Lord of Londons pleasure to recommend the Reverend Mr. Johnston to the abovesaid Parish which in Obedience to his Lordships appointment, and also the Honorable Society's recommendation and that Mr. Johnston might not be disappointed, I willing and free without the request and desire of any relinquish'd the title and interest I had to the parish of St. Philips for was all very well satisfyed of the faithfull discharge of my duty as by a Certificate I have from the Governor Council, Clergy and Parishioners appears, of which I have sent a Copy inclosed; in truth I left the Parish contrary to the Will and desire of the Parishioners.

I am now elected Rector of Christ Church Parish the Salary £50 per annum and some small Subscriptions of the Parishioners, but shall be content in any Condition so that I may be serviceable in God's Church to promote his Glory and the Salvation of Souls.

But Sir not having paid all the Charge of transporting my wife and Children hither and this removal happening at this Juncture and where I was in hopes, in a short time to have lived comfortably, has been a great trouble and Affliction to me, but God's will be done, I shall not repine but thro' his assistance shall continue faithfully to discharge the duties of my Function; I wou'd not willingly disoblige my Lord of London in any thing, nor do an Action unbecoming a Missionary.

I hope the Society will consider my Condition, I have a Wife and three Children and now but a very bare subsistance, and I readily relinquished St. Philips Parish (which is a plentifull Living, and when I had the Approbation of all the parishioners) that Mr. Johnston who came recommended by my Lord of London and them might not be disappointed, therefore hope will be pleased, to allow me something yearly for three or four years, till I be in better circumstances, if it be but a small Summ it will be very acceptable.

When first I came to Charles Town it was all in Confusion, but God be praised have been very successfull in promoting peace and unity; we have had constantly a full Church since my Arrival here, when fifty or sixty was a great Congregation (as was told before;) the Congregation encreast so fast that was necessitated to build a Gallery.

I administred the Communion here Monthly since Christmas day, had about forty Communicants constantly; I have been instrumental in bringing several dissenters to the Church, have baptised one family of Anabaptists and a Quaker Woman aged Seventy years, and she has three Sons married which have promised to come to Church and be baptised.

There is an Island near Charles Town called James Island on which is about fifty Families most of them dissenters, I preach'd there once in two Weeks, and was in hopes to have had great success, and did procure by Subscriptions One hundred pounds to build a Church on the Island, but now being removed cannot preach there as did before (being at too great a distance) and am afraid that nothing further will be done there for some time at least.

I left Charles Town with great dissatisfaction to the People, the Parishioners, seems as yet very backward to Elect Mr. Johnston, and whether will be prevail'd with I cannot at this time Judge, but at present most are very averse; I have done my endeavour (both in publick and private) to perswade to be unanimous in the electing of him; I hope the People will consider and act Prudently.

It will be great encouragement in the faithfull discharge of the duties of my Function to be taken notice of by the Honorable Society, and to understand that what I have Acted is acceptable to them; I am Honor'd Sir Your most humble and Obedient Servant.

Richd. Marsden

Charles Town, S. Carolina
23d August 1708

Copy.

[*LAM/SPG/XV*]

Vestry of Chowan to Bishop of London
1708 August 24

North Carolina the 24th August 1708

May it please your Lordship

Wee esteem it the peculiar and special blessing of heaven that wee of this poor Province are cast so happily under your Lordships patronage protection and care whose emenency in propagateing the Interest of Religion and Establishment of Church Government is Conspicuous to all mankind that knows your Lordship, not only within your Lordships Diocesse but elsewhere and Scarcely to bee parallelld.

Wee therefore (in behalfe of that part of this Province to which wee belong) in a deep sense of our duty to God and Gratitude to your Lordship do most Gladly embrace this Seasonable oppertunitie of making a due return of our humble and unfeighned thanks for the many favours your Lordship hath been pleased to Confer upon us, but more particularly for your Recommending us to the care of so Good and worthy a man whose prudent and pious Example is well worthy of our Imitation, sutable to and Adorning his profession (A blessing in no place wanted more than in this) wherefore wee conceive it our further duty to aquaint your Lordship that the Reverend Mr. Gorden is Universally Aproved on by all in Generall amongst us, whose sweettnesse of disposition and spotlesse Conversation is so highly Engaging togather with his most excellent and practicall way of preaching, as hath prevaild even with the very enemies of the Church to bee silent at his deserved aplause, Wee therefore most heartily Lament his leaveing us so soon, but hope for his speedy return (of which wee have obtaind his promise and doubt not of his performance) Assureing your Lordship that in the Interim wee will use our uttmost Endeavours to have all things relateing to the Church in a better posture for his Reception, resolveing to employ our uttmost Interest and zeal to further so Good and Excellent a work by our dilligent zeal wherein wee hope both for the blessing of heaven and the Continuance of your Lordships favour unto us, who have allready been pleased to make us so long partakers of your Lordships bounty.

May the God of all mercyes discharg the great Obligations wee of this poor Province lye under to your Lordship by Multiplying the choicest of his blessings to your Lordship in this life, in earnest of an Everlasting happiness hereafter Is the most sincere and fervent prayer of your Lordships Most affectionate Most Obliged Most Obedient and most humble servants.

John Arderne Church Warden, William Duckenfeild, Edwd. Moseley, Thos. Luton, Nicholas Crisp, Edard Smithwick, Will. Benbury, Wm. Charleton, Thomas Pollock, John Blounte, James Long, Thomas Garrett Church warden

[*Addressed*:]
These
To the Right Honourable
Henry Ld. Bishop of London

[*Endorsed*:]
(118.)
North Carolina
Vestry of Chowan
24 Aug. 1708

DS. Read at a meeting of the SPG on June 3, 1709: "Agreed that this matter be laid before his Grace the Lord ABp. the President [the archbishop of Canterbury, president of the SPG], and that all the papers relating to the ...Gentleman be also laid before his Grace at the same time." Journal of the SPG, I, 389.

[*LAM/SPG/XV*]

Churchwardens of Chowan to Secretary, SPG
1708 September 13

<12>

North Carolina
Chowan precinct the 13th Septbr. 1708

Sir

Wee beleive it our duty in behalf of the Rest of our Vestry whose names are not Subscribed to the within Letter of thanks, to signifie unto you the true reason thereof, which I do assure you proceeded not through any dislike they had to it, but would Readily have Subscribed cold they have been gott togather but liveing Remote and haveing distractions in the Government[1] cold not have the whole body togather, and therefore thought it better wee the Church Wardens alone to Subscribe in behalfe of the whole, than only to have part with us which please to Signifie unto the Right Honourable the Lds. of the Societie that they may not have reason to believe any of our Vestry Lukewarm in making a due return of there humble and unfeighnd thanks. Wee are Sir your most humble and Obliged Servants.

John Arderne Church Warden
Thomas Garrett Church warden

[*Addressed*:]
These To John Chamberlain Esqr.
Secratarie to the Honourable
Societie for the propogateing the
Gospell in Forreighn parts

[*Endorsed:*]
Church Wardens of Chowan
Precinct N. Carolina 13 Sepr. 1708.
Entered

<65>
Church Wardens of Chowan
N. Carolina 13 Septr. 1708.
Entered

LS. The document following was enclosed in the present one.

[1]The Cary Rebellion.

[*LAM/SPG/XV*]

Churchwardens of Chowan to SPG
1708 August 6

<8>

North Carolina Chowan Precinct
the 6th of August 1708

Right Honourable

That the blessed effects of your Lordships pious and Generous favours and noble distributions have found there way into this poor Province into this Remote and obscure corner of the world requires our highest Admiration and Gratitude, by which Its evident to all mankind that no part of the Christian world how mean or obscure, can possibly escape being made partakers of your Lordships bounty and care, A blessing so choice and Valuable and an Obligation so great (if duly Considerd) As might sufficiently excite the most Obdurate and Impenetrable wretches to a true sense and Knowledge of there duty.

My Lords Wee therefore conceive it the least part of our duty by this happy opportunity to pay the reasonable tribute of our humble and unfeighnd thanks for your Lordships Generous Christian and Affectionate Remembrance of us, in the present of books by the Reverend Mr. William Gorden, A Gentleman every way duly qualified to perform an embassaye from such Honourable Employers, who hath not only discharged his trust in the delivery of them, but Likewise Annext his advice thereto, And during his short stay amongst us, hath Indefatigably employd his time and Talent in promoteing the Interest of Religion throughout this Province, but more particularly in this precinct where wee have so far as in us lyes Engaged him to ourselves, and shall Impatiently wait for his return.

My Lds. Our most hearty and sincere wishes are that wee and all other partakers of your Lordships bounty may in some degree bee found worthy of so eminent blessings. May future Ages never want such Renowned Heroes to defend there Christian cause, May your Lordship bee blesst with a happy and florishing poserstie to Inherit your Lordships vertues, and since your Lordships are most dessiredly plact in honourable stations on

Earth, May the Mansions of Saints and Angells bee your portion in heaven, May one Constant scene of health and happinesse attend your Lordships throughout this Vale of tears to your Everlasting home is the most fervent prayers of My Lords your Lordships most Obliged Most humble and Most affectionate Servants.

John Arderne Church Warden
Thomas Garrett Church warden

[*Addressed*:]
These To the Right Honourable
The Societie for Propogateing
the Gospell in Forreighn parts

[*Endorsed*:]
(66)
Churchwardens of Chowain
Precinct N. Carolina 6 Aug. 1708
Entered

LS. Read at a meeting of the SPG on February 11, 1708/9. Journal of the SPG, I, 368. This document was enclosed in the one immediately above.

[*LAM/SPG/XV*]

Rev. James Adams to Secretary, SPG
1708 September 18

N. Carolina Septer. 18th 1708.

Sir

In my Last by Capt. Stuart I wrote you an account among other things what Steps I had made in order to administer the Sacrament of the Lds. Supper to Such as should be religiously dispos'd, but Our unhappy distractions[1] which immediatly followed, and the flame the Countrey has continued in ever Since broke my Measures as to that, and has made me desist till it shall please God to put an end to the Confusion and Contentions the whole province is engag'd in. I shall not trouble you with a long Narrative of the Unhappy Circumstances this Countrey at present Lyes under because Mr. Gordon can inform you by word of Mouth and, I believe, show a Coppy of the true State of this province written by Our president,[2] in whose Sincerity and Integrity you may confide, and who has been no Small Sufferer for his affection to the Church. I Shall only add that in general there are three Sorts of people among us, Many Religious and true Members of our Communion, Some Quakers, and those bred up in ignorance, who neither know nor profess any Religion at all, and of these Last its to be hop'd our Saviour has a plentiful harvest to be reap'd. The Quakers, tho not the 7th part of the Inhabitants, yet by the Assistance and Contrivance of Archdale[3] a Quaker and one of the Lords proprietors, have in a manner the Sole management of the Countrey in their hands, and of late years have at their pleasure procur'd a Revolution of Government as often as ever he that set at the helm Seem'd to favour our Church, or endeavour'd to make any provision for a Ministry, and if the grievances of the Countrey be not speedily redress'd by the proprietors the Quakers in conjunction with the Irreligious (who always, in hopes of preferment side with those who are in a Capacity to promote their Interest) will bear down the Church and in stead of Our makeing proselytes, we shall, I am afraid, be hardly able to keep what we have from being perverted and Seduc'd in this place of so great Ignorance and Enthusiasm; besides we shall be engag'd in perpetual Pereils and Quarrels (as we are at present) for Our old worthy patriots who have for many years bore rule in the Government with great applause, cannot without concern and indignation think of their being turn'd out of the Council and places of Trust, for no other reason but because they are members of the Church of England, and that shoemakers, and Several other Mechanicks shou'd be appointed in their Room meerly because they are Quaker preachers and notorious Blasphemers of the Church, Some of which have declar'd that till the Prince of Wales be prov'd a bastard the Queen Can have no pretensions to the Crown of England. We are in hopes the Lds. have been impos'd upon by Archdale, and that we shall be redress'd from England according to the Charter and Laws of Our Countrey.

In the mean time I shall by the Grace of God endeavour to behave myself with such moderation, diligence and fidelity as not in any respect to prejudice the good Cause I have in hand. That part of the Countrey where I am concern'd design'd by this Fleet to have sent an Adress of Thanks to the Society for my being Sent among them but at my request they have desisted till our Animosities and heats (which already have not been without blood) be compos'd, and I give a further proof of my Ministry. That I may punctualy observe your Instructions and Commands shall be the constant and faithfull endeavour of Sir Your most humble Servant.

James Adams

I desir'd in my Last that what instructions you shall send me at any time may be directed to the care of Mr. Wallace Minister at Kikaton in Virginia.

[*Addressed:*]
To John Chamberlayne Esqr.
at his house in petty france
Westminster London This

[*Endorsed:*]
(60.)
Mr. Adames N. Carolina
18 Sept. 1708
Entered

ALS. Read at a meeting of the SPG on February 11, 1708/9, when it was ordered "that the Secretary do write the said Mr. Adams, and desire to know the Reason of Mr. Gordon's returning from thence without leave, and of the State of the Church." Journal of the SPG, I, 368.

[1]The Cary Rebellion.

[2]William Glover.

[3]John Archdale (1642-ca. 1710), an English convert to Quakerism, acquired through purchase the Lord Berkeley of Stratton proprietary share of Carolina in 1678. He spent several years in the province in the 1680s, acting on several occasions as governor of the northern part. In 1695 he arrived in Charleston as governor, but returned to England following the sale of his proprietary share the following year. In 1705 he purchased the Sir William Berkeley share of Carolina and took an active role in proceedings at the proprietary board until his sale of the share three years later. *DNCB.*

[*SPG/A/4*]

William Glover to Bishop of London
1708 September 25

<CXIX> Governor Glover to the Lord Bp. of London

My Lord,

Besides my own Obligations of duty and Gratitude, I am ingaged by the repeated Application of many of the Inhabitants of this place to offer to Your Lordships care over us and especially in behalf of the Parish of Pascotank where an Orderly Congregation has been kept together by the Industry of a Young Gentleman[1] whom the Parish employed to read the Service of the Church as the Law of this place for want of a Minister doth direct: This Gentleman being of an unblemished life by his decent behaviour in that Office and by apt discourses from house to house according to the Capacitys of an ignorant people not only kept those he found but gain'd many to the Church in the midst of it's enemies, insomuch that the Reverend Richd. Marsden waiting here for a Passage to S. Carolina thought it convenient to administer the Sacrament of the Lord's Supper which is the first time I can learn of its being Administred in this poor Country this was done on Trinity Sunday 1706 and the same day 45 Persons infants and Adults were baptised. If any thing My Lord in this life was able to raise in my Breast a Joy without mixture it was to see unbaptised Parents with their Children in their Arms offering themselves to Christ which I have seen and therefore I ever will rejoyce. This with the adjacent Parish of Caratuck is now under the Cure of the Reverend James Adams to their general Satisfaction whom they have presented to the Small Provision of £30 per annum in each, which our Law appoints. The Reverend Wm. Gordon did not find things in so good Order in the other two Parishes of Chowan and Paquimons yet I hope the Account he will give of his reception will be in some measure satisfactory: It lyeth somewhat on me to make an Apology for the Vestry of Paquimans where I live, it is the place where Quakerism has mostly prevail'd and thereby most attended with difficultys for which Cause their vestry Adjourn'd their Meeting to have gained the little Advantage of my Company till time insensibly slipt from them whilst I was ingaged in the unhappy troubles, which the enemy, alarm'd at the coming over of these worthy Gentlemen, has raised against me under which I still labour with patience till the Lords Proprietors shall apply some Remedy to the present disorders to whom I have faithfully represented the whole matter by the Reverend W. Gordon who is the bearer hereof (whilst we bewail his absence here) Your Lordship will have a more particular Account of the State of

Affairs, as also a Copy of the Act[2] pass't here relating to the Church of which there is one great Error which was not in my power to prevent (videlicet) the Subjecting the Clergy to be judged by Laymen, altho' that Clause was never interpreted even by the most Zealous asserters of it to extend to a power of displacing those who were orderly presented and Inducted; but only such as came by chance and were Agreed with from Year to year as the manner has been formerly among our neighbours of Virginia; I shall only add further that that Clause had not bin thought of by the Composers of that Law had not the disorderly behaviour of Mr. Brett given the Occasion. I most earnestly begg Your Lordship's pardon for this trouble and yr. prayers for this poor Country and in it for me the most unworthy Your Lordships Most dutyfull and ever Bounden Servant.

W. Glover

Hampton in Virginia
25th Septemb. 1708.

Copy. Read at a meeting of the SPG on June 3, 1709. Journal of the SPG, I, 388.

[1]Not identified.
[2]Not located.

[*SPG/A/4*]

William Glover to SPG
ca. 1708 September

<LXVI> Governor Glover to the Society

My Lords.

The pious regard your Lordships have shewn to this poor remote Countrey demands a return of thankfulness as far above my Abilities as your bountifull Charity is above our deserts but how little soever we deserve our necessity was great and crying to the relief of which the help which your Lordships have sent over is so reasonable and the Labourers so worthy of their great employment that we must own the whole work to have been directed by the Lord of the Harvest who will we hope bless and defend his own work against all the Attempts of the Enemy till by your Lordships pious and noble endeavor's and in imitation of your Lordships Zeal, Wee and all who call themselves Christians laying aside all unhappy strifes and differences become one Society for propagating the Gospel of our Lord Jesus Christ which is the earnest and dayly prayers of Your Lordships Most bounden and Most humble Servant.

W. Glover.

Copy. Apparently the undated letter from Glover read at a meeting of the SPG on December 17, 1708. Journal of the SPG, I, 357.

[*SPG/A/4*]

Rev. William Gordon to Secretary, SPG
1708 December 13

<LXI> Mr. Gordon to the Secretary

Monday 13th decr. 1708.

Sir.

I am just Arrived from Carolina in a weak though hearty Condition, the distractions among the people, and other intollerable inconveniencies in that Colony has force'd me from them so soon, both against my design and inclinations; if I be able to come abroad I shall wait on the Honorable Society next Monday, in the mean time I thought it fit to send those Letters by the Bearer which please to receive and excuse these abrupt Lines from Your very Humble Servant.

Will. Gordon

Directions are
To Jno. Chamberlayne Esq.
at St. Pauls.

Copy. Read at a meeting of the Committee on December 13, 1708. Journal of the Committee of the SPG.

[*PC 31.2*]

Thomas Pollock to Rev. William Gordon
ca. 1709

A Copy of A letter to Mr. Gordon minister att Cho[wan] inclosed in Mr. Glo[ver's] letter to be sealed and delivered to him att [*torn*] by him

Sir

Since ye went from us confusion and disorder have proceeded in ther full career of which President G[lover] can give you a full account. And I doubt nott the justness of the cause. The zeall you have for [*torn*] religion And the Charity ye have for the So[uls of] the people of North Carolina who are now ec[lipsed] with the darke clouds of quakarisme, Envy, and ignorance will prompt yow to use your uttermost [en]deavore to be help full whatt ye can to dispel aforesaid clouds thatt agane wee may injoy the Sunshine of religion; justice and order which you [*torn*] should then be highly pleased to injoy the [*torn*] of your company here and yow may assure [*torn*] to command all thatt lyes in my Power. I would intreatt the favor of yow to acquant me by all [junctures] of the proceeding in thatt affaire which [*torn*] infinitly obleidge. Sir yr.

T. P.

Sir

Please to direct your letters to me to be left att Mr. Mongo Engless's att queens creek near yorke[1] River. Mr. James Wallace Minister at kocotan or Captain Ritchd. Exums house near Nansemom River. Sir yrs.

T. P.

Copy. Thomas Pollock (1654-1722), a Scot from Glasgow who arrived in the colony as a merchant and proprietary deputy in 1683, was a large landowner prominent in the colony's political life. A long-time member of the council, and on several occasions its president, he held a variety of offices over the course of his career and was also an unswerving upholder of the Anglican interest. *DNCB.*

[1]*James* written and struck through.

[*LAM/SPG/XV*]

Report
[1709 January]

<16> I being Employ'd by this Right Reverend and Honorable Society to exercise my Minesterial function in the Province of North Carolina in Septembr. 1707 did Set out from London in October following. We Sail'd from Bristoll the 27th of November but by bad weather and cross winds, were forc'd into Kingsale in Ireland Decembr. the 2d. On the 10th of Janry. 1707/8 we put to Sea again and after a very Severe passage, arriv'd within the Capes of Virginia the last day of March 1708.

As soon as I got my bookes etc. ashore and a passage for them by Sea to Carolina, I took my Jorney by Land, but before I could reach the first house in that Countrey, my horse being a Virginian, and unaccustom'd to the rugged roades of these parts, founder'd upon all foures Which put me to Some inconvenience being oblig'd either to Stay there for his recovery or pay a very extravagant rate for fresh horses and a New guid; this last I chose being equally desirous of comeing to the end of my Jorney and entering upon my bussines, So went on twenty miles further to the next house, where I was furnish'd with a new Companion who carried me to one Mr. Moseley's house upon Albemarle Sound in the Precinct of Chowan by whose Assistance I got a passage to Mr. Glover President of the Council, where I arriv'd on Saturday the 24th of Aprll. The next morning Mr. Glover went with us to Pasquetank about twelve miles from his house (the worst of roades) where at Mr. Adam's desire I preach'd to a Congregation of about a hundred People in the house of one Mr. Lamarr, Mr. Adams haveing befor read Prayers and Baptis'd Some Children. On Monday I return'd with the President finding Mr. Adams inclin'd to Setle in that Precinct (which indeed is the best in that Countrey) and from his house got passage back to Mr. Moseley's. The Sunday following I read Prayers and Preach'd in a Church about four miles distant from thence on Wednesday May the 5th I mett the Vestry at the Same place where (after many kind offers made me if I would take charge of their Precinct only) I declar'd my resolution of attending both them and Paquimans, which I did accordingly dureing my Stay, tho' I must own Summer weather made that practicable which in Winter would be impossible.

I had no other designe at first then to Stay for Some yeares in these parts. The prevaileing ignorance of the most of the People, with the just Sence Some Seem'd to have of their condition, and the good inclination attending it, not to mention particular kind offers, would easily have prevaild with me, to have continued in the Same mind had not the many inconveniencies and hardships of that Region (which I Shall not here insist upon) overballanc'd these considerations and by degrees made my life more and more uneasie, for finding and old distemper with which I have formerly been afflicted recurr upon me, my Stomach faile, my Sleep forsake me, my flesh wast and my whole constitution altered for the worse, no remedies at hand, nor a Physitian in the Countrey, I could not but dread the consequences of Such Symptoms and doe that which to the best of my judgement I thought would be for the Interest of the Honorable Society, my People and my Selfe, as for my Selfe I cannot but acknowledge I am so farr Man as to have a Sence of that common principle of Self preservation, and so farr a husband as to be affraid what Calamities might come upon my Wife after my untimely death there, And I Saw not how it could be for the Advantage of those committed to my Charge or to the Satisfaction of the Society, for me to Languish out a Sickly life in an Air destructive to my constitution, uncapable of performing any part of what might be expected from me burthensome to my People, and consequently unacceptable and expensive to the Society, when I might be better Serviceable to myself and them by a Speedy returne, whereby I might recover my health according as I Should recover the European Air, and the People might be Supplyed with a Missionary every way better qualified, and this I thought would be at once least chargeable to the Society, and most beneficial to those People. So I Left the place about the beginning of September (allmost a year after my Entering into that Service) At which time the fleet were just ready to Saile from Virginia to Great Brittain.

But this Reverend and Honorable Board haveing requir'd the reasons of my Leaveing that Province without first acquainting them and without <17> their order for my returne, I humbly crave leave to informe them that as I am very Sensible it was my duty to advertise them by all Opportunities of the Effects and Success of my mission so in this I did not willingly faile, haveing written Letters both to them and the Right Reverend Father in God Henry Lord Bishop of London which with Some others about my own private concerns, I Sent in to Virginia to be forwarded in that fleet which Sail'd about the end of June or beginning of July under convoy of her Majesties Ship Guardland Capt. Charles Stewart Commander, these Letters tho' Sent in time were either by the carelessness or forgetfullness of the Gentleman to whom I recommended them (notwithstanding his repeated promises to me) left undeliver'd and to my Surprise as well as loss they came to my hands again when I arriv'd in Virginia in order for my Passage home, and this is the true reason why not only the Honorable Society, but my friends at home had no account from me after my Arrival in the Province of Carolina.

Nor Should I have acted So Seemingly contrary to their Expectation as to have left the Station wherein I was placed by them, without their consent first obtain'd but that considering the distance between this place and Carolina, with the State of my fleeting health it seem'd more then Probable that I might be laid in my grave befor their answer to my Letter could reach the place of my residence.

As to the bringing Certificates of my Sickly condition, I must confess it did not enter into my mind, the distracted circumstances the People were in the Last part of my time, with the Presidents continuall hurry made me forget many things I have Since thought would have been both usefull and necessary but I am Sure I brought too Authentick a certificate of it in my own person, Tho' God in his mercy has restor'd me Sooner then I did or could expect, and as to the truth Of my Illness there I might very well alledge what to my friends and relations at Least is plain demonstration, Since by comeing back so soon I have acted contrary to my visible Interest, in Leaveing a Countrey (where besides the kindness of the People to me, I had a prospect of bettering my Subsistance by degrees;) By hazarding the Loss of the favourable oppinion and of incurring the displeasure of the most Venerable body of men that ever (Since the Apostles) Join'd their Endeavours in the Promotion of Religion, and Exposeing my Self to the rigours of So long and tedious a voyage in the winter Season in danger of being taken by the French on the one hand, and Loseing the Stipend allowed Me by the Society on the other. And what could prevaile with any man to do this, I cannot tell besides a desire to recover Lost health; which was not neither the only motive prevailing with me, Since I found that the service of that People and of the Society requir'd another to be put into my Station, as soon as might be, in case I Should not be able to discharge the trust repos'd in me by both according to my duty; and as I allwayes Look'd upon the Societies money to be the Price of the Soules of these poor Creatures, So I Should justly pull down a curse upon me and Mine if I did not there performe in my own Person the Offices of that Minestry which I had undertaken.

This May it please your Lordships etc. is a true Narrative of the State of my case, and of the reasons induceing me to returne Sooner then was expected, I Shall only add that as at your Commands I undertooke that voyage, and charge upon me So nothing but the preceeding considerations could have prevail'd with me to leave these pour Soules befor I had Seen Somewhat of the Good Effects, with which I was in hopes God would have bless'd my endeavours, tho' Sown in much weakness. As to my life and conversation with the constant Exercise of the Several duties of my Function upon all occasions dureing my Stay there I forbear to mention them my Selfe and therefor doe referr to the Testimonialls given of me by others. I humbly Submitting them, this Short account, and my Self to your Just and wise Consideration.

William Gordon

[*Endorsed*:]
Mr. Gordon's Case

DS. Gordon attended a meeting of the SPG on December 17, 1708, when he "was call'd in and asked the Reasons of his Returning, and after some Small Account given thereof he was directed to put in writing what he could say, against next Meeting." Journal of the SPG, I, 357. At a meeting on June 17, 1709, "The Secretary reported that he had according to Order laid before the Lord ABp. [of Canterbury] all the papers relating to Mr. Gordon and that they are now under his Graces Consideration." Journal of the SPG, I, 391.

[*SPG/Jou/1*]

Journal of the SPG
1708/9 January 21

<363> 21th January 1708-9. [...]

3. The Secretary acquainted the Bord that Mr. Gordon attended with his Case on Reasons for returning from N. Carolina (according to Order) then the said Case was read, and Mr. Gordon was call'd in and discourst about the said Matter, and the Standing Orders relating to Missionaries withdrawing themselves from the Service of the Society without leave[1] being also read: Agreed that the Salary of the said Mr. Gordon be paid till Michaelmas last being the time he left Carolina, but that the Treasurer do detain in his hands the Sum of Ten pounds, till the Society be satisfy'd that their Books are Secure. [...]

Minutes.

[1]Standing Order XV stated that "if any Missionary, in the Service of the Society, shall return from the Plantations, without Leave first had from the Society, such Missionary shall receive no farther Allowance, from the time he shall leave his Service there." *Standing Orders of the Society for the Propagation of the Gospel in Foreign Parts*, n.d., 14.

[*LAM/SPG/VIII*]

Bishop of London to Secretary, SPG
1709 March 29

<84> Sir

You know, how hard it will be in a very little time to send any Missionaryes over to the Plantations, this being the Season, when all the ships bound that way, are making what hast they can to gett off: And Since there are so many Missionaryes wanting, I think we ought to embrace this Gentleman Mr. Reynolds for one, who is so very well recommended. And therefore for the Sake of Dispatch, I could wish the weekly Committee would take him to Task for his Probation; that he may be the more easily dispatcht at the monthly meeting. I am Sir your most humble Servant.

H. London

If you could direct me, where to find Mr. Gordon, who came lately from North Carolina, it may prove to his Satisfaction and the Content of the Society.

[*Addressed*:]
For John Chamberlayne Esqr.

at his house in Petty France
Westminster

[*Endorsed:*]
(89)
Lord Bishop of London
29 March 1709
<*Entered*>

ALS.

[*SPG/Jou/1*]

Journal of the SPG
1709 April 15

<376> 15th April 1709. [...]
1. Col. Tynte the Governor of S. Carolina, and Col. Hyde[1] the Governor of N. Carolina proposed the first time for Members of the Society. [...]

Minutes.

[1]Edward Hyde (1667-September, 1712), a distant relation of Queen Anne, was apppointed by the Lords Proprietors deputy governor of Carolina in 1709. Due to the death of Edward Tynte, governor of Carolina and the other person nominated for membership in the SPG at this meeting of the Society, Hyde was unable to procure a commission upon his arrival from England in August, 1710. This lack of proper credentials helped to precipitate armed rebellion by the followers of Thomas Cary, a conflict that was not put down until July, 1711. In 1712 the proprietors erected a separate colony of North Carolina and appointed Hyde governor.

Edward Hyde and Edward Tynte were proposed for membership for a second time at a meeting of May 20, and elected at a meeting of June 3. Journal of the SPG, I, 382, 388.

[*LAM/SPG/XV*]

Testimonial
1709 May 4

These are to Certifie whom it may concern, that Jno. Urmston[1] Clerk, the Bearer hereof, hath faithfully and well discharged the Duty of Curate of East Ham in the County of Essex these three years last past, his life and conversation, hath been pious, sober and exemplar, and we verily believe hath conform'd in all things to the Rubrick of the Common Prayer Book and done all that his Function requireth of him. Witness our hands. May 4th 1709.

Stephen Robins Vicar of East Ham
John Chisenhale
Vicar of Barking

[*Endorsed:*]
[126]
Mr. Urmstone's Testim[onial]

DS.

[1]Rev. John Urmston. See appendix.

[*LAM/SPG/XV*]

Rev. William Gordon to SPG
1709 May 13

<18> I have already deliver'd to your Honorable Board a Short account of my Voyage and Journey to No. Carolina, the Effects of my Mission; and the Reasons which induc'd me to leave the Place. And Since you desire to know Something further of the State of the Countrey and condition of the People in relation to their Religion, Principles, and Practice, I Shall (by the help of the Clossest and Justest Observations I could make and the best Informations I could get dureing my travels through that Countrey) give you what Satisfaction can be reasonably Expected from So Short a Stay.

The Continent of North Carolina is part of that great tract of Land granted by King Cha. IId to several Lords Proprietors whose Successours and present Possessors are William Lord Craven, his Grace Hen. Duke of Beaufort, John Lord Carteret, Maurice Ashley Esqr. Sir John Colleton Bart. John Danson Esqr. being in Number Eight.[1]

There are few or no Dissenters in this Goverment but Quakers who have been allwayes the greatest Sticklars against, and constant opposers of the Church, and that with no small Success it will not therefore be improper to trace their Rise with the Priviledges and Immunities they Still plead and contend for at this day, to the great disturbance of the Peace of that Province, and the Hinderance of good Lawes and other proper Endeavours for its' Improvement.

From the first Setlement (I find) for Some yeares, they were but few in number and had litle or no Interest in the Goverment, untill John Archdale Proprietor and Quaker went over; by whose meanes some were made Councelors, and there being then no Ministers in the place they began to increase and grow Powerfull; For the Council granting all commissions, in a Short time they had Quaker members in most of their Courts, nay in Some the Majority were Such, who Still pushing at the Goverment were very diligent at the Election of Members of the Assembly; So that what by themselves, the Assistance of Several unthinking People, and the Carelessness of Others, they carried all in that meeting likewise, So far that no Encouragement could be obtain'd for Ministers notwithstanding Some endeavours which were us'd to procure them a very Small and inconsiderable allowance.

At Last after many Attempts the Church men Carried an Act but by one or two Votes call'd the Vestry Act,[2] by which twelve Vestry men are to be Chosen in every Precinct, who have power to build a Church in Each and to raise money from the Inhabitants for that Purpose with a Sume not Exceeding thirty pound per An. for a Minister, whom they likewise have (by that act) power, not only to disprove but displace if they See Cause, I took a Copie of it, and of Some other papers, but my Servant and trunck being Left behind by an accident they are not yet come to my hand.

The Church Party thought they had now made a good Step and therefor design'd to Improve it to the Advantage of Religion and, Setting Such a regular Church discipline as the Lords Proprietors were oblig'd by their Charter to countenance and Encourage, but herein they mett with Constant Oppisition from the Quakers, who being Still Powerfull in the Council, numorous in the Assembly, and Restless in their Endeavours, Spared neither Paine nor Expence to have this Act repeal'd or Alter'd and by there continnue Cavills and disputes Lengthen'd out the time of the Assembly's Setting to their great Trouble and Charge.

In the year 1704 the Law made in the first year of the Reign of her Present Majestie Intitled an Act to declare the Oath comeing in place of the Abrogated Oaths etc.[3] reach'd Carolina; which the Quakers refuseing to take, they were dissmissd the Council, Assembly and Courts of Justice and a Law made that none Should bear any Office or Place of Trust without takeing the Said Oaths.

Some time After the Quakers Sent Complaints against Collonell Daniel[4] then Governour deputed by Sir Nathll. Johnson[5] in South Carolina, they Prevaile, Sir Nathll. removes him and Sends one Collonell Cary[6] in his room.

The Quakers then begin their old Game, and Strive to get in to the Courts and Assembly again, this Governour hereupon tenders them the oaths which they refuseing to take are again dissmissd and an Act[7] made that whoever Should promote his own Election or Set and Act, not quallifieing him Self first by takeing the Oaths Should forfeit five Pound. This so netled the Quakers that in the year 1706 they Sent one Mr. John Porter[8] to England with fresh greivances and New Complaints to the Lords Proprietors, who by his cunning Managment and the help of Mr. Archdale a Quaker Proprietor, Obtain'd a New Commission, by virtue whereof Sir Nathll. Johnson's power in that Province was Suspended, Collonell Cary removed, and Several new Deputations Sent by the Proprietors, with Power to Choose a President among them Selves, thus Porter haveing procur'd a Deputation for him Self, and Some other Quakers, arriv'd in Carolina Octobr. 1707 about five months befor we reach'd Virginia.

And here Sir I could give you a Large account of this mans managment and the use he made of this new Commission, with his many tricks to advance the Interest of the Quaker's, and the Confusion and Disturbance of which he was the Chief Or only Occasion. But this would be as tedious as his actions were in them Selves, unwarrantable.

In Short Sir As soon as he arriv'd he calls the new Deputies together being most Quakers (without waiting for the Governour and Old Deputies presence tho' they had all appointed a day for the whole Council to Sit and Setle the Goverment according to the Lords Proprietors Instructions in that Commission) and Chooses for their President one Mr. Glover whom they imagin'd would be for their purpose, but he takeing the Same Method as the former Governours did, Dissapointed Porters Expectation, who for revenge gets a meeting with both old and new Deputies reverses Glovers Election, declaring it illegal and so void and Null tho' he was the only Promoter of it. The President and Collonell Pollock a Councelour protested against these proceedings, but Porter went on, Stricts in with Collonell Cary the Late Deputy Governour whom he had by his complaints turn'd out, chooses him President, by the votes of the very Same Councelours Who had befor chosen Mr. Glover and all this by Virtue of that very commission which removed him from the Goverment. From this Sprung the Great confusions in which I left that poor Distracted Collony, there were two Competitors for command, each drew their Party in armes to the field one man was killd befor I came away and God knowes how far they have carried these contentions Since.

I did at my Arrival in England Lay the whole State of these affaires befor the Lords Proprietors who no doubt will take a Speedy and Effectual method not only to Suppress the present, but prevent Such Dissorders for the future, and there is now a Gentleman Appointed Governour[9] of that Province who by his Prudence will in all liklyhood cool the Present heats, and lead them on gently towards a regular and Lasting Establishment to the Advantage of the Proprietors and Peace of the Countrey.

<19> And Now Sir I Shall examin a little the Quakers Pretences, who Plead that they were the first Setlers in that Countrey but this (according to the best accounts I could get) Seems false in fact, That Religion being Scarse hear'd of there 'till Some yeares after the Setlement it's true Some of the most ancient Inhabitants after George Fox went over did turne Quakers.

2d. They Alleadge they are the Cheif Inhabitants, promoters and upholders of it's interest, but this must be either by their number, riches or Prudence, as to their number they are at this time but about the tenth part of the Inhabitants and if they were more, they would be but the greater burthen; Since they contribute nothing towards its defence, neither is it by their riches, their being but few or no traders of note amongst them: besides the Levy there is rais'd per poll and not by the Estimate of Mens Estates, So that the Poorest pay as much as the Richest, and it is So farr from being by their Prudence that on the Contrary their Ignorance and obstinacy is but too remarkable upon all occassions. Of which they have given So very evident proofe by being the great Promoters of the Present Confusions of that Collony So that I see no right they have to Such a Share in the Goverment as they Pretend. The Charter[10] I am Sure grants them none, nor does it give power to the Lords Proprietors to grant any, neither have they by their Constitution[11] done any Such thing, and if there be any Priviledges granted to the Inhabitants, it is to Such only as bear armes So that it was other Dissenters not Quakers they intended to invite thither by those Indulgencies. As for Liberty of Conscience, none may more peaceably Enjoy it if they would be therewith content.

I could not but take notice of their Irreverent Carriadge in Subscribeing their Sollemn Affermation, Mr. Archdale himself has uncover'd his head to hear a foolish woman make an unaccountable Clamour befor meat at his own table, but when he Subscrib'd the oaths to be taken for putting in Execution the Lawes of trade he did it with his Hat on, which is an Error no Barclay has made an Appology for. I have observ'd amongst the worst of the other Sort when they came to the book they Show'd a reverence, and there appear'd an Awfullness upon them which Serves the great end of God and the Queen in the

Discovery of truth, whilst the careless and unseemly behaviour of these men is openly Scandalous and Profane.

I Shall now Sir Give you Some Small account of the particular Precincts you'll See by the Plain Draught[12] the Largeness of So much of the Countrey as is laid down the Bearings of the Land, and Number of tythables in each Precinct, The Roades are Generally very bad especially in Paquimans and Pasquetank which makes it a very troublesom work for one Minister to attend two Precincts.

Chowan is the Westermost the Largest and thinest Seated, they built a Church Some yeares agoe but it is Small, very Sorrily put together, and as ill lookd after, and therefor I prevail'd with them to build an other, which they went about when I came away. The Plan of it I brought over and was desir'd to procure if Possible from the Society as much glass as will be Necessary for the windowes, which by computation will amount to 325 feet.

There is I think no Quakers or any other Dissenters in this Parish, the People indeed are Ignorant there being few that can read and fewer write even of their Justices of Peace and Vestry men, Yet to me they Seem'd very Serious and well inclin'd both in Publick and Private; many of them being very ready to Embrace (as far as they could) all Opportunities of being instructed, the worst is that the narrowness of their Sence and Conceptions, occasion many differences and Quarrels amongst themselves, for which no man can find any Shadow of reason, but their ignorant mistakes of one anothers meaning, and upon this account I found these more frequent here then in any Countrey I have yet travel'd.

This Precinct was one of the two I attended and being very large, and devided by the great Sound and Severall rivers and Branches was very troublesom however I was in all the Parts of it baptis'd allmost a hundred Children, distributed those small tracts which were Sent over, Setled a Schoolmaster,[13] and gave Some books for the use of Scholars, which the Church Wardens were to See left for that use, in case the Master Should remove. The greatest difficulty I mett with was, in Some an Obstinate aversion to Godfathers and Godmothers neither Sence nor reason could prevaile with them; In this therefor I bent my Strongest endeavours, with one or two, who by their Caracter for Sence and Sobriety had Some Influence over the rest, with whom haveing prevail'd, all were convinc'd and follow'd their example and So they would often times in any thing Else without examining the Cause or troubleing themselves for reasons; This being a general rule for their Practice in all other (to them) doubtfull cases. However I am Confident they are yet by the blessing of God on the Pious care and Prudent Conduct of Some diligent Minister, in a Capacity of being made Devout Christians and Zealous Churchmen whereas if they be Let allon the Principles and (It's to be fear'd) the Practice too of Religion and Morality will be in a Short time quite defac'd.

The next Precinct is Paquimans under my care equally with the other. Here is a Compact little Church built with more Care and Expence and better contriv'd then that in Chowan it continues yet unfinish'd by the Death of one Major Swan[14] about Septembr. 1707 who Zealously promoted the Interest of Religion in general, and forwarded by his continual pains and expence the building of that Church in Particular when there was none in the Countrey, Here is no Library or other Publick bookes whatsoever.

The Quakers In this Precinct are very numerous, Extreamly Ignorant unsufferably Proud and Ambitious and Consequently very ungovernable. This made my work more difficult then it was in Chowan. They doubled their Efforts and Contrivances against my

Endeavoures; their Meetings amongst themselves were more frequent, and their Attacks upon others More furious, however as those things cost me the more Paines, So I us'd the utmost Circumspection both in Publick and Private, and If at any time I took occasion to Preach against <20> their Principles as now and then I found it necessary; I was as moderate as was possible in my Expressions free [*torn*] harsh Reflections and allwayes press'd the truth as much for it's own Sake as for [the] Church's which Profess'd it. And this I found had a better Effect then the rougher methods which it seemes had been formerly us'd with them, for by such meanes, and the Success of Some Small favoures I Shewed them in Physick, they not only became very civil but respectfull to me in their way, and have many times entertain'd me at their houses with much freedome and Kindness.

This Precinct is not So large as Chowain and tho' the roades are worse, the Jorneyes are Shorter. There are twelve Vestry-men as in the rest, but most if not all of them very ignorant, Loose in their Lives, and unconcern'd as to Religion. It was not in my Power to get one meeting with them, while I was there, notwithstanding my best Endeavours to obtain that favour. Their Ill Example and the want of Ministers and good Books has Occasion'd many who were better Dispos'd tho' Ignorant to Join with the Quakers; Being willing to embrace anything that Lookes like a Religion rather then none at all, yet I am Apt to think that Some of these poor Souls may be regain'd Several haveing told me they ow'd their first departing from the Church to the Ill Example and Imprudent Behaviour of their Ministers; And therefor it Seemes absolutely necessary, that if any Missionary be Sent thither, he Should if Possible be Endowed with more then common Prudence besides an Examplary Life, and diligent Attendance on all the Duties of his Function. He should be as well read in Men as in Books and will find as much if not more Occasion for the one than th'other. And as he will meet with unaccountable Tempers, So they will require uncommon Methods to deal with them, in order to gain Credit and Consequently an Access to their Hearts. Here and In Chowan the wayes of Liveing are much alike, both are equally destitute of good Water most of that being breakish and Muddy. They feed generally upon Salt Pork and Some times upon Beef their Bread of Indian Corn which they are forc'd for want of Mills to beat. And in this they are So Careless and uncleanly that their is but Litle Difference between the Corn in the Horse Manger and the Bread on their tables; So that with Such Provisions and Such drink (for they have no Beer) in Such a hot Countrey, you may Easily judge Sir what a Comfortable Life a man must Lead; not but that the Place is capable of Better things were it not overrun With Sloath and Poverty.

The next Precinct is Pasquotank where as yet there is no Church built, the Quakers are Here very numerous. The Roades are I think the worst in the Countrey, but it's closser Seated then the Others and better Peopled in Proportion to it's Bigness. In their way of Liveing they have much the Advantage of the rest, being more Industrious carefull and Cleanly; but above all I was Surpris'd to See with what Order Decency and Seriousness they Perform'd the Publick Worship considering how ignorant People are in the Other Parishes. This they Ow to the Care of one Mr. Griffin[15] who came there from Some Part Of the West Indies and has for three yeares past lived amongst them, being Appointed Reader by their Vestry; whose diligent Instructions and Devout Example has Improved them So far beyond their Neighbours and by his descreet Behaviour has gaind Such a general Good Caractor and Esteem; That the Quakers themselves Send their Children to his School, tho' he has Prayers twice a Day at Least and Oblig'd them to their Responses and all the Decencies of Behaviour as well as Others. After Mr. Adams was Setled here I found it Improper for Mr. Griffin to Stay, and therefor notwithstanding the Large Offers they Made him if he would continue, He consented to fix in Chowan. There I Left him, haveing Procur'd for him a Small Allowance from the Vestry; But I'm Affraid the hardships he'll meet with in that Part of the Countrey, will Discourage him if not force him from thence, Tho' he Promis'd me to hold out as Long as he Could.

Coratuck is the Eastermost Precinct includeing the Sand Banks, and Some Part of the South Side of the Sound. A very Incommodious Place for Damp Colds in Winter and Musqueeto's in Summer, I never travel'd through this Parish, So I can give but a very Litle Acct. of it. They have no Church nor ever had any bookes Sent them. Mr. Adams has at present under his care this Precinct and Pasquetank, from whom an Account at Large may be best Expected.

Bath-County Containes most of that Land which Lyes to the Southward of Albemarle Sound to Pamtico River and About thirty or forty Miles more Southerly to Nues River which (being but Lately Peopled with a few French who Left Virginia) is not Laid down in the Draught.

They have Devided the whole into three Precincts or Parishes, tho' the Inhabitants of all are but equal in number to any one of the Other, most of Which are Seated on Pamtico river and it's Branches. Here is no Church tho' they have begun to build a Town call'd Bath, it consists of about twelve houses being the Only town in the whole Province. They have a Small Collection of Books for a Library which were Carried over by the Reverend Doctor Bray, and Some Land is laid out for a Glebe. But no Minister would ever Stay Long on the Place, tho' Several has come thither from the West Indies and Other Plantations in America, And yet I must own it is not the unpleasentest part of the Countrey, Nay in all probability it will be the Center of trade, as haveing the Advantage of a Better Inlet for Shiping, and Serrounded with most Pleasant Savenna's very usefull for Stocks of Catle.

In this as in all other Parts of the Province there is no money every one Buyes and Payes with their own Commodities of which Corn Pork, Pitch and Tarr are the Chief, Pork at 45*s*. per Barrell Cont. 250 P. Weight, Pitch at 25*s*. per Barrell Corne at 20*s*. per Bushall and Tarr at 12 Shillings per Barrell which Prices (tho Rec'd. by their Lawes) they can Seldom reach for it any where else, after Considerable Expence and Risque So that by their Computation, the Difference of their Money to Sterling is as one to three. And if you buy a Plantation, there for £300 of their Pay they'll much rather take £100 in England. <21> Thus Sir I have in Obedience to your Commands give you this plain and (I'm Sensible) Imperfect acct. in North Carolina a Countrey but wild and Imperfect in its' Circumstances. And in all I have Said to the dissadvantag of the People in General I must beg Some Exceptions, as few as you please. There being here and there a Gentleman whose Substance, Sense in Manadging, And Methods of liveing Somewhat Exceed the rest, but they live at Such Distances that as by their Example they have but Litle Influence, So upon the Same Account they can as Litle Contribute to the Easiness of a Missionar's condition who is forc'd to take up with what conveniencies he can find not too many miles distant from the Churches he is oblig'd to Attend. And this will Necessitate any Minister who goes over to purchase Land, Buy Servants, Build a House and improve a Plantation, befor he can live tollerably, which will require more Expence then the Encouragement given will bear. If Sir you think this worth Communicating to the Honorable Society I Leave it to your Discretion, and Am Sir Your very Humble and Obedient Servant.

William Gordon

London May 13, 1709

[*Endorsed*:]
(105)
Mr. Gordon London
13th May 1709.

DS. At a meeting of the SPG on May 20, 1709, the secretary "acquainted the Bord that the Lord Bp. of London had directed him to lay several papers and Letters (given him by Mr. Gordon and relating to the Affaires and State of the Church in N. Carolina) before the Society.... Order'd that all the said Letters and papers be refer'd to the Committee and they to report their Opinion of the same at the next Meeting of this Society." Journal of the SPG, I, 381.

[1]Missing from this list is the proprietary share held by Joseph Blake, as well as the share in contention between Ann and Nicholas Trott, and James and Henry Bertie. Powell, *Proprietors of Carolina*, 10.

[2]This act of 1701 has not been located.

[3]1 Anne, cap. 22, "An Act to Declare the Alterations in the Oath Appointed to be Taken... for the Further Security of Her Majesty's Person and the Succession of the Crown in the Protestant Line; and for Extinguishing the Hopes of the Pretended Prince of Wales...."

[4]Robert Daniel (d. 1718), a prominent South Carolina political figure, military leader, and loyal churchman who served as deputy governor of North Carolina July, 1703-March, 1705. *DNCB*.

[5]Governor of Carolina, 1702-1708.

[6]Thomas Cary (d. ca. 1720) succeeded Robert Daniel as deputy governor of North Carolina in March, 1705. Cary was at first in alliance with the church party, and dissenters effected his replacement by William Glover as president of the council in October, 1707. Glover broke with the dissenters in 1708, whereupon Cary joined with them and became president. The arrival in Virginia in August, 1710, of Edward Hyde as deputy governor of North Carolina precipitated an armed conflict that was resolved in Hyde's favor in July, 1711. Cary's arrest and appearance before the Lords Proprietors in England came to nothing. Cary returned to North Carolina in the spring of 1713 and apparently spent his remaining years quietly there, in Bath County. *DNCB*.

[7]Not located.

[8]John Porter (1663-1712), former attorney general, justice of the General Court, and speaker of the assembly. Although descended from Quakers and acting in their behalf in this instance, Porter appears not to have been one himself. *DNCB*.

[9]Edward Hyde.

[10]The instrument by which King Charles II granted Carolina to the eight Lords Proprietors in 1665.

[11]The Fundamental Constitutions of Carolina, in theory the organic law of the province, had by this time gone through a number of versions, the last one in 1698. The "Liberty of Conscience" referred to at the end of this paragraph was one of the more noteworthy provisions of the Constitutions.

[12]Not located.

[13]Presumably the "Mr. Griffin" mentioned later in this document.

[14]Samuel Swann (1653-1707), a Virginian, removed to North Carolina ca. 1696 and served in various official capacities, including that of provincial secretary and councillor. *DNCB*.

[15]Charles Griffin (ca. 1679-ca. 1720), first known schoolteacher in North Carolina, came from the West Indies to North Carolina around 1705 and opened a highly successful school in Pasquotank Precinct. He had removed to Virginia by 1714, where Governor Alexander Spotswood employed him to teach Indian children. The last few years of his life were spent as master of the Indian school at the College of William and Mary. *DNCB*.

[*SPG/Jou/App B*]

Proposal
1709 May 16

<134.> Proposals to the Corporation pro promovendo Evangelio, for a Minister to be sent with the poor Palatines.[1] A Proposal humbly offered to the Committee of the Society for the propagation of the Gospel in foreign parts, meeting at St. Pauls Chapter house this 16th of May 1709.

The poor Palatines who are lately come over, having taken up their quarters in Aldgate and St. Catharine's Parishes, it gives me an opportunity to acquaint my self pretty well with their state and circumstances, and from what knowledge I have hitherto atteined thereof, I humbly crave leave to propose as follows.

That those who are already arrived and are expected to follow, being about nine hundred souls, if they should be sent to New-York or any other of her Majesty's Plantations, as it is said they will, a Minister who can officiate in High-Dutch may be provided with all expedition to go along with them; since it would add very much to the hardships of those poor souls, who have reckon'd it a great part of their sufferings to be deprived of their Churches and Ministers in their native Country, to be sent to a far Country there to enjoy the comfort of neither.

That these people being a mixt body of Lutherans and Calvinists, who as far as appears may be easily united upon the foot of the Liturgy of the Church of England; it be enquired whether any student in Divinity who can read and preach in high Dutch, and shall be otherwise well qualified will take orders in the Church of England; and if so, that a competent number of our Liturgie lately translated into high-Dutch by the encouragment of the King of Prussia be bought up, and sent with him for the service of his Congregation.

That if it shall be found that most of them will communicate therein a German Minister who will himself officiate according to that service be forthwith sought out to go along with them.

That he have an allowance from the Society for the Propagation of the Gospel in foreign parts, such as may subsist him comfortably in the said service.

That a considerable number of the Common Prayers translated into high Dutch be bought up and sent with them.

That this will be a Mission as honourable to our Church in general and Society in particular, as any has yet, or can be sent, and may possibly prove of equal, if not of greater advantage to the Propagation of the Gospel in foreign parts for many reasons, which may be offered.

D. At a meeting of the SPG on May 20, 1709, the secretary reported from the Committee that it had received these proposals, "which they Agreed to lay before the Society as also to move the Society that in case no Minister can be found in England fit to be sent to take care of the said Palatins that some application may be made to Professor Frank at Hall in Germany for a fitting Minister for the said people: then the said proposals being read; Agreed that the Consideration thereof be postpon'd, till the government have resolved how to dispose of the

Said palatines and that in the mean time Copies of the said Proposals be laid before the Lord ABp. of Canterbury and the Lord Bp. of London and their Opinion humbly recd. upon the same." Journal of the SPG, I, 382.

On June 3, the secretary reported to a meeting of the Society "that he had, according to Order, laid before the Lord ABp. of Canterbury and Lord Bp. of London, the Proposal about providing a Minister for the poor Palatins, and humbly ask't their Lordships advice about the same, and that both their Lordships were of Opinion, that it was not proper for this Society to meddle therein, till the Government has resolved how to dispose of 'em." Journal of the SPG, I, 388.

[1]The "poor Palatines" referred to in this document were protestant refugees driven from their homes in Germany, mainly the lower Palatinate, by warfare and harsh weather. Beginning in May, 1709, and continuing over the next two years, an estimated 13,000 entered England. The crown encouraged Palatine emigration to the colonies, and numbers of them went to New York, North Carolina, and elsewhere. The Swiss Baron Christopher Graffenried and his associates were responsible for embarking some 650 German and 100 Swiss settlers for North Carolina, the baron and associates having purchased land along the Neuse and Trent Rivers. Price, *Higher-Court Minutes, 1709-1723*, x-xi.

[*SPG/Jou/1*]

Journal of the SPG
1709 July 15

<394> 15th July 1709. [...]

2. The Secretary informing the Bord that by Mr. Gordons returning from North Carolina there was want of a Minister to supply the place of the said Mr. Gordon: Agreed that it be refer'd to the Committee to enquire after a fit Person to be sent over in the room of the said Mr. Gordon. [...]

Minutes.

[*LAM/SPG/VIII*]

Bishop of London to Secretary, SPG
1709 August 13

Aug. 13.

Sir

Let me intreat you to give my service to the gentlemen of the Committee and to present the bearer Mr. Urmstone to them, as one that desires to go abroad their missionary. If they are pleased to try him, I question not but they will be satisfyed with his performance and his future behaviour. I am Sir your most humble servant.

H. London

[*Addressed*:]
For John Chamberlain
Esqr.

[*Endorsed*:]
(138.)
Lord Bishop of London
3d August 1709

ALS. Read at a meeting of the Committee on August 15, 1709, "and the said Mr. Urmstone attending was called in and produced a Testimonial of his good behaviour in the Curacy of Eastham in the County of Essex. Signed by Mr. Stephen Robins Vicar of the said Church, and Mr. John Chisenhall Vicar of Barking, Agreed that the said Mr. Urmstone do read prayers and preach on Fryday at St. Antholines Church in Order to be a Missionary." Journal of the Committee of the SPG.

[*SPG/A/4*]

Bishop of London to Secretary, SPG
1709 August 15

<CXLVI> Ld. Bp. of London to the Secretary

15th Augst. 1709.

Sir,

I wish you had not altogether set Mr. Gordon by, till you had provided another fit for his place, which I fear you will not easily do.

The Bearer Mr. Crawford offers himself to go a Missionary and is well recommended by Mr. Chalmers: but I wou'd not Ordain him till I know your pleasure; especially since some are of Opinion to send no Missionaries, and to what then serves our Charter? I am Sir Your most humble Servant.

H. London

Directions are
To Jno. Chamberlayne Esq.

Copy.

[*SPG/Jou/1*]

Journal of the SPG
1709 August 19

<398> 19th August 1709. [...]

<399> [8.] It was reported from the Committee that Mr. John Urmstone had attended 'em with recommendations from the Lord Bp. of London in order to be employed as a Missionary, and that he had produced Testimonials signd by Mr. Roberts Vicar of Eastham, and Mr. Chisenhal Vicar of Barking and that he had read prayers and preach't according to Order, and upon the whole that it appeared to the

Committee that he was well qualifyed for the Service of the Society; Resolved that the Society dos Agree with the Committee.

[9.] The Minute relating to the supplying the room of Mr. Gordon in N. Carolina with a fit person, being considered it was moved that the abovemention'd Mr. Urmstone be appointed to North Carolina, in the sted of the said Mr. Gordon, then the said Mr. Urmstone being called in, was acquainted with the said Motion and gave his consent thereto: Agreed that Mr. Urmstone be appointed to the same Precincts in North Carolina that Mr. Gordon lately quitted with an allowance of eighty pounds Per Annum <400> commencing from this day, together with the Summ of five Pounds in small Tracts to be disposed of among his Parishioners.

10. Ordered that the Library intrusted to Mr. Gordon be deliver'd to Mr. Urmstone.

[...]

<401> [13.] Also that they having read the Minute of the Society relating to Mr. Gordon and allowed him to make his Option of Hopewell in W. Jersey vacant by the death of Mr. Moor or of Chester or New Castle in Pensylvania vacant by the Removal of Messr. Nichols and Ross and that thereupon the said Mr. Gordon had made his Choice of Chester. Agreed that the Society do approve of the Choice made by the said Mr. Gordon of Chester aforesaid, and that he have the Yearly Allowance of £60 as he had before in N. Carolina commencing from Midsummer last past in case the Lord ABp. of Canterbury approve the same. [...]

Minutes.

[*SPG/Jou/1*]

Journal of the SPG
1709 September 16

<402> 16th September 1709 [...]

1. The Secretary acquainted the Bord that Mr. Gordon has put into his hands the Copy of an Act of the Assembly in North Carolina intituled *An Act for electing of Vestrys*[1] etc. in order to be Communicated to the Society: then that Clause in the said Act relating to the turning out Ministers by the Vestry was read: Ordered that the Secretary do wait on the Lord ABp. of Canterbury with a Copy of the said Act, and at the same time lay before his Grace the Resolutions of this Society at their General Bord Meeting on 15th Febry. 1705 upon a Case of the same nature and pray his Lordships directions herein. [...]

Minutes.

[1] Not located.

[*LAM/SPG/X*]

Secretary of the SPG to Governors
1709 September 24

Westminster
24 Septemb. 1709

Honor'd Sir

The Society for Propagating the Gospel in Foreign Parts having lately made an order that all their Missionaries should correspond with the Secretary at least twice a year viz.: at Midsummer and Christmas or thereabouts; which order has been communicated to all their good Missionaries, and upon that occasion it having been represented to the said Society, that by reason of the frequent Miscarriages of Ships and other Accidents in War time, and the Distance of some of these Gentlemen from Sea-Port Towns their Correspondence has been render'd very Difficult I am commanded by the Society to pray your Excellency's Favor in promoting the Correspondence between such of the Missionaries as are setled in your Government, and the said Society by such Means and Methods as shal seem most expedient to you. Sir if I may have the Happiness to Know your Mind herein, and lay it before my Masters you will extremely oblige Honored Sir your Excellency's most Humble Servant

John Chamberlayne

[*Endorsed:*]
Septemb. 1709
Copy of my letter to all the Governors
of Plantations where the Society has sent
Missionaries Correspondence etc.

Draft.

[*LAM/SPG/X*]

Secretary of the SPG to Missionaries
1709 September 26

<77>

Petty France Westmr.
26 Septemb. 1709

Reverend Sir

Having writ to you lately, I shall not Trouble you with more at present than these few Lines to inclose the order of the Society about the Correspondence of their Missionaries with the Secretary etc.; the occasion of which you will see in the order it-self, to which referring and earnestly exhorting you to a strict Complyance with all these orders and Rules concerning your Conduct and Behaviour, which by their Direction I have from time to time communicated to you, and of which I have *ex abundanti Cantelã* sent you Duplicates by several opportunites; I remain Reverend Sir your affectionat humble Servant.

John Chamberlayne

[*Endorsed:*]
26 Septemb. 1709
Copy of a Letter to all the
Missionaries about Corresponding etc.
sent 'em via N. Engl.

Draft.

[*LAM/SPG/XV*]

Rev. John Urmston to [Secretary, SPG]
1709 September 28

Worshipful Sir

I hope my aversion to go for Carolina in the Princess Anne will not be imputed to want of Zeal for the good of Souls, when you know that I did not without difficulty prevail with my wife, sometime before I was chosen Missionary, to go with me beyond sea. She is a tender and timorous poor creature, hath never been upon the salt water and has a strange notion of my undertaking. I have lived many years in divers Foreign Countries and may, I presume, be allow'd to know what is necessary to render life abroad comfortable to my self and family. I have experienced the uneasiness and great inconveniencies which attend men, and their wives in living asunder, besides the vast and unnecessary charge of keeping two families, as I must do, if I leave my wife in Engd. We might all live for less in America, than will maintain her and three children here and except she goes with me she declares she'll never undertake such a voyage. As for my own part I should as freely expose myself to all the hazards that may attend th' aforesaid Ship in her voyage as any man, but it would be a great affliction to see my wife and little babes at the mercy of a cruel enemy, which is too much to be fear'd, did we go in her for she might as well sail along the coasts of France as go North about or round the Cape in Virginia. I know that at this time of the year there always are many Privateers lurking about Shorland, so that it is very improbable a single ship, of what force soever should escape them. The Russia and Greenland Merchants will tell them as much. I hope the Honorable Societie will have more regard for their Missionaries and their families than those forlorn poor wretches, the Palatines. I never expected to be sent with Convoy. The dangers of the sea are many in time of War and there have been those that have been carried into France, notwithstang they had a strong safegard of six or more Men of War, with them. Should the like befall me and family I should be very much condemn'd for venturing in a single Ship and 'twould undoubtedly cause regret in all that press't me to it, but if I go with Convoy I must be content with the common fate of the whole Fleet, come what will.

These, with submission, are I think urgent reasons enough, why I should desire to be excused from going now, with the Palatines and hope I shall not be worse treated than the rest of my Brethren who are appointed Missionaries in America; but if after application made to his Grace my Lord Arch-Bishop of Canterbury and others, which favour I humbly beg of you, on my behalf; the Honorable Societie will not be pleased to allow me salary from the time I was admitted, I freely submit my self to their Good will and Pleasure in this and all other matters that have relation to the Mission, as I think myself in duty bound and am Sir Your Worships most obedient and humble servant.

Jno. Urmston

East Ham
Septr. 28, 1709.

ALS. Read at a meeting of the SPG on October 21, 1709. Journal of the SPG, I, 417.

[*LAM/SPG/XV*]

Rev. John Urmston to Secretary, SPG
1709 October 3

Worshipfull Sir

Nothing doubting but mine might come to hand soon after you had dispatch't yours to me. I delay'd writing or coming till friday following, thursday being Holy day and supplies not so easily gotten in the Countrey as in Town, but on thursday in the Evening was seiz'd with a violent quotidean[1] with little or noe intermission, till this morning. This day I've spent in preparing my body for the Bark, so that after another fit which I perceive coming on this evening I hope I may be able to wait on you towards the end of the week or the beginning of the next; if should fail thro' sickness and the Ship be gone, I hope this will be an unanswerable reason above all the rest, for the old Maxim is nemo tenetur ad impossibile,[2] my going is morally so, besides upon 2d thoughts, till that pernicious Act of placing and displacing Ministers at pleasure be set aside as it was in S. Carolina 'tis uncertain whether they'll receive me or not. I've understood that two of the Districts contend mightily for having a Minister entirely to themselves, which will create great confusion and Mr. Lawson[3] moreover tells me, that 'tis impossible I should supply places so distant as Perquiminse and Bath, besides the difficulty and charge of passing the Rivers. I hope to have a favourable answer to all these things the Next Court day at St. Martin's, but if able I shall wait on you before then. In the interim I am Sir with all humble respects yr. Worships most humble servant.

Jno. Urmston

E. Ham
Oct. 3, 1709.

Pardon this scribble because written in ane trements.

[*Addressed*:]
To The Worshipfull
Jno. Chamberlayne Esqr.
in Petty France Westminstr.

[*Endorsed*:]
(13)
Mr. Urmston. E. Ham
3 Octob. 1709

ALS. Read at a meeting of the SPG on October 21, 1709. Journal of the SPG, I, 417.

[1]In the sense used here, *quotidian* means "of an intermittent fever or ague, recurring every day." *OED*.

[2]One rendering of this phrase is *no man should be held to such an impossible thing*.

[3]John Lawson (1674-1711), native of Yorkshire, explorer, surveyor, author of *A New Voyage to Carolina* (London, 1709), was in North Carolina from 1701, and in 1708 was appointed surveyor-general by the Lords Proprietors. In October, 1709, he was in England making arrangements for publication of his book, and also promoting development of the region south of Albemarle Sound. He arrived back in North Carolina in April, 1710, with several hundred Palatines, and soon had laid out the town of New Bern. In September, 1711, he was tortured and murdered by Tuscarora Indians in the opening days of the uprising known as the Tuscarora War. *DNCB*.

[*SPG/A/5*]

Rev. James Adams to Secretary, SPG
1709 October 4

<*CII.*> Mr. Adams to the Secretary.

Virginia Oct. 4th, 1709.

Sir.

I wrote April last by Mr. Glover our late president, who went as far as Virginia in order to embarque for England but being unluckily disappointed of his passage left my Letters with a friend of his who promised to be very carefull in sending them speedily and safely over, but whether or not they came to your hands I am altogether ignorant, having had no Letters from Europe since my arrival in America. I have taken this Journey into Virginia (there being never any opportunity from North Carolina) to let you hear from me again, according to my Instructions. I doubt not but Mr. Gordon inform'd you by word of Mouth, that when we came hither we found the Government in the hands of such persons as were promoters for Gods Service, and good Order and from whom we met with all reasonable incouragement in the discharge of Our Mission; But now the Case is sadly Alter'd, for the Quakers alarm'd at our Arrival did in a most tumultuous manner stir up the ignorant and irreligious who are by much the greater Number in this Colony, by bold Lies and Calumnies against both the Government and us. And we are now ruled by such as are generally friends only to Drunkenness, irreligion and prophanness, insomuch that in many places where before I met with all encouragement and Civility, I find nothing now but reproaches, threatnings and ill usage, and many who then seemed Zealous and forward are now turned quite back. Mr. Gordon had experience of these things in some measure before he went over, but now things are carried to far greater extremes; the abuses and Contumelies I meet with in my own person are but small troubles to me in respect of that great grief of hearing the most Sacred parts of Religion impiously prophan'd and redicul'd. We had a Communion lately and the looser sort at their Drunken Revellings and Caballs spare not to give about their bread and Drink in the Words of Administration, to bring in contempt that most holy Sacrament, and in derision of those few good persons who then received it, and yet such flagrant Crimes, notwithstanding of my Complaint to Our Magistrates go unpunished and unregarded. We daily expect in our new Governor;[1] who I hope will set the Country again in order, and redress our Grievances. I pray God he may prove a good Man, for upon his disposition will very much depend the further fruit of my Mission.

In the precinct of Pascotank where I chiefly resided last year are 1332 Souls whereof 900 profess themselves of the Church of England excepting some few presbyterians who now constantly joyn themselves with us in our Service have had their Children baptised by me and are willing to have them brought up in our way of Worship. There is about 11 who profess no Religion at all, 210 Quakers, and 211 Negroes some few of which last are Instructed in the Principles of the Christian Religion, but their Masters will by no means permit them to be baptised having a false notion that a Christen'd Slave is by Law free. I have baptised since I came between the parishes of Pascotank and Caratuck 213 Children and 2 Adult persons. I have administred the Sacrament of the Lord's Supper 3 times, twice in Pascotank where I first had 14 Communicants, the second time I had 24. And the last time I administred in Carratuck where I had 30 the Names of all which housekeepers, Communicants and baptised persons etc. I have by me in my Notitia parochialis according to my Instructions.

I have lately lived most in Caratuck but it is a Precinct of so large an Extent and so much divided by water, that I have not yet been able to get passages in all the extreme Corners of it.

In my next I shall send you an account of that parish which is not above half as populous as pascotank and but one profes'd Quaker in the whole bounds. Had the Government continued as we found it there had been Churches built ere now, but since the Quakers and their Accomplices have got to the helm all such thoughts are laid aside. I have not since I came to the Country received so much as to pay for my diet and Lodging and if I had not drawn Bills upon Mr. Hoar I had been in very great want. I have a very laborious Mission, the places I preach at being some of them 60 others above 70 Miles distant. I bless the Lord I have had my health well and I pray God to give me his Grace so to direct my ways in this troublesome and unsettled Country as not only to acquit myself with applause to those good Men who sent me but that I may be likewise able to give a Comfortable Account of my Stewardship at that dreadfull Tribunal where the Secrets of all hearts shall be disclosed which shall be the dayly prayer and faithfull endeavour of Sir Your most humble Servant.

James Adams

I wrote to you formerly of one Mr. Griffin who had behaved himself very remarkably in the Office of a reader and Schoolmaster he has fallen into the Sin of Fornication and joyned with the Quakers Interest which has proved a great Stumbling block to many of our perswasion.

Copy. Read at a meeting of the SPG on July 21, 1710. Journal of the SPG, I, 491. Read again at a meeting on October 20, 1710, along with another letter from Adams dated March 27, 1710, also written from North Carolina. Both letters had been considered by the Committee, who recommended to the Society "that the Case of the said Mr. Adams is worthy their Consideration." Journal of the SPG, I, 512.

[1]Edward Hyde.

[*SPG/Jou/1*]

Journal of the SPG
1709 October 21

<407> 21st October 1709. [...]

[1.] The Minute of the last Meeting, relating to the Act of Assembly of N. Carolina about Ministers being had, the Secretary reported that he had waited on the Lord Archbishop of Canterbury, according to Order and had laid before his Grace a Copy of the said Act, and of the proceedings of the Society in a like Case in Febry. 1705, and had also by his Graces directions acquainted the Lords Proprietors of Carolina with the said Proceedings; Agreed that the farther Consideration of this matter be Adjourn'd till the Lord Bp. of London has discours't with his Grace about it. [...]

<410> 11. Agreed that the Secretary do give Notice to all the Societys Missionarys that unless they give an <411> account of the State of their Church etc. at least twice a year according to the Order of the Society made at the last quarterly Meeting; their pay will be stopt and their Bills refused. [...]

Minutes.

[*SPG/Sermons*]

Standing Orders
ca. 1710

<[1]> Standing Orders of the Society for the *Propagation of the Gospel in Foreign Parts*.
I. Orders *Relating to the* Society.
<*Rules contained in the Charter.*> I. That the Society meet upon the Third *Friday* in *February* Yearly, between the Hours of Eight and Twelve in the Morning, and they, or the Major Part of such of them that shall then be present, shall choose one President, one or more Vice-Presidents, One or more Treasurers, Two or more Auditors, One Secretary, and other Officers for the Year ensuing, who shall respectively take an Oath for the due Execution of their respective Offices.

<[2]> II. That if any Officer die, or be removed, the President, or one of the Vice-Presidents, may summon the Members to meet at the usual Place of the Annual Meeting of the Society, and choose another in his Place.

III. That the Society meet on the Third *Friday* in every Month, and oftner, if Occasion requires, to transact the Business of the Society, and may, at any such Meeting, elect Persons for Members.

IV. That no Act of the Society be valid unless the President, or one of the Vice-Presidents, and Seven other Members be present.

V. That at any Meeting on the Third *Friday* in the Months of *November, February, May*, and *August* Yearly, and at no other Meetings, the Society, or the major Part then present, may make By-Laws, and execute Leases, etc.

VI. That the Society may depute such Persons as they shall think fit, to take Subscriptions, and collect Monies contributed for the Purposes of the Society.

VII. That the Society shall Yearly give an Account in Writing to the Chancellour, our Keeper of the Great Seal, the Chief Justices of the King's Bench and Common Pleas, or any Two of them, of all Monies receiv'd and laid out, and of the Management of the Charities.

<[3]>VIII. That before the Society enter upon Business, the following Prayers shall be used by one of the Clergy then present. *Prevent us, O Lord, in all our Doings, with thy most gracious Favour, and further us with thy continual Help, that in all our Works begun, continued, and ended in Thee, we may glorify thy holy Name, and finally by thy Mercy, obtain everlasting Life, through Jesus Christ our Lord.* Amen.

O Merciful God, who hast made all Men, and hatest nothing that Thou hast made, nor wouldest the Death of a Sinner, but rather that he should be converted and live; have Mercy upon all Jews, Turks, Infidels, *and* Hereticks, *and take from them all Ignorance, Hardness of Heart, and Contempt of thy Word; and so fetch them home, Blessed Lord, to Thy Flock, that they may be saved among the rest of the true* Israelites, *and be made one Fold under one Shepherd, Jesus Christ our Lord, who liveth and reigneth with Thee and the Holy Ghost, One God World without End.* Amen.

IX. That there be a Sermon preached before the Society, on the Third *Friday* in every *February*, and that the Preacher and Place be appointed by the President.

X. That the Form of the Oath to be tendered to all the Officers of the Society, before they are admitted into their respective Offices, be <[4]> as follows. *I.* A. B. *do swear, that I will faithfully and duly execute the Office of* [*blank*] *of the Society for the Propagation of the Gospel in Foreign Parts, according to the best of my Judgment*; So help me God.

XI. That the Charter and Seal of the Society, and all Writings, Instruments, Deeds, and other Papers, that are order'd to be preserved, be put into a strong Box, and lodged in the Place where the Society meets.

XII. That no Sum or Sums of Money exceeding Ten Pounds, (excepting yearly Salaries of Missionaries, etc.) be disposed of at any Meeting, unless Fourteen Members of the Society be present.

XIII. That no Book or Paper be printed and dispersed at the Charges of the Society, or admitted into the Missionaries Libraries, or sent over to them, till the said Book or Paper has been proposed and approved at a General Meeting of the Society.

XIV. That the Minutes of the last Day and the Minutes of intermediate Committees, be read before the Society enters upon new Business.

XV. That all the standing Orders be read every Third *Friday* in *May*.

XVI. That the Accounts of the Society be Audited Yearly in *January*.

<[5]> XVII. That every Minute be read over as soon as taken by the Secretary, and sign'd by the Chairman, before the Society proceed to other Business; and that the same Method be also observed at all the Meetings of the Committee.

XVIII. That the original Minutes be collated with the Books into which they are enter'd, by the Secretary or his Clerks, and that this be done at the first Meeting of every Committee, that immediately follows the General Meeting.

II. Orders *Relating to the* Committee.

I. That a Committee of the Society be appointed to receive Proposals that may be offer'd to them, for the promoting the Designs of the Society, and to prepare Matters for the Consideration of the Society.

II. That such Members of the Society as please to come, or any Three of them, be the said Committee, and that the said Committee meet at St. *Paul's* Chapter-House, the *Monday* immediately preceding the General Meeting <[6]> (and oftner, if necessary) at Four in the Afternoon.

III. That no Motion for Money or Books be originally made, or received at the Committee.

III. Orders *Relating to the* Members.

I. That no Person be admitted a Member of the Society, till he be proposed at Three several Meetings.

II. That Elections of Members, and all other Matters that are put to the Question, be determin'd by Balloting.

III. That no Persons be admitted Members of the Society, unless they consent to subscribe something Annually for the promoting the Designs of the Society, excepting such as have been Benefactors.

IV. That all the Orders relating to the Choosing Members, be read before the Society proceed to balloting.

V. That when any Person is proposed for Member of the Society, the Name of the Person that proposed him, be enter'd in the Journal at the same Time.

<[7]> IV. Orders *Relating to the* Auditors.

I. That the Auditors, in their Reports, enter the Name of all such Subscribers as have not compleated their Payments to the Quarter-Day before the Audit; and also the respective Sums then unpaid; and that the Particulars of the said Report do always lie on the Table, that every Subscriber may have the Opportunity of correcting any Mistake.

II. That the Secretary, after each Audit, do write to all such Members as are above a Year in Arrear, for their Subscriptions, taking first the Directions of the Society therein.

III. That the Auditors take an Account of all Books within the Year past, and how disposed of, and what are remaining in the Hands of the Treasurers, or any other Officer.

IV. That at every Election of Auditors, one of the former Year be always chosen, as an Auditor for the Year ensuing.

V. That every Audit be fairly enter'd into a Book kept for that Purpose by the Secretary, and examined and subscribed by the respective Auditors.

<[8]> V. Orders *Relating to the* Treasurer

I. That if the Society shall think fit to choose more than one Treasurer, neither of them be answerable for the Acts or Miscarriages of the other.

II. That the Treasurer or Collector do demand of the Members of the Society, such of their Quarterly Subscriptions as remains unpaid, on the first Meeting that shall follow the Quarter-Day after which such Subscriptions are due.

III. That the Treasurer be empower'd to pay the Charges of Porteridge, Freight, etc. of such Books and other Things as are sent from the Society to the Plantations.

IV. That all Benefactions and Entrance-Money be registred in a Book kept for that Purpose; and that at every Monthly Meeting of the Society, the Treasurer, if present, shall charge himself under his Hand in the said Book, with all such Receipts; or in the Treasurer's Absence, the Secretary shall, under his Hand, in the same Book, charge himself with such Receipts, and at the first Opportunity, shall pay the Money to the Treasurer, and take his <[9]> Discharge in the said Book; which Book, at every Audit, shall be laid before the Auditors.

V. That the Treasurer do always in his Accounts, mention the Date of the Order upon which he acts.

VI. That the Treasurer or Treasurers shall be entirely trusted with the Monies of the Society, upon his or their giving such Security as the Society approve; and that they, or either of them, shall be accountable for no more Money than actually comes to their Hands.

VII.That in Case any of the Missionaries shall draw upon the Society any Bill, payable before it becomes due, the Treasurer do accept to pay it when it becomes due, and not otherwise.

VIII. That as soon as the Treasurers Accounts are Audited, the several Vouchers and Receipts of Disbursements, for the particular Sums in the said audited Accounts, be delivered up by the Treasurer to be kept by the Society.

VI. Orders *Relating to the* Secretary.

I. That the Secretary be always present at the Audit.

II. That the Secretary do from time to time <[10]> lay before the Lord Arch-Bishop of *Canterbury*, and Lord Bishop of *London*, Copies of the Minutes taken at the Meetings of the Society, and of the Committee.

III. That the Secretary keep a Register of all the Books allow'd to Missionaries, or other Persons, in which the Missionary's or other Person's Name, the Place of his Abode, and the Time when he receiv'd the said Books, are to be entered, excepting the Society's Anniversary Sermons and other Papers, and such small Tracts, which are to be given away to their respective Parishioners.

IV. That the Secretary lay before the Committee all such Letters, or Answers to Letters, as he from time to time shall write to, or receive from any of the Missionaries or other Persons, by Order of the Society.

V. That the Secretary do furnish every new Member, and all such Persons as from time to time are sent abroad by the Society, with a Copy of all the standing Orders, with the Anniversary Sermons, and other Papers publish'd by the Society.

VI. That the Secretary do prepare an Abstract of the most material Transactions of every Year, which, after they have been approved by the Society, shall be publish'd at the end of the Anniversary Sermon.

<[11]> VII. Orders *Relating to the* Missionaries.

I. That for the greater Encouragement of such Clergymen, or others, as are willing to engage themselves in the Service of the Society, one half Year's Salary shall be advanced to them, (they giving Security that they will take the first Opportunity of a Passage) and at the Determination of the first Year, or in Case of Mortality, the remaining Part shall be paid to their Executors, or Assigns.

II. That if any Missionary, sent over to the Plantations with an Allowance from the Society to any particular Place, shall fix himself in any other Place, by the Direction of the present Governour, or otherwise, the Society will not continue the Allowance to the said Missioner, until the said Change shall be approved of by the Society.

III. That a Sum, not exceeding £10 be allowed to such Missionaries as shall be sent over by the Society, to Places where there are no Libraries, towards buying any of the Books mention'd in the Society's Catalogue.

IV. That a Sum, not exceeding £5 be allowed every Missionary sent by the Society, <[12]> to be laid out in such practical and devotional Books, as the standing Committee shall think fit, which are to be distributed *Gratis* by the said Missionary, amongst his Parishioners, according to his Discretion.

V. That no Person shall receive any Allowance from the Society, unless he produce such Testimonials as have been agreed on by the Society.

VI. That no Testimonials shall be allowed of, but such as are sign'd by the respective Diocesan of any Missionary that is to be sent over to the Plantations; and where that is not practicable, by some other Persons of Credit and Note, three at least of the Communion of the Church of *England*, and such as shall be well known to some of the Members of the Society.

VII. That all Missionaries, in Matters which they desire should be laid before the Society, do correspond only with the Secretary of the Society.

VIII. That a Letter of Recommendation, in the Name of the President for the time being, and the Society, to the Captains and Masters of Ships, in which the Society's Missionaries go over, be given to each Missionary by the Secretary, at the time of his Departure.

<[13]> IX. That all such Persons as are sent abroad by the Society, and have Half a Year's Salary advanced to them, do give the Treasurer good Security, that they will repair to their Posts as soon as they are able, or refund the Society's Money.

X. That no Person whatsoever be employ'd as a Missionary by the Society, till he has been try'd and approv'd of, as touching his Ability in Reading the Common-Prayer, and Preaching, etc., and (if not an *English-man*) particularly as to his Pronunciation.

XI. That all Missionaries, to whom Books are given, be obliged to leave a Catalogue of the said Books, and to sign a Bond, the Penalty of which, shall be double the Value of the said Books, to be accountable for the same.

XII. That one Dozen Copies of Mr. *Ostervald's* Catechism, be sent with all the Missionaries that shall be appointed by the Society into Foreign Parts.

XIII. That all such Missionaries as are sent over to Places where there are no Churches, nor Church-Books, be provided with a Bible, and Common-Prayer-Book, and Book of Homilies, and that it be left to the Discretion of the Committee, to provide the same where they shall judge necessary.

<[14]> XIV. That no Person, sent as a Missionary into the Plantations, etc. shall receive any Allowance or Books from the Society, but those only that shall bring such Testimonials, as are contained in the Society's printed Paper of Qualifications.

XV. That if any Missionary, in the Service of the Society, shall return from the Plantations, without Leave first had from the Society, such Missionary shall receive no farther Allowance, from the time he shall leave his Service there.

XVI. That no Notice be taken of any Application for Missionaries, or otherwise, unless such Application be made to the Society.

XVII. That all Missionaries sent over to the Plantations by the Society, (being married Men) be obliged to take their Wives with them, unless they can offer such Reasons as shall induce the Society to dispense therewith.

XVIII. That the Salary of every Missionary, who is not dismiss'd the Service for some Misdemeanour, shall continue one Year, and no longer, after the Society have resolved at their Board to dismiss such Person from their Service.

XIX. That if any Place or Places in the Plantations desire to have a Missionary sent to them, this Society will not send any till they know whether those Places are able and willing to contribute towards the Maintenance of a <[15]> Missionary, and that the Society will supply those Places, before others, which are most willing to contribute to such Maintenances.

XX. That no Books shall be given for the future to any other Persons, excepting to the Society's Missionaries.

VIII. Orders *Relating to the* Messenger.

I. That the Messenger for the time being, give Receipts in his own Name for the Money he shall receive upon the Account of the Society, from any of the Members thereof, and that he pay the said Monies over to the Treasurer or Treasurers, and take his or their Receipt for the same, which shall be a Discharge thereof to the said Messenger.

II. That the Messenger attend the Treasurer and Secretary alternately every Day, to make up his Accounts, and receive such Directions from them, as may relate to the Service of the Society.

Printed.

[*SPG/A/7*]

Extract from List
ca. 1710

<82.> A Catalogue of Books deliver'd and sent to the Societys Missionaries etc. [...]

To Mr. Wm. Jordan [*sic*] Missionary to North Carolina 4th Octobr. 1707	10._._
Small Tracts	5._._
12 Common Prayers in 24 Psalms plain etc.	2._.9._
To Mr. James Adams Missionary to North Carolina 4th October 1707	10._.6._
Small Tracts	5._._
Like Number of Common Prayer Books	
Book of Homilies	2._.9._ [...]
To the Use of the Missionaries in Carolina 30th Sept. 1707	
in Small Tracts	1.10._ [...]

D.

[*CO 5/289*]

Lords Proprietors to Edward Tynte
1709/10 February 9

Craven House Febry. the 9th 1709/10

Colonel Tynte.

The Bearer hereof Mr. John Urmston having been well Recommended to Us by the Lord Bishop of London as a Person of Worth and Learning and very well Qualifyed to do the Duty of a Minister in Our Province. We have agreed to send him Over to North Carolina, and Do desire you or your Deputy Governor to give him all the Encouragement and Assistance You can that he may be the better Enabled to perform his Sacred Function. We are etc.

Craven Palatin, Beaufort, J. Carteret,
M. Ashley, J. Colleton

Copy. At a meeting of the proprietary board on February 2, 1709/10, it was "Ordered, That a Lettre be wrote to Mr. Tynte to recommend Mr. John Urmston Minister to him and to give him what Encouragement he shall think proper in North Carolina, having been well recommended to Us by the Bishop of London as a person of worth and very fitly Qualifyed to be a Minister." CO 5/292, 32.

[*SPG/A/5*]

Rev. John Urmston to Secretary, SPG
1709/10 February 10

<*LXIX*> Mr. Urmston to the Secretary.

10th Feb. 1709/10

Worshipful Sir.

I am inform'd by Mr. Gordon that there are no Bibles, Common Prayer Books nor Communion Plate, Table or Pulpit Cloth and Surplices belonging to the Churches where he lately officiated in Carolina; I petition'd the Right Reverend my Lord of London for them as well as Glass windows for the New Church in Chowan, and his Lordship was pleased to answer that he had procured such ornaments and necessaries for many Churches abroad, but cou'd not do the like for all; I therefore humbly pray you to intercede with the honorable Society to allow me some if not all the things wanted as above, Bibles at least and prayer Books and a Surplice with one Set of Communion plate which may serve the whole Country. If not sent from England there's no likelihood that the People either can or will provide them and for want thereof I shall be hinder'd from doing my whole duty or else commit great indecencies. I further pray the Honorable Society to consider the great Charges I shall be at in providing necessaries for my wife and Children for the Voyage and when with Gods Assistance arrived at Virginia, in transporting them and my household goods from thence to Carolina I am Good Sir Your most Obliged.

John Urmston

Copy. Read at a meeting of the SPG on February 17, 1709/10, when it was "Agreed that such a Number of Bibles and Common prayer Books be given to the said Mr. Urmston as the Committee think fit." Journal of the SPG, I, 464.

[*SPG/A/5*]

Rev. James Adams to _____ Hoar
1710 March 27

<*CXXXVIII*> Ditto to Mr. Hoar.

Sir.

It is a very great trouble to me that I have not heard from the Society or you since my Arrival in America tho' I have taken care to write over duly according to my Instructions. We are now almost out of hopes of our New Governor[1] whom we have long expected to put an end to our Distractions. I have struggled these two Years with a Lawless and Barbarous People in general and endured more I believe than any of the Society's Missionaries ever has done before me. I am not able as the Countrey is now to hold out much longer but intend God willing next Summer or Fall to set out for Europe and shall bring such Testimonies of my Labors as shall give I hope satisfaction to you all. I hear Mr. Jenkins is dead and Mr. Black left the Society's Service, if you will be pleased to use your Interest to procure a Change of my Mission it will be an extraordinary kindness done me for I am quite tired of my life in a place where there has been neither Law nor Government since I came to it. I shall most chearfully and readily go whethersoever you agree to send me, for I am very positive I cannot go to a worse place in all respects. Were my Mission alter'd to another Government I shou'd not be fond of going for Europe these 3 or 4 Years and if the Society will be so kind as do it I doubt not but their Instructions may reach me time enough to prevent my embarking for England which I think not to do before next Fall nor without a very good passage. What little Money is due to me pray keep it in your hands and if God shall please to call me I have two Sisters the one named Janet and the other Elspet Adams living near Aberdeen in North Britain to whom I desire you may pay it, having had the News of my Fathers Death since I left Europe. I shall ever have a grateful remembrance of your kindness and friendship and always be Sir Your most Obliged and humble Servant.

James Adams

N. Carolina Currituck
27th March 1710.

Copy. Read at a meeting of the SPG on October 20, 1710. See notes accompanying the document immediately following the present one.

[1]Edward Hyde.

[*SPG/A/5*]

Rev. James Adams to Secretary, SPG
1710 March 27

<*CXXXVII*> Mr. Adams to the Secretary.

Sir.

In my last I gave you a large Account of the sad Disorder and Confusion of Our Countrey, and till Authority interposes we are likely to Continue in the same Deplorable Condition. We have long expected our New Governor but now begin to dispair of his coming. I have taken particular care to write over according to my Instructions, but have not heard from the Society since my Arrival in America, which makes me very uneasy not knowing whether or not my Letters have got to Your hands. Nothing but my true concern for so many poor Souls scatter'd abroad as sheep having no Shepherd, and my duty to those good Men who reposed this Trust in me cou'd have prevailed upon me to stay in so barbarous and disorderly a Place as this now is where I have undergone a World of trouble and misery both in Body and Mind. Had the Government continued as Mr. Gordon and I found it I doubt not but I shou'd have been able to have given a very successfull Account of my Mission, but as long as things continue as they are, I can have but small hopes of making Proselytes, and gaining over that Number, which if Backed by Authority, I by the Grace of God might probably have done. I have met with so many discouragments (of which my not hearing from you is none of the least) that I intend (please God) next Summer or Fall as a passage shall offer to embarque for Great Britain, and shall I hope produce such Testimonies of my endeavours and behaviour in every respect as shall satisfy you all well of my diligence and fidelity.

We have in this parish of Currituck 839 Souls whereof 97 are Negroes 1 Quaker and 5 or 6 of no professed Religion, the rest all joyn with me in our Church Service. I have baptised this last half year 35 Children between the Precincts of Currituck and Pascotank and some of Piequimmins. I administred the Lords Supper Christmas last and had 27 Communicants. I am with all respect Sir, Your most humble Servant.

James Adams

Currituck
March 27, 1710.

Copy. Read at a meeting of the SPG on October 20, 1710, when it was considered together with a letter from Adams dated October 4, 1709, also written from North Carolina and previously read by the Society on July 21, 1710. The Committee reported to the Society that both letters indicated that "the Case of the said Mr. Adams is worthy of their Consideration." After reading the letter from Adams to Hoar of March 27, 1710, above, it was "Agreed that Mr. Adams have notice that the Society have taken his case into their Consideration, and have thought fit to allow him the additional Salary of Twenty pounds commencing from Michaelmas last in case the Lord ABp. shall approve the same." Journal of the SPG, I, 512-513.

[*SPG/A/5*]

Rev. James Adams to Secretary, SPG
1710 September 4

<*CLXXII*> Mr. Adams to the Secretary.

Virginia 4th Septr. 1710.

Sir.

I came hither now to Virginia with a design to embark for South Britain, but not meeting with a Passage to my Mind, the advice of some of my best Friends has prevaild upon me to Continue still in Carolina till I shall hear farther from You. I was much concerned to hear by Mr. Urmston that all my Letters since Mr. Gordon have miscarryed which I am sure has not been occasion'd thro' want of pains or Cost in me which I can easily make appear, if the Society so requires. Of my two last I have sent Copies now again, and as to the Posture of Affairs here, I need add no more but that we labour still under the same dismal Circumstances, and which is worst of all the hopes of any redress by the Governor of South Carolina is now quite vanished having t'other day had the News of his death.

About a Week ago I waited upon the Honorable Mr. Hyde who was appointed Governor of our Countrey, and as far as I can learn he thinks it not adviseable, as things have happen'd to go into N. Carolina till he hears again from England, so that God only knows when our Distractions are to have an end. Tho' We be a Numerous and Considerable Body of People, yet we seem to be below the Care of the Lords Proprietors who I am afraid are abused by a Misrepresentation of the Countrey made by the Quakers and their Faction, or trust too much to the Management of Mr. Danson[1] a Proprietor of the foresaid Sect who receives his Informations from those of that party particularly one Porter a person notoriously Infamous whose practice is in Conjunction with the Quakers Adherents; when they hear of any Man's going from this Countrey who is not of their Interest, to write Scandalous lyes and Calumnies against him to the Lords Proprietors to lessen the said Person's Credit in what he shall say in relation to the State of the Countrey. Thus they served Mr. Gordon and others, and hearing of my Intentions for Europe have probably done the same by me. But I hope the Testimonies sent from the two Parishes where I have lived ever since my Arrival in the Countrey are sufficient enough to prevent all my Enemys from doing me any Mischief that way. Mr. Glover has been Sollicited by many worthy Persons in Virginia who pity the Lamentable Condition our Colony has so long been in, to write the State of the Countrey and Dedicate it to the parliament of Great Britain and Commissioners of Trade, but he is resolved to be silent till he hears the determination of the Lords Proprietors.

I have lived here in a dismal Countrey about two Years and a half where I have suffer'd a World of misery and trouble both in body and mind. I have gone through good report and evil report, and endoured as much I think as any of Your Missionarys has done before me, wherefore I humbly pray and hope the Honorable Society will now be pleased to Alter my Mission to South Carolina where I doubt not but by God's Assistance, I shall be able to do more good, and whoever succeeds me here will have this Advantage that none of the Countrey will be prejudiced to his Person (as all who adhered to the Quakers are to mine) and this in my Opinion will not conduce a little to the Success of his Labours. I have lodged above this Year past in the house of a planter an Old Man who before the Quakers got the Government in their hands was one of our Councelors; he has after his own decease and his Wife's, left a considerable Legacy for the encouragement of a Minister in the Parish where he lives, which is as followeth videlicet A very good Plantation upon which he lives, with all the houses and some household Furniture; two Slaves and their increase for ever, together with a Stock of Cows, Sheep, hoggs and Horses with their increase for ever; all which immediately upon the Old Peoples decease may Moderately be valued at £200 and in some Years after may prove a Moderate Living for a Minister in itself. The old Gentleman's Name is Sanderson.[2]

Since my last I have baptised 40 Persons, whereof 6 were Adult palatins the Number of Communicants last Easter was 25.

We have in this Precinct about 70 or 80 Indians many of which understand English tollerable well but our own distractions has hitherto prevented my thoughts of doing any great matters among them considering the bad examples we shew them.

I understand by my Lord of London's Letter that the Society has been pleased to Augment my Salary for which I desire to offer my most humble thanks. I begg you will be pleased to let me hear from you by the first opportunity and remain with all respect Sir Your most humble Servant.

James Adams

Pray direct all your Letters for me to
the Care of the Reverend Mr. Wallace
Minister of Kiquotan in Virginia.

Copy. See the note accompanying the document dated August 30, 1710, below. The three documents following were enclosed in the present one.

[1]John Danson (d. ca. 1724), Quaker and son-in-law of John Archdale, who deeded his proprietary share to Danson and his wife. Powell, *Proprietors of Carolina*, 60.

[2]Richard Sanderson, ca. 1641-1718. *DNCB*.

[*SPG/A/5*]

Testimonial
1710 August 25

<*CLXXIV*> Vestry of Caratuck to the Society.

We the Church Wardens and Vestry Men as Representatives, and at the request of the Precinct and Parish of Carahtuck in N. Carolina do desire to offer our gratefull Acknowledgments in the most humble and hearty manner to the most Reverend Father in God Thomas Lord Arch Bishop of Canterbury etc. President, and the rest of the Members of the Society for the Propagation of the Gospel in Foreign parts for their pious care in sending the Reverend Mr. James Adams amongst us; who has during his Abode here (which has been about two Years and five Months) behaved himself in all respects as a Messenger of the Mild Jesus, exemplary in his life and blameless in his Conversation; and now being bound for England we with sorrowfull hearts and true love and Affection take our leave of him. We shall ever bless that Providence that placed him among us and shou'd be very unjust to his Character if we did not give him the Testimony of a Pious and Painfull[1] Pastor, whose sweetness of temper, diligence in his Calling, and Soundness of Doctrine has so much Conduced to promote the great end of his Mission, that we hope the good Seed God has enabled him to Sow will bear fruit upwards, which has in some measure appeared already, for tho' the Sacrament of the Lord's Supper was never before his Arrival administred in this Precinct, yet we have had more Communicants than most of our Neighbouring Parishes of Virginia, who have had the Advantage of a Settled Ministry for many years. We have no more to add but begg the Honorable Society will be pleased to continue us still under their Charitable Care, for whatever our Merits be, our necessity's are great, and all the return we are able to make is, to praise God for raising up so many truly good friends to our Souls, and that heaven may prosper you in so laudable, so pious, and so Charitable a Design, shall ever be the Subject of our prayers. Given under our hands this 25th day of Augst. 1710.

Richd. Sanderson senior, John Bennet Church Wardens, John Hodgson, Wm. Stafford, Ben. Tulle, Wm. Williams, Richd. Sanderson junior, Edward Tayler, Foster Jarves, Thomas Tayler, Thomas Vandermulen, Thomas [*blank*]

Copy. This document was enclosed in the one immediately above.

[1]Painstaking, diligent, careful. *OED*.

[SPG/A/5]

Testimonial
1710 August 26

<*CLXXV.*> Pascotank Vestry to the Society.

North Carolina. To the most Reverend Father in God Thomas Lord ABp. of Canterbury etc. President and the rest of the Members of that Honorable and Noble Society for the Propagation of the Gospel in Foreign parts.

Wee the Church Wardens and Vestry Men of the Parish and Precinct of Pascotank in the Province aforesaid on behalf of ourSelves and at the earnest request of the Inhabitants of the said Precinct do in all humility and sincerity render our most hearty and unfeigned thanks and acknowledgements to the Honorable and Noble Society for that their pious and Charitable Care for the Eternal Welfare of our immortal Souls in sending the Reverend Mr. James Adams amongst us our Pastor, who by his Vigilant faithfull and painfull preaching and due Administration of the Sacraments, his Exemplary and blameless Conversation, together with his peaceable and sweet temper and deportment all the time of his residing here (which has been two Years and five Months in this Parish and Caratuck) has justly merited the Character of a faithfull painfull pastor and Orthodox Minister of our Lord and Saviour Jesus Christ.

We hope the fruits and effects of his Ministry etc. will appear abundantly in our lives and Conversations to the Honour of Almighty God and our Soul's everlasting Peace and Comfort.

Divine providence calls for his departure from us We take our leaves with great Sorrow for our loss, which we hope may be his gain; humbly begging of the Honorable and Noble Society to extend their further piety and Charity towards us, that the Work of Grace so happyly begun by the Indefatigable pains and singular piety of the Reverend Mr. Adams may be Seconded and back't with the like proceedings and Crown'd with an answerable Conclusion; and that the Honorable Society may have a Confluence of happyness heaped upon them here and hereafter shall be the dayly prayers of Your Honors most humble Supplicants whose Names are hereunto Subscribed this 26th day of Augst. 1710.

Fra. DelaMare, John Davis, Ant. Hatch, Tho. Relf, Nic. Chevin, Sam. Davis, Robt. Lowry, John Palin, Tho. Boyd, Robt. Wallis, John Jennings, Wm. Relfe

---

Copy. This document was enclosed in the letter from Rev. James Adams to the secretary of the SPG dated September 4, 1710, above.

[*SPG/A/5*]

Testimonial
1710 August 30

<*CLXXIII*> Col. Glover to the Society.

May it please Your Lordshipps.

Altho' the trouble and Confusion this unhappy Countrey has Labour'd under ever since the Arrival of your Lordships Reverend Missionaries has Compelled me to retire from all publick employments and the poor return we are able to make for Your Lordships pious Care and Charitable expences admonisheth me to lay my hand upon my Mouth and keep silent till the Lords Proprietors shall by their prudent Care have restored Order and Justice among us, under the Influence of which we hope by Gods Grace to bring forth better fruit. Altho' I say these Considerations had discouraged me from making my application until I cou'd have presented Your Lordships with a fairer prospect of Affairs, yet the inclosed Papers being put into my hands, I held my self bound to present them to your Lordships and joyn with the Subscribers in the Character they justly give of the Reverend James Adams and which I'm sure all Persons who have any respect either to Religion or Loyalty do heartily concur. I will not enter into a relation of the success his Labours have had; as to that his Reverend Successor will not, as I think he is in Justice bound not to be, silent. And for the difficultys he has met with he has waded through them under the Vigilant eyes of the Malitious enemy without committing any thing unbecoming a Minister of our Lord and Saviour Jesus Christ. What is further necessary he himself is able by word to supply if any thing be wanting in the Account he has already given by writing, wherein I know he has neither neglected opportunity nor spared Cost or pains. These Papers ought to have come under the Publick Seale but that being forceably detained in the hands of those who are the professed Enemys of the Church as well as to all good Order it cou'd not be procured on this Occasion being able therefore to give them no greater Confirmation I humbly present them to your Lordships with my hearty Acknowledgments for your Lordships Noble Bounty to this poor Country and therein especially to Your Lordships Most Obliged and humble Servant.

Wm. Glover President

North Carolina
30th Augst. 1710.

Copy. Read at a meeting of the SPG on March 22, 1710/11, when it was ordered that "Col. Glover's, and Mr. Adams's Letters, and the Addresses therein mention'd be refer'd to the Committee who are to consider what is fit to be done therein, and report their Opinion to the Society." Journal of the SPG, II, 16. At the following meeting of the Society, April 20, 1711, the Committee reported that it "had Considered the Lettres from Col. Glover and Mr. Adams together with the Addresses from the Inhabitants of Caratuck and Pascotank, to them refer'd, and had thereupon Agreed to report as their Opinion, that Mr. Adams appears to be so serviceable, in North Carolina, that he shou'd be desired to stay there, at least till the Society can find a fit person to succeed him, and till there shall be a Vacancy in South Carolina or some other Countrey." The Society agreed. Journal of the SPG, II, 19-20. This document was enclosed in the letter from Rev. James Adams to the secretary of the SPG dated September 4, 1710, above.

[*SPG/A/5*]

Rev. John Urmston to Secretary, SPG
1710 October 15

<*CLXXI*> Mr. Urmston to the Secretary.

Worshipfull Sir.

The Quakers oppose Col. Hyde, and are resolved to Maintain their usurped Authority till a power comes from England, and what that will be we cannot well tell, for their Interest is too great there. If they go on thus the Church will not continue long here. This I write in hast doubting whether 'twill reach James River 'ere the Ships Sail, and therefore cannot add save that I am Sir Your most Obliged.

Jno. Urmston

N. Carolina
Octr. 15th 1710.

Copy.

[*SPG/Jou/1*]

Journal of the SPG
1710/11 February 8

<570> 8th Febry. 1710/11. [...]

<575> 10. The Secretary acquainted the Bord that he having been formerly directed to wait on the Lord ABp. to know whether his Grace wou'd approve the increasing the Salary of Mr. Adams in N. Carolina from £60 to £80 his Lordship was pleased to tell him that he consented to the Same. [...]

Minutes.

[*SPG/A/6*]

Rev. Jacob Henderson to Secretary, SPG
1710/11 March 21

<LXXV> Mr. Henderson to the Secretary.

Kicotan in Virginia
21st March 1710/11

Dear Sir [...]

I have nothing to acquaint the Honorable Society of to you, only that Mr. James Adams the Missionary to North Carolina dyed the 30th Octr. last which I saw in a Letter to the Reverend Mr. Wallace of Kicotan from his Assistant and Fellow Labourer Mr. Urmston; there are also a Parcel of Books left with Mr. Wallace by one Mr. Gordon whom he has never heard from since he left them, they are not near the value of what are usually given by the Honorable Society, so that if they are not to be disposed of otherwise, they being all different Books from what I have, the Honorable Society may as well Order them to me, since Mr. Wallace has no use for them. [...]

I am with all immaginable respect Dear Sir Your Obliged humble Servant.

Jacob Henderson.

Copy.

[*LAM/SPG/XV*]

Christopher DeGraffenried to Bishop of London
1711 April 20

My good and Excellent Lord

The misfortune I mett withall in being unexpectedly hurried away from London, to New Castle to meet my Suissers in order to transport them into Nord Carolina after these 650 Palatines I had Send before which unlookt arrivall of them so far North gave me no time to pay my Duty to your Lordship Whom I then was told was neither in London or att fullham. I can assure Your Lordship no Suisser of any Rank is unacquainted with that great and good Caracter your Lordship has and merits, So i can make no excuse on that behalfe, butt heartily begg pardon, and att the Same time humbly request your Lordship to accept of me and my People and Receave us unto yr. Church under Your Lordship's Patronage and we shall Esteem our Selves happy Sons though of a latter Stock and I hope we shall allways behave our Selves as becomes members of the Church of England and Dutifull children to so pious and Indulgent a Father as your Lordship is to all under your Care In all obedience Craving yr. Lordship blessing to me and my Countryman here. I make bold to Subscribe My Lord Your Lordships most Dutifull and most obedient humble Servent.

C. DeGraffenried[1]

New Bern in Carolina
April the 20, 1711.

[*Addressed*:]
To The Right Honorable and Right
Reverend Father in God
Henry Lord Bishop of London.

[*Endorsed:*]
Baron de Graffenried
New Bern in N. Carolina
20 April 1711

ALS. Read at a meeting of the SPG on January 18, 1711/2, having been forwarded to the secretary by the bishop of London. The bishop gave "his opinion thereon; That if the Society will allow a Stipend for a Chaplain to read Common prayer in high dutch he will provide one for Baron de graffenrieds people etc. Collonel Nicholson acquainting the Bord that there is a report that the Setlement of Baron de Graffenried and his people have been lately destroy'd by the Indians: agreed that this matter be adjourn'd to another meeting." Journal of the SPG, II, 156-157.

[1]Christopher DeGraffenried (1661-1743), Swiss baron and guiding force in Georg Ritter and Company, which purchased nearly 19,000 acres of land on the Neuse, Trent and White Oak Rivers in 1709. The following year DeGraffenried personally supervised the settlement there of some hundreds of Palatine Germans and Swiss, as well as the establishment of the town of New Bern. The enterprise was ravaged by the Tuscarora during the war that broke out in 1711, during which DeGraffenried was captured but escaped death through the intervention of Governor Alexander Spotswood of Virginia. Plans to establish another colony in Virginia did not come to fruition; DeGraffenried mortgaged the land of Ritter and Company to Thomas Pollock and returned permanently to Switzerland in 1714. *DNCB*.

[*LAM/SPG/VIII*]

A.W. Boehm to Secretary, SPG
1711 June 30

<151> Sir

I make bold to trouble you with this Letter to Mr. Tribbeko in hopes you'l see it deliver'd to the Lady that designs to set out for these parts. Mr. Tribbeko tells me in his Letter, that the Palatines setled in New York began then whilst he was there to repair to their several districts marked out for 'em, in order to make pitch and Tar. That those in Carolina had no Minister but onely a Schoolmaster, one Rasor[1]; so that a good Preacher was highly wanted among 'em, I hope in Time one may be provided for 'em; which is the wish of Sir Yr. very humble Servant.

A. W. Boehm.

Jun. the 30th, 1711.

[*Addressed:*]
To John Chamberlaine
Esqr. at His House in Petty France.

[*Endorsed:*]
(89)
Mr. Boehm, London
30th June 1711

ALS. Read at a meeting of the SPG on July 20, 1711, when it was agreed "that Mr. Boehm's Letter be refer'd to another Meeting." Journal of the SPG, II, 80.

[1]Possibly the Martin Frederick Rasor who received two grants of land in Chowan County in 1717. Hofmann, *Province of North Carolina*, 272; Cain, *Records of the Executive Council, 1664-1734*, 69-70.

[*SPG/A/6*]

Rev. Giles Ransford to Secretary, SPG
1711 July 5

<*XC*> Mr. Ransford[1] to the Secretary.

Bury 5th July 1711.

Worthy Sir.

I presume to give you this second trouble with the same reason I had for the former, an entire tender of my Service to the Society, for being a Missionary to the Plantations. I had not been so Arrogant, as to repeat my request of going there, were I not inwardly perswaded, that you'l have no reason to complain of my services done to the Church in those parts. And since I am a Stranger altogether to the Society (at Your instance) I'le procure the Archbishop of Dublin's Letter in favour of me, I find by Mr. Hall's Letter to me that the Society may be now in a Condition of furnishing out some Missionarys, by reason of the late Collections made within the Bills of Mortality; and if so, since there's a Vacancy in S. Carolina, I hope You'l be pleased to consider me and if my qualifications may appear to be equally advantageous to the design of sending Men of my Function abroad, I hope I may depend (upon better information) on your friendship and assistance in this matter. I writ somthing (which I have shewn to some Clergymen in these parts) in favour of the Society, and which I designed to Publish, but was disswaded from it, by their reasons given me, that my Topicks I went on, were, much the same of what was already printed in Sermons to Your Society on the Occasion, tho' I never saw one of them but the last. But in a little time I shall offer at somthing else. Tho' my Lord of London's in Essex yet you may in some Measure satisfy me relating to my humble request, in Your Answer (which I take the liberty to depend on) and which I hope may be soon by reason, I'm Chaplain to a Ship which lies a Cleaning at Harwich, and to which I can't tell how soon I may be called to. I begg pardon for my Assurance but apply to you as to one whose Character is Noble, ingenuous, and obliging and Subscribe myself with all immaginable deference Sir Your most obliged faithfull humble Servant.

Giles Ransford

At Mr. Payne's House
in Bury in Suffolk.

Copy.

[1]Giles Ransford. See appendix.

[*SPG/A/7*]

Rev. John Urmston to Secretary, SPG
1711 July 7

<365> <2> Mr. Urmston's Letter. 7th July 1711.

North Carolina July 7th 1711

<*Ex.*> Honored Sir

<*In relation to that Country, and his own low Circumstances and the behaviour of the People and the ill usage he meets with from them etc.*> Since my arrivall here I have written divers Letters to you and others which I hope were laid before the Honorable Society so fraught with unpleasant Relations of my own and the Countrys Circumstances that I am almost perswaded you scarce Expected to have heard any more from me. I am almost bereft of life and the little sense I had, and after a years fatigue and almost Continual bad health, am at last together with my Familly in manifest danger of perishing for want of Food, we have <366> liv'd many a day only on a dry Crust, and a draught of Salt water out of the Sound, such regard have the People for my labours, so worthy of the Favour the Society have shewn them in provideing Missioners and sending Books, so great is their Esteem for the Ministry, and our Endeavours which I can assure you have on my part been very hearty for the most part; but they thinck I am beholden to them for coming to hear me, they will be at noe charge, nor trouble and yet expect I should give my attendance, notwithstanding in many places there are great Rivers from one, two, to Six, twelve and fifteen Miles over, no Ferry Boats, neither will they be at the trouble of setting me over. I am destitute of all help both as to house keeping and the discharge of my Duty to the Society as I would he that will answer the end of his Mission must not only have a good horse, but a large Boat, and a Couple of Experienced Watermen not knowing when the Confusions of this unhappy Country would be over, or any Settlement made for the Church and Ministry, after Seven months uneasiness in a sorry house, I at last bought a Plantation scituated on the North Side of the Sound in Chowan Precinct between Mr. Pollocks, and that which was Mr. Walkers, now Moseleys. I found a new house and a Kitchin, upon it halfe finished, twil Cost me a great deal to make it fit to live in, workmen are dear and scarce. I have about a dozen Acres of clear ground and the rest woods in all *300* Acres, had I servants and money I might live very Comfortably upon it, raise good Corne of all sorts and Cattle without any great labour, or Charges could I once be Stockt, but for want thereof shall not make any advantage of my Land. I have bought a horse some time ago; since that three Cows, and Calv's five sheep and some Fowls of all sortes, but most of 'em unpaid for, together with 14 Bushells of Wheat, for all which I must give English goods, at this rate I might have anything that either this Government or any of the Neighbouring Colonies afford, but had I stock, I need not fear wanting either Butter, Cheese, Beef or mutton of my own raising, or good grain of all sortes. Missioners as the world go's must be Planters too if they have Famillies, or starve, the Salary alone will not do; I am forc'd to work hard <367> with Ax, Hac[1] and Spade. I have not a Stick to burn for any use, but what I cutt down with my own hands. I'm forced to Digg a Garden raise

Beans, Peas etc. with the assistance of a sorry wench my wife brought with her from England, my Neighbours seem to like well of my Industry, but are farr from affording me their Assistance in anything. They love to see new Commers put to their shifts as they themselv's have been, and cannot endure to see any Body live as well as themselv's without haveing undergon the Slavish part, and learnt to live independent of others. Men are generaly of all Trades, and Women the like within their spheres Except some who are the posterity of old Planters or have been very fortunate, and have great numbers of slaves, who understand most handycraft. <*Of their Several Trades and Callings*> Men are generaly Carpenters, joyners, Wheel Wrights Coopers, Butchers, Tanners, Shoemakers, Tallow Chandlers, Watermen and what not. Women Soapmakers, Starchmakers, Dyers, etc. He or she that either cannot do all these things, or hath not slave that can, over and above all the Common occupations of both Sexes, will have but a bad time on't for help is not to be had at any rate, every one haveing buisnes Enough of his own, this makes Tradesmen turn Planters, and these become Tradesmen, no Societie Commerceth now with another but all Study to live by their own hands, of their own produce, and what they can spare goes for Foreigne Goods; <*Of their Dyet*> Nay many live on a Slender Diat, to buy Rum, Sugar, and Molassees with other such like necessaries which are sold at such a Rate, that the Planter here is but a slave to raise a Provision for other Colonies, and dare not allow himselfe to partake of his own Creatures; except it be the corne of the Country in hominy-Bread, much or otherwise of Cooking, which after all is fitter for Hoggs, than Christians, and a little Stinking Swamp Water, a Bogg or els Brackish, and sommetimes down right salt Water, and yet such a Wretch as this Shall layout 40.50 <368> it may be £60 per annum in Rum, and Suggar. You'l not wonder I should fare so ill, when I tell you that my necessity and long stay in England after chosen Missioner together with the Charges of Transporting myself and Familly hither exhausted the money advanced. I brought nothing with me but Apparell and a few goods, not halfe Enough for my occasions here. I have little or nothing, and times so Confused that I cannot say when any provision may be made for me, or any other Minister.

<*Of the Ministers Journeys and fatigue in officiateing his Ministerial Function.*> I have hitherto supplyed 3 Precincts videlicet Chowan, Pequimans, and Pasquotank, which are very remote from one another, the most Southerly place I Preach'd at is above *70* miles distant from the most Notherly, this hath been my Circuit for the year last past, without any omission on my side, if I ever failed of Officiateing on the day appointed, twas for the want of a passage, so long as I was on Terra firma, neither the badness of the Roades, broken Bridges, over dangerous places, wet or Cold weather in Winter, nor the Excessive heat even to stifling in the woods for want of Aire ever causd me to disappoint a Congregation albeit they have often fail'd to meet me, every Body would have a Church by his own door, every Sunday or not at all. The whole Precinct can never meet at one place but must have 5 or 6 Meetings in each. Except they had more Zeal for Churches, might be so fix'd as that all might meet in a few hours either by Land or wather, Except bad weather or Contrary winds prevent they will not willingly come to weekly Lectures, in regard Pasquotank is very Numerous, many Quakers, and too many loose disorderly professers of the Christian Religion, a very factious, Mutinous and Rebellious People most of them Allyed to the Quakers, and at all turns at their Back, ready to oppose either Church or State if required by them whence arise all these troubles for the 3 yeares past. This

Consideration made me to Engage my self to Preach two Sundays in 4 and twice on the week day at 4 different places for which somme of the more sober part proposed a Voluntary Subscription, but not <369> meeting with the readyness, manny at first seemed to Express, could not prevail with a third of the People to Contribute, the whole amounted to £23. 5. *2d.* whereof I recd. £13. 11*s.* 6*d.* the rest will never be paid, somme have been so plain with me as today they expected I should have been altogether in their Precinct, whereas our agreement was drawon and signed, others say they don't think they ought to be at any Charge since our Society have sent me at their own Cost and allow me what they think is fitting. This is the story of most in the Government, and are very Confident they shall have Missioners sent to every Parish, but in very deed are not Worthy of one. Pequimans began a Subscription, there is about £9 I think given for one Sunday in 4 and once a Month in the week day. I have recd. £2 11*s.* 4*d.* no more to be Expected there, without I wou'd give one halfe for gathering the other, nor that for so small a summe in Chowan. I preach'd Constantly only once a Month at the Chappel, the like on the Southside, and West Shores of the Sound till they cou'd not agree who should set me over the River, and where we should meet on the South Shoare, they gave me two Barrells of Skins and the worse pieces of Lean Beefe. On the West Shoar was Subscribed £19 5*s.* 00 Recd. £4 13*s.* 4*d.* through their fault and not mine; our meeting has been discontinued for 4 Months, so that nothing is to be had more there, at the Chappell the Congregation is pritty numerous, they have often talkd of raising somthing, but as yet nothing don, neither dare I seem pressing for fear of Reproach. I went by Land 27 miles along the Sound Side towards Virginia, where there were as they told me *40* or *50* Children unbabtized, I Babtized 14; the Season being Wett I appointed to be there again that day month but no body Came. I heard of a great many met to be merry at a Reaping of Wheat in my way. I upbraided them with the neglect of a Concern of so great a moment, they promised to appoint a day but I have not yet heard from them albeit somme Weeks are past, they Sayd as their Phrase was, they would Employ me, and <370> Imploy me and Contribute for the future, but the time past was not thought of. There are about 40 or *50* Familys at Allegator, and Scogarlong about *20* miles down the Sound towards the South. East from where I livd many marryed and have Children who never were Babtized, nor ever saw a Minister on their Shoar. I have offerred to goe thither provided they would procure me a passage, a day has been twice prefixd, But they never came for me; so indifferent are they and Cold in their Souls health, and tis to be feared live like Beasts, I have heard of monstrous doings among them. Pampliticough I have not yet visited, by reason the Roads till now were unpassible.

I intended to have gon thither this Month, but warr being revived among us, we are all in Confusion, there is no stirring abroad. Colonell Hide has don all that in him lay to bring the Country into good order, and promote Religion, but is therefore hated, and Threatened with fire and sword and all of his party which you'l Easily believe me to be of, and therefore, not only fare ill but am in somme danger. My Horse hapned to break Pasture and stray into an Enemys Ground, and when taken up somme Ruffians said had their party known whome he belonged to, they had Certainly shott him. To such a height are our Divisions brought, and when they will cease I know not, Except her Majestie takes the Government into her own hands. I have preach'd 4 times in Corritack and Administred the Sacraments, I had *86* Comunicants, and at the Severale times Babtized *10* Infants. I have Administered the Lords Supper 3 times in Pasquetank and once in Poquimans. The 1st time I had 17 Communicants, the 2d 5 the 3d Seven and the 4th nine. I have Babtized in these three Precincts *154* Children, Preach'd *77* times, the People being unacquainted with Psalmody, instead thereof I comonly Catechise, but never fail of so doing where there is a Psalm sung. People are mightily averse to God Fathers, and Godmothers and therefore many will not have their Children Babtized, others thinck no Body more fitt than their Parents. To tell them of the orders of the Church avails not, theyl not hearken to the ordinances of man, but will have Express Scripture for all <371> they are to do, or observe. There is not a Schism or Corruption Broach'd in England, but here it hath its Defenders but the most numerous are those that Dissent from every thing that is called Religion, Libertines; Men and women of loose disolute, and Scandalous Lives, and practices. Tis usualy said our Colonies are chiefly peopled by such as have been Educated at somme of the Famous Colledges of Bridewell Newgate, or the [Fleet][2] what must our Inhabitants be not being sufferred to live in other places for their Wicked Courses, many of whome after their Transportation from England, have been banished out of all or most of the other Colonies or for fear of punishment have fled hither this is a Nest of the most Notorious profligates upon the Earth. Women forsake their husbands, come in here and live with other men, they are sometimes followed, then a price is given to the husband and Madam stays with her Gallant. A Reporte is spread abroad that the Husband is dead, then they become man and Wife make a figure and pass for people of worth and Reputation, Arrive to be of the first Rank and Dignity. What to do with such I know not, nor how a Reformation can be ever hoped for. I have not been Wanting in my Endeavours. I have spoiled good Horses, Enslav'd my selfe, hazard my life, to little purpose save the discharge of my Conscience, and the hopes I have of gaining the approbation of the Society. The people you see are generaly bad, yet Carress'd by the Quakers my Irreconcileable Enemys, those Excite aid and assist nay and Joyn with them in destroying the Government and opposeing the Establishment of the Church their aim and designe is to overthrow the Church, and deface the few Footsteps there are of the Christian Religion among us; and Establish their nonsensical Tenets in the roome thereof. There were severall Quakers that Bore Arms in a late attempt upon Colonell Hide, which was Carryed on with great Cunning, Malice, and Rage, but the aggressors were happily repulsed, and what further Wickedness they are Contriveing time will shew they rove about the Countrys in great Bodys, ravage and plunder all such as are not on their side. It wou'd be too tedious to give you a Succinct Account of every thing that has past since the first begining of the Confusions of this unhappy Government all owing to the Quakers who 7 or 8 Years agoe procured one Daniel a Monster of Wickedness to be Deputy Governour, for ever since this <372> Government depended on Ashley River Governor,[3] that office was on sale, the Quakers thought they cou'd manage him, they grew saucy an he restive. They soone procured another worse than he to succeed him, one Cary, Madam Knightly a Lady of known worth can give you an account of him, she livs at Kensington neither did this answer their Expectations, they made a purs and sent one Porter a known villian the son of a Quaker, and he one in disguise to the Proprietors accused the said Cary of many things indeed gross Enough, and with a great deal of truth, sufficient to cause him to be turn'd out, accordingly he was discharged from his Office, and there being noe Governor at Ashley River then Sir Nathaniel Johnson being put out by the Whiggs this Porter brought

an order to the Councill to Chuse as was accustomary in such Cases one of their Brethern to be President till a Governor was appointed. Mr. Glover a sober, discreet, and the only man of parts in the Country was Chosen. The Quakers dislike him and by force of Arms thrust in Cary whome the Proprietors had deposed into the Presidentship here were two Presidents, one appointed by the Lords Proprietors and the other sett up by the Roguish Quakers, neither was obeyed, the honest party would not obey Cary, and the other Mr. Glover, so that for two years and upward, here was no Law, no Justice, Assembly or Courts of Judicature so that People did and said what they likt. Olivers days come again[4] Colonel Hide arrived here but through Colonel Teints Death, had no Commission, he was Chosen President by all sides after long Debates, he persists in Mr. Glovers opinion of not Sufferring the Quakers, who had Deputations either Forged, or granted by those who were not Proprietors to be of the Council or have any thing to do in the Administration. An Assembly was Called with much difficuilty, we had the Majority. As to what has been Transacted in Temporalls, I must refferr you to the President and Council their Journal,[5] if you can get a sight of it, which is layd before the Proprietors, or a Copy which I believe My Lord Rochester will have to shew the Queen, and Council, and begg your pardon and patience while I add what relates to the Interest of the Church.
<373> The Assembly was made up of a Strange mixture of men of various opinions, and Inclinations, a few Church men, many Presbyterians, Independents, but most Any-thingarians, some out of principles, others out of hopes of power and authority in the Government to the End they might Lord it over their Neighbours. All Conspired to act answerable to the desire of the President and Councill. I was at this Solemn meeting a great part of the time, they Sat, I Preached twice before them, procured a Proclamation for a generall Fast which was kept on good Fryday, which otherwise wou'd not have been observed, any more than any other day. I administred the Holy Sacraments of the Lords Supper then, and did all I cou'd both in publick and private discourse to Excite them to use their Endeavours to Establish the Church, accordingly they made a very good, and proper Act to that End, which was to this Effect, that the Worship of God and our most Holy Religion as by Law Established in England should be put in Practice, and observed here in all particulars as farr forth as is Compatible with the Circumstance of the people, a Select Vestry of *12* men in every Precinct, or parish was thereby appointed, all the Burgesses were made Members thereof. These bound in a penalty to meet in their Severall parishes on a Certain day within 6 Weeks after the publication of the Act, to Chuse Church Wardens, give them power to buy a Glebe, Build a Church or Churches, as there was occasion, houses for Ministers, provide a sufficient maintenance for them, and to use their utmost Endeavours to provide that every Parish might be supplyed by a Clergyman approved of and allowed by the Lord Bishop of London. I thought it might not be improber to be present at their Vestrys as the first that met were very much disordered with drink, they quarelled and cou'd scarce be kept from Fighting, broke up without doing any thing, Leaveing first agreed when to meet again, when the day came there only met five, we pitched upon another day, then came but two in another Precinct. The Vestry met at an ordinary where Rum was the Chief of their buisness, they were most of 'em hot headed very averse to goe upon buisness, with much ado I prevailed with them to Chuse Two Church Wardens, resolve upon Building a Church which is very much wanted, and tis a shame to be without one since the Quakers have three meeting Houses in that and as

manny in the next Precinct whereas we have neither Church nor Chappell in 3 of the Precincts, and those two we have in Chowan, and Pequinans were never finished, ready to drop down, that in the former Precinct hath neither Floor nor seats, only a few loose <374> Benches upon the sand, the Key being lost the door stood open ever since I came into the Country, all the Hoggs and Cattle flee thither for shade in summer and warmth in Winter, the first dig Holes and Bury themselves these with the rest make it a loathsom place with their Dung and Nastiness which is the Peoples regard to Churches hence you may Expect a hopefull result from the vestry I was speaking of while the Rum Bottle were about, I Entertained the Church Wardens with the Articles of visitations which Church Wardens of England are bound to answer to. I cou'd not bring them to any thoughts of raising money, either for Building the Church, buying a Glebe, or providing for a Minister that is the great Bugg bear. Here they care not to be at any Charge, nor much trouble. If I would live altogether in that Precinct they proposed first £60 per annum but some more generous than the rest were for allowing £70 per annum which is in the goods they usualy pay Ministers with the refuse. The worst pay in the Country is good Enough for us. This £70 would purchase here about £15 worth of English goods as wearing apparel and the like. I told them I thought a Missioner was not to sitt down in one Parish and Sufferr the next or as manny as he could Supply with Convenience to live in Ignorance, meer Heathens, for my part I would not, this they Imputed to avarice which provoked me to upbraid them with their Generosity the last year, well if I would Continue to come among them as I had hitherto don two Sundays in four and give them two Sermons in the Week day in order to which I must ride *100* miles and be forced to quarter in somme sorry house or other not fitt to Lodge a man in for 11 or *12* days they would be kind for the future but haveing been ill used by them already I pressed them to give me some assurance, not being willing to trust to their generosity, they very libraly offerred me £25 for the year, or proportionable till such time as they had a Minister, which I refused and am resolved if I must starve. I'le not thereunto add Slavery more than indeed I am able to performe Except the Road's were better. I had another Horse and hoped for a better accomodation both for man and Horse than we usualy mett with, they treat us with a great deal of formality and think there is noe differrence between a Gentleman and a Labourer, all Fellows at Foot Ball, they have since Hired a Reader for £15 per annum who to them is more welcom than a Minister. <375> He is little Charge and pleases as well, nay many know no difference, for these Readers bring us into Contempt and breed fanaticism. <*Of the Readers takeing upon them to preach*> I lent him a Book of Homiles, and Enjoyned him to use no other Sermons, but I hear he goes on in the old way, which is to transcribe a Sermon, and then Read it to the People which is as much say they as we of the Ministry do, tho' I believe somme of 'em have reason to think otherwise of me.

If we are like to have a Church Government I humbly pray that the Society would Send somme directions to the Governor or me about these Readers for if suffered they'l be of ill Consequence, I have seen it in one French[6] a Rascall who was at first one of these and now pretends to the Ministry uses me ill, pray's Extempore and do's much mischief, he tells People he was ordained by the vice Chancellor of Oxford, shew's them something Pasted on the Innside of a Book in Latin which he sayth are his Lettres of orders. <*Marriages by Justices of the peace.*> I think Readers should not be allowed to Read the absolutions nor the Comunion or 2d Service nor yet Baptize Children as they Comonly do. The Governors assumeing the power of granting Licenses to Justices to marry is of ill Consequence for by virtue thereof are manny Adulterous Weddings, Christians unequally yoked, with Quakers or Heathens. I have shewed Colonell Hide what the Cannons require in that behalfe, but Governors and men in power will not Easily be Informed by an Insignificant worthless Pr[iest]. Notice ought likewise to be taken of an abuse offerred to my Character, our Blessed vestrymen, who are to Establish the Church, in order thereto at the first strike at one of the Fundamentalls of our Constitution in understanding the Act of Vestry otherwise than it was intended in a former Act which the Society did not allow of, as you may remember twas sayd Expressly that the Minnister should allways be deemed a vestryman, which is highly necessary here, where they are so great Strangers to the buisnesse of a Vestry, being to mend that Act by abolishing that power of meeting annualy to hire their Minister for the year Ensuing. They have omitted that of the Minister being a Vestryman, whereupon many will have it that the Minister hath nothing to do in Vestry which is Contrary to our Establishment in England and will of Course destroy this Act too, if so understood this is the Contrivance of an Enemy, and not of a Vestry man who ought to be Examplar and pious Christians in the Parish, but those are many of them Presbyterians or Independants unfitt for such an office but being Burgesses when the Act pass'd thrust themselves into the Number of Vestry with no good intent, this you'l say is rather History than a Lettre, I begg pardon for my prolixity hopeing the subject will Palliate the irksomness thereof, but perhaps not please. I wish in my next I may have cause to Change my matter and not as hither to be oblidged to acquaint you with things more disagreeable than in my former Letters, but we are agrieved the Church presented in danger, I myselfe yr. Creature a Sufferrer my sole dependance is on the honorable Society all good Christians here begg for Protection and Assistance from you the Eys of all are upon you hoping for some Redress from that great and Honorable Body. Nothing <376.> doubting but that they who are at so great a Charge and trouble in propagateing the Gospell among them will Cherish and maintain the Same so propagated, you have here a true but brief account of the difficulties I Struggle with. The most unsportable I hope will procure Compassion and speedy relief. Hard labour and Famine cannot be born long. You See what will make me, and think that is absolutely necessary a couple of good Negro's with somme stock to begin with, and money to buy provisions with till I can raise it within myselfe, this with the £45 the price of my plantation will Exceed £30 per annum. Mr. Gordon in his request for *£100* was not so unreasonable as many thought it to be, if the Societie will not Consider my Charge I pray they may be pleased to advance me £40 over and above what will then be due upon the departure of the next virginia Fleet, which I suppose will not be before spring. I have recd. nothing from the Society since I arrived here. Fleets are so uncertain, I did hope to be honored 'ere now with a Line or two from you. I am Sir yr. humble servant.

John Urmston

<Desires the Society may Write to the Governor about Dr. Brays Library etc.> I wish the Society would write to the Governor and Council about the Library which Doctor Bray sent to Bath in Pamplicough through mistake, and being Informed that there was the seat of Government whereas it is the most obscure Inconsiderable place in the Country. I hear Colonell Codrington has been a great Benefactor to the Society if true it

will be an Easy matter to order me two Negroes from Barbadoes born there and speak English used to House work and can handle an Ax, they may be sent by way of Barmud as opportunities are frequent. N. B. The Vestry of Chowen never met at all, all things are like to remaine till the Confusions are over which will not be till Colonell Hide has his Commission if then.

Copy. Read at a meeting of the SPG on October 10, 1712. Journal of the SPG, II, 223. The same meeting notes receipt of a letter from Urmston dated December 4, 1711; this has not been located.

[1]Hatchet or axe. *OED.*

[2]Bridewell, Newgate, and the Fleet were three prisons in London.

[3]I.e., the governor at Charleston. The proprietors formally united into one colony and government the northern and southern parts of Carolina in 1691. In theory, the governor of Carolina residing at Charleston governed that part of the colony "north and east of Cape Fear" through a deputy. In reality, the northern government was for all practical purposes entirely independent of control from the south. In 1712, with the appointment of Edward Hyde as governor of North Carolina, the fiction of a unitary government for Carolina was laid to rest.

[4]I.e., the period of the Commonwealth (1649-1660) in Great Britain and Ireland, during which royal government was supplanted by republicanism and the monarch by Lord Protector Oliver Cromwell.

[5]No council journals are known to have survived between 1706 and November, 1711.

[6]Richard French (d. ca. 1716) in November, 1712, was upon the complaint of Rev. John Urmston ordered by the council to appear before it to answer Urmston's allegation that he baptised and performed marriage ceremonies "without being Duely quallifyed for the Same." Later the council charged that French presided over bigamous marriages and ordered him to cease officiating at any matrimonial services. Cain, *Records of the Executive Council, 1664-1734,* 31, 477. Someone of this name sat in the lower house of the assembly in 1715. Clark, *State Records,* XXV, 159.

[*LAM/SPG/XV*]

Rev. John Urmston to Secretary, SPG
1711 July 17

<27> Sir

Since my last of the 7th the Rebels after a shamful defeat in their wicked attempt against the Governor and Council dispersed themselves, some fled into Virga. where they will be met with others have absconded but so as to be ready at a call. The Governor of Virgn. is expected in by land with forces and Captain Smith Commander of her Majesties Ship the Enterprize Guardship in Virga. brings with him a Sloop and Marines so that thire will be search made for the enemies, they'll I hope be apprehended and disabled from ever making head again, except they are protected and assisted in their villany by Danson, their old friend, they have sent divers to him by this Fleet to make their complaint and are very confident they shall turn out Colonell Hyde and his Council and have the whole management of affairs in their own power. If the Proprietors are so negligent of us surely the Societie will interpose and engage the Queen to take us under her Protection, otherwise there will be little hopes of establishing the Church or any good order. I've been dreadfully threatned by them and if they prevail must not expect to be sufferr'd to stay here. Madam Hyde[1] the Governor his Lady with Mr. Knight[2] Secretary of this Government come over with the same Ships. She has a copy of all proceedings, as sent to the Proprietors which is to be given to my Ld. Rochestr., who will doubtless acquaint her Majestie and Privy Council therewith. I told you in my last, I think that several Quakers bore arms and more are ready so to do and if that will not do, they threaten to bring in the Indians upon us. Danson sent hither from Engd. one Roach[3] with some goods and a dozen or 14 great Guns and ammunition under pretence of building a ship, but 'tis verily believed were designd for our ruine. Many of them were mounted on board a Brigantine which was mann'd by the Rebels with small arms, but upon their dispersing was since taken by our forces with 3 men only in her and all the great guns and ammunition. This is a considerable addition to our Strength and now many who were intimidated by the audacious impudence and cruel menaces of this rascals now daily join the Governor and others who were for the Adversaries are disheartned from acting against us; so that at present things have a better face and we shall I hope, be in quiet till news from Engd. Except Collonel Hyde have a Commission from the Queen he'll either be turn'd out or not obey'd, so great is Danson's influence over the rest of the Proprietors. These are with all humble respects to the Honorable Societie from Sir yr. most humble servant.

Jno. Urmston

N. Carolina July 17, [1]711.

As for the Rebels I am not much concern'd but 'tis grievous to hear the complaints of the poor men and families who have been so long in arms that they have lost their crops and will want bread. The ravage and plunder the enemies have committed has ruind others. Another instance of the Quakers knavery I cannot omit, which concerns you to know as having been Commissioner for the Palatines. Baron Graffenried with his people must have starved, if not supplied by others here. He had an order from the Proprietors i.e. Danson, for the rest never concern themselves, to receive £1500 here for which he was to pay 1000 sterling, a great cheat, for a £1000 sterling is worth 3000 here in our pay. Danson in his letters to his Friends here bragged they should get an estate by these Forreigners. Cary the late Usurper of this Goverment and now head of the Rebels was to pay £700 on the Proprietors Dues which he had received, he was arrested and made his escape. What reason then have they to protect him? To prevent others from supplying the Baron in his great distress Roach and the Quakers reported that the Baron had no credit in Engd. nor had he any money any where. Thro' ill usage in their way hither and since their arrival, of 900 Palatines there are but 300 now alive and those ready to starve. Through th' instigation of the English who live near them the Neighbouring Indians are very troublesome to them; in the beginning of this present rebellion the Baron with the Swiss and Palatines would have join'd the Governor, but were threatn'd with fire and sword. The English and Indians design'd to destroy them and all they had. Such encouragement do the Proprietors give people to come into their Colony. I've written a very tart letter to Sir Jno. Colleton[4] a Proprietor concerning all matters. Whether pleas'd or displeasd I matter not. The Proprietors promised me all friendship and favour, but as yet never shew'd any and I believe never will.

[*Addressed*:]
To The Worshipful Jno. Chamberlayne Esqr.
Petty France Westmr.

[*Endorsed*:]
Mr. Urmston N. Carolina 17 July 1711
receiv'd 24 Octob. 1711
For want of room for a seal
put this under a cover.

ALS. Read at a meeting of the SPG on November 29, 1711, when it was agreed "that a Copy of Mr. Urmstons letter be laid before the Lds. proprietors of Carolina." Journal of the SPG, II, 129.

[1]Catherine Hyde returned to England in July, 1711. Early in the following year she sailed again for North Carolina, bearing Edward Hyde's proprietary commission as governor. *DNCB*.

[2]Tobias Knight (d. 1719), secretary of the colony 1705-07, 1712-19; member of the council 1712-19; chief justice 1717-18. Accused of being an associate of the pirate Edward Teach, "Blackbeard," Knight was tried before the council and acquitted in May, 1719. *DNCB*.

[3]Richard Roach, London merchant, probably a Quaker and a ringleader in the Cary Rebellion, came into the colony with a cargo of arms for the rebels in 1710 or early 1711. On the collapse of the insurrection, Roach was one of the half-dozen or so exempted from the general pardon issued by Governor Hyde and the council. Saunders, *Colonial Records*, I, 774-778, 795, 804, 806-807, 831-832, 873, 917-918.

[4]Sir John Colleton (1669-1754) was a wealthy merchant of Exmouth, Devonshire, who lived for a brief time in South Carolina after 1714. Sir John inherited the Colleton share of Carolina as a minor in 1679 and held it until the sale of the proprietary to the crown in 1729, the longest period of time a share was ever held by a proprietor. Powell, *Proprietors of Carolina*, 58.

[*LAM/SPG/XVII*]

Benjamin Bradly to Secretary, SPG
1711 July 26

July the 26th 1711

Sir

The barer hereof the Reverend Mr. Giles Ransford is a Gentleman from Dublin and Son of Sir Mar[*torn*] Ransford Late Alderman of that City who with My self desiers your favour and assistance to be admitted to one of those vacancies he Tells me of In Carolina or Virginia or Else where, If he Goes To virginia I will Give him a Letter to the Commissary to be kind to him for I think he well deserves it I Could never hear any thing otherwise then that he is Beheav'd himself in Ireland, where I marred my wife, as a Minister of Religion should, and was Reputed to be a Sober discreet person and I hope he does to hear If any of our Merchants are of the Society could I hear who they are I would speak to them in his behalf, this is all I have to Say and in favouring my friend In the Request he makes, will oblidge Sir your Most humble Servant.

Benja. Bradly

[*Endorsed:*]
Mr. Bradly
26 July 1711

[*Addressed:*]
To John Chamberlaine Esqr.
In Petty France
Westminster

ALS.

[*LAM/SPG/XV*]

Testimonial
1711 July 30

<28>

Chevington Parsonage
near St. Edmunds-Bury Suff.
July the 30 1711.

Worthy Sir

By a letter from Mr. Giles Ransford dated the 20th of this month, I understand, that he has design'd his service under the Acceptance of The Venerable Society, which provides for the propagation of the Xn. Faith, on this behalf to the Mission Assign'd for the American parts; in order to which he desires my Testimony, of his Qualification, as his Credentials (in part) Whereupon he may be approv'd and recommended by the justice, and his Charecter from what I know of him.

In answer to which request of his, and expectation of yrs., I do certify you, that he has been a Gremial[1] for some months in my Family, and has behaved himself very acceptably to me, and as a person of sobriety and sence, and as becometh a clergy-man, with uncommon caution, reservednesse and respect; and do beleive that he will be diligent and faithfull, to carry and expresse a winning zeal for Christianity abroad with him; and be very Conscientious in the discharge of his high and serious trust, for the souls he so chearfully undertakes the care of, to which great and Good aim, I hold his pastoral abilitys to be as proportionate, as the society can desire.

He is a man (in short) of [*illegible*] (tho it is not fit that I should Envy him to the Indies, nor Grudge (in Xts. own works) to America, yet) I averr that The Losse of such a true affection for this Church, may be Lamented at Home, As is attested by one that prayes for A blessing on the piety of yr. Society and concluds himself Sir yr. humble Servant.

Edw. Grove.

[*Addressed:*]
To The Worshipfull Thomas Chamberlain

Esqr. Secretary to The Venerable Society
for propogating The Gospel in Forreign Parts
These

[*Endorsed*:]
Mr. Grove, Chevington
near St. Edm. Bury
30 July 1711

ALS.

[1]An intimate member of a society or other group. *OED*.

[*LAM/SPG/XV*]

Testimonial
1711 August 7

<29>

Chevington-Parsonage near St. Edmunds
Bury Suffolk.
August the 7th 1711.

Worthy Sir

Having Sent you a letter, from hence, last weeke containing a just Testimonial of Mr. Giles Rainsford, who (I perceive) has designd himself as a Missionary (upon the encouragement of the Venerable Society, for the propagation of The Gospel in Forreign parts) which letter (as I finde) has miscarried. I Give you this trouble, in persuit of his charecter, tho' I have not that time to inlarge myself, on this subject as I did in that which I wrote, to you before when I was more at Leisure. And Sir I promise to yr. Society and yourself on his behalf, thus farr, that he is a person who is very Serious and refind, and of a conversation becoming a clergy-man; and one that I hope highly of, as to his future service, in the church of Christ; whither he bestows his Labours, in the bosom of this establishd Chuch or upon the Conversion of Indians; of whose abilitys [what unto] which yourselves shall Judge, I beleive you will not doubt, but that what I offer is truly from my full persuasion and Experience of his due pastoral tendernesse and Concern for the good of souls and the glory of Religion. Which I desire may be accepted; as tis Humbly tender'd to that Worthy Society by Sir yr. most humble Servant.

Edw. Grove

[*Addressed*:]
To John Chamberlain Esqr.
Secretary to The Worthy Society for
propagating The Gospel in Forreign
Parts to be left with Mr. Ransford

At the Green Dragon, in Bishop-gate
Street London These

[*Endorsed:*]
Giles Rainsford's Testimonials.
Mr. Grove Chsington
Paronage [*sic*] near St. Edmds.
Burry Suffolk 7 Aug. 1711

ALS.

[*SPG/Jou/2*]

Journal of the SPG
1711 August 17

<83.> 17th Augst. 1711. [...]

<84> 6. Mr. Mayo acquainted the Bord that one Mr. Giles Ransford attended without in order to offer his Service to <85> the Society; then the said Mr. Ransford was called in, and produced a Letter of recommendation from Mr. Grove Minister of Chivington near St. Edmds. Bury (whose Curate he had been some Months) and another from Mr. Bradley Merchant of London, as also the Testimonials from the Provost and Fellows of Dublin, and his Deacon and Priests Orders from the Bishop of Down and Connor in Ireland, and Lord Bishop of London which were read: Order'd that the said Mr. Ransford do read Prayers and Preach at St. Antholines next Monday sennight on the Text of 10 St. Luke v. 23, 24:[1] and that the Committee report his qualifications at the next Meeting of the Society. [...]

Minutes.

[1]"And he turned him unto *his* disciples, and said privately, Blessed *are* the eyes which see the things that ye see: For I tell you, that many prophets and kings have desired to see those things which ye see, and have not seen *them*; and to hear those things which ye hear, and have not heard *them*." Luke 10:23-24, Authorized Version.

[*LAM/SPG/VIII*]

Bishop of London to Secretary, SPG
1711 August 27

Aug. 27.

Sir

I received a letter from Mr. Ransford in great hast for my letter to my Lord Treasurer: but tells me not where to direct to him, which if I did he would be never the better for it:

because I give no such letter without a bond from him of another sufficient person for repayment in case of failure. [. . .] I am Sir your most humble servant.

H. London

Mr. Chamberlain.

[*Addressed*:]
Mr. John Chamberlain Esqr.
hous in Petty france Westminster.

[*Endorsed*:]
(109.)
Lord Bp. of London
Essex. 27. Aug. 1711

ALS.

[*LAM/SPG/XVII*]

Rev. Benjamin Dennis to Secretary, SPG
1711 September 3

Goose Creek Septembr. 3d, 1711

Sir

May the 23d I left Wmsburg. (in order for this place) and cross'd James River: In my passage over, discourseing with one of the Nigroes, found him to be a very Sensible Fellow; I ask'd him severall questions, amongst which I ask'd him if he believed there was a God and what his notion was of him, he answer'd he was the maker of all things both in Heaven and Earth. I ask'd him if he believed in Christ the Son of God, he said yes he did. I ask'd him if he profess'd any Religion, who replied that he did, and that when he had time he went to the Church of England, but it was seldome, his Master (who was the Whery man of that place) not Suffering him to have any time either Sundayes or other daies. I ask'd him if he was Baptized, he said not, his Master not admitting it, notwithstanding his great desire: By this time I had got over, and it being late was oblig'd to put forward having 7 or 8 mile to ride before I could get to any house, but I advis'd him to apply himself to the Minister of the Parish, and that I was shure, he would prevail with his Master, to admit him to be Baptized etc., all which the Fellow thank'd me for, and ashured me that he would the first opportunaty, and desired God to Bless and be with me for my good advise.

I met with nothing worthy remark 'till I got into No. Carolina (being the 26) which is distant about a hundred and some odd miles, where I found the People all in Confusion and disorder, every one getting their Armes and selves in a readiness, to goe down to a place call'd Pamplicoe to take one Colonell Cary, who was late President, and had got the

Lds. mony in his hands, and would neither Lodge it in the Assemblies hands, nor give 'em Sufficient Security for the indemnifying the People from the Lords. This put me to a Stand whether I had best proceed thro' such a disordered Country as I perceiv'd that was, or else to goe back, but desireing Gods protection and Blessing I resolv'd to put forward. So sending my horses and Guide back I cross'd Ronoke River, and then was oblig'd to travel 6 miles on Foot, there being no such thing as a horse to be had: at length I got one, and that night reach'd to Governor Hides, where I found abundance of men in armes: I was recd. very kindly and after the Governor had perused a Letter from the Honorable Governor Spotswood of Virginia (which was in my behalf) he told me he was design'd to Pamplicoe the morrow, and that there was an opportunaty there for my Passage for So. Carolina. The next day being Sunday the 27: the Governor with about 80 Men cross'd the Sound and went up the river Morrotto about 12 mile, and there landed his Men and 2 pieces of small Cannon. The next morning march'd his men which were then Increased to about 150, but left his Guns there. We were all oblig'd to be in the Woods that night, and the next day got to Pamplicoe (otherwise call'd Hampton) the place where Colonell Cary lived, but he having notice of our coming made his escape to a house of one Colonell Daniels, which was a Small way down the River. The Governor did not think fit to pursue him that day, but next went down with his men at which time Colonell Cary had fortifyed the house with 2 pieces of Cannon and had about 40 Men. They could not bring him to any terms that was reasonable and finding they were so well Fortifyed, marched back again without any action. There was a Young Gent. a Relation of Governor Hides kill'd by accident.

June the 10, the Governor with his men marched up in the Country again and Remain'd at Hampton waiting for my Passage, the Vessel not being then ready. Dureing my Stay here I lodg'd at one Major Gales,[1] a very civil Gent. at whose house the People met each Sunday, where a young Gent. a Lawyer was appointed to read Prayers and a Sermond, they having no Minister. I understood they had a Gent. sent 'em by the Honorable Society, but he could not live amongst such an unaccountable sort of People and was remov'd up in the Country.

Colonell Cary finding the Governor gon Infused into the People, that that Assembly was not duely Ellected and that Governor Hide was not Governor having no Commission sent him and therefore he could not comply with their Demands, and one Mr. Roach a Merchant (Sent with some goods of 2 Merchants in London which are Proprietors) backing the said Colonell Cary with ashuring the People that Colonell Hide was not designd Governor, rais'd the Affections of the People towards Colonell Cary, and Insens'd them against Governor Hide, so that about 300 men (as I was inform'd) went up the Country in order to take Governor Hide, Colonell Pollock and other Gentlemen of the Governors Council, what the end will be I know not, being oblig'd away for this place. My reason for insisting so long on this Subject is to let you see partly the Management of this Country, the Inconstancy, and unacountableness of this People who are of such a Factious temper that they are ready to follow any one that will head them, let the design be what it will, and all is purely for want of sense or Reason. I realy think there cannot be a People in the World like 'em. Indeed the Country is good pleasant and Fruitful, and if Inhabited with honest, Just and Industrious People, would excell all the Places I have as yet seen. [...]

Ben. Dennis

[*Addressed:*]
Mr. Denis. Goose-Creek
S. Carolina. 3. Septemb. 1711

ALS. Read at a meeting of the SPG on December 21, 1711. Journal of the SPG, II, 136.

[1]Christopher Gale (ca. 1679-1735), originally from Yorkshire and son of a clergyman, emigrated to Bath County ca. 1700, where he was for some years active in the Indian trade. He held various posts in the colony almost from the time of his arrival, most notably as councillor, 1712-30, and justice of the General Court 1703-08, 1712-17, 1721-24, 1725-30, being presiding justice for most of those years. Often embroiled in controversy, he was one of the most able politicians of the later proprietary period. *DNCB.*

[*LAM/SPG/VIII*]

Rev. Robert Lasinby to Rev. Dr. Butler
1711 September 20

Epsom Seper. the 20th 1711

Reverend Sir.

Mr. Ransford having sent me word, that if some report be not made The Society on fryday of the sermon which he preached at St. Antholin's by their order, his voyage will be put off for a month: and Mr. Mayo and I, who were appointed to hear him being hindered from attending the Society at that time; I beg the favour of you to acquaint them that Mr. Rainsford read prayers, very distinctly and with great Devotion, and preached a very good usefull practical sermon. This Sir is Mr. Mayo's opinion as well as mine as you will find by his letter to me, which I have here inclosed. Pray Sir excuse this trouble and believe me to be Sir Your most Humble Servant.

Robt. Lasinby

[*Endorsed:*]
(118.)
Mr. Lazinby 7br. the 20th 1711

[*Addressed:*]
For The Reverend Dr. Butler
near St. Lawrence's Parish
London.

ALS. The document following was enclosed in the present one.

[*LAM/SPG/VIII*]

Rev. R. Mayo to Rev. Robert Lasinby
1711 September 19

Reverend Sir,

I know not by what mistake it has been represented to you, that I objected against the performance of Mr. Ransford, when He preach'd at the church on Monday the 27th of August last. I did indeed inform the committee that I could difficultly hear Him, which I did to Excuse my Self, that I was not able to Speak so much in commendation of what I heard, as I desired to do but I heard so much as to be able to declare that I lik'd the discourse, and that I have a very good opinion of the Preacher, and do hope that He will answer the designs of the Society, if they think fit to employ Him in the great work, that He desires to be sent about. And that I do think by converse with Him, that there is no defect in his view, but that He is able to meet with it a far greater Audience. I fear I shall be hindred from my attendance on Friday next, I beg the favour of you therefore to give in this as my report, if there be any doubt of what I said at the committee.

I am, Sir yr. Affectionate Bro. and humble Servant.

R. Mayo

Sept. 19, 1711.

[*Addressed:*]
For The Reverend
Mr. Lazingby
These

[*Endorsed:*]
<122>
Mr. Mayo 7ber. 19th
1711.

ALS. This document was enclosed in the one immediately above.

[*SPG/Jou/2*]

Journal of the SPG
1711 October 19

<90.> 19th Octr. 1711. [...]

<106> 16. The Secretary reported from the Committee that Mr. Ransford had read Prayers and preach't, according to Order, and having perform'd to satisfaction, they Agreed to report as their Opinion, that he appears well qualifyed for the Society's Mission: The said Mr. Ransford attending was called in, and acquainted that the Society dos admit him as a Missionary and appoints him to North Carolina in the room of Mr. Adams

deceased with a Salary of £80 per Annum commencing from Michaelmas last, on Condition that he take the first opportunity of going over and £5 in Small Tracts to be dispers't among the people occasionally. [...]

Minutes.

[*SPG/Jou/Cte*]

Journal of the Committee of the SPG
1711 December 10

10 Decemr. 1711 [...]

Mr. Ransford attending desird that the Society would be pleas'd to allow him a schoolmaster to assist him in N. Carolina, and recommended a young Man that he brought with him one Charles Bradey for that purpose, and Acquainting the Board that he could procure him his passage free, The Secretary also laid before the Board a Letter from Dr. Hare recommending the said Charles Bradey. Agreed to Report the Request of Mr. Ransford to the Society. [...]

Minutes. Considered at a meeting of the SPG on December 21, 1711, when it was "Agreed that it be refer'd to consider whether it be necessary to send over a Schoolmaster, to N. Carolina, and if so, to enquire after a proper person." Journal of the SPG, II, 141. A meeting of the SPG on January 4, 1711/2, agreed with a recommendation of the Committee that "it wou'd not be proper to send a Schoolmaster into the said Country till the Society were satisfyed where he cou'd be fixed and settled." Journal of the SPG, II, 148.

[*LAM/SPG/XV*]

Rev. Giles Ransford to Secretary, SPG
1711 December 13

Sheerness dec. the 13th 1711

Honorable Sir

Last night I came to this place, where I had the satisfaction of meeting with my Ship the Bedford Gally under the command of Capt. Andrew Lee, bound for Virginia. I took the opportunity of entring myself and servant, and a little after was muster'd on board, as late as it happen'd to be. The Capt. assures me, that unless I procure an order from the Lords of the Admiralty to be discharg'd at Virginia, he'le keep me in the service, and the method I must use to obtain it, must be your letter to Mr. Burchett[1] to move the Lords for such an order in the name of the Society. This Gentleman carri'd over Mr. Umpsty[2] who us'd the same means as are now propos'd to me for his discharge. And if there be any possibility of dispensing with my not returning again to town, I shall (as I always did) think myself oblig'd both in duty and gratitude to offer up every faculty of my soul to your service. The favours you have already confer'd upon me are so numerous, that I had not presum'd to have beg'd more. Had not your former condescending goodness, embolden'd me to aspire to what my humble thoughts wou'd scarce permit me to expect. The bearer Mr. Brady will attend my Lord of London, with your letter, for his, in my behalf to the Governour of North Carolina, if you in your wisdom think it proper, and the same Messenger will convey your instructions, for me at the same time. But if you are pleas'd to order me to town, I shall instantly obey your command by personally attending you there. The reason I have for continuing here, is for fear the Ship shou'd sail to the Downs without me, and then my charges wou'd be considerable to follow her thither, I can hear of none but she and the Oxford that are appointed for the Virginia fleet. I hope Sir you'le do me what service you can to send the Bearer (if possible) a Schoolmaster to those parts I go to, since I can assure you he's every way qualifi'd for such a Mission, and it being the last request I shall make you, on this side the Water. Excuse this haste, by reason of at least thirty or more Sailours, in the same room bawling round me and no other place to be had, and believe me to be Dear Sir with all sincerity and gratitude your most oblig'd thankfull humble Servant.

G. Ransford

On Board Her Majesties ship
the Bedford Gally at Sheerness

[*Addressed*:]
To John Chamberlayne Esqr.
at His House in Petty France
Westminster London

[*Endorsed*:]
Mr. Ransford. Sheerness
13 Decemb. 1711

ALS.

[1]Josiah Burchett, secretary to the Admiralty Board.
[2]John Urmston.

[*LAM/SPG/VIII*]

Bishop of London to [Secretary, SPG]
1711 December 31

Sir

I return you the Letter from Mr. Urmston, as likewise a Letter from the Parish of Christ Church in South Carolina, who Seem to be very kindly earnest for a Minister, if we could find a proper Person for them, and the better, could we Send Such an one over by the next dispatch. You have here inclosed the Letter you desired for Mr. Ransford to carry to the D. of Beaufort.[1] I am, Sir your most humble Servant.

H. London

Fulham
Dec. 31, 1711. [...]

ALS.

[1]Henry Somerset, 2nd duke of Beaufort (1684-1714), was at this time palatine of the Lords Proprietors of Carolina. By the Fundamental Constitutions, the eldest proprietor became palatine and presided at the proprietary board, but at a meeting of the board in January, 1707/8, the proprietors resolved that palatineships were thereafter to be elective. CO 5/292, 1-2.

[*LAM/SPG/XV*]

Rev. Giles Ransford to Secretary, SPG
1711/2 January 9

<31>

Chatham Jany. the 9th 1712

Worthy Sir
I hope that you'le excuse my not writing to you sooner on the score of not having an opportunity of coming on shoar before this day with the Captain. The 3 Instant I went on board, and deliver'd your letter which I presume will be answer'd this post. On Sunday last after preaching and reading divine service I din'd with the Capt., and prevail'd with him to let me in the Afternoon catechise the boys which he very much approv'd of, and beg'd I may continue that method every Lords day. There were some Warrant Officers who kept women in their cabbins, whome by private information I found were none of their own, and upon application to the Capt. one of 'em he sent away. I shall take all the care imaginable to omit no opportunity of doing good in the present station I am in and when I leave the Nore, I'le trouble you again from the Downs. We shall leave this place to night and repair to our duty. I am Sir your most obedient humble Servant.
G. Ransford

[*Addressed*:]
To John Chamberlayne
Esqr. Petty France
Westminster London

[*Endorsed*:]
Mr. Ransford. Chatham
9 Jan. 1711/12

ALS. Read at a meeting of the SPG on January 18, 1711/2. Journal of the SPG, II, 155.

[SPG/A/6]

Bishop of London to Secretary, SPG
1711/2 January 12

<CLVIII> The Lord Bp. of London to the Secretary.

Fulham 12th Januar. 1711/12

Sir

I received your 2 letters, as likewise another from Baron de Graffenried; which I likewise Send you with them. [....] As to the letter of Barron Graffenried where by you may perceive, that they are all ready to conform to the Church of England; if the Society will be pleas'd to allow a Stipend for a Chaplain to read common prayer in high dutch, I will endevour to provide one, so soon as I have their Resolution: which I would willingly hear so soon as possible that I may Send him over with Mr. Ransford. I am Sir your most humble Servant.

H. London

Copy. See note accompanying the document dated April 20, 1711, above.

[LAM/FUL/VI]

Rev. John Urmston to Bishop of London
1711/2 January 21

<208> Rt. Reverend Father in God. May it please Yr. Lordship.

Supposing that the repeated accounts I have sent of this unhappy Country with my proceedings in my Mission might come to yr. Lordships hands either at the Board of the Honorable Societie or before deliver'd in, by the Reverend Mr. Stubs, to whom I send all my letters which concern the Societie open for that purpose, I hope my omission in not writing to yr. Lordship will not be imputed to a want of a grateful sense of yr. many favours or of due respect and duty to my Diocesan.

I need not therefore now relate what difficulties and unheard of hardships I've here struggled with: I could not have fared worse at Malabar. Our confusions have much obstructed my endeavours, which I crave leave to assure yr. Lordship have been very earnest and indefatigable. Mr. Gordon my Predecessor's request was not unreasonable. I protest were I in Engd. I would not come hither again for five times as much as is allow'd.

I pray Your Lordship to make the Societie sensible of my misfortune in being sent to such a wretched place and excite them to consider me whilst here and either provide better for me, remove me to a Christian Country or else call me home.

These with all duty and humble respects are from My Ld. Your Lordships most obedient and humble servant.

Jno. Urmston, Missionary

North Carolina
Janry. 21, 1711/12

The granting Divorces, Lisences for marriage which often cause bigamy and incest, with Letters of Administration belongs not to the secular Courts: 'tis granted to some Colonies by Charter, but as little understood and as ill managed as here, but the Proprietors of this Provice have no such power. Your Lordship ought to have an Official here that would prevent many absurd inconveniences and abuses and 'twould be a considerable advantage or benefit to the See of London.

[*Addressed*:]
To The Rt. Reverend and Rt. Honorable
My Ld. Bp. of London
present

[*Endorsed*:]
N. Carolina
Mr. Urmston 1711/12

ALS.

[*SPG/A/7*]

Rev. Giles Ransford to Secretary, SPG
1711/2 February 20

G. Ransford Letter to John Chamberlaine Esqr.

Bedford Galley rideing
at Spithead Febr. 20th 1711/12

Worthy Sir

<*Ex.*> Since my last to you from Chattam <*of the discharge of his Ministerial Function*> I have Endeavoured to discharge my Conscience (as become a Person of my Function) with a tender regard to the Ships Company, and for the uncommon Zeal and concern I sometimes shew'd in the behalf of Religion I met with nothing but base and unworthy returns.

<*Of the rude and impious behaviour of the Captain and his officers and of the ill treatment he meets with from them.*> Indeed I might have Expected no better, since Mrs. Cordiner (before I left London) gave me a Just Character of my Captain, sufficient to

deterr any Conscientious man from going to sea under such a Commander, whenever I reproove him for Swearing, he tells me my buisiness is only to Preach and read Prayers as he shall direct, and the same Wretched liberty most of the Officers take, in prejudice to the Merits of their Baptismall vows, and their hopes of Salvation in their injur'd Reedeemer. Whenever swearing is the Argument of my Complaint, tis not the Sanctity and Priviledge of holy orders can protect me from a curse, however, that God may give him and the rest (that are like him) grace to repent and live, shall ever be a subject of my devotion, when we were in the Downs. <*Mr. Phillips absent from his Ship*> I went a Board the Sorlings, and found their Chaplain Mr. Phillips had not been with 'em since his Entring himself at Woolwich and can hear nothing of Mr. Mainadier on Board the Oxford.

<*Heard Mr. Urmston is dead*> Our Captain tells me he hears Mr. Urmston is dead in North Corolina, his Information is from Deal, but how to Credit his relation I cannot tell. We only wait here for a Wind haveing been since Sunday in our passage from the Downs hither. <*Mr. Bell appointed for Virginia, his Wife and Servant not mention'd are left behind.*> One Mr. Bell, a Clergyman appointed for Virginia, had an order to Come on Board us, but his wife and Servant being not mentioned are all unfortunatly left behind. How he'le get to us is now thought Impossible, since we are to proceed directly on our Voyage. I waited on his Grace of Beaufort with My Lord of Londons letter, and gave his answer to yr. Clerk Mr. Russell which was that he would take care of the contents, so depending on yr. Prayers for my Safe Arrivall to the place I am appointed to I begg leave to Subscribe my Selfe Yr. most obliged thankfull Servant.

G. Ransford

Copy.

[*SPG/A/7*]

Rev. Giles Ransford to Secretary, SPG
1711/2 February 23

G. Ransford his Lettre to John Chamberlain Esqr. att his house in Petty France Westmr.

Bedford Galley riding in Plymouth
Sound Febr. the 23 1711/12

Worthy Sir

<*Ex.*> <*Of his being under sail for Virginia.*> I have only time to tell you that we are just under Saile for Virginia being the last Port we shall touch at in England. And send this on shore by a Hoy that brought us Provisions on Board. <*Hears nothing of Mr. Maniadier.*> I heard nothing yet of Mr. Mainadier in the Oxford or any other Ship. I troubled you with a line from Spithead but since find my Captain is a man of another temper, and begg yr. prayers for our happy and safe Arrivall to our designed for Port. <*Of the Fleet's haveing left 'em behind 24 hours sail*> The Oxford, Severn, and all the Virginia fleet have left us behind 24 hours sail, the Commodore haveing ordered us to Dartmouth

and other Ports to call for Merchant men to Convoy 'em to join the Fleet. Yours Eternally in great haste.

G. Ransford

Copy.

[*SPG/A/7*]

Secretary of the SPG to Rev. John Urmston
1712 April 29

<472.> Letter from the Secretary to Mr. Urmstone.

29th Aprill 1712

Reverend Sir
The Ships are now ready to sail, and tho' there is not time to write to you any thing Else Yet I am directed to acquaint you That at the last Anniversary Meeting of the Society 15th feb. 1711 An Order was made That Mr. Wm. Taylor[1] be Secretary of the Society and a Standing order was then made That all Letters for the future be directed in this Form videlicet To the Secretary of the Society for propagating the Gospel etc. to be left at the Lord Arch Bishop of Canterburys Library at St. Martins London. I am etc.
You will please to communicate this to all concerned near you.

Copy. An identical letter was addressed to Rev. Giles Ransford.

[1]William Taylor served as secretary until February, 1715/6.

[*SPG/A/8*]

Edward Hyde to Rev. Giles Ransford
1712 May 30

<372> <2> Mr. Hyde to Mr. Rainsford. Enclosed in Mr. Rainsfords of the 17th feb. 1712.

Chowan May the 30th 1712

Reverend Sir
I have the honour of my Lord of Londons Letter withe the favour of yours by Mr. Pugh. I am very much obliged to you for so Early Acquainting me with your Arrival, and heartily congratulate you upon that and the Mission you come about. I wish with all my heart the Country was in Such a State, as will give you no reason to repent so long a voyage, and I hope it will not, for as the work you come about is of so a Essentiall Nature so I doubt not but God will Prosper you and your Endeavour, and the People Learn to do their duty. I

will Assure you there shall be nothing wanting in me to render Every thing to you as Easy as Possible nor would I have you to be the Least discouraged by any representation you may receive (this under the Rose)[1] from Mr. Urmston which will be very Loud and Complaining, but I will be free to tell you that all or the greatest Part of it is Purely oweing to himself and his Unfortunate Temper which no ways suits with the Humours of the Naturall born People of America (This as a Caution).

When you favour me with your Company I shall give you a faithfull acct. of the Observations I have made of the People Here, and the Method that will gain them for they are not to be won by any thing but Gentle methods to what is Serious and devout and Morall and Poor Mr. Urmstons railing and Morose temper has lost them all in generall. I have recd. and am fully Satisfied with your Credentials which I have returned you back and please myself with the thoughts that a Little time will Settle this Country more to your Satisfaction and mine notwithstanding all the trouble I have met with in it. I have cut of and Took Prisoners betwixt 3 or 400 Indian Enemies[2] and am in Hopes in a Little time to have Matters so ripe as to have a Treaty of a General Peace set on foot. It is indeed by nature one of the best Countrys in the World though the People are Naturally loose and wicked Obstinate and Rebellious Crafty and deceitfull and Study to Invent slander on one another, and sow such seeds of Sedition, that they have Generally reapt them in the Plentifull Crops of Rebellion.

And now (Sir) give me leave to give you an Invitation to my house, where you shall be most Welcome as long as ever you please; nor shall you have the Occation to Complain of the Country, as Mr. Urmstone has unhappily created himself. The times have been so very troublesome that I have the more pityed Mr. Urmstone, because the Scituation of his abode is such, as I have not been able to Accomodate him with such conveniencys as otherwise I would have done. But should he complain of me in that respect I will Assure you it is groundless. I have often offered Let him but send a Canooe and hands and I would Supply him. Nay would pay a Canooe and hands would he but Procure them.

I shall take it very kindly if you let me to be free with you in relation to your kind Offer of Sugar and if you will get your Purser to let me have a barrell of his best white Sugar for my own use and 5 barrells of his Muscavado best Sugar, I will pay him in Pork out of this Government or if North Carolina Staple will not do, but that they will have mony or bills of Exchange, be so kind to give me the Credit for so much, and I will pay you in money when you <374> come in, or in good bills of Exchange or in anything in this Country that will amount to the Intrensick value of what the Sugar will come to. I wish I could Procure some few Pounds of Indigo also, but I know not how to compute, what the mony would come to or I would not have given you this trouble. I wish you safe in this Province and the Enjoyment of your health as well as I have had it without the trouble and danger I have been Exposed to. You may entirely depent that I am with all the respect and Service in my Power Reverend Sir Your most humble Servant.

Edward Hyde.

May 30th 1712

I am sorry I can hear nothing of my wife[3] and was in hopes when she missed her passage in the fleet, she had been time enough to have come in the Bedford Gally. I am a true rejoycer of your good Luck in the Prize.[4]

Copy.

[1]I.e., *sub rosa*, secret.

[2]The Tuscarora War began on September 22, 1711, when Tuscarora Indians and their allies in the Core, Pamlico, Machapunga, and Bear tribes launched a surprise attack on white settlements along the Neuse and Pamlico Rivers. During the first three days, farms were put to the torch and at least 150 colonists were killed. Animosities engendered by the Cary Rebellion, and Quaker reluctance to engage in warfare, greatly hindered the colony's effort to launch a counteroffensive. However, a force from South Carolina under the command of John Barnwell, soon dubbed "Tuscarora Jack," entered the colony in January, 1711/2, and by late February had reduced a number of Indian forts and burned six Indian towns. In April, Barnwell and a force of North Carolina militia beseiged Hancock's Fort, the main Tuscarora stronghold. Within a few weeks Barnwell had signed a truce with the Indians and secured the release of prisoners from the fort. The South Carolinian was denounced by the governors of North Carolina and Virginia for not pressing his advantage, but Barnwell claimed that his force had been inadequately supplied by the host colony. By the end of June Tuscarora Jack had returned to South Carolina, and the Indians resumed their attacks. Not until March, 1713, would Tuscarora power finally be broken with the taking of Fort Nohoroco, again with crucial assistance from South Carolina. The best account of the Tuscarora War is in Price, *Higher-Court Minutes, 1709-1723*, xxv-xxxii.

[3]Catherine Hyde had returned to England the preceding year. *DNCB*.

[4]The naval vessel on which Ransford took passage to America, the *Bedford Galley*, obviously had taken an enemy vessel at sea, and the clergyman presumably had received or was to receive a share of the proceeds from its condemnation.

[*SPG/A/7*]

Rev. John Urmston to Secretary, SPG
1712 May 30

<416> Mr. Urmstones Letter to Jno. Chambelaine Esqr.

On board the Bayly in James River
Virginia Capt. Harvy commander
May 30th 1712.

<Ex.> Sir

<*Of the Warr with the Indians.*> Our Collony is Still in great confusion and God knows how the war with the Indians will end. Tis next to a Miracle wee are not all Cutt off by them hostelities have been very Violent on both sides and if not Assisted by Neighbouring Governments wee shall not be able to withstand them. Here's so great Scarcity of Provisions that tis to be feared many will Perish for want of food.

<*Of his own Misfortunes.*> I and my poor family will be the first. You'l Scarce beleive me but I assure you Verbo Sacerdotis wee have Sufferd much by hunger. Wee find it the hardest thing in the World to keep Soul and body together. We cannot do it long so that I intend to come for England God willing and the next fleet. The Country owes me above £100 already and the longer I stay the worse it will be. Greater Poverty and heavy taxes I cannot get a penny out. I've had no Supply from England never Since I came into these parts. They who should collect my dues here say they cannot tis not to be had one of them told me he would not give 12d. in the pound[1] for it. How can it then be Expected I should continue here twill be Impossible to winter here. Tis a good time for us as well as Indians

and Hoggs while fruit is on the trees. That was last summer. Our mean dependance tho' with the Hazard of our lives by eating of trash I was Afflicted with a Violent flux for the Space of Eleven weeks. I thought I should have died. I have told you so much of my misfortunes in former Lettres that I need not add, depend on't they are worse than ever without any prospect of Amendment. I recomend myself to the Prayers of all the Pious Members of the Honorable Society and am Sir Your most Humble Servant.

Jno. Urmston

Copy. Read at a meeting of the SPG on October 10, 1712. Journal of the SPG, II, 223, 227.

[1]I.e., 5 percent.

[*SPG/A/8*]

Bond
After 1712 July 23

<29> Condition of Mr. Coopers Bond to the Society on receipt of part of Mr. Ransfords Salary. Penalty £80.

Whereas The Reverend Mr. Giles Ransford one of the Missionaries of the Abovenamed Society to North Carolina in America with the Salary from the said Society of £80 Per annum hath drawn a bill of Exchange on the said Society dated the 23d of July 1712 for £40 payable to Edmd. Kerney or order for his half years Salary due at Michaelmas 1712 which bill is duly assigned to the above bound Wm. Cooper who hath applied himself to the said Society for the payment thereof but whereas the said summ of £40 due at Michaelmas 1712 hath been heretofore duly paid by the said Society to the proper person before that time authorized by the said Giles Ransford to receive the same, and the said Society considering the Case of the said Wm. Cooper and conceiving his Demand to be reasonable have ordered that the summ of £40 be paid to the said Wm. Cooper as part of the Salary at this time due from the said Society to him the said Giles Ransford, And the said Wm. Cooper having Agreed to deliver the said Bill and to give Security to the said Society to indempnify them for such payment of the said £40 unto him as aforesaid, and the said summ of £40 being now accordingly paid by the said Society to the said Wm. Cooper and the said bill being by him delivered up in pursuance of the Agreement aforesaid. Now the Condition of this Obligation are such that if the said Wm. Cooper and Wm. Dandy their Heirs Executors and administrators do and shall from time to time and at all times hereafter well and truely save harmless and keep indempnified the said Society and their Successors for the payment of the said summ of £40 to him the said Wm. Cooper in manner aforesaid, and in Case the said Society hereafter shall be obliged to pay the said Giles Ransford his Executors or Administrators the said summ of £40 for which the said Bill of Exchange was so drawn as aforesaid, if then the said Wm. Cooper and Wm. Dandy their Heirs Executors and Administrators every or any of them do and shall forthwith upon the Society's returning back and delivering to him or them the said bill of Exchange so drawn by the said Giles Ransford as aforesaid pay to reimburse and satisfy or cause to be paid to reimbursed and satisfied unto the said Society the said summ of £40 so paid by them to the said Wm. Cooper in Manner aforesaid. That Then etc.

Copy.

[*SPG/A/7*]

Rev. Giles Ransford to Secretary, SPG
1712 July 25

<417> <*Ex.*> Mr. Ransfords Letter to John Chamberlaine Esqr.

Chowan in N. Carolina
July 25th 1712

Worthy Sir

<*Gives an Account of what relates to his mission.*> To give you a description of a 12 weeks Passage we had from the Lizard to Virginia with the many Inconveniences I Labour'd under in it would but renew in me the Melancholy Ideas of what is past as well as trouble you in reading a relation of them. I shall therefore proceed to what Imediately relates to my Mission by giving a faithfull acct. of the condition the Country's in at Present and what Good (with Gods fatherly Assistance) I may do the Society and people by my continuance among them. June the 5th I arrived at the Governors where I was most Kindly received by him as afterwards by Colonell Pollock and Squire Duckenfield[1] being the only persons of any note that I could see or hear of on that Shore and as an Instance of my duty thought I could not do better than remind 'em at that time of preparing themselves for the receiving of the Sacrament on the then Approaching festival Whitsunday. The trifleing Excuses they made sufficiently satisfied me of the Little regard they had to the Indispensible Obligations that lay on 'em to so Solemn a duty. However Severall of the People came that day to divine Service, but perfect Strangers to the Method of the Worship of our Church. Mr. Urmstone and I by a mutuall Agreement with the Approbation of the Governor are to Manage after this Manner. He proposes to Supply the North Shore at the Lower End of Chowan together with all Paspetanck provided I take Care of the West Shore (where theres no Church but a vast tract of Land to ride over and in every Instance very fategueing) which I promised to do till I hear further from the Society. But Since the whole Countrys Entituled to my labours I visited his Shoar (which I am Sorry to say) has been a long time Neglected. Mr. Urmstone is Lame and says he cannot do now what he <418> formerly he has done but this Lazy distemper has settled him (by what I hear) ever since his coming to the Country. I shall give you a faithfull acct. of his proceedings and management as I desire he may do of mine that either of us according to the Merit or Demerit of our performances may be valued or disesteem'd by the Society.

Theres a Small Chapell near an old Indian Town on the North Shore, where I preachd at June the 15th and had vast Crouds came to hear to me but Obsurv'd they Exprest very little or Rather no devotion in time of Divine Service. That day and the day following I baptiz'd 17 Children four of them Eleven year old, nine of them Six, and the other four three, and when I told Mr. Urmstone of the Neglect he excused himself by saying that he never had notice of their having Children there Unbaptizd. June the 22d I preachd at one Mr. Garrats the upper End of Chowan, but had Such numbers that I was obligd to go under a Large Mulbery Tree, where most of the People to my great satisfaction seem'd very devout the whole time of Service, and very ready in their Responces as well as in their method of Singing Praises to God. Here I baptized two Girles of the age of 16 and one boy of 10 children of one Mr. Odams, and by much importunity prevailed on Mr. Martin to lett me baptize three of his Negroes 2 Women and a boy. All the Arguments I cou'd make use of would Scarce Effect it, till Bishop Fleetwoods Sermon[2] preachd before the Society turn'd the Scale, and wherever I baptizd there I distributed a share of the Small parcell of books. Old Mr. Saunders of Curahick[3] who has Mr. Adams's books refuses to deliver 'em unless I promise to Settle and Intirely fix there which I told him I could no way do to Neglect the Greatest part of the Country to serve there, but promis'd him as much of my time as I could Possibly Spare to that district. Many of the books <419> he tells me too are lost and he pretends a Claim to keep 'em and a Watch by Virtue of a debt contracted by Mr. Adams in his life time. <*Of his Conference with a King of the Indians*> I had Several conferences with one Thoms. Hoyler[4] King of the Chowan Indians, who seems very Inclinable to embrace Christianity and proposes to send his Son to School to Sarum, to have him taught to read and write by way of foundation in order to a further proficiency for the reception of Christianity. I readily offer'd my Service to Instruct him myself he having the Opportunity of Sending him to Mr. Garats where I Lodge being but three miles distance from his Town. But he modestly declin'd it for the Present, till a General Peace was concluded between the Indians and Christians. I found he had some Notions of Noahs Flood which he came to the Knowledge of and Exprest himself After this manner—My Father told me I tell my Son. But I hope in a little time to give the Society a better acct. of him, as well as of those peaceable Indians under his Command. There's one Mr. Mashburn[5] who keeps a School at Sarum on the frontiers of Virginia, between the two Governments and Neighbouring upon 2 Indian Towns, who I find by him, highly deserves encouragement and could heartily wish, the Society would take it into consideration and be pleased to Allow him a Sallary for the good services he has done and may do for the future. What Children he has under his care can both write and read very distinctly, and gave before me such an acct. of the Grounds and Principles of the Christian Religion that Strangely Surprized me to hear it. The man upon a Small Income would teach the Indian Children gratis (whose Parents are willing to send them could they but Pay for their Schooling) as he would those of our English Familys had he but a fixt dependancy for so doing, and what Advantage this would be to Private Families in particular, and whole Colony in General is easie to determine <420> Since my comeing in the Countrey (I thank God) I have had my health perfectly well, and dureing the continuance of it shall be Indefatigable in the discharge of that great trust that is reposed in me. Observing at the same time the Societys method of Writing over Every Six Months with an account of the Services I have done, and what Larger advances I have made to the furtherance of Religion and Enlargement of Christs Kindom. As for the eating Part I have far'd but very indifferently since my Arrival in the Country, and find for the future, must with Virgil's Shepherd be Satisfied with my Mitia Poma, castaneas nuces[6] And as ordinary as I am like to live, must Give Twenty pounds yearly for my Board. I was in hopes the Assembly wou'd take care to Provide me my table free. But the Countrys so poor that I can Expect nothing of that Nature, from 'em.

I desire Sir You'le think of me the next General Meeting, that I may have an Order for my ten Pounds worth of Books which I'le take Care to Send one to wait on you for them. Dr. Brays publick Library is all disperst and lost by those wretches that don't consider the Great Benefit of so valuable a gift. I cannot forget the uncommon Civilities that were Shewn me at my first Landing at Hampton in Virginia by one Mr. Kearny a Merchant of that place. He was a perfect Stranger to me yet shewed his great readyness to Supply me with mony to buy me a Horse and to transport my Goods for Carolina, and had anything Else been wanting he would have furnished me, and only as he told me for this great consideration of Setting forwards a good work, and Serving the Society. It has one way or other cost me twenty Pound in the Country and been Expensive beyond Imagination. <*Of the Indian Warr*> I presume you are no Stranger to the Indian War, which has some time Since begun and continues in the Barbarous Massacres of so many English Inhabitans, Most Families of Pamlico hourly feeling the Effects of their Cruelty. <421> Nor Truly can the Governour promise himself one hours safety, being continually Allarm'd by the Tuskarora Spies in his Own Quarters. Colonel Boyde was the other day sent out with a Party against the Indians, but was unfortunately Shot thro' the Head, and few of his men came home, but what shar'd in his fate and fell Sacrifices in the same common Misfortune. They Sculck so in Parties in the Woods, that common prudence obliges the Inhabitants (as the surest method of preservation) to keep to their Plantations and Several of them told me, that when they lye down in their beds, (they are so often Invaded) that they can't say they shall rise to see morning. Assistance is sent for to Ashly River, and Colonel Hyde flatters us with the hopes of either cutting them of, or obliging 'em to a Peace. But alass I fear all this without reason. The People are so Impoveris'd by the War that I wonder how they pay their Quit Rents to the Proprietors, and I am sure it would be highly Charitable in the Lords to forgive them for these ten years to come. I like the Country far better than any I have hitherto seen and certainly by nature tis one of the best in the world, and were but the Inhabitants free'd from the dangers of the War, they might enjoy the blessings of plenty, as well as all other comforts of life. This is a genuine acct. of what I have done and observed in North Carolina, and shall take all oppertunitys of Serving the Society (as I'm in duty bound) to the utmost of my Power, as well as of Expressing my gratitude to you for the many undeservd favours confer'd on Sir Your most Obliged faithfull humble Servant.

G. Ransford.

Copy. Read at a meeting of the SPG on October 10, 1712. Journal of the SPG, II, 227.

[1]William Duckenfield (d. ca. February, 1721/2), councillor and justice of the General Court. An active Anglican, he served on the vestry of St. Paul's, hosted worship services in his home, offered hospitality to missionaries, and donated land for a church and glebe. *DNCB*.

[2]William Fleetwood (1653-1723), bishop of St. Asaph, 1708-1714, preached the anniversary sermon before the SPG on February 16, 1710/1, on the text "To open their eyes, and to turn them from darkness to light." Acts 26:18, Authorized Version. The sermon was published in 1711.

[3]Richard Sanderson. See Ransford's letter to Francis Nicholson, December 1, 1713, below.

[4]Undoubtedly John Hoyter, king of the Chowan. *See* Cain, *Records of the Executive Council, 1664-1734*, 48, 70, 73, 99, 637-638.

[5]Edward Mashborne, son of the proprietress of one of the most famous London coffee houses, was a schoolmaster in Virginia from the late 1690s. In 1716 he wrote the secretary of the SPG seeking employment in North Carolina, but apparently his request was never brought before the Society. See his letter to the secretary of April 25, 1716, below. Someone of this name was appointed justice of the peace in Onslow County at its erection in November, 1731, and served to at least 1739. Cain, *Records of the Executive Council, 1664-1734,* 225, and *Records of the Executive Council, 1735-1754,* 88.

[6]Ripe fruit and chestnuts.

[*LAM/FUL/VI*]

Rev. Giles Ransford to [Bishop of London]
1712 July 25

<209> Chowan in North Carolina July the 25th 1712.

My Lord

As I was appointed by the Society Missionary of North Carolina, So duty obliges me to lay before you as my Diocesan the encouragment I have met with relating to the errand I was sent about to these remoter parts of the world. At my first arrival in the countrey, I had such kind invitations from the sev'ral Inhabitants that gave me reason to believe that nothing but the Good I expected wou'd result from such a well dispos'd people as I experimentally found 'em to be. Wherever I preach'd, I had great numbers of hearers, but in time of divine service, observ'd most of 'em strangers to the method of the worship of our Church. They brought many of their Children to be Baptiz'd, and what most surpriz'd me found all of 'em prety far advanc'd in years, at their receiving the benefit of that Sacrament. I likewise Baptiz'd some of their Negro's tho' with much difficulty I obtain'd the leave for so doing from their Masters. There's one Mr. Mashburn a School master at Sarum, on the frontiers of Virginia between the two Governments that highly deserves the encouragment of the Society. The children under his care are so well disciplin'd in the Principles of our Religion, and gave before me such an account of the Grounds of it, upon examination that strangly surpriz'd me to hear 'em. He's seated between two Indian Towns and the Chowans wou'd send to him their children for instruction, had they but money to pay for their schooling. And he promises upon a small Sallary of 20 pound yearly allow'd him to teach those children as well as our English that come to him gratis. I have represented it to the Society already, and hope your Lordship will use your interest with them, for the encouragment of so pious a work. The countrey is mightily harras'd by this Indian War, and truly the people are so much impoverished that I'm so far from expecting a support from 'em, that I shou'd rather beg the Proprietors to forgive 'em their Quitrents, the better to enable 'em to carry on the War. Mr. Urmston and I, with the approbation of the Governour have so order'd it, that we manage our respective Districts to the Gen'ral satisfaction of the People. I like the countrey extream well at present, and hope the good I'm like to do in it, will continue me much longer than I thought to have stay'd. Tho' the Lords Proprietors have given two hundred Pounds to the erecting of a Church, yet the continuance of the War silences all advances to such an undertaking. Colonell Hyde our Governour, gives his Duty to your Lordship, and please to give me leave to subscribe myself what most gratefully I am, My Lord, your Lordships most obedient dutifull Son and servant.

Giles Ransford

[*Endorsed:*]
N. Carolina
Mr. Ramsford 1712

ALS. At a meeting of the SPG on November 14, 1712, "A Letter from the Lord Bishop of London dated 3 Instant was read relating to the Request of the Governour of Virginia to the Society to Assist in the Education of some Indian Children in the College there, as also the Desire of mr. Rainsford Missionary in North Carolina for the Society's Encouragement, to one mr. Washburn [*sic*] schoolmaster near the Chowan Indians, And an Extract of a Letter from the said Governour was also read; Agreed That Colonel Nicholson be desired to Enquire into this matter when he shall be in the Plantations and Report his Opinion to the Society what is proper for them to do therein." Journal of the SPG, II, 253.

[*SPG/C/7*]

Rev. Miles Gale to Archbishop of York
1712 August 26

<16>
My Lord

I am informed by letters from my eldest son Chr. Gale, who has been an Inhabitant of North Carolina these last 8 years and born several Offices in that unsetled Government, that religion in that country; is at a very low Ebb and that little Stock carryed over, in danger to be totally lost without Speedy care of sending Ministers to teach the word of truth.

That North Carolina has been inhabited by the English 18 years,[1] and in all that space they have had but one clergy-man, and he left them for want of encouragement. And that these last 8 years they have had none, so that all the children under that age remain unbaptized, of which many have been cut of, by a late Massacre. The unhappy divisions among the English into Parties, encouraged two Sorts of Indians, the Corees and the Tuskarora's to come down upon them, and cut of about 200, the rest securing themselves in small Garisons, made of private Houses. According to my Sons request I hereby acquaint yr. Grace with the present sad circumstances of that fine and fruitfull Country, not doubting of your assistance in so pious a work, as the establishment of christianity in a Heathenish Country. That yr. Grace may live long to God's glory, the worlds good, and yr. own happiness, is the hearty prayer of yr. most obedient and humble Servant.

Miles Gale

From Kighley in Craven
[Tuesday][2] Aug. 26, 1712.

[*Endorsed:*]
Mr. Gale Kighley

26th August 1712
to the Ld. ABp. of York
of the State of N. Carolina

ALS. Read at a meeting of the SPG on September 19, 1712. Journal of the SPG, II, 217-218.

[1]The Albemarle region of North Carolina had been permanently inhabited by whites since the 1650s. The Pamlico Sound area, where lived the writer's son, Christopher, had begun to be settled in the 1690s.

[2]The writer uses the planetary symbol for Mars to indicate this day of the week.

[*SPG/Jou/2*]

Journal of the SPG
1712 September 19

<216> Att a Meeting of the Society. Fryday 19th Sept. 1712 [...]

2. Reported from the standing Committee that they had agreed to Move the Society, and desire if they think it Convenient that some person or persons Members of the Society be desired to search the Treasurers Accounts and other the Books of the Society what Library of Books have been given or sent to or with Missionarys, and to send over to the Plantations and Enquire in the best Method, whether the said Librarys are kept and preserved according to the Intentions of the Society.

Agreed to by the Society, And Dr. King, and Mr. Nelson are desired to make such search and Report what they shall do therein to the Society.

3. Likewise that they Agreed to move the Society that the several Missionarys be wrote to, and in such places where there are no Missionarys To the Vestry, Church Wardens, or other proper Persons to transmit to the Society an History of the Founding and Building of the several Churches in the respective Provinces and how they have been supplyed with Ministers and that the said account be signed by the said Missionarys, Vestry Church Wardens and the principal <217.> Inhabitants of the said Parishes.

4. Agreed to by the Society with this Amendment that Letters be sent to such Places where there are or have been Missionaries of the Society or where Missionaries are desired for the purpose above mentioned.

5. And that they Agreed to move the Society that the Several Missionaries be wrote to, and put in mind of observeing the standing Order of the Society, with respect to their Missionarys sending every six Months an Acct. of the state of their respective Parishes according to the scheme there annex'd. Agreed to. [...]

Minutes.

[*LAM/FUL/VI*]

Rev. John Urmston to Bishop of London
1712 September 29

<211> May it please yr. Lordship.

My Lord
The Death of Colonell Hyde, which happen'd on the 8th inst. causeth me to take the liberty of these notwithstanding I have been so lately troublesome; I know not what may be the consequence thereof: the factious, quaking Party are not a little rejoiced, but I hope the Government is so well settled as that they will not dare to attempt any new commotions, Colonell Pollock, being the first of the Council, is chosen President, and it would be for the interest of the Proprietors, the Countrey and of the Church in particular; were he to be confirm'd Governor, having been long here, acquired a good Estate without which a Governor will not be able to subsist on a poor salary only. He is a prudent, wise Gent., hath labour'd heartily to preserve the Church and State from being ruin'd by intestine as well as a Foreign Enemy, was the great Supporter of our late Worthy President Mr. Glover and Colonell Hyde against their inveterate and irreconcilable Adversaries, hath been at a vast expence and even hazarded his life for the common safety and wellfare of us all.

I need not suggest to yr. Lordship what an influence such a Governour would have in the Propagation of our most Holy Religion to which he is so well affected and thro' whose means, I question not, but all the difficulties I have hitherto labour'd under will be removed and now in power will signalize his esteem for Our Function more than ever.

Give me leave therefore My Good Ld. to request yr. Lordships interest with his Grace the Duke of Beaufort, our Palatine on behalf of the said Gent. and to assure You that I have no other motive than as above written to presume thus much. I am My Ld. yr. Lordships most dutifull and obedient servant.

Jno. Urmston Missionary

North Carolina
Septr. 29th, 1712.

Mr. Ransford hath preach'd but once in this Goverment and I hear is bound for Engd. per the first Ship, he hath earn'd an £150 easily.

My Ld. of Beaufort was pleased to promise, upon yr. Lordship's kind recommendation, to honour me with the title of his Grace's Chaplain but did not. He may now do it as Palatine without doing his other Chaplains any damage. I also press'd some friend to procure me a Deputation[1] from Sir Jno. Colleton, which by Mr. Glover's death vacat: these favours would be no profit at all, but a great furtherance of my Mission.

We are in great danger of being destroy'd by th' Heathen the people being of quaking principles with reference to the maintaining of the Clergie and fighting.

If the Societie is not kind I shall be forced to run for't, bankrupt and not able to continue much longer here.

[*Addressed:*]
To The Rt. Honorable and Rt. Reverend
Father in God Henry
Lord Bishop of London

[*Endorsed*:]
N. Carolina
Mr. Urmston
1712

ALS.

[1]Each of the Lords Proprietors was entitled to appoint a deputy, who thereby acquired a seat on the council.

[*SPG/C/14*]

Bishop of London to Secretary, SPG
1712 October 3

<24A>
Sir

I receiv'd Letters lately from Virginia, and have in Charge from the honest and good Governour[1] to move the Society in behalf of that Colony, That they would assist them in propagating the Gospel in Such particulars, as they are not able to proceed in without their help.

1. The Governour hath obliged the Natives that are Tributary to them to send two of the Chief Men's Children out of each Town to be educated in the College, which Number, with 4 they had already, amounts to 20 where they are dieted, cloathed and Instructed in Literature and the Principles of Christianity So much to the Satisfaction of their Parents and Friends, that come frequently to See them, that they lament their own want of So great advantages in their Infancy. But all this hopefull beginning is in danger of failing for want of a Subsistance for them [and] which Mr. Boyle's Charity[2] will not near reach unto. And therefore he intreats the Assistance of the Society in a work that So evidently relates to the Propagation of the Gospel. And that,

2. For a farther carrying on of this good Work, the Society would likewise maintain two Missionaries to reside among those people, and have each of them a Chappel built and Schole House in 2 of the Principal Towns, with the allowance of a Clerk qualifyed to teach a School. He recommends Mr. Forbes who is now upon the Place, as a very fit person to make one of the Missionaryes, and who is very willing to undertake it upon the Society's Encouragement. So that both places will be Supplyed, when Mr. Andrews comes thither.

3. There's one Mr. Mashburn, a Schole Master at Sarum on the Frontiers of Virginia near North Carolina, who deserves very Highly, as Mr. Ransford, Minister at Chowan in N. Carolina informs me, the encouragement of the Society. He tells me, that the Children under Mr. Mashburn Care are So well disciplined in the Principles of our Religion, and gave before him Such an account of the Grounds of it, as strangely Surprized him. He is Seated between 2 Indian Towns, and the Chowans would Send their Children to him for Instruction, had they but money to pay for their Schooling. He promises upon a Small Salary of £20 paid yearly to teach those children that come to him gratis.

Pray lay these particulars before the Society, and desire in my Name, Mr. Nelson, Dr. Moss, Mr. Jennings, etc. to press it to them, as a Work of the greatest importance, and most likely to influence the Conversion of those poor People. I am, Sir Your very humble Servant.

H. London

Fulham
Oct. 3, 1712.

ALS.

[1]Alexander Spotswood, lieutenant governor of Virginia 1710-1722.
[2]The eminent scientist Robert Boyle (1627-91) established a fund at the College of William and Mary for the education of Indian youth. *DNB*.

[*SPG/Jou/2*]

Journal of the SPG
1712 October 17

<246> Fryday 17th October 1712 [...]

3. Mr. Cuigly named in last Minutes Attended and produced a proof taken before a proper person of the letter of Attorney therein mentiond which was read. Agreed that it is the Opinion of the Society that the Treasurer may and ought to pay the forty pounds now due to Mr. Ransford to the Said Mr. Cuigly to whom the letter of Attorney was made and who as it Appears hath Already paid and Advanced the like Summ to the Said Mr. Ransford and Orderd <247.> that the Secretary do write to the Said Mr. Ransford and Acquaint him that the Society doth highly disaprove his proceedings in drawing a bill on the Treasurer to pay a Sume of mony to one person when he had before had mony Advanced to him and given Authority to Another Person to receive the Like Sume. [...]

Minutes. At a meeting of the Society on October 10, 1712, the treasurer "acquainted the Society that a bill of Exchange from Mr. Giles Ransford for forty pounds for his Years Salary, ending the 29 Septem. last, drawn upon him, came to his hands—and one Mr. James Cuigly attending acquainted the Society, that he had a Lettre of Attorny duly executed from the said Rainsford to receive the like Summe, which he was indebted to him and had produced a Note under the hand of the said Ransford, whereby it was mentioned that he had advanc'd the said Summe to him. Agreed that the said Mr. Cuigly do make proof of the said Letter of Attorney against the next meeting of the Society, at which time the Society will take further Order therein." Journal of the SPG, II, 245.

[*SPG/A/8*]

Rev. John Urmston to John Hodges
1712 October 22

<353> <13.> Mr. Urmstone to mr. Hodges.[1]

Sir

I Acquainted the Honorable Society with the Death of my fellow Labourer the Reverend Mr. Adams late Missionary in this province per the first Opportunity after the Same And with all That being disappointed of that Library brought in per Mr. Gordon and for which I stand bound, I demanded that which belonged to Mr. Adams, which upon Enquiry I found Safe and Entire but was refused it, The precinct where the deceased last dwelt, pretending the Books belonged to them and would not part with them Except I would live with them. I am told mr. Ransford had the like Answer. Thus the Society is Abused and their Missionaries in this as well as other cases illtreated by an Ungratefull worthless people. I hope you will either cancell my Obligation or Send Me other Books instead of those lost by mr. Gordon. I aver and Testifie that those Mr. Adams brought in were at the time of his Death Safe and Entire as above and therefore See no reason his heires should Suffer but what is Since become of them perhaps neither you nor I shall ever know.

I've more than Once complained of the unjust usage I have met with in Reference to a very valuable Collection of Choice Bookes detained at Bath, now the Seat of War many of which are Spoilt and the rest will infallibly be destroyed by the Heathen, at least the Ministry will never be much better for them for whose use they were chiefly intended. That place will never be the Seat of Government nor Supply'd by an Incumbent, a remote Obscure dangerous place of it Self incapable of Subsisting a Minister and inconsistent with any other part of the Colony. I have not been favoured with a Line since I arrived here from the Society. I hope I shall be So happy within a short time and that my Requests per Colonell Quarry will be granted, otherwise you must Expect to hear I am bankrupt and forc't to run for it. Since Colonell Hide's Death the Quackers and their Adherents threaten to Act over againe the late Tragedy in Order to Settle and Establish themselves, overthrow the Church and in the End finish the Ruin of this poor Countrey, if the Indians do it not for them but these meeting with little or no Opposition cannot fail of Destroying us all. We are <354> In Expectation of Succour from Ashley River but that is very uncertaine. Our Cowardice and Quaking Principles render us the Scorn and Contempt of all our Neighbours. We are to have an Assembly on the 4th of Next Month. I hear few but Quakers and their party are Chosen Burgesses So that we may Expect but litle good. They give out already they'l have New Lords and new Laws or rather no Laws, that will best please the Generality of our Gentry. I am Good Sir Your Most humble Servant.

Jno. Urmstone Missionary.

North Carolina
Octr. 22, 1712.

Copy. Read at a meeting of the SPG on October 16, 1713, when it agreed to accept a report of the Committee that "if...the Books formerly Mr. Adams's deceased intend'd for the said Mr. Urmstone in N. Carolina cannot be delivered him that then the Bond of the said Mr. Urmstone be delivered up to him." Journal of the SPG, II, 331.

[1]John Hodges, treasurer of the SPG.

[*SPG/A/7*]

Secretary of the SPG to Rev. Giles Ransford
1712 November 6

<485> <*Ex.*> Letter from the Secretary to Mr. Ransford.

November 6th 1712

Reverend Sir

Yours of the 25th July last came to hand and has been communicated to the Society. They are glad of your safe Arrival in North Carolina and are thankfull to your good Governor for his kind reception of you, and which they desire you to let him know. They are well Pleased with the particular relation of your Proceedings since your Arrival there, but I am Sorry to Acquaint you, That very lately it Appeard to the Society by their Treasurer, that a bill was brought to him drawn by you, for the payment of a Sum advanc'd to you, by a kind Gentleman in Virginia, when at the Same time one Mr. Quigley, who had before advanced to you, here in England, the like Summ Applyed to him for the payment thereof to himself. This matter has occation'd great Trouble to the Society to Adjust this Affair, and upon Consideration of the Several Demands, they conceived it to be just, that your half Years Salary from the Society due at Michaelmass last Past, should be Paid to Mr. Quigley and have ordered the same to be paid to him accordingly. The Society very much disaprove your proceedings in this Matter, and direct me to let you know so much. You will perceive Sir and I hope be convinced, that this and the like Practices (as they shall be known) will rather hinder than Promote the Gospel of Christ. What I have now said is Enough, and it greives me to tell you so much.

I am directed to Acquaint you and others, That in Such Places in the Plantations where there are or have been Missionaries of the Society or where such are desired, They the said Missionaries (and in Such Places where there are none the Vestry, Church Wardens, or other proper persons) are desired to transmit to the Society an acct. or History of the Founding and building of the several Churches in the respective Parishes, and how they have been Supply'd with Ministers. And that the said Acct. be Signed by the said Missionaries Vestry, Church Wardens, and the Principal Inhabitants of the said Parishes.

<486> I am likewise directed to put the Several Missionaries in mind of Observing the Standing Order of the Society with respect to their Sending over Every Six months an acct. of The State of their Respective Parishes according to the Scheme there Annexed.

Her Majesty having been gratiously pleased to Appoint the Honorable Colonell Francis Nicholson her commissioner in North America for Several Purposes mention'd in his said Commission, The Society have requested and desired him (and he hath consented) when he shall be in the Plantations to make Enquiry of and concerning the Societys Missionaries, Schoolmasters, and Catechists, as also of the Present State of the Churches, Glebes, Parsonage houses and Libraries (sent by the Society) there, To the End the Society may be fully informed concerning them, and be the better enabled to discharge the great trust reposed in them. Now when Colonell Nicholson shall Signifie his Pleasure to you to Assist him in his Enquiry the Society desire and Expect that you readily and willingly comply therewith and shew all due regard to him.

I have in command nothing more to transmit to you at Present Except it be that when you write any thing to be communicated to the Society you direct your Letter to the Secretary of the Society for the propagation of the Gospell in Forreign Parts at his Grace the Lord Arch Bishop of Canterburys Library St. Martin in the Fields London. I am etc.

Copy.

[*SPG/A/7*]

Secretary of the SPG to Rev. John Urmston
1712 November 6

<483> <*Ex.*> Letter from the Secretary to Mr. Urmstone.

November 6th 1712

Reverend Sir

Yours of the 7th July 4th decembr. 1711 and 30th may last have been recd. and communicated to the Society, who as they are well Pleased with your Particular relation of things, Yet are much concerned at the confusion in North Carolina by a Warr with the Indians and the Miseries occationd thereby to the Inhabitants.

<484> I am directed to Acquaint You and others, [...][1]

Copy.

[1]The remainder of this letter duplicates the one of this date from the secretary to Rev. Giles Ransford, immediately above.

[*SPG/A/8*]

Alexander Spotswood to Rev. Giles Ransford
1712 November 14

<1> <*Carolina Papers*> Colonell Spotswood to Mr. Rainsford Enclosed in Mr. Rainsfords of the 17th february 1712.

Williamsburg Nov. 14th 1712

Sir

The business of the Assembly has obliged me to detain your Messenger a few Hours longer than I would otherwise have done to Answer your Letter which I this day received.

I do with you beleive that little encouragement can be given you in a Country from whence I have most dismal representations of their Circumstances and thereupon am the more ready to Comply with any thing that may be proposed to make a Gentleman of your function easy in this Government, but as I am restrained from Beneficing any Minister here without the Ld. Bp. of Londons Certificate, and am loath to do any thing disagreeable to the Society in relation to their Missionarys, I can only permit you to Officiate upon the best Terms you can make with the Vestrys of Hampton or Surrey Parishes (for York is already Supply'd) till you can produce to me the Ld. Bp. of Londons Certificate and (I could wish) therewith the Societys Approbation of your removal from North Carolina hither. I am Sorry for your Indisposition as being with great Truth Sir Your very Affectionate Humble Servant.

A. Spotswood.

Copy.

[*SPG/C/14*]

W. Hall to [Secretary, SPG]
1712 November 24

<26>

Fulham Nov. 24, 1712.

Sir

My Lord of London wonders, he can hear nothing from you in relation to Newbery in New-Hampshire; and is very much Surprized to find in the last Minutes, that a thing of So great Consequence, as that of the Educating of Indian Children in the College of Virginia, and by Mr. Mashburn amongst the Chowan Indians, should meet with Such unaccountable delay. He thinks so good a Work should be promoted with all imaginable Speed and Application, and desiring you would move the Committee to consider it again, and not leave it till an Account be sent from Col. Nicholson after his arrival in those Parts; least it should prove then too late to doe any Service in that kind. I am, to desire you to give an Answer the first opportunity to, Sir Your very humble Servant.

W. Hall.

There is a Gentleman lately come from Virginia; who will give the Committee a full account of these Matters, if it be thought needfull.

[*Addressed:*]
To Mr. Taylor at Cursitor's Office
in Chancery Lane

[*Endorsed*:]
44
Lord Bp. of London, 24th Novr. 1712
Concerning Educateing Indian Children
in the Colleg. of Virginia

ALS.

[*SS 845*]

Will
1712 December 17

North Carolina ss.

In the name of God Amen. I Richd. French of the Precinct of Paquimmons being at this time thro the goodness and mercy of God both in health of body and also of a perfect and Sound mind and memory do make constitute ordain and declare this last will and Testament in manner and form following hereby revoking all other wills formerly by me made.

<*Imprimis*> I commit give up and recommend my Soul into the hands of God my Creator Christ my Redeemer from whom at first I received it etc.

<*Item*> I commit my body to the earth from whence it came to be decently buryed according to the discretion of my Executrix hereafter named Provided that my wife realy and unfeignedly intends to be buryed immediately or close by me if otherwise then my will and desire is that my body be buryed somewhere alone by it self or at such convenient distance as to be seperated by it self and not in company with any other.

And after my funeral charges and lawfull debts paid and Satisfyed I give and bequeath what earthly goods it hath pleased God to intrust me with in manner following.

<*Item*> I give unto my wellbeloved wife Elizabeth French that Plantation and Tract of land containing two hundred Acres now in the Tenure and occupation of John Old and Susannah his wife to her and her Assigns for ever to be disposed of as she shall see good by her last will and Testament or otherwise.

<*Item*> I give unto my Said wife all the rest of my estate goods and chattles of what nature kind or property soever within this Government or elce where to her own proper use and behoof and afterwards to be disposed according to her own will.

<*Lastly*> I constitute ordain and appoint my Said wife Elizabeth French to be wholy and Solely the Executrix of this my last will and Testament In Wittness whereof I the Testator have hereunto set my hand and Seal this 17 day of Decembr. Annoq. Domini. 1712.

Richd. French

Signed Sealed and acknowledged in the presence of
Thomas Clitchensen
Rich. <*his mark*> Skinner Junior
Sarah <*her mark* > Evens

[*Endorsed:*]
Proved in open Court In Aprill the 13th 1716
Test. Richd. Leary Clerk Court

DS.

[*LAM/FUL/XVII*]

Representation
ca. 1713

The Case of Gideon Johnston Clerk humbly offered to the venerable Society for the propagation of the Gospel in foreign parts.

The Cure of Charlestown in S. Carolina was proposed to him in February 1706/7, which he thankfully accepted.

In pursuance to his resolution, he disposed of all his affairs in Ireland, and came to Dublin with his Family, From whence after Being detain'd there for considerable time by Privateers and contrary winds he arrived in London, July 10, 1707.

In a few daies after his arrival, he was by a Letter from his Lordship the Bp. of London recommended to the Secretary: And according to the said Secretary's directions he waited on the Committee 21st ditto. His letters of orders and letters dismissory being then perused, and an account given in of his Family, at that time 11, and now 10 in number, he was ordered to write for more Testimonials to Ireland, such as he brought with him not being thought sufficient. And it was then likewise proposed to him to go to N. Carolina, and he was directed to give his Answer to the Secretary that week.

Accordingly he wrote for more Testimonials; and accquainted the Secretary that he coud not go to N. Carolina; but that he wou'd get one, that Shoud go for him. This the Secretary accepted of; and with his approbation he wrote for the Person he proposed, who was then his Curat in Ireland, and is now emploied by the venerable Society in N. Carolina. [...]

[*Endorsed:*]
Mr. Johnston's Case

DS. Johnston goes on to complain that he went to considerable trouble in obtaining the testimonials required by the SPG, only to have the Society then decide at a meeting on September 19, 1707, that in Johnston's words, it "had nothing to do with the affairs of" South Carolina, and that therefore "farther proceedings concerning him [Johnston] wou'd be laid aside, without having any regard to his numerous family, or the expense and trouble he had been at in transporting himself thither, and in his long attendance on the venerable Society." In fact, the only reference to South Carolina in the record of the meeting was that the bishop of London informed the SPG that he intended to send Johnston to that colony, and it was then "Agreed that he [Johnston] be Discharged from his Attendance on the Society." Journal of the SPG, I, 295-296.

[*SPG/C/14*]

Bishop of London to Secretary, SPG
1712/3 January 17

<29>
Mr. Taylor

It being my unhappiness, that I can't attend the Society, as I could very gladly doe, I once again desire you to give my most humble Service and respects to them, and acquaint them, that it is my earnest request to them, that they would take into their consideration anew, what I represented to them from the Governour of Virginia; because I do believe, they have not any Affair under their Care, that more naturally regards the Trust of their Commission; when they consider, that it is most properly for the propagation of the Faith in Foreign Parts to bring up the Children of the Heathen in the Knowledge of Christianity, and to embrace So fair an opportunity of bringing over their Parents, by building a Church amongst them at their own request. I should think, we could not too greedily lay hold upon this occasion, especially when it may be done at So easy an expence; and therefore I hope they will not delay it So long, as to refer it to Col. Nicholson to report it when he arrives there, Since nothing more properly requires a Speedy Care. I am Your assured Friend.

H. London

Fulham
Jan. 17, 1712/13.

[*Addressed*:]
For Mr. Taylor at Cursitor's Office
in Chancery Lane
London

[*Endorsed*:]
Ld. Bp. of London
17 Jan. 1712
relateing to the Affair represented
by the Governor of Virginia

ALS.

[*SPG/A/8*]

Rev. Giles Ransford to Secretary, SPG
1712/3 February 17

<7> Mr. Rainsford to the Secretary.

Chowan N. Carolina
Feb. 17th 1712/13

Honorable Sir

Since my last to you on the 25th of July, with deep Concern I am forc't to tell you, That this Countrey has been miserably reduced by Indian Cruelty. The Inhabitants are brought to So low an Ebb by this Unhappy War that rather than Expose themselves to their Enemies, They have most of them quitted their plantations, and Entirely thrown themselves on the virginians for Reliefe. The Governour of South Carolina has Sent in Eleaven hundred Indians in Order to Relive this Government And Colonell Pollock our President with his Council have leavy'd five pounds on every Tithable Six Buchells of Corn, a Quarter part of all their Wheat for the Maintenance and Support of these Ashley River Indians. The Stocks of our English Inhabitants are all Destroy'd by their Coming to this Countrey And their poverty is So great That Virginia has given £1000 Sterling to Relieve them, with 900 Yards of Duffile to Cloath them So that should they Conquer their Enemies without the Charitable Support of the Proprietors they can never Afterwards be able to Subsist. This is a True Account of the Miserable State the Countrey now labours under as may Appear by Governour Spotswoods Hint in the enclosed to me. I have been already taken by the Salvages in my Journey to one Odams to preach, and after a little Conference let go but Guarded by two of them out of the Parts. There's Scarce a Man even on the North Shore of Chowan River (Which borders on Virginia) to be found, and for the Women they won't leave their Plantations to go to a house where I make an Appointment to preach, So that very little good at the present Juncture can be expected from us. Indeed I have been visited with a Terrible Seasoning[1] to the great Hazard of my Life, being given over for 3 Months together by those that beheld me but it has pleased God to restore me againe to my former health. The Danger of Liveing here at present is Such, That it has Oblidged me to petition the Governour of Virginia for a Liveing in his parts for six Months only, which upon Mature Deliberation, hoping That the Disorders of the Countrey in that time may be Composed, he has Condescended to gratifie me in but with Great Caution to the Venerable Society whose Missionaries he would no way be Supposed to remove. I am Entertain'd in Surrey parish for the time mentioned conditionally That I return to my Duty upon the first happy Opportunity of a Peace, which I have promised to doe. And by my future Diligence (I hope) shall Answer the Pious Intentions of the Society's Sending me Over. I am not So remote but a Dayes Journey will fetch Carolina, and I shall be sent for upon any Occasion (by Mr. Garrat) where my Duty calls for my Appearance. My Agreement with the people of Surrey is from the 25th of March to the Succeeding Michaelmas and no longer. And if the Society think fit to Stop my Salary for that half Year, I must acquiesce and Submit to their pleasure. A Principle of Conscience Oblidged me to lay before you my proceedings, or otherwise I must receive the Societys Money as Mr. Urmstone does who has bought a plantation on the Confines of Virginia and lives to his Satisfaction on the plentifull Income of what the Society Allows him. Were it in his power to doe the Society the Services they might Expect, Yet he has so Exposed himself to popular Hatred by his wretched way of begging and other Indiscretions. I am unwilling to mention, That no Single person in the Government will attend his Appointments on the Score of this Selfish principle. I have enclosed the late Governour Hides Letter to me before ever I had Seen him with a Designe the Society should no way be imposed upon where I have an Interest. I Desire no Missionary may be sent over here since I have no way quitted their Service. Onely being forc't to't as I may properly Say in a Time of Persecution. New Castle in Pensilvania is vacant by the Removeal of Mr. Sinclare, and Should be Extream Thankfull should the Society be pleased to Order me there. I wish Sir You would propose it at a General Meeting for I am very Uneasie to be hindred from my Duty by these Unhappy Differences. I have drawn upon Mr. Hodges our Treasurer for my half Years Salary Ending 25th March next And do almost hope I may Receive the Succeeding half Year. I mean till Michaelmas Upon Condition I'm ready to attend my Duty here on the least Notice when Occasion requires me. On the Account of my late Indisposition I have been able only to Catechise Children and baptize Six Negroes with the Advantage of what Good I might Do, thro' Gods Blessing by preaching and Conference. I might truely have Starv'd and been lost, were it not for Mr. Edmond Kearney a Merchant of Hampton I mentioned in my last, who took Great Care to Supply me with money and Necessaries in my late Sickness, which mightily reduced my Stock by Gratifieing the Phisitians and Oblidged me to take from him this half years Salary before hand. I Design to deal with him Entirely while I am in your Service and not do as some Missionaries contrive, to buy Goods in London and to neglect the True Ends of their Mission, by attending their Marketts here to the Great Scandal of their Profession. I Earnestly Request That you would please to Speak to Mr. Hodges, That my Bills may be honoured at the very Day of payment Since Mr. Kerney's Civilities to me have been almost Inexpressible. I have Nothing more to Add but that I am withall truly Christian Gratitude for favours already done me. Your most Oblidged faithfull humble Servant.

Giles Ransford

Please to Direct to me at
Hampton where care will be taken
to forward it.

Copy. Read at a meeting of the SPG on October 9, 1713. Journal of the SPG, II, 326-327.

[1]"The process by which a person becomes hardened or inured to a strange climate, acclimatization." *OED*.

[*SPG/Jou/2*]

Journal of the SPG
1713 June 19

<296> 19 June 1713 [...]

<298> 9. The Case of Mr. John Ward and Mr. Cooper with respect to their several Demands of Mr. Rainsfords Salary was read and considered. Agreed it is the Opinion of the Society That £8 10*s*. part of Mr. Rainsford Salary due at Lady day last be paid to Mr. Ward And That the Remainder viz. £31.10 be paid to Mr. Cooper, if he shall give Such Security to Indemnifie the Society As Mr. Jennings shall think fit and Approve. [...]

Minutes.

[*SPG/A/8*]

Rev. Giles Ransford to Secretary, SPG
1713 July 13

<358> <15.> Mr. Rainsford to mr. Chamberlayne.

Chowan N. Carolina
July the 13th, 1713.

Worthy Sir

<*Of the Countrey, Return from Virginia, the Invitations he meets to return Thither, of his Bills not being Answered.*> Tho' this be my Third to you, I have not been honoured with a Line from you, Since my Arrival in these parts. I Cannot help Concluding but that you have writt to me in Mr. Urmstone's packet which he received by Capt. Havey of the Bayley, notwithstanding his Silence in the matter. I need not use Repetition in describing the Miseries of the Govenment was lately Exposed to. I need only say that we Seem no[w] to enjoy peace tho Some Mischiefs are done by Scattered Indians in the remoter parts of the Colony. All due Care is taken by Colonell Pollock our President to Suppress them, and wherever they are taken they are destroyed, So that I presume in a Litle time the Countrey may be cleared of these Salvages. King Blunt[1] as they Term him has Oblidged himself to Clear the West Shore of Chowan River <359> Which he Seems to be indefatigable in. The Countrey is miserable poor, and there is nothing to be Expected from the Inhabitants, Since the Ashley River Indians destroyed their Stocks. For my part I never received the Value of a Bushel of Corn Since I was concerned here, but what I gott by Weddings. I did not continue in Virginia near two Months, and even that time my want of health Oblidged me to it. I am now at Squire Duckenfields on the West shore of the Sound, pressed on by Capt. Maul[2] our present Surveyor to Stay there Some time by reason of the Great want there is of me. I have had Severall Invitations to Virginia with great Allowances would I accept them as Appears by Col. Duke's Letter to me who is one of the Councellours of that Colony, but I Chose rather to Slight them for the Service I am Engaged in. I have Obey'd the Society's Orders to a Punctilio, in giveing you an Account of my proceedings half yearly and shall endeavour to do. So during my Continuance I am Melancholly Enough that I can have no Answer to my Bills drawn on Mr. Hodges, which I can't but think is very hard, considering I'm left destitute in this remote part of the World. You ever Appeared my good Friend in London, and dare I Presume, I should entreat you to Sollicite him to Dispatch this drawn on him now, as well as the former. I can't imagine how he thinks I can Subsist, the Countrey allows nothing and of Consequence the Society must be my Support And I hope for the future more punctual payments will be made. I Designe (God Willing) to continue here till I receive an Answer to this, and could then wish for a place of Settled Residence. The Difficulties, I have gone thro' are almost inexpressible and One Distemper or another like the Thunder and Lightning continually disturbing me. Thank God, I am Extreamly beloved by the Inhabitants which is notorious Enough, and were they in any Condition I should have their Assistance I shall never get Mr. Adams's Books from Old Sanders and therefore hope youle Consider me by remitting

me <360> Aparrell in the next Shipps that come to Virginia. Please to direct them to me at Hampton and care will be taken there to send them me up. The Choice I leave to your better Judgement Tho' I could wish for Some of Phisick, with Dr. Caves 2 Vol. of the Lives of the Fathers and all Colliers Essays and Norris's works. Dr. Leakes Single vol. would be of use. I take all Imaginable Care to discharge the great Trust thats reposed in me according to Conscience. I am Ashamed to tell you of my fare, for the whole year is one Continued Lent, Fish being the Constant Attendant on the Table. I have writt to my Good Lord of London as I am in Duty bound and also to Mr. Hodges. I beg of you Sir to Send those Books, and remind Mr. Hodges if you please to pay those Bills, for when I want money here I Send to Virginia to Mr. Edmond Kerney Merchant there and he Supplys me. I shall take no other way of payment during my Stay here it being the readiest and best. I am Sir with all imaginable Gratitude Your most Oblidged faithfull humble Servant.

Giles Ransford Missionary

Copy. Read at a meeting of the SPG on October 30, 1713. Journal of the SPG, II, 334-335. The document following was enclosed in the present one.

[1]Tom Blunt (ca. 1675-ca. 1739), principal chief or "king" of the Tuscarora in the northern part of North Carolina, did not join in the attacks on the white settlers. In addition, near the end of the war he turned over to the government the leader of the insurgent Tuscarora, Hancock, and took some thirty scalps of Hancock's followers. *DNCB.*

[2]William Maule (1690-1726), at this time deputy surveyor general of North Carolina, was later surveyor general, councillor, vice admiralty judge, and assemblyman. *DNCB.*

[*SPG/A/8*]

Henry Duke to Rev. Giles Ransford
1713 May 25

<9.> Mr. Duke to mr. Rainsford. Enclosed in Mr. Rainsford, of 13 July 1713.

May 25th 1713.

Reverend Sir

The Great Character I have heard of your parts and Eminency makes me desirous of your Acquaintance, And to take the Freedom to tell you that our parish is at present without a Minister. Its a Sweet Scented parish,[1] and Lyeth convenient for the Trade both of York and James River; on York there is generally great plenty of all Sorts of Goods; and our Sort of Tobacco in the worst of times is never less then 10*s*. per Cent now it is 2*d*. per lb. and on to 20*s*. per Cent and we always take Especial Care to pay our Minister as honorably as we can. If you'l favour us with a visit and have any thoughts of Moveing, I am confident our parish will be very fond of Entertaining a Gent. of yr. Worth. I respectfully Salute you and am Sir yr. most humble Servant.

Hen. Duke

I should be glad of a Line from you the first Oppertunity mr. Elthd. Taylor will direct how to write or Send to me.

Copy. This document was enclosed in the one immediately above.

[1]I.e., a tobacco-growing parish. *OED.*

[*SPG/A/9*]

Rev. John Urmston to Secretary, SPG
1713 November 6

<271> Mr. Urmstone to the Secretary.

Novr. 6, 1712 [*sic*]

Sir

The last of Nov. 1713 I received one from the Honorable Society by Colonell Nicholson, who Stopping at Boston forward'd it. The many true dismall but true Accounts I've given of affairs here both with Relation to my Self and the Governour required methinks with Submission a more timely and Suitable Answer if Your Missionaries are not sold to be Slaves or banished to a much worse place than ever the Giacii[1] of old were much more what they now are. This is the first I ever was favoured with Notwithstanding above 50. <272> I Have written I Shall be ready to comply with what is Expected of me with reference to the Said Gent. and accordingly upon a bare Intimation that he Expected to hear from me I have acquainted that what is required of me I can not comply with by reason that the Vestries have rejected misused and refused to do any thing for Missionaries upon a Supposition that our Sallary in England is Sufficient and that it was ne're expected by the Society that the Inhabitants should be at any charge. The plain truth is, our holy Religion (as with Sorrow I have often hinted) is totally Neglected disregarded and those who Promote the Same trampled upon. I am very miserable indeed, thro' the baseness of the People and the Mismanagement of my Sallary in England which is an accident that happens to most men that travell. This is not the first time I've been abused by one I have Intrusted and thought tho' mistaken I was Safe. So unhappy are many and if Missionaries what signifie great Sallaries, I am poorer now by far than when I came hither and were I but Able would Speedily Quit the Country. I have wrecked my Brains ever Since I Arrived to keep Soul and Body together and have been Almost continually in as much danger as in the greatest Extremity that can be at Sea in Fine Death would be welcome. The Society may perhaps Say that this my constant Stile but am perswaded when my Reports are confirmed by Colonel Nicholson they may have some further Influence with the Society. I am desirous, if Possible of Staying here till he comes among us and then Doubt not but he will Justifie my Leaving this wretched Contrey and returning to England.

Mr. Rainsford has proved another Alexander his comeing in has been of great detriment to me and no Service to the Countrey. I wish he may Stay in it as long as I've done but very much doubt it. Never any one could do it and had I been able Should have long agoe betaken me to some other place. I am Sir your humble Servant.

[Jno. Urmstone]

Copy. Although this entrybook copy is dated 1712, the reference to Francis Nicholson places the document in 1713.

[1]The Gracchi brothers (Tiberius and Gaius Gracchus) were leaders of a popular faction in Rome during the second century B.C.

[*SPG/C/7*]

Bond
1713 November 17

<21>
Noverint Universi Per presentes nos Willm. Cooper de Token House Yard London Warehouseman et Willm. Dandy de Aldermanbury London Gentleman teneri et firmiter obligari Societati pro promovend Evangel. in Partebus Transmarenis in Octogenta Libris bone et legalis Moneto Magne Britannie solvend eid Societati Successoribus vel Assign suis ad quamquid Solutionem bene et fideliter faciend Obligamus Nos utrumque nostrum Heredes Executores et Administratores Nostros, utriusque nostrorum firmites Per presentes Sigillis nostris Sigillat dat decimo Septimo die Novembris Anno Regni Domine Nostre Anne Dei Gratia nune Regine magne Brittannie etc. duodecimo Anoque Domini 1713.

Whereas the Reverend Mr. Giles Ransford one of the Missionaries of the abovenamed Society to North Carolina in America with the Salary from the said Society of Eighty pounds Per annum, hath drawn a bill of Exchange on the said Society dated the 23d of July 1712 for forty pounds payable to Edmond Kerney or order for his half years Salary due at Michaelmas 1712 which bill is duely Assigned to the abovebound Wm. Cooper, who hath Applied himself to the said Society for the payment thereof, but Whereas the said Summ of forty pounds due at Michaelmas 1712 hath been heretofore duely paid by the said Society to the proper Person before that time Authorized by the said Giles Ransford to receive the same and the said Society considering the Case of the said Wm. Cooper and conceiving his Demand to be reasonable have Ordered that the sum of forty pounds be paid to the said Wm. Cooper as part of the Salary at this time due from the said Society to him the said Giles Ransford, and the said Wm. Cooper haveing Agreed to deliver the said Bill and to give Security to the said Society to indempnify them for such payment of the said forty pounds to him as aforesaid, and the said summ of forty pounds being now accordingly paid by the said Society to the said William Cooper and the said Bill being by him delivered up in pursuance of the Agreement aforesaid. Now the Condition of this Obligation is such that if the said Wm. Cooper and William Dandy their Heirs Executors and Administrators do and shall from time to time and at all times hereafter well and truely save Harmless and keep indempnified the said Society and their Successors for the payment of the said Sum of forty pounds to him the said Wm. Cooper in manner as Aforesaid, and in Case the said Society hereafter shall be obliged to pay to the said Giles Ransford his Executors Administrators or Assigns the said sum of forty pounds for which the said bill of Exchange was so drawn as aforesaid, If then the said Wm. Cooper and William Dandy their Heirs Executors and Administrators every or any of them do and shall forthwith upon the Societys returning back and delivering unto him or them the said bill of Exchange so drawn by the said Giles Ransford as aforesaid pay to, reimburse and Satisfy or cause to be paid to reimbursed or Satisfied unto the said Society the said Sum of forty pounds so paid by them to the said Wm. Cooper in manner aforesaid, That then this Obligation shall be void or else shall remain in full force and virtue.

W. Cooper
Wm. Dandy

Sealed and delivered (the words, and William Dandy their, being first, twice interlin'd in the Condition) being duly stampt in the presence of G. Jeffries
W. Taylor

[*Endorsed:*]
33 Mr. Cooper's Bond to
indempnify the Society payment
of £40 pt. of Mr. Rainsford's Salary.

DS.

[*SPG/A/9*]

Rev. John Urmston to Francis Nicholson
1713 December 1

<289> <2> Mr. Urmston to Generall Nicholson Dec. 1 1713.

Honored Sir

The good News of your honours safe Arrivall at Boston was very welcome to most here and has rather encreased than abated our longing desire of your presence here ever Since we heard of the Lord Proprietors their good intention towards us in impowering so Honorable a person to regulate the disorders and Unacountable <290> Confusions which this Unhappy Countrey hath been so long Involved in the happy Effects of the prudent care of other Colonies when under Your command makes your coming among us look the Auspicious. If ever we shall be a people worthy the care and protection of our Mother Country, we must date it from the day of your Arrivall which God grant may be Safe and Speedy. But give me leave to tell you Your honour will have a pretty hard task on it. I beleive I need not tell you what a Strange mixture of wretched mortalls we have here many Impatient of all discipline whether Spirutual or temporal not a whit better than those St.

Paul fough with at Ephesians 9.[1] Poor Colonel Hyde dureing his Short reign was vilely puzled with them But the Honest Gentleman our now Honorable President hath met with many more difficulties not onely a refractory disobedient and gainsaying people but a potent and cruel Enemy to Struggle with when he took upon him so heavy a Burden. The Indyan War was but Just begun but by his unwearyed diligence and wise conduct hath been Carryed on with great Success. A Countrey preserved which every body that was but the least acquainted with our Circumstances gave over for lost and the Enemy forced to apease upon Honorable terms. Our Intestine Broyls and Contentions (to which all the Misfortunes which have Since Attended us are owing) are in a great Measure appeased Factions and partyes no longer heard of. And all haveing Sufficiently Smarted for their past divisions agree in their good Esteem and Approbation of his Administration his publick Spirit and earnest Endeavours for the welfare of this Government tho at the Expence of a great part of his Estate hath gained him a great Influence over all Sorts and If not blest with a plentyfull future he could never have Waded thro' so many Difficulties.

A perfect Insight into the Interest of the Countrey and a good Estate are Needfull for a Governour and are very engaging with our Folk and without that I plainly Saw in Colonell Hyde the Character will be despised and the honour due to unto it not supported.

(Sir) in Obedience to the commands of the honorable Society per your honour I make you an humble tender of my best respects and take the liberty of Assureing You I Shall allwayes have a due regard for the power wherewith you are Invested by the honorable Society with reference to us Missionaryes as well as to the Merits and repute your Indefatigable pains and generous concurrence in the promoteing our most holy Religion as by law Established hath deservedly gained you from all good men. But to give you as directed a Succint Account at present of all mattres relating to my Mission would be too tedious. At a Generall Assembly next after Colonell Hydes takeing the Government upon him, A very favourable Act was made in order to Establish our Church. But thro' the Opposition of Sectarists who are Unwearyed in Seduceing and perverting Unsetled minds and Stirring up an Aversion in all that will hearken to them against our hierarchy and by reason of the poverty Misery and calamitous Circumstances the Country is reduced to, All Essayes and Attempts have proved Abortive little or nothing done persuant to the said Act Neither know I when it can be expected there Should be for my part I despair of ever Seeing it. The Fatigues and hardships I've been continually exposed to have quite Wearyed me, my constitution which has been heretofory Healthy and Strong and Sufficiently tryed by long and repeated Journeys and Frequent change of Climates is now broken. The Air of America has been more disagreable than that of a great part of the known World besides my health and my strength are very much Impaired.

I Have Supplyed to the Utmost of my power the whole County of Albemarle which is of a great Extent above three Years and an halfe have left no Corner of it Invisible. I never was so hard put to it in all my Life to keep Soul and Body together and Subsist my poor <292> distressed Family. I have been ill used by One whom I Intrusted to receive my Sallary and lay it out in Goods which would have turned to a good account here but for want thereof have been forced to draw Bills for England to the Value of £250 Sterling of which I could easily have made a thousand pounds this countrey pay besides £45 sterling I am to pay for my Plantation when a Dispute about the title[2] is ended which I beleive will come before your honour.

My Fellow Labourer Mr. Rainsford was with us two or three days in August 1712 and returned to Virginia on pretence of Fetching in his Goods but Loitered there till the Indian War broke out which deterred him from comeing again till about a Month ago.[3] He now is Set down in my parish and Saith that when the Inhabitants have once heard him they'l forsake me and so I must be turn'd out. I fear he is of a very contentious Temper. I've seen him but once since and that was by Chance. His carryage towards me was very haughty as if I were some contemptable Inferiour. A rupture which is almost unavoidable would be of ill consequence, create Myrth and diversion among our adversaries, who are always ready with or without cause to revile and reproach us and it would be very repugnant to the business and disposition of a Missionary. I understand he expects his Salary from the commencement of his Mission albeit he hath done nothing for it. Mr. Gordon my Predecessor was not at all out of the way in demanding an hundred pounds per Annum to come back again hither. I wish I had gone where at first design'd Altho' I had paid him the Augmentation he desired. But beleive that would not have engaged a timerous man to have stay'd here so long as I have done, if your Honour would vouchsafe to prompt the Society to take into consideration my mean circumstances, the loss which I sustain in the mismagement of their Bounty the pains I have taken for want of Assistance and the little prospect of any Encouragement from the Country it shall ever be acknowledged as an extraordinary Act of your accustom'd Goodness and Charity (for in truth I am very poor) by Honoured Sir Your Honours most Obedient and at all times most humble Servant

Jno. Urmstone

North Carolina
1mo. Decr. 1713

Copy. Read at a meeting of the SPG on March 18, 1714/5. Journal of the SPG, III, 48.

[1]The New Testament book of Ephesians contains only six chapters.

[2]Court records relating to this appear not to have survived.

[3]At the meeting of the SPG at which this letter was read, the Society "Agreed that the Secretary do write to the Inhabitants where Mr. Rainsford Officiated in North Carolina to know the time he left that Place and that he Consult Genl. Nicholson thereon." Journal of the SPG, III, 48.

[*SPG/B/1*]

Francis Nicholson to Secretary, SPG
1713 December 1

Boston in New England
Decemb. 1, 1713

Sir

Your Letter to Governor Craven[1] and the Severall Missionaries of North and South Carolina with Some of Dean Kenett's Sermons Some of the Collections of Papers printed by Order of the Society and Some of the Comon Prayer Books Printed at Edinburgh from whence I had them (that the North Brittains in those parts might See how the Church of England by Law Established Succeeded there) I Sent, Those for South Carolina with the said Governor Craven To whose Favour and Protection I recommended the Society's Missionarys in our Government as per Extracts of my Letter to him (here inclosed No. 1.) not doubting of his Endeavours to Promote the Interest of the Church etc.

And those for North Carolina to Colonell Pollock (The Present Commander in Chief) to whom also I recomended the affairs of the Church etc. (as by the Extracts No. 2.) which I hope he will be a Friend to. I am Informed that Mr. Rainsford one of the Societys Missionarys there is entertained as Minister at Kicotan in Virginia in the Room of Mr. Wallis deceased (from which place I remember he Drew a Bill on the Society) and hath Presided very little in North Carolina; I don't Expect to hear from Virginia 'till the Spring But I recommend to my Brother Auditor to Examine into this Affair, which if true I think he ought to be prosecuted instead of being paid. [...]

Your Affectionate Friend and humble Servant.

Fr. Nicholson [...]

LS. The document following was enclosed in the present one.

[1]Charles Craven, governor of South Carolina 1712-1716.

[*SPG/B/1*]

Extract from Francis Nicholson to Thomas Pollock
1713 October 30

Extract. To Collonel Thomas Pollock President of the Councill in North Carolina

Boston Octobr. the 30th 1713

Honorable Sir

I herewith send you Two Letters for the Reverend Messrs. Urmston and Rainsford with an Account of their Arrears Due from the Society at Christmas last as likewise the Copy of the Societys Commission to me which I desire may be Safely Delivered to them.

I hope to have the Good Fortune of hearing from you this winter or early in the Spring as also from the said Two Reverend Gentlemen to whom pray my humble Service. I also send you Copys of the Two Librarys formerly Sent by the Society into Your Government which be pleased to Communicate to the said Gentlemen, and you will very Much Oblige to Inform me of the Circumstances of those Two Gentlemen, where they Officiate what Congregations they have And where the Said Two Librarys are.

Boston N. England Novr. 2d 1713

I have since give to Our Friend Mr. Borland Merchant here Seven Comon Prayer Books. The Black One be pleased to keep for your Self. The other Six are to be divided between the Two Ministers for the use of their Parrishes, By the Printing of these

Common Prayer Books at Edinburgh You may See how Christianity Flourisheth in that Antient Kingdom. I also herewith send you Seven Sermons Preached before the Society so That with Marble Paper Cover you may Please to keep for yourself the other Six I desire may be given to the Two Ministers for the use of their Parrishes.

Fr. Nicholson

[*Endorsed:*]
Extracts to Collonel Pollock 1713
No. (2)

Copy. This document was enclosed in the one immediately above.

[*SPG/A/9*]

Rev. Giles Ransford to Francis Nicholson
1713 December 1

<294> <4> Mr. Rainsford to Genl. Nicholson.

Chowan North Carolina
Decr. 1st 1713

I had the Honour of a Letter (which You were pleas'd to convey) from the Society deliverd me by the Hands of our most worthy President Colonel Pollock. I understand my duty in part is to inform your Excellency what Libraries there are of the Societys in General and of my own in particular in this Government. As to my own particular Share of books I recd. none; except a parcel of small tracts with Some Prayer books which I dispose of where I see most Occasion, and where the necessitys of the people require, and where I find they are ready to put 'em to the use intended by the Society. I had an Order of the Societys for the books of my Predecessor the Reverend Mr. Adams who died in Curatuck amounting to the value of ten pounds, and now in the hands of Mr. Richard Sanderson but never recd. one tho' I often apply'd for 'em. The place where I at present Officiate in is on the West Shore of Chowan River where there are a Considerable Number of Inhabitants well disposed to the Interest of our Church, as truly zealous in the Defence of the Country from the Common Enemy. Thanks be to God we have no disturbances among ourselves, but all Peoples Hearts unite and every Member of the Government is happy (as the time will admit of) under the wise and prudent administration of our good President. I heartily thank your Excellency that You were pleas'd to condescend to take Notice of me in your letter to the President, and shall readily shew my gratitude by a cheerfull and submissive Obedience to your Commands. Here is a great want of School-masters in this Government for the Instruction of Children which I hope you'l be pleased to lay before the Society as you in your Wisdom shall think fit. Please to pardon this presumption, and look upon it only as a branch of my Duty which engaged me to let you know I received your Commands and how much I am (but with all due regard to the distance between us) Your Excellencys most obliged most obedient humble Servant.

Giles Rainsford Missionary

Copy. Read at a meeting of the SPG on March 18, 1714/5. Journal of the SPG, III, 48.

[*SPG/A/8*]

Secretary of the SPG to Rev. John Urmston
1713 December 18

<460> <11> The Secretary to mr. Urmstone.

18th December 1713

Reverend Sir

Yours of the 22th Octr. 1712 to mr. Hodges late Treasurer of the Society, I have recd. and communicated the Same to the Bord. They have Agreed that if the Books formerly Sent with mr. Adams deceased, and intended for you, cannot be delivered to you as they Expected they should be for your use. That then the Bond Executed by you on that Account be delivered up and Cancelled. I am very unwilling but forced to tell you, That the Society have recd. a Complaint against you, That you are Negligent of your Duty and that Some your indiscreet Actions have Exposed <461> You to the Hatred of the people in the Province of North Carolina. I pray God this may not be true, but think it is necessary, That by your Life and Conversation there, and by proper Evidences here, you ought to clear your Self of such Imputation. The Society have lately made Some Standing Orders, which are as follow.

That whereas it is an Instruction to the Clergy employed by the Society for the propagation of the Gospel in Foreigne parts, That they Send over every 6 months An Account of the State of their respective Parishes According to the Scheme Annext, No. 11. The following particular be Added to that Scheme, videlicet VIII No. of Converts from a prophane Disorderly and unchristian Course to a Life of Christian purity Meekness and Charity.

The Society finding great Inconvenience by their Missionaries leaveing Letters of Attorney for receiveing their Salary, and afterwards Changeing the Same powers, and by their frequently drawing Bills of Exchange for their Salary during the Continuance of Such powers in force, Ordered that from and after Midsummer next, The Salary of the Society's Missionaries Schoolmasters etc. be paid only by Bills of Exchange to be by them drawn upon the Treasurers from time to time as such Salary Shall become due.

Copy.

[*SPG/A/8*]

Secretary of the SPG to Rev. Giles Ransford
1713 December 18

<461> <12> The Secretary to mr. Rainsford.

18th December 1713

Reverend Sir

Yours of the 17th February and 13th July last have been recd. and Communicated to the Society. I hope you had my last Letter by Genl. Nicholson, which may perhaps Surprize you in that Some things have of Necessity been made known to the Society which <462> Cannot prove to your Comfort or Reputation. Since that they have been put to much Trouble on your Account with one Ward, who you had when here made your Attorney, And one mr. Cooper who was possessed of a Bill of £40 drawn by you for half a Years Salary which was before paid to mr. Quigley, who had Advanced and paid the like money to your Self in England. The Society and I am Sure on my own part I have been very much fatigued to compose and Settle your Unjust proceedings of which you ought to be Ashamed. Your Accounts with the Society are that at Christmas next there will be due to you £51 10*s*. 00*d*. The Society have lately made Some Standing Orders, which are as follow. As before to mr. Urmstone.[1]

Copy.

[1]See the last two paragraphs of the document immediately above.

[*SPG/A/9*]

Rev. John Urmston to Francis Nicholson
1713/4 January 1

<293> <3> Mr. Urmstone to Genl. Nicholson.

Honored Sir

I have sometime agoe congratulated your safe arrival at Boston but in hopes still of better things dared not be so plain with you being under some obligation of shewing mine to some who perhaps might have disliked, tho' would neither contradict nor yet remedy what I could and now as heretofore for near these four years have had too much reason to complain of. This is now the time of payment whilst people have it. Vestries have been summon'd but to avoid Payment would not meet, and thus they have serv'd me ever since I came among them. So that I fear I must retire into the next Government for relief, which will be an Eternal reproach to this Government and the totall ruin of me and my poor family. If these find Your Honour at Boston and you shall think fit to intercede with our Governor and Council to provide for me till you come I shall be very glad to see you here but without Your Letter cannot hope to be so happy. I have made use of my Witts to live hitherto but now am at my Wits End. Starve nor dig I cannot and beg I am asham'd. I humbly entreat Your Honour to peruse the inclosed[1] and forward them according to Directions. These with my humble respects are from Honorable Sir Your most humble Servant.

John Urmstone

North Carolina
Jan. 1st 1713/4

Copy. Read at a meeting of the SPG on March 18, 1714/5, pp. 48-49.

[1]It cannot be determined what documents Urmston is referring to here.

[*SPG/SAP*]

Report
1713/4 February 19

<44> <*An Abstract of the Proceedings of the Society.*> [...] The Reverend Mr. *Ramsford*, in a Letter to the Secretary, dated *Chowan, North Carolina, Feb.* 17, 1712. relates, "That in their miserable State of a cruel War with the *Indians*, and having been himself taken by the Savages, and suffered other Indisposition, he had been able only to catechize and baptize Six *Negroes*. [...]

Printed. Extracted from the yearly publication containing the sermon preached at the annual anniversary meeting of the SPG, together with a review of the activities of the Society and its missionaries during the preceding year. The date above is the date of the meeting.

[*SPG/A/10*]

Vestry of Queen Anne's Creek to Secretary, SPG, and Francis Nicholson
1713/4 March 2

<66> Vestry of Queen Annes Creek To Genl. Nicholson.

At a vestry held in the Church the 2d of March 1713/14 on Queens Anne's Creek Albermarle County

Sir

Wee whose names are underwritten Vestry Men and Church Wardens of the precinct of Chowan in the County of Albermarle in the Provence of North Carolina do for our selves and on the behalfe of the Rest of the Inhabitants of the Precinct in amost gratefull manner Return our hearty Thanks to the Honorable Society etc. For their great Care of

our Souls Health in sending over Missionaries to preach the word of God and administring the Holy Sacrament among us. Wee and the whole English America ought to bless and praise the Almighty for having putt it into the Hearts of so many great and Honorable Personages to think of their poor Country Folk whose lott it hath been to come into these Heathen Countries were we were in danger of becomeing like the Indians themselves without a God in The world. Wee of this precinct with the Rest of this government in Perticular have been for some Time happy in the pious endeavours of divers of the Clergy Missionaries and others who have set up the worship of God according to the Church of England as by Law Established among us but through the Poverty of the Country unsettleness and Oppossition for those of that holy Order which wee Fear been the Occassion of their Short Stay with us none of them even abode So long here as the Reverend Mr. Urmstone hath done yet have not been So happy in him neither as we could have desired by reason that for the most part there hath been no Minister in these parts since his arrival and he seeing the Confusions and Distractions of this unhappy Colony were so great the Opposers of our Holy Church so numerous and there Endeavours to Subvert the same Indefatigable he hath made the other precincts of this County sharers with useing his Ministry his great pains and unwearied diligence to keep together those of our Church, hath had good Success and will undoubtedly be very acceptable to the Society.
<67> It were to be wished he had met with due Encouragement proportionable to the great Fatigues and Hardships which he hath undergone but Fear he hath Failed thereof.

Wee of this Precinct allowed him according to our first Act of Assembly in Favours of the Church of England (which was not obtained without hard struggling) £30 per Annum for the First year and an half hopeing the other precinct where he officiated would have done the like. We can't say we have Fullfilled our promise as for the two years last past he hath been prevailed with and Indeed been necessitated not being able to Travel any longer about the Country to confine himself to this precinct where his Residence hath Constantly been.

Wee have a large Parish many Inhabitants and those seated at a great distance from each other passages very uncertaine by reason of a broad River which Runns through the Heart of the parish and but one sorry Church on the north shore of the Sound, never Finished, no Ornaments belonging to a Church nor wherewith to Buy any Except the Bounty of the Honorable Colonel Nicholson (videlicet) Tenn Pounds Sterling part of the Thirty Pounds given to three Parishes of this County which is not as yet Expended (for want of an Addition) according to the Intent of the Donner Personage House and Glebe we have none nor a School the First Library of great Value sent in by the Direction of the Reverend Dr. Bray through an Unhappy Inscription on the back of the books (videlicet) belonging to the Parish of St. Thomas of Pamplico (in the then Riseing but now miserable County of Bath) Falsely Supposed to be the Seat of government was lodged there and by that means Rendred useless to the Clergy for whose Service 'twas cheifly Intended and in what Condition we know not. We Fear, the worse by Reason of the Late warr. The Library sent by mr. Gordon was all left with the Reverend Mr. Wallace late Minister of Kecketan in Virginia save Whitby's Annotations on the new Testament 2 Vol. Fol. and Peirson on the Creed which we have. The said mr. Wallace upon due Application refused to deliver the Books without an Order from the Society or mr. Gordon. There were missing the Collection of Cannons Beveridge on the Catechisme Bennet against the Quakers, Lucas of Happyness of 2 Vol. Colonel Eacharde Ecclesciasticall History Fol. and now the said Mr. Wallace he is dead. We Fear the like Ill Fate may attend the Rest. Those Charity books to the Value of £5 the generous gift likewise of the Society have since Mr. Gordens departure been disposed of as was Intended.

<68> What Relates to the other parishes within this Government we presume will be laid before the Society by their Respective Vestries their Necessities we believe to be very great but being under the like unhappy Circumstances beg leave only to Supplicate for our selves and to pray to the Honorable Society to Continue or Rather add to the Salary of Mr. Urmstone so that he may be Enabled to Stay with us and that they will out of their great Charity concur with our Honest but weak Endeavours Church ministry and a School with the Allowance of 10 or £15 per Annum to a Person whom we shall make Choice of to Teach our Children in this precinct and shall be bound ever that God Almighty may Increase their Store and Strengthen their Hands in the Carrying on the great work they have so piously undertaken and may with a Happy Success in That glorious Designe. So pray Yr. most Oblidged poor Country men of the Vestry aforesaid.

Jno. Urmstone Missionary
Thos. Peterson per order of Saml. Padget and Jno. Bird Church Wardens Thomas Luton, Thomas Peterson, John Blount, Wm. Duckenfeild, Robert West

Honored Sir

The Reverend Mr. Urmstone haveing acquainted us with Your Honours good Intentions towards this poor Country particularly to us of this parish and the Continuance of your generosity towards us we Humbly pray your Acceptance of our unfeigned thanks for your Favours hopeing we have complied with the orders the Honorable Society in the Enclosed we Humbly begg your Honour would be pleased <69> to Concurr with our request to the Society and promote the Interest of a poor Country which you seem to wish so well your presence here is very much desired all Honest men and Freinds of the Church are big with Expectation. The Influence your good Endeavours may have over us all to Confirme and make all the Members of our Church adhere more Zealous to the Justness thereof, silence the gainsayers, and reduce the Authors of our Late Confusions to a due obedience to all lawfull Authority in church and State. These with all unfeigned and Humble Respect are from Honored Sir Yr. Honors most oblidged poor Countrymen.

Jno. Urmstone Missionary Thos. Peterson per order of Sam. Padgett and Jno. Bird church Wardens Thos. Luton, Thos. Peterson, Jno. Blount, Wm. Duckenfeild, Robert West

---

Copy. This document was enclosed in the letter from Thomas Pollock to Francis Nicholson dated August 3, 1714, below.

[*SPG/A/9*]

Rev. Giles Ransford to Secretary, SPG
1714 March 30

<273> <9> Mr. Rainsford to the Secretary.

Chowan N. Carolina
March 30th, 1714

Worthy Sir

Since my Arrivall here I have writ Severall Lettres to the Society according to their directions half Yearly and particularly relateing to my Mission and Proceedings in this Government. I can't Suppose my Letters to have miscarried, by reason of my Bills being Protested by the Treasurer as soon as exposed to Veiw. I can't but think this Very Severe Usage, considering the Inexpressible hardships and Inconveniences it exposes me to. I need not tell you that neither Mr. Urmston nor my Selfe have ever received any thing by way of Support by the contribution of the Inhabitants. But my own particular Losses have been considerable in this Government whether I respect the Horses I have lost here the Great expence I have been at for a Guide to Inform me in the Roads (which has been no less than £20 Yearly) my everlasting Fatigue in going by water and hireing of hands and now the great misfortune of haveing my Bill protested. This last particular has almost ruined me by destroying my credit which has been upheld ever Since my Arrivall by that worthy Gentleman Mr. Edmand Kearney out of profound respect to the Society And now this very thing not onely Exposes me to want but even to the danger of a Jayle. The fatigue of being an Itenerant I am not able longer to Undergoe and have accordingly quitted the 25th of this Instant the Societys Employ I Designed Instantly home but can't possibly leave America till Mr. Kearney is ever Satisfied for the Sumes he <274> has lent me. Its well known to the Society that I left an excellent cure in England. That I came here not out of Necessity but choice not for Interest but Conscience when I entered into their Employ. And I had rather Served the Society 7 Years Gratis than to let this Gentleman Suffer for his undeserved Civility and I am now with him in order for Virginia where I shall Supply some vacant parish 'till I receive an Answer to this and accordingly have Sent those two Bills a Second time which have been once protested hopeing that Honorable Body will consider my Condition in so remote and helpless an Abode and pay them now punctually to Mr. John PorterField that I may be easier under these heavy and allmost Insupportable Circumstances. I have put the two Fourty pound Bills into One Eighty pound that it may be less troublesom to the Treasurer. There is this last halfe year due to me Still with the preceeding halfe year that I have not heard of tho' drawn for this. I shall omit drawing for 'till I see Colonell Nicholson who is expected in two Months time. I formerly mentioned my readiness to Serve the Society in any other part of America except this of North Carolina provided I may be a Setled Incumbant and have no greater difficulties to grapple with than the rest of my Brothers Employed in this Service. I now Sincerely offer my Selfe to any place the Society shall please to appoint me. I have faithfully and conscientiously discharged my duty dureing my continuance in these parts and at the first return of an Answer to this shall go for Britain unless the Society disposes of me as I propose. The Coliny is now at peace the whole Body of the Indians being entirely destroyed I never yet received a Book of Mr. Adams's Mr. Sanderson who had 'em at his death haveing disposed of them to those who neither will use them nor return them. Madam Hyde sold all the <275> Society's Books comitted to her care for Eggs Butter etc. when they were to be disposed of Gratis according to the Intent of the Society.

I can Safely Say that my Lodging for the best part of my time in this Government was in an old Tobacco House and exposed even in my Bed to the Injuries and violence of bad Weather with Infinite other inconveniences only to Settle my self where I thought I had an Opportunity of doing most good.

Mr. Urmston tells me he immediately designs home soon after the Arrivall of Colonel Nicholson. And truely I don't see how the Countrey any way deserves a Missionary among them for behave Your Self with the greatest caution and reserve and Show the Fairest example of a Christian life Yet Notwithstanding they'l traduce Slander and bely you and if you Seriously tell them of their faults they'l not onely absent themselves from Divine Service but as much as in them lyes hinder others from the performance of what God and Religion require at their hands. I once more Intreat you Venerable body the Society that my Bills may be paid in order to my future quiet. And I shall ever Acknowledge it to be highly charitable and condescending in them for so distinguishing an Act of their bounty and Goodness shewn to their Missionary as well as most gratefull most obliged thankfull humble Servant.

Giles Rainsford Missionary

I formerly writ to be discharged from this Cure and if the Society took it into consideration as I Suppose they did and discharged me at their Board there remains their bounty of a Years Sallary (as appears by their collection of papers) which I presume is intended to carry us home.

Copy. Read at a meeting of the SPG on November 19, 1714: "Agreed that the Secretary acquaint Mr. Rainsford that as to the protest of his bills it appears to the Society his Salary has been fully paid to the time he confesses by his letter to have left their Service and as to his expectation of a Years Salary to be given him by the Society, that he be informed he is not within their Rules as having quitted their Service without Leave." Journal of the SPG, III, 18. This document was enclosed in the letter from Thomas Pollock to Francis Nicholson, [April, 1714], below.

[*SPG/Jou/2*]

Journal of the SPG
1714 March 30

<367> March 30th 1714 [...]

3. Reported from the Committee for Bps. and Bishopricks that They had read the Letter from Genl. Nicholson dated Decemr. 1st last to them referred together with the Several Papers in the said Letter inclosed that they had taken short Notes thereof and had desired Mr. Stubbs to draw up an Abstract from the said Notes taken by the Committee

which he laid before them reduced under Several Heads which few now and with the Opinion of the Committee thereon and are as follows. Videlicet

I. A Call for Bps. and Bishopricks in America.

II. The great want of Missionaries and the Encouragement of [them]

III. The want of Catechists and Schoolmasters

IIII. The fixing of Libraries

V. The Great Work of the Conversion of the Indians

VI. Miscellanious Affairs [...]

<370> IV. As to the fourth head videlicet The fixing of Libraries. His Excellency informs, That two Standing ones have been sent to Braintree, one with Mr. Barclay the other with Mr. Eager, and that one of them may Serve for Naraganset to which place none ever yet has been sent No. 12. He Apprizes likewise That the Packets of Books for South and North Carolina were sent, The former to Governour Craven, the latter to Colonell Pollock to both which he recommended the Care of the Church and hopes they will be Friends to it. [...]

Minutes.

[*SPG/A/9*]

Rev. John Urmston to Francis Nicholson
1714 April 12

<296> Mr. Urmstone to Genl. Nicholson.

Honored Sir

As soon as possible after I was favour'd with one from the Society inclosed in your Honors I sent to the several Vestries within this wretched Government in number seven and exhorted them to lay hold of this Opportunity of obtaining Missioners and Schoolmasters which are much wanted. I know not how quick they may be in complying with your Commands: if I know them I am apt to believe they'l not be over forward. Such slow belly's to all that concerns Souls health, most here had rather be without them. I am sure they are not worthy of any, and were their usage of me known I am perswaded none would be so mad as ever to come among them. They'l neither pay Minister nor Schoolmaster, nay they had need to be hired to go to church or send their Children to School. I and all my Predecessors have been laden with Calumnies, Reproch and scandalous falshoods instead of wealth, nay having had the hard fortune of staying sore against my will longer with them than any of my Function ever did. I find them more prone to take from us by fraud and extortion what we bring with us and seem unwilling we shold live, tho' at our own Cost, by them.

I cannot but wonder the Society should want to be informed about the State of this sorry Country, since I have sent them so many and such dismal Accts. of it. I fear I have been abused for my Custom hath been to send my Letters open to a certain Member of the Society who either hath not deliver'd 'em or else they were not believed. I have often prayd for a Removal or rather leave to go home, and had I been able I should long 'ere this have left the Place tis very grievous to live in so great want of food and raiment and indeed all necessaries to hear the complaints of a poor Gentlewoman, I brought from her Friends who had she not been my wife would never have endured so much baseness and above all the continual danger we have been in a long time of being sacrificed by <297> the Indians. Frightful Reports of dayly murders comitted in the neighbourhood. I bless God we have escap'd with our lives but have sufferd mor than any other family in the Government for all that lost either houses goods or provisions were releived and taken care of whereas we are neglected. I have frequently beg'd both in publick and private for relief. If not Allowance as their Minister at least their Charity as being at Christian and Inhabitant but it availed nothing; many would say why did I not labour and make corn they saw no reason why I should not work as well as they.

I cannot see how it will ever be possible to settle a Ministry here the People live so scatterd and remote. The Parishes so large that they cannot be supply'd without much labour and charge. I have been often exposed to great danger and a great expence, and at last bought a Couple of Negroes and a Canoe in order to serve my cure and forced to hire a white hand to teach 'em as well as make 'em work. Weary of that charge I resolved to buy me an English Servant, was cheated with one by Thos. Jones who out of pure kindness spar'd me one whom his brother had tried for 8 Months and not being able to manage him, let me have him for £14 Sterling. He could not have found such another villain in all America. He first Robed me and at 3 weeks end ran away. I sent after him but cannot hear of him. This is the 4th White Servant I've lost since I left England. I was most abominably Cheated with a Negroe who died within ten days after I bought him. I've been very unfortunate in Cowes and horses my Salary spent in bills the worst way of Improving it. My Attorney abuses me, has suffer'd two bills to come back protested and I fear will serve other two, which I since drew upon him in like manner, so that I shall be very miserable, nothing coming in from the Country nor Credit.

We had great plenty of Corn, wheat and pork and hoped I should have had a little of each, if I had not employd my hands in the service of an ungratefull people I might have had grain of all sorts. I prest the Vestry to meet and provide for me in time but could not prevail till the Arrival of your Honors Letter, and then 'twas with great difficulty after six voyages and 10 days spent, my self and hands attending upon the Gentry. Some were for allowing me nothing, others said it was too late. The People having disposed of all the <298> provisions they could spare. They Agreed upon an Answer to your Honor and the Society. Tis order'd to be written over fair, I guess by Christmas next twill be ready to send. I would have incerted their treatment of me it might perhaps have been Encouragement for others to come from England. I do not suppose they'l let me see, much less sign it. They do not Allow me to sit in Vestry, at my first coming I prevaild with the Assembly to make an Act for Establishing the Church but was not consulted about it. The former Act offended the Society in reserving a Power to the Vestry to turn out and hire Ministers at Pleasure. I think this is of worse consequence, for now they are at their Liberty to allow any thing or nothing and accordingly they purpose to serve me. Colonel Hyde engaged this Parish to pay me £45 for the time past to Christmas 1711. Tis not much above half collected and of that I have recd. £11 odd shillings they promised me £60 per Annum ever after but now will pay me nothing. A year hence we may perhaps have another Vestry, and then the Sherriffe must Account for his mismanagement. If I have no goods from England this Spring I know not what will become of me. Mr. Rainsford acted very unfair, he would have forced me out of this Parish, no other place would please him. He offer'd to serve it Gratis and told the People the Society did not expect the country should allow any thing. That doctrine was very edifying, but in a short time he became as contemptable as he endeavour'd to render me. He is now in Virginia but will not be entertain'd. Keekotan and Nansemond rejected him. I am told the Governor has threatned the latter to compel them to receive him.

I acquainted your Honor in a former if I mistake not that the Library my Predecessor Mr. Gordon should have brought in was left with Mr. Wallace in Virginia. He is dead, and I fear the books will be lost. I have desired an Order more than once from the Society or Mr. Gordon to demand them but have no Answer to that nor a thousand other Things very material relating to my Mission; surely paper and ink must be dear in England. The Vestry of Coratuck where Mr. Adams late Missionary died detain his books on Pretence they wer at some charge in fetching them out of Virginia and will appropriate them to that Parish where no Minister will scarce ever reside. The famous Library sent in by Dr. Brays Directions is in a great measure destroy'd <299> I am told the books are all unbound and have served for some time for wast Paper.

I humbly beg of your Honor to Order £20 Sterling to be laid out as follows and sent by the bearer and I'le send you my bill upon the Treasurer, videlicet Sugar the best sort Molosses and Rumm of each a Barrel, the best pale or Slack dry'd Malt of a hhd. with hops proportionable, the three former are as precious here as gold of Arabia with them I can buy Provisions. I shall want 3 or 4 Sickles, a gallon of the best Sallet Oyl Nutmegs Oz.[1]ij Ginger lb.ij black Pepper as much, Cinamon Cloves mace each Oz.[2]iiij ink Powder two Papers and if money will hold out a barrel or two of Syder will be very welcome. I should not have taken this Liberty had I any acquaintance there. I desired the Society to give me credit there or at Barbado's £20 per Annum but am neglected. 'Twould have done me great Service. Many begin to doubt of your Honor coming hither and more do not desire you may. If you do not here will be no abiding for me. I therefore crave I may be dismiss'd if your Honor cannot do it. I entreat You to press the Society to do it. I find by vertue of an Order made since I left England 'tis not prudent to remove without leave first obtain'd. I beg pardon for my tedious long Letter and your acceptance of the most humble respects of Good Sir Your most Obedient.

John Urmstone Missionary

North Carolina
Aprl. 12th 1714

Copy. Read at a meeting of the SPG on March 18, 1714/5. Journal of the SPG, III, 48. This document was enclosed in the letter from Thomas Pollock to Francis Nicholson, [April, 1714], below.

[1]The symbol given here for apothecary weight appears to be the one for ounce, but may possibly be the one for dram. Eight drams make an ounce.

[2]Ditto.

[*SPG/A/9*]

Thomas Pollock to Francis Nicholson
[1714 April]

<289> <1> A Paragraph of a Lettre from the Honorable Col. Thomas pollock president of North Carolina to Francis Nicholson Esqr. Videlicet.

Your Lettres to the Reverend Dr. Urmston and Rainsford have delivered and hope their Lettres herewith Inclosed will give Account of the Libraryes Sent in by Mr. Gordon and Mr. Adams.

The Wars and troubles here hath much hindered them from doing that good here that otherwise they might have done.

A true Copy Fr. Nicholson

Boston May 11th, 1714

Copy. Enclosed in the letter from which this paragraph was taken was the letter from Rev. John Urmston to Nicholson, April 12, 1714, and the one from Rev. Giles Ransford to the secretary, March 30, 1714, both of which are printed above.

[*SPG/A/9*]

Francis Nicholson to Secretary, SPG
1714 May 11

<352> <5> Genl. Nicholson to the Secretary.

Boston May 11th 1714

Sir

Inclosed are copys of my two Letters to You of the 17th of February last with a Duplicate of that of the 7th Instant. I also herewith send you Letter etc. from North Carolina, by which the Society may please to see, how their Affairs are managed there and I hope they will be pleased to take particular Care about their Missionarys there for I find that tho' there be but two of them they don't agree for which I am heartily sorry and that there are such Divisions amongst the rest of the Societys Missionaries in Pensilvania Jersey and New York, but I hope in God that a Bp. will come and set all the Church Affairs to Rights, for without one I am afraid that the Church will decrease faster than it ever increased in these parts of the World. [...]

I am in dayly hopes of hearing from you in answer to the several Letters writ you by him who is Your most Affectionate Friend and faithfull humble Servant.

Francis Nicholson

Copy. Read at a meeting of the SPG on March 18, 1714/5. Journal of the SPG, III, 47.

[*SPG/A/9*]

List
1714 May 11

<379> <9> Papers inclosed in General Nicholsons Letter dated Boston May 11th 1714 In Number.

No. 1 Papers from N. Carolina

A. Paragraph of a Letter from Colonel Pollock to Gen. Nicholson.
B. Two Letters from Mr. Urmston to Gen. Nicholson <*Vide Carolina Papers No. 1, 2.*>
C. One Letter from Ditto to the Secretary <*Vide Carolina Letters No. 3.*>
D. One Letter from Mr. Ransford. Vide Carolina Papers No. 4. [...]

Copy.

[*SPG/A/9*]

Rev. John Urmston to Secretary, SPG
1714 June 12

<277> Mr. Urmstone to the Secretary.

Sir

You say in yours of Decbr. 18, 1713 which came to hand two Days agoe, that mine to Mr. Hodges dated Oct. 22, 1712 was at last Communicated to the Bord. I Wonder what is become of divers of older as well as fresher date of far greater Moment. I gave Bond for the books which Mr. Gordon should have brought in but left with the Reverend Mr. Wallace late Minister of Kicketan in James River Virginia, where greatest part of them still are. I did indeed after the decease of Mr. Adams, demand his books but was denied them, and so will every one that is not Musketta[1] proof. The Vestry pretend that they are appropriate to that Parish, so that I beleive neither Society nor their Missionarys will ever be the better for them. Theyll do by them as the Gentry of Bath have done with that famous Library the Reverend Dr. Bray sent in here of a £100 Value make Wast Paper of their Books rather than the Clergy should have them, such is their esteem of our Func[tion] as in all other Respects, were it in their Power they would deprive us of food and Raiment too. I and my Poor Family are brought to that pass. I brought £50 worth of Books with me, they are mostly destroyd in the way and thro' want of safe Custody; Apparel and Neccessarys We had sufficient, but now being forc'd to sell our Bedding, Cloths off our Backs and all the Moveable Wee could spare for a Little Provision. Wee are destitute of Goods and Naked and insted of Books Ive gotten a parcel of Tools fitt for all Trades sett up for my Library, which I am forc'd to make as much use of as I should do of Books had I leasure, contempt enough without any fault of mine. I call God and all good Men to Witness; but such is the fate of the greates part of the Ministry, thanks to the mismanagement of the Reformation and the Worldy <278> mindedness of the many who have the good fortune to be known to Great Men, and some by Merritt but more by indirect not to say unlawful ways have attain'd to great Preferments, yet the Contempt brought upon us the inferiour Rank reaches unto them their pluralities of fatt Benefitts does not screen them from Partaking with us, but they can better bear it. Nil habet in sese duruis Paupertas.[2] You say complaint has been made that some indiscreet and negligent Actions have exposed me to the hatred and Contempt of the People. It is no wonder, for twas so from my first setting foot into this Wretched hole. Tis well Ive any discretion left at all, since I am almost bereft of the little sence and Reason I was once Master of. My sacred Character is sufficient to draw hatred and Contempt upon me from a pack of Proffligate and loose People and zealous Sectarists whose whole endeavour it is to load me with reproaches. This Colony cheifly consists of such, our Vestries not excepted, however I procured after 7 Months entreaty, many long and tedious Journeys and Voyages, sometimes 3 or 4 days abroad with 3 Servants divers appointments and as many disappointments I got, I say, 7 of our Vestry Men together at last who preswaded with much difficulty to draw up an acct. of the state of this Parish, which had not been obtain'd did not they fear Colonell Nicholson would come in and be displeas'd with them, at the request of the Said Colonell I communicated both this and that from the Society to all the Parishes within this Government, but hear not of anything done save in my Parish: the great reason of our Vestry Men their unwillingness was fear of being oblidg'd to do something for me, it being then pay time and great plenty of all sorts of Provisions, yet Poor was put by, neither the 45 order'd me Decembr. 1716 and then due nor any thing from the time since that could be obtaind nor ever like to be they were forward enough to magnifie their Poverty and beg further assistance of the Society but in <279> very deed worthy of none. These Vestry Men youl say, can be no better than Enemies to me, nay two of them are Professed Anabaptists and 3 Vehement Scotchmen Presbyterians and one descended from Quakers and I Beleive never Baptiz'd and still I suspect no Friend of the Church, yet these very Men in their said acct. will take of all such Accusations alledg'd against me, tho unjust in all other respects yet have done me that Justice even before I knew I was Accused. I cannot but lay it very much to heart to see the Society so forward to hearken to the complaint of some idle Person and so regardless of the repeated Requests I've made for their assistance and directions in many difficult cases and the frequent dismal relations of my Misery which increases daily upon me. I am now in manifest danger of Starving for want of Bread and except am releived as soon as the Wheat is reap'd I know not what to do. The Sloops from N. England sweep all our provision away. We have twice as many Vessels this Year as ever were wont to Come, there are above 7 now waiting like as many Vultures for our Wheat and more daily expected, they sell their Goods at Exorbiant rates and thus Wee are rendered Poor, no marvel then I suffer, for come what will on't, lett who will go unpaid, Rum long sweetening alias Mollosses glystr.[3] sugar must be had. I've nothing to buy anything with but Bills. £20 in English goods would do me more service than my Years Salary in this way of managing, but how to come at that now I know not since Wee are not allow'd Attornys. I had one as I suppos'd a Friend but prov'd the Worst of Enemys, sent me but one remittance since I left England, but never was worthy to know what nor of what value till the other day when in a huff by reason of my complaints of ill usage he has sent an Acct. of all his Managment. I could not so much as hear from him; He charges me with the Postage of a multitude of Letters. I never wrote to him but sent one inclosed to some of the Society but fear they were not all delivered, he payd what Bills he listed and has sent others back protested, which puts me to an unnecessary charge and endless shame and disgrace; for want of goods I've been forc'd to draw upon the Treasurer supposing my friend to be dead; he saith he could not supply <280> me by reason my Salary was not duly paid, once stopped because I had left my Cure and again for drawing upon the Treasurer what must I do in such case. I've drawn more than my Salary will pay by Michaelmas next. My Plantation must be paid for or I must turn out and whither to go I know not. I have not a Morsel of either Pork or Beef against Winter, nothing to buy with nor can I draw, hard fate! Will nothing draw compassion? I was not sold a Slave to Egypt nor yet deserved to be banished to the Gyaril.[4] Must I make brick without Straw and my task be increased. I hoped for Milder Task-Masters. And after all my unparralled hardships and fatigues for 4 Years together be still told that I am idle and negligent of my Cure I challenge all the Clergy in the Church to equalize what I have done and suffered for so long time together if I continue here I hope for better encouragment or if I fail therein and am forced to come home, care will be taken of Sir Your Poor distressed friend and most humble Servant.

Jno. Urmstone Missionary

North Carolina
June the 12 1714

I shall comply with my duty and your instructions in my next Notitia Parochialis that I am preparing but have not now time to finish.

Copy. Read at a meeting of the SPG on January 21, 1714/5. Journal of the SPG, III, 29.

[1]This word can be a variant of both *musket* and *mosquito*. *OED*.

[2]"Nothing is so hard to endure as poverty."

[3]Glyster is a variant of *clyster*, which among other things can mean a nutritional substance taken in suppository form. *OED*. This may or may not bear any relationship to the word used in this instance.

[4]The meaning of this word is unknown.

[*SPG/A/10*]

Edward Moseley to Francis Nicholson
1714 July 15

Mr. Mosley to Genl. Nicholson.

Chowan No. Carolina
July the 15 1714

The Laudable designes you have constantly persued of Advansing the Intrest of the Church in America Among other Matters of your great intentions for promoteing that Service led you to bestow of your own Generosity the Sum of Thirty pounds to be distributed in three of the precincts of North Carolina which you lodged in the hands of Mr. Walker my predecessor at my Intermarriage with his Widdow. I found the money had not been applyed by Reason of his death soon after your gift tho he had <63> taken Care to have it mentioned in the Vestry book of this precinct that the part bellonging to it viz. Ten pounds should be laid out for a peice of plate for the Communion Service mentioning the Donars Gift and I preswaded my Self the like care was taken by him in the other Two precincts Pequimans and Pasquotk tho I cannot learne there is any thing appears on their books.

I have paid Pasquotanck precinct who have misapplyed the money Contrary to your Excellencys Intentions by parting with it to Satisfie such Engagements as the produce of Our Country would have been Sufficient for videlicet Some debts and how to Raise So much plate at present they know not what measur's to take.

The Same Steps were begun by the Pequimans, And I fear the Chowan money, but I lodged it in Mr. Jere. Dummers[1] hands of boston towards procureing Church plate where at present I find it lyes to wait Mr. Excellencys further Orders altho they have constrained me to give orders for the Removeale of the money with out any apparent Intentions of applying it to the Uses you so generously proposed. For those Reasons I have presumed to trouble your Excellency with these few lines to <64> Request you to give your orders to Mr. Dummer to Send it to the precincts of Chowan and Pequims. in such plate as you Shall please for the Service of the Church as you designed it. He has my Letters accompanying this to observe your orders for that purpose which if you do not so order I can hardly think the Church will be the better for so pious and Charitable a Gift. Begging your Excellencys pardon for the trouble I give you in peruseing this Scrawle and leave to present your Excellency my hearty Sincere thanks for the favours you are pleased to Show me when in Company Quarry [*sic*][2] I waited on Your Excellency in Your Government of Virginia.

I crave leave to Subscribe my Self Your Excellencys most Obliged and Obedient humble Servant.

Edward Moseley

Copy.

[1]Jeremiah Dummer, a Boston merchant trading to North Carolina.

[2]Presumably this means that the writer was in company with [Robert] Quary, who was briefly governor of South Carolina in the 1680s. Later he was judge of the vice admiralty court of Pennsylvania, and surveyor general of customs in the American colonies, 1703-1714. Andrews, *Colonial Period*, IV, 152, 200.

[*SPG/A/10*]

Thomas Pollock to Francis Nicholson
1714 August 3

<65> Colonell Pollock to Genl. Nicholson

Chowan Augt. 3 1714

May it please Your Excellency

I recd. yours by Capt. Dunming with her Majesties Speech to this Parliament for which Returne you my humble thanks. Governor Eden[1] Arived here last May all being in peace and Quietness only one or two Small parties of Enemy Indians that contine to do mischeife on our Fronteires. Colonell Cary is gon for the West India's but intends Inn againe this fall.

The Church Wardens and Vestry of the precinct of Chowan desired me to Send the two Enclosed to your Excellency, and indeed wee have very great want not only of Schoolmasters but also of Ministers, for albeit Dr. Urmston hath continued amongst us ever since his Arrivale He hath had little encouragement yet. Dr. Rainsford hath been very little time in this Country only about Two or three months about the time I recd. your first letters but hath Continued all in Virginia so that he deserves nothing of the Society, that wished for Success may Attend all your noble and glorius Undertakeings shall be Earnestly desired. Your Excellencys most Humble Servant.

Tho. Pollock

Copy. Enclosed in this document was the letter from the vestry of Queen Anne's Creek to the secretary of the SPG and Francis Nicholson dated March 2, 1713/4, p. 171.

[1]Charles Eden (1673-1722) succeeded Edward Hyde as governor of North Carolina in May, 1714, and served until his death. *DNCB*.

[*SPG/A/9*]

Rev. John Urmston to Secretary, SPG
1714 August 7

<280> <12> Mr. Urmstone to the Secretary.

N. Carolina Aug. 7, 1714

Sir

During the last ½ year the state of Religion is much the same changes for the better are not easily brought about. The People are daily more unkind. Ive baptizd 59 whereof two were Adult. We have not had the Lords Supper administred in publick durring that time. I have some hopes of better things in many respects thro the endeavours of an honest Gent. our now Governor.[1] He seems resolved to promote Church discipline being a strict observer thereof himself. He must expect to meet with many difficulties some insuperable. I wish a letter were sent to him, it would be of use. He purposes to redress many of my aggreivances, which will render life more comfortable. I am sorry We are not like to see Colonell Nicholson here if a bill for £14 payable to Thos. Jones of Virginia be unpaid I pray it may never be paid thro the perifidous dealing of my Agent at London. I am worse than I thought for, in want of many things but must not draw if my Salary had been duly paid and invested in goods I had been one of the richest in this famous Colony, whereas I am now the poorest. £30 in goods would have done me more good than thrice that has, being forc'd to give 4 or 5 hundred per Ct. for all what I give bills for. I have not recd. the Catechisms sent by Mr. Ransford. He never disposed of the gifts books value £5. He made more by his Voyage and years Salary than I've done these 5 Years and never did any thing for it. A handful of Indians who would not come into the Treaty with the rest have spilt more innocent blood than all the rest and We cannot cause Our men to goe against them nor willingly pay those that will, they rove from place to place; cut of 2 or 3 Familie's to day and within 2 or 3 Days do the like a hundred Miles of from the former they are like Dear theres no finding them. We have Men out after them to sue for peace. I am Sir with all Dutiful Respects to the Society Yr. most humble Servant.

Jno. Urmstone Missionary

I Earnestly beg all my bills to Mr. Jekyl my very good friend may be pd. in due time.

Copy. Read at a meeting of the SPG on January 21, 1714/5. Journal of the SPG, III, 30.

[1]Charles Eden.

[*SPG/A/9*]

Rev. John Urmston to Secretary, SPG
1714 September 22

<282> <13> Mr. Urmstone to the Secretary.

North Carolina Sept. 22d 1714

Sir

Since my last my hopes are blasted. Wee were then going to have an Assembly from whom, thro the Governours assistance I expected some redress of the many greivances Ive formerly laid before the Society. The loss of Bath County if not the whol Government is threatned, to prevent which our honest Gouvernor was wholly bent but after near a fortnights time spent to no purpose he was forc'd to send them home. We daily hear of families cutt of and destroy'd. 'Tis difficult to raise men to secure the frontiers but more difficult to find Provisions to subsist them. The Northern Indians Senecars[1] I think they call them, are design'd speedily to joyn our Enemies, which if true will compleat the ruin of this wretched Country. Our Confederate Indians seeing we are not able to vanquish such a handful, dayley desert us to joyn them and by the unwillingness of the rest to go out with us and get them, according to capitulations Wee may to justly fear they'l brake peace with us, and having experienc'd the Cowardice of our Quakers and their Adherrents who like other Sectarists never care to fight except it be against the Church and Crown the Indians will not dally nor trifle with us as they did at first.

Wee except [*sic*] to hear that famous City of Bath consisting of 9 Houses or rather Cottages once stil'd the Metropolis and seat of Government will be totaly deserted and yet I cannot find means to secure that admirable collection of books sent in by the Reverend Dr. Bray, for the use of the ministry of this province but it will in all Probability serve for a Bonfire to the Indians. These Indians who do us all this mischeif were at first but a handful about 30 in Number the remains of 3 small Nations who were cutt of and taken by the forces from S. Carolina, who meeting with little or no opposition encreased daily so that now Wee are forc'd to sue to them for peace but fear Wee shall not obtain it. These are from Sir your most humble Servant.

Jno. Urmstone Missioner

Copy. Read at a meeting of the SPG on January 21, 1714/5. Journal of the SPG, III, 30-31.

[1]The Seneca of New York were, like the Tuscarora, of the Iroquoian linguistic group.

[*SPG/C/7*]

Charles Eden to SPG
1714 October 8

<60>

North Carolina
Octor. the 8th 1715 [*sic*][1]

Most Honourable

The Lds. proprietors of Carolina haveing thought fitt to Honour me with the Government of that part of their Lordships Province I take leave (as I think it is my Duty) to remonstrate to you the deplorable State of Religion in this poore unhappy province. It is now about four months since I enter'd upon the Goverment when I found no Clergy man upon the place except Mr. Urmston one of your Missionarys who is realy an honest painstakeing Gentleman and worthy your Care but poore Man with utmost endeavours is not able to Serve one half of the County of Albermarle which Adjoins to Virginia, when the County of Bath of a much larger extant is wholy destitute of any Assistance I cannot find but the people are well enough inclined to embrace all oppertunitys of Attending the Service of God and to Contribute to the utmost of their Abilitys towards the Support of such Missioners as you shall in Compassion to their circumstances think fit to send amongst them but our Tedious Indian Warr has reduced the Country so lowe that without your Nursing Care the very foot Steps of Religion will in a short time be worne out, and those who retains any remembrance of it will be wholy lead away by the Quakers, whereas a few of the Clergy of a Complaisant temper and Regular lives woud not only be the darlings of the people but woud be a means in time to recover those already Seduced by Quakerisme etc.

This is what I thought my Self under an Indespensible Obligation to lay before you for your Serious Consideration and at the same time I take leave to recomend to you the person from whose hands you'l receive this (Vidilicet) Mr. Thomas Gale[2] late of Trinity

Colledge in Cambridge, who I doubt not will come otherwise recomended as a very Proper person for that Service if he shall meet with your Approbation.

There has been distroy'd by the Indians Since the beginning of the Warr above four Score unbaptised Infants and a great Number in the County of Bath even to Seaven years old are now under that Circumstance for noe other cause but want of Opertunity and as yet there are noe Quakers in that County. The groth of their Sect in it I hope the Charritable care of your Most Honourable Society will effectualy prevent. I wish I cou'd be anyways instrumental in Serving any thing Sent by you into these parts whenever any Opertunity Offers with great readiness I shall be glad to showe how much I am Most Honourable Gentlemen your most Obedient Humble Servant.

Charles Eden

Copy of a Letter sent to the most Honourable
Society for Propogating the Gospel in
Forreigne parts.

[*Endorsed*:]
Copy of a Letter from
Governour Eden dated
North Carolina 8th Octor. 1715

Copy (entirely in the writer's hand). Read at a meeting of the SPG on September 16, 1715, when it was "Agreed that Mr. Commissary [Gideon] Johnston with the Advice and Approbation of the rest of the Clergy do Appoint one of their Number a Single man and one who has been obliged to leave his Parish, to repair to North Carolina and Officiate as the Societys Missionary there and that a Letter be wrote to him accordingly." Journal of the SPG, III, 80.

[1]As is plain from the date of this letter's consideration by the SPG, 1714 is the correct year. Another copy, unaccountably dated October 8, 1717, is found in SPG/A/10,72-73.

[2]Brother of Christopher Gale. See the undated letter from Thomas Gale to the secretary, p. 203.

[*SPG/A/9*]

Secretary of the SPG to Rev. John Urmston 1714 December 17

<308> <13> To Mr. Urmstone.

17th Decb. 1714

Reverend Sir

Your three Letters of 12th June 7th August and 22th of Septemr. last have been recd. and communicated to the Society. I am sorry at the Hardships You seem <309> to complain of lying under but when You consider the Society allow to You even more than what they do even any other their Missionaries, and that they cannot Justly dispose of the charity money committed to their Management to one Place only, You will beleive They are particularly kind to You and the People under Your Care by the large Allowance of £80 per Annum. I have nothing [*blank*] as to Mr. Maule No. 3.[1]

Copy.

[1]The portion to be repeated in the present letter is contained in one from the secretary to Rev. Robert Maule in South Carolina: "I have nothing more in command specially to write to You except it be that you observe on your part all the Rules and Orders of the Society of which you have already Notice, and that you use your best Endeavours to answer this Good Design by Carefulness and Diligence in your Holy Calling and Function to promote the Glory of Almighty God and the Salvation of Souls particularly of those committed to your Care. I am etc." SPG/A/9, p. 305.

[*SPG/A/9*]

Secretary of the SPG to Rev. Giles Ransford
1714 December 17

<309> <14> To Mr. Rainsford.

17 Decemr. 1714

Reverend Sir

I have recd. Yours of the 30th March last which hath been communicated to the Society. I am directed to acquaint You, that (as to the Protest of Your Bills You complain of in the said Letter) it appear to the Society; that Your Salary hath been paid to the time You confess by your Letter to have left their Service, and as to the Expectation of a years Salary to be given You by the Society; I am Orderd to let You know that You are not within their Rules as having quitted their Service without Leave. I am etc.

Copy.

[*CO 5/293*]

Act of Assembly
1715

An Act for Establishing the Church and appointing Select Vestreys

<*This Act not only confirms the Church of England here but divides the Country into Parishes According to the Scituation and Conveniency. Appoints Church Wardens and a Vestry in Each Parish and Investeth them with Power, But as they Allow them to Raise a Levy of but 5 shilling per Poll on the Parish, Since Bills are Come into Payment it Amounts to So Little as will scarce do more (after maintaining the Poore if any) than to Pay A Reader for Reading the Common Prayer and Printed Sermon on Sundays to the People but as to* [*illegible*] *and Collation of Parsons there is so Little of it that there*

is not a Settled Parson in the Country. His Majesty's Instruction on this head I Laid before the Assembly but nothing was don about it. >[1] This Province of North Carolina being a Member of The Kingdom of Great Britain, And the Church of England being appointed by the Charter from the Crown to be the only Established Church to have publick Encouragement in it Wee Therefore to Express our gratitude to the Right honorable the Society for promoting the Christian Religion in forreign parts, and our Zeal for promoting our holy Religion by making such provision for the building of Churches and Chaples and maintainance of the Clergy as the Circumstances of this Government will admitt Doe Pray that it may be Enacted.

And be it Enacted by his Excellency the Palatin and the Rest of the true and absolute Lds. Proprietors of the Province of[2] Carolina by and with the advice and Consent of the Members of the Generall Assembly now meet at Little River for the North East part of the Province and by the authority of the Same.

It is hereby Enacted That this Province of North Carolina be Divided into Parishes according to the Divisions or Precincts hereafter mentioned that is to Say, Chowan Precinct into Two parishes to be Divided by Albemarle Sound and Chowan River and shall be Distinguished by the Names of the Eastern parish of Chowan and the South West Parish, Pasquotanck precinct into Two parishes to be Divided by Pasquotanck River and shall be distinguished by the Names of the North East parish of Pasquotanck and the South West Parish of Pasquotanck, Perquimans, Currytuck, and Hide to be parishes, and bounded by the Limits of the Several Precincts. The Remaining part of Pamplico River and the Branches thereof Commonly Called Beaufort Precinct to be One parish by the name of St. Thomas Parish, And New River and the Branches thereof by the Name of Craven parish to which all the Southern Settlements shall be Accounted as part of the Same parish untill further Divisions be made.

And be it further Enacted by the Authority aforesaid That there shall be a Vestry in Each and Every of the aforesaid Parishes or Precincts Consisting of the Minister of the parish whenever any Such shall be there Resident and twelve Men whose Names are hereafter Mentioned.

Eastern Parish of Chowan Precinct

The honorable Charl. Eden Esqr., Collonel Edwd. Moseley, Capt. Fredrick Jones, Major Thomas Luton, Capt. Nicholas Crisp, Mr. Thomas Bray,[3] Mr. James Farlow, Capt. Henry Bonner, Mr. John Blount, Mr. Samuel Padget, Mr. Thomas Garret, Mr. John Jordan

S.W. Parish of Chowan Precinct

Collonel Thomas Polluck, Collonel Will. Maule, Will. Dukenfield Esqr., Major Thos. West, Capt. John Bird, Mr. John Hardy, John Woreley Esqr., Mr. Lewis Briant, Mr. Jo. Hallbrook, Mr. Robt. Lanier, Mr. Lan Sarson, Mr. Lewis Williams.

Perquimans Parish

Fran. Foster Esqr., Collonel Mau. Moor, Collonel John Hacklefield, Thos. Harvey Esqr., Capt. Richd. Sanderson, Mr. James Mengs, Mr. Henry Clayton, Mr. Jos. Jessop, Mr. Saml. Phelps, Mr. Richd. Whitbee, Mr. Hill, Mr. John Stepney.

S.W. Parish of Pasquotank

Natha. Chevin Esqr., Collonel Thos. Boyd, Tobias Knight Esqr., Mr. John Jennings, Mr. Richd. Madren, Mr. Edmd. Gale, Mr. Antho. Hatch, Mr. John Jeacucks, Mr. John Palin, Mr. William Norris, Mr. Robt. Lowry.

No. East Parish of Pasquotanck Precinct

Thos. Miller Esqr., Mr. John Solly, Mr. John Relf, Mr. John Bell, Mr. Saml. Bernard, Capt. John Norton, Mr. Gab. Burnhame, Mr. Thos. Sawyer, Mr. Henry Sawyer, Mr. Allexr. Spence, Mr. Robert Sawyer, Mr. John Upton

Currituck Precinct Parish

Richd. Sanderson Esqr., Collonel Will. Reed, Will. Swann Esqr., Thomas [*blank*], Mr. Thos. Taylor, Mr. Will. Williams, Mr. Forster Gervice, Mr. Benja. Tull, Mr. Jos. Sanderson, Mr. Joseph Wiker, Mr. Will. Lufforrance, Mr. Will. Stafford.

St. Thomas Parish

The honorable Charl. Eden Esqr., Collonel Crist. Gale, Tobias Knight Esqr., Mr. John Porter, Danl. Richardson Esqr., Mr. Thos. Worsly, Mr. Jno. Drinkwater, Capt. John Clark, Mr. John Adams, Mr. Patr. Maule, Mr. Thos. Harding, Mr. John Lillington.

Hide Parish

Collonel Em. Cleaves, Mr. Wilb. Barrow, Mr. John Jordan, Mr. Saml. Slade, Mr. Richd. Jasper, Mr. Wilb. Cording, Mr. Hen. Slade, Mr. John Porter, Mr. Robt. Spring, Mr. Richd. Daw, Mr. Richd. Harvey, Mr. Robt. Green.

Craven Parish

Collonel Will. B[*blank*], Major Will. Hancock, Mr. John Nellson, Mr. John Slocomb, Capt. Richd. Graves, Mr. Danl. Mcfarlan, Mr. John Smith, Mr. John Makey, Mr. Thos. Smith, Mr. Joseph Bell, Mr. Mart. Frank, Mr. Jacob Sheets.

Which Said Vestrymen are to be Sumoned by the Marshall or his Deputy in each precinct or parish to meet together at the Church Chapple or Court house in Every precinct or if there be none then at such other places as the Marshall shall appoint within fourty Dayes after the publication of this Act, And if any person or persons Appointed by this Act to be Vestry Men shall fail to meet as aforesaid on Such Summons he or they shall forfeit and pay the Sume of Three pounds, or if the Marshall shall Refuse or Neglect to Summons the Vestry men as before mentioned and appointed he shall forfeit the Sum of Twenty shillings for Every Vestry Man not Summoned.

And be it further Enacted by the Authority aforesaid that all and Every person and persons who by this Act are appointed to be Vestry men without any Parish or precinct in this Government shall on or before the Easter Sunday next Ensuing the Ratification of this Act, And all and Every Such person and persons who shall at any time hereafter be Ellected a Vestryman or become a Member of any Vestry within this Government shall within One Month after his becoming a Vestryman or Member of any Vestry before Some One or more Justice or Justices of the peace within that Parish or precinct besides taking the Oaths by law Enjoyned, make and Subscribe the Declaration and Accknowledgement following Videlicet.

I A B Do Declare that it is not Lawfull upon any pretence whatsoever to take up Arms against the King, And that I will not Oppung [*sic*][4] the Liturgy of the Church of England as it is by Law Established And That all and Every Such person who shall Neglect or Refuse to Do the Same within the Respective time aforesaid shall be deprived of Such his place of Vestrymen and being a Member of Such Vestry to all Intents and purposes, and Such place shall be Actually Void. And if Such person is not a known and publick Dissenter from the Church of England he shall also forfeit the Sum of Three pounds. And that from and after Such Neglect or Refusall it shall be lawfull for the Remaining part of the Vestrymen to proceed to Elections and Nomination of Some other discreet freeholder of the Respective parish in the Room of Such person so Neglecting or Refusing as aforesaid. And if Such person so to be Elected in the Room of Such person as Neglecting or Refusing shall also neglect and Refuse to make and Subscribe the Declaration and Accknowledgement in manner and time aforesaid in Such Cases, if the Vestry shall proceed to Election within One Month after Such Vacancy, Then it shall be Lawfull to and for the present Incumbent (if any) or for want thereof the Commander in Chief of this Government for the time being, Under his hand and Seal to Elect and Nominate a Discreet freeholder in the parish in Such Vacant Room, which person so to be Elected and Nominated after making his Subscription in the manner and time aforesaid shall be Deemed and taken a Vestryman and a Member of Such Vestry as if he has been Expressly Nominated by this Act.

And be it further Enacted by the authority aforesaid That the Vestrymen of Every precinct or parish or the greatest part of them shall Choose Two persons Who are Vestry

Men to be Church Wardens, who Shall Continue in that office One year and no Longer Unless he or they shall be Willing, and Then Two Other Vestrymen shall Suceed in the Said Office for the next year and So Successively until Every Vestryman hath Served in the Office aforesaid.

And be it further Enacted by the Authority aforesaid that if any person who shall be Chosen a Church Warden shall Refuse to Execute that office without Lawfull Cause he shall forfiet and pay Thirty shillings to be Levyed on the Estate of the Person so Refusing by Order of the Vestry or the greatest part of them to be Disposed of to the use of the parish upon which Such person Shall be Excused till his turn Come again in Course. And The Church Wardens in Each Respective parish and their Successors shall have full power to Call the Vestrymen together and to Appoint the time of their meeting. And in Case of their Neglect to Do when Occasion shall require it shall be Lawfull for three or more of the Vestry to Do the Same. And if any Vestryman shall fail to give his Attendance at Such time of meeting without Lawfull Cause to be Allowed and Approved of by the Vestry or the greatest part of them he shall forfeit and pay the Sum of Tenn shillings for every Such Default to be Levyed and Disposed of in manner aforesaid.

And be it further Enacted by the Authority aforesaid That the Several Church Wardens and Vestrys or the greatest part of them shall Use their best and utmost Endeavours to procure an Able and Godly Minister Qualified According to the Ecclesiasticall Laws of England; And a person of Sober Life and Conversation to be Clerk And to Raise for him or them Such Stipends yearly as they shall think Convenient, So as Such Summ or Stipend for the Minister be not Less then fifty pounds yearly and that in the Raising thereof, and all other parish Charges the whole do not Exceed five shillings per pole on all the taxable persons in the parish. Provided always that Such Minister of whome Such monys are to be Raised yearly be Constantly Resident in the parish And Do no Ommit the Officiating at the Church or Chappell within the parish above One Sixth part of the Sundays in the year unless permitted by the Church Wardens and Vestry to Officiate in the Neighbouring parishes which are Vacant.

And be it further Enacted by the Authority aforesaid that the Church Wardens and Vestrymen or the greatest part of them in Each Respective precinct and parish aforesaid and their Successors forever shall have full power and Authority to purchase Land for a Glebe, To Build One Church and One or more Chappells in Every respective parish or precinct aforesaid as they or the greatest part of them shall think fitt and the Same as often as need shall Require to Repair, And also to provide and to take Care to Satisfy and pay all parochial Charges out of Such Gifts Goods and Chattles as shall Come to their hands for the Church or parishes Use Towards the payment of parochial Charges, all the fines and forfeitures by this Law Incurred shall be Levyed by the Church Wardens in each respective precinct or parish and by them Accordingly Applyd.

And be it further Enacted by the Authority aforesaid That for the Defraying and paying whatsoever Charges shall and may from time to time Arise by force of this Act or Which shall properly be a parish Charge altho not mentioned in this Act It shall and may be Lawfull for the Several Church Wardens and Vestrymen or the greatest part of them and their Successors in every Respective precinct or parish aforesaid to Raise and Levy money by the pole so as the same do not Exceed five shillings by the pole per annum which Summ or Summs of money so Laid Equally by a pole tax shall after Twenty Days Notice Given by the Church Wardens to the parishioners be paid by the time appointed for the payment thereof Either at the Glebe Church or Chappell or at Such other place as by the Church Wardens shall be Appointed, under the penalty of Double Disstress to be made by the Church Wardens on the Goods of Such person Refusing or Neglecting to bring the Same by the time Appointed. And be it further Enacted by the Authority aforesaid That the Church Wardens of Every precinct or parish aforesaid shall take Due Care and Order that all such Summ or Sums of money as the Vestry shall Order and Appoint be Duely Raised, and applyed and paid to Such Uses as by the Vestry shall be Directed for which the Church Wardens shall be allowed on their Accounts the Summ of three pounds per Cent and no more. And if any ChurchWarden shall refuse or neglect to perform his Duty therein he shall be Obliged to make good and pay all Such Summ and Summs so Ordered by the Vestry to Such person or persons as Should have had the Same, had the Taxes been duely Levyed and paid excepting Insolvents, And to prevent illegal and unlawfull Marriages not allowable by the Church of England but forbidden by the Table of Marriages.

Be it Enacted by the Authority aforesaid That no Minister or Priest or Majistrate (who are hereby Impowerd to Joyn persons together in Marriage in Such parishes where no Minister is Resident) Either upon Lycence or after the persons Intending to Marry have had the Banns of Matrimoney published three times by the Clerk at the usual place of Celebrating Divine Service, Or having Given publick Notice by Affixing Such their Intentions at the Court house door two Distinct Courts, Shall presume to Joyn together in Marriage any persons whatsoever Contrary to the Table of Marriages which the Church Wardens and Vestry are hereby Required to Cause to be set up in all Church and Chappels under the penalty of five pounds, Nor shall any person forbidden to Intermarry by Such Table of Marriages presume to be Joyned in marriage under the Like penalty of five pounds[5] One half in the parish for the use of the poor the Other to the Minister Resident or Incumbent, And that it shall and may be Lawfull for every Minister to take and Receive of Every person or persons by him Married the Sum of five shillings and no more Provided Such persons Come to the parish Church or Chappel at time of Divine Service, for so Solemnizing Such Marriage.

D. Although at least two previous statutes had dealt with church establishment in North Carolina, this one of 1715 is the earliest extant.

[1]These marginalia were added by Governor George Burrington in a copy of the act he sent to the Board of Trade in 1731.

[2]*North* written and struck through.

[3]Although bearing the same name as the founder of the SPG, the two are not related, as far as is known.

[4]*Oppugn*: "To be opposed to, come in conflict with, run counter to." *OED*.

[5]Another copy of this act includes here the following: *and that no Lay person in any parish where a minister or priest is resident shall join any person in Marriage under the penalty of five pounds.* BV North Carolina, Laws, p. 31, New-York Historical Society.

[*SPG/B/4*]

Abstract
1715

Abstract of the Act for Establishing the Church and Apointing Select Vestrys.

It is enacted that the Province of North Carolina be divided into Parishes videlicet Chowan Precinct into two Parishes that part of the precinct lying on the North East side of Albermarle Sound and Chowan river to be called the Eastern parish of Chowan and the other the Southerne parish. Pasquotank precinct into two Parishes and to be Divided by Pasquotank River. The Precincts of Perquimons, Courratuck and Hyde each to be a parish. Beaufort parish with the branches of pamlico River to be call'd St. Thomas's Parish, Craven precinct to be one parish til further Divission.

2. A Vestry apointed to each parish and to consist of twelve men whose names are incerted in the Act and the Minister Resident in the parish is allways to be a Vestry man.

3. Which Vestrys are to meet, upon Summons within forty days at the Church, Chappel, or Court House, under penalty of three pounds and if the Marshal shall fail to Summons the Vestry he shall forfeit 20 shillings for each Vestry man not Summoned.

4. Every Vestry man shall on or before Easter munday next before a Justice of the peace make and Subscribe the Declaration following. "I A. B. doe Declare that it is not Lawfull upon any Pretence whatsoever to take armes against the King and that I will not Oppugn the Liturgy of the Church of England as it is by Law established." And all other Vestry man hereafter to be apointed shall make and Subscribe the Same Declaration within one month after his being apointed Vestryman.

5. Vestrymen not takeing and Subscribeing the Declaration aforsaid shall be Deprived and Such place void, and if not a Knowne Dissenter from the Church of England shall forfeit three pounds.

6. Upon Neglect or refusal to make and Subscribe the Declaration the remaining part of the Vestry may Ellect a Freeholder to be a Vestry man in the roome of Such refuseing or Neglecting.

7. If the Vestrys doe not proceed to Ellection within one month after Such Vacancy, then the present Incumbent (if any) or for want of such, the Governor or Comander in Cheif under his hand and Seal may nominate a Freeholder of the parish to fill up Such Vacancy in the Vestry.

8. Two Church Wardens to be Chose out of the Vestry to Continue in that Office one yeare and not to be Obliged to Serve againe until all the Vestry men have Served Successively.

9. If any person chose to be Church Warden shall refuse to Serve he shall forfeit 30 shillings to be Levied on his Estate by Order of the Vestry and then not to be Obliged to Serve as Ch. Warden til his turne come againe in Course.

10. Church Wardens have full power to call the Vestry at Such times as they shall think necessary and if Occassion require any three of the Vestry have the Same Authority, and if any Vestry man fail to give his Attendance without lawfull cause for so doeing he forfeits ten Shillings.

11. Church Wardens and Vestry men to use their best endeavours to procure an Able and Godly Minister Quallified According to the Eccliesastical Lawes of England and a person of a Sober life and Conversation to be Clark and to allow them Such Stipends yearly as they shall think Convenient.

<*There is not a Parish in the Goverment but has Considerable more then 200 taxables, Except the Southern parishes, Bath County, which have been depopulated by the late Indian Warr and Massaccre And now Since that Warr is ended those parishes will quickly be able to make Suitable provission for Ministers.*

And it will not be very Difficult in the meane time for men of Substance in those parishes to make up by Subscriptions what the five Shillings per pole Shall fall short of £50. The Province of Maryland gave but forty pounds of Tobacco per pole to the Minister which is commonly estimated 3.4d and very often not So much. And they have Allowed their Vestrys to raise but ten pounds Tobacco per pole more for all parochial Charges, which in the whole makes but foure Shillings and Two pence.>

So as the Stipend for the Minister be not less then £50 Yearly, And that in the raising thereof and all Parish Charges the whole doe not exceed 5 shillings upon each taxable, And provided the Minister be constantly Resident and doe not omit Officiating above one Sixth part of the Sundays in the yeare, unless permited by the Vestry to Assist in Neighbouring Vacant parishes.

12. Church Wardens and Vestry have power to purchase Glebes build Churches, Chapels and to make repairs and to Cause all parochial charges to be paid and Sattisfied out of Such gifts, goods, and Chattles, as shall come to their hands for that purpose towards which all the fines and forfeitures in this Act are appropriated.

13. Church Wardens and Vestry have authority to raise mony by the pole to Sattisfy all Parochial Charges So as the Same doe not exceed 5 shillings per pole per Annum as is Aformentioned And after 20 days Notice give by the Church Wardens to the parishioners the Same shall be paid by the parishoners either at the Church Chappel or Glebe or Such other place as by the Church Wardens shall be appointed under penalty of double Distress.

14. Church Wardens shall take care that all Summs rais'd be duly applyed and paid as by the Vestry shall be directed for which they shall be allowed three per Cent and no more and if any Church Warden shall fail to performe his Duty, he shall be obliged to make good and pay all Such Summ or Summs order'd by the Vestry, as if the Taxes had been duly levied and paid excepting Insolvents.

15. And to prevent illegal and unlawfull Marraiges not allowable by the Church of England but forbiden by the table of Marraiges It is Enacted, that no Minister Priest or Majestrate, shall Joine in Marraige any person Contrary to the table of Marages under the penalty of five pounds, which table the Church Warden and Vestry are required to put up in all Churches and Chappels. Nor shall any Person forbiden to intermarry by the Table presume to be Joined in Marraige under the like penalty.

In Such parish where a Minister shall not be Resident any Majestrate is impower'd to Joine in Mattrimony any person not forbidden by the table of Marraige, So as Such person have Licence from the Governor or Comander in Cheif, or have been published three times by the Clark at the usual place of Celebrating Divine Service or have given publick Notice by Affixing Such their Intentions at the Court House Doore two distinct Courts. Any Person presumeing to Joine in marrige any persons in the parish where a Minister shall be Resident shall Forfeit five pounds, one half to the parish the other half to the Minister.

Ministers may take five Shillings for each Marraige.

[*Endorsed:*]
<2> Abstract of an Act of Assembly for
Establishing the Church in North Carolina
and for appointing select Vestrymen
Enclosed in Colonel Edens
Letter of the 10th May 1716

D. This document was enclosed in a letter from Governor Charles Eden to the secretary dated May 10, 1716, below. Although the act of which this is an abstract is printed in its entirety above, it is useful to have Governor Eden's comments on it, and also to see how he chose to summarize it for the authorities at home.

[*SPG/C/7*]

Rev. Giles Ransford to George Jefferies
1714/5 January 10

<23>

Chowan N. Carolina.
Jany. the 10th 1714/15

Worthy Sir

I lately receiv'd a letter from Mr. Taylor the Societies Secretary, wherein he has been pleas'd to lay before me the state of Accompts between the Society and myself. I have return'd my answer to both his letters by this opportunity of a Passage, with an account of the present state of the countrey, which I hope may prove satisfactory. I find there is considerably due to me, and upon that Presumption have drawn on you for twelve Pounds and five shillings Sterling. Pray make punctual payment at thirty days after the Bill is exhibited to you, for I have receiv'd the full value from Capt. William Wright of Virginia, and believe me to be Sir Your most obedient humble Servant.

Giles Rainsford Missionary

[*Addressed:*]
<5> To Mr George Jefferies
Treasurer to the Society for the
Propagation of the Gospel etc.
at the Arch-Bishop of Canterbury's
Library in St. Martins London

[*Endorsed:*]
Mr. Rainsford to the Treasurer

ALS.

[*SPG/A/10*]

Rev. Giles Ransford to Secretary, SPG
171[5] January 19

<69> Mr. Rainsford to the Secretary

Pascotank No. Carolina.
Janry. 19th 171[5]

Worthy Sir

I Received both yr. letters but that of the 18th of Decembr. came to hand but Novembr. last. I am extreemly concerned at the mortifying Consideration of my disoblidging the Society in the Business of mr. Ward and Quigley should I go about to lay before you the many Advantages they made of my necessity the Compass of a letter would not be Sufficient to unravel the Several Items of their Extortion but I am in Some measure Satisfied with the bare Consideration of what <70> Pennance I inflicted on my self for so unwise and so unwarrantable a practice. The Fault I hope is not unpardonable with the Society since this acknowledgment of my Guilt may wipe away the staines of a reproachfull Crime. The pure affects of my necessity Durum tetum necessitas[1] I found a True saying in the very Instance before me. However I am thankfull to you for yr. kind reproof which was done as the Apostle Enjoyns in the Spirit of meekness and forfearance [*sic*] as to the present State of the Government the Indian Differences are all Composed and Peace and Quietness seems to Flourish in our Land. You are pleased to give me an Account of Fifty one pounds and Tenn shillings due to me at Christmas 1713. I have drawn for the £80 Sterling some time since which was formerly protested in 2 forty pound Bills and should this I mention meet with the same Fate I Cannot tell what will become of me. But the Consideration of the last Standing Order made by the Society relating to Missionaries Bills, forbids me to suspect any such proceedings. I have now drawn on the Treasurer for twelve Pound and five Shillings Sterling which I hope Sir you will add this one trouble more to the rest you have undergone for me of seeing it paid. Protesting of Missionaries Bills, when the Salary's due to 'em brings great Scandal on the Drawer and makes us little in the eyes of these prying Animals. I have been five Months together in Chowan Indian Town,[2] and made my self almost a Master of their Language, and therefore upon my hearing of the Governour of Virginia's project of Settling four Nations of Indians at the Head of Maherring river, I offer'd myself as Missionary to 'em with the Proposal of having a hundred Pound sterling yearly paid me for my trouble. 'Tis thirty Miles beyond Inhabitants, and the great good I may do, thro' Gods Fatherly Assistance among those unenlightned Creatures may redound to Gods Great Glory and my Comfort. I have enclos'd the Governour of Virginia's answer to my Letter,[3] and hope to meet some encouragement from the Society in relation to this Affair. Charles Eden our new Governour tells me he'l acquaint the Society in this opportunity of a Passage home, of my behaviour and deportment since his arrival among us, and how indefatigable I have been in that grand concern the Care of Souls. So that I need say no more on this Head, but leave it to his Report. I shall only add that I have brought over to the Church one Patrick Lawler on Bennets Creek from a Rank virulent Papist, to be a sound Orthodox Believer. I have baptiz'd upwards of forty Negroes in this and the Neighbouring Government in the compass of this past Year. Besides (which is almost an impossibility here) Christned three Children Of one Pierce a Quaker's by the consent of the Mother tho' seemingly of that Perswasion. <71> In Nansemond County bordering on Carolina, I have sav'd upwards of two hundred Souls from embraceing Quakerism by my Preaching and conference among 'em and have made the ignorance of their Great Apostle Joseph Gloster[4] in a dispute appear to whole Multitudes. And yet their prejudice to our Establishment is such that I fear there's no possiblity to win upon 'em. I found myself oblig'd in conscience to continue for sometime with these People, by reason of their Luke warmness and indifferences to our own constitution; but by my constant Catechising and teaching they are become tolerable Proficients in the Knowledge of the Gospel. This very action occasion'd Mr. Urmstons Report of me that I do not Altogether continue in the Government I was appointed to, whereas my Commission from Mr. Chamberlayne was to be a General Itinerant in this Colony, but if I see a Sheep going astray in the wide Wilderness I must not Step out of my own Pasture to save it. Alass poor Man! I never sold the Societys Books for Butter corn and Eggs but made conscience of Dispersing them according to the true intent of the Donors. I wish I had some small Tracts remitted me with Bibles and Prayer Books which are very much wanting here. I sadly want Bennets Confutation of Quakerism, with the rest of his Works. Jones's translation of Lemborch to lend about, I cou'd wish for some good discourses on the Passion of Christ, with all the Sermons Preach'd at Boyles Lectures particularly Dr. Bentleys. Spark upon the Festivals these if stopt out of my Salary. I have not one of the Societies Collections of Papers, otherwise I shou'd take my measures according to the Instructions you were pleas'd to give me. I beseech you to pardon what is past and hope to meet suitable encouragment from the Society (the necessary reward of my future diligence) in all religious performances undertaken by Sir Your most Obedient humble Servant.

Giles Rainsford Missionary

I shall stay now in this place till I receive an answer.

Copy.

[1]This idiomatic Latin phrase indicates that the writer faces a difficult and inescapable situation.

[2]This place is shown on the Moseley map of 1733 as lying between Bennetts Creek and Trotman Creek in the south central part of present Gates County. Powell, *Gazetteer*, 106.

[3]Not included here.

[4]Not identified.

[SPG/A/10]

Rev. John Urmston to Secretary, SPG
1715 April 13

<115> Mr. Urmstone to the Secretary.

North Carolina 13 April 1715.

Sir

Ive little to add or vary from what I have formerly written. My Circumstances are little or Nothing better'd. The Vestry's very averse to meet and with much difficulty have been prevail'd to order me some money, but then no care is taken for Collecting it. The Church Warden for Pascebank precinct was orderd to Collect £30 for the first Year after my coming into this wretched Country, and hath had it in his hands these two Years and I cannot receive it without an Arrest which would cause Clamour enough. The Vestry for Chowan where I reside last December order'd me £110 for the 3 years last past, but If the time is lapsed for the Collection this Year and which was to serve me for a little Provision I know not. I've nothing to buy with and not able to raise any. If I had not with the utmost Slavery made a Little Corn, we should have all Perish'd. Ive not a morsel of any thing save corn; beef or Mutton is not eatable at this time of the Year nor can we expect any till Augst. I have been Oblig'd to pay for my Plantation at last or must have turn'd out after Improvements which amount to near £50. I have drawn a Bill for £60 sterling upon the Treasurer which I hope he will pay in time. If money be not just due, The person it is payable to will stay to take it as it becomes due. I must draw for £40 more in a Short time so that goods I must expect none from England this Year, and 'tis very hard buying necessaries here at such Exorbitant Prices. I have often prayed for some relief, if it can be had <116> Towards paying for my Expences I am at, but am not so happy. We are at Peace, thanks be to God with the Indians and among our Selves. I hope we shall have a Communion these Holy Times but fear my Congregation will be small, by reason it never was yet Administred in our Chappel. I intend to goe all over the Next Country towards the end of this Month for the first time and if I find it practicable may visit them oftner till that pt. of the Government can be better Supplied I am Sir Your most humble Servant.

Jno. Urmston Missionary

Copy. Read at a meeting of the SPG on November 13, 1715, when it was agreed to accept the recommendation of the Committee that "a Letter be wrote to the Governor of North Carolina in Answer to one recd. from him acquainting him that the Society have Ordrd a Missionary thither from South Carolina and that a Copy of Mr. Urmstones Letter be sent to him with the desire of the Society that he will Assist him as to the Matters he complains of in such manner as he shall think proper." Journal of the SPG, III, 98.

[*SPG/C/7*]

Rev. Miles Gale to Secretary, SPG
1715 April 22

<17>

Kighley[1] Apr. 22, 1715.

Honored Sir

Upon letters received from his Excellency the present Governour Eden, and My Eldest son Chr. Gale I sent for son Tho. to come over, and resolve ether to go into the West Indies (as kindly invited both by the Governour and his Eldest Brother) or write his excuse, he has chose to do the latter. The work is of that nature, as I was no hindrance to his going, and could wish to go myself, (tho now aged 67) rather then Heathenisme, or any other schisme from the Church of England should prevail 3 of my sons upon their own choice, have gone to Carolina, where two of them are well married, and one dead. I have made all the enquiry in my power after some to go as Missionaries, they like the terms but dread the Voyage, and the heat of that Climate, I heartily wish, and hope Religion may be taken care for in that Heathenish Country, by those in whose power it is. Desiring my service may be made acceptable to that Honorable Society, praying for all yr. healths and happiness I conclude Worthy Sir yr. very humble Servant.

Miles Gale Rector
de Kighley

[*Addressed:*]
To the Secretary of the Honorable
Society for propagation
of the Gospel in Forreign Parts.

[*Endorsed:*]
Mr. Miles Gale
Kighley 22 April 1715

ALS.

[1]The astronomical symbol for Friday (and Venus) is inserted here.

[*SPG/B/4*]

Rev. John Urmston to Secretary, SPG
1715 June 12

12 June 1715

Sir

I was favour'd with yours of Decembr. 17th per Captain Godfrey whom I've not yet seen, I believe he'll not be able to come so far up into the Countrey: he was but 7 weeks on the passage and I fear he is come in a wrong time, for we are in great confusion, the cause I've already given you in two letters per via Boston and Virga. this comes by S. Carolina and if the others faild, comes to advise that by an express sent from thence for our aid, we were inform'd that the Neighbouring Indians fell on Good Fryday last upon the inhabitants in the South parts of that Govt.[1] and cutt most of 'em off, after the most barbarous and inhumane murther of some of the Principals viz. Agents and Traders, who they pretend had wrong'd 'em. I wonder they should send to us, who refused to defend ourselves and had it not been for them, must have been a Sacrifice to the Enemy and stand still [indebted] to them for their kind assistance, in larg[e Summs] but equally unwilling to pay or return the kindness. If all those Nations be joyn'd I fear 'twill goe hard with us and them too: those are numerous and a warlike people: the English have taught 'em to beat their Masters.

There have been seen a body of strange Indians on our borders, some say 40 or 50 but now we hear, upwards of 200: they have pitched their camp in that part of the Tuskaruroes countrey vacated by the late war, seized on a Fort and Trenches which cost us much Blood and not demolish't, (like wise soldiers that we are) they may annoy us but not to be subdued: we have a small body ready to goe out 200, pt. Tributary Indians, 150 are bound for S. Cara. and the rest to speak with these Indians and I fear we shall catch a Tartar:[2] they have committed some hostilities against our Tributary Indians and if we attack 'em, let the success of the other Govt. be what it will, 'Tis more than probable we shall bring 'em upon ourselves and when joyn'd by their followers will finish the ruine of this wretched place, but I must not complain either here nor in Engd.; Ive had reason, too much God knows for't and you have made me the same answer in effect that I've often received from this Gentry: if you compare former letters you'll easily guess at my circumstances. My complaints have been communicated to the Proprietors who are highly incensed against me, and have represented me as a spie to the Countrey I live in and now I am treated little better, unthankful Lords but far more ungrateful vassals; our Quaking Lds. Danson and Rag[3] were mightily offended with a letter of mine to you which they say I had better have let alone except I had written more like a Missionary: they may and ought to be ashamed of their famous Countrey they would have all men doe as Lawson[4] did, write whole volumes in praise of such a worthless place: he has had his reward: all that I can say of it is: there is not the like to it under the sun, Siberia in Muscovy, where I lately was, the Gyarij[5] of old are outdone by this: but if I know the circumstances or the people I am of opinion this Heptarchy[6] cannot stand long. For Godsake use yr. endeavours with the Society to advance me one £20, and send me credit for the same at Barbadoes or Boston. Your best way of sending to me is by way of New Engd., order yours to be left with or under cover to Jno. Jekyl Esqr. Collector of the Customs at Boston. These are from Sir Yr. most humble servant.

Jno. Urmston

North Carolina
June 12 1715

[*Addressed*:]
To Willm. Taylor Esqr., at his Grace th' Arch Bishop of Cant. his Library at St. Martin's in the Fields London

[*Endorsed*:]
<13>

Mr. Urmstond
N. Carolina June 12th 1715
recd. the 20th April 1716

ALS. Read at a meeting of the SPG on November 16, 1716. Journal of the SPG, III, 178-179.

[1]Yamasee Indians attacked frontier settlements in South Carolina near Port Royal, and soon were joined by Creeks, Choctaws, and Catawbas in a general uprising known as the Yamasee War. Disaster was averted by the forging of an alliance between South Carolina and the Cherokee, and by early 1716 the worst of the danger had passed. Sirmans, *Colonial South Carolina*, 111-118.

[2]*To catch a tartar*: "to get hold of one who can neither be controlled nor got quit of; to tackle one who unexpectedly proves to be too formidable." *OED*.

[3]Presumably the writer is referring either to Samuel Wragg or his brother Joseph, both of whom were prominent South Carolinians, but neither of whom was ever a proprietor.

[4]John Lawson.

[5]The reference is unclear.

[6]Presumably the reference is to the rule of the Lords Proprietors, although there were eight proprietary shares rather than seven, as is implied by the term "heptarchy."

[*SPG/B/4*]

Rev. John Urmston to Secretary, SPG
1715 June 21

North Carolina June 21, 1715

Sir

Yours per of Xbr. 17th per Capt. Godfrey I received ten days agoe by which I understand I must not expect any addition to my salary: tis true I am allow'd more than most Missionaries but then it ought to be consider'd that my lot is such a wretched hole as is not to be paralleld, my circumstances very mean, a numerous family, obliged to buy house, land servants and stock, at the worst hand, besides abundance of necessaries which every one must have that will live here, every thing that is useful to a Farmer, with tools for divers trades and he that cannot use them himself must hire others whose demands are very exorbitant especially of me: the fate of most Clergie-men. We pay 5 or 6 hundred Per C. for all Goods imported: £2[0] [*torn*] An sent yearly in English Goods would have been of more service than my whole income at the rate I've been forced to part with it, the Countrey will never be brought to make any provision for a Minister, they have all in general imbibed a Quakerlike abhorrence of hirelings, as averse to be at any charge in the saving of their Souls as their Countreys praying and fighting they equally dislike: which are at this time like to prove pernicious Tenets, for we are now in more danger than ever of being destroy'd or driven out by the Heathen. I suppose you'll have the unwelcome news e're this arrives of the loss of a great part, if not all, South Carolina; if all the neighbouring Indians be joyn'd, the Inhabitants cannot withstand 'em; all endeavours have been used to send 'em some help, but fear our men will be attacked by the way, for the Indians are coming down upon us, have cutt off some of our friendly Indians at Cape-Fare, a small party have been seen within our Govt., so that we have too much reason to fear the worst. God knows what acct. my next may bring. I beg of you recommend us all to the Prayers of the Societie and believe me Sir Yr. unfortunate poor friend.

J. Urmston

[*Addressed*:]
To Mr. Wm. Taylor at the
ABp. of Cant. his Grace's Library
at St. Martin's in the Fields London

[*Endorsed*:]
Mr. Urmstone
N. Carolina June 21st 1715
Recd. the 20th April 1716

ALS. Read at a meeting of the SPG on November 16, 1716. Journal of the SPG, III, 178-179.

[*CO 5/971*]

[Rev. John Talbot to Rev. John Urmston]
[1715] July 17

[...] I thought you had been dead in that dismal Swamp where there is hardly any thing that is good as for those things that you Send here for I would Send them with all my heart but since you design to Remove the best way is to Come Soon here are Several Churches vacant that you may Serve and I will Ingage my Intrest with the Secretary that they shall allow your Sellary. General Nicolson Sent a letter here last post that He would be here in the Fall, I can do any thing with Him and He with the Secretary. Mr. Vesey is fled for Persecution from New York So that Church is destitute at Present only the Missionarys Serve it by Turns. Next week we are going all hands to Open the Church at New Bristol over against Burlington. I have sent to the Society for a Missionary for that and Hopewell but first Come first Serv'd, Therefore make the best of your way. [...]

Copy. Robert Hunter, governor of New York, included this extract in a letter to the secretary to the Board of Trade dated November 14, 1715. He purported it to have been written "in his own hand" by Rev. John Talbot in Philadelphia to Rev. John Urmston in North Carolina, "to be left at Mr. Blackamores in Virginia." Hunter alleged that this letter, along with another one written by Talbot, demonstrated the sinister machinations of Jacobite clergy.

[*SPG/C/7*]

Rev. Thomas Gale to Secretary, SPG
1715 ca. August

<18> <*no date*>

Honored Sir

By letters from my eldest Brother Major Christopr. Gale of Bath-Town in No. Carolina, I find myself recommended to the Honorable society for propagation of the Gospel in Forreign parts, to be sent as a Missionary into No. Carolina, and therein to the county of Bath, which at present is without any Clergy-man, and stands in great need (as my Brother's letters both to my Father the Rector of Kighley, and me Minister of Carlton nigh snathe do set forth). Now I do heartily wish the promotion of the Gospel in the Country, and had I been single, should not have excus'd myself, but as the case stands, being married into a family that will by no means hear of my leaving this country, I crave leave to be excused, wishing some one more worthy than myself may undertake that work heartily, and perform it faithfully. I pray my humble service may be given to the Honorable Society from (Sir) yr. very Humble Servant.

Tho. Gale.

[*Addressed*:]
To the Secretary of the Honorable
Society for propagation
of the Gospel in Forreign Parts.

[*Endorsed*:]
Mr. Thomas Gale
no date

ALS. Read at a meeting of the SPG on September 16, 1715. Journal of the SPG, III, 80.

[*SPG/A/10*]

Secretary of the SPG to Rev. Gideon Johnston
1715 September 16

<132> To Mr. Commissary Johnston.

Septemr. 16th 1715

Reverend Sir [. . .]

I am directed to acquaint You that the Society have lately received a Letter from Governor Eden dated from North Carolina complaining of the great Want of a Good Missionary to officiate there, there being but one Missionary videlicet Mr. Urmstone, in all that Government. The Society have consider'd thereof and being of Opinion by the Account they have recd. from your Parts that several of the Parishes in South Carolina where Missionaries have been sent, are totally deserted and not likely to be soon setled again. They have thought fit to order that You with the Advice and Approbation of the Majority of the Missionaries do appoint one of your Number (a Single Man and one who has been obliged to leave his Parish) forthwith to repair to and officiate as the Societys

Missionary in North Carolina, of which You will inform the Society by the first Opportunity, so wishing You all a happy deliverance from the troubles You lye under. I am etc.

W. T.

Copy.

[*SPG/A/10*]

Secretary of the SPG to Charles Eden
[1715] November 18

<133> To Governor Eden.

18th November 1721[*sic*][1]

Honored Sir

I received your Letter of 8th October 1714 to the Society for the propagation of the gospel in forreign Parts which hath been communicated to them for which they give you their hearty thanks. I am directed to acquaint you that they have also received a letter from Mr. Thos. Gale the person you recomend as a proper person to be Sent a Missionary to North Carolina wherein he desires for Some particular reasons to be Excused from the Mission the Society have taken into Consideration the great want of a Missionary in the County of Bath and have thereupon ordered one of their missionarys in South Carolina to repair to North Carolina and officiate there who I hope before this will be Arrived Safe. I am Commanded by the Society to Acquaint you that they have lately received a letter from Mr. Urmstone their Missionary in your Government (a Coppy of which Lettre is inclos'd) Complaining of the Difficultys he lyes under and the hardships he Suffers for want of the due payment of his Salary Settled by Act of Assembly. The Society pray you will please to Assist him for his releif as to the Matters he Complains of in Such Manner as you Shall think most proper. They present their humble Service to you.

Copy.

[1] An obvious slip of the pen by the copyist. In addition to clear internal evidence that 1715 is the correct date, this document immediately follows and precedes others of that year in the entrybook from which it is taken.

[*SPG/A/10*]

Secretary of the SPG to Rev. John Urmston
1715 November 18

<133> To Mr. Urmstone.

18th Novr. 1715

Reverend Sir

Your Lettre 13th Apr. last Wherein you complain of Some hardships you Suffer and difficultys you lye under from the unwillingness of the Vestrys to meet order and take care of the Collection of the Salary Settled by Act of Assembly towards your Support and Mentainance has been received and examined by the Society who have taken your case into Consideration and have ordrd me to write as I do by this Conveyance to Governor Eden praying him to Assist you for your releif as to the Matters you Complain of in Such manner as he Shall think most proper and that he may the Better know your Grievances they have inclosd A Coppy of your Lettre to him the Society have taken into Consideration the Great want of A missionary to Officiate in the County of Bath have ordered one of their Missionarys in South Carola. to repair thither who I hope before this time will be Safly arrived this is what I have in Command to Write to you. I am etc.

Copy.

[*SPG/A/11*]

Rev. Gideon Johnston to Secretary, SPG
1715/6 January 27

<106> Mr. Johnston. To the Secretary.

Charles Town Jan. 27, 1715.

Sir [. . .]

You will in the Clergy's Inclosed Letter See, what their Opinion is, concerning one of their Number to be put to North Carolina. It is true, none of us is, in all Respects, qualifyed for that Mission According to the most Illustrious Directions. But it being certain, that one cou'd be spar'd for some Time at Least, <111> I pressed that some of us might be appointed for that Service; and at the same Time declared my own willingness to go, if they thought I cou'd be spared from my Cure, till we received fresh Instructions from our Superiours. After this I withdrew and left them intirely to themselves; and upon a Short Debate the Choice fell upon Mr. Taylor[1] unanimously.

Whether I have acted according to the Society's Intentions in this Affair or not, I cannot tell; but sure I am, I meant well tho' I find Mr. Taylor is resolved not to goe notwithstanding all the Arguments I made Use of, to bring him to it. But not doubting, but that he will endeavour to justifye his Conduct to his Superiours, I will leave him to himself. Tho' I cannot but observe at the Same Time, that he has often prevaricated in this Affair; haveing solemnly promised before the Governour and Clergy, that he would go, more than once. And as unaccountably retracted and declined it.

The plain Truth on't is (for I dare not conceal a thing of this Importance from my most Honoured Superiours) we are all of Opinion that he would do better elcewhere than here; neither his peevish and uneasie Temper or his self conceit and Obstinious or his Way of

Preaching which is alltogether upon the Old Presbyterian Way, or his too penurious and covetous Rate of Life, being at all agreeable to his Brethren, his Parishioners, or indeed to any one in the <112> whole Country. I will only add, that he offer'd to go to N. Carolina, provided I wou'd give him the half Years Advance, which he Fancies is Bounty Mony from the Society; but I own I was a little nettled at this Proposall, as if he thought I was capable of so much Baseness as to betray my Trust, and bribe him to his Duty with the Soceity's Mony; which he is now So farr from wanting, that he is taxed at £1400 in this Country. And indeed, considering how little Use he makes of Mony, unless it be to lett it out At Interest and consequently how little occasion he has for any, I think my Self in Conscience and Duty bound to acquaint the Society, that they wou'd do well to withdraw his Salary and apply it to some better Use; And shou'd this Substraction commence from our last Meeting as a Just Punishment for his Disobedience, I am most humbly of Opinion, it wou'd not be amiss. It may perhaps be objected that he is my Convert; but I hope this never will be turn'd to my Disadvantage, in Regard I was not the only person that was deceived in him; And it is no Wonder I shou'd be mistaken this Way, Since even the wisest Men are often So. Several Articles have been exhibited against him by his Parishioners, but as what I have said concerning him is enough, to make him forfeit his Right to the Society's Favour So I will venture to Say that the whole Clergy of this Province wou'd be extreamly oblidg'd to the most Illustrious Society, <113> shou'd they by their Application to the Lord Bishop of London prevail upon his Lordship to withdraw his Licence; for I am unwilling to concern myself about him, farther, then to admonish and represent to him the Folly and ill Consequences of his Conduct, and to take Care that his Cure be supply'd by Turns till we hear from Home, provided he consent to it for none of his Parishioners will come near the Church whilst he officiates, at least preaches, tho' I have endeavoured to set them streight in this Matter, but to no purpose. The Clergy are of Opinion, that Mr. Guy[2] would do well in Mr. Taylor's Parish, shou'd he be removed, it being probable, that neither his nor Mr. Osborn's Parish will be inhabited, so as to need a constant Resident Minister, for sometime; But if Mr. Taylor goes, the Parish will choose whom they think fitt. However let the Election fall on whom it will, it will be unsafe for him to accept of it, without the Society's leave; because if he does so, he must, according to the Standing Order, forfeit both his Mission and Salary; And therefore I humbly pray for the Societies Resolution in this Matter, that none of us may be a Sufferer by it.[. . .]

And am, <116> Sir Your most humble and most Obedient Servant.

Gideon Johnston [. . .]

I hear Mr. Taylor gives out, that I have Silenc'd him; which if he has the Assurance to Say in any of his Letters, I solemnly declare it to be absolutely False, haveing only threatened him with a Suspension for not goeing off; and for the other Matters contain'd in those Articles I just now mention'd which my Lord of London has.[. . .]

Tho' I threatened Mr. Taylor with suspension <117> for his not goeing to N. Carolina, yet it was the least of my Thoughts to proceed to that Extremity with any of the Societies Missionaries, knowing well, that they wou'd upon Information, soon find a Way to chastize him more effectually, than I cou'd do, in Regard no Censure of mine cou'd Effect his Salary; but if it did, my great Respect for my Superiours in the Society wou'd never permit me to go to any Length this Way, further than to admonish and reprove him, and if that wou'd not do, to threaten him if possible, into a just Sense of his Duty. Mr. Taylor was so willing to go to N. Carolina at first, that he desir'd Mr. Guy or any other Bro. that could assist him, to supply his Cure for Some Sundays, that he might the sooner put himself in a readyness to goe off. And accordingly Mr. Guy Mr. Whitehead[3] and I supply'd his Church for three or four Sundays; But upon Changeing his Mind and refusing to go off, he wou'd have no more of our Assistance, tho' his Parishioners earnestly desir'd it; upon which wee forbore. And I am lately inform'd that he refused to come to Church or Officiate tho' sent to more than once, by his Parishioners, for that purpose.

Copy.

[1]Ebenezer Taylor (d. 1720), formerly a Presbyterian minister in South Carolina, took Anglican orders in 1711 at the behest of Gideon Johnston, commissary of South Carolina. See appendix.

[2]Rev. William Guy.

[3]Rev. John Whitehead.

[*SPG/B/4*]

Rev. John Urmston to Secretary, SPG
1716 February 14

14. Feby. 1716

Sir

I have lived these five years in hopes of some provision being made for me here, but now I plainly see they never intended it, with great difficulty and charge I prevai'ld, with seven of our Worshipfull Vestry-men to meet March 2 1713/4 in order to answer Collonel Nicholson's Letter and comply with the demands of the Honourable Societie, but, if you have that acct. they then gave of the circumstances of their Parish, you'll find no mention of what they allow'd me nor could I engage them to resolve upon anything, notwithstanding I prest 'em very earnestly. On the 3d of January following the like number with much solicitation were perswaded to meet again, but 'twas to divide the Parish and make two of it, so that they might not be at the trouble of crossing the Sound (and yet they wou'd have obliged me to doe it 3 Sundays in a month) they then endeavour'd to put me off as before, but at last agreed to allow £110 for the 3 years past. Had I officiated in another Parish alternately, as the Vestry Act impowered me, they ought to have pd. me £30 per An. in each, but the difficulty of attending upon two Parishes being great, they offer'd me the hire of 2 Parishes, provided I would go on the River, as before, which was not possible for me to do before I had a Canoe and servants and furnishings therewith, whilst abroad my family starved at home so that I was constrain'd to keep my hands at home and make corn or else we must have fasted: I was very much blamed and seing I had not answer'd their expectations, 'twas thought great generosity to give me £110. From that time to this I never could prevail with them to meet: I went and wrote to the Ch. Warden who was to collect the money divers times but to no purpose he never design'd it. Another year is expir'd and now some of the Bards tell me, I rely they did not hire me the last year nor will ever employ me more but are mustering and contriving to pay me as they have done all before me with lies and all manner of scandalous stories, lade me with reproach and contempt so that now I am in a fair way to be starved. I've no grain of any kind whatsoever or any sorte of provisions save 5 young porkers which weigh'd about Cwt. each and have nothing to buy with: no longer credit at Boston by reason of nonpayment of my bills in Engd. I was wont to have Rum, sugar and Mulosses from thence and with that I could buy provesions; we are all naked and the winter very severe; Ive lately lost a Negro he was nerely starved for want of cloths and a warm lodging and I shall be obliged to sell the other Negroe to keep us till I hear from you, which I pray may be with all speed. Here I cannot stay and therefore beg I may return home and be allow'd my salary according to the Standing Orders of the Honourable Society section 18 page 56[1] otherwise I shall not be able to procure us a passage, for my Plantation and all I have will be seized for debt, except my bills be pd. in Engd. but so many have been sent back protested that 'tis generally believed the Society will pay no more at least many here wish they may not. I have been at great charges and trouble in endeavouring to make my house fit to live in, with th' addition of a couple of little rooms, one a shop for me and the other a kitchen to dress our victual's when God sends it: it hath cost me near £100 beside diet, lodging and th' attendance of all my family for a great part of a year. This order for £110 gain'd me credit with the workmen, but being disappointed by the Ch. Wardens, have been forced to raise all the money I could, have borrowed £50 and some work is still owing for. I owe a servant made that my wife brought from Engd. upon wages for 2 yrs. service, the poor girl is almost naked. Many wonder how I came into such circumstances but 'tis easily made appear, having no support from this wretched folk I was constrain'd to anticipate or draw faster than money became due, I had but 50 per Ct. against sterling money and gave 5 or 600 per Ct. for every thing that I bought except victuals, which truly is cheap enough and generally very plentiful: we lade most yrs. 50 or 60 Sloops and other vesels with all sorts of good provisions and God knows reap small benefit by it, goods are sold at such exorbitant prices. If I could have had the money that has been due to me from the Societie invested in goods I might have lived handsomly and had a thousand pound in Pitch which would have fetcht as much in Engd. clear of all charges. I am told Mr. Rainsford is design'd for Engd. in order to be admitted Missionary again for this miserable place, I wonder at it, for he had, tho a short yet full taste of the temper and nature of these Ephesian beasts[2] and their treatment of Ministers, he had a plentiful reward for the service he did, was laden with scorn, contempt and calumny abundance of scandalouse, I hope false, stories are told of him; 'tis said, provided I could have been removed, he would have stay'd in this Parish and not have taken a farthing of them (which was a very endearing Article) for he had a sufficient support from Engd.; if true I believe he'll be of another opinion now, for he has married a sorry girl in Virga., besides his way of living [requ]ires a good Income. We have had all our laws review'd and amended where it was needful (and still they are confused and simple enough) and 'tis said they are to be sent to the Proprietors for their approbation and then be printed. It would be well if you could procure a copy of the Vestry Act, I suppose the Societie will not allow of it, for 'tis in the power of every New Ch. Warden to continue or not their Minister. Likewise it ought to be specified that the Ministers Salary be pd. in the staple Commodities of the Contrey viz.: Corn wheat, Beef, Pork and Pitch, at his dwelling house, for 'tis not worth his labour to collect it, but beware of destroying the Act for fear such another may never pass and in after ages perhaps these amendments may be made with the consent of an Assembly. I beg of you to desire the Treasurer to send me an acct. of all the money pd. to my use, since my late Attorney refused to act for me: he sent me a ballance to Sept. 29, 1713, he had then inhand 14.-16.-6. I draw'd a bill for £10 upon him since that and he sent it back protested; I long to know what is become of my money from that time; according to my draughts I shall owe but seven pounds the 25 of the next month, if all my bills were pd., but Mr. Jekyll at Boston writes me that my last bill for £20 payable to him is not pd. and there is another to Thos. Handrey Merchant for £37 come back protested, Mr. Tryon[3] said he had no effects, and yet since both these, one to Thos. Lee who went from hence for £20 was punctually pd. If my Att. has recd. any thing since his acct., he has wrong'd me: he pretended he would never be concern'd for me and accordingly in one to Mr. Hodges I revoked the power given him and desir'd no more money might be pd. to him.

I sent my Journal to Michaelmass last by way of Virga. dat Xber. 16. I should be glad to know it came safe, for 'twas kept here 3 weeks and I've great reason to suspect it was open'd, if not destroy'd, you know my seal without doubt. We have had no News a long time from S. Carolina, God knows what condition they are in, we have great reason to wish for their success. I am Sir Yr. most humble servant.

Jno. Urmston
Missionary

P.S. It is not altogether a sorry subsistance we have been forced to take up with that has brought me into debt, but the extraordinary charges I've been at, which is unavoidable for a man that has a family, and a single man will not meet with a commodious [Place to][4] board in: to give a hint at my unexpected charge

[Plantation]	£50.0.0.	
[3 Negroes]	£79.0.0	two whereof are dead.
[Repai]rs etc.	£80.0.0	
[Ho]rses	£12.0.0.	one dying of the Pole evil.[5]
Household gds.	£63.0.0.	mostly worn out and destroy'd by servants
Mill	£5.0.0.	
English servant man	£16.0.0.	run away within 10 days after I bought him beside a fellow I bought from Engd. detain'd by the Man of War I came over in.
Canoe and sails	£7.0.0.	lost in a storm.
Carts-2	£4.10.0.	all of little value if to be sold.
plow and harrow	£3.15.0.	
Plow Irons etc.	£2.10.0.	

Geer	£3.16.0.	Besides all sortes of tools; Xcut and handsaws hoes, axes, hatchets, spades and carpenter and Cowpers tools and whatsoever else requisit to set up a Farmer
	£326.11.0.	

Sir

Since the finishing this long scrowil we have bad news from Eng.[6] if tis likely to be bad times and the Enemies to the Crown, which God forbid, should prevail, I had rather be removed towards the North in or near New England, for few vessels come here, except from thence: there is no living for me in England, if Popery is like to be in fashion. Here are two small ships from Engd., one arrived in May and the other in July: the Crews have their bellies full but the ships are empty. Godfrey, by whom I recd. your last dated Xber. 19, 1714 is designd homewards by whom I intend to send this if not prevented. A copy hereof will come by Boston. Godfrey can give a full acct. of this wretched place.

N.B. in the acct. I forgott—Cows I bought whereof five are lost, with 3 calves and nine been eaten by wolves

North Carolina Febr. 14th 1715/6

[*Addressed:*]
To Wm. Taylor Esqr. at the Arch Bp. of
Canterbury his Graces Library at St.
Martins in the Fields London
Captain Godfry Q.D.C.
paid 3

[*Endorsed:*]
<15> Mr. Urmstone
North Carolina the
14th February 1715/6
recd. the 15th June 1716

ALS. Read at a meeting of the SPG on November 16, 1716, when it was agreed to accept the recommendation of the Committee that "Mr. Urmstones Request to come home be complyed with." Journal of the SPG, III, 179-181. Although the present document and the one immediately following are substantially similar, there are enough differences to justify inclusion of both in this volume.

[1]Standing Order XVIII of the orders of the SPG relating to missionaries provided that "the Salary of every Missionary, who is not dismiss'd the Service for some Misdemeanour, shall continue one Year, and no longer, after the Society have resolved at their Board to dismiss such Person from their Service." *Standing Orders of the Society for the Propagation of the Gospel in Foreign Parts*, var. eds.

[2]The reference is to the difficulties of St. Paul in his ministry in Ephesus.

[3]William Tryon, merchant of Lime Street, London, was a few years later treasurer of the SPG.

[4]Material in brackets in this document is supplied from another copy in SPG/A/11, 85-90.

[5]*Poll-evil.* "An inflamed or ulcerous sore between the ligament of the neck of a horse and atlas or first bone of the neck." *OED.*

[6] In 1715, following the death of Queen Anne and the accession of the first of the Hanoverians to the throne of Great Britain, an abortive insurrection attempted to overthrow George I and install the Stuart claimant, James Francis Edward, the "Old Pretender." Although support for "James III" was forthcoming in northern England and in Scotland, the new dynasty was never in serious danger, and by April, 1716, "The '15" had been completely crushed.

[*SPG/C/7*]

Rev. John Urmston to Secretary, SPG
1715/6 February 14

<66>

Sir

I have lived these five years in hopes of some provision being made for me here but, now plainly see they never intended it; with great difficulty and cost I prevaild with seven of the Vestry-men to meet in order to answer Collonel Nicholson's letter and comply with the demands of the Honorable Societie, but if you have that acct. they gave oft the circumstances of this Parish, you'll find no mention of what they allow'd me, nor could I engage them to resolve upon anything, notwithstanding I prest them very earnestly. This was March 2d 1713/4. Jan. following the like number with much solicitation were perswaded to meet again, but was with a design to part the Parish, so that they might not be at the trouble of crossing the River and yet they would have oblig'd me to doe it three Sundays in a month; this last Vestry was held on the 3d of Jan. 1714/5; they endeavour'd to put me off as before but at last agreed to allow me £110 for the 3 yrs. past; had I Officiated in another Parish alternately, as the Vestry Act impower'd me, they ought to have pd. me £30 per An. in each, but thro' their importunity and a promise at my first coming of both a year in this Parish alone and the extraordinary difficulty in attending two Parishes, I complied with them as long as I could, but having not been able to goe over the River as they requir'd, 'twas thought great generosity to give me the 110; from that time to this I never could prevail with them to meet again. I went and wrote to the Ch.-Warden, who was to collect the money divers times, but to no purpose, he never design'd it. Another year is expir'd and now they tell me they did not hire me the last year nor will they pay me what they order'd me before, so that I am now in manifest danger of starving. I've no manner of provisions save five hogs I kill'd this winter which weigh'd about 100 lb. a piece, and have nothing to buy with no longer credit at Boston by reason of non payment of my bills in Engd. I was wont to have Rum, sugar and Malosses from thence and with that I could buy provisions: we are all naked and the winter very severe; I've lost a Negroe this winter, he has merely starved for want of cloths and a warm lodging, and I shall be forced to sell the other Negroe, to keep us till I can hear from you, which I pray may be with all speed. Here I cannot stay and therefore beg I may return home and be allow'd my salary according to the Standing Orders of the Societie paragraph 18. p. 56, otherwise I shall not be able to pay for our passages for my Plantation and all I have will be seiz'd for debt except my bills, be pd. in Engd., but so many have been sent back protested that 'tis generally believed the Societie will pay no more; at least many wish they may not. I have been at a great charge and trouble in endeavouring to make my house fit to live in with th' additions of a couple of little rooms, it hath cost me near An hundred pounds besides diet and lodging. This order for £110 gain'd me credit with the workmen but being disappointed, have been forced to raise all the money I could have borrowd £50 and some work is still owing him for I owe a servant maid that my wife brought from Engd. for 4 years service, the poor girl is almost naked. Many may wonder how I came into these circumstances but 'tis easily made appear. Having no support from this wretched people I was constraind to draw faster than money became due, had but 50 per ct. against Sterling money and gave 5 or 600 per ct. for every thing bought save victuals which truly is cheap enough and generally very plentiful. We load most years 50 or upwards Sloops with all sorts of good provisions and God knows have but small benefit, goods are sold so excessive dear. If I could have had the money that has been due from the Society invested in goods I might have lived handsomly and had a thousand pound in Countrey goods which would have been worth as much in Engd. Our poverty has put us upon burning Pitch which now is accounted equivalent to sterling. I am told Mr. Rainsford is design'd home in order to be admitted Missionary for this place, I wonder at it, for he had a short but full taste of the peoples temper and usage of Ministers, he had a plentiful reward of scorn contempt and reproach laid on him, abundance of scandalous stories, I hope lies, told of him. They say he offerr'd to stay here, provided they would remove me to some other place and not expect a farthing from them, having a good allowance from Engd. sufficient to support any man. If true I suppose he'll be of another mind now, for he has married a sorry girl in Virga. besides his way of living requires a good Income. We have had all our laws review'd and amended where there was occasion and 'tis said they will be sent to the Proprietors for their approbation and then are to be printed, 'twould be well worth while to procure the Vestry Act, the Societie will not like divers things in it particularly that of the Ch. Wardens procuring a Minister, for they pretended to have the disposal of the Parish every year and can chuse whether they'll hire the same Minister again or not. I beg of you to desire the Treasurer to send me an acct. of money pd. to my use. My late Attorney Mr. Heald accounted with me to Michaelmass 1713. I want to know what is become of my salary, from that time; according to my draughts I shall owe but seven pounds the 25th of the next month if all my bills were paid, but here is one for £39 now come against me protested. I cannot guess of the reason of it. If my Attorney has recd. any thing since his acct., he has wronged me. He pretended he would not be concern'd any longer for me.

I am Sir yr. most humble servant.

Jno. Urmston

If report be true there's great confusion in Engd. and if troublesome times there I had rather goe to the Northward any where in or near N. Engd. We have seldom any vessels but from Chance; we have two small ships from Engd. but I believe will never come hither again if once out [and] they can say much [else].

P.S. I sent my journal to Michaelmass last by way of Virga. dated 16 Xbr. I should be glad to know it came safe for it was kept here 3 weeks and I've great reason to suspect it was open'd if not destroy'd. We have had no News this long time from South Carolina God knows what condition they are in, we have great reason to wish for their success.

N.B. It is not altogether a sorry subsistance we have been forced to take up with but the charge of Plantation which was a mere Wilderness, miserably out of repair, servants bought and others hired besides Cows, hogs, horses, Carts, plows, etc. and all things needful for a Planter and necessaries for housekeeping, together with Canoes, sails and all manner of tools, which have brought me into debt, charges unexpected, but not to be avoided by any that will live here, my horses and their Geer are worn out, two Negroes dead, a White man that I brought from Engd. left me as soon as arrived, another since that run away, who cost me £14 sterling, besides the loss of 5 cows, 3 calves, and nine sheep and a horse now dying of the Pole Evil. I've lost a canoe which cost me £10. It has cost above £6 to set up a Mill and that not good neither.

This per via Boston is a Copy of one sent by Captain Godfrey Feb. 14, 715/6. In the other I've given them a more regular acct. of my extraordinary expences since my arrival here which amounts to £32 11*d.* besides sundrys of great value with the losses I've sustain'd, so that they may be assured we have not lived riotously nor clothed gorgeously.

[*Addressed*:]
To Wm. Taylor Esqr.
Secretary to the Honorable Society for
the Propagation of the Gospel in
Foreign Parts at his Grace the ArchBp. of
Cant. Library at St. Martin's in the Fields.
<4> London
to be left with Jno. Jekyll Esqr.

[*Endorsed*:]
Mr. Urmstone
North Carolina 14th Feb. 1715/6
Duplicate

ALS. See the notes accompanying the document immediately above.

[*SPG/B/4*]

Rev. John Urmston to Secretary, SPG
1715/6 February 28

North Carolina Feb. 28 1715/6

Sir

<*I mist of the oppurtunity of sending this as was intended and therefore have sent it per via Boston.*> Since the delivery of mine per this same opportunity and the copy thereof per via Boston, I understand that a copy of our Laws is sent per Godfry, so that if the Societie think fit to procure a sight of the Vestry Act there must be no delay. I presume they'll

not approve of it; which I think most material to be added is: that it be not in the power of the Vestry to remove their Minister at pleasure, that the Minister's salary be pd. in Specie of the Country produce at his own house: that a Table of Feas belonging to the Surplice as, weddings, burials, funeral Sermons etc. be agreed on by the Vestry and made publick; that no body be buried but by the Minister nor married; that the Minister be exempt from all Taxes, Imprests or Levies upon him or any belonging to him; all liberties and priviledges, as is practised in Engd., be continued and observed, as far forth as is consistent with the Country; that the choice of one Church warden yearly be allow'd him; that the Vestry do meet at least once every Quarter, in Easter week especially and christmas. Ch. Wardens and what ever else the Honourable Societie may think fit and can be obtain'd of the Lds. Proprietors. <*Verte*> The Proprietors must be prest to use their interest with the Colony to have all such amendments made the next Assembly after the return of the Laws; for the Proprietors have not Authority enough to ratifie them without the consent of an Assembly. This sending of the Acts to be perpetuated by the Proprietors is the only step made since the settlement of this Colony to make it a Regular place. Soon after the Grant of this Colony to the Proprietors, they made several Laws and Constitutions,[1] which are in print but these have been little regarded for many years, if not quite set aside and the Lords Power of little force. They were wont to have all Acts of Assembly confirmed by the Lds. or else they were not in force above two years, but of late they never troubled the Proprietors at all but pass'd and anull'd Laws at pleasure and at the first meeting of every Biennial the old laws were confirm'd and to be continued for that or yrs. following and by that means evaded the Lords approving or disallowing their Laws according to the Power they reserved to them selves in the Fundamental Constitutions. I suppose the Lds. will scarce approve of all the Acts.

This comes per a pd. passenger in Captain Godfrys I pray you if mine by him and the Copy per Boston come to hand and the seal of Sir your humble servant.

Jno. Urmstone

ALS. Read at a meeting of the SPG on February 1, 1716/7. Journal of the SPG, III, 241.

[1]The Fundamental Constitutions of Carolina, theoretically the organic law of the colony dealing with the structure of government and society, the granting of land, and the practice of religion, were first promulgated by the Lords Proprietors in 1669. Several versions followed, the last being one of 1698.

[*SPG/A/11*]

Rev. Francis LeJau to Secretary, SPG
1715/6 March 19

<130> Dr. LeJau.[1] To the Secretary.

South Carolina Parish of St. James
near Goose Creek Mar. 19th 1715/6.

Sir [. . .]

About 9 Years agoe I had the Honour to mention to the Honourable Society a Curious Account I had from a very Ingenious and Pious good Woman Mrs. Bird now deceased, That some Traders or Travellers had assured her they had seen some Circumsised Indians not farr from us. What she said was somewhat Obscure and not to be wholely depended upon, But after much Inquiry, here is a Small Relation which I hope will please.

A week ago a good honest Man, called Kirk, a Nottingham and an Ingenious Man in his Trade which is Shipwright and Joiner and Carver, came to my House to see my Son with whom he grew acquainted in their Cherikee Expedition, and told me he had seen 3 Years ago in Renoque[2] two circumsised Indians actually sold Slaves to be transported abroad. They belonged to the Nation called maramoskeets liveing in the North of Renoque towards Virginia. That Nation consisted of 50 Family's, two of which Family's onely circumcised all their Males, but the Nation being concern'd in the Tunarora Warr were dispers'd many kill'd or sold; yet there is a Remnant of it settled not far from Renoque. He promis'd to use all Diligence in getting further Information of that Matter. I will neglect no Oppertunity on my Part, and will let you know what I can discover further about it. [. . .]

I am with due Respects Sir Yr. most humble and Obedient Servant.

Francis Le Jau.

Copy.

[1]In 1706, Rev. Francis LeJau was sent by the SPG as a missionary to South Carolina, where he served until his death in 1717.

[2]I.e., Roanoke.

[*SPG/A/11*]

Rev. Gideon Johnston to Secretary, SPG
1716 April 4

<117> Mr. Johnston. To the Secretary.

Charles Town Apr. 4°, 1716.

Sir [. . .]

Mr. Taylor continues still the Same Unhappy Man, And has added that of a Notoious and common Reviler and Slanderer of all his Parishioners and Brethren, to the rest of his good Qualities; And has been so Spitefull and Malicious as not to converse with some of his Parish or ever be in the Same Company with them at my House; tho' it was his undoubted Interest to compose and settle Things by all the mild and Christian Methods he could. He uses me very Scurvily; and threatens me as he does all the Rest of Mankind, but this, I thank God gives me not the least uneasyness. [. . .]

I am, Sir, Your most humble Servant.

Gideon Johnston.

Copy.

[*SPG/A/11*]

Rev. Ebenezer Taylor to Secretary, SPG
1716 April 18

<163> Mr. Taylor. To the Secretary.

From St. Andrews Parish In South
Carolina Aprill the 18th 1716.

Honored Sir [. . .]

Sir, Thus have I been fighting With Saint Paul's Beasts at Ephesus, and casting my Pearls before Swine for near 4 Years and they have been trampling them under their Feet and turning again upon me, and renting me all this While, and the Fight is not yet over but it is so far from this, that the Battle is now hotter then ever against me, for now my Enemies have got Mr. Commissary[1] on their Side, and he assists them mightily, and now I must unavoidably be Vanquisht and devoured, if the Society, and my Lord of London do not defend and preserve me, as I hope they will. Sir, It is since the Speciall Meeting of the Clergy in Charles Town on the 25th of Janry. last past that the Battle is grown so very hot against me, on Mr. Commissary's Part especially. At this Meeting Mr. Commissary produced and shewed us a Letter from you as Secretary of the Society, dated the 16th of September last, wherein you tell us that the Society are of Opinion by the Accountts <188> they have received from our Parts of the Indian War here, that Several of the Parishes of this Province, where Missionary's are sent are totally deserted, and not likely to be settled soon again, and that therefore they have thought fit to order Mr. Commissary, with the Advice and Approbation of the Majority of their Missionaries here, to appoint One of our Number (a Single Man, and one who has been oblidg'd to leave his Parish) forthwith to repair and officiate as the Society's Missionary in North-Carolina. Sir Though there are 2 Missionaries that are Single Men, that is, Mr. Maule[2] and Mr. Bull[3] and one that was oblidged to leave his Parish and has not been in it, since the very begining of the War unto this Day, that is, Mr. Guy, yet all the Missionaries, that were present at this Meeting, were so partiall and favourable to these 3 Missionaries, that not one of them but my self only, gave his Vote for any one of their going to North-Carolina. Indeed I told them, that I did really beleive the Society intended one of them should go, and he especially that was oblidged to leave his Parish, that is Mr. Guy. And when I had said this every one of them unamimously voted for my goeing there, tho' I am neither a Single Man, nor one that has been oblidged to leave my Parish so much as one Lds. Day, or one Week Day all this War. And now I could not forbear telling them that they had no Regard to the Societys Letter and that they Voted as directly contrary to the Society's Directions, by their Voteing for my goeing to North Carolina, as they could Vote, which Things I could not but Wonder how they <189> could be guilty of. But I perceived my Brethren had a Turn to Serve and that was to turn me out of my Parish, and so gratifye Mr. Skene and his Fellow Libellers, and now they thought they had a fair Oportunity to effect this Thing, but I think it was a very ill Thing of them so palpably to abuse this Order of the Society's, and to act quite contrary to their Directions, to accomplish such an ill design thereby. And I can't think the Society will be displeas'd at such ill Actions when they hear of them. Indeed had not the Society plainly declared in their Letter, that this was their Special Reason why they thought Fitt that one of their Missionaries here, should be sent to North-Carolina, even because they were of Opinion by the Accountts they had received from our Parts of the Indian War here, that Several of the Parishes of this Province, were Missionaries have been Sent, are totaly deserted, and not likely to be soon settled again. What can be plainer then that the Society intended one of the Missionaries of these Parishes should be sent to North-Carolina, that he may officiate theere and not live here unimployed? Indeed had the Society been pleas'd to referr it absolutely to Mr. Commissary and the Majority of the Missionaries here, to send what Missionary they thought fit, and had they not exspressly order'd us to send a Missionary that is a Single Man, and one that has been oblidg'd to leave his Parish, if there were a Missionary among us under these Qualifications. Indeed had there not been a Missionary that is a Single Man nor one that had been oblidg'd to leave his Parish, and indeed <190> if I had been either a Single Man, or one who had been oblidged to leave my Parish, and all my Brethren had unanimously voted for my goeing to North-Carolina, I could not have thought They had done me any Wrong, (tho' I might and should have thought there were other Missionaries much fitter to be sent, and, who were likely to do much more good there than I) and I would have repaired most readily with the First Oppertunity to North-Carolina, and officiated there as the Society's Missionary as faithfully, and profitably as I could.

But now that the Society hath so plainly declared that it was their Intent that one of the Missionaries of those Parishes that are totally deserted, and not likely to be soon settled again that it was their Intent that a Missionary that is both a Single Man or one that has been oblidg'd to leave his Parish, should be sent to North-Carolina. But now that there are 2 Missionaries that are Single Men and one that has been oblidg'd to leave his Parish, and now that I am neither a Single Man, nor one that has ever been oblidg'd to leave my Parish, and yet notwithstanding all these, that all the Missionaries that were present at this Meeting (at which Meeting all the Missionaries in this Province were present except Dr. LeJau, and Mr. Maule) but my self should so greatly disregard the Society's Letter, and vote so directly contrary to their Order and Directions, that they should all Vote for my goeing, and not one of them Vote for any other Missionary's going <191> to North-Carolina, I can't but wonder how Ministers, how Missionaries could be guilty of Such great Crimes as these are, and especially how they could write these Words in their Letter to the Society about this Affair, In Particular we crave leave to lay before you our ready Complyance with your Order to Mr. Commissary Johnston in Relation to one of your Missionaryes going to North-Carolina, when they shewed no Complyance with but great Disobedience to the Society's Order, by voteing quite contrary to it, by not voteing for a Missionary's goeing there that is a Single Man, tho' there are 2 such Missionaries, nor voteing for a Missionary's goeing there, who has been oblidg'd to leave his Parish, tho' there was such a Missionary, and by Voteing for a Missionary's goeing there, who is neither a Single Man, nor one that was ever oblidg'd to leave his Parish, then which Things nothing can be more Contrary to the Society's Order. And this is their ready complyance with it, which is such a ready Complyance, as, I believe, no one ever heard before. And, wee unanimously came to this Resolution, videlicet we are of Opinion, That none of the Society's Missionary's are Qualifyed according to their Directions, tho' I was never of this

Opinion, but allways thought, that especialy the Missionary that was oblidged to leave his Parish, whether he was Single or marryed, but especialy if he was Single, as Mr. Guy was, when he was oblidged to leave his Parish, was the Missionary which the Society intended should <192> go to No. Carolina, but this was not the Missionary my Brethren intended should go there but he that was neither Single, nor ever oblidg'd to leave his Parish, was the Missionary they were resolved should go there, that is myself only, and therefore I did not Subscribe this Letter. However, say they, In Obedience to your Order, and to exspress our Readyness and Zeal to promote your pious and Charitable Designs, We have thought that one of us ought to go. But yet they did think that a Missionary that is a Single Man or a Missionary that had been oblidg'd to leave his Parish ought to go, tho' the Society told them that they thought fit, and moreover ordered such a Missionary should goe there, but, as if they were resolved to affront and confront the Society's Order, And act as contrary to it as they could, they thought that a Missionary that is neither a Single Man nor one that was ever oblidg'd to leave his Parish ought to go, that is, I ought and should go, and no other Missionary, and so they tell the Society that they have chosen the Reverend Mr. Taylor, and do judge him the most proper Person (being willing) to undertake this Mission, If my Brethren had realy been of Opinion, that none of the Society's Missionary's are qualifyed accordding to their Directions, had they not resolved to make use of this Oppertunity to make me leave my Parish, and to please Mr. Skene and his Fellow Libellers, which they could do no other Ways, I am perswaded the <193> Society would have heard nothing of my Brethrens Obedience to their Order, nothing of their Readyness and Zeal to promote their charitable and pious Designes, nothing of this Thought of theirs, That one of us ought to go to North-Carolina. But now that they had Such a fine Oppertunity to make me leave my Parish, and thereby to gratifie Mr. Skene and his Fellow Libellers so cleverly, Who So Obedient to the Society's Order, if I may not Say who so disobedient to it, and who so ready and zealous to promote the Society's pious and charitable Designes, or rather, if I may say so, who so ready and Zealous to promote my going to North-Carolina, as my Brethren? If my Brethren had really been of Opinion, that none of the Society's Missionaries are qualifi'd according to their Directions, and had been Sincerely desirous to shew their Obedience to the Society's Order and the Readyness and Zeal to promote their Pious and Charitable Designs by sending one, certainly, they would have complyed with the Societys Order and Directions as near and as much as ever they could, they would have chosen a Missionary that was either a Single Man, or one that had been oblidg'd to leave his Parish, seeing there were such Missionaries, but then they would not have oblidged Mr. Skene and his fellow Libellers, and would never have chosen me, who am neither a Single Man, nor one that has ever been oblidged to leave my Parish.

But right or wrong, I was the Missionary who my Brethren were resolved Should go to North Carolina, I can't think, because they really judg'd me the most proper Person, <194> for my Age and the Pains I have been this long Time and am Still continually under and above all I being so very much Inferiour to all my Brethren in Parts and Abillityes, as I understand they themselves think me and as I readily acknowledg my self to be, make me the most improper Person of them all for this Mission. And as to my being willing to go, as they declare in their Letter I was, I must confess Mr. Commissary, Mr. Skene, and my other Libellers did make my Life so uncomfortable in my Parish, and because I saw they were resolved to make my Life as miserable as they could, therefore for a while, I own, I was willing, to ease my self of their troubleing me, to retire to North-Carolina, and imploy myself there in the Work of the Ministery, untill the Society and my Lord of London should be pleased to make known their Minde and Pleasure to us about this Matter. And now, my Brethren thought they had gain'd the Point and accomplished their Design against me, and that they should gratifye Mr. Skene and his fellow Libellers with my leaving my Parish in a little Time. I perceived my Brethren extraordinary well pleas'd with and over joy'd at this, and immediately they all became very kind to and promised they would do me all the Service they could in my Concerns here in my Absence. One of them who at my Request preach'd in my Church I think it was the very next Lords Day, could not refrain from declareing before he went out of my Parish, that if the Ministers do but once get <195> Mr. Taylor on the other side of the Bar towards North Carolina, they would take care that he should never come over again Minister of St. Andrews Parish, which one that heard him speak these Words acquainted me with, and severall others told me they were sure this was the Clergy's Designe against me. This, and the Consideration that my going to North-Carolina at that Time of the Year, which was the worst Time in all the Year might Hazard my Life, and might be very prejudiciall to my Interest here, which is pretty considerable, and that I was no Way's obliged By the Society's Letter to go, but rather exempted by from going there; and so I should rather disobey and displease; then obey and please the Society by my going there, made me alter my Mind, and resolve not to go over the Bar, but to keep Possession of my Parish, untill we receive the Societys Determination of this Matter. If I had known I should have pleased the Society and my Lord of London by going to North-Carolina, I would have embraced the very first Oppertunity, and have gone there, whatever became of my self in the Voyage, and of my Concerns here. When I acquainted the Commissary that I was resolved to keep my Parish, untill the Society and my Londn. had determined this Affair, Now the Battle grew hotter and hotter on his Part. [. . .]

At this Meeting Mr. Commissary ask'd me if I would <199> go to North Carolina, I told him I was not at all inclin'd to go there now, but was resolv'd to keep my Parish untill We knew the Society's and my Lord of London's Determination of this Matter, and I pray'd him to referr it wholely to them, who are the fittest Judges of it, and to lett me continue in my Ministeriall Work untill then, but this Kindness I could not obtain of him, but now he told me, I should preach no more, but he would Supply my Place by all the other Ministers of the Province. And if this is as not a regular, formall and Legall, it was a virtuall, real, and effectuall silenceing of me, and actually silenc'd me for 9 Weeks, in all which Time I did not preach, nor durst not preach one Sermon, for fear of disobeying and displeasing Mr. Commissary, no not those 3 Lord's Days that were vacant, as I fain would have done Now that Mr. Commissary's and my Libellers Hopes of my goeing to North-Carolina were all frustrated, they trump up their Libell again, which was laid aside, while they had any Hopes I would to go North-Carolina. [. . .]

I will add no more now but my heartiest Prayers to God for all Success and Prosperity to all the Society's glorious Designs for the Propagation of the Gospel in Forreign parts, and Subscribe myself this Most Christian Societys most Dutifull and faithfull Missionary and your most humble Servant.

Eben-Ezer Taylor.

Copy.

[1]Rev. Gideon Johnston.
[2]Rev. Robert Maule.
[3]Rev. William Tredwell Bull, later successor to Gideon Johnston as commissary.

[*SPG/Jou/3*]

Journal of the SPG
1716 April 20

<134> 20th April 1716 [. . .]

<135> 6. Reported also as the Opinion of the Committee that Mr. Guy being destitute of a Parish as appears by his own Letter of the 20th of September last by reason of the late War in South Carolina be sent to Naraganset if he be not already appointed by Mr. Commissary Johnston and the rest of the Clergy to a Mission in North Carolina, and in that case that Mr. Honyman be order'd to withdraw his Attendance from Naraganset etc. by which the Society will save £20 Per Annum allowed extraordinarily to Mr. Honyman. Agreed to by the Society. [. . .]

Minutes.

[*SPG/A/11*]

Secretary of the SPG to Rev. John Urmston et al.
1716 April 23

<221> To Messrs. Maule Taylor Hassell Bull and Urmstone.

Aprill 23d, 1716

Reverend Sir

Since you have received any Letters from the Secretary the Society [*blank*][1] Made known to you.

Copy.

[1]A letter of this date from the secretary of the SPG to Rev. William Guy was intended as a circular to him and to the missionaries named in the address line of this document: "Since you have received any Letters from the Secretary the Society have Made a Standing Order that the Severall Missionaries do Send An Account of the Founding and Building of the Churches in their Respective parishes together with an Account of the Glebes Parsonages houses etc. and how the Said Churches have been Supply'd with Ministers. The Society have further ordered Mee to Acquaint the Severall Missionaries that it is the Resolution of the Society That Mr. Francis Phillips who was Some time Since Dismiss'd their Service for his ill life and Conversation be not Suffered to or [*sic*] Officiate in Any of the Churches under their Care. I have taken this Opportunity of Acquainting you with these new Orders of the Society Which I question not but you will Show a ready Obedience upon their bein Made known to you." SPG/A/11, 220.

[*SPG/A/11*]

Edward Mashborne to Secretary, SPG
1716 April 25

<400> Mr. Mashborne. To the Secretary.

Nansemd. in Virginia
April the 25th 1716.

Most Worthy Sir

The fair Oppertunity that offers at this Juncture of the Reverend Mr. Rainsford's returning from these Parts for Great Britain, encourages me to address you after this Manner. Tho' at the Same Time I hazard a Presumption by declareing my Intentions by Letter rather than Petition. At the Arrival of Your late Missionary Mr. Rainsford in Virginia, I had the Happyness to guide him in his Way for North-Carolina, and received from him Several Small Tracts with the Societies Collection of Papers[1] which were very Satisfactory to me; and prov'd not only advantagious <401> to my Self in Particular but to the Children committed to my Care in General, some of them explaining the Church Cathecism after so familiar and easie a manner that thro' God's Assistance I have fixt not only in Children but in those of Riper Years the Fundamentals of Religion, whereby they are able to give a Rational and well grounded Accountt of the Faith they were Baptized in. Thro' this Prospect of doing further good, I took the Liberty to Send this, hopeing my well meant Intentions may be complied with. I find in the Book Intituled the Collection of Papers, the Societies readiness to entertain Such Schoolmasters as well as Ministers who are of good Repute and well recommended to 'em: and much the Sooner for their Offering themselves to them. This Indulgence gave me some Assurance of my future Acceptance with that Venerable Body. It's proper I should mention the Place of my Birth, which was in London, and am Son to the late Mrs. Loyd that kept her Coffee House in Lombard Street, who I presume may be known to Some of the Society. I have continued here in Virginia these eighteen Years a School Master, but finding the much greater Necessity there is for one of my Business in North-Carolina rather than this Place; and the lamentable Circumstances they lye under in that Government (Old as well as Young) for want of Education, I humbly presumed to offer my Self to the Society for that employ. My Character I bless God is well known to be Inoffensive, and my poor Labours have been Indefatigable. The Gentleman from whom the Inclosed Recommendation comes[2] may Satisfye as to that Particular. My Life and Deportment will bear the Test of whats' required from Schoolmasters by the Society and for my other Qualifications writing and Arithmetick and instructing Children in the Principles of Religion, the Subscribers doe testifye for me, as well as the Reverend Gentleman the Bearer. <402> If you please to communicate this to the Society I shall be very gratefull for the Honour and should they condescend to entertain me, my utmost Diligence shoud be exerted in so honorable and Religious an Undertakeing. The Condition of that Government is well known to Mr. Rainsford, and he can amply Satisfye the Society in these particulars. I shall presume to add no more, being with great Veneration Your most Obedient humble Servant.

Edwrd. Mashborne

Copy.

[1]*A Collection of Papers, Printed by Order of the Society for the Propagation of the Gospel in Foreign Parts*, var. eds.

[2]Not included here.

[*SPG/B/4*]

Charles Eden to Secretary, SPG
1716 May 10

Chowan North Carolina May the 10th 1716

Sir

I received the Honour of yours dated the 18th of November last but the other Day.

As Soon as the Vestryes can be called of the Two parishes of the precinct the place of Mr. Urmston's residence I shall in obedience to the commands of the most Honourable Society recommend that Gentleman's Case to them, and make not much doubt but the members will releive him in the affaire he complains of to your Board. And as for the precinct of pasquotank he has already received parte of that money And the residue will be paid in by Tuesday in Whitson week which is the time appointed by that vestry for it; I have particularly recommended that matter to the Secretary of this province, who I am well assured will take all necessary care of him.

If Mr. Urumston is not so happy in this place as he might have been, I doubt he has but himself to thank for it; He has been but a moderate conductor of his affairs, which I beleive has run him into many ill conveniencyes that he easily might have avoided But having spoken So largely of that Gentleman already I care not for mentioning him now, nor Should I have done it, had it not been in regard to the Country whereof I have the Honour to be Governour.

I take the liberty to inclose with this an abstract of an Act of Assembly made here the last Winter, which I beg Sir you will lay before [*torn*] Society, It may Serve to give those Gentlemen a Specimen of the Inclinations of these poor people Tennants to my Masters the Lords proprietors, which are not so black as they may have been painted but on the Contrary are as willing as any of his Majesties Subjects on the Continent to contribute to their utmost to the Subsisting of ministers that are Gentlemen of good Lives and affable behaviour and conversation, Though hitherto it has been their Misfortune to be in manner void of Such necessary Instructors. I dare not presume to ask any favour of the Gentlemen of the Society They being the only Judges how far they can extend their Nursing care to a poor uninstructed people, But if we cannot be So happy as to procure Ministers for each of our parishes, would they but please to Send us Schoolmasters qualified as mentioned in their Most Excellent rules, I verily beleive the Inhabitants would willingly pay them the greatest part of the Salaryes established by the Act for reading the Service and Catachising the Children reserving the overplus to any of your Missionaries who Should Visitt them twice or thrice in the Yeare.

In most of the parishes they have already established Two or Three Readers, who are the most capablest persons we can gett here To Some of which they allow per Annum Thirty pounds, To others Twenty pounds and to none lesse then Ten pounds.

The Gentleman[1] you mentioned to be ordered from the Southward to Bath County is not yett arrived, Whenever he does I wish he may be Such a one as they have need of, otherwise he may prove of Ill consequence by giving roome for Sectarists breaking in upon the people, who as yett have few or none amongst them, How Soon they may be furnished I know not, They beginning now to reap the benefitt of peace with the Heathen, which Since my former I have had the good luck in a great Measure to procure for them and make but little doubt of Establishing that great Blessing.

I intend in the fall to Settle at pempticough with my Family and intreat your favour with the Society, That an Honest Gentleman may be appointed thither, Where I am confident the poor people would doe anything to incourage him to discharge So great a Trust, And whilst I am Speaking for what I should esteeme my own particular happiness to have the Conversation of Such a One, So you may be assured I would lett nothing be wanting in my parte to make everything answere expectation.

I beg my Most humbly Duty to the most Honourable Society whose commands I Shal alwaies esteeme my happiness to obey whenever you communicate them to him that is with great respect Sir Yr. Most humble Servant.

Charles Eden

ALS. Enclosed in this document was the abstract of the vestry act of 1715, above.

[1]Rev. Ebenezer Taylor.

[*SPG/A/11*]

Secretary of the SPG to Charles Craven and Charles Eden
1716 May 14

<222> To Governor Craven[1] and Governor Eden.

May 14th 1716

Honors

The Society for the propagation of Gospel in Forreign parts Make it their Request to your Excelencys that you would inform them if any of their Missionarys Within You Excellencys Governments of New York and New Jersey[2] Are disaffected to the Government of his Majesty King George[3] and if there be Any Such that your Excellencys Would be pleas'd to Specifie the Matters of fact upon which the Charge of Such disaffection is Grounded And Cause A Coppy of Such Accusation to be delivered to the persons Accused before it is transmitted hither, that if they have Any thing to offer in defence of themselves they May have a Speedy Opportunity of Transmitting it to the Society. I am.

Copy.

[1]Charles Craven, governor of South Carolina.

[2]A scribal error for South Carolina and North Carolina.

[3]In the aftermath of the Jacobite insurrection of 1715, the government of the new Hanoverian dynasty attempted to ferret out anyone suspected of disloyalty.

[*SPG/A/11*]

Secretary of the SPG to Rev. John Urmston et al.
1716 May 14

<222> To Messrs. Maule, Taylor, Hassell, Bull, Jones, Urmstone, Guy and Dr. Le Jau.

May 14th 1716

Reverend Sir.

The Society have Ordered me to Acquaint you and the rest of your bretheren the Clergy with their resolution at your next meeting pursuant to the Standing Orders of the Society in order 12th[1] page 22d. You Would after Enquirey Made inform the Society if any of your Bretheren are Disafected to the Government of his Majesty King George And if there be any Such that you Would Specifie the Matter of fact upon Which Charge of Such Disaffection Are Grounded And that before it is transmitted hither you Would Cause A Coppy of Such Accusation to be delivered to the persons Accused that if they have Any thing to Offer in defence of themselves they May have A Speedy Opportunity of Transmitting it hither to the Society. The Society have Wrote to the Severall Govenors of the plantations to the Same Effect As you Will Observe by the Inclos'd which is A Coppy of that Letter.

Copy.

[1]The relevant instruction enjoins missionaries to "preserve a Christian Agreement and Union one with another...[by] keeping up a Brotherly Correspondence, by meeting together at certain Times, as shall be most convenient for mutual Advice and Assistance." *A Collection of Papers, Printed by Order of the Society for the Propagation of the Gospel in Foreign Parts*, var. eds.

[*SPG/A/11*]

Secretary of the SPG to Charles Craven and Charles Eden
1716 May 25

<223> To Governor Craven and Governor Eden.

May 25th 1716

Honored Sir

The Society for the propagation of the Gospel in Forreign parts desire the Favour of you to transmitt to them an Account what Allowance their Missionaries have by Act of Assembly in your Government and also What Voluntary Contributions their Severall Missionaries receive from their parishes And in What Manner either the Above mentioned Allowances by Act of Assembly or Voluntary Contributions are paid Whether in money or in the Commodities of the Countrey. I am etc.

Copy.

[*SPG/A/11*]

Secretary of the SPG to Rev. John Urmston et al.
1716 June 11

<223> To Messrs. Urmstone, Le Jau, Maule, Taylor Hassell, Bull, Jones.

June 11th, 1716

Reverend Sir

The Society for the propagation of the Gospel have made Lately two new orders relating to the Missionaries which I take <224> This Opportunity of Acquainting you With the first is Concerning the Matter of your Corresponding With the Secretary, which they have Ordered Should be in the following Method. That Each the Missionaries take a receipt of the Master of the Ship if it Can be Obtained for every Letter they Send to the Society Mentioning the day and year When they delivered the Same and that they keep a Coppy of all Letters And papers transmitted to the Society and send duplicates by the Next Conveniency, and therewith a Coppy of their receipt for their Originall Letter And if the place of their residence be not a Seaport they Send such Letter to one of their Bretheren Who resides at such seaport desireing him to forward the Same by the first opportunity taking the like receipt And they Shall give An Account of the time the Ships Name by Which they receive Any Letter from the Society.

The other New Order of the Society is that they Missionaries Should transmitt to the Society A Very Just and particular Account What Allowances they have by Act of Assembly And Also what Voluntary Contributions they receive from their parishes and in What Manner the Allowances by Act of Assembly or Voluntary Contribution are paid Whether in Money or in the Commodities of the Countrey.

Copy.

[*SPG/A/11*]

Secretary of the SPG to Vestries of Chowan, Pasquotank, and Elsewhere
1716 June 11

<224> To the Vestrys of Chowan, Pascotank, Charles Town, Cooper river, St. Andrews, St. James' St. Pauls Christ Church and St. Thomas.

London June 11th, 1716

Gentlemen

The Society for the propagation of the Gospell in Forreign parts desire the favour of you to Inform them what Allowance their Missionaries in your parishes have by Act of Assembly And Also What Voluntary Contributions he receives from the people and in what Manner either the abovementioned Allowances by Act of Assembly or Voluntary Contributions are paid Whether in Money or in the Commodities of the Countrey.

Copy.

[*SPG/A/11*]

Secretary of the SPG to Missionaries in Carolina
1716 July 16

<225> To the Severall Missionaries in Carolina.

July 16 1716

Reverend Sir

There have been Severall Letters from the Societys Missionaries directed to private Members and men, Laid Before the Society upon Which Occasion I have had Orders to Acquaint each of the Missionaries that it is Contrary to the Standing orders of the Society for any Missionary to Correspond with private Members in Matters they desire Should be Laid before the Society, And that the Society is not pleasd with Severall of their Missionarys Corresponding in that Manner And to Acquaint you With the Societys further directions to Correspond only with the Secretary in Such Matters as you desire Should be Laid before them. I am etc.

Copy.

[*SPG/A/11*]

Rev. Giles Ransford to Secretary, SPG
1716 August 17

<16> Mr. Rainsford. Augst. 17th, 1716. Deliverd by himself.

Augst. the 17th, 1716.

Worthy Sir

The Inclosed is a Copy of a Letter formerly sent to the Society by the Governor of North Carolina, laying before 'em the then, as well as present miserable State of the Inhabitants, for want of Missionaries to enlighten 'em with the Bright-shineing of Christianity in that Dark Corner of the Earth. His Honours meeting with no Return of his first Letter occasion'd the Trouble of this, and he beg'd of me (being formerly a Missionary there) not only to deliver it to their Secretary with my own Hands, but in his and the Country's Name to implore further Assistance from that Venerable Body in so momentous a Concern. Since my Arrival here, I have been to wait on my Lord Bishop of London with a Letter from the Governor of Virginia, relateing to my own Particular Behaviour and Management in the Plantations abroad. His Lordship upon Reading of it was pleased to exspress a great deal of Satisfaction for the good Services done by me in those Remote parts; and ordered me to waite on the Society to know their Pleasure whether they were inclined to send any further Assistance to North-Carolina the Place I formerly belonged to That poor Colony will Soon be over-run with Quakerishm and Infidelity if not Timely prevented by your sending over able and Sober Missionaries as well as shool-masters to reside among them. These two Years past ev'ry third Sunday I constantly Preach'd in Albemarle Country in North-Carolina and have engaged hundreds from going to Quakerism as can be attested by the Inhabitants While I was in the Society's Employ I serv'd 'em faithfully and to the uttermost of my Power: and Shall again, whenever there is Occasion for the Service of Sir Your most Obedient Humble Servant.

Giles Rainsford.

Copy.

[*SPG/A/11*]

Parishioners of St. Andrews to Rev. Gideon Johnston
1716 October 19

<212> Some Reason's offered by the Parishioners of St. Andrews Parish to Mr. Commissary Johnston etc. Concerning Mr. Taylor dd. to the Society 19th 8br. 1716. South Carolina.

Some Reasons humbly offered to the Reverend Mr. Commissary Johnston by the Parishioners of St. Andrews, why Mr. Ebenezr. Taylor should be no Longer Suffered to officiate in the said Parish.

1st. His uncharitable railing in his Sermons, Taxing his Parishioners, and the whole Province with the most Heinous and gross Crimes, that can be invented.

2dly. Not giveing Notice of the Fasts and Feasts of the Church, as Good fryday Whitsunday etc. and omitting the proper Service appointed for such Days.

3dly. Not Administering the Holy Sacrament on Christmas Day, or So much as reading the proper or any other Psalms on that Day.

4thly. When he is prevailed with to administer the Sacrament, he does it with so much Indency <213> that he Shocks even the most Serious and Considerate Persons present, by droping Carelessly and throwing away the consecrated Bread, As well as all other his behaviour at That Holy Ordinance.

5thly. Traduceing and Treating the Carracter of the Blessed Virgin Mary in So Scandelous a Manner as chilled the very Blood of his Hearers, and that not only in one but two Sermons.

6thly. Not keeping to the Prayers of the Church but entering into a long and unmannerly Expostulation with God Almighty, after the Method of the meanest and most ignorant of the Presbyterians.

7thly. Neglecting to pray for the Sick when desired.

8thly. Being so sordidly Covetous that he is an Offence to Modesty, not allowing himself Britches or Stockings; And endeavouring to Stop Part of his poor Clerks Salary, because himself sat the Psalm sometimes when the Clerk was impress'd and at the Camp,[1] and quarreling with Several Vestrys, for refuseing to pay him for two Sermons he preach'd 'ere he was elected, even to that Degree that no Business can be done, by Means whereof the Church is greatly out of Repair and hitherto intirely Neglected.

9thly. Removeing the Pulpit from the Proper Place <214> and placeing it before the Communion Table, and because it was removed from thence refuseing to go into it but preaching in the Desk.

10thly. In allmost all his Sermons presumeing to add even to God Almighty's own Words, and Composeing his Discourses of Non-Sensicall Repetitions.

11thly. Quarrelling with and abuseing his Parishioners calling them gross Names; As Mr. Miles whom he called Old Rogue and Old Villain. And upon the said Miles his answering that if he was so he desired to be instructed otherwise by him, the said Taylor returned, in a great Passion you are past it you are past it; And soon after, meeting Mr. Myles's Sons he told them with much Heat, if there Father and they did not dye quickly they would all be hang'd and their Souls go to Hell. He also called Mr. Wm. Cattel, Villain, Sorry pittifull Fellow, and many other Scurrilous Names at the said Cattells own House, and at Collonel Gibbe's abused Mr. James Stanyarne, and the said Cattell, in the same Manner. He likewise at Mr. Cattel's House told him, with great Heat, that all his Parishioners were a Pack of Infamous People.

12thly. Refuseing to come and pray by the Sick or to Administer the Holy Sacrament to them, <215> tho' very much pressed thereto.

13thly. Never haveing read the Thirty Nine Articles Since his comeing into the Parish to the Knowledge of any of his Parishioners.

Many other Things of this Nature cou'd Justly be laid to Mr. Taylor's Charge. So contrary, to the Doctrine and Discipline of the Church of England that they are no longer to be born, by any who have a due Regard for that Holy Religion.

Wherefore It is humbly pray'd, that Care may be taken to Supply the Cure, with some other of the Reverend the Clergy Untill the Right Reverend Father in God John Lord Bishop of London shall be pleased to give his Directions for our Relief.

And We comfort our Selves with the Assurance that soon after His Lordship is made acquainted with the Unhappy Circumstances of this Parish <216> by haveing so unqualifyed a Minister, He of his great Goodness and Piety will Ease us of the Misfortune we now labour Under.

He the said Taylor did also on the Sunday after Christmas last, Administer the Holy Sacrament to a New Indian Wench, belonging to Capt. Bull, who never was baptized or any Ways instructed and afterwards proposed to Christen her.

A. Skene, James Stanyarne, Jon. Musgrov, Manly Williamson, Wm. Cattell, Wm. Fuller, John Williams, Th. Rose, Jno. Miles, Samll. <*his mark*> Turner, Benja. Perry, Peter Cattell, Joseph folkingham, John Drayton, Lewis Morgan, Lilia Haige, Jemimah Skene, Arabella Edwards, Jane Stanyarne, Chatherine Cattell, Mary Cattell, John Mell, William Ladson, Samuell Page, Samll. page Junior, Tho. Harse, Jane Williamson, Samll. Deane

---

Copy.

[1]I.e., on military service.

[*SPG/B/4*]

Rev. John Urmston to Secretary, SPG
1716 November 13

North Carolina
9br. 13, [1]716

Sir

I've already acquainted you with the report of your letters by Captain Godfrey, (who to the great astonishment of every body is come in a 2d time with a small ship from Lond.) that to the Vestry of Pascotank was delivered but is misunderstood by them: they imagine you want to know what they are willing to allow a Missioner and intend to make as large offers as they did to me at my arrival and doubtless will be as well perform'd. That Parish is now divided into two: the poorer half proposed to furnish me with a good house, land, stock of all kinds and allow me £100 per An. if I would abide altogether on their shore and yet the whole Precinct was hard put to it to raise me £30 in five years; 'twas collected in that produce of that Countrey in the space of three yrs. and after 20 journies 50 miles on end and several Vestries I first gott £20 in paper money and about a year after with much adue the remainder in like pay. This I've formerly suggested but suppose I am not believed, and no wonder, for 'tis not credible that a Minister should be so treated by a people who would be thought Christians, and think you the Vestry will ever own it? Convince me of an untruth they cannot, I defie them.

There was a Vestry appointed for Chowan where I've resided six yrs. and a half: several Essays have been made towards a meeting, but there never a majority, at last we had eight, whereof two refused to qualify themselves as the Act (which I sent to the Society) directs and now they pretend without a new Act They are no Vestry: all t'evade paying me, hoping by this means to drive me out of the Countrey, as they have served others before me and so save their money. I offerr'd to name others in the place of those that refused to act, but was answer'd that I was never hired by the Parish and therefore not Incumbent the Governor dare not take upon him to do it, for a great part of the Colony are ready to rise against him for attempting to remove some of our Great Officers: they say they'll have him out by one means or other.

I am like to have a fine time out amidst such confusion: I took great pains this year to make divers sortes of grain: barley, wheat and Indian Corn; it pleas'd God to destroy all or most, quite through out the Goverment; we must be supplied from abroad or starve, and to compleat our ruine, we have no mast in most pts.; I did once hope to have had pork and bacon enough of my own, but shall not have a morsel, save what I feed with Indian Corn which is very scarce with me: Ive not enough to keep me with bread six months, no beef, butter nor cheese, no fat to butter our Hominy, nor make soap, no tallow to make me a few candles, so that we shall have a tedious winter, long and dark nights, hungry bellies and dirty linnen. I've nothing to buy with, let our wants be what they will: Swamp water goes down worse in winter than in summer: my credit is lost, Ive had so many bills protested, that no body will trust me, blessed circumstances! But custom makes 'em something easier, this is not the first complaint I've made, but expect I shall not be believed or not regarded, as heretofore, 'tis strange living when a man is continually wracking his brains how to gett a belly-full of meat. I was not in Lancastr., my Native Countrey, at the time of the Rebellion,[1] nor if there, should I have join'd the Rebls and why I must remain in Exile I know not, but if it be my doom, I pray I may have £40 sterling per An. in two £20 Bills of Exchange payable at Barbadoes that in W. Ind. Goods would Keep my house handsomly. I made the like suit to the Society 3 or 4 yrs. agoe and if complied with I had not needed to run into debt as I've done and draw faster than money became due. I hope I've some in bank now and will eat boild Corn and salt the year out, before Ill draw any more. I desird in divers of my former letters an acct. of my money from the time my Attorney Mr. Heald, laid down his power and clear'd with me which was to Michaelmass 1712: he own'd he had then in hand £14 odd sterling, but refuses to pay, sufferr'd a bill for £10 to be return'd protested; he has my Tickets for the Ship I came over in but either has not recd. the pay[2] or keeps it from me. When you write direct yours to be left with Mr. John Jekyl Collector at Boston. We have that way commonly in 10 or 11 weeks from Engd.

Notitia Parochialis. I travelld as soon as the heat of summer was over quite thorrow the Govt. from end to end, 100 miles Southward, beyond Neuce River 60 m. Westward towards Virga. and as far N.E. I Baptized in the last half year 279 whereof 11 were Adult Thro the parents neglect, want of passage by land and water. I left many unbaptized in my travels. I find the people of a temper throughout the Govt. very indifferent as to Religion, will be at no pains or trouble about Souls health and at the same time complain of me, as if I were bound to goe to every house. We have had no Communion Since Easter was twelvemonths; as to other matters we continue Statu quo. These with my humble respects to the Honorable Society, especially those I am known to, are from Sir Yr. most humble servant.

Jno. Urmston
Missioner

[*Addressed*:]
To Mr. Davd. Humphreys[3] at the Library near St. Martin's in the Fields London
To Mr. David Humphreys
att the Library near St. Martins In the Feilds London
[*torn*] Capt. Chandler
[*torn*] via Boston

[*Endorsed*:]
Mr. Urmstone North Carolina
13th of Novemr. 1716
Recd. the 1st of March do.
Entered

ALS.

[1]A Jacobite force was briefly active in Lancashire during the insurrection of 1715.
[2]This may refer to remuneration received by Urmston for service as chaplain.
[3]David Humphreys held the post of secretary from February, 1715/6, until his death in March or April, 1739.

[*SPG/Jou/3*]

Journal of the SPG
1716 November 16

<176> 16 Novemr. 1716 [. . .]

1. Reported from the Committee that they had read the Paper (containing some Reasons humbly offered to the Reverend Mr. Commissary Johnston by the Parishioners of St. Andrews why Mr. Ebenezer Taylor should be no longer suffer'd to officiate in the said Parish) to them referred as also part of a Letter from the Clergy of South Carolina dated 25th Janry. 1715/6 and part of two Letters from Mr. Johnston one dated Charles Town 27th of Janry. 1715/6 the other the 4th of April 1716 complaining of the behaviour of Mr. Taylor etc. and an Abstract of Mr. Taylors Letter dated St. Andrews Parish South Carolina 18th April 1716 and thereupon Agreed to Report as their Opinion that Mr. Taylor is not a proper Person to be continued Minister of St. Andrews Parish in South Carolina. The Society read a Letter from the Clergy of South Carolina acquainting the Society that in pursuance of their Order they had appointed the Reverend Mr. Taylor to go to a Mission

in North Carolina Agreed by the Society that they do confirm the said appointment of the Clergy, and do Order that Mr. Taylor be removed from South Carolina to North Carolina to succeed Mr. Rainsford with a Salary of £80 to commence from his Arrival in North Carolina. [. . .]

Minutes.

[*SPG/A/11*]

Secretary of the SPG to Rev. Ebenezer Taylor
1716 November 22

<226> To Mr. Taylor.

Novr. 22 1716

Reverend Sir

The Society for the propagation of the Gospel in Forreign parts having by their Letter to Commissary Johnson of the 16th Septr. 1715 Ordered that he with the advice of the rest of the Clergy Should Appoint one of their Number to repair to And Officiate in North Carolina. The Society have lately received A Letter from the Clergy of South Carolina dated the 25th Janry. Last Adviseing that they had Chosen you and Judge you the Most proper person to Undertake that Mission. I am therefore directed to Acquaint You that the Society do Confirm that Appointment of the Clergy and order that upon the receipt of this you do forthwith remove from South Carolina to North Carolina to Succeed Mr. Rainsford late the Societys Missionary there and that you have a Sallary of £80 Sterling per Annum to Commence from the time of your Arrival in North Carolina. I am etc.

D. H.[1]

Copy.

[1]David Humphreys.

[*SPG/B/4*]

Rev. John Urmston to Secretary, SPG
1716 December 15

Sir

In my last of Nov. 13, last past I gave you an acct. of th' extraordinary pains I had taken the last Autumn. That I had visited all the corners of the Colony, however obscure or inaccessible, I Baptized great numbers, but not all that wanted it, thrô the stupid neglect of Parents etc. and want of assistance in passages over all the petty Creeks and swamps, which are almost between every house. The humour of the people in Genl. being such that when their turn is served, they care not who goes unserved. If I must continue here I shall attempt another Progress in the Spring, God willing, provided the Society shall not think fit to send more Labourers into this uncultivated Vineyard and then possibly I may stop the mouths of many Complaints of neglect in my late endeavours.

By waiting to see what the Vestry would do and expecting an acct. of what money is due to me from the Society and all my debts paid, I am reduced to great straits, insomuch that I am now forced to draw a fresh or starve; supply I expect none from the Countrey. The Governor can due me noe service, for all are ready to kick against him and the sure way not to speed is to desire his assistance, Governors and Ministers here are generally accounted useless, burdensome and even enemies to the Country. I pray you therefore desire the Treasurer to the Society to pay to Jno. Jekyll Esqr., his Majestie's Collector of Customs at Boston in New Engd. or his Order 20 pounds Sterling (bills of equal date being produced) and if his Correspondent, the Bearer hereof, will undertake it, pay likewise 40 pounds of like money, to be invested in goods to buy me 3 or 4 Negroes in Guiney but if he refuse I beg somebody may be employ'd to engage some Guiney Capt. or Merchant to deliver to the aforesaid Jno. Jekyl or to me, 3 Negroe men of middle stature about 20 yrs. old, and a girl of about 16 yrs. Here's no living without servants, there are none to be hir'd of any [la]bour and none of the black kind to be sold good for any thing, under £50 or 60 white servants are Seldom worth keeping and never stay out the time indented for. I likewise desire a Bill of Exchange for £20 Sterling payable to me or Order at Barbadoes: I believe I have more due for according to my acct. on the 25th instant there will be an hundred pounds coming to me. I shall be glad to hear my requests are complied with and till then must struggle with a hard winter, scarcity of provisions, and [rub thorrow] any more difficulties with all the patience I am endued with and ever be Sir your most humble servant.

Jno. Urmston
Missionary

North Carolina
Xber. 15th 1716.

[*Addressed:*]
To Mr. Humphreys Secretary
to the Honourable Societie for the
Propagation of the Gospel etc. at the Library
near St. Martins in the Fields London

[*Endorsed:*]
Mr. Urmstone
N. Carolina 15th December 1716
recd. the 17th of May 1717

Entered

ALS.

[*SPG/A/11*]

Secretary of the SPG to Rev. John Urmston
1716 December 17

<226> To Mr. Urmstone.

December 17th 1716

Reverend Sir
The Society have recd. your Letters wherein you make it your request that You may return home, and at a General Meeting on the 16th of Novemr. 1716 resolved to comply with your desire and have order'd me to acquaint you with this their resolution and that you have their leave to return to England at Your own Conveniency. I am etc.
D. H.

Copy.

[*SPG/B/4*]

Charles Eden to Secretary, SPG
1716/7 January 17

<12>

North Carolina Janry. 17th 1716

Sir
I am Honoured with Two of yours one bears date the 14th of May the other the 25th 1716 to the former I can Soon make an answer there being but one Missionary (and never another Clergyman) in my Government which is Mr. Urmston whose duty and Affection to his Majesty King George I beleive the most Honourable Society need not doubt off for as to that part I think the Gent. is unquestionable and now I shall again lay hold of this opertunity to lay before your Board the great want there is of Clergymen amongst us notwithstanding this Gent. does all he is able in the discharge of his function and Spares for noe pains yet Stil there are Hundreds of Children and others unbaptized, and are like to remain soe unless Some further Charity be extended to them.

As to that of the 25th I shall Say little now haveing transmitted formerly to your Predecessor Mr. Taylor an Abstract of our Vestry Act which I hope came to hand if it has not or it is not Sattisfactory upon your accquainting me, shall Send a copy of the whole Act but I must Observe tho' that Act Seems very Speicious it is at present of little benifitt to your Missionary for the mony raised thereby as well as all other publick monys are paid in publick Bills of Creditt which are at a vast discompt whilst in truth our Vestry have not been so ready in Assisting this Gent. as they ought to have been which fault I hope will be in a little time remedied not only as to Mr. Urmston's part but towards any other person whose lot it shall fall as to come amongst us. I did myself the Honour to implore of the Society a Missionary for the County of Bath a place of much larger extent then this of Albermarle and altogether neglected hithertoo which I must again intreat you to mention to the Board if there is not one already appointed for that Service Mr. Taylor indeed mentioned a Gent. that was to come from South Carolina amongst us but I never heard anything of him, nor doe I beleive wee ever shall. I have been So full before in relation to the poore people of that County that I shall forbear any farther Addition at this time more then intreating my most Humble duty to the most Honourable Society whose Commands I shall allways Obey with great readyness which concludes as I truly am Sir Your Most humble servant.

Charles Eden

[*Endorsed:*]
Collonel Eden
North Carolina Janry. 17, 1716
Recd. 19th July 1717
Entered

ALS.

[*SPG/B/4*]

Rev. John Urmston to Secretary, SPG
1716/7 January 29

North Carolina Jan. 29 1716/7

Sir

I'm perswaded you'll never have given answer to the two letters to the Vestries and Ch. Wardens of Chowan and Pascotanck: the former is in my hands still not knowing to whom I must give it, for thrô default I may say wilful neglect in not meeting in due time, those appointed to be of the Vestry have a notion they are no longer a Vestry and have no power to meet or act till nominated a fresh by an Additional Act to that of the late Assembly and if that be ever brought into debate, 'twill be annull'd. I sent the Act inclosed in one of June 19th last past[1] which if 'tis come to hand will satisfie th' Honourable Societie in many particulars; did it take place, (but fear it never will) tis the most favourable I could obtain from the Assembly. I did not think there could have been such a construction put upon those words, which impower the Ch. Wardens to procure a Minister, which are now taking to be equivalent to that odious phrase of hiring or dismissing at pleasure yearly a Minister. I alter'd the good Old term, but dared not to goe any further pursuant to our Fundamental constitution. All our Acts were sent last Feb. to be confirm'd by the Lds. Proprietors or as the term is, perpetuated, without which no Act is in force longer than two years, but of late the people assume that power to them selves by chusing all such laws, as they think fit, to be confirm'd at the first meeting of every Bienium and Enact laws contrary and destructive of former Laws which have been perpetuated. I am of opinion divers of th' aforesaid Laws will not be allow'd by the Proprietors [*torn*][2] in danger of being laid aside The Fundamental Constitutions were intended to be inalterable, but now as little regarded as Magna Charta in Engd. This lawless people will allow of no power or Authority in either Church or State save what is derived from them a Proprietor were he here would be look't on no better than a ballad singer what then can a Governour doe or what success or Order in the great design of establishing our Church can be expected by a poor despised and contemptible Missionary?

The Governor would concur with me in appointing a New Vestry, but our Vestry-men (that should be) say I am not incumbent, because forsooth, not hired by them and his Honours appointment will not signifie any thing! He has offerr'd t' induct me in order t' entitle me to the salary allow'd by this late Act, but all in vain for twill never be paid. I hope his letter to the Societie which comes by the same opportunity will answer their demands, as to my Loyalty and Conformity to the present Govt. and King George, whom God long preserve, my endeavours in the discharge of my Duty and the treatment I've met with and like to expect whilst in this wretched corner of the world, so that I shall not need to add in reference to yr. two letters of Apr. 23, and May 14, 1716 which with one of June 11 I recd. all together per via South Carolina Decemb. 9. I have not heard of any such person as Mr. Frans. Phillips, mentiond in this last, in these parts, if he comes this way I shall obey the order sent me.

This is the 10th I've sent to the Honourable Societie within these 13 months under the several dates; ut infra; all the letters per Boston were sent under a Cover to Jno. Jekyll Esqr. Collector there, my very good friend and Old acquaintance. Ive often intimated that the quickest and safest way of sending to me was under cover to him. If these letters be come to hand and would be complied with I might hope to live something easier than I've hitherto done, but having no answer to any of them, it afflicts me sore, my misery encreasing the longer I stay. Could I dispose of my dear Plantation without much loss I would not stay a day in this Countrey, for I am in apparent danger of starving. We are threatned with famine, there's not half grain in the Goverment to subsist the Inhabitants, little or no pork; for my part if not supplied from Boston, I shall not have a morsel of any kind of food within these six weeks. I thought I should have had corn and wheat sufficient for my use, but thru bad seasons and the worm I did not reap the 10th part of what I might reasonably have expected. I had a fine stock of hogs, but am in danger of losing them all: we had no mast and for want of corn they die daily.

My kind Parishioners are in hopes I must flie and then their debt for nigh six years service is paid, whilst one is gaping after my Plantation another my servants and stock, at their own price; 'tis inconceivable nay past expression what I and my poor family have endured for all most 7 years and tis like to be worse with us than ever If money will hold out I beg I may be supplied with a little cheese of all sortes, butter and malt unground; I've not a gown to my back nor hat to my head nor indeed any other decent apparrel. I am in great want of a good and large rug and quilt a pr. of large blankets, with a good ticking for a bed, bolster and pillows. I beg some honest man may be employ'd to buy 'em for me and therewith an easie saddle and curb bridle and some paper and wax. I once made bold to hint that one common Agent for all Missionaries would be of great service to us, I had rather pay commission than by cheated by pretended friends or relations.

If the Society would be pleas'd to advance me half a years salary, 'twould be deem'd a gift and put me in a way of living that I should not need to draw so fast. In my last I desir'd 2 bills of £20 sterling each payable at Barbadoes; with W. Ind. goods to that value. I could buy provisions to serve me handsomly 12 months My good Ld. and late Rt. Reverend Diocesan, promised me, if the Society did not make any addition to my salary, that he would make me partaker of some private Benefactions, but never heard from his Lordship I recomend my self and my poor family to the Generous Bounty of the Honourable Societie, begging their prayers for us and rest. Sir yr. most humble servant.

Jno. Urmston
Missionary

Date of letters:
per via Virga. Xbr. 17, 1716.[3]
per Mr. Gray passenger in Godfrey's ship, Success, under cover to Jno. Rinet at the hand and Pen in St. Alban's street London. Feb. 14, 1715.
Copy thereof per Boston ditto 27.[4]
per Boston ditto 29.[5]
Per Mr. Porter now prisoner in the Fleet[6] Apr. 3d.[7]
Per Boston ditto 31.[8]
Per Virga. June 19.[9]
Under Mr. Chevins's[10] cover to Mr. Hoar or the Custom house Oct. 25.[11]
Per Boston Novr. 13 [*torn*] <*I am told this Brig returns with all speed.*>

Sir

The Master by whom this comes returns hither, so that you may send by him, he is to be spoken with at Jacob Atkinson's at the three Tunns on Little Tower Hill. If you can procure a gown and Cassack Ingram in Pater Noster Rowe has my measure. I should be glad of a Riding Coat for thrô want of that I've torn my gowns in the woods.

[*Addressed*:]
To David Humphreys Esqr.
at the Library near St. Martin's
in the Fields London

[*Endorsed*:]
<6>
Mr. Urmstone
North Carolina Janry. 29th 1716/7
Recd. the 17th of May 1717
Entered

ALS.

[1]Not located.
[2]Another source includes here the following: *and the vestry act will be.* SPG/A/12.
[3]Not located. Perhaps it is the one dated December 15, 1716, above.
[4]Not located. Perhaps it is the one dated February 28, 1715/6, above.
[5]Ditto.
[6]The Fleet, in London, was a prison mainly for debtors. The "Mr. Porter" referred to may possibly be Edmund Porter, the merchant and Cary rebel, subsequently councillor and admiralty judge, who from time to time made voyages to London. *DNCB.*
[7]Not located. Urmston's letter of April 13, 1715, is printed above.
[8]Not located.
[9]Not located.
[10]Nathaniel Chevin (d. ca. 1720), justice, councillor, and active Anglican. *DNCB.*
[11]Not located.

[*SPG/C/7*]

Rev. John Urmston to Secretary, SPG
1716/7 February 9

<65>

Sir

I could not see Captain Luckis and therefore have no report of th' Original at the time of his departure I was in another part of the Countrey. He returns hither very speedily, I believe directly he is to be spoken with at the Three-Tuns on Little Tower Hill. I am Sir yr. most humble servant.

Jno. Urmston Missioner
North Carolina

Feb. 9th [1]716/7.

[*Addressed*:]
To Davd. Humphreys Esqr.
at the Library near St. Martins
in the Fields London

per via Boston
in N. Engd.

[*Endorsed*:]
Mr. Urmstone, N. Carolina
29th of Janry. 1716
Duplicate

ALS.

[*SPG/A/12*]

John Jekyll to Secretary, SPG
1716/7 February 23

<434> <No. 2.> Mr. Jekyll to the Secretary.

Boston New England
23d of Febry. 1716.

Sir

Herewith I enclose a Letter of advice of a Bill of Exchange, for Twenty pounds, drawn in my Favor by Mr. Jno. Urmston Missionary In North Carolina on your Treasurer. He had sent me a sett of Bills for forty pounds but I thought his Project Impracticable and therefore return'd them to him, but as for the £20 (I now send) I have Endorsed to Edwd. Blackett Esqr. or Order, and have advanced him the money already here and Remitted him Necessary's for his <435> Winter Support. Therefore Desire your Assistance that it may meet with due Honour and that you will excuse this Fredom and Command me in these Parts as Sir Your very humble Servant.

John Jekyll

Copy.

[*SPG/B/4*]

Churchwardens and Vestry of St. Thomas's to SPG
1716/7 March 10

North Carolina Bath County
March the 10th 1716/7.

May it Please the Honourable Society.

The great design of propogating Christian Knowledge in Forreign parts having been for these many Years past carried on with such fervency and Exemplary Success by the members of Yr. Honourable Society. It Encourages us the Subscribers members of the Vestry of St. Thomas Parish in Pampicoe. Humbly to recommend our present circumstances with that of the Neighbouring Parishes in Bath county to Yr. pious care and consideration and to Implore Yr. Further Assistance.

Wee have been told that Severall of Yr. Missionarys that have Arrived in No. Carolina were ordered by Yr. Honourable Society for this and the adjacent parishes, but as yet wee have not been So happy to have one Missionary resident in all the county and of all those that have come to No. Carolina it has been very rare that they have So much as Vizited these parts, So that many of the Children of these parts are yet unbaptized even to tenn or Twelve Years of age. Notwithstanding of which the people of this county are generally kept from dissenting from the Church of England by the care which has been taken to Appoint Readers pursuant to the Act of Assembly for Establishing the church and appointing Select Vestrys, an abstract whereof is here Inclosed,[1] by that Act It may Easily be perceived how well inclined to the church of England the whole Goverment is in generall by the care taken that the Salary of the ministers shall not be less than £50.—.— per Annum although at present there are a few of the parishes where the five Shillings per pole will not fully amount to the £50.—. per Annum but this may be helped by the Annexing to such parishes as are adjacent till Such time as they come to be better Settled and able of themselves to make suitable provision.

Att present this is our unhappy circumstance, as well as of the other parishes in Bath County which have been Extreamly reduced by the late Indian warr In which many Scores of unbaptized Infants (who remainded So for want of Oppertunity only) were barbarously Murdered but Seeing that Warr is now Terminated and our County very likely to Flourish again in all other respects Except the only Necessary Videlicet That of religion, Wee therefore humbly beg Yr. Honourable Society will consider our present Deplorable State and allott Some good Devine of Exemplary Life and Conversation thô of less Learning For a Missionary to these parts and wee do assure Yr. Honours That wee will always make Such Further Suitable Allowance for the maintenance of Such a one as not only the laws of this Goverment but our own private circumstances will admitt off.

This comes by Christopher Gale Esqr. Cheif Justice of No. Carolina who has been very Serviceable to these parts in promoting religious worship by whom Yr. Honourable Society may be more fully and Truely Informed of the present State and condition of these parts then it is possible for us to do in the compass of this letter.

Wee heartily beg god Almighty to crown with Success all Yr. pious Endeavours for his glory. Wee are Yr. Honours Most Obliged and Obedient, Humble Servants.

Mau. Moore[2] Church Warden,
Thomas Worsley, Jno. Porter, John
Lillington, John Adams

May it Please yr. Honours

[*Endorsed*:]
Church Wardens and Vestry
of Bath County in North Carolina
March the 10th 1716/7

Entered

DS.

[1]Not included here.

[2]Maurice Moore (d. 1743) was a South Carolinian who remained in North Carolina after serving as a captain in the military expedition sent in 1712 by the government of South Carolina to assist in the war against the Tuscarora. Later rising to prominence as a large landowner and political figure in the Lower Cape Fear. *DNCB*. This document helps to clear up previous uncertainty regarding his place of residence at this time.

[*SPG/B/4*]

Thomas Howard to Rev. Ebenezer Taylor
1717 April 20

Reverend Sir,

I being Informed that you have Received orders from the most Illustrious the Society for Propagating of the Gospell in Foreign parts, forthwith to Depart for North Carolina, and that you have been So unfortunate hitherto as not to meet with an Opportunity. This Sir and the great Deference I have for that August Body makes me offer you the Accomadation of his Majesties Ship under my Command, and to put you on Shore In such part of Virginia as is nearest to North Carolina, I Design to Saile on Saturday next, and if you will then Come on Board you shall find me as I now am Sir Your Most Humble Servant.

Thos. Howard.

Shorham
the 20th of Aprll. 1717

[*Addressed:*]
To the Reverend Mr. Taylor

ALS.

[*LAM/FUL/IX*]

Instructions
1717 April 22

<67> The Lord Bp. of London's Instructions to the Clergy of North and South Carolina.

1. That they do in all things conform themselves to the Canons and Rubrick, and in case of any difficulty apply themselves to the Commissary for his advice.

2. That no Clergyman, the Commissary excepted, presume to officiate, or by any means concern himself in the affairs of another Parish, unless the Minister be sick, and that his consent be thereunto first had, or except he be absent, and at so great a distance from his Parish that his leave cannot be timely obtain'd; In which case any perquisite receiv'd by the Minister officiating shall be by him without the least deduction given to the Incumbent, unless he refuse to receive the same.

3. That No Minister for the time to come shall take upon him to supply any vacant Parish without a License from the Bishop to officiate in the Province of N. or S. Carolina, and the Commissary's appointment for the particular Parish; And that as to the care of such parishes, the Clergy shall govern themselves by such directions as the Commissary shall give them, 'till such time as the Bp.'s pleasure can be known.

4. That where the Banns are superseded by the Grant of a Licence, The Minister shall not join together any persons in the holy estate of Matrimony, but such as are his own

Parishioners, or at least that the Woman be so. And that when the Minister shall have married such Couple, He shall notify the same within a month after to the Commissary.

5. That the Commissary shall strictly and punctually hold a general Visitation of the Clergy each year, and that he shall visit them parochially and call them together at other times, as often as the good of the Church and the necessity of affairs shall require it. And that at all such Visitations He shall earnestly recommend to them so to frame their own Lives as may adorn the doctrine of Christ our Lord, and so to discharge all the parts of their Ministerial Office as may best lead to the Edification of those intrusted to their care.

J. L.

Somerset-house
Apr. 22, 1717

[*Endorsed*:]
Ld. Bp. of London's Instructions
to The Clergy of Carolina
1717.

D.

[*SPG/Jou/3*]

Journal of the SPG
1717 April 26

<254> 26 April 1717 [. . .]

3. The Right Honorable the Lord Carteret[1] proposed a first time for a Member of the Society by the Lord Bp. of Bristol. [. . .]

Minutes. Carteret was proposed for the second time on May 17, and for the third time on June 24, when he was elected. Journal of the SPG, III, 257, 262.

[1]John Carteret, Earl Granville (1690-1763), inherited a proprietary share of Carolina in 1695 and was palatine from 1714 until the sale to the crown of seven-eighths of the proprietary in 1729. Carteret (created Earl Granville in 1744) retained his one-eighth share, which later was laid out as the Granville District of North Carolina. A favorite of George I and George II, Carteret held the high offices of secretary of state and lord president of the council, among others. Powell, *Proprietors of Carolina*, 56-57.

[*SPG/B/4*]

Rev. John Urmston to Secretary, SPG
1717 May 1

Sir

I've nothing to add to nor alter in my last letters per Captain Luck the Commander of a Brigantine bound for London dated Jan. 29 and copy per via Boston Feb. 2d[1] last past, save that I am still strugling for life in this wretched place. If a sloop expected from New York with flowre and bisket doe not arrive within these 10 days I shall not have a morsel of bread to eat. Ive had no beef in my house these six months nor any thing alse save fat pork and that almost gone. I gott by chance a barrel which has been in salt 18 months: 'tis profitable victuals: a little goes a great way: I've no other eatables; peys and beans I am like to have some, but neither bacon nor butter to eat with 'em jovial living! The Countrey is in a miserable condition: we have lost almost all our hogs, and abundance of cattle are lately dead in all parts of the Government of the Murrain, and mine I've been a great sufferer that way: out of my poor stock, I've lost to the value of £30 very near.

If I must linger out my days here, I must have a couple of Negroes and a woman all born among the English the woman used to house work. If the Honourable Societie could spare them out of Collonel Codringtons Estate I would allow more than would buy six others newly come from Guinea; New Negroes are of new [*sic*] use to me. My Parochial acct. is very short; from Michaelmass to Lady Day I Baptised 19 infants was not able to goe abroad by land for want of a horse nor by water having no body to rowe me, nor wherewith to hire and if I had, men will not be hired. I went this winter 7 times to the Church in the Neighbourhood (i.e. 4 miles distance) and met not a Congregation so indifferent are our Gentry in their Religion. They had rather never come to Church than be obliged to pay me any thing: they cannot endure the thoughts of it: they wonder I do not leave the Countrey and then their debt would be pd.; that is the way they have treated all of my Function before me and will have the world believe they are no Changelings. This comes per via Boston under cover to Mr. Jekyl Collector there I am sir Yr. most humble servant.

Jno. Urmston

North Carolina
May 1 mo. 1717.

[*Addressed*:]
To Davd. Humphreys Esqr.
at St. Martin's Library
in the Fields London

[*Endorsed*:]
Mr. Urmstone
North Carolina May 1st 1717
recd. the 19th of July do.

Entered

Paid 4*d*.

ALS.

[1]Not located.

[*SPG/B/4*]

Rev. John Urmston to Secretary, SPG
1717 June 22

22d June 1717

Sir

Since my last per via New-Engd. dated May the first I've recd. one from you of July 16, 1716 by So. Carolina; at my first coming hither I sent divers of my letters open to a certain Member of the Society to be by him first perused and then deliver'd in at the next Board; the little good effect they had (albeit the contents I thought would have drawn pity from a heart of stone) made me suspect my friend and therefore have not been guilty of that which I now find is deem'd a fault, for many years, but perceive as little regard had to me as before; notwithstanding I ever had fresh matter of complaint and as long as I stay here I need not fear wanting that. With hard strugling we have had a Vestry at last in my Parish viz. on the North Shore of the Sound in Chowan there were but seven Vestry men and they chose in a New Member in the room of one who positively refused to qualify himself as the late Act directs by declaring under his hand that he would not Oppugn (a soft word for tender consciences instead of Conform to) the Church of Engd., for, he said, he must goe sometimes to the Quakers meeting and if he saw cause he might one time or another oppugn etc.

Th' absent members will not agree to what was then enacted and many of those present seem to dislike of what they then did, pretending they were overawed by the Governour, by whose order the Vestry was call'd, who is since gone to live in the County of Bath so that all the good his Honor intended me will come to nought. T'was proposed by the Governour and minuted down that I should be Inducted the Majority were consenting, but now unwilling to part with the power so valued by them of chusing or hiring yearly their Minister. It was than order'd that ev'y tythable in this Parish should pay me 5 shilling towards the raising £50 for the last year ending Janry. the 1st last past; the number of the Tythables is not sufficient to raise such a summe (and they have not power to levy above 5 shilling, per Tythable) for our Parish contains not a third part of the Inhabitants which are in the Precinct and aforetime were one parish. As for th' arrearages for 4 years, which said to formerly due, which by agreement ought to be £25 Sterling but was by an after Vestry reduced to £15 Sterling and order'd by the then Ch. Wardens to be collected, that can not be rais'd unless the other parish or pt. of the Precinct which before separation was equally obliged per a new Act be compelld to pay their share. In plain English 'tis to put me of from insisting upon what is my just due; neither do I think I ever shall receive what is now ordered; for notice has been given by the present Ch. Wardens according to the Vestry Act, to pay their Levy on or before the first of this month, upon pain of forfeiting double Tax, and as yet I've recd. but six pounds in paper; this paying of money, such as it is, puts me quite out of humour: they cannot endure to be at charges upon what they so little value, Religion.

I've given you an acct. informing too, of the great scarcity of provisions throughout the Country; I thank God we have with hard strugling and many an empty belly gott over it.

'Twas not so grievous to my family as many others, because accustom'd to want. Our Northern Colonies have taken advantage of our Necessity and have made us pay dear for the worst of bread and meal: what cost them but 7 shilling we have pd. 40 shilling for in pitch and tar, besides divers ways of cheating us Our Governour bought a couple of barrells of meal and one of them proved half ballast. We have hitherto had a very seasonable year, there's great prospect of plenty of grain and fruit, but if the winter affords us mast we have noe hogs, some died of poverty last winter and the black cattle are almost all destroy'd by the murrain, so that we shall not suddenly recruit. In these difficult times I've been forced to draw upon the Treasurer as often as I met with any body that knew what to doe with a bill of Exchange. I've purchased pitch to buy food with, gave more than it would sell for in Lond., some proved nought other some not full cask and in one not yet pd. and thus I've been puzzled to keep soul and body together Since the 21st of Xber. last I've drawn for £85 and am still in want: 'tis not twice £80 will maintain me here at the rate I am forced to manage £20 yearly pd. before hand in goods vendible here, would have done me more service than my salary, I never bought so much goods for £80 my necessity still obliging me t'anticipate and often draw before money became due.

These accts. are tedious I doubt and scarce believed, seing the Society require it and the Parishioners own hand, which I think not to be expected. 'Twas agreed that we should hold a Vestry every first sunday in the month, but we have had none since the first, nor I believe ever shall; the 1st sunday in this month we had one Ch. Warden and three Vestry men I deliver'd the Society's Letter dat June 11, 1716 directed to the Ch. Wardens and Vestmen of Chowan; they read and gave it me again saying they knew not what answer to return; so little regard had to so great Authority and less gratitude to so generous Benefactors: 'tis all one to them whether they have a Minister and a Church to goe to or not.

My quondam fellow Labourer the Reverend Mr. Rainsford meeting with some of my Parishioners in Virga. told one I was to be turn'd out, to another recall'd, they would be glad of either, for then the debt due to me would be pd. I've more than once desir'd the latter and if not provided with two Negroe young men and Negroe girl, all born among th' English and used to work and a bill or letter of Credit to Barbadoes for £40 yearly, as I've formerly requested, 'twill be utterly impossible for me to stay much longer here.

My unjust Att. Mr. Heald in Checkr. yd. without Aldgt. has £14-16*s*.-6*d*. of mine in his hand, which upon quitting his power of acting for me, he said he was ready to pay and yet soon after protested a bill of £10 for want of effects: he has also my pay or tickects for six seven months service in the Bedford Galley; I beg somebody may be engaged to demand the money and if the Tickets are not pd. to endeavour to get me that money as soon as may be; I wish it be not lost thrô his knavery and neglect I've written divers to him but he'll not vouchsafe an answer, other friends I've none that I know of in or about London. I am Sir Your most humble servant.

Jno. Urmston Missionary

North Carolina
June 22, 1717.

<You have another upon a different subject which I dared not to insert here of the same date and for ought I know by the same ships from Boston.>

[*Endorsed*:]
<20> Mr. Urmstone
North Carolina June 22d 1717
Recd. the 18th October do.

Entered

ALS.

[*SPG/B/4*]

Rev. John Urmston to Secretary, SPG
1717 June 22

Sir

You'll say my other letter of the same date needed no addition but cannot avoid acquainting you that by the same opportunity comes one of our great Dons upon an Embassy from the whole Country, fraught with complaints against the Governor. (I suppose I shall not escape) He is a Clergyman's son in Yorkshire, bears the great name of Gale.[1] I know not how near a kin to the late Dean of York. He has a little smack of school learning, was sometime a clark to a country Attorney at Lancastr. Th' occasion of his coming into this hiding place is unknown to me thô I suppose not uncommon with other our Worthy Patriots. A great shew of learning gain'd him great esteem among the beasts in the woodes he has past long for an Oracle, gone thru now all the Offices in the Govt. save that he is said now to push for, i.e. that of the Governour.

Upon the breaking out of th' Indian War he went to South Carola. for assistance; there he prevaild with Mrs. Blake[2] one of the Proprietors to make him her Deputy; in his return he was taken prisoner by the French and carried to Martinico: at length he came back to us, was for his good Offices and sufferings presented with a purse of money, made a Collector of Bath County, then the seat of War, but by reason of his unfitness laid that down and being deem'd learned in the Law was made Ch. Justice of the whole Province. Being arrived to the high pitch of supposed grand[*torn*] he grew very imperious; he hath often opposed me in matters relating to Church Discipline, and all the Authority he could assign was the practice of a poor Country Parson, his Father, I believe him equally knowing in every thing else he pretends to In our debates when he had no other answer, he would often appeal to his dignity and imaginary power which he thought gave authority enough to all he asserted, nay he did not stick once to rebuke me for contradicting him telling me that we were not equal's and that I ought to pay a greater defference to what he said, how false soever; as to the first I was entirely of his mind and as to the latter I cannot see why I should be born down by such a block head, when I had good authority for what I said. He intends to dethrone the Governour, this is publickly known and if he succeeds him not, then he'll come Missioner,[3] but this is only whisper'd, for if not forced, he would not be thought to take up with so mean a Station.

His complaints against the Governour, I must confess, are not altogether groundless, for his Honor has acted towards all men very arbitrarily, not to say unjustly, his treatment of me has been very base and scandalous, yet he never brake [my] head without giving me a plaister, not always healing, for after having trampled upon and prostituted me to the people in order to curry favour with them tis no such easy matter to affect a thorrow cure; what signifies such favours as subject a man to daily affronts and abuses? We have been often at variance. Ive resented his ill usage more than once, have not visited him for several months together, but the greatest difference we ever had was oweing to this Incendiary, my Ld. Ch. Just_ss and now he with a pack of knaves and seditious rascals is combin'd to set us all in flames and rather than not gain his point he'll do his utmost to subvert that little settlement we have with the greatest difficulty attain'd to in Church and Government. This is not the first voyage he has taken upon the like errand and if the Proprietors will hearken to such a Boutefeu[4] they must never hope to see this a settled Country.

I cannot say but that the Governour is a strange unaccountable man, having all that either the Land or sea service furnisheth towards the making a compleat Ruffian, besides some great accomplishments acquir'd in his voyages a long the coasts of America; a stranger to him would straight imagine upon a slight acquaintance that he had been a Boatswain's Mate who are commonly the greatest reprobates in a Man of War, fit only to co[mmand the Forecastle gang; and seeing the genius] and temper of this people are so like to the said Gentry, there cannot be a fitter man to Govern here, the Lords will suffer by the change and we shall be like the Frogs in the Fable.[5] He is well known to Collonel Handyside, late Governour of Jamaica and I believe Counsell Kettleby has some knowledg of him.

As to my particular I care not what this sower of Sedition can say against me; it has been his constant business to oppose me in everything I went about in the furtherance of the great Errand I was sent upon, this is he that chiefly hindred me from having the Library sent in by the Reverend Dr. Bray in my custody, as was intended by the Donor, this is he that first started a notion that the Societie did not expect the Country should make any provision for me, they having allow'd me a sufficient maintainance, this is the Copper Smith for he hath done me much harm; And if he applys himself to the Societie it will easily appear what a fit person he is to make a Priest of and how much he hath benefitted by that excellent collection of books which have been injuriously detain'd from me. I excuse not the Governour in many things but cannot think him so black as he'll be represented nor would I have him changed except we were assur'd of a better, who will scarce be found, to act a part in our Comedy. I am Sir your most humble servant.

Jno. Urmston Missionary

North Carolina
June 22, 1717.

<*I've gain'd mightily upon the Governour since the death of his wife, who [faded] a strange medling, troublesome, proud woman, and put him often up on doing that which he had no mind to do; I believe for the future we shall always have a good understanding. I wish he may find favour with the H[onourable] Societie so as to prevent his being turn'd out. I've heard say Counsell Kettleby was not his friend: if a member of the Societie he*

may be perswaded to act for him. Tis in his power to do the Governour good service and to stop the mouth of this ba[bler]. >

[*Addressed*:]
<3> To Davd. Humphreys Esqr. Secretary to the
Honorable Society for the Propagation of
the Gospel, etc. at the Library near
St. Martin's in the Fields London

[*Endorsed*:]
Mr. Urmstone North Carolina
June 22th 1711
recd. the 18th of Octor. do.

Entered

paid 4

ALS. Material in square brackets has been supplied from SPG/A/12.

[1]Christopher Gale.

[2]Elizabeth Blake, widow of Proprietor Joseph Blake (d. 1700) and guardian of their son, Joseph (1700-1751), who inherited his father's share of Carolina at birth. Powell, *Proprietors of Carolina*, 55-56.

[3]I.e., missionary.

[4]"An incendiary, a firebrand; one who kindles discontent and strife." *OED.*

[5]The reference probably is to the fable concerning frogs who implored Jupiter to give them a king. The god sent them in succession a log and an eel, both of which the frogs thought too inert. Jupiter, implored by the frogs to allow them a more active ruler, next sent a heron, who then proceeded to prey upon the frogs until there were none left in the lake. Townsend, *Three Hundred Aesop's Fables*, 31-32.

[*SPG/Jou/3*]

Journal of the SPG
1717 July 19

<267> 19th of July 1717 [. . .]

<268> 5. Reported from the Committee upon reading the Abstract of Dr. Le Jaus Letter of the 16th Novr. last, that it is their Opinion enquiry be made why Mr. Taylor the Societys Missionary in South Carolina has not taken his Wife with him. Order'd that Dr. Le Jau be desired to enquire of Mr. Taylor and acquaint the Society of the reason why he did not take his wife with him pursuant to the standing Order of the Society. [. . .]

Minutes.

[*SPG/B/4*]

Churchwardens and Vestry of Pasquotank to SPG
1717 August 10

10th August 1717

May itt please the Honorable Society

We recd. the Favour of Yrs. of June the 11th past, Sign'd by Yr. secretary Mr. Humphreys, and In answer their to take leave to Inform you that by an Act of the last Assembly made January 1715 the precinct of Pasquotank was devided into 2 parishes, each parish has power to rase £50 per An. by the pole, which with the Allowance made by your Honours to A Missionary wou'd be a very handsome maintenance, Cou'd we be so happy as thro yr. Charitable disposition and appointment to enjoy one, since the death of poore Mr. Adams we have been all to gather deprived of that Happyness. The p'resent Missionary Living In Chowan precinctt about 30 Miles distant from hence and seldome Coming down above once a yeare, soe that he has very Little allowance From hence save what presents he has made him upon perticular accations, which are sometimes very Considerable, As to the manner of pay In this Country, we must beg Leave to Inform Yr. Honours that there is noe runing Cash, but that to Supply that defect, all our Comodities are rated[1] and Answer the same end.

And now since yr. honourable Society has given us this Accation off addressing our selves to you we begg Leave Further to represent to you, that some years agoe His Excellency Francis Nickolson gave to this precinct (as well as Chowan and Perquimons) the some of £10 sterling to be Imployd to wards the building of A Church but thatt money Lyeing not made use of till the yeare 1708 after much sollicitation and Management by Mr. Glover and Mr. Knights, the same was lent to Mr. Glover by vertue of the vestrys order A Coppy whereof is here Inclosed, Since which Glover is dead, and his widow marryed to said Knights who by one artifice or other will In all probability deprive the parish of that money, As may Appeare by his protest to the vestry here allsoe Inclosed unless someways releived by yr. honourable society and then by representing the Case to our Lds. Proprietors whose officer he is, or otherwise, as you In yr. Wisdome shall think fitt to direct or advise. We are in all Humility Yr. Honours most humble Servants.

Edmd. Gale, Jno. Palin, Church Wardins, N. Chevin, Benja. West, Jno. <*his mark*> Jennings, Richard Madrant, Robert Lowry, John Bourne, David Baley, Antho. Hatch, W. Norris Clk.

Pasquotank Precinct
August the 10th 1717

DS. The document immediately following was enclosed in the present one.

[1]The system of "rating" was the statutory assignment of a value at which certain commodities could pass in monetary transactions, unless the amount were specified in sterling. Rating of commodities was the subject of a series of legislative enactments, the earliest surviving one being a statute of 1715. By that act, fifteen

commodities, including tobacco, corn, butter, pitch, and pork, were rated, with tobacco, for example, passing at 10 shillings per hundredweight. Clark, *State Records*, XXIII, 54-55. Rev. John Urmston and other creditors often complained that the commodities were overvalued, and Urmston had the additional hardship of having to collect them himself from individual plantations.

[*SPG/B/4*]

Vestry Minutes
1708 October 18; 1716 May 22

At a Vestry held for Pasquotank Precinct N. Carolina at the house of Mr. DeLamare 18. 8br. 1708. The Reverend Mr. James Adams Minister. Present Mr. Francis Delamare, Mr. Boyd, Mr. Wallis, Mr. Saml. Davis, Mr. Jennings, Mr. Relfe, Vestry. Mr. Thos. Relfe, Mr. Richd. Madren, Church Wardens.

Ordered that the money in Mr. Boyds hands be taken out and employed for the Honorable Wm. Glover Esqr., going for England, it being the money the Said Mr. Boyd has given a receipt for to Mr. Moseley: It being to be made good hereafter.
Copia Test.
W. Norris Clk.

Pasquotank So. West Parish. May 22d. 1716. A Vestry held at Jos. Peggs the day and year aforesaid. Nath. Chevin Esqr., T. Knight Esqr., Tho. Boyd Esqr., Mr. Jno. Jennings, Capt. Benjn. West, Mr. Autho Hatch, Mr. Richd. Madren, Vestrymen, W. Norris, Capt. Jno. Palin, Mr. Edmd. Gale Church Wardens.

Ordered that the Church wardens for the time being Use Such means for the recovery of the Ten pounds by a former Vestry taken out of Mr. Boyds hands and employed for the Honourable Wm. Glover Esqr. going to England: as to them Shall be thought most convenient and necessary.
Copia Test.
W. Norris Clk.

The Honourable T. Knight Esqr.
protested against this order

[*Addressed*:]
To Davd. Humphreys Esqr. Secretary to the
Honourable Societie for the Propagation etc. at the
Library Near St. Martin's in the Fields London

[*Endorsed*:]
Church Wardens and Vestry
of Pasquotank Precinct.
N. Carolina 10 August 1717

Entered

Copy. This document was enclosed in the one immediately above.

[*SPG/B/4*]

Rev. John Urmston to Secretary, SPG
1717 October 23

23 October 1717

Sir

In my last I acquainted you with a further hardship that I've hitherto met with. I borrow'd £30 to pay for the repairing my house, I was to pay it out of the Parish Levy, which ought to have been raised six yrs. agoe. My Creditor is now Church-Warden, and is obliged to collect my salary which will at Christmas next amount to a hundred pounds, besides £140 arrears, due from the Precinct before 'twas divided into two Parishes, it ought to have been £240, but 'twas no wonder, for their making such a defalcation was in order to cut off the whole, for unless it be to pay my dedbts, I shall never see a farthing of it, the Ch. Warden is a great Lawyer and keeps the whole Countrey in awe of him:[1] he has taken upon him to recover two other debts and has arrested me in three several Actions and threatens to seize my house and goods; all the debt is but £90 and yet he'll not take the Parish pay:[2] 'twill be very severe, not to say unjust, they say I am not their Minister because forsooth not hir'd, they are resolved to keep up that [good Old Custom] so that I am not entitled to the Salary allow'd by Law. I am blamed for not keeping constantly to my Parish; 'tis hard neither to pay me nor allow me to goe to those that would. The Governor press'd me to make the other County a Visit, hoping they would have regard to my two former journies as well as the last, but find they are all Carolina Principles. I went to a hole where I never was before: I Baptized 63 children and one adult; a young white man; they say there are more unbaptiz'd not out of principle, as a Supine neglect of parents and their own shamefacedness, and I fear not to be wrought upon; there was a great Congregation, most out of curiosity, having never seen the face of a Minister. 15 more I Baptized the last six months, I have not to add to my Notitia Parochialis, my people are as remiss as ever, a Parish Levy puts 'em quite out of conceit with the Church: I Preach often to 9 or 10 and sometimes ride five miles or more in rain not finding a Soul there. Mr. Taylor arrived here about a month agoe but is not fixed, not being able to find a house to put his head in. Theres no living here for a Clergyman except he [will] keep house. I believe he'll return [to] South Carolina he is most [unfit] man that they could have chosen, neither was it fare to send him. I understand the Societie order'd one of their Missioners whose Parish was abandon'd by reason of the War with the Heathen: he is not able to ride five miles were it to gain the world; he is aged and very infirm I have acquainted him with my usage, he insists on being chosen or inducted for life, which no Parish here will comply with. If my [late lettres] come to hand I hope for a favourable answer if not you may expect to see me next Spring: here I cannot live without servants. These with my humble duty to the Honorable Societie and earnest request for their Prayers are from Sir yr. most servant.

Jno. Urmston
Missionary

North Ca.
Oct. 23, 1717.

[*Addressed*:]
To David Humphreys Esqr.
at the Library at St. Martin's
in the Fields London
To be left at [*blotted*] at Boston in New Engd.

[*Endorsed*:]
Mr. Urmstone
North Carolina
October 23 1717
Entered

ALS. Material in square brackets has been supplied from SPG/A/12.

[1]Presumably Edward Moseley.
[2]I.e., commodity payments.

[*SPG/A/10*]

Alexander Spotswood to Rev. Giles Ransford
1717/8 January 19

<72> <No. 6.> Colonell Spotswood to Mr. Rainsford.

19th January 1717.

Sir

The Overture you have made for undertaking the Indian Mission is very acceptable to me and I shall gladly do whatever Lyes in my power to obtain you the encouragement you expect. But after this great Turn of Affairs upon the Death of the Queen[1] it is necessary to know how this Design is like to be favoured by the Crown before I ingage any farther than The Fifty pounds per Annum to the Schoolmaster and his Assistant which I have undertaken to pay out of my own Pocket. As I cannot but commend your Zeal in offering so freely your Assistance to promote this good Work, I shall have particular regard to your interests whenever I can effectually carry it on Assuring you in the mean time that this and such like pious dispositions will engage me more and more to be Sir Your most humble Servant.

A. Spotswood.

Copy.

[1]Presumably a reference to the accession of the Hanoverian dynasty and the passing of political ascendancy from the tories to the whigs. Queen Anne, the last of the Stuart monarchs, had been a notably generous supporter of the Church of England.

[*SPG/A/13*]

Rev. John Urmston to Secretary, SPG
1718 May 2

<152> Mr. Urmstone to the Secretary.

North Carolina May 2nd 1718

Sir

Since my last of October 23d last past per via Boston, I have been in Corratuck where I Baptised 35 Children and the Mother of one of them. She hath 3 sisters and 2 Brethern all adult, the sons and daughters of an anabaptizt who pretends to be a Phisiciam Fortune teller and Conjurer; always Chosen Burgess for that Precinct and a leading man in Our Assemblies.[1] A fit man you will say, for a vestry man, but we have too Many such in other Vestries whence it is we find so little favour among them. They rather oppose than promote the Interest of our Church rather than be subject to such. Mr. Taylor my fellow Labourer relies upon the voluntary contributions of a few in the Neighbourhood (I commend him not for it) but being unable to travel he keeps to One house, has the ¼ of Chamber for his Appartment and the Liberty of a Large room to Preach in. Theres one Crisp[2] my neighbour gone for Engd. I doubt not but impower'd to endeavour to procure more and better Missionaries that will enrich the people but take nothing from them, this is the squeamish Gent., who instead of Conform to would have it said in the Vestry Act every vestryman should promise not to Oppugn the Church as by Law Established and after all tho' Appointed, refused to become a vestry Man. <153> I am your Most humble Servant.

John Urmston

Copy.

[1]Not identified.

[2]Nicholas Crisp, named a vestryman for the "Eastern Parish of Chowan Precinct" by the vestry act of 1715. Clark, *State Records*, XXIII, 7.

[*SPG/A/13*]

Rev. John Urmston to Secretary, SPG
1718 September 29

<193> Mr. Urmstone to the Secretary.

North Carolina 7ber. 29 1718

Sir

Since my Last dat May 2d Iv'e little to add. I could trouble you with a repetition of some former Letters but they had so Little Effect that I forbear tho' have as much reason as before. Iv'e told the Secretary I could not Live here without Servants. There's none to be hired. Iv'e offered £20 per Annum; my son is grown up has friends in England that would provide for him. He is weary of being a Negroes. I can do no better for him tho it Causeth not a little Shame and greif. When he is gone I Shall not be able to manage at any rate with one dumb sensless Animall of a Slave. I am in hopes of Selling my plantation tho I shall be a great loser per the bargain however I shall be in a readyness to Leave the Countrey. When left destitute and helpless I hope I have a little money in the treasurer's hands but have wanted it sore. We have pinched both back and belly either to have somthing to buy Slaves with or to Come to when forced to return home.

I have had very bad health a great part of the Summer So that I have little to say as to the Notitia parochialis save that with great Difficulty and no little hardship Iv'e Visited a hole about 50 miles off where I never was before. I baptized 4 or 5 in Some 7 or 8 Children and Adult persons divers of them men and women yet notwithstanding frequent Opportunities they never thought it worth their while to Come to me but must be waited on. I have Some thoughts of going into bath County if I find I Can do it with Safety. There are eight Indians remnant of our enemies Who ravage murther and destroy the people and their Estates in So much that divers families are removing into the County. I fear the County will be Desarted. Bath Town is unpeopled there is but two families the Governour and an ordinary and yet I Cannot prevail with our Governour to have that Library I have written So Often about. Tis very hard to lose £20 worth of books in Coming into that wretched and Heathenish Corner of the world desired that Library and allowed no books as is usuall from the Society wheither there are two Librarys this at bath Town and Mr. Adamses the English books in both of them are distributed about the Countrey. Any body may be intrusted with them but me. The pretences why these book are denied are Iv'e mentioned in former Lettres more than once. I am Sir your most humble Servant.

John urmstone
Missionary

Copy. Read at a meeting of the Committee of the SPG on August 15, 1720. Journal of the Committee of the SPG.

[*SPG/A/13*]

Rev. John Urmston to Secretary, SPG
1718 October 18

<194> Mr. Urmstone to the Secretary.

North Carola. 8br. 18th 1718

Sir

My Last dated Septr. 29 I fear will never come to hand by reason the bearer Wm. Briggs late Chyrurgeon to the famous pirat Blackbeard who was bound for England having first Comply'd with the Act of grace was forced to go along with Another gang of pirats at our Inlet. They plundered the Ship he was in and Severall other Vessells, as well going out as coming into the Countrey this Ship is not as yet able to proceed on her Voyage. Another Ship from Boston designd for Ingland fared Little better and is since Lost near the barrs. Three other Shipps from London within 2 Years thro damage received on the barrs have been Condemned another detained in the Countrey 27 months for want of men. Those which Came in her having first robb'd her and then fledd into Virginia so that our Merchants are great Sufferers. Our trade from England which was Likely to have been very Advantageous to us is at an end. I gave the said Briggs a bill of Exchange upon the Treasurer for £5 for medicines Salves etc. bought of him all damaged and good for little. If Catch'd hee'll be hanged as most of his former Comrades for former piracies have been So that I desired in a former as now allso that the bill may not be paid. At the time they Surrendered the Act Could not help them and most of them return'd to their old Calling and are either taken or killed. You may have heard that bonnet[1] was taken and all his Crew by 2 Sloops fitted out from South Carola. Blackbeard alias Thache[2] was Come in again here with a Fr. Ship richly Laden having on board a Cargo of Another Ship which they turn'd adrift. Capt. Brand[3] in the pearl at the instance of Some in this government arm'd two Sloops with his men and Sent em in to Apprehend the pirats who Vigorously opposed 'em the pirats killed all the men of the first Sloop they engaged With at one Assault Save 7 and then Attackd the other boarding her at once with Sword and pistoll Killed many of the men belonging to the pearl but were at Last all Slain but three the fight was violent but soon over. Great was the resolution and Courage on both Sides nothing but that number would have Subdued the pirats all our government Could not muster So many brave stout heroes as that one Sloop had in her Command'd by the Leiutenant[4] only the Capt. being Safe on Shore.

At the same time I sent my notitia parochialis, but thro' want of paper have no Coppy by me the particulars I remember not the Summer prov'd very unhealthy. We had a great mortality thanks be to god after Long illness I Escaped. I Made one trip to a hole where I never was before about 60 miles off where I baptiz'd divers Children besides 8 or 10 adult. They were better able to have Come to me but had I not gone to seek them they would never have thought it Worth their while to Come so far. So Little Concern have our English heathen for their souls health Could I discourse with the Indians there wou'd be more hopes of them. How Mr. Rainsford Could send so gross a lie that he had Converted so Many Indians and negros I know not. I am Sure he made many Inglish to turn heathen and is now tossd from one parish to Another in virginia where a greater Apostle than he wou'd scarse please for which reason together with the unwholsome air so Many parishes are void they treat their Clergy as bad as any part of <195> America and the Climate kills many. I am Inform'd there have 9 or 10 Clergymen died in Virginia Since I Came into America and not many less in South Carola. Some are of Opinion that my life is owing under god to poore Living Sparing and ordinary diet with much Excericse and Sometimes hard Labour but age makes Me abate of the Latter so that I fear my fare will be worse if that Can be. I sett out To Morrow to a place near a hundred miles of must

Cross a broad Water near 12 miles in a Cannoo Where Mr. Keith Stopt when in the province where I hope to get a Little beef and pork. If I fail we shall ineveitably Starve and to go a begging will avail little. Iv'e tried that way more then once. My family have had little else for some time but a little boiled Corn Such as others feed their hoggs with and now and then Mush alias hasty pudding made of Indian Meal or rather water porridge such as is eaten in the north of Engd. and would be good food had we a little Salt butter to it. The Longer I stay here the poorer I grow. Apparrel and houshold Stuff wear out and how to recruit I know not. My Salary as Managed will not keep us. Nothing is to be expected from the parish. I cannot prevail with the vestry men to meet; the Governor has endeavoured to Cause them but in vain. He has Difficultys enough to grapple with; this Countrey abounds with men of all Sects and factions. Opposers of all that wish well to it the Spirit of Contradiction reigns here. They are not to be govern'd but by methods of their own Contriving like no religion but one of their own making and will be Saved in their own way. I have more then once desired that I might receive half my Salary yearly at Barbados either by bills of Exchange or Generall Letter of Credit. I want many things from thence my bill will not pass there for want of an Indorser which is wanted in other Governments. Also to my Great disapointment Goods are to be bought now in virginia at the first Cost in Engd. A Couple of good Slaves that Speak English and have been used to plantation work and a Wench for the house I want Sore; my Son is grown up and hath great offers made him in Engd. Tis not justice to make a Negro of him, as he has been for Severall years, work at hoe and ax and may Live like a Gentleman in Engd. which he must never expect to do here there being but few of that degree among us. I am denied one of the greatest Comforts of Life i.e. Conversation with either the living or the dead, the Library at pamptichoe sent in for the use of Clergymen by Dr. Bray in all Appearance will be totall destroyed that place being Abandoned and So will all the Country in a Short Time be, for fear of 7 or 8 Indians the remnant of Some of the towns we destroyd in the Late war who with the Assistance of Some from the north and South do great Mischief and threaten the whole Colony so helpless are we and a prey to every body that will attack us. The books Mr. Gordon should have brought in and did of right belong unto me were left with Mr. Wallace Late minister of Keekotan in Virginia and those Mr. Adams left at his death and demanded by me are detained by the Worshipfull Gentlemen of the Vestry who say they are Appropriated to that parish and no man shall have them except he'll reside which I would not doe for £500 per Annum. Now I beg as I have often done once more that the honorable Society may procure an order from the proprietors to the Governor and Councell for the delivery of the Said Library and those books in Corratuck which the said Mr. Adams brought in or else send me others.
<196> These Severall requests I have made more then once and if they Came to hand I cannot See why I have no Answer except the Society will Oblidge me to leave the Countrey, the people would be well pleas'd, for by that means they would Avoid paying me £340 which is due to me and were it not for hopes of receiveing that money one day, I should be Equally willing to Leave them for I am quite Weary of my Life. I was in hopes of Selling my plantation at half worth and when ever I part with it twill be at that Lay yet I must do it unless the Society will Comply with what is desired and Let me have a favourable and kind Answer with all Speed. These are from Sir your most humble Servant.

J. Urmstone Missionary

Copy.

[1]Stede Bonnet (d. 1718), the "gentleman pirate" taken in the Cape Fear River in late September, 1718, by a small force from South Carolina under the command of William Rhett, receiver-general. *DNCB*.

[2]Edward Teach, or Thatch, the most notorious of the pirates infesting the coast of the Carolinas during the second decade of the eighteenth century, resided briefly in Bath. He received a pardon from Governor Eden in June, 1718, but soon resumed his piratical career. In November, 1718, Blackbeard was killed off Ocracoke Inlet in hand-to-hand combat with the officer commanding a naval force dispatched from Virginia. *DNCB*, "Blackbeard the Pirate."

[3]Ellis Brand, commander of HMS *Pearl*.

[4]Robert Maynard, lieutenant of HMS *Pearl*.

[*SPG/SAP*]

Report
1718/9 February 20

<36> <*An Abstract of the Proceedings of the Society*.> [. . .] The Society have received Letters and other Accounts from their Missionaries, relating to the State and Condition of their Parishes, and of the Progress they make in Converting the Infidels, and of their Success in the Exercise of their Ministerial Function; and do in general give such an Account, as makes the Society hope they shall in Time overcome the great Difficulties which they meet with in the Propagation of the Gospel in those Parts. All their Missionaries represent the great and pressing Want of more Ministers to supply several Churches and Congregations; and the Society have resolved to exert themselves as far as they can, and have agreed to send several new Missionaries forthwith to *Pensylvania* and *Carolina*, *Naraganset*, and *Stratford* in *Connecticut*, where there is represented to be the greatest Want of Ministers. [. . .]

Printed. Extracted from the yearly publication containing the sermon preached at the annual anniversary meeting of the SPG, together with a review of the activities of the Society and its missionaries during the preceding year. The date above is the date of the meeting.

[*SPG/A/13*]

Rev. Ebenezer Taylor to Secretary, SPG
1719 April 23

<212> Mr. Taylor to the Secretary.

Perquimons Precinct Apl. 23d 1719

Honoured Sir

Your Letter Dated November the 22d 1716 <213> wherein is the most Excellent Society's Order for my Removeing from South Carolina to North Carolina I receiv'd the 20th of March following with the greatest Joy and Gladness, and with all thankfullness to them for this their so great a Kindness to me. I have sent you a very large Letter Dated on the 24th of March 1717, and 18,[1] by Captain Geoffrey Farmer Commander of the Ship George of London, wherein I have presum'd to give the most Noble Society an Account of the great and many wrongs and Abuses which I receiv'd in South Carolina from the 30th of June 1716 to the 23d of May 1717, which I hope you have receivd, and therefore I will say nothing of them now, in this Letter I have allsoe return'd, and soe I doe now again return my most hearty Thanks to the most wise and Good Society for having been so good and kind to me, to put such an Honourable and Comfortable End to that tedious and Vexatious fight that I had in St. Andrews Parish in South Carolina, with some of St. Pauls Beasts at Ephesus, and to my casting of some pearls before Swine, who did trample them under their feet and turn again, and Rent me for a great while, by their Ordering me to remove from that Seat of Warr to this place of Peace, where I enjoyed the first half year I lived here with <214> much more Ease and Comfort then I did in South Carolina all the while I lived there, or ever should. I think in this Letter I have allsoe made bold to beg that the most Bountifull Society would be pleas'd to be soe kind to me, Now I am their Missionary here as they were when I was their Missionary in South Carolina, and send me such a Library as I had there, which I have a great want of and would be very Beneficial to me, and that they would be so kind to my Parishoners here as they were to my Parishoners there, and send them allsoe a box of their Charity Books, who Stand in great Need of them, and I hope would make a good Use of them. From the time I receiv'd the Society's Order to goe to North Carolina, I impatiently waited for a convenient Opportunity to goe there the 25th of June following. Fearing it would be a much longer time before I should meet with a Passage directly to North Carolina (which indeed would have been the most convenient for me because of My Sores, which rendered me alltogether unfit for Travail by Land either on Foot or on Horseback) I embrac'd a Passage for Hampton River in Virginia where we arriv'd the 8th of July following, and where I was forced to stay till the 5th of September following waiting for a Passage by Water from thence to North <215> Carolina, because my Sores made it impossible for me to Travel by Land. A little before this 5th of September a dreadfull Hurricane forced severall Sloops into James's River that were bound to North Carolina and soe I met with a passage by Water there in one of those Sloops, where we Arriv'd the Ninth following and on the 25th following I got to the South west Shore of Chowan, where I Officiated the first Year, soon after I arriv'd in Virginia, I writt a letter to the Governor of North Carolina to acquaint his honour that the Society had been pleas'd to order me to remove from South Carolina to North Carolina, and that in Obedience to this their Order I was come as far as Virginia and to desire him to inform Me where it was that Mr. Rainsford did Officiate when he was in North Carolina, that I might not goe out of my way but goe Straite there; and make my Journey as Short as ever I can because of my Sores and pains. His honour was pleas'd to Answer my Letter (as he himself has told me) but I was so unhappy as not to receive his Answer. Understanding when I came to North Carolina, that Mr. Rainsford was never a Settled Minister of any Parish in this Province. Soon after I came to the South West Shore of Chowan, I writ another Letter to our Governor to desire his Honour, to let me know his pleasure as to the Parish <216> in which I should Settle, hoping the Society would be pleas'd with my resigning my self, and referring this matter to the Governor, Seeing I could not find out Mr. Rainsfords Parish, to Succeed him in it, as I would have done, according to the Society's Order, if I could have found it. His honour was pleas'd to Answer this Letter allsoe and in his Answer to tell me, That he was glad that I was at last come to North Carolina, and that if I would look for Mr. Rehoboth in the Parish and Town where he lived, he Assured me nothing should be wanting in him to make it a place of rest to me, and that he verily thought the Neighbourhood would doe their part likewise. And his honour further Saies This is the Cure I think the most Honourable Society design'd you to.

This Answer of our Governors and his further telling me That all the Gentlemen of the Vestry Saluted me, and that they would be glad to receive me presently fix'd my Resolutions to goe to Bath Town and be Minister of St. Thomas's Parish, as soon as I met with a Passage by Water for I could not then nor can't yet Travail any other way because of my Sores. Before I met with a passage our Governor came to the South West Shower of Chowan, and went on board a Sloop to goe to little River, where our provinciall Assembly then met. I went and waited on his honour aboard this Sloop, and told him that t'was impossible <217> for me to Ride to Bath Town because of many Sores and the extream Pains I was allways in. When I had told his honour this, he told me again he should be glad to Enjoy my Company at Bath Town, But he could not require Impossibilities of me. And now he charg'd me not to Settle my Self in any Parish till I heard from him from Little River, because he did not know he should meet with a Passage by Water for me there, if he did he wou'd send for me, And accordingly this his Honours Charge till he return'd from Little River to his Son in Law Collonel Maules, from whose house he writt to Collonel Pollock, with whom I then Lived, In which his honour gave me leave to Settle where I pleas'd, seeing it was impossible for me to goe to Bath Town by Land and presently after this I settled my self on the South West Shoar of Chowan for the first Year. For I am not willing to Settle in any Parish here longer then a Year, till I know what parish the Society will please to Settle me in. During my Officiateing on the South West Shore of Chowan I preach'd every Lords Day throughout this Year, and I would have Administred the Lords Supper severall times this Year, if I could but have had the small number of Communicants which our Church requires, But I could not truely get this <218> small Number, and therefore I must confesse, I did not Administer it at once. Nor I doe not know when I shall here. The people are so little inclin'd to receive it which is one thing makes me very weary of living in this place. When I give Notice of my Intentions to Administer the Holy Communion on Easter Day, A few Lords days before, a considerable person after the Publick Worship of God was ended, Said now Mr. Taylor is goeing to Damn his Parishoners, I suppose he said this, because he thought that they that would receive were very unfit for it, and would Eat and Drink Unworthily, and so eat and drink Damnation to themselves, And I must confess it, the People here generally and allmost all of them are very ignorant and very irreligious: and very Worldly wicked, and doe very little desire to be better informed, or reform'd which is another thing that makes me weary of living here. Yet I hope I may say, I did some good too this year that Officiated in the South West Shore of Chowan, that I promoted Knowledge of the best things and Religion in some there: and perswaded them to be less Worldly and Wicked then they were before. In this Year I caus'd a pretty many of the Children to learn our Catechism and Catechis'd them in publick. In this Year I Baptiz'd one Adult white young Woman and Thirty white Children, and one Adult Negroe <219> Young Man, and one Mustee Young Woman and

3 Mustee Young Children in all 36. I hope I took a Method with the Negroe Young Man and with the Mustee Young Woman, whom I Baptiz'd, which will please the Society, which was this. I made them get our Church Catechism perfectly without Book and then I took some pains with them to make them understand it, and especially the Baptismall Covenant, and to perswade them faithfully and constantly to perform the Great things they were to promise at their Baptism, and ever after to perform to God. And then I caus'd them to say the Catechise one Lords Day and the other another Lords day before a Large Congregation, without Book, which they did both distinctly, and so perfectly, that all that heard them admired their Saying it so well and with great Satisfaction to my self I baptiz'd these two persons. These two Persons were Esqr. DuckenFields Slaves (The Gentleman with whom I liv'd most of this Year, and whose House was our Church all this Year) This Gentleman had severall other Slaves, who were as Sensible and Civil, and as much Inclined to Christianity and things that are Good: as ever I knew any Slaves in any place, wherever I have been <220> and indeed soe are the Slaves generally in this Province, and many of the Slaves of this Countrey, I am perswaded would be Converted Baptiz'd and Sav'd if their Masters were not so wicked as they are, and did not oppose their Conversion, Baptism and Salvation so much as they doe. I had for sometime great hopes of being the Minister that should convert and Baptize the rest of Esqr. Duckenfilds Slaves, which I was very desirous and Ambitious to be, and I would have begrudg'd no pains, but would most freely and with the greatest Pleasure have done all I could to Promote and Accomplish this so great and so good a work, And in Order thereunto I was preparing 4 more of them for Baptisme, and had taught one of those 4 their Catechism very perfectly and the other 3 a good part of it, and now as I was about this good Work, the Enemies to the Conversion and Baptism of Slaves, industriously and very busily buzz'd into the Peoples Ears, that all Slaves that were Baptiz'd were to be set free, and this silly Buckbear so greatly Scar'd Esqr. DuckenField, That he told me plainly I should Baptize no more of his Slaves till the Society had got a Law made in England that no Baptiz'd Slave, should be set free because he is Baptiz'd and send it here, and many more are of the same mind, and soe this good Work <221> was knock'd in the head, which is a great Trouble to me, because so many Slaves are so very desirous to become Christians without any Expectation of being set free when they are Baptiz'd. I fear this good Work will not be reviv'd and prosper here till such a Law is Enacted by the Parliament of Great Britain, and this people are acquainted with it, For I perceive nothing else will satisfie them.

This and some other Rubbs that I met with, and the great need of a Church of England Minister, which the Interest of the Church of England stood in here, where there are many Quakers, who make it their Business to gain as many of our Friends over to them as they can; wherein they have been too Successfull, and leavened some of our people with their principles and practices too much and especially with Anti-baptism and Many of their Children and of themselves too are unbaptiz'd and Used commonly to goe to the Quakers Meeting because their was no publick place of Worship for them to goe to. These things were the chief Reasons of my leaving the Southwest Shoar of Choan and comeing here where I hope I shall encrease the Interest of the Church of England, and cause the Interest of the Quakers to decrease, and then I perswade my self that the most excellent Society will not be Offended at my removing here, For I should be very <222> Sorry if I should doe any thing that is displeasing to them. I have lately Preach'd a few Sermons to the Adult unbaptiz'd persons among us, wherein I prov'd it their great Duty and their greatest priviledge Interest and happiness to joyn both them and their Children to the Lord in a Baptismall Covenant perpetuall that shall not be forgotten, With some good Success I thank God for it, For since I have Baptiz'd 4 Adult persons 3 Men 2 of which descended from Quakers and one Woman, two of these I caus'd to say our Church Catechism one of the 13th of the last Month and the other on the Lords Day following, who said it so exactly perfectly and distinctly that all that heard them admir'd their Saying it so well before such large Congregations and when they said it I Baptiz'd them, I have great hopes that severall Adult persons will allsoe qualifie and make themselves fit for Baptism. I have set many of our boys and girls upon getting our Church Catechism, and I hope I shall cathechize at least either one Severall Young Man or Woman, or Boy or Girl every Lords day all this Summer, which I shall doe partly that the elder persons of my Parish may be better acquainted with our Catechise than they are, Which I can't but think they will be by their hearing it so often repeated over. I have Baptiz'd six young Children in all ten here on the Lords <223> Day, before last Easter day. I Gave Notice to my poor People here allsoe of my Intention allsoe to Administer the Lords Supper on Easter Sunday following, if three of them would be Communicants with me: and preach'd a Sacrementall discourse to them, and I Intended to Preach another on Good Fryday following if I had known of but three that would have Communicated with me, I desired those that intended to be Partakers of the Holy Communion next Lords day to come to me. And soe I am forced to live without the Lords Supper My Self and without Administring it to others Year after Year here, which is no small Trouble to me. I assure the most Christian Society I intend the Lords day next before Whitsunday or Sooner to Preach a Sacrementall Discourse or two to give my People Notice again, that I intend to Administer the Lords Supper on Whitsunday following hopeing that 3 or more will receive it then, if they won't this will make me very weary of this place allsoe, and oblige me to beg the most Christian Society to give me leave to live in a Parish in this Province where I may partake of the Holy Communion my self, and Adminster it to others, if I can find out such a Parish in this Government, or if I cant to remove me again to a province where I can. I please my self with the hopes that the Good Society <224> will be pleas'd to gratifie me herein, whenever I crave this favour of them, I will make my Scroll no longer, but will now Conclude it with my devoutest and hearty Prayers to the Divine Majesty that he would be pleas'd allways to Bless and prosper all the most Glorious and Pious Designs of the most famous Society for the Propagation of the Gospell in Forreign Parts, and Subscribe my self this most Honourable Society's most Dutifull Faithfull and most humble Missionary, and Sir your most humble Servant.

Ebenezer Taylor

Copy. Read at a meeting of the Committee of the SPG on August 15, 1720. Journal of the Committee of the SPG.

[1]Not printed in the present volume. The 2,800-word document is in SPG/A/13, 155-178.

[*SPG/A/13*]

Rev. Ebenezer Taylor to Treasurer, SPG
1719 November 20

<246> Mr. Ebenezer Taylor to the Treasurer.

Bath Town Novr. 20th 1719

Sir

Last September was 12 Months I drew three Bills of Exchange upon the Society's Treasurer for One hundred and five pounds to be paid to Mr. John Lovick[1] or his Order, which was my last half Years Salary in So. Carolina from the 25th of March 1717 to the 29th of September following and my first whole Years Salary in No. Carolina which was from the 29th of September 1717 to the 29th of September 1718 which money I doubt not is paid before this time. And now I have bold to draw 3 Bills of Exchange for One hundred and Twenty pounds upon You, bearing Date the 20th of November 1719 to be paid to my Couzin Jno. Walker or his Order, which is my Salary from the 29th day of September 1718, to the 25th of March 1720, which I intreat you to pay him at the time mention'd in my Bills. Sir I am got into such a Countrey now that it is an hard thing to meet with an Oppertunity of sending a Letter from hence to the Excellent Society, and I am afraid it is a much harder thing for their Secretary to meet with an Opporty by which he may send a Letter to me here. I have writt twice to the Society's Secretary Since I came <247> here, both which Letters I hope he has receiv'd. But I have not receiv'd one word from him since I came here, Nor I doe not know when I shall Pray Sir be soe kind to me, as to give my most humble Service to the most Noble Society and tell them I am makeing it my Business to doe all the Good I can here and by the Grace of God, this I will allways doe while I am in their Employ. I am Honored Sir yr. most humble Servant.

Ebenezer Taylor

Copy.

[1]John Lovick (d. 1733) came to North Carolina in 1713 in the entourage of Governor Edward Hyde. Over the next two decades he held various important offices, including councillor, assemblyman, secretary of the province, and vice admiralty judge. *DNCB*.

[*SPG/A/14*]

Rev. John Urmston to Secretary, SPG
1719 December 31

<63> Mr. Urmstone to the Secretary.

North Carolina Decr. 31, 1719

Sir

Since my last of July[1] per Via New York there occurrs very little worth rehearsing. We used to say, Eis repetitia placent[2] but I find I may repeat Bill Millies the old story over again before I learn whether it pleases or not I can only tell You I am more misserable than ever and harder put to it to subsist myself and poor family than I used to be, I did intend since my Letters are in Vain to have come over for England next Spring and to have made known my circumstances Vivâ Você and if I had Sped no better than my Letters have done I purposed to have sent for my family and to have taught A.B.C. in a Garrett and have tried to have got one of the many £5 Curacies, or Readers places in or about London and doubted not but to have had more comfort and Enjoy'd my self better than ever I did here. It hath pleas'd God to take to himself my dear Wife, she died of very greif and discontent, Not to say want, for truely of late we have lived very sorrily. It was Irksome and Uneasie enough to turn farmer or Planter, but am grown so great a proficient that if I had Slaves and Barns with Necessaries that must be had, I could improve my plantation raise Stock and Subsist my self and family very <64> Comfortably but to Cott[3] as I must Now do will be more tedious to me and create more trouble than all the rest. I have only a Sorry Wretch that I came by on the Ships Acct. and hath but a Year and half to serve, She knows nothing of household affairs a Notorious Whore and theif and yet preferable to any that can be hired here notwithstanding all her faults, she was bred a Trader in Spittlefields[4] but followed the Musick Houses most and other vile Courses which brought her to Bridewell and from thence transported hither, Except I can get a Sober good Woman into the house I cannot hold it any longer. I intend to send my two Youngest Children as a present to the Society hoping they will put them into some Charity School or hospitall whereby they may be Educated and provided for when they come to Age for I am not able to Maintain them. My Eldest is near twenty, and capable of helping me but is bent upon going for England so that You may guess what a rare housekeeper I am like to make with this sorry wench and a Sinceless dumb Negroe fellow. There is no boarding here, there is never a family that I know of that I would live in if they would hire Mee. My Brother Taylor[5] has had tryalls of that and has changed his about a Doz. times since he came hither, and wishes himself in South Carolina again. I can put no other construction upon the Societies not taking notice of me, but that they will force me to leave their Service and now You see I must do it, and yet considering I am aged wanting but 3 of 60 Years. I am not fond of leaving a pritty Settlement and A warm Countrey to come to seek my Bread in A cold Starving Country and therefore once more begg the Society to put me in a way how to get Negroes 3 or 4 at least recommend <65> Me to somebody at Barbados or the other Islands Virginia or New York who will take my Bills and be just to me or else will pay what is due to Me, at any of the places aforesaid, I will continue where I am; I know no body I can trust, all that I have ever dealt with me have cheated me since my tedious and dangerous fitt of Sickness. I am grown very Crazy[6] and not able to travell so that I have not baptized many this last half Year, Seven only in my Neighborhood and one in another parish the first long journey I took since my Sickness, thro' weakness and bad Rodes I was so fatigued that I desired to have my horse sent back and I hired a Canoe and two Negroes to carry me back, I was soundly wett and got a great Cold, the passage cost me 20*s*. so that besides loss of health I was out of pocket, and scarce thanks for my pains. I have had many such Chapps:[7] its a common Notion that I am obliged to serve the whole

Countrey but I must disapoint them for the time to come. With much adoe I prevailed with my vestry to meet the first time in 3 Years, they pretended to have collected for the 2 first Years after the late Act took place, they paid me in Bills £79 for £100 alledging they could raise no more and for the 2 last Years ending this day they have promised Mee £80 more and what they collect more is to pay a reader in the remote parts where I cannot attend as they say I ought to do every other Sunday, which I neither can nor would be obliged to for £50 per Annum more I must pay the Collector 2: 3 per C. so that my income is of little value. They have Entred a Memorandum in their Vestry Book that there £143 due to Me on the former acct. but when or how it will ever be raised I know not, for no man is lyable to pay more than 5*s*. per pole every Year and that You may see will not raise the Yearly allowance, what must be Come of the Arrears? In fine I <66> Find they are for keeping up the Old Custom to do what they list with Ministers. They matter not how poor we are or how Misserable we live, we shall be the first they Cheat or overeach in their dealings, ready enough to Complain upon any supposed Neglect and Yet at the same time are not for coming to Church above once in a Month or two and then they neither know nor care what they come about very Negligent and Ignorant of their duty. I have Administred the Sacrament of the Lords Supper but twice these five Years in publick, and as often to Sick persons. I pray You let me know the Sentiments of the Society in relation to this that I may begin to dispose of myself and family if so be they will not comply with my requests, I wish I could sell my House and Land at any thing near the value. I should not then be long in resolving what to do, I am Sir Yr. most humble Servant.

John Urmstone

Copy. Read at a meeting of the Committee of the SPG on August 15, 1720. Journal of the Committee of the SPG.

[1]Not located.
[2]This phrase may be rendered "repetition pleases them."
[3]*Cot*, a verb meaning "to cohabit, to dwell with one in the same house." *OED*.
[4]Spitalfields is a district in the east of London.
[5]Rev. Ebenezer Taylor.
[6]Undoubtedly in the sense of "broken down in health; diseased; infirm." *OED*.
[7]*Chap*, a noun meaning "a stroke, knock, rap." *OED*.

[*CO* 5/293]

Act of Assembly
1720

<*An Aditional Act to the Vestrey Act.*> An Additional Act To the Act Intituled an Act for Establishing the Church and appointing Select Vestrys.

Whereas by the said Act the Government is divided into parishes and Twelve Men Nominated in each division a Parish to serve after Such qualifications by the said Act is Provided as a Vestry Man, and it appearing that the persons appointed by the said Act to Serve for the S.W. parish of Chowan and Craven precinct a Parish in the County of Bath did not proceed to Qualify themselves at time nor manner and form as in and by the said Act was appointed and required neither have done the same since by which the said Vestry in the said precincts are fallen and termined so as there can be no lawfull or regular Tax or Levy of money on the pole in the said precinct for the payment of Ministers, buildings or repairing of Churches, or relief of the poor, for Remedy whereof and prevention of the Same for the future.

Be it Enacted by his Excellency the Palatin and the rest of the True and Absolute Lords Proprietors of Carolina by and with the Advice and Consent of the rest of the Members of the Generall Assembly now mett at the Generall Court house at Queen Ann's Creek in Chowan Precinct for the N.E. part of the said province. And we pray that it may be Enacted that the Marshall or Deputy for the said Precincts or Parishes of Craven, and South West parish of Chowan do within forty days from the ratification hereof under the penalty in the said Act Provided Summons the Severall persons by the said Act appointed to Serve as Vestry Men in the said Parishes to appear and Qualify themselves at Such place and in such manner in their Severall parishes under the penalty in the said Act mentioned.

And be it further Enacted by the Authority aforesaid, That the Members of Each parish here mentioned so meeting and qualifying themselves shall have full power and good Authority on a Vacancy either of Death Removal or nonconformity of any person appointed by the said Act to Serve as Vestrymen in the parish to Choose and Elect some other person or persons Freeholders in their said parishes to serve in the room of that Persons so dead, removed, or not conforming to meet at such time and place as they or the greatest part of them shall appoint to qualify themselves, and after due qualification to be held, deemed and esteemed of equal Dignity to Act and do in all things relating to Vestrymen to all Intents and purposes as if they had been Named and appointed in the said Act.

And Whereas at the time of passing the aforesaid Act there was due from the precinct of Chowan to Mr. John Urmston Minister the Sum of One Hundred and Ten pounds which for want of proper provision being made in the said Act at the same time of Division of the said precinct into two Parishes cannot now be Levyed and Collected without Authority of the Assembly. Therefore be it Enacted by the Authority aforesaid That the Vestry men of the N.E. Parish of Chowan do sometime on or before the 25th day of Novr. next Ensuing the Ratification of this Act Levy and Collect, or Cause to be Levyed and collected upon each and every Tythable person in the said respective parishes so much per pole as shall pay unto the said Reverend Jno. Urmston the aforesaid Sum of One Hundred and Ten pounds over and above the 5 Shillings per pole mentioned in the said Act anything in the Act contained to the contrary thereof Notwithstanding.

And be it further Enacted by the Authority aforesaid that each and every Vestry or the greatest part of them in the severall precincts in the said Act appointed shall in case of Vacancy by death, or removal of any Member or Members of Vestry in any of the Severall precincts or parishes have full power from time to time and at all times hereafter to Elect or Choose one or more freeholders of their said parish or precinct in such Vacancys, and Such persons so Elected after qualifying themselves according to Law to be held, deemed Esteemed and Enabled to Act as Vestry men to all Intents and purposes as if they had been by the said Act Nominated and Appointed.

And Whereas That Notwithstanding the falling the said Vestry as aforesaid the Inhabitants of the S.W. parish of Chowan Precinct have Employed a Minister and a Reader. The Salary have been paid by some particular Persons of said parish.

Be it therefore Enacted by the Authority aforesaid That the said Vestry have and they are hereby Impowered to raise and Levy such a pole Tax on the Inhabitants of the said Parish as to reimburst and pay such persons the Severall Summs before by them paid to the uses aforesaid any thing in this Act contained to the contrary in anywise Notwithstanding.

And Whereas in the Vestry Act Sufficient power is not given to the Church Wardens for the Levying of all such fines and forfeitures as by that Act shall become due according to the intent and meaning thereof.

Be it therefore Enacted by the Authority aforesaid That where any distress fines or forfeitures shall become due by increase of the aforesaid Act that the Church Wardens in each and every of their Respective Parishes and precincts within this Government have full power and Authority (either by himself or Warrant under his or their hand directed to the Constable or some other proper person) to Levy and make Distress on the Estates of all and every person within their severall Limits and districts for all such failures fines and forfeitures as by the said Vestry Act shall become due and the same to dispose of as in and by the said Act is Provided any Thing contained in the said Act to the contrary to anywise Notwithstanding.

D.

[*SPG/A/14*]

Rev. John Urmston to Secretary, SPG
1719/20 February 15

<67> Mr. Urmstone to the Secretary.

North Carolina Febr. 15 1719/20

Sir

I Received from You a Letter Dated Xr. 17 1716 per Via Boston on the 7th Instant wherein You say the honorable Society at A General Meeting Novr. 16 of the same Year resolved that I should have their leave to return to England. I wish Yours had come to hand in due time. I hope there's some Mistake in the date and that I may be entitled <68> To their bounty as in their Standing Orders relating to Missionaries page 56 and 16.[1] I Joyfully accept their leave for its worse with me than Ever having lost my poor Wife who died last Year Oct. 18 without any previous Sickness. Not many hours before her death she declared before several Neighbours that her heart was broken thro' our ill usage and Comfortless way of living. She prest me sore for divers

Years either to quitt this wretched Countrey, or give her leave to go home with her Children. I wish I had done ither it might have pleased God to have Continued her to me many Years longer. I propose to take my passage in the Next Shipp that I can hear of going from Virginia for England and therefore Countermand my request to the Society in mine of the Ult. Decr. last past per Via New York. I shall be a great Sufferer by leaving this place and Yet I would rather undergoe that than suffer and get nothing whereas I hope to End my days with some Comfort in my Native Country if the Society will not be pleased to do something better for me; for I had rather be Vicar to the Bear Garden[2] than Bp. to No. Carolina these are from Sir Yr. most humble Servant.

John Urmstone

Copy. Read at a meeting of the Committee of the SPG on August 15, 1720. Journal of the Committee of the SPG.

[1]Presumably this refers to Standing Order XVIII, "That the Salary of every Missionary, who is not dismiss'd the Service for some Misdemeanour, shall continue one Year, and no longer, after the Society have resolved at their Board to dismiss such Person from their Service." "Standing Orders of the Society for the Propagation of the Gospel in Foreign Parts," 14. Urmston's page reference is unclear.

[2]"A place originally set apart for the baiting of bears, and used for the exhibition of other rough sports." *OED*.

[*SPG/SAP*]

Report
1719/20 February 19

<51> <*An Abstract of the Proceedings of the Society.*> [. . .] From Mr. *Urmstone* at *Chowan, North-Carolina*, That he has visited some People about 50 Miles from thence, where he never was before, where he baptiz'd four or five Persons in a House, and in some seven or eight, many of which were Men and Women. [. . .]

Printed. Extracted from the yearly publication containing the sermon preached at the annual anniversary meeting of the SPG, together with a review of the activities of the Society and its missionaries during the preceding year. The date above is the date of the meeting.

[*SPG/A/14*]

Rev. John Urmston to Secretary, SPG
1720 April 25

<71> Mr. Urmstone to the Secretary.

North Carolina Aprill 25 1720

Sir

Yours of Decemr. 17th 1716 I received per Via Boston on the first Instant wherein You say that the Honorable Society at a Genl. Meeting Novr. 16 1716 resolved that I should have leave to return to England, I wish Yours had come to hand in due time, however I hope my Salary will be continued to mee till I arrive as it is intended by their Standing Orders Page 56 par. 18. I thankfully accept of their leave, for its now worse with me than Ever, having lost my poor Wife who died last Octr. 18 without any previous Sickness, saving a loosness and Vomiting which lasted not many hours, and to all appearance was happily stopt by proper means the Evening before. The next morning that she was Strucken with death and all that day in an Agony Not many hours before her departure she declared to Severall Neighbours that her heart was broke thro' the ill Usage we have met with and our uncomfortable way of living. She prest me sore for many Years either to leave the Countrey or let her go home with her Children. I wish I had done either it might have pleased God to have continued her to me for many Years longer. I shall be a great looser by leaving this wretched Countrey, Yet had rather Submit to that than suffer on and get nothing. I am little the better for what the Society is pleasd to allow me and my dependance on this people very inconsiderable, whereas if I find Favour from the Society, I hope Yet to spend the remainder of my days with Comfort.

P.S. Mr. Taylor my fellow labourer after having tryed many places in the Countrey and Endured much went last Autumn to the other County where he was much wanted but meeting with <72> No better usage at Bath Town the place he first set down in was for Shifting as he had done here from place to place and in his way to Choe-Sound[1] the Southernmost Settlement in the Goverment went on Shore on Harbour Island which is not inhabited about 30 Miles from any Inhabitants in the mouth of Neuse River where after having been ten days and Nights in an open Boat he perished thro' Cold last February. There were some people on the Island hunting for Hoggs that had been placed there, who with those that went with him buried him and then rifled his Chests and divided the Spoile and are not to be brought to any Acct.[2] Some of them have been purged by Oaths but that is of little force with a North Carolina Man (such Executors a man must Expect that dies here) Nay when alive and leaves the Country and leaves any thing behind him will fare little better, for upon my resolving to come home I treated with severall about my plantation and was like to have been Bubbled.[3] It's hoped I shall leave it unsold and then I may expect a blessed account of it as well as the Money that is due to Mee this precints owes me £243. £80 whereof was due last New Years day but as Yet not paid nor do I know when will, the rest has been due these 5 Years but its pretended it cannot be raised without a new power Additional to the Act of Vestry which must be done by the Assembly which was to have met the first Week in May next, but I understand it will be Prorogued for reasons of State: I suppose to see the event of the Revolution in South Carolina who have revolted from the Lords proprietors and will own no power but that of the King.[4] Rather than come away before I have tried the Uttmost I am willing to stay tho' I hazard my health another Summer, but come what will I am resolved to Quitt next Spring if God spare me life and health.

<73> I shall continue to labour in this fruitless Vineyard till then and hope that my staying longer than I either care or am obliged will not be deemed a fault. The sober thinking part of the people which God knows are but few are very much disatisfied with my thoughts of leaving them quite destitute after having brought the Countrey into a little Order. It will be a great greif to them say some not to go to hearing and to Enjoy the other Rites of the Church as to have their Children Baptized etc., and truely its a Melancholy, dejecting thought, but till better provission be made and more regard to our Function there is no remedy. They are for trying to bring the generallity of the Inhabitants to make some new overtures which You may be assured I shall promote for the sake of our Successors, but I do not Expect they will be such as will detain mee and cause me to alter my intentions.

I should be glad to have a line or two from You could it come in less time than the last did, there are frequent oppertunities to Boston in New England and the like from thence hither, Except in the depth of Winter.

The Collector there Mr. Jekyll is my Correspondent and will take care of all Letters to as well as from Sir Your most humble Servant.

John Urmstone

Be pleased to cause the
inclosed[5] to be deliver'd Safe

Copy.

[1]Core Sound, in present Carteret County.

[2]In November, 1720, a prosecution was brought against one James McDaniel "for Felloniously taking Some money belonging to Eben-Ezer Taylor." McDaniel escaped from jail and fled the colony, and the bench of the March, 1721, term of the General Court dismissed the action. Price, *Higher-Court Minutes, 1709-1723*, 228, 245.

[3]From a verb meaning to delude or cheat. "Also *to bubble* (any one) *of*, *out of*, or *into* a thing." *OED.*

[4]The "Revolution" of 1719 was a virtually bloodless coup d'état in which the Commons House of Assembly of South Carolina declared itself a convention "delegated by the People, to prevent the utter Ruin of this Government," and prominent rebels proclaimed a new governor appointed by themselves. In 1720 the Privy Council in London granted the rebels' request that the crown assume the government of the colony. North Carolina did not take part in any of these proceedings. Sirmans, *Colonial South Carolina*, 126-131.

[5]It is not known what this refers to.

[*SPG/A/15*]

Rev. John Urmston to Secretary, SPG
1720/1 February 5

<42> Mr. Urmstone to the Secretary.

North Carolna. Febry. 5th 1720/1

Sir

Since my last of Xber. 22d[1] nothing of Any Moment Occurs save that I am still detained Sore Against my Will in this Wretched Countrey in hopes of Getting my Money but

Greatly Suspect I shall be disapointed. I was to have had £120 the first of the Last month and got but £54 and the £122 due Six years agoe is not yet raised. Notwithstanding an Act of Assembly which I obtain'd With great Strugling last Augt. for the payment of it on or before 25th of Novr. Last Nor do I believe I Shall ever have it. I will Wait till May And if there be no more Likelyhood than I see at present I think to Come home. I did hope to have had Something to have Come home to but am forced to draw bills for every thing I want. I was not very happy in my late wives days upon divers Accounts but I am now quite weary of My life And Worse put to it than ever to Subsist what Ive received from the parish is all Gone towards paying for a Negroe Within ten days after I bought him and A White Man Who ran Away within the Like time. If I had not received the Money I verily beleive I never should have had a peny from the parish. I endured 4 or 5 Arrests to Make me give Bills of Exchange but being restive My Creditors were Oblidged to take parish pay With the Advance of £150 per Ct. in lieu of Sterling money.

I Desired in my Last as I now doe that if Any one Came to the Society or Treasurer that Called himself my Son that no notice should be taken of him. I have been forced to turn him Adrift for his Undutifullness in Combining With my Servants to ruine me. He gott A Servant Wench With Child Who had 2 Years to Serve rendered her not only Useless but even A Burthen to Mee Yet am forced to keep her not knowing where to get A better Being in Great want of provisions. I sent a bill of Exchange for £20 to Coll. Heathcoat at New York but after, divers since the date thereof Which was July 15 1719 I Cannot hear from him I pray you or the treasurer to Acquaint Whether it was ever tendered or paid. I hear he is poore which makes me fear my Money is Lost. We are Inform'd Our Late good for Nothing proprietors have Sold their Interest in these parts to 3 Quakers[2] if so the Church is Like to Flourish. Others Say We Are under the Crown. I Cannot hear from Ingland. I am Buried Alive in this hell of a hole. The last from you Was dated Novr. 16th 1716. Sir pray favour me with a line Or 2 Which you may direct to Mr. Jeykill Collector at Boston in the Next heell forward it to Sir your Most humble Servant.

J. Urmstone

Copy.

[1]Not located.
[2]This rumor was untrue.

[*SPG/A/15*]

Charles Eden to Secretary, SPG
1721 April 12

<43> Governor Eden to the Secretary.

North Carolina Aprill 12 1721

Sir

The Unhappy State this Colony is Left in for want of A Missionary, Mr. Taylor being dead And Mr. Urmstone having after the most Unaccountable manner imagniable left his Mission some Twenty days since without Acquainting My Self or Any of the Councell or Vestry of the parish Where he resided Save one Mr. Moseley a person not the happiest in his Character for behaviour Towards Government or good Order Who he has Left to take Care of his Affairs which no wise required his deserting them, but rather might have Encouraged his Contin[uing] but not having made the Least Application to Me for Credentials. I shall forbear giving Character of the Gentleman that is now Comeing before your August Assembly Where I pray My Humble duty May be received and your interest and Charitable Care of Nine parishes Consisting of Upwards of Twenty five hundred White Souls intirely Left destitute of Any Assistance in Religious Affairs but What their readers give them Who are not So able As I Could Wish Amongst a people perfectly Well Affected to the Church and Very desireous of giving Encouragement to Ministers of A Courteous And Affable behaviour to reside Amongst them Could they have the good fortune to be Supplied with Such and unless Some due Care be taken this person Leaving his Flock so intirely deserted may Give Occasion for Quakerism to Spread Amongst us Those being the Only Sect of Dissenters worth minding in the Government. I am Confident if this finds Credence with the Most Honorable Members of your Society Whatsoever Gentleman shall be sent to us will have no Occasion to repent themselves And hope nothing that Mr. Urmstone May have to Offer in Justification of his own Mismanagement Will make Impression with his Grace of Canterbury and the rest of that Venerable body to the prejudce of these neglected people Who howsoever formerly ill represented deserve well now To Take up more of your time would be Needless So not doubting of your Favour On this Lamentable Occasion I beg Leave to Subscribe as with great respect and Esteem I am Your most humble and obedient Servant.

Charles Eden

Copy. Read at a meeting of the SPG on November 17, 1721, when it was agreed to concur in a recommendation of the Committee "that this Letter be reconsider'd upon Mr. Urmstones makeing any Application to the Society; and that a Letter be wrote to Governor Eden Thanking him for the Favour he expresses to the Society and their Missionaries, and acquainting him that the Society have already sent one Missionary, and will, as soon as conveniently may be, send another to North Carolina." Journal of the SPG, IV, 182-183.

[*SPG/A/15*]

Rev. John Urmston to Secretary, SPG
1721 May 10

<44> Mr. Urmstone to the Secretary.

Sir

You may perhaps understand by Advice for 2 or 3 Bills Iv'e been forced to draw before I could get out of this expensive Countrey and that Im bound for London with Gods Leave. I Left North Carolina March 26th After divine Service hopeing to a Sail'd in a week or ten days but Ships are tedious and Long in Breaking Ground. My Stay and fitting out with mine Will Cost me dear but it Could not be Avoided. I purposed to have Come home Last Summer but was perswaded to Stay till the Meeting of An Assembly with hopes of Great Matters. I was Assisted by My Friends in procureing an Act for the payment of the part of My Arrearages but after obtained Little Came of it t'was all Labour Lost. I Could Stay no longer Nor do I think of returning Except I Can hope to Live with more Comfort than I have hitherto done. I wish this Voyage may Not prove dangerous. We are 5 or 6 Ships in Company ready to Sail but Understanding by a Ship Newly Come in who Was ill Used by two pyrates off of the Wasts[1] of Great force Who Expected to be Joyned by a Ship of 40 Guns and 400 Men design'd to plunder this Government in revenge for the Execution of Some Give out they will not Spare man woman or Child we dare not put out to Sea, here are preparation Making for the defence of the Countrey, but I fear to Little purpose Except there were Ships Capable of Carrying Men and Guns. Ships might be had but such an Equipage will not be provided in hast. What Will be the event God Knows I wish We were an hundred Leagues out. I beleive the Ship by Which this Came will Steal out in the night. She being a good Sailor and May possibly Escape the Rogues. I dread falling into their hands. These With All due Respects are from Your Most humble Servant.

John Urmstone
Missionary

James River May 10, 1721

Copy.

[1]Obsolete form of *waist* (as well as *waste* and *west*). *OED*. The reference presumably is to the narrows of the James River.

[*SPG/A/15*]

Anonymous to Secretary, SPG
1721 May 26

<45> A letter Without Name to the Secretary.

about Mr. Urmstone
dated May 26th 1721

I have given you the trouble of these few Lines that the honorable Society might be somewhat Acquainted of the Character of Mr. Urmstone that is Lately gone for England and intends he Says to return again to north Carolina, if the Society thinks fit to Send him But indeed he is a very Unfit Missionary for that or any other place, his Life is So Wicked and Scandalous notorious Drunkard and Swearing and Lewdness is also what he is ocupied of for these and others of his vices he was so much disliked of the people he was Among that Scarce any of them come to hear him and it is what one shall hear Almost from everyones Mouth that knows him that it is a pitty that he Shou'd ever come into these parts Any More Except he reforms his Life and bad Example doing More hurt then ever his preaching did good, there are Many Quakers in Carolina and to be without a Minister gives them Great Advantage. What I have Writt You Assure the Honorable Society it is not out of any prejuduce to Mr. Urmstone or Self Interest but purely that their Christian Charity and pious Intent Might be better Answered With respect to that place and those poor Ignorant people better provided for by a person Sent Capable of doing Good Amongst them which is the Hearty Wish of Sir etc.

Copy.

[*T 1/234*]

Bishop of London to Treasury Board
1721 June 23

My Lords,

The Bishop of London was by K. Charles II entrusted with the care of provideing and Sending Ministers to the Colonies and Islands in America, and was afterwards by His late Majesty K. William directed to apply to the Treasury for the Summ of £20 to each Missionary to defray his passage. This charitable Bounty being at first readily paid upon each application, was of great benefit to those Missionaries. Afterwards it was oft times delayed, and become thereby much less usefull, many of the Missionaries having by too long attendance been reduced to great Straits. I am now told that upon their application at present the answer given them is, that Severall to whom that Bounty has been given did not proceed on the Mission, and therefore Your Lordships make a difficulty to grant the same any longer. I have heard that the like remark was made in my Predecessors time, for which I hope there was little or no Grounds: but for my own part I can assure Your Lordships that thô in <*Lords Commisioners of the Treasury.*> this case I once lost £20 of my own money, yet I have not been so unfortunate as to lose any of His Majesties, except in one Instance, where the Party appointed to go fell into madness and was not suffered to proceed. Perhaps it may have given occasion to the Reflection now made, that two persons who lately had the £20 did not proceed; but this will be clear'd by acquainting Your Lordships that after their dispatch at the Treasury they got preferment at home and one of them refunded the £20, which I forthwith applied to the use of another Missionary without troubling Your Lordships; the other has paid back the one half and I dayly expect the Remainder, which I shall also apply in the like Manner.

But if, (as there seems to be some reason to apprehend) Your Lordships think it not fit to trust me any longer with this Dispensation of the Crown's money, You will, I presume, move His Majesty to employ some other person, for I cannot believe Your Lordships will ever advise His Majesty to retrench this Bounty, since without it, it will be impossible for any whatsoever to get those Colonies supplied. In that case I shall willingly acquiesce in the Conviction of my own mind, that I have faithfully and honestly done my Duty. This comfortable Reflection has hitherto, and will continue to relieve me against the malicious Slanders of some, and the mistakes of others both at home and abroad; especially considering that I shall thereby be freed from a great and vexatious trouble, which has no

Connexion with the Duty of a Bishop of London, and yet putts him to a considerable charge, without the profit of one penny a Year. I am My Lords, Your Lordships, most humble and obedient Servant.

John London

Jun. 23 1721.

[*Endorsed*:]
Bishop of Londons Lettre
about the £20 Bounty to Missionaries
1721.

LS.

[*SPG/A/15*]

Rev. John Urmston to Secretary, SPG
1721 July 21

<52> Mr. Urmstone to the Secretary.

London July 21 1721

Sir

My Coming home Cannot Seem Strange to any who have perusd my Letters from the time of my Arrival in North Carolina, you Acquainted me in one of yours that the honorable Society had granted me Leave to return, but that good news did not Come to hand till Decr. 19th 1719 which Was three years and Odd Months after upon, receipt Whereof, I resolved to leave the Countrey Last Summer, which I should have done had I not been perswaded by some friends to stay for the Meeting of An Assembly which was by purogation put off from time to time but a Last met in Octobr. Last. The Last vestry act was deficient having no regard to the Arrears due to me to the time of passing the Same, the Vestry by that Act had not power to levy More than 5*s*. per Poll Which wou'd scarce pay the Yearly Salary. I obtained With much entreaty and Solicitation An Additional Act to impower the Vestry to lay Such Levy as Wou'd pay me the Arrears Aforesaid. This prov'd ineffectual too for tis pretended that the vestry are enabled but not Compelled by Any penalty to Comply with it notwithstanding it was Enacted that I should be paid on or before the 25th of Novr. Following the debt Was £222 but by what means or for what reason the Assembly made a Defalcation of £112 is too tedious now to incert. There was further due £116 for part of the 3 Years last past Ending primo Janr. last, besides Sundry Small debts all which I Saw no Appearance nor Grounds of hopes ever to receive the Same tis all Lost so that I was not able to Subsist nor endure such treatment any Longer. I am now Blessed be god Safe Arrived after a Tedious and expensive Voyage. I hope not without Leave in order to go back Again on Such Terms as are absolutly Necesary and expedient, or rather to end my days in my Native Countrey And withall Submission to my

Superiours I think it most reasonable after having Served the Church 27 Years been Missionary well nigh 12 thereof Among an inGratefull people Strugled with great inconveniencys of Liveing in Such an Obscure Corner of the world inhabitted by the dreggs and Gleanings of all other Inglish Colonies and a very unhealthy Countrey which have driven many Clergy men out of it not being able to Stay So many months as I have years And brought others to their Graves Seeing then it hath pleased Almighty God to prepare me a body to endure more than Any of my Function ever did or I am perswaded ever will. I see no reason I shou'd be doom'd to Exile. I hope I shall find favour for Altho' Aged I have Still Sufficient Strength of body the Lord be praized some Share of Sence and abillity to Serve my God and his holy Church the remains of a Liberall Education Long Travells and Scraps of the French And Italian Tongues and am of Opinion Employment may be found for such a one this I pray you Lay before the honorable Society this Meeting at the door attends your etc.

John Urmstone

Copy.

[*SPG/Jou/4*]

Journal of the SPG
1721 July 21

<164> 21 July 1721 [. . .]

<166> 9. Order'd that the Treasurer pay the Reverend Mr. Urmstone Thirty pounds on Account of his Salary and that his Case be referr'd to the Committee to consider and Report their Opinion thereon to the Society. [. . .]

Minutes.

[*SPG/C/7*]

Testimonial
1721 September 12

<116> This is to Certifie whom it may Concern that We whose Names are Underwritten have known the Reverend Mr. Thomas Newnam[1] for some Years and do beleive to be a Person of an Exemplary Life and sober Conversation, and that he is Orthodox as to his Principles according to the Doctrine of the Church of England and that we do beleive him to be very well affected to our present Establishment both in Church and State. In Witness whereof we set our hands this twelth day of September 1721.

Tho. Gillesbey L.L.B.
Tho. Sheppard M.A.
Tho. Clendon M.A.

[*Endorsed*:]
7
Mr. Newnams Testimonial
approv'd by the Society the
28 Septemr. 1721

Copy.

[1]See appendix.

[*SPG/Jou/4*]

Journal of the SPG
1721 September 28

<174> 28th Septemr. 1721 [. . .]

<175> 3. Also that the Reverend Mr. Newnam had laid before them his Deacons and Priests Orders, that they gave him a Text videlicet the 30th Verse of the 17th Chapter of the Acts,[1] and desired Mr. Arch Deacon Stubbs and Mr. Lasinby to hear him read Prayers and Preach, and directed him to lay his Testimonials before the Society. Mr. Newnam attending was called in and laid his Testimonials before the Board, which were read and approvd, and Mr. Arch Deacon Stubbs acquainting the Society that he had heard him read Prayers and Preach which he performed to his Satisfaction: Agreed that he be received the Societys Missionary and be sent to North Carolina with a Salary of Eighty pounds Per Annum to commence from Michaelmas next, and that he be provided with a Church Bible, Common Prayer book, and book of Homilies, a Library of Ten pounds and five pounds worth of Small Tracts.

4. Also that the Reverend Mr. Urmstone late Missionary in North Carolina attending was called in, and acquainted the Committee that there was due to him at Ladyday last the time he left Carolina £120.12.6, and pray'd that he may be paid the Ballance of his said Account, after the Bills drawn by him and paid by the Treasurer are deducted, which appears by the Account deliver'd by the Treasurer to amount to £38.12.6, that thereupon they agreed as their Opinion that the Treasurer do pay the said £38.12.6 to Mr. Urmstone in full of his Salary, and that it be submitted to the Society to Judge of the 21st Rule relating to Missionaries,[2] Mr. Urmstone <176> being of Opinion that he is entituled to a years Salary according to that Rule. Agreed that the Treasurer do pay to Mr. Urmstone what was due at Ladyday last, and that the consideration of the Sense of the 21st Rule relating to Missionaries be postpon'd to some fuller Meeting. [. . .]

Minutes.

[1]"And the times of this ignorance God winked at, but now commandeth all men everywhere to repent." Acts 17:30, Authorized Version.

[2]Presumably Urmston is here referring to a standing order relating to missionaries: "[T]he Salary of every Missionary, who is not dismiss'd the Service for some Misdemeanour, shall continue one Year, and no longer, after the Society have resolved at their Board to dismiss such Person from their Service." In the set of standing orders printed above and dated ca. 1710, this rule is number 18.

[*T 60/11*]

Order
1721 October 23

<108> <*James Mac Sparran*> Order etc. this 19 day of Novr. 1720 By Virtue of his Majestys General Lettres Patents Dormant bearing date the 14th of Augt. 1714 <*Confirm'd by Warrant dated 15th May 1721 Vide Money Book 29 p. 11.*> That you deliver and pay of such his Majestys Treasure as remains in your Charge unto James Mac Sparran or to his Assigns the Sum of Twenty pounds without Account towards Defraying the Charges of his passage to New England whither he is going a Minister. And these etc. £20, J.A., G.B., Cha. Turner [...]

<*Thomas Newman*> A like Order for £20 for his passage to North Carolina whither he is going a Minister Dated 23d Octobr. 1721. Sign'd R. Walpole, Cha. Turner, R. Edgcumbe, H. Pelham [...]

D.

[*SPG/A/15*]

Secretary of the SPG to Charles Eden
1721 November 7

<73> Carolina Letters from the Society. Anno 1721. To Governor Eden.

London Novemr. 7th 1721

Honored Sir

The Society for the Propagation of the Gospel in Foreign Parts have recd. your Letter of the 12th of April last, and upon your representation of the great Want of Missionaries to supply the several vacant Parishes in your Government have (for the present) appointed the bearer the Reverend Mr. Newnam to succeed Mr. Urmstone, and will as soon as may be send another to the other Parishes where there is the greatest want of them. Mr. Newnam has been very well recommended to the Society, and I doubt not but he will by a faithfull discharge of his Holy Function endear him self to the People, so as to meet with all suitable encouragement from them; and the Society do hereby earnestly recommend him to your Honour for your favour and Countenance, which they have reason to hope for from the great zeal you have always shewn for the Prosperity of the Church in your Government. I am etc.

D. H.

Copy.

[SPG/A/15]

Secretary of the SPG to "Vestry of Chowan"
1721 November 7

<74> To the Vestry of Chowan North Carolina.

London Novr. 7th 1721

Gentlemen
The Society for the Propagation of the Gospel in Foreign Parts have thought fit to appoint the Reverend Mr. Thomas Newnam to be their Missionary among You, he has been very well recommended to the Society, and they have reason to hope that by his Piety and diligence in the discharge of his Holy Function he will engage your Affections to his Person, and that you will not be wanting on your Parts to do what you can for his comfortable Support and Maintenance among you. I am etc.
D. H.

Copy.

[*CO 323/8*]

Order in Council
1721 November 11

At the Court of St. James's the 11th of Novbr. 1721 Present The Kings most Excellent Majesty in Councill.

<*Octobr. 25th 1721.*> Upon Reading this day at the Board a Representation from the Lords Commissioners of Trade and Plantations with four Draughts of Additionall Instructions to his Majesty's Governors of New York, New Jersey, Carolina and Barbadoes pursuant to an Order in Councill of the 26th of Septbr. last in Relation to the Bishop of Londons power of Licensing Ministers and School Masters in the Plantations, His Majesty in Councill taking the same into Consideration, Is pleased to approve the said four Draughts of Additionall Instructions, Which are hereunto annexed,[1] And to Order as it is hereby Ordered, That the Rt. Honourable Lord Carteret one of his Majesty's principall Secratarys of State do prepare the same for his Majesty's Royall Signature.
a true Copy.
Edward Southwell

[*Endorsed*:]
Plantations Genl.
Copy
Order of Council, of 11th Novbr. 1721,

Approving the Draught of an Additional
Instruction to the Governors of Barbadoes,
New-York, New Jersey and Carolina, relating
to the Bishop of London's Power of Licensing
Ministers and Schoolmasters in the Plantations.

Received 23d
Read 24th April 1722.

L:26.

D.

[1]Not present.

[*SPG/C/7*]

Rev. Benjamin Pownall to the SPG
ca. 1722

To the Honorable and Reverend Society for the Propagation of the Gospel in foreign Parts.

Benjamin Pownall Clerk humbly offer's his Service to be employ'd as one of the Society's Missionary's in either of the Carolinas and is with Stedfast duty and obedience Your faithfull Servant.

[*Endorsed*:]
4
Mr. Pownall's Petition

D. By ca. 1725, Rev. Benjamin Pownall had been removed almost three years from a parish in Virginia to one in South Carolina. Manross, *Fulham Papers in the Lambeth Palace Library*, 139.

[*SPG/Jou/4*]

Journal of the SPG
1721/2 January 19

<192> 19 January 1721-2. [. . .]
<194> 11. Agreed that the Case of Mr. Urmstone late the Societys Missionary in North Carolina be referr'd to the Committee. [. . .]

Minutes.

[*SPG/SAP*]

Report
1721/2 February 16

<40> <*An Abstract of the Proceedings of the Society.*> [. . .] The *Society* have this Year supply'd the following Places with Missionaries, who have been well recommended to them both for their Abilities and pious Life and Conversation, and to be duly qualified to answer the Ends of the Mission. [. . .] <41> To *North Carolina*, in the Room of Mr. *Urmstone*, who is return'd from that County, the Reverend Mr. *Thomas Newnam*, with a Salary of *Eighty Pounds per Annum*: [. . .]

Printed. Extracted from the yearly publication containing the sermon preached at the annual anniversary meeting of the SPG, together with a review of the activities of the Society and its missionaries during the preceding year. The date above is the date of the meeting.

[*SPG/Jou/4*]

Journal of the SPG
1721/2 February 16

<195> At Bow Vestry 16th February 1721-2. [. . .]

<196> 3. Also that they had taken into consideration the Case of Mr. Urmstone late the Societys Missionary in North Carolina to them referr'd, and that it appeard to the Committee that Mr. Urmstone had leave to come home on the 16th of November 1716, but that Notice thereof (as he signifys in his Letter from thence) did not come to his hand till three years afterwards, after which time he used his endeavours to settle his Affairs to come over as soon as possible but as the Committee conceive without an Intention of returning; Whereupon the Committee agreed as their Opinion that the Society be moved to determine how far his Case comes within the Equity of the XVIII and XXI Rules relating to Missionaries. Agreed that forty pounds be given to Mr. Urmstone, in full of all demands he hath or may have on the Society. [. . .]

Minutes.

[*SPG/C/7*]

Rev. John Urmston to Secretary, SPG
1722 June 15

<67A>
Sir

Not being able to find employment here I must goe where it can be had and finding I cannot hope for health in this Climate, I am desirous of going to a warmer. I am afraid I shall have a lame acct. of my interest in North Carolina, which is very considerable and there being great want of a Minister in Bath County, in the Province aforesaid where Mr. Taylor was for a short time, I pray the Honorable Societie would be pleased to send me thither; being inclined to end my daies there; I am assur'd of being well received and am resolved and fully purposed to use all diligence and care to discharge my duty with a good Conscience as becometh Sir yr. most humble Servant.

Jno. Urmston

Attending at
the door June 15, 1722

[*Addressed*:]
To Davd. Humphreys Esqr.
Secretary to the Honorable Societie
for the Propagation of the Gospel in Foreign Parts.

[*Endorsed*:]
7
Mr. Urmstones Petition
15th June 1722

read and rejected

ALS. Read at a meeting of the SPG on June 15, 1722, when it was "Agreed that he be acquainted that the Society have provided for North Carolina and shall have no Occasion for his Service." Journal of the SPG, III, 222.

[*SPG/B/4*]

Rev. Thomas Newnam to Secretary, SPG
1722 June 29

<9> North Carolina. June the 29th 1722.

Sir

After a long and fatigueing Voyage of above 4 Months from Decembr. the 1st to April the 10th my self and little family (bless'ed be God) are safely arriv'd at Carolina. The late Governor Eden being dead, I thought it my Duty then to waite upon the President[1] (who is a very Worthy Gentleman) and communicate my affairs to him; he read my Credentialls, declar'd himself well satisfied and received us with all imaginable respect. He has settled me where I hope to be able to do abundance of Good: as for Labour I shall spare none, (God granting me health) as is Evident from the Journeys, the Vestrymen have already laid out for me. The 1st Sunday, I preach going by Water and Land some few Miles at Esqr. Duckenfeild's House large enough to hold a great Congregation, till we have built a Church which is hereafter to be call'd Society Church; and in order to it we are now Making a Collection thro' the Whole Parish. The 2d Sunday, I take a Journey up to a Place call'd Maherin, about 40 Miles off, where there are abundance of Inhabitants, who also are making a Collection to build a Chappel forthwith. 3d Sunday, I perform Divine Service again at Esqr. Duckenfeild's. 4th Sund. I go up to a place call'd Wicacon about 30 Miles Journey. 5th Sund. I cross the Sound to go to Eden Town, where the Vestry there have also purpos'd to have a Church built out of hand. 6th Sund. I go to the Chappell upon the South shore, about 12 Miles by Water and so the 7th Sund. begin again ut supra; except once every Quarter, I go up to a Place called Ronoke about 80 Miles Journey. And the 5 last Sundays of the Year, the Vestrys do give me that I may go my Rounds and visit the remote parts of the Country, where the Inhabitants live some 150 Miles off: people who will scarcely ever have the Opportunity of hearing me or having their Children baptis'd, unless I go to and amongst them. The people in Generall are well pleas'd with my Coming, and are not willing to lose any Opportunity of being Instructed; for all our Congregations are very full and numerous: they are indeed (I mean the Inferiour Sort) very Ignorant, and by Consequence liable to any Impression made upon them; but at present, we are not apprehensive of any Danger of their being seduc'd or brought over to any Sect: because we have very few Dissenters of any Sort amongst us. There are Some Scatterring Quakers about us but I hope there will never be such a Number of them as able to do the least Mischeif. As for Rom. Catholicks, we have not I beleive of that Perswasion 12 in the Government. So that with care and pains I am in great hopes, we shall ever have the Liturgy of the Church of England perfectly establish'd amongst us without Interruption from any Quarter by Sectaries of any kind whatever. The Indians at present are not very numerous, not exceeding 300 fighting men, they live in 2 Towns by themselves, very quiet and peaceable; but as to the Converting them to the Christian Faith, it is a thing that I almost despair of ever seeing effected whilst amongst them. The Number of Children, I have baptiz'd are 193. Boys 102. Girls 91. five of which were adult Persons at least 20 Years of Age and 2 of which were married Women; they could give but very little Account of their Faith: I gave them all the Assistance I could, recommending a few of the Societies Books to them. As to Marriages, I have but little Business in this Affair, by reason People live at a great distance from me and cannot afford time as well as Expence to waite upon me; so that they go to the Justices of Peace in their Neighbourhoods, who are by an Act of Assembly priviledg'd to perform that Office. As to Burialls we have but very few, and those I cannot conveniently all attend being sometimes 60, 80 and 100 Miles off. This is all the Account that can at present be given of our Ecclesiastick Constitution here by Sir Your most Obedient and Humble Servant.

Thos. Newnam

My Humble Duty to the Society.

[*Addressed*:]
To The Secretary of the Honourable
Society for the Propagation of the Gospel
in Foreign Parts, to be left at the Archbishop
of Canterbury's Library at St. Martin's London
These

[*Endorsed:*]
Mr. Newnam. No. Carolina
June 29th 1722.

ALS.

[1]Thomas Pollock.

[*SPG/SAP*]

Report
1722/3 February 15

<49> <*An Abstract of the Proceedings of the Society*.> [. . .] The Reverend Mr. *Newnam*, in *North-Carolina*, [advises] That he officiates at six or seven Places in that Government, where he has very full and numerous Congregations; that the People in general are well pleased at his coming amongst them, and are not willing to lose any Opportunity of being instructed; that he has baptized 193 since his Arrival there, five of which were at least twenty Years of Age, and two of them married Women. [. . .]

Printed. Extracted from the yearly publication containing the sermon preached at the annual anniversary meeting of the SPG, together with a review of the activities of the Society and its missionaries during the preceding year. The date above is the date of the meeting.

[*SPG/B/4*]

Rev. Thomas Newnam to Secretary, SPG
1723 May 9

North Carolina May the 9th 1723.

Sir

Since my last Letter to you dated June the 29th 1722 I and my little Family have laboured under a severe fitt of Sickness the Feaver and Ague commonly known by the name of the Seasonings incident to all new Comers here; it holding me from the beginning of August to the latter end of December made me incapable in the mean time of performing my Duty as I could have wish'd; but by the blessing of God we are all now Perfectly recovered, and I have pursued my Journeys since to the severall respective places as usuall: but I intend in a short time to confine my Self a little more to the Town[1] than I have done for I find that place does now more immediately require my particular Attendance, it beginning to grow very populous: All the Publick Officers being oblig'd by an Act of Assembly to reside there will occasion it to be the very Seat of Government; and I am also desir'd by the President and the rest of the Gentlemen to settle there my Self, but at the same time so as not to neglect other places, which will very much want my

Assistance till some other Gentleman is sent by the Society to supply those more distant parts and in order to give a Generall Satisfaction I shall reserve a Sufficient and Seasonable time of the year, (it being extremely troublesome to travell far in this hott Country in the Summer Season) that I may visit the most remote Quarters. For whilst I am well and in health I will never be remiss in doing my Duty and giving Satisfaction to the people. Since my last Account sent June the 29th of the No. of Children baptiz'd, I have baptiz'd two hundred and Sixty nine more, whereof Boys 120, Girls, 149 besides 1 adult woman 3 adult men, who gave me a very good Account of their Faith, and 2 Negroes who could say the Creed, the Lord's prayer and 10 Commandments and gave good Sureties for their further Information. Tho we have a great Number of Quakers, yet I live very quiet and peacsable and undisturb'd by them, the Government here not countenancing them any further than they well can avoid: the No. of Dissenters here is inconsiderable and those of the Roman Persuasion very Small. We waite the Arrival of our New Governour,[2] and then I hope to see here a large and beautifull Brick Church go forward; at present indeed all things seem to stand in Statu quo with relation to Church Buildings as they did when I first arrived; by reason the Publick Buildings are now in hand such as the Courthouse the Councill room prison etc. but as soon as these are finished, I am persuaded that there'll be not one but what will readily and willingly contribute his part towards a beautifull Church The Number of Titheables here and the Levies generally Laid upon them, I hope to be better able to acquaint you with per the next.

This last Easter I administred the B. Sacrament to those who thought themselves fit Communicants; indeed the Number was very small but I hope against the next Opportunity to find persons better disposed. To morrow I do designe to sett out for Bath County where I am Greatly Wanting, there are at least as I am inform'd 300 Children waiting my Coming among them to be baptiz'd, it is some Years since the late Mr. Urmstone visited those parts which now occasions greater Labour and paines to be taken by myself.

We are in the utmost peace and tranquillity meeting with no Disturbance from the Indians within (who indeed are very inconsiderable for their Number) and enjoying a flourishing a Trade abroad.

This is the State of our Affairs here and as Soon as any thing Materiall offerrs it shall be Communicated to you by Sir Yr. most Humble Servant

Tho. Newnam

[*Addressed:*]
To The Secretary of the Honorable Society for
Propagating the Gospel in forreign
parts to be left at the Archibishop of
Canterbury's Library at St. Martins. Westminster
These

[*Endorsed:*]
<3>
Mr. Newnam

North Carolina May 9th
1723

Entered

ALS.

[1]Edenton, named in honor of Governor Charles Eden (1673-1722). A town was authorized to be laid off at the site in 1712, and the first lot was sold in 1714. The settlement was known as the Town on Queen Anne's Creek until 1722. Powell, *Gazetteer*.

[2]George Burrington (ca. 1682-1759), originally from Devonshire, was an officer in the army before being appointed governor of North Carolina by the Lords Proprietors in February, 1722/3. He arrived in January of the following year, and his disputatious nature led to stormy political confrontations throughout his tenure. He was replaced by Sir Richard Everard after only eighteen months, but returned in February, 1730/1, as first governor of the royal colony of North Carolina. His service to the crown was also punctuated by bitter conflict, and in November, 1734, his successor, Gabriel Johnston, arrived in the province and assumed the governorship. *DNCB*.

[*SS* 853]

Will
1723 September 21

North Carolina sc. In Dei Nomine amen.

I Thomas Newnam Clerk now residing at Edenton in North Carolina as Missionary from the Honorable the Society for Propogating the Gospell in Forreign parts being Sick and weak in body but of Sound and perfect memory Blessed be Allmighty God Doe make and Ordaine this my Last Will and Testament in manner and forme following. That is to Say

<*Imprimis.*> I committ my Soule into the hands of God who gave it and my body to the earth to be decently interrd, at the discretion of my Executrix herein afternamed and as to Such worldly Estate as it hath pleased God to bless me withall (my Debts and funerall Expences being first fully Satisfied and paid) I give Devise and Bequeath the Same both reale and personall be it of what nature or kind soever or where Soever either within this Government of North Carolina or within the Kingdom of Great Brittaine or Elsewhere, and whether the same be in my possession, or in Expectation or Reversion, by Legacys, or otherwise due or to become due, unto my Loving Wife Frances Newnam and to her Heirs Executors Administrators and Assignes for Ever.

And I do hereby nominate constitute and appoynt my Loving Wife Frances Newnam my Sole and whole Executrix of this my last Will and Testament hereby revoking all former and other Wills by me made.

In Testimony whereof I have hereunto Sett my hand and Seale this twenty first day of September Anno Domini One thousand Seven hundred and twenty three.

Tho. Newnam

Signd, Seald, publisht, Declard
to be the last Will and Testament of

Thomas Newnam in the presence of Us.

C. Gale
Sarah Lloyd
John Fryars

North Carolina sc.

Memorandum: the aforewritten Will was duly proved by the Oaths of Sarah Lloyd and John Fryars before me this 22d day of Novr. Anno Domini 1723.

C. Gale C.J.

DS. An attested copy of this will was read at a meeting of the SPG on August 21, 1724. Journal of the SPG, IV, 318.

[*SPG/A/17*]

"Vestry of Edenton" to Secretary, SPG
1723 November 18

<111> Vestry of Eden Town[1] to the Secretary.

North Carolina Novr. 18th 1723.

Sir

This brings you the melancholly News of Your worthy Missionary Mr. Newnams Death, on whose Charrector and prudent Deportment we shou'd think it our Duty to be here in very particular did not the resolve of this days Vestry (Copy whereof is herewith enclosed) sufficiently shew our Concern for so great a Loss which Ocasions us again to be petitioners to Your Honorable Body that You wou'd still continue Your favors towards us by filling that vacancy with some person of equall Meritt and unblameable conversation a thing to be wished for rather than expected.

We heart'ly recomend his Widow to Your Consideration of her Slender Circumstances occasion'd by the endeavors he was making to settle himself amongst us the Circumstances of our parish not admitting us to do more then what We have done and so not doubting but the same Charitable disposition which has hitherto occasion'd Your particular notice of us will so continue that Religious worship <112> within this province may wholy owe its advance to Your benign Influence. We have not now one Clergyman in the whole province tho' it consists of eleven parishes, which unhappy State is humbly Submitted to the Consideration of the Honorable Society by Nich. Crisp Jno. Jordan Tho. Luten Saml. Pagett Jno. Blunt Henry Bonner Thos. Garrett Junior W. Badham Thos. Rowntree C. Gale E. Moseley Ad. Cockburne.

Mr. Newman died Novr. 6th 1723.

At a Vestry held at Edenton for the North Parish of Chowan the 18 day of Novr. 1723.

Present Thos. Garret Junior Church Warden. The Honorable Colonell Xtopher Gale, Colonell Edwd. Moseley, Major Thomas Luton, Captain Nicholas Crisp, Captain

Henry Bonner, Capt. Saml. Paget, Mr. Thomas Rountree, Adam Cockburn Esqr. and Mr. William Badham.

The Reverend Mr. Newnam Missionary having officiated but the one halfe Year and being departed this Life, the Vestry in Consideration of the said Mr. Newnams pious and good behavor during the time of his Mission among us, and also being willing to Contribute towards the accomodation of his Widdows intended voyage to Great Brittain.

It is order'd That the whole Years Sallary be paid to his Widow notwithstanding his decease.

Copy. Read at a meeting of the SPG on September 18, 1724. Journal of the SPG, V, 4.

[1]Properly speaking, this letter was from the vestry of the Northeastern Parish of Chowan Precinct.

[SPG/A/17]

**Proceedings of the General Assembly
1723 November 20**

<158> Minutes of the Assembly in No. Carolina. Novr. 20th 1723. Relating to Mrs. Newnam. Began 4th day of Novr. 1723. Held at Edenton In the upper House. Present The Honorable Wm. Reed Esqr. President etc. Christopher Gale, Richd. Sanderson, John Lovick, Thos. Pollock, Maur. Moore, Esqrs. Lords proprietors Deputies. <159> Wednesday Novr. 20th.

Then Was read the following Resolve from the Lower House Videlicet.

This House taking into Consideration the Case of Mrs. Newnam the Widow of the Reverend Mr. Newnam Missionary late decd. designed to depart this Government for Great Brittaine and being willing to Contribute towards her better accomodation in her intended Voyage.

Resolved

That the Summ of £40 be paid by the publick Treasurer to the said Mrs. Newnam.

Sent to the upper house for their Concurence per order of the House.

R. Hicks Cler. Dom. Con.

Which being read was Concurr'd with and then the following messuage was sent to the lower house Videlicet

Mr. Speaker and Gentlemen of the house of Burgises.

Your Resolve for Assisting the late Widow of the late Missionary Mr. Newnam hath the intire Concurrence of this House.

J. Lovick Secretary

Minutes. This document was enclosed in the letter from John Lovick to the secretary to the SPG, November 28, 1723, below.

[*SPG/A/17*]

John Lovick to Secretary, SPG
1723 November 28

<113> Mr. Lovick to the Secretary.

North Carolina Novr. 28th 1723

Sir
On the 5th of this Instant our Missionary The Reverend Mr. Newnam departed this life and left this poor unhappy Country consisting of above 10000 Christian Souls without one Minister of the Gospel, so that we are intirely deprived of any Spiritual Comfort, Mr. Newnam was a person whose behavor in his holy Station was very examplary and Blameless and he was very agreeable to the People, The poor Gent. hath left a Widdow amongst us in circu'stances indifferent enough but the parish where he resided to Shew their Gratitude to the decd. as well as to follow the Example of So truly pious and Christian Society as the Gentlemen that sent him hither are, have order'd the Widow the whole Years Salary tho' when he died he had not officiated above five Months and had been incapable of performing Divine Service most of that time, And our assembly upon my representing to them the Case of the poor Widdow unanimously voted her £40 towards forwarding her voyage home to her Friends, a Copy of which order, as well as the vestrys resolve, is now sent You, which I beg you'l lay before the Honorable Society, and at the same time recommend the Deplorable Condition of this Country to them, and as we have often experienced their goodness and Care of us, So I doubt not of their Charitable Care and assistance now, I humbly intreat You'l present my Duty, and give me leave to Assure You I am with the greatest truth and Esteem Sir your most obedient etc.
J. Lovick

Copy. Read at a meeting of the SPG on September 18, 1724. Journal of the SPG, V, 4. Enclosed in this document was the extract from the journal of the assembly dated November 20, 1723, above.

[*LAM/FUL/VI*]

Memorandum
ca. 1724
John Baptista Ashe to Rev. William Tredwell Bull [Extract]
1723 April 6

<213> Memorandum Concerning the Endowment of the Church In North Carolina.

It appears by Doctor Trott's Collection of the Laws of America relating to the Church etc.[1] page 84.

That the Province of North Carolina is devided into Nine Precincts or Parishes, <*In Some letters to the Society lately come from thence, 'tis Said there are Eleven Parishes.*> and that the Church Wardens and Vestry Men of Each Parish are empowered to procure an able and Godly minister qualified according to the Ecclesiastical Laws of England and to raise for him such an yearly Stipend as they shall think Convenient so as Such Summ or Stipend be not less than fifty pounds, and that in the raising thereof and all other Parish Charges the whole do not exceed five shillings per pole on all the taxable inhabitants in the Parish.

They are also impowered to purchase lands for a Glebe and to build a Church, and one or more Chapels in every Parish or Precinct and the same as often as need shall repair.

N.B. It doth not appear by any Accounts yet come to the Society, that there any Glebes purchased, or any Churches or Chapels built.

The said five shillings per pole is in the Currency of that Province, and at present not worth above Eighteen pence Sterling, altho' at the passing of the Law <*N.B. The Law was passed in the year 1715. Charles Eden Esqr. Governor*> it was <214> of the value of three shillings and four pence, or at least so intended; and if this deficiency was made good, or the five Shillings advanced to Sterling, It would be but a very moderate Tax, and yet afford such a comfortable subsistence for a Single Person as might be Sufficient encouragement to worthy Persons to accept of a Mission thither.

Extract of a Letter from John-Baptist Ashe[2] Esqr. dated Bath in No. Carolina April 6th 1723. To the Reverend Mr. Bull[3] in So. Carolina, which not coming to hand before Mr. Bull left Carolina, lay so long in the hands of his Correspondent, that 'twas [not] received 'till but about the month of June 1724.

You desire me to give you an Acct. of the State of Religion in this Province. My Time is too short at present, let it suffice to say, that we are almost altogether destitute of Ministry, having only one Parish in the whole Province Supplied, viz. by the Reverend Mr. John Newnam. It would be a christian charitable Action to represent (as you well know how) our case hence of which I shall give you a much larger acct. quickly, to those who are capable and well disposed to assist such as are indeed both very ignorant, and very negligent and wanting to themselves, as to what may conduce to their future happiness.

[*Endorsed*:]
Endowment of the
Church in N. Carolina
Bull
A Letter from Mr. Ashe
of N. Car. to Mr. Bull
1723

D. Presumably this document was prepared for the bishop of London.

[1]Nicholas Trott (1663-1740) was a South Carolinian who served as attorney general, chief justice, and speaker of the Commons House of Assembly. *DAB*. The work referred to is *Laws of the British Plantations in America Relating to the Church and the Clergy, Religion and Learning*..., 1721.

[2]John Baptista Ashe (d. 1734), large landowner and holder of various important offices, including speaker of the assembly and member of the council. *DNCB.*

[3]Rev. William Tredwell Bull (1683-1738) served as second commissary of the Carolinas from ca. 1719 to 1723. He resided in Charleston. George W. Williams, ed., "Letters to the Bishop of London from the Commissaries in South Carolina," *South Carolina Historical Magazine*, 78 (January, 1977), 11, 16.

[*SPG/C/7*]

Richard Hewitt to SPG
[1724]

Most Worthy and Honoured Sirs

It being notify'd to me That this Honourable Society are determin'd to send some [*illegible*] selfe to this Society's favour I being resolv'd in all things to Obey yr. Orders If I'm thought worthy to be employ'd in so good and pious a Work. I humbly hope that Testimonials from my Lord of Londn. of my being already ordaind Deacon by his Lordship and shall, by Gods Admission, recieve Priest's Orders on Sunday next. I am Honour'd Gentlemen yr. Honours most Dutifull and most Faithfull Servant.

Richd. Hewitt

[*Endorsed*:]
Mr. Richard Hewitts
Certificate. 1724

ALS.

[*SPG/A/18*]

Power of Attorney
1724 March 26

<105> Mrs. Newnams Power of Attorney to Mr. Lovick.

Know all Men by these presents that I Frances Newnam Relict Widdow and Sole Executrix of the last Will and Testament of Thomas Newnam Clerk Missionary from the honorable the Society for propagating the Gospel in Foreign Parts, have Constituted ordained and made and by these presents Do Constitute ordain and make and in my Stead put Hugh George Lovick of the City of London in the Kingdom of Great Britaine Haberdasher to be my true sufficient and lawful attorney for me and in my Name and Stead and to my use to ask demand Sue for recover and receive of and from any person or persons whatsoever the same shall or may Concern any Sum or Sums of money Debts goods Wares Merchandize effects and things whatsoever and wheresoever especially any Sum or Sums of money or Salary that shall appear to be due from the honorable the Society for propagating the Gospel in foreign parts to the said Thomas Newnam Missionary as aforesaid Giving and hereby Granting unto my <106> said attorney My full and whole power Strength and Authority to ask demand Sue for recover and receive any Legacy or Legacies or shall hereafter become due to the said Thoms. Newnam decd. and the same to receive for me in my aforesaid Capacity and to take and use all due Course and process in the Law for the obtaining and recovering of the same and receipts thereof in my Name to make Seal and execute and for the premisses to appear and the person of me the Constituent to represent before any Judge Minister or officer in the Law whatsoever in any Court of Judicature and there in my behalf to answer defend and reply unto all Actions Causes matters and things whatsoever relating to the premisses with full power to make and Substitute one or more Attorneys under him my said Attorney and the same againe at pleasure to revoke and Generally to say do act Transact Determine accomplish and finish all matters and things whatsoever relating to the premisses as fully amply and Effectually to all Intents and purposes as I my Self ought or cou'd do if personally present altho' the matter should require more especial Authority than is herein Comprized. I the said Constituent Ratifying allowing and holding firm and Valid all and whatsoever my said Attorney or his Substitutes shall lawfully do or cause to be done in and about the premisses by Virtue hereof, In Witness whereof, I have hereunto set my hand and Seal the 26th day of March Anno Domini 1724.

Frances Newnam (Seal)

Signed Sealed and
Delivered in presence of us (The word Hugh being first interlined)
D. Beckman
Forster

<107> No. Carolina ss. George Burrington Esqr. Governor Captain General and Admiral of the said province.

To all to whom these presents shall come or may Concerne. Greeting.

These may Certify that Mrs. Frances Newnam widow and Relict of the Reverend Mr. Thomas Newnam late Missionary in this province did in my presence and in the presence of the persons who are Evidences Sign Seal and execute the annexed procuration or power of Attorney for the uses therein mentioned.

In Testimony whereof I have hereunto set my and Caused the Seal of the Colony to be affixed at Edenton the 26th day of March Anno Domini 1724, and in the tenth Year of his Majesties Reign.

Geo. Burrington

Lovick Secretary

Copy.

[*SPG/Jou/4*]

Journal of the SPG
1724 August 21

<317> 21st August 1724 [...]

<319> 10. An Abstract of a Letter from Mr. Moseley dated Chowan in North Carolina 3d Febry. 1723[1] was read advising that he hath sent a bill of Exchange of Ten pounds Sterling to the Secretary of the Society which he desires may be laid out to purchase 12 Common Prayer books of about 2*s*.6*d*. each. 12 Whole Dutys of Man about the same Price, 12 Dr. Nichols <320> Paraphrase on the Common Prayer and 12 Dr. Hornecks great Law of consideration together with some of Bishop Beveridges Sermons of the usefullness of the Common Prayer, Dorringtons familiar Guid and such like helps and that they should be markt with the Impression of the Societys Seal, and wrote upon, to be lent in the North East Parish of Chowan and be deliver'd to the twelve Vestrymen for the use of themselves and neighbours. That he has inclosed a Catalogue[2] of some books which he desires the Society to accept of towards forming a Provincial Library at Edenton on Queen Annes Creek, and hopes the Society will readily promote so usefull and necessary a work, by sending such Books as they shall think fit for that purpose. That if the Society would be pleas'd to employ £150 per Annum towards the support of three Missionaries in that Government it would be as usefull a peice of their Charity as could be, and that fifty pounds together with the Allowance given by their Laws (seldom less than fifty pounds per annum their money) and other advantages they generally have would make a handsome Living and such as with good and frugal management, something might be annually laid up by them: and in such Case he proposes that they should be settled as follows; One for Bath County, another for that part of Albemarle County lying to the Westward of Little River, and a third for that part lying to the Eastward of Little River, which would make the Division near equal, and tho' they resided chiefly in one part of their division, yet by frequent visiting the rest they might give abundance of Satisfaction and receive <321> large Gratuities for such their Visits, and might have at least £100 Per Annum that money each for their Sundays Service only; the People being very ready to assist, and to do all the good Offices in their power to a Minister who behaves himself well.

The Secretary now acquainting the Board that he has provided the Books desired by Mr. Moseley:[3] Order'd that the Impression of the Societys Seal be put thereto, and that a Letter be wrote to Mr. Mosely to know whether, if the Society comply with his Proposal of sending three Ministers, they may be assured of the whole Salary allow'd by the Government for the support of a Minister in each Parish, tho' he shall alternately officiate in several Parishes; and agreed that a Missionary be in the mean time sent in the room of the late Mr. Newnam deceased. [...]

Minutes.

[1]Not located.

[2]This document is printed in Saunders, *Colonial Records*, II, 583-584, where it is stated to be "From [the] North Carolina Letter Book of [the] S.P.G." A few years later, in 1896, it was also printed in the *Annual Report of the American Historical Association for the Year 1895*, 189-191, in the article "Libraries and Literature of North Carolina." The author of the article, Stephen B. Weeks, asserted that "The list has come down to us woefully corrupted by carelessness and ignorance of copyists," and in this corrupted form had been printed in the *Colonial Records*. Weeks then went on to state that Rt. Rev. Joseph Blount Cheshire, Jr., bishop of North Carolina, with the assistance of Rev. John Humphrey Barbour, former librarian of Trinity College, Hartford, had "corrected and annotated" the list, and that the corrected version was the one printed in Weeks's article. It is not made clear whether it was based on an examination of the original list or on inferences made from the list

as printed by Saunders. In any event, the document appears to be no longer among the records of the SPG. The following is the version printed by Weeks.

FOLIOS.

Pool, Matthew. Synopsis Criticorum. 5 volumes.
Augustinus, S. Opera. Col. Agrip. 1616. 10 volumes.
Sanchez (or Sanctius), Caspar. In quartuor libros Regum. Lugd., 1623.
—In Jeremiam. Lugd., 1618.
—In Ezechielem. Lugd., 1619.
[Polanus, Amandus?] Syntagma theologiae Christianae. [Hanoviae, 1615?]
Leigh, Edward. Body of Divinity, in 10 books. 1654 or 1662.
Deodatus, Giovanni. Annotations on the Holy Bible. Lond., 1648.
Eusebias, Socrates, Evagrius; Ecclesiastical Histories of. [Camb., 1683 or 1692?]
Simson, Patrick. History of the Church. [Third edition, London, 1634?]
Cartwright, Thomas. Harmonia Evangelica. [About 1630.]
Notationes in totam Scripturam Sacram.
[Fuller, Thos.?] Church History of Britain. [Lond., 1655.]
26 folio volumes.

QUARTOS.

Bilson, Bp. Thomas. True difference between Christian Subjection and unchristian rebellion. Oxon., 1585.
Ball, John. Answer to two treatises of Mr. John Carr, the first...Necessity of seperation [*sic*] from the Church of England....the other, a stay against straying;...unlawfulness of hearing the ministers of the Church of England. Lond., 1642.
Birkbeck, Simon. Protestant's Evidence. Lond., 1634.
Rainolds, John. De Romanae Ecclesiae Idolatria. Oxon., 1596.
Pierce, Thomas. The Sinner impleaded in his own Court. Lond., 1679.
Heinsius, Daniel. Exercitationes sacrae ad Novum Testamentum. Lugd., Bat., 1639; Camb., 1640.
Cartwright, Thomas. Commentarii in Proverbia Solomonis. Amst., 1638.
Usher, Achbp. James. Britanicarum Ecclesiarum Antiquitates. Dubl., 1639.
—Answer to a challenge made by a Jesuite. Dublin.
Buridan, John. Quaestiones super viii libros Politicarum Aristotelis. Oxon., 1640.
Prideaux, John. Fasciculus controversiarum Theologicarum. Oxon., 1652.
Ball, John. Friendly Trial of the grounds tending to Seperation [*sic*]. Camb., 1640.
12 quarto volumes.

OCTAVOS.

Francisco Le Rees. Cursus Philosophicus, 2 p.
Tertia Pars Sum. Philos & quarta.
Piccolominaeus. Universa Philos. de Moribus.
Davidis Parei Exercitationes Philosophicae.
Buxtorf's Lexicon.
Dialogue in answer to a Popish Catechism.
Augustinus (S.). De Civitate Dei, 2 vols.
Greek Grammar.
Hunnius; De Scripto Dei Verbo.&c.
—Comment. in Evang. secundum S. Matt.
Eustachii a Sancto Paulo Summa Philosophiae quadripartita.
Scheibleri Liber Comment. Topicorum.
Schiekard's Horologium Hebraicum.
Melancthonis Chronicon Carionis.
Calvin's Institutiones Christianae Religionis.
Davidis Parei Corpus Doctrinae Christianae.
Aristotelis Organon.
Heckerman's Systema S. S. Theologica.
—Systema Logica.
Leusden's Clavis Graeca Novi Testamenti.
Baronii Metaphysica Generalis.
Dounam's Comment. in Jet. Rami Dialect [?].

Joh. Regii Commentarii ac Disputationes Logacae.
Sallii Ethica.
Buxtorf's Epitome Gramatices Hebraeae.
Heyselbein's Theoria Logica.
Amesius de Divina Predestinatione.
Baronis. Annales Ecclesiasticae.
Hugo Grotius. Defensio Fidei Catholicae.
Augustini (S.) Confessiones.
Amesii Medulla Theologica.
—Rescriptio Scolastica ad Grevinchovium de Redemptione Generali.
—Technometria.
Wendelini Christiana Theologia.
Lactantii Divinae Institutiones.
Petri Cunaei de Republica Hebraeorum.
Hebrew Psalter.
38 octavo volumes.

This list as printed in Saunders is followed by what obviously is the body of a letter, but the addressee and writer are not stated, nor is the date or source. The letter, which Weeks said was included among the records of the SPG with a date of 1725, is no longer there. The document as rendered by Saunders is as follows:

"In the year 1720 Mr. Edwd. Moseley sent a bill of Exchange for 10£ Sterlg. to the Secy. of the Honble. Society drawn by their Missionary The Revd. Mr. Urmstone & it was his desire that that sum should be laid out in the following Books and that they should be marked with the impression of the Society's Seal & wrote upon; ""To be lent to the Northeast Parish of Chowan"" & they should be delivered out to the 12 Vestrymen for the use of themselves & Neighbours—viz.—

"12 Common prayer Books of about 2/6 each
"12 Whole duty of [M]an near the same Price
"12 Dr Nicholl's Paraphrase on the Common Prayer
"12 Dr. Horneck's Great Law of Consideration
"Bishop Beveridges' Sermons of the usefulness of Common Prayer and such like helps.

"But my friend receiving no account of what was done in this affair he wrote again to the Secry. in April 1723 with a second bill of the Draught, with request to the Secry. that the money should be laid out in the books afore mentioned, or such as should be judge most useful, & he also sent a catalogue of such books as he had purchased desiring the Honble. Society would be pleased to accept of them towards a Provincial Library for the Govt. of North Carolina to be kept at Edenton, which is the Metropolis of that Province. But has never to this day had any intelligence from the Secretary of the Society altho' they have had the Revd. Mr. Newnam their Missry. come amongst them since his first letter & their Govr. since his last."

[3]Nothing more is known of this library. As this passage makes plain, the Society responded favorably to Edward Moseley's request, thereby proving erroneous the statement of Weeks that "We have, unfortunately, no evidence that the generous gift of Moseley was ever accepted by the Society." Weeks is, however, correct in noting that the absence of any relevant provincial legislation suggests strongly that no public lending library ever eventuated from the Moseley gifts of money and books. More problematical, however, is Weeks's hypothesis that the volumes offered by Moseley were from a variety of sources: books brought into the province by Moseley on his first arrival; part of the library of Rev. James Adams; Rev. John Urmston's missionary library; and a portion of the library at Bath. Stephen B. Weeks, "Libraries and Literature in North Carolina," *Annual Report of the American Historical Association for the Year 1895*, 192-193.

[*SPG/C/7*]

Th. Bradley to Bishop of London
1724 August 22

Bolingbrooke, Aug. 22nd, 1724.

My Lord,

I have by this days Post, a Letter from Mr. Hewit late Schoolmaster here wherein He compleins of the Misfortune of being out of Business at present. He tells me he [*illegible*] to yr. Ld.Ships and you were pleas'd to encorege him to believe that you'd use yr. Good Endeavours to promote him, provided, I cou'd give a good Account of him during the time of his being here.

My Ld. I can give you Testimony in the behalf of Mr. Hewit that he was a Master very well approv'd of by the Parish Neighbourhood, Sober and industrious and otherwise qualify'd to the general Content of Such as he had to deal with in quality of Schoomaster; if the concurrent Testimony of the Gentlemen and Clergy in the Neighbourhood may be of further Satisfaction to yr. Ld.Ships I make no difficulty to procure [*illegible*] in the behalf of Mr. Hewit; I only beg leave to add that I am, My Ld., your Lordships Most Oblig'd and Humble Servant.

Th[*illegible*] Bradley

Aug. 31st 1724
[*illegible*]
Given of Mr. [*illegible*]
Edmd.

[*Addressed*:]
To The Right Reverend Edmund Lord
Bishop of London in [*illegible*]

ALS.

[*SPG/Jou/5*]

Journal of the SPG
1724 October 16

<7> 16th October 1724 [. . .]

2. It was reported from the Committee that they had taken into consideration the Petition of the Vestry of King Williams Parish above the Falls of James River in Virginia, to them referr'd and the Secretary acquainted them that the Lord Bishop of London had recd. a Letter from the Governor of Virginia earnestly recommending the Case of the said Parish to the consideration of the Society; The Committee agreed to Report that it appears to them that the Society have not hitherto since their first establishment maintaind any Missionaries in the Governments of Maryland and Virginia, they having an establishment by Law for the Support of their Clergy and because there were poorer Governments unable to make a setled Provision for their Ministers, which the Society thought, ought first to be supply'd; and since the Society have intentions of establishing three Missionaries in North Carolina which whole Province is now entirely destitute of any Minister of the Church <8> of England, the Committee agreed to report as their Opinion that it may not be proper to engage in any new constant Expence for the support of a Missionary in

Virginia. Agreed to by the Society, but that Enquiry be made by the Committee whether that Parish has any Establishment by Act of Assembly. [. . .]

Minutes.

[*SPG/Jou/5*]

Journal of the SPG
1724 December 18

<18> 18 December 1724 [. . .]

<20> 9. Petitions of Mr. Walter Jones and Mr. Richard Hewitt offering their Service to be employed as Missionaries in North Carolina were read, and their Testimonials were also laid before the Board and read: Orderd that they read Prayers and Preach on the 8th Verse of the 2d Psalm, upon the first Sunday in January, Mr. Jones at 10 in the forenoon at Mr. Spatemans Church, in the hearing of the Master of the Charterhouse and Mr. Spateman; and Mr. Hewitt at St. Michael Basishaw in the afternoon in the hearing of Dr. Mayo and Mr. Baker. [. . .]

Minutes.

[*SPG/SAP*]

Report
1724/5 February 19

<37> <*An Abstract of the Proceedings of the Society*.> [. . .] From *North-Carolina* it has been represented, That there are eleven Parishes in that Province, containing near ten thousand <38> Christian Souls, without one Minister of the Gospel to officiate among them. [. . .]

Printed. Extracted from the yearly publication containing the sermon preached at the annual anniversary meeting of the SPG, together with a review of the activities of the Society and its missionaries during the preceding year. The date above is the date of the meeting.

[*SPG/Jou/5*]

Journal of the SPG
1724/5 February 19

<27> At Bow Vestry Fryday the 19th of February 1724 [. . .]

<33> 15. Mr. Shelton[1] Secretary to the Lords Proprietors of Carolina attended and being called in laid before the Board a Clause in their Charter[2] whereby the Right of

Nomination to the several Parishes in Carolina is vested in the said Lords Proprietors, and recommended from their Lordships the Reverend Mr. Barnes[3] and the Reverend Mr. Blacknall[4] to be <34> sent over as Missionaries to North Carolina, and desired the Society would be pleased to make them Annual Allowance: Mr. Shelton was acquainted that the Society are ready to receive any Proposal from the said Lords Proprietors signifying what Salary shall be allow'd by the Government or People of North Carolina to the Missionaries which may be sent thither in order to the Societys appointing a Salary for their further Support. [. . .]

Minutes. At a meeting of the Lords Proprietors on February 17, 1724/5, "Two Clergemen attended to desire their Lordships Recommendation to the Bishop of London to be sent to North Carolina." The proprietors then "Ordered that the Secretary attend the board for the Propagation of the Gosple, and in the Lds. Proprietors' Names to recommend the abovesd. Clergymen to be sent to N. Carolina." CO 5/292, 150.

[1]Richard Shelton, secretary to the Lords Proprietors from 1709 to 1727. Paschal, "Proprietary North Carolina," 148.

[2]The charter of 1665 from King Charles II to the Lords Proprietors included a grant of "the Patronages and Advowsons of all the Churches and Chapels which...shall happen hereafter to be erected." Parker, *Charters and Constitutions*, 92.

[3] Not identified.

[4]Rev. John Blacknall. See appendix.

[*SPG/Jou/5*]

Journal of the SPG
1725 April 16

<39> 16 April 1725 [. . .]

3. It was reported from the Committee that Sir Richard Everard[1] Governor of North Carolina being present acquainted them in pursuance of the Minute of the 19th February last, that the Lords Proprietors of Carolina have agreed to build a house and lay out 300 Acres of Land for a Glebe for a Minister of the Church of England to be sent over thither, and that what he is further to expect must arise from the Voluntary Contributions of the Inhabitants, and that Mr. Blacknall one of the Persons recommended by the Lords Proprietors attended, and the Committee apprehending they were not impowerd to admit him as a Missionary from the Society, they agreed to move the Society to make such Gratuity and Annual allowance <40> to the said Mr. Blacknall as they shall think proper. The Society taking this matter into consideration Agreed that a Salary of Fifty pounds Sterling per Annum be allowed to Mr. Blacknall from Ladyday last provisionally that he do Officiate every other Sunday at Edenton, and the other Sundays Alternately at the Two next Parishes; that he enjoy the full Allowance already setled by Act of Assembly on those Parishes, and that the People of Edenton do by a Voluntary Contribution raise twenty pounds Sterling Per Annum more: and Order'd that half a years Salary be advanced to him and that five pounds worth of Small Tracts and One dozen of Ostervalds Catechisms be given him. [. . .]

Minutes.

[1]Sir Richard Everard (1683-1733), an English baronet, was the last proprietary governor of North Carolina, serving from July, 1725, to February, 1730/1. *DNCB*.

[*SPG/B/4*]

Rev. Brian Hunt to [Francis Nicholson]
1725 May 12

Charles Town
S. Carolina
May 12 1725.

May it please your Excellency
Sir!

Having, with the rest of my brethren had large and Expected instances of your Excellencys regard and generosity to me as a clergyman of the Church of England, and a missionary to this province, for which I beg your Excellency to accept of my most humble thanks.

I am bold to entreat your Excellency to represent for me to the honorable the society that I having four Children and an encreasing family, and the allowance here not permitting to lay up any thing for them They would be pleas'd to remove me to North Carolina with the salary the allowd to their former Missionaries viz. 80 pounds sterling per annum. [. . .]

I am Sir,

Your Excellencys most [*illegible*]
[Brian Hunt][1]

ALS.

[1]Rev. Brian Hunt, a former Lincolnshire vicar and naval chaplain, came to South Carolina in 1722 and returned to England ca. 1728. Weis, *Colonial Clergy of Virginia, North Carolina and South Carolina*, 80.

[*SPG/A/19*]

Rev. Brian Hunt to Secretary, SPG
1725 May 12

<73> <15> Mr. Hunt to the Secretary.

St. Johns So. Carola.
May 12 1725

Reverend Sir

His Excellency our Governor Genl. Nicholson coming over to Engld. for a small time I took the opportunity which his Excellencys goodness offer'd to give my Duty to the Honorable Society and therewith the present Acct. of the State of St. John as follows.

The Church is in good repair, so is the Rectory house. On my representing to the Parishioners the necessity of the Minister for the time being his having Negro's as well to serve in the House as on the Glebe they were pleas'd to Subscribe for five one is dead the other 4 are well and one is employ'd in the kitchen and the other 3 in the field to raise Corn for my Familys support, they cost the parish in all £150 Sterling. I have at present about twenty five constant Comunicants. I preach once every Sunday and design to begin to Catechise the Children next Sunday after Whitsontide as I did last Year, Sir altho I like my parish very well and many of the Parishioners have been very kind to me yet the Salary here and at home not admitting of my laying up any money for my numerous Family, I humbly beg leave to be remov'd to North Carola. (which province we are here inform'd wants a Missionary) providing the honorable Society please to allow me the same Salary as they did to their former Missionarys which was £80 Sterling per annum. If my honorable Masters please to indulge me in this request I believe I may be able to lay up somewhat for my poor little ones and whenever I remove hence I shall have the Satisfaction of leaving St. Johns in a better Condition for the Support of a missionary than any other of this province. If the honorable Society have any other Mission <74> more advantagious for a Missionary with (as mine is) a large Family I am willing to serve to any such place they please to appoint me, I humbly beg your Interest in my favor and am Reverend Sir Your most respectful humble Servant.

Brian Hunt

ALS. Read at a meeting of the SPG on August 20, 1725, when it was agreed to accept the recommendation of the Committee that "the Society do not send any Missionaries at present to North Carolina." Journal of the SPG, V, 53.

[*SPG/A/19*]

Secretary of the SPG to Rev. Brian Hunt
1725 October 2

<116> <6> To the Reverend Mr. Hunt at St. John's.

London October 2d 1725

Reverend Sir

I have laid before the Society your Letter to them dated St. Johns So. Carolina the 12th of May 1725 wherein you desire them to remove you from your present Cure, to North Carolina, with the Allowance of £80 per Annum, given to former Missionaries. The Society have order'd me to acquaint you, that they do not intend at present to send any

Missionaries to North Carolina, and therefore they cannot condescend to your request. I am etc.

D. H.

Copy.

[*LAM/FUL/VI*]

Affidavit
1725 December 3

<215> North Carolina ss.

On this Third day of December *1725*, Before me Edward Moseley Personally came and Appeared George Burrington Esqr. who on his Oath on the Holy Evangelists taken Saith That on Monday the 22d of November last The Reverend Mr. Thomas Baylye[1] came to this Deponents Lodgeings in Edenton and told this Deponent that Christopher Gale Esqr. Chiefe Justice of this Province had granted a Warrant against him, and that he was then in Custody of a Constable, and desired him, to go with him before the Chiefe Justice, which he this Deponent readily did, That there present with the Said Chiefe Justice there in the House of Mr. William Badham in Edenton, Sir Richd. Everard Barronett Governor of North Carolina John Lovick Secretary and Others; That they Questioned the Aforemention'd Mr. Baylye concerning his preaching the Day before; to which Questions Mr. Baylye gave Modest Answers Notwithstanding the Said Sir Richard Everard Governor Christopher Gale Chiefe Justice and John Lovick Secretary did very much Insult the Said Mr. Baylye, treating him with Base and Scurrilous Language Such as this Deponent Saith he never heard given to a Clergyman by any Magistrate before. The Said Mr. Baylye was also threatned to be Sent to Prison if he would not give Security to appear at the General Court; And this Deponent verily believes they would have So Served him, if Bail had not been Given.

Geo. Burrington

Sworne Before me the Day and Year first Abovewritten.

E. Moseley

Also Arthur Goffe Esqr. Mr. James Winright and Mr. Jerome Armor came before me and made Oath that they were present at the Examination of the Reverend mr. Baylye in the above Deposition mentioned and they also give the like Testimony of the Treatment Mr. Baylye met with as mr. Burrington has above declared.

A. Goffe
Jams. Winright
Jer. Armor

Sworne Before me
E. Moseley

[*Endorsed:*]
Affidavitt relative to
Mr. Baylye 1725

Copy.

[1]Rev. Thomas Baylye. See appendix.

[*LAM/FUL/VI*]

Statement
ca. 1726

<224> The Ninth of November Sir Richard Everard came up to the house where I lived in Bertie precinct where I had Two dayes Conference with Sir Richard in my Own Chamber and Sir Richards discourse being Stuffd very much with Unusual Reflections on our late Governor Mr. Burrington; I Show'd a dislike whereupon Sir Richard took upon him with abundance of heat and Warmth to reflect upon my Selfe by telling me that I not only Stood precarious as a Minister here but that it was in his power to prevent me preaching here to the people. I humbly Answer'd him that I had done Nothing unbecomeing my Ministerial Function but had more diligently attended in the Precinct then any former Minister ever had done by Collecting more Numbers of People and Baptizeing more People and Children: neither had I been wanting to acquaint his honour in time of the Reasons of my Comeing to North Carolina, that the Vestry of Bertie Precinct had sent me an Invitatory letter with promises of great Encouragements which letter I shew'd to him and told him that before I sat down with them I Exhibited to our former Governor Mr. Burrington to Colonell Moseley and Divers Others of the Government when there was no Minister in the Government who together with the Publick approv'd of my Residence with them under which Governor I liv'd very peaceably and added there was many People daily at Church. Upon which Sir Richard became more moderate but still levelling his discourse against Mr. Burrington. I Express'd an Uneasieness by telling him that I knew of no harm of Mr. Burrington and that I could not Speak with Other Mens Tongues and I told Sir Richard that if I could not Obtain his Countenance without Speaking Evill of any man that I know no Evil of I must despair of Obtaining it. Sir Richard then was very Calm and Invited me and my Wife to his house at Edenton accordingly the Monday following I Set out for Edenton, and Arriv'd there Thursday Morning. The Saturday following I met with the Reverend Mr. Blacknall. I asked leave of his pulpit he Answer'd, I was Welcome to his Pulpit; Soon after I met with Sir Richards Son told him I intended to preach to morrow; he told me his father Invited me to a dish of Chocolate in the Morning. I Answered I wou'd waite upon Sir Richard and accordingly did, where I met with a free Access good Entertainment Exceptions Only some Scandalous and gross Reflections on Mr. Burrington. I told Sir Richard I was not susceptible of such Egregious Reflections on a Gentleman of So vast a Character among both Rich and poor as Mr. Burrington alway's did and does to this support, Immediately enter'd a Beavy of Ladies to breakfast with Sir Richard, We broke off our discourse, took my leave, and departed

Expecting Sir Richard and the Ladies to come to Church at the time Appointed; And after I had taken a walk about an hour and halfe meeting with mr. Parriss he ask'd me whether it was not time for Church or no. I Answer'd in the Affirmative asking him who kept the Key, who Answer'd mr. Badham and that he would go for it and Immediately did, and as soon return'd telling me the Governor had Sent for it, at which I was very much Surprised. The Congregation being ready for their devotion there was a great murmuring from which I understood that the door would be Broke Open, I desired them not to do it, for I would go to Sir Richard for the Key my Self rather then any Violence should be used, And Accordingly I Approach'd Sir Richard after this manner, (who was then in Company only with Doctor Allen[1] a man of a Vile Character and lately Condemn'd at Williamsburg for Curseing King George and Mr. Drysdale who is Governor of Virginia) Sir Richard The Congregation waits to go to Church, and I beg that yr. Honour will please to let me have the Key. He takeing the Key then up in a great Rage, thus Express'd himself, Sirah I will make you know who is Governor. I answered I knew that his Honour was Governor and I hoped that his Honour knew likewise who was Priest, he reply'd I should not preach to day, I told him that I would and that unless his Honour would please to Send the Key I was Assur'd by what I heard that the Door would be Opened, he Said he would put me in Prison if I did preach. I Answered however I would try that not doubting but God would defend me. I then departed and came to Church where the Door was Open, I went in read Divine Service and gave the People a Sermon. The next Morning a Warrant was <225> sent by the Constable from Justice Gale which is as follows.

When I came before the Justice he Examining me demanded Security or Wou'd order me to Prison. I demanded Security of him for his Libel which denomination I gave the Warrant, Information being given by a person Notoriously disaffected to King George and lately arrain'd for Publickly Curseing the King and Government and by many Evidences was Convicted, Condemn'd and fin'd, also recorded at within the Capitol at Williamsburg for the Same yet Notwithstanding this to Prison I must have went had not mr. Burringtons Compassion and love to the Clergy prevented by offering himself Baile which was accepted.

Thos. Baylye

Vera Copia

Copy.

[1]Dr. George Allen, a physician of Edenton, was presented by the grand jury of the General Court in March, 1726, for "Cursing King George" in Edenton the preceding November. The presentment was later quashed on a technicality. Cain, *Higher-Court Minutes, 1724-1730*, 224, 229-230.

[*LAM/FUL/VI*]

Richard Everard to Bishop of London
1725/6 January 25

<217>

Edenton North Carolina
Jan. 25 1725

My Lord

We have one Thos. Bayley who calls himself a Missionary. He formerly was in Philadelphia and turned out there for a Scandelous drunken man Came into Virginia and turned there likewise out for his vile Actions then Came into my Province where if he could gett mony or Creditt would be continually Drunk and break Windows or be Fighting. This Bailey lately came into Edenton where I reside and for two Days kept himself much disordered in Liquor on the next Day being on a Saterday he Spoke to my Son to desire him to procure my leave for him to Preach which I possitively denyed him at which he was very uneasie and by the instigation of Burington the late Governour he came to me on Sunday about 12 'a Clock and demanded the key of the Courthouse which I also refused on which he told me If the Court house Door was not opened for him it shall be broke open and immediately went to the Door and broke it open. In this Court house are keept all Records and the Jornalls of the Assembles on which the Chief Justice bound him over to our Generall Court Mr. Burington is his bail. He's as Im inform'd in a Distant Part of this Country calld Pasquatank a Preaching up Rebellion and begg Your Lordship if I prosecute him according to our Laws here for his Enormous Crimes and his Acting out of his sphere your Lordship will Pardon me I'm well asured. Mr. Baileys life and Carrecter is paralell if not Superlative to Mr. Nathaniell Gentry on Whom Your Lordship executed the greatest Justice. I'm greatly oblidged to your Lordship for oblidging me with my Request and admitting the Reverend Mr. Blacknall to come with me to Carolina. He is a Gent. that's a very good Preacher a Gent. perfectly Sober beloved by all but by Mr. Buringtons Party. He has made about one hundred and Sixty Christians Since he has been here and I don't in the least doubt but he'l double that number before he has been here a twelve Month. I beg Your Lordship will oblige us with three other Missionarys one for Bertie, another for Bath and a Third for Pasquatank. We are a most Heathenish Part of America and have no Sect amongst us but Quakers who daily Encrease. I thought it Proper to acquaint <218> yr. Lordship of this that the Society may Favour us with Sober and pious men if not having such a man as Mr. Bailey he will be dispised and Rideculed. I must beg your Lordships Pardon in Writing in so great a Hurry not knowing of this oppertunity till within this two Days and my Secretary so sick he cant put Pen to Paper. I am forced to write all my dispatches my self therefore begg You'l excuse all interlineation and Errors in My Lord Your Lordships Most Faithfull Humble Servant.

Richd. Everard

[*Endorsed*:]
[*Illegible*]ow N. Carolina
<*Philadelphia, Virga.*> Scandalous
charrecter of Bayly
Burrington Supports him
disaffected
3 more missionaries
good acct. of Backnall

Backnall's deposition about Baily
1725/6

ALS.

[*LAM/FUL/VI*]

Affidavit
1725/6 January 27

<219> No. Carolina sc. Before Sir Richard Everard Barronet Governor Capt. General and Admiral of said Province.

The Reverend Mr. John Blacknell being Sworn on the Holy Evangelists Saith

That on the Twentyeth day of November last being designed on a Journey to the Indian Towne to Preach, he accidentily met with Mr. Thomas Bailey (a Clergy-man) at Edenton who addressing himself to this Deponent amongst other things. They had some discourse of this Deponents Journey Whereupon he the said Bailey told the Deponent that he had been with the Governor and was then going to him again, and believed that Sir Richard would ask him to Preach and begg'd of this Deponent if he had the Governors approbation to give him the use of his Pulpit but this Deponent having heard a very vile and infamous Charecter of the said Bailey, and knowing Sir Richard was apprised of the Charecter he had, only told him that if he had the Governors leave, he this Deponent had nothing to say against it.

Jno. Blacknall

Taken this 27th day of January
Anno Domini 1725.
Richd. Everard

[*Endorsed*:]
Blacknall's Affidavit
relative to Bailye 1725

DS.

[*SPG/SAP*]

Report
1725/6 February 18

<33> <*An Abstract of the Proceedings of the Society.*> [. . .] The Society have this Year appointed [. . .] The Reverend Mr. *Blacknall* to *North Carolina*, with the like Salary;[1] [. . .]

Printed. Extracted from the yearly publication containing the sermon preached at the annual anniversary meeting of the SPG, together with a review of the activities of the Society and its missionaries during the preceding year. The date above is the date of the meeting.

[1]I.e., £50.

[SPG/Jou/5]

Journal of the SPG
1726 April 15

<85> 15 April 1726 [. . .]

<87> 10. Upon reading a Letter from Sir Richard Everard Governor of North Carolina dated August the 18th 1725[1] representing the great want of Missionaries and Schoolmasters there; and the Minutes of the Society relating to the sending Missionaries thither: Ordered that a Copy of the Resolutions of the Society be delivered to Mr. Shelton to be laid before the Lords Proprietors, and that their Lordships be informed that the Society are willing to proceed so far towards supplying the Parishes there with Ministers and that this is the utmost they are able to do. [. . .]

Minutes.

[1]Not located.

[LAM/FUL/VI]

Rev. Thomas Baylye to Bishop of London
1726 May 12, 25

<220> May It please your Lordship?

Tis from that Paternal care and great concern yr. Lordship has In advancing the Kingdome of Christ by an orthodox ministry abroad as well as at home, and the zealous desire of yr. unworthy Missionary to be Instrumental In the converting of Souls from Athiesm and Infidelity to the true religion that we presume yr. recommendation to the Honourable Society for propogation of the Gospel In America whereby we may obtain the usual gratuity (by yr. Lordship favour and benediction) for our Minister.

This is the 3d year that with great Labour and much pains I have Officiated in North Carolina and baptized above four hundred Children many adult persons; three Adult Indians with many negros and have brought many to the Sacrament of the Lords Supper and should it please God to continue me by your Lordships favour, I doubt not but the Poeple under my care (which is one half of North Carolina) will by regular Christian lives and conversations take off a reproach too Justly by their neighbouring Colonys hitherto cast upon em which has ben for want of the ministry to Instruct em in the Institutes of the Christian religion.

The Salary and perquisites here run so low as renders my Life extreamly uncomfortable, that I shall be obliged to embark for England or else where, unless encouraged by the Society who have allow'd eighty pounds per annum for the supply of this place; and being Invited into this Goverment by the cheif men thereof (as one Mr. Porter an Agent for this Country who is embarkt for England[1] and has promised to wait on yr. Lordship in my favour can Inform you). It was expected long before this time the Salary to have been affixed: for the want thereof I have been a great Sufferer and in some measure the whole body of the Church, in regard the exigences of myself, wife and four small children have these three years last past loudly Invoked for what was absolutely necessary to support the honour and dignity of The Ministry.

But one cheif reason of my removing from the place of my mission was my wife's having lost the use of her Limbs by the Gripes, a distemper very common in some parts of America, but (blessed be God) since we came Into Carolina shes almost restored to her former health, her long sickness with four small children have extorted this Epistle, which weighed in yr. Lordships Charitable schales I hope will not be thought troublesome, Since another opportunity of exercising the greatest of virtues in the illumination of the Ignorant by Divine providence is offered and In the assistance of yr. Petitioner is humbly Implored.

Our Late Governour Mr. Burrington together with the Assembly have sent to the Lords Proprietors (as they have Informed me) on my behalf, of which yr. Lordship may be acquainted with by the general receiver Mr. Goffe,[2] who is presumed to be now in London, and from mr. Edmond Porter two Agents for the Country, the latter whereof has promised me to wait on yr. Lordship in my favour, a man of great Integrity and resolution capable of carrying on any negotiation with the Divine assistance he takes in hand. Neither has our present Governour Sir Richard Everard been wanting in his promises of sending home to the same purpose, but whether the two great troubles he is engaged in att present has prevented any steps towards it, I cannot affirm: however this I can with boldness affirm, that most of the refractoriness of this country is owing to the want of ministers being setled upon a good foundation; they having but seldom the opportunity of hearing the Gospel, and that sometimes by the Presbiterian, one whereof is now setled at Neuse River, not farr from Bath town, where the Poeple are pretty populous, Their Present Minister Mr. Clemens[3] an Irish Gentleman of good learning and conversation and complying with the Rubrick, and nothing hinders his total conformity to the established Church of England but the want of Imposition of hands to which purpose I have advised him to Embark for Europe, who is willing, but thro exegency of circumstances not able. Here are also at Pasquotank and Pacquimmins many Quakers; but my preaching there and Baptizing as often as opportunity permits hinders the further growth and Encrease of em; the first time I visited em, In those two Parishes I baptized above an hundred and fifty Children and Adult persons a few.

This part of yr. Lordships Diocess is for extention as Large as that at whome, even that which is at present under my care, tho' nothing so populous, and the same zeal which moves yr. care there, descends as from the fountains into a little River actuating mine here, Oh! may it ever flow to the enlarging of our Zion, In the exterpation of heresy and scism and to the illuminations of Pagans and Infidels both at home and abroad, till the calling of the Jews and advancment of the gentiles be accomplished. Tis the glory of some missionaries that the Preaching the cross of Christ is not so much a stumbling block and foolishness to this Ignorant part of the world as it was to learned Greeks and more obstinate Jews In other Parts <222> And should God of his Infinite mercy make the Purest Prelacy of the world those of great Brittain and Irland the happy Instruments of sending missionary (with feet shod with the preparation of the Gospel of Peace) to Asia and Affrica, we should hope that Paganism Mahomatism[4] and Judaism would like dark metors dissappear (if not be ecclipsed) at the transcendant light of Christianity.

Doctor King present Master of the Charter house where I preach'd my Missionary Sermon and of whome I have requested his favour In this affair may acquaint yr. Lordship of my Charecter. He was Instrumental In my first comming abroad. I would have paid my duty in person; but the circumstances of my wife and small children, adunated to my tender affection, under the most absolute necessity confines me with em; I have been fourteen years In America, the most part whereof In Maryland have laboured abundantly in the Gospel and Suffer'd very much by the Romans;[5] all which being left to yr. Lordships more Judiciary consideration, as In duty bound I subscribe my self Yr. Lordships most humble most devote and obedient Servant.

Thomas Baylye.

Bath Town, North Carolina
May the 12 1726

Poscript

And because many wolves have crept into the church and have received benefit therefrom in sheeps cloathing in these parts as well as to prevent yr. Lordships Trouble of a Retrospection, I here Subscribe the time and place in the words of the ordination I received of the Bishopp of London. Die dominico decima quinta scilicet die mensis Junii Anno domini millesimo septing[ent]essimo duo decimo In Capella Intra Palatium nostrum de fillam Middlesex.[6] And by a letter demissery of H. London the same Bishop to Ric. Bpp. of Peterborough, some few years before I was ordained Deacon at Westminster namely in the year 1705 and am now enterd into the three and fortieth year of my age. I hope yr. Lordship will consider the great difficulty I undergoe the many miles I weekly ride, which once a month is not less than three hundred in circumferance, besides other casual Journeys, and the present circumstances of my own family and of this part lately by a Barbarous Indian warr lately wasted but now Blessed be God in a fair way of Becoming a good Settlement, being disposed to receive the Gospel of Christ of which I presume under yr. Lordship favour and recommendation to be the happy tho' unworthy Instrument And therefore I take Leave once More Most Reverend Father In God In all humility to Subscribe myself yr. most Dutyfull Son and meanest of Servants.

Thomas Baylye.

May the 25, 1726
Bath Town North Carolina

[*Endorsed*:]
To The most Reverend Father In God The

Bishop of London and
of his Majesties plantations In America
1726 Most Humbly present
A Letter from Mr. Baylie

ALS.

[1]Edmund Porter was one of three men chosen by the General Assembly in 1726 to go to London in order to represent to the authorities the assembly's displeasure with Governor Richard Everard. *DNCB.*

[2]Arthur Goffe (d. by June, 1737) took the oaths as receiver general and member of the council in January, 1723/4. Within two years he had vacated the receiver general's post, and with the accession of Richard Everard as governor in April, 1725, he ceased to be a councillor. *DNCB.*

[3]Probably the John Clement suspended from the Presbyterian ministry in New Jersey in 1721 for being "at diverse times overtaken with Drink [and] chargeable with very abusive Language and Quarrelling and . . . stabbing a Man." Klett, *Minutes of the Presbyterian Church*, 49.

[4]I.e., *Mahometanism*, an archaic spelling of *Mohammedanism.*

[5]I.e., Roman Catholics.

[6]"On Sunday that is the fifteenth day of the month of June in the year of the Lord 1712. In the Chapel within our Palace [Fulham] in the village of Middlesex."

[*LAM/FUL/VI*]

Petition
1726 May 25

May 25 1726.
Bath Town North Carolina.

May It please yr. Lordship

To receive with Clemency the Humble Petition of the Church wardens, Vestry, and Gentlemen of St. Thomas parish Bath town North Carolina In the behalf of Mr. Baylye our Pious and Examplary Minister, Who was recommended to us by our Late Governour Colonel George Burrington and has been in these parts almost three years, Long Expecting the usual Salary from the Royal Society, which we presume afore this time would have been Afixed had not his recommendations been Intercepted. The Sense we have of Mr. Baylye's Administration in the Gospel and the great pains and care he hath taken Since he hath been Amongst us obligeth us on this Occation to Acknowledge the benefitt this Province has Enjoyd from the same. And since his desires of Continuing with us; if Asisted with the Usual Salary from the Honourable Society for the Propogation of the Gospel in North Carolina, as well as in Other parts of America, a place wanting the Blessed benefit of the Gospel, More than any Other part of yr. Lordship Most extensive Diocess, and his Majesties Dominions Abroad. We beg Leave therefore together with our Neighbouring Vestry and Parish humbly to Petition Your Lordship to Recommend the Reverend Mr. Thos. Baylye our Able and worthy devine to the Honourable Society for the Eighty pounds per Annum, which our former ministers have been poseled [*sic*] with. Assureing your Lordship that we shall now be wanting to provide for him, as Honourable a Support as possibly we can, Butt for as

much as the Late Indian Wars has rendered us unable to raise a Sufficient Subsidy for a Decent Maintainance of the Ministry.
<223> We Unamously and Humbly Petetion yr. Lordships Asistance in the setling so pious and Able a man as Mr. Baylye amongst us under Whose Ministry we Esteem our selves very happy and your Petetioners as in Duty bound shall Ever Pray.

James Leigh judge of the court, Gyles Shute Justice, Seth Pilkington, Abraham Adams, Robt. Turner Justice, Wm. Snoad Justice, John Adams, John Adams clerk of Vestry, Josiah Jones, Matt. Roan, Thomas Worlsey Justice of peace, Simon Alderson Justice, Joshua Porter Justice

The Commissioners of the Vestry of Hide Parish Who were Authorized by Order of the Vestry to Meet and joyne with the Gentlemen of the Vestry of St. Thos. parish have mett the same day and doe Most Humbly Supplicate the same from your Lordship And shall ever Pray.

Robt. Peyton Barronett,[1]
Joseph Tart
Sam. Slade

[*Endorsed:*]
[*Illegible*]
Hyde Parrish, in favour
of Mr. Bayly
1726 North Carolina

D. The names appended to this petition appear to be forgeries. Although the document gives the superficial appearance of an original rather than a copy, and apparently is intended to convey this impression, a comparison of a number of the "signatures" (those of Thomas Worsley, James Leigh, Gyles Shute, Seth Pilkington, Abraham Adams, Robert Turner, John Adams, and Joseph Tart) with those on relevant wills reveals without question that they are not the same.

[1]As far as is known, Robert Peyton was not a baronet.

[*LAM/FUL/XXXVI*]

Nathaniel Duckenfield to "Reverend Sir"
1726 October 3

Reverend Sir

I was Sorry I was disappointed of Seeing you which Obliged me to leave the papers[1] for your perusall and Since not having an Opportunity of waiting on you I am Engaged to write And to desire you wou'd give me your Advise what I Should do with them. My thoughts are to have them laid before my Lord Bishop of London as the most probable Way of getting this Grievance Redressed for to lay them before the Proprietors I Apprehend that they have So little of Church Affairs at Heart that I Should find little Reliefe there. And if the Clergy must be so Basely Insulted by those who Should rather be the greatest Encouragement of them It will not only be an Utter discouragement for any to go Over but will be the Ruin of the Province Therefore to put a Stop to this Abominable Evil I wou'd Willingly take those Methods as may Effectually Crush this Vile practice of Abuseing the Clergy in that part of the World where they are So much wanted. I have prodigious Complaints in Civill Affairs So that the [Inhabitants] thereof labour under Intolerable Grievances by their Officers which I Shall lay before the Proprietors.

If you Apprehend the giving of those papers to the Bishop I could wish and Should take it as a favor if you wou'd Either deliver them or Send them to him so that you wou'd let me know your thoughts what I Should do.

My Spouse Joins with me in Humble Service to Mrs. Sears and Mrs. M[*illegible*] to His [*illegible*] Daughter and to Mr. Charles [*illegible*] Son and to your Self.

I have Enquired after the [Piermont Dates] and I am told it is to be had at One Smith Apothecary in Cannon Street at 14*s*. per Bottle. I Rest hopeing you all Enjoy a Comfortable State of health and I am Yr. Most Obedient Humble Servant.

N. Dukinfield

Edmonton
Octob. 3d 1726 pardon hast

[*Addressed*:]
The Reverend [*torn*]

[*Endorsed*:]
Duckingfield [*illegible*]
Sir Richd. Everett
Barrington
Bayly
3d. Octr. 1726
Sir N. Duckinfield

[*Postscript*:]
[*Illegible*]
about the [Dates] before the End
of last Week Else Should have
given Sooner Notice of it.

LS.

[1]This reference is unclear.

[*NYHS*]

Extract from Act of Assembly
1727

<312> An Act to appoint the Northwest part of Barte Precint[1] a District by the Name of the Northwest parish of Bartie Precint and for appointing Vestry men for the said Parish And to appoint Commissioners in Every Parish in this Government to Call the Churchwardens and Vestry to Accompt for the Parish Money by them received.

[. . .] And be it further Enacted by the Authority aforesaid that it Shall and may be Lawfull for the Parishoners of the said Parish and of all other Parish in this Government to Choose at each and every Bienniel Election Two Men to inspect into the Vestry books and adjust the Accompts and Such adjustment Shall Publish at the Chapple under the Penalty of One hundred pounds and if any of the Parish money be found Applyed to private uses by the Churchwardens or any of the Vestry men which have been now are or hereafter Shall be Appointed It Shall and may be Lawfull for Such persons so nominated by the Parishoners to Sue the said Church Wardens or Vestrymen in the name and for the use of the Parish in an Action of Accompt render and Judgment and Execution thereof to [have] and to and for the use of the Parish for and in whose name Such Action Shall be brought.

And be it Further Enacted by the Authority aforesaid that it Shall and may be Lawfull for the Parishoners of each parish to meet at the next Court in Each and every Precint in this Government which Shall be next after the Ratification of this Act to Choose Two men <314> who Shall be Invested with Same Powers and Subject to the Same penalty as before in this Act is provided for Such two Men as Shall be Chosen for Each and Every parish in this Government at the next Biennial Election which persons so Chosen at the Precinct Court Shall continue and remain invested with the said Powers and be Lyable to the said penalty 'til the next Biennial Election and no longer.

D.

[1]Bertie Precinct.

[*SPG/A/21*]

Rev. John LaPierre to Secretary, SPG
1728 October 25

<19> Mr. LaPierre,[1] to the Secretary.

So. Carolina October 25th 1728

Reverend Sir

I humbly crave leave to inform the Honourable Society, that I am the man who twenty years ago or longer was sent by the late Right Reverend Bishop of London, to a French Congregation in South Carolina, during which time I have been lying under great Straights, as the Honourable Society has been made Sensible of, Witness their Bounty granted to me from time to time, and in such a Case, as my Parish was intermixt with that of the Reverend Mr. Hazel, I have now and then shared my Ministerial functions between the English and the French, which my Parishioners not approving, I have desired them therefore, to provide me themselves with Necessaries, but since <141> I am amongst them, they have not so much as furnished me with a Parsonage and Glebe and yet they required me, to be always ready to serve them at the first Call, which I have endeavoured to do, to the best of my Ability, till I have seen that I could live no longer amongst them. For besides the want of their due help, a certain man of the French and belonging to another Parish hath taken upon himself, to sett my Parishioners against me, and the Said Parishioners consented to be led by him, therefore withall boldness, he contradicts whatsoever I propose in Church, I made the Journal of their Proceedings and have sent it to the Clergy; and more than that, they have lately procured a Letter from an outragious Presbyterian, containing all manner of reproachfull reflections against the Church and State. I have Shewed this likewise to the Clergy. This I may look upon as a Consequence of their none Conformity in one of our Cheif ordinances, for they rather Chuse to exclude themselves from the holy Sacraments than to receive the same with the posture of humility required; these are they Reverend Sir who did once already renounce our Church when they called for Mr. Stoup in my Stead before he had taken Episcopal Orders, but they soon fell out with him and I came to resume my functions amongst them, this is that Gentleman whom the Honourable Society have made Since one of their Missionaries at New Rochel, in New York, and now Sir I could find an Opportunity if it seem good to the honourable Society, to grant me leave to go and Edify a poor dispersed multitude of People residing up and down Cape fear, I have been already with them at my own Cost to baptize Several of their Children and to preach to them at three several times, with the honour of their approbation which I conceive to proceed from their urging want of the word of God; I humbly crave of the Honourable Society Reverend Sir out of regard to my reasons, and to the State of my Poor Families consisting of my Wife that is blind and of 3 Children to honour me with their indulging favour upon this design that I may always be ready to shew my Self, their most devoted and humble Servant and yours.

John LaPierre

Copy. Read at a meeting of the SPG on March 21, 1728/9, when it was agreed to concur in the opinion of the Committee "that this matter doth not immediately relate to the Society." Journal of the SPG, V, 197.

[1]Rev. John LaPierre. See appendix.

[CO 5/293]

Act of Assembly
1729

An Act for Regulating Vestrys in this Government and for the better Inspecting the Vestrymen and Church Wardens Accounts of Each and Every Parish within this Government.

Whereas many Complaints are made by the Inhabitants of Several Parishes in this Government of the misapplication of the parish Taxes and of the Connivance of the Vestrymen in settling the Church Wardens Accounts which has arisen by evil Disposed and averitious persons getting into Vestrys For preventing the Like abuses for the future and giving the fullest satisfaction to the Inhabitants of the Several parishes in this Government

Be it Enacted by his Excellency the palatine etc. And it is hereby Enacted that the Inhabitants Freemen in each and every Parish in this Government may and are hereby Impowered to meet the first Easter Munday after the Ratification of this Act and at every Easter Monday that shall be Every Two Years after at the Court house in Every Parish and if there be none at such other place as by this Act is Appointed (Videlicet) in North East parish of Pasquotank precinct at the Chappell at Sawyers Creek in Society parish, in Bertie precinct at the Chappell at Ducking Run, in St. Andrew's parish in Tyrrell precinct at South shore Chappell untill the Court house for the precinct be built in Hyde precinct at William Websters, then and there to Elect and Choose twelve good and Sufficient Freeholders to Serve as Vestrymen for the Ensuing two years which Vestrymen so Chosen shall be Summoned by the Constable to meet within twenty dayes at the place aforesaid under the Same penaltys and forfietures already provided in the Act for Establishing the Church and appointing Select Vestrymen and the said Vestrymen so Chosen shall meet and Qualifie themselves under the same penaltys and forfietures and in the Same manner as in the said Act for Establishing the Church and appointing Select Vestrys is appointed.

And be it further Enacted by the Authority aforesayd that the Vestrymen so Chosen shall have full power and authority to call any former Church Warden or Vestryman to account for the use of the parishes money and if any Church Warden or Vestryman so Called upon shall neglect or Refuse within Twenty dayes Notice given by the Vestrymen for the time being to Deliver a true perfect and fair account on Oath of all the Sum and Sums of money Collected and Disposed of by them or any of them heretofore or hereafter to be Collected or Received for Such their neglect or refusal of Rendring their Accounts aforesaid in the time aforementioned, that then each and Every Church Warden and Vestryman so Refusing shall forfiet the Sum of One hundred pounds One half of the Said forfietures, to and for the use of the said Parish where the Default shall be made and the other half to the Church Wardens Suing for the Same to be Recovered by Action of Debt bill plaint or Information in any Court of Record within this Government wherein no Essoign Protection or Wager of Law shall be allowed or admitted of.

And Be it further Enacted by the authority aforesaid That if it shall appear to the said Church Wardens or Vestrymen for the time being upon the Exhibiting the said Account that any of the Parish shall be found to have been Applyed or hereafter to be applyed to private uses by the Church Wardens or Vestrymen which have been, now are, or hereafter shall be, that then it shall and may be Lawfull for the Church Wardens or Vestrymen for the time being which have been, now are, or hereafter shall be Appointed, that then it shall and may be Lawfull for the Church Wardens or Vestrymen for the time being to Recover the said moneys so misapplyed by Action of Debt Bill plaint or Information in any Court of Record within this Government wherein no Essoign protection Injunction or Wager of Law shall be allowed or Admitted off to be applyed to, and for the use of the parish, and for which their trouble the said Church Wardens or Vestrymen for the time being shall be allowed out of the so received tenn per Cent with Costs.

And be it further Enacted by the authority aforesayd that the Vestry men and Church Wardens for the time being in Every parish shall have full power and authority to Call any Justice of the peace or other person or persons whatsoever to account on Oath for what Sum and Summs of money they shall have received at any time as fines for Adultery fornication, Breach of Sabbath or any other forfietures, that part thereof or all should be applyed to and for the use of the Parish, and which does not appear to be so applyed or accounted for already which said Justices or other persons shall account with the Vestrymen or Church Wardens for the time being, in the Same manner and under the Like penaltys as is in this Act provided for the Vestrymen and Church Wardens accompting, and the forfietures to be in the Same manner applyed.

And be it further Enacted by the Authority aforesaid That the Vestrymen for the time being are hereby authorized and Impowered within forty Days after Every Easter Monday to appoint what parish Levy shall by them appear needfull for the better Enabling them to Maintain a Minister and Defray the Contingent Charges of the Parish any Law Custom or useage heretofore to the Contrary Notwithstanding.

And be it further Enacted by the authority aforesaid That the freemen Inhabitants of Each parish shall on every Easter monday appointed by this Act for Electing and Choosing Vestrymen first Elect and Choose some Certain person to take the Votes of the freemen for Electing the Vestry which person so Chosen shall take the Votes in Like manner and under the same penalty as is provided for the Election of Burgesses for this province and Return the Vestrymens Names so Elected within Six days after the Election to the Church Wardens or Clerks of the Vestry then in office who are hereby Directed and Required to Record the Same and Deliver to the Constables a Copy of the Said Returns within twelve days after the said Election so as the Constable may thereby be Enabled to Summons the Vestrymen so chosen as is Directed in this Act, which said Church Wardens or Clerk of the Vestry neglecting to give the Constable a List or Copy of Such Returns within the time aforesaid shall forfiet for Such Neglect the Sum of Ten pounds to be recovered by Action of Debt Bill Plaint or Information in the precinct Court the one half to the Informer the other half to and for the use of the parish. Whereas the Southern Settlements of this province hath been very much Increased by the Settlement of Cape Fear

Be it Enacted by the Authority aforesayd that the Southern Part of this Province be Divided from the Haul over between Little Inlett, and new River Inlett, and the Southermost Boundary of this Province into a Distinct Precinct Called New Hanover with all and every the Rights priviledges and other benefitts and Advantages whatsoever as any other of the precincts of Bath County Can or may have use or Enjoy.

And be it further Enacted by the Authority aforesaid That the precinct of New Hanover as now bounded by the Haul over between Little and New River Inletts and the Southermost Boundary of the Province shall be and is hereby appointed a Separate and Distinct parish by the Name of St. James' parish and that The said Parish shall Enjoy all Such Liberties and priviledges as any other Parish within this Government can or may be.

And Be it Further Enacted by the authority aforesaid That the following persons are hereby appointed to be present Vestrymen for the Said Parish Videlicet Colonel Maurice Moore, Mr. Saml. Swann, Mr. Jos. Waters, Mr. Cornl. Harnet, Roger Moore Esqr., Mr. Natha. Moore, Mr. Edwd. Hyrne, Mr. John porter, Mr. John Grange, Mr. John Bapt. Ashe, Mr. John Swann, Mr. Richd. Nixon.

And Be it Enacted by the authority aforesayd That the Church Court house and Goal for the Said Parish and precinct shall be Erected and Built on a parcell of Land that is already Laid out apart and Designed for a Towne on the West Side of Cape Fear River Lying Over against the upper haleover and Called Brunswick.

And Be it Further Enacted by the Authority aforesayd That the Justices of the Said precinct are hereby Impowered and Required to Raise money for Building the Court house and Goal by a pole Tax to be then assessed on the Tythable persons Residing within the said Precinct, to be Levyed and Collected by the Marshal of the Said precinct so as for the Defraying the Charges of the Said Buildings no greater Tax to be Laid on the Inhabitants than five shillings per pole for Two years.

D. This act is here printed for the first time. It was not included in the ones edited by Walter Clark and published in the *State Records*, XXIII, XXV.

[*LAM/FUL/IX*]

Clergy of South Carolina to Bishop of London
1728/9 January 24

<227> <*Duplicate*> 1728/9

Mayt please your Lordship

As it is our Duty to acquaint your Lordship of all extraordinary Occurrences in Ecclesiastical Affairs here, We now accordingly beg leave to acquaint you of these following (viz.) The Deaths of two of our Brethren; the Resignation of his Parish by a third, the Removal of a fourth out of his Setlement; And a fifth's being dismissed by the Parish he was sent to for his ill Behaviour.

The two first were the reverend Messrs. Ludlam of Goose Creek and Standish of St. Paul's; who died, the former the 11th of 8ber. the later the 26 of 9ber. last. The 3d is the reverend Mr. Hunt; who resigned his Parish at St. John into the hands of the Churchs Commissary here, sometime last month. The 4th is the reverend Mr. Lapierre; who remov'd from hence about a month ago, to a New Setlement, calld Cape fear, bounding on this and North Carolina, but under neither, nor any Government. The 5th is the reverend Mr. Winteley; who was dismissed by the Parish of Christ Church from supplying that Cure last Michaelmas for his frantick and immoral Behaviour.

The truth is, the Behaviour of this unhappy Brother has been so long, openly, and against all Admonition, exceptionable; that we are quite both sorry and ashamd that we can say nothing in his Behalf.

These several Parishes will doubtless make all proper Application to your Lordship and the honorable Society with respect to their Several Vacancies; which meantime we shall not fail to supply as much as possibly we can.

We shall only further add that we humbly crave your Lordships Blessing and that we are Mayt please your Lordship Your most dutiful sons and obedient humble Servants.

W. Guy, F. Varnod, A. Garden, L. Jones, Tho. Hasell, John Lambert

So. Carolina
Charlestown Janry. 24th 1728/9

[*Addressed:*]
To The right reverend Father in God
Edmund Lord Bishop of London These

LS. Read at a meeting of the SPG on May 16, 1729. Journal of the SPG, V, 204.

[*LAM/FUL/VI*]

Richard Everard to [Bishop of London]
1729 April 14

May it please yr. Lordship.

Tis with no smal concern I send this to inform You that our Church is not built nor is it like to be gon about for those men that were appointed Commissioners for the Building it and have Six hundred pounds in their hands are now the only opposers of Building one I was, in order to the laying the Foundation chose Church warden as one Mr. Moseley we had Several meetings to consult about building it but could not agree being always hindred by our Secretary one Mr. Jo. Lovick a man of no Religion Fears nor God nor man believes neither seldom seen at any place of devine worship his mony is his God ridicules all Goodness whilst such a man is in Power no good can be expected. His Original was bred a barber brought up a Footboy and a Pimp to him of my Predecessors but enough of his Carecter. I lately mett with Gent. who informs me one <226> Mr. Sanderson who died about ten Years agoe left a Will and bequeathed Several hundred Acres of Land ten Cows and calves ten sows and Piggs Sheep and Several houshould Goods to maintain a Clergy man in the Precinct of Curratuck in this Province but these a Embezled by the Managment of Lovick and others of his Stamp by Setting the Will aside the Gent. promised me the Coppy which as soon as it comes to hand shall be sent to Your Lordship who shall Comand all the Assistance that lyes in the Power of my Lord Your most Dutifull Son and Humble Servant.

Richd. Everard

No. Carolina
Apr. 14th 1729

[*Endorsed*:]
N. Carolina

ALS.

[*LAM/FUL/XII*]

Rev. James Blair to [Bishop of London]
1729 June 28, 30

<134>

Williamsburgh June 28, 1729.

My Lord [. . .]

Mr. Baylie, one of those Clergymen that was censured in Governour Drysdales time, is now going for England. No parish here, nor in Maryland or North-Carolina will receive him. I would willingly have been silent about him; but I thought your Lordship would think it strange in me to let such a man <135> surprize you and I say nothing of it. He, or his wife (who is almost as bad as himself) pretend they have friends in England that will take care of them.

And (now that I have mentioned North-Carolina) it is a most shameful thing that in a Christian Countrey as that is, there is not one Minister in all the Countrey. I hope, now that the King has purchased S. and N. Carolina from the Proprietors, (if our news is true) some better care will be taken of them as to Religion. Your Lordships reminding the Ministry of these things will go a great way; but I fear the people themselves have got such an habit of irreligion, and are so afraid of a little charge, that they will not much stir in this affair themselves. If nothing can be done any other way, surely the Society for Propagation of the Gospel will think it worthy of their care. The most effectual way at present is to send Governours that are good men and have a respect for the church and religion. I know your Lordships Endeavours will not be wanting. I heartily pray to God to bless them; and am My Lord Your Lordships most obliged servant.

James Blair[1] [. . .]

[*Endorsed*:]
Blair
Colle.-Chapel Letter about
Smith-Bayley-N. Caro.

ALS.

[1]Rev. James Blair (1655-1743), founder and first president of the College of William and Mary, came to Virginia as a missionary in 1685. In 1689 he was appointed commissary to the bishop of London, in which capacity he wrote this letter. *DAB*.

[*LAM/FUL/XII*]

Rev. James Blair to [Bishop of London]
1729 July 5

<138>

Williamsburgh July 5, 1729.

My Lord

Since I sent away my Letters I had your Lordships packet with the Commission,[1] in which I observe one alteration viz. that Bermuda is added to Virginia. That Island lyes so out of my way that it will but deceive your Lordship to depend on me for it. There is one word in the end of your Lordships letter; you desire to know where Baylie and Worden are. Worden died in South Carolina. Baylie goes to England in this fleet. I have said enough of him in another letter to your Lordship. Marsden is fled out of this Countrey for debt. If it had been known that he was under censure, I dare say the Governour would not have admitted him here. [. . .]

I am My Lord your Lordships most obliged and most obedient Servant.

James Blair. [. . .]

[*Endorsed*:]
Blair, Bayley, Worden
Answer'd

ALS.

[1]This undoubtedly refers to Blair's commission as commissary.

[*LAM/FUL/XII*]

Rev. James Blair to [Bishop of London]
1729 September 8

<142>

Williamsburgh Sept. 8, 1729.

My Lord [. . .]

Mr. Marsden is fled out of this Countrey for debt. I believe he is the same man your Lordship writes of. He had not been so civilly received here, if we had known any thing of his circumstances; besides he showed some respectful letters he had both from my Lord of Canterbury and from your Lordship which I believe were genuine; for I think I know both your hands very well. [. . .]

I beg your prayers and blessing, and am My Lord Your Lordships most obedient and most obliged Servant.

James Blair.

[*Endorsed*:]
Comission—Marsden-Chapel
Dawson Transfer

ALS.

[*SPG/Jou/5*]

Journal of the SPG
1729 September 19

<214> 19 September 1729 [. . .]

<217> 13. A Petition[1] from the Reverend Mr. Baylie was read and referred to the Committee to consider what Services he hath done in North Carolina: Ordered that Ten pounds be given Mr. Baylie in the meantime by way of Charity. [. . .]

Minutes.

[1]Not located.

[*LAM/FUL/VI*]

Richard Everard to [Bishop of London]
1729 October 12

<228>

My Lord

When I find Quakers and Baptist Flourish amongst the North Carolinians it behoved Me that am the Governour Here to enquire and look into the originall Cause which on the Strictest examination and nicest Scrutiny I can make find that owing to the want of Clergiemen amongst us We in this great Province have never a One and truly my Lord both Quakers and Baptists in this vacintiy are very busy making Proselites and holding Meetings dayly in every Part of this Goverment.

Indeed our New Country next Virginia is well supplyd by the indefatiguable Pains and Industry of the Reverend Mr. Jones[1] of Nansemond who has the Carecter of a Pious good and worthy Man but He is Old and Infirm. My Lord when I came first here there were no disenters but Quakers in the Goverment and now by the means of one Paul Palmer[2] the Baptist Teacher he has gained hundreds and to prevent it tis impossible when I have a Secretary One John Lovick that makes a Jest of all Religion and values not nor God, Man, nor Divel a true Enthusiast when I posed building the Church He was the only man that hindred it laid so many Stumbling Blocks in the way it was impossible to go about it then. And I very much Fear whilst he is in the Goverment none will be built. He may truly be called the Remora to all Religion and Goodness. His Original was a Footboy to the Former Governour Mr. Hide[3] and by making Friends gott also to be recomended to Mr. Eden who in the Affair of Thacth the Pirate made him Act the Part of an Affidavite Man[4] but that being before my Time don't Personably know it but have it credibly attested by Honest Living Evidences of good veracity this is the Man that at present Rules every thing Yea even our Religion etc. but hope thro Your Lordships assistance to throw off this heavy Yoak and Banish him to a Place where he may have less Power to perpretrate his Roguerys and we have the free Liberty of a Good Clergie and our Religion and Freedome which is the Sencere and hearty Prayer of my Lord Your Lordships Most Dutifull and most obedient Son and Humble Servant.

Richd. Everard

Edenton Octbr. 12th 1729

[*Endorsed:*]
Sir Richd. Everard
against Lovick
want of Clergy in Nth. Car.

ALS.

[1]Rev. Nicholas Jones came to Virginia in 1723 and settled in Nansemond County in 1728. Weis, *Colonial Clergy of Virginia, North Carolina and South Carolina*, 28.

[2]Paul Palmer (d. 1742?) was a Baptist clergyman who appeared in Perquimans Precinct prior to March, 1719. In 1729 he was active in Chowan Precinct and northeastern Pasquotank Precinct. *DNCB*.

[3]Lovick was in the retinue of Governor Edward Hyde when Hyde arrived in Virginia in August, 1710. The Virginian William Byrd, Lovick's fellow commissioner in running the boundary between North Carolina and Virginia in 1728, called him "Shoebrush" in his journal of the dividing line. Byrd found Lovick to be "a merry good humor'd Man" who had "learnt a very decent behaviour from Governour Hyde, to whom he had been Valet de Chambre, of which he still carry'd the marks by having his coat, wast-coat & Breeches of different Parishes." Boyd, *William Byrd's Histories of the Dividing Line*, 47.

[4]I.e., one who falsely swears an affidavit, a perjurer.

[*SPG/Jou/5*]

Journal of the SPG
1729 October 17

<218> 17th October 1729 [. . .]

3. It was reported from the Committee that they had read the Petition[1] of the Reverend Mr. Thomas Baylie to them referred and also a Certificate said to be signed by the Church Wardens and Vestry of St. Thomas's Parish in Bath County and the Commissioners of the Vestry of Hyde Parish North Carolina, setting forth his Services among them, but the Committee observing that he was not employed nor sent by the Society, and that he had been formerly before this Society, and was discharged from any dependance on them for some irregularites, and the Committee also taking Notice that there has not been any Precedent for the Society paying Clergymen for serving abroad unless they have been first approv'd of or sent by the Society, The Committee agreed to report as their Opinion, that the Society have been very Charitable in giving him Ten pounds at last Meeting, and that it doth not seem fit to make any farther Gratuity to him. Resolved that the Society do agree with the Committee. [. . .]

Minutes.

[1]Not located.

[*LAM/FUL/IX*]

Rev. Alexander Garden to Bishop of London
[1729 November 24]

<*Duplicate*>

My Lord [. . .]

Mr. Marsden is gone from Cape Fear for Lisbon in Portugal, as I intimated to your Lordship he intended sometime ago. A man who has certainly provd a very great Scandal to his holy Function in these parts, and as I am informd, is very well known to no better Advantage [to his] Character in several parts of England particularly [in] and about the City of Coventry. [. . .]

I am My Lord your Lordships most obedient Son and humble Servant.

A. Garden[1]

ALS.

[1]Rev. Alexander Garden (1685-1756) was the third cleric appointed commissary for the Carolinas by the bishop of London. Serving in this capacity from 1729 to 1749, Garden, like his predecessors, Rev. Gideon Johnston and Rev. William Tredwell Bull, resided in Charleston and apparently never visited North Carolina. George W. Williams, ed., "Letters to the Bishop of London from the Commissaries in South Carolina," *South Carolina Historical Magazine*, 78 (January, 1977), 12.

[*SPG/C/14*]

Daniel Kidlye to "Sir"
ca. 1730

<40>

Sir
I have been thrice at your house Saturday last to wait on you, (Understanding that Mr. Baylye my son in Laws buisness is agen referred to his Grace the Arch Bp.) to acquaint you that he has been very much abused concerning the calumny that arose against him, of which upon strict enquiry he is found altogether Innocent, therefore I hope this will be a Motive to Incline your favour towards him, in so doing you will lay a very great Obligation on your most humble Servant.

Daniel Kidlye

ALS.

[*LAM/FUL/XXXVI*]

Bishop of Meath to [Bishop of London]
1729/30 January 31

My very Good Lord
I hope you will pardon the liberty I take of troubling yr. Lordship once more in favour of Mr. Lennon, who has serv'd a Cure 19 years in My Diocese, with great Credit, and good example. His Income is small, and His Family large and I am so indifferent a Patron (most of My Livings, being in the Crown) that I know not how long it may be before I may have it in my power to do for him. This has determind Mr. Lennon to think of going to the W. Indies, particularly to North Carolina. But without yr. Lordships encouragement, He can by no means attempt it; and He humbly hopes that yr. Lordships Goodness to him, will not only extend to a Nomination for that place, but likewise to a Recommendation of him to the Society for propagating the Gospel in forreign parts, without whose Assistance He will not be able to go the voyage, or undertake the Cure; He has been invited there by a Merchant, who trades to this place and promises him much Friendship; but his Chief relyance must be on yr. Lordship and the Society.

I beg leave again to assure yr. Lordship that Mr. Lennon is a Clergyman of very good Character somewhat advanc'd in years, and has always behav'd himself regularly in his duty, and to the great satisfaction of all those who have been under his Care, and I am convinc'd, will discharge his duty in such parts to yr. Lordships full pleasure, and expectation.

I must pray yr. Lordship at yr. leisure to let me know if This [*illegible*] be agreeable to you and whether you are pleasd to send him to North Carolina on the terms here proposd to yr. Lordship. He only waits yr. Commands to be gone.

I intreat yr. Lordship to forgive these importunities and to believe me with the utmost esteem My Lord yr. Lordships most oblig'd and obedient Servant.

Ralph Meath

Janry. 31st 1729. Dublin

ALS.

[*SPG/A/23*]

Petition
1730 Easter Monday

<242.> Right Reverend Father in God.
Sir

We the Vestry Men and Church Wardens of St. James Parish on New Hanover River alias Cape Fair do as in duty bound humbly pray your pious Affection and Religious Regard towards us in this Remote Part of the World; We are a New Settlement upwards of Fifteen Hundred Souls, and have had no Minister but what is some hundred of Miles distance from us, till the Reverend and Worthy Mr. John La'Piere out of his great Goodness and pious Concern for us at our most earnest entreaties was prevailed with to leave his Benefit of five hundred pounds Per Annum which he recd. for Ministring to a French Congregation in the Parish of St. Thomas in South Carolina to whom he was sent above Twenty Years agoe by your Predecessor The old People being dead and their Children Speaking English, the end he was then sent for ceased which inclined him to consent and bring his Wife and three Children and resides among us where he constantly and Cheerfully Officiates his holy Function notwithstanding all the hardships a New Settlement is exposed to. We therefore humbly pray for your approbation and Assistance to the Honorable Society for Propagating the Gospel in Foreign Parts to whom we have now wrote. That he may be admitted one of their Missioners here and receive the Benefit of their Pious Bounty faithfully promising Reverend Sir, that we will make such provision for the <243> Maintenance of our Minister as we hope will always encourage Godly Divines to live among us and forever pray for your health and prosperity here and Eternal happiness hereafter who are Reverend Sir Your dutiful and Obedient Humble Servants.

Richd. Marsden, M. Moore, R. Moore, Nathl. Moore, Corns. Harnett, Edwd. Hyrne, Saml. Swann, Chr. Bevis, Edwd. Smith

At the Vestry held in New Hanover
River Easter Monday 1730.

[*Endorsed*:]
To the Rt. Reverend Father in God
Edmund Lord Bishop of London.

Copy. Read at a meeting of the SPG on June 19, 1730, and referred to the Committee. Journal of the SPG, V, 255. No further action on this petition is recorded in the minutes.

[*CO* 5/323]

Instructions
1730 December 14

<37> G. Rex. Instructions For Our Trusty and Welbeloved George Burrington Esqr. Our Capt. General and Governor in Chief, in and over Our Province of North Carolina in America, Given at Our Court at St. James's, the Fourteenth Day of Decembr. 1730, in the Fourth Year of Our Reign. [...]

74. You are to permit a Liberty of Conscience to all Persons (except Papists) So as they be contented with a Quiet and Peaceable Enjoyment of the Same, not giving Offence or Scandal to the Government.

75. You Shall take especial care, that God Almighty be Devoutly and Duly Served, throughout Your Goverment, the Book of Common Prayer as by Law establish'd, Read each Sunday and Holyday, and the Blessed Sacrament Administred according to the Rites of the Church of England.

76. You shall take care that the Churches already built there, be well and orderly Kept, and that more be built, as the Province Shall by Gods Blessing be improved; And that besides, a Competent <78> Maintenance to be Assigned to the Minister of each Orthodox Church, a convenient House be built at the common Charge for Each Minister, and a competent proportion of Land Assigned him for a Glebe, and Exercise of his Industry.

77. And You are to take care that the Parishes be So limitted and Settled as You Shall find most convenient for Accomplishing this Good Work.

78. You are not to prefer any Minister to any Ecclesiastical Benefice in the Province, without a Certificate from the Right Reverend Father in God the Lord Bishop of Lond., of his being Conformable to the Doctrine and Discipline of the Church of England, and of a good Life and Conversation. And if any person already preferred to a Benefice, Shall Appear to You to give Scandal either by his Doctrine or his Manners, You are to Use the proper and usual Means for the Removal of him, and to Supply the Vacancy in Such manner, as We have Directed.

79. You are to give Orders forthwith (if the Same be not already done) that every Orthodox Minister within Your Government, be One of the Vestry, in his respective Parish, and that no Vestry be held without him, except in Case of Sickness, or that after Notice of a Vestry Summond he Omit to come.

<79> 80. You are to Enquire whether there be any Minister within Your Government, who preaches and Administers the Sacrament in any Orthodox Church or Chappel without being in due Orders, and to give an Acct. thereof, to the Ld. Bishop of London.

81. And to the end, the Ecclesiastical Jurisdiction of the Lord Bishop of London may take place in that Our Province, So far as conveniently may be; We doe think fit that You doe give all Countenance, and Encouragement to the Exercise of the Same excepting

only the collating the Beneficies, Granting Licences for Mariages and Probat of Wills, which We have reserv'd to You Our Governor and to the Commander in Chief of Our Said Province for the time being, as far as by Law We may.

82. And We do further direct, that no Schoolmaster be henceforeward permitted to come from this Kingdom, and to keep School in that Our Said Province, without the Licence of the said Lord Bishop of London. And that no other Person now there, or that Shall come from other Parts, Shall be admitted to keep School in North Carolina, without Your Licence First Obtained.

83. And You are to take Especial care, that a Table of Marriages, Established by the Canons of the Church of England be hung up <80> in every Orthodox Church, and duly Observed; And You are to Endeavour to get a Law passed in the Assembly of that Province (if not already done) for the Strict Observation of the Said Table.

84. Having been Graciously pleased to Grant unto the Right Reverend Father in God, Edmund Lord Bishop of London a Commission, under Our Great Seal of Great Britain, whereby he is impowered to Exercise Ecclesiastical Jurisdiction, by himself or by Such Commissaries as he Shall Appoint in Our Several Plantations in America; it is Our Will and Pleasure that You give all Countenance and due Encouragement to the Said Bishop of Lond. his Commissaries in the Legal Exercise of Such Ecclesiastical Jurisdiction, according to the Laws of the Province under Your Government, and to the Tenour of the Said Commission a Copy whereof is hereunto Annex'ded And that You doe, cause the Commission, to be forthwith Registred in the publick Records of that Our Province.[1]

85. The Right Reverend Father in Gód, Edmond Ld. Bishop of London, having presented a Petition to his Said late Majesty,[2] humbly beseeching him to Send Instructions to the Governors of all the Several Plantations, in America, That they cause all Laws already made against Blasphemy, Prophaness Adultery, Fornication, Bigamy,[3] Incest Prophanation <81> of the Lords Day, Swearing and Drunkenness, in their respective Governments, to be Vigorously executed; And We thinking it highly just, that all Persons who Shall Offend in any of the particulars aforsaid, Should be prosecuted and punished for the Said Offences. It is therefore Our Will and Pleasure, that You take due care, for the punishment of the fore mentioned Vices, and that You earnestly recommend to the Assembly of North Carolina; to provide Effectual Laws for the Restraint and punishment of all Such of the fore menetioned Vices, aganst which no Laws are as Yet provided. And also You are to Use Your Endeavours, to render the Laws in being more Effectual by providing for the punishment of the afore mentioned Vices, by presentments upon Oath to be made to the Temporal Courts by the Churchwardens of the Several Parishes at proper times of the Year, to be Appointed for that purpose; And for the further Discouragement of Vice and Encouragement of Virtue, and good living, that by Such Example the Infidels may be invited and perswaded to Embrace the Christian Religion. You are not to Admit any Person to publick Trusts or Employments in the Province under Your Goverment, whose ill Fame and Conversation may occasion Scandal. And it is Our further Will and Pleasure, that You recommend to the Assembly, to Enter upon proper Methods for the Erecting and maintaining of Schools, in Order to the <82> training up of Youth to Reading, and to a necessary knowledge of the principles of Religion; And You are also with the Assistance of the Council and Assembly to find out the best Means to facilitate and Encourage the Conversion of Negroes, and Indians to the Christian Religion. [...]

D. Clauses relating to the established church were not included in any set of instructions from the Lords Proprietors to their governors and deputy governors in North Carolina. The king's instructions to George Burrington, the province's first royal governor, do, however, address the establishment, and the relevant clauses were retained, mostly unaltered, in those issued to Burrington's successors.

[1]This clause is included in instructions issued in 1733 to the next governor, Gabriel Johnston, but entirely omitted in those to Johnston's successors.

[2]George I.

[3]*Bigamy* is changed to *polygamy* in instructions to Burrington's successors.

[*CO 5/308*]

George Burrington to Duke of Newcastle 1731 July 2

July 2d 1731

North Carolina. To the Duke of Newcastle One of His Majesty's Principal Secretarys of State

May it Pleasure Your Grace [...]

75th and 76th Instructions I laid before the Assembly concerning Churches and the Publick Worship but I Could not Observe much Sence of Religion among them or that any Notice was taken, This Country has no Orthodox Minister legally Settled, those that formerly have been here Generally Proved so Very bad that they gave People Offence by their Vicious Lives, The Country is Divided into Parishes and their are in Each Parish Church Wardens and a Vestery who have power to raise Money by a Poll Tax not Exceeding 5 sh./ in Bill Money on Tythable Persons, which now the Bills are So low, amounts to a Small Summ, this is put to Maintain the Poor if any or Paying some Neighbouring Minister for Comeing out of Virginia, and to pay Readers there being one or Generally More at a Small Stipend Hired Annually to Read the Common Service of the Church on Sundays, and Some Printed Sermon at a Chapple House were there is any or in some Publick Place, Several Parishes having by Contributions or otherwise built Chapples at Convenient Places.

85th Instruction, for Laws to Punish and Restrain Vice, There are Already Good and Wholsome Ones in the Country Provided for that Purpose, as may be Seen in the Book of Laws, which I Can only Say have been better Framed than Executed, But shall for the future Recommend a more Exact Observance of them. I Intend pursuant to this Instruction when the Assembly is Disposed to doe Business very Heartily Recommend the Establishing Schools for the Education of Youth, so much wanted here and So Necessary for the Early Implanting Knowledge and Virtue. And as for making Laws for the Conversion of Negroes and Indians, I Cannot Expect much will be done that way Soon since so little Regard is God [*sic*] Even among the English, to promote the Publick Worship and Divine Service. [...]

I am My Lord Duke with all Duty and Submission Your Grace's Most humble Most Obedient And Most Devoted Servant.

Geo. Burrington

LS.

[*SPG/Jou/5*]

Journal of the SPG
1731 August 20

<304> 20th August 1731 [. . .]

<305> 9. A Memorial[1] of Mr. John Gale[2] concerning sending an Itinerant Missionary to North Carolina was read, and referr'd to the Committee: And the Reverend Mr. Nutkins[3] offering to goe on the said Mission: Agreed that he lay his Testimonials before the Committee. [. . .]

Minutes.

[1]Not located.
[2]Not identified, but perhaps of the family that included Christopher Gale.
[3]Not identified.

[*SPG/C/7*]

Petition
[1732]

<142> To The Society for the Propogation of the Gospell in forreign parts. The Representation and Petition of John Boyd[1] Sheweth

That your Petitioner hath Lived for some time in North Carolina and is well acquainted with the country that there is no minister of the Church of England residing in any Part of that Government for want of which many of the People are drawen away By Presbiterian anabaptist or other Dissenting teachers many of their children unbaptized and the administration of the Sacrament of the Lords Supper wholly Neglected.

That Your Petitioner being recommended by many of the Gentlemen of that country is come over to England to Obtain holy orders and to return as a Missionary from this venerable Society if they shall think fitt to receave him into their service.

That if he shall Be receaved by the society as their missionary he Proposes to Preach and to administer the Sacraments through the whole Country twice a year and administer the sacraments and Constantly to serve two Precincts By which means he hopes to have a settlement according to Law and Divisions made by the country which they will never endeavour till there is a minister among them.

That He shall keep a constant Journall of all his Proceedings and yearly transmitt the same to the society.

John Boyd

[*Endorsed:*]
Entered
Petition of John Boyd
read the 15th Septemr. 1732

DS. Read at a meeting of the SPG on September 15, 1732, when it was agreed "that when he shall be in priests Orders he be appointed Missionary to North Carolina with a Salary of Eighty pounds per Annum to commence from Midsummer last, and that the Lord Bishop of London be desired to give him a Text, and to appoint some Member or Members of the Society to hear him read Prayers and Preach, and upon the report of his Lordship that he perform'd to such Members satisfaction, the Secretary give him the necessary dispatch in Order for his Proceeding on his Mission." Journal of the SPG, VI, 37.

[1]Rev. John Boyd. See appendix.

[*LAM/FUL/IX*]

Rev. Alexander Garden to [Bishop of London]
1731/2 February 25

<262> My Lord [. . .]

The No. of your Lordships *Pastoral Letters*[1] I recd. for North Carolina, I have sent thither by a good Opportunity: Part of which I orderd into the hands of the reverend Mr. *Lapierre*, for the use of the new setled part of that Colony at *Cape-Fear*, and the rest into the hands of Collonel *Mosely*, for the *Old Setlements*; whose Care and Discretion in Dispersing them I coud best depend upon.

<263> Mentioning of *Cape Fear* puts me in mind to give your Lordship some further Account of Mr. *Marsden*. My last Account of him was, that he was gone from *Cape Fear* to *Lisbon*, to which I now add that from thence he soon after returnd back to *Cape Fear* again, with a *Cargo of Goods*, to the Value of £1500 Sterling, which he had found Means to be credited with 'mongst the English Merchants at *Lisbon*, on his own *Bills of Exchange* (not worth six pence) to *London*. His protested Bills soon followd him; but to no Purpose; he was got into a *place of Sanctuary*, and which he had made more so to himself by Means of his *Cargo*; so that the Gentlemen of this place intrusted to sue him, have not been able to touch either his *Person*, or one Shilling of his *Effects* to this Day. With the *Produce* of this Adventure he has setled a *Plantation* there, and now employs himself in that and a peddling sort of Merchandizing. He is not employd by the people there as a *Minister*; only, I'm informd, he preaches sometimes, to those that will come to hear him, at his own House. [. . .]

I humbly crave your Lordships Blessing, and am My Lord Your Lordship's most dutiful son and obedient humble Servant.

A. Garden.

So. Carolina

Charlestown
Feb. 25th 1731/2

[*Endorsed:*]
Garden/Lesly
Visitation
Pastoral Letters 2d, and 3d
Hooper-£200—Provid.
Commission
Marsden

Recd. Apr. 25, 1732
Answered

ALS.

[1]Not located.

[*LAM/FUL/VI*]

George Burrington to [Bishop of London]
1731/2 March 15

<230>

N. Carolina the 15th of March 1731/2.

My Lord.

I was not able to prevail with the last Assembly to make necessary provision to subsist a convenient number of Clergymen, but have a very good expectation the ensueing one will come into the measures I proposed.

Doctor Marsden continues in the South part of this Province, he sometimes preaches, Baptiseth Children, and marrieth when desired.

The Reverend Mr. Beville Granville nephew to the Lord Lansdown is also here, he was going to Maryland but wee have hopes he will continue with us, if your Lordship will procure the usual allowance from the Society.

These are all the ministers of the Church of England now in this Government. There is one Presbyterian minister who has a mixt audience; and there are four Meeting houses of Quakers. Mr. John Boyd (the Gentleman who delivers this letter) was bred att the University of Glasgow, has practised Physick in the Colony of Virginia seven years, is now desirous to take orders; several Gentlemen of my Acquaintance in this Country, give him the character of a worthy conscientious man, well qualifyed for the Ministry, they are desirous of haveing him for their Pastor, and earnestly requested me to recomend Mr. Boyd to my Lord Bishop for Orders, a certificate, and an allowance from the Society the better to support him, if your Lordship thinks him deserveing; as I belive Mr. Boyd's designs are purely to do good in takeing the ministry upon him, and not out of any view of gain, I humbly recomend him to your Lordship for Orders and a Certificate. I am My Lord Your Most humble And Most Obedient Servant.

Geo. Burrington

ALS.

[*LAM/FUL/XII*]

Testimonial
1732 April 4

<173> To the Right Reverend Father in God Edmund by divine permission Lord Bishop of London and to all our beloved in Christ to whom thes presents shall Come Greeting.

As it is a general point of Justice and our Christian duty to bear witness to the truth, so it is in a more particular manner when we are thereunto specially required. And for as much as John Boyd of the County of King Willm. in the Colony of Virginia being desireous to be admitted into Holy Orders hath desired that our Letters testimonial concerning the praiseworthiness of his life and Conversation may be granted him by us. We therefore whose names are hereunto subscribed do testifie that we have for these three years last past personally Known the Said John Boyd, all which time he lived among us, and piously, Religiously and Soberly led his life and seriously applied himself to his Studies, and furthermore as to the things which pertain to Religion never held or believed any thing that was not Consonant to the Christian and Catholick Verity and what the Church of England approves and maintaines. In Testimony whereof we have hereunto Sett our hands and Seals this 4th Day of Apl. 1732.

Zach. Brooke of St. Pauls Parish in Hanove. County Clk. (Seal), Jno. Brunskill of St. Margarets parish in Kg. Willm. County Clk. (Seal), Fra. Peart of St. Stepns. parish in Northumberland County Clk. (Seal), Daniell Coleman Churchwarden of St. Margarets Parish (Seal), Rolf Parish Church Warden of St. Margarets Parish (Seal), John Douner Vestryman (Seal)

[*Endorsed*:]
Boyd
Testimonial Canons

DS.

[*LAM/FUL/VI*]

Christopher Gale to Bishop of London
1732 April 6

<232>

Edenton In No. Carolina.
Apr. the 6th 1732.

My Lord,

Yr. Lordship haveing been so Good as Permitt me to address you on the Account of the State of Religion in North Carolina: And not meeting with any one in London whilst I was there, whome yr. Lordship thought fitt to send upon such A Mission I take leave to Inform yr. Lordship That here is now at Edenton one Mr. Bevil Granvill, who seems to have the general Approbation of the Inhabitants, and was design'd for Maryland at the request and by direction of the Lord Baltimore. But falling in here in his passage thither, The Governour has prevaild with him to stay for one year: And he so well likes the place, that he promises to continue with us; in case he has Encouragement to support him.

For this Year the people have made verry considerable Subscriptions to his Satisfaction; but as those methods of Support are too precarious to be Depended on for Continuance: If yr. Lordship <*Lord Bishop of London*> thinks fitt to approve of him for the Mission upon the footing I laid down to the Society, He sais he shall verry willingly accept of it, and make his aboad amongst us. But as he is under the misfortune of not being known to yr. Lordship, yet being senceable of that tender care in not Approveing of any Missionarys but such as are well recommended He beggs leave to referr yr. Lordship for his Character to The Lord Ducy, and Lord Lansdown, who (he sais) Know him verry well. As for my self, I have but once heard him perform Divine Service or preach but I must say he did both in so Devout and Gracefull A manner that I cannot forbear mentioning of it to yr. Lordship. But as I presume his Excellency the Governour may have writt to you on his Account. Nothing but the Duty I owe your Lordship, and the Concern I have for the yet unhappy State of Religion in this <233> province, wou'd have Occation'd you this trouble from My Lord Yr. Lordships most Devoted humble Servant.

C. Gale

P.S. My Lord,

Since yr. Lordship was pleas'd to talk with me on Carolina Affaires in general, and being in Council, when the petition of Mr. Smith[1] Ch. Justice against our Governour and others was read; I hope yr. Lordship will not take amiss my Informing you, That the Facts in that petition, now I am upon the Spott, appeare to me more notoriously not only to be false and Scandalous, as I said in London, but to be formd only by himself and one or two busy fellows, without any Authority that I can learn from the several bodys of people he pretends to represent. His Accusation against the Gentlemen he mentions and his pretence of the Governour's Screening them is equally groundless.

And as little truth is there in his Represention of the Governour's Conduct, who has acted with remarkable Caution and temper.

Yr. Lordships etc.

C. G.

[*Endorsed:*]
Gale
Granvil
N. Carolina

ALS.

[1]William Smith (d. 1743) held several high offices in the colony of North Carolina, most notably chief justiceship of the General Court, 1731, 1734-1743.

[*LAM/FUL/XII*]

Rev. Francis Peart to "Sir"
1732 April 15

<175> Sir

Having an opportunity to write by Mr. Boyd the bearer hereof, I thought it my duty to Acquaint you, that to my great satisfaction I am successfully settled in a Parish in Virginia; which I must own was very much owing to your interest with and introduction to my Lord of London, and gratitude will ever oblige me to Acknowledge your other repeated favours. Experience has fully Convinced me that it is the entire disposition of your Nature to good offices and therefore with the more boldness I take upon me to recommend Mr. Boyd to your Care whose business is to wait upon my Lord on the Same Account as I formerly did and to be introduced to his Lordship by you may be of Singular service to him. He is a Gent. whose employment in Virga. has been in the practice of Physick, and having too good a conscience to use that exorbitant extortion which most of our practicioners do, chooses rather to take upon him the ministry. I have been severall years acquainted with him and think him both as to his parts (of which my Lord will be a Judge upon Examination) and his Morals deserving of a Good Character. But I need not enlarge upon this, for reference being had to his other Testimonials his character will more at Large appear. [. . .]

Please to present my humble and dutifull respects to his Lord and accept of the same yourself from Sir Your most obliged Humble Servant.

Fra. Peart Clk.

Virginia April 15th 1732

ALS.

[*LAM/FUL/VI*]

Rev. Bevill Granville to [Bishop of London]
1732 May 6

<234>

Edenton No. Carolina
May the 6th 1732.

My Lord

From Ld. Baltimores frequent sollicitations to leave England and settle in Maryland, and upon his promise to provide for me in the best manner that that Province would allow, I took Shipping from Dublin in order to go there; landing in No. Carolina, I accidentally mett Mr. Burrington, who earnestly entreated and perswaded me to stay in this province there being so great occasion for Ministers, as your Lordships will Judge when I assure you that I Baptized near a Thousand Children, and person's in a very Short time after my coming in. As Mr. Burrington and Mr. Gale are pleas'd to write in my behalf, I thought it my Duty (tho' personally unknown to you) to acquaint your Lordship how willing I am to fix in a Country where the Clergy is so much wanted, and where so few care to Settle; Hoping that (as unworthy a Member as I am) I may be of Some service to that Church whereto I belong. Being well assur'd of one thing, that lest my abillity's be never so poor, yet the name of a Minister will hinder the growth of Various dangerous sects willing and ready to over-run the whole province.

Should Your Lordship think me worthy of the Mission You shall always hear that I am industrious in the Service of God and these people, and that I shall act in such a manner I hope as to deserve yr. Lordships approbation, and as becomes the person indulg'd with the Friendship of the aforemention'd Gentlemen.

I am My Lord Your Lordships most Dutyfull and Obedient Servant.

Bevill Granville

[*Endorsed*:]
Granville
N. Carolina

ALS.

[*SPG/C/7*]

Rev. Brian Berks to Secretary, SPG
1732 May 9

<141>

May 9 1732

Reverend Sir

Dr. Mangey was so kind as to let me have your Book,[1] that Relates to the incorporated Society etc. Upon perusing of it, I find that North Carolina is the properest Place in the World, for a Clergy Man to go to that is either weary of his Life; or fit to appear no where else. Dr. Mangey would have me go to South Carolina, and thank him, I believe will do what he can for me; He will sollicit for me at the next meeting I hope and procure me the 80 Pounds per An. which I was to have had, had I gone to North Carolina. I humbly beg that you with him, will promote my Interest in this Affair to the utmost of your Power and be assurd, I shall thankfully acknowledge the Obligation. I desire that you will Favor me with a Line after the Meeting, and that you will be so good as to tell me what to do. Be pleasd to direct to me at the Reverend Mr. Berks's Rector of Bilsthorp near Mansfield Nottinghamshire.

I am Reverend Sir your most obedient humble Servant.

B. Berks

P.S. I have made strict Enquiry for a Ship this 2 or 3 Months, and cannot hear of one that goes to North Carolina Ergo Ter. Incog.

N.B. I coud not possibly stay to wait upon the Society, my Father having sent man and Hope for me.

[*Addressed*:]
To The Reverend Dr. Humphreys
in Warwick Court
Warwick Lane near Newgate

[*Endorsed*:]
<1> <late>
Mr. Brian Berks
May 9th 1732
Answer'd the 13th June

ALS.

[1]David Humphreys, D.D., *An Historical Account of the Incorporated Society for the Propagation of the Gospel in Foreign Parts*...(London: Printed by Joseph Downing in Bartholomew-Close near West-Smithfield, 1730). The work of the Society in North Carolina is discussed on pp. 128-143.

[*LAM/FUL/VI*]

George Burrington to [Bishop of London]
1732 May 10

<236>

N. Carolina the 10th of May 1732.

My Lord

I did my self the honour to address a letter to your Lordship sometime since by Mr. Boid, wherein the Reverend Mr. Granville is mentioned, this Gentleman I prevail'd with to stay in this Country one year, a subscription has been made for him by particular Persons, more adequate to the circumstances of the contributors then to Mr. Granville's merits, who is incessant and indefatigable in his endeavours to promote the service of the Church of England, allready has Christened about one thousand Children, and is now on a progress in which he will Baptize some hundreds. Wee fear Mr. Granville will leave us when his year is expired, unless your Lordship with the Society think proper to establish him a Missionary in this Province.

Mr. La Pierre a French Clergyman has an allowance from some People att Cape Fear in this Government which is renew'd, when I wrote the former letter was told, he had quitted that place, but after was certainly inform'd had agreed to stay another year. Doctor Marsden officiates gratis, att a place call'd Onslow Fourty miles from his own habitation, and a Clergyman beneficed in Virginia[1] preaches once in a Month in a precinct named Bertie on the borders of this Country, this is My Lord the condition wee are att present in respect to Ministers.

Mr. Gale who came from England lately brought a copy of complaints against me to his Sacred Majesty by William Smith, the said Mr. Gale inform'd me, an order of Council passed for the complainer to examine wittnessess to make good his charge, which I think he will not attempt; because he knows the chief part to be false, as those complaints lye in the Council office, if my adversary doth not proceed in a little time, I will send my Answer (allmost finisht) till it is seen I hope Your Lordship nor any Lord of the Council will entertain an ill opinion of me, being very wrongfully calumniated as I shall in due time make appear.

I beg your Lordship's pardon for presumeing to write the fore-going paragraph, and leave to subscribe my self as realy.

I am (With all due respect) My Lord Your Most humble And Most Obedient Servant.

Geo. Burrington.

ALS.

[1]Presumably Nathaniel Jones.

[*LAM/FUL/VI*]

William Hay to [Bishop of London]
1732 September 25

<238>

My Lord

Yesterday in the afternoon, I heard Mr. Boyd (the Societys Missionary to North Carolina) read prayers, and preach on St. Matt. 5 and 9th[1] And he performd both very well.

I am My Lord Your Lordships most obedient humble Servant.
Wm. Hay

Monday
Septr. 25, 1732

[*Endorsed*:]
Boyd
Hay

ALS.

[1]"Blessed are the peacemakers, for they shall be called the children of God." Matthew 5:9, Authorized Version.

[*SPG/Jou/6*]

Journal of the SPG
1732 October 20

<39> 20th October 1732. [. . .]

<42> 8. The Secretary also acquainted the Board that Mr. Griffith Hughes and Mr. John Boyd having recd. Priests Orders had read Prayers and Preached, which they performed to the satisfaction of the Persons desired by the Bishop of London to <43> hear them, and that he had thereupon, according to the Orders of the Society, provided them with the books appointed by the Standing Rules, and given them the other necessary dispatches for their proceeding on their Missions to which they were severally appointed by the Society. [. . .]

Minutes.

[*LAM/FUL/VI*]

Rev. John LaPierre to Bishop of London
1732 November 29

<240>

My lord

As I am one who in Queen Ann's Reign 1708 was by your Lordship's most worthy predecessour sent to South and north Carolina, to officiate in both at Several times as minister of the Church of England under the royal and Episcopal protection; having for the full space of twenty years shared my office between a french Parrish named St. Denis, and an English parrish Called St. Thomas under the reverend Mr. Hazel the rector of the Same; I was at last called from this former province to the next adjacent Contrey Named

Cape fear or New Hannover belonging to North Carolina where I have already been four Years, following my functions and now I See my Self under the Sad necessity of Superseading them for the reasons I shall Acquaint your Lordship with; the people of my Charge did at the first carry a fair correspondence with me; till one Mr. *Richard Marsden* Came amongst us, with a Commission as he said from the Bishop of London and from the Honorable Society for the propagation of the Gospel in foreign parts, to be an Inspector over the Clergy in these parts of the north, tho I could never Hear that your Lordship had any other commissary besides the Reverend Mr. Garden in South or North Carolina. Moreover the Said Mr. Marsden since that time has forsaken such pretensions, having taken upon him to be a publick merchant and traffickant, Since his late voyage to Lisbon in portugal and follows it daily amongst us, and thinks it no way inconsistent with the Sacred orders, for he it is, who has set my hearers against me, with his proffers of serving them gratis; which was the reason why my Subscribers have not paid me According to their promise in writing and thereby have disabled me to wait upon them as their minister And Compelled me by the same means to work as a slave in the field for my living, after gratifying them with Eight months of my time, and the same mr. Marshden him self who had made the people of Cape fear such generous proffers has left them since having made intrest with Governour Barrington for the new parrish of *Core Sound and new river tho'* not as yet settled but he is contented with the private Acknowledgements of the inhabitants of that place. I have already laid before your Lordship the first obstacle to my going foreward in my office: but there is still another My lord, of no less consequence viz., the great misunderstanding between the great men of the place and Governour Barrington; for having at his first arrival applied to his Excellency on the behalf of their church, in order to recommend it to the Societie's bounty and to your Lordship's protection: his excellency return'd them this answer, from both: that this could not be done till their church can be Erected into a parrish, and till they could allow to their Minister a Parsonage and a glebe, a thing they have not as yet thought upon but have endeavoured to shew in opposition to the Governours words that it was a Parrish and their vestry is gone so far that way as to Assess the countrey for my last payment which was before consisting of private Subscriptions: but they alter'd it at their pleasure without the Governour's consent, So that at this time I am the Sufferer depending upon nó manner of Certainty and not daring to take the bare word of those who have already Sufficiently imposed upon my Simplicity. Therefore, My Lord, as I account myself happy in following your Commands, Suffer me likewise to desire the favour of your paternal Advice tending to the preservation of My Lord your Lordships most dutiful and obedient Servant.

John Lapierre

Cape fear alias new Hannover
November the 29th 1732

[*Addressed*:]
To the Right Reverend
Father in God Edmund Bishop of London
at his Pallace of Fullham
These

[*Endorsed:*]
Lapiere
Cape fear
Received Febr. 17, 1732/3

ALS.

[*LAM/FUL/XXXVI*]

Bishop of London to Governments in Colonies
ca. 1733

Having receiv'd information that one Marsden, a Clergyman, goes about in the Plantations, pretending to be my Commissary General for Visiting the Churches and Clergy in the several Governments there; I have thought it necessary to signify[1] to the several Governments[2] that I have made no such appointment, and that if he produce any Commission from me to that purpose, it is forg'd; and further, that I am credibly inform'd,[3] that the said Marsden is a person of very ill character.

Edmd. London

Draft.

[1]*Send a circular letter* written and struck through.
[2]*To signify* written and struck through.
[3]*By persons on whom I can depend* written and struck through.

[*CO 5/294*]

George Burrington to Board of Trade
1732/3 January 1

To the Right Honourable the Lords of Trade and Plantations.
May it Please your Lordships.

I do my self the Honour to Send the Lords of Trade, an account of the Present State, and condition of North Carolina; [...]

There is not one Clergyman of the Church of England, regularly settled in this Government. The former Missionarys were so little approved off; that the Inhabitants seem very indifferent, whither any more come to them.

Some Presbyterian, or rather Independent Ministers from New England have got congregations, more may follow; many of them being unprovided with liveings in that country; where a Preacher is seldom pay'd more, then the value of twenty Pounds Sterling a year by his Parishioners.

The Quakers in this Government are considerable, for their Numbers, and substance; the regularity of their Lives, hospitality to Strangers, and kind offices to New Settlers Induceing many to be of their Persuasion. [...]

Your Lordships Most humble and Most obedient Servant

Geo. Burrington

No. Carolina the
1st of January 1732/3

LS.

[*SPG/SAP*]

Report
1732/3 February 16

<62> <*An Abstract of the Proceedings of the Society.*> [. . .] The Society have this last Year received very earnest Application from several Places for Missionaries; from *New Town* and *Reading* in *Connecticut* Government, in *New England*; from *North Carolina*, which whole Province was entirely destitute of any Minister; from *Kent County* in *Pensylvania*; from *Scituate* in *New England*; from *Providence*, the chief of the *Bahama* Islands; all which Islands are without a Minister; and also from the Trustees for settling a Colony in *Georgia*, in *South Carolina*. The Society have resolved to establish new Missions in all these Places; being fully persuaded, there is a great Want of Missionaries for the Instruction <63> of such great Bodies of People, who have lived several Years without the Celebration of Publick Divine Worship. [. . .]

And the Reverend Mr. *Boyd* hath also been appointed, and is gone over Missionary to *North Carolina*, which whole Country had no Minister. And the Society having had Application made to them by several Persons for the other Missions, they will be very soon supply'd with Ministers. [. . .]

Printed. Extracted from the yearly publication containing the sermon preached at the annual anniversary meeting of the SPG, together with a review of the activities of the Society and its missionaries during the preceding year. The date above is the date of the meeting.

[*LAM/FUL/XII*]

Certificate
1732/3 March 17

<188>

Williamsburgh Mar. 17, 1732-3.

Whereas the Reverend Mr. John Garcia[1] dessyning to remove himself and his family into North-Carolina is desirous of a Certificate from me of his life and Conversation during his continuance in this Country of Virginia; These are to certify to all persons concerned that during the time of his Ministry in this Government (which is now near nine years) as far as I know he has been a person of a good life and conversation, and sober and diligent in the Exercise of his Ministerial function.

James Blair. Commissary.

Wms.burgh June 27th 1733

The above Certificate is given to Mr. Garzia by the Bishop of London's Commissary.

William Gooch[2]

DS.

[1]Rev. John Garzia. See appendix.

[2]Sir William Gooch (1681-1751), governor of Virginia 1727-1749. *DAB*.

[*LAM/FUL/XII*]

Rev. John Boyd to Bishop of London
1733 April 5

<201>

Virginia Apr. 5 1733

My Lord

Upon my arrivall in Virginia I waited on Mr. Commissary Blair, in order to clear up my character to him, which I have done very much to his satisfaction concerning which he will write to your Lordship by this opportunity.

I shall if your Lordship thinks fitt and require it, yearly transmitt a testimoniall of my life and conversation from the People among whom I reside, and it shall alwayes be my endeavour (by divine assistance) to live up to the Character I have assumed; that none may have any thing to say to my charge.

Mr. Granville has removed from Carolina to maryland: I am Now removing what effects I have in Virginia there[1] where the People are very willing to receive and Give me all the encouragement they can.

I shall By another opportunity be able to give a full and satisfactory account of the state of the country. I Hope your Lordship when you have received Mr. Blairs Letters will allou me to have my Priests orders and Licence from Mr. Paulett. Begging your Lordships Blessing and Protection I am your Lordships Most Obedient and Most Humble servant.

John Boyd

[*Addressed*:]
To The Right Reverend Father
In God Edmund Lord Bishop of London

[*Endorsed*:]
Blair, Boyd
Recept Jul. 6, 1733.

ALS.

[1]I.e., North Carolina.

[*LAM/FUL/XII*]

Rev. James Blair to [Bishop of London]
1733 May 5

Williamsburgh May 5, 1733.

My Lord

I have received your Lordships by Mr. Pedin; but before it came to my hand I discovered the abuse which had been put upon me by some of Mr. Boyds Enemies, who with abundance of artifice had laid a train to give me a very bad character of him. I was confirmed in this bad character after I understood that Mr. Boyd had been in this towne where I live, and never came near the Governour nor my self, tho' at that time he was resolved to go to England for orders. I have had opportunities since of informing my self more particularly concerning his character, and theirs likewise from whom I had my information concerning him, and am sensible he was very grossly abused, and with a malicious design to do him a prejudice. Had I had the least acquaintance with him I could not have represented the matter from fame and hearsay as I did. I am now fully satisfied after I have had him five or six weeks at my house, that he is both a man of good parts and Learning, and of a sober life and Conversation suitable to the character of a clergyman. And therefore I must now, to do him right, as much interceed for your Lordships favour to him, as I did formerly caution you against him. He is now a removing his family to North Carolina, where I hope he may do a great dale of good both to their Souls and Bodies; for he is a good Surgeon and Physitian, and as good a Divine as most that come abroad are, and dayly improving. I am very glad your Lordship observed so justly of him your self, and put him in orders. But the more I enquire of the other man Cotton, I find his Character worse and worse. I took care to inform the Commissary of Maryland of Mr. Wrights character so soon as he fled out of this Country, which hindred his fixing there, and now that we have a post set up it will be more easy for us to give notice of irregular persons all over the Continent. I beg your Lordships good prayers and Blessing, and am My Lord Your Lordships most obedient much obliged Servant.

James Blair.

[*Endorsed*:]
Blair, Boyd
Recept. Jul. 6, 1733.

ALS.

[*LAM/FUL/VI*]

Rev. Richard Marsden to [Bishop of London]
1733 June 20

<242>

Brunswick Cape Fear in North Carolina
June the 20th, 1733

May it please yr. Lordship

I have for some time been under very great Inquietude and concern and I have neglected to write to your Lordship since I left Jamaica on the death of the late duke of Portland;[1] but I have this satisfaction that it has not been from forgetfulness or disregard for I have always affected a Reputation (since I had the Honor to be Known to your Lordship) of having the utmost deference and Esteem for you. I was sensible yr. Lordship had recd. many Impressions to my disadvantage, and I must confess this made me ashamed to appear before you, or to address you but I cannot any longer find in my self the means of satisfieing the passion I feel in me to do my duty in this particular to your Lordship. I will not presume to say anything to Excuse the errors laid to my charge in Jamaica, Either in whole or in part; however with the strictest sincerity I make bould to assert to you, that I cannot Express the Insupportable trouble and grief of mind I sustain under a serious and great sense, and awakened apprehension, of haveing committed a crime[2] there, heniously reflecting on my holy Character, and whereby I have Incurred your displeasure. I had run through many changes and varieties in this uncertain state, and met with many losses and disapointments but I can with a good Conscience declare that the General bent of my Resolutions, and the constant course and tenor of my life and conversation has been pious, and strictly conformable to the Ghospel of Christ; and I have always discharged the ministerial function with an affectionate zeal and unwearied diligence in the several places where I have officiated, and as may appear by authentic certificates, which I hope may in some measure apologize for me. I presume to throw my self upon yr. Lordships compassion which being a virtue so agreeable to yr. nature I hope I shall not be an unfortunate Instance of Imploreing it. I humbly beg yr. pardon, and you ought to forgive me when I assure you I shall never forgive my self for any miscarriage I have been guilty of, or for haveing done anything to Incurr your dislike, or to forfeit your good opinion. When I arrived in England from Jamaica I had a statute of Banckrupt taken out against me and was striped of all I had and reduced to great want and obliged to throw my self upon the goodness of my cheif creditor who was so Kind as to assist me to go over to North America, and I have been settled at Cape Fear above three years, where I have been very servicable in promoteing the Interest of this new settlement, and with laborious diligence [I] have discharged the duties of my function, traveling from place to place, very often above a hundred miles distant from my habitation and that without any consideration of reward from any person, and I hope not without good success, but what ever success I have had I hope I shall receive the reward of an honest Endeavour from him who Estimates our pains not by their events (which are not in our power) but by their Natural tendencies and Sincere Intentions. The Goverment of North Carolina is at least three hundred miles in length and none of his majesties Plantations are in so great want of the Ghospel as this, and that which is most deplorable is this, that tho they want the Ghospel, they are not sensible of the want nor of the comfort and refreshment of ordinances.

When I came to Cape Fear I found one Mr. Lepear a French man that had for some time officiated to a French Congregation in the Goverment of South Carolina, and the Gentelmen here out of their Generosity provided him a house and Plantation and contributed to his support; I was chosen one of the vestry and gave him all the Encouragment I could on all occasions, and as the Parish was very large and t[he] Inhabitants dispersed at a great distance I preach'd very often in the most distant parts where he was uncapable of Supplys, as well as five or Six times a year traveling to some of the farthest parts of the Goverment where there was no Minister, as there is not any at present in the Goverment but in this settlement without the desire of receiving anything for my trouble for I had by the goodness of some got a Plantation, and by the Generosity of my greatest creditors and by my own Industry in the managment of my affairs, and in Improveing what assistance he had condescend to give me, I have procured a few servants which maintains me; But Mr. Leapear being of a very unsettled temper, and haveing done several things to disoblige his friends (after he had taken his solem leave of the People in a sermon) I was solicited to be their minister which I for some time refused hopeing Mr. Leapear would repent of his rashness, and they came into a temper of tenderness towards him; but last Easter Monday (Mr. Leapear not haveing preachd at the usual place in five months before) after a new vestry was chosen by the Inhabitants (as is usual in this Goverment on Easter monday) I was Elected their minister, and they agreed to allow me four hundred pound this Currency, and am to Preach two Sundays in three in the town of Brunswick, and the other Sunday sometimes up the North East branch of this river, and sometimes up the North west, which places are at a vast considerable distance, and gives me a very great fateague, but I was not willing to be confined to the town as Mr. Leapear was, because I had not so great opportunity of doing good as I heartily desired. What we call Cape Fear has not been settled above seven or Eight years; but we have daly a vast Increase of Inhabitants from diferent parts, and some persons of good substance, so that I believe we have at this Instant near fifteen hundred Inhabitants with negroes, and this must be a vast thriveing place because of the goodness of navigation for there is not any othere place in North Carolina capable of receiving ships of so great a burthen as this; our Bar is far better than that of Charles town, we have lately had a man of war here which is the first that was ever in any port in this Goverment, and the Capt. I am confident will do Justice to the place, and make a report agreeable to Justice and the goodness of the harbour; and it must in a short time be the Seat of Goverment. I am sensible of yr. Lordships favourable Inclinations to countenance and protect any clergy man who Endeavours with laborious diligence to discharge the duties of his function. I beseech you to retain a favourable opinion of me and if you condescend to receive me into favour it will be a grace I shall Endeavour to deserve by all the actions of my life. I have confidence of doing good in this place and amongst this people for I have their affections and nothing shall be wanting in my power by doctrine and Example to farther their Salvation. I have a great compassion for their souls and my labour in the ministry is now (I can truly say) my recreation altho I am near Sixty years old. I have no book, besides the Bible common prayer Book and Burket on the new testament, if your Lordship will be pleased out of yr. great goodness to Influence the Society to send me a few Books for my use, and some to be lent amongst the Inhabitants of Cape fear it will be recd. as a great and sensible favour and the books shall be taken care of according to any direction I shall receive. I have a great family to provide for, and the Sallery that have agreed to allow me is but precarious, and will but go a little way in provideing for a family as goods are sold here so that my cheif dependence will be on my Plantation, Except yr. Lordship out of your tenderness and compassion will be pleased to procure me a small Sallery from England, there is not any place in his majesties Collonies that requires the Societies consideration more than this does at this time. I have a daughter come over to me last year by the Kind assistance of my cheif friend and creditor mentioned before, who paid her passage; his name is John Eaton dodsworth, a Gentelman in London, and if I had it in my power I would have all my Children with me, but my ability will not alow me to send for them as yet. I hope I shall Experience yr. Lordships condescention of goodness towards me, and if you can forgive me the miscariage I was guilty of you shall never have reason to repent of what you may do for me, and I shall readily obey yr. commands in anything; and if yr. Lordship desires it I will get, and transmit to you and the Society a particular and Exact acct. of all the parts of this Goverment on all necessary points. I shall with a great deal of Impatience presume to Expect an answer from you. I shall conclude with beging yr. Lordships blessing and with assureing you that I am and to the last moment of my life shall be ambitious of being yr. Lordships most obedient and most Humble Servant.

Richd. Marsden

ALS.

[1]Henry Bentinck, 1st duke of Portland, was governor of Jamaica from 1721 to 1726. Marsden was chaplain to Portland from 1723 until the duke's death in 1726. Fleming James, "Richard Marsden, Wayward Clergyman," *William and Mary Quarterly*, Third Series, XI (October, 1954), 583-585.

[2]Presumably this refers to Marsden's bigamous marriage in 1724 to a wealthy Jamaican widow. C11/1781/25 (Chancery), Public Record Office, Kew, Surrey, England.

[*CO 5/342*]

Proceedings of the General Assembly
1733 July 4

At a General Assembly begun and held for His Majestys Province of North Carolina at Edenton the 4th day of July 1733. Present His Excellency George Burrington Esqr. Governour etc., The Honorable Nath. Rice, Jno. Bapta. Ashe, John Lovick, Edmd. Gale, William Owen Esqrs. Members of His Majestys Council.

His Excellency the Governour Commanded the Attendance of the Lower House, who came in a full body and presented Colonel Edward Moseley their Speaker, who His Excellency approved of and there delivered His Speech which is in these following Words Videlicet.

Gentlemen of Both Houses [...]

I am commanded by the 75th and following Instruction to take Especial Care that the publick Service of the Church of England be only maintained and that a Competent Provision be made for the Ministry Lands assigned them for Gleebs, and convenient Houses built thereon; The Little Provision hitherto made for supporting the Publick Worship seems to be a Reproach to the Country and prevents many good People from coming here to settle. It certainly becomes you to provide some more decent means to maintain the Clergy, and to appropriate money for the Building a Church or Chappel in Every parish, which in most places are now wanting [...].

Minutes. The upper house did not make formal reply to this speech. The lower house replied on July 6 that "By the Laws pass'd in 1729...We think a very good Provision was made for establishing the several Vesteries, to build Churches, purchase Gleebs, and to make ample provision for the Clergy," and that it would do nothing further until the royal pleasure had been expressed concerning the act. Governor Burrington replied sarcastically on July 17: "If I understand the intended Law in 1729 for enabling Vestries to build Churches purchase Gleebs and make provision for the Clergy, the true Meaning of it is, that None of those Good things should be effected."

[*T 56/18*]

Warrant
1733 August 4

<437> <*Gabl. Johnston*[1] *Esqr. Governor of North Carolina Chapple Plate.*> These are to Signify unto your Lordship his Majestys Pleasure that you provide and deliver to Gabriel Johnston Esqr. Governor of North Carolina 2 little Flaggons 1 Chalice a Paten and Receiver to take the Offerings in for the use of his Majestys Chappel there[2] not exceeding the Value of £80. And for so doing this shall be your Lordships Warrant Given under my hand this 4th day of Augst. 1733 In the 7th year of His Majesty's Reign.

Grafton

To the Lord Lynn etc.

This Warrant will come to £80 or thereabouts.

Robt. Sedgwick.

Let this Warrant be executed.
Whitehall Treasury Chambers
4th Septr. 1733.

R.W., W.C., G.O.

Copy. It is not known whether or not Governor Johnston ever received the items mentioned here, and if he did, what became of them.

[1]Gabriel Johnston (1699-1752), second royal governor of North Carolina, took the oaths of office in November, 1734, and served from then until his death.

[2]What, if anything, is meant by "his Majestys Chappel there" is unknown. Most probably it is simply an example of misapplication of a stock phrase.

[*LAM/FUL/VI*]

Rev. John LaPierre to Bishop of London
1733 October 9

<244>
My lord

As I had the honour to have been ordained by your Lordships predecessour in the year Seventeen hundred and Seven, who recommended me to the Governour of South Carolina Sir Nathanael Johnston, to Entitle me to a parrish Called the parrish of St. Dennis, in a french Colony which I was to Serve till the death of the old Settlers who did not understand the English tongue. So In the time of the new generation who understood the Said tongue in which they were born, I became an assistant to the Reverend Mr. Hazel in the parrish of St. Thomas next to my parrish, hoping of the two nations to make but one and the Same people; tho they were a distinct parrish they indifferently followed the English church and the french as well acquainted with both languages. And then Seeing that my ministerial functions were not Essentially required from a french minister, and hearing besides that in a province of North Carolina Called Cape fear, alias new Hanover they wanted a minister, the inhabitants of that place Sent for me and the Reverend Mr. Garden your Lordships Commissary in Concurrence with the rest of the Clergy did actually Consent that I should go and Settle the divine Service where it had never been, I readily Complied to go thither, with the proviso that they would inform your lordship Concerning my removeal but things Succeeded otherwise than I expected; the first year I was regarded and respected of the Inhabitants as St. paul was at the first by the Galatians; Every one readily Subscribed towards my Salary; and tho' it fell Short of near one hundred pounds yet was I Satisfied, out of Consideration to a new countrey, which owed it's good beginning less to the provision made by human laws than to the good discretion of some Conscientious inhabitants. The Second year, the Gentlemen of the vestry thought fitt to lay an assessement upon the parrish, that private Subscribers Should not be overburthened, but this proved of none Effect upon a mistake; because what was Called a parrish was in reality no parrish by law or act of publick assembly, therefore I was entirely left to the good discretion of the Several inhabitants against whom the vestry had no power of Compulsion therefore I fell short of my Sallary a Second time; the third year, the vestry I Confess did me that Justice to engage that Satisfaction to me that might be denied by the publick, accordingly they promised me a Certain Sum to lessen my loss but this fell a great deal Short of my necessary living;

after the third year I Served the people of Cape fear Six months longer; but received nothing for it, onely this answer: Who put you to work? Then I thought it was time to ask for my discharge, which after three Times asking they granted me at last, and took in my stead one Mr. Richard Marsden now actually performing the divine Service among them, a man whose whole Study always was to undermine me; now My lord I am left to my own shifting and I am forced to work in the field for my living and for fear this people of my former Charge should in any wise endeavour to impose upon your lordship's probity, as I hear that they petition for a new minister; So I think my Self in conscience bound to declare my mind, that any Clergyman that has a mind to Come hither at their request will find a lawless place, a Scattered people, no Glebe, no parsonage to receive him, without which Governour Barringtown told them that no minister should Ever be sent to them from the Society nor from your Lordship. However My Lord there is a Certain Collony in this province that requires my help upon promise of Subscribing towards my maintainance; with whom I will with your lordships good leave comply upon any reasonable terms. Sooner than to see the country destitute of the light of the Gospel; the bearear my Lord Can testify the truth of what I do here Set forth before your Lordship whose must [*sic*] obedient servant And dutiful Son I ever profess to be in the Gospel of Christ.

John Lapierre

New Brunswick In Cape fear alias
Cape fear October the 9th 1733.

[*Addressed*:]
To The Right Reverend father in God,
Edmund Lord Bishop of London
at his Palace in Fulham Near London
These p.A.Q.D.C.

[*Endorsed*:]
Lapiere
Cape fear N. Carola.

marsden

Recd. Decr. 2, *1733*.

ALS.

[*SPG/A/25*]

Rev. John Boyd to Secretary, SPG
1734

<102> Mr. Boyde to the Secretary.

North Carolina 1734

Reverend Sir

This comes with an account of my Mission since I was Employd by the Honorable Society. I arrived in Virginia in Janry. 1732 and went Immediatly for Carolina and waited on the Governour with your Letter, and Designed to Settled at Edentown and from thence visit the Country according the Design of my Mission, but by reason of Differences that Subsist, between the Governour and some Gentlemen there it was Impossible without giving Umbrage to Some Party. I therefore went into the Country and Agreed with the Vestry men of North west Parish in Bertie Precinct for 10 months reserving 2 months for Visiting the other parts of the Country; I have resided there ever Since and visiting the other parts. I am oblidged to Ride Upwards of 200 miles in a Month for serving the Parish in Preaching at the Stated places of Worship, by Reason of the Vast Extent of the Parish. I have only received £39 of their Currency, which is at the Rate of 10 for one. I have Baptized since my Arrivall 800 Children when I administred the Holy Communion. I never Had above 4 Communicants. If there are any farther Instructions from the Society pray transmitt them and they Shall be punctually observed by Reverend Sir Your most humble Servant.

John Boyd

Copy. Read at a meeting of the SPG on January 17, 1734/5, when it was "Orderd that a Letter be wrote to Mr. Boyd acquainting him that he doth not answer the design of his Mission by residing Ten Months in a year in one Parish, he being appointed to Preach and administer the Sacraments thro' the whole Country twice a year. Order'd also that a Letter be wrote to the Governour of North Carolina acquainting him with the difficulties Mr. Boyd meets with in his Mission, and that the Governour be desired to use his endeavours to remove any Obstructions Mr. Boyd may meet with in discharging the Duty of his Mission according to the Societys intention." Journal of the SPG, VI, 199.

[*LAM/FUL/VI*]

Rev. John LaPierre to Bishop of London
1734 April 23

<246>

New Hannover alias Cape fear in No. Carolina April 23d, 1734.

My Lord

I had the honour in my last to inform your Lordship, about the present State of Cape fear both Civil and Ecclesiastical. I was the first minister of the church of England that came to these places to preach, which I did during three years and a half, and at last frustrated of the best part of my Salary, was obliged to ask for my discharge, then forced to work in the field to help to maintain my family, afterwards compelled by necessity to Sell my house and land and lastly my moveables, so that at this time I am no better than a mendicant. I have been three years out of place, depending and living upon my own substance, but every now and then Exercising my functions gratis among some of the dispersed families; 'tis true, my Lord I had Several invitations from abroad for vaccancies to be Supplied, but the letters directed to me fell into the hands of our gentlemen who made no Scruple to Suppress them as I have found it out Since, lest my complaints of their proceedings should reach too far, last of all I went further northward to a new Colony called New River consisting of above one hundred families; all poor people, but very desirous to have the holy worship Sat up amongst them. Governour Burrington and one Mr. John Williams beeing the chief Encouragers. It is a thriving place, and likely in few years to become a flourishing parrish. There is a vast number of children among them to be instructed; and if this place falls to my Lot; I shall make bold My lord, to send you a larger and more Satisfactory account, both of Cape fear and of that new place. Your lordship's pastoral letters my lord which the Reverend Mr. Garden sent me, I dispersed among the people of Cape fear: but too little purpose, for some of the chief inhabitants had already been secretly Seduced by the favourers of, one Chub,[1] and by means of such seducers and underhand dealers, many have learn'd to quibble and cavill about the holy Scripture: and as their belief, so is their manner of life: in publick incest or polygamy (a first of which in a great man, was the first occasion of my gradual depression and degradation in their mind, when I spoke against it! Till att last they Substituted in my room, after I took my discharge,) one Mr. Richd. Marsden formerly a preacher in Charlestown in Sth. Carolina who declined appearing before Commissary Johnson and the rest of the Clergy to shew his credentials: afterwards my lord Portlands chappelain in Jamaica. Then an incumbent in virginy in a parrish called princess Ann and of late a traficant to Lisbon and Sometimes after his return promoted by few gentlemen to be minister of Cape fear without any popular Election. A man of an indifferent Character and Causing by the violence of assessements great murmurings among the people, before they can get a qualified vestry; and the said Richard Marsden, belonging to Leverpool pleads that he was, ordained by one of your Lordships predecessours much about the time that I was sent to So. Carolina under Queen Ann 1707. One Mr. Hall being the Bishop's Secretary, And the Cape fear gentlemen had since agreed to send to your Lordship for a minister and to have him qualified a missionary by the honorable Society, this My Lord is left to the prudent discretion of that honorable Body and to your Lordships mature consideration, that their bounty should not be misapplied, nor a clergyman ensnared by their fair words, there beeing no rules, nor laws in the place for Church or State; and the people being most of them stated men and very substantial planters, but unwilling to contribute towards the building of churches, and glebe houses, or to the handsome maintainance of a minister; all Captains of Ships who have been here will depose the Same, My Lord, as your Lordship's most humble Servant and most dutyful son in the Gospel.

John Lapierre

[*Addressed*:]
To the right Reverend Father in God
Edmond Lord Bishop of London
att his Palace of Fulham near London
These

[*Endorsed*:]
Lapiere
Acct. of Cape fear

New River in N. Cara.
Marsden
Sheppard

ALS.

[1]Not identified.

[*LAM/FUL/IX*]

Rev. Alexander Garden to [Bishop of London]
1734 June 8

<*Duplicate*>

My Lord

Nothing but what I take to be my indispensable Duty in Discharging the Trust your Lordship has been pleased to repose in me, shou'd prevail with me to trouble you so often with my Letters.

My last to your Lordship was by Mr. *Oglethorp*; and the trouble of this is to acquaint you, that there is Since arrived here a certain Clergyman directly from *Ireland* without any Licence from your Lordship, nor so much as pretending that his coming abroad to *America*, was with your Approbation or Privity. His name is *Laurence Oneill*. His Credentials are only *Letters* of his *Ordination* (for the Order of Presbyter) under the Hand and Seal of *William* late Archbp. of *Dublin*, dated 9ber 16th 1719; and Letters *Dimissory* (in the common Form) under the Hand and Seal of John the present Archbishop of the same See, dated 9ber 20th 1733.

Your Lordship will receive a Copy of a Paper herewith inclosed (the Original of which, inclosed with my Letter of which this is a Duplicate, I hope will come safe to hand) containing his Answers to some Queries: which I hope will afford sufficient Light for your Lordship's further Enquiry, and obtaining satisfactory Accounts concerning him. I truly wish that every thing may appear as represented in that Paper; but the two or three following Particulars have occasion'd me some Apprehensions to the contrary.

Some Slips of Behavior here already 2.) That such as the Paper is, yet was it not without Difficulty that I obtained it from him. 3.) That as his *Letters Dimissory* are from the present Archbp. of Dublin, so he at first told me that His Grace had also promised to recommend him to your Lordship; but afterwards he receded from that assertion, and wou'd not mention him in his Paper.

Your Lordship will be pleased to signify your Directions as soon as may be concerning this Gentleman; whom meantime I shall barely permit to officiate in the vacant parish of Christchurch on his good Behaviour.

I humbly crave your Lordship's Blessing and am My Lord your Lordship's most dutiful and obedient Son and humble Servant.

A. Garden

So. Carola.
Charlestown
June 8th 1734

P.S. Mr. Oneill has not brought any Family with him; says he is a Widower, and has got two Children in Ireland.

[*Endorsed*:]
Garden
Lawrence ONeill
Received Sept. 11, 1734.

ALS. The document following was enclosed in the present one.

[*LAM/FUL/IX*]

Answers
1734 June 13

<307>

June the 13th 1734.

The Reverend Mr. Garden Commissary to the Right Reverend the Ld. Bishop of London; His Queeres to Lau. Neill Clerk M. A.

Sir What Diocess or diocesses Parish or Parishes have you served in since the year 1719 in which year yr. Letters shew you was ordained?

Answer. I was ordained in that year a priest by his Grace Dr. William King, Lord Arch Bp. of Dublin to the Service of the Cure of St. Michaels Church Dublin and licensed thereto, Mr. Francis Higgins Preebendary thereof, then Removed to St. Lukes Church Dublin Dean Dopping Curat the Salary better than that of St. Michaels, Then to Donoghmore and Served that Cure for three preebends thereof Successively viz. the Reverend Mr. James King Curat of St. Bridgets Dublin the Reverend Zacharias Norton the Reverend Mr. Thos. Feathersone who now resides in said Diocess on which acct. I took out Letters dismissory and recommendatory dated the 20th day of Nov. 1733 and then Came aboard ship for America.

Sir What were the Grounds and Motives of yr. Comeing Heere; what Encouragment was promised you and by whom?

[Answer.] Immediately I was Apply'd to by Bp. Maul Bishop of Dromore in Ireland to Goe with Captain Rowan[1] one of his Majesties Councell in North Carolina who tould the Bishop and me In that province I shou'd find Good Encouragement and might do vast Service in the propogation of the Gospell.

Sir who were yr. Perswaders to Come directly from Ireland without any application to, or license from the Bp. of London?

[Answer.] The Bp. of Dromore Tould me he wou'd secure all proper Encourgement for me from the Bp. of London, the Arch Bp. of Casshell allso the 30th of Novr. last Declar'd he wou'd recommend me to the Bp. of London (and Many others in Dublin) If I wou'd Goe etc. and I approved the Clime and wou'd settle there.

[Sir] How Came you to South Carolina when you proposed to Goe to No. Carolina.

[Answer.] After I resolved to Goe to North Carolina in Captain Rowans ship by Distress of weather we put in at Charles town in the South and findeing a better prospect of Doeing Good heere Both to the church as well as a better provision for my self and family I doe desire on proper application made to the Bp. of London to settle Heere, Beside there is no provision for a Clergyman in North Carolina.

Reverend Sir These your Queestion's I hope have answerd to yr. Satisfaction Who am yr. obedient Humble Servant.

Lau. Neill

DS. This document was enclosed in the one immediately above.

[1]Matthew Rowan (d. 1760), an Ulsterman, was in North Carolina from at least 1726. A merchant and planter, as well as holder of major offices such as surveyor general and receiver general, he was a councillor from 1731 until his death. *DNCB*.

[*LAM/FUL/VI*]

Petition
1734 October 10

<251> To The Right Reverend Father in God Edmund Lord Bishop of London. The Humble Petition of the Church:wardens, Vestry:men and other Inhabitants of St. Thomas's parish on pamplico River in the province of North Carolina

Humbly Sheweth

That whereas Your Petitioners (notwithstanding the many sects and parties in Religion Settled amongst us) have had the happiness of being brought up in the protestant Communion, but have been destitute of means (ever since our first Settlements) to allow a decent maintenance for a protestant Minister by reason of our poverty (to which our indigence and incapacity the late Massacre, and severe persecution of the Savage Indian Nations bordering upon us have not a little contributed).

And Whereas That ever since the first day of January 1733[1] (out of an ardent Zeal to encourage the protestant Religion as it is now Establish'd) we have entertain'd the Worthy and Reverend Mr. John Garzia who (in pursuance to your Lordship's Licence) had preach'd the Gospel and Acted as a parish Minister in Virginia for nine years past; By which Licence together with a Certificate from Dr. Blear Commissary of, and Attested by the Governor of Virga. setting forth his diligence in his function and good behaviour, And having had upwards of one and twenty months Experience, we are encourag'd to retain the said Reverend Minister; but to our extream Grief, the maintenance that we by reason of our poverty can afford him, is far short of our inclinations in Supporting decently a man of his worth and merit.

And Whereas we were also encourag'd to retain the said Mr. John Garzia with hopes of having due provisions made for the Clergy pursuant to his Majesties Instructions to our Governor and Council, which provisions have not yet, nor is there any visible appearance of any to be made, we find our expectations therein defeated, by which means the inhabitants in general are deprived of having the Gospel preach'd amongst them and very often as well Antient, as young persons die without Baptism.

And Whereas (as well by the frequent applications of the said Reverend Mr. Garzia as our own free and earnest inclinations to carry on so good a work) we are now building at our own proper Costs a Small Church[2] (being the only one in the whole province) but we fear that our Abilities will be far short of compleating and adorning the same as becomes the temple of God. We therefore your Petitioners most humbly pray that your Lordship (as our Diocesan) will use your best endeavours in assisting and forwarding the Petition Annext[3] and to do Such other Acts of Charity in our favour as to your Lordship shall seem meet And your Petitioners (as in duty bound) shall ever pray.

Robt. Turner, Edward Salter, church wardens, Thos. Jewell, Wm. Willis, John Barrow, Simon Alderson, James Singellton, Charles Odeon, John Odeon

[*Endorsed:*]
<250> The humble Petition of the
church-wardens and Vestry of St. Thomas's
parish in the province of North Carolina in America
October the 10th 1734.

DS.

[1]In light of the reference later in this paragraph to "one and twenty months Experience," it would appear that January, 1732/3 is meant, rather than 1733/4.

[2]St. Thomas's Church, Bath, is the "oldest Episcopal church building in North Carolina." London and Lemmon, *Episcopal Church in North Carolina, 20.*

[3]Presumably the petition dated May 8, 1735, pp. 357-358, below.

[*SPG/SAP*]

Report
1734/5 February 21

<63> <*An Abstract of the Proceedings of the Society.*> [. . .] Besides the Missionaries sent to particular Places, the Society have appointed several Itinerant or travelling Missionaries, who are obliged to visit many Places in large Districts, and at Times officiate among all the Inhabitants of the Country. In the Year *1732*, they appointed the Reverend Mr.

Boyd to be Itinerant Missionary to *North-Carolina*. The Society had observed with much Concern, there was not one Minister of the Church of *England* in that whole Province, containing a great Body of People; and being not able to send several Missionaries, they yet resolved to send one Itinerant Missionary, the Rev. Mr. *Boyd*, who should travel thro' all that large Country, and at Times officiate in every Part of it. And the Society have lately received an Account from Mr. *Boyd*, that he arrived in *Virginia Jan. 1732*, and went immediately to his Mission to *North-Carolina*; that he deliver'd a Letter from the Society to the Governor at *Eden-Town*; but on Account of some Difficulties arising there, he went soon after to *North-West* Parish in *Bertie* Precinct, and had agreed with the Vestrymen there to <64> continue ten Months among them, and to employ two Months in visiting the other Parts of the Country. He says he is obliged to ride upwards of 200 Miles in a Month, in serving that Parish, and preaching at the stated Places of Worship, by reason of the vast Extent of that Parish; that he hath baptised since his Arrival 800 Children, but when he administred the Holy Sacrament he had not above 4 Communicants. The Society have lately order'd a Letter to be wrote to him, directing him to travel thro' the whole Country, and distribute his Labours among all the People. [. . .]

Printed. Extracted from the yearly publication containing the sermon preached at the annual anniversary meeting of the SPG, together with a review of the activities of the Society and its missionaries during the preceding year. The date above is the date of the meeting.

[*SPG/Jou/6*]

Journal of the SPG
1734/5 March 21

<218> At St. Martins Library 21st March 1734 [. . .]

<220> 12. A Bill drawn by the Reverend Mr. Boyd Missionary in North Carolina dated Virginia September 24th 1734 payable to Mr. James Buchanan for *Eighty three*, without <221> mentioning the word *Pounds* was laid before the Board, and a Letter to the Treasurer of the same date sign'd by Mr. Boyd advising that he hath drawn bills for 83, was also laid before the Board and read: Order'd that the Treasurer do pay the said Bill. [. . .]

Minutes.

[*LAM/FUL/VI*]

Rev. John Boyd to [Bishop of London]
1735 April 12

<252>

Northwest Parish. North Carolina.
April 12, 1735.

My Lord

I was very sorry to hear from our Governour that my Letters to your Lordship had miscarryed for since my arrivall in this Place, I have done my self the honour to write to your Lordship 4 Severall times.

Upon my coming here I waited upon Governour Burrington, and delivered a Letter directed to him from the Honorable society; He received me very kindly, and promised to doe me all the service Lay in his Power. From thence I went up into the country and agreed with the vestry of Northwest Parish in Albermarle County for 10 months reserving two months for visiting the other Parts of the country. They were to pay me £400 of their currency (which att tenn for one is not a parr with sterling) and I have not yett received fifty.

The Parish I Live in is of a vast extent being upwards of One Hunderd miles in Length and fifty in breadth. I preach in 7 different Places which obliges me to ride every month 260 miles. I have Baptized about a 1000 Infants and 30 Adults. The first time I administred the Blessed sacrament of the Supper I had only four communicants the Last time 20. We have as yett no Church or Chappell in this Parish but since my coming the Parishioners have raised by private subscriptions enough to build four. We are very happy in having no different sects or opinions in this part of the Country but I have great reason to Complain of a Laodicean Lukewarmnes and immorality; But Lower down in the Country there are a great many Quakers and anabaptists in my Last Journey I had a great many of them my Auditors and I Baptized five Adults that formerly proffessed Quakerism, and I Believe were there a minister settled among them, they would mostly come over to the church and a Better way of thinking.

There are two ministers in the more southern Parts. Mr. Garzia from Virginia in Pamplicoe and Mr. Marsden in Cape fair.

I never Could Gett any of the library that was left here by Dr. Newnam.

I Begg Leave to Assure your Lordship (By the Blessing of God) That I will faithfully to Discharge the ends of my Mission in Propogating the knowledge <253> Of the Christian faith to the utmost of my Power. I am My Lord Your Lordships Most Humble and Most Obedient servant.

John Boyd

[*Endorsed*:]
Boyd Accounts of himself read at the Society 17th Octr. 173[5] Order'd that Copies of Mr. Boyds Letters be sent to the Governour of North Carolina and that he be desired to give the Society his Opinion in what place or places Mr. Boyd [may] be employed so as to be most service in the discharge of the Duty of his Mission.

ALS. Read at a meeting of the SPG on October 17, 1735, when it was agreed that "Copies of these Letters [including also a letter from Boyd of August 24, 1735] be sent to the Governour of North Carolina, and that he be desired to give the Society his opinion in what Place or Places Mr. Boyd may be employed so as to be most serviceable in the discharge of the Duty of his Mission." Journal of the SPG, VI, 286.

[*LAM/FUL/VI*]

Petition
1735 May 8

<254> To the Right Honourable the Society for propogateing the Gospel in Foreign parts.

The Humble Petition of John Garzia Minister of St. Thomas's parish in Beaufort precinct in North Carolina.

Humbly Sheweth.

That your petitioner about twelve years ago was sent and licenced to preach the Gospel in Virginia, in which time your Petitioner receiv'd Instructions from your honourable Board (By the hands of Doctor Thomas Bray) in order to Baptize and instruct the Negroes in that Colony. And that your Petitioner pursuant thereto did (having made report thereof some years ago to the said Dr. Bray in order to be comunicated to your Board) Baptize and instruct severall Negroes as [it] appears by the List hereunto annext,[1] And Whereas there was an allowance to have been made by your honourable Society for the same, your Petitioner therefore humbly prays, that your Honourable Board will be pleased to transmitt for the said service such an allowance As to you shall seem meet.

And your petitioner (as in duty bound) shall ever pray for your Honour's prosperity and Remain your Diligent and Most Obedient humble Servant.

John Garzia

[*Endorsed*:]
The humble Petition of John
Garzia Minister of St. Thomas's
parish in No. Carolina America
May 8th, 1735

DS.

[1]Not present.

[*LAM/FUL/VI*]

Petition
1735 May 8

<255> To the Right Reverend Father in God Edmund Lord Bishop of London.

The Humble Petition of John Garzia Minister of St. Thomas's parish in North Carolina in America.

Humbly Sheweth

That whereas your Petitioner hath been minister of this parish for almost three years last past, and having used my best Endeavours with the vestry and Parishioners to

Undertake the building of a Brick Church (the walls and roof whereof is just now finished). And Whereas your petitioner finds the inhabitants in Generall well dispos'd to carry on so good a work, but that their disabilities must put a stop to their good intentions at least for some years. Your Petitioner therefore thinks it his bounden duty to lay this their poor Condition and willingness before your Lordship, and humbly to petition your Lordship to intercede with the Society in our behalf, in order to obtain for us the Severall necessaries annext hereunto, and your Petitioner (as in duty bound) shall always pray for your Lordships Prosperity and Remain Your Lordships Most Obedient Humble Son and Servant.

John Garzia

A Bible
2 Common Prayer Books
1 Book of Homilies
(Some Monitors against Profaneness etc.
to be distributed among my parishioners)
A Font
A pulpit Cloth and Cushion
A Carpet for the Comunion table
Other conveniencies as your Lordship shall think
proper (all being wanting).

[*Endorsed*:]
The humble Petition of John
Garzia Minister of St. Thomas's
parish in No. Carolina in America

May 8th, 1735

DS.

[*LAM/FUL/VI*]

Rev. John Garzia to Bishop of London
1735 May 8

<256> May it please your Lordship.

Haveing been Licenced by your Lordship for about twelve years past to preach the Gospel in Virga., and having done my duty, with that Sincerity (I hope) as becomes a minister of the Establish'd English church as will appear by a Certificate from Mr. Comissary Blair, and Attested by the Governor of that colony; And having also comply'd with the instructions of the society by doctor Thomas Bray deliver'd to me in your Lordship's presence to instruct and Baptize the Negroes in Virginia; And having remov'd from thence into this province with my family in hopes to be further serviciable to the church, and the Labourers being few, and the harvest too great, appears to me to want the assistance of more of my Brethren. Notwithstanding for almost three years I have done my duty in this province not only in my own parish, but in severall others as mov'd with compassion to see them as sheep without a shepherd (as more at Large you Lordship will be inform'd by the Governor) and all this time supporting my self and family out of the small stock I saved in Virgia. notwithstanding the misfortune of being cast away in my passage hither, My Salary here not exceeding 24 or 25 sterling, I humbly move your Lordship (as being very willing to continue here) to intercede with the Society in my behalf, and to cause a remission to be made to the Governor as well for my past services, as for my future maintenance in consideration of my great poverty. Well remembring your Lordships Goodness to me heretofore, emboldens me to implore your charitable assistance for the future, and Conclude praying for your Lordships health, prosperity and God's blessing; these are the wishe's of your Lordship's Most dutiful son and most Obedient Humble Servant.

John Garzia

North Carolina
Bath May 8, 1735.

[*Endorsed*:]
The humble Petiton of John
Garzia Minister of St. Thomas
parish in No. Carolina in America

May 8th, 1735

ALS.

[*LAM/FUL/VI*]

Rev. Richard Marsden to Bishop of London
1735 July 7

<258>
My Lord

In a short time after I was determined to settle at Cape Fear I presumed to write to your Lordship, for I always thought it Incumbent on me to give yr. Lordship an acct. how I Employed myself and I was under very great Inquietude that I had at all neglected the performance of my duty in that particular, but I had this satisfaction that it was not from forgetfullness or disregard for I always affected a reputation of haveing the utmost deference and Esteem for you, but I was sensible you had recd. some Impressions to my disadvantage, and I must confess it was this made me ashamed to appear before yr. Lordship but I could not any longer satisfie myself in defering to acquit myself of this obligation.

I recd. Sundry strong Evidences of yr. Lordships good will towards me whilst I was in England, when yr. Lordship was Bishop of Lincoln, and I Embraced the first opportunity from Jamaica after I was Informed of yr. translation to the See of London to Congratulate you on his late Majesties favour to you and yr. Lordship was pleas'd to Condescend to Honor me with a most kind and obligeing Answer. It has been an Inexpressible grief to me that I have since fallen into any misdemeanor whereby I have Incurred yr. Lordships displeasure. In my abovementioned Letter from this place I Humbly Implored yr. Lordships pardon and sincerely assured yr. Lordship that I should never forgive myself for any miscarriage I had been guilty of, and cast myself upon yr. Compassion which being alwaies so agreeable to yr. nature I flattered myself I should not be an unfortunate Instance of yr. denyeing it when Earnestly Implored. If yr. Lordship had been pleased at that time to have Intimated to me the favourable Inclinations towards me, in an answer to my letter, it would have been a singular Support to me under the great labour and pains I take in this new settlement In the faithfull discharge of the offices of my function, and I should have recd. it as a great and sensible favour and I should on all occasions Expressed my utmost Gratitude; But I recd. a Letter from his Excellency Gab. Johnston our Governor from Edenton at the time of the Sitting of the Assembly there which struck me In an Extraordinary manner, for he was pleas'd to acquaint me in it that he had lately recd. a Letter from yr. Lordship wherein there was a Postscript Relateing to me whereby yr. Lordship seems to be misinformed as to my Behaviour and Conduct, but that he Intending to lay yr. Lordships Letter before the assembly he had ordered his secretary to make out a Coppy of it which he would sign to attest the truth of, rather than send in the original with the Postscript to my disparagment, and was pleased also to assure me that he would set yr. Lordship right in his answer, and in the most Effectual manner do me Justice to yr. Lordship.

The Gentelmen of the vestry of St. James Parish in Cape Fear sometime since recommended me in a letter to the Honorable Society for the Propogation of the Ghospel makeing application to them in my favour for an additional stipend as with that of the Parish might be sufficient to support me; but I was advised to defer sending of it till his Excellencys arrival who was then daily Expected, haveing good reason to believe that when his Excellency was truly Informed of my behaviour, state and Circumstances would also readily condescend to recommend me. I have presumed in this to send a coppy to yr. Lordship of the Letter for yr. perusual but his Excellency assureing me of his best offices in my favour to yr. Lordship and that I might depend I had no occasion of the vestrys recommendation, or to make any other application therefore I did not send the original at this time.

There is a time when a man may be the Subject of his own discourse and give full relation of things he has worthyly done as well as other truths when used by way of Apology to remove a Calumny or accusation. I have been at cape Fear near seven years and I can truly say that Earnestly Imploreing the devine assistance I have from my heart and soul done my utmost to promote the glory of God; and the general bent of my resolutions and the constant course and tenor of my Conversation has been strictly conformable to the Ghospel of Christ, for I have always been under apprehension and fear least any thing in or from my self should hinder the success of the Ghospel which I teach. Frailty is so conspicuous and Epidemical that there are few men free from faults Either in conduct or principles but with respect to my ministry my Conscience clears me of all unfaithfulness and neglect of duty Four years I preached freely at my own house without demanding or

Expecting anything for my pains and gave the greatest part of my Congregation every Sunday a dinner and did not receive in all any consideration; and with Laborious diligence I traveled some weeks 60 or 70 miles to preach and Baptize; and I hope it was not simply unlawful for me to Endeavour to subsist myself by Imploying what little I had in trade or in an honest way to Increase it where many of the Inhabitants here are in such mean circumstances that they cannot maintain a minister; and if I had Insisted on a maintenance at my first settlement it would have hindered the progress of the Ghospel hereby hindering the people from coming under the Preaching of it finding it would be chargeable to them and therefore I was willing to give them a convinceing demonstration that I sought not [*illegible*]. But haveing met with various losses and disapointments the vestry aforesaid, came to a resolution to allow me a sallary as mentioned in their Letter to the society in my favour but have not received to the value of one hundred pound this Currency which is not above £20 proclamation mony and have no certain prospect when I shall receive the remainder there being no care taken at present to Collect it, and I am certain I cannot but in necessary Charges, when I preach at Brunswick and in traveling to the different places where I am called to officiate have spent in the last two years above two hundred pound this Currency besides being often obliged to take two negroes for three or four days in a week to transport me where I am necessitated to preach, to the great neglect of my Plantation which would be a Certain maintenance if I could allow myself to continue at home and mind the business of it and not be solicitious to do what good I can in this new settlement, as his Excellency our Governour is fully Convinced of and therefore I hope will not fail to do me Justice to yr. Lordship. I have often declared, and it is a true assertion that if yr. Lordship was on any acct. to suspend me from Exerciseing my ministerial function it would be as great a service as you could do me If I was to continue here. I am bould to say that there is not a Clergyman in the west Indies or in this part of america that has a better title to the Societies favour than I have as I can make fully evident, I have never acted from worldly advantages, and I go through more fateague and labour in the discharge of my office than any three of them and love is the spring and fountain of all my performances and I have met with little Consideration for my pains and diligence but have run myself into a great many Inconveniences, and I am now in an advanced age, and under dificult circumstances and not capable to performe a very toilesome and troublesome service but however I shall ever be sparing of myself for fear of shorting my days for I am truly sensible that the lamp of my life can never burn out better than in Endeavouring to light others to heaven, and shall never Judge any labour or pains too great; [*illegible*] contending with the Errors and sins of men sufficient in order to bring them unto God by Conversion and repentance. My behaviour here for above six years must have convinced all reasonable persons that I have a true Compassion for the souls of the people of this new settlement and a fervent desire to farther their salvation; and whatever success I have had I hope I shall receive the reward of an honest Endeavour from him who Estimates our pains not by their events but by their natural tendencies and sincere Intentions; and I hope I shall meet with yr. Lordships approbation and Generous Encouragment. Pray lay asside all displeasure against me and make me so happy as to assure me that you retain a favourable opinion of me. Your Lordship has always Encouraged the honest Endeavours of the meanest of the Clergy. I beg of you let not me be the only unfortunate Instance of your denieing it. If yr. Lordship out of your great goodness and compassion will condescend to procure me a yearly allowance from the Honorable Society I shall ever acknowledge the favour and you may depend shall never have the least cause to repent of any Kindness shewn to me. I have no Books besides the Bible common prayer Book and Burket on the new testament; and truly my Ld. there are very few Bibles, common prayer Books or Books of devotion etc. in this Province. It would be a great act of Charity, without delay to supply this part of the Country with good Books, there are many families that have been furnished some way or other with the Independent Wigg,[1] Jubb and Wolston on our Saviors Miracles and are Industerously Lent about, if yr. Lordship will condescend to prevail with the [Society] favour to this place to send what books you shall Judge proper and order them to my care you shall receive from me all possible satisfaction in the discharge of my duty and the prudent distrabution of the books that shall be sent.

I have Endeavoured as much as may be to get an Exact Knowledge of the Inclinations dispositions, state and Condition of the Inhabitants of north Carolina and if yr. Lordship requires an acct. from me I will not fail to send you as perfect an one as I can. I am well Known in all the parts of this Goverment, and I have Baptized in it above thirteen hundred men women and Children, and never recd. the least Consideration on that acct. and I always Endeavoured to guard myself from Contempt and have procured a moderate reputation to myself in the severall parts of this Province.

I will not be any farther troublesome to yr. Lordship at this time but Conclude with beging your blessing and Encouragement, and Let me assure yr. Lordship that no one can declare with greater Chearfulness, or greater fidelity or with more respect and regard than myself that I am yr. Lordships most Humble and most obedient Servant.

Richd. Marsden

Cape fear north Carolina
July the 7th, 1735

This is a Coppy of what I writ to you per Capt. Bradfor and will be delivered to yr. Lordship by my son if he be in London he intends to come to cape Fear In a short time.

[*Addressed*:]
To The Right Reverend Father in God
Edmond Ld. Bishop of London

[*Endorsed*:]
Cape fear
Recd. Mar. 9, 1735/6

ALS.

[1] I.e., *Whig*.

[*SPG/Jou/6*]

Journal of the SPG
1735 October 17

<278> 17th October 1735 [. . .]

<285> 6. It was also reported from the Committee that they had read a Letter from the Reverend Mr. Boyd to the Secretary dated Eden Town North Carolina August the 24th 1735[1] Acquainting <286> that he had received the Secretary's of the 29th of January last;[2] and giving his reasons for taking up his Residence in Northwest Parish for ten Months in the year, videlicet, That there are in that Province two Counties Albemarle and Bath, the first contains about four fifths of the Inhabitants. In Bath there were two Orthodox Ministers, so that County (in which the fewest Inhabitants were) was tollerably well supplyed, while Albemarle was quite destitute, which was the only reason why he resided so long in Northwest Parish; which part he supplyed at the extraordinary fatigue of riding above 250 Miles every Month, besides meeting the People on Week days to Catechise and Instruct them; But as soon as he received the Secretary's Letter, he quitted his residence, and will endeavour to perform his Mission according to what the Secretary wrote, till otherwise order'd by the Society. Agreed that Copies of these Letters[3] be sent to the Governour of North Carolina, and that he be desired to give the Society his Opinion in what Place or Places Mr. Boyd may be employed so as to be most serviceable in the discharge of the Duty of his Mission. [. . .]

Minutes.

[1]Not located.
[2]Not located.
[3]Including also one from Boyd dated April 12, 1735, printed above.

[*SPG/SAP*]

Report
1735/6 February 20

<48> <*An Abstract of the Proceedings of the Society.*> [. . .] The Reverend Mr. *Boyd*, Itinerant Missionary in *North-Carolina*, writes an Account of his Labours there: He says, the Parish he lives in is of a vast Extent, being upwards of one hundred Miles in length, and fifty in breadth; he preaches in seven different Places, which obliges him to ride every Month 260 Miles, besides meeting the People on Week-Days to catechize and instruct them, in order to prepare them to receive the blessed Sacrament. He says the Heats in Summer, and Colds in Winter in that Climate, are so excessive, that it renders it impossible for the best of Constitutions to endure the Hardships of constantly travelling, over a Country that in some Parts is almost destitute of the Necessaries of Life. He hath, since his Arrival there, baptized 1000 Infants, and 50 Adults. At the first time of administring the <49> Holy Sacrament he had but 4 Communicants, but at the last time 20. [. . .]

Printed. Extracted from the yearly publication containing the sermon preached at the annual anniversary meeting of the SPG, together with a review of the activities of the Society and its missionaries during the preceding year. The date above is the date of the meeting.

[*CCR 192*]

Memorandum
1735/6 March

North Carolina ss. March Genl. Court 1735.
Memorandum

That John Garzia Clerk as well in behalf of himself as of the poor of the Parish of St. thomas's in Beaufort precinct informs and giveth this Court to understand that Henry Crofton of the Said precinct gent. (in custody of the Marshal) on or about the Sixteen day of April 1734 in St. thomas Parish and precinct aforesaid did as a Justice of the peace Join Andrew Lathinhouse and Patience Smith together in the holy state of Matrimony in the Parish and precinct aforesaid, he the Said John an orthodox Minister of the church of England upon the day aforesaid being resident and Incumbent in the Said Parish, Contrary to the act of Assembly[1] in that case made and provided by which Illegal proceedings he the Said henry hath by virtue of the Said act forfeited the Sum of five pounds Currency Mony one half thereof to the use of him the Said John as a m[inister] and the other half to the use of the Said Parish yet he the Said henry, the Said Sum of five pound or any part thereof to him the Said John or for the use of the poor of the Said parish hath not paid altho often thereto requested but to pay the Same hath hitherto refused, he the said John as well in behalf of himself as the poor of the Said parish therefore prays the aid of this Court and that what the law requires may be done in the Premisses.

J. Montgomery.[2]

[*Endorsed*:]
[*torn*]a qui tam vs. Craffton Information sur. stat
We of the Jurey find for the plantif
five pounds.
James Brodgdol for man.

DS.

[1]The 1715 "Act for Establishing the Church and Appointing Select Vestrys," printed above, provided that "no Lay person in any parish where a minister or priest is resident shall join any person in marriage under the penalty of five pounds One half to the parish for the Use of the poor and the other to the Minister resident or incumbent."

[2]John Montgomery (d. 1744) was at this time attorney general of the province. Later, he was an assemblyman and chief justice. *DNCB*.

[*LAM/FUL/VI*]

Rev. John Garzia to [Bishop of London]
1735/6 March 19

<260>

May it please yr. Lordship

In the month of May 1735 I made bold to send to your Lordship two Petitions at the request of my vestry, one to your Lordship and the other to the Society for propagating the Gospell in foreign pts. humbly begging your Lordships intercession with the society to enter me into the list of Missionaries in order to help this poor parish to support me their minister, their poverty being so great that of themselve's, they are not able. I have also petitiond yr. Lordship for a church bible and two church Common Prayer books etc. for the use of our new church being the only one in this Government; and have also sent the attestation of Mr. comissary Blair and the Governor of Virga. as touching my life and conversation during my abode there for about nine years, together with an account of my proceedings pursuant to the instructions of the society by doctor thos. Bray in relation to the instructing and baptizing the negros in Virga. their Number being upwards of three hundred as by the said account appears; I hope, that the said Petitions and letters are come to your Lordship's hands, but not having heard any thing about them, Embolden's me thus to reiterate my indigence and necessity, as having but £200 of this currency which answers about £20 sterling, which is far short to support me and my family, (cloathing being very scarce and dear) and my self at present very much in want; Our present Governor Mr. Johnston has ever since his first coming (pursuant to your Lordships letter to him) used his best endeavours to have a Competent maintenance settled on the clergy, but the majority of the assembly being so ill dispos'd that he cant but lament his incapacity, as yet to compleat so good a work. I humbly beg your Lordship answer directed to his Excellency the Governor and craving your Lordship blessing, and praying for your Lordships prosperity as well spirituall as temporall, (well remembring the past Kindness and benefits I recd. at your Lordships hands) I remain your Lordship's Most dutifull Son, and Most obedient humble Servant.

John Garzia

No. Carolina, Bath town
St. thos. parish March 19th, 1735.

[*Endorsed*:]
[*Illegible*]
Received June 1736
read at the Society 17 Septr. 1736
Orderd a Church Bible and Common
Prayer book be sent him, and that he
be acquainted the Society are not in
a condition to establish New Missions.

ALS.

[*SPG/B/4*]

Rev. John Garzia to Secretary, SPG
1735/6 March 19

19 March 1735/6

Reverend Sir

In the month of May 1735 at the Request of my vestry I sent two petitions Sign'd by them to the Society, representing the poverty of this my parish, and beging the honorable Society to enter me into the List of Missionaries that by that means I might be supported, but have not as yet heard any thing in answer thereto I humbly beg the favour of you to Signifie to me the resolution of the Society in relation to that affair. I humbley beg you will excuse me for this Liberty who Am Reverend Sir Your unKnown humble and Most obedient Servant.

John Garzia

No. Carolina, Bath town
St. thos. parish March 19th 1735.

[*Endorsed:*]
<12.> Entered
Mr. Garzia. Bath Town
North Carolina Mar. 19th 1735
recd. 18th July 1736.

Directed to the Reverend Dr. David
Humphey in Warwick street
Warwick Lane London.

ALS. At a meeting of the SPG on September 17, 1736, a report on this letter was received by the Society, "Whereupon the Secretary acquainted the Committee, that he never received either of the Petitions mentioned in the foregoing Letter, nor does he know any such Person as Mr. Garzia. And a Letter from Mr. Garzia to the Lord Bishop of London of the same date and to the same purpose being now read, and desiring also the Society to send him a Church Bible and common Prayer for the use of the New Church there: Agreed that a Bible and common Prayer be sent to him; and that he be acquainted that the Society are not in a condition to establish any New Missions." Journal of the SPG, VII, 51-52.

[*LAM/FUL/VI*]

Rev. Richard Marsden to Bishop of London
1736 August 16

Augt. the 16th 1736.

I have flattered myself for some time with an Expectation that your Lordship would condescend to favour me with an answer to the Letter I presumed to write to you. I always Esteemed myself Obliged to have a peculiar Regard for yr. Lordship and always thought it an Incumbent duty on me to give you a true acct. how I spent my time and I was under great Inquietude that I had at all neglected the performance of my duty in this particular, and I could not satisfie myself in defering to acquit myself of this obligation. I was very sensible your

Lordship had received some Impressions to my disadvantage and it was this made me ashamed for sometime to appear before your Lordship. In my Letter to you I have in the sincerity of my heart assured yr. Lordship that it has been a real affliction to me and a heavy pressure upon me that I have fallen into any misdemeanor whereby I have incurred your displeasure, and the thoughts of it continues to give me a very great torment, perhaps greater than your forgiveing nature would Know how to Inflict on the greatest offender, and I trust in God I shall never forgive myself for any discredit or dishonour to Religion or offence to yr. Lordship I have Humbly Implored yr. pardon and cast myself upon yr. tenderness and Compassion which being so agreeable to your nature I promised myself (with the utmost confidence) that I should not be an unfortunate instance of yr. denying it when Implored. Your Lordship cannot but be sensible that I have been a very great sufferer and treated with very little candor; but God be praised he has out of his Infinite Goodness Enabled me with chearfulness to bear up under pressures, calamities and distresses of Life and with zeal and diligence to pursue the great End of my ministry for this Eight Years with as much pains and fatigue in this new settlement, where there is a want of many of the Conveniencies and necessaries of life, with a very mean or no allowance but Cheifly at my own Expence as I could have done under the greatest plenty of outward Encouragement and if I am conceited enough to fancy that I deserve a little better treatment, I thank God I have more grace than to Quarrel with Christianity because I am not sufficiently rewarded.

My last Letter to your Lordship was dated (I believe) aprl. the 13th 1734[1] in which was Inclosed a Coppy of the vestry for this parish recommendation of me to the Honorable Society for Propagating the Ghospel in Forreign parts, and was as I am informed delivered to yr. Lordship by Mr. Thoms Hunter a Considerable dealer in Black Friars London; I did not send the original because his Excellency our present Governor assured me of his best offices in my favour to yr. Lordship and that I had no occasion to send it, or to make any other application; I depend his Excellency has had a due regard to his kind offer and promis and Condescended to do me justice to your Lordship.

Mr. Hunter has been pleased to Intimate to me in a Letter lately received from him that yr. Lordship had laid asside displeassure and had condescended to promis to lay my case before the Honorable Society and to Endeavour to obtain some allowance for me; This was very agreeable news to me and I presume to render yr. Lordship my most [*torn*] thanks for yr. goodness and kind Intentions towards me; But I cannot but Express a Concern that yr. Lordship did co[nde]send to assure of this in a Letter, for without that Satisfaction I shall continue under apprehensions and fears lest your Lordships displeasure is not Entirely removed, and therefore I have presumed to procure a letter to your Lordship from the Inhabitants of this Parish supplicating you in the most humble manner in my behalf and giveing your Lordship a most Just representation of my case and Circumstances, and also what my doctrine and manner of Conversation has been from the time of my Settling here, and I would humbly hope that this will fully Satisfie your Lordship of the diligent and faithfull discharge of my duty as a minister and of the regularity of my life; and I trust I shall never for the future be guilty of anything that may render me unworthy of your Lordships countenance and protection. I have freed my self as much as possible I can from all worldly Incumberances which might in the least hinder me in the performance of the offices of my function dedicateing my whole time to the carring on the work of the Ghospel and my heavenly fathers business there is a time when a man may be the subject of his own discourse, when used by way of apology to remove any ill apprehensions that may be Entertained of him to his prejudice. When first I came to Cape Fear seeing the necessity of the Inhabitants my heart did warm most tenderly towards them and I soon resolved through Gods assistance to render them the most Important service in my power, for none of his Majesties Plantations are in so great want of the Ghospel as this and that which I thought most deplorable is that tho they want the Ghospel, yet many of them are not sensible of their want. The Inhabitants on this River, also New River and White Oak River have not any of them been settled above 11 years but there is such a large Continual Increase of people every year into these new settlements that they are become very numerous but there is not many of them as yet in circumstances to Contribute sufficiently to the Maintenance of a minister and as I have been ready on all occasions to assist the necessities of the people Inhabiting these Rivers which are by act of assembly made three Parishes and Contains a very great Extent at Least 150 miles in Length; I was willing to give them a Convinceing proof that I sought not theirs but them, for I never in the least Insisted on a maintenance or of any allowance for my Expences not even when I have traveled at the distance of a 100 miles and have Baptiesed many Children [*illegible*] whom for if I should have Insisted on any Consideration I was apprehensive I should have but small success in my labours, and therefore as I expected nothing of them I desired nothing from them; for let a minister be never so laborious in his office and inoffencive in his life I have found by Experience that if he Expect but a moderate allowance there are many that will open their mouths against him that Expects it. There is a Law of this Province Impowering the vestry of Each parish to assess the Inhabitants for the maintenance of a minister not Exceeding 10*s*. Each tytheable and accordingly the vestry of [*torn*] Parish where I reside and Cheifly officiate did lay a Levie of 10*s*. a head this Currency in my favour for the last four years but I found it caused to much discontent and uneasiness that I would not have it Collected with Rigour but was willing rather to fling up all pretensions to a recompence and renounce all hopes of receiveing my Property out of the hands of those that are unwilling to pay the assessment and [*illegible*] I am Entirely Indifferent tho my strait circumstances requires special assistance for I am much reduced by various losses and disapointments I have suffered, and the Continual expence I [*illegible*] in traveling from place to place and my constant labour and great fateauge has broke my Constitution very much of late and I am in advanced age (59 next octobr.) and by the Course of nature cannot Expect to stay long in the world. The people here are Entirely disposed in affection to me and God be praised I do see some success of my Labours in the hearts and lives of my people and I have the happyness to meet with some very Exemplary Christians and I began to see a new face of things from Gods blessing on my faithful Endeavours, for I have endeavoured as much as in me lay to Engage men to be sound and thorough Christians, and it is this that is matter of unspeakable consolation to me, makeing my ministerial work my delight, Chearfully Embraceing all offers, not Excepting against time or distance; and last week I was Earnestly Solicited to go to Preach at least 70 miles distant from this place Informeing me that there would be at least 40 Children to be Baptized, and I have really Baptized above the number of Infants and adult that is mentioned in the Letter Inclosed to yr. Lordship and that without receiving any offering or Consideration; wherefore everything duly weighed and considered my case is peculiar and even singular and therefore I think I may with modesty Challenge some little regard. Your Lordship has always Encouraged the honest Endeavours of the meanest of the Clergy and I humbly hope I shall not be the only unfortunate Instance to have my case overlooked and disregarded. I beseech your Lordship most humbly and most Earnestly to condescend to recommend my case and the case of the Inhabitants here, without delay (as your Lordship shall think proper) to the Honorable Society and to be solicitous with the worthy members to obtain an Immediate assistance for me, as some small reward for former services; and you may depend they will Encourage me to go on to more Labour, and diligence (if possible) and if it shall be Improved (through Gods assistance) as an help and advantage for carrying on the work of the Ghospel and the interest of Religion, and the Parishioners with me will have abundant cause to bless almighty God for yr. Lordship and Jointly Lie under the greatest obligations to the Honorable Society for affording us their charitable assistance. I presumed in my last letter to yr. lordship to Intimate that I had not any books but the Bible Comprayer Book and Burkes on the new testament there are I am sensible Some publick spirited Gentelmen that if they was made acquainted of my want this way they would condescend to furnish me with a few necessary Books for the discharge of my duty.

And truly my Lord there are few Bibles, common prayer Books, Books of devotion etc. It would be a great act of Charity Speedaly to Supply this new settlement with what Books might be Judged proper, and if was directed to my care you should receive from me all possible satisfaction in the prudent distribution of yr. books you shall send. I have Endeavoured as much as may be to get an exact Knowledge of the Inclinations [*illegible*], State and Condition of North Carolina and if yr. Lordship desires an acct. from me I will [*torn*] to send it as soon as possible. We have here no place Set apart my lord to a Religious use so as to be Entirely free from all common use of life nor in any part of this new settlement; I here fitted up my own house in Brunswick and furnished it with pues and Benches and made it as decent as possible at my own Charge and the vestry proposed to allow me £100 this Currency a year but I have not received anything on that acct. and I preach in it commonly two Sundays a month. I have several things to represent to yr. Lordship but I have trespassed too long already on yr. Lordships patience.

I make bould to send this packet to yr. Lordship under Cover to Mr. Hunter also, requesting the favour of him to wait on yr. Lordship with it; I am informed he is a substantial Gentleman and a Considerable dealer and if anything be determined in my favour he may be confided in to direct it to me. I beseech yr. Lordship most Earnestly to favour me with a Letter to let me know how far I may depend on the Honorable Societyes Support, and make me so happy as to assure me that you retain a favourable opinion me [*sic*] and that I shall meet with yr. Encouragement and regard. I have really subsisted without a sallary as long as I can, and I beg leave to represent to your Lordship that if this supplication proves in Effectual I shall be obliged to leave this place for some time and Entirely throw my self into yr. Lordships hands in London, and with your favour present my own case, the trouble fateague and Expense I have been at to keep up the face of religion here. I cannot help takeing notice to your Lordship that I am informed that I am the peculiar mark of a Gentelmans spleen in South Carolina[2] and that he does me all the Ill offices he can with yr. Lordship Endeavouring to defame and misrepresent me, if he does not think such behaviour unbecoming his Character I think it below me to take notice of it and shall only say that the Inclosed Letter I presume to hope will be Judged by yr. Lordship a Sufficient vindication from any aspersions cast on my Conduct for the time I have resided here. I shall desist from troubling yr. any further but conclude with beging yr. Lordships Blessing and Encouragement and with assureing yr. Lordship that I shall always be tender that no dishonour be reflected on the name or the cause of the lord whom I serve and I Humbly Intreat yr. Lordship to believe me always with the utmost duty and Submission yr. Lordships most Humble and most obedient Servant.

Richd. Marsden

[*Addressed*:]
To
Right Reverend Father in God
Edmond Lord Bishop of London

[*Endorsed*:]
Society
Received Dec. 31, 1736.

ALS.

[1]Not located.
[2]Undoubtedly Commissary Alexander Garden is meant.

[*CO 5/344*]

Proceedings of the General Assembly
1736 September 22

North Carolina ss. At a General Assembly begun and held at Edenton on Tuesday the 21st day of September 1736. Present The Honorable William Smith Esqr. President, Nath. Rice, Robt. Halton, Math. Rowan, Edwd. Moseley, Cullen Pollock Esqrs. Members of the upper house of Assembly. [...]

Wednesday Septr. 22d.
The house met according to Adjournment [...]
His Excellency[1] came to the Upper house, and by a Messenger, requir'd the Attendance of the House of Burgesses; who came in a full body, and presented William Downing Esqr. their Speaker, whom his Excellency was pleased to Approve of; And then Delivered his Speech to both houses in the following words, Videlicet.
Gentlemen of the upper house; Mr. Speaker And Gentlemen of the House of Burgesses.
[...]
I shall begin with Observing the Deplorable and almost Total want of Devine Worship throughout the province. I Believe it is Impossible to Instance in any Country, I'm Sure it is, in any Colony belonging to a Christian Nation; where some Effectuall provision has not been made; for paying in Publick and at Stated times, That Adoration and Homage to Almighty God, so highly Becoming all Rational Creatures; and for Instructing the People in their Duty to the Supream Author of their Being, to one Another and to themselves.

After Observing this, no body will be Suprized at the many disorders which have always Prevailed among us; Especialy when it is Considered how little care there is taken of the Education of Youth.

In all Civilized Societys of Men it has allways been looked upon as a Matter of the Greatest Consequence to their peace and Happyness, to Polish the minds of Young Persons with some degree of Learning, and Early to Instill into them the Principles of Virtue and Religion; and that the Legislature has never yet taken the least care to Erect one School, which deserves the name, in this Wide Extended Country, must in the Judgment of all thinking men be Reckoned one of Our greatest Misfortunes. [...]

Minutes. On September 25, the upper house replied that "We lament very much the want of Divine Publick worship (a crying scandal in any, but more especially in a Christian Community;) as well as the general neglect in point of education, the main sources of all disorders and Corruptions, which we should rejoice to see removed and remedeyed, and are ready to do our parts, towards the reformation of such flagrant and prolifick Evils." The lower house apparently made no formal reply to the governor's speech, but instead presented him with a list of various grievances on October 7. On the same day, Johnston rejected the grievances and went on to comment derisively that "In any other Country besides this I am satisfied they [the assembly committee drawing up the grievances] would have taken notice of the want of divine worship, the neglect of the education of youth, the bad state of your Laws and the impossibility to execute them, such as they are Grievances which will deserve redress, but these it seems are not reckoned grievances in this part of the world." On October 12, the governor prorogued the assembly after the lower house refused to obey his command to attend him in the chamber of the upper house. At the next session of the General Assembly the following March, Johnston reiterated his desire that it enact legislation "for maintaining and establishing the public Worship of Almighty God." No statutes relating to the church were passed during the session, however. Saunders, *Colonial Records*, IV, 239, 271.

[1]Governor Gabriel Johnston.

[*LAM/FUL/VI*]

Rev. Richard Marsden to [Bishop of London]
1736 November 8

<264>

Brunswick Cape Fear
Novembr. the 8th, 1736.

My Lord

My last Letter to yr. Lordship was dated Augt. the 16th and sent in a ship from this Port bound for London; and I presumed to Inclose in it a Letter to you from the most considerable in Habitants in this New settelment, Supplicateing yr. Lordship in my behalf and giveing you a Just representation of myself and Circumstances, and what my doctrine and manner of Conversation has been for Eight years the time of my Setteling here and I made bould to Inclose it in a Letter to Mr. Tho. Hunter a Considerable dealer in Black fryars London (the gentelmn that condescended in my behalf to wait on yr. Lordship with my Letter of the 13th of Apll. 1734,[1] in which was Inclosed a Coppy of a Letter from the vestry of St. James Parish recommending me to the Honorable Society for Propogation of the Ghospel in forreign Parts) and presumed to beg the favour of him to deliver it to yr. Lordship, and I was in hopes you would have received it before this time, but I have been Informed that the Commander Captin Quince was obliged by distress to put in at New york in order to refit the ship before he could proceed on his voiage; this news has given me some uneasiness but I hope my Letter will be delivered safe to your Lordship tho at a much longer distance of time than I Expected. It has been a real affliction to me, and a heavy pressure upon my heart that I have done anything to Incur your Lordships displeasure; But I recd. the agreeable news in a Letter from Mr. Hunter that yr. Lordship had now Entertained a more favourable opinion of me, and had been pleased to promis to lay my case before the Honorable Society and to Endeavour to obtain some allowance for me from them. I assure yr. Lordship I shall always retain the most Grateful sense of yr. Lordships goodness and Kind Intentions towards me; but I shall continue under apprehensions and fears that your displeasure against me is not Entirely removed 'till I am Honored with a Letter from yr. Lordship to assure me of it, which would be an unexpressible satisfaction and Encouragment to me; but if my Letter of the 16th of Augt. with the Inclosed comes safe to yr. hands I am confident will fully satisfie yr. Lordship as to the diligent and faithful discharge of my duty as a minister and the regularity of my life and Entirely remove any Prejudice you may have received against me and if I find after some time that those Letters are not arrived I will not fail to send a duplicate of the Letters from the Inhabitants to your Lordship attested by the Governor and under the seal of the Collony. I have rendered this place all the Important service in my power and Endeavoured as much as in me Lay to Engage men to be sound and thorough Christians, and hitherto all my sermons tended, and God be praised I do see some success of my labours in the hearts and lives of my people. I have had no other motive for my Preaching here but a passionate regard for the Glory of God; my ministerial work is my delight, my heart is always in it Chearfully Embraceing all offers not Excepting against time or distance, and have been Exemplary in my whole deportment, and am possessed of a General Esteem, but I have met with small requital for my pains and diligence but I rest satisfied in the secret testimony, and siolent applaus of my own Conscience. Most of the Inhabitants here are poor and have been at great Expence in setteling in this uncultivated place only some few that are for makeing disturbances and will neither pay the King nor the minister what may reasonably be Expected from them and therefore I have gone on Chearfully in the discharge of the offices of my function at my own great Expence to Support the face of Religion in this new settelment. Whereby I have brought my self into great straits and dificulties, and have really subsisted without a sallery as long as I can. I have the most low thoughts of myself and performances, but my case viewed in all its circumstances seems to me to deserve some little regard and I trust yr. Lordship out of yr. paternal tenderness will be disposed to use yr. good offices with the Society to settle a sallery on me and to send me some few useful Books. I most humbly submit myself and desires to yr. Lordships wisdom and goodness but if I am to meet with no Encouragment, and the recomendations sent home have not success in my favour it is my firm Resolution to come to London without delay and throw myself at yr. Lordships feet let the Consequence be what it will, and resign myself Entirely to your Lordships pleasure. I will give yr. Lordship no farther trouble at this time flattering my self that my Letter of the 16th of Augt. with the Inclosed will come safe to yr. hands and that I shall be Honored with a Letter from your Lordship to direct me in my Conduct. I am with the utmost Esteem and regard yr. Lordships most humble and most dutiful Servant.

Richd. Marsden

If yr. Lordship Condescends to favour me with a Letter, if you will be pleased to send it to John Eaton dodsworth Esqr. in Mansel Street one of the directors of the Bank or to Mr. thomas Hunter at the Golden Head in Black Fryars will be sent by the first opportunity to me.

[*Endorsed:*]
Marsden
Cape fear
sollicits a Salary
will come home

ALS.

[1]Not located.

[*SPG/Jou/7*]

Journal of the SPG
1736 December 17

<84.> 17 December 1736. [...]
<87.> 4. It was also reported from the Committee that they had read a Letter from the Reverend Mr. Boyd Itinerant Missionary in North Carolina dated Edentown July 24th 1736[1] In which he acquaints, that he did not receive the Secretary's of the 17th September 1735[2] till the last of May, and should have waited on the Governor according to the Society's directions, but he was above 300 Miles to the Southward and dayly expected, tho' he has not seen him yet. That in his last of the 24th March[3] he Acquainted the Society with his Journey into the other County, since which time he hath served in the North East Parish of Chowan and North west of Bertie; that in the North East Parish of Chowan there are Abundance of Anabaptists and Quakers, most of them entirely ignorant of the Fundamentals of Our Religion, several of them have already become his Auditors, and this year besides a great Number of Infants, he hath baptized 4 Quakers. That he hath not this year recd. any of their Country Allowance having freed himself from all engagements; since he recd. the Secretary's of the 29th January 1734,[4] so that his whole dependance is upon his Allowance from the Society. He renews his request to the Society for a Library in so remote a Place, having used his utmost diligence in seeking after the Books that were left by Mr. Newnam <88.> but can hear nothing of them; and if the Society would be pleas'd to send a Parcell of Small Tracts, they would be very Serviceable and well accepted there. Agreed by the Society that 5 pounds worth of small Tracts be sent to Mr. Boyd, to be distributed among the People, and that ten pounds worth of Books be sent him for a Library for the Missionary appointed by the Society to North Carolina. [...]

Minutes.

[1]Not located.
[2]Not located.
[3]Not located.
[4]Not located.

[*SPG/Jou/7*]

Journal of the SPG
1736/7 February 18

<106.> At Bow Vestry 18th February 1736. [. . .]

<107.> It was also reported from the Committee that they had read a Letter directed to the Lord Bishop of London, dated Cape Fear, North Carolina July 1736[1] and signed by the Principal Inhabitants of the Parish of St. James's on Cape Fear River, Members of the Church of England; praying his Lordship to use his good Offices with the Society, that the Reverend Mr. Marsden their worthy Pastor, may obtain a Mission from them, that he may be thereby enabled to proceed in the Work of the Ministry among them. They set forth that their Settlement is very new, perhaps the newest, except Georgia, in His Majesty's Dominions. They represent that Mr. Marsden hath recd. little more than what the Gentlemen of the Vestry, and a few others have voluntarily given him; that the Parish is very far extended, and the Expence of Water Passages very great, in so much that in attending the several Parts of his Cure, he <108.> hath really expended considerably more than he hath recd.; That during the Eight Years of his Ministry there his life hath been unblameable. They therefore Humbly pray his Lordship to recommend their Case to the Society.

Whereupon the Committee agreed to report, that as the Society have come to a former Resolution not to create any new Missions, and as they do already support the Reverend Mr. Boyd an Itinerant Missionary in North Carolina, that they should not Establish a New Mission at Cape Fear, but the Committee Agreed to recommend the said Mr. Marsden to the favour of the Society for a Gratuity. Agreed by the Society that a Gratuity of £20 be given to Mr. Marsden for his Service at Cape Fear. [. . .]

Minutes.

[1]Not located.

[*SPG/Jou/7*]

Journal of the SPG
1737 April 15

<134.> 15th April 1737. [. . .]

<142.> A Petition[1] to the Society from Mr. William Davidson was read. In which he sets forth that the People of North Carolina are very desirous of having more Missionaries, and will contribute towards their Support according to their Abilities. And Mr. William Davidson Offers his Service to be employed as a Missionary from the Society in North Carolina. Agreed by the Society that Mr. Davidson be acquainted that they are not in a Condition to send any new Missionaries there at present. But that when the Society shall be informed the People of North Carolina have built a Church in some Convenient place, and Setled a Salary for a Minister, the Society will make some further allowance towards his better support, if wanted. [. . .]

Minutes.

[1]Not located.

[*LAM/FUL/X*]

Rev. Alexander Garden to Bishop of London
1737 September 6

<76> <*Duplicate*>

My Lord

I have lately receiv'd a Letter from his Excellency the Governor of Nth. Carolina, of which the Following is a Paragraph, Concerning the ill Behaviour of Mr. Boyd, the Honorable Society's Missionary in that Colony.

After having expressed much Concern, that no farther assistance was to be expected from the Honorable Society, towards the Propagating of Religion in that Colony, than the one Missionary already there; His Excellency Subjoins concerning him and Says.—"But what makes the matter still worse is that this very Missionary is one of the Vilest and most Scandalous Persons in the Government. I gave you some Hints of his Idleness and Inclination to Drunkeness, when I had the pleasure of Seeing you at Edenton; But Since that time, I have heard such accts. of his behaviour as are realy Shocking. Particularly that on a Sunday, this Spring, at noon day, he was seen by many Persons Lying dead Drunk and fast asleep on the Great Road to Virginia, with his Horses Bridle tyed to his Leg; this I have been assur'd of by Several Persons of the best Credit. As he is under your Inspection I hope you will take some notice of such horrid practices."

I have also receiv'd a Letter, on the same Subject, from another very worthy Gentleman, a Member of his Majestys Council, and Collector of his Quit Rent's in that Province.[1] Concerning Mr. Boyd he Saith.—"Whose life and Conversation would be Scandalous in a Layman, much more So in one of his function. Drunkeness in a most open manner is his frequent practise; and I was told, by the Chief Justice,[2] when I was last at Edenton, that he was found on a Sunday in that Condition, fast asleep, on the Road nigh the Town. In Short he is, I thinck, a Man in all respects of as bad principles, as any I have ever Seen, Considering his Education; from whence you will form a Judgement, how the Interest of Religion is caried on under his Ministry."

I am so far from putting the Least Doubt to the truth of the above Informations, that they would have met with entire Credit from me, had they come from persons of much less Known honour and Integrity than they do. For when, about two years ago, I came thro' that Province, in my way from N. England to So. Carolina I had such Intimations given me, not only by the Government [and] the People of Barty County in General of Mr. Boyd's ill behaviour, with Respect to Drunkeness and Neglect of duty, that I should Certainly have then made a Legal Enquiry unto it; but that neither had I my Commission with me nor could I spare so much time (the Winter at hand and at that Distance from home) as would have been necessary for that purpose. And as tis now Impraticable for me to leave my Charge and go to Edenton, (distance from hence 400 Miles) to make Such Enquiry; All I can do in the Case is, thus to transmit it, in the best light I can to the Honorable Society, not without hope, that they will Soon decide upon it, to Discharge that unworthy Missionary from their Service, or rather from adding to the real Disservice he has already done them.

The Governor and Council of that Colony have it much at Heart to obtain a Legal Establishment of a Competent Maintainance for the Clergy; but the unhappy Discord Subsisting twixt them and the Common House of Assembly, about Civil Concerns, has hitherto obstructed it. Meantime <77> they thinck, that the Pension of £80 per Annum allow'd Boyd by the Honorable Society would be apply'd to the best advantage, if £25 a piece were given to the two Clergymen, at Bath Town and New-Berne, who are in great Poverty; and the remaining £30 to Some Sober Clergyman, to be Sent over to Bladen Precinct, where the Governor is settled, and where he assures me, his Neighbourhood are well disposed to join with him, for making it up a handsome maintainance.

I humbly crave your Lordships Blessing, and am My Lord Your Lordship's most dutiful and Obedient humble Servant.

A. Garden

So. Carola.
Charlestown
Septr. 6th 1737

[*Endorsed*:]
<*Answered*>
Boyd
Duplicate.

LS. An identical letter addressed to the secretary was read at a meeting of the SPG on January 20, 1737/8, when it was agreed to concur in a recommendation of the Committee "that enquiry be made into Mr. Boyds conduct, and that a letter be wrote to him, requiring him to answer to the Charge laid against him." Journal of the SPG, VII, 202.

[1]Eleazer Allen (1692-1750), Harvard graduate and political ally of Governor Gabriel Johnston, at various times held numerous important offices in the colony, including that of receiver general of quitrents, chief justice, and provincial treasurer.

[2]William Smith.

[SS 841]

Will
1737 October 9

In Nomine Dei Amen. I John Boyd of Chowan Precinct Clerk Being in health of Body and of Perfect sense and sound Memory doe make and ordain this my Last will and Testament.

Imprimis. I Give my Body to the earth and my spirit I resign to God (when He shall think fitt to call me hence) in full and assured hopes of a resurrection of Both Body and soul and for what Estate I have I Leave it in manner and form following.

I Desire and ordain that my Beloved wife Lydia Boyd may have the sole use and Benefitt of my whole estate real and Personall of what Kind or Quality soever during her widowhood or Naturall Life, and that During her widowhood she shall have the sole Power, of Dividing my estate as she shall think fitt amongst my four children William Anne Marion and Lydia Boyds and I further Desire that she may not be obliged to give security as the Law prescribes only to return to the secretary office a full inventory of the same I further Desire that if she marrys again she may resign the whole according to the inventory Given and I Doe hereby Impower my executors to take the same out of her hands and manage it to the Best advantage for my children but I further Desire she may still have the tuition of my children and the Power of Distributing to them their severall shares and I Doe hereby Constitute and appoint my Wife Mr. Philip Aylett In Virginia and Andrew Irving My Executors In Wittnes Whereof I have hereunto sett my hand and seal this 9th of Octobr. 1737.

John Boyd

Signed sealed and Published in Presence of us.
John Rowsom
Jas. Williams
Edward (his mark) Silk

North Carolina Chowan ss. July Court Anno Domini 1738. Present His Majestys Justices.

These may Certifie that James Williams and Edward Silk Two of the Subscribing Evidences to the within Will Appeared in Open Court and Made Oath on the Holy Evengelists that they were present and Saw John Boyd Sign Seal Publish and Declare the within to be and Contain his Last will and Testament and that the Said John Boyd was there and at that time of Sound and Disposeing Memory and that they also See John Roussham the Other Subscribing Evidence Sign his Name thereto at the Same time. Then also Appeared Lydia Boyd an Executrix in Open Court and took the Executors Oath in due form of Law, Ordered that the Honorable Nathl. Rice Esqr. Secretary of this province have Notice thereof that Letters Testamentory Issue thereon as the Law Directs.

Test. Jams. Craven Clerk Car.

[*Endorsed:*]
Jno. Boyds Will
Indorced fees Not paid
Letters testamentary Issued May the 23d 1739
per J. Craven
Recorded

DS.

[*SPG/B/12*]

Rev. Alexander Garden to Rev. John Garzia
ca. 1738

<122a> Your 2d Letter, concerning a Box of Books for you from the Society, is come to hand, in which you mention 3 former ones you had wrote me, one of which only I have recd., desiring me to find an Opportunity of sending the said Box to Edenton consigned to Governor Johnson.

The said Box has been in my Custody nigh a 12 month and you may wait 7 years before any such opportunity offers as from hence to Edenton. And I must acquaint you, that it must be your Business to look after for such Opportunity from that Place Hither, and by such to send me your Order for the Delivery to some particular Person.

I am Your very humble Servant.

A. Garden.

[*Addressed:*]
<7> To The Reverend Mr. Garzia Minister
at Bath town
North-Carolina

ALS.

[*SPG/B/7*]

Account
[1738]

<207> North Carolina. A True Account of the Number of People Baptized by me [Rev. John Garzia] In this Province from the Year of Our Lord 1733 to this Present 1738 with the Names of the Parishes and Precincts.

Anno 1733

From January the 1 to the 19 in Several places	Males	58	Females	62
In Roanoke Island and there Abouts before and After I was Cast Away, going to Virginia for My Family from Aprill the 27 to May the 5	Males	9	Females	3
Coming up Albumar Sound upon the South Shore from May the 10 to the 14	Males	24	Females	16
In the Lower part of Saint Andrews Parish Calld Cuscopnung River from the 14 of May to the 15	Males	75	Females	32
Up the Sound from the 16 to the 17	Males	11	Females	13
In Edenton Parish Chowan Precinct At the House of Abrahams Hills June the 2d	Males	9	Females	17
At the Norwest Landing Septr. the 3d	Males	8	Females	4
In the Old and New Mattummuskete Septr. the 9 10 11	Males	5	Females	4

Anno 1734

In Society Parish Bartie Precinct from March the 24 to the 28	Males	33	Females	27
In Edenton Parish Aprill the 21	Males	9	Females	14
In Newbern Town Craven Precinct June the 23d	Males	14	Females	22
In St. Andrews Parish Tarrel Precinct July the 28 and in Perquimons	Males	18	Females	13
Belonging to Hide Precinct July the att Sundry times	Males	9	Females	11
In Saint Andrews Parish N. Coratico Chappel at the House of Mr. Hordinson, Septr. the 29 to Octobr. the 3d	Males	24	Females	24
In Cuscopnung River Octr. the 27	Males	21	Females	29
<208>In Society Parish Bertie Precinct Octr. the 30	Males	57	Females	19
In Edenton Parish Chowan Precinct Novembr. 3	Males	5	Females	8

Anno 1735

In Newbern Town Craven Precinct March the 16	Males	21	Females	29
In Edenton parish Chowan Precinct Aprill 27th	Males	5	Females	7
In Society Parish Berties Precinct at the Chappel And at the Houses of Mr. Win and Mr. Garret from May the 10th to the 16th	Males	58	Females	47
In St. Andrews parish Tarrell Precinct at the Chappel and at the House of Mr. Smetick August the 3d	Males	45	Females	48
In Edenton Parish Chowan Precinct Novembr. 2d	Males	6	Females	4
In Cuscopnung River St. Andrews Parish Tarrel Precinct Novembr. the 30th	Males	28	Females	11

Anno 1736

In Edenton Parish Chowan Precinct March the 29	Males	4	Females	6
In Society Parish Bertie Precinct Aprill 5 to the 9 At the Chappel and at the Houses of Mr. Win and Mr. Garret	Males	51	Females	47
In Saint Andrews Parish Cuscopnung River, and At Mr. Fraleys House Septr. the 6 to the 10	Males	30	Females	34
In St. Andrews Parish Tarrel Precinct at the Houses of Mr. Fraley and Mr. Smeticks from Octr. the 3th to the 7th	Males	42	Females	34
In Edenton Parish Chowan Precinct Octr. the 30th	Males	5	Females	7
In St. Johns Parish Carteret Precinct from Novembr. the 21 to the 26	Males	11	Females	18

Anno 1737

<209>In Aligator Creek in St. Andrews Parish March the 6th	Males	23	Females	20
In Hide Parish Hide Precinct March the 27th	Males	22	Females	18
In St. Andrews Parish Tarrel Precinct May the 1st to the 3	Males	31	Females	39
In Society Parish at the Chappel and at the Houses of Mr. Win and Mr. Garret from July the 24th to the 29th	Males	57	Females	51
In Edenton Parish Chowan Precinct July the 30th to August the 5th	Males	7	Females	6
In Saint Andrews Parish Tarrel Precinct In that Part of Cuscopnung River and at Moratico Chappel from Octor. the 2d to the 4th	Males	30	Females	28

Anno 1738

In Carteret Precinct Saint Johns Parish Febuary the 5 and in Aprill 2d 3d	Males	10	Females	15
In the Newhannover Precinct from Aprill the 27 to May the 16	Males	6	Females	12
In OnsLow Precinct St. Jnos. Parish May the 21th	Males	11	Females	16
			Males In All	918
			Females In All	839
			And In All	1757

And in My parish St. Thos. In Bath Town Beaufort Precinct from Jany. the 1 1733 to this 1738	Males	279	Females	242

And Among those three Quaker families one of 7 in family, one of 6, one of three. More on Indian and Elleven Negros

D.

[*LAM/FUL/VI*]

Rev. Richard Marsden to Bishop of London
1737/8 March 13

<266>

Monday March 13th 1737.

May it please yr. Lordship

It was very shocking to me to be Informd by the Gentelmen that waited on you with my Letter to acquaint yr. Lordship of my arrival from Cape Fear that I had suffered so much in yr. Esteem that you was utterly averse to see me. I do with great Injenuity and sorrow confess that I have given yr. Lordship great cause to be offended with me, but I can with a good Conscience declare that I have sincerely repented of every miscarriage that my memory can recollect and shall never be partial to myself but ready on all occasions to declare my detestation and abhorrance of every neglect of duty.

I Humbly beg yr. Lordship will Judge Charitably and candidly of me and if you will not be graciously pleased to Interest yr. self so far in my favour as to recommend my case to the Honorable Society I Humbly Supplicate yr. Lordship to Condescend to deliver to the secretary of the Society the Letter you recd. from the Inhabitants of Cape Fear in my favour from the hands of Mr. Hunter and to Inform him that you have recd. a Letter from Governor Johnston confirming from his own Knowledge the Character given of me by my Parishioners.

I desire to live to no other End than to do service to Gods Church; and Conscience of my own good Intentions and desires suggests to me many flattering hopes of doing God and his Church good service at Cape Fear if I meet with sutable Encouragment.

I subscribe myself yr. Lordships most Humble and most obedient servant.

Richd. Marsden

Capt. Wimble[1] Intreats
yr. Lordship to accept of this map
of North Carolina

[*Addressed*:]
<267>
To The Right Reverend Edmond
Ld. Bishop of London

[*Endorsed:*]
Marsden
Cape fear

ALS.

[1]James Wimble (1696/7-ca. 1744), sometime resident of North Carolina, merchant, privateer, early promoter of Wilmington, and cartographer, published in 1738 "the best coastal chart of North Carolina before the closing years of the eighteenth century." Cumming, "Turbulent Life of Captain James Wimble," *North Carolina Historical Review*, 1-18.

[*SPG/Jou/7*]

Journal of the SPG
1737/8 March 17

<218.> 17th March 1737. [. . .]

<228.> Mr. Marsden made his Application to the Board to be Employed as Missionary at Cape <229.> Fear North Carolina. Agreed that he be acquainted, that the Society are not in a condition at present to create a New Mission. [. . .]

Minutes.

[*SPG/Jou/7*]

Journal of the SPG
1738 April 21

<230.> 21st April 1738. [. . .]

<241.> 34. A Representation of the Reverend Mr. Marsden to His Grace the Arch Bishop of Canterbury was read, and referred to the Committee to make Enquiry concerning Mr. Marsdens Character, and also to consider the State of the Mission in North Carolina. [. . .]

Minutes.

[*SPG/Jou/7*]

Journal of the SPG
1738 May 19

<242.> 19th May 1738. [. . .]

<244.> It was reported from the Committee that they had taken into consideration the Reference to them of the State of the Mission in North Carolina and to make Enquiry

concerning Mr. Marsdens Character. And Agreed to Report as their Opinion, that two Settled Missionaries would answer the ends of the Society more Effectually in North Carolina than one Itinerant Missionary.

Also that they had read several Papers relating to Mr. Marsdens Character, and after mature consideration of the same it appears to them, that he had been setled at Cape Fear in North Carolina for above 7 Years last past, and hath occasionally done considerable Services as a Clergyman in that Province, and appears to have maintained a good Character for that time.

<245.> Agreed by the Society that the Mission in North Carolina be divided into two Missions with a Salary of £50 per Annum to each Missionary to Commence from Midsumer next, and that Mr. Richard Marsden be appointed one of the Missionaries, and that his Residence be at the Hermitage[1] at Prince Georges Creek. Ordered that he read Prayers and Preach on the 4th Ver. of the 5th Chapter of St. Mathews Gospel[2] on Sunday, Sennight, and that Dr. Roper be desired to hear him, and upon his making a Report to his Grace of Canterbury that he hath perform'd the same to his Satisfaction, that the Secretary give him the necessary dispatch to proceed on his Mission.

And that it be referred to the Committee to settle the Bounds of the two districts where the two Missionaries are to Officiate, and to make their Report thereon to the Society. [. . .]

Minutes.

[1]Marsden's plantation.

[2]"Blessed are they that mourn: for they shall be comforted." Matthew 5:4, Authorized Version.

[SPG/Jou/7]

Journal of the SPG
1738 June 16

<249> 16th June 1738. [. . .]

<250.> 6. It was also reported from the Committee that they had taken into consideration the Reference to them to settle the Boundaries of the two districts where the two Missionaries in North Carolina are to Officiate. And Agreed as their Opinion that the Proper place for Mr. Marsden to reside, is at his own Plantation, the Hermitage in St. James's Parish in Hannover Precinct, and that he do duty at Brunswick and Newtown,[1] and that he do as Opportunity offers, visit all that part of North Carolina lying South West of the River Newse. And that the other Missionary do reside at Chowan and officiate at the two Chappels there, till the Church at Edington, now Building, be finished, and do as Opportunity offers, visit all those Parts <251.> of North Carolina lying on the North Eastside of the said River Newse. Resolved that the Society do agree with the Committee. [. . .]

<256.> 15. It was also reported from the Committee that they had read a Letter from the Reverend Mr. John Boyd dated August 24th 1737,[2] In which he writes, that in May last he received a Box of Books by the way of Virginia, but no letter, Invoice or

Catalogue with them, further that he chiefly resides in the North East Parish of Chowan, where there are a great many misled Anabaptist Preachers, that he hath used his utmost Endeavours to reclaim them from their Error, by Sending for their Teachers and convincing them, and by adapting his Publick Discourses to their Capacity which, by Gods Blessing hath had a good Effect and a great many who professed that Sect, have left their Meetings and are become his constant hearers. He writes, that there are in that Parish two Chappels about 35 Miles apart, and there is <257.> now Building a large Brick Church at Edenton. Says he shall reside in that Part of the Parish till the Society Order otherwise, that he hath no Country allowance, and only some few Marriage Fees. Agreed that the Secretary do write to Mr. Boyd and acquaint him that the Society have divided the Mission in North Carolina into two Missions, and that he do inform him what the District of his Mission, is, and that his Salary from Midsummer next will be £50 a year, and no more. [. . .]

Minutes.

[1]A few years later Newtown, or Newton, was renamed Wilmington.
[2]Not located.

[*SPG/B/7*]

Gabriel Johnston to SPG
1738 June 30

North Carolina June 30, 1738.

<211> To The Honorable the Lords and Gentlemen of the Society for propagating the Christian Religion in forreign parts.

The Reverend Mr. John Boyd the Missionary for this Province having dyed the 19 or 20th Day of May and having in this Province a worthy and Religious poor Minister the Reverend John Garzia of St. Thomas's Parish Pamptico Incumbent who before my coming to this Province the People of that Parish induced by fair Promises to come from Virginia and live among them and at present they are willing to Starve with his Wife and three Children by not paying him his little Sallery for Two Years and a half past which knowing and likewise his indefatiguable care in going often from Parish to Parish preaching the Word of God and Baptizing as will appear by his Report In Consideration of which I do recommend him to yr. Honorable Society to be appointed a Missionary for this Province being not only a fit person but the Same will be an Act of Charity to the relief of him from the Oppression he labours under and if So I desire an Answer to inform him of his Duty therein.

Yr. Honors Most Obedient Servant.

Gab. Johnston

[*Addressed:*]
To The Honourable The Society
for propagating the Gospell in
Forreign parts London

[*Endorsed:*]
Governour Johnson's of North Carolina
his Letter to the Society dated June 30th 1738
Read 11th June 1739.

LS. This document was enclosed in the one immediately following and was read at meetings of the SPG on May 18 and June 15, 1738. On the former date it was agreed "that Mr. Garzia be appointed Missionary to North Carolina in the Room of Mr. Boyd deceased with a Salary of £50 per Annum, to Commence from Michaelmas last." The meeting of June 15 agreed with the report of the Committee "that this matter was fully setled at the last Meeting of the Society." Journal of the SPG, VIII, 51, 54.

[*SPG/B/7*]

Rev. John Garzia to Secretary, SPG
1738 July 20

<203>

St. Thomas' Parish No. Carolina.
July 20th 1738.

Reverend Sir

I received your letter Dated the 18th of September 1736 and have since received the Bible and Common Prayer Book for the use of the Church and I heartily thank the Honorable Society for the Same. My humble request to you Sir is that you'll be pleased to lay the inclosed Lettres before the Society immediately after arrival by reason they concern both my duty and Interest and hope Good Sir you'll contribute to forward the same. One is in my behalf from our Governor the other as I know, tis my Duty is from myself containing my Report of, my behaviour in my Function. I am Reverend Sir with my hearty and Sincere prayers for yr. wellfare Your Most Obedient Servant.

John Garzia.

P.S. The Sallary that the parish has [sett]led on me is no more than £225 in the money of this province being paper money which is not in value above £20 Sterling and that not paid, by which you may perceive in what manner my family is supported, and hope Sir you will Communicate the same as well to the Bishop [as] to the Society.

LS. The documents immediately above and immediately following, as well as the account above, pp. 378-381, were enclosed in this letter. Read at a meeting of the SPG on June 15, 1739, at which it was agreed that "this matter was fully setled at the last Meeting of the Society"; the previous meeting (May 18, 1739) had agreed "that Mr. Garzia be appointed Missionary to North Carolina in the room of Mr. Boyd deceased with a Salary of £50 per Annum, to Commence from Michaelmas last." Journal of the SPG, VIII, 51, 54.

[*SPG/B/7*]

Rev. John Garzia to SPG
1738 July 20

<335>

No. Carolina
July 20th 1738.

To the Honorable the Lords and Gentlemen of the Society for propagating the Gospell in Forreign Parts.

My Lords and Gentlemen the enclosed is a Letter from his Excellency our Governor, representing to you the real State of my present condition in this remote part of the World, which I hope you'll be pleased to consider off and extend your Charity towards my relief as recommended by the Governor. I thought it my duty to acquaint you of my behaviour since I am in this Province thereupon have sent you my Report which I hope will meet with your approbation. I most heartily thank your honours for your piety in sending the Bible and Common prayer Book for the use of our Church I am with continuing my prayers for your Honours wellfare. Your most Obliged Most Obedient and Most humble Servant.

John Garzia

Bath Town in St. Thomas' Parish No. Carolina.
July 20th Day 1738.

LS. This document was enclosed in the one immediately above.

[*SPG/Jou/7*]

Journal of the SPG
1738 July 21

<260.> 21st July 1738. [. . .]

<263.> It was also reported from the Committee that they had read a Letter from the Reverend Mr. Marsden dated Feckenham near Alcaster Warwickshire July 14th 1738[1] acquainting that on his Application to the Lord Bishop of London for his Licence to proceed on the Mission to North Carolina, he had not obtained his Lordships Licence. Ordered by the Society that the Secretary do attend the Lord Bishop of London and lay before his Lordship the Report of the Committee concerning the Appointment of Mr. Marsden to be Missionary, and what was done by the Society upon the said Report; And that he do acquaint his Lordship that if he desires to see the Testimonials of Mr. Marsden upon which the Committee moved the Society to appoint him Missionary, they shall be laid before his Lordship as soon as they can be received from Mr. Marsden who is now in the Country, and hath been wrote to for that purpose. [. . .]

Minutes.

[1]Not located.

[*SPG/Jou/7*]

Journal of the SPG
1738 August 18

<265.> 18th August 1738. [. . .]

6. Mr. Henderson, in the Absence of the Secretary, Reported to the Board, that he had waited on the Lord Bishop of London with the Report of the Committee concerning the Appointment of Mr. Marsden, <266.> and what was done by the Society upon the said Report, and had also acquainted his Lordship that if he desired to see Mr. Marsdens Testimonials they should be laid before him, who said, He should be glad to see them. Mr. Henderson also acquainted that he had wrote twice to Mr. Marsden since the last Meeting of the Society, according to his own directions, but had received no Answer. [. . .]

Minutes.

[*SPG/Jou/7*]

Journal of the SPG
1738 September 15

<274.> 15th Septemr. 1738. [. . .]

<278.> 10. The Secretary acquainted the Board that according to the directions of the Society he had waited upon the Lord Bishop of London and laid before his Lordship an Attested Copy of the Reverend Mr. Marsdens Testimonials under the Seal of the Province of North Carolina, And his Lordship had directed him to acquaint the Board that he should not obstruct Mr. Marsden's being sent Missionary to North Carolina, but thought he could not properly give him a Licence till he had heard concerning his Character from his Commissary there.

Agreed that the Secretary do give Mr. Marsden the proper dispatches to proceed on his Mission in <279> North Carolina. Ordered that a Library of ten pounds be allowed him with a Bible and Common Prayer Book and five Pounds worth of Small Tracts and one doz. of Ostervalds Catechisms to be distributed among the Poor People there as usual. [. . .]

Minutes.

[*SPG/Jou/7*]

Journal of the SPG
1738 November 17

<292.> 17th November 1738. [. . .]

<300.> 9. It was also Reported from the Committee that they had Read a Petition[1] from Mrs. Eleanor <301.> Bayley Widow of the Reverend Mr. Thomas Bayley late Curate of the Parish of St. Mewan in the County of Cornwall Setting forth, that her late Husband had been for 17 Years a Missionary at Carolina, and other His Majesty's Plantations abroad, and that for four Years and a half preceding his death, he had no other Subsistance or Income to Support his Family than £30 a year for serving the Cure of St. Mewan, by which means he left the Petitioner in very low and mean Circumstances, altogether Friendless and helpless. Agreed as the Opinion of the Committee that it appearing Mr. Bayley never was Employ'd as a Missionary by the Society therefore his Widow is not Intitled to any Gratuity from them. Resolved that the Society do agree with the Committee. [. . .]

Minutes.

[1]Not located.

[*SPG/B/7*]

Rev. John Fordyce to Secretary, SPG
1738/9 February 1

<229> Frederick Parish, Winyaw
South Carolina Feby. 1st 1738/9

Reverend Sir

Yours of date 25th July 1737 came to hand the 26th of Octr. Last, with a Copy of a Minute relating to the Behavior of Mr. Boyd Missionary in N. Carolina, desiring me to make what Enquiry I coud in his genl. Conduct. I wrote to Mr. Eliazr. Allen of Cape Fear, as a person capable to inform me, whose answer I recd. this day and Runs Thus: I recd. yours, (relating to Mr. Boyd,) In Answer to which I cou'd have said much, as to the Subject you write about, but the Man is gone to give account before the Supreme Judge of all his Conduct either in his private Capacity, or that of his Minister Function. To him we must leave him, et de Mortuis Nil nisi Bonum.[1] [...]

At the Request of some Gentlemen at Cape fear N. Carolina, as well as the Reverend Mr. Garden, (Having obtain'd leave from my parish) I went and preach'd at Brunswick on Trinity Sunday last, to a large Congregation of people, well affected to the Church of England, and gave Notice of the Holy Sacrament the Sunday following, which I Administrat to 20 Communicants and Baptised five Infants. Here, they are at a great Loss for want of a Minister, being good Religious people, and ready to contribute to the Building of a Church and the Maintainance of a Minister. They have yet greater need of a Missionary towards Eden-Town, as I was Credibly informed w[*torn*] at [*torn*] that those who ought to be promoters of R[*torn*] <230> and Ignorant of their Duty to God; their Neighbour; and Loyalty to their Prince, or those then in authority under him. In so much that they have oppos'd, and prevented those Religious people that are among them from Building a Church, or Chapel, for the Publick Worship of Almighty God. So regardless are they, and Irreligious.

Having nothing further necessary I remain Reverend Sir The Honorable Societies most Dutiful and Obedient humble Servant.

John Fordyce [. . .]

Baptized at Cape Fear and upon the Road going there.	
Infants at C. F.	5
Lockwoods Folly	
Infants	2
Married Adult Women Baptized	2
At Little River 9 and west End long Bay 1, in all	10

ALS. Read at a meeting of the SPG on May 18, 1739. Journal of the SPG, VIII, 47.

[1]"And of the dead nothing but good [we will speak]."

[*CO 5/344*]

Proceedings of the General Assembly
1738/9 February 8

North Carolina ss. At a General Assembly begun and held at New Bern, the Sixth day of Febry. One thousand seven Hundred and thirty Eight and in the twelfth year of the Reign of Our Sovereign Lord George the Second by the Grace of God of Great Britain France and Ireland King etc. being the first Session of this present Assembly. [...]

Thursday the 8th of Febry. 1738.

The House met According to Adjournment. [...]

Gentlemen of the House of Burgesses. [...]

The Establishment of the publick worship of Allmighty God as it is the Great Foundation of the Happiness of Society and without which you Cannot expect his protection deserves your Earliest care that in Such a Wide Extended province as this Inhabited by British Subjects by persons Professing themselves Christians there Should be but two places where divine Service is Regularly Perform'd is realy Scandalous it is a Reproach peculiar to this part of his Majesty's Dominions which you Ought to remove without loss of time. [...]

Minutes. Governor Gabriel Johnston addressed these comments to a joint sitting of the General Assembly. The upper house replied later that same day that "We are of opinion with your Excellency that the Establishment of the worship of Almighty God in this Province merits our chiefest care. We shall therefore apply ourselves to consider the most proper methods, to make farther provision for the maintaining of any orthodox clergy among us." The following day the lower house replied in identical language, and a week later sent to the upper house a bill "for the better support of the Clergy of this Province." The upper house took no action on the bill, however.

[*SPG/SAP*]

Report
1738/9 February 16

<58> <*An Abstract of the Proceedings of the Society*.> [. . .] <*North-Carolina.*> The Society taking into particular Consideration the Condition of *North-Carolina*, hath judged proper to divide it into two Missions, the one on the North-East Side, and the other on the South-West Side of the River *Newse*; and hath appointed the Reverend Mr. *Marsden* to the South-West Mission, and designed the Reverend Mr. *Boyd*, at that time their Itinerant Missionary there, for the North-East Mission; but Mr. *Boyd* is since reported to be dead. [. . .]

Printed. Extracted from the yearly publication containing the sermon preached at the annual anniversary meeting of the SPG, together with a review of the activities of the Society and its missionaries during the preceding year. The date above is the date of the meeting.

[*LAM/FUL/X*]

Rev. Alexander Garden to Bishop of London
1739 May 4

<54>

(May 4, 1739)
(from Mr. Garden Minister
of Charlestown S. Carola.)

My Lord

I have recd. the Honour of your Lordship's Letter of the 14th July 1738; and am quite astonished at the Society's employing a Person of so notoriously vile a Character as *Marsden* for their Missionary. Let the Society inquire, my Lord, whether he has not fled almost every Colony in *America* for Crimes? Let them inquire whether when in *Barbadoes*, he was not accused of some very foul Actions, and particularly respecting one Mr. *Beresford*, a Brother Clergyman there? Whether in *Jamaica*, during the Government of the late *Duke of Portland*, he did not marry a second Wife, his former still living in England? And whether he fled not that Island on the Discovery? Let them inquire his Character of the Clergy of *New-England*, *Maryland*, and *Virginia*; and what his Behaviour was when in those Colonies? Let them inquire 'mong the *Lisbon* Merchants (I mean of the English Factory there) whether in the year 1729 he, the said *Marsden*, did not fraudulently obtain a Cargo of Goods from some of them, to the amount of £1500 Sterling for which he drew Bills of Exchange on such Persons in London as either knew nothing of him or had no Dealings with him, and which were all returned back protested? Let them inquire, whether Meantime he was soliciting the Society's Mission for *Cape-Fear*, he was not at Work also, in his usual Way, to defraud one Mr. *Austin* of *Liverpool* or *Chester* (but who keeps a large Warehouse in *London*) of Goods to a considerable Value, as also <*Mr. Garden-Moir*> two poor Milleners in *London* of considerable Sums for which he was pursued, endeavouring to make his Escape, arrested, and imprisoned at *Chester*? In a word, my Lord, let them inquire his Character of his own Wife and Children in or near *Whitby* in Yorkshire, if I mistake not the Name of the Place. I cannot conceive by whom he can be recommended to the Society; I'm sure not by any Clergy, or Layman of any Character, in *America*. And if, by the Populase at *Cape Fear*, I'm satisfied, that any one may take a hundred hands[1] 'mong them, to any Certificate he shall desire, for a single Bowl of Punch.

The Bearer of this is one Mr. *Moir*[2] who came into this Province, a Missionary from the Kirk of Scotland, about six years ago, has ever since preached to a Congregation of that Persuasion, in a Place here called *Edisto*, in the Parish of St. John in Colleton County; as in that Station has behaved himself in such manner, as very well to deserve the Certificate he brings with him from his Brethren here, who stile themselves a Presbytery. He always shewed a great Regard and Inclination towards the Church of England, and now waits upon your Lordship to receive her Holy Orders; and of which as I take leave to add my Testimony of his moral Character, so I hope that with Respect both to his Principles and Learning, your Lordship <55> will find him not unworthy. [. . .]

Boyd of No. Carolina is dead; and as the Governor there writes me, *he died in the same Beastly Manner he lived*. I have no Answer from the Society to my Letters concerning him; [. . .]

I humbly crave your Lordship's Blessing and am My Lord Your Lordship's most dutyful and obedient humble Servant.

A. Garden.

So. Carolina
Charlestown
May 4th 1739

[*Addressed*:]
To The Right Reverend
Bishop of London
St. Barthws. Parish
Thomson

[*Endorsed*:]
Mr. Garden
Marsden
Moir

ALS. This document was enclosed in the letter from the bishop of London to the secretary of the SPG dated July 13, 1739, below. Read at a meeting of the SPG on July 20, 1739, when it was "Agreed that Mr. Marsden be dismissed from being a Missionary to the Society; And Mr. Moir attending and offering his Service to be employed as a Missionary of the Society. Agreed that he attend the Committee with his Testimonials." Journal of the SPG, VIII, 67.

[1]I.e., obtain sworn statements.
[2]Rev. James Moir. See appendix.

[*LAM/FUL/VI*]

Minute; Secretary of the SPG to Bishop of London
1739 May 18, 21

<268> At a Meeting of the Society for the Propagation of the Gospel in Foreign Parts at St. Martins Library May 18th 1739.

The Secretary laid before the Board a Letter from The Lord Bishop of London dated April 27th 1739[1] recommending the Reverend Mr. Garzia of North Carolina to the Favor of the Society. Allso a Letter from Gabriel Johnson Esqr. Governor of North Carolina dated North Carolina June 30th 1738 to the same Purpose.

Agreed, that Mr. Garzia be appointed missionary to North Carolina, in the room of Mr. Boyd deceased with a Salary of £50 per annum to commence from Michaelmas last.

The Lord Bishop of St. Davids reported, and paid the Treasurers a Benefaction of £25, which his Lordship had received from The Lord Bishop of London, being a Gift to the Society transmitted to his Lordship by a Person unknown.

My Lord

I am ordered by the Society to return your Lordship their Thanks for your Care and Trouble about the abovementioned Benefaction and I hope your Lordship will accept the minute about Mr. Garzia, as a token of my Obedience to your Lordship's Commands, which will allways with pleasure be observed by My Lord Your most Dutifull Humble Servant.

Philip Bearcroft.[2]
Secretary.

Charterhouse
May 21st 1739.

[*Endorsed*:]
[*Illegible*]
Society—Garzia

Copy.

[1]Not located.
[2]Rev. Philip Bearcroft was secretary to the SPG from April, 1739, until his death in October or November, 1761.

[*SPG/B/7*]

Rev. Richard Marsden to Secretary, SPG
1739 June 6

Reverend Sir

The last Letter I was Honored with by order of the Honorable Society for Propagation of the Ghospel in Foreign parts was in part to Inform me that on my giveing Bond for the repair to my mission by the first Conveniency the Honorable Society would advance me half a years sallery I recd. yours at the City of Chester In Septembr. last and was not Inclined to repair to London for that End, it being my setteled resolution to make all the dispatch possible in my affairs that might without delay fully answer the Societys Expectations from me. I have met with many disapointments and delays on several accounts but this is to acquaint you that I am now arrived (God be praised) in Virginia and expect in three or four days to be within the bounds of my mission, and with zeal pursueing the duties of my function (as I shall not fail by every opportunity to give you, and the Society a Just acct. of my succeedings and progress) but I am obliged from necessity to give my Bills of Exchange on you at 60 days after date for thirty pounds Sterling which I beg may be Honorably Complied with the twenty fourth of this month there being a years sallery due to me by the Appointment of the Society. I am Reverend Sir yr. most obedient Humble Servant.

Richd. Marsden

June the 6th 1739
Hampton In Virgia.

[*Addressed*:]
<4>
To The Reverend david Humphreys
Secretary to the Honorable Society
for Propagation of the Ghospel in
foreign parts.
Warwick Court Warwick Lane

[*Endorsed*:]
Virginia
Mr. Marsden
June 6th 1739

N. Carolina
Recd. 14th Janry. 1739.

ALS.

[*LAM/FUL/X*]

Rev. Alexander Garden to Bishop of London
1739 June 12

<56> My Lord

My last Letter to your Lordship was of the 8th ultimo;[1] in which, 'mong other things, I took leave to certify your Lordship concerning the Bearer Mr. Moir, that he had served in this Province, as a Missionary from the Kirk of Scotland, for some years; and had behaved without any Exception to his moral Character, etc. This was doing the Gentleman but a Piece of common Justice, especially as he declared his Intention of applying to your Lordship for Church of England Orders. [*Torn*] is a very exceptionable thing with his late Congregation here, and who have therefore done all they can to prejudice the Church of England People against him, as a lucrative Man, and One that is come over to the Church, not out of Principle, but for the sake of a Better Provision. How false and uncharitable soever this Insinuation, it yet answers the End: For the Vestry of the Parish of St. John in Colleton Country (a Parish lately divided from St. Paul's, and has lately applied to your Lordship and the Society for a Missionary) have sent to me, to know, whether I have recommended the said Gentleman to be appointed Missionary for that Parish, and to signify, that he will not be acceptable there.

I have assured them that I have not recommended him to be appointed for theirs, nor any particular Parish in the Province; but only certified his Character in general as it appeared to me and against which they have none other than the above pretended Objection. But however best the Society should be minded [to] favour that Parish with a Missionary, and on such Recommendation as procures him Orders at your Lordships hand should appoint that Gentleman for the Service, I have thought it necessary to acquaint your Lordship as above, that I apprehend it will not be adviseable for him to accept of any Missi[on] [*torn*] of the Prejudice gone out against him.

I humbly crave your Lordship's Blessing, and am My Lord Your Lordship's most dutiful and obedient humble Servant.

A. Garden.

So. Carola.
Charlestown
12th June 1739

[*Endorsed*:]
Vestry
Moir
Moving of Clergy

ALS.

[1]Presumably the letter of May 4, 1739, above, is meant.

[*SPG/B/7*]

Bishop of Chester to Secretary, SPG
1739 June 20

<263> Chester June 20, 1739.

Reverend Sir

I have yours of May 29th relating to Mr. Marsden. It is true, that he was confind in this City, and that he has made his escape; but in a very dishonourable manner, by grosly imposing on the Jailor, and leaving him in the lurch for £80. I had compassion for him for some time after his imprisonment, and by what I saw from the Society, and other Credentials, hop'd his unhappy Circumstances were owing altogether to misfortunes. But it was not long before some ugly Stories were told of him; and now I fear every one of them are too true. I sent to Liverpool (since I had your letter,) from whence many of them came, where he was well known formerly, and where he has some Relations. His immoralitys on many accounts are attested; and as that Town has great correspondence with the American Countrys his bad behavior there is confirmd, as well as in his Native one, He is as artful man, and has made use of that talent for many years to deceive the board. With my humble favor to The Society, and with my Sincere Prayers for their good success I am Reverend Sir yr. very Affectionate Brother and humble servant.

Saml. Cestricus.

P.S. I have talkd with some Persons in this City, who confirm his ill Character from their own knowledge; but did not Speak of him While he was in Prison.

[*Endorsed*:]
Lord Bp. of Chester to the Secretary
dated June 20th 1739.
answered July 24th 1739

ALS. Read at a meeting of the SPG on July 20, 1739, when it was "Agreed that Mr. Marsden be dismissed from being a Missionary to the Society." Journal of the SPG, VIII, 67.

[*SPG/B/7*]

Bishop of London to Secretary, SPG
1739 July 13

<265> Fulham Jul. 13 1739

Good Sir,

I inclose Mr. Garden's Letter to me, which I mention'd to you yesterday. The occasion of his writing it, was a Letter from me, to acquaint him that Mr. Marsden had obtain'd an appointment from the Society to be one of their Missionaries, but that I had forborn to grant him my Licence, because he brought no Letter Testimonial of his good behaviour from him, as my Commissary; and I also remember'd, that he had given me a very ill character of him some years since, in a Letter which I think I laid before the Society. I did not know but he might have repented, and became a new man Since, but thought my self obliged to refuse him a Licence, till I could hear from Mr. Garden; and, as things have come out, I am very glad I did. I am, Sir your assured friend and Brother.

Edmd. London

I desire you either to return the inclos'd or a Copy of that part which relates to Mr. Moir.

[*Addressed*:]
For The Reverend Dr. Barecroft
at the Charterhouse
London

ALS. Enclosed in this document was the letter from Rev. Alexander Garden to the bishop of London, May 4, 1739, above.

[*SPG/Jou/8*]

Journal of the SPG
1739 August 17

<69> 17th August 1739. [. . .]

<79.> It was Reported from the Committee that Mr. James Moir had Attended and laid before them his Testimonials which were Approved, and it was Agreed by the Committee to Recommend Mr. Moir to succeed Mr. Marsden in his late Mission in North Carolina, if Mr. Moir shall produce at the next Meeting of the Society Mr. Commissary Gardens Recommendation of him to the Lord Bishop of London, or a Recommendatory Letter from his Lordship; And Mr. Moir having brought to the Board Mr. Commissary Gardens Recommendatory Letter to the Lord Bishop of London.

Agreed that Mr. James Moire be Appointed Missionary to North Carolina in the Room of Mr. Marsden, with a Salary of £50 a Year to Commence from Midsummer last, provided the Lord Bishop of London will be pleased to Ordain him. [. . .]

Minutes.

[*SPG/B/7*]

Secretary of the SPG to Rev. John Garzia
1739 August 28

<296> To the Reverend Mr. Garzia of North Carolina.
Reverend Sir

The Society for the Propagation of the Gospel in Foreign Parts hath rec'd. your Petition to succeed Mr. Boyd in his Mission together with the Acct. of yr. religious Services in North Carolina and out of regard to them and the recommendation of Governor Johnson hath appointed you to succeed Mr. Boyd in his Mission with a Salary of £50 per Annum to commence so far Back as Michaelmas last, so that you may draw as soon as you please for what Salary is due to you on Messrs. Wm. and Thos. Tryon Merchants in Crutched Fryers Treasurers, to the Society, the Society some time since appointed Mr. Moir their Missionary, when he shall arrive in the Province you will shew all Brotherly Love and Kindness to him, and jointly as well as separately endeavour to the very best of your Power to propagate and promote the most Holy Religion of our great Lord and Saviour Jesus Christ. I have inclosed a Notitia Parochialis to which you are to conform, as far as the Circumstances of yr. Mission will permit and transmit every half Year an Account of yr. Labours to Sir

P. B.

Aug. 28th 1739.

Copy.

[*SPG/B/7*]

Secretary of the SPG to Gabriel Johnston
1739 August 28

To Gabriel Johnson Esqr. Governor of North Carolina.
Sir

The Society for the Propagation of the Gospel in Foreign Parts out of Regard to yr. Recommendation, and the good Services of Mr. Garzia have appointed him one of their Missionaries in North Carolina with a Salary of £50 per Annum to comence so far back as Michaelmas last, the Society some Time since took the religious State of yr. Province under Consideration, and divided it into 2 Missions to be separated from each other by the River Neuse, the one to comprehend all that Part of yr. Province lying on the North East Side of the River Neuse and to which Mr. Garzia is now appointed and to reside at Chowan untill the Church of Edenton is finished, and the other Mission to comprehend all the other part of yr. Province lying to the So. West Side of the River Neuse, and to which the Society some Time since appointed Mr. Marsden, that hath a Plantation called the Hermitage in St. James's Parish in Hanover Precinct but upon his misbehaviour and a further Inquiry into his Character the Society have dismissed him their Service and on the 18th of this Month appointed to Succeed him Mr. Jas. Moir lately a Teacher to a Presbyterian Congregation in So. Carolina, but now desirous upon full Conviction to enter into the holy Orders of our Church and strongly recommended to the Society by the Commissary and Clergy of So. Carolina, as soon as he shall be ordain'd he will take the first Opportunity to present him self to you. I have taken the Liberty to send under yr.

Cover a Letter to Mr. Garzia, humbly intreating yr. Excellency's Countenance and Protection to Mr. Garzia and Mr. Moir in the Exercise of their Ministerial Functions, and wishing you all happiness and Success in yr. Government. I am.

P. B.

Charterhouse Aug. 28th 1739

Copy.

[*SPG/Jou/8*]

Journal of the SPG
1739 September 21

<81.> 21st Septemr. 1739. [. . .]

<82.> Ordered that Mr. James Moire attend the Board at their next Meeting. [. . .]

Minutes.

[*SPG/B/9*]

Vestry and Churchwardens of St. James's Parish to Archbishop of Canterbury
1739 October 3

<148> To his Grace the most Reverend John Lord Arch Bishop of Canterbury and the rest of the Members of the Honorable Society for the Propagation of the Gospel in Foreign Parts.

We the Church Wardens and Vestry of St. James's Parish in New Hanover County take this Opportunity to return You our hearty and unfeigned thanks, for Your favour in answering the request of us, and the principal Officers and Inhabitants of this Parish by appointing the Reverend Mr. Marsden Your Missionary in these Parts.

He arrived in North Carolina the Twelfth of June last past, and with great diligence repair'd to us, doing the Office of his Ministry at Sundry Places in his Journey, he has his Residence on his own Plantation the Hermitage on Prince George's Creek. He Officiates att Brunswick and Newton, and at other places Occasionally in the discharge of his Mission to our great Satisfaction. Wee are thanfull for the Salary of Fifty pounds Sterling you have been pleased to order Your Said Missionary, as he has for many Years formerly as well as since his late arrival given us manifest proof of his unwearied diligence in the Ministerial Function and led a reputable Life among us. Wee promise to do what shall be in our power in addition to the Salary you have fixed on him to make his time Comfortable to him in the Discharge of his Mission. He has made known to us your pious Care in ordering Ten pounds worth of Books as a Missionary's settled Library for St. James's Parish at Cape

Fear together with a Bible and Common Prayer book, also Five pounds worth of small Tracts, and one Dozen of Osterwalds Catechisms to be distributed among the poor parishoners. For this and all other the marks of your Tender Regard for this Young Settlement Wee are sincerely thankful.

Wee are Your most Obedient Humble Servants.

Rog. Moore, E. Moseley, M. Moore, Jno. Swann, Edwd. Hyrne, Jno. Porter, Geo. Ronald, Corn. Harnett, Nath. Rice, Wm. Dry

Oct. 3d 1739

[*Addressed*:]
To
The most Reverend John Arch Bishop
of Canterbury

Copy. Enclosed in a letter from Richard Marsden to the archbishop of Canterbury, December 10, 1740, below. Marsden states there that he enclosed the original in a letter to the secretary of the SPG, but it is not among the surviving records of the Society.

[*SPG/Jou/8*]

Journal of the SPG
1739 October 19

<83.> 19th October 1739. [. . .]

<92.> Mr. James Moir attended and laid before the Board his Deacon and Priest Orders. Agreed that Mr. Moir do Read Prayers and Preach on the 3d Ver. of the 5th Chap. of St. Mathews Gospel,[1] and that the Reverend Dr. Moore be desired to hear him and upon Dr. Moor's Report to His Grace the Lord Arch Bp. of Canterbury that he hath performed the same to his Satisfaction, Order'd that the Secretary do give him the necessary dispatch in order to his proceeding on his Mission and that half a years Salary be advanced him by the Treasurers. Order'd also that a Library of Ten pounds be allowed him with a Bible and Common Prayer Book, and five pounds worth of Small Tracts, and one dozen of Ostervalds Catechisms, to be distributed among the Poor People as usual.

Ordered that he do duty at Brunswick and New Town, and that he do, as opportunity offers, Visit all that part of North Carolina lying South West of the River Neuse and that his Residence be fixed as the Governor shall think proper. [. . .]

Minutes.

[1] "Blessed are the poor in spirit: for theirs is the kingdom of heaven." Matthew 5:3, Authorized Version.

[*SPG/Jou/8*]

Journal of the SPG
1739 November 16

<98> 16th Novemr. 1739. [. . .]

<100.> It was also Reported from the Committee that they had read a Certificate dated 31st of May 1739, of Lydia Boyd Widow of the late Reverend Mr. John Boyd, who died one of the Missionaries of the Society, on or about the 19th day of May 1738, that she was left Executrix of the last Will of her late Husband and had duly proved it, and she therefore prays the payment of the Salary due at the decease of her said Husband, and that she may be permitted to keep the Society's Books, in possession of him at his death, for her private use and comfort. Agreed to recommend to the Society to direct the Treasurers to pay Mr. Boyds Salary up to Midsumer 1738.

Resolv'd, that the Society do agree with the Committee. [. . .]

Minutes.

[*SPG/B/18*]

Secretary of the SPG to the Inhabitants of St. Paul's Parish, Chowan, and Elsewhere
1739 November 19

<(172)> London, Warwick Court,
Warwick Lane, Nov. 19 1739

Gentlemen,

I am directed by the Incorporated Society for the Propagation of the Gospel in Foreign Parts to acquaint you, that they have appointed the Reverend Mr. John Garzia to be one of their Missionaries in North Carolina, and that he Officiates in Chowan Precinct, and in all other Places as Occasion require to the North East side of the River Neuse. The Society do hereby Recommend him to yr. favour, and as he is very sufficently Recommended to them, more Especially by his Excellency Gabriel Johnston Esqr., they conceive good hopes he will answer the End of his Mission; and they do Expect you will Contribute, according to the best of yr. Ability, towards his better Support, and Recommend it to you to procure him a Passage Toll-Free, in the Several Ferries over the Rivers within his Mission. Praying, that you may make a right Use, of having the great blessing of Gods word administred to you, and that it may Shine forth in yr. Lives and Conversations.

I am, Gentlemen, Yr. Humble Servant.

Philip Bearcroft

[Plea]se to Direct thus,
The Inhabitants of St. Paul's Parish,

Chowan, and of all other Places where
I [*sic*] shall officiate.

Copy. This letter was laid before the lower house of the assembly on August 7, 1740. On August 11 the house passed a resolution "that all Missionaries within this Province pass free from paying any moneys for their ferriage over the Rivers within their respective Missions and that the several persons who keep [said] ferrys shall have a claim on and be paid by the publick for such service." The upper house concurred on August 21. Saunders, *Colonial Records*, IV, 549, 560-562, 571.

[*LAM/FUL/VIII*]

Rev. Gabriel Talck to Bishop of London
ca. 1740?

<86> May it please Your Lordship

Seven years and something more are now past, since your Lordship and the honourable Society for the propagating of the gospel, from their bounty were pleased to favour me with £20 sterling; compassionately considering the damage I suffered, by being shipwrecked at my coming over to the American shore to preach the gospel and publish the glad tidings of Jesus Christ to poor souls in vacant places being destitute of any setled ministry, was even at the same time from your Lordship, laid to my charge. Wich I afterwards, according to that abilitie God Almighty hath been pleased to bestow upon a weak instrument, have done my constant duty. Having gone through the new setlements of Pensilvany Maryland, North-South Carolina and Georgia. Several small Chapels have even been erected under the same time of my abode in the remote new setlements Two in the colony of Virginy; one near the river Shonadoor, the other not far from a Creek called Opechon. Four places and houses to worship God in, according to the canons of the Church have even been under the same time fixed and builded in the province of Pensilvany. Your Lordship please from this conclude that hier are more vacant places among us then one single person for their great distance is able sufficiently to supply. Which cannot but be a great grieve to see poor souls go astray and starve for want of a shepherd to lead them in a good pasture and feed them with the heavenly manna. Particularly doth North Carolina labour under this calamity Where in the whole province I did not find more then two ministers professing themselves to the Church of England. <87> God Almighty grant that this distemper could be cured and true labourers send out to plant a vineyard, wherein trees of righteousness might grow up to the praise and glory of God.

The 10 Chapter of St. Mathew hath been my rule and comfort in this my Apostleship and blessed be God and our Lord Jesus Christ who even hath fulfilled his promise upon me his unworthy servants. And though I desire not to be unloosed from that yoke which is laid upon me, yet little relief and support under my burden should be very agreable, by sending over some more fellow labourers and little assistance from the generasity of the venerable and illustrious society for buying some books and other necessary things. God Almighty bless your Lordship and the honourable Society to continue shining lights for ever, whereby all darkness of errors and heresie may be dispelled, and the true Light wich lighteth every man that come into the world, more and more glorified all the world over amen, Lord Jesus, am your Lordships most obedient

Gabriel Talck

[*Endorsed:*]
Talck
Pensylvania

ALS.

[*CO* 5/333]

Act of Assembly
1740

<8.> An Act to enable the Comissioners herein after appointed to erect and finish a Church in Newbern in Craven County and parish in the province aforesaid and for the better regulating the said Town and other Purposes therein mentioned.

Whereas the late Vestry of Craven Parish in the Province aforesaid in the year one thousand seven hundred and thirty Nine laid a levy on all and every the Tithables in the said Parish for and towards the building and finishing a Church in Newbern in the aforesaid parish and appointed Commissioners to manage and carry on the same and to apply such levy to that purpose which said Comissioners have made one hundred Thousand Bricks and have been at other expences towards building the said Church but the said levy not amounting to a Sufficient Sum to Compleat the said work and the present Vestry refusing to Assist therein and thereby the money allready expended and laid out for that purpose will be lost and so good and laudable a design frustrated and in order to raise a Sufficient Summ for the finishing and compleating the Same. We pray it may be enacted.

And be it Enacted by his Excellency Gabriel Johnston Esqr. Governor by and with the Advice and Consent of his Majesty's Council and the General Assembly of the said province And it is hereby Enacted by the Authority of the same that a Tax of one Shilling and Six pence proclamation money for two years next ensuing the ratification of this Act be laid and it is hereby laid on each and every Tithable person within the said parish or County <9> of Craven to defray the expence and Charge of Compleating and finishing the said Church to be paid yearly in such Comoditys as are herafter rated videlicet: Pork good and merchantable dry Salted per Barrel thirty Shillings proclamation money Beef dry Salted per Barrel good and merchantable Twenty Shillings proclamation money Indian drest Deer Skins two Shillings and Six pence proclamation money per pound Tallow four pence per pound Bees Wax ten pence half penny per pound Rice per hundred ten shillings to be paid at such times and places as are directed for the receipt of his Majesty's Quit Rents in and by an Act Intituled an Act for providing his Majesty a Rent roll for Securing his Majesty's Quit Rents for the remission of Arrears and Quit Rents and for quieting the Inhabitants in their possessions etc. which said Tax shall be annually Collected and received by John Bryan Gent. he first giving Security in the Sum of four Hundred pounds proclamation money to the Justices of the County Court of Craven for the faithfull discharge and payment of the same who shall be allowed four per Cent for Attending receiving and paying the same and that upon receipt of any Commodity or Commoditys Summ or Summs of Money for the use aforesaid the same shall be by him paid to the Commissioners or the Majority of them or their order for the use aforesaid.

And be it further Enacted by the Authority aforesaid that each Inhabitant in the said Parish who shall not pay or cause to be paid each and every Year the tax herein before mentioned at the times and places aforesaid to the said John Bryan as in and by this Act is directed such person or person so failing shall for each default forfeit and pay the Summ of four Shillings proclamation money for each Tithable besides Costs to be levied by a Warrant from under the hand and Seal of one or more Justices of the peace for the County aforesaid upon the goods and Chattles of the delinquent which forfeiture shall be paid to the said John Bryan or any other Person appointed by the said Commissioners or the Major part of them and by them to be Applyed towards the building and Compleating of the said Church.

And be it further Enacted by the Authority aforesaid that George Roberts William Wilson George Bold William Herritage and Adam Moore Gentlemen are hereby appointed Commissioners to receive the said levys from the said John Bryan when by him received and Collected and to contract and agree with fit and proper Persons for finishing the said Church in a Neat and workmanlike manner and the said John Bryan shall and is hereby directed to account with the Commissioners aforesaid when required for the Several Comoditys and Sums by him Collected and received in manner aforesaid.

<10> And be it further Enacted by the Authority aforesaid that all Persons that shall Subscribe to pay any Sum or Sums of Money for and towards the Building of the aforesaid Church that upon refusal of payment of the said Sum or Sums mentioned to be paid by such Subscription such Person or Persons shall be liable for the same and the Commissioners or the major part of them for the time being are hereby Authorized to sue for the Same in the same manner as any Person can be sued for nonpayment of money due by a promisory Note.

And whereas the late vestry of Craven Parish laid a levy in the year one thousand seven hundred and thirty Nine on all the Tithables in the said Parish towards building and Compleating the said Church which said Levy is found insufficient to carry on and Compleat the said Work a Considerable part of which is yet paid and uncollected.

Be it Therefore Enacted by the Authority aforesaid that the Several Persons who have not allready paid the said Tax or levy are hereby Commanded and required to pay the said Levy in Current Bills as laid by the said Vestry in the same manner and at the same times and places and to the same Person as before mentioned and under the same Penalties as in and by this Act is before directed.

And be it further Enacted by the Authority aforesaid that all Persons who have been heretofore Church Wardens or that now are Church wardens or that have been heretofore Commissioners and all persons whatsoever who have any parish money in their hands for the use aforesaid do forthwith after the Ratification of this Act account with the Commissioners aforesaid or the Majority of them and pay to them or their order on demand all Such Sum or Sums of Money that shall appear to be due owing and in under the penalty of ten pounds proclamation money over and above the Sum due owing and in Arrear to the parish aforesaid to be recovered by Action of Debt Bill plaint or information in the General or County Court.

And be it further Enacted by the Authority aforesaid that on the death or removal out of the County aforesaid of any of the aforesaid Commissioners the Majority of the said Commissioners are hereby authorized and empowered to appoint a proper person or persons who shall be deemed duly Qualified to Act in his or their room and stead.

And Whereas there have been great differences and disputes about the bounds and limits of the said Town of Newbern which hereafter may be of Pernicious Consequences to the freeholders of the said Town as well as a discouragement for others to settle therein

Be it Enacted by the Authority aforesaid that the Justices of the Court of Craven County at the Court to be held for the said County next after the ratification of this Act or at any other Subsequent Court shall and they are hereby required to appoint a day whereon the freeholders of the said Town shall meet at the Court House in the said Town and whereof the said freeholders shall have Notice and with a Sworn Surveyor for that purpose by the said Court appointed shall admeasure and lay out the Meets and bounds of the said Town pursuant to an Act of the General Assembly of this Province Intituled an Act for the better Settling the Town of Newbern in the Precinct of Craven and shall lay out the Streets and affix marks at the corner of each and every lot allready taken up and saved at the Costs and Charge of each and every freeholder of the said Town which Charges shall be assessed by the President or Chairman of the said Court with two other of the Justices of the peace of the said County and two freeholders to be appointed by the Court next Succeeding such admeasurement laying out and marking of the said Streets and Lotts or any other Subsequent Court which Charges Assessed as aforesaid shall be paid by the freeholders of the said Town respectively in proportion to the Number of the saved Lotts that he she or they shall hold in the said Town to the said Justices to defray the said Charge of Admeasuring laying out and marking as aforesaid and on default or nonpayment of their respective proportion of the Charges so Assessed within ten days after such Assessment and demand of the same the said Assessment shall be levied by a warrant from any one Justice for the said County of the goods and Chattles of such Delinquent and Sold at Vendue five days after such distress rendering the overpluss if any Charges first deducted to the owner. And whereas in and by the aforesaid Act of Assembly there was a Lot laid out in the said Town for a Church which said Lot being insufficient and not so comodious for the said use and all the adjacent lots being taken up and Saved therefore the said Vestry have taken up four lots more convenient and comodious for Erecting a Church on for a Church yard and other parish uses.

Be it therefore Enacted by the Authority aforesaid that as soon as the said Church shall be fit to Celebrate Divine Service in the said four Lotts shall be saved to the Parish for the purposes aforementioned in as full and ample a manner as if the said Parish had erected a house on each of the said lots of the Quality and dimentions prescribed by the said Act for saving Lots in the said Town.

And be it further Enacted by the Authority aforesaid that the Commissioners aforesaid are hereby impowered to make Sale and dispose of the above mentioned lot at Publick Vendue after four days Notice given to be applyed towards the building of the said Church any law to the contrary notwithstanding.

J. Hodgson Speaker
Will. Smith President
Gab. Johnston

D.

[*SPG/B/7*]

Statement; Bill of Exchange; Protest
ca. 1740 January

<215> Whereas on the 19th of March last the Reverend Mr. Richard Marsden Clerk of the Precinct of Brumsick in the south part of North Carolina came to me Paul Smith in Crane Lane of the City of Dublin Glazier by the Title and Charecter of Missionary by the Authority of the Society of the Gentlemen in London for Promoting Christian Knowledge in Foreingn parts.

The said Richd. Marsden affirmd to me that he has been from the aforesaid pps. 12 Months Eleven of Which he Resided in England, and one in the Isle man, from the Latter he was Reccomended to me as a Stranger to Dublin, and to help him to a good Quiet Lodging, in the Isleland he had a Deacon ordaind By the Bishop of Sodor and man (whose name I cant remember) to be an Assistant as he pretended to him in the aforesaid parts, and from whence he had three boys bound apprentices to him by the consent of their parents.

His buissines in Dublin as he told me was, to gett some Honest famillys to go along with him to Carolina. He shewed me several Credentials Sign'd by the Lord Bishop of London and the Society of Gentlemen for Promoting of Christian Knoledge in Foreign parts, Authorizing Said Richd. Marsden as Missionary in the aforesaid parts, with a Sallery of £80 per Annum. Likewise a Lease from the Lord Carteret of 2000 Acres of Land in the aforesaid parts to him said Richd. Marsden.

Upon these presumtions the 29th of March last I Endors'd a bill of Exchange For him, said Richd. Marsden, of Fifty pounds Sterling English money, directed to Mr. Jacob Bonell Merchant in Great Kerby street Hatton Garden London, for payment of the said sum, but no such person as said Jacob Bonell was To be found (as the protest anex'd will make appear) the bill was Return'd For non payment and to the great Detriment of my Trade and Familly was obligd to pay fifty five pounds Eight Shillings and nine pence Sterling Irish money for Said Richd. Marsden.

<216> I Therefore make it my Humble Request to the Reverend Dean Cooping to Inquire whether he the said Richd. Marsden be the person he pretends to be that I may apply To the Honorable Gentlemen of the Society in London for promoting

Christian Knowledge in Foreign Parts For Repayment which will be most Gratefully Accknowledg'd By your most Humble and most Obedient Servant.

Paul Smith

Mr. Richd. Marsden is a full bodied man between 60 and 70 years of Age near Six Foot high a Stoop in his Shoulders a Swarthy Complexion and mark'd with the small pox.

<217> A True Coppy of The Protest.

Dublin march 29, 1739

Ea £50.

At twenty one days sight pay this my first for Exchange To Mr. Paul Smith or order fifty Pound Sterling Value Received am advis'd by.

Richard Marsden

To Mr. Jacob Bonell Merchant
in great Kerby Street Hatton Garden
London

Pay the Contents to the order of Mr. Edmd. Huband Value Received march 29th 1739.

Paul Smith

Pay the Contents to Messrs. Ker and Elms or order.

Edmund Huband

On this Day the first of may anno Domini 1739 at the Request of Messrs. Ker and Elms of London Merchants, I Anthony Wright Notary Publick by lawfull authority admitted and sworn dwelling in London Went with the Original bill of Exchange whereof the Copy is here above written, to great Kerby Street Hatton Garden London, where the said bill is derected, To Mr. Jacob Bonell on whom the same is drawn, in order to demand payment of the Contents of the said bill, but having Enquired of several persons, and at several houses in and about the said Street, for the said Mr. Jacob Bonell and not finding any person that Knew him or could tell where the said Mr. Jacob Bonell dwelt, or that could Inform me where I might apply for payment of the said bill (the twenty one days therein mentioned being Elaps'd since my endeavoring to find out the said Mr. Jacob Bonell in order to procure acceptance thereof tho without Effect), I therefore Enquired at the General Post Office At the Bank of England on the Royal Exchange and at divers other publick places of this City for the said Mr. Jacob Bonell, but not being able after all Dilligence used to hear of him or to find any person that woud take Cognezance of the said bill so as to pay for him. I the said Notary ded Thereupon at the Request aforesaid protest and by these presents do protest as well against the drawer of the said bill, as all Others whom it doth or may Concern, for Exchange and Reexchange costs damages and Interest Suffered and to be suffered, for want of payment of the said bill Thus protested In the precence of Robt. Payne and John Mason Wittnesses.

Anthony Wright N. P.

[*Endorsed*:]
This Manuscrict was sent to H. Newman by Mr. Dean Copping in a Letter dated at Dublin 10th of Jany. 1739/40.

Mr. Marsden's wife is said to be now living as Housekeeper to the Reverend Dr. Legh vicar of Halifax.

D.

[*SPG/SAP*]

Report
1739/40 February 15

<53> <*An Abstract of the Proceedings of the Society.*> [. . .] <*North Carolina.*> The Publick were informed in the Abstract of the last Year, that the Society had taken into particular Consideration the Religious State of *North Carolina*, and divided it into two Itinerant Missions; <54> one on the North-East Side of the River *Newse*, to which they appointed Mr. *Boyd*, then the only Missionary of the Society in that Province; and the other Mission on the South-West Side of the same River, to which they appointed the Reverend Mr. *Marsden*, upon the Recommendation and earnest Petition of the Inhabitants of St. *James's* Parish in that Province, where Mr. *Marsden* had a Settlement, and being a Clergyman of the Church of *England* had for some Years officiated. But not long after these Appointments, the Society received a Letter, dated *June* 30th, from *Gabriel Johnston*, Esq.; Governor of *North Carolina*, to inform them, that Mr. *Boyd* died on the 19th of *May* preceding; and to recommend to succeed to his Mission the Reverend Mr. *Garzia*, a Worthy and Religious poor Minister, whom the Inhabitants of St. *Thomas's* Parish, *Pamplico*, had induced by fair Promises to come from *Virginia* to them, and were starving with his Wife and three Children, by not paying him his poor Salary, (20 Pound sterling *per Annum*) for two Years and an half past; and the Lord Bishop of *London* was likewise pleased to testify his good Opinion of, and to recommend Mr. *Garzia*. Whereupon the Society on the 18th of *May*, 1739, appointed Mr. *Garzia* to succeed Mr. *Boyd* in the Itinerant Mission, on the North-East Side of the River *Newse*, with a Salary of £50 *per Annum*. And out of Regard to his good Services (it appearing by an authentick Certificate, that from the Year 1733 to the Year 1738, he had baptized in the Parish of St. *Thomas* 279 Males, and 242 Females; and in <55> other Parts of the Country, 918 Males and 839

Females, in all 2278 Persons) and to his poor Circumstances ordered his Salary to commence from *Michaelmas* preceding.

And before Mr. *Marsden* was established a Missionary under the Seal of the Society, there appearing some Reasons to suspect his Character, there was a further Inquiry made about him; and the Society being at length but too well assured of his bad Behaviour, disclaimed all further Intercourse with him, and dismissed him their Service; and upon the Recommendation of the Reverend the Commissary and Missionaries of *South Carolina* of Mr. *Moir*, a Person of good Life and Learning, who had resided six Years among them; the Society hath appointed Mr. *Moir* to succeed Mr. *Marsden* in the Itinerant Mission on the North-West Side of the River *Newse*, and he having been ordained Deacon and Priest in *England* is now on his Voyage to *North Carolina*.

The Society takes the Liberty on this Occasion to desire the Publick, and more especially their Friends in *America*, to be so just to them, when a Clergyman of the Church of *England* appears of bad Morals in our Plantations, to examine into his Name and Circumstances, as far as may be, and by whom he was sent thither; and to inspect the publick List of the Names of all the Missionaries of the Society; and they are fully persuaded it will generally appear, that these unworthy Wretches are such, whom their own bad Conduct and desperate Fortunes have carried thither on their own Heads; and if at any time it appears, that one <56> such proves to have been sent thither by the Society, (and can human Prudence always prevent it?) they intreat their Well-wishers in the sacred Name of Christ to inform them, and they will *put away from them the wicked Person*. [. . .]

Printed. Extracted from the yearly publication containing the sermon preached at the annual anniversary meeting of the SPG, together with a review of the activities of the Society and its missionaries during the preceding year. The date above is the date of the meeting.

[*SPG/B/9*]

Rev. James Moir to Secretary, SPG
1740 October 29

<145>
Reverend Sir

Upon my Arrival at Cape-fear in May last, I soon perceived this South-west Mission to be so widely extended, that, in Order to transmit a just Account to the venerable Society, it was necessary I should travel to some of the remotest Parts of it; which I did accordingly last Summer, and then returned to Wilmington (formerly called Newtown) the usual Place of my Residence at the time. And being here inform'd that there was a Ship in the River getting ready to sail for England, I very chearfully embrac'd this Opportunity of returning you my humble and sincere Thanks for all your Kindnesses and Civilitys to me at London, and professing to make it my constant Study to act agreeably to the manifold Obligations I am under. Be pleased to know then, Reverend Sir, that, as far as I am yet capable of judging, this Part of the Province where I have the Honour to be appointed Missionary is about one hundred and fifty Miles in Breadth along the Coast, and in some Places they have settled upwards of one hundred and fifty Miles back from the Sea. The Inhabitants are very much scattered and in many Places live at a vast Distance from one another, which renders it impossible for me to serve them as I could wish. The Generality of them are extremely ignorant but willing to be instructed, which has encouraged me Sometimes to officiate twice in the Week. I have baptized two hundred and ten Children. And the kind Reception I meet with from some in my travels, together with their repeated Entreatys to discharge the Sacred Function in a greater Variety of Places than I can comply with, give me Ground to hope that my Endeavours shall not prove altogether unsuccessfull. There is nothing as yet which can be reckoned a tolerable Support for a regular Ministry among them. They engage in Party Affairs with so much Zeal, that I am apprehensive, a thing of this Nature will meet with the greatest Difficultys at present, notwithstanding several of the leading Men of both Sides have promised to assist me in it to the utmost of their Power. However I am resolved to push it, as soon as a favourable Opportunity offers, and to prevent any Obstacle my Conduct might give Occasion to, shall make it my Business as it is my Duty to oblige them all; and so much the rather, because I am fully sensible that if the Attempt should not succeed; there will be but very little Encouragment to send Missionarys among them. That the generous Intentions and pious Labours of the venerable Society, may be always crown'd with Success, is the sincere Desire of Reverend Sir Your most humble and much obliged Servant.

James Moir

Wilmington Octr. 29th 1740

[*Endorsed*:]
North Carolina
Mr. Moir Oct. 29 1740
Read 11 May 1741.

ALS. Read at a meeting of the SPG on May 15, 1741. Journal of the SPG, VIII, 246.

[*SPG/Jou/Cte*]

Journal of the Committee of the SPG 1740 October 30

At a Special Committee 30th Octor. 1740. Present. The Reverend Dr. Moore, Mr. Montague Wood, Mr. Paris, Dr. Roper. Dr. Moore in the Chair. Prayers.

The Committee proceeded to review the Catalogue of the Missionaries Library etc. and Agreed to recommend the following Books to be added thereto, Videlicet.

B. Bishop Bulls Works, Bishop Blackhalls Sermons, Blairs Sermons, Bennet against the Quakers, Binghams Works, Bp. Berkley's Minute Philosopher, Bp. Butlers Analogy of Natural and Revealed Religion, Bullocks Sermons.

C. Bp. Chandlers Defence of Christianity, Vindication of the same, Dr. Cudworths Intellectual System, on Morality, Coneybears Defence Religion, Chapmans Eusebius.

D. Dupins Canon of Scripture.

F. Fleetwoods Works, Fiddes's Body of Divinity.

G. Goodmans Penitent pardoned, Bp. Gastrells Christian Institutes, Bp. Gibsons Pastoral Letters.

H. Humphrey's Historical Account of the Proceedings of the Society of the Propagation of the Gospel in Foreign Parts.

I. Jenkins's Reasonableness of Christianity.

K. Bp. Kennets American Library, Kennet on the Creed, ArchBishop King on the Origine of Evil.

L. Losotho on the Prophets, Bp. Long's Boyles Lectures, Lelands Answer to Christianity as Old as the Creation.

M. Marshall's Chronological Tables, Mapletofh Principles and Duties of the Christian Religion.

N. Nourse on the Homilies.

P. ArchBishop Potter on Church Government, Prideaux's Connexion of the Old and New Testament, Preservation against Popery 2 Volumes fo., Pococks Works.

R. Rymer on Revealed Religion, Rogers Visible and invisible Church.

S. Bp. Sherlock on Prophecy, Bp. Smaldridg's Sermons, Bp. Smallbrook's Vindication of the Miracles of our Blessed Saviour, Bp. Stillingfleets unreasonableness of Separation, Scots Christian Life, Smiths Preservative against Quakerism, Shuckfords Connexion of Sacred and Prophane History.

T. Bp. Taylor's Ductor Dubitantium, Life of Christ, Trap against Popery.

W. Wollaston's Religion of Nature delineated, Welshman on the 39 Articles, Wheatley on the Common Prayer, Wall's the Defence of Infant Baptism, Bishop Wilson's Essay towards the Instruction of the Indians Waterlands Importance of the Trinity, on the Eucharist.

Minutes.

[*SPG/B/9*]

Rev. Richard Marsden to [Archbishop of Canterbury]
1740 December 10

Brunswick North Carona.
decembr. the 10th 1740

May it please yr. Grace

It is with all Humility, and very great regard that I presume to write to your Grace at this time, and I humbly beg yr. pardon for the bouldness I take, for it is no Little concern to me that I am oblige to have recourse to you in this Exigency of my affairs.

Inclosed is a Coppy of a Letter from the vestry and Church wardens of the Parish of St. James in Cape Fear North Carolina (to which place I was appointed a missionary the 19th of May 1738 with a sallery of £50 per annum to commence from midsummer next following) to return yr. Grace and the Honorable Society thanks for answering their request in appointing me Missionary here and for the marks of yr. tender regard for this New settelment.

The Original I sent Inclosed in a Letter to dr. Humpreys by a ship for London, with an account concerning the Spiritual state of my Parish and as far as my mission Extended; and have not neglected to send an account also every six months as required, but I have not been favoured with an answer. I am Certain my services here deserve highly some notice to be taken of them, for I have not Indulged myself, but faithfully discharged my duty in labours more abundant; and I can truly affirm that have recommended my self to every mans Conscience in the sight of God. But I cannot avoid representing to yr. Grace that a Gentleman is arrivd here and Appointed missionary in my place,[1] and gives out that I am dischargd but notwithstanding I must confess I cannot fully give credit to it because I have received no advise of my dismission, nor cannot account for it, but that I am Informed he was recommended by my Ld. of Londons commissary in St. Carolina[2] that has for some time without any Just Cause been prejudiced against me, But I must say if the report be true I think I am wronged and hardly dealt with.

Your Grace was made acquainted with the misfortunes I fell under soon after I was appointed missionary and of the delay given me by the Bishop of London refuseing me his Licence, because I had not a recommendation of his commissary before mentioned, and of my confinement in the City of Chester, which took up a considerable time before I could Extricate my self out of these dificulties. I heartily lamented my loss of time in England and was under continual anxiety on that acount, for I had a true Compassion for the souls of the Inhabitants in this new settelment and a fervent desire to farther their salvation; and therefore as soon as I was a liberty, my zeal and resolution to serve them, determined me to hasten to Cape Fear as soon as possible without coming to London to receive my dispatches, to give Bond according to the Societys method and receive half a years sallary and the Books allotted for me; And yr. Grace will find after my Arrival in Virginia with what diligence I repaired to the place Appointed by the Honorable Society for my residence. A dispensation is committed to me and woe is me if I preach not, and I trust according to my mean ability I shall always Endeavour by a prudent holy and unblamable Conduct to keep up the dignity and Influence of my ministry. I have Just reason to fear that I have been injustly assesed on some account or other for I beleive many think themselves at Liberty to censure the wanting and necessitated, but whatsoever causeless or groundless censure any person may Entertain concerning my person I can fully Justifie myself from any considerable blemish, and in this settlement here is many Gentelmen of worth and Honor (if required) that will Justifie me for having done my duty and will condemne those that have any ways been Instrumental to hinder the good Effort of it.

I Humbly Intreat yr. Grace to take my case into your consideration, I relye Entirely on yr. Goodness, and I do not Question but yr. Generous, Innate disposition will

Influence you to compassionate my condition and condescend to favour me with yr. protection and Encouragment; and if any Errors in my conduct can be laid to my Charge I beg yr. Grace will put a favourable construction of them. I hold myself bound in point of Integrity and duty not to dissert this people who continue to shew a disposition to Encourage me, before I hear from the Honorable Society. It is reasonable for me to Expect that my case should be considered by them, and I think I may promis myself some relief adapted to the Circumstances of my condition, I shall with patience wait the Issues of Providence by the course of nature I can not live long, but I trust in God It will be my business wile I live to benifit others, and I am sure yr. Grace wishes success to every hand Engaged in the service for Propagation of the Ghospel in Forain parts.

When the Honorable Society agreed to give me the proper dispatches to proceed on my mission, they was pleased to order ten pounds worth of Books for a missionaries setteld Library at Cape Fear, and five pounds worth small tracts etc. to be distributed among my Poor Parishioners and also a Bible and Common Prayer Book, I humbly desire that these marks of the Societys regard for this new settelment may not on any account be frustrated, and if I be Judged worthy to receive their commands concerning them I will carefully observe their Instructions and faithfully answer their good design.

There has been a Large Subscription by the Inhabitants of Brunswick and some Neighbouring Gentelmen, towards Building a Brick Church in town for me, and I can assure yr. Grace that it will be finished next summer. I presume to flatter myself that yr. Grace will condescend to give directions that I may know yr. pleasure, and what the Honorable society is pleased to determine in my case. I shall always pay the utmost regard to yr. Grace and I trust in God I shall always behave so as to do nothing unworthy yr. Countenance and Protection.

May I please yr. Grace I Humbly crave leave to Subscribe myself yr. Graces most obedient and Most Humble Servant.

Richd. Marsden

If a Letter be directed to me under Cover to the Honorable Roger Moor Esqr.[3] one of majestys Counsellors for North Carolina and delivered to Mr. Joseph Wragg merchant In London It will be sent by the first opportunity and come safe to my hand.

ALS. Enclosed in this document was a letter purportedly from the vestry and churchwardens of St. James's Parish to the SPG dated October 3, 1739, above. Read at a meeting of the SPG on May 15, 1741, when it was agreed to concur in the recommendation of the Committee "that the Secretary be directed to acquaint Mr. Marsden, that before he was confirmed the Society's Missionary, they received such a Character of him, that they could not think fit to Employ him, and therefore immediately appointed the Reverend Mr. Moir to be Itinerant Missionary to all that part of North Carolina lying South West of the River Newse." Journal of the SPG, VIII, 247.

[1]Rev. James Moir.

[2]Rev. Alexander Garden.

[3]Roger Moore (1694-1751) removed from South Carolina to the Cape Fear region ca. 1725, becoming a large landowner and promoter of the development of Brunswick as a port and urban center. Moore held numerous offices, including assistant justice of the General Court, and councillor from 1734 until his death. *DNCB*.

[*Swann's Revisal*]

Act of Assembly
1741

<151> *LAWS of* North-Carolina. <*A.D. 1741.*> [...] CHAP. XIX. *An Act, the better to enable the Commissioners appointed for building a Church at* Newbern, *to erect the same, and to impower them to demand and receive, of any Person or Persons, all Parish Levies already laid and not appropriated; and for other Purposes therein mentioned.*

<*Private.*> I. WHEREAS by an Act of Assembly of this Province, passed the last Session, enabling the Commissioners therein appointed to erect and build a Church in *Newbern,* and the better to enable them to carry on and finish the same, they were impowered to levy a Tax of One Shilling and Six Pence, for the Two then ensuing Years, on each Tythable in the said Parish; and the said Tax being found insufficient to finish the said Church: And whereas there was laid by the late Vestry, on the Inhabitants of the said Parish, a Tax of Fifteen Shillings *per* Poll, on each Tythable, for paying a Minister for the ensuing Year, and the succeeding Vestry not thinking fit to employ a Minister, the said Tax thereby remains, as yet, unappropriated to and for any Parish Use.

II. WE therefore pray that it may be Enacted, *And be it Enacted, by his Excellency* Gabriel Johnston, *Esq.; Governor, by and with the Advice and Consent of his Majesty's Council, and General Assembly of this Province, and by the Authority of the same,* That the said Tax of Fifteen Shillings, shall be appropriated to and for the building and finishing the said Church.

III. *AND be it further Enacted, by the Authority aforesaid,* That the Churchwardens of the said Parish shall, on or before the First Day of *May* next, after the Ratification of this Act, account for and pay to the Commissioners appointed by the before-recited Act, all such Sum or Sums of Money as they shall have received on <152> Account of the aforesaid Tax or Levy of Fifteen Shillings, under the Penalty of One Hundred Pounds, Proclamation Money; to be sued for and recovered; in the General Court of this Province, by Action of Debt, Bill, Plaint, or Information, (wherein no Essoign, Injunction, or Wager of Law, shall be allowed or admitted of,) by any Person who will sue for the same; to be applied to the Use of the said Church: And all Persons who have not paid the aforesaid Tax or Levy to the Churchwardens as aforesaid, shall, on or before the last Day of *May* next, after the Ratification of this Act, pay the same to the said Commissioners, or to such Person whom the Majority of them shall appoint to receive the same, under the Penalty of double Distress; to be levied by a Warrant from One Justice of the Peace for the said County, and to be applied as aforesaid.

IV. AND whereas the said Commissioners have made One Hundred Thousand Bricks, towards building the said Church; and some of the said Bricks being deemed insufficient for the said Work; *Be it therefore further Enacted, by the Authority aforesaid,* That the said Commissioners, or the Majority of them, may sell or dispose of any such Bricks as the said Commissioners shall judge not fitting or sufficient for the building of the said Church, and apply the Money arising by such Sale, to the Uses aforementioned.

Printed.

[*Swann's Revisal*]

Act of Assembly
1741

<156> *LAWS of* North Carolina. <A.D. 1741.> [. . .] Chap. XXIII. *An Act, for Establishing the Church, for appointing Parishes, and the Method of electing Vestries; and for directing the Settlement of Parish Accompts throughout this Government.*

<*Government divided into Parishes.*> I. *BE it Enacted, by his Excellency* Gabriel Johnston, *Esq.; Governor, by and with the Advice and Consent of his Majesty's Council, and General Assembly of this Province, and it is hereby Enacted, by the Authority of the same,* That this Government be and it is hereby divided into distinct Parishes, in the Manner following; that is to say, St. *Paul's* Parish, in *Chowan* County, *Berkely* Parish, in *Pequimons* County, St. *John's* Parish, on the *Southwest* Side of *Pasquotank* River, and St. *Peter's* Parish, on the *Northeast* Side of *Pasquotank* River, in *Pasquotank* County, *Currituck* Parish, in *Currituck* County, *Northwest* Parish, and *Society* Parish, in *Bertie* County, St. *Andrew's* Parish, in *Tyrell* County, St. *Thomas's* Parish, in *Beaufort* County, St. *George's* Parish, in *Hyde* County, *Christ's-Church* Parish, in *Craven* County, St. *John's* Parish, in *Onslow* County, St. *James's* Parish, on the *East* Side of *Cape-Fear* River, in *New-Hanover* County, and St. *Phillip's* Parish, on the *West* Side of *Cape-Fear* River, in *New-Hanover* County, from the <157> Mouth of the said River, runing up the *Northwest* River to the Bounds of the County, inclusive of the Island at the Mouth of the *Northwest* and *Northeast* Rivers, in the said County, commonly called *Eagle's Island,* lying to the *South* of the Thoroughfare, St. *Martin's* Parish, in *Bladen* County, and *Edgcomb* Parish, in *Edgcomb* County.

<*Inhabitants of every Parish to choose Vestrymen, who shall be summoned by a Constable to meet and qualify themselves.*> II. *AND be it further Enacted, by the Authority aforesaid,* That the Inhabitants of every Parish aforesaid, being Freeholders, shall, and they are hereby directed and impowered, to meet together on the First *Monday* next after the Ratification of this Act, and on every *Easter Monday* every Two Years thence after, at a Court-house, or where there is no Court-house, at the most usual Place of Public Worship, in every Parish, then and there to choose and elect Twelve Freeholders, to serve as Vestrymen for the Two next ensuing Years: Which Vestrymen so chosen, shall, by the Constable or Constables, be summoned to meet at the Church, and where there is no Church, then at the Court-house, or where there is no Court-house, at the most usual Place of Public Worship as aforesaid, in each respective Parish, within Forty Days next after such Choice, and then and there to Qualify themselves according to the Directions, and under the Penalty hereafter mentioned; and if the said Constable or Constables, or

any of them, shall neglect or refuse to summon the Vestry as aforesaid, he or they so offending, shall forfeit and pay the Sum of Twenty Shillings, Proclamation Money, for each and every Vestryman not summoned as aforesaid, who shall reside within the District of such Constable; to be levied and applied as herein after is directed.

<*Vestrymen to take the Oaths, etc. on Penalty of £3 and if any refuse, major Part to choose others.*> III. *AND be it further Enacted, by the Authority aforesaid,* That no person shall be admitted to be of any Vestry within this Government, that doth not take the Oaths by Law appointed to be taken, for the Qualification of Public Officers and subscribe the following Declaration, *viz. I* A. B. *do declare, That I will not oppose the Liturgy of the Church of* England, *as it is by Law established*: And all and every Vestryman who shall neglect or refuse to do the same, shall (if he be not a known Dissenter from the Church of *England,*) forfeit and pay the Sum of Three Pounds, Proclamation Money; to be levied and applied as herein after is directed. And if any Person or Persons, chosen as a Vestryman or Vestrymen, shall neglect or refuse to take and subscribe the said Declaration, the Vestry of which such Person or Persons was or were elected a Member, or the major Part of them, are impowered and required to elect and choose another or other Freeholder or Freeholders, to be Vestryman or Vestrymen in the Room and Stead of the Person or Persons neglecting or refusing as aforesaid. And if it shall happen that the Vestry of any Parish within this Government, shall not elect and make Choice of another or others in the Room and Stead of <*Vestry neglecting to choose others in the Room of those refusing to qualify, Minister may appoint; if no Minister, the Governor may.*> such Vestryman or Vestrymen neglecting or refusing to qualify as aforesaid, within one Month next after such Neglect or Refusal, that then and in such Case it shall and may be lawful for the Minister of such Parish, or for Want of such, the Governor or Commander in Chief for the Time being, under his Hand and Seal, to appoint some Freeholder or Freeholders to supply such vacant Place or Places in such Vestry.

<*Vestrymen to choose Churchwardens; if they elected refuse to act, to pay 40s., and Vestry to elect others.*> IV. *AND be it further Enacted, by the Authority aforesaid,* That the several Vestries of this Government shall, within Forty Days after *Easter Monday*, Yearly and every Year, elect and choose out of the said Vestry, Two Persons, to execute the Office of Churchwardens in each and every respective Parish; and if the Persons elected and chosen Churchwardens as aforesaid, or either of them, shall refuse to execute the said Office, he or they so refusing, shall forfeit and pay Forty Shillings, Proclamation Money; to be levied and applied as herein after is directed; and the Vestry shall immediately proceed to elect and choose another Churchwarden or Churchwardens out of the Vestrymen, in the Room of him or them so refusing to act.

<158> <*No Person obliged to serve more than 1 Year.*> V. *PROVIDED always*, That no person whatsoever, shall be obliged to serve as Churchwarden in any Parish within this Government, for more than One Year, unless he consent thereto.

<*Churchwardens, or three of the Vestry, may call a Vestry.*> VI. *AND be it further Enacted*, That the Churchwardens, or in Case they refuse or neglect, any Three or more of the Vestry in each and every Parish in this Government, shall have full Power and Authority to call the Vestry together, at the Places as are in this Act heretofore directed, at any Time, and upon any Occasion, they shall judge necessary, by Warrant or Warrants under their Hands, directed to the several Constables of the respective Districts and

Parishes, who shall be obliged to execute the same according to the Tenour thereof, under the Penalty of Ten Shillings, Proclamation Money, for each and every Vestryman in such Warrant mentioned, who shall not be summoned; to be levied and applied as herein after is directed. And every Vestryman who shall neglect or refuse to attend the Vestry agreable to such Summons, shall forfeit and pay the Sum of Ten Shillings, Proclamation Money, for such Offence, unless he can shew sufficient Cause for his so doing, to be admitted of by the Vestry, or the major Part of them, at their next Meeting; to be levied and applied as herein after is directed.

<*On Death or Removal of Church wardens, or Expiration of Time of Service, Vestry to choose others.*> VII. *AND be it further Enacted, by the Authority aforesaid,* That the Vestries of the several Parishes of this Government, shall have full Power and Authority, upon the Death or Removal out of their respective Parishes of any Churchwarden or Churchwardens, before the Time limitted for the executing the said Office be expired, to elect and chuse, out of the Vestry, another Churchwarden or Churchwardens, in the Room and Stead of the Person or Persons dead, or removing out of the Parish as aforesaid; which Churchwarden or Churchwardens so elected and chosen, shall serve until the Time appointed by this Act for the Election and Choice of Churchwardens: Any Thing herein contained to the contrary, notwithstanding.

<*Vestry to lay a Tax, to defray Parish Charges.*> VIII. *AND be it further Enacted, by the Authority aforesaid,* That the Vestries of each respective Parish within this Government, shall have full Power and Authority, and they are hereby directed and required, within Forty Days next after every *Easter Monday*, Yearly, and every Year, to appoint and order such Sum of Money as they shall judge necessary, to pay and satisfy the Expence and Charge of their respective Parish, for the then current Year, to be raised by the Poll, and collected in the same Manner by the Sheriff as other Taxes.

<*Deducting three per Cent for Churchwardens Trouble.*> IX. *AND be it Enacted, by the Authority aforesaid,* That the Churchwardens of each and every respective Parish in this Government, shall deduct, out of the Money arising from all Parish Taxes by them received, the Sum of Three *per Cent*, as a Reward for their Trouble, and no more.

<*Churchwardens to pay all Parish Monies to the Vestry, on Penalty of £20.*> X. *AND be it further Enacted, by the Authority aforesaid,* That the Churchwardens of each and every respective Parish in this Government, shall, the first Vestry to be held in each Parish after every *Easter Monday*, Yearly, and ever Year, on Oath, account with their respective Vestries for all Parish Monies in their Hands, of what Kind or Denomination soever, that now are or hereafter shall become due, by Virtue of any Law for that Purpose, or otherwise, and shall pay the same to the Vestry, or their Order. And if any Churchwarden or Churchwardens which now is or are, or that hereafter shall be, in any of the respective Parishes in this Government, shall neglect or refuse to account for and pay to the respective Vestries, or their Order, the Money in his or their Hands, belonging to the Parish for which he or they are Churchwardens, within Twenty Days next after Notice, in Writing, given to him or them, to account for and pay the Parish Money aforesaid, <159> he or they so offending, shall severally forfeit and pay Twenty Five Pounds, Proclamation Money; to be recovered by Action of Debt, Bill, Plaint, or Information, in the Name of the Churchwardens, in any Court of Record within this Province, wherein no Essoign, Injunction,

Protection, or Wager of Law, shall be allowed or admitted of; to be applied by the Vestry to the Use of the Parish.

<*Proviso.*> XI. *PROVIDED always*, That nothing in this Act shall be construed to repeal any Clause, Matter, or Thing, in Two several Acts, passed last Session, at *Edenton*, for the finishing a Church at *Edenton*, and for erecting, building, and finishing a Church at *Newbern*.

<*Vestry may call Justices to Account for Parish Money.*> XII. *AND be it further Enacted, by the Authority aforesaid*, That the Vestry and Churchwardens of each and every Parish in this Government, shall have full Power and Authority to call any Justice of the Peace or other Person or Persons whatsoever, to account, upon Oath, for the Monies in the Hands of them or any of them belonging to their respective Parishes, or accruing and becoming due to the same, by Virtue of any of the laws of this Government. And if any Justice or Justices or other Person or Persons, shall refuse to appear and account as aforesaid, such Justice or Justices, or any other Person or Persons so refusing or neglecting, shall forfeit and pay the Sum of Twenty Pounds, Proclamation Money; to be recovered by the Churchwardens of the Parish where such Monies become due, or where payable, by Action of Debt, Bill, Plaint, or Information, in any Court of Record within this Government, wherein no Essoign, Protection, Injunction, or Wager of Law, shall be allowed or admitted of; to be applied to the Use of the Parish.

<*Vestry to lay a Tax, for building Church, Glebe-house, etc.*> XIII. *AND be it further Enacted, by the Authority aforesaid*, That the Vestry of each and every Parish in this Government, shall have full Power to raise Money, by the Poll, for building a Church, Chappel, or Chapples, to purchase Lands for a Glebe, to erect convenient Buildings thereon, and to keep the aforesaid Edifices in Repair, as Need shall be, from Time to Time, and to buy Books and Ornaments for the Church and Public Worship, and for the Care and Support of the Poor, and all other Parish Charges as they shall judge necessary for the respective Parishes; which said Poll-Tax shall be collected and levied as in this Act before is directed, and shall not exceed Five Shillings, Proclamation Money, *per* Poll, in any one Year, for all the Purposes in this Act before mentioned.

<*Vestry to procure a Minister, and Clerk, and allow them Salaries.*> XIV. *AND be it further Enacted, by the Authority aforesaid*, That the several Churchwardens and Vestries of the several and respective Parishes of this Government, or the greatest Part of them, shall use their best and utmost Endeavours, to procure an able and Godly Minister, qualified according to the Ecclesiastical Laws of *England*, and a Person, of a sober Life and Conversation, to be Clerk; and may raise him or them such Stipends, Yearly, as they shall think convenient, so as such Stipend for the Minister be no less than Fifty Pounds, Proclamation Money, Yearly.

<*Minister to be resident in the Parish, etc.*> XV. *PROVIDED always*, That such Minister for whom such Monies are so to be raised, be constantly resident in the Parish, and doth not omit officiating at the Church or Chappels within the Parish, unless permitted by the Churchwardens and Vestry to officiate in such neighbouring Parish which may be vacant, or disabled by Sickness, or other unavoidable Accident.

<*Minister guilty of Immorality, Vestry may withdraw his Salary.*> XVI. *AND be it further Enacted*, That if any Minister who shall have a Cure in any Parish by Virtue of this Act, shall be notoriously guilty of any scandalous Immorality, it shall and may be lawful

for any Number of the Vestry not less than Nine, agreeing thereto, to withdraw the Stipend by this Act allowed to such Minister.
<160> <*Minister may bring Suit for his Salary, and Vestry may plead their Order.*> XVII. *PROVIDED always*, That after such withdrawing of the Stipend, such Minister shall be at Liberty to bring Suit, in the General Court of this Province, against the Churchwardens of his Parish, for the Recovery of his Stipend; in which Suit the Churchwardens may, in Bar of the Action, plead the Order of the Vestry, and shall set forth the particular Facts for which the Vestry withdrew the Stipend of such Minister: <*If Jury find for the Minister, he shall have his Salary; but if not, another Minister may be appointed.*> And in Case the Jury shall find for the Minister, then he shall recover his Stipend, with Costs of Suit, and enjoy his Benefice; but in Case the Jury find for the Churchwardens, then, and in such Case, the Vestry of the Parish are hereby impowered to elect another Minister in his Room and Stead.

<*Minister to keep his Glebe in Repair, and suffer no Waste, or be liable to the Action of the Churchwardens.*> XVIII. *AND be it further Enacted, by the Authority aforesaid*, That every Minister within this Government, shall, during his Incumbency, keep and maintain the Mansion-house, and all other the Out-houses and Conveniencies that shall be erected on his Glebe, in tenantable Repair, and shall so leave the same at his Death, or Removal out from the said Parish, (the Accidents of Fire and Tempest only excepted,) and shall not suffer any Waste, by cutting down of Timber, or otherwise, to be committed on his said Glebe, except for necessary Repairs, Fences, or other Improvements, and Fire-wood, to be used thereon. And in Case any Minister shall fail to keep his said Glebe, and the Buildings thereon, in tenantable Repair, or shall suffer any Waste to be committed thereon as aforesaid, such Minister, his Executors, and Administrators, shall be liable to the Action of the Churchwardens of the Parish for the Time being, whereby the Value of such Repair or Waste shall be recovered, in Damages, with Costs of Suit; and the Damage so recovered shall be laid out, according to the Directions of the Vestry and Churchwardens, in making necessary Repairs upon the Glebe.

<*Forfeitures how to be recovered and applied.*> XIX. *AND be it further Enacted, by the Authority aforesaid*, That the several Sums of Money, arising and becoming due by Reason of the Forfeitures by this Act inflicted, and for which no Method of Recovery or Application is directed before in this Act, shall be levied, within one Week next after they shall become due, by Warrant of Distress, and Sale of the Offenders Goods, from one or more of his Majesty's Justices of the Peace within the County where the Default shall be made, (Regard being had to the Jurisdiction of the said Justice or Justices, returning the Overplus, if any, to the Owner,) and paid to the Churchwardens, for the Use of the Parish, and by them to be accounted for and paid as herein before is directed.

<*Vestry appointed for St. Philip's Parish.*> XX. AND whereas a Vestry and Churchwardens will be wanting, for the Parish of St. *Philip's*, in *New-Hanover* County, before the Time limited by this Act, for the Election of Vestrymen for the several Parishes within this Province; *Be it Enacted, by the Authority aforesaid*, That *Nathaniel Rice, Eleazer Allen, Matthew Rowan, Roger Moore, William Forbes, James Hasel, Richard Eagles, John Davis, Archibald Hamilton, George Ronald, Cornelius Harnet*, and *George Moore*, be, and are hereby appointed Vestrymen for the said Parish of St. *Philip's*, until the next Election of Vestrymen, as by this Act directed: Which said Vestry shall have full Power to

choose Churchwardens, and to do and perform every other Matter and Thing, which other Vestrymen may do by Virtue of this Act, and shall be liable to the same Penalties and Forfeitures as in this Act is before mentioned; any Law, Custom, or Usage, to the contrary, notwithstanding.

<*Repealing Clause.*> XXI. *AND be it further Enacted, by the Authority aforesaid*, That all and every other Act and Acts, and every Clause and Article thereof, (except as before excepted,) heretofore made, so far as relate to the establishing the Church, appointing Parishes, and select Vestries, and for directing the Settlement of Parish <161> Accounts, is and are hereby repealed and made void, to all Intents and Purposes, as if the same had never been made.

Printed. This act was disallowed by the Privy Council in 1754. *Acts of the Privy Council*, IV, 807.

[*SPG/SAP*]

Report
1740/1 February 20

<65> <*An Abstract of the Proceedings of the Society.*> [. . .] The Society hath received no Letters this year from *North Carolina*; [. . .]

Printed. Extracted from the yearly publication containing the sermon preached at the annual anniversary meeting of the SPG, together with a review of the activities of the Society and its missionaries during the preceding year. The date above is the date of the meeting.

[*SPG/B/9*]

Churchwardens of St. James's Parish to Secretary, SPG
1741 March 30

<144>

Wilmington St. James's Parish
30 March 1741

Reverend Sir

The Vestry of this place meeting to day for the first time since the arrival of the Reverend Mr. James Moir, Were Very glade to find by your Letter which he was pleased to lay before us That he was appointed Missionary here, and Agreed to embrace this Oppertunity of returning the Venerable Society their hearty and Sincere Thanks for sending him among them. And beg leave to acquaint the Society that they don't doubt but, as his Morals, Learning and Dilligence in the Discharge of his Sacred Ofice have hitherto given General Satisfaction, so he will continue to do all he can for Promoting the Interest of true Relegion among us. And do assure you that he shall have all the encouragement we are capable of giving in our present low Circumstances. We are Reverend Sir Your most humble Servants.

Robt. Walker
Thos. Clark, Church Wardens

Copy. Read at a meeting of the SPG on September 18, 1741; the date of the document is there mistakenly given as June 30, 1741. Journal of the SPG, VIII, 263.

[*SPG/B/9*]

Rev. John Garzia to Secretary, SPG
1741 April 16

<149> Bath Town No. Carolina
April the 16th 1741

Sir

The 26th of May 1740 I sent a Letter to yr. Reverence by the way of South Carolina, in which in the first place I begg'd of you to offer my humble Thanks to the Honorable Society for propagating the Christian Knowledge in Forreign parts, having appointed me one of their Missionarys for this Province; and made my Report according to Order, and the Notitia Parochialis but the 7th Day of February Last I understand by a Letter from my Friend in So. Carolina, that the Ship in which my Letter for you was Sent, was taken by the Spaniards; wherefore I humbly hope, it will not be imputed to me as a Neglect of Duty; and according to Gratitude I desire the favour of you, to return my humble and hearty thanks to their Lordships and Honors the Honorable Society, for having appointed me their unworthy Chaplin a Missionary for this Province; and likewise for their great Charity in appointing me Sallery for the Preceding Years. I inclose here to you my Reports not only as a Missionary, but what happend between my last Report and my Mission.

His Excellency orderd me according to Instructions, to fix my Residence in the Parish to which he had before Inducted me, That is to Say, at Bath Town in St. Thomas's Parish in the County of Beaufort. I have demanded of Mrs. Boyd Relict of my Predecessor the Books belonging to the Mission, according to order; but received only a Bible in Folio, a Common Prayer Book, the Book of Homelies and Doctor Tillotsons Sermons Three Volumes; for which I gave a Receipt, as for the rest She can only say, that her Husband frequently lent them out, and all her Endeavours to find them Seem ineffectual, which is a great Injury done to the distressed Widdow of a Clergyman and worthy of yr. Compassion and Notice. The Thirtyth Day of July last I received yr. Last Letter to me by order of the Society dated the 19th of November 1739 the Contents of it I communicated to his Excellency the Governor and the Assembly then Siting at Edenton, his Excellency orderd me to wait upon the Kings Attorney, one of the Members, to introduce yr. Letter to the House: which done the House orderd me to have Passage Ferry free, over the Severall Rivers and Creeks within my Mission, at the Expence of the Publick.[1] I have read yr. Letter in the Several places I have officiated in Since, without any effect: So far (I am sorry to say it) are the People here from contributing to the Advancement of the Glory of God under the auspicious protection of the Honorable Society. Manageing in the most frugall Manner my traveling Expences will not be less than five pound Sterling per Annum in a Country where a Bate for a Horse to a Missionary is not to be had without pay. I pray you Sir to recommend to their Lordships and Honors to Send me Some Monitors against Swearing, Drunckeness, and breach of the Sabbath also preparatorys for worthyly approching the Lords Table; and if possible a few Spelling Books for the Erudition of poor Children within my Mission; and farther pray, that a Silver Cup with the Hutch and Plate of any other Proper Metal, for the decent Administring the Lords Supper, may be added, at my own Expence payable out of my Sallery, with the Name of the Donor. I recommend my Self to the Prayers of our Fathers the Prelates and the rest of the Honorable Society and yr. own Reverend Sir likewise My prayers for all my Benefactors and Masters cease not as I always shall be Reverend Sir Their and your most obliged and Most humble Servant.

John Garzia

P.S. As this Place has no direct Correspondence but to the Ports of Bristole and Liverpoole I pray an Order for makeing my Reports by the way of either as oppertunity shall happen.

LS. Read at a meeting of the SPG on September 18, 1741, at which time it was agreed to concur with a recommendation of the Committee that the Society "send Mr. Garzia 40*s*. worth of the Tracts desired." The SPG also ordered "that the said Letter be referred back to the Committee for their further Consideration, and that it be referred to the said Committee to consider of a more Effectual Method for the better preservation of the Libraries of the Missionaries." Journal of the SPG, VIII, 262-263. For the recommendation of the Committee, see the journal entry dated October 16, 1741, below.

The document following was enclosed in the present one.

[1]See the editorial note accompanying the letter from the secretary dated November 19, 1739, above.

[*SPG/B/9*]

Notitia Parochialis
[1741 April 16]

<150> The Report of John Garzia Missionary

The Number of Men Women and Children within my Parish and Mission is computed to be	9000
Number Baptized within my Parish and Mission Since appointed Missionary	519
Adult Persons formerly Quakers	011
Actual Communicants in my Parish Twenty Seven	
Within my Mission Exclusive of my parish Seventy Two	099
To be more exact I referr for the Number of the Church of England to my next Report	

The Number of Dissenters refer'd to my next but Papists in my Parish Nine, out of my Parish yet discover'd but Three.	012
The Number of Infidels by Information not above Two Hundred.	200
Of Converts etc. Eleven	011
For Two years before I was a Missionary Baptized 247 and Three Negroes in all	250

John Garzia

[*Addressed*:]
To The Reverend Phillip Barecroft D. D.
Secretary to the Honorable Society for propagating
the Christian knowledge in forreign Parts
In Warwick Court Warwick Lane London
per Capt. Howan for Leverpool

[*Endorsed*:]
North Carolina
Mr. Garzia April 16, 1741

DS. This document was enclosed in the one immediately above.

[*SPG/B/9*]

Rev. James Moir to Secretary, SPG
1741 May 25

<146>
Reverend Sir

Having this Opportunity of acknowledging my Duty to the venerable Society; I beg Leave to acquaint them, That since October last I have travelled twice betwixt Cape-fear River and the Neuse, and performed the Dutys of my Function in several Places. I baptiz'd three hundred and six white Children, and one Adult; seven Negroe Infants and two Adults. The Number of Communicants is but small, the Generality of the People being ignorant to the last Degree, and very little Provision made for defraying the necessary Charges of such as might be willing to instruct them. The Assembly of this Province is to meet here September next, and not a few of the Members have promised me to use their utmost Endeavours to put the Clergy on a better footing than they have been heretofore. Whether this Attempt should prove successfull or not, you may next Winter expect a more full and exact Account of the State of this Country in Regard to Religion from Reverend Sir Your most humble and much obliged Servant.

James Moir

Wilmington May 25th 1741

ALS. Read at a meeting of the SPG on October 16, 1741. Journal of the SPG, VIII, 272-273.

[*LAM/Misc. 1123*]

Rev. George Whitefield to Bishop of Oxford
1741 July 28

<(29)> On board the May and Ann bound from London to Scotland. July 28th 1741.

My Lord
Want of leisure, not respect has been the occasion of my not sending Your Lordship my letter which I promised some time agoe. Being now on board in my way to Scotland, I have time to write my thoughts more freely. I wd. first then observe to Your Lordship that You have too good an Opinion of the Missionaries in general, that are employed by the Honourable Society. Your Lordship says Page 31st "that it hath been pretended indeed, that immoral and negligent men are employed as Missionaries." This can be too easily proved. I could mention several instances. Whether this be for want of such care I will not take upon me to determine, but that it frequently and commonly happens is certain. I have lately recd. a letter from Jonathan Belcher Esqr. late Governour of New-England wherein He writes thus "It is now about 37 Years ago that I dined with the late Dr. Compton (then Bishop of London) at his Palace, at Fulham, and there were several Bishops and other dignifyed Clergy at table, and knowing me to be a Young Gentleman of Interest and Figure in my Country, they urged me much to conform to their Church, and ask'd me how the Church of England got forward in New England. I told their Lordships, that they were greatly deceived in what mony was sent hither, in that service, for that the general rise of the Church in New-England, was from Dissolute Livers, and such as quarrelled, with their Ministers, but that it was Raraavis in terrâ, for any man to go over to the Church, from a principle of Religion and conscience or to improve himself in a Pious serious life, and this really Sir (adds this worthy Gentleman) is the case of this "Country at this day." I hope this will have more wait with Your Lordship as coming from a Gentleman without my knowing any thing of it; [a] Gentleman also of figure and good report, and who declares himself unprejudiced in another part of his letter. For speaking of a particular thing He writes thus, not that I have any squeamish prejudices against that Excellent Church (meaning the Church of England) altho' I have been born and bred a Dissenter. And pray what do we differ is in Doctrine? Would they preach and live their Articles, there would be a more general Coalition among them and the Dissenters. And He afterwards says, "From long observation I find no persons going from our Church to that of the Church of England who thereby become more Vitally pious. If I found they did, I should I hope from a wise and Judicious Choice, immediately conform." Thus for the Worthy Governour Belcher. And indeed my Lord, this is too true. Those at a distance cannot well conceive how contemptible [the] Church is abroad, and that owing to the Unworthy, Immoral, and Negligent lives of the Generality of the Missionaries, Several of whom have come over to us because they could not stand trial among [the] Dissenters, or had lived too loosely among them. Your Lordship is pleased to say, Page 32nd "That the most earnest requests the most sober Adjurations are sent, that all who can, would give any useful intelligence relating to them." This is certainly right and good. But I fear Your Lordship hath been misinformed if Your Lordship was told "that great Regard is *always*

paid to such intelligence." For I have sent over two letters to the Honourable Society [*illegible*] no regard has been paid to them. If Your Lordship please I will send You copies of them both. I could not but further [*illegible*] looking over the list of the Missionaries, that there are no less than twenty employed in preaching and teaching school in [the Province] of New England (where certainly the Gospel is preached to greater purity than at home) and but two settled Missionaries in all North-Carolina and one of those viz. Mr. Garzia, can scarce speak English. Does not this look too much like making a Party of Religion?

I have a letter now by me somewhere amongst my papers, wrote by Dr. Mather to the late Lord Chancellour King in which He gives sad proofs of the immorality of our Missionaries, and also complains of this seeming partiality. If the people of New England impose taxes upon the Members of the Church of England whilst others are exempted it is certainly wrong. But as the first settlers went over there to worship God in their own way, Independency I think may well be reckoned the Establish'd worship there as well as Presbytery the Establish'd worship in Scotland. And surely it wd. more answer the design of the institution of the Honourable Society to send Missionaries to North Carolina, where there are Inhabitants enough and nobody to teach them, than to New England, where they have a Minister of their own every five or ten miles. Your Lordship I am persuaded is more noble than to be Offended at this plainess of speech. The Searcher of hearts knows from what principle I write. Your Lordship is pleased to say page 31st "that exact Accounts are received from the Missionaries twice a Year; of what duty they do, and what Progress they make." This is right. But are these Accounts my Lord brought in twice a Year? And when they are brought in what accounts do they generally give? That they have baptised many and had so many Communicants. A poor account this. In other respects so very bad that when I was last at Philadelphia many that were really friends to the Church upon reading the Accounts were ashamed to see how the Honourable Society was imposed upon by the Account of the *Pious Labours* of the Missionaries. Indeed Your Lordship says, page 17th and I doubt not but Your Lordship was informed so, "that multitudes of Negroes and Indians have been brought over to the Christian faith." This for all as I know to the contrary may be matter of fact. I pray God it may be found true at the Great Day. But Your Lordship says page 9th the success of one of the Catechists has been "so great in the Plantation belonging to the Society, that out of two hundred and thirty, at least seventy are now Believers in Christ." I should be glad to know what Plantation Your Lordship means. That seventy may have learnt to repeat their Creed, the Lords prayer and ten commandments in the Vulgar tongue and been baptized, is probable enough. But that seventy are now *Believers in Christ*, I cannot help questioning. I fear Your Lordship hath been misinformed. And now I am mentioning the Negroes. I beg leave to Object against the method lately proposed for their Conversion. I mean especially in the Province of Carolina, where the Governours are so exceeding jealous over any that shall undertake publickly to teach them. I believe it will be a work of a long time to find out two or three Young Negroes, and to instruct them as to qualify them to instruct others. Besides few I believe will readily submit to be taught by a Young Negroe. I question whether the Assembly will permit a slave to learn to write. And after all, the way of converting them will only be teaching them to write and read.

These are good things. But without setting over them truly pious people, that may have more Authority over them than of Young Negroes whatsoever, and may lead them to a knowledge of themselves and God, however good the intention of the Honourable Society may be, I fear their good intention will prove Abortive and of none Effect. Pensylvania in my Opinion is far prefarable to Carolina for the instruction of the Negroes. The Quakers however blameable in other respects, are certainly praise worthy in this. I mean their lenity to their Poor Slaves. Your Lordship is pleased to urge these peoples forbidding to asist his Majesty (whom I truly love and honour) as one reason why Missionaries should be sent over to instruct the people in better principles. But at the same time Your Lordship takes notice of "many other pernicious Errors, that took early root in the Provinces abroad, that are not yet extirpated, and perhaps in part newly revived: Some dissolving the Obligations of Moral Duties: Some, destroying the inward peace of very pious and good persons, and making life gloomy and uncomfortable: Some leading men to ascribe every folly or wickedness that possesses the fancy to Divine inspiration: Some inconsistent with our present happy Establishment." All these my Lord are Errors. And as Your Lordship hath been pleased so particularly to mention the Quakers, would it not have been right in Your Lordship to have pointed out the others also who are thus Erroneous that people might the better beware of and so avoid them? I suppose Your Lordship has been informed of the persons that broach such Errors, otherwise I suppose Your Lordship wd. not have mentioned them. And if so, I wd. humbly submit it to Your Lordship judgement, whether You are not bound in conscience, to write to them, or plainly name them, that they may either clear themselves, or take shame for holding and preaching things contrary to the Gospel of the Ever blessed Jesus. Thus, my Lord, I have freely wrote to your Lordship what was upon my heart. I think I have no sinister end in view. I think I write purely out of a Zeal for God, and the good [of] souls. I heartily pray for the coming of Christ's kingdom, and therefore wd. willingly have all things taken out of the way, that may obstruct its progress. I am persuaded Your Lordship would not wilfully continue in any error, nor be above receiving [in]formation from the meanest Servant of Jesus Christ. This persuasion encouraged me to write to Your Lordship. You may depend on it my Lord that I shall not mention what I have wrote and if Your Lordship is so condescending as to send me a line by way of answer, it shall be kept quite secret by, My Lord, Your Lordship's dutyful Son and Servant.

George Whitefield[1]

P.S. I hope to be in London in about six weeks. If Your Lordship pleases to direct a letter to me as before, it will come to hand. The Lord be with Your spirit!

ALS. This document, and the one following, are included in their entirety in this volume because of their usefulness as analyses of Anglican missionary activity in America. The passages of writing to which Whitefield alludes are contained in the anniversary sermon preached to the SPG by the bishop of Oxford on February 20, 1740/1, and printed later that year. The page citations differ from those in the printed version, and perhaps refer to a manuscript. See *A Sermon Preached before the Incorporated Society... by Thomas Lord Bishop of Oxford* (London, 1741).

[1]Rev. George Whitefield (1714-1770) was one of the principal founders of Methodism, although he later became a rigid Calvinist and broke with John Wesley. Whitefield was sporadically in America from his arrival in Georgia in 1738 until his death, and his evangelistic fervor and powerful preaching contributed much to the religious ferment known as the Great Awakening. *DAB*.

[*LAM/Misc. 1123*]

Bishop of Oxford to Rev. George Whitefield
1741 September 17

<(30)>

Cuddesden, Sept. 17, 1741.

Sir

It being now about the time that you proposed to be in London, I send this to return you Thanks for your last Letter. I am not sufficiently acquainted with Governor Belchers Character to know how far his Account of his own Impartiality may be relied on. We often deceive our selves in that Matter: and all Sects of Christians are too apt to think hardly of those who are not of their own Church and especially of those who leave it. And as there is but too much Room for all parties to reproach one another with Want of inward Religion, very well meaning persons may mistake in making Comparisons. To his Testimony you add your own: and I believe you speak as you think. But you must permit me to say, and I do it with sincere good will to you, that I am persuaded you are much too severe in what you have printed concerning your Brethren of the Clergy in this nation, and therefore you may have been too severe in what you have written concerning those abroad; especially as I find, that many Accounts, different from yours, are sent to the Society, concerning their missionaries, by persons in all Appearance well deserving Credit. Still what you and the Governor have said may, and I hope will, give Occasion for stricter Inquiries: but you cannot think it reasonable, that we should pay Regard to your Accounts only. I have seen one if not both your Letters to the Society. They consist, as I remember, of general Charges, without mentioning any particulars: and therefore all that can be done upon them is to inquire. Your Objections against the Number of Missionaries in New England I have endeavoured to answer in my Sermon: and if they can be proportioned better, I wish they were. But I have always understood, that the Reason of there being only two in North Carolina was the bad Reception of those who were sent; of which you may read very discouraging Accounts in Humphreys's History of the proceedings of the Society,[1] and the Difficulty of finding persons to undertake that mission which Difficulty, I suppose must have been the Reason of sending a person, not sufficiently acquainted, by your Account, for I know not the Fact, with our Language. I believe the Accounts of the missionaries are as regularly sent to the Society, as can be expected from that Distance; or proper notice taken of the Neglect. They may indeed, and frequently, if not constantly, do give further Accounts than of their Baptisms and their Communions; which however are such marks of Christian profession, as deserve to be particularly mentioned: nor do the Accounts, which we publish, by any means consist of these only. But it may be very improper for us to print every thing, which it may be proper for them to write. If any part of their Information, which we print, is false; we designedly put it in the power of all abroad who are really Friends of our Church, or of Religion, to prevent our being imposed on by it: and if they will not, the Blame is not ours. For making these things the Subject of their Discourse instead of informing us, is only doing Harm. But I hope all good persons will consider, how very licentious common Discourse upon such Subjects usually is; and will therefore examine carefully before they take up Accusations. The only plantation belonging to the Society, I mean as their property, is in Barbadoes: and when I say, that 70 of the Negroes there are Believers in Christ, I use that Expression, as I apprehend it is commonly used in speaking of Countries where different Religions are professed to signifie, that so many profess themselves Christians. I do not see Reason to suspect their being Hypocrites in that profession: and I hope their Faith produces good Fruits. The Method lately proposed for instructing Negroes continues to appear to me very promising: at least highly fit to be tried. There is a prospect, that the young Negroes, designed for Teachers, will by the Blessing of God on their Education, become truly pious as well as qualified in other respects. The Disadvantage of their Youth will be lessening every Day: their Countreymen, it may be expected, will hearken to them more readily for being such: and they will gain Authority by Degrees if they are duly supported. It is not, that I know of proposed that their Scholars should learn to write: and I do not at all understand why you say that this Method will be only teaching them to write and read. Whether Pensylvania is preferable to Carolina for Instruction of the Negroes, I know not: but wish it were tried every Way. What Errors took early Root in our Colonies, and are not yet extirpated, you may see in Humphreys: And as I have only spoken doubtfully concerning the Revival of any of them; and that not upon any Intelligence communicated particularly to me, but from such Accounts as lie before the Society, I do not apprehend my self obliged to go further than I have done in this Matter. I have accused no persons, nor designed to make any person otherwise thought of, than he was before. If I have given Occasion to any one to ask himself, whether he is blameable or not, I have only put him upon doing what we all ought to do frequently: and God grant we may do it to his Glory and our own Good. I am, Sir, your loving brother and Servant.

Tho. Oxford.

Mr. Whitefield

ALS.

[1]David Humphreys, D.D., *An Historical Account of the Incorporated Society for the Propagation of the Gospel in Foreign Parts*...1730. The work of the Society in North Carolina is discussed on pp. 128-143. Humphreys was secretary to the SPG from 1716 to 1739.

[*SPG/Jou/8*]

Journal of the SPG
1741 September 18

<260.> 18th September 1741. [. . .]

<262> The 4th Letter was from Mr. Marsden to His Grace the Lord Arch Bishop of Canterbury, dated Hermitage near Brunswick in North Carolina 4th June 1741.[1] [. . .]

Minutes.

[1]Not located.

[*SPG/Jou/8*]

Journal of the SPG
1741 October 16

<266.> 16th October 1741. [. . .]

<277.> Also that they[1] had taken into Consideration the reference to them[2] for providing a more Effectual Remedy for the Security of the Missionaries Libraries for the use of their Successors, and have also looked into the 13th Standing Order relating to Missionaries, and are of opinion, that, that Order should be inlarged, and that every Missionary who goes over, should procure some person to be bound with him in the Bond, for the leaving of the Books he takes with him, in case he takes any with him, or in case he goes to a place where a Library has been already sent, then for Sending over by the first Conveyance after his Arrival an Account of what Books shall come to his hands, and for the leaving the same for his Successors, and that the Society should also please to order, that, upon every Missionaries death, £10 out of what shall remain due to him be stopped, untill the said Bond be Complied with.

Agreed, that the affair of the Missionaries Libraries be deferred till the next Meeting of the Society. [. . .]

Minutes. At the next meeting of the SPG on November 21, 1741, it was agreed that this recommendation of the Committee "be appointed as one of the Standing Orders of the Society relating to Missionaries." Journal of the SPG, VIII, 291.

[1]The Committee.
[2]See the letter from Rev. John Garzia to the secretary, April 16, 1741, above.

Edmund Gibson, bishop of London from 1723 to 1748. Bishop Gibson took little interest in North Carolina, aside from persuading the SPG to withdraw its appointment of Rev. Richard Marsden as missionary to the colony. This portrait is from the collection of the Bodleian Library, Oxford University, and is by an unknown artist. Reproduced in Norman Sykes, *Edmund Gibson, Bishop of London, 1669-1748: a Study in Politics and Religion in the Eighteenth Century* (London: Oxford University Press, 1926).

THE

GROUNDS and PRINCIPLES

OF THE

Chriſtian Religion,

Explain'd in a

CATECHETICAL DISCOURSE,

FOR THE

Inſtruction of Young People.

Written in *French* by

J. F. OSTERWALD, Paſtor of the Church of *Neufchatel*, and Author of a Book, Entituled, *A Treatiſe concerning the Cauſes of the preſent Corruption of Chriſtians, and the Remedies thereof.*

To which is added, A

LITURGY : *Or, Form of publick Prayers*,

Which are ſaid in the Church of *Neufchatel* every *Saturday* at Five of the Clock in the Evening, and were Eſtabliſh'd in the Month of *May*, 1702.

Rendred into *Engliſh* by Mr. *HUM. WANLEY*: And Revis'd by *GEO. STANHOPE*, D.D.

LONDON, Printed by *W. Sayes*, for *William Hawes*, at the *Roſe* in *Ludgate-Street*, 1704.

"Osterwald's Catechism," as this work was usually termed, was for many years a staple of the literature supplied by the SPG and the SPCK to missionaries and churches. Jean-Frederic Osterwald (1663-1747) was a Swiss theologian. Reproduced from a copy in the British Library, London.

196. 6 June 1712

Present

Earl of Clarendon, Lord Bp of Bangor
Lord Bishop of Chester, Lord Bishop of
Worcester, Dr Marshal, Dr Gutteridge
Dr Loriano, Dr King, [illegible]
Mr Shute, Mr Stubbs, Mr Postlethwait
Coll. Nicholson, Maj Shute, Mr
Chamberlayne Mr Tayleure, Mr
Edwards, Mr Jennings.

Prayers

1. Coll. Cleland, and Mr Rowland Tryon propos'd a second time Members of this Society

2. Coll. Nicholson propos'd the honble Arthur Moor Esq. a first time Member of this Society.

3. Mr Shute propos'd Mr William Treacher a Barbadoes Merchant, a first time Member of the Society

4. Upon reading ye Minute of last Meeting relating to Mr Menadier, the Society was acquainted that he has returned the Small Tracts but not ye Library delivered to him as he was ordered, and part of a letter from ye Lord Bp of London dated ye 3d Jus. relating to Mr Menadier were read. Agreed that when Mr Menadier has returned ye sd Library Dr King and Dr Marshall be desired to attend his Lopp and acquaint him with ye reasons that induced the Society to dismiss Mr Menadier.

Ord.

First page of fair minutes of a monthly meeting of the SPG. From the SPG papers in Rhodes House Library, Oxford University. Reproduced by permission.

Henry Compton, bishop of London from 1675 to 1686 and 1688 to 1713. Bishops of London had at least nominal ecclesiastical jurisdiction in British America throughout the colonial era. Bishop Compton took this responsibility seriously, as evidenced by correspondence printed in this volume. This portrait is by Sir Godfrey Kneller, from the collection of the National Portrait Gallery, London. Reproduced in Edward Carpenter, *The Protestant Bishop, Being the Life of Henry Compton, 1632-1713, Bishop of London* (London and New York: Longmans, Green, 1956).

This is to Certifie whom it
may Concern that We whose Names are –
Underwritten have known the Reverend Mr:
Thomas Newnam for some Years & do believe
to be a Person of an Exemplary Life & sober
Conversation & that he is Orthodox as to his
Principles according to the Doctrine of the
Church of England & that we do believe him
to be very well affected to our present Estab:
:lishment both in Church & State – In Witness
whereof we set our hands this twelfth day
of September – 1721

Tho: Gillesby LL B.
Tho: Sheppard M:A:
Tho: Clendon M:A:

Document attesting the good morals, orthodox religious principles, and political trustworthiness of Rev. Thomas Newnam. See p. 276, below.

The Liberty of the Gofpel explained, and recommended.

A

SERMON

Preached before the

Incorporated SOCIETY

FOR THE

PROPAGATION of the GOSPEL in Foreign Parts;

AT THEIR

ANNIVERSARY MEETING

IN THE

Parifh Church of St. *Mary-le-Bow*, On *Friday* the 15*th* of *February*, 1716.

By *THOMAS HAYLEY*, A. M. Canon Refidentiary of *Chichefter*, and Chaplain in Ordinary to His Majefty.

LONDON,

Printed by *Jofeph Downing*, in *Bartholomew-Clofe* near *Weft-Smithfield*, 1717.

A sermon by an eminent divine was an established feature of each annual meeting of the SPG. The sermons were printed, along with a report on the work of the society and its missionaries during the preceding year. From the SPG papers in Rhodes House Library, Oxford University. Reproduced by permission.

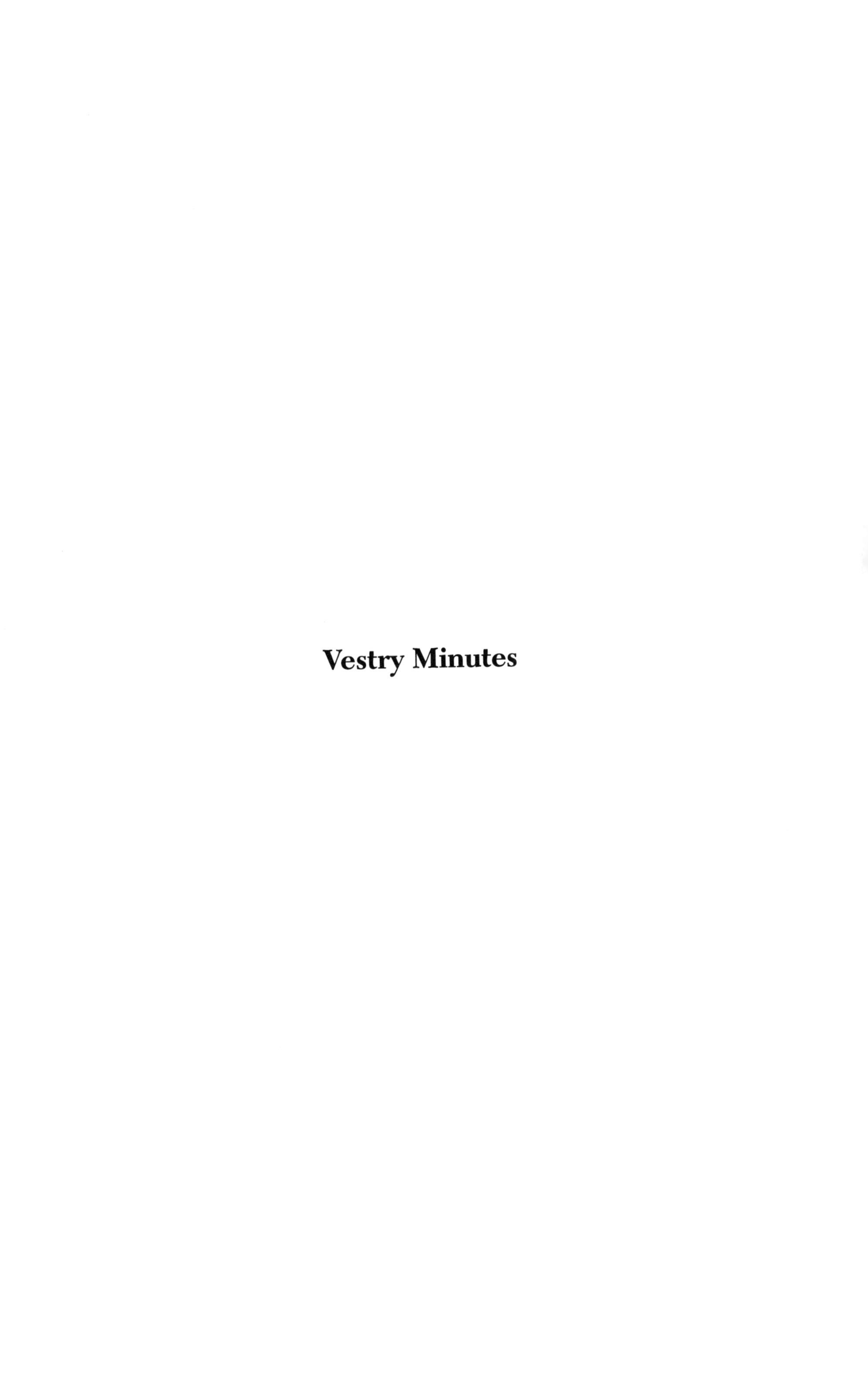

Vestry Minutes

Att a Vestrey Mett and held at The Indian Town Chappell the 18th day of Aprill 1741 Pr.

Mr. Isaac Hunter Mr. William Speight Mr. Jacob Butler Cls.
Mr. Thos. Walton Mr. Edwd. Hair
Mr. Richd. Bond Mr. William Skinner

Ordered that Mr. Thos. Walton and Mr. Richard Bond Serve as Church wardens for this Insuing year 1741

Ordered That Demsey Sumner as Late church warden Lay his acct. Before the next Vestrey to be held for this parrish and acct. for ye Same

Ordered That James Egerton be allowed and payed the Sum of Twenty pounds by the Church wardens for his Trouble and Care in Keeping and maintaining of a poore child Sarah Lewy by name

Ordered That the church wardens pay unto John Sumner Ten pounds for his Trouble in Serveing as clerk of this Vestrey for the year 1740

Ordered That the church wardens pay unto Capt. Thos. Garrett the Sum of Twenty five pounds for his Trouble and Charge in Keeping & maintaining Margett Rodgerson from ye first day of June 1740 untill ye first day of aprill 1741

Ordered That a Tax or Levey of Two Shillings proclamation money be Levied on Every Tythable in this Parish for the Insueing year 1741 for Towards the Defraying the Contingent charges of this Parish and Towards the Building of two chappells Each to be Thirty five foot long and Twenty two foot and a halfe wide and to Stand one at James Costans or their abouts and the other to Stand at James Braddeys or near their abouts

Ordered That Mr. Richd. Parker Mr. Isaac Hunter Mr. Thos. Walton and John Sumner doe Imploy or hire work men for to build two Chappells in chowan Parish Viz. at James Costans or their abouts as they Shall Think fitt and the other at James Braddeys or near their abouts and The Dementions as here mentioned Vizt. Thirty five foot Long and Twenty two foot and a halfe wide Eleven foot in the pitch betwen Sill and plate and a Roof workman like near a Squear and to be a Good frame Gott out of Good Timber and covered with Good Sipress Shingles and weather boarded with [illegible] Edged plank nine Inches broad with Good Lapp of two Inches at the Least and Good Sleepers and flower of Good plank of Inch and a qt. thick and Sealed with Good plank with [illegible] three windows two Dores Suitable with a pulpitt Suitable for Such a house or houses and all things Suitable according to the Vew of the Sd. Richard Parker Isaac Hunter Thos. Walton and John Sumner

(Turn forward)

First page of vestry minutes for St. Paul's Parish, Edenton, April 18, 1741. No known minutes are extant for other North Carolina parishes prior to April 30, 1742.

Vestry Minutes

[*St. Paul's Episcopal Church, Edenton*]

Vestry Minutes, St. Paul's Parish 1701-1741

1701

<*Anno Domini 1701.*> Chowan Precinct Sc. In Obedience to an Act of Assembly made November the 2[9] 1701[1] appointing a Vestry for this precinct Consisting of The Honorable Henderson Walker Esqr., Colonell Thomas Pollock, William Duckenfield Esqr., Mr. Nicholas Crisp, Mr. Edward Smithwick,[2] Mr. John Blount,[3] Mr. James Long, Mr. Nathaniel Chevin, Mr. William Banbury, Colonell William Wilkinson,[4] Capt. Thomas Leuten,[5] Capt. Thomas Blount.[6] Who being all present at the House of Mr. Thomas Gillam Dec. the 15th 1701.

It being debated where a Church Should be built Mr. Edward Smithwick undertakes to give one Acree of Land upon his old planta[tion] and to give a Conveyance for the Same to the Church Wardens hereafter appointed for the Use and Service of the precinct to build a Church upon and for no other Use and to acknowledge the Same in open Court. The Choice of Church Wardens.

It is appointed that Colonell William Wilkinson and Capt. Thomas [Leuten] shall be Church Wardens for the following Year who shall agree with [a] Workman for building a Church 25 feet long [*blank*] posts in the Ground [*blank*] and held to the Collar Beams and to find all manner of Iron to[ols] Videlicet Nails and Locks etc. with full power to contract and agree with Said Workman as to their Discretion shall Seem meet and convenient.

It is agreed that Nathaniel Chevin shall be Clerk of the Vestry and keep a Book of the proceedings of the Vestry for which he Shall be allowed 10 Shillings per Day for every Day he attends upon the Vestry or Church Wardens.

Ordered that the Church Wardens aforesaid having agreed with a Workman for the Building of a Church as aforesaid, Whatsoever Ch[arge] shall accruee for and towards the building of the aforesaid Church or other Charge relating to the Same altho' not here particularly mentiond by the Said Church-Wardens be levied by the pole upon the Tythables of the precinct, the Church-Wardens first Endeavouring to raise the Said Money Contribution, and in Case of Failure to raise it by the pole as aforesaid to agree with a Collector or Collectors to receive the Same with power to destrain in Case of Refusal.

[Ordered that the Church Wardens] [*illegible*] [pro]vide a Reader and Shall agree with Him for his Service And that each [Vestry] Man shall do his Endeavour to enquire for a Reader and give thereof an Account to the Church-Wardens if any presents.

Ordered that the Inhabitants of the So. West Shore build a Chappel of Ease[7] on their Shore at the Charge of the precinct after the aforesaid Church be built and that they may there have a Reader at their own Cost and Charge and be excused from paying any thing to a Reader on the North Shore.

And that either the Honorable Colonell Thomas Pollock or William Duckenfield Esqr. agree with the Said Reader.

Ordered that Twelve pence be levied on every Tythable in the precinct and that Eight pounds be paid out of it to Christ. Buttler towards the Supply and maintainance of Robert Willson. And that Francis Wells Collect the lower part of the precinct as high as Mr. Crisp's and William Early from thence Upwards On the West Shore by William Jones On the South Shore by John Walker, And Shall render an Account of the Same to the Church-Wardens, and the Said Church-Wardens shall pay out of it to Christopher Buttler Eight pounds and shall give Account of the Remainder to the Vestry. And the Constable of each District shall deliver the Copy of this Order to the respective Collector. And if any of the aforesaid Collectors Shall refuse the Same, the Constable or Constables of their District shall bring them before the Honorable Henderson Walker Esqr. etc. or before the Honorable Thomas Pollock Esqr. to answer their Contempt.

D. St. Paul's Parish, Chowan County, was erected by the vestry act of 1701, and the vestry appointed by that legislation met within a few weeks of its passage. Although gaps are evident in these minutes, they are the only ones extant for any North Carolina parish before 1742, and with those of St. John's, Carteret County (from 1742), St. George's, Northampton County (from 1773), and Dobbs Parish (from 1756), constitute the only ones known to exist for the colonial period. The St. Paul's minutes, laminated and rebound by the North Carolina State Archives, remain in the custody of the vestry of St. Paul's Episcopal Church, Edenton, by whose kind permission they are here published.

[1]Not located.

[2]Edward Smithwick (ca. 1649-1716) was at various times justice of the peace, member of the council, and assemblyman. *DNCB*.

[3]John Blount (1671-1726) was after this time appointed to the bench of Chowan County, and also later became a justice of the General Court and councillor. *DNCB*.

[4]William Wilkinson (ca. 1645-1706), originally from Maryland, was at this time justice of the General Court, having previously been a member of the council and speaker of the assembly. *DNCB*.

[5]Thomas Luton (d. 1731) in 1701 was provost marshal of the General Court, and at other times held the posts of justice of the General Court and Chowan Precinct Court, and member of the assembly, among others. *DNCB*.

[6]Thomas Blount (d. 1706) at this time was justice of the General Court, and previously had been a member of the council and an assemblyman. *DNCB*.

[7]A place of worship built for the convenience of parishioners living far from the parish church.

1702

At a Vestry holden the 30th of June 1702 at the House of Thomas Gillam. Present Colonell William Wilkinson, Capt. Thomas Leuten, Capt. Thomas Blount, William Duckenfield Esqr., Mr. Edward Smithwick, Mr. Nicholas Crisp, Mr. William Banbury, Mr. James Long, Nathl. Chevin.

In Obedience to a late Act of Assembly made in March last[1] impowering the Vestry of each precinct to provide a Standard for Weights and Measures. And it being debated how the Said Weights and Measures shall be procured.

Agreed that the Church-Wardens shall Use their Utmost Endeavour by the first Convenience to Send for Weights and Measures as the <*Anno Domini 1702.*> Law directs, and agree with some person for that purpose at as Cheap a Rate as possible, and also one fair and large Book of Common Prayer One Book of Homilies.

Ordered that the Church Wardens Shall agree with and pay the Collector or Collectors for Collecting the precinct Levies.

And then the Meeting broke up.

At a Vestry held at Thomas Gillam's October the 13th 1702. Present The Honorable Henderson Walker President, Colonell Wm. Wilkison, Capt. Thomas Leuten, Church-Wardens, Mr. Nicholas Crisp, Mr. John Blount, Capt. Thomas Blount, Mr. Edward Smithwick, Mr. William Banbury.

Whereas at the last Vestry it was ordered that there Should be a Standard of Weights and Measures Sent for the Use of the precinct in Obedience to the Act of Assembly, the Charge whereof with the Best [*sic*] of the [*illegible*] Charge being as followeth. Videlicet.

	£ Shillings *d.*
To building the Chappel to Mr. John Porter	25. 0. 0
To Richard Curten Reader	7.10. 0
To the Standard for the precinct	12.10. 0
To clearing an Acree of Ground and flooring the House to Mr. Smithwick	2.10. 0
To Nathaniel Chevin acting as Clerk	1.10. 0
To the Joiner for Windows Table Forms and Benches	6. 0. 0
To Thomas Gillam for Trouble of his House	1.10. 0
To the poor of the precinct	8. 0. 0
To John Tyler for Attendance	0. 1. 0
To Sallery for Collecting at 10 per Ct.	6. 8. 0
The Total amounts to	70.19

The List of Tythables in the precinct being taken is found to be 283 in the Sum.

Ordered that the Church-Wardens collect from each Tythable person in the precinct five Shillings And Colonell William Wilkinson [*faded*] undertake [*torn*] Collection [*torn*].

<*Anno Domini 1702.*> Ordered that Colonell William Wilkinson do collect upon all and every [*faded*] Tythables within this precinct (a List whereof is delivered to him under the [*illegible*] of the Clerk of the Vestry) five Shillings per pole and for non payment thereof to make Distress according to Law and likewise to pay unto the Several persons

aforementioned the Several Sums due to them and allotted by this Vestry and He together with the other Church-Wardens do provide and pay for the other things mentioned in the aforesaid Order and render an Account of the Same to this Vestry to be holden the last Tuesday in April next and finish all the Collection.

Let it be remembred that Colonell William Wilkinson on his own Behalf and Mr. Nicholas Crisp on Behalf of the Said Wilkison do oblige themselves their Heirs etc. to this Vestry in the penal Sum of one hundred pounds Sterling to Collect the aforesaid Money and render a perfect Account of the Said Collection and payment at the Vestry the last Tuesday in April next at the House of Mr. Thomas Gillam.

Ordered that a Warrant be directed for the Summoning of the Several Collectors hereafter named to appear at the next Meeting of the Vestry at the House of Mr. Thomas Gillam the 15th Day of December next to give an Account of their Several Collections the two last Years And accor[*blank*] the whole Vestry does pray the Honorable the president to direct his Warrant unto William Bush, Francis Perrot Capt. Thomas Blount Nicholas Symmons And for the present Year last past Francis Wells William Early William Jones and John Walker.

Ordered that the Vestry meet to Morrow Morning to view the Chappel.

October the 14th 1702.

The Vestry being met and having viewed the Chappel the Major part of the Vestry do declare their Dislike of the ceiling of the Chappel by Reason of the Boards being defaced.

Ordered that Mr. Edward Smithwick and Mr. Nicholas Crisp on Behalf of the Vestry do Choose one indifferent Man that is Skilled in building and Mr. John Porter shall choose another who shall meet at the Chappel the Second Saturday in November to give their Judgment whether the Boards be fit for ceileing Such an House. And if these two persons chosen as aforesaid cannot agree in their Opinions, then they Shall choose an Umpire and what Opinion he the Said Umpire Shall give Shall be a full and final Determination of the Matter about the ceiling and Boards and the Agreement between the Church-Wardens and Mr. John Porter shall be thence.

<*1702.*> At a Vestry holden at the House of Mrs. Sarah Gillam [*torn*] the Day of December 1702. Present Colonell Wm. Wilkinson, Capt. Thos. Leuten, Church Wardens, Mr. Wm. Duckenfield, Mr. Edward Smithwick, Mr. Nicholas Crisp, Capt. Thomas Blount, Mr. William Banbury, Mr. Nathl. Chevin, Mr. James Long.

The Several Collectors being Summoned to render an Account of the Several Collections which being duly examined there is found to be due to the Church-Wardens for the Use of the precinct these following Sums of Money.

	£ *s*. *d*.
In the Hands of Colonell Thomas Pollock	1.12. 2
In Christopher Buttler's Hands	0. 6. 0
In William Earley's Hands	2.12.
In John Walker's Hands	1.18. 6
	£6. 8. 8

Colonell William Wilkison and Capt. Thomas Leuten having Served [one] Year in the Station of Church-Wardens and the Choice of New Church Wardens being debated.

Mr. Williams Duckenfield and Mr. Edward Smithwick are approved Church-Wardens for the ensuing Year.

There being found the abovesaid Sums of Money due to the precinct and also the Reader being gone whereby the Publick Charge of the precinct is lessened and abated.

Therefore ordered that the Collector collect from every Tythable person in the Precinct four Shillings per pole.

The Chappel being this Day viewed by all the Vestry here present and are Satisfyed therewith and do receive the House and Keys from Mr. John Porter [him] promising to provide So much Lime as will Wash the Ceiling of the Chappel [and] the Vestry to be at the Charge of a Workman to do the Same.

---

[1]Not located.

1703

<1703.> April the 24th 1703. At a Vestry holden at the House of Mrs. Sarah Gillam.

Present The honorable Henderson Walker Esqr., Mr. William Duckenfield, Mr. Edwd. Smithwick, Church-Wardens, Colonell Wm. Wilkinson, Capt. Thomas Leuten, Capt. Thomas Blount, Mr. Nicholas Crisp, Mr. Wm. Banbury, Nathl. Chevin.

The Church Wardens etc. having agreed with Colonell Wm. Wilkinson for the Sending for a Standard of Weights and Measures for this precinct and he having received the Same from Boston comes and produces an Account of the Same from under the Hand of Mr. William Welstead Merchant of Boston as followeth, Videlicet.

	£ shillings *d.*
5 ½ Cts. one Qr. Ct. one 14 lb. at 20 *sh.* per Ct.	2.17.6
One Brass Yard 25 shilling One Iron Do. at 2 shilling	1. 7.0
Three Brass Weights, Videlicet 4 and 2 etc.	0.14.0
One pair of Brass Scales	0.16.0
One Wine Gallon pewter pot	0.18.0
One pottle[1] and one Quart Do.	0.15.0
One/2 Bushel and one peck	0. 5.0
paid the Town Sealer for Sealing the Weights etc.	0. 3.8
paid porterage to the Vessel	0. 1.0
First Cost	£ 7.17.2

Ordered that Colonell William Wilkinson deliver to Mr. Edward Smithwick the aforesaid Weights and Measures who is impowered to keep the Same by Act of Assembly etc. And that Mr. Edward Smithwick give a Receipt for the Same.

Whereas Robert Wilson who was kept by William Brethell for the Space of 2 or 3 Months upon the precinct Charge, and is dead and Colonell Wilkinson declaring that he has paid unto the Said Brethell for the Care and keeping of the Said Willson the Sum of Eight pounds, which was the full Consideration for one whole Year.

Ordered that William Brethell Shall reimburse Colonell William Wilkinson the aforesaid Eight pounds except So much as he Shall make appear to have disburst for his Burial and the time he kept Him.

It being debated for a Reader to be agreed with to read Divine Service.

It is agreed that the Church-Wardens shall make Choice of a Reader who shall remain until the next Vestry and if approved of by the Vestry <*1703.*> Shall remain and if not Shall be paid for his Time and discharged.

Information being made by Capt. Thomas Blount that Elinor Adams [*faded*] of Infirmity and Indigence is in great Danger of being lost for want of [*illegible*].

The Same being taken into Consideration.

Ordered that Capt. Thomas Blount treat with Doctor Godffrey Spruill in [order] to her Cure and that Doctor Godffrey Spruil be paid for his physick and Cure [by] the Church-Wardens five pounds, and Capt. Thomas Blount is requested [*torn*] Vestry to endeavour to oblige the Said Elenor to Serve the Doctor for the [*torn*] of his House and nursing.

There being three Church Bibles intended for this Country one which belongs to this precinct and the Same being Sent for to Williamsburgh by William Jones.

Ordered that the Church-Wardens pay one third of the Charge for fetching in the Said Bibles.

There being Want of Some Letters for the Stamping the Weights and Measures for the Standard. And Capt. Thomas Blount undertakes to make a Small Letter C for Stamping the styllyards and potts and Weights etc. and Larger C for the half Bushell and peck.

At a Vestry holden at the Chappell the 6th Day of October [1703.] Present The Honorable Henderson Walker Esqr., Mr. Wm. Duckenfield, Mr. Edward Smithwick, Church-Wardens, Colonell Wm. Wilkinson, Capt. Thos. Blount, Capt. Thomas Leuten, Mr. John Blount, Mr. Nicholas Crisp, Mr. Wm. Banbury, Nathl. Chevin.

In pursuance of a former Order.

Ordered that the Church-Wardens shall immediately Account with William Brethell for eight pounds paid him by Colonell Wm. Wilkinson and if he Shall refuse to deliver and pay the Same, that they Commence an Action against Him for the Recovery thereof.

Ordered that the Church-Wardens shall with all possible Speed [*faded*] the Windows of the Chapell finished and that Glass may be Sent for [and] purchased here if possible.

---

[1]An archaic liquid measure equivalent to two quarts.

1704

<*1703.*> At a Vestry met at the Chapel the 9th Day of March 1703/4. Present The Honorable Henderson Walker Esqr., Colonell Wm. Wilkinson, Wm. Duckenfield Esqr., Mr. Edward Smithwick, Mr. Nicholas Crisp, Mr. John Blount, Mr. Wm. Banbury, Nathl. Chevin.

William Duckenfield Esqr. and Mr. Edward Smithwick being appointed Church Wardens for the Last Year and having Served a Year the 15th of December last, and they having failed of Calling the Vestry together at that time in Order to be discharged.

Ordered that they Serve another Year in that Station.

Whereas Dr. John Blair presenting himself before the Vestry, as a Minister of the Gospel and having the Approbation of the D. Governour,[1] he is received as a Minister of the Gospel and the Church-Wardens for and in Behalf of the Vestry do assume to pay to the Said Dr. John Blair 30 pounds (as the Law provides) per Annum. The Year to begin the first of this Instant March.

The Choice of a Reader and Clerk of the Church being debated and Daniel Leigh presenting himself for that Office.

It's agreed that Daniel Leigh Serve in that Station and that he keep the Keys of the Church and keep the Church clean, and keep the Woods fired at the time of the Year round the Chappel also to provide Water for the baptizing of Children, and to attend the Chappel every Lords Day, when the Minister is here to officiate as a Clerk, and when the Minister is absent to read divine Service, and a Sermon etc. to keep the Vestry Journal and to attend the Vestry at their Meetings. He promising to the Vestry to lead a Sober and exemplary Life in his Station his Year to begin this Day.

Whereas his Excellency Francis Nicholson Esqr., his Majesty's Lieutenant and Governour of the Colony of Virginia hath been pleased to contribute the pious and Charitable Gift of ten pounds Sterling for the Use of the Church in this our precinct and parish of St. Paul's and for a perpetual Memorial of his pious and Charitable Gift it is

Ordered that the ten pounds in pieces of Eight wt. 17 p.wt. shall be Sent to Boston to purchase a Chalice for the Use of the Church with this Motto Ex Dono Francis Nicholson Esqr. her Majesty's Lieutenant Governour of her Majesty's Colony and Dominion of Virginia.

Ordered that the Church-Wardens do Speedily agree with a Workman to make pulpit and pew for the Reader with Desks fitting for the Same and in as decent a Manner as may be and what they shall agree for the Vestry do oblige themselves to See paid. And that they put a former Order in Execution for the Getting the Windows put up and to get Glass and have it put up forthwith.

Ordered [. . .][2]

<1703.> the Vestry Colonell Wm. Wilkinson having accepted of the Ballance in his [*faded*] the Insolvents.

The Publick Charge is as followeth. Videlicet.

	£ sh. *d.*
To Doctor Spruil for Curing [*blank*] Adams	5.[*faded*]
To Luke Meazle's Services	0. 9.[*faded*]
To Colonell Wilkinson a Barrel of Tarr	0.[*faded*]
To Danl. Leigh for tarring the Chapell and fetching the Tarr	1. 0[*faded*]
To Nathl. Chevin Clk.	2.[*faded*]
To Sallery for collecting at 15 per Ct.	1.10[*faded*]
	£ 11.[*faded*]

Ordered that the Collector collect of every Tythable in the precinct the Sum of One Shilling and Eight pence with power to destrain in Case of Refusal to be collected by the Church-Wardens or their Deputies and the afor[esaid] Church Wardens do undertake for the faithfull Collection and true accounting for the Same in the Sum of fifty pounds Sterling to be levied upon their Goods and Chattells in Case of Default.

At a Vestry held at the Chappel the 26th of May 170[*faded*].[3] Present Colonell Wm. Wilkinson, Wm. Duckenfield Esqr., Mr. Edward Smithwick, Mr. Nicholas Crisp, Mr. Nathl. Chevin, Mr. John Blount, Mr. Wm. Banbury, Capt. Thomas Luten.

Ordered that Mr. John Ardern[4] Serve as Vestry Man in the Room of the Honorable Henderson Walker deceased.

Ordered that three pound be paid Richard Booth towards the Maintainance of an Orphan Child left destitute per Stephen Preston.

The Reverend John Blair Serving as Minister of the Gospel out of his Charitable Gift hath given what Sallery is due to him to the poor for which the Gentlemen of the Vestry return him thanks.

---

[1]Robert Daniel.

[2]At least two pages of the manuscript are missing at this point.

[3]Undoubtedly this is 1704, since Henderson Walker, whom John Arderne replaced as vestryman in the entry below, died in April, 1704.

[4]John Arderne (d. ca. 1710) served in the lower house of assembly in 1703, and was appointed to the council in 1705. *DNCB.*

1705

<*Anno Domini 1704.*>[1] At a Vestry mett at the Chappel the 9th Day of Sept. 1705. Present Colonell Thomas Pollock, John Ardern Esqr., Wm. Duckenfield Esqr., Capt. Thomas Luten, Mr. John Blount, Mr. Nicholas Crisp, Mr. Wm. Banbury, Mr. Nathl. Chevin, Mr. Edward Smithwick.

Mr. Henry Gerrard[2] presenting himself to the Vestry as a Minister of the Gospel and he having the Honorable Deputy Governor's Approbation is received by the Vestry into this precinct and the Said Mr. Henry Gerrard declaring that by Reason of the great Distance betwixt this precinct and pequimins and the Dirtyness of the Roads he is not able to Serve in the two precincts, and therefore is willing to attend in this precinct wholy and decline his Intentions of Serving in pequimons.

And the Church-Wardens for and in Behalf of the Vestry do undertake to pay to the aforesaid Mr. Henry Gerrard thirty pounds per Annum as the Law directs besides these Voluntary Subscriptions hereafter mentioned to which the Several persons have Subscribed Videlicet.

	£ *s. d.*
Colonell Thomas Pollock	4. 0. 0
Wm. Duckenfield Esqr.	4. 0. 0
John Ardern Esqr.	3. 0. 0

Mr. Edwd. Moseley	5. 0. 0
Capt. Thomas Luten	1. 0. 0
Mr. Nicholas Crisp	1. 5. 0
Mr. Edward Smithwick	1. 0. 0
Mr. John Blount	1. 0. 0
Mr. Wm. Banbury	0. 8. 0
Mr. Nathl. Chevin	1. 0. 0
John Wheatly	0.10. 0
Richd. Rose	0.10. 0
John Linnington	0.15. 0
Capt. David Henderson	0.10. 0
Henry Bonner	0.10. 0
	£ 25. 8. 0

It is agreed that a third part of the thirty pounds be levied and raised in the precinct in December next.

And the Vestry agrees to meet the 15th of December next.

<*1705.*> At a Vestry meet at the Chappel Decembr. the 16, 1705. Present Colonell William Wilkinson, John Ardern Esqr., Wm. Duckenfield Esqr., Mr. John Blount, Mr. Edward Smithwick, Capt. Thomas Leuten, Mr. Nichol. Crisp, Mr. Wm. Banbury, Mr. Nathl. Chevin.

Ordered and agreed that Colonell Thomas Pollock and Mr. John Blount Shall be Church Wardens for the ensuing Year.

And there being not a full Vestry it's agreed that the Vestry meet the Second Day of January next.

[1] *Sic.* It seems likely that *1705* is meant, and that the September 9, 1705, date given in the first paragraph is the correct one. It is, however, impossible to know for certain from internal evidence or from the sequence of sittings which year is correct.

[2] See appendix.

1706

At a Vestry met at the Chappel the 3d Day of Janry. 1705. Present Colonell Wm. Wilkinson, Capt. Thomas Luten, John Ardern Esqr., Wm. Duckenfield Esqr., Capt. Thomas Blount, Mr. John Blount, Mr. James Long, Mr. Edward Smithwick, Mr. Nathl. Chevin, Mr. Wm. Banbury.

It being debated whether the Publick Account shall be examined Colonell Pollock being absent, who is appointed one of the Church Wardens therefore the Church-Wardens who have Served the Last Year cannot render their Accounts, because one of them is absent as aforesaid and so the Account cannot be made up.

<*And he brings an Acct. for his Work Six pounds.*> Also debated the payment of John Dicks for Work about the pulpit the Said Work not being finished, whether he Shall be

paid before the Work be done, He alledging that he could not finish it for Want of Nails and Boards.

Ordered that John Dicks be paid one pound Seventeen Shillings Nine pence besides what he has been paid and that he finish the Work then Account with the Vestry.

Whereas several Scandalous Reports has been Spread abroad in the Government of the Reverend Mr. Henry Gerrard of Several Debauched practices which (if true) tends highly to the Dishonour of Allmighty God and the Scandal of the Church.

<*1705.*> It is debated whether he shall be continued.

Ordered that he continue in this precinct as a Minister till the first of May next in which time it is expected by the Vestry that he Use his Utmost Endeavours to clear himself of these black Calumnies laid to his Charge or else he may expect a Dismission.

It's agreed that if Colonell Thomas Pollock refuse to Serve as a Church-Warden he paying the Fine shall be excused and Nathaniel Chevin Shall Serve in his Stead with Mr. John Blount as aforesaid.

It is agreed by the Vestry, Mr. Gerrard agreeing thereto, that Mr. Gerrard Shall once in two Months be fetcht over to the South Shore by a Canoe and two Hands from thence to begin the first Monday in February, and So the first Monday in the Month every two Months, which Men shall be paid by the publick.

Ordered that Richard Booth be paid three pounds towards the Maintainance of an Orphan Child left destitute by Stephen Beston. Ordered that the Collector of each District in this precinct Collect of every Tythable in their and either of their Districts two Shillings and Six pence with power in Case of Refusal and the Church-Wardens do undertake for the faithfull Collection and accounting for the Same in the Sum of fifty pounds Sterling to be levied upon their Goods and Chattels in Case of Refusal.

1707

Memorandum December the 15th 1707.[1]

Then the Church-Wardens John Blount Esqr. and Nathl. Chevin having legally Summoned the Vestry and none appearing. Since Mr. William Banbury and the aforesaid Church-Wardens having before encouraged Mr. James Beaseley to attend this Vestry in Order to be established a Reader and he appearing in order thereunto, and there being no Vestry, he is willing to Officiate in the Station of a Reader of Divine Service untill a Vestry shall meet and approve off and agree with him.

[1]The gap of twenty-three months between this entry and the one immediately preceding is worth noting, and cannot be explained by internal evidence. The present entry immediately follows the one of January 3, 1705/6 on the same page. Although it is possible that the vestry did not meet during this time, a more likely explanation is that meetings did in fact take place, but that the rough minutes made at the time were unavailable to the clerk when these fair minutes were compiled.

1708

<*Anno Domini 1708.*> At a Vestry at the Chapell the 18th Day of April 1708. Present Wm. Duckenfield Esqr., John Ardern Esqr., Capt. Thomas Luten, Mr. Nichl. Crisp, John Blount Esqr., Mr. Edward Smithwick, Mr. Wm. Banbury, Mr. Nathl. Chevin.

Mr. Nathl. Chevin being now removing out of this precinct and being debated who shall Serve instead of him.

Agreed that Thomas Garret Esqr. shall Succeed in the Room and Stead of Nathl. Chevin.

Also it being debated who Shall Succeed in the Room and place of Capt. Thomas Blount deceased.

Resolved that Edward Moseley Esqr. shall Succeed in the Vestry in the place of Capt. Thomas Blount.

It is also voted who Shall Succeed as a Vestry Man in the place of Colonell William Wilkinson.

It is agreed that Wm. Charlton Esqr. shall Succeed as a Vestry man in the place and Stead of Colonell Wm. Wilkinson.

And accordingly Thomas Garret and Wm. Charlton Esqrs. took their places in the Vestry.

Richard Booth having had an Allowance of three pounds per Annum for maintaining an Orphan Child of Stephen Bessons comes here and Assumes to keep and maintain the Child without any further Charge.

This Day William Duckenfield Esqr. and Mr. Edward Smithwick made up their Accounts in the time of their being Church-Wardens. And upon adjusting their Accounts it appears that there is due

	£ *s*. *d*.
Mr. Duckenfield from the Vestry the Sum of	4. 5. 0.
And Mr. Smithwick stands indebted to the Vestry	1. 2. 6.
Ordered that Mr. Smithwick pay the Same to Wm. Duckenfield Esqr. and then there will be due to him from the Vestry	5. 2. 6.
John Blount Esqr. and Nathl. Chevin this Day producing their Accounts of the publick Accounts. Upon adjusting the Accounts there appears be due to the publick the Sum of	6. 6. 8.

Ordered that Mr. Crisp be paid for the Use of his Canoe two Shillings and Six pence per Nathl. Chevin.

So the Account Stands thus.

	£ *s*. *d*.
John Blount and Nathl. Chevin Church-Wardens Stands Debtors to the publick for the Years 1706 and 1707	6. 0. 0
<*Anno Domini 1708.*> By Mr. Crisp	6. 2. 6

By Mr. Moseley	1. 2. 6
By Mr. Duckenfield	3. 2. 6
	£ 4. 7. 6

Ordered that Phillis Dicks Widow of John Dicks be paid by the publick the Sum of two pounds besides what he hath been allowed and paid by the publick for his Work on the Chapel.

On the petition of William Walston Shewing that Elenor Kirkham was accommodated at the petitioner's Eighteen Days being Sick and impotent and there died and was buried at the petitioner's Charge having no Estate prays Allowance etc.

And he presenting No account.

Ordered that he appear at the next Vestry and present his Account.

On petition of Madam Mary Blount for accommodating a poor indigent Man named Thomas Wright at her House in his Sickness one Week, whereof he died and was buried at her Charge, prays Allowance.

Ordered that She be paid by the publick forty Shillings.

Ordered that the Honorable Colonell Thomas Pollock and John Ardern Esqrs. shall be Church-Wardens for the Year ensuing.

Ordered that Mr. Nicholas Crisp agree with [*blank*] to officiate as a Reader in the Chapel for nine pound per Annum to execute in that Office and also as Clerk of the Vestry, And Mr. Nichl. Crisp doth promise to give Notice to the Inhabitants of the Time when he shall begin upon that Employment.

<*Anno Domini 1708*> At a Vestry met at the Chappel on Wednesday the 5th of May 1708. Present William Duckenfield Esqr., Edward Moseley Esqr., Capt. Thomas Luten, Mr. John Blount, Mr. William Banbury, Mr. Wm. Charlton, Mr. John Ardern, Church Wardens.

In Observance to a late Act of Assembly intitled an Act for electing Vestrys, the Said Act being first read, the Vestry made Choice of the Reverend Mr. William Gordon the Honorable presidents[1] Approbation being Signified, to officiate in this precinct as a Minister of the Gospel.

It having this Day been Signified to the Vestry that the Honorable Thomas Pollock declines the Office of a Church-Warden.

Ordered that Mr. Nicholas Crisp officiate in his Room and that the Honorable Colonell Thomas Pollock pay his Fine As appointed by the Act.

Mr. William Walston having this Day brought in his Account for the Interment of Ealinor Kirckum and demanding thirty Shillings for his Trouble and Charge therein, being thought a Reasonable Demand is therefore allowed the Same to be paid by the publick.

It is ordered that a full Vestry pay their Attendance at the Chapel on Tuesday the 11th of this Month for the further Settling of Matters relating to the Church.

At a Vestry Met at the Chappel on Tuesday the 11th Day of May 1708. Present William Duckenfield Esqr., Edward Moseley Esqr., Mr. Edward Smithwick, Capt. Thomas Luten, Mr. John Blount, Mr. Nicholas Crisp, Mr. William Banbury, Mr. Thomas Garret, John Ardern Esqr.

<*Anno Domini 1708.*> Mr. Nicholas Crisp being present and refusing to perform the Office of a Church-Warden.

Ordered that he pay his Fine pursuant to the Act and that Mr. Thomas Garret be Church Warden in his Room.

It having this Day been debated (for the better Encouragement of a Minister for this precinct only) which is the most proper place to purchase for a Glebe, it's unanimously agreed upon that the plantation now belonging to Mr. Frederick Jones[2] whereon the Church now Stands is the fittest place can be thought on for that Use: the Tract of Land in Quantity containing five hundred Acres.

It is therefore the humble Request of the Vestry that Edward Moseley Esqr. (having now Business into Virginia) will please to treat with Mr. Frederick Jones concerning the purchase of the Said Land and agree with him for the Same provided he exceed not an Hundred pounds in Country Commodities.

Ordered that the Church-Wardens endeavour to have the pulpit finished with all possible Speed as likewise the Desk and what other things belong to it, As likewise to have the Church Floor laid with Brick, but upon further Debate of the Matter, it's agreed upon that the Floor Shall be laid with plank as being the Cheapest and Most expeditious way of having it done.

There appearing upon the Adjousting of Mr. John Blount's and Mr. Nathaniel Chevin's Accounts to the Vestry on the Eighteenth of April last, Mr. Chevin remains Debtor to the publick

Ordered that the Said £ 1. 19*s*.2*d*. be paid to Mrs. Mary Blount in part of forty Shillings due to her by a former Order.

Ordered that the Vestry Meet at the Chapell the following Day to our next precinct Court.

<(17)> <*1708*> At a Meeting at the Chapell of Edward Moseley Esqr., Capt. Thomas Leuten and Mr. John Blount on Wednesday the 7th of July 1708. As likewise of John Ardern the Rest of the Vestry not appearing.

Ordered that a full Vestry make their Appearance at the Chapell on Sabbath Day next being the 11th of this Instant.

Memorandum. The Vestry having been legally Summoned to make their Appearance at the Chapell on Sunday the Eleventh of July 1708, but none appearing except Edward Moseley Esqr. Mr. Edward Smithwick Mr. Nicholas Crisp John Ardern and William Banbury there being no Majority no Bussiness could be accomplisht.

Ordered that a full Vestry make their Appearance at the Chapell on Sunday the 25th of July 1708.

At a Meeting of the Vestry holden at the Chapell on Sunday the 25th of July 1708. Present. Edward Moseley Esqr., William Duckenfield Esqr., Capt. Thomas Luton, Mr. Nicholas Crisp, Mr. Edward Smithwick, Mr. William Banbury, Mr. William Charlton, John Ardern Esqr.

Whereas the Reverend Mr. William Gordon is Speedily designed for England hath therefore recommended unto this precinct for a Reader Mr. Charles Griffin of whom he renders a good Character the Said Mr. Griffin being likewise made known to Some Gentlemen of the Vestry.

It's unanimously approved of to accept of the Said Mr. Griffin for our Reader in Mr. Gordon's Absence and to allow for his Officiating as Such and performing the Office of a Clerk to the Vestry twenty pounds per Annum to be paid by the publick.

<(18)> <*Anno Domini 1708.*> Whereas it hath been taken into our mature Consideration the many and great Inconveniences which attend the Chappell which is already built both in Respect of it's ill Situation Smallness and rough and unfit Workmanship.

We therefore to Shew our true Zeal for the Glory of God and propogating So good a Work do unanimously agree that a Church of forty Feet long and twenty four wide fourteen Feet from Fenant to Fenant for Hight, the remaining part of the Work to be proportionable, the Roof to be first plankt and then Shingled with good Cypress Shingles and the whole to be ceiled with plank and floored with plank for the Speedy accomplishment of which Said Work, it's the Earnest Request of the present Members of the Vestry that Edward Moseley Esqr. and Capt. Thomas Leuten will undertake to See the Same performed, they living convenient, and to agree with Workmen at as easy Rates as may be. It being well and Substantially performed.

There appearing to this Board that Eight pounds are due to the Reverend Mr. William Gordon for Officiating as a Minister in this precinct.

Ordered that the Said Eight pounds be paid to the Reverend Mr. Gordon or his Order by the publick.

[1] William Glover.

[2] Frederick Jones (d. 1722), merchant and large landowner, moved into the colony from Virginia in 1710. He thereafter served in the assembly and on the council, and as chief justice of the General Court. *DNCB.*

1709

At a Vestry held at the Chapell on Thursday the 27th of Febry. 1708/9. Present John Ardern Esqr., Mr. John Blount, Capt. Thomas Luten, Capt. Nichl. Crisp, Capt. James Long, Mr. Thomas Garret, Mr. Edwd. Smithwick, Mr. Wm. Banbury, Mr. Wm. Charleton, Mr. Edward Moseley.

<(19)> <*Anno Domini 1708.*> Thomas Garret and John Ardern being this Day dismist from the office of Church-Wardens adjusted their Accounts with the Vestry which Stands as followeth. Videlicet.

Publick	
Dr.	£ *s. d.*
Widow Dicks Claim	2. 0. 0
Per Wm. Walston	1.10. 0
By Mrs. Blount	2. 0. 0
By John Ardern Sterling	0. 5. 0
Per Mr. Gordon	8. 0. 0
Per a late Demand of Mr. Gordon	1. 0. 0

Per Mr. Gordons Expences about the Books	0.15. 0
Per Richd. Booth	3. 0. 0

Cr.	£ *s*. *d*.
Per Currituck and Pasquotanck Fines	1.10. 0
Per Ballance of Widow Dicks's Account	1.19. 2
By 500 feet of Inch Board by Mr. Smithwick towards laying the Floor	2.10. 0

But if the payment of the Said three pounds be found a Mistake, It's to be refunded back.[1]

	£ shillings
Per Mr. Griffin	20. 0.0

Ordered that the Collector of this precinct do collect from each Tythable the Sum of two Shillings and Nine pence which rise Sufficient to pay the publick Debts here mentioned and will advance the Sum of twelve pounds towards the beautifying of the Chapell over and above the Charge of the Collection.

Ordered that Mr. Edward Smithwick do with all reasonable of expedition deliver the Standard now in his Custody into the Care of Mr. Nicholas Crisp he living more convenient to the precinct.

Ordered that Mr. John Linnington be constituted Clerk of the Vestry and be allowed for each Days Attendance five Shillings to be paid by the publick.

Ordered that the Way and Method of beautifying the Church be left to the Descretion of the Church Wardens for the Year ensuing Videlicet enlarging repairing etc.

Ordered that Edward Moseley Esqr. and Major Luten be appointed Church Wardens for the Year ensuing and have taken their places accordingly.

<*Anno Domini 1708.*> The Proceedings of the Vestry for the precinct of Chowan in the County of Albemarle in the province of North Carolina met at the Honorable Colonell Hyde's then president. Present The Honorable Edwd. Hyde Esqr. President, The Honorable Thomas Pollock Esqr., William Duckenfield Esqr., The Honorable Thos. Peterson Esqr., Mr. Thomas Luten, Mr. Edward Smithwick, Mr. Jno. Bird, Mr. Thomas Lee, Mr. John Walker.

Ordered Imprimis.

That there be allowed and raised in the Said precinct of Chowan forty five pounds and paid by the hereafter named and appointed Church-Wardens to the Reverend Mr. Urmston for having Officiated in this precinct from the Time of his first Coming into this Government till the 25th Instant in the Commodities appointed by the Vestry Act.

Ordered that the Honorable Thomas Peterson Esqr. and Mr. Thomas Lee be and are hereby chosen and appointed Church-Wardens for the Year ensuing the Date hereof and that they levy raise and Collect all Sums appointed to be raised for the Use of the parish and that they be allowed for their So doing after the Rate of £20 per Ct.

That the Ten pounds Sterling given by Colonell Nicholson and now in the Hands of Mr. Edward Moseley be demanded and received by the aforesaid Church Wardens.

That for want of the Act of Assembly for regulating of Vestries Establishing the Church and Making provision for Ministers, and the Vestry Book with the Late Church-Wardens Accounts. Another Vestry be held at the Honorable the presidents the first Day of Janry. next ensuing and that the late Church Wardens be warned to attend there and then to give up their Accounts.

Edwd. Hyde, Thos. Pollock, Thos. Peterson, Thos. Leuten, Edward Smithwick, John Bird, Thomas Lee, John Walker.

[1]This sentence apparently refers to the entry for Richd. Booth, above.

1712

<(21)> <*Anno Domini 1711.*> Chowan Precinct. At a Vestry held at the Honorable the President's[1] the 1st day of Janry. 1711/12. Present The Honorable the President, The Honorable Thos. Pollock Esqr., The Honorable Thos. Peterson Esqr., Wm. Duckenfield Esqr., Mr. Edwd. Smithwick, Mr. Jno. Bird, Mr. Thos. Lee, Mr. Jno. Walker.

Ordered then that the Honorable the President be humbly requested to issue his Warrant to the Several Constables of this precinct to take a List of the Tythables within their Charge and bring in the Same or make Return of the Same to the Honorable the president within the Space of one Month after the Date hereof.

Ordered that the Honorable Thomas Peterson Esqr. together with Mr. Thomas Luten be desired to take Mr. Moseley's Account of late Office of Church Warden for this precinct.

Ordered that the Reverend Mr. Urmston be allowed for officiating in this precinct the Year following commencing from the twenty fifth of December last past at the Several Times and Places hereafter mentioned, Seventy pounds to be levied and paid as the Act of Assembly for establishing the Church and making provision for Ministers doth appoint and direct dated March the 12th 1710/11[2] Videlicet One Sunday on the South Shore the two next Sundays on the Western Shores alternately, provided always that he officiate the fourth Sunday on the other Side opposite to that where he officiated the two foregoing Sundays, and that he provide a passage at his own Cost and Charge.

Jno. Urmston Missionary, Edward Hyde, Tho. Peterson, Tho. Lee, Church Wardens, William Duckenfield, Thomas Pollock, John Bird, John Walker, Edward Smithwick

<*Anno Domini 1711.*> At a Vestry held at the Honorable the president's Febry. the 6th 1711/12.

Whereas there is no Constable appointed for the lower District of the North Shore from Edward Standings lower down the precinct the Church Wardens or either of them are hereby impowered to hire a fit person to take a List of the Tythables within the Said District and after having received all the Several Lists of all the Districts within this precinct to assess and collect or cause to be Collected the aforesaid Sum of forty five pounds and the Additional Charge for collecting the Same to be raised equally per pole.

Item that whereas the Honorable Thomas Peterson Esqr. and Mr. Thomas Luten have not been able to take and receive Mr. Moseley's the late Church Warden's Account of his Said Office according to the Order of the last Vestry, It is hereby ordered that they demand and take and lay the Same before the next Vestry.

Thos. Peterson Church-Warden, John Bird, Samuel Patchet, Leonard Lofftess, William Duckenfield, Thos. Luten, Edward Hyde, Thos. Pollock, John Urmston Missionary, Thos. Lee Church Warden, John Walker

[1] Edward Hyde had been president of the council since January of the previous year.
[2] Not located.

1713

At a Vestry held at the Honorable Thomas Pollock's Esqr. president at his House on the West Shore in the precinct of Chowan in the province of North Carolina Febry. the 6th 1712/13.

It was then ordered that in pursuance of an Act of Assembly dated March the 12th 1710[1] and likewise by an Order of Vestry met at the House of the Honorable Edward Hyde Esqr. president dated December the 18th 1711[2] appointing the Collection of forty five pounds <(23)> <*Anno. 1712*> with the Charge of Collecting the Said Sum to be paid to the Reverend Mr. John Urmston Missionary.

These are therefore to impower You John Hardy to collect and receive of every Tythable person in the precinct of Chowan twenty pence in the Staple Commodities of the Country and to lodge the Same in places convenient upon the Water giving the Said Mr. Urmston Notice and order to receive it, and for the So doing You shall receive fifteen per Cent out of the Said Collection Given under our Hands this 6th Day of Febry. 1712/13.

Ordered upon Complaint of Mr. Thomas Lee that Mr. Edwd. Moseley had bought of him the Said Thomas Lee fourteen hundred feet of plank on pretence of laying a Floor and repairing the Church on the North Shore in this precinct and now refused to pay for the Same and therefore upon Application made 'twas then to be entred in the Vestry Book that We the Vestrymen for the Said precinct are of Opinion the Said Mr. Moseley is indebted and obliged to pay for the Same and not the parish, there appearing no order of

Vestry for the purchase of the Said plank, neither hath it been applyed as pretended but is wasted or destroyed and rendred Useless.

That Mr. Edward Moseley refund the three pounds received of the Vestry on Account of Richard Booth to the Church-Wardens for this Year the Same appearing not due to the Said Richard Booth.

That Mr. John Bird and Mr. Samuel Patchet be and are hereby chosen and appointed to be Church Wardens of this precinct for the Year ensuing.

Ordered that Thomas West be Clerk of the Vestry and be allowed as formerly.

Ordered that the Church Wardens for the Year ensuing demand of the Executor of Mr. Robert Fendall deceased twelve pounds which the Said Robert Fendall collected for the Use of this precinct and in Case of Refusal to Sue him for the Same.

That the Bible now in the Custody of Mr. Nicholas Crisp be delivered to Major Thos. Luten, he obliging himself to See it forthcoming the Gift of the Honorable Society de propaganda etc. by the Reverend Mr. Urmston.

That the Bible now in the Custody of Mr. Thomas Lee be delivered to the Vestry when demanded.

<*Anno Domini 1712*> That the Standard of Weights and Measures is committed into the Custody of Mr. Thomas Peterson and that he demand and receive the Same wherever they be and that the Said Mr. Thomas Peterson give an Account thereof to the next Vestry.

That Capt. Robert West[3] and Capt. David Henderson be and are hereby chosen Vestrymen in the Room of the Honorable Edward Hyde Esqr. our late Governor and Mr. John Walker deceased.

That Mr. Thomas Peterson and Mr. Thomas Lee do Sue Mr. Edward Moseley pursuant to a former Order of Vestry for the Money in his Hands, which was given for the purchase of Church plate.

Thomas Peterson, Thomas Lee,
William Duckenfield, John Bird,
Thomas Pollock, Thomas Leuten,
Leonard Loftin

[1] Not located.

[2] Not located.

[3] Robert West (1677-1743) in later years was an assemblyman and member of the council, and also held various lesser offices. *DNCB*.

1714

<*1713.*> At a Vestry met at the Church on the North Shore of the Sound in Chowan Precinct March the 2d 1713/4. Present The honorable Thoms. Pollock Esqr. President, William Duckenfield Esqr., Thomas Peterson, Thomas Luten, Thomas Lee, Leonard Loftin, Samuel Patchet.

And They having taken into Consideration the Letters from the Honorable Society[1] by the Honorable Colonell Nicholson together with one from his Honor the following Answers to the Said Letters were ordered.

To Honorable Society de propogandâ etc.
Sirs

We whose Names are here underwritten Vestrymen and Church Wardens of the precinct of Chowan in the County of Albemarle <(25)> <*Anno Domini 1713.*> in the Province of North Carolina, do for our Selves and on Behalf of the Rest of the Inhabitants of this Said Precinct in a most Gratefull Manner Return our hearty Thanks to the Honorable Society etc. for their great Care of our Soul's Health in Sending over Missionaries to preach the Word of God and Administer the Holy Sacraments among Us. We and the whole English America ought to bless and praise the Allmighty for having put it into the Hearts of so many Honorable and Great persons to think of their poor Country Folks whose Lot, it hath been to come into these Heathen Countries, Where We are in Danger of becoming like the Indians themselves, without a God in the World. We of this precinct with the Rest of the Goverment in particular have been for Some time happy in the pious Endeavours of divers of the Clergy Missionaries and others who have Set up the Worship of God according to the Church of England by Law established amongst Us, but by the poverty of the Country, Unsetledness and Opposition of Sectaries, We never Yet were able to make due provision for those of that holy Order, which hath We fear been the Occasion of their Short Stay with Us. None of them ever abode So long here as the Reverend Mr. Urmston hath done, Yet have not been So happy in him neither as he would have desired, by reason that for the most part there hath been no other Minister in these parts Since his Arrival; and Seeing the Confusions and Distractions of this Unhappy Colony were So great, the Opposers of the holy Church so numerous and their Endeavors to Subvert the Same indefatigable, he hath made the other precincts Sharers with Us in his Ministry. His great pains and unwearied Dilligence to keep together those of our Church hath had good Success and will undoubtedly be very acceptable to the Society. It were to be wished he had met with due Encouragement proportionable to the great Feteagues and hardships, which he hath Undergone, but fear he hath failed thereof. We of this precinct allowed him according to our first Act of Assembly in Favour of the Church of England (which was not obtained without hard Strugling) £30 per Annum for the first Year and half hoping the other precincts where he officiated would have done the like, We cannot Say we have fullfilled our promise As for the two Years last past he hath been prevailed with, and indeed Necessitated, not being able to travel any longer about the Country, to confine himself to this precinct, where his Residence hath constantly been. We have a large parish many poor Inhabitants and those Seated at a great Distance from each other, passages very Uncertain by Reason of a broad River which runs through the Heart of the parish near 100 Miles in length and in many places broad, and but one Sorry Church on the North Shore of the Sound never finished, no Ornaments belonging to a Church nor wherewith to buy any except the Bounty of the Honorable Colonell Nicholson Videlicet 10 pounds part of the £30 given by him, when Governor of Virginia to three parishes <(26)> of this County, which is not Yet expended for want of an Addition according to the Intention of the Donor Parsonage House and Glebe we have none nor a School the first Library of great Value Sent Us by the Direction of the Reverend Dr. Bray, thro' an Unhappy Inscription on the Back of the Books or Title page Videlicet Belonging to the parish of St. Thomas of pamplico, in the then rising but now miserable County of Bath, falsly Supposed to be the Seat of the Government was lodged there and by that means rendred Useless to the Clergy, for whose Service it was chiefly intended, and in what Condition We know not, We fear the worst by Reason of the late War. The Library Sent in by Mr. Gordon was all left with Mr. Wallace late Minister of Keketan in Virginia, Save Wilby's Annotations on the New Testament 2. Vol. Fol. and pearson on the Creed, which We have, the Said Mr. Wallace upon due Application refused to deliver the Books, without an Order from the Society or Mr. Gordon. There were missing Collection of Cannons, Beveridge on the Catechism, Bennet against the Quakers, Lucas of Happiness 2 Vol. 8vo. Eachards Ecclesiastical History fol. and now the Said Mr. Wallace is dead, we fear the like ill Fate may attend the rest: those Charity Books to the Value of £5 the generous Gift likewise of the Society have been Since Mr. Gordon's Departure disposed off as was intended. What relates to the other parishes within this Government, we presume will be laid before the Society by their respective Vestries, their Necessity We believe to be great, but being under the like unhappy Circumstances beg leave only to Supplicate for our Selves, and to pray the Honorable Society to continue or rather add to the Salary of Mr. Urmston to the End he may be ennabled to Stay with Us, and that they will out of their great Charity concurr with our Honest but weak Endeavours to establish a Church, Ministry and a School, with the allowance of 10 or £15 per Annum to a person whom We shall make Choice of to teach our Children in this precinct and we shall be bound ever to pray that God Allmighty may encrease their Store and Strengthen their Hands in the carrying on the great Work they have So piously Undertaken and may meet with happy Success in that their Glorious Design.

So prays Sirs, Your most obliged poor Countrymen of the Vestry aforesaid.

<(27)> To the Honorable Colonell Nicholson.
Honoured Sir

The Reverend Mr. Urmston having acquainted Us with your Honours good Intentions towards this poor Country, particularly Us of this parish, and the Continuance of Your Generosity to Usward. We humbly pray your Acceptance of Our unfeigned thanks for all your Favours, Hoping We have complied with the Orders of the Holy Society in the enclosed. We humbly beg your Honour would be pleased to concurr with our Request to the Society and promote the Interest of a poor Country which You seem to wish so well. Your presence here is very much desired, all honest Men and Friends of the Church are big with Expectation of the great Influence your good Endeavours may have over Us all, to confirm and make all the Members of our Church adhere more Zealously to the Interest thereof, Silence the Gainsayers and reduce the Authors of our late Confusions[2] to a due Obedience to all lawfull Authority in Church and State. These with all unfeigned and humble Respects are from Honoured Sir Your etc.

Upon Complaint from Mr. Urmston that the Sherriff Jno. Hardy had failed in the Collection of forty five pounds ordered to be paid to the Said Mr. Urmston December the 10th Anno 1711.

Ordered that the Said John Hardy do give an Account to the Church Wardens, who ordered him to Collect the Same of all he hath received and paid on that Account on or before the last of this Month.

Ordered that the present Church-Wardens pay James Bea[sley] for a Desk in the Church as Soon as it can be raised.

Ordered that Doctor Spruill be paid for the Cure of Eben. Aldridge his Claim of twelve Pounds by the present Church Wardens as Soon as money can be raised.

Ordered that Mr. Moseley be allowed forty Shillings for the Be[nefit] of the Said Eben. Aldridge for four Months by the present Church Wardens as Soon as Money can be raised.

That Mr. Edward Moseley's Request for an Allowance toward his Loss in the plank bought for the Use of the Church be referred to the Consideration of the Next Vestry.

Thos. Lee, Leonard Loftin, Thos. Peterson, Thos. Pollock, Wm. Duckenfield, Thos. Luten

---

[1]I.e., the Society for the Propagation of the Gospel in Foreign Parts.
[2]I.e., the Cary Rebellion.

1715

<(28)> <*Anno Domini 1714/15.*> At a Vestry met at the Church on the North Shore of the Sound in Chowan Janry. the 3d 1714/5.

It was then Ordered.

Imprimis that in the place of Mr. Thos. Peterson deceased the Honorable Charles Eden Esqr. Governor etc. be and is hereby chosen Vestry Man and in the Abscence of Mr. Thos. Lee Colonell Edward Moseley hereby is Chosen Vestryman.

Item upon Mr. David Henderson's declaring himself a Dissenter from the Church and that it is Contrary to his Conscience to act as a Vestryman He the Said David Henderson is hereby dismissed from being a Vestryman and in his place Mr. John Hardy be and is hereby chosen a Vestryman.

Item that at the Request of Mr. Edward Smithwick to be dismissed by Reason of his Age and Infirmity, He be and is hereby dismist from being a Vestryman and in his place Capt. Henry Bonner be and is hereby Chosen one of the Vestry.

Item that Mr. Hardy do attend and lay before the next Vestry his Account of the Collection made by him for the Use of the parish by Order of Mr. Thos. Peterson deceased and Mr. Thos. Lee the then Church Wardens.

Item that Colonell Moseley be allowed and paid by the present Church Wardens three pounds for and in Consideration of the Loss Sustained in plank, which he provided for the Use of the Church.

Item it is resolved by the Vestry now present that the next Assembly be petitioned by Colonell Moseley on behalf of the Vestry to divide this parish and make two parishes of it.

Item ordered that Capt. Nichl. Crisp be desired to demand of the Widow Peterson and all others who have any part or parcel of the Weights and Scales and Measures belonging to the Standard for the Use of this parish and keep the Same.

Item that the Church-Wardens pay to Thomas Luten Junior Ten Shillings for the Writing two Letters.

Ordered that the Church Wardens do Collect or Cause to be collected the Sum of two Shillings and Six pence of every Tythable Person in this precinct.

And that after the Comissioners for Receiving the other Debts of the precincts are paid, the Remainder be paid to the Reverend Mr. Jno. Urmston in part of the one hundred and ten pounds which is due to him for Officiating 'till last New Years Day.

<(29)> Ordered that Capt. Thomas West Robert West and Mr. Leonard Loftin be Church Wardens 'till next New Years Day.

Jno. Patchet, Samll. Patchet, Edwd. Smithwick, Wm. Duckenfield, Thomas Leuten, Jno. Blount, Robt. West, Edwd. Moseley, Henry Bonner

1717

Chowan Sc. At a Vestry held at the Chappel on the North Shore the 4th of May 1717. Present The Honorable Charles Eden Esqr. Governor etc. Edward Moseley, Nichl. Crisp, Thomas Luten, John Jordan, Henry Bonner, Samll. Patchet, of the Vestry.

Who qualified themselves according to an Act of Assembly in that Behalf made and provided.

Mr. James Beasley is received into the Vestry in the Room of Mr. James Farlow, who refuseth to Qualify himself as a Vestry Man.

Colonell Edward Moseley and Mr. James Beasley are Chosen Church Wardens.

It is agreed by this Vestry that So Soon as the Accts. of the former Collectors are made up, that the Vestry will then proceed to pay the proportionable part of Such Sums of Money As were due from the parish of the precinct of Chowan to the time of the Division of that parish into the Eastern parish and the South West parish. And that Mr. Hardy and the other Collectors be desired to lay before this Vestry the Account of their Severall Collections between this Time and the first Sunday in the Next Month.

Ordered that the Church Wardens do receive of Each Tythable person in this parish the Sum of five Shillings per pole being for the parish Taxes due last New Years Day. Out of which Sum they are ordered to pay to the Reverend Mr. John Urmston Missionary the Sum of fifty Pounds for his Officiating in this parish 'till last New Years Day.

<*Anno Domini 1717.*> The honorable the Governor moving that the Reverend Mr. John Urmston Missionary Should be inducted.

The Vestry did not allow thereof.

But it is ordered that the Said John Urmston be paid the Sum of fifty pounds on or before the first of Janry. next.

Provided the Said Mr. Urmston does give his Attendance and officiate every third Sunday at Some Convenient place near the Indian Town and the Remaining Sundays at the Chappell.

It is also ordered that each Tythable person in the parish do bring to the Church Wardens or either of them the Sum of five Shillings on or before the first of Janury. next being the Tax for the present Year.

At a Vestry held at the Chappel the 15th Day of Septembr. 1717. Present Nicholas Crisp, James Beasley, Thos. Luten, Samll. Patchet, Henry Bonner.

Capt. Frederick Jones and Mr. John Blount qualifyed themselves as Vestry-men.

Ordered that the Vestry meet this Day Sennight.

At a Vestry held at the Chappel the 22d Day of September 1717.

Mr. James Farlow qualifyed himself as a Vestry-man by taking and Subscribing the Several Oaths by law appointed and is taken into the Vestry in the Room of the Honorable the Governor who is removed to Bath County.

Mr. John Urmston having failed to receive the parish Tax due from Such of the Inhabitants as live near the Indian Town which he had Undertaken to do at Such Times as he was appointed to preach there.

It is ordered that the Church Wardens do cause the Collection to be compleated with all Expedition, imaginable and payment to be made the Said John Urmston according to Order.

<(31)> <*Anno Domini 1717.*> This Day Edward Moseley one of the Church Wardens laid before the Vestry a Letter from the Society for propogation of the Gospell in forreign parts dated June the 11th 1716 which the Said Edward Moseley declared he had received open from John Urmston.

It is ordered that the Church Wardens with Such other of the Vestry as can conveniently meet together do prepare an Answer thereto and that in the doing thereof they have regard to the Several Others passed in the Vestry of Chowan And that the honorable Society be informed of the State of Religion in these parts.

Fred. Jones, E. Moseley, Jno. Farlow, James Beaseley, Nichl. Crisp

1719

Chowan Sc. At a Vestry held at the House of the Honorable Fred. Jones Esqr. the 16th Day of August 1719. Present The honorable Fred. Jones Esqr., Edwd. Moseley, James Beaseley, Church Wardens, Nichl. Crisp, John Jordan, James Farlow.

Mr. Thomas Garret Senior is quallified as a Member of the Vestry by taking and Subscribing the Several Oaths by Law appointed.

Ordered that Thomas Garret Junior be appointed a Member of the Vestry in the Room of Mr. Thomas Bray. The Said Thomas Garret took and Subscribed the Several Oaths by Law appointed for his Qualification.

Robert Hicks Collector of the two five Shilling pole Taxes due the first Day of Janry. 1717 made Up his Accounts of the Same which are here incerted and it appearing that there is due to the parish the Sum of Eighty Nine pounds Excepting Such Insolvents as shall be returned by the Said Hicks.

It is ordered that the accounting for the Said Eighty Nine pounds be referred 'till the Reverend Mr. John Urmston can attend.

	£ *s*. *d*.
Commissions for receiving £100	3. 0. 0

Paid Thomas Luten his Claim	0.10. 0
Mr. Beasley for a reading Desk	0.10. 0
Mr. Moseley for allowed by a former Vestry	2. 0. 0
Mr. Moseley for Loss of plank	3. 0. 0
By 189 Tythables 1716/7	47. 5. 0
By 215 Tythables 1717/8	53.15. 0
	101
	12
	89.

	£ *s*. *d*
<(32)> <*Anno Domini 1719.*> Edward Wood for looking after Mary Gent and burying her	3. 0. 0

Edward Moseley and James Beasley Church Wardens having made up their Accounts and desiring to be discharged of their Office.

It is ordered that Mr. Nicholas Crisp and Mr. John Jordan be Church-Wardens in their Room And that they do collect five Shillings parish Tax due last Janury.

It is further ordered that for the Ease of the Church Wardens in their Collections the parish be divided into two Districts by Rockahock Creek and that Branch of it that runs by tattering Bridge.

Ordered that Robt. Hicks be allowed forty Shillings for his Attending as Clerk to the Vestry and that it be paid out of the Eighty Nine pounds.

Ordered that the Vestry meet at the Church this Day fortnight and that the Reverend Mr. John Urmston be desired to attend there.

Chowan Sc. At a Vestry held at the Chappel the 20th Day of August 1719. Present Nicholas Crisp, Jno. Jordan, Church Wardens, The honorable Fred. Jones Esqr., Colonell Edward Moseley, Major Thomas Leuten, John Blount, Thomas Garret Senior, James Farlow, Thomas Garret Junior, Capt. Henry Bonner, James Beazley.

John Sivers having maintained Elizabeth Muns for Eight Months past and has engaged to maintain her 'till new Years Day next.

Ordered that he be allowed and paid the Sum of Six pounds. It is further ordered that the Church Wardens do take Care to provide for the Said Elizabeth Muns necessary Apparel.

This Vestry viewing the Church Wardens Certificate of the Collection of the £20*s*. pole Tax upon the precinct of Chowan for paying the Sum of 45 pounds in the Year 1711, do find that of that Sum of 45 pounds the Money raised amounts to but £32.10*s*.0*d*. whereby there Remains unpaid to the Said Doctor Urmston the Sum of £12.10*s*. 0*d*. It is therefore agreed by this Vestry <(33)> <*Anno Domini 1719.*> that they will cease the proportionable part of the Same to be paid by the parish when the Rateable part of the hundred and ten pounds is levied by the parishes as the Same Stands due to the Said Doctor Urmston by a form in Order Dated the 3d Day of Janury. 1714/5.

It appearing to the Vestry that the Ballance in the late Church Wardens Hands amounts to no more than the Sum of £79.

It is ordered that the Same be paid to the Reverend Mr. John Urmston Minister in full of what is due to him from this parish to the first of Janry. 17[*faded*] with which he is content. And in Regard that the Said Minister hath not officiated in the parts near the Indian Town according to the former Order of the Vestry.

It is agreed that the Said Minister be paid the Sum of Eighty pounds for the two Years to be compleat and ended Next New Years Day, the Minister being content therewith and promising that for the Remainder of the time 'till New Years Day, he will Officiate every third Sunday at Some convenient place near the Indian Town.

It is ordered that the Church Wardens do agree with Some proper person to build a Chappel at the most convenient place for the People of the upper parts of the parish and that the Charge thereof be defrayed out of the Monies that Shall be collected for the last Year and this present Year So as the whole Charge of building the Said Chappel do not exceed thirty pounds out of the two Years Collections.

Mr. Paul Phillips having Served as a Reader near the Indian Town from the first of June 'till this present and offering to officiate 'till New Years Day coming.

It is ordered that he be paid for the Same after the Rate of Sixteen pounds per Annum.

It is ordered that the Church Wardens do with all Convenient Speed after the first Day of Janury. next Levy and collect the Sum of five Shillings per Pole upon all the Taxables in this parish to defray the Charges of this present Year.

1720

<(34)> No. East Parish of Chowan Sc. At a Vestry held at the Chappel the 18th Day of April 1720. Present Nicholas Crisp, John Jordan, Church Wardens, The honorable Fred. Jones Esqr., Major Thos. Luten, Capt. Henry Bonner, Capt. Samll. Patchet, Mr. James Farlow, Mr. Thos. Garret Senior, Mr. Thos. Garret Junior.

Ordered that Mr. Thomas Roundtree be a Vestry Man in the Room of Mr. James Beaseley deceased.

Ordered that the Clerk of the Vestry do keep a fair Book and Enter the Lists of Tythables Yearly.

Ordered that Mr. John Jordan do place Elisabeth Muns with Such a person as he Shall think proper and that She be allowed and paid as formerly Six pounds per Annum.

Ordered that Mr. Paul Phillips be continued Reader at the Indian Town upon the Same Allowance as he was formerly paid.

No. East parish of Chowan Sc. At a Vestry held at the Chappel the 10th Day of December 1720. Present Nicholas Crisp, John Jordan, Church Wardens, Fred. Jones Esqr., Capt. Henry Bonner, Capt. Samll. Patchet, Mr. James Farlow, Thomas Garret Junior.

Thomas Rountree took and Subscribed the Several Oaths for his Qualification as a member of this Vestry.

Mr. John Jordan Church Warden for the Upper District from Tottering Bridge and Upwards made up his Accounts Videlicet.

John Jordan
Dr.

	£ s. d.
211 Tythables at 5*s*. each is	52.15. 0
	54. 2.11
Due to Mr. Jordan	1. 7.11

<(35)> And is Dr. for 6 Tythables 2 Years.
Cr.
Per Contra

Paid Paul Phillips for reading at the Indian Town from 1st of June to the 1st of Janry. last	9. 6. 8
Paid Edwd. Wood for keeping Mary Gent	3. 0. 0
Paid John Sivers for keeping Elizabeth Muns	6. 0. 0
To Building the Chappel	30. 0. 0
Commissions at 3 per Cent	1.11. 0
Cloths to Elisabeth Muns	4. 5. 3
	54. 2.11

Robert Hicks Collector of the parish Dues in the lower part of the North Shore of Chowan made up his Accounts for 228 Tythables at 5 Shillings each £55.5*s*.0*d*. and paid the Same to the Reverend Doctor Urmston.

Ordered that the Sum of £24.15*s*.0.*d*. be paid to the Reverend Doctor Urmston out of the ensuing Years Collection.

Ordered that Mr. Jordan be paid the Ballance of his Account out of his Delinquents.

Ordered that Capt. Henry Bonner and Mr. James Farlow be appointed Church Wardens for this Year.

Ordered that Thomas Matthews be paid the Sum of 15 pounds for keeping etc. Elisa. Harris.

Ordered that the Church Wardens Sue William Branch for the Money paid by this Vestry for keeping Elisa. Harris She being wounded at the Said Branches House and in his Service.

Ordered that Thomas Yates be allowed £3.10*s*.0*d*. and Thomas Muns £2.10*s*.0*d*. for maintaining Elisa. Muns And that the Church Wardens do further provide for her as they See Necessary.

Ordered that Mathew Bryan be allowed £50*s*. for maintaining Wm. Jones.

Ordered that the Sum of £40 be paid to the Reverend Doctor Urmston for this present Year.

Ordered that the Church Wardens do levy and Collect the Sum of five Shillings on every Tythable person in this parish on or before the first of Janury. next being the Levy due for this present Year.

1722

No. East Parish of Chowan. At a Vestry held at the Chappel the 7th Day of May 1722.

Present Capt. Henry Bonner, James Farlow, Church Wardens, Colonell Edward

Moseley, Major Thos. Luten, Mr. Jno. Blount, Mr. Thos. Garret Senior, Mr. Thos. Garret Junior, Capt. Samll. Patchet, Mr. Jno. Jordan.

Ordered that Christopher Gale Esqr. be appointed a Member of the Vestry in the Room of Frederick Jones Esqr. deceased.

There appearing to be due to the Reverend Mr. Jno. Urmston the Sum of one hundred thirty Eight pounds five Shillings for the Time he has officiated in this parish including the one half of the Money that was due to the Said Mr. Urmston before the Division of the precinct into two parishes.

Ordered that the Church Wardens for the Year 1720 do upon making up their Accounts for the Same Year pay the Ballance in their Hands towards paying that Sum due to the Said Mr. Urmston.

It is also further Ordered that the Said Church Wardens do Collect of each Tythable in the parish the Sum of 7*s*.6*d*. per pole for the Year 1721 And Pay the Ballance of the Said Collection or payment to the Said Mr. Urmston as part of the Money due to him. And that what Shall appear to remain unpaid of the aforesaid £138.5*s*.0*d*. to the Said Mr. Urmston when the two payments are made shall be raised and Collected out of the parish Tax to be Collected for this present Year.

Ordered that for the more Speedy and easy payment of the aforesaid 7/6 Tax the Church Wardens or Such as shall be appointed by them do collect the Same by going from house to House in Regard that timely and convenient Notice can't well be given to the Inhabitants to bring in their Taxes and that there is no List of Tythables taken for which They be allowed on their Accounts ten per Cent.

Ordered that a Vestry be appointed at the Chappel on Sunday next the 13th of this Inst.

1723

<(37)> At a Vestry held at Edenton for the No. East Parish of Chowan the 9th Day of March 1722/3. Present Colonell Edward Moseley, Mr. Jno. Blount, Major Thos. Leuten, Capt. Nichl. Crisp, Capt. Samll. Patchet, Mr. Thos. Garret Senior, Mr. Thos. Garret Junior, Mr. Jno. Jordan.

Capt. Henry Bonner Church Warden for the Lower District made up the Accounts of his Collections as followeth. Videlicet

Dr.	£ *s*. *d*.
To 139 Tythables at 5 shillings for the Year 1720 deducting 10 per Cent for Commissions	31. 5. 6
To 173 Tythables at 7*s*./6*d*. for the Year 1721 deducting Commissions	58.17. 6
To Fines Nt. Proceeds	17.02. 0
	107. 5. 0
	29. 1.10
Ballance due	78. 3. 2

Cr.	
Paid Matthews for keeping Elisebeth Harris	15. 0. 0
To Matthew Bryan for burying etc. Wm. Jones	2.10. 0
To Thos. Yates for Widow Muns	3.17. 6
To Henry Bonner for clearing Church Lotts etc.	3. 0. 0
To Henry Bonner for burying Thomas Favour	2.10. 0
	26.17. 6
Paid Clerk's Fees for prosecuting the Suit against Branch	2. 4. 4
	29. 1.10

Which was all paid to Mr. Moseley in part of the Money due to the Reverend Doctor Urmston pursuant to a former Order of the Vestry.

Mr. James Farlow Church Warden for the Upper District his Accounts are thus Stated. Videlicet

Dr.	£ *s*. *d*.
To 135 Tythables at 5 shillings for the Year 1720 Nt. proceeds	30. 7. 6
To 114 Tythables at 7/6 for the Year 1721	38.10. 0
To Fines	1. 2. 6
	70 .0 .0
	49. 0. 6
Ballance Due is	20.10. 6
Cr.	
Paid Paul Phillips for 2 Years Reading	32. 0.
To Thomas Muns for maintaining of the Widow Muns and Cloathing her excepting the last 9 Months when discharged	13. 8.
To Copeland for Cleaning round the Chappel and one Years keeping it clean	1.10. 0
To John Champion in part for the Chappel Floor	1.10. 0
To Mr. Jordan	0.12. 6
	49. 6. 6

Which Said Ballance of £20 19*s*.6*d*. is also paid to Mr. Moseley in part of the Money due to Mr. Urmston So that there Remains now due to the Said Doctor Urmston £29. 2*s*. 4*d*.

There appearing to be less Tythables in Mr. Farlows List of Tythables for the Last Year than is in the first Years List.

Ordered that he do account for the Tythables uncollected in the last Years List.

There appearing to be due to Dr. Godfry Spruil the Sum of £12 for his Cure of an Indigent person.

Ordered that the Sum of 4 pounds be paid by this parish which is their proportionable part thereof.

There appearing to be due from the parish these Sums following Videlicet.

	£ shillings *d.*
To Doctor Urmston	29. 2. 4
To Doctor Newnam	10. 0. 0
To Mr. Jordan for Paul Philips	4. 0. 0
To Godfrey Spruil	4. 0. 0
To Thomas Muns	4.10. 0
To Robert Hicks	4.17. 6
	56. 9.10

Ordered that Mr. John Blount and Mr. Thos. Garret Junior be appointed Church Wardens and that they Levy and collect the Sum of three Shillings from every Tythable person in this parish for this present Year which ends the 25th of this Instant March.

Ordered that a Meeting of the Vestry be appointed on the first Day of May next.

<(39)> At a Vestry held at Edenton the first Day of May 1723. Present Thomas Newnam Missionary, Thos. Garret Church Warden, Colonell Chrs. Gale, Colonell Edward Moseley, Major Thomas Luten, Capt. Henry Bonner, Mr. James Farlow, Mr. Thomas Rountree.

The honorable Christopher Gale Esqr. paid to this Vestry forty Shillings the Fines of John Charlton and William Charlton Junior.

Also fifty Shillings for the Lapse of Lotts in Edenton deducting 5 per Ct. Commissions makes the Sum Total £4. 5*s*. 6*d*.

Capt. Henry Bonner paid in 10 shillings for the Fines of David Ambross and William Sadler. Also accounted for five pounds Edward Howcotts Fine four pounds of which was paid to John Harlow towards the Maintainance of Sarah Simpsons Bastard Child. The Sum in the whole deducting Commission at 5 per Cent was £1. 5*s*. 0*d*.

Robt. Hicks Collector of the parish Dues made up his Accounts for 370 Tythables at 3 shillings per pole deducting Commissions at 15 per Cent made the Sum of £46.3.6 which together with £5.10*s*.0*d*. paid in by Colonell Gale and Capt. Bonner made the whole to be £51.14*s*.0*d*. in the Hands of the Said Robt. Hicks. Which the Said Robert is ordered to pay According to the Orders of the last Vestry.

Ordered that the Reverend Mr. Newnam Missionary be paid the Sum of ten pounds out of the next Years Collection to make good the Sum of twenty pounds which was promised by the Vestry for his Officiating part of the last Year in this parish.

Ordered that the Sum of Sixty Pounds shall be paid to the Reverend Mr. Newnam out of the next Years Collections in Consideration that the Said Mr. Newnam officiate in this parish for one whole Year to Commence from this Day, That is to Say, twenty Sundays in the Said Year at Edenton and ten Sundays in the Same Year at the Chappel near the Indian Town the other Sundays in the Year being allowed the Said Missionary for his Attendances on other parts of the Government.

Ordered that Mr. Rountree be paid the Sum of five pounds for his Reading at the Chappel near the Indian Town.

<(40)> Mr. James Farlow by Reason of Age and Infirmity praying to be discharged from his Attendance as a Vestry Man.

Ordered that he be discharged.

Ordered that Adam Cockburn Esqr. be appointed a Member of the Vestry in the Room of Mr. James Farlow, who was present and took and Subscribed the Declaration according to Law.

Ordered that William Copeland be paid the Sum of twenty Shillings out of the next Years Collection for this last Years looking after the Chappel at the Indian Town.

At a Vestry held at Edenton the 18th Day of Novbr. 1723. Present Thomas Garret Junior Church Warden, The honorable Colonell Christr. Gale, Colonell Edward Moseley, Major Thomas Luten, Capt. Nichl. Crisp, Capt. Henry Bonner, Capt. Samll. Patchet, Mr. Thomas Rountree, Adam Cockburn Esqr.

Mr. Thomas Garret Senior by Reason of Age and Infirmity prays to be discharged from any further Attendance as a Vestryman.

Ordered that he be discharged and that Mr. William Badham be appointed a Member of the Vestry in the Room of Mr. Thomas Garret who took and Subscribed the Oaths and Declaration by Law appointed for his Qualification.

Colonell Christopher Gale paid into the Vestry the Sum of £3.18*s*.6*d*. which he received for Fines and Sales of Lotts.

The Reverend Mr. Newnam Missionary having officiated but one half of the Year and being departed this Life, the Vestry in Consideration of the Said Mr. Newnam's pious and good Behaviour during the Time of his Mission among Us and also being willing to contribute towards the Accommodation of his Widows intended Voiage to Great Britain.

It is Ordered that the whole Years Sallary be paid to his Widow notwithstanding his Decease.

Ordered that a Letter be prepared to be Sent to the Society for propagating the Gospel in Forreign Parts humbly requesting to Send another Missionary to this province.

Edenton in North Carolina
Novembr. the 18th 1723

Sir

This brings You the Melancholy News of your worthy Missionary Mr. Newnam's Death on whose Character and prudent Deportment We should think it our Duty to be herein very particular did not the Resolve of this Days Vestry (a Copy whereof is herein inclosed) Sufficiently Shew our Concern for so great a Loss; which occasions Us again to be petitioners to Your honourable Board, that You would Still continue Your Favours towards Us by filling that Vacancy with Some person of equall Meritt and unblamable Conversation, a thing to be wished for rather than expected. We heartily recommend his Widow to Your Consideration of her Slender Circumstances occasioned by the Endeavours he was making to Settle himself amongst Us (the Circumstances of our parish not admitting Us to do more than what We have done) So not Doubting but the Same Charitable Disposition which has heitherto occasioned Your particular Notice of Us, will So continue, that Religious Worship within this province may wholy owe it's Advance to your benign Influence. We have now not one Clergy Man in the whole province, tho' it consists of Eleven parishes which unhappy

State is humbly Submitted to the Consideration of the Honorable Society by Your most obliged and most obedient humble Servants.

1724

At a Vestry held at Edenton the 11th Day of June 1724. Present Mr. Thos. Garret Church Warden, Capt. Nichl. Crisp, Major Thos. Luten, Capt. Henry Bonner, Capt. Samll. Patchet, Mr. John Jordan, Mr. Thos. Rountree, Mr. Adam Cockburn.

Ordered that Mr. John Blount and Mr. Thomas Garret Church Wardens do levy and collect the Sum of five Shillings from every Tythable Person in this Parish for the 1723.

<(42)> The Choice of a Reader being debated and Mr. Robert Route presenting himself for that Office.

It is agreed that the Said Mr. Robert Route do Serve in that Office And that he be allowed the Sum of fifteen pounds per Annum his Year to begin from the first of this Instant.

Ordered that there be a Meeting of the Vestry on the last of September next.

At a Vestry held at Edenton the 31st Day of November 1724. Present Thos. Garret, Jno. Blount, Church Wardens, Colonell Edward Moseley, Major Thos. Luten, Major Henry Bonner, Mr. Adam Cockburn, Capt. Samll. Patchet, Mr. Wm. Badham.

Ordered that the Church Wardens do collect the Sum of 5 shillings from every Tythable person in this parish for the Year 1724.

Ordered that Mr. Robert Jeffrys be paid the Sum of fifteen pounds per Annum for his Officiating as a Reader at Edenton to commence from the first of July last.

Ordered that Mr. Thomas Rountree be paid the Sum of ten pounds per Annum for his Officiating as a Reader at the Chappel at the Indian Town to commence from the last Year he was allowed five pounds.

Ordered that the Widow Copeland be paid the Sum of 20 shillings per Annum for keeping Clean the Chappel and Ground belonging to it at the Indian Town.

Ordered that the Church Wardens desire the Commissioners for building the Court House etc. to draw out of the Hands of the Lords proprietors Receiver General the Sum of two hundred pounds Sterling and also the Sum of two hundred pounds out of the Hands of the publick Treasurer the Same being appropriated for the Building a Church at Edenton, And that the Commissioners be desired to proceed on the Same Building.

<(43)> Pursuant to the Act of Assembly entitled an Act for Settling the Titles and Boundaries of Lands.[1] The Vestry proceed to lay out this parish into Six Cantons or Districts as followeth. Videlicet.

The first being the Eastermost part of the parish from Drummond point to that part of Queen Ann's Creek whereon Hoskins's Bridge Stands inclusive for which Wm. Stuart and Wm. Haughton are appointed processioners.

The Second District from that Branch of the Creek to the other Branch whereon the Long Bridge commonly called Luten's Bridge inclusive for which Thomas Luten Junior and John Charlton are appointed processioners.

The third District from the last mentioned Creek to Indian Town Creek whereon Ballards Bridge Stands inclusive for which Francis Branch and William Holsey are appointed processioners.

The fourth District from the Said Indian Creek to Catharine Creek all the Lands inclusive for which John Parker and John Jordan Junior are appointed processioners.

The fifth District from Catharines Creek to Bennets Creek all the Lands inclusive for which Aaron Blanchard and Richd. Minshaw are appointed processioners.

The 6th all the Lands to the Northward of Bennets Creek for which John Collins and Jacob Oadham are appointed processioners.

Ordered that the Vestry be appointed to meet the third Tuesday in April next.

---

[1]This act, passed in 1723, provided that every three years the boundaries of the landholdings in each parish were to be "processioned," or paced off, and the boundary marks renewed. The vestry was directed to divide the parish into districts and appoint two processioners for each. Clark, *State Records*, XXIII, 104.

1725

At a Vestry held at Edenton the 18th Day of Augt. 1725. Present Thomas Garret Church Warden, Colonell Christopher Gale, Colonell Edward Moseley, Major Thomas Leuten, Capt. Nichl. Crisp, Capt. Samll. Paget, Major Henry Bonner, Mr. Wm. Badham.

The Honorable Sir Richard Everard Barronet is appointed a Member of this Vestry who was accordingly qualified.

<(44)> Also the Reverend Doctor John Blacknal who is received Minister Resident was Accordingly qualified.

The honorable Christopher Gale Esqr. paid in £3.15*s*.0*d*. he received for Fines.

Ordered that Major Thomas Leuten and Mr. Wm. Badham be appointed Church Wardens in the Room of the former Church Wardens and that they Settle and receive the Accounts from the late Church Wardens.

This Vestry being acquainted that the Society expects that the Sum of fifty pounds Sterling or the Value thereof Should be raised by the three parishes wherein the Reverend Mr. Blacknal Shall officiate.

It is ordered that he be paid for his Officiating in this parish the Ballance of the Church Wardens Accounts after the contingent Charges of the parish are deducted.

1726

At a Vestry held at Edenton the 15th Day of Janury. 1725/6. Present Major Thos. Luten, Mr. Wm. Badham, Ch. Wardens, Sir Richd. Everard Bart., Christr. Gale Esqr.,

Edwd. Moseley Esqr., Major Henry Bonner, Capt. Nichl. Crisp, Thos. Rountree, The Reverend Jno. Blacknal Missionary.

Colonell Christopher Gale paid in the Sum of three pounds which he received for Fines and the Sale of Lotts in Edenton.

Major Henry Bonner paid in the Sum of Seven pounds which he received for Fines.

Information being made to the Vestry that there is Several Sums of Money in the Hands of Major John Worley.

<(45)> Ordered that he do Account with the Church Wardens for Such Moneys as are due to this parish before the Division of the parish.

Information being made to the Vestry that there is Several Sums of Money in the Hands of Mr. William Charleton and Thos. Matthews due to this parish.

Ordered that they do Account with the Church Wardens for the Same.

Ordered that the Sum of five Shillings be levied and collected from every Tythable person in this parish for the Year 1725.

Capt. Nicholas Chrisp having paid the Sum of five pounds to Mr. Bailey for this parish.

Ordered that the Same be paid him by the Vestry.

At a Vestry held at Edenton for the No. East Parish of Chowan the 10th of July 1726. Present Major Thos. Luten, Mr. Wm. Badham, Ch. Wardens, The honorable Sir Richd. Everard Bart., Colonell Christr. Gale, Colonell Edwd. Moseley, Capt. Nichl. Crisp, Capt. Samll. Patchet, Major Henry Bonner.

Mr. Wm. Little[1] is appointed a Vestry Man in the Room of Mr. John Blount deceased who took and Subscribed the Oaths and Test by Law appointed for his Qualification.

There being a Vacancy of a Reader and Mr. Samuel Warner offering himself.

Ordered that he be appointed to read at Edenton and that he be allowed the Sum of Sixteen pounds per Annum.

Ordered that there be a Meeting of the Vestry on the Second Sunday in August Next and that the Collector of the parish Tax make up his Accounts and lay the Same before the Vestry.

---

[1]William Little (1692-1734), a native of Massachusetts and convert to Anglicanism, was a merchant and public official who served as attorney general and receiver general in the 1720s, and as chief justice of the colony from 1732 until his death. *DNCB.*

1727

<(46)> At a Vestry held at Edenton the 5th Day of Janury. 1726. Present Wm. Badham Church Warden, The honorable Sir Richd. Everard Bart., Colonell Edward Moseley, Colonell Christr. Gale, Capt. Nichl. Crisp, Major Henry Bonner, Mr. Wm. Little.

It being reported that Mr. Rountree who is a Member of this Vestry is turned Anabaptist.

Ordered that the Clerk of the Vestry make Enquiry and report thereof to the next Vestry and that Mr. Rountree be then desired to give his Attendance.

Ordered that the Sum of 2/6 be levied and collected from every Tythable person in this parish being the parish Tax for the Year 1726.

May the J D D[1]

At a Vestry held at Edenton the 23d Day of July 1727. Present Major Thos. Luten, Mr. Wm. Badham, Church Wardens, The honorable Sir Richd. Everard Bart., Colonell Christr. Gale, Major Henry Bonner, Mr. Wm. Little, Mr. Thos. Garret.

Thomas Hobbs an Indigent person and an Inhabitant of this parish praying to be relieved by this Vestry for his Maintainance.

Ordered that the Church Wardens enquire into the Circumstance of his Sons and report to the next Vestry if they are able to maintain him and that in the mean time the Said Thomas Hobbs be allowed by the Vestry fifteen Shillings per Month for Maintainance to be paid by the Church Wardens.

<(47)> Upon the petition of Wm. Weston praying to be allowed for maintaining one Francis Perigreen who lay Sick five Months who was delivered of two Children and then dyd with her Children.

Ordered that he be allowed and paid five pounds for the [*faded*] and Trouble of Burial.

Ordered that Mr. Thomas Rountree be allowed and paid Sixteen pounds per Annum for the Time he has read and Shall continue to Officiate in the Office of a Reader at the Chappel at the Indian.

Ordered that Mr. Samll. Warner be paid the Sum of Sixteen pounds for Officiating in the Office of a Reader at Edenton for the last Year and that he be continued in the Said Office.

Ordered that Mr. Edmond Gale[2] be appointed a Member of this Vestry in the Room of Mr. Nichl. Crisp deceased who was accordingly qualifyed.

Mr. Thomas Rountree moving to the Vestry by Colonell Gale and Mr. Garret to be excused from being a Member of this Vestry.

Ordered that he be excused and that Jno. Lovick Esqr. be appointed a Member of the Vestry in his Room.

---

[1]The meaning of this entry is unknown.

[2]Edmund Gale (d. 1738), a native of Yorkshire and brother of Christopher Gale, served in the assembly at various times from 1716, and was a justice of the General Court (1722-1726) and councillor (1725-1728, 1731-1734). *DNCB*.

1728

At a Vestry held at Edenton the 20th Day of Febry. 1727/8. Present Major Thos. Luten, Mr. Wm. Badham, Church Wardens, The honorable Sir Richd. Everard Bart., Colonell Chrr. Gale, Colonell Edwd. Moseley, Mr. Edmd. Gale.

Jno. Lovick Esqr. qualifyed himself a Member of this Vestry.

Colonell Christr. Gale paid to the Church Wardens forty five Shillings arising by the Sale of 5 Lotts in Edenton Commissions deducted.

<(48)> The Honorable Sir Richard Everard Barronet and Colonell Edward Moseley are appointed Church Wardens in the Room of Major Luten and Mr. Badham. Colonell Edward Moseley made a present to the parish of a Silver Chalice and Plate with his own Name Engraven thereon.

Ordered that the Former Church Wardens make up their Accts. in Easter Week next.

At a Vestry held at Edenton the 22d Day of April 1728. Present Mr. William Badham Church-Warden, The Honorable Sir Richd. Everard Bart., Colonell Edward Moseley, Colonell Christr. Gale, Jno. Lovick Esqr., Wm. Little Esqr., Major Henry Bonner, Capt. Samll. Paget.

Mr. Wm. Badham Church Warden delivered his Accounts and there is a Ballance due to the parish of £2.10*s*.0*d*. which is allowed him for the Maintainance and Care of Mary Johnson.

Robt. Hicks delivered his Accounts of the Collections of the parish Tax and there appeared in Ballance due to the parish £14.18*s*.6*d*. which is ordered to be paid to Mr. Warner towards his Sallary from July last.

Ordered that if the Inspectors of the parish Accts. desire to See the Accounts of the parish that the Clerk of the Vestry lay the Same before them and Suffer them to take Copy thereof in his presence if required.

Mr. Badham late Church Warden delivered the Chalice and plate to the Honorable the Governor now one of the Church Wardens.

The former Church Wardens having made up their Accounts are discharged. The Honorable the Governor and Colonell Edward Moseley now Church Wardens enter upon their Office.

<(49)> Mr. John Jordan praying to be excused from attending as a Member of this Vestry by Reason of Age and Infirmity.

Ordered that he be excused and that Mr. Thomas Leuten Junior be a Member of the Vestry in his Room.

The No. East parish of Chowan in No. Carolina to William Badham Church-Warden.

	£ shillings *d*.
Dr.	
<*1725.*> For Doctor's Fees for attending Alexander Goreham	1. 0. 0
<*Sept. 12th*> For Expences and Funeral Charges on the Said Goreham	5. 0. 0
<*Decbr. 24th*> Paid for Sweeping and adorning the Church	0. 5. 0
For Bread and Wine for the Sacrament	1. 0. 0
For Bread and Wine for the Sacrament the Easter following	1. 0. 0
<*1726.*> Pd. to Elijah News for Making Benches	1. 0. 0
<*Decbr. 24th*> Pd. for Sweeping and adorning the Church	0. 5. 0
<*1727.*> For Bills pd. to Abraham Hobbs for Relief	1. 0. 0
<*June the 10th Sept. 28th.*> To Wm. Pearce for keeping the Said Hobbs from the 20th of July last	2. 5. 0
<*Octobr. 12th. Decbr. the 24th.*> To Do. for keeping the Said	

Hobbs from the Said Day to the 22d of April 1728	6. 5. 0
For Sweeping and Adorning the Church	0. 5. 0
To Mary Tanner for cleaning the Same Sundry Times	0.10. 0
To an Abatement by the Vestry of Wm. Sadler it being allowed to his Widow	0.10. 0
Ballance due to the parish and is allowed to the Said Badham for maintainance and Care of Mary Johnson and Indigent person in the Said Parish	2.15. 0
	£23. 0. 0

Except Errors the 22d April 1728 per William Badham Church Warden.

Per Contra. Cr.

	£ *s*. *d*.
<*1725 Sept. the 13th.*> By a Fine Received from Jno. Norcomb for fighting	0.10. 0
By Do. from Bat. Scott for fighting and being drunk	0.15. 0
<*Octbr. the 18th.*> By Do. of Wm. Day for Sabbath-breaking	0.10. 0
<*Janry. 25th.*> By Do. of Geo. Allen for beating Mr. Marston	0.10. 0
<*March the 22d.*> By Do. of Mrs. Ruston for her Maid's Fornication	2.10. 0
<*1726.*> By Do. of Luke White the 9th Instant for Fornication	2.10. 0
<(50)> <*April the 4th.*> By Do. of Mr. Everard Rowden and Cittern for fighting	1.10. 0
<*May the 5th.*> By Do. of Wm. Sadler and Peter Young for fighting	1. 0. 0
<*Do. 9th.*> By Do. of Peter Osburn for Beating Jane Taylor	0.10. 0
<*Do. 14th.*> By Do. of Catharine Denevan for beating little Judith	0.10. 0
<*Do. 26th.*> By Do. of Bat. Scott for beating Thos. Betterly	0.10. 0
<*Janury. 6th.*> By Do. Luke White for Fornication.	2.10. 0
<*March the 11th.*> By Do. of Bat. Scott for beating Cath. Denevan	0.10. 0
<*1727*> <*May the 29th.*> By Do. of Judith Slade for Fornication	2.10. 0
<*June the 24th.*> By Do. of Mr. Everard for Beating Mrs. Lloyd	0.10. 0
<*Do. the 27th.*> By Do. of Jno. Symons for Fornication	2.10. 0
<*Novbr. the 1st.*> By Do. of Mr. Jones and Michael Ryan for fighting	1. 0. 0
By Colonell Gale received 45 shillings for Sale of Lotts in Edenton	2. 5. 0
	£23. 0. 0

<*1725*> The No. East parish of Chowan Precinct to Robt. Hicks Collector of the Parish Levys.

Dr.

	£ *s*. *d*.
To the Commissions for the Collecting £157 5*s*.11*d*.	22 . 2. 6
Paid Major Bonner	4. 0. 0
Paid Mr. Rountree	5. 0. 0
Paid Thos. Munns	10. 2. 0
For Copys of the Laws for the processioners	1.10. 0
Over paid to the parish by Mistake last Year	7.10. 0

Attending the Vestrys	3. 0. 0
Paid Mr. Spruil	4. 0. 0
Paid the Widow Copeland	2. 0. 0
Paid Jno. Champion	15. 0. 0
Paid Mr. Newnam	70. 0. 0
Paid Mr. Jeffrys Reader	16. 5. 0
	£160. 9. 6

Per Contra Cr.

By the Collection of 590 Tythables at 5 shillings each including the Years 1723 and 1724	147.10. 0
By received of Colonell Gale for Fines and Sale of Lotts in Edenton	3.15. 0
<(51)> By received of Major Bonner	7. 0. 0
By received of Colonell Gale	3. 0. 0
	£161. 5. 0
	160. 9. 6
Ballance due to the parish	£ .15. 6

Except Errors per Robt. Hicks Collector.

<*1726*> The No. East parish of Chowan precinct to Robt. Hicks Collector of the parish Levys.

Dr.

	£ *s*. *d*.
Paid Mr. Blacknall	54.10. 0
Paid Do. by Major Bonner	1. 0. 0
Paid Do. by Edward Standing	0.12. 6
Paid Do. by Mr. Rountree	0.10. 0
Paid Mr. Crisp	0. 5. 0
Paid Mr. Rountree for Reading	2.10. 0
Pd. Widow Copeland	2.10. 0
Pd. Reading at Indian Town Chappel 3 Months	4. 0. 0
Attending and Summoning Vestrys	3. 0. 0
To Commissions of £97.15*s*.6*d*	14.13. 3
	£87.15. 9

Per Contra Cr.

By Ballance of My last Accts. as above	0.15. 6
By the Collection of 391 Tythables at 5 Shillings Each for the Year 1725	97.15. 0
	£98.10. 6
	87.15. 9
Ballance due to the parish	£10.14. 9

Except Errors per Robt. Hicks Collector.

<(52)> <*1726*> The No. East parish of Chowan to Robt. Hicks Collector Dr.

	£ *s*. *d*.
To Commissions of £49.12*s*.6*d*	7. 9. 0
Pd. Mr. Warner for Reading to July last	16. 0. 0
Pd. Mr. Rountree for Reading to this 22d of April 1728	16. 0. 0
Pd. Wm. Weston	5. 0. 0
Pd. the Widow Copeland	1. 0. 0
	£45. 9. 0

Per Contra Cr.	
By Ballance of last Accounts	10.14. 9
By 397 Tythables at 2/6 each for the Year 1726	49.12. 6
	£60. 7. 3
	45. 9. 0
	£14.18. 3

Except Errors this 22d Day of April 1728.

Per Robt. Hicks Collector.

1729

At a Meeting of the Vestry for the No. East parish of Chowan at Edenton the 23d of Febry. 1728/9. Present E. Moseley Church Warden, Jno. Lovick Esqr., Colonell Chrs. Gale, Edmond Gale Esqr., Wm. Little Esqr., Major Henry Bonner, Capt. Samuel Patchet.

Ordered that the Sum of twelve pounds be paid unto Colonell Edwd. Moseley for Moneys by him Expended for the parish Service Videlicet

Five pounds to the Reverend Mr. Fountain.[1]

Five pounds to the Reverend Mr. Marsden.

For their Officiating at Edenton and forty Shillings pd. to the Reverend Mr. Marsdens Clerk who attended him.

<(53)> Also Sixteen pounds to Mr. Warner Reader for the present Year ending the 17th of July next 'till which Time he is to officiate for it.

Also to Mr. Wm. Williams £6.17*s*.6*d*. for Expences and attendance on Margaret Scott during her Sickness And for Coffin and Funeral Charges.

Also to the Reader of the Upper Chappel as usual.

Ordered that there be a parish Tax of 2/6 on Every Tythable person in the parish to be Collected by the person that Collects the publick Tax, if he will undertake it, at a Rate not exceeding 10 per Ct., and if the Collector of the publick Tax will not undertake the Collection, then the Church Wardens are to agree with Such person as they Shall think proper for which Collection Security is to be given to the Church Wardens.

And that Edmond Gale Esqr. and Mr. Thos. Luten be Church Wardens for the next ensuing Year.

Ordered that the Reader at Edenton be Clerk of the Vestry.

Ordered that all Moneys Fines etc. be brought to the Vestry by Easter next.

Then the Vestry adjourned untill Easter Monday Next.

E. Moseley, Church Warden, Chrs. Gale, Edmond Gale, Jno. Lovick, Henry Bonner, Wm. Little, Samuel Patchet

<(54)> At a Meeting of a Vestry for the No. East parish of Chowan at Edenton the 7th of April 1729. Present Edmd. Gale Esqr. Ch. Warden, Major Henry Bonner, Capt. Thos. Luten Ch. Warden, Christr. Gale Esqr., Jno. Lovick Esqr., Wm. Little Esqr., Mr. Wm. Badham.

Mr. Thomas Leuten Junior having been formerly chosen a Vestryman this Day appeared and qualifyed himself according to Law and took his place in the Vestry accordingly.

Edmond Gale Esqr. and Mr. Thomas Luten Junior having been named for Church-Wardens by the last Vestry are now elected and Chosen Church-Wardens for this parish for the Year ensuing.

Ordered that another Vestry meet on Whitson Monday next and that the Clerk of the Vestry give Notice of the Said Meeting to the late Church-Wardens that they may prepare to make up their Accounts to the Vestry and that in the mean while the Honorable the Governor be desired to deliver up the Chalice and plate to the Clerk of the Vestry to be delivered to either of the present Church-Wardens.

It is ordered that the present Church Wardens make Enquiry for the Standards for Weights and Measures that belong to the parish and make Report thereof to the next Vestry.

And that the Clerk Search the old Orders of the Vestry to See what Standards were bought for the Use of the parish, and return an Account thereof to the Next Vestry.

Mr. Hicks the former Clerk being ordered to transcribe the old Orders of the Vestry into a Bound Book and he failing therein It is ordered that the present Clerk do the Same.

Edmond Gale, Thos. Luten Junior, Ch. Wardens, Christr. Gale, Jno. Lovick, Wm. Little, Henry Bonner, Wm. Badham

<(55)> At a Meeting of a Vestry for the No. East parish of Chowan at Edenton the 2d Day of Novbr. 1729. Present Edmd. Gale Esqr., Mr. Thos. Leuten Junior, Ch. Wardens, Jno. Lovick Esqr., Chrs. Gale Esqr., Mr. Wm. Little, Mr. Wm. Badham.

Ordered that the Child be returned to Charles Wilkins that was left by Him at Mr. Thos. Luten's, and that the Said Charles appear the next Vestry.

Ordered that there be a Meeting of the Vestry the Sunday next ensuing.

Chowan Sc. At a Meeting of the Vestry for the No. East parish of Chowan at Edenton the 9th Day of Novbr. 1729. Present Edmond Gale, Capt. Thos. Luten, Church Wardens, Jno. Lovick Esqr., Colonell Christr. Gale, Mr. Wm. Badham, Major Henry Bonner, Mr. Wm. Little Esqr.

Ordered that there be a parish Tax of Two Shillings and Six pence on every Tythable person in the parish to be collected by the Church-Wardens with the Arrears due last Year.

Ordered that Charles Wilkins be paid for Expences and Funeral Charges on the Account of Ann Peter £9.5.0.

<(56)> Ordered that Edmond Gale Esqr. receive from Charles Wilkins all the Cloaths and other things belonging to Ann Peter deceased, he giving Bond to indemnifie the parish of the Said Ann Peter's Child and that he also receive Six pounds more Advance.

Major Henry Bonner paid into the Church Wardens Hand Six pounds which he received from Mr. Wm. Charlton Senior for Fines the Said Wm. Charlton had formerly received.

And the Said Money was then paid to Edmond Gale Esqr. being the Six pounds allowed on Account of his taking the Child aforementioned.

Wm. Little, Wm. Badham, Henry Bonner, Edmond Gale, Thos. Luten Junior, Jno. Lovick, Christr. Gale

---

[1]Rev. Peter Fontaine (1691-1757), a Huguenot refugee and rector of Westover Parish in Charles City County, Virginia, acted as chaplain to the party surveying the boundary between North Carolina and Virginia in 1728. Dubbed "Humdrum" by William Byrd in his diary of that expedition, Fontaine in March visited Edenton, where, according to Byrd, he "preach't in their Court house, there being no Place of Divine Worship in that Metropolis." He also "Christen'd 19 of their Children, & pillag'd them of some of their Cash." Boyd, ed., *William Byrd's Histories*, 101.

1731

At a meeting of the Vestry for the No. East Parish of Chowan Easter Munday 1731. Present Edmd. Gale Esqr., Mr. Thos. Luten, Church Wardens, John Lovick Esqr., Ed. Moseley Esqr., Major Hen. Bonner, Mr. Richd. Parker, Wm. Little Esqr.

Ordered that the tax this year be so much per Poll as with the Last years order will make in the Whole two Shillings and Six pence per Annum for the last and the Present year.

Order'd that Mr. Warner be paid twenty five Shillings the Ballance of Accts. due to him and that the said Acct. be enter'd in the Vestry book.

Order'd that the Parish Accts. be made up as Soon as may be and when the Same are ready to be laid before the Vestry, that the Clerk of the Vestry doe summons the Vestry to Meet.

Order'd that John Champion be paid for singling [*sic*] the Chappel.

Ed. Moseley, Jno. Lovick, Emd. Gale, Thos. Luten, Hen. Bonner, Richd. Parker, Wm. Little

Parish of Chowan held at Edenton July the [*faded*] 1731. Present Edmd. Gale Esqr., Mr. Thos. Luten, Church wardens, John Lovick Esqr., Ed. Moseley Esqr., William Little Esqr., Henry Bonner Esqr., Capt. Samuel Paggeth, Major Thos. Lowick, and Mr. Willi. Hinton.

Edmund Gale Esqr. and Mr. Thos. Luten former Church Wardens made up their Accts. of what money they had Received and Pay'd, which Accts. are as here followeth. Which are Ordered to be entered at [*faded*] in the Parish Book; the ballance Due to the Parish being 10 Shillings and 6 pence.

Ordered that John Arline be continued and Paid for Attending the Chappel

The following List of Weights and Measures belonging to the parish were given in by the Late Clerk, and Said to have been Lodged in the hands of Nicholas Crisp deceas'd videlicet as per list.

5 ½ Ct. one Qr. Do. one 14

One brass Yard

One Iron Do.

3 brass Weights Videlicet 4 lb. and 2 lb. etc.

One Pair of brass Scales.

One Wine Gallon pewter

One Pottle and one Quart Do.

One half Bushell.

One Peck.

Ordered that the Church Wardens do demand and Receive the Said Standard weights and Measures of the Executors of Nicholas Crisp.

Mr. Luten Church warden is allowed a demand on the Parish of 10 Shillings and 6 pence; which is Allowed and ballences the Acct. of Said former Church Wardens.

<(58)> Dr.

To Sundry payments made per Order viz. to Mr. Luten Church Warden		39.15. 0
To Mr. Gales Acct. Church Warden viz. to Mr. Jeffryes	12.00. 0	
To himself	25.00. 0	
To Ditto	2.00. 0	
To Ditto	18.10. 0	
To Ditto	20.10. 0	
	78.00. 0	78. 00. 0
To William Branch per Order		1.10. 0
To pd. to Mr. Claxton per Order		1.00.
To Mr. Warner etc.		1.05.
To Ditto		3.02.
To Mr. Thos. Rountree		5.09.
To Mr. Warner the Collections he Received		10.00.
To Colonell Moseley pd.		3.05.
To Commission on 170.12.6 at 15 per Ct.		25.12.
To Ballence Due to Church Wardens		168.18.
To Commission on Mr. Porters Levyes and Mrs. Veals		00.17
		169.15

	6.11
	176.07
Cr.	
By Levyes received for the year 1728 being 661 Tythables at 2*s*. 6*d*.	82.[*faded*]
By Levyes for the year 1729 being 704 at 2*s* /6 per head	88.[*faded*]
By Mr. Porter's Levyes	03.[*faded*]
By Mrs. Veals Ditto	02.[*faded*]
	176.[*faded*]
To Edmund Gale Esqr. and Mr. Thos. Luten Churchwardens.	
Dr.	
To Commission allowed Ednd. Haucot for Collecting £176.7.6	25.12
To money paid to Mr. Thos. Roundtree per Ed. Haucot	05.[*faded*]
To Mr. Warner in Mr. Haucots acct.	10.00.
To Ditto	03.02.
To Ditto	01.05.
To Collonel Moseley per Ditto	03.
To More Commissions allowed Mr. Haucot	00.17.
To Ditto's Acct. pd. Mr. Claxton 20*s*. and Wm. Branch 30*s*.	02.10.
To Jeffryes for keeping the Butcher	12.00.
To Mary Stone £2.5*s*.0*d*. Judith Slade 20*s*.	03.05.
To Mr. Wm. Arkill for Boarding Rachel Doldrige	12.15.6
To Wm. Branch 20*s*. per Thos. Luten 20*s*. Ditto per Ed. Gale	02.00.
To Rachell Doldrige	01.00.
To John Parker for burying Abraham Hobby	06.05.0
To Mr. Williams for Marget Scot	06.17.
To John Flowers for Rachel Doldrigde	02.15.
To boarding John Williams	01.00.
To Lining and Making pair Breeches for Ditto	00.17.6
To Carrying him to Tarripin-hill	00.05.0
To the Reverend Mr. Marsden for a Sarmon	05.00.0
To the Reverend Mr. Robinson[1] for a Sarmon	05.00. 6
To the Butcher Sundries	01.12.0
To Mr. Jeffryes More for John Williams	02.13.0
To Charles Wilkins per Order	02.05.0
To Bills paid Mr. Warner	25.15.0
To John Williams 5*s*.	00.05.
To Linnen and Shirt made for Ditto	01.07.
To Ditto Britches and Making	00.15.
To 3 ½ yards Dowless[2] for Ditto	01.09.
To the Reverend Mr. Jones[3] for a Sermon	05.00.
To Collonel Mosley what he Advanced for the Parish	08.15.
To ballance Due to the Parish	00.10.
	187.04.

<(60)> Cr.

	£ *s*. *d*.
By the Collections for the Years 1728 and 1729 per Mr. Ed. Haucot videlicet £176.7*s*.6*d*.	176. 7. 6
By Judith Slade fine	1. 5. 0
By Mary Jones fine	1. 5. 0
By William Cutts fine	2.10. 0
By Rebecca Hile	1. 5. 0
By bills of Christor. Gale Esqr. for Lots Sold	2.17. 6
By Anne Hill a fine	1. 5. 0
By Mr. Williams a fine	0.10. 0
	137.04. 0

Made up July 3d 1731.

Mr. Thos. Lowick and Mr. Richard Parker having been Chosen Church-Wardens to Succeed Mr. Gale and Mr. Luten when they made up their Accts., which they having now done the Said Church Wardens for the year Coming are now Confirmed, and for the future to Act and on Sittling Accts. of the Parish it Appears that the Parish Levy of 2*s*. and 6*d*. for the Year 1730 is Unpay'd, and also for the present Year the Levy of 2*s*. and 6*d*. to be Collected next Season by Law Appointed for Collections; but there being Money Due to Mr. Sagg for his Reading it is Order'd that the Church Wardens Impower Mr. Sagg to Collect in the Neighbourhood So much of the Year 1730 Due as will pay him, and give in the Acct., And Mr. Rountrees Acct. is Referred till the Collections Come to be made, and then what Shall Appear Due to him to be paid.

Order'd that Mr. Rountree Read One Sunday at the Chappell and another about Mr. Abraham Hills till further Order. And his Acct. is Settled and that their is due to him £42.11*s*.0*d*. for being Reader till Aprill the 22d 1731. And that the Church wardens Impower him to Collect in his Neighbourhood so much for the Year 1730 as to pay him.

Edmund Gale, Thos. Luten, Church Wardens, John Lowick, Wm. Little, Hen. Bonner, Thos. Lowick, Samll. Paggeth, Ed. Moseley, Wm. Hinton

[1]Not identified.

[2]Dowlas is a coarse linen, much used in the seventeenth century. *OED*.

[3]Probably Rev. Nicholas Jones, minister in Nansemond, Virginia.

1732

<(61)> Att a meeting of the Vestry for the North East Parish of Chowan on Easter Munday 1732. The following Persons were voted and allowed to be of the Vestry viz. Christopher Gale Esqr., Edward Moseley Esqr., Edmund Gale Esqr., William Little Esqr., Henry Bonner Esqr., Mr. Thos. Luten, Capt. Samuell Paggeth, Thos. Lovick Esqr., Mr. William Hinton, Mr. Isaac Hunter, George Martin Esqr., Mr. John Perry Senior.

Easter Monday 1732. Present of the Vestry Edward Moseley, Edmond Gale, William Little, Henry Bonner, Thomas Luten, Thomas Lovick, Samuel Paggith, George Martin.

The following Persons were Chosen Churchwardens for the year Ensuing. George Martin Esqr., Mr. William Hinton, Church Wardens.

It was agreed that a Parish tax be layed on all the tythables of this Parish of five Shillings per tythable to be levyed for this Current year to be paid to the Church wardens for the Use of the Parish.

The Reverend Mr. Granvile having performed Divine Service in this Parish begining one forthnight before Easter Sunday and the Vestry being willing to encourage him to Continue as well as that he be pay'd for the time past.

It is Ordered that he be paid from the said Time he began for One year the aforesaid Sum to be raised by the Parish Tax, now Lay'd excepting Sixteen pounds per Annum to be allowed to Mr. Rountree for Continuing as Reader and the Same to Mr. Sagg to Continue Reader and what other accidental Charges Shall arise in the Parish. And that the said Mr. Granvile be Allowed pro rato for the time he Officiates, if he Serves less then a year. And that he Officiate two Sundays out of five in the upper Parts of the Parish viz. one at the Chappell and [*faded*] Sunday in the five at or near Abraham Hills and the Remaining S[*faded*] at Edenton; And the Church wardens Shall get what Subscriptions further [*faded*] the Said Mr. Granvill they can procure for the encouraging him to Stay amongst us.

Ordered that the late Church wardens make up their Accounts with the Present Church wardens as Soon as they Can to be laid before the next Vestry.

1733

At a Vestry held at Edenton for the North East Parish of Chowan in the year 1733 March 26th. Present George Martyn, Mr. Hinton, Church Wardens, William Little Esqr., Edmd. Gale Esqr., Henry Bonner Esqr., Thomas Lovick Esqr., Mr. Thomas Luten, Capt. Samuel Padget, Mr. John Perry, Mr. Isaac Hunter.

Mr. Thomas Lovick former Church Warden now produced his Accounts which are ordered to be Entered by the Clerk and the Ballance of his Account was £29.6.10 ½ and the Account being Examined it appeared that Mr. Roundtree has been paid as Reader till April 1732 and Mr. Sagg till Febry. 1732 and that Mr. Roundtree collected of the Parish dues above Ballards bridge £105.7.0 and Mr. Sagg below Ballards Bridge in the whole the Sum of £59.9.0. The Ballance is ordered to be paid to the Succeeding Church Wardens and accordingly was paid down £29.2.6 to George Martyn Esqr. Church Warden.

Mrs. Williams Executrix to William Williams of Edenton deceased of Eight pounds five Shillings due from the Parish for Keeping Abraham Perkins and the same is allowed and Ordered to be paid by the Church Wardens.

Mr. Hinton Church Wardens Account.

<63> Dr.
Parish to Mr. Hinton

To money paid Videlicet	
To cleaning the Chappel 5 Year and Eight Months	£5.17. 6
For burying Anthony Mackeel	3.—.—
Table for the Parish	1.10.—
Plank for the Chapple	3.—.—
For burying Tro. Gulliver	6. 7. 6
To John Champion for burying a man	5.—.—
To Commissions on 116 at 15 per Cent	17.18.—
	42. 2.—
Due to Ballance	73.18.—
	116.—.—
	73.18.—
John Freeman for reading 6 Months till Lady day 1733	8.—.—
Due	65.18.—

Cr.

By money received by Sundry Collections Tythables above Ballards bridge	497
Insolvents	33
	464 at 5/£116.—.—

According the Sum of £65.18.— was paid to the Vestry and put into the Hands of Capt. Martyn and the Eight pounds due to Mr. Roundtree for the former Six months of this last Year he officiated, he is to be paid out of the Levyes due in 1730 which he undertook to collect.

John Freeman is continued Reader for the upper parts of the Parish for the year Ensuing on the same terms Mr. Roundtree officiated.

The Vestry Ordered a Levy to be raised in the Parish the year Ensuing of five Shillings per pole.

<64> Thomas Lovick to the North East Parish of Chowan Precinct

Dr.

For fines arising and becoming due to the said parish and were delivered into his hands by Joseph Jenoure Esqr.	5.—.—
For Ditto Recd. of Mr. Thomas Jones and Mr. Samuel Swann for fighting in Edenton	1.—.—
For Do. recd. of W. Jones for fighting as aforesaid.	1.—.—
For Do. received from I. Vanpelt for prophane swearing	—.15.—
For Parish Levys Collected by Mr. Sagg as by his List appears	56. 1. 6
For Parish Levys collected by Mr. Roundtree as by his several Lists will appear	105. 7.—
For more parish Levys recd. by Mr. Sagg as by his Account appears	3. 7. 6
	172.11.—

Cr.

By Cash paid for boarding of John Williams from the 20th Augo. 1731 till the 12th of April 1732 being 7 Months and 22 days at 30/per Month	11.12. 6
By Do. paid for 7 yds. of Ozinbrigs to make him two shirts also pd. for making and thread	3.—.—
Ap. 10, 1732, by ditto paid Thomas Roundtree pursuant to two Orders of Vestry as by Rect. will appear	58.11.—
<*pd. to Apl. 10, 1731*> By ditto paid to Mr. Sagg as by his Account appears	45.—.—
By Commissions for Collecting of 161.8.6 at 15 per Cent	24. 4. 6
Ballance due to the said parish	29. 6.10
By Commissions for receiving and Collecting the £3.7.6	—.10. 1
	172.11.—

Except Errors March the 14th 1732.
Per Thos. Lovick.

1734

<65> At a Meeting of the Vestry for Chowan Parish held at Edenton March 25, 1734. Present George Martyn, Willm. Hinton, Church Wardens, Edwd. Moseley, Henry Bonner, Saml. Padget, Thomas Luten, Jno. Perry, Isaac Hunter.

By the Account exhibited by Mr. Martyn, it appears that he hath accounted for 318 Tithables and by Mr. Hintons Account he hath collected 464 Tithables for the year 1732, both which Collections, togather with the Sum of £29.2.6 recd. from the former Church Warden Mr. Thomas Lovick appear to have been paid away as by the Accounts now exhibited more fully appear.

Ordered that the Minutes of the Late Vestry held March the 26, 1733 togather with several Accounts above specified, be Entered in the Vestry Book And that for the future all Proceedings and orders of Vestry as well as Accounts of the Church Wardens and Collectors be Entered in the Vestry Book as soon as may be.

Ordered that Mr. William Macky be paid the Sum of Eight pounds for the Burial of Francis Fletcher.

Ordered that Mr. Edwd. Howcot be paid the Sum of five pounds for sundry Expences concerning his care and Maintainance and other Charges about Christian Newton.

Moseley Vail is appointed Clerk of the Vestry.

E. Moseley, Henry Bonner, Isaac Hunter, T. Luten, Saml. Patchet, J. Perry, Geo. Martyn, Wm. Hinton.

The No. East Parish of Chowan.
Dr.

<*1732. Sepr.*> To pd. Jno. Ballard for boarding of Jno. Williams	£4.10.—

To pd. the Widow Williams by the Vestry's order	8. 5.—
<*Apl.*> To pd. Doctor Blackhall for sallavating[1] Eliz. Powers	25.—.—
To pd. Mr. Sagg for Attendance	1.—.—
To pd. for 11 yds. Ozenbrigs for Francis Jones	4. 2. 6
To pd. for washing Doctor Boyds Surplice	—.10.—
<*May*> To pd. Robt. Kingham for boarding Eliz. Powers	28. 8.—
To pd. Mary Stacy for boarding Eliz. Powers	20. 5.—
To pd. Doctor Granvile ½ the Nt. Levy for last Year	52.17.—
To pd. Robt. Kingham for Christian Newton	7.10.—
To pd. Doctor Boyd for Preaching	5.—.—
<*1733*> To pd. Doctor Blackhal in part for Christian Newton	10.—.—
To pd. Jno. Robinson part of his Account for F. Jones	5.14. 6
	173. 7.—

Per Contra
Cr.

By fines recd. for fighting in Town	£1.—.—
By Do. Recd. from Colonel Bonner and Mr. Badham	3.15.—
By Do. from Colonel Bonner	1. 5.—
By Do. from Vanpelt	3.15.—
By Do. from Mr. Badham for Mr. Gale	—.10.—
By 2 levys from Doctor Blackhal	—.10.—
By Bills received of Mr. Thomas Lovick	29. 2. 6
By Do. of Mr. Hinton	65.10.—
By Do. of Robt. Kingham the last year Levys	67.11. 6
	173. 7.—

Errors Excepted.
Geo. Martin Mar. 25th 1734.

<67> April the 15th 1734 being Easter Monday.

The Vestry and Parishioners having met proceeded to choose a New Vestry agreeable to Law and by pole chose Edward Moseley Henry Bonner Thomas Luten Jno. Montgomery George Alleyn Samuel Padget Wm. Hinton John Perry Isaac Hunter Jno. Sumner Thomas Walton Senior and William Luten to Serve as Vestrymen for the Ensuing year and these Parishioners chose Edmd. Porter, Henry Baker, Inspectors.

The Same day. Present Henry Bonner, Thos. Luten, Saml. Padget, Jno. Mongomery, Wm. Hinton, Isaac Hunter, Wm. Luten, Geo. Alleyn and choose George Alleyn and Isaac Hunter Church Wardens for the Ensueing year.

Ordered That the late Church Wardens do appear before the Vestry on the last Satturday in May next And account for the Parish money by them received the last year past.

I do declare that I do beleive there is not any transubstantiation in the Sacrament of the Lords Supper or in the Elements of Bread and Wine at or after the consecration thereof by any person whatsoever.

Jno. Montgomery, Henry Bonner, Thos. Luten, Wm. Luten, Isaac Hunter, Samll. Pagett, Geo. Alleyn, William Hinton

<68> At a Vestry held at the Court house in Edenton the 25th of May Anno Domini 1734. Present George Alleyn Isaac Huntor Ch. Wardens, John Montgomery Esqr., Colonel Henry Bonner, Capt. Saml. Padget, Mr. Thos. Luten, Mr. William Luten, Mr. Thomas Walton.

Ordered That John Parker be paid the Sum of Twenty five pounds out of the Arrears now due and of the present year for his keeping and looking after Francis Jones.

Ordered that John Robinson be paid the Sum of Twenty one pounds Tenn Shillings and Six pence ballance of his Accounts for Entertaining Francis Jones.

Ordered That Mr. James Trotter be paid the Sum of Eight pounds for sundry Charges in burying David Smith.

Ordered That Thomas Roundtree be paid the Sum of Seven pounds fifteen Shillings for maintaining of Francis Jones and that his Charge for reading be post poned till the next meeting.

Upon Information of Capt. Saml. Padget that the Chalice and plate is in the hands of Colonel Christopher Gale Ordered That it be Delivered to the Clerk.

Ordered That there be a parish Tax of Five Shillings for Every Tithable person in the parish to be collected by the Church Wardens.

Ordered That Colonel Henry Bonner and Mr. William Luten be impowered to receive the Taxes due for the Last Year and all Arrears and Accounts for the Same at their Meeting in July.

Ordered That the Vestry meet on the Third Thursday in July next.

John Montgomery, Henry Bonner, Saml. Padget, Thos. Walton, William Luten, Geo. Alleyn, Isaac Huntor

<69> At a Vesty held at Edenton for the N. East parish of Chowan the 19th day of July 1734. Present Doctor George Alleyn Mr. Isaac Huntor Church Wardens, Colonel Edward Moseley, Mr. John Montgomery, Colonel Henry Bonner, Mr. Thomas Luten, Mr. Thomas Walton, Mr. William Luten, Mr. William Hinton, Mr. Saml. Padget.

Pursuant to the Order of the Last Vestry Colonel Henry Bonner, produced an Account of his Rect. of 137 Tithables for the year 1733. Also he delivered into the Vestry a List of such Tithables who have not paid.

Mr. William Luten who produced his Account of the Rect. of 189 Tithables for the year 1733.

The aforegoing Lists of Colonel Henry Bonner and Mr. Wm. Luten being for the Lower part of the Parish from Ballards Bridge.

Mr. William Hinton who was to Account for the upper part of the parish from Ballards Bridge, not being ready to produce his Accounts by reason Mr. Richd. Kensky who was his Collector has failed to appear. It is Ordered That Mr. Hinton do cause his Accounts to be laid before the Vestry with all convenient Speed.

Colonel Bonner and Mr. Luten with their Accounts delivered into the Church Wardens the Sum of £51.5.6 being the Balance due from them.

Ordered That their Accounts be Entered in the Vestry Book.

Ordered That Moseley Vail as Clk. be paid the Sum of Five pounds for his Entring in the Vestry Book the former proceedings, and for his Attendance as Clerk including this day.
<(70)> Ordered that the Church Warden be allowed on their Account 45/ per Month for the care of Elisabeth Powers.

Ordered That a Vestry be held the third Thursday in Octr. next.

Geo. Alleyn, Isaac Hunter, Church Wardens, E. Moseley, J. Montgomery, Henry Bonner, Thos. Luten, Thos. Weston, Willm. Hinton

At a Vestry held the 17th day of October Anno Domini 1734 at the Court House in Edenton. Present Colonel Edwd. Moseley, Colonel Henry Bonner, Mr. S. Padget, Mr. Thos. Walton, Mr. Isaac Huntor, Mr. John Perry, Mr. Thos. Luten, Mr. W. Luten.

Mr. Hinton not attending this Vestry according to Orders of the last Vestry.. Ordered that he attend and make up his accounts the next Vestry.

It is agreed that Mr. Isaac Huntor be reader for the upper part of the parish and that he be paid for the time he officiates.

Henry Bonner, Wm. Luten, Isaac Huntor, T. Walton, T. Luten, E. Moseley, J. Perry, Saml. Padget

<(71)> Colonel Bonner 137, W. Luten Tithables at 5/	£81.10.
Commissions 15 per Cent	£12. 4. 6
pd. to James Trotter	8.—.—
to Henry Bonner for	3.—.—
to Ed. Moseley for Do.	5.—.—
to Geo. Alleyn Do.	2.—.—
pd. in at the Table to Dr. G. Alley Ch. Warden	51. 5. 6
	£81.10. 0

[1]*Salivation* was a medical treatment consisting of the stimulation of a copious flow of saliva through the administration of mercury. *OED.*

1735

<(72.)> At a Meeting of the Vestry for Chowan Parish at Edenton March the 29, 1735. Present, Isaac Hunter Ch. Warden, E. Moseley, Jno. Montgomery, Henry Bonner, Saml. Padget, Thos. Luten, and Wm. Luten.

Doctor George Alleyn, one of the Church Wardens being dead, and the time of Collecting the Parish dues being near expiring Mr. William Luten is appointed Church Warden to continue till Esther Monday in the year 1736.

Isaac Hunter, J. Montgomery, Henry Bonner, Thos. Luten, E. Moseley, Saml. Paget, W. Luten.

At a meeting of the Vestry for Chowan parish the 3d day of May Anno Domini 1735.
Present Mr. Isaac Huntor, Mr. William Luten Ch. Wardens, Colonel Henry Bonner, Mr. Sam. Padgett, Mr. Thomas Walton, Mr. William Hinton, Mr. J. Perry, Mr. Thos. Luten.

Ordered That Mr. John Champen be paid the Sum of Fifteen pounds for his finding Nails and Shingling the Indian Town Chappel formerly.

Mr. John Richards Executor of the Estate of Doctor George Alleyn late Church Warden not being ready to make up the said Alleyns account now; it is ordered that he attend the next Vestry and make it up.

Ordered That Mrs. Butler be paid the Sum of Six pounds fifteen Shillings for Three months board of Elizabeth Powers.

<(73)> Mr. William Hinton former Church Warden now produced his account and there appeared to be due to the parish the sum of Twenty Eight pounds Seventen Shillings and three pence. Ordered that he pay the said Sum to Mr. Huntor Present Church Warden.

Ordered That Mr. Charles Westbeere be paid the Sum of Thirty Shillings for part of the Expences in burying Mary Reed.

Ordered That John Parker be paid the Sum of Twenty Seven pounds five Shillings for the Board and maintainance of Francis Jones.

Ordered That Hannah Walton be paid the Sum of Eighteen pounds Tenn Shillings for maintainance of Will Weston.

Ordered that Robert Kingham be paid the Sum of Three pounds Seven Shillings and Six pence for the board of Eliza. Powers.

Ordered That Mr. James Potter be paid the Sum of Three pounds for makin a Coffen to bury a man that dyed on the parish.

Ordered That there be a parish tax of Five Shillings Levied on the Tithables of Five Shillings.

Ordered That Mr. William Luton and Mr. Isaac Huntor make up their Accounts the next Vestry.

Ordered That Moseley Vail be paid the Sum of Five pounds for acting as Clerk.

Isaac Huntor, Will. Luten, Thos. Luten, Saml. Padget, Jno. Perry, Henry Bonner, Thos. Walton, Will. Hinton

By order
Moseley Vail Clk.

<(74)> William Hinton Church Warden to the No. East parish.

Dr.

<*1733*> To 497 Tithables at 5/ per Tithable	124. 5. 0
To Mary Brodys fine for a Molatto Bastard	3.—.—
To Eliz. Reeds fine for Two Do.	6.—.—
To Olive Morgans fine for Fornication	1. 5.—

To Eliza. Jinns fine for Do.	1. 5.—
To Eliza. Daniels fine for Do.	1. 5.—
To Josiah Brodys fine for Do.	1. 5.—
	138. 5. 0
	109. 7. 9
The Ballance due to the parish is	£28.17. 3

Cr.	
Commissions at 5 per Cent	18.12. 9
pd. John Arline	1.10.—
pd. John Robinson for keeping Frans. Jones	21.10.—
pd. Jno. Freeman for reading	16.—.—
pd. John Champen	3.—.—
pd. Jno. White by order of John Parker	4.10.—
pd. Jno. Champen by order of Jno. Parker	20.10.—
pd. E. Howcott for Expences on Ch. Newton	5.—.—
pd. Thos. Roundtree for Expences on Frans. Jones	18.15.—
	109. 7. 9

1736

<(75)> April the 26th day 1736 Being Easter Monday.

The Vestrey and parishners having mett proceeded to Chuse a new Vestrey agreeable to Law and by pole Chose William Smith Esqr. John Montgomery Esqr. Robt. Forster Esqr. J. Hodgson Esqr.[1] Henry Bonner Thos. Luten Edmund Gale, Abraham Blackall Jos. Anderson Henry Baker John Sumner Samll. Padgett.

Duely quallifyed themselves as Vestrey Men by taking the Oathes By law directed.

And Chosed Abram. Blackall and Henry Baker Church Wardens for The Ensueing year.

And then the Vestrey by plurality of Votes Chose Henry Bonner Junior Clerk of the vestrey who was duely quallifyed by Taking the publick Oaths by law directed.

Itt is Ordered by the Vestrey that the Said Henry Bonner have And receive the Sum of Thirty pounds Current Money per annum As a Salary for his Service as Clerk of the Vestrey.

And the Church Wardens of this parish are Authorized And directed to pay the Said Sume of Thirty pounds per annum to the said Henry Out of the parish Levies which Shall by them be Collected from The Inhabitants of this parish.

Itt is Ordered that a Vestrey be held at Edenton this day fortnight and the late Church Wardens do make up their accounts and lay them before the Vestrey on that day.

The Church wardens are directed to pay Twenty Shillings per week for the Support of [*blank*] Thompson till the Next Meeting of the Vestrey.

Itt is Ordred that the Clerk of the Vestrey give Notice to Henry Baker and John Sumner Gentlemen, that they are Chosen Vestrey Men of this parish and that it is Expected by the Vestrey that they appear at Edenton this day fortnight and quallifie themselves for that office and the Said Baker quallify and accept of the Office of Church Warden.

Abraham Blackall Church Warden

<(76)> Chowan Sc. Att a Vestry held for the No. East Parish of Chowan Prcinct att Edenton the tenth day of May 1736. Present Mr. Abraham Blackall Ch. Warden, The Honorable Wm. Smith Esqr., John Montgomerey Esqr., John Hodgson Esqr., Joseph Anderson, Edmd. Gale, Henry Bonner, Thos. Luten, Robt. Forster.

The late Church Wardens Being Called on to Make up their Accounts and Mr. Hunter One of them appeard But was Not Ready Not having finished his Collection Whereupon a further day is given them to Monday the 24th day next At Which time they are Ordered to be ready with their accounts to be then Made up.

Ordred that the Clk. serve each of the Said Late Church wardens with a Copy of this Order.

Orderd that the Same Allowance be Continued to Mrs. Thompson till the Sitting of the Next Vestrey.

A letter from the Reverend Mr. Boyd being Read And Ordred that it Lie for a further Consideration at the Next Vestrey.

An Order from the Reverend Mr. Garzia for five pounds payable to Mr. Slaughter[2] for divine Service. Ordred that Mr. Wm. Luten the Late Church Warden pay the Same and Charge it in his account.

Ordred that to Contribute towards defraying the Expences of Building a Church at Edenton for Support of the poor and other Contingent Charges of the parish a taxx or levey Of twenty Shillings per pole be levied on Each Tythable in the parish for the Ensuing year.

<77> Chowan Precinct. At a Vestry Held at Edenton the 24th day of May 1736. Mr. Abraham Blackall Church Warding, John Montgomery Esqr., John Hodgson Esqr., Joseph Anderson, Edmund Gale, Thos. Luten, Henry Bonner.

The Late Church Wardens haveing produced their accounts According to the Order of the last Vestrey.

Ordred that Mr. Anderson and Mr. Luten suspect [*sic*] the Said Accounts and Make Report thereof at the Next Vestry And that the Said Late Church Wardens then Attend.

Ordred that the Vestry Meet on Tuesday the first day of June Next and that Such persons as have been Chosen and Not quallifyed have Notice then to Attend.

At a Vestry held at Edenton the first day of May 1736. <*Present.*> Mr. Abraham Blackall Church Warden, Wm. Smith Esqr., John Montgomery Esqr., John Hodgson Gent., Edmd. Gale Gent., Joseph Anderson, Henry Bonner, Tho. Luten, Samll. Padgett.

Mr. Anderson and Mr. Luten returned their Report of the late Church Wardens Accounts and Stands dated as follows.

<(78)> No. Carolina September the 20th 1735.

These are to Certifie that William Badham And Martha Mooney were Lawfully Married per me.

John Boyd

William Badham the son of Willm. Badham and Martha his wife was Born November 22, 1736.

William Badham Deceased Octobr. the 29, 1736.

Thos. Ecleston the Son of Thos. Ecleston was Born the 7th day Octobr. 1736.

Henry Bonner Clk. Vestry

May 1736. Mr. W. Luten late Church Warden to the No. East Parish.

Dr.	
For 462 tithables @ 5 *s.* per tithable due for the year 1734	£115.10. 0
For 384 tithables @ 5 *s.* per tithable due for the year 1735	96.—.—
For fines due to Said parrish	3.10.—
	215.—.—

Mr. Isaac Hunter to the above Said parish

Dr.	£
For 510 tithables @ 5 per tithable due for the year 1734	£127.10.—
For 505 tithables @ 5 per tithable for the year 1735	141. 5.—
For fines Due to the Said parish	8.—.—
For Money Received of W. Hinton late Church Warden	28.17.—
	520.12. 0
Cr.	403. 9. 3
The Ballance Due to the parrish is	£117. 2. 9

<(79)> By Credit

To the Commissions of 215 tithables @ 15 per Cent	£32. 5.—
To Robt. Fullington for Boarding Chrisr. Nuten	32.—.—
To Mary Butler for Boarding Eliz. Powers	6.15.—
To Caleb Calleway and W. Wathum for Buring Danll. Williams	8.—.—
To Robt. Kingham for boarding E. Powers	3. 7. 6
To James Potter for a Coffin	3.—.—
To Doctor Blackall for Sallevating C. Nuten	25.—.—
To Robt. Fullington for Boarding C. Nuten In her Salevation	10.—.—
To Robt. Kingham for Board of E. Powers	4.10.—
To Said Kingham for Boarding the Said Powers	8.—.—
To Moseley Vail for Being Clark of the Vestery	5.—.—
To Parson Garzia	5.—.—
To W. Mackey for board of Frans. Fletcher	8.—.—
To Parson Garzia five Pound	5.—.—
To the present Church Wardens	10.—.—
	165.17. 6

By Credit

To the Commissions of £305.12 @ 15 per Cent	45. 1.
To John Parker for Boarding F. Jones	21. 5.—
To Hanah Walton for Barding W. Weston	18.[*faded*]

To John Champin for Repairing the Chapil	15.[*faded*]
To Hanh. Walton for Boarding the Said Weston in a Sickness	7.[*faded*]
To Michll. Ward for Boarding the Said Weston 3 Months	6. [*faded*]
To Richd. Reiner for Boarding the Said Weston 2 Months and ½	5. [*faded*]
To 23 yds. of Ozinbrigs @ 6 per yd. for Said Jones, and Weston	6.[*faded*]
To 3 pair of Shoose @ 25 per pr. for Said Weston.	[*faded*].15.
To Making Two shirts and two pr. Britches for Do.	1. [*faded*]
To 3 ½ yds. kersey 1 dozen butens and 1 Sliphair and pr. Stocks for Jones	[*faded*]
To one Qt. of Brandey @ 8*s*. and one Course hatt @ 2*s*. 4 for said Weston	[*faded*]
To My Self boarding the Said Weston 5 Months and ½	13. [*faded*]
To My Reading In the Uper parts of the parish; @ £16 per year	32. [*faded*]
To John Arline for Looking after the Chapel 2 year	03.
To John Parker Boarding F. Jones 1 year and 8 days	[*faded*]
And Making him a Cearsey Coat	[*faded*]
To Money Paid to the presant Church Wardens	[*faded*]
Cr.	[*faded*]

<(80)> North Carolina ss. May the 29th 1736.

Wee the Subscribers persuant to an Order of the Vestry for the No. East parish of Chowan held at Edenton the 24 of This Instant May have duly Examined the Accounts of Wm. Luten and Isaac Hunter Late Church Wardens and find that Mr. Luten on the Ballance of his account is Indebted to the parish The Sum of £49.2.6 and that Mr. Hunter is the Sum of £81.15.3 Out of which ballance an article in the Said Hunters account for of W. Weston five Monthes and half the allowance of Which When ascartained by the Vestry to be [*illegible*]educed.

Jos. Anderson
Thos. Luten

Which Report being Read and approvd of It is ordered that an Allowance of £13.15.0 be Made unto Isaac Hunter for the boarding of W. Weston which reduces the ballance of his acct. to £68.0.3 and it is further ordered that the Said Wm. Luten and Isaac Hunter Late Church Wardens forthwith pay the Ballance of their Respective accounts to the presant Church Wardens.

Ordred that Francis Jones and W. Weston have an allowance of foarty pounds Each per anum for their maintainance for this Ensuing Year.

Ordred that the Constable do Summons Mr. Henry Baker and Mr. John Sumner to attend at a vestry to be held on Tuesday the 15 of June Next.

Mr. Wm. Luten late Church Warden Paid to Mr. A. Blackal presant Church Warden the Sum of twenty Nine pound five Shillings in part of the ballance of his account.

<(81)> At a Vestrey held for the No. East parish of Chowan the 19th of August 1736. Mr. A. Blackall Church Warden, W. Smith Esqr., J. Montgomery Esqr., J. Hodgson Esqr., J. Anderson Gent., E. Gale Gent., H. Bonner [*illegible*], Thos. Luten Gent.

Ordred that Mr. Edmund Gale and Henry Bonner Examine and Settle the Account of Doctor George Alleyn formerly Church Warding With John Richards Executor to the Said Alleyn and Make their Report at the Next Vestrey.

Ordred that Walter Droghen be Allowed reasonable and Nessessary Charges in Cloathing W. Weston for the Ensuing Time.

Ordred that the Church Wardens do demand and Receive of Mr. W. Badham and Mrs. Penelope Little Executrix of W. Little Esqr. Deceased the Several and Respective Sums Lodged in him the Said W. Badhams hands as also Mr. Little Deceased Towards Building a Church at Edenton and that Upon Refusal of Nonpayment of the Same Respectively They the said Church Wardens Commence Suit against them the Said Mr. Badham and Mrs. Little or Eyther of Them that the Same May be applyed to the Use that the Same was Intended.

[1]John Hodgson (ca. 1705-1747) was attorney general of the colony from 1734 to 1741, and was elected to the assembly at various times from 1735, serving as speaker 1739-1740. He was also provincial treasurer of the northern district from 1740 until his death. *DNCB*.

[2]The ambiguous wording suggests that "Mr. Slaughter" conducted the service, but it is more likely that Rev. John Garzia did this and ordered his payment to be given to Slaughter. One Michael Slaughter was an Edenton tailor and keeper of the jail there at about this time. *See* Cain, *Records of the Executive Council, 1664-1734*, 319-320.

1737

<(82)> At a Vestry held for the No. East Parish of Chowan the 11 day of April 1737.

Mr. Abraham Blackall Church Warden, W. Smith Esqr., J. Montgomery Esqr., Jo. Hodgson Esqr., Jos. Anderson Gentleman, Edmd. Gale Gent., Henry Bonner, Thos. Luten.

Ordred that Mr. John Sumner be Summonsed to meet At Edenton to quallify As a Vestry Man.

It is Certifyed that Robt. Forster Esqr. Vestry man of this Parrish Is Departed this goverment. And that Mr. Isaac Hunter be quallifyed As Vestry Man In his Stead.

It being Moved by Mr. A. Blackall Church Warden that an Order passed Last Vestry Impowering the Church Wardens to Call in Such Sums of Money as is Now Due to this parish Towards Building a Church at Edenton and the Said Church Wardens Setting forth the difficulty of getting a full Vestry when Need Requirs It is thereupon Ordered that Mr. Edmund Gale be a Commissioner to Receive and Call in the Said Money he giving good and Sufficient Security to the Church Wardens And their Successors for the Same to and for the Use of this Parrish And further that the said Commissioner be Impowered to Disburse from time to time Such Part of the Said Money as is Nessessary towards Building the Said Church and that the Said Commissioner Account with the Church warden or wardens for the time being for Such Disbursements As Aforesaid when Ever thereto Required.

Ordred that Mr. Isaac Hunter Pay to John Parker forty Pounds in part of the Ballance of his Account for the Maintainance of Francis Jones.

Ordred that the Six Pounds being the Ressidue of Mr. Hunters Account be paid to Walter Droughen in part for the Maintainance of Will Weston.

<(83)> At a Meeting of the Vestry held for the No. East Parish of Chowan the 27 day April [*torn*]. Mr. A. Blackall, Mr. Henry Baker Church Wardens, W. Smith Esqr., J. Hodgson Esqr., Mr. Samll. Padgett, Mr. Isaac Hunter, Mr. Henry Bonner.

Ordred that Towards defraying the Expences of a Church at Edenton and Repairing the Indian Town Chappell and other Continget Charges of the parrish a Tax or Levey of Ten Shillings per pole be leveyed On Each Tithable of the parish for the Ensuing Year.

Ordred that Henr. Bonner Continue Clerk of the Vestry for the Same lowance for this Ensuing year.

Ordred that Ten persent be allowed for Collecting the said levey.

Henry Baker Church Warden

<(84)> At a Meeting of the Vestry held for the No. East Parish of Chowan the 12 of August 1737. Mr. Abraham Blackall Church Warden, W. Smith Esqr., J. Hodgson Esqr., J. Montgomery Esqr., Jos. Anderson Gent., Edmd. Gale Gent., Henry Bonner Gent.

Ordred that the money Arrising from the Parish Leveys the readers Salleryes Money Nessessaryes for the Support of the poor and Other Incident Charges Occruing deducted be paid into the Hands of Mr. Jno. Hodgson to be by him Aplyed to the building of the Parish Church at Edenton and the Church Wardens are hereby Ordred to pay the Same Into his hands for that Purpose.

1738

Easter Monday April 3d 1738.

The freeman of The parish of Chowan Mett at The Court house In Edenton and There Did Elect for Vestrey men Videlicet Richd. Parker, Isaac Hunter, Robt. Hunter, John Alston, Thos. Luten, John Sumner, Willm. Arkill, Edwd. Hare, Charles King, Jacob Butler, John Blunt, Will. Spight.

The Same Day the Freemen Did Chuse Will Battle and Thos. Pearce Inspecters.

To [*faded*] Continued Clerk [by] the [*faded*]

<(85)> And On The 17th Day of Apreill 1738 Mett at the Court House in Edenton The Said Mr. Richd. Parker, Mr. Robet. Henter, Colonell John Aulstone, Capt. John Sumner, Mr. Edwd. Hare, Mr. William Spight, Mr. Isaac Hunter, Mr. John Blount, Mr. Thos. Luten, Mr. Willm. Arkill, Mr. Jacob Butler.

They being Qalified by Taking the Publick Oaths Do appoint and Chuse Mr. John Blount and Capt. John Sumner to be Ch. Wardens for this Year.

It is this Day Ordered that the Late Ch. Wardens Doctor Abraham Blackhall and Capt. Henry Baker do lay their accounts before the Vestry at their Next meeting Which is by appointmen to be Next at the Court house in Edenton on the 12th day of may Next.

Ordered That Mr. John Blount Ch. Warden Demand of Mr. Heny. Bonner The Vestry Book and all papers Relaiting to The parish affaires Which is in his possession to be had at the Next Vestry.

At a Vestry Held for the parish of Chowan at the Court house In Edenton the 12th day of May 1738. Present Mr. John Blount, Capt. John Sumner, Ch. Wardens, Mr. Richd. Parker, Mr. Isaac Hunter, Colonell John Aulston, Mr. Thos. Luten, Mr. Edward Hare, Mr. William Spight, Mr. Robet. Hunter, Mr. Willm. Aakell, Mr. Jacob Butler.

Mr. Charls King this day Qalified as a Vestry man and took his place accordingly.

Ordered that for and towards the Defraying all Neasessary Charges and Expenses of this parish a tax or Leavey of ten Shillings per pole Be Leavied on Each Tithable of the parish for the Ensuing Year.

<(86)> Doctor Abrm. Blackhall one of the former Ch. Wardens prodused his accounts to this Vestry and it is Ordered that Mr. John Blount Capt. John Sumner Mr. Jacob Butler and Mr. Richd. Parker Inspect and Settle the Said accounts and make report of the Same to the Next Vestry.

Ordered that the Ch. Wardens be allowed on their accounts fifty Shillings per Mounth for the Support of Elizah. Thompson a pore Wooman, till the Next Vestry.

Ordered that the readers Continu till the Next Vestry.

Capt. Henry Baker Late Ch. Warden haveing failed to Lay his accounts before this Vestry pursuant to an Order of the Last Vestry It is this day Ordered that the Said Henry Baker make up his accounts and Lay them before the Vestry at their Next Meeting.

By Consent of the Whole Vestry John Luten Is appointed Their Clark. It is Orered that the Ch. Wardens pay him ten pounds Currant Money for this Year for his Servises as Clark of the Vestry.

Ordered that there be a Vestry held at the Indian town Chappell on the first Saterday in July Next.

John Blount, John Sumner, Ch. Wardens Wm. Arkill, Wm. Spight, Edwd. Hair, Richd. Parker, Charles King, John Aulston, Isaac Hunter, Robet. Hunter, Thos. Luten, Jacob Butler

Att a Vestrey held for the Parish of Chowan at the Indian Town Chappell on the first day of July 1738. Present Colonell John Alstone, Mr. Isaac Huntor, Mr. Robt. Huntor, Mr. Thos. Luton, Mr. Jacob Butler, Mr. Willm. Arkill, Mr. Willm. Speight, Mr. Edwd. hair, Mr. Richd. Parker, Mr. John Blunt, John Sumner, Church Wardens.

Persuant to an order of Last Vestrey Capt. Henry Baker Late Ch. wardin Laid his accountts before this Vestrey and on Examination there appeairs to be dew to this parish £128.3*s*.3*d*. He then paid £24 to Jno. Sumner which Reduceth the Ballance due to the Parish to 104.3.3 which he is ordred to pay to the present Church wardens.

Ordred that Eliza. Tompsons allowance of fifty Shillings per month be Continued tell next vestrey. Ordred that Willm. Luton pay to Mr. Jno. Blunt Present Church warden his Ballance of acountts due to Mr. Abraham Blackall Late Church warden.

Ordered that Willm. Walton be allowed for Keeping Willm. Weston and Fra. Joanss [fo]rty pounds per annum Each or in perportion per month.

Ordred that Jno. Luton Receive of Mr. Edmd. Gale the Chalis and plate which belongs to this Parish and produce it to the [*torn*].

<(87)> <*1738*> [It] was ordered that Mr. John Blunt and John [*torn*] Inspect and Settle the accountts of Abra. Blackale one of [*torn*] Church wardens and [*torn*] Reporte thereof to the next vestrey and they do Report that they Cannot Settle the said accountts for [*torn*] the said Church Warden hath Given in but part of the Lists of Tythables, on Reading their Report it is ordred that the said Blackale Doe appeair before John Blunt and Thos. Luton at the Court hows in Edenton on the 15th day of this Instant July and their make up his accountts According to the Severall Lists of the Tythables Between Ballards Bredge and yawpim Rever which are for the years 1736 and 1737 and they to make Report of the Same to the next vestrey.

Ordred that Robt. Rodgers be payd five pounds Current money for Looking after Eliza. Hart one month in her Sickness and Decently Buriing her Corps.

Mr. Edmond Gale being by an order of a former vestrey appoynted a Commissioner to Receive and Call in Severall Sums of money that was Dew towards Building a Church at Edenton and by the Same order the said Commissioner is obledged to accoumpt with the Church wardens for the time Being for the Same it is ordred that the present Ch. warden or Ch. wardens Call upon the Said Commissioner to Render to him or them an account of all Sums of money Recd. by him and how he hath applied the Same.

Ordred that the Readers Continue untill the next vestrey.

Ordred that the Vestrey meet the 22d day of this Instant July at the Indian Town Chappell.

At a vestrey held for the parrish of Chowan at the Indian Town Chappell the 22d of July 1738 present John Alston, Isaac Huntor, Robt. Huntor, Thos. Luton, Richd. Parker, Edwd. Hair, Charles King, John Blunt Church Warden, John Sumner Church Warden.

Persuant to an Order of a vestrey held the first day of July 1738 appoynting us the Subscribers to inspect and Settle the accountts of Doctor Abra. Blackall Late Ch. warden and wee have Carefully Examoned the Said accountts and find that their is due to the Parish acording to the Severall Lists of Tythables for the years 1736 and 1737 Videlicet for 496 Tythables for the year 1736 at 20*s*. per Tythable is £496 and for 496 Tythables in the year 1737 at [*torn*] per Tythable is £248 which is in all £744.

Dr.

By Cash Recd. of Several persons as per his accountt	80.10.
	824.10.
	223. 4.
	£601.06.0

The Ballance which is Dew to the Parish £601.6*s*.0*d*

Given under our hands the 22d day of June 1738

Per Credit

By the Commissions 744 at [*torn*]	74. 8.
By Cash pd. the Parish	148.16.
	£223. 4.

John Williams proposed to this vestrey to take and Keep of the Parish a Child Born of the Body of one Mary Vann Single woman of this County and Parish (She being Dead) for the Consideration of the Sum of fifteen pounds paid him by the parish and have the Child bound to him till it Cums of age. It is Considered and ordred that the Ch. wardens pay the Said Williams fifteen pounds and bind the said Child to him according to the Direction of the Laws in Such Cases made and provided.

Ordred that the Church wardens Collect the Parish Leveys for this Present year and that they be allowed ten per Ct. for the Same.

Ordred that the Late Ch. wardens Abra. Blackall and Hen. Baker pay to the Parish forty pounds or Deliver to the present Ch. wardens a mullatter boy by them pretended to be bound to one Sarah Readeng.

Ordred that the present Church wardens Receive and Collect all the moneys now due to the parrish.

Ordred that all the moneys that is properly Parish moneys after the Past Debts that is now Dew is payd Except the Levey for this present year be payd into the hands of Thos. Luton to be by him applyed towards Compleating a Church now begun at Edenton he giveing Security to the Ch. wardens in the behalfe of the Parish to Render to the vestrey an accountt thereof when Required.

Ordred that Robt. Fullerton be payd fifty nine pounds two Shillings and Six pence for nursing and boarding Christian Nuton from the 12d of febuary 1736 to the 22. of July 1738.

Ordred that Mrs. Mary freeman be payd Eighteen pounds for Keeping Margrett Rodgerson 9 Months.

Ordred that Willm. Hews be payd £20 for Keeping Margrett Rodgerson 12 months.

Ordred that the former Readers be Continued.

Ordred that Eliza. Thompsons allowance of fifty Shillings per month be Continued till next Vestrey.

1739

At A Vestrey Held on Easter Munday Aprill The 23, 1739 at Mary Freemans Hows.

Present John Alstone, Jacob Butler, Isaac Huntor, William Arkeele, William Speight, Robert Huntor, John Blunt Church Warden, Jno. Sumner Church Warden.

Ordered That the Church wardens pay unto William Walton Seventy four pounds fifteen Shillings for Keeping Wm. Wesson and Francis Joanes untell the 10th day of Aprill 1739.

Ordered That the Church wardens pay unto William Skinner fifteen pounds for Reading at three Several places untell This Day Being one year.

Ordred that the Church wardens pay unto Mary Freeman Twelve pounds for Keeping John foard a poor man from the 20th day of January to the 20th of Aprill 1739.

Ordred that the Church Wardens pay unto Mr. William Arkeele five pounds for Burring of Mr. Wicks.

Ordred John Sumner and Thomas Luton Serve as Church wardens for this present year 1739.

Ordred that Colonell John Alston take Joyce Daughter of Mary Braddy and Keep her untill the next vestrey to be held for this parrish and to Return her to the Said vestrey their to be Dealt with according to Law.

Ordred that the vestrey Meet at Mrs. Mary Freemans Hows The first day of June Next.

<(89)> At a Vestrey Held at the hows of Mary Freeman the first day of June 1739. Present John Alstone, Jacob Butler, William Arkeel, William Speight, Robert Huntor, Isaac Huntor, Edward Hare, Charles King, John Sumner Ch. Warden.

Ordred That the Church wardens Take the Scailes waits and Measures Belonging to this Parrish into their Care and Keep the Same untill further orders.

Ordred that Capt. Thos. Garrett Take Margrett Rodgerson and Keep her at the Rate of Twenty pounds per year according to a greement.

Ordred that the Church wardens pay unto Capt. Thos. Garrett Twenty Eight pounds for Keeping Margrett Rodgerson and makeing two Shifts one Coat and Jackett, untill the first day of June 1739.

Ordred that the Church wardens pay unto Mary Freeman fifty Shillings for Keeping and Looking after John Foard a poor man and makeing Cloathes for him untill the first day of June 1739.

Ordred that the Church wardens pay unto Elizabeth Tomson forty Shillings per month from the first Day of June 1739 untill further Orders.

Ordred that Benjamin Talburt and William Skinner Continue Reading Devine Service at the Rate of fifteen pounds per year according to former orders.

Ordred that the Church wardens pay unto Mary Freeman five pounds for Charges of the Vestrey at her hows.

1740

<(90)> On Easter Munday April the 7th Day 1740.

The Freeman of Chowan County Did Meet at the Court Hows and Chuse Benjamin Talbot as Clark for Takeing the pole for vestrey men and then and their did Elect and Chuse for Vestrey men the following persons Videlicet John Blunt, John Sumner, Demsey Sumner, Richard Parker, Thomas Walton, John Benbuary, Jacob Butler, William Skinner, Isaac Huntor, William Speight, Edwd. Hare, Richard Bond.

And mett on the 18th day of Aprill 1740 at the Court Hows in Edenton the Said John Blunt, John Sumner, Demsey Sumner, Richard Parker, Thomas Walton, John Benbuary, Jacob Butler, William Skinner, Isaac Huntor, William Speight, Edward Hare.

They Being Quallified by Takeing The publick Oaths Do appoint and Chuse Mr. Jacob Butler and Mr. Demsey Sumner to be Church wardens for this Insueing year.

Itt is ordered that the Church wardens or Either of them Demand the vestrey Book of Mr. John Luton and all papers Relateing to the Parish affairs which is in his possession To be had at the Next vestrey.

Ordred that the Late Church wardens make out their Collections and Lay their accounts before the next vestrey held for this Parrish.

Ordred that the Church wardens pay unto Benjamin Talbot forty Shillings for his Takeing the pole at the Collection.

Ordred that a Levey of five Shillings per pole be Leveyed on all the Tythables in the parrish of Chowan for and Towards the Defraying all Nessary Charges and Expences of the Said Parish for the Insueing year.

Ordred that the vestrey meet at Mr. Thos. Waltons at Cathrian Creek the first Saturday in August Next.

Jacob Butler Ch. Warden
Demsey Sumner Ch. Warden

<(91)> Att a vestrey mett and Held at Mr. Thomas Waltons Hows the 10th day of May 1740. Present Jno. Sumner, Richd. Parker, Isaac Huntor, Thos. Walton, Wm. Speight, Richd. Bond, Edwd. Hare, Wm. Skinner, Demsey Sumner, Jacob Butler, Church wardens.

Ordred That the Church wardens pay Each and Every person which produces a Sertificate for a Lawfull Claim Relateing to the vermine act[1] when the Parish money is Collected as the Law Directs.

Ordred That the Ch. wardens pay unto Precilla Perry by order of Eliza. Thompson five pounds it being for the Support of the Said Eliza. Thompsons Maintainence.

Ordred that the Ch. wardens pay unto Isaac Huntor Sixteen pounds and to Willm. Skinner fifteen pounds for Reading devine Service from Aprill 23, 1739 to Aprill 23, 1740.

Ordred Isaac Huntor and Willm. Skinner Continue Reading Devine Service according to former orders.

Ordred that Mr. Jacob Butler appoynt a Readör for the Lower part of this Parish at the Rate of fifteen pounds per year.

Ordred that the Ch. wardens pay unto Thomas Walton Seventy pounds and fourteen Shillings for His Charges with Weston and Joanes in Keeping and Decently Buriing of them.

Demsey Sumner
Jacob Butler

<(92)> Att a vestrey Mett and held at Mr. Thos. Waltons Hows The 25 day of October 1740. Present videlicet John Sumner, Willm. Skinner, Thos. Walton, Richd. Parker, Isaac Huntor, Edwd. Hare, Demsey Sumner Ch. Warden.

This Day John Sumner Layd his accountt Before this vestrey as Being Late Church warden and it is ordred that Demsey Sumner Richard Parker and Isaac Huntor inspect and Settle the Said accountt and they Report that the Ballance of the Said accountt dew to the Said John Sumner is Nineteen Shillings and three pence which he is ordred to be payd per the Present Church warden.

Ordred that Capt. Thos. Garrett be allowed at the Rate of Thirty Pounds per year for Keeping Margrett Rodgerson from the first day of June Last.

Ordred That the Church warden be allowed for a Doctors Bill or accountt for a Cure or Trouble with Fleete Cooper, a poor Boy which is now Lame.

Ordred That Mr. John Blunt Settle his accountts as Being Late Church warden at the next vestrey to be held for this Parish.

Ordred that Mr. Thos. Walton be allowed and payd forty Shillings for his Trouble and Charge in provideing and Gitting a Coppy of the vermin act which act is Ordred to be Kept for the Use of the vestreys with the Vestrey Book.

Ordred that the Vestrey meet at Mr. Thos. Waltons hows on fryday the 28th day of November next to appoynt possessioners to possession Every Mans Land in this Parish.

Demsey Sumner Church Warden, John Sumner, Willm. Skinner, Richd. Parker, Isaac Huntor, Thos. Walton, Edward Hare

<(93)> Att a vestrey mett and held at Mr. Thos. Waltons Hows for Chowan Parish the 28 day of November 1740. Present John Sumner, Isaac Huntor, Thomas Walton, Edwd. Hair, William Skinner, William Speight, John Blunt, Richard Bond, Jacob Butler Ch. Warden.

This Day Mr. John Blunt Layd his accountt Before this vestrey as Being Late Church warden which accountt was Inspected and Settled and the Ballance of the said accountt dew to the Parish is two hundred and twe[nty] pounds and Eighteen Shillings whereof he pays down to Demsey Sumner Present Ch. warden Seventy Seven pounds and to Jacob Butler Present Ch. warden Seventy five pounds whereof there is Remaining Dew to this Parish fifty pounds and Eighteen Shillings. It is therefore Ordred that Mr. John Blunt pay the Ballance of his accountt Being fifty pounds and Eighteen Shillings into the hands of Mr. Jacob Butler Present Ch. warden for the Use of this Parish and that he the said Butler accountt for the Same With the vestrey.

Ordred that the Church wardens pay Mr. Benja. Talbott Ten pounds fifteen Shillings for Reading Devine Service from the first day of June 1739 to Easter munday following.

Jacob Butler Church Warden

---

[1]The 1738 "Act for Destroying Vermin within this Province" provided that anyone claiming a bounty for killing a panther, wolf, wildcat, or squirrel was to take the animal's head or scalp to a magistrate. The certificate issued by the magistrate could then be presented to the vestry and churchwardens of the parish in which the killing had taken place for payment of the bounty. CO 5/333, fols. 29b-30.

1741

Att a Vestrey mett and Held at the Hows of Mr. Thos. Waltons for the Parish of Chowan March 30 day 1741. Present Mr. Edwd. Hair, Mr. Willm. Speight, Mr. Thos. Walton, Mr. Isaac Huntor, Mr. Richard Bond, Mr. William Skinner, Mr. Jacob Butler Church Warden.

	£ *s*. *d*.
Ordred That the church wardens pay to Lodwick Mircler	16. 5. 0
Ordred That the church wardens pay Mr. Isaac Huntor for Reading two years at £16 per annum	32. 0. 0
Ordred That the Church wardens pay to Mr. Wm. Skinner for Reading one year	15. 0. 0
Ordred That the Church wardens pay to Mr. Benja. Talbot for Reading one year	15. 0. 0

Ordred that Mary Havil be alowed and payed by the Church wardens Twenty Shillings per month from March the 30th 1740.

Jacob Butler Church wardin Laid his accountt before the vestrey and was Examined and allowed of £83.4*s*.10*d*. it being moneys dispusted for the use of the poor.

Ordred that the vestrey meet at the Indian town Chappell the 18th day of Aprill 1741.

Jacob Butler Ch. Warden

<(94)> Att a Vestrey Mett and held at The Indian Town Chappell the 18th day of Aprill 1741. Present Mr. Isaac Huntor, Mr. Thos. Walton, Mr. Richd. Bond, Mr. William Speight, Mr. Edwd. Haire, Mr. William Skinner, Mr. Jacob Butler Church Warden.

Ordred that Mr. Thos. Walton and Mr. Richard Bond Serve as Church wardens for this Insueing year 1741.

Ordred that Demsey Sumner as Late church warden Lay his accountt Before the next vestrey to be held for this parrish and accountt for the Same.

Ordred That James Eggerton be allowed and payed the Sum of Twenty pounds by the Church wardens for his Trouble and Care in Keeping and maintaining of a poore child Sarah Lacey by name.

Ordred That the church wardens pay unto John Sumner Ten pounds for his Trouble in Serveing as clerk of this vestrey for the year 1740.

Ordred That the church wardens pay unto Capt. Thos. Garrett the Sum of Twenty five pounds for his Trouble and Charge in Keeping and maintaining Margett Rodgerson from the first day of June 1740 untill the first day of Aprill 1741.

Ordred That a Tax or Levey of Two Shillings proclamation money be Leved on Every Tythable in This Parish for the Insueing year 1741 for and Towards the Defraying the Contengent charges of this Parish and Towards the Building of two chappells Each to be Thirty five foot Long and Twenty two foot and a halfe wide and to Stand one at James Costans or their abouts and the other to Stand at James Braddeys or near their abouts.

Ordred That Mr. Richd. Parker Mr. Isaac Huntor Mr. Thos. Walton and John Sumner doe Inploy or hire work men for to build two Chappells in chowan Parish videlicet at James Costan's or their a bouts as they Shall Think fett and the other at James Braddeys or near their a bouts and The Dementions as here mentioned videlicet Thirty five foot Long and Twenty two foot and a halfe wide Eleven foot in the pitch betwee Sill and plate and a Roof workman Like near a Squear and to be a Good fraim Gott out of Good Timber and coverd with Good Siprus Shingles and weather boarded with feather Edged plank nine inches broad with Good Lapp of two Inches at the Least and Good Sleapers and flower of Good plank of Inch and a quarter thick and Sealed with Good plank with three windows Suitable for Such a hows or howses and two Doars Suitable with a pulpitt and all things Suitable according to the vew of the Said Richard Parker Isaac Huntor Thos. Walton and John Sumner.

<(*Turn forrad*)>

<(95)> Ordred that the Church wardens pay unto Mr. Jacob Butler the Sum of fifty Shillings for the Like Sum payd Robt. Fulerton Towards the maintainance of Christian Nuton.

Ordred that John Sumner Keep the vestrey Book this Insueing year and act as Clark of the vestrey and to be allowed Ten Pounds for the Said Service untill next Easter munday.

Ordred that the vestrey meet at the Indian Town Chappell the Last Satterday in June next.

Jacob Butler

Att a Vestrey mett and held at Mr. Thos. Waltons Hows The 8th day of August 1741.

Present Mr. Isaac Huntor, Mr. Richd. Parker, Mr. Edward Haire, Mr. Demsey Sumner, John Sumner, Mr. Thos. Walton, Mr. Richd. Bond Church wardens.

Ordred that Mr. Richd. Bond be allowed and payd the Sum of forty Shillings for the Like Sum pd. by him to Rachell Pervine a poore woman in Great wont of assistance from the parish.

Ordred That Richard Bond and Jonathan Parker Be allowed and payd by this Parish the Sums of money by them a greed for by this vestrey for the building of Two Chappells when their work is Done according to their a greement.

Ordred that Precilla Perry be allowed and payd by the Ch. wardens the Sum of Thirty two pounds for her Trouble and Charge in Keeping and maintaining of Eliza. Tompson Eight months.

Ordred that the Ch. wardens pay unto Capt. Thos. Garrett the Sum of five pounds fifteen Shillings for his Trouble in Keeping Margett Rodgerson from the first day of Aprill to the Tenth day of June 1741.

Appendix

APPENDIX

Listed here are the seventeen known clergymen of the Church of England appointed to serve in North Carolina during the period 1699 through 1741, most of whom were employed by the Society for the Propagation of the Gospel in Foreign Parts (SPG). Information concerning them has been taken from the present volume and from sources cited at the end of entries. Ministers such as Rev. George Keith and Rev. John Talbot, neither of whom held an appointment to a parish or to a mission district in North Carolina, have not been included.

James Adams (d. 1710) received his ordination in 1701. From 1702 to 1707 he was curate in the parishes of Castlemore, Kilmovee, and Killcolmon, Ireland. In 1707 Adams received a missionary appointment to North Carolina from the SPG and traveled to the colony with Rev. William Gordon, also appointed to North Carolina. In March, 1708, the pair arrived at Lynnhaven Bay, Virginia. Adams wrote in September of the disruptions caused by the Cary Rebellion, by which time he was officiating in the parishes of Currituck and Pasquotank. Adams died at Currituck, October 30, 1710, after writing to the SPG in the preceding month that he had "lived here in a dismal Country about two Years and a half where I have suffer'd a World of misery and trouble both in body and mind."

Thomas Baylye (ca. 1684-before November, 1738). According to Baylye, he was ordained deacon at Westminster in 1705, and licensed for service in Maryland around 1712. He resigned a parish on the western shore ca. 1717, "upon some distaste to his Parishioners," following complaints about his drunkenness, swearing, and quarrelling. In 1721 Governor Spotswood of Virginia said that Baylye had "thrust himself" into livings at two parishes, without the governor's approval. In 1724 Rev. James Blair, commissary in Virginia for the bishop of London, wrote that Baylye had scandalized the colony by his continual drunkenness and fighting. Spotswood removed him from his parish (Newport), but gave him another on Baylye's promise of reform. In 1724 or 1725 Baylye appeared in North Carolina, officiating in Pasquotank and Perquimans precincts. In 1725-26 he became involved as a partisan of George Burrington in the bitter political warfare between the governor, Sir Richard Everard, and his predecessor, Burrington. Commissary Blair gave Baylye funds to go home to England, since no parish in Maryland, Virginia, or Carolina would have him. He returned to England in 1729, leaving two young sons behind in the colony. Shortly after his arrival there, Baylye solicited funds from the SPG, presenting a forged petition purportedly from the vestries of Hyde Precinct and St. Thomas's, Bath, extolling his services to them. The SPG gave him £10, noting that it had no obligation to him since he had never been in their service. In 1738 his widow unsuccessfully petitioned the Society for a donation, claiming that for four and a half years before his death, Baylye had been curate of St. Mewan, Cornwall. Manross, *Fulham Papers in the Lambeth Palace Library*, 28, 29, 168-170, 173, 180, 181.

John Blacknall (ca. 1690-1749). Upon the request of the lords proprietors, Blacknall was appointed missionary to North Carolina by the SPG in April, 1725. He went there with the new governor, Sir Richard Everard, and was received as minister of St. Paul's, Edenton, the following August. Blacknall was a minor and unwilling participant in the bitter political warfare waged between his patron, Everard, and former Governor George Burrington. By July, 1726, Blacknall had removed to Virginia, where he ministered for the remainder of his life. *DNCB*.

John Blair (fl. 1703-1704) was ordained in April, 1703, and sent to North Carolina under the sponsorship of Thomas Thynne, Viscount Weymouth. Blair arrived in the colony in January, 1703/4, where he was received as minister at St. Paul's, Edenton. He remained only a few months. The vessel on which Blair was returning to England was taken by the French in August, 1704, and he was in London by November of that year.

John Boyd (d. 1738). In March, 1731/2, Governor George Burrington stated that John Boyd had been educated at the University of Glasgow and had practiced medicine in Virginia for the preceding seven years. Later that year Boyd travelled to London for ordination and licensing, even though Commissary James Blair wrote the bishop of London from Virginia that Boyd had a "very scandalous" reputation. Boyd was ordained in October, 1732, and assigned by the SPG to North Carolina as an itinerant missionary. At the time of his appointment, there were no Anglican clergy in the province, and Boyd was expected by the Society to "officiate in every Part of it"—a patently impossible hope. In May of the following year, Blair wrote that Boyd had been with him for five weeks and had favorably impressed the commissary. Blair surmised that the bad reports concerning Boyd had been due to malice. Boyd resided in the Northwest Parish of Chowan (Bertie Precinct) until late 1735 or early 1736, when he moved to Edenton at the behest of the SPG. The SPG received a report from Commissary Alexander Garden in Charleston that Governor Gabriel Johnston and other officials had complained of Boyd's drunkenness and neglect of duty. Even so, when the Society in June, 1738, divided the mission field of North Carolina into two parts, Boyd was assigned the one north and west of the Neuse River. He never took up the new appointment, having died on May 19, 1738, "in the same Beastly Manner he lived," according to Governor Johnston. He bequeathed his estate to his wife, Lydia, and four children. *DNCB*.

Daniel Brett (fl. 1700). The first missionary regularly assigned to North Carolina spent at most two years the colony, then departed under a heavy cloud of opprobrium. Apparently sent under the auspices of the Society for the Promotion of Christian Knowledge, with his salary provided by the earl of Guildford, Brett probably arrived in the colony early in 1701. He left sometime before January, 1702/03, having served mainly in the Pamlico region. The nature of the offense driving him from the colony in disgrace was never stated explicitly by his detractors, but epithets applied to him at the time ("Scandalous Beast," "the Monster of the Age," "the worst ... that ever came over") indicate that it was rather more than trivial. Brett's subsequent history is unknown. Clark, *State Records*, XXII, 733.

John Garzia (ca. 1700-1744). Thought to have been a native of Spain, John Garzia had converted to Anglicanism from Roman Catholicism by 1723. He may have been a former priest. In August of that year he received the king's bounty for passage to the Bahamas as a clergyman. Departing London for the Bahamas, he was detained at Cork, Ireland, and charged with the theft of a chalice from a Catholic place of worship with which he had formerly been associated. The difficulty apparently was resolved, and in April, 1724, Garzia again received the royal bounty—this time for Virginia, where he arrived later in the year. Garzia served there until his departure for North Carolina in 1733. He officiated at St. Thomas's, Bath, until 1739, when the SPG appointed him missionary to the district north and east of the Neuse River. John Garzia retained a strong foreign accent to the end of his life, which came in November, 1744, after a fall from a horse. Garzia was frequent supplicant for increased financial assistance from the SPG, and he left his widow, Mary, in a destitute condition. *DNCB*.

Henry Gerrard (fl. 1700-1710). In September, 1705, Henry Gerrard presented himself to the vestry of Chowan as a minister approved of by the deputy governor, Thomas Cary. The vestry accepted him, but in the following January demanded that he clear his name of allegations that he had engaged in "Several Debauched practices." At the same time it ordered him to attend the South Shore of Albemarle Sound once every two months. Between January, 1706, and September, 1707, Gerrard appeared in Charleston, having also been in the Bahamas, where he had been plundered by the French. His destitution was relieved by a gift of £20 from the South Carolina Commons House of Assembly in October. Nicholas Trott, chief justice of South Carolina, wrote the SPG in September, 1707, that Gerrard was in South Carolina by virtue of a shipwreck, and that he had spent much of his life in traveling. Trott also noted that the cleric was skilled in Latin, Greek, Italian, Spanish, and French, but offered the opinion that his spoken delivery was "mean," and that "his preaching will not much take with the people here." Trott recommended Gerrard as a missionary to the Yamassee Indians, but the SPG deferred action and he apparently did not receive the appointment. Henry Gerrard was dead by April, 1716. Manross, *SPG Papers in the Lambeth Palace Library*, 142, 146; Manross, *Fulham Papers in the Lambeth Palace Library*, 131; A. S. Salley (ed.), *Journal of the Commons House of Assembly of South Carolina, October 23, 1707-February 12, 1707/8* (Columbia, S.C.: Historical Commission of South Carolina, 1941), 10.

William Gordon (b. 1683 or before) spent at least part of his life in Scotland before migrating to London. After three years there, he received from the SPG an appointment as a missionary to North Carolina. Gordon arrived in the colony in April, 1708, in company with Rev. James Adams, both of whom arrived just prior to the opening skirmishes of the Cary Rebellion. Gordon served the precincts of Chowan and Perquimans for only some five months before returning to England, pleading ill health. Rev. John Urmston reported that Gordon demanded £100 per year to return to the colony. Although the Society expressed its displeasure at his abandoning his post without leave, it soon dispatched Gordon to another charge at Chester, Pennsylvania. Manross, *SPG Papers in the Lambeth Palace Library*, 11.

Bevil Granville (fl. 1732-1733), nephew of George Granville, baron Lansdowne, arrived in the colony in 1732 from Dublin, on his way to a clerical post in Maryland. At the insistence of Governor Burrington and Christopher Gale, the former chief justice,

Granville decided to remain in Chowan Precinct instead. Granville claimed to have baptised nearly a thousand children and adults in a remarkably brief period, and private subscriptions were raised for his salary. The vestry of St. Paul's agreed to pay him for one year from Easter Monday, 1732, with Granville to officiate in Edenton and outlying areas of the parish. By early April, 1733, Granville had taken permanent leave of the province. *DNCB*.

John LaPierre (1681-ca. 1755) was the son of a Huguenot clergyman who migrated with his family from France to London around 1700. In 1701, LaPierre enrolled at Trinity College, Dublin, receiving an A.B. in 1706. He was ordained in 1707, and the following year went to South Carolina as a missionary of the SPG. For the next twenty years he served several parishes there with sizeable numbers of French speakers. In 1728, he moved to the new settlement on the Lower Cape Fear, thereby becoming the first Anglican minister to settle in the region. An insufficient maintenance, due to the competition of Rev. Richard Marsden, led him to remove to Craven (later Christ Church) Parish in 1734-35. He resided in New Bern for the remainder of his life. It is unclear whether or not he was ever installed as minister at Christ Church, New Bern, but he was active until his death in conducting services and establishing chapels throughout the parish. *DNCB*.

Richard Marsden (ca. 1675-1742) was one of the more colorful and controversial clerics to serve in colonial North Carolina, and certainly the most traveled. A native of Yorkshire, he emigrated to Maryland, became a lay reader, and in 1700 returned to England for ordination. Marsden went again to Maryland and served as a minister there until 1706. He then went to South Carolina by way of North Carolina, where he held a communion service and baptised a number of people. After serving in South Carolina until 1709, Marsden spent indeterminate periods in England and Barbados before proceeding to Pennsylvania in 1714 to teach school. After two years Marsden returned to England, obtained an appointment from the duke of Portland as his domestic chaplain, and accompanied the duke to Jamaica when he became governor there in 1721. The duke's death in 1726 led to more wandering by Marsden, this time to New England and Virginia. In the latter colony he, in 1727, became the incumbent of Lynnhaven Parish, on the border with North Carolina. In 1729 Marsden appeared in the Cape Fear region, just beginning to be settled. He claimed, falsely, to hold a commission as an itinerant missionary and inspector of clergy. After making a commercial voyage to Lisbon, Portugal, Marsden returned to the Cape Fear, where he quickly became a popular figure and in time effectively usurped the position of Rev. John LaPierre as minister in the area. In 1738, the SPG tentatively appointed Marsden missionary of that part of the colony south of the Neuse River, but opposition from the bishop of London led to withdrawal of the appointment. Marsden's attempts over the next few years to have it reinstated were unsuccessful, and apparently he never again held a clerical appointment. Richard Marsden's lengthy career was periodically punctuated with unsavory incidents that did little to enhance his reputation. His fellow minister in South Carolina, Francis LeJau, judged that Marsden's "itching for trading, which he does not understand[,] has been the cause of his misfortunes." These misfortunes included drawing fraudulent bills of exchange, having to flee to escape prosecution for debt, and imprisonment for defrauding several trusting merchants of a cargo of goods. Commercial failings were not the only ones chargeable to Marsden. While in Jamaica he contracted a bigamous marriage with a wealthy widow, a fact that in time became widely known. Nevertheless, Marsden was liberally gifted with talents highly useful to the pursuit of a clerical career. Francis Le Jau, while decrying Marsden's commercial adventurism, considered that "in the main he is a sober man and has an art of pleasing the common people." Marsden also drew complimentary comments from Virginians William Byrd and Commissary James Blair, and the Cape Fear councillor James Murray considered that Marsden was "the best minister that I have heard in America." *DNCB*. Nina Moore Tiffany, *Letters of James Murray, Loyalist* (Boston: Printed not Published, 1901), 26.

James Moir (ca. 1710-1767) emigrated from Scotland to South Carolina as a missionary of the Church of Scotland around 1733. In 1739 he undertook a voyage to London for ordination as an Anglican minister, after which the SPG assigned him the district south and west of the Neuse River. Initially, Moir officiated mainly in Wilmington and Brunswick, although several times he undertook an itineration throughout his large district. In 1747, the Society granted his request to be transferred to Edgecombe (later St. Mary's) Parish. In 1762 Moir moved to St. George's, Northampton County, although he continued to serve St. Mary's as well. In 1766, he traveled to the northern colonies for his health, but died before he could accomplish his plan to return permanently to England in 1767. Moir and Gov. Arthur Dobbs became implacable enemies, excoriating each other in the harshest terms in letters to the SPG. The reasons for this enmity remain obscure, but probably resulted from Moir's support of the councillor James Murray, a fellow Scot, in his struggle with the governor. *DNCB*; Vol. XI of the present series, forthcoming; *Robbins Papers*, Massachusetts Historical Society.

Thomas Newnam (d. 1723) received an appointment from the SPG as missionary to North Carolina in September, 1721, arriving there with his "little family" the following April. He served the Southwest Parish of Chowan Precinct and also Society Parish, Bertie Precinct, when that precinct was erected in 1722. He made a trip to Bath County in order to baptize hundreds of children. Newnam was well regarded for his diligence in the performance of his clerical duties, but he was in the colony for less than two years, succumbing to illness in November, 1723. The assembly made his widow a gift of £40 to assist her passage home. *DNCB*.

Giles Ransford (b. 1679, d. after 1726) was born in Dublin, Ireland, the son of an alderman. Educated at Trinity College, Dublin, and St. John's College, Cambridge, he was ordained in 1702, and may have gone to Jamaica in that year or shortly after. In 1711, while curate of Chivington, Suffolk, he sought appointment as a missionary in South Carolina. The SPG appointed him to North Carolina instead, where he arrived in May, 1712. Ransford and Rev. John Urmston divided Chowan Precinct between them, with the former taking the "West Shore." The two missionaries quickly conceived a hearty dislike for one another, each accusing the other of malingering and other failings. Less than a year after his arrival, Ransford was seeking appointment to a parish in Virginia, and the governor there granted him one in Surry County. In 1714 he secured a parish in

Nansemond County, while still occasionally visiting North Carolina. In March, 1714, he resigned as an SPG missionary, furious at having several of his bills of exchange refused by the Society. Until he returned to England for good in 1727, he served a succession of parishes in Virginia and Maryland. *DNCB*; Manross, *Fulham Papers in the Lambeth Palace Library*, 32-33, 36, 38, 40-41, 166.

Ebenezer Taylor (ca. 1660-1720) went from England to South Carolina as a Presbyterian minister, but in 1711 returned to England for Anglican ordination. Going back to South Carolina, he proved unpopular both with his congregation and with his brother clergy, who voted to have him sent to North Carolina to replace Rev. Giles Ransford. Taylor arrived in the colony in September, 1717, and spent his first year at the southwest shore of Chowan. Finding little interest there in his ministry, Taylor removed to Perquimans Precinct, where he enjoyed even less support. By November, 1719, he was in Bath Town, to which place he had been invited by the governor and vestry of St. Thomas's. Finding insufficient encouragement here as well, Taylor resolved to go to Core Sound, at that time the southernmost limit of settlement in the colony, which was a few years later erected into Carteret Precinct. Hiring an open boat to take him there, he was said to have died from exposure to the harsh winter weather and to have been buried on Cedar Island. There is a possibility that Taylor was murdered, since his traveling chest was plundered of a sizeable sum of money.

John Urmston (1662?-1731) had a varied career prior to his coming to North Carolina. Born in Lancashire, England, Urmston is supposed to have spent "many years" in various foreign countries before being ordained in London in 1695. For most or all of the next seven years he operated a boarding school in Kensington, London, where he taught Greek, Latin, French, and perhaps Italian, in addition to arithmetic, writing, and drawing. In 1701 he served for six months as chaplain aboard an English warship, then was employed by the Russia Company as chaplain in Moscow and Archangel. In 1706 he took the curacy of East Ham, Essex, England, and in 1709 entered the service of the SPG as missionary to North Carolina. Arriving in the colony in 1710 with his wife, three children, and two servants, Urmston spent the next eleven years there. Although his plantation and the larger part of his ministry were in Chowan Precinct, he appears to have visited Pasquotank and Currituck Precincts every year, and Bath County in 1716 and 1717. Urmston kept up a barrage of lengthy letters to the SPG complaining bitterly of the ungenerous treatment of him by his vestries, often reducing him and his family to the direst straits. The Society in 1716 granted his request to return to England, but Urmston did not receive the letter announcing it until 1720. Departing the colony in 1721, Urmston subsequently served tempestuous missions in Pennsylvania and Maryland, dying in a fire in the latter colony. *DNCB*.

INDEX

Index

Proper names and subjects are entered in this index. For persons, one spelling of each individual's name has been selected from the spellings appearing in the manuscripts, with variant spellings provided in parentheses following the main entry for each name. A cross reference to the selected spelling is given for each variant of the surname. Cross references also are provided between names known or thought to refer to the same person. Where a distinction, such as place of residence or date of death, can be determined between or among individuals of the same name, it is indicated in parentheses following each surname entry. For personal entries, the designation "clergyman" was not given to individuals until they were in orders. Names of authors are entered when the indexer was certain of the authorship of a work. The work itself is given as it appears in the document, and is enclosed within brackets when it is not its complete title. Brief biographical sketches of clergymen appearing in the volume are indicated by italicized page numbers following their name. Modern spellings are used for place names unless the indexer has been unable to identify the place, in which case the spelling is one appearing in the documents. Variant spellings are given in parentheses, and cross references to the spelling used in the entry are provided under all variants except those closely resembling the modern spelling. Subject entries are in modern spelling. Titles of books do not appear as main entries, but are included following the names of their authors. Where a subject or name is mentioned intermittently throughout four or more consecutive pages, the term "passim" follows the final page number in the sequence.

The index was prepared by Robert J. Cain, Dennis L. Isenbarger, Leigh Anna Lawing and Susan M. Trimble.

_____, Charles, greeting to, 311
_____, Charles, Mr. *See* _____, Charles
_____, Thomas
  testimonial by, 108
  vestryman, 108, 190
Aakell, Willm. *See* Arkill, William
Aberdeen, Scotland, 105
Abstract, to be made, 175
Acadia. *See* Nova Scotia
Accomack County, Virginia, marriage ceremonies in, xv*n*
Account render, action of, may be used to recover parish funds, 312
Accounts, 312, 314, 413, 439, 445
  audited, examined, inspected, xxxi, 100, 474, 477, 482, 484, 486-488, 491-493
  bond to render, 489
  by attorney, 182
  civil list, 14
  for building church, 440
  for burial of indigent, 442
  justices of the peace to present, 417
  not presented, 442
  of arrears, 167
  of churchwardens, xxxii, xxxvii, 474
  of clergyman, 170
  of collector, 403, 432, 451-454 passim, 463
  of collector of parish taxes, xxxii, 450
  of commissioner, 485
  of Dr. Bray, 4-5, 14-15
  of messenger, SPG, 102
  of parish funds, xxxi-xxxii, 414, 416
  of payment for missionary voyage, 14
  of SPG, 99-100, 196
  of treasurer, SPG, 147
  parish, inspectors of, 465
  requested, 210, 231, 234
  sheriff to present, 178
  SPG to present, 98
  vestry to present, 4
  See also Acts of assembly—on parish accounts; Churchwardens—accounts of
Action, lawsuit, xxxiv*n*
  bar to, 418
  brought against clergyman, 252
  brought by churchwardens, 436, 485
  brought by vestry, 458
  by complaint, 314-315
  costs of, 418
  evidence in, xv
  for failure to maintain glebe, 418
  may be brought by clergy, 415
  permitted in General Court, 404, 413
  to collect subscriptions for church construction, 403
  to recover parish funds, xxxi
  to recover stipend, 415
  to recover tax funds, 413, 448
  See also General Court—dismisses action; Information; Qui tam—action of
Acts, 19
  American, relating to church, 289
  on church establishment, 296-297
Acts of assembly, xxx*n*, 304, 402, 490
  abstract of, 193-196 passim, 223, 235, 241
  alarm dissenters, xxv
  amendments to, 210, 215
  book of, 327
  concerning church, 224, 371*n*
  confirmed by assembly, 215
  confirmed by lords proprietors, 215, 236-237
  copy of, procured, 466, 492
  criticized, xxviii
  dates of, uncertain, xxvi
  defective state of, 371*n*
  define tithable, xxvii*n*
  disallowed, xxv-xxvi, 419*n*
  do not permit removal of clergy, xxxviii
  erecting parishes, xxxiii, 368
  fail to address state of religious observance, xlviii
  for holding lottery, xxx
  for sale of booty, xxx
  for sinking fund, xlvii*n*
  incorporating British statutes, xxvii
  missing, xxvii
  not confirmed by lords proprietors, 28
  objected to by SPG, 177
  of limited duration, 236
  of Maryland, 15
  of New York, xxiii*n*
  of South Carolina, xxvi
  of Virginia, xxiii*n*, 10
  on appointing vestries, 188-196 passim
  on binding in servitude, 489
  on blasphemous behavior, 326
  on church construction, xxii, xxiv, 22, 82, 119, 189, 195, 290, 346, 402-405, 413-414, 417
  on church establishment, xx, xxii-xxiv, xxvii*n*, xxviii, xxxi, xxxiii, xxxv-xxxvii, xxxvii*n*, xxxviii, xlix, 22-23, 74, 82, 87, 119, 121, 165, 172, 177, 188-193 passim, 194-196, 208-210, 212-215 passim, 231, 235, 239, 241, 245, 250, 254, 265-267, 269, 275, 290, 293, 298, 314, 328, 346, 364, 414-419 passim, 431-433, 443, 446, 449, 452

on collection of parish tax, 473
on commodity payments, 86
on conversion of Negroes and Indians, 327
on displacing ministers, 94
on election to assembly, 82
on establishment, xlviii
on fornication and adultery, xxxiv*n*
on glebes, 346*n*
on immoral behavior, xxxiii-xxxiv, xlv, 326
on killing vermin, xxxv*n*, 491-492
on land, 461, 462*n*
on libraries, 15, 15*n*
on marriage, xxxi, 283, 364, 364*n*
on New Bern, 404
on parish accounts, xxxi, 11, 57, 72, 81, 312, 314, 316*n*, 414, 419
on parish taxes, 447
on payments to clergy, xv, xxiv, xxvii*n*, xxxi*n*, 28, 65, 73, 205-206, 226-227, 245, 266-267, 268*n*, 269, 271, 273, 437-438
on poverty, xxxv-xxxvi
on processioning, xxxv, 466
on procuring clergy, xxvi*n*, 97
on public worship, 371*n*
on Queen's College, xlviii
on quitrents, 402-403
on rating commodities, 250
on readers, 73
on regulation of town, xxxiv
on sabbath observance, xxxiii-xxxiv
on seat of government, 284
on servants and slaves, xxix
on taxation, xxviii
on taxation by vestry, xxxvi, 368
on towns, 402, 404
on vestries, xxii, xxviii-xxix, xxix*n*, 91, 236, 314, 316*n*, 445, 481
on vestry accounts, xxxii
on vestry elections, xxvi*n*, 442, 477
on vestrymen, 469
on weights and measures, xxxiv-xxxv, 435
parish formed without, 347
proposed, 326
proposed, on table of marriages, 326
published, 191
Quakers and, 151
read, 442
repealed, 215, 419
revised, 209, 213
sent to Board of Trade, 153
sent to lords proprietors, 22, 209, 213
struggle to obtain, 449
to be printed, 209, 213
to be read publicly, xxxiv*n*
See also Fundamental Constitutions of Carolina—on acts of assembly; Lords proprietors— statute enacted in name of
Acts of Parliament
on bankruptcy, 343
on Book of Common Prayer, 325
on church, xiii, xxvii, xxix, 194, 290
on encouraging settlement of protestants, 32
on oaths, 82, 87*n*
on officeholding, xxvi
on pardon for piracy, 256
on trade, 83
proposed, on baptism of slaves, 261
Adam, Mr. *See* Adams, James
Adams, Abraham
petitioner, 309-310
signature of, forged, 310*n*
Adams, Elinor (Elenor), 436
to serve physician, 436
treated by physician, 437
Adams, Elspet, brother of, 105
Adams, James, *497*
arrival of, 64, 86
behavior of, 108
books of, 151, 160, 169, 175, 180, 255, 257
character of, 53-55, 57*n*, 109-110, 110*n*, 112, 151, 168-169, 178, 251, 295*n*
clergyman, xiv
curate, 53*n*
debtor, 143
deceased, 112, 131-132, 151, 151*n*, 168-169, 178, 180, 250, 257
difficulties of, 104, 107
journey of, 62
letter from, 60-65, 71-72, 95-97, 97*n*, 104-106, 106*n*, 107, 109*n*, 110*n*
letter to, 72*n*
library of, 295*n*
library sent by, 179
ministerial ability of, 60
ministry of, 65, 73, 76, 96, 105-107
missionary appointment of, xiv, 53-54, 57, 61-62, 86, 108, 110*n*, 112
offers service to SPG, 56
payment to, 103
qualifies as missionary, 60
recommendation of, 57*n*
refuses to deliver books, 143
salary of, 106*n*, 111
sisters of, 105
testimonial in behalf of, 53-54
warrant to, 5*n*
Adams, Janet, brother of, 105

Adams, John
clerk, 310
letter from, 240-241
petitioner, 309-310
signature of, forged, 310*n*
vestryman, 190, 241
Adams, John, petitioner, 309-310
Adams, Mr. *See* Adams, James
Adams, Reverend Mr. *See* Adams, James—clergyman
Adams. *See* Adams, Elinor
Administrator, administratrix, 418
See also Will
Admiralty Board, 132
secretary to, 133
Adultery. *See* Crime—adultery, fornication
Affidavit, deposition
by governor, 301
concerning clergyman, 301-302, 305
Affirmation, by Quakers, 83
Africa, 308
Afterlife, belief in a requirement for land ownership, xix
Agent
appointed by General Assembly, 309*n*
for colony, 307
of lords proprietors, 164
See also Clergy, clergyman—agent for, suggested; agent of; Indians—agents of
Ague. *See* Disease, illness, affliction—ague
Aime, Mr. *See* Amy, Thomas
Albany, New York, clergyman appointed to, 45, 48
Albemarle (region)
precincts in, xxiv
religious services in, xv
Albemarle (Albumar) Sound, 86, 95*n*
clergyman at, 76, 160
ministry at, 379
parish boundary at, 189, 194
precincts north of, 65*n*
settlement along, xxiii
settlements north of, xiii
vestry meeting near, 245
Albemarle court. *See* County Court—Albemarle
Albemarle Precinct, County, xvii*n*, 147*n*, 171, 186, 236, 293, 363, 445, 449
clergyman in, xl, 53*n*, 165, 228, 356
government of, xxi, xxi*n*
letter from, 449-451
library in, 9
parish of, xxviii
religious condition of, 363
Albemarle, County Court of, justice of, 4*n*
Albumar Sound. *See* Albemarle Sound
Alcaster. *See* Alcester, England
Alcester (Alcaster), England, 386
Alderman, of Dublin, 124
Aldermanbury, London, 163
Alderson, Simon
desires to retain minister, 353-354
justice of the peace, 310
petitioner, 309-310, 353-354
vestryman, 354
Aldgate Parish, London, palatines in, 88
Aldgate, London, attorney near, 246
Aldridge, Eben.
maintained by parish, 451
medical treatment of, 451
Alexander, _____, arrival of, 162
Allegiance. *See* Oath—of allegiance
Allen (Alley, Alleyn), George (G., Geo.)
allegedly curses officials, 303, 303*n*
character of, 303
churchwarden, 477-480 passim
debtor, 466
executor of estate of, 480, 485
oath taken by, 477-478
payment to, 479
physician, 303, 303*n*, 478-480, 485
vestryman, 477-478
Allen, Doctor. *See* Allen, George
Allen, Eleazer (Eliazr.)
chief justice, 376*n*
Harvard graduate, 376*n*
letter to, 388
receiver general, 376*n*
treasurer, 376*n*
vestryman, 418
Allen, William, author, 8, 35
Allestree, Richard, author of [*Whole Duty of Man*], 6, 9, 34, 36, 295
Alley, G. *See* Allen, George
Alleyn, George (Geo.). *See* Allen, George
Alligator Creek, ministry at, 380
Alligator River, religious condition along, 117
Alston (Alstone, Aulston, Aulstone), John
guardian, 490
vestryman, 486-490 passim
Alstone, John. *See* Alston, John
Amboy. *See* Perth Amboy, New Jersey
Ambross, David, debtor, 459
Ames (Amesii), William, author, 295
Amesii. *See* Ames, William
Amesius, _____, author, 295
Amusements, games
at reaping of wheat, 117

bear baiting, 268*n*
football, 120
Amy (Aime), Thomas (Tho.)
information by, 28
letter from, 3
letter to, 14
proposed for SPG membership, 13, 13*n*
proprietor, xl*n*, 3, 4*n*, 13, 13*n*, 14
to attend meeting, 14
Amy, Mr. *See* Amy, Thomas
Anabaptist. *See* Dissenters—Baptist, Anabaptist
Anderson, Joseph (J., Jos.)
account signed by, 484
to report to vestry, 482
vestryman, 481-482, 484-486
Anderson, Mr. *See* Anderson, Joseph
Andrews (Andrews), Lancelot, author, 34-35
Andrews, Bishop. *See* Andrewes, Lancelot
Andrews, Mr., missionary appointment of, 149
Ann, Queen. *See* Anne, queen of England
Annapolis, Maryland, lack of clergy in, 20
Anne (Ann), queen of England, xxvi, 18, 26, 80*n*, 87*n*
bounty of, 27
deceased, 212*n*, 253
reign of, 18, 337
speech by, 184
zealous church supporter, 254*n*
Anniversary Sermon. *See* Sermon, homily—at meeting of SPG
Apoquiniminck, Delaware, clergyman appointed to, 48
Apostle's Creed, recited by Negroes, 285
Apothecary. *See* Occupation, trade, profession—apothecary
Apprentice, binding of, 405
Aquinas, Thomas, *Saint*
author, 33
author of [*Tertia Pars Sum*], 294
ArchBp. of Cant. *See* Canterbury, archbishop of
Archdale Precinct, 65*n*
Archdale, John, 72, 83
governor, xxi*n*, xxxiv*n*, 73*n*
instructions to, xxi*n*
land deeded by, 108*n*
proprietor, xxxiv*n*, 71, 81-82
purchases proprietary land, 73*n*
Quaker, 71, 73*n*, 81-82
refuses to take oath, 83
son-in-law of, 108*n*
Archdale, Mr. *See* Archdale, John
Ardern, John. *See* Arderne, John
Arderne (Ardern), John
assembly member, 438*n*
churchwarden, 68-69, 71, 442
Council member, 438*n*
dismissed as churchwarden, 444
letter from, 68-71
payment to, 444
subscription by, 438
vestryman, 438, 438*n*, 439, 441-444 passim
vestryman, absence of, 443
Arian, author, 34-35
Aristotelis. *See* Aristotle
Aristotle (Aristotelis), author, 294
Arkeel, William. *See* Arkill, William
Arkeele, William. *See* Arkill, William
Arkill (Aakell, Arkeel, Arkeele), William (Wm., Willm.)
allowance of, 472, 490
vestryman, 486-487, 489-490
Arline, John
allowance of, 471, 484
payment to, 481
Armor, Jerome. *See* Armore, Jerome
Armore (Armor), Jerome (Jer.)
testimonial by, 301
witness, 301
Arms, armaments, ordnance, 83, 129
cannon, 129
in Cary Rebellion, 123, 124*n*, 128
musket, 182*n*
needed for defense against pirates, 273
oath not to use against king, 191
of militia, xxxvi*n*
of pirates, 273
pistol, 256
sword, 256
Army, British, governor former officer in, 286*n*
Arnauld, Antoine
author of [*Ars Cogitandi sive Logica In qua praeter Vulgares Regulae plura nova habentur ad Rationem dirigendam utilia*], 9
author of [*The Art of Speaking by Messieurs du port Royal*], 8
Arrest, 31
contemplated, 199
of clergyman, 252, 271, 391
of Thomas Cary, 23
Ashe, John (Jno.) Baptista (Bapt., Bapta., Baptist.)
assembly member, xlv
Council member, 291*n*, 346
letter from, 289-290
speaker of the assembly, 291*n*
to render account, xlv

vestryman, 316
Ashe, Mr. *See* Ashe, John Baptista
Asheton, Dr. *See* Assheton, William
Ashleworth, England, 21, 24
Ashley River. *See* Charleston, South Carolina
Ashley, Maurice (M.)
letter from, 3, 103
proprietor, 4*n*, 81
Ashton, Dr. *See* Assheton, William
Asia, 308
Assheton (Asheton, Ashton), William, author, 9, 35, 38
Atheism, irreligion, 17, 95-96, 105, 256, 260, 306, 389
habitual, 318
secretary accused of, 317, 321
Athias, Joseph, author, 6
Atkinson, Jacob, meeting place of, 238
Attorney, 252
clergy not allowed to employ, 181
English, 247
of clergyman, xv, 170, 177, 210, 213, 231, 246, 272
See also Occupation, trade, profession—attorney
Attorney general, 364*n*, 463*n*, 485*n*
of South Carolina, 290*n*
Porter, John, 87*n*
Augustine (Augustini, Augustinus), *Saint*
author, 294-295
Augustini, S. *See* Augustine, *Saint*
Augustinus, S. *See* Augustine, *Saint*
Aulston, John. *See* Alston, John
Aulstone, John. *See* Alston, John
Austin, Mr.
allegedly defrauded, 391
merchant, 391
of Liverpool, 391
Autumn, fall, 224, 233, 269
Francis Nicholson to arrive in, 203
Axe. *See* Tools, equipment—axe
Aylett, Philip
executor, 377
of Virginia, 377
B., P. *See* Bearcroft, Philip
B_____, Will., vestryman, 191
Backnall. *See* Blacknall, John
Bacon. *See* Food, diet—bacon
Badham, Martha, husband of, 483
Badham, Mr. *See* Badham, William
Badham, William (W., Wm.)
account signed by, 466
allowance of, 465
churchwarden, 462-466 passim
debtor, 477
delivers elements for Eucharist, 465
dismissed as churchwarden, 465
house of, 301
lawsuit against, 485
letter from, 287-288
marriage of, 482
oath taken by, 460
possesses key, 303
presents account to vestry, 465
replacement for, 465
son of, deceased, 483
to return money, 485
to settle account, 462
vestryman, 288, 460-462, 469-470
wife of, 483
Badham, William, [Jr.]
deceased, 483
parents of, 483
Bahama Islands, 340
commissary for, xliv
Baile. *See* Baylye, Thomas
Bailey, Mr., allowance of, 463
Bailey, Mr. *See* Baylye, Thomas
Baily. *See* Baylye, Thomas
Bailye. *See* Baylye, Thomas
Baker, Henry (Hen.)
churchwarden, 481-482, 486-487, 489
inspector, 477
to attend vestry meeting, 484
to settle account, 486-487, 489
vestryman, 481
Baker, Mr., to review missionary's performance, 297
Baker, Richard, author, 6
Baley, David
letter from, 250
vestryman, 250
Ball, John, author, 294
Ball, Samll.
churchwarden, 53
testimonial by, 53
Ballard's Bridge Creek (Ballard's Bridge), 462, 478, 488
Ballard's Bridge. *See* Ballard's Bridge Creek
Ballard, Jno., allowance of, 476
Ballast, 246
Ballinletter (Ireland), prebendary of, 55
Ballykean (Ireland), rector of, 55
Baltimore, Ld. *See* Calvert, Charles, 5th baron Baltimore
Banbury, William (Wm.)
encourages reader, 440
subscription by, 439

vestryman, 431, 433-436 passim, 438-439, 441-444 passim
Bands. *See* Clothing, jewelry—bands
Banishment. *See* Penalty, punishment—banishment
Bank of England, 406
director of, 373
Bank of England, London, 406
Bankruptcy, insolvency, 148, 193, 195, 437, 453, 475
act of Parliament on, 343
of clergyman, 343
Baptism, 264, 304, 361, 384, 407-408
absence of, 354
and Tuscarora War, 187
book about, xlii, 16, 410
by readers, 120
certification of, 407
denied slaves, 96, 128, 261
hinders growth of Quakerism, 307
instruction in, 41
instructions concerning, 357-358
not undertaken, 32, 143, 146, 231, 328
of adults, 44, 66, 73, 96, 107, 184, 231, 254, 262, 268, 283, 285, 302, 306-307, 334, 356, 362-363, 368, 389, 421-422
of Indians, xiii, xv*n*, xlvi-xlvii, 230, 381, 406
of married women, 283
of mustee, 260
of Quakers, 356, 373, 381, 421
of slaves, xlvi-xlvii, 143, 145, 159, 171, 198, 260, 285, 306, 357-358, 365, 381, 422
of Virginia Dare, xiii, xv*n*
rumored to free slaves, 261
statistics of, 378-380, 421, 424, 426
to be reported, 42
unlawful, 122*n*
vestrymen lack, 181
vows taken at, 137
See also Child, children—baptism of, not baptized; Church, chapel, meeting-house—baptisms in
Baptist. *See* Dissenters—Baptist, Anabaptist
Bar, (The), harbor at, 220
Barbados, 122, 279-280
clergyman desires credit in, 178, 201, 231, 234, 238, 246, 257, 264
clergyman in, 390
settlers from, xvii
SPG plantation in, 427
Barber. *See* Occupation, trade, profession—barber
Barbour, John Humphrey
clergyman, 293*n*
librarian, 293*n*
Barclay (Barklay), Robert (Robt.)
author, 17
polemicist, 19*n*
Barclay, Mr., library sent by, 176
Barecroft, Dr. *See* Bearcroft, Philip—clergyman
Barecroft, Phillip. *See* Bearcroft, Philip
Bark. *See* Medicine, medical treatment—bark
Barking (England), vicar of, 80, 90, 90*n*
Barklay, Robt. *See* Barclay, Robert
Barley. *See* Food, diet—barley
Barmud. *See* Bermuda
Barn. *See* Building—barn
Barnaby, Mr., merchant, 16
Barnes, Mr.
clergyman, 298
recommended for SPG service, 298
Barnwell, John
force of, inadequately supplied, 140*n*
leads military expedition, 140*n*
signs truce with Indians, 140*n*
Baron (Baronii), Robert, author, 294
Baronet, 310, 310*n*, 462, 464-465
Baronii. *See* Baron, Robert
Baronio (Baronis), Cesare, author, 295
Baronis. *See* Baronio, Cesare
Barrel. *See* Container—barrel
Barrington. *See* Burrington, George—governor
Barrow, Dr. *See* Barrow, Isaac
Barrow, Isaac, author, 6, 34-35
Barrow, John
desires to retain minister, 353-354
petitioner, 353-354
vestryman, 354
Barrow, Wilb., vestryman, 190
Barte. *See* Bertie Precinct, County
Bartholomew Close, London, printer in, 39, 335*n*
Barty. *See* Bertie Precinct, County
Bastard, bastardy, 459, 489
mulatto, 480
Bates, William, author, 7
Bath (Bath Town), 94, 263, 290, 308, 359, 365-366, 376, 386, 420
chapel, church in, 354*n*
clergyman appointed to, 204, 420
clergyman in, 269, 307, 378
clergyman traveling to, 260
depopulation of, 255
description of, 86, 186
erected, xiii
established, xxi

lack of clergy in, 186, 304
library in, xli, 86, 121, 151, 180, 255, 295*n*
ministry in, 380
official in, 204
petition from, 309-310
pirate in, 258*n*
selling of town lots benefit vestry in, xxix
Bath and Wells (England), bishop of, 34
Bath County, 65*n*, 241, 265, 316
clergyman appointed to, 204, 224
clergyman in, xlv, 285, 322
description of, 32, 86
governor in, 245, 453
Indian wars in, 185, 187, 195, 241, 255
lack of clergy in, 186, 205-206, 236, 240, 282, 293
leader of rebellion in, 87*n*
library in, 9*n*, 44, 172, 449
official in, 130*n*, 204*n*, 247
parish in, xxviii
petition from, 32-33
religious condition of, 187, 224, 363
vestryman in, 453
Bath Town. *See* Bath
Bathe Palatine. *See* Grenville, John, 1st earl of Bath—palatine
Battle, Will, inspector, 486
Baxter, Richard, author of [*Dr. Edwards against the Socinians*], 34, 36
Bay. *See* Long Bay; Lynn Haven Bay, Virginia
Bayley (ship), 140, 160
Bayley, Mr. *See* Baylye, Thomas
Bayley, Thomas (Thos.). *See* Baylye, Thomas
Bayley. *See* Baylye, Thomas
Baylie, Mr. *See* Baylye, Thomas
Baylie, Thomas. *See* Baylye, Thomas
Baylie. *See* Baylye, Thomas
Bayly, Mr. *See* Baylye, Thomas
Bayly. *See* Baylye, Thomas
Baylye (Bayley), Eleanor
gratuity for, denied, 388
husband of, 388
petitioner, 388
widow, 388
Baylye (Baile, Bailey, Baily, Bailye, Bayley, Baylie, Bayly), Thomas (Thos.), 311, *497*
affidavit regarding, 301-302
attends meeting, 302-303
bail provided for, 304
behavior of, 301-304 passim
character of, xlix, 304-305
clergyman, xlvi, xlix, 301, 302*n*, 304-305, 309, 320, 322, 388
clergyman, censured, 318
curate, 388
deposition regarding, 305
employment of, questioned, 388
family of, 308
father-in-law of, 323
invitation to, 302
letter from, 306-309
letter regarding, 318-319
ministry of, xlvi, 306-308
missionary appointment of, 388
ordained as deacon, 308
payment to, 320, 322
petitioner, 320, 322
petitioner in behalf of, 309-310
recommendation of, 309
returns to England, 318-319
salary of, 307
statement by, 302-303
treatment of, 301
unable to secure parish, 318
warrant against, 301
wife of, 302, 318, 388
Baylye, Mr. *See* Baylye, Thomas
Beans. *See* Food, diet—beans
Bear baiting, 68*n*
Bear Indians. *See* Indians—Bear
Bearcroft (B., Barecroft), Philip (P., Phillip)
clergyman, 392*n*
letter from, 392, 397-398, 400-401
letter to, 395-396
report to, 421-422
secretary to the SPG, 392, 392*n*, 422
Beaseley (Beasley, Beazley), James
churchwarden, 452-453
deceased, 455
dismissed as churchwarden, 454
payment to, 450, 454
reader, 440
vestryman, 452-454
Beasley, James. *See* Beaseley, James
Beaufort, selling of town lots benefit vestry in, xxix
Beaufort Parish, erected, xxviii, 194
Beaufort Precinct, County, 65*n*
clergyman in, 357, 364, 420
library for, 15*n*
marriage in, 364
ministry in, 380
parish in, 189, 414
petition from, 357
Beaufort, D. of. *See* Somerset, Henry, 2nd duke of Beaufort

Beaufort, Ld. of. *See* Somerset, Henry, 2nd duke of Beaufort
Beaufort. *See* Somerset, Henry, 2nd duke of Beaufort
Beazley, James. *See* Beaseley, James
Beckman, D., witness, 292
Bed, bedding. *See* Household furnishings—bed, bedding
Bedford Galley (naval vessel), 139
  chaplain of, 246
  transports clergy, 132-133, 136-138, 140*n*
Bedford, Mr., clergyman, 60
Bedlam. *See* Hospital of St. Mary of Bethlehem
Beef, 85, 115, 182, 199, 231, 244, 257
  payment in, 117, 402
  staple commodity, 209
  See also Food, diet—beef; Price, value, cost—of beef
Beer. *See* Drink—beer
Beeswax. *See* Commodity payments—beeswax; Price, value, cost—of beeswax
Belcher, Governor. *See* Belcher, Jonathan—governor of New England
Belcher, Jonathan
  character of, 426
  governor of New England, 423, 426
Bell, John, vestryman, 190
Bell, Joseph, vestryman, 191
Bell, Mr.
  clergyman, 137
  leaves family, 137
Benbuary, John, vestryman, 490
Benbury, Will.
  letter from, 68-69
  vestryman, 68
Benefaction, 44, 107
  for construction of churches, 12, 15, 22
  for support of clergy, 241
  of Alexander Spotswood, 253
  of archbishop of Tuam, 58
  of Colonel [Christopher] Codrington, 121
  of Francis Nicholson, 172-173, 183, 250, 437, 449
  of Robert Boyle, 149
  of viscount Weymouth, 4, 15, 28-31, 46
  promised, 238
  to SPG, 12*n*, 14, 99-100, 392
Benefice, 418
  collation to, xliii-xliv, 188, 326
Bennet (Bennett), Thomas, author, 10, 34-35, 173, 409
Bennet, John
  churchwarden, 108
  testimonial by, 108
Bennett. *See* Bennet, Thomas
Bennetts Creek, 198*n*
  former Catholic at, 198
  ministry on, 198
  parishioner at, 198
  processioners for, 462
Bentinck, Henry, 1st duke of Portland
  chaplain of, 350
  deceased, 343, 345
  governor of Jamaica, 345*n*
Bentinck, Henry, 2nd duke of Portland, deceased, 390
Bentley, _____, lecture by, 198
Bentley, Dr. *See* Bentley, Richard
Bentley, Richard, author, 35
Beoregii. *See* Beveridge, William
Berenclow, Mr., house of, 59
Beresford, [Richard], clergyman, 390
Beresford, Mr. *See* Beresford, [Richard]
Berkeley (Berkley), George, bishop of Cloyne, author, 409
Berkeley Parish, erected, 414
Berkeley, John, baron Berkeley of Stratton
  proprietary land of, sold, 73*n*
Berkeley, William, proprietary land of, sold, 73*n*
Berkley, Bp. *See* Berkeley, George, bishop of Cloyne
Berks, Brian (B.)
  letter from, 334-335
  rector, 335
Berks, Mr. *See* Berks, Brian
Bermuda (Barmud, Bromudas), 28, 122, 319
Bernard, Saml., vestryman, 190
Bertie (Barte, Barty) Precinct, County, xxx, 312*n*
  clergyman in, 302, 336, 349, 355, 373, 376
  erected, xxxiii
  lack of clergy in, 302, 304
  meeting place for vestrymen, 314
  ministry in, 379-380
  parish in, 312, 373, 379-380, 414
Bertie, Henry, proprietor, 87*n*
Bertie, James, proprietor, 87*n*
Besson, Stephen. *See* Preston, Stephen
Beston, Stephen. *See* Preston, Stephen
Betterly, Thos., beaten, 466
Beveridge (Beoregii), William
  author, 9, 33-35, 38-39, 173, 295
  author of [*Sermons*], 35
Beveridge, Dr. *See* Beveridge, William
Bevis, Chr.
  petitioner, 324
  vestryman, 324

Bible. *See* Books, tracts—Bible
Bigamy. *See* Crime—bigamy, polygamy
Bill, 465, 472
  in General Assembly, 390
  of complaint, 413, 416-417
  of credit, xlviii*n*, 212
  of exchange, 96-97, 100, 139, 141, 150, 150*n*, 152, 159-161, 163, 165, 167, 169-170, 174-175, 175*n*, 178, 181-182, 184-185, 188, 196-197, 199, 209-210, 213, 231, 234, 238, 240, 246, 256-257, 263-264, 271-272, 277, 293, 329, 355, 390, 393, 405-407
  of physician, 492
Bill plaint, money to be recovered by, 404
Bills of mortality, collection solicited within, 114
Bilson, Thomas, author, 294
Bilsthorpe (England), rector of, 335
Bingham, Joseph, author, 409
Biography, books concerning, xlii
Birckbek (Birkbeck), Simon, author, 294
Bird, John (Jno.)
  churchwarden, 173, 448
  letter from, 171-173
  signature in behalf of, 173
  vestryman, 189, 445-448 passim
Bird, Mrs., deceased, 215
Birds, fowls, 115
Birkbeck, Simon. *See* Birckbek, Simon
Birket. *See* Burkitt, William
Birth, recorded, 483
Biscuit. *See* Food, diet—biscuit
Bishop, archbishop, 3, 49, 101, 374, 423
  certificate from, 21, 330-331
  committee for, 175
  jurisdiction of, in colony, 325
  needed in colonies, 18, 46, 176, 179
  nonjuring, 5*n*
  of Bristol, 243
  of Canterbury, xl, 3*n*, 19, 39*n*, 56-57, 60, 69*n*, 79*n*, 89*n*, 91, 94, 97, 100, 106*n*, 108-109, 111, 138, 153, 196, 201, 203, 211, 214, 272, 283, 285, 320, 323, 382-383, 398-399, 399*n*, 410-412, 427
  of Carlisle, 47
  of Cashel, 353
  of Chester, 395
  of Chichester, 33*n*
  of Down and Connor, 127
  of Dromore, 352-353
  of Dublin, 114, 351-352, 410
  of Elphin, 53-54, 57*n*
  of Gloucester, 21, 49
  of Lincoln, 359
  of London, xiv-xv, xxii, xxvii, xliii-xlv, xlix, 13*n*, 18-19, 19*n*, 21-23, 23*n*, 27, 39, 47-48, 51-53, 55-57, 57*n*, 58, 63, 66-69 passim, 73-74, 79, 87*n*, 89, 89*n*, 90, 90*n*, 97, 100, 103, 103*n*, 104, 107, 112, 113*n*, 114, 119, 127, 133, 135, 138, 145-146, 146*n*, 147-149, 154-156, 156*n*, 157, 161, 207, 216, 220, 279-280, 306-309 passim, 311, 313, 316-319 passim, 319*n*, 320-322, 322*n*, 323-326 passim, 329, 329*n*, 330-339 passim, 348, 352, 357-362 passim, 364-366, 366*n*, 367-376 passim, 381, 385-387, 390-391, 391*n*, 392, 394-396, 401, 405, 407, 410-411, 423
  of Meath, 323-324
  of North Carolina, 268, 293*n*
  of Norwich, 49
  of Oxford, 423, 425
  of Sodor and Man, 405
  of St. Asaph, 144*n*
  of St. David's, 392
  of Tuam, 57-58
  of York, 146-147
  palace of, 348, 350
  prerogatives of, xxxviii
  report to, 366, 366*n*
  suffragan, 3, 18, 49
  See also License—from archbishop of Dublin, from bishop of London
Bishopsgate Street, London, 127
Black, Mr. *See* Black, William
Black, William
  arrival of, 65
  clergyman, 47*n*, 65*n*
  letter regarding, 55
  missionary appointment of, 47*n*, 48
  resigns as missionary, 104
Blackal, A. *See* Blackall, Abraham
Blackale, Abra. *See* Blackall, Abraham
Blackall (Blackal, Blackale, Blackhal, Blackhall), Abraham (A., Abra., Abram., Abrm.)
  churchwarden, 481-482, 484-489 passim
  debtor, 477
  payment to, 477, 483-484
  physician, 477, 483, 486-488
  to appear before vestry, 488
  to settle account, 486-489 passim
  vestryman, 481
Blackall (Blackhall), Offspring, author, 35, 409
Blackall, Doctor. *See* Blackall, Abraham—physician
Blackamore, Mr.
  letter to be left with, 203*n*
  of Virginia, 203*n*
"Blackbeard." *See* Teach, Edward

Blackett, Edwd., endorsement to, 240
Blackfriars Road, London, merchant in, 367, 371, 373
Blackhal, Doctor. *See* Blackall, Abraham—physician
Blackhall, Abrm. *See* Blackall, Abraham
Blackhall, Bishop. *See* Blackall, Offspring
Blackhall, Doctor. *See* Blackall, Abraham—physician
Blackhall, Doctor. *See* Blackall, Abraham—physician; Blackall, Offspring—author
Blackhall. *See* Blackall, Abraham
Blacknal, John. *See* Blacknall, John
Blacknal, Mr. *See* Blacknall, John
Blacknall (Backnall, Blacknal, Blacknell), John (Jno.), *497-498*
  attends meeting, 298, 302, 463
  character, 304
  clergyman, xlvi, xlix, 5*n*, 298, 298*n*, 302, 304-305, 462-463
  deponent, 305
  mentor of, xlix
  ministry of, 305
  missionary appointment of, xlvi, 298, 304-305
  payment to, 467
  recommended for SPG service, 298
  salary of, 298, 305, 462
  warrant to, 5*n*
Blacknall, Mr. *See* Blacknall, John
Blacknell, John. *See* Blacknall, John
Bladen Precinct, County
  lack of clergy in, 376
  parish in, 414
Blair (Blear), James
  author, 409
  certification by, 341, 353, 358
  clergyman, xlvi, 319*n*
  commissary, xliv, 319*n*, 341, 353, 358, 365
  commission of, 319*n*
  founder of College of William and Mary, 319*n*
  letter from, 318-319, 319*n*, 320, 341-343
  notes shortage of clergy, 318
  president of College of William and Mary, 319*n*
  testimonial by, 365
Blair (Bleare), John, *498*
  allegedly convenes vestry, xxiv
  clergyman, xiv, xxiv-xxv, xxvi*n*, 5*n*, 30, 30*n*, 31, 437-438
  debtor, 30-31
  difficulties of, 31
  donates salary to poor, 438
  letter from, 31-32
  ministry of, 27-29, 46
  missionary appointment of, xiv
  prisoner, 30
  salary of, 437
  salary of, delinquent, 31
  statement by, xxv
  travel of, 30
  warrant to, 5*n*
Blair, Mr. Commissary. *See* Blair, James—commissary
Blair, Mr. *See* Blair, John
Blaire, Mr. *See* Blair, John
Blake, Elizabeth
  proprietor, 247
  son of, 249*n*
  widow, 249*n*
Blake, Joseph, Jr.
  inherits proprietary land, 249*n*
  parents of, 249*n*
Blake, Joseph, Sr.
  proprietor, 4*n*
  son of, 249*n*
Blake, Mrs. *See* Blake, Elizabeth
Blanchard, Aaron, processioner, 462
Blanket. *See* Household furnishings—blanket
Blasphemy. *See* Crime—blasphemy, swearing
Blear, Dr. *See* Blair, James—clergyman
Blessed Virgin Mary, character of, vilified, 229
Blessing (of food), by Quaker, ridiculed, 83
Blindness. *See* Disease, illness, affliction—blindness
Blome, Richard, author of [*The Art of Heraldry in two parts comprehending all Necessary Rules; And Giving a full Account of the Priviledges of the Gentry of England*], 8
Blount (Blunt), John (Jno.)
  letter signed by, 173
  vestryman, 189, 441-442, 444
Blount (Blunt), John (Jno.)
  churchwarden, 486-489 passim, 492
  payment to, 487
  presents account to vestry, 487-488, 492
  to retrieve parish books, 487
  vestryman, 486, 490, 492
Blount, John (Jno.)
  churchwarden, 440-441, 459, 461
  Council member, 432*n*
  county court justice, 432*n*
  debtor, 441
  deceased, 463
  General Court justice, 432*n*
  letter from, 287-288

letter signed by, 173
presents account to vestry, 441, 443
subscription by, 439
to collect parish tax, 459, 461
vestryman, 68, 173, 431, 433, 436, 438-439, 441-442, 444, 452-454, 457
Blount, Mary
allowance of, 443-444
petitioner, 442
Blount, Thomas (Thos.)
assembly member, 432*n*
Council member, 432*n*
deceased, 441
General Court justice, 432*n*
information from, 436
replacement for, 441
standardizes weights and measures, 436
vestryman, 431, 433-436 passim, 439
warrant to, 434
Blounte, John, letter from, 68-69
Blunt, John (Jno.). *See* Blount, John
Blunt, King. *See* Blunt, Tom—Tuscarora Indian chief
Blunt, Tom
cooperation of, 160, 161*n*
Tuscarora Indian chief, 160, 161*n*
Board of Trade
act sent to, 193*n*
instructions from, to governors, 279
report to, xlix
report to, proposed, 107
secretary of, 203*n*
Boards, planks, 32, 440, 443
flooring of, 445
for church, chapel, 444, 447-448, 451, 475, 493
reimbursement for, 451, 454
Boat, ship, 123, 129, 213, 335
at Virginia, 161
attacks pirates, 256
boatswain's mate of, 248
brig, 238
brigantine, 123, 243
cabin, 60
canoe, 29, 139, 177, 208, 210, 214, 257, 264, 440-441
captain, master of, 39, 50, 60-61, 63, 64*n*, 65, 65*n*, 71, 77, 92, 94, 101, 132, 134, 136-137, 140, 160, 200, 202, 226, 230, 232, 234, 238-239, 242-243, 256, 258*n*, 259, 350, 353, 362, 372
chaplain of, xv*n*, 114, 246, 299*n*
clergy takes passage on, 39, 50, 55-56, 132-133, 138, 148, 231, 268, 273, 423
clergyman dies on, 269
construction of, 32, 123
crew of, 39, 136, 211
empty, 211
ferry, 115
for England, 408
for London, 243, 371, 411
forecastle gang of, 248
French, 256
from Boston, 246, 435
from Boston, lost, 256
from England, 211
from London, 230, 256, 259
from New England, 181, 211
from New York, 244
hired, 66, 264
lacks crew, 256
large, at Brunswick, 344
lieutenant of, 256, 258*n*
lost in storm, 210
mast of, 32
merchantman, 138
name of, to be noted, 226
naval, 32, 55, 64, 64*n*, 65, 65*n*, 77, 93, 122, 132, 136, 140*n*, 210, 242, 248, 256, 258*n*
naval, at Brunswick, 344
passenger on, 39, 60-61, 215, 238, 345
pirate, 273
privateer, xxx, 93, 156
purser of, 139
refitting of, 372
sails, rigging of, 32, 214
sloop, 63, 122, 209, 213, 244, 256, 259-260
supplies for, 32
taken by pirates, 256
taken by Spanish, 420
to plantations, 79
transports servant, 264
warrant officers of, 134
wrecked, 359, 379, 401
See also Bayley, Bedford Galley, Burlington, Enterprize, Garland, George, Mary and Ann, Oxford (naval vessel), *Oxford* (ship), *Pearl, Princess Anne, Severn, Shoreham, Success*
Bodin (Bodini), Jean, author, 9
Bodini. *See* Bodin, Jean
Boehm, A. W., letter from, 113, 113*n*
Boehm, Mr. *See* Boehm, A. W.
Boid, George, commissioner, 403
Boid, Mr. *See* Boyd, John
Bolingbroke (stately home, Lincolnshire, England), 295
Bolster. *See* Household furnishings—bolster

Bolton, Theophilus, archbishop of Cashel
to recommend missionary, 353
Bond, Richard (Richd.)
churchwarden, 493-494
payment to, 494
vestryman, 490-493 passim
Bond, security, surety, 303-304, 489
for books, 180, 428
for collection of tax, 403, 468
not required, 377
of churchwardens, 434
of clergy, 47, 101, 128-129, 141-142, 151, 151*n*, 163-164, 169, 301, 393, 411, 428
of SPG treasurer, 100
to indemnify parish, 470
to receive funds, 485
Bonell, Jacob
bill of exchange to, unpaid, 405-406
merchant, 405-406
Bonner, Capt. *See* Bonner, Henry
Bonner, Colonel. *See* Bonner, Henry
Bonner, Henry (H., Hen., Heny.)
allowance of, 458
churchwarden, 456-457
letter from, 287-288
oath taken by, 477-478
payment by, 467, 470, 479
payment to, 458, 466, 479
pays find to vestry, 459, 463, 467, 477
presents account to vestry, 457, 478-479, 485
subscription by, 439
to collect parish tax, 459, 478
to return parish books, 487
vestryman, 189, 288, 451-452, 454-455, 459-465 passim, 468-471 passim, 473-474, 476-482 passim, 484-486
Bonner, Henry (Henr.), Jr.
allowance of, 486
clerk, 481, 483, 486
oath taken by, 481
salary of, 481
Bonner, Major. *See* Bonner, Henry
Bonnet, Stede
captured, 256, 258*n*
pirate, 258*n*
Bonnet. *See* Bonnet, Stede
Book of Common Prayer, xv, 80, 102-103, 188, 345, 362, 365, 369, 412
act of Parliament on, 325
churchwardens to provide, 433
gift of, xlii, 13, 39, 104*n*, 167-168, 277, 385-387, 399
in German, 88, 135
kept by widow of clergyman, 420
lacking, 104
printed at Edinburgh, 166
pupils to use, 43
requested, 16, 358, 366*n*
royal instruction concerning, 325
scarcity of, 198
to be purchased, 293
to be read, xliii
treatise on, 410
Books, tracts, 335
against drunkenness and breach of sabbath, xlii, 421
against Quakerism, xlii
against swearing, xlii
allegedly sold, xlii
Bible, xlii, 4, 13, 18, 40-41, 43, 58, 83-84, 98-99, 102, 104, 104*n*, 118, 127, 127*n*, 144*n*, 166*n*, 277, 345, 358, 362, 365, 369, 386-387, 399, 412, 420, 436, 448
bond for, 180, 428
by Quakers, 17
catalog of, lacking, 384
catalog, list of, 5-10 passim, 33-39 passim, 39*n*, 102-103
claimed by vestry, 151, 180
consigned to governor, 378
destroyed by Indians, 151
detained by vestry, 178
expenses concerning, 445
for clergy, xlii, xlv, 33-39 passim, 56, 100, 102-103, 161, 186, 378, 409-410
for entry of tithables, 455
for readers, 28
from SPG, 450
gift of, xli-xlii, 4-5, 9, 13, 16-18, 22, 26, 44, 70, 84, 91, 100-101, 115, 132, 143, 172, 176, 185, 198, 222, 293, 298, 337, 383, 386-387, 398-399, 411, 448
in Latin, 120
inscribed, 449
invoice for, lacking, 383
kept by clergyman's widow, 420
lack of, 85, 362
loaned, 9, 44, 79, 293, 345, 362, 420
lost, 143
none sent to Currituck, 86
of clergy, 65, 76, 112, 143-144, 151*n*, 160-161, 168-169, 175, 180
of homilies, 102-103, 120, 277, 358, 409, 420, 433
of vestry orders, 469
on baptism, xlii, 16, 410
on episcopacy, 16
on spelling, 421

publication of, 95*n*
receipt for, 420
requested, 15-16, 44, 198, 362, 365, 369, 372
requested by clergyman, 257, 259, 345, 401
requested for poor children, xlii, 421
search for, 373
secular, xlii
shortage of, 369
sold, 175, 198
to be distributed, 84
to be given to poor, 387, 411
to be lent, 41
to be purchased by vestry, 417
vestry detains, 178
widow of clergyman asks to keep, 400

Bookseller, clergy to lodge with, 39

Booth, Richard (Richd.), 446*n*
account of, settled, 448
allowance of, 438, 440-441
guardian, 438, 440-441
payment to, 445

Borland, Mr.
books sent to, 167
merchant, 167

Boston, Massachusetts, 12, 166-167, 179-180, 200, 211, 214, 232, 237-240 passim, 243, 246, 253-254, 256, 267, 269-270
clergyman in, 13
clergyman's debts in, 209-210, 212
customs collector in, 201, 210, 231, 234, 237, 244, 271
governor of Virginia in, 162, 164, 170
merchant in, 183, 183*n*

Boundary
diary of running of, 470*n*
of canton, 461-462
of mission, 383, 393
surveyed, 470*n*
with Virginia, 3*n*, 321*n*, 470*n*
See also Land—processioning of

Bounty
paid to clergy, 4, 15, 24, 27, 166, 175, 267, 274-275, 278, 350
payment of, for killing vermin, 492*n*
sought by church, 338

Bourne, John
letter from, 250
vestryman, 250

Boursrough, _____, author, 35

Bovel. *See* Bovet, Richard

Bovet (Bovel), Richard, author, 8

Bow vestry. *See* St. Mary-le-Bow, London

Bowl. *See* Household furnishings—bowl

Box. *See* Container—box

Boyd, Anne
legatee, 377
parents of, 377

Boyd (Boid, Boyde), John (Jno.), 343, *498*
arrival of, 341
attends University of Glasgow, 330
awaits missionary appointment, 328-329, 356, 363
behavior of, 375-376, 376*n*, 388
bill of exchange from, 355
books delivered to, 383
certification by, 482
character of, 333, 342
children of, 377
clergyman, xlv, 5*n*, 329*n*, 336, 340, 354-355, 363, 374, 377, 383-384, 388, 390, 400, 477, 482
deceased, 384, 385*n*, 390-392, 400, 407
delivers letter, 336, 355
desires to become missionary, 330
difficulties of, 349*n*
enemies of, 342
letter from, 341-342, 348-349, 355-356, 356*n*, 363, 363*n*, 373, 383
letter to, 384
ministry of, 349, 355-356, 363
missionary appointment of, 340, 349, 354-355, 356*n*, 363, 374, 390, 407
moves to North Carolina, 341
of Virginia, 331
ordination of, 337
payment to, 477
performance of, 336
performs marriage, 482
petitioner, 328-329
physician, 333, 342
recommendation of, 330, 333
requests books, 373
salary of, 329*n*, 376, 384, 385*n*, 392
salary of, delinquent, 356, 400
successor as missionary, 397
testimonial in behalf of, 331
warrant to, 5*n*
wife of, 377, 400
will of, 377-378

Boyd, Doctor. *See* Boyd, John—clergyman

Boyd, Lydia
legatee, 377
parents of, 377

Boyd, Lydia
certificate from, 400
children of, 377
executrix, 377, 400
husband of, 377

legatee, 377
letters testamentary issued to, 377
requests delinquent salary, 400
widow, 400, 420
Boyd, Marion
legatee, 377
parents of, 377
Boyd, Mr. *See* Boyd, John; Boyd, Thos.
Boyd, Mrs. *See* Boyd, Lydia
Boyd, Reverend Mr. *See* Boyd, John—clergyman
Boyd, Thos. (Tho.)
money of, reallocated, 251
petitioner, 44-45
testimonial by, 109
vestryman, 45, 109, 190, 251
Boyd, William
legatee, 377
parents of, 377
Boyde, _____
killed during expedition, 144
militia colonel, 144
Boyde, John; Boyde, Mr. *See* Boyd, John
Boyl, Mr. *See* Boyle, Robert
Boyle (Boyl), Robert
author, 8
establishes college fund, 149, 150*n*
lectures of, 34-38 passim, 410
scientist, 150*n*
Boyle, _____, sermon by, 198
Boyle, Mr. *See* Boyle, Robert
Braddey, James, land of, 493
Braddy, Joyce
guardian of, 490
mother of, 490
Braddy, Mary, daughter of, 490
Bradey, Charles. *See* Brady, Charles
Bradfor, _____
delivers letter, 362
shipmaster, 362
Bradfor, Capt. *See* Bradfor, _____ —shipmaster
Bradfor, Mr., memorial presented by, 23
Bradford, Dr. *See* Bradford, Samuel
Bradford, Samuel, author, 35
Bradley, Mr. *See* Bradley, Benja[min]
Bradley, Mr. *See* Bradly, Benja.
Bradley, Th.[*illegible*]
letter from, 295-296
letter to, 296
testimonial by, 296
Bradly (Bradley), Benja.
letter from, 124-125
letter of recommendation by, 127
merchant, 127
of London, 127
Brady (Bradey), Charles
requested as schoolmaster, 132-133
to deliver letter, 133
Brady, Mr. *See* Brady, Charles
Brady, Nicholas, author of [*Introductions of the New Version of Psalms*], 10
Bragg. *See* Bragge, Francis
Bragge (Bragg), Francis, author, 35
Braintree, Massachusetts, library in, 176
Branch, Francis, processioner, 462
Branch, William (Wm.)
lawsuit against, 456, 458
maintains parish member, 456
payment to, 471-472
Brand, Capt. *See* Brand, Ellis—ship commander
Brand, Ellis
confrontation with pirates, 256
ship commander, 256, 258*n*
Brandy. *See* Drink—brandy
Brass, weighing and measuring devices of, 435, 471
Bray, Dr. *See* Bray, Thomas—clergyman
Bray, Mr. *See* Bray, Thomas
Bray, Reverend Doctor (Dr.). *See* Bray, Thomas—clergyman
Bray, Thomas (thos.), 52
account of, 4-5, 14-15
act of assembly sent to, 22-23
author, 6, 9-10, 16, 22, 34-35
author of [*Catecheticall Discourses*], 9
author of [*Ch. Catechisms with Prayers and Graces*], 10
author of [*Expositions of the Ch. Catechisms with Scripture proofs*], 10
author of [*Pastoral Letters shewing the necessity and Advantage of an Early Religion*], 10, 38
books delivered to, 26
clergyman, xxii, xxv-xxvi, xxxix, 3, 3*n*, 10, 22, 121, 172, 178, 180, 186, 248, 257, 357-358, 449
commissary, xliv, xlv*n*, 3, 3*n*, 22, 23*n*
delivers letters, 12*n*
fails to visit North Carolina, xlv*n*
founder of SPCK, xxxix, xliv, 3*n*
founder of SPG, xl, xliv, 3*n*
instructions delivered by, 357-358
instructions given by, 365
letter from, xxv
library delivered by, 86
library of, 144

library sent by, xli, 22, 65, 121, 172, 178, 180, 186, 248, 257
method of, criticized, 16
recommendation by, 31
recommendation of, xxii
requested as minister, 66
statement by, xxvi
suffragan, 3
unaware of clergyman's character, 22
visit by, 22
Bray, Thomas
replacement for, 453
vestryman, 189
Bread, consecrated, 96
profaned, 229
See also Food, diet—bread
Breakfast, 302
Breeches. *See* Clothing, jewelry—breeches
Bret. *See* Brett, Daniel
Brethell, William
maintains parishioner, 435-436
to reimburse parish, 436
Brett (Bret), Daniel (Dan., Danll.), 5*n*, *498*
behavior of, 15, 22, 74
clergyman, xxxix-xl, 4*n*, 5, 9*n*, 12*n*, 15, 15*n*, 22
leaves colony, 20
library sent by, 9*n*
library sent to, xxxix, xli, 5
missionary appointment of, xxxix-xl
opinion of, xxxix
payment to, 4
warrant to, 5
Brett, Mr. *See* Brett, Daniel
Brett. *See* Brett, Daniel
Brewster, Samuel, author of [*Christian Schollars In Rules and Directions for children and youth*], 10
Briant, Lewis, vestryman, 189
Brick
for floor of church, 443
to be sold, 413
See also Building—brick; Church, chapel, meetinghouse—brick
Bridewell (London prison), 118, 122*n*, 264
Bridge, 454, 461-462, 474-475, 478, 488
broken, 116
Bridge, Mr., character of, 52
Bridge. *See* Hoskins Bridge; Luten's Bridge, Tottering Bridge
Bridle. *See* Horse—bridle for
Brig. *See* Boat, ship—brig
Brigantine. *See* Boat, ship—brigantine
Briggs, Wm.
bill of exchange to, 256
kidnapped, 256
surgeon, 256
Bristol (England), bishop of, 243
Bristol (New Bristol), Connecticut, 203
Bristol, Bp. of. *See* Smalridge, George, bishop of Bristol
Bristol, England, 60-62, 76, 421
Britain. *See* Great Britain
Brodgdol, James, 364
Brody, Josiah, debtor, 481
Brody, Mary, debtor, 480
Bromudas. *See* Bermuda
Brooke, Zach.
clergyman, 331
testimonial by, 331
Brumsick. *See* Brunswick Precinct, County
Brunskill, Jno.
clergyman, 331
testimonial by, 331
Brunswick (Brumsick) Precinct, County
clergyman from, 405
Brunswick (New Brunswick), 343, 348, 371, 410, 427
chapel, church in, 369, 412
clergyman appointed to, 344, 383, 399
clergyman in, 361, 388, 398
development planned for, 316
early promoter of, 412*n*
Bryan, John
collects tax, 403
security by, 403
Bryan, Matthew (Mathew), allowance of, 456, 458
Buchanan, James, bill of exchange to, 355
Bugg, Francis, author of [*The Quakers set in the true Light*], 6
Builder. *See* Occupation, trade, profession—builder
Building
barn, 264
brick, 285, 402
capitol, 303
coffeehouse, 222
cottage, 186
Council room, 285
courthouse, 191, 193-195, 266, 285, 304, 312, 314, 316, 404, 414, 461, 470*n*, 478-479, 486-488, 490
customhouse, 238
door of, 119, 303-304, 493
floor of, 120
glebe house, 350

house, xxii, xxvii-xxxviii, xliii, 17, 20, 45, 55, 59, 66, 76, 80, 85-87, 107, 114-115, 119-120, 128-129, 133, 137, 139, 158, 172, 177, 186, 202, 209, 213, 215-216, 229-230, 232-233, 244, 251-252, 254, 257, 260-261, 265, 265*n*, 268, 282, 298, 301-302, 323, 325, 329, 342, 344, 346, 349, 360, 369, 379-380, 404, 406, 418, 431, 433-435, 442, 447, 449, 453, 456-457, 489-494 passim
key to, 119
kitchen, 115, 300
palace, episcopal, 348, 350, 423
parsonage, rectory, 125-127, 152, 221*n*, 300, 313, 338, 348
payment for flooring of, 433
prison, jail, xxi, 264, 270*n*, 285, 303, 316
schoolhouse, 149
seats in, 120
state house, xxi
to be maintained by clergymen, 418
tobacco house, 175
warehouse, 291
windows of, 433
See also Church, chapel, meetinghouse; Occupation, trade, profession—builder, carpenter, glazier, joiner; Price, value, cost—of addition to house
Building materials, 431, 434, 440, 443-444
lime, 435
nails, 431, 440, 480
shingles, 444, 470, 480, 493
See also Boards, planks; Brick
Bull, _____, slave of, 230
Bull, Bishop. *See* Bull, George
Bull, Dr. *See* Bull, George
Bull, George, author, 7, 409
Bull, Mr. *See* Bull, William Tredwell
Bull, William Tredwell
clergyman, 217, 221*n*, 291*n*
commissary, xliv-xlv, 221*n*, 291*n*, 322*n*
instructions to, 225
leaves Carolina, 290
letter to, 221, 225-226, 290
order to, 226
rector, xliv
resides in Charleston, 322*n*
Bullingbrooke, Jon., testimonial by, 55
Bullock, Thomas, author, 409
Burchett, Josiah
letter to, 132
secretary to the Admiralty Board, 133*n*
Burchett, Mr. *See* Burchett, Josiah
Burgess, Thomas
clergyman, 5*n*
warrant to, 5*n*
Burial, 155
of indigent, 436, 442, 454, 458, 464-465, 472, 475, 478, 480, 483, 488, 490-491
Buridan, Jean (John), author, 294
Burington, Mr. *See* Burrington, George
Burington. *See* Burrington, George
Burkitt (Birket), William, author, 35
Burlington (naval vessel), transports clergy, 65
Burlington, New Jersey, 17, 203
clergyman in, 45
Burnet, Bp. *See* Burnet, Gilbert
Burnet, Gilbert
author, 7-8, 35
author of [*Life of Bp. Bedle*], 7
Burnhame, Gab., vestryman, 190
Burrington (Barrington, Barringtown, Burington), George (Geo.), 311
advice from, 348
arrival of, xliii
character of, 286*n*
criticizes assembly, xlviii
deponent, 301-302
encourages missionary, 350
fails to encourage proselytizing of slaves, xlvii
governor, xvi, xxi*n*, xliii, xlvii-xlix, 193*n*, 286*n*, 292, 302, 304, 307, 309, 325, 327*n*, 338, 346, 346*n*, 348, 350, 356
instructions to, xxi*n*, xliii, 325-326, 327*n*
lays instructions before assembly, 327
letter from, 327-328, 330-331, 335-336, 339-340
letter to, 356
military officer, 286*n*
notes condition of Presbyterian ministers, 339
notes Quaker population, 340
notes shortage of clergy, 339-340
of Devonshire, England, 286*n*
power of attorney proved before, 292
provides bail, 304
recommendation by, 309
reply by, 346*n*
reports status of religion, xlix
request by, 334, 336
request by, denied, 338
supports missionary, 304
testimonial of, 334
Burrington, Governor. *See* Burrington, George—governor
Burrington, Mr. *See* Burrington, George
Bury St. Edmunds (Bury), England, 114, 125-126

clergyman from, 127
minister in, 127
Bury. *See* Bury St. Edmunds, England
Busbaei. *See* Busby, Richard
Busby (Busbaei), Richard, author, 8
Bush, William, warrant to, 434
Butcher. *See* Occupation, trade, profession—butcher
Butler_____
clergyman, 130
letter to, 130
Butler, Bp. *See* Butler, Joseph, bishop of Bristol—author
Butler, Jacob
allowance of, 494
churchwarden, 490-493 passim
signs vestry minutes, 494
to appoint reader, 491
to settle account, 487
vestryman, 486-487, 489-490
Butler, Joseph, bishop of Bristol, author, 409
Butler, Mary, allowance of, 480, 483
Butler, Reverend Dr. *See* Butler, _____—clergyman
Butler, Samuel, author of [*Hudibrass 1t and 2d parts*], 7
Butter, 115
as rated commodity, 250
books traded for, 175
See also Food, diet—butter
Buttler, Christopher (Christ.)
allowance of, 432
debtor, 434
Buttons. *See* Clothing, jewelry—buttons
Buxtorf (Buxtorifij), Johann, author, 8-9, 294-295
Buxtorifij. *See* Buxtorf, Johann
Byrd, William
boundary commissioner, 321*n*
denounces colonists, xiv
diary of, 470*n*
of Virginia, xiv, 321*n*
Calleway, Caleb, allowance of, 483
Calvert, Charles, 5th baron Baltimore
request by, 332, 334
Calvin, John, author, 294
Calvinism, 425*n*
among Palatines, 88
Cambridge University, 186-187
Cambridge, England, clergyman from, 187
Camp, military, 229
Campbell, Jno., letter to be delivered to, 61
Candles. *See* Household furnishings—candles
Cannon. *See* Arms, armaments, ordnance—cannon
Cannon Street, London, apothecary in, 311
Canoe. *See* Boat, ship—canoe
Canons, book on, 450
See also Church of England—canons of
Cant. *See* Canterbury, archbishop of
Canterbury (Cant.), archbishop of, 19, 39, 39*n*, 57-58, 69, 79*n*, 89*n*, 91, 94, 97, 100, 272, 320, 382-383, 399, 399*n*, 427
letter to, xi, 398-399, 410-412
library of, xl, 138, 153, 196, 201, 203, 211, 214, 232, 234, 238-239, 244, 249, 251, 253, 283, 285, 355, 392
meeting held in library of, xl
testimonial to, 108-109
Canterbury, John Arch Bishop of. *See* Potter, John, archbishop of Canterbury
Canterbury, prebendary of, 13
Canterbury, Thomas Lord Arch Bishop of. *See* Tenison, Thomas, archbishop of Canterbury
Canton, parish divided into, 461
Cape Fair. *See* Cape Fear; Cape Fear River
Cape Fare. *See* Cape Fear
Cape Fear (Cape Fair, Cape Fare, Lower Cape Fear)
boundary at, 122*n*
clergyman in, 317, 322, 329, 336, 338, 344, 348-350, 356, 359-360, 368, 374, 381-383, 388, 391, 408, 411
growth of, 315-316, 344
Indians attacked at, 202
lack of clergy in, 347, 350
library for, 345, 398-399, 412
ministry in, 313, 344, 389
official in, 241*n*, 412*n*
pastoral letters in, 329, 350
settlement in, xiii
vestry in, xxiii
See also New Hanover Precinct, County
Cape Fear (Cape Fair, New Hanover) River
ministry near, 422
parish along, 324, 374, 414
petition from, 324
pirate captured in, 258*n*
privateer captured in, xxx
town near, 316
Caranza. *See* Carranza, Arturo
Caratuck. *See* Currituck Parish; Currituck Precinct, County
Carlile, _____, missionary appointment of, 47
Carlisle (England), bishop of, 47
Carlton, England, minister in, 204

Carolina (Carolinas), xvii, 12, 63, 78, 112, 180, 243, 278-280, 298, 332, 405
  books for, 103
  clergyman appointed to, 4-5, 21, 298
  clergyman in, xxvi*n*, 4-5, 45, 51, 75, 79, 104, 106, 200, 277, 280, 282, 304, 307, 341, 349, 388
  clergyman traveling to, 65, 76, 93, 144, 158, 349
  commissary for, xliv, 290-291, 291*n*, 322*n*
  deputy governor of, 80*n*
  description of, 252
  disorder in, 46
  divided, 122*n*
  established religion affected in, xix
  established religion in, xviii, xx
  form of government in, xxi
  governor of, xxxiv*n*, 80*n*, 87*n*, 122*n*
  granted to Lords Proprietors, 87*n*
  instruction of negroes in, 424-425, 427
  lack of chapel, church furnishings in, 104
  lack of clergy in, 113, 258
  letter to clergymen in, 227
  ministry near, 198
  oath of allegiance in, 82
  pirates in, 258*n*
  proprietary share of, 73*n*, 124*n*, 243*n*, 249*n*
  Quakers in, 82
  toleration of religion in, xvi
  united, 122*n*
  See also South Carolina
Carolinas. *See* Carolina; South Carolina
Carpenter. *See* Occupation, trade, profession—carpenter
Carpet, 358
Carranza (Caranza), Arturo, author, 33, 35
Cart, 210
  of clergyman, 214
Carteret Precinct, County, xxxvi
  ministry in, 380
  parish in, 432*n*
  sound in, 270*n*
Carteret, John (J.), Earl Granville
  land leased by, 405
  land of, 243*n*
  letter from, 3, 103
  palatine, 243*n*
  president of Privy Council, 243*n*
  proposed for SPG membership, 243, 243*n*
  proprietor, xl*n*, 3*n*, 81
  secretary of state, 243*n*, 279
Carteret, John Lord. *See* Carteret, John, Earl Granville
Carteret, John, 2nd baron Carteret. *See* Carteret, John, Earl Granville
Carteret, Lord. *See* Carteret, John, Earl Granville
Carteret, Roanoke Island, laws concerning morality in, xxxiv
Cartographer. *See* Occupation, trade, profession—cartographer
Cartwright, Thomas, author, 294
Carver. *See* Occupation, trade, profession—carver
Cary Rebellion, xxvii*n*, xxxviii, 65*n*, 69, 70*n*, 71, 72*n*, 73, 75, 78, 80*n*, 83, 87*n*, 122-123, 124*n*, 128, 140*n*, 239*n*, 451*n*
  legislation during, xxvi
  put down, 122
Cary, Colonel. *See* Cary, Thomas
Cary, Thomas
  appears before Lords Proprietors, 87*n*
  arrest of, 87*n*
  deputy governor, 82-83, 87*n*, 118
  escape of, 129
  president of Council, 83, 87*n*, 128
  rebellion leader, 80*n*, 87*n*, 123, 128-129
  removed from office, 82, 118-119
  residence of, 129
  travel of, 184
Cashel (Ireland), archbishop of, 353
Cashell, archbishop of. *See* Bolton, Theophilus, archbishop of Cashel
Cask. *See* Container—cask
Casshell, archbishop of. *See* Bolton, Theophilus, archbishop of Cashel
Cassock. *See* Clothing, jewelry—cassock
Castlemore Parish, Ireland, clergyman from, 53
Castlereagh, Ireland, 53, 57*n*
Catawba. *See* Indians—Catawba
Catechism, catechizing, xlii, 16, 22, 39, 41, 43, 101, 118, 159, 185, 198, 222, 224, 260, 262, 298, 300, 363, 387, 399
  book on, 450
  Negroes and, 261, 424
Catechists, 224
  shortage of, 176
  See also Indians—catechist to
Caterbury, A. Bishop of. *See* Tenison, Thomas, archbishop of Canterbury
Catharine (Cathrian) Creek
  parish boundary at, 462
  vestry meeting held at, 491
Cathrian Creek. *See* Catharine Creek
Cattel, Mr. *See* Cattell, Wm.
Cattel, Wm. *See* Cattell, Wm.

Cattell, Chatherine
letter from, 228-230
parishioner, 230
Cattell, Mary
letter from, 228-230
parishioner, 230
Cattell, Peter
letter from, 228-230
parishioner, 230
Cattell, Wm.
house of, 229
letter from, 228-230
parishioner, 230
verbal abuse of, 229
Cattle, 115, 120
die from murrain, 245
eaten by wolves, 211
in Bath County, 86
loss of, 214, 244
of clergyman, 214
Causin. *See* Caussin, Nicolas
Caussin (Causin), Nicolas
author, 6
author of [*The Penitent or Entertainments for Lent*], 8
Cave, William, author, 33-35
Certificate, certification
exonerates clergyman, 343
for killing vermin, 491, 492*n*
from bishop of London, 330-331
from commissary, 340-341, 353, 358, 394
from Presbyterian congregation, 391
from widow of clergyman, 292, 391, 400
of baptisms, 407
of marriage, 482
of tax collection, 454
See also Churchwardens—sign certificate; Clergy, clergyman—certificate concerning; certificate for, required; certificate on behalf of
Cestricus, Saml. *See* Peploe, Samuel, bishop of Chester
Cha. IId. *See* Charles II, king of England
Chalice, 346, 465, 469, 478
of parish, 488
to be purchased at Boston, 437
Chalmers, Mr., recommendation by, 90
Chambelaine, Jno. *See* Chamberlain, John
Chamberlain (Chambelaine, Chamberlaine, Chamberlayne), John (Jno., Thomas)
issues commission, 198
letter from, 58, 92-93
letter to, 19-21, 24, 46, 48-49, 51-52, 55, 57, 61-67, 69-72, 75, 79-80, 89-90, 93-97, 113-130, 132-138, 140-144, 160-161
secretary to the SPG, 19*n*, 20, 125-126
Chamberlain, Thomas. *See* Chamberlain, John
Chamberlaine, John. *See* Chamberlain, John
Chamberlane, John. *See* Chamberlain, John
Chamberlayne, Edward, author of [*Angliae Notitia sive praesens status Angliae Succincte Enucleatus*], 9
Chamberlayne, John. *See* Chamberlain, John
Chamberlayne, Mr. *See* Chamberlain, John
Champen, John (Jno.). *See* Champion, John
Champin, John. *See* Champion, John
Champion (Champen, Champin), John (Jno.)
allowance of, 475
payment to, 458, 467, 470, 480-481, 484
Chancellor, of England, 98
Chancery Lane, London, 154, 157
Chandler. *See* Occupation, trade, profession—tallow chandler
Chandler, _____
delivers letter, 232
shipmaster, 232
Chandler, Bp. *See* Chandler, Edward—bishop of Durham
Chandler, Edward, bishop of Durham, author, 410
Chaplain. *See* Clergy, clergyman—chaplain
Chapman, John, author, 410
Charity, in poor relief, xxxvi
Charles City County, Virginia, rector of, 470*n*
Charles II, K. *See* Charles II, king of England
Charles II, king of England, 4, 274
charter from, 298*n*
charter granted by, xvi
land grant by, 81, 87*n*
Charles Town. *See* Charleston, South Carolina
Charleston (Ashley River, Charles Town), South Carolina, xliv, 67, 206, 216, 232, 299, 317, 330, 344, 352, 376, 390-391, 394
clergyman appointed to, 51-52
clergyman from, 350
clergyman in, 66-67, 156, 353
commissary in, 291*n*, 322*n*
effort to uplift moral behavior in, xxxiv*n*
governor in, 73*n*, 118, 122*n*
Indians from, 158, 160
island near, 67
letter to vestry of, 227
military assistance from, 144, 151
ministry in, 67
opposition to clergyman in, 217

rector of, 66
settlement founded, xviii*n*
Charleton, William (Wm.). *See* Charlton, William
Charlotte, xlviii
Charlton, John
debtor, 459
processioner, 462
Charlton (Charleton), William (Wm.)
churchwarden, 442
debtor, 470
letter from, 68-69
to present account to vestry, 463
vestryman, 68, 441, 443-444
Charlton, William, Jr., debtor, 459
Charterhouse, London, 297, 392, 396, 398
clergyman at, 308
master of, 308
Charters
and church establishment, 189
grant of powers by, xxii, 136
grant of to Charleston, urged, xxxiv*n*
of Carolina, xvi, xxviii, 72, 83, 87*n*
of Carolina, religious powers granted by, xvi
of SPG, 39, 90, 97-98
toleration clauses of, xvii
Chatham, England, 134
Checker Yard, London, attorney in, 246
Cheese. *See* Food, diet—cheese
Cherokee. *See* Indians—Cherokee
Cherokee expedition, 216
Cheshire, Joseph Blount, Jr., bishop of North Carolina
corrections made by, 293*n*
Chest. *See* Container—chest, trunk
Chester (England), bishop of, 34
letter from, 395
Chester, bishop of. *See* Gastrell, Francis; Peploe, Samuel, bishop of Chester
Chester, England
clergyman in, 391, 393, 411
merchant from, 391
Chester, Pennsylvania, 17
clergyman appointed to, 91
Chevin, Mr. *See* Chevin, Nathaniel
Chevin, Nathaniel (N., Nath., Natha., Nathl., Nic.)
account of, 441, 443
Anglican, 239*n*
churchwarden, 440-441
clerk, 431, 433, 437
Council member, 239*n*
debtor, 441, 443
justice, 239*n*
letter from, 250
letter to, 238
moves from precinct, 441
payment to, 433, 437
replacement for, 441
subscription by, 439
testimonial by, 109
vestryman, 109, 190, 250-251, 431, 433-436 passim, 438-439, 441
Chevington Parsonage (Chivington, Chsington Paronage), Suffolk, England, 125-126
minister in, 127
Chichester (England), bishop of, 33*n*
Chichester, Bp. *See* Williams, John, bishop of Chichester
Chief justice. *See* Justice, chief justice
Child, children, 23, 44, 86, 117, 267, 324, 345, 391, 407, 409
baptism of, 13*n*, 14*n*, 19, 28-30, 47*n*, 49*n*, 53-54, 58-59, 66, 72-73, 76, 84, 96, 105, 117-118, 120, 125, 135, 141-143, 145, 181, 184, 198, 204, 222, 224, 233, 244, 252, 254-257 passim, 260, 262, 268, 270, 277, 283, 285-286, 302, 306-307, 313, 330, 334, 336, 349, 355-356, 362-363, 368, 373, 388-389, 409, 422, 437, 470*n*
bastard, 459, 489
birth of, 464
books requested for, xlii, 421
bound as servant, apprentice, xxx, 489
catechized, 159, 224, 260, 262
death of, 464
education of, 11, 42, 54, 143, 145, 168, 176, 222, 350
in poverty, xxxv-xxxvi, xlii, 492-493
killed in Tuscarora War, 187, 241
lame, 492
mulatto, 489
mustee, 261
Negro, 43, 87*n*
not baptized, 32, 117-118, 143, 146, 191, 235, 240-241, 252, 328
of clergy, 93, 104, 264, 268-269, 299, 307-308, 352, 377, 384
of indigent, 470
of planters, 116
of servant, xxx, 271
orphan, 438, 440-441
returned, 469
school for, 176
Virginia Dare, baptized, xiii, xv*n*

See also Education, instruction—of Indian children; Indians—children of; Servant—child bound as
Chillingworth, William, author, 6, 35
China, 7
Chisenhal, Mr. *See* Chisenhall, John
Chisenhale, John. *See* Chisenhall, John
Chisenhall (Chisenhal, Chisenhale), John
testimonial by, 80-81, 90, 90*n*
vicar, 80, 90, 90*n*
Chivington. *See* Chevington Parsonage, Suffolk, England
Choan. *See* Chowan River
Chocolate. *See* Food, diet—chocolate
Choctaw. *See* Indians—Choctaw
Choe Sound. *See* Core Sound
Chowan (Choan) River
clergyman at, 168, 259-261
disorder along, 158
governor at, 259-260
Indians along, 160
ministry at, 260
parish boundary at, 189, 194
religious conditions at, 261
Chowan County, court. *See* County Court—Chowan County
Chowan County Courthouse, meeting of freemen at, 490
Chowan Indian Town
chapel, church at, 142, 452, 459-461
clergyman in, xxxvii-xxxviii, xlvi, 142, 197, 305, 452-453, 459
reader in, 455-456, 459, 461
Chowan Parish
clergyman in, 73
salary for clergyman of, xxxi*n*
tax levied in, 491
vestry meeting held for, 471, 476, 479-480, 487-488, 492
vestry of, xii, xxxvii
vestrymen of, 486
Chowan Precinct, County, xxxvi-xxxvii, xlvi, 65*n*, 138, 145, 158, 160, 168, 174, 182, 196, 223, 293, 401
clergyman appointed to, 142, 383, 397, 400
clergyman in, 76, 86, 115-117, 149, 250, 266, 268, 321*n*
collection of taxes in, 445, 452, 454, 456
collector of dues for, 456
construction of chapel, church in, xxv
court. *See* County Court—Chowan
description of, 84-85, 116-117
difficulty for clergyman in, 199, 236
disorder in, 171
divided, xxxiii
divided into parishes, 189, 194
donation for chapel, church in, 250
donation toward chapel, church in, xxx
glebe in, xxv
inability to fund construction/maintenance of chapel, church in, xxx
Indians in, 143
indifference of vestry in, 122, 231, 246
lack of chapel, church furnishings in, 104, 120, 183
lack of clergy in, 184
land grant in, 114*n*
lay reader in, xxv
letter from, 68-71, 171-173, 449-450
letter to, 75, 227, 279, 400
meeting of freemen in, 490
ministry in, 143, 268, 379-380
official in, 432*n*
parish in, xxiv-xxv, xxvi*n*, xxvii*n*, xxviii, 414, 432*n*
vestry meeting held in, 245, 287, 431, 445-446, 448, 451-454 passim, 482
vestry of, xxiv-xxv, xxvi*n*, xxvii*n*, xxviii
will from, 377-378
Chowan Precinct, eastern parish of
erected, xxviii, 189, 194, 452
vestrymen of, 189, 254*n*
See also St. Paul's Parish
Chowan Precinct, northeastern parish of, 288*n*
accounts for, 455-459, 466-468, 476-477, 480-481, 483-484
churchwarden in, 465, 480, 483
clergyman in, 373
collector for, 466-468, 475
library for, 293, 295*n*
ministry in, 373, 384
religious groups in, 373, 384
tax levied in, 266
vestry meeting held for, 455-457, 463, 468-470, 473-474, 478, 482, 484-486
vestrymen of, 456-457, 463, 468-470, 474-476, 478, 482, 484-486
Chowan Precinct, northern parish of
vestry meeting held for, 287
vestrymen of, 287-288
See also St. Paul's Parish
Chowan Precinct, southern parish of, erected, xxxiii, 194
Chowan Precinct, southwestern parish of, 267, 452
erected, xxviii, 189
salary for clergyman in, xxx
vestry act concerning, 265

vestrymen of, 189
See also Society Parish
Chrisp, Nicholas. *See* Crisp, Nicholas
Christ Church Parish
clergyman in, 351
erected, 414
letter to, 227
Christ Church Parish, South Carolina
clergyman in, 67
lack of clergy in, 133
minister dismissed, 317
Christ Church, Philadelphia, 25
Christmas, 106, 167, 170, 177-178, 197, 229-230, 252
clergy ordered to write at, 92
proposal for vestry to meet at, 215
Chsington Paronage. *See* Chevington Parsonage, Suffolk, England
Church of England, xiii, 101, 200
acts of Parliament on, 194, 290
and marriage, 195
assisted little by lords proprietors, xxi
canons of, 40, 121, 242, 326, 401
communicants of, 96, 107-108, 117-118
conformity to, 254, 423
conversion to, 17-18, 46, 72, 105, 112, 126, 135, 151, 198, 207, 258, 261, 283, 306, 326, 422
conversion to, criticized, 423
discipline of, 184, 230, 247, 325
disregarded, 162
doctrine of, xlii-xliii, 40, 44, 50, 62, 108, 230, 276, 325, 423
endowment of, 289-290
established, xiii, xviii-xix, xxii-xxiii, xxvii*n*, xxviii, xxxi, xxxiii, xxxvi, xl, xlix, 59, 118-119, 121-122, 126, 165, 167, 172, 188, 307, 327*n*, 415, 449
established by charter, 189
established in Virginia, xvii
establishment of urged, 119
fasts and feasts of, 229
French congregation in, 313
Fundamental Constitutions and, xviii
liturgy, rubrics of, xxix, 16, 40-41, 88, 96, 191, 194, 242, 270, 283, 415
maintenance of, xix
members of, xiii, 173, 421
members of, taxed, 424
not referred to in instructions, xliii
not securely established, xlviii
opposed, 449
prayers of, 229
royal instruction concerning rites of, 325, 346
slave attends services of, 128
supported by Queen Anne, 254*n*
See also Acts of assembly—on church establishment
Church of Scotland
established, 424
missionary of, 391, 394
Church, chapel, meetinghouse, xliii, 173, 309, 338, 354*n*, 384, 432*n*, 433
absence of, xiii-xv, 17, 58, 64, 470*n*
assembly to build, xviii
at, near Indian town, xxxvii, 459-461, 464, 486-488, 493-494
baptisms in, 379-380
beautifying of, 445
benches for, 369, 433
bequest for construction of, xxx
Bible for, 365
books for, 386
books for, requested, 365
brick, 285, 358, 384, 413
ceiling of, 434-435, 444
chapel of ease, 432, 432*n*
chapter house of, xl
cleaning, decorating of, 465-466, 475
clergyman to officiate at, 192, 383
collar beams for, 431
commissary visits, 339
communion table carpet for, requested, 358
considered unsuitable, 444
construction of, xxii*n*, xxiv-xxv, xxvii, xlix, 17-18, 28, 84, 285, 354, 358, 375, 388, 401, 403, 405, 412-414, 431, 456, 482, 485-486, 488-489, 493
construction of, planned, xxx, xxx*n*, 65
construction of, proposed, 321, 325, 346
construction of, proposed for Indians, 149, 157
construction specifications for, 431
contract for construction of, 403, 431
contributions for construction of, xxii, xxxi, 12, 15, 327
cushion for, requested, 358
desk for, 229, 437, 443, 450
dimensions of, 493
doors of, 493
failure to contribute to construction of, 350
fines applied to use of, 413
floor of, 443-445, 447, 458, 493
font for, requested, 358
frame, 493
funds available for construction of, 317

furnishings for, 354, 417, 433, 437, 449, 454
gift to, 107
Holy Communion not administered in, 199
in disrepair, xxii*n*, 172, 229, 266
in good repair, 290
indifference to attendance at, 246
insufficient funds to construct, 266, 403
irreligious prevent construction of, 389
keys to, 303, 435, 437
lack of, 85-86, 96, 102, 120, 142, 317, 369
lacks furnishings, 104
land for construction of, 144
library in, xl
lime for, 435
lottery for construction of, xxx
minister refuses to officiate in, 208
neglected, 66
no minister for, 203, 258
not completed, 449
on plantation, 443
order concerning location of, 493
parish accounts to be published at, 312
payment for clearing town lots of, 458
payment for construction of, 433, 494
payment for maintaining grounds of, 458
payment for maintenance of, 460, 471, 484
payment for work on, 442
pew for, 369, 437
planks for, 451, 475, 481
plate of, 493
posts for, 431
preaching in, 20, 90*n*, 117, 131, 142, 220
proprietors may build, xvi
proprietors promise funds for construction of, xxi
pulpit cloth for, requested, 358
pulpit for, 437, 439, 443, 493
Quaker, 330
reader to clean, 437
repairs to, 447, 484, 486
report on history of, requested, 147
roof of, 358, 444, 493
royal, 347*n*
royal instruction concerning, 325
service conducted at, xxxiv, 283, 327
service in, not attended, 244
shingled, 444, 470, 480
sill of, 493
specifications of, xxii, 444, 493
subscription for construction of, 67, 145, 250, 282-283, 356, 403, 412, 432
table for, 433, 475
table of marriages to be displayed in, 326
tarred, 437
taxation for building of, 417, 432
taxes to be brought to, 193, 195
to be constructed, xliii, 192, 283, 455, 461
to be maintained, xliii
town lots for, 404
under construction, 383-384, 397, 402-405 passim
vestry elections to be held at, 314
vestry may compel services at, xxix
vestry may construct, xxix
vestry meets in, 171, 436, 438-439, 441-444 passim, 451-452, 454-455
vestry to meet in, 191, 194
vestry views, 434-435
walls of, 358
windows of, 84, 433, 436-437, 493
yard of, 404
See also Chevington Parsonage, Suffolk, England; Christ Church, Philadelphia; Indian Town Chapel; North Currituck Chapel; Roanoke Chapel; St. Antholin, London; St. Benet Paul's Wharf, London; St. Briget's, Dublin; St Dunstan in the West, London; St. Luke's, Dublin; St. Martin-in-the-Fields, London; St. Mary-le-Bow, London; St. Michael Bassishaw, London; St. Michael's, Dublin; St. Paul's Episcopal Church; Society Church
Churchhill. *See* Churchill, Winston
Churchill (Churchhill), Winston, author, 6
Churchwardens, 53, 63, 246, 251, 287, 433-439 passim, 443-448 passim, 454, 457-459, 461-462, 464-465, 468, 470-471, 478-479, 482, 484-486, 491-492, 494
accounts of, xxxii, 193, 314, 435-436, 438-439, 441, 443-445, 447-448, 454-459, 462-463, 465-469, 471-477, 479-488, 491-493
accounts to be given to, 450
accused, 314
agreement with builder, 434
allowance to, for collecting taxes, 445
appointed, xxvii, 119, 188, 192, 215, 431, 435, 437, 439, 442, 445, 448, 452, 454, 456, 459, 462, 465, 469, 473-474, 477, 479, 481-482, 486, 490, 493
ask to be discharged, 454
bond of, 434
building of church and, 317
collect tax, 445, 452, 454, 456-457, 459, 461, 470, 474, 476, 478-479, 489, 491
conveyance to, for building church, 431
death or removal of, 416, 479-480
dismissed, 444

estates of, 194
fail to attend meeting, 479
fail to produce accounts, 487
fail to summon vestry, 437
fine, forfeiture, for refusal to serve, 142, 415, 440, 442-443
fined for refusal to fulfill duties, xxix
former, order to, 489
hold funds of minister, 199
letter from, 69-71, 171-173, 184, 411, 419-420
levy fines and forfeitures, xxviii*n*, xxxi, 267
may be sued, 312, 418-419, 440
may bring suit, 418, 485
may contract for building of church, 431
may distrain, 438
may hire list taker, 447
may impose tax, 327
office of, origins, xxviii*n*
order collection of arrears, 245
order collection of tax, 451
ordered to make payment, 493-494
parish accounts and, 315
payment to, 483
payments by, xxxv, 434, 436, 451
petition from, 309, 353-354
powers of, summarized, 290
refuse to raise funds, 120, 208-209, 212
refuse to serve, 442-443
replaced, 440
responsible for collection of tax, 432-433, 440
sell services of servants, xxix
sign certificate, 322
subject to action against, 440
summon vestry, 440
sums due to, 434
tenure of ministers and, 209, 213
term of service of, xxviii*n*, 192, 194, 415
to account for parish funds, 312
to account for taxes collected, 413, 440, 488
to account with commissioners, 403
to be appointed by vestry, 415-416
to beautify church, 445
to bind out children, xxx
to bring action, xlv, 456
to collect salary of clergyman, 252
to employ reader, 432, 436
to employ workman, 437
to give parish funds to vestry, 416
to inquire about weights and measures, 469
to keep weights and measures, 438, 490
to oversee distribution of books, 84
to pay clergyman, 438
to pay for burial, 490
to pay for killing of vermin, 491
to pay for procuring Bibles, 436
to pay physician, 451
to prosecute vice, 326
to provide Book of Common Prayer, 433
to provide clothing, 454
to receive gift from Francis Nicholson, 445
to receive parish funds, 416
to receive portion of taxes collected, 416
to recover forfeitures, 417
to render account, xxxvii
to report on indigent, 464
to secure vestry records, 487, 491
to seek accounting of fines, 315
to serve extra year, 437
to summon vestry, 415
vestry to choose, xxviii*n*, 419
See also Bond, security, surety—of churchwardens; Fine, forfeiture—for refusal to serve as churchwarden

Churchwardens and vestry
letter from, 240-241, 250, 398
letter to, 236, 250
may call justices to account, 417
may dismiss clergyman, 236
may procure clergyman, xxix, 236
may purchase land, 192
may summon vestry, 192, 194
notice by, 193
payments made by, 195
punished for refusal to serve, 192
to make report on parish, 152
to procure clergy, 122, 194, 236, 417
to procure clerk, 417
to provide lots for church, 404
to seek accounting of fines, 315

Cider. *See* Drink—cider
Cinnamon. *See* Spices—cinnamon
Circumcision, reported among Indians, 216
Cittern, _____, debtor, 466
Civil War, English, religious turmoil during, xviii
Clagett, Nicholas, bishop of St. David's, report by, 392
Clark, John, vestryman, 190
Clark, Thos.
churchwarden, 420
letter from, 419-420
Clark, Walter, editor, 316*n*
Clark. *See* Clarke, Samuel
Clarke (Clark), Samuel, author, 7, 35
Class, social, ranks of not observed, 120
Claud. *See* Claude, Jean

Claude (Claud), Jean, author, 6
Claxton, Mr., payment to, 471-472
Clayton, Henry, vestryman, 190
Cleaves, Em., vestryman, 190
Clemens, Mr. *See* Clement, John
Clement (Clemens), John
  behavior of, 309*n*
  clergyman, 307
  clergyman, suspended, 309*n*
Clendon, Tho., testimonial by, 276-277
Clergy, clergyman, xxiii*n*
  absence of, xxxi, 242
  accused, xlii, 390
  accused of crimes, 309*n*
  accused of drunkenness, 304, 309*n*
  accused of misconduct, 15, 19-20, 22, 74, 85, 102, 273
  act of assembly concerning, xlviii, 11, 94, 97
  admits guilt, 345
  agent for, suggested, 238
  agent of, 185
  agreement with vestry, 356
  alleged Jacobite, 203*n*
  angry at magistrates' marrying, xxxi
  answers queries, 351
  appointed, hired, xxii, xxix, 63-64, 91, 121, 145, 209, 212, 231, 238, 245, 252, 305, 329*n*, 383, 385*n*, 392-393, 396-398, 400, 407-408, 411, 418-420, 442
  approves act of assembly, xxvii*n*
  archdeacon, 49, 277
  arrested, 252, 271, 391
  asks protection of archbishop of Canterbury, 412
  attorney of, 170, 177, 210, 213, 272
  bankrupt, 151, 343
  behavior prescribed, 40
  benefaction for support of, 241
  beneficed, 154
  bequest to, 317-318
  bishop of London refuses to see, 381
  bishop of London to approve, xxvii
  books entrusted to, 9, 172-173
  books of, xlii, xlv, 33-39, 56, 65, 76, 100, 102, 112, 143-144, 151, 160-161, 168-169, 175, 180, 186, 378
  borrows money, 209, 252
  bounty for, requested, 324
  buried, 269
  buys goods for resale, 159
  can be removed by vestry, 91, 215
  captured by Indians, 171
  cattle of, 214
  censured, 317
  certificate concerning, 25, 27, 57, 57*n*, 58, 66, 78, 80, 154, 322, 343
  certificate for, required, xliii, 325
  chaplain, xvi*n*, 4-5, 14, 39, 45, 54, 113-114, 135, 137, 148, 232*n*, 246, 299*n*, 345*n*, 350, 420, 470*n*
  churchwardens and vestry to procure, 192, 194, 236, 417
  churchwardens to procure, 236
  commissary, xliv-xlv, xlv*n*, 3, 3*n*, 22, 23*n*, 52, 124, 187*n*, 204, 208*n*, 217-219, 221, 221*n*, 228-229, 232-233, 242-243, 291*n*, 317, 319, 319*n*, 322, 322*n*, 326, 338-342 passim, 347, 350, 352-353, 358, 365, 370*n*, 387, 394, 396-397, 408, 411
  contributions to, 226-227
  corn of, 177
  crimes of, 343, 345*n*, 360, 367, 390-391
  criticized, accused, xxxi, xli, xlv, xlix, 20, 107, 120, 139, 142-143, 152, 158, 162-163, 166, 169-170, 176, 181, 184-185, 197-198, 206-207, 209, 213, 216, 220, 223, 229-232 passim, 234, 246, 252, 256, 272-274, 304-305, 317-318, 322-323, 327, 338-339, 342-344, 348, 369, 375, 376*n*, 390-391, 394-397 passim, 408, 411, 412*n*, 423-424, 426-427, 440
  curate, 53*n*, 54, 57*n*, 59, 80, 90*n*, 127, 156, 264, 323, 352, 388
  deacon, 127, 277, 291, 308, 399, 405, 408
  dead, 101, 104, 112, 132, 151, 151*n*, 167, 172-173, 178, 180, 250, 256-257, 269, 272, 276, 287-289, 292-293, 316, 319, 384, 385*n*, 388, 390-392, 400, 407, 418, 425*n*, 428, 460
  dean, 13, 54-55, 247, 405, 407
  debts of, 24, 27, 143, 209-210, 212, 214, 231, 234, 252, 271, 286, 318-320
  denied seat on vestry, xxviii
  difficulty of, in speaking English, 424, 426
  disciplining of, xxxviii
  dismissal of, legislation allowing, xxvi
  dismissal of, threatened, 440
  dismissal of, urged, 376
  dismissed, 90, 102, 221*n*, 268*n*, 277*n*, 316-317, 322, 325, 391*n*, 395, 408
  disobedience of, 207
  displaced, 82
  dissenter, 11, 18, 208*n*, 307, 309*n*, 321, 321*n*, 328, 330, 339, 384 , 397, 424
  do little to convert heathen, xlvi
  drunkenness of, 375
  early, in colony, xv
  education of, 276, 376

elderly, 219, 252, 256, 264, 276, 321, 323, 345, 361, 368, 412
elected, 66-67, 207, 229, 344, 418
escapes from prison, 395
executor, administrator of, 101, 286, 397
exempt from militia service, xxiii, xlviii
expenses of, 87, 104
faces bankruptcy, 148
fails to proceed to mission, 274
fails to reply to letter, 387
fee to, for marriage, xxiii, 195
flees, 342, 391
for Palatines, 88, 89*n*
forced to sell personal goods, 180
French, 336
funeral of, 286
German, 88
gift from, 438
gift to, 317
glebe not provided for, xlviii
governor interrogates, 301
governor to designate residence of, 399
governor to recommend, 367
hardship of, xiv, xxiv, xl-xli, 12, 27, 29, 96, 104, 107, 110, 115-124 passim, 135-136, 140, 142, 151, 156, 156*n*, 158, 160, 162, 166, 170-172, 174-177 passim, 180-182, 184-185, 187, 197, 199, 201-202, 205-206, 208-209, 212, 214, 219, 223, 230-231, 234, 237, 244-246, 248, 252, 255-257, 259-260, 264-265, 267-269, 271, 274, 276, 307, 313, 338, 343-344, 347-349, 349*n*, 350, 361, 363, 365, 367-369, 372, 384-386, 411, 449
health of, 26, 40, 61, 65, 77-78, 96, 107, 115, 139, 142-143, 154, 158, 160, 165, 242, 252, 255-256, 269, 276, 281-282, 284-286, 311, 321, 325, 417
higher, members of SPG, xl
house not provided for, xlviii
house of, xxvii, xxxviii, xliii, 87, 230, 344, 418
house to be built for, xxii
Huguenot, 470*n*
immoral, xxxviii-xxxix, 417
imprisoned, 391, 395, 411
in custody of constable, 301
Independent, 18, 339
induction of, 237, 420, 452
inquiry concerning character of, 382-383, 388, 391, 397, 408
instruction to, 39-42, 60, 95-97, 104, 169, 357-358
insulted, 301, 311
judged by laity, 74
keeps shop, 209
lacks credit, 209, 212, 231
lacks license, 351
lacks provisions, 209
learns Indian language, 197
leaves post without permission, 79, 79*n*, 174, 175*n*
lends books, 420
letter from, 13, 15-21, 24, 31-32, 50, 60-67, 71, 73-74, 81-87, 93-97, 103-106, 106*n*, 107, 109*n*, 110*n*, 111-112, 114-124, 130-133, 135-138, 140, 142-151, 157-160, 162, 164, 166*n*, 168-171, 174-179, 179*n*, 180-182, 184-187, 187*n*, 196-203, 203*n*, 204-208, 212, 214-221, 227, 230-234, 236-239, 243-249, 252-265, 267-273, 275, 281-286, 299-300, 306-309, 312-313, 316-320, 329-330, 333, 341, 356, 363, 365-366, 366*n*, 367-373, 378, 381, 383, 385-386, 388, 390-391, 393-396, 399*n*, 401-402, 407-412, 419-425, 427, 428*n*, 482
letter to, 15-16, 50, 114, 130-131, 152-154, 161-162, 167, 169-171, 176, 179, 187, 188*n*, 203, 203*n*, 204-206, 225-227, 233, 235, 237, 242, 253, 267, 355, 363, 372, 378, 396-398
library of, xli-xlii, 33-39, 39*n*, 98, 147, 151, 168, 178, 409, 412, 421*n*, 428
license for, 279-280, 341, 387
list of, 424
list of, sponsored by SPG, 408
loan to, 174
loyalty of, asserted, 235, 237, 276
madness of, 274
marriage performed by, xv, 193, 193*n*, 195, 242-243, 330
married, 21, 24, 77, 93, 102, 204, 209, 213, 217, 219
may appoint to vestry, xxix, 415
may be dismissed by vestry, 91, 215
may be removed by laymen, xxvi*n*
may hold office and serve in assembly, xx
may nominate to vestry, 191, 194
may not appoint to vestry, xxxi
may not be member of assembly, xix
may not hold civil office, xix
may return to England, 211*n*, 235, 267, 269
may serve neighboring parishes, xxxvii
may sue in General Court, xxxviii, 418
may sue to recover stipend, 415
meeting of, 206-207, 216, 218
meets governor, 349
member of vestry, 121, 189
mercantile activities of, 209, 329, 390

method of corresponding with secretary, SPG, 226
neglects district, 455
none among Roanoke Island settlers, xvi*n*
none to be sent to North Carolina, 300, 300*n*, 301
not elected, 350
not permitted to employ attorney, 181
not to leave post without permission, 178
not well received in colony, 426
observations on, solicited, 423
of Church of Scotland, 391, 394
of Virginia, xv-xvi
offers services, 114, 124-127 passim, 131-132, 280, 282, 291, 297, 298*n*, 328, 334, 365-366, 375, 382, 391, 437-438
officiates often, 409
ordination of, 18, 27, 54, 57, 66, 88, 90, 120, 208*n*, 277, 291, 308, 325, 328, 330-331, 337-338, 341-342, 347, 350-352, 391, 394, 396-397, 399, 408
patronage for, 323
perquisite of, 242
physical description of, 406
plan to obtain, 176
plentiful, 20
praised, 172, 228, 288-289, 342
prebend, prebendary, 13, 55, 352
president of college, 319*n*
proposes Indian mission, 253
proposes to keep journal, 329
proposes transfer, 300
proprietors may appoint, xvi
protection from governor requested, 398
provides meal to congregation, 361
publishes writings, 426
qualifications needed as, xxix
qualifications of, xxxvii, 11, 21, 39-40, 51-52, 56, 60, 85, 91, 102-103, 103*n*, 114, 125, 131, 192, 194, 206, 218, 241, 290, 325, 330, 342, 417
quarrels with parishioners, 229, 259
received by vestry, xxvi*n*
receives no letters from SPG, 104, 121, 151, 160, 162, 178, 237, 257, 263, 366, 411
recommended, xxii, xlv, 48-49, 51-52, 54-56, 57*n*, 58-60, 66-68, 79, 89*n*, 90, 101, 103, 103*n*, 124, 127, 186-187, 204-205, 278-279, 281, 298, 309-310, 323, 330-331, 333-334, 341, 347, 360, 367, 371, 374, 384, 386, 391-392, 394, 396-397, 400, 405, 407-408, 411
recruited by SPG, xli
rector, xliv-xlv, 66-67, 200, 204, 335, 337, 470*n*
reduction in salary of, xxxvii-xxxviii
refugee, 470*n*
refused permission to preach, 304
refuses service in colony, xli
refuses to officiate, 208
removal of, xxxviii, xliv-xlv
repentence of, 381
report by, xlix, 76, 363, 421, 426
report on state of, xliv
report on, requested, 225-226
requested, 23, 32, 66, 102, 133, 146, 186, 228, 236, 240-241, 287, 289, 293, 318, 340, 401, 460
requests discharge from post, 348
requests letter from secretary, SPG, 270
residence for, specified, 420
resigns, 316-317
resolution of, 218
returns to England, 275, 318-319
robbed, 269
rumors concerning, 395
salary, allowance, maintenance, xiv-xv, xviii, xxiii-xxv, xxvii, xxvii*n*, xxviii*n*, xxix-xxx, xxx*n*, xxxi-xxxvii, xli, xli*n*, xliii, 5, 12, 14*n*, 31, 44-46, 48, 51, 56, 58, 63, 73, 78-79, 79*n*, 81-82, 86, 88, 91, 94, 96-98, 101-102, 105, 106*n*, 107, 111, 113*n*, 115, 117, 119-121, 132, 135, 141, 148-150, 150*n*, 151-152, 158-166 passim, 169-170, 172-174, 175*n*, 176-177, 181-182, 185-189 passim, 192, 194-199 passim, 201-202, 205-210 passim, 211*n*, 212-213, 215, 223-224, 226-227, 230-231, 232*n*, 233, 237-238, 240-241, 244-246, 248, 250, 252, 257, 263, 265, 276-277, 277*n*, 279, 281, 288-291, 293, 296, 298, 300, 305, 307, 309-310, 315, 323-325, 329*n*, 330, 335-336, 339, 344-350 passim, 353-354, 356-357, 359-362 passim, 365, 367-369, 372-376 passim, 383-385, 385*n*, 388, 389*n*, 392-393, 396-400 passim, 405, 407, 409, 411, 413, 417-418, 420-421, 437-438, 444-446, 449, 452, 454-460 passim, 462, 468, 470*n*, 474, 483
seizure of house and goods of, threatened, 252
shipwrecked, 359, 379, 401
shortage, lack of, xiii-xiv, xxxix, 3-5, 10-12, 12*n*, 13*n*, 15, 19-20, 22, 24-25, 29, 44-45, 47, 51, 58, 72, 81, 84-86, 89, 113, 117, 129, 130*n*, 146, 172, 176, 184, 186, 189, 204, 206, 223, 227, 235, 240, 250, 258, 261,

270, 272, 274, 278, 282, 285, 287, 289-290, 296-297, 300, 302, 306-307, 318, 321, 324, 327-328, 330, 334, 336, 339-340, 344, 355-356, 363, 388, 401, 424, 449, 460
son of, xvn
speaks French, 347
speaks German, 88
standing orders concerning, xl, 101
subscription for, 195, 332, 336, 338, 344, 347-348
sued, 252
summons vestry, xxiv
surplice of, 104, 477
suspicions concerning, 351
taken by Indians, 158
taxed, 207
teaches, 198
testimonials concerning, 25-26, 49, 51, 52*n*, 53-55, 56*n*, 57, 57*n*, 58, 60, 78, 80-81, 90*n*, 101-102, 107-110 passim, 125-127, 156, 156*n*, 276-277, 291, 296-297, 328, 331, 333, 341, 386-387, 391*n*, 396
threatened, 122
threatened with imprisonment, 174, 301
threatened with suspension, 207-208
to answer accusations, 440
to attend meeting of committee, 398
to be member of vestry, xxix, xliii, 194, 325
to catechize pupils, 43
to correspond with secretary, SPG, 42, 92-93
to keep glebe in repair, 418
to maintain house and land, xxxviii
to make periodic reports, 42, 96, 147, 152, 169, 174
to meet together, 41-42, 225, 243
to meet with vestry, 454
to pay for passage on ferry, 446
to reside constantly in parish, xxxvii, 417
to visit parishioners, 41
tobacco owed to, xv
trade of, 209, 327, 390
travel, voyage of, xlvn, 3-4, 12, 14-17 passim, 20, 20*n*, 26-31 passim, 39-40, 44-45, 46*n*, 47, 51, 55-56, 57*n*, 60-63 passim, 64*n*, 65-66, 75-77, 78*n*, 79, 81, 84, 86, 89, 93, 95-96, 101-102, 104-108 passim, 116-117, 128-129, 132, 137-138, 140*n*, 142, 148, 152, 156, 156*n*, 158, 160, 162, 165, 170, 172, 174-175, 177, 181, 185, 200, 205-206, 208-209, 212, 220, 222, 230-231, 233, 242, 244, 250, 252, 254-260 passim, 264, 268-269, 272-273, 275-276, 278, 281-285 passim, 305, 307-308, 316-317, 323, 328-330, 332, 334, 336-338, 340-342, 344, 349, 352, 355-356, 358, 361, 363, 368, 373, 376, 379-381, 383, 393, 398-401 passim, 408-409, 411, 419, 421-422, 425*n*, 428, 440, 443, 446, 449, 459, 470*n*
unable to perform duty, 284
unmarried, 204, 217-219, 290
vestry and churchwardens to appoint, xxxvii
vestry may specify residence and duties, xxix
vestry may withhold salary from, 417-418
vicar, 80, 90, 90*n*, 268, 299*n*
violence of, alleged, 304
visitation of, by commissary, xlv
wants goods for resale, 181, 185, 202, 231, 234, 238, 246, 257
wants servants, slaves, 234, 237, 244, 246, 253, 255, 257, 264, 300
wife of, dies, 264
wife, widow of, 42, 267, 269, 271, 286-289 passim, 291-292, 302, 307-308, 318, 324, 377, 384, 388, 390-391, 400, 407, 420, 460
wishes to return to England, 211*n*, 212, 235, 271, 281
Clerk, takes election poll, 490
Clerk of court, 156, 377
Clerk of vestry. *See* Vestry—clerk of
Clitchensen, Thomas, witness, 155
Cloth, fabric, yarn
dowlas, 472
duffle, 158
kersey, 484
linen, 231, 472, 473*n*
osnaburg, 476-477, 484
thread, 476
Clothing, jewelry, 16, 40, 116, 120, 180, 237, 257, 485
bands, 16, 31
breeches, 229, 321*n*, 472, 484
buttons, 484
cassock, 31, 238
clergyman forced to sell, 180
coat, 321*n*, 484, 490
expensive, 365
girdle, 16
gown, 31, 237-238
hat, 31, 83, 237, 484
jacket, 490
made, 472
of clergy, 16, 31, 40, 65, 104, 161, 177, 237
of indigent, 454, 456, 458, 470, 472, 490
riding coat, 238
shift, 490
shirt, 16, 31, 472, 476, 484
shoes, 16, 31, 484
shortage of, 177, 365

slipper, 484
stockings, 31, 229
stocks, 484
surplice, 104, 477
waistcoat, 321*n*
washing of, 477
See also Occupation, trade, profession—dyer, haberdasher, milliner, shoemaker, tailor, tanner
Coach. *See* Travel, transportation—by coach
Coat. *See* Clothing, jewelry—coat, riding coat, waistcoat
Cock Pit, London, warrant from, 5
Cockburn (Cockburne), Adam (Ad.)
letter from, 287-288
oath taken by, 460
vestryman, 288, 460-461
Cockburne, Ad. *See* Cockburn, Adam
Codrington Estate, slaves from, requested, 244
Codrington, [Christopher]
benefactor, 121
estate of, 244
Codrington, Colonel. *See* Codrington, [Christopher]
Coffee house, 145*n*, 222
Coffin, 483
payment for, 480
See also Indigent—coffin for
Cold. *See* Disease, illness, affliction—cold
Coleman, Daniell
churchwarden, 331
testimonial by, 331
Collector of customs, 237, 244, 247
at Boston, 201, 231, 234, 270-271
Collector, collection
contempt by, 432
for building church, 282-283
of parish tax, 432-433, 435, 438, 440, 445, 447-448, 450-454 passim, 456, 459, 463-468 passim, 473-474, 476, 478, 481-482, 489, 491
See also Customs—collection of
College of Virginia. *See* College of William and Mary, Virginia
College of William and Mary (College of Virginia), 155
founder of, 319*n*
Indian school at, 87*n*, 150*n*, 154
professor at, 26, 87*n*
Colleton County, South Carolina, xliv
clergyman in, 291
clergyman rejected in, 394
Colleton, John (J., Jno.)
agent for, 4*n*
baronet, 81
deputation by, 148
letter from, 3, 103
letter to, 123
merchant, 124*n*
of Devonshire, England, 124*n*
proprietor, 81, 124*n*
Collings, William
petitioner, 44-45
vestryman, 45
Collins, John, processioner, 462
Comber, Dr. *See* Comber, Thomas
Comber, Thomas, author, 9, 16, 16*n*, 34-35, 39
Commander-in-chief, 167
Commissary. *See* Clergy, clergyman—commissary
Commissary, Mr. *See* Johnston, Gideon—commissary
Commission (appointment), 320, 330
as commissary, 319, 319*n*
as governor, 80*n*, 82-83, 119, 122-123, 124*n*, 129
forged, 339
from bishop of London, 338
from SPG, 338
to bishop of London, 326
Commission (body of commissioners), given power over church, xxv-xxvi
Commission (allowance for transacting business)
on collection of fines and forfeitures, 459, 481
on sale of town lots, 459, 464
on tax collection, 437, 447, 453, 457, 459, 466-468, 471, 475-476, 479, 481, 483, 486, 489
See also Salary, wage, payment
Commissioner
for building church, xxx, 317, 402-405 passim, 413-414, 461
for building courthouse, 461
for delineating boundary, 321*n*
for establishing school, xlviii
for Palatines, 123
for receiving debts, 452
of library, 15*n*
royal, 152-153
to receive and disburse funds, 485, 488
under Church Act, 66
Commodities, 213
rated, 250, 250*n*, 251*n*
staple, 209
beef, 402

beeswax, 402
deerskins, 402
for land, 443
payments in, 65, 86, 117, 120, 165, 183, 215, 226-227, 230, 250, 253*n*, 403, 445, 44
pork, 86, 139, 402
refusal to accept, 252
rice, 402
tallow, 402
to clergy, xxiv, xxvii
See also Acts of assembly—on commodity payments; Corn; Money
Commons House of Assembly (South Carolina), 270*n*
speaker of, 290*n*
unlikely to allow slaves to be educated, 424
Commonwealth, in Britain and Ireland, 122*n*
Communicants, statistics of, 421-422, 424, 426
Company Quarry. *See* Quary, [Robert]
Complaint, action by, 314-315
Compton, Bp. *See* Compton, Henry, bishop of London
Compton, Dr. *See* Compton, Henry, bishop of London
Compton, Henry, bishop of London
address to, 63
assigns missionary, 313
author, 35
certificate by, 154
commissary to, 3, 52*n*
deceased, 423
directions by, 87*n*
encourages missionary, 53
information from, 156*n*
instructions from, 39
letter from, 45, 47-49, 51-52, 55-57, 79-80, 89-90, 127-128, 133-135, 137-138, 146*n*, 149-150, 156-157
letter to, 22-23, 66, 68-69, 73-74, 77, 112-113, 135-136, 145-149 passim, 161
minutes laid before, 100
opinion of, 97, 113*n*
ordination by, 13*n*
petition to, 44-45, 104
presents paper to the Board, 47
proposals laid before, 89*n*
recommendation by, 90, 103, 103*n*, 156
request by, 157
tenure, 19*n*
testimonial to, 25, 53-54
to approve clergyman, 119
to assign missionary, 21
Concessions and Agreement, issued, xvii
Coneybear. *See* Conybeare, John
Confirmation, 18,
lack of, 17
Connecticut
description of, 11
lack of clergy in, 258, 340
Constable
clergyman in custody of, 301
not appointed, 447
serves warrant, 303
to deliver order of vestry, 432
to patrol streets, xxxiv
to receive election returns, 315
to summon freeholders, 414-415
to summon vestrymen, 314-315, 416, 484
warrant to, 267
Container
barrel, xxxvi, 86, 117, 139, 178, 244, 246, 402, 437
box, 98, 378, 383
cask, 246
chest, trunk, 16, 82, 269
Contract
churchwardens may enter into, xxvii*n*
for construction of church, 403, 431
Conveyance, of land, 431
Convicts, transportation of, 118
Conybeare (Coneybear), John author, 410
Cooper. *See* Occupation, trade, profession—cooper; Tools, equipment—of cooper
Cooper River, South Carolina, letter to vestry of, 227
Cooper, Anthony Ashley, 1st earl of Shaftesbury
associate of, xvi
flees England, xix
proprietor, xvii, xix
Cooper, Fleete, maintained by parish, 492
Cooper, Mr. *See* Cooper, William
Cooper, William (W., Wm., Willm.)
bill of exchange delivered by, 141
bill of exchange of, 170
bond by, 141, 163-164
demand of, 159
salary of, 141-142, 159, 163
Cooping, _____. *See* Copping, _____
Copeland, Mrs.
payment to, 461, 467-468
widow, 461, 467-468
Copeland, William
payment to, 458
salary of, 460
Copeland. *See* Copeland, William
Copper. *See* Occupation, trade, profession—coppersmith

Copping (Cooping), _____
dean, 405
delivers protest, 407
request to, 405
Coratico. *See* North Currituck Chapel
Cordiner, [William]
letter regarding, 55
missionary appointment of, 48, 55
Cordiner, Mr. *See* Cordiner, [William]
Cordiner, Mrs., information from, 136
Cording, Wilb., vestryman, 190
Core. *See* Indians—Core, Coree
Core (Choe) Sound, 270*n*
clergyman in, 269, 338
Corn, 85, 115-116
bequest of, to poor, xxxvi
for hogs, 257
levy of, 158
of clergyman, 177
payment in, 86, 198
raised, 199, 208, 231, 237, 300
rated commodity, 209, 250
value of, 86, 160
See also Horse—corn for
Cornbury, Lord. *See* Hyde, Edward, 3rd earl Clarendon
Cornwall, England, clergyman from, 388
Corritack. *See* Currituck Precinct, County
Corvinus, Johannes Arnold, author of [*Chassanaei Enchiridion Jurus Civilus*], 9
Cosin (Cousin), John, author, 33, 35
Costan, James, land of, 493
Cotelerius. *See* Le Clerc, Jean
Coton, William, testimonial by, 53
Cotton, _____, character of, 342
Council, 66, 122, 170, 332, 413-414
and Cary Rebellion, 122
Anglicans displaced from, 72
applied to by settlers, 32
as upper house of General Assembly, 346
assigns clergy, 64
complaint against, 32
enactment by, 402
governor fails to make recommendation to, xlvii
issues pardon, 124*n*
journals of, 119, 122*n*
letter to, 3, 121
member of, xxx, 4*n*, 25*n*, 65*n*, 76*n*, 83, 87*n*, 107, 124*n*, 129, 130*n*, 144*n*, 149, 161*n*, 239*n*, 263*n*, 291*n*, 309*n*, 352, 353*n*, 375, 412, 432*n*, 438*n*, 444*n*, 448*n*, 464
not informed of clergyman's departure, 272
of South Carolina, 66
of Virginia, 160
order of, 279
president of, xiii, xxiv, xxxix, 12, 12*n*, 14, 64-65, 65*n*, 66, 71, 76, 76*n*, 78, 82-83, 87*n*, 95, 110, 119, 128, 148, 158, 160, 165, 167-168, 176, 179, 282, 284, 288, 370, 405, 433-434, 442, 445-447, 447*n*, 448
Quakers on, 72, 81-82
reader appears before, 122*n*
to be consulted by governor, xlvi
to encourage conversion of Negroes and Indians, 326
trial before, 124*n*
See also Building—Council room
County. *See* Albemarle Precinct, County; Beaufort Precinct, County; Bertie Precinct, County; Bladen Precinct, County; Brunswick Precinct, County; Carteret Precinct, County; Charles City County, Virginia; Chowan Precinct, County; Colleton County, South Carolina; Craven Precinct, County; Currituck Precinct, County; Devonshire, England; Edgecombe Precinct, County; Essex, England; Gates County; Hanover County, Virginia; Hyde Precinct, County; Kent County, Delaware; King William County, Virginia; Lancashire, England; Lincolnshire, England; Meath, Ireland; Middlesex, England; Nansemond County, Virginia; New Hanover Precinct, County; Northampton Precinct, County; Northumberland County, Virginia; Nottinghamshire, England; Onslow Precinct, County; Pamlico Precinct, County; Pasquotank Precinct, County; Perquimans Precinct, County; Princess Anne County, Virginia; Roscommon, Ireland; Suffolk, England; Sussex County, Delaware; Tyrrell Precinct, County; Tyrrell Precinct, County
Court, 292, 326
absence of, 119
clerk of, 156
conveyance to be acknowledged in, 431
costs of, 403
county, xxxv, 404
does not assist indigents, xxxv*n*
higher, xxxv
notice to be given at, 193
of chancery, xv
of record, 314-315, 416
order of, 49
powers of, 136
precinct, 315, 377

Quaker justices on, 81-82
record of, xlv, 166
will proved in, 156
See also Court of Admiralty, Vice Admiralty; General Court
Court at St. James. *See* St. James's Palace, London
Court of Admiralty, Vice Admiralty
judge of, 161*n*, 183*n*, 239*n*, 263
of Virginia, 3*n*
Cousin. *See* Cosin, John
Coventry, England, 322
Cows, calves, 115
gift of, to church, 107
gift of, to clergy, 317
of clergy, 177
Cox, Nicholas, author of [*The Gentleman's Recreation in 4 parts videlicet Hunting, Hawking, Fowling, Fishing*], 7
Craffton. *See* Crofton, Henry
Crane Lane, Dublin, glazier in, 405
Craven (Yorkshire, England), 146
Craven court. *See* County Court—Craven
Craven Hill (Craven House), London, 103
Craven House. *See* Craven Hill, London
Craven Palatin. *See* Craven, William, 2nd earl of Craven—palatine
Craven Parish
erected, xxviii, 189
tax levied in, 402
vestry act concerning, 266
vestrymen of, 191
Craven Precinct, County, 65*n*
act concerning settlement in, 404
chapel, church in, 402
inability to fund construction/maintenance of chapel, church in, xxx
ministry in, 379
parish in, 194, 414
tax levied in, 402-403
vestry act concerning, 265
Craven, Charles
books sent to, 176
governor of South Carolina, 166-167, 167*n*, 176, 224-225, 225*n*
letter to, 166, 224-226
Craven, Governor. *See* Craven, Charles—governor
Craven, Jams. (J.)
clerk, 377
issues letters testamentary, 377-378
palatine, 103
Craven, William Lord. *See* Craven, William, 2nd earl of Craven
Craven, William, 2nd earl of Craven
letter from, 3, 103
palatine, 103
proprietor, 3*n*, 81
Craven. *See* Craven, William, 2nd earl of Craven
Crawford, Mr., recommendation of, 90
Creeds, 16
book on, 410, 450
Negroes and, xlvi, 424
See also Apostles' Creed
Creek. *See* Alligator Creek; Ballard's Bridge Creek; Bennetts Creek; Catharine Creek; Goose Creek, South Carolina; Indians—Creek; Indian Town Creek; Opequon Creek, Virginia; Sarum Creek; Sawyers Creek; Trotman Creek
Crime, 343
adultery, fornication, xxxiii-xxxiv, xxxiv*n*, xlv, 118, 121, 315, 466, 480-481
against morality, xlv, 326
bearing bastard child, xxxiv
bigamy, polygamy, xlv, 121, 122*n*, 136, 327*n*, 345*n*, 350, 390
blasphemy, swearing, xxxiv, xlv, 96, 475
breaking sabbath, xxxiii-xxxiv, xlv, 315, 466
cohabitation, xxxiii-xxxiv
cursing king, 303, 303*n*
drunkenness, xxxiv, xlv, 466
embezzlement, 317
fighting, 466, 475, 477
forgery, 339
fraud, 391
incest, xlv, 136, 326, 350
libel against government, xxvi
misdemeanor, 277*n*
murder, 177
of clergyman, alleged, 304, 309*n*
parishioners accused of, 229
perjury, 321*n*
sedition, xxvi
theft, robbery, 16, 264, 269, 270*n*
trial for, 270*n*
See also Clergy, clergyman—crimes of; Information; Marriage—unlawful
Crisp (Chrisp), Nicholas (Nich., Nichl., Nichol.)
awaits delivery of weights and measures, 445
churchwarden, 442, 454-455
clerk, 442
debtor, 441
deceased, 464, 471
declines office of churchwarden, 443

executors of estate of to return weights and measures, 471
letter from, 68-69, 287-288
payment to, 441, 463, 467
reader, 442
salary of, 442
subscription by, 439
to choose builder, 434
to collector parish tax, 434, 454
to deliver Bible, 448
to render account, 434
to retrieve weights and measures, 451
travel of, 254
vestryman, 68, 189, 254*n*, 287, 431, 433-436 passim, 438-439, 441-444 passim, 452-453, 457, 460-463 passim
Crisp, Mr. *See* Crisp, Nicholas
Crisp. *See* Crisp, Nicholas
Crofton (Craffton), Henry
debtor, 364
illegally performs marriage, 364
Crofton, Henry, Crown v., 364
Cromwell, Oliver (Lord Protector), 119, 122*n*
Crop
attacked by worms, 237
failure of, 231
lost in Cary Rebellion, 123
See also Food, diet
Crown, purchases Carolina, xvi, 318
See also King
Crown v. Crofton, Henry, 364
Crutched Friars, London, merchant in, 397
Cuddesdon, England, 426
Cudworth, Dr. *See* Cudworth, Ralph
Cudworth, Ralph, author, 410
Cuigley (Cuigly, Quigley), James, 197
attends SPG meeting, 150, 150*n*
salary of, 152, 170
to produce letter, 150*n*
Cuigly, Mr. *See* Cuigley, James
Culpepper, [Thomas], establishes parish, 10
Culpepper, Ld. *See* Culpepper, [Thomas]
Cumberland, Bp. *See* Cumberland, Richard
Cumberland, Richard, bishop of Peterborough, 308
author, 35
Cunaei, Petri. *See* Cunaeus, Petrus
Cunaeus (Cunaei), Petrus (Petri), author, 295
Curahick. *See* Currituck Precinct, County
Curate. *See* Clergy, clergyman—curate
Currituck (Caratuck) Parish
clergyman in, 73, 96
description of, 96
erected, xxviii, 189, 414
ministry in, 96
testimonial from vestry, 108
Currituck (Caratuck, Corritack, Curahick) Precinct, County
clergyman in, 64, 109
death of clergyman in, 168, 178
description of, xiv, 86
fines from, 445
glebe in, 317
library in, 143, 178, 257
ministry in, 65, 105, 117, 254
parish in, 194, 414
population in, 105
vestry in, xxiv
Cursitor's Office, London, 154, 157
Curten, Richard
payment to, 433
reader, 433
Cuscopnung River. *See* Scuppernong River
Custom House, London, 238
Customs, 32
collection of, 12, 24
See also Building—customhouse
Cutts, William, debtor, 473
D. H. *See* Humphreys, David
Damages
action to recover, 418
on protested bill of exchange, 406
Dandy, William (Willm., Wm.), bond signed by, 163-164
Daniel, Colonel. *See* Daniel, Robert
Daniel, Eliza., debtor, 481
Daniel, Robert, 438*n*
complaint against, 82
governor, deputy governor, 82, 87*n*, 118, 437
of South Carolina, 87*n*
Daniels, _____, 129
Danson, John
complaint to, 122
father-in-law of, 108*n*
influence of, 123
letter from, 123
order from, 123
proprietor, 81, 106, 108*n*, 123
Quaker, 108*n*, 201
Danson, Ld. *See* Danson, John
Dare, Virginia
birth of, xiii
christened, xiii, xv*n*
Dartmouth, England, 137
Davidson, Mr. *See* Davidson, William
Davidson, William
missionary appointment of, delayed, 375

petitioner, 375
Davis, Hugh, author, 6
Davis, John
petitioner, 44-45
testimonial by, 109
vestryman, 45, 109, 418
Davis, Samuel (Sam., Saml.)
petitioner, 44-45
testimonial by, 109
vestryman, 45, 109, 251
Daw, Richd., vestryman, 190
Day, Wm., debtor, 466
De Graffenried, Baron. *See* De Graffenried, Christopher, baron
De Graffenried, Christopher (C.), baron
captured by Indians, 113*n*
lacks credit, 123
land purchased by, 89*n*, 113*n*
leads palatine colonization, 89*n*, 112, 113*n*, 123
letter from, 112-113, 135
returns to Switzerland, 113*n*
settlement of, destroyed, 113*n*
De Seipso, Antonius (Antoniu.), author, 34-35
Deacon. *See* Clergy, clergyman—deacon
Deal, England, 137
Dean. *See* Clergy, clergyman—dean
Deane, Samll.
letter from, 228-230
parishioner, 230
Death, recorded, 483
Debt, 30-31, 155, 456
action of, 314-315, 404, 413, 416-417
clergyman flees from, 319-320
of clergy, 24, 27, 286
owed to South Carolina, 201
See also Clergy, clergyman—debts of; Commissioner—for receiving debts; Plantation, farm—seized for debt
Declaration
against opposing Anglican liturgy, xxix
against transubstantiation, xxviii*n*, 191, 460, 477
on liturgy, 415
Deerskins. *See* Commodity payments—deerskins
Defense, Quakers and, 83
Delamare (De Lemar), Francis (Fra.)
petitioner, 44-45
testimonial by, 109
vestry held at house of, 251
vestryman, 45, 109, 251
DeLamare, Mr. *See* Delamare, Francis
Delaware (The Lower Counties)
clergyman in, 47*n*
description of, 11
Denevan, Catharine (Cath.)
assaulted, 466
debtor, 466
Denevan, Judith, assaulted, 466
Denis, Mr. *See* Dennis, Ben.
Dennis, Ben.
clergyman, 128-130
difficulties of, 129
letter from, 128-130
ministry of, 128
Deodatus, Giovanni, author, 294
Deputation
as member of Council, 148, 149*n*
from lords proprietors, 119
Deputy governor. *See* Governor, deputy governor
Desk, for church, 229, 437, 443, 450
Devonshire, England
governor, 286*n*
merchant from, 124*n*
Diary, of boundary survey, 470*n*
Dicks, John
payment to, 439-440
widow of, 442
Dicks, Phillis
account of, 445
payment to, 442, 444
widow, 442, 444-445
Dicks, Widow. *See* Dicks, Phillis
Digby, Simon, bishop of Elphin
letter to, 53-54
letters dimissory from, 57*n*
testimonial by, 54
Dinner, provided by clergyman, 361
Diocese, xliv
of Elphin, 54
of Killala, 54
of London, 307, 309
of Tuam, 54
Disease, illness, affliction, 24, 65, 77-78, 154, 159, 210, 211*n*, 214, 264, 265*n*, 284, 304, 442, 484, 488
ague, 95*n*, 284
blindness, 313
cold, 264
communion not administered to sufferers from, 229
cured, 437, 458, 492
damp cold, 86
fever, 95*n*, 284
flux, 141
gripe, 307

lameness, 492
madness, 274
mortal, 256
murrain, 244, 246
of clergyman, 286, 417
of clergyman's wife, 267, 269
of horses, 210, 211*n*, 214
of pregnant indigent, 464
prayers refused for sufferers from, 229
quotidian, 94, 95*n*
seasoning, 158, 159*n*, 284
smallpox, 406
sores, 259
treatment of, by salivation, 477, 483, 485*n*
tremor, 94
vestry pays for treatment of, 436, 451, 468, 477, 483-484, 488-489
See also Clergy, clergyman—health of; Health; Holy Communion—administered to sick; Winter—illness in
Dish. *See* Household furnishings—dish
Dissenters, 11, 16*n*, 18-19, 22, 42, 67, 84, 118, 181, 224, 241, 257, 328, 334, 353, 423-424, 426
attend Anglican services, 384
Baptist, Anabaptist, xxxix, 17-18, 67, 181, 254, 261, 320-321, 328, 356, 373, 384, 463
book against, 450
dislike act of assembly, xxv
dismissed from vestry, 451
doctrine of, 423
enrollment of, required, xviii
excluded from office, xxvi
few in number, 283, 285
growth in numbers of, xxxviii-xxxix
impede growth of church, 449
in East Jersey, 11
in Maine, 11
in Massachusetts, 11
Independent, 18, 119, 121, 339, 424
Lutheran, 88
may not tax members, xx
may tax members, xix
Methodist, 425*n*
none in parish, 356
on vestry, xxix, 181, 191, 194, 266, 415, 463
oppose legislation, xxviii
position of, in Fundamental Constitutions, xviii
Presbyterian, xxxix, 11, 18, 28, 96, 119, 121, 181, 207, 208*n*, 313, 329-330, 339, 391, 394, 397
Puritans, xvii
Quaker, xxiii, xxv-xxxviii, xlii, 11, 13*n*, 16-19 passim, 19*n*, 20, 20*n*, 22-23, 27-28, 42, 44, 46, 66-67, 71-73, 73*n*, 75, 81-83, 85-86, 87*n*, 95-97, 105-107, 108*n*, 111, 116, 118-119, 121, 123, 124*n*, 140*n*, 148, 151, 181, 185-187, 198, 202, 211, 228, 245, 261-262, 271-272, 274, 283, 285, 304, 307, 320-321, 330, 340, 356, 373, 381, 409-410, 421, 425
replace governor, 87*n*
statistics of, 422
toleration of, xvi, xix, xx*n*, xxvii, xliii, 83, 325
toleration of, not practiced in England, xvi
See also Roman Catholics
Distraint, 267, 404, 413, 432, 438
levied for nonpayment of fine, forfeiture, xxxi
levied for nonpayment of tax, 433
warrant of, 413, 418
See also Penalty, punishment—double distress
Divorce, granting of, 136
Dobbs Parish, 432*n*
Doctrine. *See* Church of England—doctrine of; Dissenters—doctrine of
Dodsworth, John Eaton
bank director, 373
letter to be delivered to, 373
passage paid by, 345
Dodwell, Henry, Sr.
author, 26, 26*n*
scholar, 26*n*
theologian, 26*n*
Dodwell, Mr. *See* Dodwell, Henry, Sr.
Doldrigde, Rachel. *See* Doldrige, Rachel
Doldrige (Doldrigde), Rachel (Rachell) maintained by parish, 472
Donoughmore, Ireland, clergyman in, 352
Door. *See* Building—door of
Dorrington, Theophilus
author, 9
author of [*Familiar Guide*], 38
Dounam. *See* Downame, George
Douner, John
testimonial by, 331
vestryman, 331
Dowlas. *See* Cloth, fabric, yarn—dowlas
Down and Connor (Ireland), bishop of. *See* Smith, Edward, bishop of Down and Connor
Downame (Dounam, Downham), George
author, 6, 294
Downham. *See* Downame, George
Downing, Joseph

author of [*Catalogue of Small Tracts etc.*], 38
printer, 39
Downing, William
speaker of the house, 370
speech by, 370-371
Downs, (The), England, 133
clergyman at, 134, 137
Drayton, John
letter from, 228-230
parishioner, 230
Drelincourt (Drellingcourt), Charles author, 7, 36
Drellingcourt. *See* Drelincourt, Charles
Drink, 40
beer, 85, 178
brandy, 484
cider, 178
milk, 27
punch, 391
rum, 116, 119-120, 178, 181, 209, 212
water, 27, 85
water, salt, 115-116
water, swamp, 116, 231
wine, 435
See also Wine—for communion
Drinkwater, Jno., vestryman, 190
Dromore (Ireland), bishop of, 352-353
Droughen (Droghen), Walter, allowance of, 485-486
Drummond's Point, parish boundary at, 461
Drunkenness, 95-96
fine for, 466
of clergyman, 375
of vestry, 119
See also Books, tracts—against drunkenness and breach of sabbath; Clergy, clergyman—accused of drunkenness; Crime—drunkenness
Dry, Wm.
letter from, 398-399
vestryman, 399
Drysdale, [Hugh]
censures clergyman, 318
governor of Virginia, 303, 318
publicly cursed, 303
Drysdale, Governor. *See* Drysdale, [Hugh]—governor of Virginia
Drysdale, Mr. *See* Drysdale, [Hugh]
Du Moulin, Pierre, author of [*Pet. Molinaei Anatome Arminianismi*], 6
Dublin, Archbp. of. *See* King, William—archbishop of Dublin
Dublin, Ireland, 127, 324, 353, 406-407
archbishop of, 114, 351-352
bishop of, 34
chapel, church in, 352
clergyman from, 124
clergyman in, 156, 334, 352, 405
glazier in, 405
Duchy, Lord. *See* Moreton, Matthew Ducie, Lord Ducie, Baron Moreton
Duckenfeild, Esqr. *See* Duckenfield, Nathaniel
Duckenfeild, William. *See* Duckenfield, William
Duckenfield (Duckenfeild, Duckinfield, Duckingfield, Dukinfield), Nathaniel (N.)
church supporter, xxii
house of, 282
letter from, 310-311
slaves of, baptized, 261
Duckenfield (Duckenfeild, Dukenfield), William (Williams, Wm.)
account by, 441
agreement by, 432
Anglican, 144*n*
churchwarden, 435-437, 441
Council member, 144*n*
debtor, 441-442
General Court justice, 144*n*
land donated by, 144*n*
letter from, 68-69, 171-173, 450-451
missionary visits, 160
payment to, 441
receives clergyman, 142
subscription by, 439
vestryman, 68, 144*n*, 173, 189, 431, 433-434, 438-439, 441-443, 445-448 passim, 451-452
DuckenField, _____. *See* Duckenfield, Nathaniel
Duckenfield, Mr. *See* Duckenfield, William
Duckenfield, Squire. *See* Duckenfield, William
Ducking Run (Bertie County)
chapel, church at, 314
meeting of vestryman at, 314
Duckingfield. *See* Duckinfield, Nathaniel
Dudley, Colonel. *See* Dudley, Joseph
Dudley, Joseph, colonial governor, 10, 11*n*
Duffle. *See* Cloth, fabric, yarn—duffle
Dugard, Samuel, author, 8
Dugdale, William, author of [*Monasticum Anglicanum Epitomiz'd*], 6
Duke Street, London, 59

Duke, Col. *See* Duke, Hen[ry]
Duke, Hen[ry]
describes parish, 161
invitation by, 161
letter from, 160-162
Virginia Council member, 160
Duke, Mr. *See* Duke, Hen[ry]
Dukenfield, Wm. *See* Duckenfield, William
Dukinfield, N. *See* Duckenfield, Nathaniel
Dummer, Jeremiah (Jere.)
merchant, 183*n*
of Boston, 183*n*
payment to, 183
Dummer, Mr. *See* Dummer, Jeremiah
Duncan, Alexander, merchant, xxx
Dunming, _____
delivers letter, 184
shipmaster, 184
Dupin. *See* Ellies-Dupin, Louis
Dupis, [Sarah], petitioner, 32-33
Dyer. *See* Occupation, trade, profession—dyer
Eachard (Eacharde, Earhard), Laurence author, 33, 36, 173
Eager, Mr., library sent by, 176
Eagle's Island, parish boundary at, 414
Eagles, Richard, vestryman, 418
Earhard. *See* Eachard, Laurence
Earley, William. *See* Early, William
Early (Earley), William
debtor, 434
to collect parish tax, 432
warrant to, 434
East Ham, England, 94-95
clergyman from, 80, 90*n*
vicar of, 80, 90
East Jersey. *See* New Jersey
Easter, Easter Monday, 107, 191, 262, 314-315, 324, 344, 414-416, 465, 469, 473, 477, 479, 492, 494
Holy Communion administered at, 232, 260, 285
vestry to meet at, proposed, 215
Ecleston, Thos., [Sr.], son of, 483
Ecleston, Thos., [Jr.], father of, 483
Eden Town. *See* Edenton
Eden, Charles (Charl.), 185*n*
arrival of, 184
associates with pirate, 321
comment by, 196*n*
deceased, 184*n*, 282
encourages perjury, 321
governor, xxi*n*, 184, 184*n*, 196*n*, 197, 204, 206, 224-225, 258*n*, 271, 272*n*, 278, 282, 286*n*, 290, 451-452
instructions to, xxi*n*
invitation by, 200
letter from, 186-187, 196, 196*n*, 200, 204-205, 223-224, 235-236, 271-272
letter to, 205, 223-226 passim, 272*n*, 278
notes shortage of clergy, 204
pardons pirate, 258*n*
recommendation to, 321
reports state of religion, 186
request to, 224-226
town named in honor of, 286*n*
vestryman, 189-190, 451-452
Eden, Colonel. *See* Eden, Charles
Eden, Governor. *See* Eden, Charles—governor
Eden, Mr. *See* Eden, Charles
Edenton (Eden Town, Edington, Town on Queen Anne's Creek), xi, xxiv, 292, 304, 332, 334, 360, 363, 431-432, 432*n*, 460
chapel, church in, xxii, xxx, 383-384, 397, 417, 461, 485-486, 489
clergyman in, xxii, xxxvii, 283, 286, 298, 301, 304-305, 331*n*, 332, 349, 355, 373, 375, 459, 468
commissary in, 375-376
description of, xiv-xv
erected, 286*n*
general assembly held in, 346, 370
lack of clergy in, 388
letter from vestry, 287-288
library for, 293, 295*n*, 378
lots in, 459, 463-464, 466-467
minister visits, 470*n*
ministry in, 379, 380
physician in, 303*n*
reader in, 463-464
salary for clergyman in, 298
school in, xlviii
selling of town lots benefits vestry in, xxix
tailor and jail keeper in, 485*n*
vestry meeting held in, 287-288, 457, 459-465 passim, 468, 471, 474, 476, 478-479, 481-482, 484,
will from, 286-287
Edenton Courthouse, vestry meeting held at, 478, 486-488, 490
Edgcumbe, R., order signed by, 278
Edgecombe Parish, erected, 414
Edgecombe Precinct, County, parish in, 414
Edinburgh, Scotland, book from, 166, 168
Edington. *See* Edenton
Edisto, South Carolina, clergyman in, 391
Edmonton, England, 311

Edmundson, William, Society of Friends proselytizer, xxiii
Education, instruction, 24, 43, 84, 173, 264, 363
  by clergyman, 198
  in charity school, 264
  in hospital, 264
  in religion, 222, 370
  lack of, 222
  neglected, 371, 371*n*
  not encouraged, 422
  of clergyman's children, 377
  of Indians, 145, 146*n*, 149, 150*n*, 154-155, 410
  of Presbyterian minister, 391
  parishioners willing to receive, 409
  slaves unlikely to be allowed, 424
  See also Child, children—education of; Clergy, clergymen—education of; Negroes—instruction of; Schoolmaster, teacher; School, schools
Edwards, Arabella
  letter from, 228-230
  parishioner, 230
Eel, in fable, 249*n*
Eggerton, James
  allowance of, 493
  guardian, 493
Eggs. *See* Food, diet—eggs
Egypt, 182
Election
  of auditors, 99
  of burgesses, 315
  of inspectors of parish accounts, 312, 477
  to assembly, 82, 129, 315
  to SPG, 13, 13*n*, 80, 98-99
  See also Act of assembly—on election to assembly; Clergy, clergymen—elected; Constable—to receive election returns; Vestry—elected
Elizabeth Town, New Jersey, 48
Ellesby, James, author of [*Sick Christian's Companion*], 38
Ellies-Dupin, Louis, author, 410
Ellis, J., author, 34, 36
Elms, Mr.
  merchant, 406
  of London, 406
  payment to, 406
  protest by, 406-407
Elphin (Ireland), dean of, 55, 57*n*
Elphin, Diocese of, Ireland, 54
Elphin, bishop of. *See* Digby, Simon, bishop of Elphin
Elphin, S. *See* Digby, Simon, bishop of Elphin
Embezzlement. *See* Crime—embezzlement
Emigration, immigration
  by Christopher Gale, 130*n*
  by Palatines, 89*n*
  by Scots and Scotch-Irish, xxxix
  deterrent to, xlviii
  into England, 89*n*
England (South Britain), xix, xxvii*n*, xxxv, xlii-xliii, 11, 16, 19, 28, 32, 44, 66, 72, 86, 88*n*, 93, 105-106, 118-120, 124, 135, 137, 152, 170, 177, 192, 194, 209, 211, 213-215, 231, 235, 237, 255, 257, 261, 264, 267-269, 290, 307, 322, 342, 390, 408, 417, 443
  arms shipment from, 123
  church officials in, xlix
  clergyman from, 174
  clergyman in, 25-27, 30, 83, 116, 328, 334, 343, 359, 405, 411
  clergyman requests salary from, 345
  clergyman returns to, xxvi*n*, 26, 267, 299*n*
  clergyman sailing to, 95, 108, 148, 251, 273, 318-319
  clergyman's debts in, 165, 209, 212
  colonial agent returns to, 307
  commissary from, xliv
  commissary returns to, xlv
  deputy governor from, 80*n*
  disorder in, 212*n*, 213
  ecclesiastical laws of, xxix, xxxvii
  explorer in, 95*n*
  governor returns to, 73*n*, 300
  governor's wife returns to, 124*n*, 140*n*
  lack of support from, 18, 104, 111, 140, 162, 178, 181, 199, 271
  laws of, xxvii
  leader of rebellion in, 87*n*
  official from, 336
  palatines in, 89*n*
  Quaker representative in, 82
  religion affected by politics in, xvii, xix
  religious intolerance in, xvi
  religious strife in, xviii-xix
  surgeon sailing to, 256
  vestryman sailing to, 254
  See also Great Britain
Engless, Mongo, letter to be delivered to, 76
English (language), 324
  clergyman has difficulty with, 424, 426
  French settlers and, 347
Enterprize (naval vessel), 122
Epictetus, author, 7
Episcopacy, book on, 16
Epsom, England, 130

Essex, county of, (England), 114, 128
clergyman from, 80, 90*n*
Essoin, plea of, 314-315, 413, 416-417
Estate, of churchwarden, 194
Eucharist. *See* Holy Communion
Europe, xv, 95, 104-105, 107, 307
Eusebias, author, 294
Eustachii. *See* Eustachius a Sancta Paulo Eustachii
Eustachius a Sancta Paulo Eustachii, author, 294
Evagrius, author, 294
Evans, Evan, memorial presented by, 57
Evens, Sarah, witness, 155
Everard (Everett), Richard (Richd.), 311
affidavit sworn before, 305
approbation of, required, 305
attends meeting, 298, 302
baronet, 299*n*, 301, 305, 462-465 passim
churchwarden, 465
denies request, 304
governor, xv, xxi*n*, xxxix, xlix, 286*n*, 298, 299*n*, 301, 305-307, 309*n*, 320, 465
instructions to, xxi*n*
letter from, xv-xvi, xlix, 303-306 passim, 317-318, 320-321
notes shortage of clergy, 321
protégé of, xlix
questions clergyman, 301
requests missionaries, 304
son of, 302, 304
tenure, 299*n*
vestryman, 462-465 passim
warns of increasing numbers of dissenters, xxxix
Everard, Governor. *See* Everard, Richard
Everard, Mr., debtor, 466
Everett, Richd. *See* Everard, Richard
Exchequer of Receipt, 4-5
Exclusion controversy (Great Britain)
Fundamental Constitutions and, xviii-xix
Execution, on judgment to recover parish funds, 312
Executor, executrix, 155, 291, 400, 418, 448, 480, 485
of clergyman, 101, 286, 377
paid for keeping indigent, 474
to deliver weights and measures, 471
Exmouth, England, lord proprietor from, 124*n*
Expedition, military, 12*n*
Exum, Ritchd., letter to be delivered to, 76
Fable, 248
Falkner, William, author, 7
Fall, autumn, 104-105
Family, family relationships, 39-40, 54-55, 58-59, 93, 115-116, 125, 129, 140, 156, 156*n*, 165, 170, 177, 180, 202, 204, 208-210, 237-238, 246-247, 257, 264-265, 282, 284, 299-300, 308, 313, 323, 328*n*, 341, 345, 349-350, 352-353, 358-359, 365, 379, 381, 385, 388, 395, 405
brother, 163*n*, 177, 187, 200, 202*n*, 204, 254, 464*n*
children, 66-67, 313
cousin, 263
daughter, 15, 254, 311, 345, 490
father, 143, 204, 229, 247, 249*n*, 302, 335
flees Indian depredations, 255
husband, widower, 77, 118, 352, 388, 420
Indian, 216
mother, 198, 254
nephew, 330
of governor, 224
parents, xiii, 117-118, 143, 149, 231, 233, 252, 405
relative of Queen Anne, 80*n*
sister, 254
son, xv*n*, xix, 58, 67, 118, 124, 128, 130*n*, 143, 145*n*, 146, 147*n*, 200, 216, 222, 229, 247, 249*n*, 254, 257, 271, 302, 304, 311, 362, 464, 483
son-in-law, 260, 323
wife, widow, xlii, 21, 24, 66-67, 77, 102, 104, 107, 108*n*, 116, 118, 122, 124, 137, 139, 155, 177, 183, 209, 248-249, 249*n*, 264, 311, 313, 324, 345*n*, 377, 390-391, 407, 442, 444, 458, 460, 466-468, 477, 483
Farlow, James (Jno.)
churchwarden, 456, 458
dismissed as vestryman, 459
list of tithables of, 458
presents account to vestry, 458
refuses to qualify as vestryman, 452
replacement for, 460
vestryman, 189, 453-455, 459
Farlow, Jno. *See* Farlow, James
Farlow, Mr. *See* Farlow, James
Farmer. *See* Occupation, trade, profession—farmer
Farmer, Geoffrey
ship captain, 259
to deliver letter, 259
Farming, planting, by clergyman, 208
Fasting, proclamation on, 119
Favour, Thomas, burial of, 458
Featherstone, Thos., clergyman, 352
Feckenham, England, 386
Fees

for conducting funeral service, 215
for marriage, 193, 195, 384
of clerk, 458
on will, 378
table of, 215
See also Salary, wages, payment
Fence, 66, 418
Fendall, Robert
deceased, 448
executor of estate of, 448
money collected by, 448
Ferry, 27, 115
clergyman to pay for passage on, 446
free passage on, for clergy, 400, 401*n*, 420
Fever. *See* Disease, illness, affliction—fever
Fiddes, Richard, author, 410
Fighting. *See* Crime—fighting; Fine, forfeiture—for fighting
Fine, forfeiture, 315, 413, 459, 467, 473
churchwardens subject to, 419
churchwardens to levy, xxvii*n*, xxxi, 267
collected, xxxii, 445, 457-460 passim, 462-463, 466, 470, 475, 480-481
for breaking sabbath, 466
for damage to glebe, 418
for drunkenness, 466
for failure to account for taxes collected, 440
for failure to render accounts, 417
for failure to summon vestry, 415
for fighting, 466, 475, 477
for fornication, 466, 480-481
for giving birth to mulatto, 480
for illegal marriage, xxxi, 364, 364*n*
for infringement of vestry act, xxxvii
for nonpayment of tax, 403
for refusal to fulfill duties, xxix
for refusal to make declaration, 191
for refusal to serve as churchwarden, xxxi, 192, 415, 440, 442-443
for refusal to serve as vestryman, xxix, xxxi
for swearing, 475
of marshal, 191
of vestrymen, 191-192
to provide militia arms for poor, xxxvi*n*
vestry to receive, xxix, xxx*n*, 469, 483
See also Parish—receives portion of fine to aid poor
Fire, at house, 418
Fish. *See* Food, diet—fish
Fitzroy, Charles, 2nd duke of Grafton, warrant by, 346
Five Nations. *See* Indians—Five Nations
Fleet, The (London prison), 118, 122*n*, 238, 239*n*
inmate of, 238, 239*n*
Fleetwood, Bishop. *See* Fleetwood, William, bishop of St. Asaph
Fleetwood, William, bishop of St. Asaph
author, 410
sermon by, 143, 144*n*
Fletcher, Francis (Frans.)
burial of, 476
maintained by parish, 483
Flour. *See* Food, diet—flour
Flowers, John, allowance of, 472
Flux. *See* Disease, illness, affliction—flux
Foard, John
clothes for, 490
maintained by parish, 489-490
Folkingham, Joseph
letter from, 228-230
parishioner, 230
Font, baptismal, 358
Fontaine (Fountain), Peter
clergyman, 468, 470*n*
ministry of, 470*n*
payment to, 468
Food, diet, 83, 116, 180
aboard ship, 137
bacon, 231, 244
barley, 231
beans, 116, 244
biscuit, 244
bread, 85, 123, 181, 231, 244, 246, 264
butter, 198, 231, 237, 244, 257
cheese, 115, 231, 237
chocolate, 302
eggs, 175, 198
fish, 161
flour, 244
fruit, 141, 145*n*, 245
grain, 237, 245
hasty pudding, 257
hominy, 231
hominy bread, 116
inexpensive, 209, 213
malt, 178, 237
meal, 246
meat, 231
molasses, 116, 178, 181, 209, 212
mush, 257
mutton, 115, 199
nuts, 145*n*
of clergy, 27, 31, 40, 96, 115, 121, 134, 143-144, 161, 180-182, 198-199, 208-209, 212-213, 244, 256
peas, 116, 244

pork, 182, 231, 237, 244, 257
porridge, 257
salad oil, 178
salt, 231, 244
shortage of, 115-116, 140, 177, 181-182, 234, 237, 245, 257
sugar, 116, 139, 178, 181, 202, 212
See also Beef; Butter; Corn; Drink; Grain; Pork; Spices
Football. *See* Amusements, games—football
Forbes, Mr., recommended as missionary, 149
Forbes, William, vestryman, 418
Fordyce, John
clergyman, 388-389
letter from, 388-389
letter to, 388
ministry of, 388-389
Forged document, 310*n*
Forgery. *See* Crime—forgery
Fornication. *See* Crime—adultery, fornication; Fine, forfeiture—for fornication
Forster, _____, witness, 292
Forster, Robt.
leaves colony, 485
vestryman, 481-482, 485
Fort Nohoroco, 140*n*
Fort, fortification, 129
in Tuscarora War, 146
Indian, 140*n*, 201
Foster, Fran., vestryman, 190
Fountain, Mr. *See* Fontaine, Peter
Fourcroy, abbe de, author of [*A new and Easy method to Understand the Roman History with an Exact Chronology of the Reign of the Emperors for the Use of the D. of Burgundy*], 8
Fowler, Edward, bishop of Gloucester, letter from, 49
Fox, George, Society of Friends proselytizer, xxiii, 22, 83
Fraley, Mr., house of, 380
France, xlvi, 93, 389
clergyman held captive, 30-31
Frank, Mart., vestryman, 191
Frank, Professor, application to, 88*n*
Franklin, Mr., notes shortage of clergy, 24
Fraud. *See* Crime—fraud
Freamene, Diocese of, Ireland, 55
Frederick I, king of Prussia, 88
Frederick Parish, South Carolina, 388
Freeholders
may be elected to vestry, xxix, xxxii, xxxvi, 314
may elect vestries, xxxvi
may fill vacancies on vestry, xxxi, 415
nomination of, to vestry, 191, 266
to elect vestry, 414
to examine parish accounts, 312
Freeman, John (Jno.)
allowance of, 475, 481
reader, 475, 481
Freeman, Mary
allowance of, 489-490
house of, 490
Freemen
elect inspectors of accounts, 486
elect vestry, xxxii, 314-315, 486, 490
may not vote in vestry elections, xxxvi
French (language), 276, 313, 337, 347
French (nationality), 336, 344
clergyman, 347
congregation of, 324, 344, 347
settle in Bath County, 86
settlement of, 347
See also Huguenots
French, Elizabeth
executrix, 155
husband of, 155
legatee, 155
French, Richard (Richd.)
assembly member, 122*n*
character of, 120
clergyman, 122*n*
order to, 122*n*
performs bigamous marriages, 122*n*
wife of, 155
will of, 155-156
French. *See* French, Richard
Frogs, in fable, 248, 249*n*
Frontier
attacked by Indians, 184-185
of South Carolina, 202*n*
Fruit. *See* Food, diet—fruit
Fryars, John
oath taken by, 287
witness, 287
Fulerton, Robt. *See* Fullerton, Robt.
Fulham Palace, London, 48-49, 51, 56-57, 112, 134-135, 150, 154, 157, 309*n*, 338, 348, 350, 395, 423
Fuller, Thomas (Thos.), author, 294
Fuller, Wm.
letter from, 228-230
parishioner, 230
Fullerton (Fulerton, Fullington), Robt., allowance of, 483, 489, 494
Fullington, Robt. *See* Fullerton, Robt.
Fundamental Constitutions of Carolina

address status of slaves as church members, xviii
changes in, xviii-xx
church establishment in, xviii-xx
disregarded, xvii, 237
favors Church of England, xix-xx
intended for southern Carolina, xvii*n*
liberty of conscience provided by, 87*n*
not accepted in South Carolina, xxi
not fully implemented, xx
not promulgated in North Carolina, xxi
on acts of assembly, 236
on palatineship, 134*n*
position of freemen, property owners, residents in, xvii
powers granted by, 83
prohibits ridiculing of religion, xviii
provisions concerning oath-taking, xviii
provisions concerning religion, xviii-xix, 215
provisions concerning religion, revised, xvii-xix
provisions concerning worship, xviii
revises characterization of Church of England, xix
suspended, xxi
Funeral
expenses of, 155, 465, 470
fee for, 215
few performed by clergyman, 283
for indigent, 468, 470
of clergyman, 286
G., C. *See* Gale, Christopher
Galai. *See* Gale, Thomas
Gale (G.), Christopher (C., Chr., Christopr., Christor., Christr., Chrr., Chrs., Crist., Xtopher.), 249*n*
brother of, 186, 187*n*, 200, 204
chief justice, 130*n*, 241, 287
clerk, 247
collector of customs, 247
complaint by, 248
Council member, 130*n*, 288
delivers papers, 24, 336
father of, 146, 147*n*, 200
General Court justice, 130*n*
government official, 146
invitation by, 200
letter from, 200
of Yorkshire, England, 130*n*
request by, 146
testimonial of, 334
travel of, 247
vestryman, 190, 287, 468-469
will proved before, 287
witness, 287
Gale (Galai), Thomas (Tho., Thos.)
author, 7
brother of, 187*n*, 200, 204
clergyman, 204-205
delivers letter, 186
invitation to, 200
letter from, 187*n*, 203-205
recommended for SPG service, 186-187
request by, 204
Gale, Colonel. *See* Gale, Christopher
Gale, Edmond (E., Ed., Edmd., Edmund, Emd.)
allowance of, 470
assembly member, 464*n*
bond by, 470
brother of, 464*n*
churchwarden, 250, 469-473 passim
commissioner, 485, 488
Council member, 346, 464*n*
debtor, 477
General Court justice, 464*n*
letter from, 250
oath taken by, 464
of Yorkshire, England, 464*n*
payment by, 472
presents account to vestry, 471
to return Eucharist silver, 488
to settle account, 485, 488
vestryman, 190, 464, 468, 470, 473-474, 481-482, 484-486
Gale, John, memorial by, 328
Gale, Justice. *See* Gale, Christopher
Gale, Major. *See* Gale, Christopher
Gale, Miles
letter from, 146-147, 199-200
rector, 200
son of, 146
Gale, Mr. *See* Gale, Edmond
Gale. *See* Gale, Christopher
Gambling, clergy to avoid, 40
Garat, Mr. *See* Garrett, Thomas, Sr.
Garcia, John. *See* Garzia, John
Garden, 66, 115
Garden, Alexander (A.)
clergyman, 338, 347, 350, 388, 390, 396*n*, 412*n*
commissary, xliv-xlv, 322*n*, 338, 347, 352, 370*n*
letter from, 316-317, 322, 329-330, 350-352, 375-376, 378, 390-391, 394-395, 396*n*
letter to, 375, 390
pastoral letter from, 350
questions clergyman, 352

recommendation by, xlv
recommendatory letter by, 396
rector, xliv
request by, 388
resides in Charleston, 322*n*
tenure, 322*n*
Garden, Mr. Commissary. *See* Garden, Alexander—commissary
Garden, Mr. *See* Garden, Alexander
Gardner, Bp. *See* Gardner, Samuel
Gardner, Samuel, author, 36
Garland (naval vessel), transports clergy, 64, 77
Garret, Mr., house of, 379-380
See also Garrett, Thomas, Sr.
Garret, Thomas (Thos.). *See* Garrett, Thomas, Jr.; Garrett, Thomas, Sr.
Garrett (Garat, Garrat, Garret), Thomas (Thos.), Sr.
churchwarden, 68-69, 71, 443, 461-462
dismissed as churchwarden, 444
excused as vestryman, 460, 464
letter from, 68-71 passim
service held at house of, 143
to collect parish tax, 461
to relay message, 158
vestryman, 189, 441-442, 453-455, 457, 464
Garrett (Garret), Thomas (Thos.), Jr.
allowance of, 490, 492-494
churchwarden, 459-460
letter from, 287
to collect parish tax, 459
vestryman, 453-455, 457
Garzia (Garcia), John, *498-499*
books delivered to, 385-386
certification of, 341
character of, 341
clergyman, xlv, xlvii, 341, 341*n*, 353-354, 356-358, 364, 378, 384, 385*n*, 400, 407, 421, 424, 428*n*, 482, 485*n*
deponent, 364
expenses of, 421
family of, 384
instructions to, 357
letter from, 358-359, 364-366, 366*n*, 378, 385-386, 420-421, 428*n*
letter to, 378, 397-398, 420
ministry of, xlvii, 407-408
missionary appointment of, 353, 356, 385*n*, 392, 397-398, 400, 407
notitia parochialis from, 421-422
of Virginia, 356
order by, 482
payment to, 421*n*, 483
petitioner, 357-359, 365-366, 397
recommendation of, 384, 392, 400, 407
report by, 385-386, 420-422
salary of, 359, 397
salary of, delinquent, 384-385, 407
testimonial in behalf of, 353, 358
Garzia, Mr. *See* Garzia, John
Garzia, Parson. *See* Garzia, John
Gastrell (Gastril), Francis, bishop of Chester, author, 36, 410
Gastrell, Bp. *See* Gastrell, Francis
Gastril, Dr. *See* Gastrell, Francis
Gates County, 198*n*
Gavin, Antonio, author of [*Observations on a Journey to Naples wherein the frauds of Romish Monks and Priests are Discovered*], 8
General Assembly, 144, 254, 413-414
absence of, 119
and lawmaking, 237
Anglicans dominate, xxvi
appoints agent, 309*n*
asked to build schools, xlvii
assists widow of clergyman, 288-289
clergy may be members of, xx
clergy may not be members of, xix
commends clergyman, 307
committee of, 371*n*
composition of, 119
contents of letter communicated to, 420
creates school fund, xlvii
criticized, xlviii, 275
criticized by governor, 346, 370-371
displeased with governor, 309*n*
does not provide for clergymen, 330
encourages education, xlviii
fails to erect schools, xlvii, 371
favors Church of England, xxiv
financial support to Church by, xix
governor addresses, 370, 389*n*
governor attends, 260
governor fails to make recommendation to, xlvii
governor to make recommendation to, 327
House of Burgesses, 389
instructions laid before, 189, 327
journal of, xxiv, 304, 345-346
levies tax for church construction, xxx
lower house of, 346*n*, 371*n*, 376, 389*n*, 401*n*
lower house of, refuses to obey order of governor, 371*n*
meets, 28, 273
member of, xxvii, xlv, 25*n*, 122*n*, 161*n*, 254, 263*n*, 364, 370, 422, 432*n*, 444*n*, 448*n*, 464*n*, 485*n*

member of lower house of, 438*n*
members of, appointed to vestries, xxvii*n*
messenger of, 370
must authorize taxation, 266
of Virginia, 153
proceedings of, 288, 370, 389
promised funds by proprietors, xxii
prorogued, 185, 275, 371*n*
provisions concerning, in Fundamental Constitutions, xviii
Quakers in, 22, 28, 81-82, 151
refuses to increase salary of clergy, 365
responsible for construction of churches, xviii
responsible for maintenance of clergy, xviii
sits at Edenton, 360
speaker of lower house of, 25*n*, 87*n*, 291*n*, 346, 405, 432*n*, 485*n*
summoned, 119
to be consulted by governor, xlvi
to be petitioned, 451
to be prorogued, 269
to build churches, xviii
to maintain clergy, xviii
to meet, 151
to meet in Wilmington, 422
upper house of, 346*n*, 370*n*, 371*n*, 389*n*, 401*n*
urged to enact legislation concerning morals, xlv
urged to encourage conversion of Negroes and Indians, 326
urged to repeal act, xxv
See also Acts of assembly; Election—to assembly; Governor, deputy governor—speech to assembly; Resolution—by lower house of assembly
General Court
action permitted in, 404, 413
clergy may bring suit in, 418
clergy may sue in, xxviii
clergyman bound over to, 304
clergyman ordered to appear before, 301
dismisses action, 270
provost marshal of, 432*n*
See also Grand jury—of General Court; Justice, chief justice—of General Court
General Post Office, London, 406
Gent, Mary, maintained by parish, 454, 456
Gentleman (term used), 120, 124
Gentry, Nathaniell, character of, 304
Geography, books concerning, xlii
George (ship), 259
George I, king of England, 212*n*, 224, 235, 243*n*, 327*n*
instructions from, 189
publicly cursed, 303, 303*n*
George II, king of England, 243*n*, 389
letter to, 424
quitrent of, 402
Georgia, 340, 474
clergyman in, 401, 425*n*
German (language), 88
reading, preaching in, 88, 113*n*
service conducted in, 135
German (nationality), settlers, 89*n*, 113*n*
Germany (the lower palatinate), 88*n*
refugees from, 89*n*
Gerrard, Henry, *499*
allegation against, 440
clergyman, 438, 440
difficulties of, 438
future of, debated, 440
salary of, 438
Gervice, Forster. *See* Jarves, Foster
Giacii. *See* Gracchus, Gaius; Gracchus, Tiberius
Gibbe, _____, house of, 229
Gibbe, Colonel. *See* Gibbe, _____
Gibson, Bp. *See* Gibson, Edmund, bishop of London
Gibson, Edmund (Edmd., Edmond), bishop of London
alleged commission by, 338
author, 38, 410
awaits commissary's action, 396
commission to, 326, 341
delivers benefaction, 392
denies commission, 339
letter from, 339, 391*n*, 392, 395-396
letter to, 295-296, 303-309, 316-324, 329-339, 341-345, 347-352, 355-356, 358-362, 364-366, 366*n*, 367-376, 381-382, 390-392, 394, 396*n*, 401-402
ordination by, 308
papers to be laid before, 311, 386
permission of, awaited, 353
petition to, 324, 353-354, 357-358
petitioner, 326
queries given to, 352
recommendation by, 407
refuses to grant missionary license, 386-387, 396, 411
testimonial by, 291
testimonial to, 331, 387
transferred to London, 360
Gibson, Edmund, bishop of Lincoln, 359

Gillam, Sarah, house of, 434-435
Gillam, Thomas
  house of, 431, 433-434
  payment to, 433
Gillesbey, Tho., testimonial by, 276-277
Gillingham, [Richard], letter to, 15-16
Gillingham, Mr. *See* Gillingham, [Richard]
Ginger. *See* Spices—ginger
Girdle. *See* Clothing, jewelry—girdle
Gl. Sh. *See* Gloucester, England
Glasgow, Scotland, official from, 76*n*
Glasgow (Scotland), University of, clergyman from, 330
Glass, for church, chapel windows, 84, 104, 436-437
Glazier. *See* Occupation, trade, profession—glazier
Glebe, 66, 144*n*, 449
  act of assembly on, 346*n*
  land for, 192, 325, 443
  not provided, xiv, xlviii, 120, 172, 313, 338, 348
  payment of taxes at, 193
  provided, xxv, xliii, 28, 86
  purchase of, 119
  subscription for purchase of, 300
  to be kept in repair, xxxviii, 418
  to be provided, 195, 325, 346, 443
  to be provided by proprietors, xxii, 298
  vestry may purchase, xxix, 290
  See also Report—on glebes
Glebe house, 350
  clergyman to keep in repair, xxxviii, 418
  taxation for construction of, 417
  See also Building—parsonage, rectory
Gloster, Joseph, apostle, 198
Gloucester (England), bishop of, 21, 49
Gloucester (Gl. Sh.), England, 21, 24
Gloucester, bishop of. *See* Fowler, Edward, bishop of Gloucester
Glover, Col. *See* Glover, William
Glover, Governor. *See* Glover, William—governor
Glover, Mr. *See* Glover, William
Glover, President Mr. *See* Glover, William—president of Council
Glover, William (Wm.), 73*n*, 444*n*
  awaits Proprietors' decision, 107
  borrows money, 250
  Council member, 65*n*
  deceased, 95, 148, 250
  election of, nullified, 83
  letter from, 73-75, 110*n*
  opinion of, 119
  president of Council, 65*n*, 75-76, 82, 87*n*, 95, 110, 119
  supporter of, 148
  testimonial by, 110
  travel of, 95, 251
Glover. *See* Glover, William
Godefroi (Gothofridi), Denys, author, 7
Godfrey, _____
  account to be given by, 211
  delivers letter, 200, 202, 211, 214-215, 230
  shipmaster, 200, 202, 211, 214-215, 230, 238
Godfry, Captain. *See* Godfrey, _____—shipmaster
Godfry. *See* Godfrey, _____
Godparents, objected to, 28, 84, 118
Goffe, Arthur (A.)
  Council member, 309*n*
  receiver general, 307, 309*n*
  testimonial by, 301
  witness, 301
Goffe, Mr. *See* Goffe, Arthur
Golden Head, (The), London, merchant at, 373
Goldsmith, Ed, dean of Elphin
  certification by, 57*n*
  testimonial by, 54-55
Gooch, William
  governor of Virginia, 341*n*
  witness, 341
Good Friday, 119, 229, 262
  Indians attack on, 200
Goodman, John, author, 6-7, 410
Goose Creek, South Carolina, 128, 130, 215
  death of minister in, 316
Gorden, Mr. *See* Gordon, William
Gorden, William. *See* Gordon, William
Gordon. *See* Gordon, William
Gordon, Mr., payment to, 444-445
  See also Gordon, William
Gordon, Patrick
  books sent to, 13
  clergyman, 13*n*, 14
  deceased, 13*n*, 14*n*
  letter from, 13
  payment to, 14
Gordon (Gorden, Jordan), William (W., Will., Wm.), 106-107, *499*
  absence of, 444
  appears before the Board, 79
  arrival of, 64, 75-76
  attends meeting, 78*n*
  books delivered by, 112, 257
  character of, 57, 59, 68

clergyman, xiv, xxii*n*, xxvi*n*, 56, 58, 68, 70, 73, 75, 103, 135, 178, 442-443, 450
departure of, 57*n*, 68, 72*n*, 173, 443, 450
derides church building, xxii*n*
difficulties of, 76, 95-96
finding replacement for, difficult, 90
information from, 71, 91, 104
leaves mission, 77, 79, 89
letter delivered by, 87*n*
letter from, 61, 63-64, 75, 81-87
letter to, 75-76
library of, 91
library sent by, 172, 178-180, 450
ministerial ability of, 60
ministry of, 61-62, 65, 73
missionary appointment of, xiv, 56*n*, 57, 60-61, 76, 91
officers service to SPG, 56
paper relating to, 79*n*
payment to, 103
qualifies as missionary, 60
recommendation of, 56
refuses to deliver books, 151
replacement for, 91
report by, 76-78
requests salary, 121, 166
returns to England, xxvi*n*
salary of, 91, 444
salary of, withheld, 79
testimonial in behalf of, 57-59
testimonial in behalf of, delayed, 57*n*
to procure testimonial, 56*n*
Goreham, Alexander, maintained by parish, 465
Gothofridi. *See* Godefroi, Denys
Government, royal, request for, 32
Governor and Council
desire maintenance for clergy, 376
letter from lords proprietors to, xxi
order to, requested, 257
petition to, xxxii
royal instructions to, 354
Governor, deputy governor, 4, 12, 20, 65*n*, 101, 119-120, 123, 133, 162, 170, 249, 299*n*, 305, 359, 361, 363, 413-414, 426
addresses assembly, 370, 389*n*
affidavit sworn before, 305
agitated, 302-303
and Cary Rebellion, 122
applied to by settlers, 32
appointed, 80*n*, 122*n*, 186
appointment by, xlvi
approves minister, xxvi*n*, 78, 436-438
approves mission districts, 145
approves speaker of House of Burgesses, 370
arrival of, expected, 285
assembly displeased with, 309*n*
at meeting of SPG, 298
at risk, 144
attempts to increase salary of clergy, 365
attestation of, 372
bequest by, for poor, xxxvi
books consigned to, 378
calls vestry, 245
calumnies against, 336
cannot persuade vestry to meet, 257
capable one needed, 318
chosen vestryman, 451
clergyman fails to wait upon, 373
commended, 184
commends clergyman, 307
comments on clergy from Virginia, xvi
complaints against, 32, 247-248, 336, 338
conflict with clergyman, 303
contents of letter communicated to, 420
criticized, 29, 248, 302
criticizes assembly, xlviii, 346, 370-371
criticizes clergyman, xlix, 272, 391
death of, 148, 151, 282
denounces truce, 140*n*
desire to be appointed as, 247
difficulties of, 257, 307
disputatious, 286
duty of, toward church, xlii-xliii
elected to SPG, xl, xl*n*, 80
enactment by, 402
encourages new settlement, 350
fails to encourage conversion of heathen, xlvi
fails to make recommendation, xlvii
fails to support church, 29
footboy of, 317, 321
friendliness toward clergyman, 356
in British army, 286*n*
inducts clergyman, xliii, 420
instructions to, xx-xxi, xxi*n*, xxxiv, xlii-xlvii, 189, 279-280, 325-327, 327*n*, 346
interrogates clergyman, 301
issues pardon, 124*n*
letter from, xv, xlix, 14, 22-23, 138-139, 158, 186-187, 196, 196*n*, 199*n*, 200, 204-205, 223, 227, 235-237, 259, 271, 278, 303-306, 317, 320-321, 327, 335, 339, 360, 375, 381, 384-386, 391, 407
letter to, 3, 92, 129, 199*n*, 206, 224-226, 259, 278, 355-356, 363, 397
letter to be written to, 349*n*
licenses justices, 121

lodgings of, 301
lower house of assembly refuses to obey order of, 371*n*
may appoint to vestry, xxix, 415
may nominate to vestry, 191, 194
may not appoint to vestry, xxxi
meets clergyman, 349
not allowed to hire or dismiss clergy, xxvi
not involved in selection of minister, xxix
of Barbados, 279-280
of Carolina, 122*n*
of Jamaica, 248, 345*n*
of Massachusetts, 11
of New England, 10, 423
of New Jersey, 17, 279-280
of New York, 203*n*, 279-280
of South Carolina, 12, 12*n*, 66, 80, 82, 103, 106, 118, 158, 166-167, 167*n*, 176, 183*n*, 206, 224-225, 225*n*, 300, 347
of Virginia, xxxi, 10-11, 12*n*, 15, 25, 27, 113*n*, 122, 129, 140*n*, 146*n*, 150*n*, 157-158, 197, 228, 253, 296, 303, 318, 341*n*, 342, 353, 358, 365, 449
of Virginia, gift from, xxxii, 437
on vestry, 448
opinion of, sought, 356
opposed by chief justice, xlix, 332
opposition to, 231, 234, 349
order from, 420
pardon from, 258*n*
perquisites of, 326
persuades clergyman to remain in colony, 332-333, 336
political ally of, 376
proceeds against rebels, 129
proclaimed by rebels, 270*n*
promises assistance to clergyman, 307
proposes induction of minister, 452
prorogues assembly, 371*n*
protection by, desired, 398
Quaker, 73*n*
qualifications needed as, 165
receives clergyman, 142, 152
receives parish silver, 465
recommended to SPG, 248
recommends clergyman, 309, 385-386, 392, 397, 400
reputation of, defended, 333
resides in Bath Town, 255
retinue of, 321*n*
royal, 327*n*
salary of, 148
secretary of, 304, 360
seditious remarks against prohibited, xviii
sees dissenters as threat, xxxix
signs act, 405
speech to assembly, 346, 370, 371*n*
takes oaths of office, 347
to assist clergyman, 185
to deliver church silver, 469
to designate place of residence of clergyman, 399
to grant letters of probate, xliv
to grant marriage licenses, xliv
to make recommendation to assembly, 327
to receive chapel plate, 347, 347*n*
to recommend clergyman, 367
to recommend placement of missionary, 356, 356*n*
to report to bishop of London, xliii
town named in honor of, 286
travels to assembly meeting, 260
unable to establish church, 237
urges clergyman to make visit, 252
urges construction of parsonage, 348
widow of, xlii
willing to appoint vestry, 237
See also Affidavit, deposition—by governor; Commission (appointment) as governor
Governour, D. *See* Daniel, Robert—governor
Gown. *See* Clothing, jewelry—gown
Grabe, Johann Ernst, author, 36
Gracchi. *See* Gracchus, Gaius; Gracchus, Tiberius
Gracchus (Giacii), Gaius, 163*n*
Gracchus (Giacii), Tiberius, 163*n*
Graffenried, Baron (Barron). *See* De Graffenried, Christopher
Grafton. *See* Fitzroy, Charles, 2nd duke of Grafton
Grain, 115, 177, 209
barley, 231
wheat, 181
See also Food, diet—grain; Mill—lack of, for grain
Grange, John, vestryman, 316
Granvil, Mr. *See* Granville, Bevil
Granvile, Doctor. *See* Granville, Bevil—clergyman
Granvile, Reverend Mr. *See* Granville, Bevil—clergyman
Granvill, Bevil. *See* Granville, Bevill
Granvill, Mr. *See* Granville, Bevill
Granville District, 243*n*
Granville, Bevil (Belvil, Belville), *499-500*
arrival of, 334
clergyman, 330, 331*n*, 336, 474, 477
letter from, 334

letter regarding, 336
ministry of, 334, 336, 474
missionary appointment of, 331*n*, 332, 341
payment to, 477
salary of, 474
testimonial in behalf of, 334
uncle of, 330
Granville, George, baron Lansdowne
nephew of, 330
to testify for clergyman, 332
Granville, Lord. *See* Grenville, John, 1st baron Granville of Potheridge
Granville, Mr. *See* Granville, Bevil
Graves, Richd., vestryman, 191
Gray, Mr., delivers letter, 238
Great Awakening, 425
Great Britain (Britain), xiv, xxvi, xxviii, xxviii*n* xli, 77, 105, 107, 174, 189, 261, 286, 291, 294, 308, 326, 389
books sent to, 26*n*
clergyman returns to, 222
clergyman's widow sailing to, 288
colonial monetary policy of, xxxvii*n*
Commonwealth in, 122*n*
disorder in, 212*n*
See also Aberdeen; Alcester; Ashleworth; Barking; Bath and Wells; Bilsthorpe; Bristol; Bury St. Edmunds; Cambridge; Canterbury; Carlisle; Carlton; Chatham; Chester; Chichester; Cornwall; Coventry; Cuddesdon; Dartmouth; Deal; Devonshire; Downs; East Ham; Edinburgh; Edmonton; England; Epsom; Essex, county of; Exmouth; Feckenham; Glasgow; Glasgow, University of; Gloucester; Halifax; Harwich; Keighley; Kensington; Lancashire; Lancaster; Lincoln; Lincolnshire; Liverpool; London; Mansfield; Middlesex; Newcastle; Norwich; Nottinghamshire; Oxford; Peterborough; Plymouth; Portland; Portsmouth; Rochester; Scotland; Sheerness; Shoreham; Spitalfields; Spithead; Suffolk; Warwickshire; Whitby; Windsor; Woolwich; Worcester; York; Yorkshire
Great Kirby Street, London, merchant in, 405-406
Greeks, 308
Green Dragon, (The), London, 127
Green, Robt., vestryman, 190
Greenland, 93
Grenville, John, 1st baron Granville of Potheridge
father of, xix
influence of, xxiv
palatine, xix, xxiv
zealous church supporter, xix, xx*n*
Grenville, John, 1st earl of Bath
letter from, 3
palatine, xix, 3
proprietor, 3*n*
signatory, 3
son of, xix
Griffin, Charles
allowance for, 86, 444-445
character of, 444
proselytizer, 97
reader, 85, 97, 443-444
schoolteacher, 85-86, 87*n*, 97
Griffin, Mr. *See* Griffin, Charles
Gripes. *See* Disease, illness, affliction—gripes
Grot. *See* Grotius, Hugo
Grotij, Guilielmi. *See* Grotius, William
Grotius (Grot.), Hugo
author, 7, 34, 36, 295
author of [*Whole Duty of a Christian*], 38
Grotius (Grotij), William, author, 8-9
Grove, Edw.
clergyman, 127
letter from, 126-127
letter of recommendation by, 127
testimonial by, 125-126
Grove, Mr. *See* Grove, Edw.
Guide, 76
for clergyman, 129, 174, 222
necessity for, 27
Guilford, Ld. *See* North, Francis, 2nd baron Guildford
Guillim, John, author, 6
Guinea, Africa, 234, 244
Gulliver, Tro., burial of, 475
Guy, Mr. *See* Guy, William
Guy, William (W.)
abandons parish, 217, 219
clergyman, 207-208, 208*n*, 217, 219, 221*n*
instructions to, 225
lacks parish, 221
letter from, 221, 316-317
letter to, 221*n*, 225
missionary appointment of, 207
order to, 221*n*
to assist missionary, 208
Haberdasher. *See* Occupation, trade, profession—haberdasher
Hac. *See* Tools, equipment—hac
Hacklefield, John, vestryman, 190
Haige, Lilia
letter from, 228-230

parishioner, 230
Hair, Edwd. *See* Hare, Edward
Haire, Edward (Edwd.). *See* Hare, Edward
Hale, Matthew, author, 34, 36
Halifax (England), vicar of, 407
Hall, Bishop. *See* Hall, Joseph
Hall, Joseph, bishop of Norwich, author, 34, 36
Hall, Mr.
letter from, 114
secretary to bishop, 350
Hall, W., letter from, 154-155
Hallbrook, Jo., vestryman, 189
Halle, Germany, 88*n*
Halton, Robt., Council member, 370
Hamilton, Archibald, vestryman, 418
Hammond, Dr. *See* Hammond, Henry
Hammond, Henry, author, 6, 33, 36
Hampton (Kecketan, Keekotan, Keketan, Kicketan, Kicotan, Kikaton, Kiquotan, Kocotan, Riquotan), Virginia, 65, 65*n*, 74, 111, 159, 161, 393
clergyman in, 144, 167
clergyman rejected at, 178
library in, 112, 172, 180, 257, 450
merchant in, 144, 159
minister in, 72, 76, 107, 112, 167, 172, 180, 257, 450
Hampton Parish, Virginia, 154
Hampton River, Virginia, clergyman at, 259
Hancock, insurgent Tuscarora leader, 161*n*
Hancock's Fort. *See* Hancock's Town
Hancock's Town (Hancock's Fort), 140*n*
Hancock, Will., vestryman, 191
Hand and Pen, The, London, 238
Handasyd (Handyside), [Thomas], governor of Jamaica, 248
Handrey, Thos.
bill to, protested, 210
merchant, 210
Handyside, Colonel. *See* Handasyd, Thomas
Hanove. *See* Hanover County, Virginia
Hanover County, Virginia
parish in, 331
vestryman in, 331
Hanover, house of, 212*n*, 225*n*, 254*n*
Hanover. *See* New Hanover Precinct, County
Hanoverian dynasty, 212*n*, 254*n*
fears Jacobites, 225
Hanoverian. *See* Hanover, house of
Harbor, at Brunwick, 345
Harbour Island, clergyman at, 269
Harding, Thos., vestryman, 190
Hardy, John (Jno.)
sheriff, 450
to collect parish tax, 447
to present account to vestry, 450-452
vestryman, 189, 451
Hardy, Mr. *See* Hardy, John
Hare (Hair, Haire), Edward (Edwd.)
letter from, 132
vestryman, 486-488, 490-494 passim
Harlow, John, allowance for, 459
Harnet, Cornelius (Cornl.). *See* Harnett, Cornelius
Harnett (Harnet), Cornelius (Corn., Cornl., Corns.)
letter from, 398-399
petitioner, 324
vestryman, 316, 324, 399, 418
Harris, Elisebeth (Elisa.)
maintained by parish, 456, 458
wounded, 456
Harrow. *See* Tools, equipment—harrow
Harse, Tho.
letter from, 228-230
parishioner, 230
Hart, Eliza.
burial of, 488
maintained by parish, 488
Hartford, Connecticut, librarian in, 293*n*
Harvard University, 376*n*
Harvey, Richd., vestryman, 190
Harvey, Thomas
bequest of, xxxvi
Council member, 4*n*
county court justice, 4*n*
deputy governor, 3, 4*n*
General Court justice, 4*n*
letter to, 3
will of, xxxvi
Harvey, Thos., vestryman, 190
Harvy, _____
letter delivered by, 160
shipmaster, 140, 160
Harwich, England, clergyman in, 114
Hasel, James. *See* Hasell, James
Hasell (Hasel), James, vestryman, 418
Hasell (Hassell, Hazel), Thomas
assistant, 347
clergyman, 313, 347
instructions to, 225-226
letter from, 316-317
letter to, 221, 225-226
rector, 337
Hassell, Messr. *See* Hassell, Thomas
Hasty pudding. *See* Food, diet—hasty pudding
Hat. *See* Clothing, jewelry—hat
Hatch, Antho. (Ant., Autho.)

letter from, 250
testimonial by, 109
vestryman, 109, 190, 250-251
Hatchet. *See* Tools, equipment—axe, hatchet
Hatton Garden, London, merchant in, 405-406
Haucot, Ednd. (Ed.). *See* Howcot, Edward
Haucot, Mr. *See* Howcot, Edward
Haughton, Wm., processioner, 461
Haul Over (Upper Haleover), 316
Havey, Capt. *See* Harvy, _____—shipmaster
Havil, Mary, allowance of, 493
Hay, Wm.
letter from, 336-337
reviews clergyman's performance, 336
Hazel, Mr. *See* Hasell, Thomas
Headig, _____, author, 36
Heald, Mr.
attorney, 213, 231, 246
discontinues power of attorney, 246
refuses to pay debt, 246
Health, 71, 276
and climate, xli
See also Clergy, clergyman—health of; Disease, illness, affliction
Heath[cote], (Heathcoat), [Caleb]
bill of exchange to, 271
of New York, 271
Heathcoat, Col. *See* Heath[cote], [Caleb]
Hebrew, professor of, xlvii
Heckerman. *See* Keckermannus, Bartholomaeus
Heinsius, Daniel, author, 294
Helvici. *See* Helvicus, Nicolaus
Helvicus (Helvici), Nicolaus, author, 33, 36
Henderson, David
dismissed as vestryman, 451
dissenter, 451
subscription by, 439
vestryman, 448
Henderson, Jacob, letter from, 111-112
Henderson, Mr.
letter from, 387
reports to Board, 387
See also Henderson, Jacob
Henter, Robet. *See* Hunter, Robert
Herbert, George, author, 34, 36
Heresy, heretics, 18-19, 98, 307
Hermitage, (The), (New Hanover County plantation), 427
clergyman at, 383, 397-398
Heron, 249*n*
Herritage, William, commissioner, 403
Hewit, Mr. *See* Hewitt, Richard
Hewitt (Hewit), Richard (Richd.)
clergyman, 5*n*
letter from, 291, 296
petitioner, 297
schoolmaster, 296
testimonial in behalf of, 296
to perform service, 297
warrant to, 5*n*
Hewitt, Mr. *See* Hewitt, Richard
Hews, Willm., allowance of, 489
Heyselbein, _____, author, 295
Hickey, Connor
churchwarden, 53
testimonial by, 53
Hickman, Henry, author, 7
Hicks, R., resolution signed by, 288
Hicks, Robert (Robt.)
clerk, 454, 469
presents account to vestry, 465
salary of, 454
to collect parish tax, 453, 456, 459, 466-468
Hide, Colonel. *See* Hyde, Edward
Hide, Governor. *See* Hyde, Edward—governor
Hide, Mr. *See* Hyde, Edward
Higgins, Francis, prebendary, 352
Hile, Rebecca, debtor, 473
Hill, Abraham
house of, 379
land of, 474
reader, 473
Hill, Anne, debtor, 473
Hill, Mr., vestryman, 190
See also Hill, Samuel
Hill, Samuel, author, 7
Hinton, Mr. *See* Hinton, William
Hinton, William (W., Will., Willi., Willm., Wm.)
account of, 474, 476
churchwarden, 474, 476, 480, 483
oath taken by, 477-478
payment by, 477, 480, 483
presents account to vestry, 479
to appear before vestry, 478
unable to present account to vestry, 478
vestryman, 471, 473, 477-480
History, books concerning, xlii
Hoadly, Benjamin, author, 34
Hoar, Mr. *See* Hoare, Hen.
Hoare (Hoar), Hen.
information to, 64
letter to, 104-105, 106*n*, 238
loan by, 96
Hobbs (Hobby), Abraham

burial of, 472
maintained by parish, 465-466
Hobbs, Thomas, maintained by parish, 464
Hobby, Abraham. *See* Hobbs, Abraham
Hodges, John
bill presented to, 160
letter to, 150-151, 161, 169, 180, 210
treasurer to the SPG, 151*n*, 159, 169
Hodges, Mr. *See* Hodges, John
Hodgson, John (J., Jo., Jno.)
act signed by, 405
assembly member, 485*n*
attorney general, 485*n*
payment to, 486
speaker of the assembly, 405, 485*n*
testimonial by, 108
treasurer, 485*n*
vestryman, 108, 481-482, 484-486
Hodson, Samll.
prebendary, 55
testimonial by, 55
Hoe. *See* Tools, equipment—hoe
Hogs, 116, 141, 209
corn for, 257
foul church, 120
gift of, to church, 107
gift of, to clergy, 317
killed, 212
loss of, 244, 246
mast for, 231, 237, 246
on island, 269
Holder, Dr. *See* Holder, William
Holder, William, author, 8
Holland, 29
Holsey, William, processioner, 462
Holy Communion, 41, 65, 71, 142, 349*n*
administered, 13*n*, 44, 66-67, 73, 96, 106, 108-109, 117-119, 172, 262, 285, 306, 349, 355-356, 363, 388, 449
administered to Indian woman, 230
administered to sick, 265
book about, 410, 421
furnishings for, 104
not administered, 184, 199, 229, 232, 260, 262, 328
notice concerning, 260
payment for elements of, 465
preparation to receive, 421
profaned, 229
proposal concerning, 328
readers and, 120
refused, 313
ridiculed, 96
royal instruction concerning, xliii, 325
seldom administered, 265
table for, 229
wine for, 96
See also Chalice; Declaration—against transubstantiation; Silver, silverware
Hominy. *See* Food, diet—hominy
Honyman, Mr.
certificates relating to, 57
order to, 221
salary of, 221
Hooker, Richard, author, 34, 36
Hooper, _____, 330
Hoornbeek (Hornbect), Johannes, author, 6, 34
Hopewell, New Jersey, 91
lack of clergy in, 203
Hops, 178
Hordinson, Mr., house of, 379
Hornbect. *See* Hoornbeck, Johannes
Horneck, Anthony, author, 36, 295
Horneck, Dr. *See* Horneck, Anthony
Horse, 76, 117
accomodation for, 120
bridle for, 237, 375
corn for, 85
disease of, 210, 211*n*, 214
gear for, 214
gift of, to church, 107
hired, 244
injured, 118
need for, 115, 244, 421
of clergy, 129, 144, 174, 177, 214, 259, 264
purchased, 27
saddle for, 237
scarcity of, 129
Hoskins Bridge (Chowan County), parish boundary at, 461
Hospital of St. Mary of Bethlehem (Bedlam), London, 19, 19*n*
House. *See* Building—house
House of Lords, petition to, 32-33, 33*n*
Household furnishings, 104, 107, 257
bed, bedding, 144, 175, 180, 237
blanket, 237
bolster, 237
bowl, 391
candle, 231
chest, 16
dish, 302
gift of, to clergy, 317
pillow, 237
pot, 435
quilt, 237
rug, 237

table, 104
See also Container—chest, trunk
Howard, Thos., letter from, 242
Howcot (Haucot, Howcott), Edward (E., Ed., Ednd., Edwd.)
account by, 472
allowance of, 476, 481
commission to, 472
debtor, 459
payment by, 472-473
Howcott, Edward. *See* Howcot, Edward
Howel. *See* Howell, James
Howell (Howel), James, author, 6
Howell, William
author, 38
author of [*Common Prayer book best Companion*], 39
Hoyler, Thoms. *See* Hoyter, John
Hoyter (Hoyler), John (Thoms.)
king of Chowan Indians, 143, 144*n*
receptive towards Christianity, 143
Huband, Edmund (Edmd.)
order by, 406
payment to, 406
Huet (Huetij), Peter Daniel, author, 7
Huetij. *See* Huet, Peter Daniel
Hughes, Griffith, ordination of, 337
Huguenots
clergyman of, 470*n*
petition from, 33*n*
settle, 33*n*
See also French (nationality)
Humphey, David. *See* Humphreys, David
Humphreys (H., Humphey, Humpreys), David (D., Davd.), 233*n*
author, 410, 426-427, 427*n*
clergyman, 335*n*
deceased, 232*n*
letter from, 221, 224-227, 233, 235, 250, 278-279, 300-301
letter to, 214, 220, 222-224, 228, 230-240, 243-249, 251-265, 267-276, 281-285, 287-289, 299-300, 312-313, 334-335, 348-349, 365-366, 385, 388-389, 393, 411
secretary to the SPG, 232*n*, 234, 249-251, 282, 393, 427*n*
Humphreys, Dr. *See* Humphreys, David
Humphreys, Mr. *See* Humphreys, David
Humpreys, Dr. *See* Humphreys, David
Hunger, 231
during Tuscarora War, 140
See also Food, diet—shortage of
Hunnius, Aegidius, author, 294
Hunt, Brian
arrival of, 299*n*
clergyman, xli*n*, 299, 299*n*
letter from, 299-300
letter laid before the Society, 300
letter to, 300-301
ministry of, 300
naval chaplain, 299*n*
of Lincolnshire, England, 299*n*
request of, denied, 300-301
requests new missionary appointment, xli*n*, 300
requests salary, 299-300
resigns as clergyman, 317
returns to England, 299*n*
vicar, 299*n*
Hunt, Mr. *See* Hunt, Brian
Hunter (Huntor), Isaac
account of, 483-484, 486
allowance of, 479, 484, 491, 493
churchwarden, 477-480 passim, 484
oath taken by, 477-478
payment by, 484-485
reader, 479, 491, 493
to oversee chapel construction, 493-494
to present account to vestry, 480, 482, 491
vestryman, 473-474, 476-478, 485-494 passim
Hunter (Huntor), Robert (Robet., Robt.)
allegation by, 203*n*
governor of New York, 203*n*
vestryman, 486-490 passim
Hunter, Mr. *See* Hunter, Thomas
Hunter, Thomas (Tho., Thoms.)
delivers letter, 367, 372, 381
merchant, 367, 369-371, 373
to deliver letter, 369, 371, 373
Huntor, Isaac. *See* Hunter, Isaac
Huntor, Mr. *See* Hunter, Isaac
Huntor, Robert (Robt.). *See* Hunter, Robert
Hurricane. *See* Weather, climate—hurricane
Hyde Parish, 322
erected, xxviii, 189
meeting of vestrymen from, 310
ministry in, 380
vestrymen of, 190
Hyde Precinct, County, 65*n*
meeting place for vestrymen in, 314
ministry in, 379-380
parish in, 194, 414
Hyde, Catherine
delivers commission, 123, 124*n*
returns to England, 124*n*, 140*n*
sells books, 175

wife of governor, 122
Hyde, Colonel. *See* Hyde, Edward
Hyde, Edward (Edwd.), 87*n*, 97*n*, 105
allegedly sells books, xlii
arrival of, 119, 321*n*
churchwarden, 446
commission to, 123, 124*n*
deceased, 148, 151, 158, 448
governor, deputy governor, xxi*n*, xl*n*, xlii, 80, 80*n*, 87*n*, 106, 122, 122*n*, 124*n*, 129, 145, 165, 184*n*, 263*n*, 321, 321*n*, 448
house of, 447
information to, 121
instructions to, xxi*n*
letter from, 138-139, 158
letter to, 129
missionary visits, 129
obtains missionary pay, 177-178
offers encouragement, 144
opposition against, 111, 117-118, 129
pardon issued by, 124*n*
president of Council, 119, 445-447, 447*n*
promotes religion, 117
proposed for SPG membership, 80, 80*n*
supporter of, 148
unable to procure commission, 80*n*, 129
vestryman, 445-447
widow of, xlii
Hyde, Edward, 3rd earl Clarendon, governor of New York, 17
Hyde, Governor. *See* Hyde, Edward—governor
Hyde, Lawrence, 1st earl of Rochester
proceedings sent to, 123
to lay journal before Privy Council, 119
Hyde, Madam. *See* Hyde, Catherine
Hyde, Mr. *See* Hyde, Edward
Hyrne, Edwd.
letter from, 398-399
petitioner, 324
vestryman, 316, 324, 399
Illiteracy. *See* Vestry—illiteracy in
Immorality, 260
act of assembly on, 326-327
clergyman complains of, 356
converts from, 169
of clergyman, 417
See also Crime—against morality; Morals; Society for the Propagation of the Gospel in Foreign Parts—seeks information on immoral clergy
Impressment
by warship, 210
of clerk, 229
Incest. *See* Crime—incest
Independent. *See* Dissenters—Independent
Independent Whig (publication), 362
Indian Creek. *See* Indian Town Creek
Indian Town Chapel, 467, 486
vestry meeting held at, 487-488, 493-494
Indian Town Creek (Indian Creek), district boundary at, 462
Indian Town. *See* Chowan Indian Town
Indians, 50, 172
agents of, 201
assist whites, 160-161, 185
at Cape Fear, 202
baptism of, xiii, xv*n*, xlvi-xlvii, 230, 306, 381
baptism of, doubted, xlvi*n*
Bear, 140*n*
book about instruction of, 410
called godless, 449
Catawba, 202*n*
catechist to, 46*n*
Cherokee, xlvii, 202*n*
children of, 43, 87*n*, 146*n*, 149, 150*n*, 154-155, 157
children of white women and, xxx
Choctaw, 202*n*
Chowan, 143, 144*n*, 146*n*, 149, 154
circumcised, 216
civilized, 29
clergyman taken by, 158
communion administered to, 230
continue warfare, 160, 184-186
Core, Coree, 140*n*, 146
Creek, 202*n*
cruelty of, 158
deerskins dressed by, 402
depredations by, following Tuscarora War, 255, 257
destroy books, 151
destroy Palatine settlement, 113*n*
difficulties of settlers with, 32
endanger missionaries, 177
expected to burn library, 186
expedition against, xlvii
few in number, 283
Five Nations, 21, 23-24, 45
forts of, 140*n*, 201
French influence among to be discouraged, xlvi
Iroquoian, 186
kill settlers, 144, 200-201
killed, 216
king of, 143, 160, 161*n*
language of, xlvi, 197

lords proprietors urge kindness toward, xx*n*
Machapunga, 140*n*
Mattamuskeet, 216
military strength, xlvi, 283
not baptized, 230
numerous, xlvi, 201
of Maine, 11
of South Carolina, 201
Pamlico, 140*n*
peace with, 175, 184-186, 224
peaceful, xlvi, 197, 199, 283, 285
prisoners, 139
project to settle, 197
proposal for mission to, 253
religion of, xxiii
religious conversion of, xlvi, 29, 126, 150, 157, 176, 256, 424
religious conversion of, not broached, xlvii
religious conversion of, to be encouraged, xx*n*, xlvi, 326
religious conversion of, unlikely, xlvi, 283
send gift to Queen Anne, 18
Seneca, 185-186
sent from South Carolina, 158, 160
slaves, 216
small numbers of, xlvi
speak English, xlvi
threatened use of, 123
to be instructed, 43, 87*n*
town, xxxvii, xlvi, 29, 140*n*, 142-143, 145, 149, 197, 257, 283, 305, 452, 455, 459-461, 464, 467, 480, 486-488, 493-494
town of, destroyed, 257
trade with, 130*n*, 201, 216
tributary, 201
troublesome to Palatines, 123
Tuscarora, 95*n*, 113*n*, 140*n*, 146, 161*n*, 186
understand English, 107
warlike, 201
Yamasee, 202*n*
Indictment, presentment, 326
Indigent
child of, 470
coffin for, 468
death of, 442
illness of, cured, 458
prays relief from vestry, 464
pregnant, 464
See also Burial—of indigent; Clothing, jewelry—of indigent; Funeral—for indigent; Poverty
Indigo, 139
Induction, of clergyman, 237, 420, 452
Inett, John, author of [*Guides to a Christian*], 9
Infidels, heathens
colony acquires reputation for containing, xiv
statistics of, 422, 449
to be enticed to become Christians, xlvi
Information
action by, 314-315, 364, 413, 416-417
money to be recovered by, 404
on clergyman, 303
Injunction, plea of, 315, 413, 416-417
Ink, 178
Inlet. *See* Little Inlet; Lockwoods Folly Inlet; New River Inlet; Ocracoke Inlet
Insolvency. *See* Bankruptcy, insolvency
Inspector of parish accounts, xxxi, 312, 477, 486
See also Accounts—audited, examined, inspected
Instructions
clauses concerning religion included in, xliii-xliv
concerning moral behavior, xxxiv
concerning religion, 325-327
from bishop of London, xlv, 242
from Board of Trade, 279
from king, xlvi-xlvii, 325, 327, 327*n*, 346
from lords proprietors, xx-xxi, xxi*n*, xxxiv, xlii-xliii, 327*n*
from SPG, 15, 39-43, 349, 357-358, 365
no reference to church matters in, xxi
See also Clergy, clergyman—instructions to
Interest
on money lent, 207
on protested bill of exchange, 406
Invoice, for books, lacking, 383
Ireland, 62, 76, 308, 389
bishop in, 127, 352
clergyman from, 53*n*, 57*n*, 124, 156, 351-353
Commonwealth in, 122*n*
See also Ballinletter; Ballykean; Cashel; Castlereagh; Donoughmore; Down and Connor, bishop of; Dromore; Dublin; Elphin; Freamene Diocese; Killala Diocese; Kinsale; Meath; Roscommon; Tuam
Irish, Presbyterian minister, 307
Iron
wanted for vessels, 32
yard made of, 471
See also Tools, equipment—of iron
Iroquois. *See* Indians—Iroquois

Irving, Andrew, executor, 377
Island. *See* Bahama Islands; Eagle's Island; Greenland; Harbour Island; Isle of Man; Long Island, New York; Roanoke Island; James Island, South Carolina; West Indies
Isle of Man (Man), clergyman in, 405
Italian (language), 276
Jacket. *See* Clothing, jewelry—jacket
Jacobites
  clergymen alleged to be, 203*n*
  insurrection by, 212*n*, 225, 231, 232*n*
Jailer. *See* Occupation, trade, profession—jailer
Jamaica
  clergyman in, 343, 350, 360, 390
  governor of, 248, 345*n*
James III. *See* Stuart, James Francis Edward ("Old Pretender")
James Island, South Carolina, ministry on, 67
James River, Virginia, 76*n*, 111, 161, 273*n*
  clergyman at, 128, 140
  hurricane near, 259
  library at, 180
  parish near, 296
Japan, 7
Jarves (Gervice), Foster (Forster)
  testimonial by, 108
  vestryman, 108, 190
Jasper, Richd., vestryman, 190
Jeacucks, John, vestryman, 190
Jefferies (Jeffries), George (G.)
  treasurer to the SPG, 196
  witness, 164
Jeffries, G. *See* Jefferies, George
Jeffryes, Mr. *See* Jeffrys, Robert
Jeffrys (Jeffryes), Robert
  allowance of, 461, 467, 471-472
  payment to, 471-472
  reader, 461, 467
Jeffrys, Mr. *See* Jeffrys, Robert
Jekyl, John (Jno.). *See* Jekyll, John
Jekyl, Mr. *See* Jekyll, John
Jekyll (Jekyl, Jeykill), John (Jno.)
  bill of exchange to, 234
  bill of exchange to, unpaid, 185, 210
  collector of customs, 201, 231, 234, 237, 270-271
  letter delivered to, 214, 237
  letter from, 240
  of Boston, Massachusetts, 201, 210, 231, 234, 237, 271
Jekyll, Mr. *See* Jekyll, John
Jenkin (Jenkins, Jenkyns), Robert, author, 8, 410
Jenkins (Jenkyns), Thomas
  arrival of, 65
  clergyman, 65*n*
  deceased, 104
  letter regarding, 55
  missionary appointment of, 48
Jenkins, Mr. *See* Jenkins, Thomas
Jenkins. *See* Jenkin, Robert
Jenkyns, Mr. *See* Jenkins, Thomas
Jenkyns. *See* Jenkin, Robert
Jennings, John (Jno.)
  authority of, 159
  influence of, 149-150
  letter from, 250
  petitioner, 44-45
  testimonial by, 109
  vestryman, 45, 109, 190, 250-251
Jennings, Mr. *See* Jennings, John
Jenoure, Joseph, fine paid by, 475
Jersey. *See* New Jersey
Jessop, Jos., vestryman, 190
Jewell, Thos.
  desires to retain minister, 353-354
  petitioner, 353-354
  vestryman, 354
Jews, 17-18, 308
  prayers for, 98
  tolerated, xvi, xx*n*
Jeykill, Mr. *See* Jekyll, John
Jinn, Eliz., debtor, 481
Joanes, Francis. *See* Jones, Francis
Joans, Fra. *See* Jones, Francis
John (slave), 155
John_____, archbishop of Dublin, letters dimissory from, 351
Johnson (Johnston), Nathaniel (Nathll., Nathanael)
  deputation by, 82
  governor, xxi*n*
  governor of South Carolina, 347
  instructions to, xxi*n*
  powers of, suspended, 82
  removed from, 118
Johnson, Commissary. *See* Johnston, Gideon—commissary
Johnson, Gabriel. *See* Johnston, Gabriel
Johnson, Governor. *See* Johnston, Gabriel—governor
Johnson, Mary, maintained by parish, 465-466
Johnson, Mr. *See* Johnston, Gideon
Johnston (Johnson), Gabriel (Gab., Gabl.)

act signed by, 405
address by, 389*n*
books to be delivered to, 378
criticizes assembly, xlviii
deceased, 347*n*
enacts tax, 402
encourages establishment of free schools, xlvii
Eucharist silver for, 346
fails to encourage proselytizing of slaves, xlvii
governor, xlvii-xlviii, 286*n*, 327*n*, 346, 347*n*, 360, 365, 371*n*, 376*n*, 378, 381, 385, 389*n*, 397, 400, 402, 407, 413-414
instructions to, 327*n*
letter from, 360, 381, 384-385, 392, 407
letter to, 397-398
professor of Hebrew, xlvii
prorogues assembly, 371*n*
recommendation by, 384, 397, 400
rejects grievances, 371*n*
supporter of, 376*n*
Johnston (Johnson), Gideon, 58*n*
assistant to, 53*n*
bars minister from preaching, 220
character of, 58
clergyman, 52*n*, 53, 53*n*, 66-67, 156, 221*n*
commissary, xliv, 52*n*, 187*n*, 204, 208*n*, 217-221 passim, 228-229, 232-233, 322*n*, 350
complaint by, 156*n*
deceased, 52*n*
dismissed from duty, 156*n*
letter from, 206-208, 216, 232
letter to, 156, 204-205, 217, 228-230, 232-233
missionary appointment of, 52, 52*n*, 58, 156
order to, 218
reassigns missionary, xlv
rector, xliv
representation by, 156
resides in Charleston, 322*n*
support of, 217
testimonial by, 53, 55
to appoint missionary, 187*n*, 204-205, 217-218, 233
travel of, 156
Johnston County, parish formed in, xxxiii
Johnston, Mr. Commissary. *See* Johnston, Gideon—commissary
Johnston, Mr. *See* Johnston, Gideon
Joiner. *See* Occupation, trade, profession—joiner
Jones (Joanes, Joans), Francis (Fr., Fra. Frans.)
burial of, 491
clothes of, 477, 484
maintained by parish, 477-478, 480-481, 483-485, 488-489, 491
Jones, [Gilbert]
instructions to, 225-226
letter to, 225-226
Jones, Frederick (Fred., Fredrick)
assembly member, 444*n*
chief justice, 444*n*
churchwarden, 453
Council member, 444*n*
deceased, 457
land of, 443
merchant, 444*n*
vestryman, 189, 453-455
Jones, Josiah, petitioner, 309-310
Jones, L., letter from, 316-317
Jones, Mary, debtor, 473
Jones, Mr., debtor, 466
Jones, Mr. *See* Jones, Nicholas; Jones, Walter
Jones, Nathaniel, clergyman, 336*n*
Jones, Nicholas
clergyman, xvi, 321, 321*n*, 472, 473*n*
missionary appointment of, xvi, 321*n*
of Nansemond, Virginia, 321, 473*n*
payment to, 472
Jones, Reverend Mr. *See* Jones, Nicholas—clergyman
Jones, Thomas, debtor, 475
Jones, Thos.
bill of exchange to, unpaid, 184
of Virginia, 184
servant of, 177
Jones, W., debtor, 475
Jones, Walter
clergyman, 5*n*
petitioner, 297
to perform service, 297
warrant to, 5*n*
Jones, William
sends for Bibles, 436
to collect parish tax, 432
warrant to, 434
Jones, Wm.
burial of, 458
maintained by parish, 456
Jordan, John (Jno.)
churchwarden, 454-455
excused as vestryman, 465
letter from, 287-288
payment to, 456, 458-459
presents account to vestry, 455
to assist parish member, 455

to collect parish tax, 454
vestryman, 189-190, 287, 452-453, 457, 461
Jordan, John, Jr., processioner, 462
Jordan, Mr. *See* Jordan, John
Jordan, Wm. *See* Gordon, William
Judge, 20, 125, 292, 310
of Court of Vice Admiralty, 161*n*, 183*n*, 239*n*, 263
Judgment, for recovery of parish funds, 312
Jurieu, Pierre, author, 7
Jury, verdict by, 364
Jury, grand
indictments and presentments by, 303*n*
of General Court, 303*n*
Jury, petit, 418
Justice of the peace, xxxii, 20, 310, 377, 403, 432*n*
declaration to be sworn before, 194
fails to act, 96
illegally marries, 364
illiterate, 84
in Onslow County, 145*n*
marriages performed by, xxxi, 28, 120-121, 193, 195, 283
may be called before vestry, 315, 417
oaths and declarations to be taken before, 191
to assess charges, 404
to certify killing of vermin, 492*n*
to pay forfeiture, 417
to present accounts, 417
to summon freeholders, 404
warrant from, 403, 414, 418
Justice, chief justice, 124*n*, 364*n*, 376*n*, 463*n*
appointment of, 247
binds over clergyman, 304
criticized, 248
issues warrant of arrest, 301
of England, 98
of General Court, 4*n*, 25*n*, 87*n*, 130*n*, 144*n*, 241, 303, 332, 333*n*, 375, 412, 432*n*, 444, 444*n*, 464*n*
of South Carolina, 290*n*
See also Governor, deputy governor—opposed by chief justice
Justimus. *See* Justinus, Martyr, *Saint*
Justinus, Martyr, *Saint*, author, 7
Juvenalis, Decimus Junius, author, 8
K., Mr. *See* Keith, George
Kearney (Kearny, Kerney), Edmond (Edmand, Edmd.)
bill of exchange to, 141, 163
generosity of, 144, 159, 161, 174
merchant, 144, 159, 161
Kearney, Mr. *See* Kearney, Edmond
Kearny, Mr. *See* Kearney, Edmond
Keckermann (Heckerman), Bartholomaeus author, 294
Keekotan. *See* Hampton, Virginia
Keighley (Kighley), England, 146, 204
Keith (K.), George
arrival of, 15
assistant to, 13
associate of, 20
author, 6, 9, 17, 34, 36
author of [*Serious Invitations of the Quakers to return to Christianity*], 10
books sent by, 13, 18
certificate in behalf of, 25
clergyman, 13*n*, 17, 25
converted Quaker, 46
letter from, 13, 19-20
memorandum, 27
ministry of, 17, 20, 25, 257
ordained, 13*n*
professor, 26
Society of Friends member, 13*n*
travel of, 13*n*, 20
visits North Carolina, xl
Keith, Mr. *See* Keith, George
Keketan. *See* Hampton, Virginia
Ken, Thomas, author, 9
Kenett, Dean, sermon by, 166
Kenn, Bp. *See* Ken, Thomas
Kennet, Basil, author, 410
Kennet, Bp. *See* Kennett, White, bishop of Peterborough
Kennett (Kennet), White, bishop of Peterborough, author, 410
Kensington, England, 118
Kensky, Richd., fails to appear before vestry, 478
Kent County, Delaware (Kent County, Pennsylvania), lack of clergy in, 340
Kent County, Pennsylvania. *See* Kent County, Delaware
Ker, Mr.
merchant, 406
protest by, 406
Kerney, Edmond (Edmd.). *See* Kearney, Edmond
Kerney, Mr. *See* Kearney, Edmond
Kersey. *See* Cloth, fabric, yarn—kersey
Kettleby, [Abel], landgrave, 248
Kettlewel. *See* Kettlewell, John

Kettlewell (Kettlewel), John, author, 6-7, 34, 36
Key
 to church, chapel, 303, 435, 437
 to courthouse, 304
Kicotan. *See* Hampton, Virginia
Kidder, Bp. *See* Kidder, Richard, bishop of Bath and Wells
Kidder, Richard, bishop of Bath and Wells
 author, 36
Kidlye, Daniel
 letter from, 323
 son-in-law of, 323
Kighley. *See* Keighley, England
Kikaton. *See* Hampton, Virginia
Kilcolman Parish, Ireland, clergyman from, 53
Killala Diocese, Ireland, clergyman from, 54
Kilmovee Parish, Ireland, clergyman from, 53
King
 and bishop of London, 274
 assumes government of South Carolina, 270*n*
 authority of, acknowledged, 269
 colony of, 286
 creates Church of England, xiii
 cursed, 303, 303*n*
 dues to, not paid, 372
 in fable, 249*n*
 instructions from, 189, 327, 327*n*, 354
 oath of loyalty to, xxviii, 191
 patronage of, 323
 rebellion against, unlawful, 194
 rumored transfer of Carolina to, 271
 See also Crown
King William County, Virginia, 331
 clergyman in, 331
 parish in, 331
 vestryman in, 331
King William's Parish, Virginia, 296
King's attorney, member of assembly, 420
King's Province. *See* Rhode Island
King, _____
 clergyman, 308
 master of the charterhouse, 308
 report to be given by, 147
King, Bp. *See* King, William—archbishop of Dublin
King, Charles (Charls.), vestryman, 486-488, 490
King, Doctor. *See* King, _____—clergyman
King, James, curate, 352
King, Peter, author, 36
King, William, archbishop of Dublin
 author, 9-10, 34, 36, 410
 letter from, 114
 ordination by, 352
Kingham, Robert (Robt.)
 allowance of, 477, 480, 483
Kingsale. *See* Kinsale, Ireland
Kinsale (Kingsale), Ireland, 62, 76
Kiquotan. *See* Hampton, Virginia
Kirckum, Ealinor. *See* Kirkham, Elenor
Kirk, _____
 occupation of, 216
 of Nottingham, 216
Kirkham (Kirckum), Elenor (Ealinor)
 burial of, 442
Kitchen. *See* Building—kitchen
Knight, Mr. *See* Knight, Tobias
Knight, Tobias
 alleged associate of, 124*n*
 chief justice, 124*n*
 controls money for church, 250
 Council member, 124*n*
 marriage of, 250
 protest by, 251
 secretary, 122, 124*n*
 vestryman, 190, 251
Knightly, Madam, 118
Knights, Mr. *See* Knight, Tobias
Kocotan. *See* Hampton, Virginia
L'Comle, Love. *See* LeComte, Louis Daniel
L., J. *See* Robinson, John
La Pierre, Mr. *See* LaPierre, John
La'Piere, John. *See* LaPierre, John
Labor
 hired, 202
 scarcity of, 116, 244
Laborer. *See* Occupation, trade, profession—laborer, workman
Lacey, Sarah
 guardian of, 493
 maintained by parish, 493
Lactantii. *See* Lactantius
Lactantius (Lactantii), author, 295
Ladson, William
 letter from, 228-230
 parishioner, 230
Ladyday, 159, 244, 277, 298
Lake Mattamuskeet (Old Mattummuskete, New Mattummuskete), ministry at, 379
Lamarr, Mr., house of, 76
Lambert, John, letter from, 316-317
Lambert, Ralph, bishop of Meath
 letter from, 323-324

Lameness. *See* Disease, illness, affliction—lameness
Lancashire, England, Jacobites in, 232*n*
Lancaster, England, 247
  clergyman from, 231
Land, 64, 142, 265
  act of assembly on, 461, 462*n*
  bearings of, 84
  belief in afterlife a condition of owning, xix, xix*n*
  clergyman settles on, xv
  conveyance of, 431
  dissenters may tax, xix
  donated for church building, 431
  donated to church, 144*n*
  for clergy, xxvii, 87, 230
  for glebe, 192, 325, 443
  granted, 81, 114*n*, 215*n*
  improved, 32, 87
  instructions concerning, xxi
  laid out for town, 316
  leased, 405
  mortgaged, 113*n*
  owner of, xxii, xlv, 76*n*, 241*n*, 291*n*, 412*n*, 444*n*
  ownership, requirement concerning, xix
  payment for clearing of, 433
  processioning of, xxxv, 461-462, 462*n*, 466, 492
  purchased, 87, 89*n*, 113*n*, 202
  sale of, 349
  settled, 32, 81, 83, 86, 147*n*, 315, 317, 324, 346
  taxation of, xix
  vestry may purchase, 192, 290
  See also Commodity payments—for land; Town, city, settlement—lots in, lots sold in
Landing, 379
Lanier, Robt., vestryman, 189
Lansdown, Lord. *See* Granville, George, baron Landsdowne
Lapiere. *See* LaPierre, John
LaPierre (La'Piere, La Pierre, Lapiere, Leapear, Lepear), John, *500*
  assistant to clergyman, 347
  clergyman, xiv, xxx, 313*n*, 317, 324, 329, 336, 344
  denounces colonists, xiv
  difficulties of, 349
  family of, 313, 324
  Frenchman, 344
  letter from, 312-313, 337-338, 347-351
  ministry of, 313, 347-349
  missionary appointment of, xxx, 313, 317, 336-338, 344
  pastoral letter to, 350
  refuses to preach, 344
  replacement for, 348
  salary of, 324, 347, 349
  temper of, 344
  to deliver letter, 329
  wife of, blind, 313
Lasinby (Lazinby, Lazingby), Rob[er]t
  letter from, 130
  letter to, 131
  opinion of, 130
  to observe missionary, 277
  to report to SPG, 130
Lasinby, Mr. *See* Lasinby, Rob[er]t
Lathinghouse, Andrew, marriage of, 364
Laud, William, author, 6
Law
  absence of, 119, 350
  ecclesiastical, canon, 121, 192, 417
  membership in religious body necessary for protection of, xviii
  status of slave church member in, xviii
Lawler, Patrick, proselytizer, 198
Lawrence, Stephen, testimonial by, 53
Lawson, John, 202
  author, 95*n*, 201
  information from, 94
  murder, 95*n*
  of Yorkshire, England, 95*n*
  surveyor-general, 95*n*
Lawson, Mr. *See* Lawson, John
Lay reader. *See* Reader
Lazingby, Mr. *See* Lasinby, Rob[er]t—clergyman
Lazingby, Reverend Mr. *See* Lasinby, Rob[er]t—clergyman
Le Clerc (Le Clerk), Jean, [Cotelerius, J.B.], author, 33
Le Comte (l'Comle), Louis (Love), author, 7
Le Grand, Antoine, author, 6
Le Rees, Francisco, author, 294
Leapear, Mr. *See* LaPierre, John
Leary, Richd., clerk, 156
Lectures, published, 410
Lee, Andrew, shipmaster, 132
Lee, Thomas (Tho., Thos.)
  churchwarden, 445-447, 451
  complaint by, 447
  letter from, 450-451
  sues former churchwarden, 448

vestryman, 445-446, 448, 451
Lee, Thos., payment to, 210
Legh, _____, vicar, 407
Legh, Dr. *See* Legh, _____
Leigh, Daniel (Danl.)
clerk, 437
payment to, 437
reader, duties of, 437
Leigh, Edward, author, 294
Leigh, James
justice of the peace, 310
petitioner, 309-310
signature of, forged, 310*n*
Leiutenant. *See* Maynard, Robert—lieutenant
LeJau (Le Jau), Francis
absent from meeting, 218
clergyman, 216*n*
instructions to, 225-226
letter from, 215-216, 249
letter to, 225-226
to make inquiry, 249
LeJau, Dr. *See* LeJau, Francis—clergyman
Leland, John, author, 410
Lennon, Mr.
character of, 323
clergyman, 323
desires missionary appointment, 323
Lepear, Mr. *See* LaPierre, John
Leslie (Lesly, Lessley), Charles, 16*n*
author, 7, 10, 16, 34
author of [2. *Satan Disrob'd. 3 The History of Sin and Heresy. 4 A Paralell betwixt the Faith and Doctrine of the present Quakers, and the chief Hereticks in all Ages.*], 6
author of [*A Religious Conference between a minister and Parishioners concerning the Practice of Baptizing Infants by powring water on their Faces with a Vindication of Godfathers and Godmothers*], 6
author of [*An Easy method with the Deists and Jews*], 8
author of [*Discourses shewing who they are who are now Qualify'd to Administer Baptism and the Ld's. Supper*], 10
author of [*Five Discourses of the Author of the Snake in the Grass*], 7
author of [*Paralell of the Doctrine of the Quakers with the Primitive Hereticks*], 10
author of [*Pastoral Letters*], 9
author of [*Primitive Heresy Reviv'd*], 10
author of [*The Defence of the Snake*], 7, 10
Lesly, _____, 330
Lesly, Mr. *See* Leslie, Charles
Lessley. *See* Leslie, Charles
Letter, 95, 133, 135
abstract of, 232, 249
cover for, 238
difficult to send, 263
dismissory, 156, 351-352
duplicates of, to be sent, 226
express, 200
form of, prescribed, 138
from "Planter," 47, 49-50
from Alexander Spotswood, 153-154, 253
from anonymous correspondent, 273
from archbishop of Canterbury, 320
from benefactor, 46
from bishop of Chester, 395
from bishop of Elphin, 53
from bishop of London, 45, 47-49, 51-52, 55-57, 89-90, 107, 127-128, 133, 135, 137-138, 146*n*, 149-150, 274, 320, 329-339, 342, 390, 391*n*, 392, 395
from bishop of Meath, 324
from bishop of Oxford, 426
from Christopher DeGraffenried, 112-113
from Christopher Gale, 46, 332
from churchwardens and vestry, 250, 398
from commissary, 322, 396
from Dr. Bray, xxv
from Edward Mashborne, 222-223
from Edward Moseley, 182, 293
from Francis Nicholson, 171, 175, 177, 179, 203, 208, 212
from governor, xv
from governor of Virginia, 146*n*, 149, 197, 228, 296
from inhabitants of Cape Fear, 381
from John Baptista Ashe, 289-290
from John Lovick, 289
from lords proprietors, xxi-xxii, 3, 22, 103
from member of Council, 375
from Nathaniel Duckenfield, 310-311
from parishioners, 228
from president of Council, 66, 73-74, 110, 110*n*
from Richard Hewett, 291, 296
from schoolmaster, 296
from Thomas Howard, 242
from Thomas Pollock, 173*n*, 178*n*, 179-180, 183-184
from vestry, 68-69, 288*n*, 302, 361, 367, 371, 411, 450
from vestry and churchwardens, 242, 412*n*, 449
mentions Dr. Bray, xxv

miscarries, 106
not received from colony, 419
of administration, 136
of attorney, 150, 150*n*, 169, 246, 291-292
of credit, 246, 257
of ordination, 156, 351-352
of probate, xliv
open, 245
pastoral, 329-330, 350
payment for writing of, 451
postage for, 182
private, from clergy to members of SPG, 227
published, 410
receipt to be obtained for, 226
requested, 184, 369
sent under cover, 237
to archbishop of Canterbury, 398-399, 399*n*, 427
to archbishop of Tuam, 57-58
to archbishop of York, 146-147
to bishop of London, xv, xlv, 22, 47, 68-69, 73-74, 77, 79-80, 112, 135-136, 145-149, 303-305, 316-325, 329-339, 341-345, 347-351, 358-362, 364-376, 381, 392, 396
to bishop of Oxford, 423
to Brian Hunt, 300-301
to churchwardens, 147
to churchwardens and vestry, 246, 250
to Council, 3
to duke of Newcastle, 327
to Edward Moseley, 293
to establish new missions, 340
to Francis Nicholson, 168-173, 176-178, 178*n*, 179, 179*n*, 180, 182-184, 184*n*, 299
to General Assembly, xxii
to governor and Council, 3, 121
to lord chancellor, 424
to lord proprietor, 14
to lord treasurer, 127
to president of Council, 168
to William Tredwell Bull, 289-290
written from Roanoke, 11-12
Letters patent, 278
Letters testamentary, 377-378
Leusden, Johannes, author, 294
Leuten, Thomas (Thos.). *See* Luton, Thomas
Leuten, Thomas, Jr. *See* Luten, Thomas, Jr.
Leverpool. *See* Liverpool, England
Lewis, _____, author, 36
Lewis, John, author of [*Church Catechism explain'd*], 38
Libel, chief justice accused of, 303
Library
account of, 179
act of assembly on, 15, 15*n*
at Bath, 86, 186
books of, lost, 144
catalog of, 5-10, 10*n*, 13, 15*n*, 39*n*, 101, 293, 409
clergyman cannot obtain books from, 356
commissioners of, 15*n*
destroyed, 5, 28, 44, 178, 180
dispersed, xlii, 255
dispute over, xlii
establishment of, 176
gift of, xli, 9, 22, 65, 98, 101, 121, 144, 167-168, 172, 178, 257, 277, 293, 409, 449
gift of SPCK, xxxix
gift to, 26, 398
in Pamlico, 65
keeper of, 15*n*
lacking, 84
layman's, xli, 9
lending, xli
of archbishop of Canterbury, xl, 138, 153, 196, 201, 203, 211, 214, 232, 234, 238-239, 244, 249, 251, 253, 283
of no use to clergy, 450
parochial, 4-5
payment for, 15
report on, 152
requested, 373
requested by clergyman, 255, 259
titles to be added to, 409
withheld from clergyman, 248
See also Books, tracts; Clergy, clergyman—library of; Price, value—of library
License
clergyman lacks, 351
denied, 387
from archbishop of Dublin, 352
from bishop of London, xliv, 207, 242, 341, 353, 386, 411
not granted, 396
to marry, xliv, 121, 136, 195
to preach, 357-358
See also Clergy, clergyman—license for
Lillington, John
letter from, 240-241
vestryman, 190, 241
Lilly, William, author of [*The Oxford Grammar*], 7
Limborch, Philippia (Phillippus) Van (A.) author, 6
Lime Street, London, merchant in, 211*n*
Lincoln, (England), bishop of, 34, 359
Lincoln, bishop of. *See* Gibson, Edmund, bishop of Lincoln

Lincolnshire, England, clergyman from, 299*n*
Linen. *See* Cloth, fabric, yarn—linen
Linnhaven Bay. *See* Lynn Haven Bay, Virginia
Linnington, John
  salary of, 445
  subscription by, 439
  vestry clerk, 445
Lisbon, Portugal, clergyman in, 322, 329, 338, 350, 390
Literacy
  in New England, 11
  low level of, 84
Literature
  distributed by SPCK, xxxix
  distributed by SPG, xli
  instruction in, 149
Little Inlet, precinct boundary at, 316
Little River
  General Assembly at, 189
  governor at, 260
  lack of clergy in, 293
  ministry at, 389
Little Tower Hill. *See* Tower Hill, London
Little, Mrs. *See* Little, Penelope
Little, Penelope
  executrix, 485
  lawsuit against, 485
  to return money, 485
Little, William (W., Wm.)
  Anglican, 463*n*
  attorney general, 463*n*
  chief justice, 463*n*
  executrix of estate of, 485
  merchant, 463*n*
  oath taken by, 463
  of Massachusetts, 463*n*
  receiver general, 463*n*
  vestryman, 463-465, 468-471, 473-474
Littleton, Adam, author, 6
Liturgy. *See* Church of England—liturgy, rubrics of; Translation—of liturgy
Liverpool (Leverpool), England, 395, 421-422
  clergyman from, 350
  merchant from, 391
Livestock, 237
  bequest of, xxx
  for clergy, 28, 121, 230
  of clergyman, 264
  purchased, 202
Lizard Point (The Lizard), Cornwall, England, clergyman at, 142
Lizard, The. *See* Lizard Point, Cornwall, England
Lloyd, Mrs., beaten, 466
Lloyd, Sarah
  oath taken by, 287
  witness, 287
Lock, 431
Locke, John
  associate of, xvii
  philosopher, xvii
  secretary to proprietary board, xvii
Lockwoods Folly Inlet (Lockwoods Folly), ministry at, 389
Lockwoods Folly. *See* Lockwoods Folly Inlet
Lodging, 27, 31, 39-40, 59
  of clergy, 96, 107, 120, 129, 175, 209, 213, 405
  of governor, 301
Loftin (Lofftess), Leonard
  churchwarden, 452
  letter from, 450-451
  vestryman, 451
Log, in fable, 249*n*
Lombard Street, London, 222
Londn. *See* Robinson, John, bishop of London
London, bishop of, xxv
  approves clergymen, xxvii
  authority of, xliv
  commissaries report to, xliv
  correspondence of, xlv
  encourages missionary relief, xiv
  governors to report to, xliii
  instructions from, xlv
  letter to, xv-xvi, xlix
  license issued by, xliv
  petition to, xxv
  Privy Council member, xlix
  recommendation to, xxii
  report to, xlix
London, bishop of. *See* Compton, Henry; Gibson, Edmund; Robinson, John
London, Edmd. *See* Gibson, Edmund, bishop of London
London, England, xxv-xxvi, 3-4, 7, 10, 14, 20-21, 24, 31, 34-35, 50, 59, 62-65 passim, 72, 87, 113, 127, 130, 133-134, 138, 153, 157, 159-160, 163, 196, 201, 203, 211, 214, 227, 230, 232, 234, 238-239, 243-244, 249, 251, 253, 256, 264, 270*n*, 272, 275, 278-279, 283, 300, 329, 348, 350, 362, 366, 369, 371-372, 385, 393, 396, 400, 405-406, 411, 422, 425-426
  arms supplier from, 124*n*
  banker in, 345
  baron in, 112

clergyman debts in, 390
clergyman from, 391
clergyman in, 31, 58, 76, 136, 156, 408
district in, 265*n*
haberdasher in, 291
hospital in, 19*n*
lack of support from, 185, 246
merchant in, 211*n*, 367, 371, 405-406, 412
milliners from, 391
notary public in, 406
official in, 332
prison in, 122*n*, 239*n*
receiver general in, 307
representative sent to, 309*n*
schoolmaster from, 145*n*
ship from, 259, 423
SPCK founded in, xxxix
SPG founded in, xl
supplies for rebels from, 129
London, H. *See* Compton, Henry, bishop of London
London, Henry Lord Bishop of. *See* Compton, Henry, bishop of London
London, John. *See* Robinson, John, bishop of London
London, Lord of. *See* Robinson, John
London, See of, 136, 360
Long Bay, ministry at, 389
Long Island, New York, Quakers in, 20
Long, Bp., author, 410
Long, James
letter from, 68-69
vestryman, 68, 431, 433-434, 439, 444
Lord president of Privy Council, 243*n*
Lord protector, 122*n*
Lord treasurer, letter to, 127
Lord's Prayer, 16
recited by Negroes, xlvi, 285, 424
Lord's Supper. *See* Holy Communion
Lords proprietors, 3*n*, 4*n*, 24, 25*n*, 32, 134*n*, 148, 202*n*, 248, 249*n*
accused of negligence, 122
act sent to, 22, 209, 213
appearance of Thomas Cary before, 87*n*
appointments by, 80*n*, 95*n*, 186, 286*n*
Cary Rebellion and, 123
charity from, urged, 158
charter to, xxii, xxviii, 82-83, 297, 298*n*
church and, xvi, xix-xxi, xxiii, 82, 311
clergyman commended to, 307
complaint to, 106-107, 118, 201, 311
confirm acts of assembly, 215, 236-237
create unitary colony, 122*n*
criticized, 123
deputies of, 76*n*, 119, 149*n*, 247, 288
dislike clergyman, 201
disorders and, 72-73
disregarded in colony, 237
donate funds for church, 145
elected to membership in SPG, xl, xl*n*, 13, 243
erect colony, 80*n*
expected to restore order, 110
extreme protestant among, xix
fail to confirm act, 28
glebe to be provided by, 298
government of, ends, xxi
governor appointed by, 299*n*
grant of Carolina to, 215
informed of action of SPG, 97
instructions from, xxxiv*n*, xlii-xliii, 82, 327*n*
issue Concessions and Agreement, xvii
lack interest in North Carolina, xxii, 106
land granted to, 81
laws and constitutions of, 215
letter to be laid before, 124*n*
may grant concessions to dissenters, xvi
may nominate to livings, xxii, 298, 298*n*
meeting of, 134*n*, 298*n*
merchants, 129
named, 81
order from, requested, 257
palatine, xix, xxiv
powers of, 136
promise funds for buildings, xxi-xxii
promulgate Fundamental Constitutions, 215*n*
proposal concerning, 215
proposed as member, SPG, 243
proprietary share held by, 243*n*, 249*n*
purchase of proprietary share, 73*n*
Quaker, 71, 81-82, 108*n*, 201
Quaker deputies of, 82-83
quitrents of, 245
recommend clergymen, xxii, 298
remove governor, 119
resolutions of SPG to be laid before, 306
revenues of, 123, 129, 144
revolution against, 269, 270*n*
rumored to have sold Carolina, 271
sale of shares, 124*n*
secretary to, xvii, 298*n*
sell Carolina, 243*n*, 318
sell province, xvi
send agent, 164
Shaftesbury forced to flee, xix

share of proprietary held by, 243*n*, 249*n*
statute enacted in name of, 189, 266, 314
strife during rule of, xlix
Temporary Laws and, xx
tenants of, 87*n*, 223
to contribute to building of church, 461
urge kindness toward Indians, xx*n*
urged to disallow act, xxv
See also Acts of assembly—not confirmed by lords proprietors; Letter—from lords proprietors
Losotho, author, 410
Lottery, for building church, xxx
Lovick (Lowick), John (J., Jno., Jo.)
alleged fiscal mismanagement by, 317-318
arrival of, 263*n*
assembly member, 263*n*
behavior of, 321*n*
bill of exchange to, 263
boundary commissioner, 321*n*
character of, 317
Council member, 263*n*, 346
hinders church building, 317
insults clergyman, 301
letter from, 288*n*
oath taken by, 464
perjurer, 321
secretary, 263*n*, 288, 292, 301, 317, 321
vestryman, 464-465, 468-471 passim, 473
vice admiralty judge, 263*n*
Lovick (Lowick), Thomas (Thos.)
account of, 475
account signed by, 476
churchwarden, 473-474
payment by, 475, 477
presents account to vestry, 474
vestryman, 471, 473-474
Lovick, Hugh George
of London, 291
power of attorney to, 291
Lovick, Mr. *See* Lovick, John
Lower Cape Fear. *See* Cape Fear
Lower Counties, The. *See* Delaware
Lower Palatinate, The. *See* Germany
Lowick, John. *See* Lovick, John
Lowick, Thos. *See* Lovick, Thomas
Lowry, Robert (Robt.)
letter from, 250
testimonial by, 109
vestryman, 109, 190, 250
Loyd, Mrs.
coffee house owner, 222
deceased, 222
son of, 222
Lucas, Richard, author, 34, 36, 173
Luckis (Luck), _____
delivers letter, 243
shipmaster, 239, 243
Ludlam (Ludlum), [Richard]
clergyman, 316
deceased, 316
Ludlum, Messr. *See* Ludlam, [Richard]
Ludwell, Philip
governor, xxi*n*
instructions to, xxi*n*, xxxiv*n*
Lufforrance, Will., vestryman, 190
Luten (Luton), William (W., Will., Willm., Wm.)
account of, 483-484
churchwarden, 479-480, 483-484
debtor, 484
oath taken by, 477-478
payment by, 482, 484, 487
presents account to vestry, 478-479
to collect parish tax, 478
to present account to vestry, 480
vestryman, 477-480 passim
Luten's Bridge (Chowan County), district boundary at, 462
Luten, Jno. *See* Luton, John
Luten, Major. *See* Luton, Thomas
Luten, Mr. *See* Luton, Thomas, Jr.
Luten, Thomas. *See* Luton, Thomas, Jr.
Luten, Thos. *See* Luton, Thomas
Lutheran. *See* Dissenters—Lutheran
Luton (Leuten, Luten), Thomas (T., Thos.), Jr.
account signed by, 484
allowance for, 471
churchwarden, 469-473 passim
oath taken by, 469, 477-478
payment by, 472
payment to, 451, 471-472
presents account to vestry, 471
processioner, 462
vestryman, 173, 431, 465, 474, 476-478
Luton (Luten), John (Jno.)
clerk, 487
salary, 487
to retrieve Eucharist silver, 488
to return vestry book, 491
Luton (Luten), Thomas (Thos.)
awaits delivery of Bibles, 448
churchwarden, 431, 433-435, 445, 462-464, 490
county court justice, 432*n*
General Court justice, 432*n*
General Court provost marshal, 432*n*

guardian, 469
letter from, 68-69, 287-288, 450-451
letter signed by, 173
payment to, 454, 489
security by, 489
subscription by, 439
to oversee church construction, 444
to present account to vestry, 446-447, 462, 482, 488
vestryman, 68, 173, 189, 287, 433, 435-436, 438-439, 441-448 passim, 451-452, 454-455, 457, 459-462 passim, 474, 479-482 passim, 484-488 passim
Luton, William. *See* Luten, William
Lynn Haven Bay (Linnhaven Bay), Virginia, 64
clergyman in, 63
Lynn, Lord, warrant to, 346
M_____, Mrs., greeting to, 311
Mac Sparran, James
clergyman, 278
missionary appointment of, 278
order to, 278
Mace. *See* Spices—mace
Machapunga. *See* Indians—Machapunga
Mackeel, Anthony, burial of, 475
Macky (Mackey), William (W.), payment to, 476, 483
Madeira (Maderas), Spain, ship lost at, 65
Maderas. *See* Madeira, Spain
Madrant, Richard. *See* Mardron, Richard
Madren, Richard. *See* Mardron, Richard
Magistrate. *See* Justice of the Peace
Magna Carta, disregarded, 237
Maherring River. *See* Meherrin River
Maid. *See* Servant—maid
Mainadier, Mr., fails to communicate, 137
Maine (Mayn), description of, 11
Makey, John, vestryman, 191
Malabar, India, 135
Maldonaldo (Maldonatus), Juan, author, 6
Maldonatus. *See* Maldonaldo, Juan
Malt. *See* Food, diet—malt
Man. *See* Sodor and Man—bishop of
Mandey, Venturus, author, 8
Manger. *See* Mauger, Claude
Mangey, _____
clergyman, 335
loans book, 335
Mansell Street, London, banker in, 373
Mansfield, England, 335
Manteo, christened, xiii, xv*n*
Indian, xiii
Map, plan, chart, 63, 84, 86
by Edward Moseley, 198*n*
of church, 84
of coast, 382*n*
of colony, 381
Mapletofh. *See* Mapletoft, John
Mapletoft (Mapletofh), John, author, 410
Mardron (Madren, Madrant), Richard (Richd.)
churchwarden, 45, 250-251
letter from, 250
petitioner, 44-45
vestryman, 190, 250-251
Markham, Gervase, author of [*A Way to gett Wealth Containing six principal Vocations*], 6
Maro, Publius Vergilius, author, 7
Marriage, xv*n*, 28, 117-118, 124, 200, 283, 377
act of assembly on, xxvii*n*, xxxi, 283, 364, 364*n*
banns of, 193, 195, 242
by clergy from Virginia, xvi
by magistrate, xxxi, 120
ceremonies in Perquimans Precinct, xvi*n*
certified, 482
fees, 193, 195, 384
license for, xliv, 136, 193, 195, 242, 326
of clergyman, 209
of Edward Moseley, 183
prohibited between races, xxvii*n*
table of lawful and unlawful, 193, 195, 326
unlawful, xxxi, 122*n*, 193, 195, 364, 364*n*
See also Clergy, clergyman—angry at magistrates' marrying; fee to—for marriage; marriage performed by, married; Fine, forfeiture—for illegal marriage
Marsden (Marshden), Richard (Richd.), 348, 351, 382, *500-501*
accusation against, 390-391
age of, 345
alleged commission to, 338
alleged ordination of, 350, 405
alleged persecution of, 411
application of, rejected, 382
arrival of, 66, 343
behavior of, 361, 395, 397
bigamist, 345*n*, 390
bill of exchange from, 390, 405-406
bill of exchange from, unpaid, 405
censured, 319
character of, 339, 350, 382-383, 390, 408, 412*n*
clergyman, xlv, 5, 5*n*, 44, 73, 330, 336, 339, 344, 345*n*, 350, 356, 374, 383, 386-387, 390, 393, 398, 405, 468, 472

clerk of, 468
daughter of, 345
debtor, 319-320, 395
difficulties of, 361, 368, 411
dismissed as missionary, 391*n*, 395*n*, 397, 408
escapes from jail, 395
flees country, 319-320, 322, 329
friend of, 345
gratuity given to, 374
lack of compensation, 344
leases land, 405
letter from, 66-67, 343-345, 359-362, 366-373, 381-382, 386, 393, 399*n*, 410-412, 427
letter regarding, 395
letter to, 360, 387, 393
library for, 412
license of, withheld, 387
merchant, 338
ministry of, 44, 66-67, 330, 344, 360-362, 368, 398
missionary appointment of, 356, 359-360, 383, 387, 390, 395-397, 407, 411
missionary appointment of, pending, 386
notes population increase, 344, 368
notes shortage of books, 362, 369
notes shortage of clergy, 368
orders library, 398-399
payment to, 5, 468, 472
petitioner, 324
physical description of, 406
plantation of, 383
poses as commissary, 339
recommendation of, 360, 367, 371, 374, 407
rector, 67
refuses to appear before commissary, 350
repents for behavior, 381
replaces minister, 348
representation by, 382
request by, 361-362, 372
resides in England, 405
salary of, 67, 383, 393, 405, 411
salary of, delinquent, 374
successor as missionary, 396-397, 408
testimonial in behalf of, 387
to furnish testimonial, 386
travel of, 350, 393
vestryman, 324
wife of, 407
Marsden, Doctor. *See* Marsden, Richard—clergyman
Marsden, Mr. *See* Marsden, Richard
Marsden. *See* Marsden, Richard
Marsh, Narcissus, author, 37
Marshal, deputy marshal, 364
fined, xxix
to summon vestry, 191, 194, 266
Marshall, Benjamin, author, 410
Marshden, Mr. *See* Marsden, Richard
Marston, Edward, removed as clergyman, 66
Marston, Mr., beaten, 466
Martin (Martyn), George (Geo.)
account of, 476
account signed by, 477
churchwarden, 474, 476
fees collected, 475
vestryman, 473-474
Martin, Mr., slaves of, baptized, 143
Martinico. *See* Martinique
Martinique (Martinico), official in, 247
Martyn, Capt. *See* Martin, George
Martyn, George. *See* Martin, George
Martyn, Mr. *See* Martin, George
Mary and Ann (ship), clergyman aboard, 423
Mary, queen of England, 5*n*
Maryland (Piscataway), 12, 342, 390
clergyman appointed to, 332, 334
clergyman in, 3*n*, 4, 20, 20*n*, 66, 308, 330, 341, 401
clergyman rejected in, 318
commissary for, xliv
commissary in, xlv*n*, 23*n*
description of, 10
lack of clergy in, 20, 296
library for, 15, 17, 26*n*
official from, 432*n*
Quakers in, 19-20
salary for ministers in, 195
Mashborne (Mashburn, Washburn), Edward (Edwrd.)
justice of the peace, 145*n*
letter from, 145*n*, 222-223
mother of, 222
of London, 222
performance of, 149
schoolmaster, 143, 145, 145*n*, 146*n*, 149, 154, 222
Mashborne, Mr. *See* Mashborne, Edward
Mashburn, Mr. *See* Mashborne, Edward
Mason, John, witness, 407
Massachusetts
description of, 11
governor of, 11*n*
official from, 463*n*
Mast. *See* Hogs—mast for
Mather, [Samuel]

complaint by, 424
letter from, 424
Mather, Dr. *See* Mather, [Samuel]
Mattamuskeet. *See* Indians—Mattamuskeet
Matthews, Thomas (Thos.)
allowance of, 456, 458
to present account to vestry, 463
Mauger, Claude, author, 9
Maul, bishop of Dromore. *See* Maule, Henry, bishop of Dromore
Maul, Capt. *See* Maule, William
Maule (Maul), William (Will.)
assembly member, 161*n*
Council member, 161*n*
father-in-law of, 260
surveyor, deputy surveyor general, 160, 161*n*
vestryman, 189
vice admiralty judge, 161*n*
Maule, Colonel. *See* Maule, William
Maule, Henry, bishop of Dromore
encourages missionary, 352
to secure permission, 353
Maule, Mr. *See* Maule, Robert
Maule, Patr., vestryman, 190
Maule, Robert
absence of, 218
arrival of, 66
clergyman, 66, 188*n*, 217, 221*n*
instructions to, 225-226
letter to, 188, 188*n*, 221, 225-226
Mauric. *See* Maurice, Henry
Maurice (Mauric), Henry, author, 8
Mayn. *See* Maine
Maynard, Robert, Royal Navy lieutenant, 256, 258*n*
Mayo, Dr. *See* Mayo, R.
Mayo, Mr. *See* Mayo, R.
Mayo, R.
information from, 127
letter from, 131
opinion of, 130-131
to report to SPG, 130
to review missionary's performance, 297
McDaniel, James
alleged theft by, 270*n*
flees justice, 270*n*
Mcfarlan, Danl., vestryman, 191
Meal. *See* Food, diet—meal
Meat. *See* Food, diet—meat
Meath, Bishop of. *See* Lambert, Ralph, bishop of Meath
Meath, Ralph. *See* Lambert, Ralph, bishop of Meath
Meazle, Luke, payment to, 437
Mechanic. *See* Occupation, trade, profession—mechanic
Mede, Joseph, author, 6
Mediation, 3
Medicine, medical treatment, 269, 311
bark, 94
book concerning, 161
by clergyman, 85
for clergyman, 256
payment for, 436-437, 465, 477
salivation, 477, 483, 485*n*
See also Occupation, trade, profession—apothecary, physician, surgeon
Meets and bounds, of New Bern, 404
Meherrin, collection for chapel, church in, xxx
Meherrin (Meherring) River
clergyman at, 283
resettlement of Indians on, 197
Melanchthon (Melancthonis), Philipp, author, 294
Melancthonis. *See* Melanchton, Philipp
Mell, John
letter from, 228-230
parishioner, 230
Memorandum
by vestry, 440, 443
on unlawful marriage, 364
Memorial, petition, representation, 57, 222, 282, 325*n*, 354, 366*n*
for care of indigent, 442
for minister, 32-33, 33*n*, 44-45, 68-69, 348
for money, 23
for reimbursement of aid to indigent, 464
forged, 310*n*
from clergyman, 150*n*, 156, 280, 282, 320, 357
from Huguenots, 33*n*
from vestry and churchwardens of Pasquotank, 44-45
from vestry of Pasquotank, 66
from vestry of St. Thomas's, 365
to bishop of London, 44-45, 63, 68-69, 309-310, 310*n*, 324, 348, 353, 365
to divide parish, 451
to governor of Virginia, 158
to House of Lords, 32-33, 33*n*
to king, 326
to SPG, 23, 280, 282, 296-297, 320, 322, 328-329, 357, 365-366, 375, 397, 460, 461
to standing committee, SPG, 31, 51-52
to Thomas Pollock, 76, 167

to treasurer, SPG, 263
to Treasury Board (England), 274
to vestry, 147, 176, 227
to vestry and churchwardens of Chowan, 236
to vestry and churchwardens of Pasquotank, 236
to vestry of Chowan, 279
See also Churchwardens—petition from
Mengs, James, vestryman, 190
Merchant. *See* Occupation, trade, profession—merchant
Mercury, salivation induced by, 485*n*
Methodism, founder of, 425*n*
Methodist. *See* Dissenters—Methodist
Michaelmas, 106*n*, 132, 141, 152, 158-159, 163, 182, 210, 213, 231, 244, 277, 385, 392, 397
Middlesex, England, 308-309, 309*n*
Middleton, A., curate, 59
Midsummer, 169, 329*n*, 396, 411
clergy to write at, 92
Miles (Myles), Jno.
letter from, 228-230
parishioner, 229-230
verbal abuse of, 229
Militia, military forces, 122
arms for, xxxvi*n*
camp for, 230*n*
captain in, 241*n*
clergy exempt from service in, xxiii, xlviii
difficulty of raising, 185
from South Carolina, 140*n*, 241*n*, 258*n*
in Tuscarora War, 140*n*
marines, 122
muster, xlviii
supplies for, 140*n*
See also Cary Rebellion; Tuscarora War; War, warfare
Milk. *See* Drink—milk
Mill, 210
cost of, 214
lack of, for grain, 85
Mill, Mr. *See* Milne, Francis
Miller, Thos., vestryman, 190
Milliner. *See* Occupation, trade, profession—milliner
Milne (Mill), Francis
clergyman, 53*n*
instructions to, 52*n*
missionary appointment of, 52, 53*n*
Minister. *See* Clergy, clergyman
Minshaw, Richd., processioner, 462
Mircler, Lodwick, payment to, 493
Missionary. *See* Clergy, clergymen
Mohammedanism, 308, 309*n*
Moir (Moire), James (Jas.), *501*
accepted into SPG service, 391*n*
arrival of, 408, 419
attends SPG board meeting, 398-399
character of, 394, 408
clergyman, xlv, 5*n*, 391, 392*n*, 394, 397, 408, 412*n*, 419
delivers letter, 394
lays testimonial before committee, 396
letter from, 408-409, 422
letter regarding, 396
library of, 399
ministry of, 408-409, 422
missionary appointment of, 391, 396-399 passim, 408, 412*n*, 419
missionary of Church of Scotland, 391
recommendation of, xlv, 396, 408
salary of, 396, 399
to conduct service, 399
to furnish testimonial, 391*n*
to order library, 399
travel of, 408
warrant to, 5*n*
Moir, Mr. *See* Moir, James
Moire, James. *See* Moir, James
Molasses. *See* Food, diet—molasses
Money, xix, 16, 66-67, 99-100, 102, 107, 116-117, 121, 141-142, 144, 148-150, 150*n*, 159-160, 173, 178, 181, 183-184, 227, 432, 437-454 passim, 456-459 passim, 461-462, 464, 466-467, 470-471, 474-482 passim, 485-494 passim
action to recover, 448
bills, 188, 265, 473, 477
charity, 187
due from forfeitures, 418
due precinct, 435
for building of church, 317
held by vestry, 251
lent, 207, 250
of Great Britain (sterling), xxii, xxiv, xxxvii*n*, xli, xli*n*, xlii, 15, 18, 23, 27-28, 30-31, 45-48 passim, 52, 56, 58, 63, 65, 67, 79, 91, 98, 101, 106*n*, 111, 123, 132, 140, 145, 158, 163, 165-166, 168, 170, 172, 177-178, 196-197, 199, 213-214, 231, 233-234, 238, 245, 250, 250*n*, 271, 290, 293, 298-300, 329, 339, 355, 359, 365, 373-374, 383-385, 385*n*, 388, 390, 392-393, 395-399 passim, 401, 405-407, 411, 421, 428, 434, 437-438, 440, 444-445, 461-463

of Ireland, 405
of lords proprietors, 129
of North Carolina, xxxvi, xxxviii*n*, 28, 73, 82, 123, 158, 235, 290, 327, 344, 349, 356, 361, 364-365, 368-369, 373, 385, 403, 481, 488
paper, 230, 245
pieces of eight, 437
presented to Christopher Gale, 247
proclamation, xxx, xxxvi-xxxvii, xxxviii*n*, 361, 402-403, 413, 415-417, 493
raised by sale of bricks, 414
rate of exchange of, xxxviii*n*, 86, 120, 123, 209, 213, 290, 327, 349, 356, 361, 365, 385
recovery of, sought by vestry, 251
shortage of, 145, 250
to be raised by parish, 416
wanted for trade, 139
See also Commodity payments; Interest—on money lent
Mongomery, Jno. *See* Montgomery, Jno.
Montgomerey, John. *See* Montgomery, John
Montgomery (Mongomery, Montgomerey), John (J., Jno.)
assembly member, 364*n*
attorney general, 364*n*
chief justice, 364*n*
memorandum by, 364
oath taken by, 477-478
vestryman, 477-482 passim, 484-486
Mooney, Martha, marriage of, 482
Moor, Dr. *See* Moore, _____ —clergyman
Moor, Mr.
deceased, 91
of Hopewell, New Jersey, 91
See also Moore, Thorogood
Moor, Roger. *See* Moore, Roger
Moore (Moor), _____
clergyman, 399, 409
committee chairman, 409
to review missionary's performance, 399
Moore (Moor), Maurice (M., Mau., Maur.)
churchwarden, 241
Council member, 288
leads military expedition, 241*n*
letter from, 240-241, 398-399
military officer, 190, 241*n*, 316
of South Carolina, 241*n*
petitioner, 324
vestryman, 190, 316
Moore (Moor), Roger (R., Rog.)
assistant justice, General Court, 412*n*
Council member, 412*n*
deceased, 412*n*
letter from, 398-399
letter to be delivered to, 412
of South Carolina, 412*n*
petitioner, 324
vestryman, 316, 324, 399, 418
Moore (Moor), Thorogood
attempts to settle among Indians, 45
clergyman, 46*n*
deceased, 46*n*
ministry of, 46*n*
missionary appointment of, 45
Moore, Adam, commissioner, 403
Moore, Dr. *See* Moore, _____ —clergyman
Moore, George, vestryman, 418
Moore, Nathl. (Natha.)
petitioner, 324
vestryman, 316, 324
Morals, concern for, xxxiii, 44, 84, 118, 134
See also Immorality
Moratico. *See* Roanoke Chapel
Moreton, Matthew Ducie, Lord Ducie, Baron Moreton, to testify for clergyman, 332
Morgan, Lewis
letter from, 228-230
parishioner, 230
Morgan, Olive, debtor, 480
Morrotto. *See* Roanoke River
Moseley (Mosely, Mosley), Edward (E., Ed., Edwd.), 253*n*
account by, 446-447
address by, 346
affidavit sworn before, 301
allowance of, 451
assembly member, 25*n*
attends meeting, 302
bill of exchange from, 295*n*
books of, 295*n*
cartographer, 198*n*
chapel of, 443
character of, 272
chief justice, 25*n*
churchwarden, 317, 445-447, 452-453, 465, 468-469
complaint by, 447
contributes to parish, xxxii
Council member, 25*n*, 370
debtor, 442, 447-448
deponent appears before, 301-302
deputy secretary of South Carolina, 24
dismissed as churchwarden, 454
expresses need for minister, 24
gives gift to parish, 465
house of, 76

land of, 115
lawsuit against, 448
letter from, 68-69, 182-183, 287-288, 293, 398-399
letter to, 293, 453
marriage of, 183
payment to, 454, 458, 468, 471-472, 479
petitioner, 451
receipt for, 251
request by, 293, 451
speaker of the assembly, 25*n*, 346
subscription by, 439
surveyor general, 25*n*
testimonial sworn before, 301
to deliver letter, 329
to negotiate to buy land, 443
to oversee chapel construction, 444
to return money, 445, 448
treasurer, 25*n*
vestryman, 68, 189, 287, 399, 441-444 passim, 451-454 passim, 456-457, 459-465 passim, 468, 470-471, 473-474, 476-480 passim

Moseley, Mr. *See* Moseley, Edward
Mosely, Colonel. *See* Moseley, Edward
Mosely, Mr. *See* Moseley, Edward
Mosley, Mr. *See* Moseley, Edward
Mosquitoes, 86, 182*n*
Moss, _____, influence of, 149-150
Mountjoy, Lord. *See* Stewart, William, 2nd viscount Mountjoy
Mulatto
child of white woman and, xxx
fine for giving birth to, 480
taxed, xxvii*n*
vestry order concerning, 489
Munns, Tho. *See* Muns, Thomas
Muns, Elizabeth (Elisa., Elisabeth)
clothes of, 454-458 passim
maintained by parish, 454-456, 458
widow, 458
Muns (Munns), Thomas (Thos.)
allowance for, 456, 458
payment to, 459, 466
Muns, Widow. *See* Muns, Elizabeth—widow
Murder. *See* Crime—murder
Murrain. *See* Disease, illness, affliction—murrain
Muscovy. *See* Russia
Musgrov, Jon.
letter from, 228-230
parishioner, 230
Mush. *See* Food, diet—mush
Music house, 264
See also Singing
Musket. *See* Arms, armaments—musket
Mustee
baptism of, 260
catechized, 261
children, 261
Mutton. *See* Food, diet—mutton
Myles, Mr. *See* Miles, Jno.
Nagg's Head, (The), London, 61
Nails. *See* Building materials—nails
Nansemond County, Virginia, 76
clergyman from, xvi
clergyman in, 321*n*
ministry in, 198
Nansemond Parish, Virginia, xv*n*
Nansemond River, Virginia, 76
Nansemond, Virginia, 222
clergyman in, 321, 473*n*
clergyman rejected at, 178
Naples, Italy, 8
Narragansett, Rhode Island
clergyman appointed to, 221
clergyman dismissed from, 221
library for, 176
Narragansett. *See* Narrangansett, Rhode Island; Rhode Island
Navy, Royal. *See* Boat, ship—naval
Negroes
baptism of, xlvi-xlvii, 143, 145, 159, 171, 198, 261, 306, 357-358, 365, 381, 422
baptism of, doubted, xlvi*n*
catechized, 261, 424
children, 42, 87*n*
children of white women and, xxx
conversion of, xlvi, 256, 424, 427
conversion of, to be encouraged, 326
denied baptism, 96
free, xxvii*n*
instruction of, 43, 96, 357-358, 365, 424-425, 427
instructors, 424-427 passim
number of, 96, 105
questioned concerning religion, 128
recitations by, 285
religious conversion of, not broached, xlvii
thefts by, 16
See also Acts of assembly—on conversion of Negroes and Indians
Neill (Oneill, ONeill), Laurence (Lau., Lawrence)
answers queries, 352-353
clergyman, 351-352

lacks proper credentials, 351
ordination of, 352
widower, 352
Nellson, John, vestryman, 191
Nelson, Mr., influence of, 149-150
to report to Society, 147
See also Nelson, Robert
Nelson, Robert, author, 34, 37
Neuse (News, Nues) River, 86
clergyman at, 231, 269, 307, 390, 397, 399-400, 407-408, 412*n*
Indian attacks on, 140*n*
land purchased on, 89*n*, 113*n*
ministry near, 422
mission boundary at, 383, 390, 397, 407
settlement along, xiii
New Bern (Newbern Town), 112-113
bonus for clergyman at, 376
chapel, church in, xxx, 402, 413, 417
development of, 95*n*, 404
establishment of, 113*n*
General Assembly held at, 389
ministry in, 379
school in, xlviii
New Bristol. *See* Bristol, Connecticut
New Brunswick. *See* Brunswick
New Castle, Delaware (Pennsylvania), 15, 17
vacancy in, 91, 159
New England, 34, 93, 166-167, 201, 211, 213, 239-240, 245, 253, 270, 390, 426
account from governor of, 10
books for, 13
clergyman in, 13, 17, 278
commissary in, 376
customs collector in, 234
description of, 11, 423-424
governor of, 423
lack of clergy in, 340
ministers from, 339
Quakers in, 19-20
trade with, 181
New Hampshire, 154
description of, 11
New Hanover Precinct, County, 338, 349
chapel, church in, xxx
clergyman in, 338, 347, 383, 398
erected, xxxiii, 316
letter from, 398-399
ministry in, 380
parish in, 316, 414
plantation in, 383, 397
salary for clergyman in, xxx
vestrymen for, 418
See also Cape Fear
New Hanover River. *See* Cape Fear River
New Jersey (East Jersey, Jersey, West Jersey), 46*n*, 179, 279-280
books for, 13
clergyman in, 20*n*, 46*n*
description of, 11, 17
governor of, 17
minister in, 309*n*
notice regarding disaffected missionaries in, 224
Quakers in, 19-20
vacancy in, 91
New Mattummuskete. *See* Lake Mattamuskeet
New Providence (Providence), Bahamas
lack of clergy in, 340
New River, 351
clergyman at, 338, 350
description of settlement, 350, 368
parish at, 189
New River Inlet, precinct boundary at, 316
New Rochelle, New York, clergyman in, 313
New Town. *See* Wilmington
New Year's Day, 269
New York, 12, 16, 25, 179, 244, 264, 268, 279-280, 313, 372
books for, 13
chapel, church in, 25
clergyman in, 20*n*, 46*n*, 203
creditor in, 271
description of, 11
established religion in, xxiii
governor of, 203*n*
Indians from, 186*n*
legislation in, xxiii*n*
notice regarding disaffected missionaries, 224
palatines in, 88-89, 89*n*, 113
Quakers in, 19-20, 20*n*
Newbern Town. *See* New Bern
Newbury, New Hampshire, 154
Newcastle (England), duke of, letter to, 327-328
Newcastle, England, 112
Newgate (London prison), 118, 122*n*
Newgate Street, London, 335
Newman, Samuel, author of [*The Cambridge Concordance*], 6, 38
Newman, Thomas. *See* Newnam, Thomas
Newnam (Newman), Thomas (John, Tho., Thoms., Thos.), *501*
appears before the board, 277
attends vestry meeting, 459
behavior of, 288-289

books of, 373
character of, 276, 460
clergyman, xxx, xxxvii, xlvi, 5*n*, 276-278, 281, 284, 286-293 passim, 295*n*, 459-460
deceased, 287-289, 292-293, 460
incapable of performing duty, 284
letter from, 282-286
library of, 356
ministry of, xlvi, 282-285 passim, 459
missionary appointment of, xxxvii-xxxviii, 279, 281
order to, 278
payment to, 467
performance by, 277
recommendation of, 278
salary of, 281, 459-460
salary paid to widow of, 288-289
testimonial in behalf of, 276-277
travel of, 282
voyage to widow paid for, 460
warrant to, 5*n*
widow of, 286, 288-289
will of, 286-287, 291
will of, proved, 287
Newnam, Doctor. *See* Newnam, Thomas—clergyman
Newnam, Frances
executrix, 286, 291
husband of, 286, 288
legatee, 286
power of attorney of, 291-292
salary paid to, 288
widow, 291-292
Newnam, H., protest sent to, 406-407
Newnam, John. *See* Newnam, Thomas
Newnam, Mr. *See* Newnam, Thomas
Newnam, Mrs. *See* Newnam, Frances
News River. *See* Neuse River
News, Elijah, payment to, 465
Newscastle, Duke of. *See* Pelham-Holles, Thomas, 1st duke of Newcastle
Newton (Nuten, Nuton), Christian (C., Ch., Chrisr.)
maintained by parish, 476-477, 481, 483, 489, 494
medical treatment of, 483
Newton. *See* Wilmington
Newtown, Connecticut, lack of clergy in, 340
Nicholl's Dr. *See* Nicholls, William
Nicholls, William, author, 295
Nichols, Messr., removed as missionary, 91
Nicholson (Nicolson, Nickolson), Francis (Fr.)
account sent by, 154
arrival of, 164, 170, 174-175
benefactor, 12, 12*n*, 22
bounty of, 172, 449
British Army officer, 12*n*
builds church, 15
commission to, 152
confirmation by, 162
duties of, 152
gift by, 250, 437, 445
governor, xxx-xxxii, 10, 12, 12*n*, 22, 300, 437, 449
inquiry by, 146*n*
leads military expedition, 12*n*
letter delivered by, 170
letter from, 162, 166-168, 175, 179-180, 203, 208, 212, 448
letter to, 144*n*, 164-166, 168-173, 173*n*, 175*n*, 176-178, 178*n*, 179, 179*n*, 180, 182-184, 184*n*, 450-451
report by, 113*n*
request by, 179
returns to England, 300
testimonial by, 25-26
to deliver report, 157
Nicholson, Bp. *See* Nicholson, William
Nicholson, Colonel. *See* Nicholson, Francis
Nicholson, Gov. *See* Nicholson, Francis
Nicholson, Governor Genl. *See* Nicholson, Francis
Nicholson, William, author, 34
Nickolson, Francis. *See* Nicholson, Francis
Nicolson, General. *See* Nicholson, Francis
Nixon, Richd., vestryman, 316
Nobbs Crook Creek, xv*n*
minister settled at, xv
Nobility, members of SPG, xl
Norcomb, Jno., debtor, 466
Nore, (The), England, clergyman at, 134
Norris, William (W.)
churchwarden, 251
clerk, 250-251
letter from, 250
vestryman, 190
North Britain. *See* Scotland
North Currituck (Coratico) Chapel
ministry at, 379
North, Francis, 2nd baron Guildford, 5*n*
payment to, 4
Northampton Precinct, County, parish in, 432*n*
Northeast Cape Fear (Northeast) River
parish boundary along, 414
Northeast Parish. *See* Chowan Precinct, northeastern parish of

Northeast River. *See* Northeast Cape Fear River
Northumberland County, Virginia
 parish in, 331
 vestryman in, 331
Northwest (Norwest) Landing, ministry at, 379
Northwest Parish, 355
 clergyman in, 349, 356, 363, 373
Northwest River, parish boundary along, 414
Norton, John, vestryman, 190
Norton, Zacharias, clergyman, 352
Norwest Landing. *See* Northwest Landing
Norwich (England)
 bishop of, 49
 dean of, 13
Norwich, bishop of. *See* Trimnell, Charles, bishop of Norwich
Norwich, dean of, proposed for SPG membership, 13
Notary. *See* Occupation, trade, profession—notary public
Notitia parochialis, 182, 420-422
 form of, 42, 397
 of James Adams, 96
 of John Urmston, 213, 231, 244, 252, 255-256
 to be sent every six months, 42
Nottinghamshire, England, 216, 335
Nourse, Peter, author, 410
Nova Scotia (Acadia; Port Royal, Acadia), 12*n*
Nues River. *See* Neuse River
Nuten, Chrisr. (C.). *See* Newton, Christian
Nutkins, Mr., clergyman, 328
 desires missionary appointment, 328
 to produce testimonial, 328
Nutmeg. *See* Spices—nutmeg
Nuton, Christian. *See* Newton, Christian
Nuts. *See* Food, diet—nuts
Oadham, Jacob, processioner, 462
Oak, for construction of ships, 32
Oath, accounts to be rendered under, 314-315, 417
 acts of Parliament on, 82, 87*n*
 against taking arms against king, xxviii
 against using arms against king, 191
 concerning examination of clergyman, 301
 concerning insults to clergyman, 301
 concerning liturgy, 415
 of allegiance, 5*n*, 87*n*
 of clerk of vestry, 481
 of executor, 377
 of notary public, 406
 of office, xxvii, xxviii*n*, 97-98, 309*n*, 347*n*, 453
 of vestryman, xxviii, 191, 455, 460, 463, 481, 486-487, 490
 on rendering accounts, 416
 proves will, 287, 377
 provisions of Fundamental Constitutions concerning, xviii
 purgation by, 269
 Quakers refuse to take, 82
 subscribed, 83, 305, 392*n*, 453, 455, 463
 sworn to falsely, 321, 321*n*, 391
 See also Affidavit, deposition; Affirmation
Occupation, trade, profession
 apothecary, 311
 attorney, 12
 barber, 317
 builder, 403, 434
 butcher, 116, 472
 carpenter, 116
 cartographer, 382*n*
 carver, 216
 collector of quitrents, 375
 conjurer, 254
 cooper, 116
 coppersmith, 248
 director of bank, 373
 dyer, 116
 explorer, 95*n*
 farmer, planter, 107, 115-116, 202, 214, 350, 353*n*
 footboy, 317, 321
 fortune teller, 254
 glazier, 405
 haberdasher, 291
 jailer, 395, 485
 joiner, 116, 216, 433
 laborer, workman, 120, 174, 177, 209, 213, 431, 435, 437, 444, 493
 librarian, 293
 maid, 466
 master of Charterhouse, 297, 308
 mechanic, 72
 merchant, xxx, xxxvi, xl, 76*n*, 83, 93, 124, 124*n*, 127, 129, 144, 159, 161, 167, 183*n*, 210, 211*n*, 234, 239*n*, 256, 264, 323, 329, 338, 350, 353*n*, 361, 367, 369, 371, 382*n*, 390-391, 397, 405-406, 412, 435, 444*n*, 463*n*
 milliner, 391
 notary public, 406-407
 overseer, 177
 peddler, 329

physician, surgeon, 77, 254, 303, 303*n*, 330, 333, 342, 436-437, 451, 458, 465, 477-480 passim, 485-488 passim, 492
privateer, 382*n*
professor, xlvii
sailor, 133, 248
scientist, 150*n*
shipwright, 216
shoemaker, 72, 116
soapmaker, 116
starchmaker, 116
surveyor, 95*n*
tailor, 485*n*
tallow chandler, 116
tanner, 116
tavern keeper, xxxiv
town sealer, 435
valet, 321*n*
waterman, 115-116
wheelwright, 116
wherryman, 128
See also Boat, ship—boatswain's mate of, chaplain of, captain, master of, purser of, warrant officer of; Clergy, clergyman; Schoolmaster, teacher
Ocracoke Inlet, 258*n*
Odam, _____, 158
Odam, Mr., children of, baptized, 143
Odeon, Charles
desires to retain minister, 353-354
petitioner, 353-354
vestryman, 354
Odeon, John
desires to retain minister, 353-354
petitioner, 353-354
vestryman, 354
Official, 463*n*
must be member of religious body, xviii
not to engage in scandalous behavior, xlvi, 326
Oglethorp, Mr., delivers letter, 351
Old Mattummuskete. *See* Lake Mattamuskeet
"Old Pretender." *See* Stuart, James Francis Edward
Oliver. *See* Cromwell, Oliver (Lord Protector)
ONeill, Lawrence. *See* Neill, Laurence
Oneill, Mr. *See* Neill, Laurence
Onslow Precinct, County
clergyman in, 336
justice of the peace in, 145*n*
ministry in, 380
parish in, 414
Opequon Creek, Virginia, 401
Order. *See* Vestry—order of
Order in council, 279
Order of Privy Council, 336
Ordinary. *See* Public house, ordinary, tavern
Ordination, 313
by imposition of hands, 307
readers lack, xvi
See also Clergy, clergyman—ordination of
Ordnance. *See* Arms, armaments, ordnance
Orphan, vestry pays for maintenance of, 438, 440-441
Osborn, Mr., missionary appointment of, 207
Osborn. *See* Osborne, Francis
Osborne (Osborn), Francis, author, 7
Osburn, Peter, debtor, 466
Osnaburg. *See* Cloth, fabric, yarn—osnaburg
Ostervald (Osterwald), Jean Frédéric, author, 34, 37, 39
Osterwald. *See* Ostervald, Jean Frédéric
Overseer. *See* Occupation, trade, profession—overseer
Owen, William, Council member, 346
Oxford (England), bishop of
letter from, 426-427
letter to, 423-425
Oxford (naval vessel), 137
transports clergy, 133
Oxford (ship), 65
Oxford University. *See* Vice chancellor, Oxford University
Oxford University (England), vice chancellor of, 120
Oxford, bishop of. *See* Secker, Thomas, bishop of Oxford
Oxford, Tho. *See* Secker, Thomas, bishop of Oxford
Pacquimmins. *See* Perquimans, Precinct, County
Padget, Samuel (S., Saml.). *See* Pagett, Samuel
Padgett, Sam. *See* Pagett, Samuel
Page, Samll., Jr.
letter from, 228-230
parishioner, 230
Page, Samuell
letter from, 228-230
parishioner, 230
Paget, Samll. (Saml.). *See* Pagett, Samuel
Pagett (Paget, Paggeth, Paggith, Patchet), Samuel (Saml., Samll., Samuell)
churchwarden, 448
information from, 478
letter from, 287-288

oath taken by, 477-478
signature in behalf of, 173
vestryman, 189, 287-288, 447-448, 452, 455, 457, 460-463 passim, 465, 468-469, 471, 473-474, 476-482 passim, 486
Paggeth, Samuel (Samll., Samuell). *See* Pagett, Samuel
Paggith, Samuel. *See* Pagett, Samuel
Pagit. *See* Pagitt, Ephraim
Pagitt (Pagit), Ephraim, author, 6
Paine, John
bequest of, xxxvi
merchant, xxxvi
Palace. *See* Fulham Palace, London; St. James's Palace, London; Whitehall Palace, London
Palatines, 89*n*, 93-94
arrival of, 95*n*, 123
baptized, 107
Calvinists among, 88
in New York, 113
Lutherans among, 88
make pitch and tar, 113
minister for, 88, 88*n*, 89*n*
mortality among, 123
refugees, 88, 89*n*, 113*n*
settlement of, destroyed, 113*n*
voyage of, 112
Palin, John (Jno.)
churchwarden, 250
letter from, 150
testimonial by, 109
vestryman, 109, 190, 251
Palmer, Paul, Baptist clergyman, 321, 321*n*
Palmyra, 7
Pamlico. *See* Indians—Pamlico
Pamlico (Pampicoe, Pamplicough, Pampliticough, Pamptichoe, Pamptico, Pempticough) Precinct, County
clergyman in, xl, 12, 15, 117, 129, 356, 384, 407
division of, 64
governor in, 129, 224
Indian massacres in, 144
lack of clergy in, 240
library in, 5, 26, 44, 65, 257
name inscribed on parish books, 172, 449
surrounding area described, 29
uprising in, 128
Pamlico (Pamplico, Pampticoe) River
Indian attacks on, 140*n*
library for, 121
mouth of, xiii
parish on, 86, 194
petition from, 32-33, 353-354
settlement along, xiii
settlement described, 32
Pamlico Sound, 147*n*
settlement along, xxiii
Pampicoe. *See* Pamlico Precinct, County
Pamplico. *See* Pamlico River
Pamplicough. *See* Pamlico Precinct, County
Pampliticough. *See* Pamlico Precinct, County
Pamptichoe. *See* Pamlico Precinct, County
Pamptico. *See* Pamlico Precinct, County
Pampticoe River. *See* Pamlico River
Pamtecough Precinct, 65*n*
Panther
act of assembly on killing of, 492*n*
bounty paid on killing of, xxxv
Paper, 15
writing, 238, 256
Paquimons. *See* Perquimans Precinct, County
Pardon
for Cary rebels, 124*n*
for pirate, 258*n*
Parei, Davidis. *See* Pareus, David
Pareus (Parei), David (Davidis), author, 294
Paris (Parris), Mr.
SPG committee member, 409
Paris (Parriss), Mr., attends meeting, 303
Parish, parishes, xiii, 221, 223, 346, 352, 383, 403, 411, 468, 473
abandoned, 221
account of baptisms in, 378-380
clergyman to reside constantly in, 417
colony divided into, xxxviii, 290, 327, 414
contingent charges of, 315
created, xxxiii, 432*n*
depopulated, 195
deserted, 217-218
divided, xxxiii, 208, 230, 266, 394, 452, 454, 457
divided into cantons, 461-462
erected, xxviii, 86, 188-189, 194, 265, 311, 316, 338
expenses of, 195
French-speaking, 313
funds of, 312, 403
funds of, misapplied, xxxii, 312, 314-315
gift of books to, xlii, 167-168
gift of library to, 172
gift to, 192, 465
gift to, misapplied, 183
improperly formed, 347
in East Jersey, 11

in England, 88, 130
in Ireland, 53
in Maryland, 10, 66
in South Carolina, 66-67, 204, 280*n*, 394
in Virginia, xv, xvn, 10, 53, 161, 280*n*, 331
incidental charges of, 474
large, 65, 84, 96, 344, 349, 355-356, 363, 374, 449
merged, xxxiii
named, 189-190
no dissenters in, 356
not liable for payment, 447
petition to divide, 451
population of, 421
poverty of, 460
proceeds from forfeitures to benefit, 418
proposal to consolidate, 241
readers in, 224
receives portion of fine, 314-315
register of, 42
report from, requested, 227
report on, 181, 212, 300
revenue to, from sale of town lots, 459-460, 463-464, 466, 473
size of, xli, xliii, 41, 85, 172, 177
South Carolina, 313, 347
supply for, requested, 230
taxables, tithables in, 195, 432-433
taxation by, 447
to pay minister, 177-178
to support clergyman, 400
vacant, 242, 278
vestry appointed for, 431
vestry in, 82
See also Acts of assembly—erecting parishes, parish formed without; Aldgate Parish, London; Beaufort Parish; Berkeley Parish; Bond, security, surety—to indemnify parish; Castlemore Parish, Ireland; Chowan Parish; Chowan Precinct, eastern parish of; Chowan Precinct, northeastern parish of; Chowan Precinct, northern parish of; Chowan Precinct, southern parish of; Chowan Precinct, southwestern parish of; Christ Church Parish; Christ Church Parish, South Carolina; Craven Parish; Currituck Parish; Dobbs Parish; Edgecombe Parish; Frederick Parish, South Carolina; Hampton Parish, Virginia; Hyde Parish; Kilcolman Parish, Ireland; Kilmovee Parish, Ireland; King William's Parish, Virginia; Northwest Parish; Notitia parochialis; Pasquotank Parish; Pasquotank Precinct, northeastern parish of; Pasquotank Precinct, southwestern parish of; Perquimans Parish; Poverty—in parish; Princess Anne Parish, Virginia; St. Andrew's Parish; St. Andrews Parish, South Carolina; St. Bartholomew's Parish; St. Denis Parish, South Carolina; St. George's Parish; St. James's Parish; St. John's Parish; St. John's Parish, South Carolina; St. Katherine's Parish, London; St. Lawrence's Parish, London; St. Margaret's Parish, Virginia; St. Mewan's Parish, England; St. Michael's Parish, Maryland; St. Paul's Parish; St. Paul's Parish, South Carolina; St. Paul's Parish, Virginia; St. Peter's Parish; St. Philip's Parish, South Carolina; St. Phillips's Parish; St. Stephen's Parish, Virginia; St. Thomas's Parish; St. Thomas's Parish, South Carolina; Society Parish; South Shore Parish; Surrey Parish, Virginia; Westover Parish, Virginia; York Parish, Virginia
Parish, Rolf
churchwarden, 331
testimonial by, 331
Parker, John (Jno.)
allowance of, 472, 478, 480, 483-485
order by, 481
processioner, 462
Parker, Jonathan, payment to, 494
Parker, Richard (Richd.)
churchwarden, 473
to oversee chapel construction, 493-494
to present account to vestry, 487, 491
vestryman, 470, 486-488, 490-492, 494
Parker, Samuel, author, 6
Parliament, Queen's speech to, 184
report to, proposed, 107
See also Acts of Parliament; House of Lords
Parriss, Mr. *See* Paris, Mr.
Partisanship, political, 409
Pasebank. *See* Pasquotank Precinct, County
Pasor (Passor), Georg, author, 8
Paspetank. *See* Pasquotank Precinct, County
Pasquotank Parish
ministry in, 73, 96
mishandled funds in, xxxii
petition from, xxv, 44-45
vestry minutes of, xii
Pasquotank (Pascebank, Paspetanck) Precinct, County, xv, xvn, 45, 65*n*, 110*n*, 197
clergyman in, 76, 86, 105, 142, 223, 230, 304
construction of chapel, church in, xxv
description of, xiv, 85, 116, 230

difficulty for clergyman in, 199, 236
disorder in, 304
divided into parishes, 189, 194, 250, 414
fines from, 445
glebe in, xxv
lack of chapel, church furnishings in, 183
lack of chapel, church in, 64
lack of clergy in, 63, 66, 304
lay reader in, xxv
letter from, 250
letter to vestry of, 227
meeting place for vestrymen in, 314
ministry in, 96, 105, 118
Quakers in, xxiii, xxxviii-xxxix, 304, 307
roads in, 84
school in, 87*n*
sparse population in parishes of, xxxiii
testimonial from vestry of, 109
vestry in, xxiv
vestry minutes of, 251-252
vestrymen of, 251
Pasquotank Precinct, northeastern parish of
clergyman in, 321*n*
erected, xxviii, 189
vestrymen of, 190
Pasquotank Precinct, southwestern parish of
erected, xxviii, 189
vestry minutes of, 251
vestrymen of, 190, 251
Pasquotank River, xv*n*
parish boundary at, 189, 194, 414
Passage money, 345
See also Bounty—paid to clergy
Passor. *See* Pasor, Georg
Patchet, Jno., vestryman, 452
Patchet, Samll. *See* Pagett, Samuel
Paternoster Row, London, 238
Patrick, Bp. *See* Patrick, Simon
Patrick, Simon, author, 8, 34, 37
Paulett, Mr., license from, 341
Payn, Dr. *See* Payne, William
Payne (Payn), William, author, 7
Payne, Mr., house of, 114
Payne, Robt., witness, 407
Pearce, Thos., inspector, 486
Pearce, Wm., allowance of, 465-466
Pearl (naval vessel), 256
Pearse, Edward, author of [*Preparation for Death and Judgmt.*], 38
Pearson (Peirson), John, bishop of Chester, author, 6, 34, 36, 172
Pearson, Bishop. *See* Pearson, John, bishop of Chester
Peart, Fra.
clergyman, 331, 333
letter from, 333
recommendation by, 333
testimonial by, 331
Peas. *See* Food, diet—peas
Peddler. *See* Occupation, trade, profession—peddler
Pedin, Mr., delivers letter, 342
Pegg, Jos., vestry held at house of, 251
Peirc. *See* Pierce, Thomas
Peirson, Bp. *See* Pearson, John, bishop of Chester
Pelham-Holles (H.), Thomas, 1st duke of Newcastle
letter to, 327
order signed by, 278
secretary of state, 327
Pempticough. *See* Pamlico Precinct, County
Penalty, punishment
banishment, 118, 162
churchwardens subject to, 419
double distress, 193, 413-414
execution, 273
for bearing bastard child, xxxiv
for cohabitation, xxxiv
for drunkenness, xxxiv
for failure to attend vestry meetings, 194
for failure to display information on unlawful marriages, 193
for failure to make declaration, 194
for failure to pay debt owed parish, 404
for failure to present accounts, xxxvii, 416
for failure to publish parish accounts, 312
for failure to qualify as vestryman, 314
for failure to render account, 314, 413
for failure to summon vestry, 266, 314, 416
for fornication, xxxiv, xxxiv*n*
for laboring on Sunday, xxxiv
for performing unlawful marriage, 193*n*, 195
for pupils, 43
for refusal to serve as churchwarden, 194
for refusal to take qualifying oath, 415
for using profanity, xxxiv
for vestries, 194
not imposed, 96
transportation, 118
urged, 326
See also Fine, forfeiture; Distraint
Pennsylvania, 12, 17, 179
books for, 13, 26*n*
clergyman in, 20*n*, 401

description of, 11
instruction of negroes in, 425, 427
lack of clergy in, 258
Quakers in, 19
vacancy in, 91, 159
Pension, 376
Peploe, Samuel, bishop of Chester
letter from, 395
letter to, 395
Perigreen, Francis
deceased, 464
maintained by parish, 464
Perjury. *See* Crime—perjury
Perkins, Abraham, maintained by parish, 474
Perquimans (Pacquimmins, Paquimons, Piequimmins, Poquimans) Precinct, County, xvi*n*, 65*n*, 258
clergyman in, 77, 94, 321*n*
construction of chapel, church in, xxv
court minutes of, xxxv*n*
description of, 84
donation to poor in, xxxvi
glebe in, xxv
lack of chapel, church furnishings in, 120, 183
lack of chapel, church in, 250
lay reader in, xxv
marriages in, xvi
ministry in, 106, 116-118, 379
parish in, 194, 414
Quakers in, xxiii, xxxviii-xxxix, 307
roads in, 84, 438
vestry in, xxiv
will from, 155-156
Perquimans (Paquimons) Parish
clergyman in, 73
erected, xxviii
Quakers in, 73
Perrot, Francis, warrant to, 434
Perry, Benja.
letter from, 228-230
parishioner, 230
Perry, John (J., Jno.), vestryman, 474, 476-477, 479-480
Perry, John, Sr., vestryman, 473
Perry, Precilla, allowance of, 491, 494
Perth Amboy (Amboy), New Jersey, 17
Pervine, Rachell, maintained by parish, 494
Peter, Ann, burial of, 470
Peterb. *See* Peterborough, England
Peterborough (Peterb.), England, 38
Peterborough (Petriburg), (England), bishop of, 308
Peterborough, Richard, bishop of. *See* Cumberland, Richard, bishop of Peterborough
Peterson, Mrs.
to return weights and measures, 451
widow, 451
Peterson, Thomas (Tho., Thos.)
churchwarden, 173, 445-447, 451
deceased, 451
letter from, 450-451
letter signed by, 173
possesses weights and measures, 448
sues former churchwarden, 448
to present account to vestry, 446-448
vestryman, 173, 445-446, 448, 451
Petri Martyris. *See* Vermigli, Pietro Martire
Petriburg. *See* Peterborough, England
Petty France, London, 19-21, 24, 48, 50, 55, 58, 62-64, 72, 80, 92, 95, 113, 124-125, 128, 133-134, 137
Pew, 369, 437
Pewter
pot made of, 435
weighing and measuring devices made of, 471
Peyton, Robert (Robt.)
baronetcy of, fabricated, 310*n*
claims baronetcy, 310
vestry commissioner, 310
Phelps, Saml., vestryman, 190
Philadelphia, Pennsylvania, 12, 16-17, 19-20, 25
clergyman in, 203*n*, 304, 424
Philips, Paul. *See* Phillips, Paul
Phillips (Philips), Paul
allowance of, 455, 458-459
payment to, 456
reader, 455, 458
Phillips, Francis (Frans.)
dismissed as missionary, 221*n*
mentioned in letter, 237
Phillips, Mr.
absence of, 137
chaplain, 137
Physician. *See* Occupation, trade, profession—physician, surgeon
Piccolominaeus, author, 294
Piequimmins. *See* Perquimans Precinct, County
Pierce (Peirc), Thomas, author, 7, 294
Pilkington, Seth
justice of the peace, 310
petitioner, 309-310
signature of, forged, 310*n*

Pillow. *See* Household furnishings—pillow
Pirates, 124*n*
  act of Parliament on, 256
  arms, armaments of, 273
  at coastal inlet, 256
  captured, 256
  executed, 273
  off Virginia, 273
  pardon for, 258*n*
  slain, 256, 258*n*
  See also Bonnet, Stede; Teach, Edward (Blackbeard)
Piscataway. *See* Maryland
Pistol. *See* Arms, armaments, ordnance—pistol
Pitch, 32, 209
  as commodity, 209, 250
  burning of, 213
  made by Palatines, 113
  payment in, 86, 246
  purchased, 246
Plank. *See* Church, chapel, meetinghouse—planks for
Plantation, farm, 107, 431
  bequeathed, 155
  bequest of, xxx
  church on, 443
  destroyed, 140*n*
  disputed title to, 165
  during Tuscarora War, 144, 158
  of clergyman, 25, 158, 210, 212, 214, 255, 257, 264, 269, 329, 344-345, 361, 383*n*, 397-398
  owned by SPG, 424, 427
  price of, 121, 165
  purchased, 115, 182, 199
  seized for debt, 209
  tithes collected from, 251*n*
Planter. *See* Occupation, trade, profession—farmer, planter
"Planter's Letter", 50
  presented to SPG, 47
  read to SPG, 49
Plough. *See* Tools, equipment—plough
Plymouth, England, ship at, 137
Pocock, Edward, author, 410
Polanus, Amandus, author, 294
Pollock (P., Polluck), Thomas (T., Tho., Thoms., Thos.), 284*n*
  absence of, 439
  acting governor, 167
  agreement by, 432
  character of, 148
  churchwarden, 439, 442
  collectors to be brought before, 432
  Council member, 76*n*, 83, 288
  debtor, 434, 442
  declines office of churchwarden, 442
  delivers letter, 168
  fine levied by, 158
  land mortgaged to, 113*n*
  land of, 115
  letter from, 68-69, 75-76, 173*n*, 175*n*, 178*n*, 179-180, 183-184, 450-451
  letter to, 167-168, 260
  library sent to, 167, 176
  merchant, 76*n*
  of Glasgow, 76*n*
  opposition against, 129
  possible replacement for, 440
  president of Council, 76*n*, 148, 158, 160, 167-168, 179, 445-448 passim
  proprietary deputy, 76*n*
  protests election nullification, 83
  receives clergyman, 142
  subscription by, 438
  vestry held at house of, 447
  vestryman, 68, 189, 431, 438, 445-448 passim, 451
Pollock, Colonel. *See* Pollock, Thomas
Pollock, Cullen, Council member, 370
Polluck, Thomas. *See* Pollock, Thomas
Pool, Math. *See* Poole, Matthew
Poole (Pool), Matthew (Math.), author, 6, 8, 33, 37, 294
Population
  concentration of, 363
  increase in, xxiii, xxxviii, 344, 368
  numerous, 307, 355
  statistics of, 297, 324, 421
Poquimans. *See* Perquimans Precinct, County
Pork
  of clergy, 177
  payment in, 86, 139, 402
  salt, 85
  staple commodity, 209, 250
  See also Food, diet—pork
Porridge. *See* Food, diet—porridge
Port, 92
  direct communication with, 421
  See also Bristol—port of; Brunswick, port of, promoted as port; Liverpool—port of
Port Royal, Acadia. *See* Nova Scotia
Port Royal, South Carolina, Indian attacks near, 202*n*
Porter, Edmund (Edmd.)

admiralty judge, 239*n*
agent, 307, 309*n*
appears before Proprietors, 118
Cary rebel, 239*n*
Council member, 239*n*
imprisoned, 238
inspector, 477
merchant, 239*n*
order delivered by, 118-119
travel of, 307
Porter, John
attorney general, 87*n*
authority of, 434
complaint by, 82
deputation of, 82
General Court justice, 87*n*
payment to, 433
relinquishes keys, 435
speaker of the assembly, 87*n*
to choose builder, 434
Porter, John (Jno.) (Bath)
letter from, 240-241
vestryman, 190, 241
Porter, John (Jno.) (New Hanover)
letter from, 398-399
vestryman, 316, 399
Porter, John (Hyde Parish), vestryman, 190
Porter, Joshua
justice of the peace, 310
petitioner, 309-310
Porter, Mr., levy imposed by, 471-472
See also Porter, Edmund
Porter. *See* Porter, John
Porterage, 435
PorterField, John, payment to be remitted to, 174
Portland, Duke of. *See* Bentinck, Henry, 1st duke of Portland
Portmanteau, 16
Portsmouth, England, clergyman in, 27, 31
Portugal, clergyman in, 322, 338
Postage, 182
Postal service, 134, 296
in colonies, 203, 342
Pot. *See* Household furnishings—pot
Potter, James, payment to, 480, 483
Potter, John, archbishop of Canterbury
author, 410
awaits report, 399
letter to, 398-399, 399*n*, 427
representation to, 382
Poverty, xxxv*n*, 83, 85, 165-166, 173, 181, 182*n*, 213, 265-266, 271, 302, 387, 399, 412, 460
arms provided to those in, xxxvi*n*
books requested for children in, xlii, 421
caused by war, 144-145, 310, 353
child in, xxxv, 492-493
deaths from, 246
due to high prices, 181
during Tuscarora War, 158
gift from clergyman for relief of, 438
gift from governor for relief of, xxxvi
hinders procurement of clergy, 172
impedes growth of church, xxviii, 449
in Cary Rebellion, 123
in parish, 181, 364, 364*n*, 365-366
of clergy, 140, 162, 359, 376, 384, 407
of Palatines, 88, 88*n*, 89*n*
of settlers, 350, 372
prevents payments to minister, 353-354, 361
prevents purchase of books, xlii
relieved by charity, xxxv*n*
relieved by vestry, xxiii-xxiv, xxxv-xxxvi, 188, 193, 327, 417, 432-433, 435-436, 438, 440-442, 454-456, 458, 464-466, 468, 470, 472, 476-479 passim, 481-484 passim, 486-494 passim
Power of attorney, relinquished, 231
See also Letter—of attorney
Powers, Elizabeth (E., Elisabeth, Eliz., Eliza.)
maintained by parish, 477, 479-480, 483
medical procedure of, 477
Pownall, Benjamin
clergyman, 280, 280*n*
missionary appointment of, 280*n*
petitioner, 280
Pownall, Mr. *See* Pownall, Benjamin
Pratt, James, testimonial by, 53
Prayers, 40, 43, 57*n*, 60, 71, 76, 86, 90, 90*n*, 127, 129-130, 386, 425
aboard ship, 137
at meeting of SPG, 98
at meeting of standing committee of SPG, 409
by candidate for orders, 329*n*, 383, 399
by reader, xvi, 28, 120
criticized, 229
for Turks, 98
of Church of England, 229
order to read, 297
printed, 39
Quaker dislike of, 202
read, 277, 336
refused for sick, 229
requested, 141, 203, 253, 421
See also Jews—prayers for

Preaching, 19-20, 25, 28, 39, 44-45, 53, 57*n*, 60, 65-67, 76, 85, 90, 90*n*, 109, 113, 117-118, 127, 130-131, 134, 142-143, 144*n*, 145, 148, 159, 172, 207, 220, 252, 254, 260, 262, 274, 277, 282, 297, 299*n*, 300-302, 305, 308, 313, 329, 329*n*, 330, 332, 336-337, 339, 344, 349, 349*n*, 350, 355-358 passim, 360-361, 363, 368-369, 372, 383-384, 388, 391, 401, 411, 423-425, 425*n*, 449, 470*n*
aboard ship, 68, 137
before General Assembly, 119
by candidate for orders, 399
clergyman forbidden to engage in, 303
governor refuses to allow, 304
hinders growth of Quakerism, 198, 228, 307
in German, 88
in private house, 76, 158
interrogation concerning, 301
payment for, 477
proposal concerning, 328
Quaker, 72
to Indians, xlvi
under tree, 17
urged, 41
See also Sermon, homily
Prebendary. *See* Clergy, clergyman—prebendary
Precinct, precincts, xxxiii, 28-29, 65*n*, 83, 172, 467
account of baptisms in, 378-380
Bible for, 436
collector for, 445
colony divided into, 64
divided, 250, 252
Pregnancy, of indigent, 464
Presbyter, ordination as, 351
Presbyterian. *See* Dissenters—Presbyterian
Presbytery, in South Carolina, 391
Preston (Besson, Beston), Stephen, orphan of, 438, 440-441
Price, value, cost, 55, 78, 144, 199, 209, 213, 361
of addition to house, 213
of beef, 402
of beeswax, 402
of boarding, 472
of books, 101, 112, 168, 173, 185, 255, 277, 293, 298, 373, 398-399, 412, 421*n*, 450
of bread, meal, 246
of breeches, 472
of building chapel, 433, 455
of burial, funeral, 155, 465, 470, 472, 475
of canoe, 214
of cargo, 329, 390
of church furnishings, 433
of clearing land, 433
of clergyman's property, 237
of cloth, 472, 477, 484
of clothing, 120, 172, 472
of commodities, 250*n*
of copies of act, 466
of corn, 86, 160
of deerskins, 402
of elements for Holy Communion, 465
of flooring house, 433
of gift to church, 107
of goods, 391
of guide, 174
of horses, 27, 76
of house repairs, 418
of imported goods, 202
of improvements to plantation, 199
of laundering, 477
of library, 180, 277, 387, 399, 449
of lost livestock, 244
of maintaining church, chapel, 465-466, 475
of making benches, 465
of making shirts, 476
of medicine, 31
of mill, 214
of passage, 264
of pitch, 86
of plantation, 86, 121, 165, 257, 265
of pork, 86, 402
of rental of canoe, 441
of rice, 402
of servant, 214, 234
of shoes, 16, 484
of silver, 346
of slaves, 300
of table, 475
of tallow, 402
of tar, 86, 437
of tobacco, 161, 195
of tracts of land, 373, 399, 421*n*, 443
of travel, 421
of use of house, 433
of weights and measures, 433, 435
of wife, 118
of workmen, 115
See also Salary, wage, payment; Slaves—price of
Prideaux, Humphrey (Humfrey)
author, 410
proposed for SPG membership, 13
Prideaux, John, author, 294
Priest. *See* Clergy, clergyman

Prince George's Creek
  clergyman at, 383, 398
  plantation on, 383, 398
Princess Anne (ship), 93
Princess Anne County, Virginia, lack of clergy in, 20
Princess Anne Parish, Virginia, clergyman in, 350
Printing, publishing, 17, 39
  by clergyman, 426
  by SPG, 98
  of acts of assembly, 209, 213
  See also Book of Common Prayer—printed at Edinburgh; Lectures—published; Sermon, homily—printed
Prison, jail, 118
  clergyman escapes from, 395
  clergyman threatened with, 174, 301
  for debtors, 239*n*
  in Edenton, 485*n*
  in London, 122*n*, 238, 239*n*
  proprietors promise funds for construction of, xxi
  See also Building—prison, jail; Fleet Prison; Occupation, trade, profession—jailer
Prisoner, escapes, 270*n*
  See also Clergy, clergyman—imprisoned; Fleet Prison—inmate of
Prisoner of war, 30-31, 247
  in Tuscarora War, 140*n*
Privateer. *See* Boat, ship—privateer
Privy Council of England, 119, 123, 270*n*
  disallows act, 419
  member of, xlix, 336
  office of, 336
  order in, of, 279, 336
Prize of war, 140*n*
  taken, 139
Processioner, processioning, xxxv, 461-462, 462*n*, 466, 492
Proclamation
  for fast, 119
  on money, xxxvii*n*
Profanity, swearing, decried, 96, 137
Promissory note, 150*n*, 403
Prostitution, servant accused of, 264
Protection, plea of, 314-315, 417
Providence Plantation. *See* Rhode Island
Providence, Bahamas. *See* New Providence, Bahamas
Provost, 127
Provost marshal
  of General Court, 432*n*
  tax collected by, 316
Prussia, king of, 88
Psalmody, 118
Psalms, not read, 229
Public house, ordinary, tavern, 49, 61, 127
  clergy not to lodge in, 39-40
  in London, 373
  vestry meets in, 119
Pugh, Mr., letter delivered by, 138
Pullin, William, testimonial by, 55
Pulpit
  clergyman offered use of, 302
  cloth for, 358
  denied clergyman, 305
  removal of, 229
  to be built, 437, 443, 493
  work on, 439, 443
Punch. *See* Drink—punch
Quaker. *See* Dissenters—Quaker
Quarry, Colonel. *See* Quarry, [Robert]
Quary (Quarry), [Robert], 183
  governor of South Carolina, 183*n*
  payment to, 15
  Pennsylvania vice admiralty court judge, 183*n*
  request delivered by, 151
  surveyor general, 183*n*
Queen. *See* Anne, queen of England
Queen Anne's Creek
  district boundary at, 461
  general assembly at, 184, 266
  letter from, 171
  library at, 293
Queen's College, Charlotte, established, xlviii
Queen's Creek, 76
Queen. *See* Anne, queen of England
Qui tam, action of, 364
Quigley, Mr. *See* Cuigley, James
Quilt. *See* Household furnishings—quilt
Quince, _____
  forced to refit ship, 372
  ship commander, 372
Quitrents, 245, 402
  collector of, 375
  during Tuscarora War, 144
  of lords proprietors, 145
  receiver general of, 376*n*
Quorum, vestry lacks, 439, 443
Quotidian. *See* Disease, illness, affliction—quotidian
Rag. *See* Wragg, Joseph; Wragg, Samuel
Rainolds, John, author, 294

Rainsford, Dr. *See* Ransford, Giles—clergyman
Rainsford, Giles. *See* Ransford, Giles
Rainsford, Mr. *See* Ransford, Giles
Ramsford, Mr. *See* Ransford, Giles
Ransford (Rainsford, Ramsford), Giles (G.), 114*n*, *501-502*
answer by, 151
appears before Board, 127
arrival of, 174
authorizes payment, 163
behavior of, 166, 178
bill of exchange from, 150*n*
character of, 125-126
clergyman, xlvi, xlvi*n*, 124, 140*n*, 141, 163, 166, 166*n*, 167, 179, 179*n*, 184, 196, 222, 233, 246, 259
commission of, 198
compliment by, 253
debtor, 174
delivers letter, 228
desires new assignment, 159
difficulties of, 142, 158, 160, 174
embellishes report, 256
fails to send catechism, 185
father of, 124
information from, 130, 149, 162
lacks certification, 154
letter delivered to, 126
letter from, 114, 125, 127, 132-134, 136-138, 142-144, 144*n*, 145-146, 152-153, 157-161 passim, 168-169, 171, 174-175, 179*n*, 180, 188, 196-198, 228
letter of attorney from, 150*n*
letter of recommendation for, 127
letter to, 138-139, 150, 152-153, 153*n*, 154, 158, 160-162, 170, 179, 188, 197, 253
marriage of, 209
ministry of, xlvi, 134, 142-143, 145, 148, 159, 171, 198
missionary appointment of, 131, 141-142, 145, 149, 167, 209, 213
of Dublin, Ireland, 124
parish of, unknown, 259
payment to, 196
performance of, 130-131
petitioner, 158
received by governor, 142
receives proceeds, 140*n*
request by, 133, 145, 146*n*
resigns as missionary, 174-175, 188
returns to England, 222
salary of, 132, 141, 148, 150, 159, 163-164, 175*n*, 188
salary of, delinquent, 174
successor of, 233
testimonial by, 126
testimonial in behalf of, 125-127
to accompany chaplain, 135
to deliver letter, 133
to perform service, 127
verbal abuse of, 137
wife of, 213
work ethic of, 185
Ransford, Mar[*torn*]
alderman, 124
son of, 124
Ransford, Mr. *See* Ransford, Giles
Raonoak. *See* Roanoke
Rasor, Martin Frederick, land grant of, 114*n*
Rasor. *See* Rasor, Martin Frederick
Rawlet, John
author, 7, 34, 37
author of [*Christian Monitors B.*], 9, 38
Readeng, Sarah, alleged servant of, 489
Reader, xvi, 28, 86, 224, 478
act of assembly on, 73
appointed, 85, 120, 265, 267, 327, 437, 440, 442, 444, 461, 463, 479
baptism by, 120
becomes Quaker, 97
books for, 28
churchwardens to provide, 432
collects parish tax, 474
continued, 475, 487-491 passim
criticized, 120, 272
departs, 435
desks for, 437
duties of, 437
for chapel of ease, 432
for Indian Town, 455-456
German-speaking, 88
in London, 264
keeps keys of church, 437
may collect tax, 473
paid, xxv, xxx, 188, 224, 433, 455-456, 458-459, 461, 463-465, 467-468, 474-475, 477, 479, 481, 484, 486, 489-493 passim
payment due to, 473
pew for, 437
prevents growth of dissent, 241
recommended, 443
to be clerk of vestry, 469
to be employed, xxiv, 436
to clean church, 437
to conduct worship service, 440
to provide baptismal water, 437
to provide fire for church, 437

See also Council—reader appears before; Holy Communion—readers and; Will—of reader
Reading, Connecticut. *See* Redding, Connecticut
Reahemaine, Thos., testimonial by, 55
Rebellion, declaration against, 194
See also Cary Rebellion; Governor, deputy governor—proceeds against rebels; Jacobites; Oath—against using arms against king
Receipt, 100, 102
for correspondence, 226
for weights and measures, 435
Receiver general, 309*n*, 353*n*, 461, 463*n*
of quitrents, 376
of South Carolina, 258*n*
presumed in London, 307
to deliver funds for construction of church, xxii
Records, public
document to be registered as, 326
kept in courthouse, 304
Rector. *See* Clergy, clergyman—rector
Rector, Mr., letter to, 47
Rectory. *See* Building—parsonage, rectory
Redding (Reading), Connecticut, lack of clergy in, 340
Reed, Eliz., debtor, 480
Reed, Mary, burial of, 480
Reed, Will[iam] (Will., Wm.)
president of Council, 288
vestryman, 190
Reformation, 181
Refugees
Huguenot clergyman, 470*n*
Palatine, 89*n*
Regii, Joh. *See* Regius, Johannes
Regius (Regii), Johannes (Joh.), author, 295
Rehoboth, Mr., 260
Reiner, Richd., allowance of, 484
Relf, John, vestryman, 190
Relf, Tho. *See* Relfe, Thomas
Relfe (Relf), Thomas (Tho., Thos.)
churchwarden, 45, 251
petitioner, 44-45
testimonial by, 109
vestryman, 109
Relfe (Relph), William (Wm.)
petitioner, 44-45
testimonial by, 109
vestryman, 45, 109, 251
Relfe, Mr. *See* Relfe, William
Religion
Fundamental Constitutions and, 215*n*
indifference toward, 231
Relph, William. *See* Relfe, William
Renoque. *See* Roanoke
Report, 29, 40-41, 65-66, 114, 120, 129-130, 220, 385-386, 421
from bishop of St. David's, 392
from clergy, xliv, 42, 96, 147, 152, 169, 174, 359, 421, 424, 426
on accounts, 482, 484-485, 488
on baptism of Negroes, 357
on baptisms, 384
on building churches, 221*n*
on Cape Fear, 349
on Cape Fear, promised, 350
on Church in colony, xlv, xlix, 11-12, 27-30 passim, 47, 66, 73, 76, 81, 87*n*, 110, 147, 171, 179, 184, 186, 258, 268, 281, 283-284, 289-291, 297, 305, 332, 340, 354, 363, 382-383, 390, 407, 419
on Church in North America, 10-11, 26
on circumcised Indians, 215-216
on clergy, xlix, 31, 60, 78*n*, 198, 387
on clerical qualifications, 56, 396
on colony, 81-87 passim, 107, 176, 196-197, 211, 285, 332, 339, 341, 345, 362, 369
on disaffected clergy, 224-225
on glebes, 221*n*
on harbor, 344-345
on houses for clergy, 221*n*
on indigent, 464
on mission, 420
on mission boundary of districts, 383
on mission station, 285, 349, 408
on missionary libraries, 39*n*
on parish, 42, 152, 258, 411
on petition, 388
on potential missionaries, 14*n*, 131
on recovery of standard weights and measures, 448
on religion in colonies, 10-11
on religion in precinct, 453
on request of clergyman's widow, 400
on schools, 43
on services of clergyman, 397
on settlement at New River, promised, 350
on shortage of clergy, 45
on South Carolina, 204
on SPG, xl, 258, 258*n*, 268, 281, 284, 297, 305-306, 340, 354, 363, 390, 407, 419
on Yamasee War, 217-218
printed, xl
published, 426

read, 327
to archbishop of Canterbury, 399
to bishop of London, xliv
to Board of Trade, xlix
to Board of Trade, proposed, 107
to secretary of state, xlix
to SPG, xlix, 49, 110*n*, 259, 298, 363, 385, 426-427
to vestry, 463
See also Clergy, clergyman—letter from; Letter; Notitia parochialis
Resolution, by lower house of assembly, 401*n*
Revolution, against lords proprietors, 269, 270*n*
Reynolds, Mr., recommended for SPG service, 79
Rhett, William
leads military expedition, 258*n*
receiver general of South Carolina, 258*n*
Rhode Island (King's Province, Narragansett, Providence Plantation)
description of, 11
lack of clergy in, 258
Quakers in, 20
Rice. *See* Commodity payments—rice
Rice, Nathaniel (Nath., Nathl.)
Council member, 346, 370
letter from, 398-399
secretary, 377
vestryman, 399, 418
Richards, John, executor, 480, 485
Richardson, Danl., vestryman, 190
Richardson, John, author, 7
Rinet, Jno., letter to, 238
Riquotan. *See* Hampton, Virginia
Ritter, Georg, and Company, purchases land, 113
River
crossing of, 27
impedes travel, 84, 94, 172
See also Alligator River; Cape Fear River; Chowan River; Cooper River, South Carolina; Hampton River, Virginia; James River, Virginia; Little River; Meherrin River; Nansemond River, Virginia; Neuse River; New River; Northeast Cape Fear River; Northwest River; Pamlico River; Pasquotank River; Scuppernong River; Shenandoah River; Trent River; Wiccacon River; White Oak River; Yeopim River; York River, Virginia
Roach, Mr. *See* Roach, Richard
Roach, Richard
Cary rebel, 124*n*, 129
delivers arms, 123
exempted from pardon, 124*n*
merchant, 124*n*, 129
of London, 124*n*
report by, 123
Roach. *See* Roach, Richard
Roads
guide for, 174
poor condition of, 27, 29, 48, 76, 84-85, 116-117, 120, 438
Roan, Matt. *See* Rowan, Matthew
Roanoke (Moratico) Chapel, ministry at, 380
Roanoke (Morrotto) River
clergyman at, 129
governor at, 129
Roanoke (Raonoak, Renoque), xvi*n*, 12*n*
christening in, xiii
clergyman appointed to, 23-24
clergyman in, 12, 12*n*, 283
Indians near, 216, 216*n*
Roanoke Island, xiii
ministry on, 379
See also Carteret, Roanoke Island
Robbery. *See* Crime—theft, robbery
Roberts, George, commissioner, 403
Roberts, Lewis, author of [*The Merchants Map of Commerce*], 6
Roberts, Mr., to attend SPG committee meeting, 47
Roberts, Mr. *See* Robins, Stephen
Robins (Roberts), Stephen
testimonial by, 80-81, 90, 90*n*
vicar, 80, 90, 90*n*
Robinson, John (J. L.), bishop of London
application to, 207
encouragement by, 217
instructions from, 242-243
letter from, 228, 274-275
opinion of, 220, 230
Robinson, John (Jno.) (Chowan), allowance of, 477-478, 481
Robinson, Mr.
clergyman, 472
missionary appointment of, 48
payment to, 472
Rochester (England), bishop of, 34
Rochester, Lord. *See* Hyde, Lawrence, 1st earl of Rochester
Rochestr., Ld. *See* Hyde, Lawrence, 1st earl of Rochester
Rockyhock Creek, district boundary at, 454
Rodgers, Robt., allowance of, 488
Rodgerson, Margrett (Margett)

clothes for, 490
maintained by parish, 489-490, 492-494
Rogers, John, author, 410
Rogers, Thomas, author, 34, 37
Rolf Parish, Virginia, vestryman in, 331
Roman Catholics, 308, 309*n*
book against, 410
duke of York, xviii-xix
excepted from religious toleration, xliii, 325
few adherents in parish, 283, 285
former, 198
leave Virginia, xvii
may not be taxed by Catholic Church, xix
not taxed, xix
statistics of, 422
tolerated, xvi
Rome, xix, 163*n*
Ronald, George (Geo.)
letter from, 398-399
vestryman, 399, 418
Roof. *See* Church, chapel, meetinghouse—roof of
Roper, _____
committee member, 409
to review missionary's performance, 383
Roper, Dr. *See* Roper, _____
Roper, Mr. *See* Roper, _____
Roscommon, Ireland, 57*n*
Rose, Richd., subscription by, 439
Rose, Th.
letter from, 228-230
parishioner, 230
Ross, Messr., removed as missionary, 91
Roundtree, Mr. *See* Rountree, Thomas
Roundtree, Thomas. *See* Rountree, Thomas
Rountree (Roundtree, Rowntree), Thomas (Thos.)
account of, deferred, 473
allowance of, 459, 461, 464, 468, 474, 478, 481
Anabaptist, 463
collects parish tax, 474-475
excused as vestryman, 464
letter from, 287-288
oath taken by, 455
payment to, 466-467, 471-472, 476
reader, 459, 461, 464, 468, 473-475
to attend vestry meeting, 463
vestryman, 288, 455, 459-461, 463
Rountree, Mr. *See* Rountree, Thomas
Route, Robert
allowance of, 461
reader, 461
Rowan (Roan), Matthew (Math., Mathew, Matt.)
accompanied by clergyman, 352
Council member, 353*n*, 370
deceased, 353*n*
merchant, 353*n*
occupation of, 353*n*
of Ulster, Ireland, 353*n*
petitioner, 309-310
receiver general, 353*n*
ship of, distressed, 353
surveyor general, 353*n*
vestryman, 418
Rowan, Captain. *See* Rowan, Matthew
Rowden, _____, debtor, 466
Rowntree, Thos. *See* Rountree, Thomas
Rowsom, John, witness, 377
Royal Exchange, London, 406
Rug. *See* Household furnishings—rug
Rum. *See* Drink—rum
Russell, Mr., clerk to bishop of London, 137
Russia (Muscovy), 93
clergyman in, 201
Ruston, _____, debtor, 466
Ruston, Mrs. *See* Ruston, _____
Ryan, Michael, debtor, 466
Rymer, Thomas, author, 410
S. Cara. *See* South Carolina
Sa, Manuel de, author of [*Notationes in totam Scripturam Sacram*], 294
Sacrament. *See* Baptism; Holy Communion
Saddle. *See* Horse—saddle for
Sadler, William (Wm.)
debtor, 459, 466
payment to widow of, 466
Sagg, Mr.
allowance of, 473-474
collects parish tax, 473-475
payment to, 476-477
reader, 473-474
Sailor. *See* Occupation, trade, profession—sailor
St. Albans (England), archdeacon of, 49*n*
St. Albans Street, London, 238
St. Andrew's Parish
clergyman in, xlv
erected, xxxiii, 414
meeting place for vestrymen in, 314
ministry in, 379-380
See also South Shore Parish
St. Andrews Parish, South Carolina, 217
letter from, 228-230
letter to vestry, 227

opposition to clergyman in, 220, 229, 232, 259
St. Andrews, University of, governor a former professor at, xlvii
St. Antholin, London, clergyman at, 90*n*, 127, 130
St. Asaph, Bp. of. *See* Beveridge, William
St. Bartholomew's (St. Barthws.) Parish, 391
St. Barthws. *See* St. Bartholomew's Parish
St. Benedict's, Paul's Wharf. *See* St. Benet Paul's Wharf, London
St. Benet, Paul's Wharf (St. Benedict's Paul's Wharf), London, 59
St. Bridget's, Dublin, curate of, 352
St. Carolina. *See* South Carolina
St. Catherine's Parish. *See* St. Katherine's Parish, London
St. Davids, Lord Bishop of. *See* Clagett, Nicholas, bishop of St. David's
St. Denis (St. Dennis) Parish, South Carolina
clergyman in, 337, 347
St. Dunstan in the West, London
clergyman at, 57*n*
St. Edmunds Bury. *See* Bury St. Edmunds, England
St. George's Parish, 432*n*
erected, 414
St. James's Palace (Court at St. James), London, 325
St. James's Parish, 215, 371, 374, 411, 412, 412*n*
clergyman in, 360, 383, 407
erected, xxxiii, 316, 414
letter from, 398-399, 419-420
letter to vestry, 227
library for, 398
lottery in, xxx
petition from, 324
plantation in, 397
St. John's Parish, 432*n*
clergyman in, 391
consolidated, xxxiii
erected, 414
financial assistance from, xxxvi
ministry in, 380
St. John's Parish, South Carolina
clergyman in, 300, 317
clergyman rejected in, 394
letter from, 299-300
religious condition of, 300
St. Katherine's (Catherine's) Parish, London
palatines in, 88
St. Lawrence's Parish, London, 130
St. Luke's, Dublin, clergyman in, 352
St. Margaret's Parish, Virginia, vestryman in, 331
St. Martin's Library. *See* Canterbury, archbishop of—library of
St. Martin's Parish, erected, 414
St. Martin's. *See* St. Martin-in-the-Fields, London
St. Martin-in-the-Fields (St. Martin's), London, 138, 153, 196, 201, 203, 211, 214, 232, 238-239, 244, 249, 251, 253, 283, 285, 355, 392
chapel, church in, xl
St. Mary-le-Bow (Bow Vestry), London, 23, 297, 374
St. Mewan Parish (Cornwall, England), clergyman from, 388
St. Michael Bassishaw, London, 297
St. Michael's Parish, Maryland, clergyman in, 66
St. Michael's, Dublin, clergyman in, 352
St. Patrick's Parish, erected, xxxiii
St. Paul's Parish, South Carolina
clergyman in, xliv
death of minister in, 316
divided, 394
St. Paul's Parish, Virginia, 331
St. Paul's Parish
description of chapel, church in, xxii*n*
erected, 414, 432*n*
financial assistance from, xxxvi
letter to inhabitants, 400-401
letter to vestry, 227
vestry minutes, xi, 431-494
vestryman in, 144*n*, 331
vestry of, xi, xxii, xxiv
See also Chowan Precinct, eastern parish of
St. Pauls' Chapterhouse, London, xl, 25*n*, 32, 39, 75, 88, 99
St. Peter's Parish
consolidated, xxxiii
erected, 414
St. Philip's Parish
erected, 414
lottery in, xxx
vestrymen for, 418
St. Philip's Parish, South Carolina, clergyman in, xliv, 66-67
St. Stephen's (St. Stepns.) Parish, Virginia vestryman in, 331
St. Stepns. *See* St. Stephen's Parish, Virginia
St. Thomas's (St. Thomas, St. Thos.) Parish, 310, 322, 354, 359, 365-366, 385-386
clergyman in, 260, 337, 358, 384, 407, 420

erected, 189, 194, 414
inscribed on parish books, 172, 449
lack of clergy in, 240
letter to vestry, 227
library in, xli, 5, 9*n*, 44
marriage in, 364
ministry in, 380, 407
petition from, 309-310, 353-354, 357-358
vestrymen of, 190
St. Thomas's Church, 354*n*
St. Thomas's Parish, South Carolina, clergyman in, 324, 347
St. Thos. *See* St. Thomas's Parish
Salary, wage, payment
for building chapels, 494
for burial of indigent, 442, 454, 458, 464-465, 468, 470, 472, 475, 478, 480
for clearing land, 433
for clerk of vestry, 229, 431, 433, 437, 445, 448, 479-480, 483, 486, 493-494
for collecting taxes, 433
for conducting worship service, 485*n*
for gift to indigent, 494
for keeping indigent, 432, 435-436, 438, 440-442, 454-455, 458, 464-466, 472, 476-484 passim, 486-494 passim
for maintaining, repairing church, chapel, 460, 465-466, 484
for making church furnishings, 440
for making clothes, 472, 484, 490
for making coffin, 480
for making desk, 450, 454
for medical treatment, 436-437, 465, 477
for nursing indigent, 493
for obtaining copy of act, 492
for preaching, 477
for serving vestry, 467
for shingling chapel, 480
for summoning vestry, 467
for tarring chapel, 437
for transporting clergyman, 440
for use of house for vestry meeting, 490
for washing surplice, 477
for work on pulpit, 439
of clerk of vestry, 481, 487
to churchwardens, 483
to clerk, 468
to widow, 468
to workmen, 444
See also Clergy—salary, allowance, maintenance; Reader—paid
Salem, Massachusetts, 48
Salivation. *See* Disease, illness, affliction—treatment of, by salivation; Medicine, medical treatment—salivation
Sall (Sallii), Andrew, author, 295
Sallii. *See* Sall, Andrew
Salt. *See* Food, diet—salt
Salter, Edward
churchwarden, 354
desires to retain minister, 353-354
petitioner, 353-354
Sanchez, Caspar. *See* Sanctius, Gasparus
Sanctius (Sanchez), Gasparus (Caspar) author, 294
Sand Banks (Currituck County), 86
Sanders, Old. *See* Sanderson, Richard
Sanderson (Sanders, Saunders), Richard (Richd.), Sr., 108*n*, 144*n*
bequest by, xxx, 107, 317
churchwarden, 108
Council member, xxx
deceased, 175
refuses to return books, 143, 160, 168, 175
testimonial by, 108
vestryman, 108, 190
Sanderson, Bp. *See* Sanderson, Robert, bishop of Lincoln
Sanderson, Jos., vestryman, 190
Sanderson, Mr. *See* Sanderson, Richard, Sr.
Sanderson, Richd., Jr.
Council member, 288
testimonial by, 108
vestryman, 190
Sanderson, Robert, bishop of Lincoln, author, 7, 34, 37
Sanderson. *See* Sanderson, Richard
Sandford Hen[ry], letter from, 53-54, 57*n*
Sandford, Mr. *See* Sandford, Hen[ry]
Sarson, Lau, vestryman, 189
Sarum Creek
school at, 143, 145
schoolmaster at, 149
Sarum. *See* Sarum Creek
Saunders, Mr. *See* Sanderson, Richard
Savanna, 86
Saw. *See* Tools, equipment—saw
Sawyer, Henry, vestryman, 190
Sawyer, Robert, vestryman, 190
Sawyer, Thos., vestryman, 190
Sawyers Creek, meeting place for vestrymen at, 314
Scales. *See* Weights and measures—scales for
Scheibler (Scheibleri), Christoph, author, 294
Scheibleri. *See* Scheibler, Christoph

Schickard (Schiekard), Wilhelm, author, 294
Schiekard. *See* Schickard, Wilhelm
School, schools, 17, 176
  assembly creates fund for, xlvii
  assembly neglects, 371, 371*n*
  charity, 264
  desired, 173
  dissenter, 11
  encouraged by SPG, 43
  established by SPCK, xxxix
  for Indians, 87*n*
  free, xlvii
  fund for, diverted, xlvii
  governor to recommend establishment of, xlvii, 327
  in New Bern, Edenton, xlviii
  lack of, 172
  none erected at public expense, xlviii
  of Charles Griffin, 86
  public, xlvii
  Queen's College, xlviii
  royal instruction concerning, xliv, 326
  to be encouraged, 42
  Trinity College, Cambridge University, 186-187
  University of Glasgow, 330
  University of St. Andrews, xlvii
  See also College of William and Mary, Virginia; Trinity College, Cambridge, England; Trinity College, Hartford, Connecticut; University of Glasgow, Scotland
Schoolmaster, teacher, 11, 86, 87*n*, 132*n*, 133, 145, 146*n*, 149
  act concerning, 11
  becomes Quaker, 97
  bounty for, 4
  for Indian children, 42, 87*n*
  German, 88*n*
  instructions for, 42-43
  letter from, 296
  license required for, xliv
  licensed, 279-280
  plan to obtain, 176
  qualifications of, 222-223
  recommended, 132
  report on, 152
  requested, 227
  salary for, 48, 145, 149, 169, 173, 176, 253
  salary for, requested, 143
  seeks employment, 222
  settled, 84
  shortage, lack of, 168, 176, 184, 306
  to be licensed, 326
  to report to SPG, 43
  with Palatines, 113
  See also Mashborne, Edward—schoolmaster; New England—school in; Virginia—school in
Science, natural, books concerning, xlii
Scientist. *See* Occupation, trade, profession—scientist
Scituate, Massachusetts, lack of clergy in, 340
Scogarlong River. *See* Scuppernong River
Scot. *See* Scott, John
Scotch-Irish, 353*n*
  increase in numbers of, xxxix
Scotland (North Britain), xix, 8, 105, 212*n*, 424
  clergyman from, 391, 394
  clergyman in, 59, 423
  ship sailing to, 423
  See also Great Britain
Scots, 76*n*
  dissenter, 181
  in Carolinas, 167
  increase in numbers of, xxxix
Scott (Scot), John, author, 8, 410
Scott (Scot), Margaret (Marget), maintained by parish, 468, 472
Scott, Bat., debtor, 466
Scott, Dr. *See* Scott, John
Scougal, Henry, author of [*Life of God in the Soul of Man*], 36
Scripture, 329*n*
  complaint concerning, 350
  passage of, 165, 277, 277*n*, 337*n*, 383*n*, 401
  preaching on text from, 297, 337, 383, 399, 399*n*
  See also Books, tracts—Bible
Scuppernong (Cuscopnung, Scogarlong) River
  description of inhabitants on, 117
  ministry at, 379-380
Seal, sealed instrument, 26, 110, 123, 164, 191, 194, 210, 215, 286, 292, 326, 331, 377, 387, 403
  for weights, 435
  of archbishop of Dublin, 351
  of colony, 372
  of governor, 415
  of SPG, 293, 408
Sears, Mrs., greeting to, 311
Season, wet, 117
  See also Autumn, fall; Spring; Summer; Winter
Seasoning. *See* Disease, illness, affliction—seasoning
Secker, Thomas, bishop of Oxford

compliments teaching method, 427
letter from, 425-427
letter to, 423-425
Secretary of state (Great Britain), 243*n*, 327
report to, xlix
to prepare instructions, 279
Secretary, secretary's office, 124*n*, 223, 263, 292, 377
accused of embezzlement, 317
accused of irreligion, 317, 321
hinders construction of church, 317
interrogates clergyman, 301
inventory of estate to be returned to, 377
Sedgwick, Robt., authorizes warrant, 346
Seller, Abednego, author, 7
Seneca. *See* Indians—Seneca
Sermon, homily, 17, 344, 372, 472
at meeting of SPG, xl, xl*n*, 98, 100-101, 144*n*, 168, 228, 230, 238, 242, 258, 268*n*, 274-275, 281*n*, 284*n*, 290*n*, 291, 296, 297*n*, 298*n*, 303-305, 306*n*, 340*n*, 354, 355*n*, 363*n*, 390*n*, 408*n*, 419, 419*n*, 425*n*
book of, 102-103, 120, 277, 358, 409, 420, 433
by missionary, 116
criticized, 228-229
fee for, 215
of bishop of Oxford, 425*n*, 426
printed, xl, 229, 281, 293, 303, 308, 327, 410, 425
read, xvi
to be read, 28, 120, 327, 437
See also Preaching
Servant, xxx*n*, 82, 115, 208, 234, 237, 436
accusations against, 264, 271
act of assembly concerning, xxix
bears child, xxix-xxx
child bound as, xxx, 489
child of, 271
hired, 214
indentured, 234, 264
injured by master, 456
maid, 466
of clergyman, 344
payments for capture of runaway, xxxv
pregnant, 271
purchased, 87, 177, 202, 213
robbery by, 177
runs away, 177, 210, 214, 271
services sold by churchwarden, xxix
ungovernable, 177
wages owed to, 209, 213
See also Acts of assembly—on binding in servitude; Clergy, clergyman—wants servants, slaves
Severn (naval vessel), 137
Shaftesbury, Lord. *See* Cooper, Anthony Ashley, 1st earl of Shaftesbury
Sharp, ABp. *See* Sharp, John, archbishop of York
Sharp, John, archbishop of York
author, 37
letter to, 146-147
Sheep, 115
gift of, to church, 107
gift of, to clergy, 317
loss of, 214
Sheerness, England, clergyman in, 132-133
Sheets, Jacob, vestryman, 191
Shelton, Mr. *See* Shelton, Richard
Shelton, Richard
lays charter before board, 297-298
secretary to the Lords Proprietors, 297, 298*n*
to appear before Lords Proprietors, 306
Shenandoah (Shonadoor) River, Virginia
chapel, church near, 401
Sheppard, _____, 351
Sheppard, Tho., testimonial by, 276-277
Sheriff
complaint against, 450
to collect parish tax, xxxvii, 416
to render account, 178
Sherlock, Bp. *See* Sherlock, Thomas, bishop of London
Sherlock, Richard, author, 8
Sherlock, Thomas, bishop of London, author, 410
Sherlock, William, author, 7, 37
Shift. *See* Clothing, jewelry—shift
Shingle. *See* Building materials—shingles; Church, chapel, meetinghouse—shingled
Shipping, freight, 197
by London fleet, 65, 72
by Virginia fleet, 55, 77, 121-122, 133, 137-140 passim
fleets for, uncertain, 121
from Virginia, 111
inlet for, 86
lack of, 44
of arms, 124*n*
of books, 100
of clergyman's goods, 144
of household effects, 104

to plantations, 79
Shipwright. *See* Occupation, trade, profession—shipwright
Shirt. *See* Clothing, jewelry—shirt
Shoemaker, cobbler. *See* Clothing, jewelry—shoes; Occupation, trade, profession—shoemaker
Shoes. *See* Clothing, jewelry—shoes
Shonadoor. *See* Shenandoah River, Virginia
Shoreham (naval vessel), transports clergy, 242
Shuckford, Samuel, author, 410
Shute, Gyles
justice of the peace, 310
petitioner, 309-310
signature of, forged, 310*n*
Shute, Mr.
brother of, 60
report by, 60
Siam. *See* Thailand
Siberia, 201
Sickle. *See* Tools, equipment—sickle
Signature. *See* Witness—to signature
Silk, Edward
will proved by, 377
witness, 377
Silver, silverware
communion cup, 421
flagon, 346
for church, 488
for Holy Communion, 104, 183, 346
offering receiver, 346
paten, 346
plate, 448, 465, 478, 493
value of, 346
See also Chalice; Governor, deputy governor—to deliver church silver, to receive chapel plate
Simon, Richard (H.), author, 7
Simplicius, author, 34
Simpson, Sarah, child of, maintained by parish, 459
Simson, Patrick. *See* Symson, Patrick
Sinclare, Mr., removed as missionary, 159
Singellton, James
desires to retain minister, 353-354
petitioner, 353-354
vestryman, 354
Singing, 143
Sivers, John, allowance of, 454, 456
Skene, A.
betrays clergyman, 217, 219-220
letter from, 228-230
parishioner, 230
Skene, Jemimah
letter from, 228-230
parishioner, 230
Skene, Mr. *See* Skene, A.
Skinner, Rich., Jr., witness, 155
Skinner, William (Willm., Wm.)
allowance of, 489-491, 493
reader, 489-491, 493
vestryman, 490-493 passim
Skins and furs, payment in, 117
Slade, Hen., vestryman, 190
Slade, Judith
debtor, 466, 473
payment to, 472
Slade, Saml. (Sam.)
vestry commissioner, 310
vestryman, 190
Slaughter, Michael
keeper of jail, 485*n*
of Edenton, 485*n*
payment to, 482, 485*n*
tailor, 485*n*
Slaughter, Mr. *See* Slaughter, Michael
Slaves, xxx*n*, 116, 162, 338, 344
act of assembly concerning, xxix
bequest of, xxx
conversion of, encouraged, xlvi
death of, 177, 210, 214
desire baptism, 261
destroy goods, 210
gift of, to church, 107
hired, 264
Indian, 216
lack clothing, 209, 212
master of, 128
masters oppose baptism of, xlvii, 261
numbers of, xxiii
of clergy, 28, 82, 121-122, 132, 137, 177, 181, 208-210, 212-213, 255, 264, 271, 300, 344, 361
owners oppose instruction of, 424
price of, 300
purchase of, 255, 271
Quakers lenient toward, 425
requested from Codrington Estate, 244
runaway, xxxv, 214, 271
sold for church construction, xxx
starve, 212
status of as church members, xviii
tithables, xxvii*n*
to be sold, 209, 212
Slipper. *See* Clothing, jewelry—slipper
Slocomb, John, vestryman, 191
Sloop. *See* Boat, ship—sloop

Smalbroke (Smallbrook), Richard, bishop of St. David's, author, 410
Smallbrook, Bp. *See* Smalbroke, Richard, bishop of St. David's
Smallpox. *See* Disease, illness, affliction—smallpox
Smalridg, Bp. *See* Smalridge, George, bishop of Bristol
Smalridge (Smalridg), George, bishop of Bristol, author, 410
Smetick, Mr., house of, 379-380
Smith, _____, shipmaster, 122
Smith, Charles (Ch.)
  letter from, 21, 24
  letter to, 25
  memorial by, 23
  mission proposed for, 23
  payment to, 23
  wife of, 21
Smith, David, burial of, 478
Smith, Edward, bishop of Down and Connor, 127
Smith, Edwd.
  petitioner, 324
  vestryman, 324
Smith, John, vestryman, 191
Smith, Mr. *See* Smith, William
Smith, Patience, marriage of, 364
Smith, Patrick, author, 410
Smith, Paul
  bill of exchange to, 406
  of Dublin, Ireland, 405
  statement by, 405
Smith, Thos., vestryman, 191
Smith, William
  act of assembly signed by, 405
  chief justice, 332, 333*n*
  complaint by, 336
  petitioner, 332
  president of Council, 370, 405
  vestryman, 481-482, 484-486
Smithwick, Edward (Edard, Edwd.)
  account of, 441
  assembly member, 432*n*
  churchwarden, 435-437, 441
  Council member, 432*n*
  debtor, 433, 441
  dismissed as vestryman, 451
  donates land for church, 431
  health of, 451
  justice of the peace, 432*n*
  letter from, 68-69
  payment by, 445
  receipt from, 435
  subscription by, 439
  to choose builder, 434
  to deliver weights, 445
  vestryman, 68, 431, 433-434, 438-439, 441-446 passim, 452
Smithwick, Mr. *See* Smithwick, Edward
Snoad, Wm.
  justice of the peace, 310
  petitioner, 309-310
So. Carola. *See* South Carolina
Soap, 231
  See also Occupation, trade, profession—soapmaker
Society Church, clergyman at, 282
Society for the Promotion of Christian Knowledge (SPCK)
  and education, xxxix
  founded, xxxix, xliv, 3*n*
  literature distributed by, xlii
  sees North Carolina as mission field, xxxix
  supported, 49*n*
Society for the Propagation of the Gospel in Foreign Parts (SPG), xxii, xlix, 318, 335, 335*n*, 348, 370, 374, 381, 396, 405, 411-412, 419, 451*n*, 462
  abstract of proceedings of, 101, 171, 258, 268, 281, 284, 297, 305, 340, 354, 363, 390, 407, 419
  account delivered to, 14
  accounts to be audited, 99
  alleged inspector of clergy for, 338
  allowance for German minister requested from, 88
  and conversion of slaves, xlvi
  annual meeting of, xl
  asked to repay debt of clergyman, 406
  auditor of, 97, 99-100, 167
  bond to, 163-164
  book on history of, 426-427, 427*n*
  books from, xlii, 180, 378
  books of, 198
  bylaws of, 98
  case to be laid before, 372
  chairman of, 99
  charter to, 39, 90, 97-98
  clergy members of, xl
  clergyman asks protection of, 216
  clergyman recommended to, 367, 371
  clergyman wants case referred to, 381
  commission from, 157
  committees of, 99
  contribution from, requested, 322
  criticized, 390
  dependence on, 77, 117, 121

discontinues assistance, 375
dismisses missionary, 211*n*, 268*n*
efforts of, to educate Negroes, 424-425
election to, 13, 13*n*, 80, 98-99
fails to reply to letter, 391
founded, xl, xliv, 3*n*
founder of, 193
gift from, 22, 173, 313, 322, 365, 401, 448, 450
gift from, requested, xlii, 84, 104, 181, 306, 310, 323-324, 358, 362, 365, 369
gift to, 4, 58, 98-100, 114, 121, 392
governor member of, xl
grants leave to return to England, 211*n*, 267, 269
gratitude toward, xxviii
historical account of, published, 410
instructions from, 39-43, 198, 349, 357-358, 365, 412
journal of, 13-14, 23, 25, 30-31, 39*n*, 45-47, 49-51, 51*n*, 52*n*, 56*n*, 57*n*, 59-60, 62-63, 65*n*, 71*n*, 72*n*, 74*n*, 78*n*, 79-80, 87*n*, 89, 89*n*, 90-91, 94*n*, 95*n*, 97, 97*n*, 106*n*, 110*n*, 111, 113*n*, 122*n*, 127, 130*n*, 131-132, 132*n*, 134*n*, 141, 144*n*, 146*n*, 147, 147*n*, 150, 150*n*, 156*n*, 159, 159*n*, 161*n*, 166*n*, 171*n*, 175, 175*n*, 178*n*, 179*n*, 182*n*, 185*n*, 186-187, 199, 202*n*, 203*n*, 204*n*, 211*n*, 215*n*, 221, 232, 243, 243*n*, 249, 272*n*, 276-277, 280-281, 282*n*, 287-289, 292, 296-298, 300*n*, 306, 313*n*, 317*n*, 320, 322, 325*n*, 328, 337, 349*n*, 355, 356*n*, 362, 366*n*, 373-374, 376*n*, 382-383, 385-389 passim, 391*n*, 395-396, 398-400, 409, 409*n*, 412, 420*n*, 421*n*, 422, 427-428, 428*n*
leases of, 98
letter from, 162, 166, 168, 176, 199, 218, 226, 246, 355, 448, 453
letter from secretary of, 25*n*, 42, 57-58, 63, 72*n*, 92-93, 100, 147, 150, 152-153, 153*n*, 166, 169-170, 175*n*, 187-188, 188*n*, 196-197, 200, 204-206, 217, 221*n*, 223-227, 230, 233, 235, 245, 250, 258, 263, 267, 269, 278-279, 300-301, 349, 349*n*, 363, 373, 385, 392, 396-397, 400-401, 420-421
letter to, xl, 12, 31-32, 45, 51, 56, 66, 70-71, 81, 108, 110, 182, 228, 237, 250, 258, 291, 300, 361, 384-386, 391, 398, 412*n*, 424, 426, 449
letter to secretary of, 13, 17-21, 24, 46-52, 55, 57, 57*n*, 58-67, 69, 71, 79-80, 89-90, 93-97, 100-101, 103-107, 109*n*, 111-113, 113*n*, 114-128, 132-135, 137-138, 140-144, 145*n*, 149, 153-155, 157, 160, 162, 166-167, 171-175, 177, 179-182, 184, 184*n*, 185-187, 187*n*, 196*n*, 197-200, 202-204, 206, 208, 212, 214-224, 228, 230-240, 243-249, 252-265, 267-273, 275, 281-287, 288*n*, 289, 296, 299-300, 312-313, 334, 348, 363, 365-366, 366*n*, 376*n*, 385, 388, 391*n*, 393, 395, 399*n*, 408-409, 419-422, 428*n*
letter to treasurer of, 196, 263
letter to, not answered, 228
literature distributed by, xli-xlii
meeting of, 12*n*, 14*n*, 23-24, 25*n*, 30, 33*n*, 39*n*, 47, 58, 64, 64*n*, 65*n*, 69*n*, 71*n*, 72*n*, 74*n*, 75, 78*n*, 80*n*, 87*n*, 88*n*, 89*n*, 94*n*, 95*n*, 97, 97*n*, 98, 103, 104*n*, 106*n*, 110*n*, 113*n*, 122*n*, 124*n*, 130*n*, 132*n*, 134*n*, 138, 141*n*, 144, 144*n*, 146*n*, 147, 147*n*, 150*n*, 151*n*, 156*n*, 159, 159*n*, 161*n*, 166*n*, 171*n*, 175*n*, 178*n*, 179*n*, 182*n*, 185*n*, 186*n*, 187*n*, 199*n*, 202*n*, 203*n*, 204*n*, 211*n*, 215*n*, 235, 255*n*, 262*n*, 267, 272*n*, 282*n*, 287-289, 300*n*, 313*n*, 317*n*, 325*n*, 329*n*, 349*n*, 356*n*, 366*n*, 376*n*, 385*n*, 389, 391-392, 395, 409*n*, 412*n*, 420*n*, 421*n*, 422, 428*n*
member of, 245, 248
merchant in, 124
merchants members of, xl
messenger of, 102
minutes of meetings of, 99-100
missionary of, criticized, 423
nobility members of, xl
obligations of missionaries toward, 42
order of, 14*n*, 172, 178, 188*n*, 205, 223, 226-227, 232-233, 235, 242, 249, 258-260, 272*n*, 276-277, 293, 297, 298*n*, 349*n*, 355-356, 363, 365, 383-384, 386, 398-399, 412*n*, 420, 421*n*, 450
papers, 98
petition, memorial to, 23, 280, 282, 296-297, 320, 322, 328-329, 357, 365-366, 375, 397, 460-461
plantation of, 424, 427
prayers of, requested, 203
president of, 39*n*, 69*n*, 97-98, 101, 108-109
printed papers of, 39, 166, 198
private letters to members of, prohibited, 227
promises to send missionary, 272*n*
proposal to, 88, 88*n*, 89, 89*n*, 99, 149
proprietor member of, xl
quorum for meetings of, 98
receives no letters from colony, 419

recruits clergy, xli
refuses assistance, 388
regulations of, xl
report from secretary of, 78*n*, 87*n*, 88, 89*n*, 91, 97, 111, 131
report on, xl, xl*n*, 258*n*
report requested by, 226
report to, xl, xlix, 83, 87, 89, 106, 106*n*, 130, 132, 143, 146*n*, 151*n*, 152, 160, 162, 179, 206, 224-225, 227, 232, 276, 296, 298, 322, 337, 366, 374, 383, 386-388, 399*n*, 400, 408, 426
representation to, 29-30, 156
requested to obtain passage of act, 261
resolutions of, 306
seal of, 98
secretary of, xxvi*n*, xl, 19*n*, 25, 60, 64*n*, 65*n*, 79, 97, 100-102, 138, 138*n*, 203, 232*n*, 293, 297, 329*n*, 383, 386-387, 392*n*
secretary of, pities colony, xiv
secretary of, to take minutes, 99
secretary writes history of, 427*n*
seeks information on immoral clergy, 408
services offered to, 114
standing committee of, xl, 4, 13, 14*n*, 25, 25*n*, 30-32, 33*n*, 39*n*, 46*n*, 47*n*, 48-51 passim, 51*n*, 52, 52*n*, 56, 56*n*, 57*n*, 59-60, 62*n*, 75*n*, 79, 87*n*, 88, 88*n*, 89-90, 90*n*, 91, 97*n*, 99*n*, 100, 101*n*, 102, 104*n*, 106*n*, 110*n*, 127, 131-132, 132*n*, 147, 151*n*, 154, 156, 199*n*, 211*n*, 221, 232, 249, 255*n*, 262*n*, 265*n*, 268*n*, 272*n*, 276-277, 280-281, 296-298, 322, 325*n*, 328, 363, 366*n*, 373-374, 376*n*, 382-383, 385-388 passim, 391, 398, 399*n*, 400, 409, 412*n*, 421*n*, 428*n*
standing orders of, xl, 51, 79, 79*n*, 97-102, 138, 147, 152, 169-170, 188*n*, 197, 207, 209, 211*n*, 212, 221*n*, 225, 227, 249, 267, 268*n*, 269, 277, 277*n*, 337, 428
standing rules of, 281
testimonials for, 54, 90, 156*n*
thanked, 189
to assist missionaries, 298
to contribute to building of church, 461
to send books, 43
treasurer of, 23, 79, 97, 99-102 passim, 147, 150, 150*n*, 151*n*, 152, 159, 169, 174, 178, 182, 196-197, 199, 210, 211*n*, 213, 234, 240, 246, 255-256, 263, 271, 276-277, 355, 392, 397, 399-400
urged to seek royal government for Carolina, 122
vestry seeks relief from, 250
vice-president of, 97-98
Society for the Reformation of Manners, 19
Society Parish
collection for chapel, church in, xxx
erected, 414
meeting place for vestrymen in, 314
ministry in, 379-380
See also Chowan Precinct, southwestern parish of
Socrates, author, 294
Sodor and Man, bishop of. *See* Wilson, Thomas, bishop of Sodor and Man
Solly, John, vestryman, 190
Somerset House, London, 243
Somerset, Henry, 2nd duke of Beaufort
letter from, 103, 137
letter to, 133
palatine, 134*n*, 148
promise by, broken, 148
proprietor, 81
Sothel, Seth
deceased, 13*n*
land of, 13*n*
proprietor, 13*n*
Sound (body of water)
impedes travel, 84
plantation on, 115
See also Currituck Precinct—sound in
Sound. *See* Albemarle Sound; Core Sound; Pamlico Sound
South Britain. *See* England
South Carolina (Carolinas, S. Cara., So. Carola., St. Carolina), xliv, 94, 110*n*, 130, 166, 199*n*, 200, 210, 213, 215, 217, 225*n*, 228, 236-237, 256, 299-300, 312, 317-318, 329, 352, 376, 388, 390-391, 394, 420
alliance between Cherokee and, 202*n*
chapel, church act of, xxvi
clergyman appointed to, 24, 107
clergyman dismissed from, 232-233, 258-259
clergyman from, 205-206, 236, 252, 264, 344, 350
clergyman in, 5*n*, 14*n*, 25, 44, 51-52, 52*n*, 66, 73, 129, 156, 188*n*, 208*n*, 216*n*, 221, 249, 259, 280*n*, 299*n*, 313, 324, 335, 337, 347, 350, 353, 376, 397, 401, 408
commissary in, xlv, 208*n*, 290-291, 291*n*, 338, 411-412, 412*n*
death of clergyman in, 319
death of governor, 106
depopulation of, 204

deputy governor from, 87*n*
description of, 10, 256
form of government in, xxi, xxi*n*
French congregation in, 313
governor of, 80, 82, 158, 167*n*, 183*n*, 225*n*
Indian attacks in, 202, 202*n*
instructions for clergy of, 242
lack of clergy in, 133, 340
letter from clergy of, 316-317
library in, 26*n*, 167, 176
lord proprietor in, 124*n*
military assistance from, 140*n*, 158, 186, 201, 241*n*, 247, 256, 258*n*
official in, 247
opposition to clergyman in, 232, 259, 369
receiver general from, 258*n*
salary for clergyman in, 263
SPG and, 156*n*
uprising in, 269-270, 270*n*
vacancy in, 114
vestry act of, xxvi
South Shore Parish, meeting of vestrymen at, 314
See also St. Andrew's Parish
South, Robert, author, 7
Southwell, Edward, order in council signed by, 279
Spade. *See* Tools, equipment—spade
Sparrow, Anthony, author, 6, 38
Spateman, Mr.
church of, 297
to review missionary's performance, 297
Speech, of Queen, 184
Speight (Spight), William (Will., Willm., Wm.), vestryman, 486-487, 489-493 passim
Spence, Allexr., vestryman, 190
Spices
cinnamon, 178
ginger, 178
mace, 178
nutmeg, 178
Spight, William (Will., Willm., Wm.). *See* Speight, William
Spitalfields, England, 264-265, 265*n*
Spithead, England, ship at, 136-137
Spotswood, Alexander (A.)
compliment by, 253
governor, lieutenant governor of Virginia, 87*n*, 113*n*, 129, 150*n*, 158
intervention by, 113*n*
leads military expedition, 129
letter from, 129, 153-154, 253
Spotswood, Colonel. *See* Spotswood, Alexander
Spotswood, Governor. *See* Spotswood, Alexander
Sprat (Spratt), Thomas, bishop of Rochester, author, 7, 37
Sprat, Bp. *See* Sprat, Thomas, bishop of Rochester
Spratt, Bp. *See* Sprat, Thomas, bishop of Rochester
Spring (body of water), 375
Spring (season), 167, 178, 234, 253, 264, 269
Spring, Robt., vestryman, 190
Spruil, Doctor. *See* Spruill Godfry—physician
Spruil, Godfry. *See* Spruill, Godfry
Spruil, Mr. *See* Spruill, Godfry
Spruill (Spruil), Godfry (Godffrey, Godfrey)
payment to, 436-437, 451, 458-459, 467
physician, 436-437, 451, 458
Spruill, Doctor. *See* Spruill, Godfry—physician
Squirrel
act of assembly on killing of, 492*n*
bounty paid on killing of, xxxv
Stacy, Mary, allowance of, 477
Stafford, Will. (Wm.)
testimonial by, 108
vestryman, 108, 190
Standing, Edward
land of, 447
payment to, 467
Standish, [David]
clergyman, 316
deceased, 316
Standish, Messr. *See* Standish, [David]
Stanhope, Dean. *See* Stanhope, George, dean of Canterbury
Stanhope, George, dean of Canterbury, author, 8, 37
Stanley, William, author of [*The Faith and Practice of a Church of England Man*], 9, 34, 36, 38
Stanyarne, James
letter from, 228-230
parishioner, 230
verbal abuse of, 229
Stanyarne, Jane
letter from, 228-230
parishioner, 230
Starch. *See* Occupation, trade, profession—starchmaker
State house, proprietors promise funds for construction of, xxi
Statement, concerning treatment of clergyman, 302

Stephans, Henry, author of [*Scapula Lexicon Graco Latinum Elzi viri et Hackij Ludg. Bat. 1652*], 6
Stepney, John, vestryman, 190
Stewart (Stuart), Charles
brother of, 60
delivers letter, 65, 71
royal navy captain, 77
shipmaster, 60, 71, 77
Stewart, William, 2nd viscount Mountjoy
brother of, 60
Stillingfleet, Bp. *See* Stillingfleet, Edward, bishop of Worcester
Stillingfleet, Dr. *See* Stillingfleet, Edward, bishop of Worcester
Stillingfleet, Edward, bishop of Worchester
author, 6-7, 34, 37
author of [*On the Sufferings and Satisfaction of Christ 2*], 7, 410
Stockings. *See* Clothing, jewelry—stockings
Stocks. *See* Clothing, jewelry—stocks
Stone, Mary, payment to, 472
Storm. *See* Weather, climate—storm
Stoup, Mr.
clergyman, 313
disapproval of, 313
Stratford, Bp. *See* Stratford, Nicholas, bishop of Chester
Stratford, Connecticut, lack of clergy in, 258
Stratford, Nicholas, bishop of Chester, author, 37
Stratton, England, 73*n*
Street. *See* Bartholomew Close, London; Bishopsgate Street, London; Blackfriars Road, London; Cannon Street, London; Chancery Lane, London; Crane Lane, Dublin; Crutched Friars, London; Great Kirby Street, London; Lime Street, London; Lombard Street, London; Mansell Street, London; Newgate Street, London; Paternoster Row, London; St. Albans Street, London; Warwick Court, London; Warwick Lane, London; West Smithfield, London; Wine Close, London
Strype, John, author of [*The Life of Sir Thomas Smith*], 7
Stuart, Capt. *See* Stewart, Charles
Stuart, house of, 254*n*
Stuart, James Francis Edward ("Old Pretender"), xxviii*n*, 212*n*
Stuart, Wm., processioner, 461
Stuart. *See* Stuart, house of
Stubbs (Stubs), Philip
archdeacon, 49*n*, 277
author of [*Gods Dominion over the Seas*], 38
clergyman, 135
letter delivered by, 135
observes missionary, 277
report by, 49
SPG and SPCK supporter, 49*n*
to supply abstract, 175
Stubbs, Mr. *See* Stubbs, Philip
Stubbs, William, author of [*Visitation Charges of the Bps. of Dublin, Worcester, Bath and Wells, Lincolns, Rochester, Chester*], 34
Stubs, Mr. *See* Stubbs, Philip
Stuck, Richd., testimonial by, 53
Student, pupil
books for, 84
of divinity, 88
religious instruction for, 43
See also Schoolmaster, teacher
Subscription, donation
for construction of church, 67, 145, 250, 282-283, 356, 403, 412, 432
for payment of clergy, xxx, 438-439, 474
for purchase of glebe, 300
See also Clergy, clergyman—subscription for
Success (ship), 238
Suffolk, England, 114, 125-127
Sugar. *See* Food, diet—sugar
Summer, 86, 104-105, 120, 141, 231, 255, 269, 273, 275, 285, 363, 408, 412
unhealthy, 256
Summons, to vestry, vestrymen, 194, 484
Sumner, Dempsey (Demsey)
churchwarden, 490-493 passim
payment to, 492
to present account to vestry, 491, 493
vestryman, 490, 494
Sumner, John (Jno.)
allowance of, 493-494
churchwarden, 486-490 passim
clerk, 493-494
payment to, 487, 491
summoned, 485
to attend vestry meeting, 484
to oversee chapel construction, 493-494
to present account to vestry, 487, 491
vestryman, 477, 481, 486, 490-492, 494
Surgeon. *See* Occupation, trade, profession—physician, surgeon
Surplice. *See* Clothing, jewelry—surplice
Surrey Parish, Virginia, clergyman in, 154, 158

Survey, of boundary, 470*n*
Surveyor, to lay out New Bern, 404
See also Occupation, trade, profession—surveyor
Surveyor general of customs, 183*n*
Surveyor general, surveyor general's office, 25*n*, 95*n*, 353*n*
deputy, 160, 161*n*
See also Lawson, John—surveyor general
Susannah (slave), 155
Sussex County, Delaware, clergyman in, 47*n*
Swan, Major. *See* Swann, Samuel
Swann, John (Jno.)
letter from, 398-399
vestryman, 316, 399
Swann, Sam[ue]l
petitioner, 324
vestryman, 316, 324
Swann, Samuel
Council member, 87*n*
deceased, 84
finances church building, 84
of Virginia, 87*n*
provincial secretary, 87*n*
Swann, Samuel , (Chowan), debtor, 475
Swann, Will., vestryman, 190
Swiss
baron, 113*n*
settlers, 89*n*, 112, 113*n*, 123
Switzerland, 113*n*
Sword. *See* Arms, armaments, ordnance—sword
Symmons, Nicholas, warrant to, 434
Symons, Jno., debtor, 466
Symson (Simson), Patrick, author, 294
Synge, Edward, author of [*Answers to all the Excuses, and Pretences which men ordinarily make for their not coming to the Communion*], 9-10
T., J. *See* Talbot, John
T., W. *See* Taylor, William
Table. *See* Church, chapel, meetinghouse—table for, table of marriages to be displayed in; Household furnishings—table
Tailor. *See* Occupation, trade, profession—tailor
Talbot (T., Talbott), John (J.)
appears before the SPG, 49
arrival of, 15
assistant to clergyman, 13
character of, xxxix
character of, unknown, 46
clergyman, xxxix, 13*n*, 17, 203*n*
letter from, 15-19, 45, 203*n*
ministry, 17, 20
missionary appointment of, 45
salary of, delinquent, 45
travel of, 13*n*, 20*n*
visits North Carolina, xl
Talbot (Talbott, Talburt), Benjamin (Benja.)
allowance of, 490-493 passim
clerk, 490
reader, 490, 492-493
Talbot, Mr. *See* Talbot, John
Talbott, Benja. *See* Talbot, Benjamin
Talbott, Mr. *See* Talbot, John
Talburt, Benjamin. *See* Talbot, Benjamin
Talck, Gabriel
clergyman, 401
difficulties of, 401
letter from, 401-402
salary of, delinquent, 401
Tallow, 231, 402
Tanner. *See* Occupation, trade, profession—tanner
Tanner, Mary, payment to, 466
Tar, 32
made by Palatines, 113
payment in, 86, 246
purchased by vestry, 437
Tarrel. *See* Tyrrell Precinct, County
Tarripin Hill. *See* Terrapin Point
Tart, Joseph
signature of, forged, 310*n*
vestry commissioner, 310
Tate, Nahum, author of [*Introductions of the New Versions of Psalms*], 10
Tattering Bridge. *See* Tottering Bridge
Tavern. *See* Public house, ordinary, tavern
Tax, 327, 451, 455
allowance for collecting, 445
bond for collection of, 403, 468
churchwardens to collect, 455
churchwardens to receive, 452
collected by provost marshal, 316
collected by reader, 474
collected by sheriff, xxxvii, 416
collection, payment of, 403, 450, 467-468
collection, payment of, certified, 454
collector of, 432-434, 454, 465-466, 479, 489
collectors of, summoned, 434
county, xxxv
dissenters may levy, xix
dissenters may not levy, xx
for constructing church, xxx, xxx*n*
insufficient to build churches, xxx

not collected, 458
notice to pay, 457
on land, xix
place of payment of, xxvii, 193, 195,
proposal to exempt clergy from, 215
to create sinking fund, xlvii*n*
vestry refuses to levy, 402
Taxation
by dissenters, xix-xx
by justices, 316
by vestry, xxiv-xxv, xxvii-xxix, xxxi*n*, xxxv-xxxvii, 81-82, 140, 188, 192-193, 241, 250, 252, 265-266, 275, 285, 290, 314-315, 327, 338, 347, 368, 402-403, 413, 416-417, 433, 438-440, 445, 451-452, 456-457, 459, 463-464, 466-468, 470, 473-476 passim, 478-482 passim, 486-487, 491, 493
by vestry, illegal, xxxiii
district for, 454
during Tuscarora War, 158
for constructing church, xxiii, 417, 432
for constructing public buildings, 316
not permitted, xix-xx
of Anglicans, 424
of clergyman, 207
of dissenters, xix-xx
of free blacks and mulattoes, xxvii*n*
of slaves, xxvii*n*
permitted only to support own church, xix
Roman Catholics and, xix
See also Commission—on tax collection; Tithables
Tayler (Taylor), Thomas (Thos.)
testimonial by, 108
vestryman, 108, 190
Tayler, Edward
testimonial by, 108
vestryman, 108
Taylor (T.), William (W., Willm., Wm.)
letter from, 138, 152-153, 169-170, 187-188, 196, 202, 204-206
letter to, 149-150, 152-155, 157-159, 162-163, 166-167, 171-175, 179-182, 184-186, 197-204, 206-214
secretary to the SPG, 138, 138*n*, 157, 196, 214
witness, 164
Taylor, Bp. *See* Taylor, Jeremy, bishop of Down and Connor
Taylor, Brother. *See* Taylor, Ebenezer
Taylor, Ebenezer (Eben-Ezer, Ebenezr.), *502*
arrival of, 252
barred from preaching, 220
behavior of, 229-230, 232
bill of exchange from, 263
character of, 206-207, 216
clergyman, xxxi, xlv, 208*n*, 219, 224*n*, 232, 235, 242, 265*n*, 269, 272
complaint by, 217-218
cousin of, 263
deceased, 272
desires new missionary appointment, 264
fails to include wife, 249
fails to report for duty, 236
instructions to, 225-226
letter from, 217-220, 232, 258-263
letter of complaint against, 228-230, 232
letter to, 221, 225-226, 233, 242, 258
ministry of, 229-230, 252, 254, 260-262
missionary appointment of, xlv, 206-207, 217, 219, 224, 232-233, 242, 282
money of, stolen, 270*n*
ordained, 208
physical condition of, 252, 259
refuses missionary appointment, 206-207, 220
requests assistance, 208
salary of, 233, 263
threatened with suspension, 207
travel of, hampered, 259-260
Taylor, Elthd., directions from, 162
Taylor, Jane, beaten, 466
Taylor, Jeremy, bishop of Down and Connor, author, 6, 410
Taylor, Mr. *See* Taylor, Ebenezer
Teach (Thache, Thacth, Thatch), Edward
alleged associate of, 124*n*
deceased, 258*n*
pardoned by governor, 258*n*
pirate, 124*n*, 256, 258*n*, 321
resides in Bath, 258*n*
Teint, Colonel. *See* Tynte, Edward
Temple Church, London, minister of, 60
Temporary Laws, xx, xxi*n*
no reference to church matters in, xxi
Ten Commandments, 16
recited by Negroes, xlvi, 285, 424
Tenancy. *See* Lords proprietors—tenants of
Tenison (Tennison), Thomas, archbishop of Canterbury
act of assembly laid before, 91, 97
application to, 94
author, 37
instructions from, 39
letter laid before, 69*n*
library of, 138, 153, 196, 201, 203
memorial laid before, 57
minutes laid before, 100

opinion of, awaited, 111
order by, 58
papers laid before, 79*n*
proposals laid before, 89*n*
recommendation laid before, 39*n*
testimonial to, 108-109
to approve salary, 91, 106*n*
Tennison, Thomas (A-Bp.). *See* Tenison, Thomas
Terrapin Point (Tarripin Hill) (Bertie County), 472
Testimonials. *See* Clergy, clergyman—testimonials concerning
Thache. *See* Teach, Edward
Thacth. *See* Teach, Edward
Thailand (Siam), 7
Thatch, Edward. *See* Teach, Edward
Theft. *See* Crime—theft, robbery
Thirty-nine Articles, 16, 40, 423
not read by clergyman, 229
Thomas, John, delivers letter, 20
Thomas, Samuel (Samll.)
missionary appointment of, 5*n*, 14, 14*n*
payment to, 14
warrant to, 5*n*
Thompson (Tompson, Tomson), Elizabeth (Eliza., Elizah.)
allowance of, 482, 487, 489-490
maintained by parish, 481, 487, 491, 494
Thompson, _____. *See* Thompson, Elizabeth
Thompson, Mrs. *See* Thompson, Elizabeth
Thornburg, Wm. *See* Thornburgh, William
Thornburgh, William (Wm.)
agent, 4*n*
letter from, 3
signatory, 3, 3*n*
Thorndick. *See* Thorndike, Herbert
Thorndike (Thorndick), Herbert, author, 6
Thorpe, George
prebendary, 13
proposed for SPG membership, 13
Thread. *See* Cloth, fabric, yarn—thread
Three Tuns (tavern), 238-239
Thynne, Thomas, 1st viscount Weymouth
application to, 46
benefactor, 30
bounty of, 27-29
complaint by, xxvi*n*
debtor, 31
letter from, 46
library given by, xli
of London, England, 27
payment from, 4, 15
sponsors clergyman, 31
supports nonjuring bishops, 5*n*
tory, 5*n*
Tillotson, ABp. *See* Tillotson, John
Tillotson, John, author, 34, 37
Timber
cutting of, 418
frame constructed from, 493
Tithables, 158, 195, 403, 413, 432, 438, 440, 445, 455
defined by statute, xxvii*n*
list of, 433, 455, 458, 478, 488
list of, to be taken, 447
list of, unavailable, 457
number of, 84, 245, 285, 433, 454, 456-459 passim, 467-468, 475-476, 478-480, 483, 488
tax not collected from, 458
taxed, xxiv, xxvii, xxix, 192, 266, 316, 327, 402, 435, 451-452, 456-457, 459, 461, 463-464, 467-468, 470, 474-476, 478-480, 482-483, 486-487, 491, 493
See also Taxation
Tobacco, 162*n*
as rated commodity, 250-251
payment in, xv, 195
price of, 161, 195
See also Building—tobacco house; Virginia—tobacco in
Tockesey, Phil.
petitioner, 44-45
vestryman, 45
Token House Yard, London, 163
Toleration, religious. *See* Dissenters—toleration of
Tompson, Eliza. *See* Thompson, Elizabeth
Tomson, Elizabeth. *See* Thompson, Elizabeth
Toole, B., book delivered by, 26
Toole, Mr. *See* Toole, B.
Tools, equipment, 202, 214
axe, hatchet, 115, 122, 122*n*, 211, 257
hac, 115
harrow, 210
hoe, 211, 257
of carpenter, 211
of clergyman, 180, 211
of cooper, 211
of iron, 431
plough, 210, 214
saw, 211
sickle, 178
spade, 115, 211
Tory, 254*n*

Tottering (Tattering) Bridge, (Chowan Precinct, County), 455
district boundary at, 454
Touchet, George, author of [*Historical Collections out of several Grave Protestant Historians concerning the Changes of Religion in the Reigns of Hen. 8 Ed. 6 Queen Mary and Q. Elizab.*], 8
Tower Hill (Little Tower Hill), London, 238-239
Towerson, Gabriel, author, 6
Town on Queen Anne's Creek. *See* Edenton
Town, city, settlement, 344
absence of, xiv, xli, 58
act for regulation of, xxxiv, 402
act of assembly on, 404
bounds of, 404
church in, 404, 412
construction of church proposed in, xxii
established, xiii, xxi, 286
establishment of encouraged, xxi
founded, 113*n*
growth of, 284
land laid out for, 316
lots in, 404-405, 458, 473
lots sold in, xxix, xxx*n*, 286, 459-460, 463-464, 466-467, 473
proposed, xxxiv
ridiculed, xiv
seaport, 92
streets of, xxxiv, 404
streets of patrolled, xxxiv
See also Aberdeen, Scotland; Albany, New York; Bath; Boston, Massachusetts; Braintree, Massachusetts; Bristol, Connecticut; Brunswick; Burlington, New Jersey; Bury St. Edmunds, England; Charleston, South Carolina; Chatham, England; Chester, England; Chowan Indian Town; Coventry, England; Dartmouth, England; Donoughmore, Ireland; Edenton; Elizabeth Town, New Jersey; Epsom, England; Glasgow, Scotland; Gloucester, England; Goose Creek, South Carolina; Hampton, Virginia; Hancock's Town; Keighley, England; Indians-town; Kinsale, Ireland; Lancaster, England; Lisbon, Portugal; Liverpool, England; London, England; Madeira, Spain; Malabar, India; Nansemond, Virginia; Naples, Italy; Narragansett, Rhode Island; New Bern; Newbury, New Hampshire; Newcastle, England; Newcastle, Pennsylvania; New Providence, Bahamas; New Rochelle, New York; Newtown, Connecticut; Perth Amboy, New Jersey; Peterborough, England; Philadelphia, Pennsylvania; Port Royal, South Carolina; Portsmouth, England; Redding, Connecticut; Roanoke; Salem, Massachusetts; Scituate, Massachusetts; Spithead, England; Stratford, Connecticut; Williamsburg, Virginia; Wilmington; Windsor, England; Winyaw, South Carolina; Woolwich, England; Worcester, England; York, England
Trade, shipping, xxxiv, xxxiv*n*, 12, 116, 123, 329, 345, 391
act of Parliament on, 83
cargo taken by pirates, 256
convoy for, 93-94
damage to, by action of clergyman, 405
flourish, 285
of Bath County, 32
of clergyman, 209, 327, 390
of Virginia, 161, 257
possibility of, 86
to Greenland, 93
to Russia, 93
with Boston, 435
with England, 256
See also Clergy, clergyman—buys goods for resale, wants goods for resale; Indians—trade with; Money—wanted for trade; Occupation, trade, profession—merchant, peddler
Translation
of Book of Common Prayer, 88
of liturgy, 88
Transubstantiation. *See* Declaration—against transubstantiation
Trap. *See* Trapp, Joseph
Trapp (Trap), Joseph, author, 410
Travel, transportation, 29, 95, 113, 116, 130, 164, 200, 239*n*
by coach, 18
by foot, 259
by sea, 248
by water, 260, 282-283
difficulty of, xli, 27, 29-30, 94, 96, 172, 206, 233, 264, 438, 449
in Chowan Precinct, 85
of governor's wife, 140*n*
of Palatine settlers, 112
of widow of clergyman, 288-289
to England, 251, 460
See also Boat, ship; Cart; Clergy, clergyman—travel, voyage of; Convicts—trans-

portation of; Occupation, trade, profession—waterman; Roads
Treasurer, provincial, 25*n*, 376*n*, 461, 485*n*
to pay clergyman's widow, 288
vestry requests funds from, xxii
Treasurer, SPG. *See* Society for the Propagation of the Gospel in Foreign Parts—letter to treasurer of, treasurer of
Treasury Board (Great Britain)
letter to, 274
order of, 278, 346
reluctant to pay bounty, 274
Treasury Chambers, London, 346
Treaty, with Indians, 185
Tree, 141
mulberry, 143
Tremor. *See* Disease, illness, affliction—tremor
Trent River, land purchased on, 89*n*, 113*n*
Tribbeko, Mr.
letter from, 113
letter to, 113
Trimnell, Charles, bishop of Norwich, testimonial by, 49
Trinity Church, New York, 25
Trinity College, (Hartford, Connecticut), librarian at, 293*n*
Trinity College, Cambridge University, 186-187
Trotman Creek, 198*n*
Trott, Ann, joint shareholder of proprietary share, 87*n*
Trott, Doctor. *See* Trott, Nicholas
Trott, Nicholas
attorney general of South Carolina, 290*n*
books of, 289-290
chief justice of South Carolina, 290*n*
joint shareholder of proprietary share, 87*n*
of South Carolina, 290*n*
speaker of Commons House of Assembly, 290*n*
Trotter, James, payment to, 478-479
Truce, with Indians, 140*n*
Trunk. *See* Container—chest, trunk
Trustee, for school, xlviii
Tryon, Mr. *See* Tryon, William
Tryon, Thos., merchant, 397
Tryon, William (Wm.)
merchant, 211*n*, 397
treasurer to the SPG, 211*n*
unable to pay bills, 210
Tuam (Ireland), archbishop of, letter to, 57-58
Tuam, Archdiocese of, Ireland, 54
Tull (Tulle), Benja. (Ben.)
testimonial by, 108
vestryman, 108, 190
Turks, prayers for, 98
Turner, Cha.
churchwarden, 354
desires to retain minister, 353-354
justice of the peace, 310
order signed by, 278
petitioner, 309-310, 353-354
signature of, forged, 310*n*
Turner, John, author, 8
Turner, Samll.
letter from, 228-230
parishioner, 230
Turretini. *See* Turrettini, Francois
Turrettini (Turretini), Francois, author, 6
Tuscarora. *See* Indians—Tuscarora; Tuscarora War
"Tuscarora Jack." *See* Barnwell, John
Tuscarora War, 95*n*, 113*n*, 140*n*, 143-144, 146, 151, 153, 158, 165-166, 171, 185, 216, 308
assistance sought from South Carolina, 247
causes poverty, xxviii, 144-145, 310, 353
colonists killed in, 140*n*
depopulates parishes, 195, 241
effect on religion, 186
endangers library, 450
ends, 160
fate of library in, 172
infants killed in, 187, 241
letter concerning, 140
levies during, 158
losses in, 177
prisoners taken in, 139
prospective treaty during, 139
Quakers refuse to fight in, 148
troops from South Carolina in, 140*n*, 241
See also Fort, fortification—in Tuscarora War; Hunger—during Tuscarora War; Indians—depredations by, following Tuscarora War; Taxation—during Tuscarora War; Women—in Tuscarora War
Tyler, John, payment to, 433
Tynte (Teint), Edward
deceased, 80*n*, 119
governor, xxi*n*
governor of South Carolina, 80, 80*n*
instructions to, xxi*n*
letter to, 103*n*
proposed for SPG membership, 80, 80*n*
Tynte, Col. *See* Tynte, Edward
Tynte, Mr. *See* Tynte, Edward
Tyrrell (Tarrel) Precinct, County

erected, xxxiii
meeting place for vestrymen in, 314
ministry in, 379-380
parish in, 414
Umpire, 434
Umpsty, Mr. *See* Urmston, John
Upper Haleover. *See* Haul Over
Upton, John, vestryman, 190
Urmston (Umpsty, Urmstond, Urmstone), John (J., Jno.), 133*n*, 171*n*, *502*
abandons parish, 272
allegedly sells books, xlii
application by, 272
behavior of, 158
bill of exchange from, 240, 271
bill of exchange to, 234
bond to be delivered to, 151*n*
books to be delivered to, 104*n*, 151*n*
case of, referred to committee, 280
character of, 80, 103, 103*n*, 139, 142, 273
children of, 264
clergyman, xiv, xxii, xxvii-xxviii, xxviii*n*, xxxi, xxxi*n*, xxxvii, xxxix, xlii, xlvi*n*, 5*n*, 80, 81*n*, 103*n*, 112, 122*n*, 136, 148, 151, 167, 172-173, 178-179, 179*n*, 182, 184-186, 203*n*, 204-205, 232*n*, 235-236, 238-240, 246, 248, 251*n*, 257, 266, 272-274, 276-278, 280-281, 295*n*, 445-450 passim, 452-456 passim
complaint by, xxxix, 122*n*, 185, 251, 450
death of wife of, 264, 267, 269
debtor, 209, 252
deceased, 137, 285
delivers letter, 246
demands return of books, 180
denied a vestry seat, xxviii
denounces colonists, xiv
describes country's temper, 164-165
desires postponement of assignment, 93-94
desires to be paid with books, 295*n*
destitution of, 170-171, 180-182, 185, 199, 202, 212, 231, 237, 244
difficulties of, 115-121 passim, 140-141, 148, 162, 172, 177, 180-182, 199, 206, 208, 212-213, 223, 231, 237, 244, 246, 251*n*, 252-253, 255-256, 264, 267-268, 271
doubts clergyman's claim, xlvi*n*
excuse by, 143
fails to receive catechism, 185
fails to receive support, 174
instructions to, 225-226
intention of, 175
leave of, granted, 235, 267, 269, 275
letter from, 93-95, 103-104, 111-112, 115-122, 122*n*, 123-124, 124*n*, 133, 135-136, 140-141, 147-151, 153, 160, 162-167, 170-173, 176-178, 179*n*, 180-182, 184-186, 198-199, 199*n*, 200-203, 203*n*, 208-215, 230-239, 239*n*, 243-249, 252-257, 263-265, 267-273, 275-276, 281-282, 453
letter regarding, 273-274
letter signed by, 173
letter to, 138, 153, 167, 169, 179, 187-188, 205-206, 221, 225-226, 235, 237, 245, 267, 269
library of, 91, 295*n*
ministry of, 115-120 passim, 172, 184, 186, 208, 231-233, 252, 254-257 passim, 265, 268, 449, 455
missionary appointment of, 91, 142, 446, 452-453
order to, 169-170, 277*n*
payment to, xxxi*n*, 232*n*, 447, 459
petitioner, 104, 281-282
physical condition of, 142, 255
purchases plantation, 115, 158
recommendation of, xxii, 89-90, 103
regret of, 269
report by, 177, 198
request by, 202, 211*n*, 238
residence of, 223, 231
returns to England, 281
salary advanced to, 240
salary of, xxxvii, 91, 173, 187-188, 257, 265-266, 276-277, 281, 445-447, 449, 452, 455-458 passim
salary of, delinquent, 162, 234, 237, 245, 252, 269-271, 275, 450, 454, 458
son of, 255, 271
testimonial in behalf of, 80-81, 90, 90*n*
to attend vestry meeting, 453-454
to make application, 272*n*
to perform service, 90*n*
travel of, 272-273
vestry refuses membership to, 452
warrant to, 5*n*
Urmston, Doctor. *See* Urmston, John—clergyman
Urmston, Mr. *See* Urmston, John
Urmstond, Mr. *See* Urmston, John
Urmstone, Mr. *See* Urmston, John
Usher, A.Bp. *See* Ussher, James
Usserii. *See* Ussher, James
Ussher (Usher, Usserii), James, author, 7, 33, 37, 294
Vail, Moseley

allowance of, 479-480, 483
clerk, 476, 479-480, 483
Valet. *See* Occupation, trade, profession—valet
Vandermulen, Thomas
testimonial by, 108
vestryman, 108
Vann, Mary
deceased, 489
guardian of child of, 489
Vanpelt, I., debtor, 475, 477
Varen (Varenij), Bernard, author, 7
Varenij. *See* Varen, Bernhard
Varet, Alexander-Louis, author of [*The Christian Education of Children, according to the Maxims of the Sacred Scripture, and the Instructions of the Fathers of the Church*], 8
Varnod, F[rancis], letter from, 316-317
Veal, Mrs., debtor, 471-472
Vendue, 418
distrained goods to be sold at, 404
town lot to be sold by, 405
Verdict, 364
Vermigli, Pietro Martire, author, 6
Vermin, to be killed, xxxv*n*, 491, 492*n*
Verstegan, Richard, author, 8
Vesey (Visey), Mr.
leaves parish, 203
letter from, 58
Vestry, 344, 350, 364*n*, 374
accounts of, xxxi-xxxii, 311
aged and infirm member of, dismissed, 451, 459-460, 465
agreement of, with clergyman, 355-356
agreement with, 349
allowance from, 86
and parish accounts, 314
and poor relief, xxiii, xxxv, 266
appointed, xxvii-xxviii, xxxiii, 119, 188-191 passim, 265-267, 312, 316, 418, 431, 432*n*, 448, 453, 455, 457
appointed by act of assembly, xxiv
appoints minister, 267, 442
assemblymen members of, xxvii, xxviii*n*, 119, 121, 254
assists widow of clergyman, 288-289
book of proceedings of, 183, 265, 431-494 passim
books claimed by, 151, 180
books detained by, 178
books for members of, 293
brings action, 458
chosen, xxxii
churchwardens to render accounts to, xxxvii
clergy as members of, xxix, xliii, 121, 189, 194, 325
clergy may appoint to, xxix, 415
clergy may not appoint to, xxxi
clergyman denied seat on, xxviii
clergyman quarrels with, 229
clerk of, 250, 310, 417, 437, 442, 444-445, 448, 455, 458, 463, 465, 469-471, 474, 476, 478-479, 481, 483, 486-487, 493-494
comments on struggle to establish church, xxiv
commissioners of, 310
controls appointment of clergyman, 177, 237
criticized, xli, 120, 170, 176, 180-181, 208, 212, 230-231, 234-235, 237, 254, 257, 265, 338
death of member of, 455
declaration required of members of, 191
difficult to secure quorum of, 485
dissenter dismissed from, 451
dissenters on, xxix, xxxix, 181, 266
elected, xxix, xxxii, xxxvi, 191, 194, 266, 314-315, 344, 414-415, 418, 442, 473, 477, 481, 486, 490
erected, xlix
fails to employ clergyman, 413
fails to levy sufficient tax, xxx
fails to meet, 122, 246, 440
fails to qualify, 265-266
falls, 266-267
illiteracy in, 84
in Virginia, 154, 296
lacks quorum, 439, 443
letter from, 171-173, 184, 184*n*, 287-288, 288*n*, 361, 367, 371, 411, 450
letter to, 176, 227, 230, 236, 279, 453, 482
may be summoned by members of, 415
may fill vacancies, xxxi, 415
may impose tax, xxxvi-xxxvii, 327
may procure clergyman, 194
may purchase land, xxix, 192
may remove clergy, 91, 215
meets, 28, 208, 212, 234, 245, 251, 265-266, 287, 419, 431-494
meets in courthouse, 478-479, 486-488, 490
meets in house, 431, 433, 489-492 passim, 494
member of, 246, 254, 254*n*, 447, 469
member of, chosen, 245
member of, criticized, accused, 85, 120-121, 162, 314
member of, dies, 441, 451, 457, 463-464

member of, dismissed, 464
member of, fined, xxviii-xxix, 191
member of, may be sued, 312
member of, refuses to qualify, xxviii-xxix, 231, 245, 254, 452
member of, replaced, 438, 438*n*, 441, 457, 460, 463-465, 485
members of, not baptized, 181
members of, opposed to establishment, xxvii*n*
members of, ordered to attend, 482
members of, qualify, 452
members of, summoned, 484
members of, to be freeholders, xxxi-xxxii, 314
members of, to hire workmen, 493
members of, to qualify themselves, 314
members of, to take oath, 415
membership in, excused, xxix*n*
memorandum of, 443
minister cannot sit on, 177
minutes of, 251, 431-432, 432*n*, 433-494
minutes of, scarce, xlix
named, 194
not informed of clergyman's departure, 272
not lawfully constituted, xxxiii
not summoned, 437
oath of member, 191
order of, xxxvii, 193-194, 250-251, 418, 431-479 passim
ordered to meet, 194
orders attendance, 451
orders money refunded, 448
orders of, to be transcribed, 469
payment to clerk of, 433, 437, 454
payments by, xxvii*n*, 195, 434
pays bounties, xxxv
pays for looking after chapel, 460
pays for maintenance of bastard child, 459
pays for maintenance of orphan, 438, 440
penalty for failure to attend meeting of, 416
penalty for failure to summon, 416
petition from, xxv, 296, 309-310, 324, 353-354, 365-366
plans itineration for missionary, 282
plans to build church, 283
powers of, xxv-xxix, 290, 419
processions land, xxxv
promises support for clergyman, 369
proposal concerning meetings of, 215
proposal to set fees by, 215
protest against order of, 251
protest to, 250
receives clergyman, xxvi*n*
receives gifts, xxx
recommends clergyman, 360, 367
records of, demanded, 487, 491
records of, scarce, xxiv
refusal of, to fill vacancy, 415
refuses to accept clergyman, 394
refuses to meet, 206, 236, 257
refuses to tax, 402
reluctant to meet, 199
requests funds, xxii
secular duties of, xxxiv-xxxv
signs certificate, 322
summoned, xxiv, 191, 223, 245, 443
table of, 479
takes oath, 490
to account for parish funds, 312
to appoint churchwardens, 415
to approve reader, 436
to be summoned, 266, 314, 415
to consider reimbursement, 451
to declare loyalty to king, 194
to make report on parish, 152
to provide weights and measures, xxxiv, 433
to purchase books, 417
to qualify, 266
to receive proceeds from sale of service, xxx
to report to SPG, 173
to seek reader, 432
uncertainty concerning organization of, xxiv
urged to construct church, 357-358
urged to provide for clergy, 177
vacancy on, xxix, xxxi, 194, 266
vestry may nominate to, 191, 194
views chapel, 434-435
welcomes clergyman, 260
Vestry Act. *See* Act of assembly—on church establishment
Vestry and churchwardens
certificate to be presented to, 492*n*
complain about Edward Moseley, xxxii
letter from, 412*n*, 449
may permit clergy to officiate in other parishes, xxxvii
petition governor and Council, xxxii
suspicions concerning, xxxi-xxxii
thank SPG, 449
to procure minister, xxxvii
Vicar. *See* Clergy, clergyman—vicar
Vicars, John, author of [*England's Worthies, or the Lives of the most Eminent person from Constantine to the present Time*], 8
Vice-chancellor, Oxford University, 120
Virgilius. *See* Maro, Publius Vergilius

Virginia, xvn, 25-26, 51, 55, 65, 72, 74, 77, 95, 106-107, 111, 113n, 121, 133, 149, 152, 154, 158, 161, 183, 186, 200, 203n, 210, 213, 238, 242, 256-258, 258n, 264, 268, 304, 319, 327, 359, 365, 377
books needed in, 17
boundary between North Carolina and, 3, 3n, 321, 470n
chapel, church in, 401
clergy from, xv-xvi, 160, 280n, 336, 336n, 356, 384, 407
clergyman appointed to, 137
clergyman in, 5n, 15, 20, 25, 27, 53n, 64-65, 76-77, 82, 95, 104, 106, 140, 144, 160, 166-167, 178, 184, 209, 213, 222, 246, 256, 259, 304, 319n, 331, 333, 341, 349-350, 353, 355, 357-358, 365, 390, 393, 401, 411
clergyman near, 158
clergyman traveling to, 62, 95, 132, 137, 142, 174, 231, 375, 379
college in, 26
commissary for, xliv
Court of Admiralty in, 3n
creditor in, 183, 196
deputy governor of North Carolina in, 87n
description of, 10, 256
established church in, xxiii
fear of privateers in, 93
fleet of, 137
governor of North Carolina in, 321n
governor, lieutenant governor of, xxxi, 12n, 15, 22, 113n, 122, 129, 140n, 146n, 150n, 157, 197, 228, 296, 303, 341n, 353, 365, 449
Indians near, 216
lack of clergy in, 20, 296-297
legislation in, xxiiin
letter to governor of, 157-159
library in, 172, 178, 180, 257, 383, 450
merchant in, 144, 161
ministry in, 72, 107-108, 117, 167, 172, 180, 231, 257, 321, 321n, 365, 450, 473n
naval forces marshaling in, 122
official from, 65n, 95, 444n
parish in, xv, 296, 350
physician in, 330, 333
Quakers in, 19-20
rebels in, 122
rector in, 470n
religious intolerance in, xvi
school near, 143, 145, 149
schoolmaster in, 87n, 145n, 222
settlers from, 86
ship in, 122, 132, 140
support from, 158
testimonial from governor, 25-26
vacancy in, 124
Visitation, by commissary, xlv, 243
Vorst (Vorstii), Conrad, author, 34, 37
Vorstii. *See* Vorst, Conrad
Wade, John
petitioner, 44-45
vestryman, 45
Wager of law, 413, 417
not allowed, 417
plea of, 314-315
Wake, Dr. *See* Wake, William
Wake, William, author, 7, 38
Wake, William, archbishop of Canterbury
letter from, 320
letter to, 323-324
library of, 211, 214, 283, 285
Wales, Prince of, 72
Walker, [Robert], letter regarding, 55
Walker, Governor. *See* Walker, Henderson—governor
Walker, Henderson
bequest of, xxxvi
church supporter, xxiv
churchwarden, 433, 435-436
collectors brought before, 432
comments on legislation, xxiv
deceased, 438, 438n
governor, xxx, xxxiii, xxxvi, 23
land of, 115
letter from, 14, 14n, 22-23
president of Council, xiii, xxiv, 12, 12n, 14, 433
statement by, xv
supports Anglican establishment, 12n
to obtain grant, 12
vestryman, 431
widow of, remarries, 183
Walker, Jno.
cousin of, 263
payment to, 263
Walker, John (Jno.) (Chowan), 432
debtor, 434
deceased, 448
to collect parish tax, 432
vestryman, 445-447
warrant to, 434
Walker, Mr. *See* Walker, Henderson
Walker, President. *See* Walker, Henderson—president of Council
Walker, Robt.
churchwarden, 420

letter from, 419-420
Wall, William, author, 410
Wallace, James
clergyman, 65, 65*n*, 72, 76, 107, 112, 172, 180, 257, 450
deceased, 167, 172, 178, 257, 450
letter delivered to, 65, 72, 76, 107
letter to, 112
library delivered to, 65, 72, 76, 107
library in possession of, 178, 180
missionary appointment of, 65, 72, 76, 107, 112, 167, 172, 178, 180, 257
refuses to return books, 450
Wallace, Mr. *See* Wallace, James
Wallis, James. *See* Wallace, James
Wallis, Mr. *See* Wallis, Robert
Wallis, Robert (Robt.)
petitioner, 44-45
testimonial by, 109
vestryman, 45, 109, 251
Walpole, R[obert], order signed by, 278
Walston, William (Wm.)
allowance of, 442, 444
petitioner, 442
Walton, Hannah (Hanah, Hanh.), allowance of, 480, 483-484
Walton, Thomas (T., Thos.)
allowance of, 491-492
churchwarden, 493-494
to oversee chapel construction, 493-494
vestry held at house of, 491-492, 494
vestryman, 478-480, 490-493 passim
Walton, Thomas, Sr., vestryman, 477
Walton, William (Willm.), allowance of, 488-489
Wanley, Humfrey
information to, 64
letter from, 59
Wanley, Mr. *See* Wanley, Humfrey
War of the Spanish Succession, causes inconvenience to clergy, 55, 55*n*
War, warfare, 92
against pirates, 258*n*
causes poverty, 144
feared by clergyman, 93
hinders work of missionaries, 179
in Cary Rebellion, 83, 117
in Palatinate, 89*n*
Quakers participate in, 118-119, 123
Quakers reluctant to engage in, 140*n*
See also Civil War, English; Tuscarora War; War of the Spanish Succession; Yamasee War
Ward, John
attorney, 170
demand of, 159
salary of, 159
Ward, Michll., allowance of, 484
Ward, Mr., 197
See also Ward, John
Warehouse. *See* Building—warehouse
Warner, Mr. *See* Warner, Samuel
Warner, Samuel (Samll.)
allowance of, 463-464, 468
payment to, 470-472
reader, 463-464, 468
salary of, 465
Warrant
for chapel silver, 346
from chief justice, 303
from churchwardens, 267
of distress, 413, 418
royal, 278
served by constable, 303
to levy assessment, 404
to levy forfeiture, 403
to pay passage money, 5
to summon collectors, 434
to summon vestry, 415-416
to take list of tithables, 446
Warwick Court, London, 335, 393, 400, 422
Warwick Lane, London, 335, 366, 393, 400, 422
Warwick Street, London, 366
Warwickshire, England, 386
Washburn, Mr. *See* Mashborne, Edward
Water
for baptism, 437
impedes travel, 96
poor quality of, 85
travel by, 174
See also Drink—water
Waterland, Daniel, author, 410
Waterman. *See* Occupation, trade, profession—waterman
Waters, Jos., vestryman, 316
Wathum, W., allowance of, 483
Wax, sealing, 238
Weather, climate, 61-63, 65, 76-77, 85-86, 89*n*, 116, 137, 156, 165, 175, 353
cold, 264, 363
forces ship into Charleston, 353
hot, warm, 200, 264, 285, 363
hurricane, 259
rain, 252
storm, 210, 418
unhealthy, xli, 256, 281
Webster, William, land of, 314

Wedding, fee for, 215
  See also Marriage
Weeks, Stephen B.
  historian, xxv
  opinion of, mistaken, xxvi
Weeks. *See* Weeks, Stephen B.
Weights and measures
  acre, xix, xxii, 298, 405, 431, 433, 443
  act of assembly on, xxxv, 435
  brass, 435, 471
  bushel, 86, 115, 158, 160, 435-436, 471
  churchwardens to keep, 490
  dram, 178
  feet, 431, 444-445, 447, 493
  fraudulent, xxxv
  gallon, 178, 435, 471
  hundredweight, 251*n*, 435, 471
  inch, 493
  list of, 471
  miles, 409
  ounce, 178, 178*n*
  payment for, 433
  peck, 435-436, 471
  pottle, 435, 471
  pound, 435, 471
  quart, 435, 471, 484
  receipt for, 435, 471
  scales for, 435, 490
  stamped, 436
  standard of, 433, 435, 448, 469
  standard of, to be surrendered, 445
  steelyards for, 436
  to be demanded, 451
  yard, 471-472, 476-477, 484
Weimouth, Lord. *See* Thynne, Thomas, 1st viscount Weymouth
Welchman (Welshman), Edward, author, 410
Wells, Francis
  to collect parish tax, 432
  warrant to, 434
Wells. *See* Bath and Wells—bishop of
Welshman. *See* Welchman, Edward
Welstead, William
  merchant, 435
  of Boston, Massachusetts, 435
Wendelin, Marcus Frederik, author, 295
Wendelini. *See* Wendelin, Marcus Frederik
Wesendunck, Mr., 52
Wesley, John, founder of Methodism, 425*n*
West Indies, 58, 86, 125, 200, 231, 238, 361
  clergyman from, 85, 87*n*
  clergyman in, 4, 323
  rebel leader in, 184
West Jersey. *See* New Jersey
West Smithfield, London, printer in, 39, 335*n*
West, Benja. (Benjn.)
  letter from, 250
  vestryman, 250-251
West, Robert (Robt.)
  assembly member, 448
  churchwarden, 452
  Council member, 448*n*
  letter signed by, 173
  vestryman, 173, 448, 452
West, Thomas
  churchwarden, 452
  clerk, 448
  vestryman, 189
Westbeere, Charles, allowance of, 480
Westminster (Westmr.), London, 19, 21, 24, 48, 50, 55, 58, 62-64, 72, 80, 92, 95, 124-125, 128, 133-134, 137, 285
  deacon at, 308
Westmr. *See* Westminster, London
Weston (Wesson), Will[ia]m (W., Will., Willm., Wm.)
  burial of, 491
  by parish, 480, 483-486 passim, 488-489
  clothes of, 484-485
  payment to, 468
  petitioner, 464
Weston, Thos., vestryman, 479
Westover Parish, London, printer in, 39, 335*n*
Westover, Virginia, xiv
Weymouth, Lord. *See* Thynne, Thomas, 1st viscount Weymouth
Weymouth. *See* Thynne, Thomas, 1st viscount Weymouth
Weymouthe, Lord. *See* Thynne, Thomas, 1st viscount Weymouth
Whaley, Nathanael, author, 7-8
Wharton (Whartoni), Henry, author, 7
Whartoni. *See* Wharton, Henry
Wheat, 115, 231, 237
  levy of, 158
  of clergy, 177
  reaping of, 117
  staple commodity, 209
Wheatley, _____. *See* Wheatly, Charles
Wheatly (Wheatley), Charles, author, 410
Wheatly, John, subscription by, 439
Wheelwright. *See* Occupation, trade, profession—wheelwright
Wherryman. *See* Occupation, trade, profession—wherryman
Whery, _____, slaveowner, 128

Whig, 118, 254*n*
Whiston, William, author, 7
Whitbee, Richd., vestryman, 190
Whitby, Daniel, author, 33, 38, 172
Whitby, England, 391
White Oak River
  description of settlement on, 368
  land purchased on, 113*n*
White, Jno., payment by, 481
White, Luke, debtor, 466
Whitefield, George
  calvinist, 425*n*
  clergyman, 425*n*
  complaint by, 426
  founder of Methodism, 425*n*
  letter from, 423-425
  letter to, 423, 426-427
  objects to teaching method, 424
  travel of, 423
Whitefield, Mr. *See* Whitefield, George
Whitehall Palace, London, 346
Whitehead, John
  assists missionary, 208
  clergyman, 208, 208*n*
Whitehead, Mr. *See* Whitehead, John
Whitsun, 142, 229, 262
Whole Duty of Man (book), 293
Wiccacon River, clergyman on, 283
Wickham Precinct, 65*n*
Wicks, Mr., burial of, 490
Wiker, Joseph, vestryman, 190
Wildcat
  act of assembly on killing of, 492*n*
  bounty paid on killing of, xxxv
Wilkins, Bp. *See* Wilkins, John, bishop of Chester
Wilkins, Charles
  allowance of, 470
  child of, to be returned, 469
  payment to, 472
  to appear before vestry, 469
  to return clothes, 470
Wilkins, John, bishop of Chester, author, 6-7, 34, 38
Wilkinson (Wilkison), William (Wm.)
  churchwarden, 431, 433-435
  Council member, 432*n*
  General Court justice, 432*n*
  of Maryland, 432*n*
  payment by, 435-436
  replacement for, 441
  speaker of assembly, 432*n*
  to be reimbursed, 436
  to collect parish tax, 433-434
  to deliver weights and measures, 435
  to present account to vestry, 434, 437
  vestryman, 431, 433, 435-436, 438-439
Wilkinson, Colonel. *See* Wilkinson, William
Wilkinson, Henry
  governor, xxi*n*
  instructions to, xxi*n*
Wilkison, Wm. *See* Wilkinson, William
Will, 310*n*
  clergy benefits from, 317-318
  funds for church construction included in, xxx
  includes bequest to poor, xxxvi
  of clergyman, 286-287, 287*n*, 377-378, 400
  of reader, 155-156
  proved, 287, 326, 400
  See also Administrator, administratrix
Willi, Dr. *See* Willis, Richard
William and Mary, College of. *See* School, schools—College of William and Mary
William III, king of England, 5*n*
  deceased, 18, 274
  order by, 274
William, K. *See* William, III, king of England
Williams, Bp. *See* Williams, John, bishop of Chichester
Williams, Danll., burial of, 483
Williams, James (Jas.)
  will proved by, 377
  witness, 377
Williams, John (Jno.)
  allowance of, 472, 489
  clothes of, 472
  guardian, 489
  maintained by parish, 472, 476
Williams, John (New Hanover)
  encourages missionary, 350
Williams, John (St. Andrews Parish)
  letter from, 228-230
  parishioner, 230
Williams, John, bishop of Chichester
  author, 34, 38-39
  presents petition to the Board, 33*n*
Williams, Lewis, vestryman, 189
Williams, Mr.
  allowance of, 472
  debtor, 473
Williams, Mrs.
  executrix, 474
  payment to, 477
  widow, 477
Williams, Will. (Wm.) (Currituck)
  testimonial by, 108

vestryman, 108, 190
Williams, William (Wm.) (Chowan)
allowance of, 468
allowance paid to estate of, 474
deceased, 474
executrix of estate of, 474
Williamsburg (Wmsburgh.), Virginia, 153, 303, 318-320, 340-342
books requested from, 436
clergyman in, 128
Williamson, Jane
letter from, 228-230
parishioner, 230
Williamson, Manly
letter from, 228-230
parishioner, 230
Willis (Willi), Richard, author, 9-10, 38
Willis, Dean. *See* Willis, Richard
Willis, Wm.
desires to retain minister, 353-354
petitioner, 353-354
vestryman, 354
Wilmington (Newton, New Town), 384*n*, 409, 419, 422
clergyman in, 398-399, 408
early promoter of, 382*n*
merchant in, xxx
street patrols in, xxxiv
Wilson (Willson), Robert
deceased, 435
maintained by parish, 432, 435-436
Wilson, Bishop. *See* Wilson, Thomas, bishop of Sodor and Man
Wilson, Thomas, bishop of Sodor and Man
author, 410
ordination by, 405
Wilson, William, commissioner, 403
Wilson. *See* Wilson, Robert
Wimble, Capt. *See* Wimble, James
Wimble, James
cartographer, 382*n*
gift from, 381
merchant, 382*n*
privateer, 382*n*
Win, Mr., house of, 379-380
Windows, in church, 84, 433, 436-437, 493
Windsor, England, SPG secretary at, 58
Wine, for communion, 96
See also Drink—wine
Wine Close (Wine Street), London, 61
Wine Street. *See* Wine Close, London
Wingate, Edmund, author, 7-8
Winright, James (Jams.)
testimonial by, 301
witness, 301
Winteley, [John], dismissed as clergyman, 317
Winteley, Mr. *See* Winteley, [John]
Winter, 78, 116, 120, 140, 167, 182, 223, 231, 234, 240, 244-245, 270, 363, 376, 422, 587
difficulty of travel in, 27
hogs killed in, 212
illness in, 86
severe, 209, 212
Winyaw, South Carolina, 388
Witness, 303
to be examined, 336
to signature, 377
Wmsburgh. *See* Williamsburg, Virginia
Wolf
act of assembly on killing of, 492*n*
bounty paid on killing of, xxxv
destroys cattle, 211
Wollaston, William, author, 410
Women
aboard naval vessel, 134
exercise various skills, 116
in Tuscarora War, 158
Wood, Alexander
clergyman, 51, 51*n*
deceased, 51*n*
ministry of, 51*n*
missionary appointment of, 51
recommendation of, 51
rector, 66
Wood, Edward (Edwd.), allowance of, 454, 456
Wood, firewood, 418
Wood, John
appoints attorney, xv
attends Oxford University, xv*n*
clergyman, xv
performs marriages, xv*n*
salary of, delinquent, xv
Wood, Montague, committee member, 409
Wood, Mr. *See* Wood, Alexander
Wood, Mr. *See* Wood, John
Woods, xxxviii, 115-116, 129
Woodward, Dr. *See* Woodward, Josiah
Woodward, Josiah
author, 38
author of [*Earnest Exhortations to the Religious Observation of the Lord's Day*], 9
author of [*Seamans Monitor*], 38
author of [*Souldiers Monitor*], 38
Woolwich, England, chaplain in, 137
Worcester, England, 38
bishop of, 34
Worden, _____, deceased, 319

Woreley, John. *See* Worlcy, John
Worley (Woreley), John
  to present account to vestry, 463
  vestryman, 189
Worlsey, Thomas. *See* Worsly, Thomas
Worship, worship services, 16, 40-41, 43, 85, 96, 105, 134, 142-143, 145, 172, 195, 260, 283, 303, 332, 346, 348, 389*n*, 404, 417, 432*n*, 449, 460, 474, 485*n*
  absence of, 340, 370
  acts concerning, unlikely to be passed, 327
  attended, 186
  clergyman incapable of conducting, 289
  conducted by reader, 437, 440
  desired by new settlers, 350
  disturbance of, prohibited, xviii
  for fasts and festivals, 229
  in house, 144*n*, 283
  lack of, xlviii, 371*n*, 389
  not attended, 244
  payment for conducting of, 482
  places of, 349, 355
  promoted by Christopher Gale, 241
  provisions of Fundamental Constitutions concerning, xviii
  read, 327
  refusal to attend, 175
  royal instruction concerning, 327
  secretary seldom attends, 317
  seditious remarks prohibited during, xviii
  shortage of places to conduct, 261, 389
  See also Acts of assembly—on public worship
Worsley, Thomas. *See* Worsly, Thomas
Worsly (Worlsey, Worsley), Thomas (Thos.)
  justice of the peace, 310
  letter from, 240-241
  petitioner, 309-310
  signature of, forged, 310*n*
  vestryman, 190, 241
Wotton, William, author, 7
Wragg (Rag), Joseph
  brother of, 202*n*
  letter delivered to, 412
  merchant, 412
  of South Carolina, 202*n*
  Quaker, 201
Wragg (Rag), Samuel
  brother of, 202*n*
  of South Carolina, 202*n*
  Quaker, 201
Wright, Anthony
  notary public, 406-407
  protest brought before, 406-407
Wright, Mr.
  character of, 342
  flees country, 342
Wright, Thomas
  burial of, 442
  maintained by parish, 442
Wright, William
  of Virginia, 196
  payment by, 196
Yamasee. *See* Indians—Yamasee
Yamasee War, 221, 259
  depopulates parish, 252
  report on, 217-218
  South Carolina assisted in, 202, 202*n*
Yates, Thomas (Thos.), allowance for, 456, 458
Yawpim Rever. *See* Yeopim River
Yeopim River (Yawpim River), 488
York (England), archbishop of, letter to, 146-147
York (England), duke of, xix, 247
York Buildings, London, 59
York Parish, Virginia, 154
York River, Virginia, 63, 76, 161
York, dean of, deceased, 247
York, Ld. ABp. of. *See* Sharp, John, archbishop of York
Yorkshire, England, 391
  explorer from, 95*n*
  official from, 130*n*, 247, 464*n*
Young, Dean. *See* Young, Edward
Young, Edward, author, 34
Young, Peter, debtor, 466